D1379428

Technical Market Indicators

WILEY TRADING ADVANTAGE

Technical Market Indicators

Analysis & Performance

Richard J. Bauer Jr.
Julie R. Dahlquist

John Wiley & Sons, Inc.

New York • Chichester • Weinheim • Brisbane • Singapore • Toronto

This book is printed on acid-free paper. ∞

Copyright © 1999 by Richard J. Bauer Jr. and Julie R. Dahlquist. All rights reserved.

Published by John Wiley & Sons, Inc.
Published simultaneously in Canada.

No part of this publication may be reproduced, stored in a retrieval system or transmitted in any form or by any means, electronic, mechanical, photocopying, recording, scanning or otherwise, except as permitted under Section 107 or 108 of the 1976 United States Copyright Act, without either the prior written permission of the Publisher, or authorization through payment of the appropriate per-copy fee to the Copyright Clearance Center, 222 Rosewood Drive, Danvers, MA 01923, (978) 750-8400, fax (978) 750-4744. Requests to the Publisher for permission should be addressed to the Permissions Department, John Wiley & Sons, Inc., 605 Third Avenue, New York, NY 10158-0012, (212) 850-6011, fax (212) 850-6008, E-Mail: PERMREQ@WILEY.COM.

This publication is designed to provide accurate and authoritative information in regard to the subject matter covered. It is sold with the understanding that the publisher is not engaged in rendering professional services. If professional advice or other expert assistance is required, the services of a competent professional person should be sought.

Library of Congress Cataloging-in-Publication Data:

Bauer Jr., Richard J., 1950–
     Technical market indicators : analysis & performance / Richard J.
     Bauer Jr. and Julie R. Dahlquist.
          p.   cm. — (Wiley trading advantage)
     Includes bibliographical references and index.
     ISBN 0-471-19721-1 (alk. paper)
     1. Investment analysis.   I. Dahlquist, Julie R., 1963–
     II. Title.   III. Series.
     HG4529.B38   1998
     332.6—dc21   98-23564

Printed in the United States of America.

10 9 8 7 6 5 4 3 2 1

This book is dedicated with love and affection to the memory of
Kenneth R. Dahlquist
and
Jo-Katherine Bauer

Preface

This book is a reasonably unbiased objective study of the performance of various technical analysis indicators. We say reasonably unbiased because everyone has biases of some sort. However, we have no particular ax to grind one way or the other with respect to technical analysis. Because our primary job duties are in the academic world, we came to our study with a healthy skepticism regarding technical analysis. The academic literature has, for the most part, given technical analysis a bad name. On the other hand, we have been aware that many market participants use technical analysis in their decision making and were puzzled as to why this would be so if technical analysis truly had no value. We suspected the truth might be somewhere in between. We were right.

Technical analysts have often been called *chartists*. Even though we describe and test sixty different technical indicators in this book, we have used few charts. Most of our results are summarized in the form of tables. In today's world, there are various ways to approach technical analysis. The tremendous increase in the availability of powerful computing has made charting both easier to do and perhaps unnecessary. Technical analysis software packages such as OmniTrader, by Nirvana Systems, Inc., which we used to help perform our analysis, have dazzling graphics. Investors can follow a strictly graphical visual approach to decision making, treating the decision making as somewhat of an art, or combine visual analysis with numeric analysis to arrive at a decision. Another approach is to let the computer calculate numbers based on various relationships, many of which could be portrayed graphically, and then let the numbers dictate decisions. With the latter approach, an investor can use technical methods without ever consulting a chart. This is the approach we have taken. Readers will note the absence of traditional technical analysis charts in this book.

A picture can often be worth a thousand words. However, for the analysis we have performed, tabular presentation seemed the best way to provide detailed results. Tabular data may take a little more effort to understand, but we think the details that are possible with this presentation are worth the effort. We hope you will agree. The tables contain a wide range of information that will allow you to do some additional analysis on your own, if you wish.

The best overall investing advice we can give is: Investor, beware! Many losses result from ignorance or improper understanding. The horror stories surrounding derivatives, the now infamous d-word of finance, are good examples of where a lack of understanding can lead. We hope that perhaps we have pointed out, even for experienced technical analysts, some issues not previously considered. We think we have given the average user of technical analysis quite a bit to think about. If you are new to technical analysis and are eager to try it out, we hope you will read our book, and others, before you dive in.

RICHARD J. BAUER JR.
JULIE R. DAHLQUIST

San Antonio, Texas
October 1998

Acknowledgments

Like most work that reaches publication, this book has a story about how it came to be. My first book, *Genetic Algorithms and Investment Strategies*, also published by John Wiley & Sons, was released in the Spring of 1994. This led to various opportunities for me, such as speaking at the New York Society of Financial Analysts' Fourth Annual Leading Investment Technologies Conference, in December 1994. In the Spring of 1995, I received a call from F. Gregory Fitz-Gerald, who had read my book and wanted to talk. I learned that, after 15 years on Wall Street as an investment banker, he had spent 15 years in senior management positions: executive vice president and CFO of Merrill Lynch, executive vice president at Primerica, and executive vice president and treasurer of American Express. He probed my interest in trying to develop my ideas as part of a commercial venture. After numerous phone conversations and e-mail exchanges, we finally met in person. The positive traits of a successful investment banker and senior executive were quickly apparent with Greg. We hit it off well and I have since formed the ANSR Company LLC, a firm devoted to developing trading software based on evolutionary computation techniques. Through Greg, I met Ed Downs, president of Nirvana Systems Inc., which sells one of the leading technical analysis software packages, OmniTrader. Greg suggested that we explore technical indicators, using OmniTrader in combination with some evolutionary computation techniques. This project is still in progress.

Greg Fitz-Gerald is, therefore, the person most responsible for this book. He has offered tremendous encouragement and many other forms of support. Thanks from both of us, Greg.

Family members have been a special source of encouragement and support. I thank my father, Richard J. Bauer, for his love and encouragement. My two older daughters, Amy and Mary, seem to take pride in my accomplishments, which helps spur me on. They have blessed and continue to bless me in innumerable ways. Katherine, my youngest daughter, doesn't understand what this is all about yet, but her smile and laugh always recharge my batteries and keep me focused on the things that are of more ultimate importance than this book. My late mother, Jo-Katherine Bauer, always took genuine interest in whatever I was doing and gave it unqualified support. At times, mildly put out with her close questioning, I replied, "No, Mom, I haven't gotten any more done with that yet." Now, I miss those inquiring calls. My grandmother, Pearl Ogden, now well into her tenth decade, continues to honor me with her enthusiastic loyalty.

My coauthor, my wife, has earned special praise. When we would mention that we were writing a book together, people would shake their heads and say, "I don't think I could do that with my spouse." But, it has been a great experience. I married Julie for many reasons, including her tremendous integrity, razor-sharp mind, and dependability. These traits, and many more, have made the task of writing as partners infinitely easier than a solo effort. Despite an incredibly stressful year, Julie has been wonderful to work with. The book has brought us closer together, and I feel very grateful to be her husband.

R. J. B.

My life and my work have been blessed by family members. From my late father, Kenneth Dahlquist, I seem to have received the gift of an interest in the financial markets. His life's work was far removed from that arena, and only after his death I discovered, in his desk drawer, his meticulous daily records and charts of stock prices. His entries, all done by hand, spanned years. Every market day was recorded, up to the day before his death. I can only imagine what he would have done with the data and computer resources I have had available while writing this book. I also want to thank Kirk Billedeaux of Merrill Lynch for sharing how he and my father talked several times each day about the stock market activity. Special thanks go to all of those who worked with my father and have told me how proud he was of me.

My mother, Averytt Dahlquist, who shudders at hearing the words "stock market," often asks how she can have a daughter who "watches those little numbers going across the television screen" and writes a book like this. I may not have received from her the gift of being interested in finance, but I thank her for giving me a love of books—a love great enough to undertake writing one.

My late grandmother, Marion Ruth Parnell, was instrumental in nurturing my gifts and supporting my education.

My daughter, Katherine, has brought a special joy into my life. Her beautiful smile and contagious laugh are a constant reminder of what life is really all about. Somehow she seems equally content watching Alan Greenspan or Barney on TV, and equally intrigued by the *Wall Street Journal* or Dr. Seuss.

Thanks go to my sisters, Carrie and Katie, for sharing life's ups and downs with me.

My coauthor is much more than my colleague and husband. He is a friend and confidant, my greatest cheerleader, and a true companion. I thank him for his support and understanding; for his confidence, trust, and respect;

for sharing parenting with me; for challenging me and working with me on this project.

Many others, too numerous to mention, have touched my life over the years. Each played her or his own part in making me the person I am today. From play school to college, from Sunday school to ballet lessons, my teachers have been an inspiration. Many friends have shared special parts of my life. Many students have been both a joy to teach and source of encouragement. And, of course, I thank those colleagues who, over the years, shared the ideals of honesty and integrity, responded to the call to lead a responsible and ethical life, and supported equal treatment of women.

J. R. D.

Together, we especially thank Ed Downs, president of Nirvana Systems, who has provided us with software and software support, and has answered many questions over the phone and via e-mail. This book would have been extremely difficult to write without OmniTrader and Ed's assistance. Besides being a great source of encouragement, Ed exemplifies how someone connected with the world of finance can be both personable and unselfish. We also thank Ruhong Cai at Nirvana, for quick and complete answers to our questions.

The idea for this book really began to take off at a John Wiley & Sons authors' reception in San Francisco, where we discussed the basic concept with Myles Thompson. Myles put us in touch with Pamela van Giessen, our encouraging, understanding, and patient editor. For most authors, "calling your editor" is probably not at the top of the list of fun things to do. Pamela is exceptional; she is fun to call.

Many others deserve our thanks for various reasons. Some may be surprised to see their names here, but we have listed them to show our sincere appreciation. They are: Jim and Janie Worth; Jeff Wood; Cathy Leary; the Koinonia class and other friends from First Presbyterian Church; Fr. Willis Langlinais; Peter McLean; our friends in Innsbruck, Austria; Teri and the Neighborhood Nanny teachers; Carl and Gabi Dimetman; Julie and Robert Rodriguez and their precious children; Sid and Becky Atkinson and their family; and Drew and Terri Heard.

R. J. B.
J. R. D.

Contents

Chapter 5   Divergence Indicators   **187**

Chapter 6   Trend Indicators   **238**

Chapter 7   Patterns   **303**

Technical Market Indicators

Chapter

1

The Technical Analysis Controversy

The weekly meeting of the investment committee for a large life insurance company was in progress. Fourteen senior research analysts and portfolio managers were gathered around a conference table discussing market conditions in the autumn of 1983. Roger, who was in his early sixties, was a veteran of such meetings. Jim, a relative newcomer, had attended his first meeting of this group one week earlier. In his late twenties, Jim had recently earned his Chartered Financial Analyst (CFA) designation and had just been promoted to senior analyst. Because Roger had been traveling the week before, this was the first time both of them were present at the weekly meeting.

Jim was surprised at the discussion's lack of structure. People just seemed to jump in with statements at will. Several people were noting recent trends in employment data. Others were focused on the Fed's monetary policy actions and their implications for inflation and interest rates. Overall, the mood was fairly bullish. Then Roger spoke up. "The advance–decline line and on-balance volume both look very negative to me." He reached into a folder and pulled out several charts. "Here, look at this. The market is clearly topping out. We're due for a real correction here. There just isn't any support for a Dow above 1300."

Jim had thought that this was a pretty serious group. But now he realized his colleagues had a sense of humor. He decided to chime in with a little humor of his own. "I know this farmer with a few extra goats. I think we could get one cheap. Let's get one, cut it open at the next meeting, and look at the entrails. What do you think, Roger?"

Complete silence fell over the room. Jim had thought Roger would appreciate his follow-up to Roger's joking remarks. But now he saw Roger's face turning pure crimson. Everyone else looked down at the table. Then Jim realized what he had done. Roger had not been joking about his charts; Roger was a technical analyst.

Jim's story is true. It was one of the most embarrassing moments of his life. Why did it happen? Was he just incredibly naive, or stupid? His company didn't think he was dumb; he was promoted to Chief Investment Officer just four years later. Where did he develop such a disdain for technical analysis?

Technical analysis has been out of favor with academics and many institutional analysts for many years. The academic community has been quite skeptical of technical analysis and has communicated its skepticism to students. Many institutional analysts have shared this view and have focused on fundamental analysis. In addition, the Chartered Financial Analyst (CFA) curriculum has, for many years, encouraged a fundamentalist approach to investing.

However, the landscape is now changing. Recent academic articles have suggested that technical analysis may indeed have value. Talking about technical analysis has become more respectable. The December 1997 issue of *Technical Analysis of Stocks and Commodities* contained an interview with Andrew Lo, Harris and Harris Group Professor of Finance at the Massachusetts Institute of Technology's (MIT) Sloan School of Management. Lo, a prominent academic, discussed some of the violations of the random walk model of market efficiency that he and others had uncovered. Discussing this, he stated:

> The predictability may not be simple, but there is definitely something there. That's what opens the door for methods such as technical analysis to be effective in providing useful information about future price movements.

The basic purpose of this book is to explore, in an unbiased and rigorous manner, whether many commonly used technical analysis indicators do or do not work. We examine the performance of many different indicators for many different stocks over a prolonged time period. The underlying concepts of the various indicators are described, and their methods of calculation are explained. We report the results of our testing of these indicators from many different angles, and we look at which indicators seem to work best. There are many side issues to understand along the way.

However, before we present our testing, it will be helpful to understand more fully why technical analysis has been so contentious over the past several decades. Let's begin by looking at some of the basic ideas behind stock trading.

The Basics of Stock Trading

Making money in stocks is based on one sound, simple, and straightforward principle: Buy low and sell high. Merely following that one rule will result in profitable investing. You should buy a stock when its price is low and sell it when its price rises to yield a high profit. No investor, financial analyst, or economist would disagree with this principle.

Understanding the rule is easy. Implementing it, however, is not so easy. Many economists would argue that it is impossible for an investor to predict consistently the market moves that will yield the benefits of this strategy. However, practitioners spend countless hours attempting to pinpoint, at least within certain limits, market lows and highs. Despite academics' disbelief, numerous claims of predictive success have come from these practitioners.

One of the tools they use is technical analysis, the focus of this book. Traders have used technical analysis throughout this century and before, but the academic literature in the past quarter century has contained heavy criticism of and arguments against its use. Meanwhile, the practitioner literature and the widespread use of technical analysis suggest benefits to its use. Thus, a "Technical Analysis Controversy" exists. One strong camp, composed mainly of academics, opposes the use of technical analysis. The other camp, composed mainly of practitioners, supports its use. In this book, we look at the arguments, both pro and con, and attempt to bring the two camps together through systematic testing of technical trading rules.

We begin by looking at what technical analysis is and examining some of the tools technical analysts use. We will then turn our attention to the pro and con arguments for using technical analysis. The chapter ends with some discussion of previous testing of these arguments.

What Is Technical Analysis?

When using technical analysis, analysts examine prior price and volume data, sometimes coupled with other market-related indicators. From these past data, market technicians attempt to determine past price trends. Their goal is to forecast the patterns and timing of future trends, based on the trends they uncover.

Charles Dow, the founder of the Dow Jones Company and the editor of *The Wall Street Journal*, is considered the grandfather of technical analysis in the Western world. He developed the Dow theory around the turn of the century. Over the years, his ideas have been refined by other market technicians.

In their classic book *Technical Analysis of Stock Trends*, Robert D. Edwards and John Magee[1] explain how technical analysis is based on these assumptions:

1. Market value is determined solely by the interaction of demand and supply.
2. Although there are minor fluctuations in the market, stock prices tend to move in trends that persist for long periods of time.
3. Shifts in demand and supply cause reversals in trends.
4. These shifts in demand and supply can be detected in charts.
5. Many chart patterns tend to repeat themselves.

From these assumptions, we see that technical analysis is rooted in basic economic theory. A stock's price is set through the interaction of demand and supply. A downward trend in stock prices can be caused by weakening demand or increasing supply. Likewise, stock prices rise whenever demand for the stock increases or the supply of the stock decreases.

A technical analyst does not need to know *why* demand or supply is shifting. To trade profitably, investors need only recognize a shift in the trend and position themselves appropriately. Technical analysts rely heavily on charts to detect these shifting trends. In fact, technical analysts are sometimes called "chartists" because of their ubiquitous use of charts of underlying stock data.

The Use of Charting

How can a chart of past stock prices be used to determine a trend? The original Dow theory is built on the premise that there are three major movements in the market: (1) daily fluctuations, (2) secondary movements, and (3) primary trends. Daily fluctuations in stock prices are not of particular importance. Neither are secondary movements, which cover a time period of up to one month, except to the extent that they reflect the market's long-term primary trend. The long-term primary trend, which *is* important, can be either bullish, indicating long-term price appreciation, or bearish, indicating long-term price depreciation.

The chart of stock price data in Figure 1.1 will help to better understand these terms. The chart plots a stock's closing price, on consecutive business days, for a period of time. This allows us to see the stock price movement and

---

[1] References cited throughout the text can be found in the Bibliography, beginning on page 411.

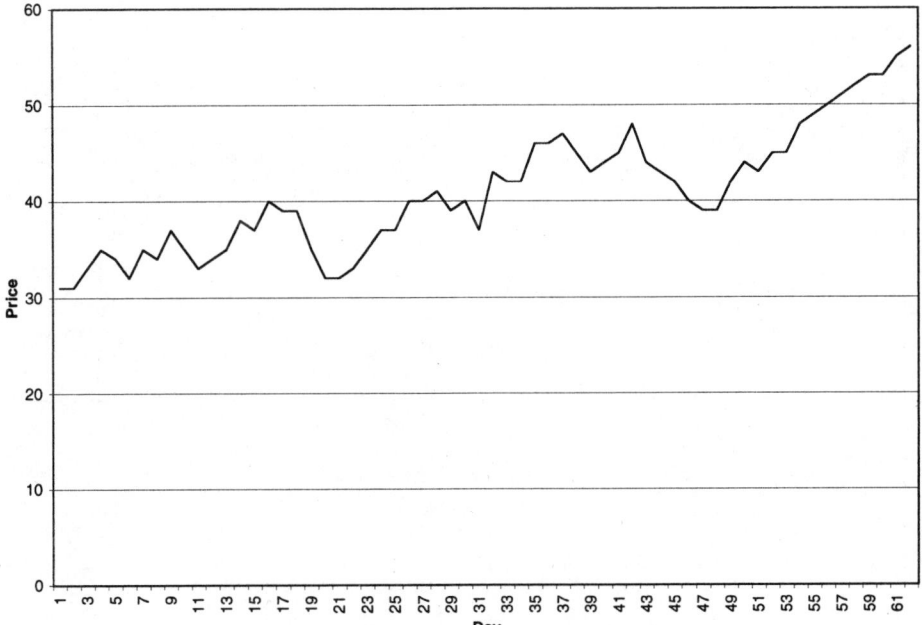

Figure 1.1   Stock prices.

fluctuation. The underlying trend has been for this stock price to increase. Therefore, we see a bullish primary trend. This does not mean that the stock's price has increased every day. In fact, two downward secondary movements occurred during this time period.

Remember that one of the basic assumptions of the Dow theory is that trends continue *for a long period.* The theory would warn traders not to become confused by the downward secondary movements. The chart helps investors distinguish the long-term primary trend and keeps them from being sidetracked by the shorter-term movements.

An old saying warns: "What goes up must come down!" The upward movement for the stock price will eventually end. The market will reverse direction, and the primary trend for the market will be downward.

Often, a stock price will fluctuate within a given range. The lower end of this trading range is called a support level, and the upper end is a resistance level. Figure 1.2 shows the price of a stock fluctuating within a trading range, between a resistance and a support level. When the stock price falls to the support level, many traders see this as an excellent buying opportunity. The stock is trading at its lowest price in recent history. When many traders begin taking advantage of this opportunity, demand for the stock increases, driving up the price. As the price rises and hits the resistance level, investors who bought the stock when the price previously reached the resistance level may decide to sell, taking the opportunity to break even on their purchase.

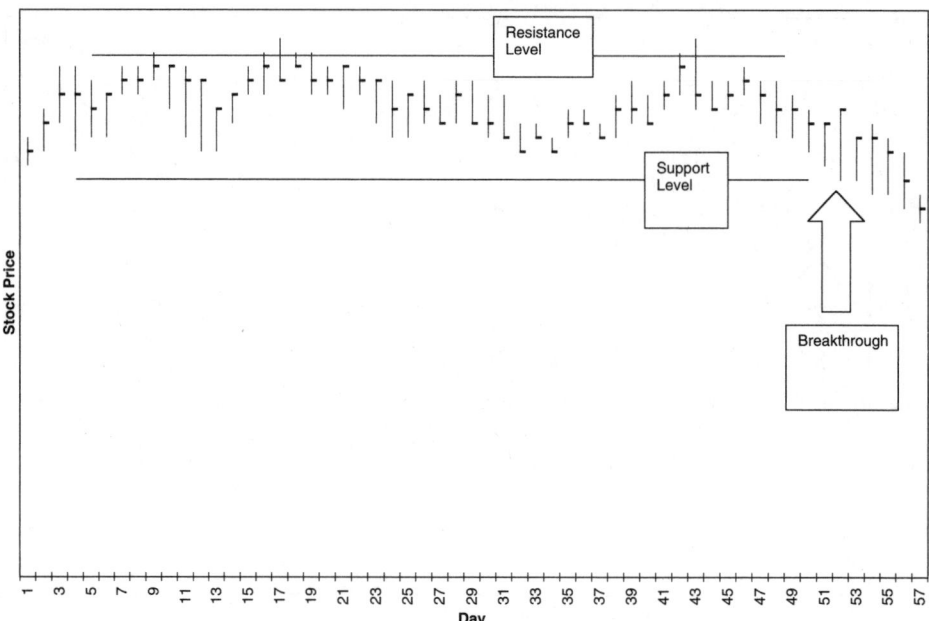

Figure 1.2   Support and resistance levels.

Other investors, noting that this is the stock's highest price in recent history, may take this opportunity to sell at a profit.

Whenever the price of a stock rises above the resistance level or falls below the support level, a breakout occurs. The occurrence of a breakout is significant. The stock has broken out of its old trading range and is now in a new trading range. Investors now expect higher (or lower) stock prices.

Figure 1.2 shows the occurrence of a breakout to the downside. Because the stock price has fallen below the support level, investors will now expect even lower stock prices to occur.

Volume

Many technical analysts consider the volume of stock trading, in addition to the direction of price movement, to be an important consideration. Volume is considered the fuel for a bullish market rally or a bearish market decline. For example, when a new high for a stock is accompanied by heavy volume of trading, the market is considered to be bullish. On the other hand, when a new high is associated with light volume, analysts assume that, because there is not much fueling the rally, the increase in price may be a temporary move.

When a new low occurs with light volume, the light volume indicates low investor participation in the stock price drop. This type of drop is not viewed as significant. However, when a new low occurs with heavy volume, many investors are trading at this lower price. This increased volume is seen as fuel for a downward trend in the market and is extremely bearish.

Bar Charts and Candlestick Charts

The chart that we looked at in Figure 1.1 is a line chart. Consecutive daily closing prices for a stock are connected with a line. Technical analysts produce many types of charts to help them visually recognize stock price patterns. Two of the most common types are bar charts and candlestick charts. In these charts, more than one stock price is recorded for each day.

A bar chart shows the high and low prices for a stock on a given day. Figures 1.2 and 1.3 are examples of bar charts. The high and low price for the day are connected by a vertical line. A horizontal dash, or tick, along the line indicates the closing price.

A candlestick chart shows four prices for a stock on a given day: (1) the opening price, (2) the closing price, (3) the daily high, and (4) the daily low. As on a bar chart, the daily high and daily low prices are connected by a vertical line. A horizontal line crosses this vertical line to indicate the opening price for the day, and another horizontal line crosses the vertical line to indicate the closing price. These horizontal lines are used to form a rectangle, or the body

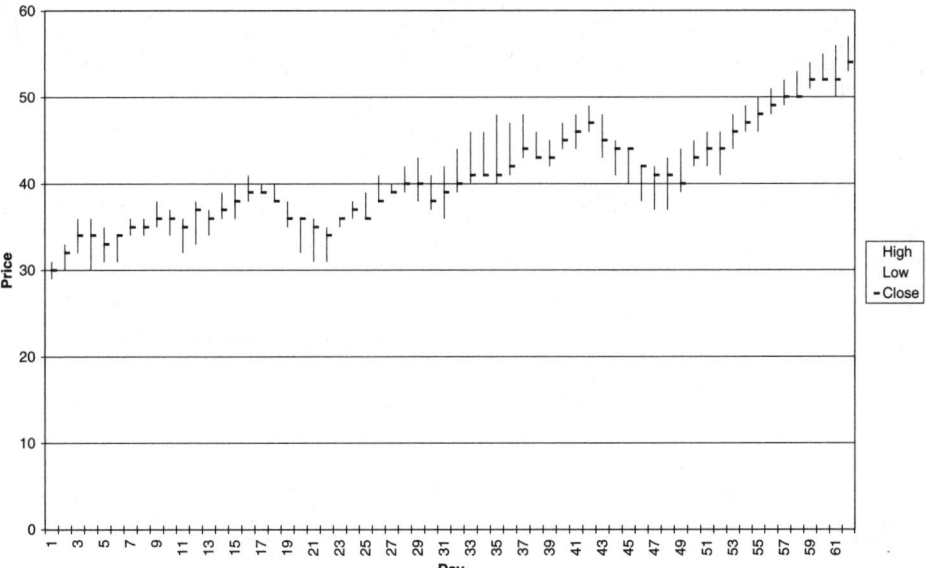

Figure 1.3   Bar chart.

of the candlestick. If the closing price of the day is higher than the opening price, the body of the candlestick is open, or left as white space. If the closing price falls below the opening price, the candlestick is closed, or is filled in as a black area. The vertical line, representing the daily trading range, is the stem of the candlestick. Figure 1.4 is an example of a candlestick chart.

Chart Construction

For many years, traders who relied on technical analysis kept handwritten worksheets on which they recorded daily information such as a stock's opening, high, low, and closing prices. This information was transferred to graph paper, on which a chart, or picture, of the stock prices was constructed. This tedious and time-consuming process was a significant factor in stereotyping technical analysts as being hunched over their desks and constantly focusing on their charts.

Today, however, most of these tasks have been simplified. Computer power has eliminated many of the tedious hours of chart construction. Now, technical analysts can easily store daily stock data in a spreadsheet program. Many of the popular software programs, such as Excel®, will take these daily data and create various types of charts, including line, bar, and candlestick

Figure 1.4 Candlestick chart.

charts. Other software programs that are especially designed for technical analysis are also available. Programs such as OmniTrader allow technicians great flexibility in designing charts. With these programs, analysts can choose various time frames and levels of detail, overlay several types of charts, and backtest trading strategies. Today, technicians can focus much more attention on analysis of the indicator charts and much less on the charts' actual construction.

The Technical Analysis Controversy

Technical analysis is both highly controversial and widely used; some practitioners also claim that it is profitable. They say that historical technical figures, such as the past behavior of a stock's price, give them foresight into future price movements. One study, by Robert Strong, showed that the majority of investment professionals believe that using technical analysis enhances investment performance.

According to reports, the use of technical analysis is widespread. For example, *The Journal of International Money & Finance* reported the results of a survey conducted by the Bank of England among chief foreign exchange dealers based in London in November 1988. At least 90 percent of the respondents placed some weight on technical analysis when making forecasts, and technical analysis was particularly popular when short investment horizons were considered. Many dealers viewed technical and fundamental analysis as complementary, rather than opposing, forms of analysis. Samuel Cherian and I. Malakkal, in November 1989, discussed the emerging idea that fundamental and technical analyses are complementary tools.

Many others, however, claim that the practice of looking at past technical data to help predict the future is outlandish; these opponents liken technical analysis to astrology. Most academics fall into this latter group. Robert Strong's study showed that over 60 percent of PhD's do not believe that technical analysis can be used as an effective tool to enhance investment performance.

Let's turn our attention to the reasons that each of these groups takes an opposing position. We will look first at the arguments supporting the use of technical analysis and then at the arguments against it.

The Pro Camp

As humans, we seem to have a preoccupation with rhythms and cycles. We seem to be hard-wired to expect certain cycles, because we experience cycles all around us. We expect morning always to follow night. Unless we're in the tropics or the far north, we expect hot summer days to be followed by crisp fall weather. We expect the crispness to turn into the cold of winter. We expect the harshness of winter to be thawed by the warmth of spring. We expect the cycle of the seasons to continue.

Whenever a cycle is broken, the event captures our attention. We experience the beauty of a 70 percent sunny day in January much differently than the same type of day in April. The thought of eating pizza at 8:00 A.M. does not sit very well with us. Eating pancakes and sausage at 6:00 P.M. seems odd, but occasionally we find a change in pace—doing something out of cycle—refreshing.

Attraction to cycles and curiosity about their being broken are evident even in infants. A ten-month-old baby appears to expect certain cycles. Tap on a table in a certain broad pattern and the baby will watch and listen intently. Change the pattern of the tapping and the infant will look bewildered, wondering what has happened to the expected cycle of taps.

Technical analysts, such as Roger in our opening scenario, believe that cycles are present in the financial markets. These analysts assume that when investors are faced with situations similar to those they have faced before, they will behave the way they behaved before. The proponents of technical analysis believe that it is inherent in human nature to expect that cycles will recur and to react accordingly. This expectation of recurring cycles influences investors' attitudes, which, in turn, determine stock prices. Thus, technicians view the future as a repetition of the past.

Some technical analysts believe that stock prices have cycles just like those of other phenomena. These technicians view the expectation of cycles as being part of human nature, and they realize that expectations determine the supply and demand for securities. Others take this one step further and claim that the same patterns that scientists—physicists, for example—have discovered in nature are duplicated in the stock market. These analysts believe that cycles have a scientific, not just an emotional, basis. For example, in the 1930s, R. N. Elliot, an accountant, claimed that the basic harmony found in nature occurs in the stock market. Thus, he used mathematical relationships similar to those used by scientists to describe and predict the stock market. This began an entire school of thought, the Elliott Wave Theory, that adheres to the principle that stock price movement forms discernible wave patterns. These analysts believe that basic laws, nearly as exact as the laws of physics, underlie economics and the financial markets.

Within the group of those who would consider themselves technical analysts, there are some subdivisions. Some technical analysts consider technical analysis to be an art form. Martin Pring, a leading technical analyst and president of The International Institute for Economic Research, states in his book *Technical Analysis Explained:*

The art of technical analysis—for it is an art—is to identify trend changes at an early stage and to maintain an investment posture until the weight of the evidence indicates that the trend has reversed.

John J. Murphy, another well-known technician, had earlier shared the view that chart reading is an art. In his book, *Technical Analysis of the Futures Markets,* Murphy discussed how charting is very subjective. He pointed to instances when even experienced chartists disagree on interpretations. He also emphasized how different technicians, practicing their art, will enter the market at a different time and in a different way, even though they may agree on the same market forecast.

Those who view technical analysis as an art form see the trader as being intimately involved with the forecasting model and the predicted outcome. These analysts are artists and designers. They are creative. They search for new insights. They nurture their talents and gifts. Profitable trading systems are their creations. Each technician's actions are unique.

Others view technical analysis more as a science. For example, Edwards and Magee defined technical analysis as:

> . . . the study of the action of the market itself as opposed to the study of the goods in which the market deals. Technical analysis is the science of recording, usually in graphic form, the actual history of trading (price changes, volume of transactions, etc.) in a certain stock or in "the averages" and then deducing from that picture history the probable future trend.

Those who tend to view technical analysis as a "science" claim to be able to deduce future stock price movement from stock price history. They say they do not need to know anything about the company, the industry, or the economic environment to be able to predict future movements. They need only the past data, pictured in a chart, to make their predictions. These analysts may even complain that outside distractions, such as the weather, may influence their scientific prediction. They therefore attempt to minimize any outside influences. Some technical analysts prefer to do their predictions in isolation, in small rooms with no windows, to minimize any biases that their emotions may bring into play. These analysts consider their job merely a mechanical process. They set their emotions aside and follow the rules of the indicator.

Edwards and Magee went further in their description of the scientific technical analyst:

> He may offer to interpret the chart of a stock whose name he does not know, so long as the record of trading is accurate and covers a long enough term to enable him to study its market background and habits.

He may suggest that he could trade with profit in a stock knowing only its ticker symbol, completely ignorant of the company, the industry, what it manufactures or sells, or how it is capitalized . . . if your market technician is really experienced at his business he could, in theory, do exactly what he claims.

Whether it is science or art—whether it represents true, unbiased predictions based on natural laws or a useful tool used by broad-minded, creative traders—technical analysis is indeed frequently used by practitioners.

The Con Camp

Opponents of technical analysis say that using technical analysis to trade stocks is like driving a car while looking into a rearview mirror. A rearview mirror shows you where you have been but it won't warn you about upcoming hazards in the road. If there is a barricade in the middle of the road because of temporary construction work, the view of where you have been gives you no warning to avoid the barricade. The only way to avoid the barricade is to look ahead and see that there has been a fundamental change in the road you are traveling on. Once this fundamental change is recognized, you can change your driving path.

Technical analysis uses only data that show where the market has been before. There is no recognition of fundamental changes in the market. The road ahead is expected to follow the same path and be in the same condition as the road already traveled.

Opponents of technical analysis agree that there may be patterns that, ex-post, can be fitted to stock price movements. However, they argue that we cannot expect this past experience to predict the future. Past patterns cannot be exploited to gain above-average returns in the stock market, for two reasons.

1. There may be some underlying patterns, but the economic environment and the marketplace are always being affected by new factors. For example, we see a business cycle occurring over and over again, so we can expect an expansionary period to follow a recession. But each of these business cycles is unique; they vary in intensity and length.

The stock market has been compared to a pendulum. It swings back and forth from bear market to bull market. However, its movement is more like that of a child on a swing than of the pendulum of a clock, which swings from side to side with perfectly timed precision. Each swing of a pendulum is predictable for its distance and timing. A child on a swing moves forward and back in a cyclical pattern, but sometimes higher and sometimes lower. If the child makes a movement, if a wind gusts, if someone pushes the child, the height of the swing changes. The forward-and-backward cycle still continues but at a different speed and height, and these are not perfectly predictable. Outside sources cause them to vary in type, timing, and intensity.

2.   If we are indeed capable of gathering, from past stock market statistics, information that aids us in predicting future stock market movements, this information will still not allow us to earn abnormal, above-average returns in the stock market. This conclusion is reached because of the assumption of market efficiency—a belief that is widely held throughout the economic and finance communities, especially among the academics in these communities. From these academics, financial analysts such as Jim, in our earlier scenario, learn to be skeptical of *any* use of technical analysis.

In their book, *Investments*, Zvi Bodie, Alex Kane, and Alan J. Marcus explain this rationale:

> The efficient market hypothesis implies that technical analysis is without merit. The past history of prices and trading volume is publicly available at minimal cost. Therefore, any information that was ever available from analyzing past prices has already been reflected in stock prices. As investors compete to exploit their common knowledge of a stock's price history, they necessarily drive stock prices to levels where expected rates of return are exactly commensurate with risk. At those levels one cannot expect abnormal returns.

For these reasons, many people, especially academics, have dismissed the use of technical analysis. The academics' views have been spread throughout society to such a degree that some individuals consider it slanderous to be called a technical analyst. In fact, as Jerry Helzner says, in a *Barron's* article, "they could easily be depicted as rodents scurrying around frantically trying to turn up a tasty morsel, poking here and there in an effort to make a few hundred or a few thousand dollars." In an interview for the December 1997 issue of *Technical Analysis of Stocks and Commodities*, Andrew Lo, Harris & Harris Group Professor of Finance at the Massachusetts Institute of Technology's Sloan School of Management, director of MIT's Laboratory for Financial Engineering, and founder of Sloan's Track in Financial Engineering, admits that he is a "black sheep in the academic community" because of his interest in technical analysis.

In his popular book, *A Random Walk Down Wall Street*, Burton Malkiel makes similar negative comments about those who call themselves technical analysts:

> On close examination, technicians are often seen with holes in their shoes and frayed shirt collars. I, personally, have never known a successful technician, but I have seen the wrecks of several unsuccessful ones.

Malkiel also questions the methods by which technical analysts promote their trade. He claims that when technical analysts make money, it is not from following their own technical advice but because they receive lucrative commissions from customers who follow their advice:

> Though chartists are not held in high repute in Wall Street, their colorful methods, suggesting an easy way to get rich quick, have attracted a wide following.

Let's look a little more closely at the efficient market theory, which claims that the stock market follows a random walk. A random walk occurs when future steps cannot be predicted by past actions. Flipping a coin produces a random walk. If you flip a coin once and it lands on heads, this information gives you no insight to predict whether the coin will land on heads or tails the next time it is thrown. For the stock market, a random walk means that future stock price movements cannot be predicted by past stock price movements because stock prices do not follow a trend.

The random walk theory was popularized in Paul Cootner's book, *The Random Character of Stock Market Prices*, published in 1964, and given further credence by Eugene Fama's seminal article, "The Behavior of Stock Market Prices," published in the *Journal of Business* the following year. The random walk theory is based on the efficient market hypothesis, that stock prices fluctuate randomly around their intrinsic value. If this hypothesis is valid, then any attempt to beat the market will be futile.

The efficient market hypothesis has a great following in the academic community. In fact, academics have taken this hypothesis even further by creating three versions of the efficient market theory: (1) a weak form, (2) a semistrong form, and (3) a strong form. If markets are weak-form efficient, no abnormal profits can be earned by examining past price and volume patterns. Weak-form efficiency rules out the use of technical analysis, which relies solely on past stock market data to predict future stock prices.

If markets are semistrong-form efficient, then no abnormal profits can be earned by using publicly available information. The rationale behind this conclusion is that traders immediately react to any publicly available information, and these actions immediately eat up any potential profits. For example, if it is announced that SuperDrug, Inc. has just discovered a drug that cures diabetes, everyone will assume that SuperDrug will be making lots of money selling this new drug. SuperDrug's higher income will mean more net income for the shareholders and higher earnings per share for the company's stock. Investors will be willing to pay more for a share of SuperDrug's stock. So, in an attempt to buy low and sell high, investors begin buying SuperDrug's stock. As the demand for the company's stock increases, so does the price of the stock. The theory of market efficiency tells us that this increased demand will happen immediately as savvy investors rush to buy the stock at the lowest possible price. Thus, the stock price rises quickly to a new, higher level. Because past stock price history is readily available public information, semistrong market efficiency would rule out the use of technical analysis for earning abnormal returns.

If financial markets are characterized by semistrong market efficiency, economists would argue that the only way to earn abnormal profits would be to act on information that is not publicly available. For example, if you are the research scientist who discovers the diabetes cure, your insider information would enable you to profit by buying the stock before the information is made available to the general public. However, the strong-form market efficiency theory says that even with this type of insider information, it is impossible for an investor to earn abnormal returns.

For many years, the academic community has thought of the market as at least weak-form efficient, if not semistrong-form efficient. Therefore, academics have given little credence to the use of technical analysis.

Testing of Technical Analysis

The pro camp seems to have convincing arguments favoring the use of technical analysis, but the con camp has equally convincing opposing arguments. As with any controversy of this nature, we begin to turn to empirical investigation to determine who is correct.

Most of the testing by academics has focused directly on the efficient market hypothesis. Many academics reason that if markets are efficient, then technical analysis has no value. Therefore, actually testing to see whether trading with technical analysis leads to abnormal profits would be a waste of time. The efficient market hypothesis, or randomness in stock market prices, can be proved only by failing to find any trend in stock market prices. Academics have mainly focused their efforts on using highly sophisticated statistical techniques, and these have failed to uncover any systematic patterns in price action. Practitioners who use technical analysis adhere to the belief that just because academics, using fancy statistics, have not been able to discover the presence of some underlying patterns, real proof that these patterns do not exist is still lacking. These technicians argue that empirical observation and practical experience yield better evidence that stock price patterns exist than the academics' sophisticated statistical models. In a nutshell, practitioners favor empirically testing technical trading techniques to see whether they are profitable, and academics prefer developing statistical techniques that describe the nature of markets and will lead them to conclusions about whether technical analysis could work.

A study by J. Austin Murphy did empirically test whether the use of technical analysis could lead to abnormal profits. After studying sixteen purely technical futures funds during the period from May 1980 to April

1985, Murphy found no statistically significant evidence that any of the technical funds could outperform a simple buy-and-hold investment strategy. He concluded that these findings supported the idea that the futures markets are efficient.

In an entertaining article in the *Sloan Management Review*, Maurice Joy discussed some of the academics' testing of the efficient market hypothesis. He likened the search for market inefficiencies to hunting for the snark, a mysterious, rarely seen beast that is the subject of a Lewis Carroll poem. Hunters do not know whether a snark really exists; investors do not know whether market inefficiencies exist. Some hunters have claimed that they have seen a snark, just as some technicians claim to have seen market inefficiencies; but neither group can produce firm evidence of its sightings. Snarks and market inefficiencies are elusive, but great rewards await someone who is able to capture one.

In another article, in the *Journal of Portfolio Management*, Joy claimed that the usefulness of technical analysis has not been adequately tested. He suggested that the presence of stock market anomalies can lead to superior investment strategies, regardless of the explanation of why these anomalies exist. Finally, he concluded that until there is incontrovertible knowledge of the true state of market efficiency, trading strategies such as technical analysis should be considered. Joy encouraged readers to continue to look for the elusive snark until they could be absolutely sure it did not exist.

Although many academic treatises have supported the efficient market hypothesis, recent studies have uncovered patterns in stock prices. In one of these studies, reported in the *Quarterly Journal of Economics*, Bruce Lehmann observed that when a stock falls by a sizable amount one week, the stock price experiences a sizable rise the following week. This pattern did not always occur for all stocks, but the frequency of the pattern was high enough for Lehmann to conclude that the pattern does create many profit opportunities for traders.

In another study, published in the *Journal of Finance*, Jegadeesh also found predictable patterns in stock prices. In reviewing monthly returns over a long time period (1934–1987), he observed that stocks that had large losses in one month tended to have strong gains in the following month. Conversely, the stocks that had large gains in one month tended to experience large declines in the following month.

Stephen Pruitt and Richard White tested the profitability of a trading system called CRISMA and reported their results in the *Journal of Portfolio Management*. The CRISMA acronym is derived from the names of the system's three component parts: cumulative volume, relative strength, and moving average. These writers claim that trading with this system achieves profitable results that are greater than can be expected by chance alone. Thus, they argue that the market may not be as efficient as many, especially academics, believe it to be.

Claims that top traders rely heavily on technical analysis are common. For example, in 1987, Dinesh Desai, a commodity trading adviser at Desai & Co., managed seven of the top eight performing public futures funds. Desai claimed to have made 85 percent of his trades based on technical analysis. Another trader, Sharhokh Nikkah, is reported to have earned above-average returns for his clients in the volatile energy markets, relying 95 percent on technical analysis. Two of the traders selected in the *Futures* fourth annual emerging commodity trading adviser hunt reported using technical analysis.

Reports claiming that traders have successfully used technical analysis to beat the market generally cover a short time period and a limited market application. Those who believe in the efficient market hypothesis say that these above-average returns should be attributed to luck, not to technical analysis. However, especially over the past decade, more and more people in the investments community seem to be at least considering the idea that technical analysis may have some merit.

In a 1991 article, Neftci suggested that moving average technical indicators may provide some informational content that is useful to traders. In a 1988 interview, Arthur A. Merrill, founder and publisher of the weekly newsletter *Technical Trends*, claimed that technical indicators can be used to identify bear and bull markets. He suggested following 40–50 indicators for optimal results, believing that this type of diversification helps prevent investors from becoming emotionally attached to any one indicator. In a 1987 *Business Week* article, Jeffrey Laderman pointed to an increased interest in technical analysis by fundamental researchers. In *InterMarket*, John Murphy discusses the significant role that technical analysis has played in market linkages.

Thus, the technical analysis controversy continues. Some practitioners are adamantly opposed to its use. Some are strong believers. More and more writers are beginning to question whether technical analysis may serve as one tool available to those who want to trade profitably in the market. And this is the whole reason for this book—to try to shed additional light on this controversy through systematic and unbiased testing of a variety of technical indicators over a long time period.

Chapter

2

Evaluating Indicator Performance

In this chapter, we will employ a big-picture perspective and present some aggregate results from our testing. The in-depth results for each individual indicator will follow in subsequent chapters. Our overall conclusion is: Technical analysis does generally seem to provide some information that can be of value in trading decisions; however, there are various potential pitfalls, as we will point out later in the chapter. Our first task is to explain in detail the tests that we performed. The book contains many tables of results, so it is important to understand exactly what we have done. Our readers come from different backgrounds and we hope that our descriptions of our tests raise some issues not previously considered.

Performance Criteria

How do we tell whether an indicator has any value? This sounds like an easy question that could be answered with: "When we make money with it, stupid!" But, the answer is not that easy. To understand why, we need to explore the question from several different angles and evaluate the criteria that could be used to gauge the worthiness of any particular indicator.

Assume that Fred approaches you with a certain investment opportunity and tells you that it will be a great deal. As evidence, Fred says:

> This has done great over the past four years. A $10,000 investment in the first year would have left you with $22,000 at the end of the year, giving you a +120 percent return on your investment for the year. This is a volatile investment, however. It seems to do really well every *other* year, but the good years are far better than the bad years. The return in the second year was −40 percent, but that was followed by years of +80 percent and −60 percent. There will be some ups and downs with this investment, but on average it is a BIG winner. The average over the past four years was +25 percent, which you can calculate for yourself by just adding the four annual returns and dividing by four.

After checking the average yourself, you are intrigued. This sounds pretty good. Fred seems to be honestly discussing the past results. However, the phrase *volatile investment* sticks in your mind. Something about that worries you. After all, one way of thinking about risk is to consider volatility as risk. Is there some risk here that lies under the surface?

You begin to think about things in another way. You say to yourself: "Fred said how much I would have at the end of the first year, but not how much I would end up with after the fourth year. Maybe I need to look at that."

"If I have $22,000 at the end of the first year and then have a −40 percent return, I will have $13,200 at the end of year two. That's still not bad. If I have $13, 200 at the end of the second year and then have a +80 percent return, I will have $23,760 at the end of year three. That's fantastic. If I have $23,760 at the end of the third year and then have a −60 percent return, I will have $9,504 at the end of year four. That's less than I'm starting with; I would lose money! That bum! Where is Fred's phone number?"

The numbers in the above scenario are correct. The average return is +25 percent over the four years, and yet you end up with less than you start with. This illustrates a major danger with a simple average. A better average to use is what is called the *geometric mean return*. This can be calculated in two different ways. Assume that a certain stock performs as follows over three time periods:

Time Period	Return (%)	Wealth
0		$10,000
1	15%	11,500
2	−5	10,925
3	10	12,018

Time period 0 is the beginning time period. The 15 percent return in the first time period represents the change from the beginning through the end of the first period. The Wealth column shows the impact of the returns on the total wealth of the investment.

There are two different ways to calculate a geometric mean return from the above information. Consider the change in wealth for the first year. The $11,500 is calculated by taking one plus the period return and multiplying by the initial wealth. So, we are multiplying 1.15 times $10,000. In the next period, we would multiply 0.95 (1.00 minus .05) times $11,500 to get $10,925. In the last period, we would multiply 1.10 times $10,925 to get $12,018. One way to calculate a geometric mean return is to multiply the "one-plus" numbers together, take the nth root, where n is the number of time periods, and subtract 1. In other words, we would first multiply 1.15 times 0.95 times 1.10, which gives us 1.202. We would then take the third root of 1.202 and get 1.063. Subtracting 1 from 1.063 leaves 0.063, or 6.3 percent. The 6.3 percent final result is the geometric mean return. The second method for calculating geometric mean return uses the ratio of ending wealth to beginning wealth. We divide the ending wealth of $12,018 by $10,000 to get 1.2018, or 1.202 as a rounded value. Not coincidentally, this is the same number we arrived at in calculating geometric mean return by multiplying the "one-plus" values. Once again, we take the third root to get the final answer of 6.3 percent.

Here are a few calculation details for those who are interested. If you are wondering how to take an nth root of a number, there are some easy ways to do it. If you are using a calculator, you just raise the number to the $1/n$ power. (See the "Exponentiation" or "Powers and Roots" section of your calculator manual for specifics.) In an Excel spreadsheet, to take the third root of 1.202, you would enter $= 1.202^{\wedge}(1/3)$ into a cell. If you have a calculator with financial functions, you could have entered 10,000 as PV, 12,018 as FV, and 3 as N, and then solved for %I. The labeling (PV, FV, N, %I) may vary in some calculators, but should be similar. All we are really doing here is solving for a compound return.

In any discussion of geometric mean return, the important fact is that the strategy having the highest terminal wealth will have the highest geometric mean (or compound) rate of return. Using terminal wealth as a measure to compare two strategies is intuitively appealing and is better than comparing average returns that have been computed as arithmetic mean returns.

One common logical benchmark for comparison is the return or terminal wealth that could have been earned with a buy-and-hold strategy. Buy-and-hold is just what it says; you buy the stock and hold it until the end of the investment horizon—the period under consideration for the investment. The investment horizon could be one month, one quarter, one year, or any other time period. Let's say you buy Digistock on January 1 at a price of $100 per share. With a $10,000 initial investment, you would have purchased 100 shares. Assume that on March 30 the price is $115 per share. Your 100 shares would then be worth $11,500. Your buy-and-hold return for the three months (one quarter) would have been 15.0 percent. The 15 percent increase can be seen by comparing either (1) the final price of $115 per share to the beginning price of $100 per share or (2) the ending value of $11,500 to the initial investment of $10,000. The numbers in this example are easy to follow, but the same idea could be applied to any initial investment and share prices. Notice that this return is not stated in annual terms. If you could do this repeatedly for four quarters, the compounded rate of return would be 74.9 percent. We can compute buy-and-hold returns as if we were buying the stock, holding it for the relevant period, and then selling it at the end of the period. We can then talk about the buy-and-hold return for the period, even though we did not actually perform those steps. Transactions costs (e.g., brokerage commissions) could be factored into the calculation, but we will ignore them for now. We will discuss the impact of transactions costs later.

Now, let's say we want to analyze the performance of a system for investing in Digistock stock, based on a technical indicator. The indicator gives us signals for when to buy and when to sell. We need to make some assumption here about what we are doing with our money when it is not invested in the stock. We will assume that a *cash* position is the other alternative—that is, the money will be kept in a non-interest-bearing account. Sometimes, in investment literature, *cash* is assumed to be an investment in money market securities. In actual practice, this is probably what most investors would be doing. Brokerage accounts often provide that proceeds from the sale of stock are immediately swept into a money market account so that interest is earned. However, we will assume no interest is earned when our hypothetical investor is "out" of the stock. This assumption does not affect the basic conclusions from our tests. See conclusion 9 in Chapter 10 for additional discussion regarding interest and transaction costs.

The buy–sell signals from the technical indicators lead to a switching strategy. The investor switches in and out of two positions: (1) holding the stock and (2) cash. Possible short positions will be discussed later. As an example, let's assume a very simple set of signals. We will return to the hypothetical Digistock numbers used earlier, with a few additional details. Once again, we will assume an investment horizon of one quarter.

Suppose the technical indicator gives a buy indication on January 1, a sell indication on February 1, and a subsequent buy signal on March 1. Further assume that Digistock's stock price on January 1, February 1, March 1, and March 30 was $100, $110, $105, and $115, respectively. With an initial $10,000 investment, how much would the investor have at the end of the investment horizon? On January 1, 100 shares could be purchased with the initial $10,000 investment. If these shares are sold on February 1 at a price of $110 per share, then the proceeds would be $11,000. We will assume that this

$11,000 is held in a non-interest-bearing checking account until March 1. On March 1, the $11,000 is used to buy 104.76 shares of Digistock at $105 per share. In computing our hypothetical returns, we will assume that it is possible to purchase fractional amounts of shares. On March 30, we assume that the 104.76 shares are sold at a price of $115 per share. The terminal wealth from this switching strategy was $12,047, for a one-quarter return of 20.47 percent (or 110.6 percent annually).

If we compare this result to the previously discussed buy-and-hold strategy, the switching strategy looks good: the ending terminal wealth is $12,047 vs. $11,500. The outperformance of the switching strategy is due to the fact that the switching strategy recommended being out of the stock from February 1 to March 1, which was when the price was falling from $110 to $105. We can summarize the comparison in one number by dividing $12,047 by $11,500 to get 1.048. We will refer to numbers of this type as *relative terminal wealth*. Relative terminal wealth values greater than 1.0 mean that the strategy under consideration is outperforming a buy-and-hold strategy. Numbers less than 1.0 mean the strategy is underperforming a buy-and-hold strategy. Using relative terminal wealth as a comparison measure answers a commonsense question: Would we be better off using a switching strategy? It is also fairly easy to calculate.

Relative terminal wealth is straightforward and has intuitive appeal, but it also has a subtle drawback. If a stock's price is generally rising, a buy-and-hold strategy is inherently difficult to beat. If a stock's price is falling, then a buy-and-hold strategy is easier to beat. To understand this point, consider a switching strategy that is governed by flipping a coin. Assume you have a fair (unweighted) coin—the kind you would normally get in change at the grocery store. At the beginning of each day, you flip the coin. If it comes up heads, you either buy shares of Digistock, or you continue holding your shares of Digistock. If it comes up tails, you either sell your shares of Digistock and hold the proceeds as cash, or you continue holding cash. So, heads means you're in the stock, and tails means you're out of the stock. The coin is providing you signals for your switching strategy.

How would you expect the coin-flipping switching strategy to perform? It will perform well when Digistock's price is generally falling, and poorly when Digistock's price is generally rising. Why? On average, the signals will say to be in 50 percent of the time and out 50 percent of the time. If Digistock's price is generally rising, this strategy will make you miss many good days to be in the stock. If the price is generally falling, you will miss more of the bad days than a buy-and-hold strategy would miss. Therefore, for this coin-flipping strategy, we would expect relative terminal wealth greater than 1.0 during periods when the stock is generally falling in price, and relative terminal wealth less than 1.0 when the stock is generally rising in price.

You may still wonder, "So what?" The problem is that if we test some strategy and it generally does well when the stock's price is falling and generally does poorly when the stock's price is rising, then we may effectively be using a strategy that is providing no more guidance than we could get from flipping a coin. The application in this book is that we really want to know whether technical indicators are providing better guidance than we could get from a coin. To do that, we will need to be cautious when we use relative terminal wealth as a performance measure.

A more basic approach to gauging the performance of a technical indicator is to examine the number of correct long signals and the number of correct cash signals. The correctness of a given signal is determined by how the stock's price actually changed. With two possible switching signals (*long* or *cash*) and two possible price change conditions, there are four possible outcomes. We will say that the price change can either be negative or nonnegative. (Nonnegative includes a 0 percent change.) If the indicator signals to go long and the price change is nonnegative, we should be pleased. If the indicator signals to go into cash and the price change is negative, we should also be pleased. If the indicator signals to go long and the price change is negative, we are unhappy because that strategy would cause us to lose money. If the indicator signals to go into cash and the price change is nonnegative, we are unhappy because we have missed an opportunity (assuming the return is nonnegative and positive).

The percentage of correct calls, known as the *hit rate*, can be calculated by dividing the number of correct calls by the total number of calls. For example, assume we have 50 long signals and 30 of these correctly signaled when it would be advantageous to be long. The hit rate would be 30/50, or 60 percent. A no-change condition in the stock's price is lumped together with price increases. The rationale here is that a signal to be *long* the stock when there is no change in price is basically harmless.

The hit rate measure has the disadvantage that it doesn't adjust for the magnitude of the price change. In other words, a correct long signal when the stock rises 1 percent is given the same weight as a correct long signal when the stock rises 2 percent. Therefore, the indicator could be giving long signals that are right about 60 percent of the time, but missing all the big upward moves in stock price. This is just a potential problem to keep in mind. However, one advantage of this approach is its ability to separate the accuracy of the long signals from the accuracy of the cash signals. Some indicators may provide better long signals than cash signals, or vice versa.

Another performance measure is the average return. We can calculate the average return for long signals and compare it to the average return for short signals. We want indicators that have significantly higher returns for long signals. We can also compare them to the average return of a buy-and-hold strategy. Consider the following example:

Day	Signal	Return
1	Long	1%
2	Long	2
3	Cash	0
4	Cash	-2
5	Long	3

The sum of the five returns is 4 percent, so the buy-and-hold daily average is 4 percent divided by 5 days, for an average of 0.8 percent. The average return for the long signals is 2 percent, obtained by adding 1 percent, 2 percent, and 3 percent, and then dividing by 3 days. Similarly, the average return for the cash signals is −1 percent. Results of this type are what we would like to see for long signals. The average return when the indicator says "Go long" exceeds the average buy-and-hold return. In other words, the long signals are saying that we can expect a better-than-average day. Similarly, the cash signals are marking good days for having our money parked in cash, waiting for better times.

In the earlier part of this chapter, we discussed the superiority of a geometric mean return over the arithmetic mean return. In our tables we use both measures of return. The geometric mean return is reported indirectly in the terminal wealth figures. The arithmetic mean is shown as "average return." Why use both? The terminal wealth figures give a truer picture of what will happen to an investment over time. However, it is useful to compare, for example, the average return for long calls versus the average return for cash calls because it reveals whether or not the indicator is accurately discriminating between better-than-average and worse-than-average return days.

Testing Methodology

Our approach straightforwardly follows what an investor might do to implement a technically based trading system. We examine the performance of 60 different technical indicators for 878 stocks over a 12-year period, using daily data. The indicators, data sources, stock selection, and performance calculations are explained below.

There are hundreds of possible technical indicators that a trader might use. New indicators appear frequently in magazines such as *Futures*. Many are variations on the same basic idea or theme. We used 60 indicators that are part of the OmniTrader Version 3.0 Release 9, a popular software package developed and sold by Nirvana Systems, Inc. The package allows traders to examine the historical performance of many technical indicators. It integrates with many different data sources, provides many graphics, and allows the tracking of user-defined portfolios. The tests we conducted could be done by any Omni-Trader user, but they were greatly facilitated by the fact that we obtained a proprietary modification to the standard package that allowed us to capture large batch results in a data file that we analyzed separately.

Nirvana classifies indicators into the following five categories: (1) oscillators, (2) moving averages, (3) patterns, (4) trends, and (5) divergences. The list of technical indicators, with their abbreviated symbols arranged in alphabetical order, is shown in Table 2.1.

Daily stock prices for the 1985–1996 period were the Telescan 2000 prices obtained from Worden Brothers, Inc., one of the leading popular data vendors. The daily prices include open, high, low, and close prices. The starting list of stocks to be examined included all stocks in the S&P 500, Mid-Cap 400, and Small-Cap 600 as of May 1997. Stocks in these indexes are familiar to many investors. Stocks without continuous price data over the entire period were eliminated. This reduced the sample to 878 stocks: 408 stocks in the S&P 500, 240 in the Mid-Cap 400, and 230 in the Small-Cap 600. This particular sample was chosen merely to provide a good mix of industries and company sizes.

To explain the performance calculations, we need to first describe the signals produced by OmniTrader and how those are linked to the return calculations. OmniTrader produces signals that tell when to initiate and exit long and short positions in individual stocks. Some indicators use only closing prices; others may use some combination of the open, high, low, and close. Let's assume that it is Wednesday evening and the user has stock prices for that day and all needed previous days. The system then generates a trading recommendation. If the recommendation is to initiate a long position, then we assume that the stock is purchased at Thursday's opening price. Daily returns from long positions are computed from daily open to daily close. Returns for short positions were the negative of long position returns. The only possibilities were "in" (long or short) or "out" (in cash). For the "out" positions, possible interest on a cash investment was ignored. Transactions costs were also ignored. The existence of transactions costs and the inability to execute at the prices used would tend to lower the returns that would actually be achievable.

One commonly used benchmark is the return from a buy-and-hold (labeled Buy/Hold in the tables) strategy. We used quarterly holding periods and assumed a $10,000 initial investment. The buy-and-hold strategy is just what it says; it assumes that you hold the stock every day. We compare this to a switching strategy based on the signals produced by the technical indicators. To compute the returns for the switching strategy, we also assume a $10,000 initial investment. Daily returns for long positions were computed as described above; returns to cash were zero. The terminal wealth from the switching strategy can be divided by the terminal wealth from the buy-and-hold strategy

Table 2.1
The Sixty Technical Market Indicators Employed

ADX-B	Average Directional Index Breakout
BND-C	Trading Band Crossover
BOL-C	Bollinger Band Crossover
BOL-T	Bollinger Band with ADX
CCI-C	Commodity Channel Index +100/-100 Crossover
CCI-D	Commodity Channel Index Divergence
CCI-FP	Commodity Channel Index Fibonacci Peaks
CCI-P	Commodity Channel Index Peaks
CHA-D	Chaikin Level Divergence
CHA-P	Chaikin Level Peaks
CN-BH	Candle Belt Hold
CN-CA	Candle Counterattack
CN-DS	Candle Doji Star
CN-EL	Candle Engulfing Lines
CN-HAM	Candle Harami Pattern
CN-HMR	Candle Hammer
CN-IHM	Candle Inverted Hammer
CN-MES	Candle Morning-Evening Star
CN-PL	Candle Piercing Line
DMI-C	Directional Movement Crossover
GAP-B	Gap Breakout
KBA-C	Kirshenbaum Bands
MAC-D	Moving Average Convergence/Divergence
MAC-M	Moving Average Convergence Crossover
MFR-B	Money Flow RSI Breakout
MFR-C	Money Flow RSI Crossover
MFR-D	Money Flow RSI Divergence
MOM-P	Momentum Peaks
MV2-C	Moving Average Crossover
ROC-C	Rate of Change Crossover
ROC-D	Rate of Change Divergence
ROC-X	Rate of Change +6/-6 Crossover
RSI-C	Relative Strength Index Crossover
RSI-D	Relative Strength Index Divergence
RSI-P	Relative Strength Index Peaks
RWI-B	Random Walk Breakout
SAR-C	Stop and Reverse Crossover
STO-C	Stochastic +80/+20 Crossover
STO-D	Stochastic Divergence
STO-M	Stochastic Moving Average
STO-P	Stochastic Peaks
TLN-BL	Trendline Break—Long Term
TLN-BM	Trendline Break—Medium Term
TLN-BS	Trendline Break—Short Term
TLN-RL	Trendline Reversal—Long Term
TLN-RM	Trendline Reversal—Medium Term
TLN-RS	Trendline Reversal—Short Term
TRU	Trend Rule Trading
TRX-D	TRIX Divergence
TXM-FP	TRIX Momentum Fibonacci Peaks
TXM-P	TRIX Momentum Peaks
VAP-B	Volume Accumulation Percent Breakout
VAP-C	Volume Accumulation Percent Crossover
VAP-D	Volume Accumulation Percent Divergence
VOL-C	Volume Climax
VOL-T	Volume Trend
VTY-B	Volatility Breakout
WLR-C	Williams %R Crossover
WLR-D	Williams %R Divergence
WLR-P	Williams %R Peaks

to get a relative terminal wealth measure. Values of relative terminal wealth greater than 1.0 signify that the switching strategy outperformed the buy-and-hold strategy in the given time period. We report values of relative terminal wealth in the tables.

Major Results

Does technical analysis work? Yes, technical analysis does work, but with some qualifications. It does not work from a certain perspective. These seemingly contradictory statements may be why technical analysis has been so controversial. The ultimate conclusion you reach about technical analysis depends on how you look at it. We will explain what we mean by this statement later in the chapter.

The big picture has various levels of detail. As a starting point, let's look at the percentages of short, cash, and long signals.

	Short	Cash	Long
Optimal	45.2%	9.2%	45.6%
Sixty Indicators	28.7	43.4	27.9

The line labeled Optimal shows the most advantageous distribution of signals, based on the actual distribution of negative, zero, and positive return days for all stocks during the entire testing period. The line labeled Sixty Indicators shows the distribution of signals from all sixty technical indicators. The high proportion of cash signals for the technical indicators is quite striking. The technical indicators appear to be, in a sense, somewhat conservative. More will be said about this shortly.

The highest levels of results are shown in Tables 2.2 and 2.3. Let's analyze the results one step at a time. In Table 2.2, we report summary results for all sixty indicators for long signals. The figures shown are averaged across all stocks and all quarters for the time period studied. The column labeled "%Long" shows the number of long signals as a percentage of the total. The average for all indicators is 27.9 percent. In other words, the indicators signal to go long on about 27.9 percent of the trading days. This can be compared to the optimal figure of 45.6 percent, meaning that positive returns occurred on 45.6 percent of the days. The fact that long signals from the indicators appear somewhat infrequently may seem worrisome. It is. More will be said about this later.

The average relative terminal wealth from following the long signals is 0.9747. This means that following the long signals from the indicators causes one to underperform a buy-and-hold strategy by about 2½ percent

Table 2.2
Indicator Performance Summary Long Signals
(Average of all stocks 1985–1996)

Indicator	Name	% Long	Relative Terminal Wealth	Long Average Return
ADX-B	Average Directional Index Breakout	59.0%	0.9850	0.056%
BND-C	Trading Band Crossover	39.5%	0.9784	0.056%
BOL-C	Bollinger Band Crossover	44.7%	0.9808	0.060%
BOL-T	Bollinger Band w/ADX	13.4%	0.9701	0.078%
CCI-C	Commodity Channel Index Crossover	22.4%	0.9719	0.061%
CCI-D	Commodity Channel Index Divergence	4.8%	0.9659	0.077%
CCI-FP	Commodity Channel Index Fibonacci Peaks	41.6%	0.9795	0.059%
CCI-P	Commodity Channel Index Peaks	40.6%	0.9787	0.057%
CHA-D	Chaikin Level Divergence	8.8%	0.9668	0.058%
CHA-P	Chaikin Level Peaks	27.6%	0.9720	0.046%
CN-BH	Candle Belt Hold	36.4%	0.9883	0.110%
CN-CA	Candle Counter Attack	0.6%	0.9641	0.091%
CN-DS	Candle Doji Star	0.5%	0.9639	0.063%
CN-EL	Candle Engulfing Lines	25.7%	0.9754	0.074%
CN-HAM	Candle Harami Pattern	17.8%	0.9711	0.069%
CN-HMR	Candle Hammer	5.9%	0.9657	0.055%
CN-IHM	Candle Inverted Hammer	22.8%	0.9724	0.061%
CN-MES	Candle Morning-Evening Star	1.1%	0.9641	0.057%
CN-PL	Candle Piercing Line	2.3%	0.9647	0.073%
DMI-C	Directional Movement Crossover	22.3%	0.9771	0.100%
GAP-B	Gap Breakout	37.8%	0.9757	0.044%
KBA-C	Kirshenbaum Bands	45.8%	0.9815	0.059%
MAC-D	Moving Average Convergence Divergence	3.5%	0.9654	0.076%
MAC-M	Moving Average Convergence Crossover	50.3%	0.9822	0.058%
MFR-B	Money Flow RSI Breakout	56.1%	0.9838	0.057%
MFR-C	Money Flow RSI Crossover	35.2%	0.9765	0.058%
MFR-D	Money Flow RSI Divergence	39.5%	0.9799	0.060%
MOM-P	Momentum Peaks	40.3%	0.9802	0.067%
MV2-C	Moving Average Crossover	56.2%	0.9859	0.062%
ROC-C	Rate of Change Crossover	37.5%	0.9775	0.060%
ROC-D	Rate of Change Divergence	3.4%	0.9649	0.055%
ROC-X	Rate of Change +6/-6 Crossover	38.4%	0.9770	0.055%
RSI-C	Relative Strength Crossover	42.4%	0.9786	0.056%
RSI-D	Relative Strength Divergence	6.5%	0.9662	0.063%
RSI-P	Relative Strength Peaks	41.0%	0.9790	0.060%
RWI-B	Random Walk Breakout System	56.2%	0.9865	0.064%
SAR-C	Stop and Reverse Crossover	53.1%	0.9860	0.068%
STO-C	Stochastic Crossover	24.7%	0.9714	0.051%
STO-D	Stochastic Divergence	7.7%	0.9670	0.071%
STO-M	Stochastic Moving Average	41.4%	0.9782	0.055%
STO-P	Stochastic Peaks	41.0%	0.9798	0.060%
TLN-BL	Trendline Break Long-term	43.2%	0.9813	0.060%
TLN-BM	Trendline Break Medium-term	47.7%	0.9834	0.064%
TLN-BS	Trendline Break Short-term	53.1%	0.9836	0.060%
TLN-RL	Trendline Reversal - Long-term	5.9%	0.9657	0.054%
TLN-RM	Trendline Reversal - Medium-term	7.1%	0.9662	0.058%
TLN-RS	Trendline Reversal - Short-term	11.0%	0.9681	0.064%
TRU	Trend Rule Trading	49.7%	0.9840	0.063%
TRX-D	TRIX Divergence	3.7%	0.9659	0.095%
TXM-FP	TRIX Fibonacci Peaks	46.9%	0.9846	0.071%
TXM-P	TRIX Peaks	45.8%	0.9831	0.068%
VAP-B	Volume Accumulation Percent Breakout	2.0%	0.9646	0.070%
VAP-C	Volume Accumulation Percent Crossover	0.9%	0.9641	0.066%
VAP-D	Volume Accumulation Percent Divergence	5.7%	0.9659	0.064%
VOL-C	Volume Climax	3.7%	0.9648	0.050%
VOL-T	Volume Trend	6.1%	0.9647	0.027%
VTY-B	Volatility Breakout System	53.6%	0.9880	0.069%
WLR-C	Williams %R Crossover	44.7%	0.9802	0.057%
WLR-D	Williams %R Divergence	1.6%	0.9647	0.097%
WLR-P	Williams %R Peaks	44.2%	0.9799	0.057%
	Average	**27.9%**	**0.9747**	**0.064%**

Table 2.3
Indicator Performance Summary Short Signals
(Average of all stocks 1985–1996)

Indicator	Name	% Short	Relative Terminal Wealth	Short Average Return
ADX-B	Average Directional Index Breakout	41.0%	0.9514	0.053%
BND-C	Trading Band Crossover	45.5%	0.9493	0.058%
BOL-C	Bollinger Band Crossover	51.9%	0.9479	0.054%
BOL-T	Bollinger Band w/ADX	9.7%	0.9615	0.039%
CCI-C	Commodity Channel Index Crossover	27.2%	0.9546	0.058%
CCI-D	Commodity Channel Index Divergence	10.3%	0.9614	0.038%
CCI-FP	Commodity Channel Index Fibonacci Peaks	50.4%	0.9475	0.057%
CCI-P	Commodity Channel Index Peaks	50.2%	0.9471	0.059%
CHA-D	Chaikin Level Divergence	11.5%	0.9605	0.047%
CHA-P	Chaikin Level Peaks	41.5%	0.9474	0.067%
CN-BH	Candle Belt Hold	40.1%	0.9585	0.021%
CN-CA	Candle Counter Attack	0.6%	0.9635	0.061%
CN-DS	Candle Doji Star	0.5%	0.9636	0.050%
CN-EL	Candle Engulfing Lines	22.8%	0.9551	0.064%
CN-HAM	Candle Harami Pattern	20.6%	0.9580	0.047%
CN-HMR	Candle Hammer	0.9%	0.9634	0.064%
CN-IHM	Candle Inverted Hammer	0.0%	0.9637	0.000%
CN-MES	Candle Morning-Evening Star	0.8%	0.9635	0.041%
CN-PL	Candle Piercing Line	2.7%	0.9631	0.036%
DMI-C	Directional Movement Crossover	21.0%	0.9618	0.015%
GAP-B	Gap Breakout	31.5%	0.9529	0.057%
KBA-C	Kirshenbaum Bands	49.0%	0.9480	0.057%
MAC-D	Moving Average Convergence Divergence	4.0%	0.9628	0.041%
MAC-M	Moving Average Convergence Crossover	49.6%	0.9486	0.052%
MFR-B	Money Flow RSI Breakout	43.3%	0.9495	0.055%
MFR-C	Money Flow RSI Crossover	48.2%	0.9480	0.057%
MFR-D	Money Flow RSI Divergence	33.4%	0.9522	0.061%
MOM-P	Momentum Peaks	43.3%	0.9501	0.055%
MV2-C	Moving Average Crossover	43.7%	0.9515	0.046%
ROC-C	Rate of Change Crossover	52.4%	0.9477	0.055%
ROC-D	Rate of Change Divergence	7.6%	0.9619	0.040%
ROC-X	Rate of Change +6/-6 Crossover	51.6%	0.9458	0.061%
RSI-C	Relative Strength Crossover	49.7%	0.9468	0.060%
RSI-D	Relative Strength Divergence	7.3%	0.9611	0.061%
RSI-P	Relative Strength Peaks	49.7%	0.9487	0.054%
RWI-B	Random Walk Breakout System	43.8%	0.9521	0.044%
SAR-C	Stop and Reverse Crossover	46.9%	0.9522	0.041%
STO-C	Stochastic Crossover	29.3%	0.9541	0.057%
STO-D	Stochastic Divergence	8.4%	0.9603	0.068%
STO-M	Stochastic Moving Average	53.5%	0.9462	0.058%
STO-P	Stochastic Peaks	49.9%	0.9481	0.055%
TLN-BL	Trendline Break Long-term	38.2%	0.9511	0.055%
TLN-BM	Trendline Break Medium-term	40.8%	0.9527	0.046%
TLN-BS	Trendline Break Short-term	46.0%	0.9503	0.051%
TLN-RL	Trendline Reversal - Long-term	3.7%	0.9623	0.066%
TLN-RM	Trendline Reversal - Medium-term	5.2%	0.9622	0.051%
TLN-RS	Trendline Reversal - Short-term	10.0%	0.9612	0.043%
TRU	Trend Rule Trading	40.0%	0.9527	0.046%
TRX-D	TRIX Divergence	4.3%	0.9628	0.034%
TXM-FP	TRIX Fibonacci Peaks	44.1%	0.9529	0.043%
TXM-P	TRIX Peaks	42.6%	0.9520	0.048%
VAP-B	Volume Accumulation Percent Breakout	1.5%	0.9634	0.034%
VAP-C	Volume Accumulation Percent Crossover	0.5%	0.9636	0.053%
VAP-D	Volume Accumulation Percent Divergence	9.0%	0.9610	0.051%
VOL-C	Volume Climax	5.5%	0.9619	0.056%
VOL-T	Volume Trend	31.6%	0.9531	0.057%
VTY-B	Volatility Breakout System	46.4%	0.9537	0.039%
WLR-C	Williams %R Crossover	51.5%	0.9470	0.058%
WLR-D	Williams %R Divergence	3.0%	0.9630	0.039%
WLR-P	Williams %R Peaks	54.2%	0.9468	0.055%
	Average	**28.7%**	**0.9551**	**0.050%**

per quarter. This is very disappointing. Suppose you choose a certain group of indicators and a certain group of stocks, and then automatically follow all the long signals from those indicators for one quarter. Our results suggest that, on average, you will underperform a buy-and-hold strategy. Some indicators work better than others. Some stocks seem to be better suited to technically based trading than others. Results are better in some time periods than in others, so you might possibly do better than the average result. However, our results throw up a giant caution flag; the average result will probably be disappointing. But, not all the news concerning the technical indicators is bad.

The last column in the table is labeled "Long Average Return." This is the average daily return for the days when the indicator signal is "Go long." The grand average is 0.064 percent. For this to have any meaning, a yardstick is needed. A logical yardstick is the average daily return for a buy-and-hold strategy, which is 0.055 percent. This is good news! When the technical indicators signal "Go long," the advice tends to be favorable. On those days, you will probably earn a return that is better than the average daily return (0.064 percent vs. 0.055 percent). So, the indicators do seem to contain information. When you see a long signal from one of the technical indicators, it probably means that a positive return will follow.

If the long signals are generally good, then why is the relative terminal wealth less than 1? The answer is found in the "%Long" column. We have noted that the long signals contain information and generally signal good days to be long. The problem is that they occur relatively infrequently: only 27.9 percent of the time versus an optimal value of 45.6 percent. Many positive returns are being missed by following the technical indicators.

The results for each indicator will be examined in great detail in subsequent chapters. However, a few summary observations may be useful now. The results vary considerably from one indicator to the next, as can be seen in Table 2.2. The long average return ranges from a high of 0.110 percent for the Candle Belt Hold (CN-BH) indicator to a low of 0.027 percent for the Volume Trend (VOL-T). The %Long figure varies from a high of 59.0 percent for Average Directional Index Breakout (ADX-B) to a low of 0.5 percent for the Candle Doji Star (CN-DS).

The quality of the long signals, as evidenced by the long average return, is extremely good for many of the indicators. Five of the indicators—Candle Belt Hold (CN-BH), Directional Movement Crossover (DMI-C), Williams %R Divergence (WLR-D), TRIX Divergence (TRX-D), and Candle Counter Attack (CN-CA)—have long average returns that are above 0.090 percent, which is more than 50 percent greater than the average buy-and-hold daily return. Only six of the sixty indicators have long average returns lower than the average buy-and-hold daily return.

The difficulty with the five indicators with the highest long average returns is that some generate few long signals. Three of these indicators signal to be long less than 4 percent of the time. So, when they say "Go long" it is generally very good advice but it doesn't happen very often. The other way to look at things is from the cash position. If we are only "in" the stock about 4 percent of the time, then we are "in" cash about 96 percent of the time. This is one of the reasons why the relative terminal wealth figures are lower than desired.

The basic difficulty here is that when the indicators say "Go long" they are generally right, but there are many days when they effectively say, "We don't know—just put your money in cash." Generally, the indicators seem to be providing useful information. How to capitalize on this information is an interesting question that will be discussed in some detail later in this chapter.

The results for the short signals, shown in Table 2.3, are more troubling. The major problem is that they all have a positive average return. If we want to go short, we want the return to be negative, not positive. The signals here are, in a sense, perverse. The relative terminal wealth figure was calculated assuming that if we go short, we are earning the negative of the actual price change. When we are not short, we are invested in cash, earning nothing. The average relative wealth figure is 0.9615, which is worse than the average for the long signals. If the short signals are generally providing bad guidance whereas the long signals are generally providing good guidance, albeit infrequently, then the fact that the average relative terminal wealth is lower than that for the long signals makes sense.

We might be tempted to conclude that the short signals are basically worthless. However, that is not true. The short average return is 0.050 percent, which can be compared to the long average return of 0.064 percent and the buy-and-hold return of 0.055 percent. The short signals seem to point out days when the return will probably be lower than the average for all days. So, the signals do seem to contain some valuable information, but that information is not as good as we would like it to be.

Ignoring the Candle Inverted Hammer (CN-IHM), which does not generate short signals, the indicator with the lowest short average return is Directional Movement Crossover (DMI-C). This indicator is, in a sense, reasonably good. The average short return is positive, which is undesirable, but it is fairly low at 0.015 percent and occurs 21.0 percent of the time. Therefore, this indicator is doing a fairly good job of pointing out days that are going to have lower-than-average returns. This information would seem to have some value. The question is: How do we capitalize on it? We will address this question in Chapter 10.

What is the bottom line here? Earlier, we said that the conclusions reached about technical analysis depend on how one looks at it. Suppose 1,000 investors each start with a $10,000 initial investment, and each decides on one technical indicator to use for trading just one stock. Our results show that the average outcome for these investors will be worse than they would obtain by following a buy-and-hold strategy. This is true for two reasons. First, our aggregate results show that the average relative terminal wealth for all stocks for all quarters was 0.9747. Second, our calculations ignore transactions costs and are, in many ways, best-case scenarios. Actual results will probably be worse. Notice that we have used the term *average outcome*. Some of the 1,000 investors will probably do well, depending on the indicator and the stock they choose. But the odds still favor the buy-and-hold approach. From this vantage point, technical analysis does not work.

However, there is another vantage point. The signals from the technical indicators do, on average, provide valuable information. When the indicators signal long, it is generally desirable to be long. When they signal to go short, it is generally desirable to go short. The complicating factor is that these signals tend to occur somewhat infrequently, leading to many days of simply maintaining a cash position. Because returns, on average, are positive, this strategy leads to many missed opportunities and accounts for the poor relative wealth result described above. The question becomes: How do we capitalize on the information, which is generally good, being provided by the indicators?

To understand the issue better, let's enlist a more general perspective. The one-day return for every stock is positive, negative, or zero. Our problem is that we don't know, with certainty, which of the three outcomes is going to happen. We would like to have some method of obtaining a signal that would tell us which of the three outcomes is most likely. Let's call this the *direction problem*. Being somewhat greedy, we would also like to know something about the magnitude of the positive and negative outcomes. Let's call this the *magnitude problem*. Overall, we are looking for methods that give us good signals concerning which stocks to buy and when to buy them. But, there are many different possibilities for *good* signals. Some methods might be good at solving the direction problem, but not give us much guidance concerning the magnitude issue. Other methods might be great regarding magnitude, but not be good discriminators concerning the direction issue. Our results for technical indicators are more like the latter situation; they tend to signal larger movements, but are often silent regarding smaller movements.

In addition to the direction and magnitude problems, we also face a *portfolio management problem*. Over the longer term, how do we actually exploit methods that provide good signals? Consider, once again, the buy-and-hold strategy. The signal is simple: Always go long! This is not a very good discriminator on either the direction or magnitude dimensions, so why does it perform fairly well? Because, on average, stocks do well. However, this strategy really shines with respect to the portfolio management problem. From a portfolio management perspective, the only strategy that would be simpler would be to never buy at all.

We began this chapter by asking: How do we tell whether an indicator is any good? We know now that this is not an easy question to answer. Our results show that many of the technical indicators are *good*, but exploiting this good information is not easy. Portfolio management for the buy-and-hold strategy is straightforward and easy. Portfolio management that attempts to exploit generally correct but infrequent trading signals is not straightforward. This problem will be addressed in Chapter 10.

Before dealing with more complicated issues, we need to examine the test results in more detail. This will be done in Chapters 3 through 7. The indicator results are grouped by major category, and the results for each category are the subjects of separate chapters.

Chapter

3

Moving Average Indicators

The moving average is one of the oldest and most popular tools used by technical analysts. Because daily fluctuations in stock prices can be great, analysts use moving averages to tone down fluctuations. Moving averages smooth erratic data, making it easier to view the true underlying trend. This allows analysts to look at a smooth trend and to deemphasize daily, distorting fluctuations.

The most commonly used moving average is the simple moving average, sometimes referred to as the arithmetic moving average. It is constructed by adding a set of data, such as the closing prices of a security, and then dividing by the number of observations in the period. For example, to calculate a 21-day simple moving average for a hypothetical company, HypoTech, you would begin by summing the closing stock prices for HypoTech for the past 21 days. Then you would divide this sum by 21 to give you the mean closing stock price for HypoTech for the past 21 days. In the example given for this hypothetical company in Table 3.1, the moving average on Day 21 would be the mean of the closing stock price for the company for Days 1 through 21, or 100.24.

On Day 22, the moving average changes. To calculate the moving average for Day 22, the mean closing stock price for Days 2 through 22 is calculated. The stock price for Day 1 is dropped from the data set, and the stock price for Day 22 is added.

Table 3.1
Moving Average Calculation: HypoTech

Day	Closing Stock Price	Simple Moving Average	Exponential Moving Average
1	102		
2	100		
3	103		
4	101		
5	98		
6	96		
7	100		
8	102		
9	104		
10	103		
11	100		
12	99		
13	97		
14	95		
15	99		
16	104		
17	102		
18	101		
19	100		
20	101		
21	98	100.24	
22	94	99.86	99.67
23	95	99.62	99.42
24	97	99.33	99.38
25	103	99.43	99.67
26	102	99.62	99.66
27	99	99.76	99.56
28	101	99.81	99.87
29	102	99.81	100.01
30	100	99.62	99.83
31	104	99.67	100.02
32	102	99.76	99.88
33	97	99.67	99.51
34	94	99.52	99.15
35	93	99.43	98.93
36	94	99.19	98.94
37	91	98.57	98.45
38	95	98.24	98.25
39	96	98.00	98.03
40	95	97.76	97.73
41	98	97.62	97.78
42	97	97.57	97.56
43	98	97.76	97.61
44	99	97.95	97.87
45	102	98.19	98.32
46	100	98.05	98.35
47	103	98.10	98.50
48	103	98.29	98.54
49	102	98.33	98.62
50	100	98.24	98.48
51	98	98.14	98.22
52	106	98.24	98.86
53	105	98.38	98.85
54	103	98.67	98.80
55	105	99.19	99.24
56	102	99.62	99.45
57	100	99.90	99.65
58	101	100.38	100.00
59	97	100.48	100.07
60	99	100.62	100.34

Calculation of the simple moving average gives equal weight to each daily price. The information that is contained in the closing price for each of the past 21 days is given equal importance. In certain situations, more recent observations may contain more relevant information than earlier observations; the theory is that the most recent day's price has more bearing on a security's future price direction. Weighting data in favor of the most recent observation gives this recent observation more importance in the moving average calculation. Calculating an exponential moving average gives the most recent day's stock price more weight.

Let's refer to the example in Table 3.1. The simple moving average on Day 21 was 100.24. The stock price on Day 22 was $94, far below the mean price for the previous 21 days. In calculating the mean price, or the simple moving average, the stock price of each of the 21 days has an equal weight of 1/21, or 4.76 percent. To calculate the exponential moving average for Day 22, we use the 21-day simple moving average for Day 21 and the stock price for Day 22. Now we are including 22 days of stock price information. Instead of each stock price having an equal weight of 1/22, or 4.55 percent, the latest stock price, the stock price of Day 22, has a greater weight. If we want the stock price of Day 22 to have a weight twice as great as it would have in a simple moving average, it would have a weight of 2/22, or 9.09 percent. Because the total of all of the weights in the calculation of the exponential moving average must sum to 100 percent, this leaves 100 percent − 9.09 percent, or 90.91 percent weight to be placed on the 21-day moving average.

Thus, the general formula for determining the weight of the current day's stock price when calculating an exponential moving average is:

$$\text{WEIGHT}_{sp} = 2/(\text{number of days in simple moving average} + 1).$$

In this case, the calculation gave us $\text{WEIGHT}_{sp} = 2/(21 + 1) = 9.09$ percent. The general formula for determining the weight given to the simple average is:

$$\text{WEIGHT}_{sma} = 100 \text{ percent} - \text{WEIGHT}_{sp}.$$

In this example, we have $\text{WEIGHT}_{sma} = 100$ percent − 9.09 percent = 90.91 percent.

The formula for calculating the exponential moving average is:

$$\text{EMA}_{\text{Day 1}} = \text{WEIGHT}_{sp} \cdot \text{Stock Price}_{\text{Day 1}} + \text{WEIGHT}_{sma} \cdot \text{Simple Moving Average}_{\text{Day 0}}.$$

For Day 22, this calculation is $\text{EMA} = 9.09$ percent $\cdot$ 94 + 90.91 percent $\cdot$ 100.24 = 99.67.

The exponential moving average for Day 22 is 99.67; the simple moving average for Day 22 is 99.86. Notice that the stock price for Day 22 is $94, far below the mean price for the previous 21 days. A new stock price observation below the previous mean value will bring the new mean value calculation down; on Day 22, the simple moving average drops from 100.24 to 99.86. In the exponential moving average calculation, this new stock price observation is given additional weight, causing the exponential moving average to be pulled down even more than the simple moving average.

Many technical indicators are based on the idea of a moving average. Now that we have seen what moving averages entail, let's focus our attention on the performance of the indicators we include in this chapter. In all, we will look at twelve of these moving average indicators.

Trading Band Crossover

The Trading Band Crossover (BND-C) system is based on trading bands, sometimes called envelopes, and on the principle that a stock's price tends to oscillate, by a fixed percent, around the moving average of that stock's price. The moving average represents the center of the stock price trend, and the bands represent the maximum divergences from this center. Thus, the bands outline the boundaries of the stock's normal trading range. Drawing two symmetrical lines parallel to the moving average, one above and one below, constructs these boundaries.

The rationale for this system is that overzealous buyers and sellers push the price of a security to extremes (the levels of the bands). The price then stabilizes and moves to a more realistic level within the bands. For example, as a stock price approaches the upper band, or the stock's resistance level, investors see the stock price as a relatively high price that has not been surpassed in recent times. Skittish investors who have been contemplating selling begin to liquidate their holdings to lock in their gains. As these investors begin selling, there is downward pressure on price. As the price falls and approaches the lower band, or the stock's support level, investors who have been wanting to purchase this stock hurry to take advantage of this buying opportunity. This drives the price back up toward a more realistic level.

Construction

First, calculate a moving average. Typically, a 21-day exponential moving average is used. Next, draw exact copies of this moving average a fixed percentage (usually, 5 percent) above and below the moving average. This creates bands that are drawn parallel to the 21-day exponential moving average.

Trades are triggered whenever price moves outside the bands but the close for the day is inside the bands. A long signal is generated when the stock price falls through the lower band, but the close for the day is within the band. A short signal is triggered on a day when the stock price has broken through the upper band but closes within the band.

Results

On balance, the Trading Band Crossover indicator works as well as the typical indicator in the sixty-indicator sample we tested. The long hits rate averages 61.4 percent (Table 3.2a), and the average short hits rate is 60.7 percent (Table 3.2b).

The BND-C long average shows that the system makes long calls 39.5 percent, slightly less often than the average optimal long call rate of 40.0 percent. If the indicator says to favor a long position over a cash position, the advice is generally correct. The average return for long signals is 0.056 percent, compared to an average stock return of only 0.055 percent for cash signals. Therefore, when the Trading Band Crossover makes a long call, the indicator is, on average, performing only slightly better than the average return.

With an average long hits rate of 61.4 percent and with the return for long calls exceeding, on average, the return of cash calls, an investor is receiving good advice from this system. However, a trader trading long with this system will, on average, earn a lower quarterly rate of return than an investor who follows a simple buy-and-hold strategy. In fact, the trader following the Trading Band Crossover will have terminal wealth that is only 97.8 percent of that of the buy-and-hold investor. Even though the trader is in the correct position the majority of the time, the trader is in an incorrect cash position 24 percent of the time. Therefore, almost one out of every four days, the trader is out of the market and foregoing a positive return, which on average is 0.055 percent. The losses this trader is avoiding by being in a correct out-of-the-market position 36.5 percent of the time are not large enough to justify missing out on the positive return days when the Trading Band Crossover incorrectly calls a cash position.

When the choice is between a short position and cash, the indicator tends to provide poor guidance. The Trading Band Crossover system makes short calls 45.5 percent of the time. This puts the investor in a short position much more often than the optimal rate of 39.4 percent of the time.

The short return results shown in Table 3.3 reveal a problem: the average return for short signals is 0.058 percent compared to 0.053 percent for cash signals. The average return on days when a short position is recommended is positive, not negative. Thus, the short signals tend to indicate days on which the market has above-average positive price movement. The positive average price movement for these short calls results in declining wealth for a trader who follows the short calls of this system. In fact, an investor beginning with a $10,000 investment and trading short with the Trading Band Crossover system for a quarter would, on average, have a terminal wealth of only $9,850 at the end of the quarter. Treat the short signals for this indicator with a degree of caution!

Overall, the Trading Band Crossover indicator seems to provide a small degree of useful information when it comes to making decisions to go long. However, the Bollinger Band Crossover indicator, discussed next, performs even better at making long calls.

Bollinger Band Crossover

John Bollinger has developed a trading system based on the Trading Band Crossover that was described in the previous section. The trading bands in the Bollinger Band Crossover (BOL-C) system contract and expand according to market forces rather than lying a fixed percentage above and below the exponential moving average. These trading bands respond to the volatility of the stock's price: they expand when volatility increases and contract when volatility decreases. The bands are self-adjusting; they automatically widen during periods of extreme price changes and automatically become narrow during periods of small price changes. The automatic widening allows the bands to be more "forgiving" of price changes during more volatile markets. Likewise, when stock price volatility is low, relatively small changes in price can be significant, resulting in a need for tighter bands. Thus, the system identifies overbought and oversold levels on the basis of observed volatility of the stock's price.

Bollinger notes that a price move that originates at one band usually travels all the way to the other band. This observation is helpful when setting price targets. Bollinger also observes that band tightening, associated with shrinking volatility, is often followed by a sharp price move.

Construction

As with the Trading Band Crossover, a P-period exponential moving average is calculated and plotted. To construct the bands, standard deviation (SD) is used to measure volatility. Standard deviation is calculated as follows:

If

P = number of periods considered in the exponential moving average, and

EMA = P-period exponential moving average of the stock's close,

then

$$SUM = (Close_1 - EMA)^2 + (Close_2 - EMA)^2 + \ldots + (Close_p - EMA)^2, \text{ and}$$

$$SD = (\text{Square root of SUM})/P.$$

Table 3.2a
Trading Band Crossover (BND-C) Long Hit Analysis
(Average of all stocks)

Qtr	Optimal Long	BND-C Long	Long Hits	Cash Hits	Total Hits	Long Right	Long Wrong	Cash Right	Cash Wrong
85:1	32.1%	19.6%	66.6%	68.8%	68.3%	13.1%	6.6%	55.3%	25.1%
85:2	30.2%	31.0%	65.2%	70.0%	68.5%	20.2%	10.8%	48.3%	20.7%
85:3	26.3%	35.7%	61.6%	75.2%	70.4%	22.0%	13.7%	48.4%	15.9%
85:4	36.6%	31.7%	69.0%	64.3%	65.8%	21.9%	9.8%	43.9%	24.3%
86:1	44.2%	25.0%	66.1%	55.8%	58.4%	16.5%	8.5%	41.9%	33.2%
86:2	39.7%	32.6%	62.0%	60.6%	61.1%	20.2%	12.4%	40.9%	26.5%
86:3	37.0%	51.3%	57.8%	63.4%	60.5%	29.6%	21.6%	30.9%	17.8%
86:4	38.5%	49.6%	62.5%	63.0%	62.8%	31.0%	18.6%	31.7%	18.7%
87:1	44.7%	24.6%	66.0%	55.5%	58.1%	16.2%	8.4%	41.9%	33.5%
87:2	40.0%	50.5%	60.8%	61.9%	61.3%	30.7%	19.8%	30.7%	18.9%
87:3	39.5%	36.0%	61.1%	60.6%	60.8%	22.0%	14.0%	38.8%	25.3%
87:4	37.9%	52.0%	55.0%	62.0%	58.4%	28.6%	23.4%	29.8%	18.2%
88:1	41.3%	29.8%	64.8%	59.8%	61.3%	19.3%	10.5%	42.0%	28.2%
88:2	39.3%	36.8%	63.3%	61.4%	62.1%	23.3%	13.5%	38.8%	24.4%
88:3	35.9%	36.9%	62.7%	64.3%	63.7%	23.1%	13.8%	40.6%	22.5%
88:4	36.3%	39.8%	63.8%	64.0%	63.9%	25.4%	14.4%	38.5%	21.7%
89:1	39.0%	30.9%	64.9%	61.1%	62.2%	20.1%	10.8%	42.2%	26.9%
89:2	40.2%	26.8%	65.7%	59.8%	61.4%	17.6%	9.2%	43.7%	29.5%
89:3	39.9%	26.5%	65.6%	60.2%	61.6%	17.4%	9.1%	44.3%	29.2%
89:4	38.3%	55.0%	60.5%	62.7%	61.5%	33.3%	21.7%	28.2%	16.8%
90:1	36.9%	54.8%	59.7%	64.6%	61.9%	32.7%	22.1%	29.2%	16.0%
90:2	39.2%	41.6%	63.4%	61.4%	62.2%	26.4%	15.2%	35.8%	22.5%
90:3	33.5%	58.6%	53.9%	66.1%	59.0%	31.6%	27.0%	27.4%	14.0%
90:4	40.8%	44.5%	63.1%	59.2%	60.9%	28.1%	16.4%	32.9%	22.6%
91:1	44.1%	23.2%	66.6%	55.8%	58.3%	15.4%	7.7%	42.9%	34.0%
91:2	39.7%	31.7%	61.3%	60.5%	60.8%	19.5%	12.3%	41.3%	27.0%
91:3	40.4%	39.6%	61.3%	59.7%	60.3%	24.3%	15.3%	36.1%	24.4%
91:4	41.2%	45.9%	59.3%	58.4%	58.8%	27.2%	18.7%	31.6%	22.5%
92:1	40.0%	27.5%	54.9%	59.2%	58.0%	15.1%	12.4%	42.9%	29.6%
92:2	38.6%	43.2%	57.7%	61.6%	59.9%	25.0%	18.3%	34.9%	21.8%
92:3	40.3%	43.3%	61.0%	59.7%	60.3%	26.4%	16.9%	33.9%	22.8%
92:4	41.9%	38.0%	62.7%	57.9%	59.7%	23.8%	14.2%	35.9%	26.1%
93:1	42.5%	37.2%	60.6%	57.4%	58.6%	22.6%	14.7%	36.0%	26.8%
93:2	42.1%	46.7%	59.1%	57.9%	58.5%	27.6%	19.1%	30.9%	22.4%
93:3	42.5%	42.7%	60.6%	57.5%	58.8%	25.9%	16.8%	32.9%	24.4%
93:4	41.5%	46.2%	58.6%	58.5%	58.5%	27.1%	19.1%	31.5%	22.4%
94:1	40.4%	42.0%	56.5%	58.9%	57.9%	23.8%	18.3%	34.1%	23.8%
94:2	40.6%	58.0%	57.8%	59.5%	58.5%	33.5%	24.5%	25.0%	17.0%
94:3	41.8%	43.7%	61.0%	58.5%	59.6%	26.6%	17.0%	33.0%	23.4%
94:4	39.5%	50.2%	57.9%	60.9%	59.4%	29.0%	21.2%	30.3%	19.5%
95:1	43.1%	41.8%	61.8%	57.5%	59.3%	25.9%	16.0%	33.4%	24.7%
95:2	43.7%	34.2%	61.5%	56.3%	58.1%	21.1%	13.2%	37.0%	28.8%
95:3	43.9%	31.6%	62.4%	56.1%	58.1%	19.7%	11.9%	38.4%	30.0%
95:4	43.4%	42.4%	59.9%	56.5%	58.0%	25.4%	17.0%	32.5%	25.0%
96:1	45.5%	35.8%	62.0%	54.5%	57.2%	22.2%	13.6%	35.0%	29.2%
96:2	42.1%	35.4%	58.4%	57.9%	58.0%	20.7%	14.8%	37.4%	27.2%
96:3	42.6%	51.8%	59.6%	58.1%	58.9%	30.9%	20.9%	28.0%	20.2%
96:4	44.3%	40.9%	61.0%	55.9%	57.9%	24.9%	16.0%	33.0%	26.1%
AVG	40.0%	39.5%	61.4%	60.4%	60.6%	24.0%	15.4%	36.5%	24.0%

Table 3.2b
Trading Band Crossover (BND-C) Short Hit Analysis
(Average of all stocks)

Qtr	Optimal Short	BND-C Short	Short Hits	Cash Hits	Total Hits	Short Right	Short Wrong	Cash Right	Cash Wrong
85:1	34.3%	57.5%	68.1%	66.2%	67.3%	39.2%	18.3%	28.1%	14.3%
85:2	34.6%	48.3%	71.4%	65.9%	68.6%	34.5%	13.8%	34.1%	17.6%
85:3	38.6%	45.3%	76.2%	61.6%	68.2%	34.5%	10.8%	33.7%	21.0%
85:4	33.1%	52.7%	65.0%	67.9%	66.3%	34.2%	18.5%	32.1%	15.2%
86:1	35.2%	57.1%	56.0%	65.6%	60.1%	32.0%	25.2%	28.1%	14.7%
86:2	39.8%	52.2%	60.7%	61.2%	60.9%	31.7%	20.5%	29.2%	18.6%
86:3	42.7%	37.1%	64.2%	58.0%	60.3%	23.8%	13.3%	36.5%	26.4%
86:4	38.7%	40.1%	63.4%	62.3%	62.7%	25.4%	14.7%	37.3%	22.6%
87:1	36.9%	62.1%	55.5%	64.5%	58.9%	34.5%	27.7%	24.4%	13.4%
87:2	40.0%	39.4%	62.3%	60.4%	61.1%	24.5%	14.9%	36.6%	24.0%
87:3	40.4%	52.2%	60.7%	60.3%	60.5%	31.7%	20.5%	28.8%	19.0%
87:4	45.3%	26.6%	63.6%	55.0%	57.3%	16.9%	9.7%	40.4%	33.0%
88:1	36.7%	62.5%	59.6%	64.1%	61.3%	37.2%	25.2%	24.1%	13.5%
88:2	37.4%	53.5%	61.4%	63.2%	62.3%	32.8%	20.6%	29.4%	17.1%
88:3	38.4%	51.9%	64.1%	62.0%	63.1%	33.3%	18.6%	29.8%	18.3%
88:4	37.0%	48.7%	64.2%	63.6%	63.9%	31.3%	17.4%	32.6%	18.7%
89:1	36.2%	54.2%	61.2%	64.1%	62.5%	33.1%	21.0%	29.4%	16.4%
89:2	35.9%	54.1%	60.4%	64.7%	62.4%	32.7%	21.4%	29.7%	16.2%
89:3	36.4%	53.1%	60.9%	64.5%	62.6%	32.3%	20.8%	30.3%	16.6%
89:4	39.0%	30.3%	63.1%	60.9%	61.6%	19.1%	11.2%	42.4%	27.2%
90:1	40.1%	32.8%	64.6%	60.1%	61.6%	21.2%	11.6%	40.4%	26.8%
90:2	37.8%	45.2%	61.4%	63.1%	62.3%	27.8%	17.5%	34.5%	20.2%
90:3	45.7%	26.1%	66.5%	54.1%	57.3%	17.4%	8.8%	40.0%	33.9%
90:4	37.6%	42.1%	58.7%	63.0%	61.2%	24.7%	17.4%	36.5%	21.4%
91:1	36.7%	58.7%	55.5%	64.6%	59.2%	32.6%	26.2%	26.7%	14.6%
91:2	40.4%	54.3%	60.6%	60.7%	60.6%	32.9%	21.4%	27.7%	17.9%
91:3	39.8%	46.5%	60.0%	61.3%	60.7%	27.9%	18.6%	32.7%	20.7%
91:4	40.5%	39.7%	58.4%	59.5%	59.0%	23.2%	16.5%	35.9%	24.4%
92:1	43.2%	55.7%	58.9%	55.7%	57.5%	32.8%	22.9%	24.7%	19.6%
92:2	42.9%	44.8%	61.7%	58.1%	59.7%	27.7%	17.2%	32.1%	23.1%
92:3	39.5%	43.5%	59.6%	60.9%	60.3%	25.9%	17.6%	34.4%	22.1%
92:4	37.5%	45.0%	57.7%	62.7%	60.5%	26.0%	19.0%	34.5%	20.5%
93:1	39.4%	45.6%	58.0%	60.8%	59.6%	26.4%	19.1%	33.1%	21.3%
93:2	40.9%	38.1%	58.4%	59.3%	58.9%	22.2%	15.9%	36.7%	25.2%
93:3	39.4%	40.6%	57.5%	60.8%	59.4%	23.3%	17.2%	36.1%	23.3%
93:4	41.7%	38.6%	58.2%	58.2%	58.2%	22.4%	16.1%	35.8%	25.7%
94:1	43.7%	41.8%	58.8%	56.0%	57.2%	24.6%	17.2%	32.6%	25.6%
94:2	42.7%	29.6%	59.7%	57.6%	58.2%	17.7%	11.9%	40.6%	29.8%
94:3	39.8%	43.4%	58.7%	60.6%	59.8%	25.5%	17.9%	34.3%	22.3%
94:4	42.8%	36.8%	61.3%	57.6%	58.9%	22.6%	14.2%	36.4%	26.8%
95:1	38.7%	46.0%	57.8%	61.6%	59.8%	26.6%	19.4%	33.3%	20.7%
95:2	38.9%	48.7%	56.6%	60.7%	58.7%	27.6%	21.1%	31.2%	20.1%
95:3	38.9%	47.7%	56.9%	61.8%	59.5%	27.1%	20.6%	32.4%	20.0%
95:4	40.5%	38.0%	57.8%	60.2%	59.3%	21.9%	16.0%	37.4%	24.7%
96:1	38.9%	46.9%	54.9%	61.5%	58.4%	25.8%	21.2%	32.7%	20.4%
96:2	42.4%	48.3%	58.0%	57.6%	57.8%	28.0%	20.3%	29.8%	21.9%
96:3	40.8%	35.2%	58.0%	59.2%	58.8%	20.4%	14.8%	38.4%	26.4%
96:4	39.8%	43.7%	56.1%	60.7%	58.7%	24.6%	19.2%	34.2%	22.1%
AVG	39.4%	45.5%	60.7%	61.1%	60.7%	27.5%	17.9%	33.2%	21.4%

Table 3.3a
Trading Band Crossover (BND-C) Long Return Analysis
(Average of all stocks)

Qtr	BND-C Terminal Wealth	Buy/Hold Terminal Wealth	Relative Terminal Wealth	BND-C Long Avg Ret	BND-C Cash Avg Ret	BND-C Long-Cash Avg Ret	Buy/Hold Avg Ret
85:1	10094	10142	0.995	0.069%	-0.009%	0.078%	0.006%
85:2	9899	9700	1.021	-0.070%	-0.069%	0.000%	-0.069%
85:3	9678	8889	1.089	-0.157%	-0.231%	0.074%	-0.205%
85:4	10327	10763	0.960	0.151%	0.086%	0.064%	0.107%
86:1	10353	11428	0.906	0.229%	0.223%	0.006%	0.225%
86:2	10246	10414	0.984	0.119%	0.041%	0.078%	0.066%
86:3	9658	9175	1.053	-0.105%	-0.152%	0.047%	-0.128%
86:4	10359	10413	0.995	0.115%	0.024%	0.091%	0.069%
87:1	10555	11929	0.885	0.355%	0.273%	0.082%	0.293%
87:2	10241	10196	1.004	0.081%	-0.006%	0.087%	0.038%
87:3	10218	10408	0.982	0.098%	0.052%	0.046%	0.068%
87:4	8616	8087	1.065	-0.415%	-0.130%	-0.284%	-0.278%
88:1	10485	10989	0.954	0.265%	0.119%	0.146%	0.163%
88:2	10315	10593	0.974	0.142%	0.075%	0.067%	0.100%
88:3	10082	10050	1.003	0.040%	-0.003%	0.043%	0.013%
88:4	10120	10196	0.993	0.053%	0.026%	0.028%	0.037%
89:1	10237	10698	0.957	0.126%	0.106%	0.020%	0.112%
89:2	10231	10772	0.950	0.139%	0.116%	0.023%	0.122%
89:3	10288	10833	0.950	0.173%	0.116%	0.057%	0.131%
89:4	10082	9904	1.018	0.026%	-0.056%	0.081%	-0.011%
90:1	10042	9980	1.006	0.016%	-0.013%	0.029%	0.003%
90:2	10249	10459	0.980	0.100%	0.060%	0.039%	0.077%
90:3	9012	8526	1.057	-0.294%	-0.210%	-0.084%	-0.259%
90:4	10408	10889	0.956	0.152%	0.142%	0.010%	0.146%
91:1	11010	12477	0.882	0.391%	0.292%	0.099%	0.315%
91:2	10161	10244	0.992	0.085%	0.027%	0.058%	0.045%
91:3	10231	10429	0.981	0.093%	0.047%	0.046%	0.065%
91:4	10249	10497	0.976	0.092%	0.073%	0.019%	0.082%
92:1	9962	10324	0.965	-0.027%	0.076%	-0.103%	0.048%
92:2	9902	9723	1.018	-0.041%	-0.054%	0.013%	-0.048%
92:3	10215	10392	0.983	0.074%	0.043%	0.032%	0.057%
92:4	10355	10963	0.945	0.144%	0.145%	-0.001%	0.144%
93:1	10190	10527	0.968	0.079%	0.080%	-0.001%	0.080%
93:2	10194	10340	0.986	0.066%	0.039%	0.027%	0.052%
93:3	10279	10686	0.962	0.099%	0.102%	-0.003%	0.101%
93:4	10133	10255	0.988	0.042%	0.027%	0.014%	0.034%
94:1	9949	9954	0.999	-0.022%	-0.003%	-0.019%	-0.011%
94:2	10026	9994	1.003	0.004%	-0.017%	0.022%	-0.005%
94:3	10281	10613	0.969	0.098%	0.083%	0.015%	0.089%
94:4	9999	9836	1.017	-0.002%	-0.057%	0.055%	-0.029%
95:1	10375	10706	0.969	0.141%	0.088%	0.053%	0.110%
95:2	10292	10873	0.947	0.134%	0.134%	0.000%	0.134%
95:3	10341	10853	0.953	0.166%	0.115%	0.050%	0.131%
95:4	10240	10445	0.980	0.086%	0.053%	0.033%	0.067%
96:1	10431	11027	0.946	0.191%	0.141%	0.050%	0.159%
96:2	10138	10367	0.978	0.062%	0.057%	0.005%	0.059%
96:3	10218	10298	0.992	0.067%	0.027%	0.040%	0.047%
96:4	10341	10817	0.956	0.128%	0.118%	0.010%	0.122%
AVG	10152	10377	0.978	0.056%	0.055%	0.001%	0.055%

Table 3.3b
Trading Band Crossover (BND-C) Short Return Analysis
(Average of all stocks)

Qtr	BND-C Terminal Wealth	Buy/Hold Terminal Wealth	Relative Terminal Wealth	BND-C Short Avg Ret	BND-C Cash Avg Ret	BND-C Short-Cash Avg Ret	Buy/Hold Avg Ret
85:1	9996	10142	0.986	0.013%	-0.002%	0.015%	0.006%
85:2	10347	9700	1.067	-0.099%	-0.042%	-0.057%	-0.069%
85:3	10799	8889	1.215	-0.251%	-0.167%	-0.084%	-0.205%
85:4	9753	10763	0.906	0.082%	0.135%	-0.053%	0.107%
86:1	9254	11428	0.810	0.227%	0.222%	0.005%	0.225%
86:2	9850	10414	0.946	0.051%	0.083%	-0.033%	0.066%
86:3	10467	9175	1.141	-0.198%	-0.086%	-0.113%	-0.128%
86:4	9950	10413	0.956	0.017%	0.105%	-0.088%	0.069%
87:1	9003	11929	0.755	0.278%	0.318%	-0.040%	0.293%
87:2	10014	10196	0.982	-0.005%	0.065%	-0.070%	0.038%
87:3	9821	10408	0.944	0.053%	0.085%	-0.033%	0.068%
87:4	10320	8087	1.276	-0.203%	-0.305%	0.103%	-0.278%
88:1	9479	10989	0.863	0.134%	0.211%	-0.077%	0.163%
88:2	9742	10593	0.920	0.077%	0.126%	-0.050%	0.100%
88:3	9973	10050	0.992	0.006%	0.020%	-0.014%	0.013%
88:4	9945	10196	0.975	0.016%	0.056%	-0.041%	0.037%
89:1	9617	10698	0.899	0.120%	0.104%	0.016%	0.112%
89:2	9599	10772	0.891	0.120%	0.125%	-0.006%	0.122%
89:3	9642	10833	0.890	0.111%	0.153%	-0.042%	0.131%
89:4	10137	9904	1.024	-0.075%	0.017%	-0.091%	-0.011%
90:1	10050	9980	1.007	-0.025%	0.017%	-0.042%	0.003%
90:2	9835	10459	0.940	0.059%	0.091%	-0.032%	0.077%
90:3	10371	8526	1.216	-0.227%	-0.270%	0.043%	-0.259%
90:4	9592	10889	0.881	0.155%	0.140%	0.016%	0.146%
91:1	8915	12477	0.715	0.325%	0.301%	0.024%	0.315%
91:2	9891	10244	0.966	0.027%	0.068%	-0.041%	0.045%
91:3	9897	10429	0.949	0.039%	0.087%	-0.048%	0.065%
91:4	9808	10497	0.934	0.082%	0.081%	0.001%	0.082%
92:1	9726	10324	0.942	0.084%	0.002%	0.082%	0.048%
92:2	10214	9723	1.050	-0.073%	-0.029%	-0.044%	-0.048%
92:3	9904	10392	0.953	0.041%	0.069%	-0.028%	0.057%
92:4	9558	10963	0.872	0.162%	0.130%	0.032%	0.144%
93:1	9791	10527	0.930	0.080%	0.080%	0.000%	0.080%
93:2	9931	10340	0.960	0.033%	0.063%	-0.030%	0.052%
93:3	9741	10686	0.912	0.109%	0.096%	0.014%	0.101%
93:4	9923	10255	0.968	0.038%	0.032%	0.006%	0.034%
94:1	10006	9954	1.005	0.003%	-0.021%	0.024%	-0.011%
94:2	10061	9994	1.007	-0.031%	0.006%	-0.038%	-0.005%
94:3	9762	10613	0.920	0.093%	0.086%	0.007%	0.089%
94:4	10165	9836	1.033	-0.070%	-0.006%	-0.064%	-0.029%
95:1	9763	10706	0.912	0.087%	0.130%	-0.043%	0.110%
95:2	9578	10873	0.881	0.147%	0.122%	0.024%	0.134%
95:3	9685	10853	0.892	0.111%	0.149%	-0.038%	0.131%
95:4	9938	10445	0.951	0.030%	0.089%	-0.059%	0.067%
96:1	9580	11027	0.869	0.152%	0.165%	-0.013%	0.159%
96:2	9811	10367	0.946	0.067%	0.051%	0.016%	0.059%
96:3	9914	10298	0.963	0.043%	0.050%	-0.007%	0.047%
96:4	9687	10817	0.896	0.117%	0.126%	-0.009%	0.122%
AVG	9850	10377	0.949	0.058%	0.053%	0.004%	0.055%

Adding SD to the EMA will give an upper band that lies one standard deviation above the exponential moving average. Subtracting SD from the EMA will give a lower band that lies one standard deviation below the exponential moving average. Larger bands can be created by adding multiples of the SD to the EMA.

Some programs, such as OmniTrader, use a variant of this calculation. Instead of using the exponential moving average of the closing stock price, two exponential moving averages are calculated—one of the daily high (EMA_{High}) and one of the daily low (EMA_{Low}). A separate standard deviation is then calculated for each of these moving averages. The upper band is constructed by adding SD_{High} to EMA_{High}; the lower band is constructed by subtracting SD_{Low} from EMA_{Low}.

Whenever the price moves outside the lower band ($EMA_{Low} - SD_{Low}$) but closes within the bands, a long signal is generated. Short signals occur when the price moves outside the upper band ($EMA_{High} - SD_{High}$) but closes within the bands.

Results

The results presented in Tables 3.3 and 3.4 indicate that the Bollinger Band Crossover system does indeed outperform the Trading Band Crossover system for long calls. When choosing between long and cash positions, both systems are correct 61.4 percent of the time. Long signals occur 44.7 percent of the time in the Bollinger Band Crossover system, compared to 39.5 percent for the Trading Band Crossover. The main advantage of the Bollinger Band Crossover system is that it seems to be better than the Trading Band Crossover at distinguishing the best times to be long. As shown in Table 3.5a, the average return when the indicator says to be long is 0.060 percent, compared to an average return of only 0.052 percent when a cash position is favored over a long position.

Comparing the short results for these two systems is not as straightforward. The short hit analysis presented in Table 3.4b suggests that the more sophisticated Bollinger Band Crossover system is inferior to the Trading Band Crossover system when it comes to making short calls. The hit rate for the Bollinger Band system of 60.5 percent (Table 3.4b) is slightly below the hit rate of 60.7 percent (Table 3.2b) for the Trading Band Crossover system. Another disadvantage of the Bollinger Band Crossover system is that it makes too many short calls. This system chooses a short position over a cash position, on average 51.9 percent of the time (Table 3.4b), much more frequently than the optimal short position rate of 39.4 percent.

However, the short signals in the Bollinger Band Crossover system give information superior to that of the Trading Band Crossover system. As shown in Table 3.5b, the average return when the signal is short (0.054 percent) is less than the average return when the signal is cash (0.056 percent).

Thus, the Bollinger Band Crossover system is making short calls on days when the market tends to have below-average price appreciation. However, because there is usually price appreciation on these days, being in a short position will lead to losses. In fact, trading short with this system will lead to a terminal wealth of only 94.8 percent of the terminal wealth of a buy-and-hold strategy. Worse yet, the investor trading short with this system would have losses. The ending amount would be lower than the initial amount.

Because using adjusting-width trading bands seems to improve trading results with the long positions, let's turn our attention to another system that uses these types of bands—the Kirshenbaum Bands indicator.

Kirshenbaum Bands

Kirshenbaum Bands (KBA-C) are similar to Bollinger Bands in that the width of the trading bands varies with market volatility. Developed by Paul Kirshenbaum, a mathematician with a PhD in economics from NYU, this model uses the standard error of linear regression lines of the closing stock price to determine band width. This has the effect of measuring volatility around the current trend, rather than measuring volatility for changes in trend.

The idea behind the Kirshenbaum Bands is that the width of trading bands should be tied to the predictability and volatility of the stock's price. During periods in which the closing prices for a stock lie in a reasonably straight line, the closing stock prices for any particular day can be estimated with a fairly high degree of accuracy. A tight trading band is desirable during these periods, and any deviation outside of this band would be of particular significance.

On the other hand, during periods of high volatility in the closing prices of a stock, a wider trading band is desirable. Because many of the closing stock prices will lie farther away from a straight line drawn to represent the general trend in closing stock prices, it is more difficult to estimate the closing stock price for any particular day with a high degree of accuracy. The stock price can fluctuate to a larger degree with the wider trading bands before the price fluctuation is viewed as significant.

Construction

First, calculate a P-period exponential moving average of the close. Then, for each day, calculate the L-period linear regression line, using today's closing price as the endpoint of the line. This linear regression line can also be referred to as the "least squares" or "best fit" line. The linear regression calculation results in a line that best fits a plot of the data set of closing prices, but many of the actual closing prices will not lie directly on the regression line.

Table 3.4a
Bollinger Band Crossover (BOL-C) Long Hit Analysis
(Average of all stocks)

Qtr	Optimal Long	BOL-C Long	Long Hits	Cash Hits	Total Hits	Long Right	Long Wrong	Cash Right	Cash Wrong
85:1	32.1%	33.6%	65.8%	68.6%	67.6%	22.1%	11.5%	45.5%	20.8%
85:2	30.2%	39.8%	66.0%	70.3%	68.6%	26.2%	13.5%	42.4%	17.9%
85:3	26.3%	49.2%	61.4%	75.3%	68.5%	30.2%	19.0%	38.3%	12.5%
85:4	36.6%	32.2%	69.0%	63.1%	65.0%	22.2%	10.0%	42.8%	25.0%
86:1	44.2%	32.3%	66.4%	55.5%	59.0%	21.5%	10.9%	37.6%	30.1%
86:2	39.7%	44.0%	62.3%	61.4%	61.8%	27.4%	16.6%	34.4%	21.6%
86:3	37.0%	52.2%	58.2%	63.1%	60.6%	30.4%	21.8%	30.2%	17.6%
86:4	38.5%	47.4%	62.6%	62.1%	62.3%	29.6%	17.7%	32.7%	20.0%
87:1	44.7%	31.8%	67.1%	56.7%	60.0%	21.3%	10.5%	38.6%	29.6%
87:2	40.0%	52.5%	61.0%	61.8%	61.4%	32.0%	20.5%	29.4%	18.2%
87:3	39.5%	45.4%	60.3%	61.0%	60.7%	27.4%	18.0%	33.3%	21.3%
87:4	37.9%	66.7%	55.9%	64.4%	58.7%	37.3%	29.4%	21.5%	11.9%
88:1	41.3%	30.8%	63.7%	59.2%	60.6%	19.7%	11.2%	41.0%	28.2%
88:2	39.3%	46.5%	63.2%	61.2%	62.1%	29.3%	17.1%	32.8%	20.8%
88:3	35.9%	49.3%	61.9%	64.6%	63.3%	30.5%	18.8%	32.7%	18.0%
88:4	36.3%	45.7%	63.7%	63.7%	63.7%	29.1%	16.6%	34.6%	19.7%
89:1	39.0%	39.0%	64.9%	61.4%	62.8%	25.3%	13.7%	37.5%	23.5%
89:2	40.2%	32.6%	65.4%	59.8%	61.6%	21.3%	11.3%	40.3%	27.1%
89:3	39.9%	41.6%	65.3%	60.8%	62.7%	27.1%	14.4%	35.6%	22.9%
89:4	38.3%	53.6%	61.1%	61.7%	61.3%	32.7%	20.9%	28.6%	17.8%
90:1	36.9%	52.7%	61.1%	64.5%	62.7%	32.2%	20.5%	30.5%	16.8%
90:2	39.2%	43.0%	63.8%	60.7%	62.1%	27.4%	15.5%	34.6%	22.4%
90:3	33.5%	66.4%	54.5%	66.7%	58.6%	36.2%	30.2%	22.4%	11.2%
90:4	40.8%	44.7%	62.7%	58.4%	60.4%	28.1%	16.7%	32.3%	23.0%
91:1	44.1%	33.2%	66.3%	56.6%	59.8%	22.0%	11.2%	37.8%	29.0%
91:2	39.7%	42.4%	61.6%	61.2%	61.4%	26.1%	16.3%	35.3%	22.3%
91:3	40.4%	48.3%	61.0%	60.2%	60.6%	29.4%	18.8%	31.1%	20.6%
91:4	41.2%	49.1%	59.3%	58.7%	59.0%	29.1%	20.0%	29.9%	21.1%
92:1	40.0%	39.0%	55.8%	58.8%	57.6%	21.7%	17.2%	35.9%	25.1%
92:2	38.6%	50.5%	57.4%	61.8%	59.6%	29.0%	21.5%	30.6%	18.9%
92:3	40.3%	44.6%	60.6%	59.5%	60.0%	27.1%	17.6%	33.0%	22.4%
92:4	41.9%	40.8%	63.2%	58.1%	60.2%	25.8%	15.0%	34.4%	24.8%
93:1	42.5%	41.4%	61.7%	57.9%	59.5%	25.5%	15.9%	33.9%	24.7%
93:2	42.1%	50.6%	59.6%	58.1%	58.9%	30.1%	20.4%	28.7%	20.7%
93:3	42.5%	41.5%	60.8%	57.5%	58.8%	25.2%	16.3%	33.6%	24.9%
93:4	41.5%	48.4%	58.0%	57.9%	58.0%	28.1%	20.3%	29.9%	21.7%
94:1	40.4%	45.7%	56.8%	59.3%	58.2%	25.9%	19.7%	32.2%	22.1%
94:2	40.6%	56.3%	57.8%	59.7%	58.6%	32.5%	23.7%	26.1%	17.6%
94:3	41.8%	45.0%	60.7%	58.6%	59.5%	27.3%	17.7%	32.2%	22.8%
94:4	39.5%	55.9%	57.1%	60.5%	58.6%	31.9%	24.0%	26.7%	17.4%
95:1	43.1%	38.5%	61.6%	56.8%	58.6%	23.7%	14.8%	34.9%	26.6%
95:2	43.7%	36.3%	61.4%	56.1%	58.0%	22.3%	14.0%	35.8%	27.9%
95:3	43.9%	37.6%	61.6%	55.8%	58.0%	23.2%	14.4%	34.8%	27.6%
95:4	43.4%	46.5%	59.2%	55.6%	57.3%	27.5%	19.0%	29.8%	23.8%
96:1	45.5%	45.1%	61.2%	54.4%	57.4%	27.6%	17.5%	29.9%	25.1%
96:2	42.1%	46.9%	57.5%	57.6%	57.6%	26.9%	19.9%	30.6%	22.5%
96:3	42.6%	48.9%	59.0%	57.3%	58.1%	28.8%	20.1%	29.3%	21.8%
96:4	44.3%	40.0%	60.0%	55.3%	57.2%	24.0%	16.0%	33.2%	26.8%
AVG	40.0%	44.7%	61.4%	60.4%	60.6%	27.2%	17.4%	33.3%	22.0%

Table 3.4b
Bollinger Band Crossover (BOL-C) Short Hit Analysis
(Average of all stocks)

Qtr	Optimal Short	BOL-C Short	Short Hits	Cash Hits	Total Hits	Short Right	Short Wrong	Cash Right	Cash Wrong
85:1	34.3%	60.9%	68.3%	65.7%	67.3%	41.6%	19.3%	25.7%	13.4%
85:2	34.6%	56.1%	70.1%	65.8%	68.2%	39.4%	16.8%	28.9%	15.0%
85:3	38.6%	46.7%	75.1%	61.6%	67.9%	35.0%	11.6%	32.9%	20.5%
85:4	33.1%	62.0%	62.8%	67.9%	64.7%	39.0%	23.1%	25.8%	12.2%
86:1	35.2%	62.5%	55.7%	65.8%	59.5%	34.8%	27.7%	24.7%	12.8%
86:2	39.8%	53.0%	61.5%	62.1%	61.8%	32.6%	20.4%	29.1%	17.8%
86:3	42.7%	43.6%	63.4%	58.1%	60.4%	27.6%	16.0%	32.8%	23.6%
86:4	38.7%	50.5%	62.1%	62.4%	62.2%	31.4%	19.2%	30.9%	18.6%
87:1	36.9%	63.9%	56.7%	66.1%	60.0%	36.2%	27.7%	23.8%	12.3%
87:2	40.0%	44.9%	62.0%	60.8%	61.3%	27.8%	17.0%	33.5%	21.6%
87:3	40.4%	51.3%	61.2%	60.1%	60.7%	31.4%	19.9%	29.3%	19.4%
87:4	45.3%	29.3%	65.1%	55.7%	58.5%	19.0%	10.2%	39.4%	31.3%
88:1	36.7%	66.0%	59.0%	63.1%	60.4%	38.9%	27.1%	21.4%	12.6%
88:2	37.4%	50.7%	61.3%	63.1%	62.2%	31.1%	19.6%	31.1%	18.2%
88:3	38.4%	47.8%	64.6%	61.7%	63.1%	30.9%	16.9%	32.2%	20.0%
88:4	37.0%	51.4%	63.8%	63.6%	63.7%	32.8%	18.6%	30.9%	17.7%
89:1	36.2%	57.6%	61.4%	64.3%	62.6%	35.4%	22.2%	27.3%	15.1%
89:2	35.9%	63.4%	59.9%	64.8%	61.7%	38.0%	25.4%	23.7%	12.9%
89:3	36.4%	55.4%	61.0%	64.9%	62.8%	33.8%	21.6%	29.0%	15.6%
89:4	39.0%	43.2%	61.9%	61.0%	61.4%	26.7%	16.5%	34.7%	22.1%
90:1	40.1%	44.5%	64.6%	61.0%	62.6%	28.8%	15.7%	33.9%	21.6%
90:2	37.8%	53.6%	60.8%	63.4%	62.0%	32.6%	21.0%	29.4%	17.0%
90:3	45.7%	28.5%	67.3%	54.5%	58.1%	19.2%	9.3%	39.0%	32.5%
90:4	37.6%	51.2%	58.4%	62.5%	60.4%	29.9%	21.3%	30.5%	18.3%
91:1	36.7%	62.0%	56.5%	65.5%	59.9%	35.0%	26.9%	24.9%	13.1%
91:2	40.4%	55.0%	61.2%	61.4%	61.3%	33.7%	21.3%	27.7%	17.4%
91:3	39.8%	49.0%	60.3%	60.8%	60.6%	29.5%	19.4%	31.0%	20.0%
91:4	40.5%	47.4%	58.7%	59.2%	59.0%	27.9%	19.6%	31.1%	21.4%
92:1	43.2%	57.2%	58.9%	55.7%	57.5%	33.7%	23.5%	23.8%	19.0%
92:2	42.9%	46.7%	61.9%	57.4%	59.5%	28.9%	17.8%	30.6%	22.7%
92:3	39.5%	52.4%	59.6%	60.5%	60.0%	31.3%	21.2%	28.8%	18.8%
92:4	37.5%	55.4%	58.0%	62.9%	60.2%	32.1%	23.3%	28.1%	16.6%
93:1	39.4%	55.5%	58.0%	61.4%	59.5%	32.2%	23.3%	27.3%	17.2%
93:2	40.9%	46.7%	58.3%	59.5%	58.9%	27.2%	19.5%	31.7%	21.6%
93:3	39.4%	55.4%	57.5%	60.6%	58.9%	31.9%	23.6%	27.0%	17.6%
93:4	41.7%	48.4%	58.1%	58.0%	58.1%	28.1%	20.3%	30.0%	21.7%
94:1	43.7%	51.7%	59.4%	56.6%	58.0%	30.7%	21.0%	27.4%	21.0%
94:2	42.7%	41.6%	59.9%	57.7%	58.6%	24.9%	16.7%	33.7%	24.7%
94:3	39.8%	52.2%	58.6%	60.5%	59.5%	30.6%	21.6%	28.9%	18.9%
94:4	42.8%	41.2%	60.5%	56.9%	58.4%	24.9%	16.3%	33.5%	25.3%
95:1	38.7%	58.7%	56.8%	61.4%	58.7%	33.3%	25.4%	25.3%	16.0%
95:2	38.9%	60.6%	56.1%	61.1%	58.1%	34.0%	26.6%	24.1%	15.3%
95:3	38.9%	59.0%	55.8%	61.4%	58.1%	32.9%	26.1%	25.2%	15.9%
95:4	40.5%	49.6%	55.5%	58.9%	57.2%	27.6%	22.1%	29.7%	20.7%
96:1	38.9%	52.4%	54.3%	61.0%	57.5%	28.5%	23.9%	29.0%	18.5%
96:2	42.4%	50.8%	57.7%	57.4%	57.5%	29.3%	21.5%	28.2%	20.9%
96:3	40.8%	48.2%	57.2%	58.8%	58.0%	27.6%	20.6%	30.5%	21.4%
96:4	39.8%	56.1%	55.2%	59.7%	57.2%	31.0%	25.1%	26.2%	17.7%
AVG	39.4%	51.9%	60.5%	61.1%	60.5%	31.3%	20.6%	29.2%	18.9%

Table 3.5a
Bollinger Band Crossover (BOL-C) Long Return Analysis
(Average of all stocks)

Qtr	BOL-C Terminal Wealth	Buy/Hold Terminal Wealth	Relative Terminal Wealth	BOL-C Long Avg Ret	BOL-C Cash Avg Ret	BOL-C Long-Cash Avg Ret	Buy/Hold Avg Ret
85:1	10049	10142	0.991	0.017%	0.001%	0.016%	0.006%
85:2	9928	9700	1.024	-0.047%	-0.084%	0.036%	-0.069%
85:3	9501	8889	1.069	-0.175%	-0.234%	0.060%	-0.205%
85:4	10299	10763	0.957	0.136%	0.093%	0.043%	0.107%
86:1	10467	11428	0.916	0.238%	0.218%	0.020%	0.225%
86:2	10396	10414	0.998	0.142%	0.007%	0.136%	0.066%
86:3	9681	9175	1.055	-0.092%	-0.166%	0.074%	-0.128%
86:4	10312	10413	0.990	0.106%	0.037%	0.069%	0.069%
87:1	10931	11929	0.916	0.458%	0.216%	0.242%	0.293%
87:2	10300	10196	1.010	0.095%	-0.025%	0.119%	0.038%
87:3	10279	10408	0.988	0.099%	0.043%	0.057%	0.068%
87:4	9109	8087	1.126	-0.192%	-0.451%	0.259%	-0.278%
88:1	10402	10989	0.947	0.213%	0.140%	0.073%	0.163%
88:2	10372	10593	0.979	0.132%	0.072%	0.061%	0.100%
88:3	10072	10050	1.002	0.028%	-0.002%	0.031%	0.013%
88:4	10129	10196	0.993	0.049%	0.026%	0.024%	0.037%
89:1	10309	10698	0.964	0.129%	0.102%	0.027%	0.112%
89:2	10291	10772	0.955	0.144%	0.112%	0.033%	0.122%
89:3	10410	10833	0.961	0.158%	0.112%	0.047%	0.131%
89:4	10019	9904	1.012	0.009%	-0.034%	0.043%	-0.011%
90:1	10127	9980	1.015	0.045%	-0.044%	0.089%	0.003%
90:2	10229	10459	0.978	0.091%	0.066%	0.025%	0.077%
90:3	9014	8526	1.057	-0.257%	-0.264%	0.007%	-0.259%
90:4	10370	10889	0.952	0.145%	0.148%	-0.003%	0.146%
91:1	11304	12477	0.906	0.412%	0.267%	0.145%	0.315%
91:2	10244	10244	1.000	0.096%	0.008%	0.088%	0.045%
91:3	10265	10429	0.984	0.087%	0.044%	0.044%	0.065%
91:4	10286	10497	0.980	0.101%	0.063%	0.038%	0.082%
92:1	9921	10324	0.961	-0.035%	0.101%	-0.135%	0.048%
92:2	9879	9723	1.016	-0.041%	-0.056%	0.015%	-0.048%
92:3	10172	10392	0.979	0.057%	0.056%	0.001%	0.057%
92:4	10403	10963	0.949	0.154%	0.138%	0.016%	0.144%
93:1	10303	10527	0.979	0.113%	0.056%	0.057%	0.080%
93:2	10181	10340	0.985	0.060%	0.043%	0.017%	0.052%
93:3	10283	10686	0.962	0.105%	0.098%	0.008%	0.101%
93:4	10058	10255	0.981	0.016%	0.051%	-0.035%	0.034%
94:1	10000	9954	1.005	-0.004%	-0.018%	0.014%	-0.011%
94:2	10028	9994	1.003	0.005%	-0.018%	0.023%	-0.005%
94:3	10282	10613	0.969	0.096%	0.083%	0.013%	0.089%
94:4	9884	9836	1.005	-0.034%	-0.023%	-0.011%	-0.029%
95:1	10300	10706	0.962	0.125%	0.101%	0.024%	0.110%
95:2	10308	10873	0.948	0.134%	0.134%	0.001%	0.134%
95:3	10340	10853	0.953	0.143%	0.124%	0.020%	0.131%
95:4	10145	10445	0.971	0.048%	0.083%	-0.035%	0.067%
96:1	10475	11027	0.950	0.167%	0.153%	0.014%	0.159%
96:2	10126	10367	0.977	0.043%	0.073%	-0.030%	0.059%
96:3	10109	10298	0.982	0.036%	0.058%	-0.021%	0.047%
96:4	10239	10817	0.947	0.094%	0.141%	-0.048%	0.122%
AVG	10178	10377	0.981	0.060%	0.052%	0.008%	0.055%

Table 3.5b
Bollinger Band Crossover (BOL-C) Short Return Analysis
(Average of all stocks)

Qtr	BOL-C Terminal Wealth	Buy/Hold Terminal Wealth	Relative Terminal Wealth	BOL-C Short Avg Ret	BOL-C Cash Avg Ret	BOL-C Short-Cash Avg Ret	Buy/Hold Avg Ret
85:1	10017	10142	0.988	0.008%	0.004%	0.004%	0.006%
85:2	10323	9700	1.064	-0.080%	-0.056%	-0.024%	-0.069%
85:3	10734	8889	1.208	-0.230%	-0.183%	-0.047%	-0.205%
85:4	9610	10763	0.893	0.106%	0.108%	-0.002%	0.107%
86:1	9216	11428	0.806	0.219%	0.234%	-0.015%	0.225%
86:2	9979	10414	0.958	0.007%	0.133%	-0.126%	0.066%
86:3	10490	9175	1.143	-0.174%	-0.092%	-0.082%	-0.128%
86:4	9871	10413	0.948	0.036%	0.103%	-0.066%	0.069%
87:1	9172	11929	0.769	0.223%	0.416%	-0.193%	0.293%
87:2	10078	10196	0.988	-0.028%	0.092%	-0.120%	0.038%
87:3	9869	10408	0.948	0.038%	0.101%	-0.063%	0.068%
87:4	10825	8087	1.339	-0.452%	-0.206%	-0.246%	-0.278%
88:1	9369	10989	0.853	0.151%	0.185%	-0.033%	0.163%
88:2	9780	10593	0.923	0.068%	0.132%	-0.064%	0.100%
88:3	9991	10050	0.994	0.000%	0.024%	-0.024%	0.013%
88:4	9916	10196	0.973	0.023%	0.050%	-0.027%	0.037%
89:1	9623	10698	0.900	0.109%	0.116%	-0.007%	0.112%
89:2	9556	10772	0.887	0.112%	0.139%	-0.027%	0.122%
89:3	9621	10833	0.888	0.113%	0.153%	-0.040%	0.131%
89:4	10111	9904	1.021	-0.045%	0.015%	-0.059%	-0.011%
90:1	10129	9980	1.015	-0.049%	0.044%	-0.094%	0.003%
90:2	9779	10459	0.935	0.067%	0.088%	-0.022%	0.077%
90:3	10487	8526	1.230	-0.272%	-0.254%	-0.018%	-0.259%
90:4	9505	10889	0.873	0.156%	0.136%	0.020%	0.146%
91:1	9039	12477	0.724	0.274%	0.382%	-0.108%	0.315%
91:2	9960	10244	0.972	0.007%	0.092%	-0.084%	0.045%
91:3	9882	10429	0.948	0.043%	0.086%	-0.044%	0.065%
91:4	9816	10497	0.935	0.061%	0.101%	-0.040%	0.082%
92:1	9657	10324	0.935	0.101%	-0.023%	0.125%	0.048%
92:2	10172	9723	1.046	-0.056%	-0.041%	-0.015%	-0.048%
92:3	9819	10392	0.945	0.058%	0.055%	0.003%	0.057%
92:4	9519	10963	0.868	0.143%	0.146%	-0.003%	0.144%
93:1	9828	10527	0.934	0.055%	0.111%	-0.056%	0.080%
93:2	9901	10340	0.957	0.040%	0.062%	-0.023%	0.052%
93:3	9664	10686	0.904	0.102%	0.100%	0.001%	0.101%
93:4	9870	10255	0.962	0.047%	0.022%	0.025%	0.034%
94:1	10058	9954	1.010	-0.015%	-0.007%	-0.008%	-0.011%
94:2	10072	9994	1.008	-0.024%	0.009%	-0.034%	-0.005%
94:3	9732	10613	0.917	0.088%	0.091%	-0.003%	0.089%
94:4	10049	9836	1.022	-0.017%	-0.038%	0.021%	-0.029%
95:1	9635	10706	0.900	0.104%	0.118%	-0.014%	0.110%
95:2	9513	10873	0.875	0.135%	0.133%	0.002%	0.134%
95:3	9550	10853	0.880	0.127%	0.136%	-0.009%	0.131%
95:4	9738	10445	0.932	0.090%	0.044%	0.045%	0.067%
96:1	9512	11027	0.863	0.156%	0.162%	-0.006%	0.159%
96:2	9779	10367	0.943	0.072%	0.045%	0.027%	0.059%
96:3	9812	10298	0.953	0.064%	0.031%	0.033%	0.047%
96:4	9499	10817	0.878	0.147%	0.091%	0.056%	0.122%
AVG	9836	10377	0.948	0.054%	0.056%	-0.002%	0.055%

Measure the distance from the regression line to the closing price for each day. Let's call this distance, from the regression line to the closing for Day i, d_i. This d_i is a measure of error; it tells us how far off the regression line was from estimating the real close.

Next, calculate the average of the square of these errors (AE) over the time period L:

$$AE = (d_1^2 + d_2^2 + d_3^2 + \ldots + d_n^2)/L.$$

Take the square root of this value to derive the standard error (SE):

$$SE = \text{square root of AE.}$$

Then, using a chosen number, N, of these standard errors, the band width (BW) is determined by:

$$BW = N \cdot SE.$$

Add this band width to the exponential moving average to arrive at today's value for the upper band. Subtract this band width from the exponential moving average to derive today's lower band.

A long signal is triggered when the stock price moves below the lower band during the trading day but closes inside the bands. When the stock price exceeds the upper band but closes within the bands, a short signal is triggered.

Results

The test results presented in Tables 3.6 and 3.7 are very similar to the test results presented in Tables 3.4 and 3.5 for the related Bollinger Bands system. The average long hit rate for the Kirshenbaum Bands system is 61.2 percent and the short average hit rate is 60.2 percent; the hit rates for the Bollinger Band system were slightly higher at 61.4 percent and 60.5 percent, respectively (Table 3.4). The Kirshenbaum Bands system generates long calls 45.8 percent of the time (Table 3.6a) and short calls 49.0 percent of the time (Table 3.6b). The Bollinger Bands system generates long calls slightly less often—44.7 percent of the time (Table 3.4a)—and short calls slightly more often—51.9 percent the time (Table 3.4b).

In our test sample (Table 3.7a), the average return in the market is 0.059 percent whenever the system trades long. Whenever the system chooses a cash position over a long position, the market return is only 0.052 percent. The average return of the market whenever a short position is called is 0.057 percent (Table 3.7b). Whenever a cash position is taken over a short position, the average market return is 0.054 percent. Thus, the short calls of the Kirshenbaum

Bands system are perverse in that they are associated with times of above-average market returns rather than the desirable, below-average, negative market returns for short positions.

If either the long-cash strategy or short-cash strategy is followed, terminal wealth is lower than the terminal wealth of a buy-and-hold strategy. The information provided by this indicator does not prove to be superior to the information provided by the Bollinger Band system. Because the Bollinger Band system is easier to construct, traders may choose to use it over the Kirshenbaum Bands system.

Directional Movement Crossover

In his book *New Concepts in Technical Trading Systems*, Welles Wilder develops and defines the directional movement concept. Directional movement compares a stock's trading range for one day to the trading range on the previous day. Positive directional movement occurs when today's high is greater than yesterday's high. The amount of the positive directional movement is today's high less yesterday's high. If today's low is below yesterday's low, negative directional movement has occurred. The value of this negative directional movement is the difference between the two lows.

Sometimes, today's trading range will be much larger than yesterday's trading range. This can lead to both a higher high (positive directional movement) and a lower low (negative directional movement). When this situation occurs, the greater difference wins.

The Directional Movement Crossover (DMI–C) is one of the few systems that identifies trend using the difference between two oscillators. Whenever positive directional movement exceeds negative directional movement, the market is trending upward. Likewise, whenever negative directional movement exceeds positive directional movement, the market is trending downward.

Construction

Two directional movement indicators, a positive directional movement indicator (+DI) and a negative directional movement indicator (–DI), are plotted. These indicators are based on the average of positive and negative directional movement over a certain time period. To calculate these directional movement indicators, let $+DM_i$ represent the positive directional movement for Day i and $-DM_i$ represent the negative directional movement for Day i.
Then

$$+DM_i = H_i - H_{i-1} \ \{if \ H_i > H_{i-1}\}$$
$$-DM_i = L_{i-1} - L_i \ \{if \ L_i < L_{i-1}\}.$$

Table 3.6a
Kirshenbaum Bands (KBA-C) Long Hit Analysis
(Average of all stocks)

Qtr	Optimal Long	KBA-C Long	Long Hits	Cash Hits	Total Hits	Long Right	Long Wrong	Cash Right	Cash Wrong
85:1	32.1%	36.6%	66.9%	68.0%	67.6%	24.5%	12.1%	43.1%	20.3%
85:2	30.2%	43.0%	65.8%	70.0%	68.2%	28.3%	14.7%	39.9%	17.1%
85:3	26.3%	49.2%	61.1%	74.4%	67.9%	30.1%	19.1%	37.8%	13.0%
85:4	36.6%	35.6%	68.1%	62.4%	64.4%	24.2%	11.3%	40.2%	24.2%
86:1	44.2%	35.4%	65.6%	55.8%	59.3%	23.2%	12.2%	36.1%	28.6%
86:2	39.7%	45.5%	61.8%	61.2%	61.4%	28.1%	17.4%	33.3%	21.2%
86:3	37.0%	50.3%	58.5%	62.4%	60.5%	29.5%	20.9%	31.0%	18.7%
86:4	38.5%	48.6%	62.7%	61.8%	62.3%	30.5%	18.1%	31.8%	19.6%
87:1	44.7%	37.6%	65.5%	56.4%	59.8%	24.6%	13.0%	35.2%	27.2%
87:2	40.0%	54.3%	60.1%	60.6%	60.3%	32.6%	21.7%	27.7%	18.0%
87:3	39.5%	44.9%	60.0%	60.6%	60.3%	27.0%	18.0%	33.4%	21.7%
87:4	37.9%	66.0%	56.4%	63.9%	59.0%	37.2%	28.7%	21.8%	12.3%
88:1	41.3%	32.2%	64.4%	58.9%	60.7%	20.7%	11.5%	40.0%	27.8%
88:2	39.3%	51.2%	62.8%	61.1%	62.0%	32.2%	19.1%	29.8%	18.9%
88:3	35.9%	50.0%	61.7%	64.4%	63.0%	30.8%	19.1%	32.2%	17.8%
88:4	36.3%	46.6%	64.0%	63.4%	63.7%	29.8%	16.8%	33.9%	19.5%
89:1	39.0%	39.6%	64.5%	61.1%	62.4%	25.5%	14.0%	36.9%	23.5%
89:2	40.2%	36.5%	65.2%	59.7%	61.7%	23.8%	12.7%	37.9%	25.6%
89:3	39.9%	42.8%	64.8%	60.7%	62.5%	27.7%	15.1%	34.7%	22.5%
89:4	38.3%	55.7%	60.7%	60.8%	60.7%	33.8%	21.8%	26.9%	17.4%
90:1	36.9%	52.3%	61.2%	63.8%	62.4%	32.0%	20.3%	30.4%	17.3%
90:2	39.2%	43.5%	63.8%	60.8%	62.1%	27.8%	15.7%	34.3%	22.2%
90:3	33.5%	58.9%	54.3%	65.7%	59.0%	32.0%	26.9%	27.0%	14.1%
90:4	40.8%	47.2%	62.4%	58.1%	60.1%	29.5%	17.7%	30.7%	22.1%
91:1	44.1%	35.8%	65.8%	56.8%	60.0%	23.6%	12.2%	36.4%	27.8%
91:2	39.7%	44.1%	60.7%	61.0%	60.9%	26.8%	17.3%	34.1%	21.8%
91:3	40.4%	50.3%	60.9%	59.9%	60.4%	30.6%	19.7%	29.8%	19.9%
91:4	41.2%	49.9%	59.7%	58.8%	59.3%	29.8%	20.1%	29.5%	20.6%
92:1	40.0%	41.3%	55.9%	59.0%	57.7%	23.1%	18.2%	34.6%	24.1%
92:2	38.6%	50.2%	57.5%	61.5%	59.5%	28.8%	21.3%	30.7%	19.2%
92:3	40.3%	47.0%	60.0%	59.2%	59.6%	28.2%	18.8%	31.3%	21.6%
92:4	41.9%	42.0%	62.9%	57.9%	60.0%	26.4%	15.6%	33.6%	24.4%
93:1	42.5%	42.0%	61.1%	57.8%	59.2%	25.7%	16.4%	33.5%	24.5%
93:2	42.1%	49.8%	59.3%	57.7%	58.5%	29.5%	20.3%	29.0%	21.3%
93:3	42.5%	42.6%	60.7%	57.6%	58.9%	25.9%	16.8%	33.1%	24.3%
93:4	41.5%	49.4%	58.0%	58.0%	58.0%	28.7%	20.7%	29.3%	21.3%
94:1	40.4%	46.1%	56.5%	59.1%	57.9%	26.1%	20.0%	31.9%	22.0%
94:2	40.6%	54.5%	57.6%	59.3%	58.4%	31.4%	23.1%	27.0%	18.5%
94:3	41.8%	47.2%	60.6%	58.6%	59.5%	28.6%	18.6%	30.9%	21.9%
94:4	39.5%	55.1%	57.1%	60.5%	58.7%	31.5%	23.6%	27.2%	17.7%
95:1	43.1%	39.8%	61.6%	56.8%	58.7%	24.5%	15.3%	34.2%	26.0%
95:2	43.7%	38.0%	61.6%	56.2%	58.2%	23.4%	14.6%	34.8%	27.1%
95:3	43.9%	41.1%	61.3%	55.5%	57.9%	25.2%	15.9%	32.7%	26.2%
95:4	43.4%	46.3%	59.1%	55.7%	57.3%	27.4%	18.9%	29.9%	23.8%
96:1	45.5%	45.7%	61.2%	54.6%	57.6%	28.0%	17.7%	29.7%	24.7%
96:2	42.1%	46.9%	57.8%	57.8%	57.8%	27.1%	19.8%	30.7%	22.4%
96:3	42.6%	50.2%	59.4%	57.3%	58.3%	29.8%	20.4%	28.5%	21.3%
96:4	44.3%	41.3%	60.0%	55.3%	57.2%	24.8%	16.5%	32.5%	26.2%
AVG	40.0%	45.8%	61.2%	60.2%	60.4%	27.9%	17.9%	32.5%	21.7%

Table 3.6b
Kirshenbaum Bands (KBA-C) Short Hit Analysis
(Average of all stocks)

Qtr	Optimal Short	KBA-C Short	Short Hits	Cash Hits	Total Hits	Short Right	Short Wrong	Cash Right	Cash Wrong
85:1	34.3%	54.6%	67.6%	66.3%	67.0%	36.9%	17.7%	30.1%	15.3%
85:2	34.6%	50.9%	69.8%	65.5%	67.7%	35.5%	15.3%	32.2%	17.0%
85:3	38.6%	45.0%	74.5%	61.4%	67.3%	33.5%	11.5%	33.8%	21.3%
85:4	33.1%	54.8%	61.9%	66.7%	64.1%	33.9%	20.9%	30.2%	15.0%
86:1	35.2%	55.6%	55.8%	64.5%	59.7%	31.0%	24.6%	28.7%	15.7%
86:2	39.8%	50.0%	61.3%	61.4%	61.4%	30.7%	19.3%	30.7%	19.3%
86:3	42.7%	42.6%	62.7%	58.2%	60.1%	26.7%	15.9%	33.4%	24.0%
86:4	38.7%	48.2%	61.8%	62.4%	62.1%	29.8%	18.4%	32.3%	19.5%
87:1	36.9%	56.1%	56.4%	64.4%	59.9%	31.6%	24.4%	28.3%	15.7%
87:2	40.0%	41.5%	61.0%	60.1%	60.5%	25.3%	16.2%	35.1%	23.3%
87:3	40.4%	49.8%	60.8%	59.5%	60.1%	30.2%	19.5%	29.9%	20.3%
87:4	45.3%	28.2%	64.7%	56.0%	58.5%	18.2%	9.9%	40.2%	31.6%
88:1	36.7%	63.2%	58.7%	63.5%	60.5%	37.1%	26.1%	23.4%	13.4%
88:2	37.4%	45.0%	61.2%	62.7%	62.0%	27.6%	17.4%	34.4%	20.5%
88:3	38.4%	46.6%	64.5%	61.5%	62.9%	30.0%	16.5%	32.9%	20.6%
88:4	37.0%	49.1%	63.5%	63.7%	63.6%	31.2%	17.9%	32.4%	18.5%
89:1	36.2%	55.5%	61.0%	63.8%	62.3%	33.9%	21.6%	28.4%	16.1%
89:2	35.9%	56.7%	59.7%	64.2%	61.7%	33.9%	22.8%	27.8%	15.5%
89:3	36.4%	52.5%	60.8%	64.2%	62.4%	31.9%	20.6%	30.5%	17.0%
89:4	39.0%	39.0%	61.1%	60.7%	60.8%	23.8%	15.2%	37.0%	24.0%
90:1	40.1%	43.7%	63.9%	61.0%	62.3%	27.9%	15.8%	34.3%	21.9%
90:2	37.8%	51.4%	60.6%	63.1%	61.8%	31.2%	20.2%	30.7%	17.9%
90:3	45.7%	32.4%	66.4%	54.3%	58.2%	21.5%	10.9%	36.8%	30.9%
90:4	37.6%	46.5%	57.9%	62.3%	60.2%	27.0%	19.6%	33.3%	20.2%
91:1	36.7%	56.7%	56.7%	64.6%	60.1%	32.1%	24.6%	28.0%	15.3%
91:2	40.4%	52.0%	61.1%	60.3%	60.7%	31.8%	20.2%	29.0%	19.1%
91:3	39.8%	46.1%	59.9%	60.7%	60.3%	27.6%	18.5%	32.7%	21.2%
91:4	40.5%	44.9%	59.0%	59.5%	59.3%	26.5%	18.4%	32.8%	22.3%
92:1	43.2%	53.4%	59.0%	55.8%	57.5%	31.5%	21.9%	26.0%	20.6%
92:2	42.9%	45.8%	61.6%	57.4%	59.3%	28.2%	17.6%	31.1%	23.1%
92:3	39.5%	49.2%	59.2%	60.1%	59.7%	29.1%	20.0%	30.5%	20.3%
92:4	37.5%	52.0%	57.5%	62.2%	59.8%	29.9%	22.1%	29.9%	18.2%
93:1	39.4%	53.3%	57.7%	60.8%	59.2%	30.8%	22.5%	28.4%	18.3%
93:2	40.9%	46.5%	57.7%	59.0%	58.4%	26.9%	19.7%	31.5%	21.9%
93:3	39.4%	52.5%	57.6%	60.4%	58.9%	30.2%	22.2%	28.7%	18.8%
93:4	41.7%	45.9%	58.1%	57.9%	58.0%	26.7%	19.2%	31.3%	22.8%
94:1	43.7%	50.0%	59.1%	56.3%	57.7%	29.6%	20.5%	28.1%	21.8%
94:2	42.7%	41.8%	59.6%	57.6%	58.4%	24.9%	16.9%	33.6%	24.7%
94:3	39.8%	48.9%	58.5%	60.4%	59.4%	28.6%	20.3%	30.8%	20.3%
94:4	42.8%	40.1%	60.7%	57.2%	58.6%	24.3%	15.7%	34.3%	25.6%
95:1	38.7%	56.2%	56.6%	61.1%	58.6%	31.8%	24.4%	26.8%	17.0%
95:2	38.9%	57.4%	56.0%	60.9%	58.1%	32.1%	25.3%	26.0%	16.7%
95:3	38.9%	53.8%	55.5%	60.9%	58.0%	29.9%	24.0%	28.1%	18.1%
95:4	40.5%	47.5%	55.8%	59.0%	57.5%	26.5%	21.0%	31.0%	21.5%
96:1	38.9%	50.3%	54.5%	60.8%	57.6%	27.4%	22.9%	30.3%	19.5%
96:2	42.4%	49.4%	57.6%	57.5%	57.6%	28.5%	20.9%	29.1%	21.5%
96:3	40.8%	44.8%	57.0%	58.9%	58.0%	25.6%	19.3%	32.5%	22.7%
96:4	39.8%	52.7%	55.2%	59.6%	57.2%	29.1%	23.6%	28.2%	19.1%
AVG	39.4%	49.0%	60.2%	60.8%	60.3%	29.4%	19.6%	30.9%	20.1%

Table 3.7a
Kirshenbaum Bands (KBA-C) Long Return Analysis
(Average of all stocks)

Qtr	KBA-C Terminal Wealth	Buy/Hold Terminal Wealth	Relative Terminal Wealth	KBA-C Long Avg Ret	KBA-C Cash Avg Ret	KBA-C Long-Cash Avg Ret	Buy/Hold Avg Ret
85:1	10069	10142	0.993	0.019%	-0.001%	0.019%	0.006%
85:2	9909	9700	1.022	-0.050%	-0.084%	0.034%	-0.069%
85:3	9469	8889	1.065	-0.190%	-0.220%	0.030%	-0.205%
85:4	10248	10763	0.952	0.099%	0.111%	-0.012%	0.107%
86:1	10533	11428	0.922	0.246%	0.213%	0.034%	0.225%
86:2	10350	10414	0.994	0.120%	0.022%	0.098%	0.066%
86:3	9692	9175	1.056	-0.092%	-0.164%	0.072%	-0.128%
86:4	10320	10413	0.991	0.106%	0.035%	0.071%	0.069%
87:1	11000	11929	0.922	0.414%	0.220%	0.194%	0.293%
87:2	10174	10196	0.998	0.057%	0.016%	0.041%	0.038%
87:3	10260	10408	0.986	0.093%	0.048%	0.045%	0.068%
87:4	9371	8087	1.159	-0.135%	-0.555%	0.420%	-0.278%
88:1	10462	10989	0.952	0.234%	0.129%	0.105%	0.163%
88:2	10353	10593	0.977	0.115%	0.083%	0.032%	0.100%
88:3	10065	10050	1.001	0.024%	0.001%	0.024%	0.013%
88:4	10113	10196	0.992	0.045%	0.029%	0.015%	0.037%
89:1	10304	10698	0.963	0.125%	0.104%	0.020%	0.112%
89:2	10312	10772	0.957	0.137%	0.114%	0.023%	0.122%
89:3	10447	10833	0.964	0.164%	0.106%	0.058%	0.131%
89:4	9925	9904	1.002	-0.019%	-0.001%	-0.018%	-0.011%
90:1	10127	9980	1.015	0.045%	-0.043%	0.088%	0.003%
90:2	10278	10459	0.983	0.107%	0.054%	0.053%	0.077%
90:3	9054	8526	1.062	-0.277%	-0.233%	-0.044%	-0.259%
90:4	10328	10889	0.948	0.120%	0.170%	-0.049%	0.146%
91:1	11356	12477	0.910	0.404%	0.265%	0.138%	0.315%
91:2	10227	10244	0.998	0.085%	0.014%	0.071%	0.045%
91:3	10245	10429	0.982	0.077%	0.052%	0.025%	0.065%
91:4	10327	10497	0.984	0.103%	0.060%	0.043%	0.082%
92:1	9991	10324	0.968	-0.006%	0.086%	-0.092%	0.048%
92:2	9840	9723	1.012	-0.054%	-0.043%	-0.011%	-0.048%
92:3	10157	10392	0.977	0.048%	0.064%	-0.016%	0.057%
92:4	10380	10963	0.947	0.140%	0.148%	-0.008%	0.144%
93:1	10274	10527	0.976	0.100%	0.065%	0.034%	0.080%
93:2	10163	10340	0.983	0.050%	0.053%	-0.003%	0.052%
93:3	10315	10686	0.965	0.113%	0.092%	0.021%	0.101%
93:4	10078	10255	0.983	0.023%	0.045%	-0.022%	0.034%
94:1	9977	9954	1.002	-0.013%	-0.010%	-0.003%	-0.011%
94:2	10009	9994	1.002	-0.002%	-0.008%	0.006%	-0.005%
94:3	10294	10613	0.970	0.092%	0.087%	0.006%	0.089%
94:4	9895	9836	1.006	-0.032%	-0.026%	-0.006%	-0.029%
95:1	10311	10706	0.963	0.125%	0.100%	0.026%	0.110%
95:2	10298	10873	0.947	0.124%	0.140%	-0.016%	0.134%
95:3	10336	10853	0.952	0.129%	0.133%	-0.004%	0.131%
95:4	10149	10445	0.972	0.048%	0.083%	-0.034%	0.067%
96:1	10503	11027	0.952	0.173%	0.147%	0.025%	0.159%
96:2	10151	10367	0.979	0.052%	0.064%	-0.012%	0.059%
96:3	10149	10298	0.986	0.047%	0.047%	0.000%	0.047%
96:4	10271	10817	0.950	0.102%	0.137%	-0.035%	0.122%
AVG	10185	10377	0.982	0.059%	0.052%	0.008%	0.055%

Table 3.7b
Kirshenbaum Bands (KBA-C) Short Return Analysis
(Average of all stocks)

Qtr	KBA-C Terminal Wealth	Buy/Hold Terminal Wealth	Relative Terminal Wealth	KBA-C Short Avg Ret	KBA-C Cash Avg Ret	KBA-C Short-Cash Avg Ret	Buy/Hold Avg Ret
85:1	9996	10142	0.986	0.011%	0.001%	0.010%	0.006%
85:2	10289	9700	1.061	-0.078%	-0.060%	-0.017%	-0.069%
85:3	10699	8889	1.204	-0.227%	-0.187%	-0.040%	-0.205%
85:4	9570	10763	0.889	0.132%	0.076%	0.055%	0.107%
86:1	9300	11428	0.814	0.223%	0.227%	-0.004%	0.225%
86:2	9932	10414	0.954	0.020%	0.112%	-0.092%	0.066%
86:3	10473	9175	1.142	-0.176%	-0.091%	-0.085%	-0.128%
86:4	9892	10413	0.950	0.032%	0.104%	-0.073%	0.069%
87:1	9244	11929	0.775	0.231%	0.372%	-0.142%	0.293%
87:2	9985	10196	0.979	0.004%	0.062%	-0.058%	0.038%
87:3	9829	10408	0.944	0.052%	0.084%	-0.032%	0.068%
87:4	10952	8087	1.354	-0.539%	-0.176%	-0.364%	-0.278%
88:1	9428	10989	0.858	0.144%	0.196%	-0.052%	0.163%
88:2	9766	10593	0.922	0.082%	0.114%	-0.033%	0.100%
88:3	9992	10050	0.994	0.000%	0.023%	-0.023%	0.013%
88:4	9915	10196	0.972	0.025%	0.047%	-0.022%	0.037%
89:1	9623	10698	0.899	0.114%	0.110%	0.003%	0.112%
89:2	9572	10772	0.889	0.120%	0.124%	-0.004%	0.122%
89:3	9647	10833	0.890	0.109%	0.155%	-0.047%	0.131%
89:4	10013	9904	1.011	-0.008%	-0.013%	0.004%	-0.011%
90:1	10119	9980	1.014	-0.045%	0.040%	-0.086%	0.003%
90:2	9807	10459	0.938	0.062%	0.093%	-0.031%	0.077%
90:3	10539	8526	1.236	-0.258%	-0.259%	0.001%	-0.259%
90:4	9485	10889	0.871	0.181%	0.116%	0.064%	0.146%
91:1	9107	12477	0.730	0.280%	0.361%	-0.081%	0.315%
91:2	9934	10244	0.970	0.016%	0.077%	-0.061%	0.045%
91:3	9850	10429	0.944	0.053%	0.075%	-0.022%	0.065%
91:4	9812	10497	0.935	0.059%	0.101%	-0.042%	0.082%
92:1	9722	10324	0.942	0.092%	-0.002%	0.094%	0.048%
92:2	10140	9723	1.043	-0.047%	-0.050%	0.003%	-0.048%
92:3	9799	10392	0.943	0.066%	0.047%	0.019%	0.057%
92:4	9494	10963	0.866	0.161%	0.127%	0.034%	0.144%
93:1	9793	10527	0.930	0.067%	0.094%	-0.027%	0.080%
93:2	9855	10340	0.953	0.053%	0.051%	0.002%	0.052%
93:3	9707	10686	0.908	0.095%	0.108%	-0.013%	0.101%
93:4	9893	10255	0.965	0.042%	0.027%	0.015%	0.034%
94:1	10021	9954	1.007	-0.005%	-0.018%	0.013%	-0.011%
94:2	10055	9994	1.006	-0.020%	0.006%	-0.026%	-0.005%
94:3	9729	10613	0.917	0.092%	0.086%	0.006%	0.089%
94:4	10077	9836	1.024	-0.028%	-0.030%	0.002%	-0.029%
95:1	9629	10706	0.899	0.111%	0.109%	0.001%	0.110%
95:2	9490	10873	0.873	0.149%	0.114%	0.035%	0.134%
95:3	9551	10853	0.880	0.139%	0.122%	0.016%	0.131%
95:4	9754	10445	0.934	0.087%	0.049%	0.038%	0.067%
96:1	9529	11027	0.864	0.156%	0.161%	-0.005%	0.159%
96:2	9784	10367	0.944	0.073%	0.045%	0.028%	0.059%
96:3	9828	10298	0.954	0.063%	0.035%	0.028%	0.047%
96:4	9538	10817	0.882	0.145%	0.097%	0.047%	0.122%
AVG	9837	10377	0.948	0.057%	0.054%	0.003%	0.055%

TR_i represents the "true range" for the stock on Day i and is calculated as follows:

$$TR_i = H - L \ \{if \ L_{i-1} \geq L_i\}$$
$$H_i - H_{i-1} \ \{if \ L_{i-1} < L_i\}$$
$$L_{i-1} - L_i \ \{if \ H_i < H_{i-1}\}.$$

The positive directional movement for P periods is calculated as:

$$+DI = (+DM_1 + +DM_2 + \ldots + +DM_p)/(TR_1 + TR_2 + \ldots + TR_p).$$

The negative directional movement for P periods is calculated as:

$$-DI = (DM_1 + -DM_2 + \ldots + -DM_p)/(TR_1 + TR_2 + \ldots + TR_p).$$

The +DI crossing the −DI to the upside generates a long signal. A short signal is generated when the +DI crosses through the +DI to the downside.

Results

The results for this indicator are shown in Tables 3.8 and 3.9. In testing this indicator, we find an average hit rate of 61.0 percent for long calls (Table 3.8a) and a hit rate of 60.2 percent for the short calls (Table 3.8b). Generally, if the indicator favors a long position or a short position rather than a cash position, the call is correct.

The average daily return for long signals is 0.100 percent. The average daily return for the market when a cash position is favored over a long position is only 0.042 percent (Table 3.9a). The indicator also tends to provide helpful information when looking at short versus cash positions. When the indicator signals short positions, the average return in the market is only 0.015 percent compared to an average market return of 0.066 percent when cash signals occur (Table 3.9b). Therefore, when the indicator recommends a short position over cash, the market return is likely to be lower than when the indicator recommends staying in cash, but the market return is, on average, still positive.

The terminal wealth following either the long recommendations or the short recommendations is higher than the terminal wealth of a buy-and-hold strategy during quarters when the buy-and-hold average return is negative. Thus, this indicator tends to give good signals during market declines. However, on average, the terminal wealth resulting from following either the long recommendations or the short recommendations from this system is less than the buy-and-hold terminal wealth.

Like many of the other indicators, this system tends to be conservative in firing signals. On average, long signals are fired only 22.3 percent of the time (Table 3.8a) and short signals are fired only 21.0 percent of the time (Table 3.8b). Because these call rates are far below the optimal call rates, this is a significant shortcoming.

MAC-D

The Moving Average Convergence/Divergence (MAC-D) is a popular indicator that was originally developed by system writer Gerald Appel, publisher of *Systems and Forecasts*. MAC-D is based on a divergence of the difference between two moving averages and price. MAC-D is calculated by subtracting the 26-day moving average of a stock's price from the 12-day moving average of the stock's price. This results in a value that oscillates above and below zero. An MAC-D value greater than zero indicates that the average stock price during the past 12 days exceeds the average stock price in the past 26 days. A negative MAC-D indicates just the opposite.

Whenever the MAC-D is moving in the opposite direction, or diverging, from the direction of price movement, a trading signal occurs. For example, if an upward trend in price is accompanied by a falling MAC-D, a bearish signal occurs. Bullish, long signals occur when a stock's price is falling but the MAC-D is rising.

Construction

First, calculate a 12-period exponential moving average and a 26-period exponential moving average of a stock's closing price. Then, to construct the MAC-D, plot the difference between a 12-period exponential moving average and a 26-period moving average. Thus, $MAC\text{-}D = EMA_{12} - EMA_{26}$.

Next, the MAC-D is compared to the stock's price trend. The price trend is determined using a Pivot Point algorithm. When a divergence in the MAC-D and the stock price movement is noticed, a trading signal is generated.

Results

This trend-following momentum indicator is designed conservatively. Traders keep on the right side of the market by sacrificing early signals. Our test results in Tables 3.10 and 3.11 show just how conservative this indicator is. Not

Table 3.8a
Directional Movement Crossover (DMI-C) Long Hit Analysis
(Average of all stocks)

Qtr	Optimal Long	DMI-C Long	Long Hits	Cash Hits	Total Hits	Long Right	Long Wrong	Cash Right	Cash Wrong
85:1	32.1%	20.1%	67.1%	68.9%	68.5%	13.5%	6.6%	55.0%	24.9%
85:2	30.2%	23.4%	65.0%	70.4%	69.2%	15.2%	8.2%	53.9%	22.6%
85:3	26.3%	19.3%	61.4%	73.7%	71.3%	11.8%	7.4%	59.5%	21.2%
85:4	36.6%	24.0%	67.4%	63.2%	64.2%	16.2%	7.8%	48.1%	27.9%
86:1	44.2%	20.9%	66.1%	56.1%	58.1%	13.8%	7.1%	44.3%	34.7%
86:2	39.7%	23.2%	61.2%	60.7%	60.8%	14.2%	9.0%	46.6%	30.2%
86:3	37.0%	19.3%	57.4%	63.1%	62.0%	11.1%	8.2%	51.0%	29.8%
86:4	38.5%	25.7%	61.0%	61.8%	61.6%	15.7%	10.0%	45.9%	28.4%
87:1	44.7%	23.1%	65.6%	56.2%	58.3%	15.2%	8.0%	43.2%	33.7%
87:2	40.0%	23.6%	59.6%	60.1%	60.0%	14.1%	9.5%	45.9%	30.5%
87:3	39.5%	21.3%	60.4%	60.8%	60.7%	12.8%	8.4%	47.9%	30.9%
87:4	37.9%	15.4%	57.4%	62.4%	61.6%	8.8%	6.6%	52.7%	31.8%
88:1	41.3%	23.2%	62.0%	58.8%	59.6%	14.4%	8.8%	45.2%	31.6%
88:2	39.3%	25.4%	62.1%	61.0%	61.3%	15.8%	9.6%	45.5%	29.1%
88:3	35.9%	21.5%	59.8%	64.0%	63.1%	12.9%	8.6%	50.2%	28.3%
88:4	36.3%	22.2%	62.8%	63.7%	63.5%	14.0%	8.3%	49.5%	28.2%
89:1	39.0%	21.8%	63.7%	61.2%	61.8%	13.9%	7.9%	47.9%	30.3%
89:2	40.2%	21.2%	64.1%	59.9%	60.8%	13.6%	7.6%	47.2%	31.6%
89:3	39.9%	22.8%	64.3%	60.7%	61.6%	14.7%	8.1%	46.9%	30.3%
89:4	38.3%	20.6%	61.8%	62.0%	62.0%	12.7%	7.9%	49.2%	30.2%
90:1	36.9%	22.2%	60.3%	63.6%	62.9%	13.4%	8.8%	49.5%	28.3%
90:2	39.2%	22.1%	63.5%	61.2%	61.7%	14.1%	8.1%	47.6%	30.2%
90:3	33.5%	14.0%	55.4%	66.6%	65.0%	7.8%	6.3%	57.3%	28.7%
90:4	40.8%	23.8%	61.3%	59.1%	59.6%	14.6%	9.2%	45.0%	31.2%
91:1	44.1%	20.8%	66.4%	56.8%	58.8%	13.8%	7.0%	45.0%	34.2%
91:2	39.7%	21.9%	59.6%	60.6%	60.4%	13.1%	8.8%	47.3%	30.8%
91:3	40.4%	26.0%	59.6%	59.6%	59.6%	15.5%	10.5%	44.1%	29.9%
91:4	41.2%	24.1%	60.9%	59.6%	59.9%	14.7%	9.4%	45.2%	30.7%
92:1	40.0%	20.3%	56.6%	60.0%	59.4%	11.5%	8.8%	47.9%	31.8%
92:2	38.6%	21.5%	56.4%	61.4%	60.3%	12.1%	9.3%	48.2%	30.3%
92:3	40.3%	24.3%	60.1%	59.8%	59.9%	14.6%	9.7%	45.3%	30.4%
92:4	41.9%	23.4%	63.4%	58.4%	59.5%	14.8%	8.5%	44.7%	31.9%
93:1	42.5%	23.1%	61.1%	57.7%	58.5%	14.1%	9.0%	44.4%	32.5%
93:2	42.1%	23.0%	59.5%	57.9%	58.3%	13.7%	9.3%	44.6%	32.4%
93:3	42.5%	22.5%	61.7%	57.9%	58.8%	13.9%	8.6%	44.9%	32.6%
93:4	41.5%	22.1%	58.4%	58.6%	58.6%	12.9%	9.2%	45.7%	32.2%
94:1	40.4%	22.3%	55.6%	59.5%	58.6%	12.4%	9.9%	46.2%	31.5%
94:2	40.6%	21.1%	57.2%	59.5%	59.0%	12.1%	9.0%	46.9%	32.0%
94:3	41.8%	23.9%	60.3%	58.5%	58.9%	14.4%	9.5%	44.5%	31.6%
94:4	39.5%	22.9%	57.7%	60.7%	60.0%	13.2%	9.7%	46.8%	30.3%
95:1	43.1%	24.0%	61.6%	57.1%	58.2%	14.8%	9.2%	43.4%	32.6%
95:2	43.7%	23.8%	61.4%	56.5%	57.6%	14.6%	9.2%	43.0%	33.2%
95:3	43.9%	22.8%	61.0%	56.1%	57.2%	13.9%	8.9%	43.3%	33.9%
95:4	43.4%	21.3%	60.0%	56.8%	57.5%	12.8%	8.5%	44.7%	34.0%
96:1	45.5%	24.6%	61.0%	54.7%	56.2%	15.0%	9.6%	41.2%	34.2%
96:2	42.1%	22.5%	58.0%	58.2%	58.1%	13.1%	9.5%	45.0%	32.4%
96:3	42.6%	23.9%	59.8%	57.6%	58.1%	14.3%	9.6%	43.8%	32.3%
96:4	44.3%	21.7%	60.9%	55.9%	57.0%	13.2%	8.5%	43.7%	34.5%
AVG	40.0%	22.3%	61.0%	60.4%	60.6%	13.6%	8.7%	47.0%	30.8%

Table 3.8b
Directional Movement Crossover (DMI-C) Short Hit Analysis
(Average of all stocks)

Qtr	Optimal Short	DMI-C Short	Short Hits	Cash Hits	Total Hits	Short Right	Short Wrong	Cash Right	Cash Wrong
85:1	34.3%	19.2%	67.9%	65.9%	66.3%	13.0%	6.1%	53.3%	27.5%
85:2	34.6%	19.9%	69.4%	65.4%	66.2%	13.8%	6.1%	52.4%	27.7%
85:3	38.6%	24.7%	73.2%	61.9%	64.7%	18.1%	6.6%	46.6%	28.7%
85:4	33.1%	14.1%	66.0%	66.5%	66.5%	9.3%	4.8%	57.1%	28.7%
86:1	35.2%	15.6%	56.1%	64.6%	63.2%	8.7%	6.8%	54.5%	29.9%
86:2	39.8%	22.6%	59.4%	60.2%	60.0%	13.4%	9.2%	46.6%	30.8%
86:3	42.7%	25.4%	64.0%	57.8%	59.4%	16.2%	9.1%	43.2%	31.5%
86:4	38.7%	21.9%	60.3%	61.2%	61.0%	13.2%	8.7%	47.8%	30.3%
87:1	36.9%	13.9%	55.2%	62.9%	61.9%	7.7%	6.2%	54.2%	31.9%
87:2	40.0%	22.9%	60.1%	60.3%	60.2%	13.7%	9.1%	46.5%	30.6%
87:3	40.4%	23.0%	60.5%	59.7%	59.9%	13.9%	9.1%	46.0%	31.0%
87:4	45.3%	26.7%	63.8%	56.1%	58.2%	17.0%	9.6%	41.1%	32.2%
88:1	36.7%	19.2%	55.5%	63.0%	61.6%	10.6%	8.5%	50.9%	29.9%
88:2	37.4%	21.7%	60.1%	62.6%	62.0%	13.1%	8.7%	49.0%	29.3%
88:3	38.4%	23.2%	63.5%	61.8%	62.2%	14.7%	8.5%	47.5%	29.3%
88:4	37.0%	21.8%	64.2%	63.4%	63.6%	14.0%	7.8%	49.6%	28.6%
89:1	36.2%	20.0%	59.5%	63.5%	62.7%	11.9%	8.1%	50.8%	29.2%
89:2	35.9%	15.2%	59.8%	63.9%	63.3%	9.1%	6.1%	54.2%	30.6%
89:3	36.4%	20.9%	58.1%	63.3%	62.2%	12.1%	8.7%	50.1%	29.1%
89:4	39.0%	21.8%	61.2%	61.1%	61.1%	13.3%	8.4%	47.8%	30.5%
90:1	40.1%	22.5%	65.4%	60.7%	61.7%	14.7%	7.8%	47.0%	30.5%
90:2	37.8%	21.3%	62.4%	62.5%	62.5%	13.3%	8.0%	49.2%	29.5%
90:3	45.7%	21.4%	66.5%	54.5%	57.1%	14.3%	7.2%	42.8%	35.7%
90:4	37.6%	17.3%	58.4%	62.2%	61.6%	10.1%	7.2%	51.5%	31.2%
91:1	36.7%	16.8%	56.7%	63.3%	62.2%	9.5%	7.3%	52.6%	30.6%
91:2	40.4%	23.3%	59.8%	59.5%	59.5%	13.9%	9.4%	45.6%	31.1%
91:3	39.8%	22.6%	59.0%	60.3%	60.0%	13.3%	9.3%	46.6%	30.7%
91:4	40.5%	22.0%	61.0%	60.0%	60.2%	13.4%	8.6%	46.8%	31.2%
92:1	43.2%	19.6%	59.5%	56.8%	57.3%	11.6%	7.9%	45.7%	34.7%
92:2	42.9%	24.1%	61.0%	57.2%	58.1%	14.7%	9.4%	43.4%	32.5%
92:3	39.5%	21.3%	59.0%	60.5%	60.1%	12.6%	8.8%	47.6%	31.1%
92:4	37.5%	19.2%	58.8%	62.7%	62.0%	11.3%	7.9%	50.7%	30.1%
93:1	39.4%	21.1%	57.0%	60.7%	60.0%	12.0%	9.1%	47.9%	31.0%
93:2	40.9%	23.6%	58.1%	59.2%	59.0%	13.7%	9.9%	45.2%	31.2%
93:3	39.4%	20.6%	57.9%	60.9%	60.3%	11.9%	8.7%	48.4%	31.1%
93:4	41.7%	21.5%	59.0%	58.5%	58.6%	12.7%	8.8%	45.9%	32.6%
94:1	43.7%	23.1%	59.8%	56.3%	57.1%	13.8%	9.3%	43.3%	33.6%
94:2	42.7%	23.7%	59.3%	57.5%	57.9%	14.0%	9.6%	43.9%	32.5%
94:3	39.8%	21.8%	58.5%	60.5%	60.1%	12.7%	9.0%	47.4%	30.9%
94:4	42.8%	22.1%	60.3%	57.2%	57.8%	13.3%	8.8%	44.5%	33.4%
95:1	38.7%	19.6%	57.2%	61.3%	60.5%	11.2%	8.4%	49.3%	31.1%
95:2	38.9%	18.8%	55.3%	60.7%	59.7%	10.4%	8.4%	49.3%	31.9%
95:3	38.9%	20.0%	56.4%	61.0%	60.1%	11.3%	8.7%	48.8%	31.2%
95:4	40.5%	20.1%	56.8%	59.6%	59.0%	11.4%	8.7%	47.6%	32.3%
96:1	38.9%	22.1%	54.1%	61.0%	59.5%	11.9%	10.1%	47.5%	30.4%
96:2	42.4%	23.7%	58.2%	57.8%	57.9%	13.8%	9.9%	44.1%	32.2%
96:3	40.8%	21.0%	58.9%	59.7%	59.5%	12.4%	8.6%	47.1%	31.9%
96:4	39.8%	19.8%	56.3%	60.3%	59.5%	11.2%	8.7%	48.3%	31.9%
AVG	39.4%	21.0%	60.2%	60.8%	60.7%	12.7%	8.3%	48.1%	30.9%

Table 3.9a
Directional Movement Crossover (DMI-C) Long Return Analysis
(Average of all stocks)

Qtr	DMI-C Terminal Wealth	Buy/Hold Terminal Wealth	Relative Terminal Wealth	DMI-C Long Avg Ret	DMI-C Cash Avg Ret	DMI-C Long-Cash Avg Ret	Buy/Hold Avg Ret
85:1	10146	10142	1.000	0.114%	-0.021%	0.135%	0.006%
85:2	9987	9700	1.030	-0.012%	-0.087%	0.075%	-0.069%
85:3	9805	8889	1.103	-0.166%	-0.214%	0.049%	-0.205%
85:4	10189	10763	0.947	0.121%	0.102%	0.019%	0.107%
86:1	10369	11428	0.907	0.291%	0.207%	0.083%	0.225%
86:2	10195	10414	0.979	0.132%	0.047%	0.085%	0.066%
86:3	9900	9175	1.079	-0.082%	-0.138%	0.056%	-0.128%
86:4	10140	10413	0.974	0.088%	0.063%	0.025%	0.069%
87:1	10613	11929	0.890	0.424%	0.254%	0.170%	0.293%
87:2	10084	10196	0.989	0.061%	0.031%	0.030%	0.038%
87:3	10166	10408	0.977	0.126%	0.053%	0.074%	0.068%
87:4	10057	8087	1.244	0.067%	-0.341%	0.408%	-0.278%
88:1	10198	10989	0.928	0.146%	0.168%	-0.022%	0.163%
88:2	10188	10593	0.962	0.123%	0.092%	0.031%	0.100%
88:3	10011	10050	0.996	0.010%	0.013%	-0.004%	0.013%
88:4	10051	10196	0.986	0.040%	0.036%	0.005%	0.037%
89:1	10222	10698	0.955	0.165%	0.098%	0.068%	0.112%
89:2	10174	10772	0.945	0.130%	0.120%	0.010%	0.122%
89:3	10266	10833	0.948	0.186%	0.115%	0.071%	0.131%
89:4	10044	9904	1.014	0.036%	-0.023%	0.060%	-0.011%
90:1	10073	9980	1.009	0.056%	-0.012%	0.069%	0.003%
90:2	10184	10459	0.974	0.136%	0.060%	0.077%	0.077%
90:3	9854	8526	1.156	-0.167%	-0.274%	0.107%	-0.259%
90:4	10153	10889	0.932	0.107%	0.158%	-0.051%	0.146%
91:1	10622	12477	0.851	0.492%	0.269%	0.223%	0.315%
91:2	10108	10244	0.987	0.079%	0.036%	0.043%	0.045%
91:3	10094	10429	0.968	0.055%	0.068%	-0.013%	0.065%
91:4	10233	10497	0.975	0.153%	0.059%	0.094%	0.082%
92:1	10080	10324	0.976	0.064%	0.044%	0.020%	0.048%
92:2	9916	9723	1.020	-0.063%	-0.044%	-0.018%	-0.048%
92:3	10095	10392	0.971	0.058%	0.056%	0.001%	0.057%
92:4	10263	10963	0.936	0.177%	0.134%	0.043%	0.144%
93:1	10151	10527	0.964	0.104%	0.072%	0.031%	0.080%
93:2	10095	10340	0.976	0.062%	0.049%	0.013%	0.052%
93:3	10196	10686	0.954	0.136%	0.091%	0.045%	0.101%
93:4	10091	10255	0.984	0.065%	0.025%	0.039%	0.034%
94:1	9983	9954	1.003	-0.014%	-0.011%	-0.003%	-0.011%
94:2	10013	9994	1.002	0.008%	-0.008%	0.017%	-0.005%
94:3	10173	10613	0.959	0.113%	0.082%	0.031%	0.089%
94:4	9979	9836	1.014	-0.017%	-0.033%	0.016%	-0.029%
95:1	10196	10706	0.952	0.130%	0.104%	0.026%	0.110%
95:2	10233	10873	0.941	0.154%	0.128%	0.026%	0.134%
95:3	10206	10853	0.940	0.143%	0.128%	0.016%	0.131%
95:4	10138	10445	0.971	0.104%	0.057%	0.047%	0.067%
96:1	10272	11027	0.932	0.177%	0.153%	0.024%	0.159%
96:2	10121	10367	0.976	0.088%	0.050%	0.039%	0.059%
96:3	10124	10298	0.983	0.083%	0.036%	0.046%	0.047%
96:4	10229	10817	0.946	0.165%	0.110%	0.054%	0.122%
AVG	10139	10377	0.977	0.100%	0.042%	0.057%	0.055%

Table 3.9b
Directional Movement Crossover (DMI-C) Short Return Analysis
(Average of all stocks)

Qtr	DMI-C Terminal Wealth	Buy/Hold Terminal Wealth	Relative Terminal Wealth	DMI-C Short Avg Ret	DMI-C Cash Avg Ret	DMI-C Short-Cash Avg Ret	Buy/Hold Avg Ret
85:1	10048	10142	0.991	-0.038%	0.017%	-0.055%	0.006%
85:2	10108	9700	1.042	-0.079%	-0.067%	-0.012%	-0.069%
85:3	10386	8889	1.168	-0.239%	-0.194%	-0.046%	-0.205%
85:4	9925	10763	0.922	0.085%	0.110%	-0.025%	0.107%
86:1	9783	11428	0.856	0.230%	0.224%	0.006%	0.225%
86:2	9906	10414	0.951	0.065%	0.067%	-0.001%	0.066%
86:3	10388	9175	1.132	-0.243%	-0.088%	-0.155%	-0.128%
86:4	9867	10413	0.948	0.099%	0.061%	0.038%	0.069%
87:1	9736	11929	0.816	0.315%	0.289%	0.026%	0.293%
87:2	9973	10196	0.978	0.017%	0.044%	-0.027%	0.038%
87:3	9952	10408	0.956	0.031%	0.079%	-0.048%	0.068%
87:4	11121	8087	1.375	-0.681%	-0.131%	-0.550%	-0.278%
88:1	9675	10989	0.880	0.276%	0.136%	0.141%	0.163%
88:2	9859	10593	0.931	0.104%	0.099%	0.005%	0.100%
88:3	10026	10050	0.998	-0.020%	0.022%	-0.042%	0.013%
88:4	10027	10196	0.983	-0.022%	0.053%	-0.075%	0.037%
89:1	9874	10698	0.923	0.103%	0.115%	-0.012%	0.112%
89:2	9892	10772	0.918	0.111%	0.124%	-0.013%	0.122%
89:3	9824	10833	0.907	0.135%	0.130%	0.005%	0.131%
89:4	9967	9904	1.006	0.021%	-0.020%	0.041%	-0.011%
90:1	10145	9980	1.017	-0.105%	0.034%	-0.139%	0.003%
90:2	10003	10459	0.956	-0.004%	0.099%	-0.102%	0.077%
90:3	10346	8526	1.213	-0.262%	-0.258%	-0.004%	-0.259%
90:4	9788	10889	0.899	0.192%	0.137%	0.056%	0.146%
91:1	9750	12477	0.781	0.248%	0.329%	-0.081%	0.315%
91:2	9952	10244	0.971	0.030%	0.050%	-0.020%	0.045%
91:3	9910	10429	0.950	0.065%	0.065%	0.000%	0.065%
91:4	9978	10497	0.951	0.011%	0.102%	-0.090%	0.082%
92:1	9960	10324	0.965	0.032%	0.052%	-0.019%	0.048%
92:2	10104	9723	1.039	-0.069%	-0.042%	-0.027%	-0.048%
92:3	9914	10392	0.954	0.064%	0.055%	0.009%	0.057%
92:4	9886	10963	0.902	0.094%	0.157%	-0.063%	0.144%
93:1	9914	10527	0.942	0.067%	0.083%	-0.017%	0.080%
93:2	9974	10340	0.965	0.016%	0.063%	-0.047%	0.052%
93:3	9930	10686	0.929	0.056%	0.113%	-0.057%	0.101%
93:4	10005	10255	0.976	-0.002%	0.044%	-0.046%	0.034%
94:1	10063	9954	1.011	-0.039%	-0.003%	-0.036%	-0.011%
94:2	10038	9994	1.004	-0.024%	0.001%	-0.025%	-0.005%
94:3	9920	10613	0.935	0.061%	0.097%	-0.037%	0.089%
94:4	10025	9836	1.019	-0.017%	-0.033%	0.015%	-0.029%
95:1	9880	10706	0.923	0.099%	0.113%	-0.013%	0.110%
95:2	9800	10873	0.901	0.173%	0.125%	0.048%	0.134%
95:3	9848	10853	0.907	0.126%	0.132%	-0.007%	0.131%
95:4	9938	10445	0.951	0.051%	0.071%	-0.019%	0.067%
96:1	9808	11027	0.889	0.142%	0.164%	-0.021%	0.159%
96:2	9936	10367	0.958	0.042%	0.064%	-0.021%	0.059%
96:3	10012	10298	0.972	-0.008%	0.062%	-0.070%	0.047%
96:4	9882	10817	0.914	0.096%	0.129%	-0.033%	0.122%
AVG	9980	10377	0.962	0.015%	0.066%	-0.051%	0.055%

Tabale 3.10a
Moving Average Convergence Divergence (MAC-D) Long Hit Analysis
(Average of all stocks)

Qtr	Optimal Long	MAC-D Long	Long Hits	Cash Hits	Total Hits	Long Right	Long Wrong	Cash Right	Cash Wrong
85:1	32.1%	1.3%	69.5%	68.0%	68.0%	0.9%	0.4%	67.1%	31.6%
85:2	30.2%	3.1%	65.2%	69.9%	69.7%	2.1%	1.1%	67.7%	29.2%
85:3	26.3%	3.3%	59.5%	73.7%	73.2%	2.0%	1.4%	71.2%	25.4%
85:4	36.6%	3.6%	68.1%	63.3%	63.5%	2.4%	1.1%	61.1%	35.4%
86:1	44.2%	1.8%	67.3%	55.8%	56.0%	1.2%	0.6%	54.8%	43.4%
86:2	39.7%	2.2%	61.5%	60.2%	60.2%	1.3%	0.8%	58.9%	38.9%
86:3	37.0%	3.7%	59.9%	63.0%	62.8%	2.2%	1.5%	60.7%	35.7%
86:4	38.5%	4.4%	64.0%	61.6%	61.7%	2.8%	1.6%	58.9%	36.7%
87:1	44.7%	1.8%	66.5%	55.3%	55.5%	1.2%	0.6%	54.3%	43.9%
87:2	40.0%	3.9%	63.1%	60.1%	60.2%	2.4%	1.4%	57.8%	38.3%
87:3	39.5%	1.7%	62.9%	60.5%	60.5%	1.1%	0.6%	59.4%	38.8%
87:4	37.9%	8.6%	59.5%	62.5%	62.3%	5.1%	3.5%	57.1%	34.2%
88:1	41.3%	1.9%	66.6%	58.8%	58.9%	1.2%	0.6%	57.7%	40.5%
88:2	39.3%	3.2%	64.3%	60.8%	60.9%	2.0%	1.1%	58.8%	38.0%
88:3	35.9%	3.3%	62.2%	64.1%	64.0%	2.1%	1.3%	62.0%	34.7%
88:4	36.3%	3.1%	63.8%	63.7%	63.7%	2.0%	1.1%	61.7%	35.2%
89:1	39.0%	2.3%	64.1%	61.0%	61.0%	1.4%	0.8%	59.6%	38.2%
89:2	40.2%	2.2%	68.7%	59.8%	60.0%	1.5%	0.7%	58.5%	39.3%
89:3	39.9%	2.2%	66.8%	60.1%	60.2%	1.4%	0.7%	58.8%	39.1%
89:4	38.3%	5.6%	60.7%	61.6%	61.5%	3.4%	2.2%	58.1%	36.3%
90:1	36.9%	5.2%	63.2%	63.2%	63.2%	3.3%	1.9%	60.0%	34.9%
90:2	39.2%	3.4%	65.0%	60.7%	60.9%	2.2%	1.2%	58.7%	38.0%
90:3	33.5%	5.7%	50.1%	66.3%	65.4%	2.9%	2.8%	62.5%	31.8%
90:4	40.8%	8.5%	62.6%	59.2%	59.5%	5.3%	3.2%	54.2%	37.3%
91:1	44.1%	2.0%	65.9%	55.9%	56.1%	1.3%	0.7%	54.7%	43.2%
91:2	39.7%	2.1%	59.5%	60.3%	60.3%	1.3%	0.9%	59.0%	38.8%
91:3	40.4%	3.9%	59.1%	59.5%	59.5%	2.3%	1.6%	57.2%	38.9%
91:4	41.2%	4.3%	59.9%	58.8%	58.9%	2.6%	1.7%	56.3%	39.4%
92:1	40.0%	2.9%	55.7%	60.0%	59.9%	1.6%	1.3%	58.3%	38.8%
92:2	38.6%	5.1%	57.7%	61.5%	61.3%	2.9%	2.2%	58.4%	36.5%
92:3	40.3%	4.2%	58.3%	59.7%	59.7%	2.4%	1.7%	57.2%	38.6%
92:4	41.9%	3.0%	60.9%	58.1%	58.2%	1.8%	1.2%	56.3%	40.6%
93:1	42.5%	2.2%	57.3%	57.4%	57.4%	1.2%	0.9%	56.2%	41.7%
93:2	42.1%	4.2%	58.3%	57.9%	57.9%	2.5%	1.8%	55.4%	40.3%
93:3	42.5%	3.1%	61.5%	57.6%	57.7%	1.9%	1.2%	55.8%	41.1%
93:4	41.5%	3.9%	57.8%	58.6%	58.5%	2.3%	1.7%	56.3%	39.8%
94:1	40.4%	3.0%	55.1%	59.5%	59.4%	1.6%	1.3%	57.7%	39.3%
94:2	40.6%	6.3%	58.1%	59.4%	59.3%	3.6%	2.6%	55.7%	38.1%
94:3	41.8%	3.5%	59.8%	58.2%	58.3%	2.1%	1.4%	56.2%	40.3%
94:4	39.5%	5.2%	57.0%	60.6%	60.4%	3.0%	2.2%	57.4%	37.3%
95:1	43.1%	3.3%	60.6%	56.8%	57.0%	2.0%	1.3%	54.9%	41.7%
95:2	43.7%	2.4%	59.8%	56.2%	56.3%	1.4%	0.9%	54.9%	42.8%
95:3	43.9%	2.3%	60.6%	56.0%	56.1%	1.4%	0.9%	54.7%	43.0%
95:4	43.4%	3.3%	58.7%	56.6%	56.6%	1.9%	1.3%	54.7%	42.0%
96:1	45.5%	2.5%	63.0%	54.5%	54.7%	1.6%	0.9%	53.1%	44.4%
96:2	42.1%	3.2%	57.1%	57.9%	57.9%	1.8%	1.4%	56.0%	40.8%
96:3	42.6%	3.9%	59.2%	57.3%	57.4%	2.3%	1.6%	55.1%	41.0%
96:4	44.3%	2.6%	60.7%	55.7%	55.8%	1.6%	1.0%	54.2%	43.2%
AVG	40.0%	3.5%	61.4%	60.1%	60.2%	2.1%	1.4%	58.0%	38.5%

Tabale 3.10b
Moving Average Convergence Divergence (MAC-D) Short Hit Analysis
(Average of all stocks)

Qtr	Optimal Short	MAC-D Short	Short Hits	Cash Hits	Total Hits	Short Right	Short Wrong	Cash Right	Cash Wrong
85:1	34.3%	3.5%	67.8%	65.7%	65.7%	2.4%	1.1%	63.3%	33.1%
85:2	34.6%	4.2%	68.8%	65.4%	65.5%	2.9%	1.3%	62.6%	33.2%
85:3	38.6%	4.1%	72.8%	61.6%	62.0%	3.0%	1.1%	59.0%	36.9%
85:4	33.1%	1.7%	57.0%	66.8%	66.7%	1.0%	0.8%	65.7%	32.6%
86:1	35.2%	5.8%	54.0%	64.7%	64.1%	3.1%	2.7%	60.9%	33.3%
86:2	39.8%	7.0%	59.3%	60.3%	60.2%	4.2%	2.9%	56.1%	36.9%
86:3	42.7%	3.2%	64.2%	57.4%	57.7%	2.0%	1.1%	55.6%	41.2%
86:4	38.7%	3.1%	62.5%	61.5%	61.5%	1.9%	1.2%	59.6%	37.4%
87:1	36.9%	3.8%	56.6%	63.2%	62.9%	2.1%	1.6%	60.8%	35.4%
87:2	40.0%	5.3%	59.5%	60.2%	60.1%	3.1%	2.1%	57.0%	37.7%
87:3	40.4%	3.9%	58.2%	59.5%	59.5%	2.3%	1.6%	57.2%	38.9%
87:4	45.3%	2.6%	65.7%	55.0%	55.2%	1.7%	0.9%	53.5%	43.9%
88:1	36.7%	3.7%	60.0%	63.3%	63.2%	2.2%	1.5%	61.0%	35.3%
88:2	37.4%	5.3%	57.9%	62.4%	62.2%	3.0%	2.2%	59.1%	35.6%
88:3	38.4%	3.6%	62.6%	61.7%	61.7%	2.2%	1.3%	59.5%	36.9%
88:4	37.0%	3.4%	62.8%	63.0%	63.0%	2.1%	1.3%	60.9%	35.7%
89:1	36.2%	4.0%	59.0%	63.8%	63.6%	2.4%	1.6%	61.3%	34.7%
89:2	35.9%	4.5%	59.0%	64.0%	63.8%	2.7%	1.9%	61.1%	34.3%
89:3	36.4%	5.5%	56.3%	63.5%	63.1%	3.1%	2.4%	60.0%	34.5%
89:4	39.0%	3.4%	59.2%	61.0%	61.0%	2.0%	1.4%	58.9%	37.6%
90:1	40.1%	2.2%	64.8%	59.9%	60.0%	1.5%	0.8%	58.6%	39.2%
90:2	37.8%	2.8%	59.9%	62.2%	62.2%	1.7%	1.1%	60.5%	36.7%
90:3	45.7%	3.1%	66.6%	54.4%	54.8%	2.0%	1.0%	52.7%	44.2%
90:4	37.6%	1.7%	58.4%	62.4%	62.3%	1.0%	0.7%	61.4%	37.0%
91:1	36.7%	4.6%	56.7%	63.5%	63.2%	2.6%	2.0%	60.6%	34.9%
91:2	40.4%	7.5%	59.3%	59.4%	59.4%	4.4%	3.0%	55.0%	37.5%
91:3	39.8%	3.8%	56.7%	60.1%	60.0%	2.1%	1.6%	57.9%	38.4%
91:4	40.5%	4.0%	56.3%	59.4%	59.3%	2.3%	1.8%	57.0%	39.0%
92:1	43.2%	4.3%	62.2%	56.9%	57.1%	2.7%	1.6%	54.4%	41.3%
92:2	42.9%	4.1%	61.4%	57.2%	57.4%	2.5%	1.6%	54.9%	41.0%
92:3	39.5%	3.5%	58.0%	60.5%	60.4%	2.0%	1.5%	58.3%	38.1%
92:4	37.5%	3.7%	56.8%	62.5%	62.2%	2.1%	1.6%	60.1%	36.2%
93:1	39.4%	6.4%	55.7%	60.6%	60.3%	3.6%	2.9%	56.7%	36.9%
93:2	40.9%	5.2%	56.0%	59.1%	59.0%	2.9%	2.3%	56.0%	38.7%
93:3	39.4%	3.6%	57.3%	60.6%	60.5%	2.1%	1.5%	58.4%	37.9%
93:4	41.7%	3.6%	58.2%	58.3%	58.3%	2.1%	1.5%	56.2%	40.1%
94:1	43.7%	4.6%	58.6%	56.3%	56.4%	2.7%	1.9%	53.7%	41.7%
94:2	42.7%	2.4%	56.7%	57.3%	57.3%	1.4%	1.1%	55.9%	41.7%
94:3	39.8%	3.0%	59.1%	60.2%	60.2%	1.8%	1.2%	58.4%	38.6%
94:4	42.8%	3.2%	60.3%	57.2%	57.3%	2.0%	1.3%	55.4%	41.4%
95:1	38.7%	3.7%	55.4%	61.3%	61.1%	2.1%	1.7%	59.0%	37.2%
95:2	38.9%	5.3%	54.4%	61.0%	60.7%	2.9%	2.4%	57.8%	36.9%
95:3	38.9%	5.4%	55.9%	61.1%	60.9%	3.0%	2.4%	57.9%	36.8%
95:4	40.5%	3.9%	56.2%	59.5%	59.4%	2.2%	1.7%	57.2%	38.9%
96:1	38.9%	4.4%	54.6%	61.1%	60.8%	2.4%	2.0%	58.4%	37.2%
96:2	42.4%	4.7%	58.6%	57.7%	57.8%	2.8%	1.9%	55.0%	40.3%
96:3	40.8%	2.9%	62.7%	59.4%	59.5%	1.8%	1.1%	57.7%	39.4%
96:4	39.8%	3.6%	55.6%	60.2%	60.1%	2.0%	1.6%	58.0%	38.3%
AVG	39.4%	4.0%	59.5%	60.7%	60.6%	2.4%	1.6%	58.3%	37.7%

Table 3.11a
Moving Average Convergence Divergence (MAC-D) Long Return Analysis
(Average of all stocks)

Qtr	MAC-D Terminal Wealth	Buy/Hold Terminal Wealth	Relative Terminal Wealth	MAC-D Long Avg Ret	MAC-D Cash Avg Ret	MAC-D Long-Cash Avg Ret	Buy/Hold Avg Ret
85:1	10018	10142	0.988	0.209%	0.004%	0.206%	0.006%
85:2	9989	9700	1.030	-0.061%	-0.070%	0.009%	-0.069%
85:3	9960	8889	1.121	-0.198%	-0.205%	0.007%	-0.205%
85:4	10031	10763	0.932	0.139%	0.106%	0.034%	0.107%
86:1	10022	11428	0.877	0.206%	0.225%	-0.019%	0.225%
86:2	9995	10414	0.960	-0.031%	0.069%	-0.099%	0.066%
86:3	9985	9175	1.088	-0.065%	-0.130%	0.065%	-0.128%
86:4	10049	10413	0.965	0.178%	0.064%	0.114%	0.069%
87:1	10045	11929	0.842	0.400%	0.291%	0.109%	0.293%
87:2	10027	10196	0.983	0.113%	0.035%	0.079%	0.038%
87:3	10020	10408	0.963	0.185%	0.066%	0.119%	0.068%
87:4	10116	8087	1.251	0.205%	-0.324%	0.529%	-0.278%
88:1	10055	10989	0.915	0.472%	0.157%	0.315%	0.163%
88:2	10023	10593	0.946	0.116%	0.099%	0.017%	0.100%
88:3	10016	10050	0.997	0.076%	0.010%	0.066%	0.013%
88:4	10009	10196	0.982	0.048%	0.036%	0.012%	0.037%
89:1	10011	10698	0.936	0.078%	0.113%	-0.035%	0.112%
89:2	10022	10772	0.930	0.167%	0.121%	0.046%	0.122%
89:3	10031	10833	0.926	0.228%	0.129%	0.100%	0.131%
89:4	9987	9904	1.008	-0.038%	-0.009%	-0.028%	-0.011%
90:1	10020	9980	1.004	0.063%	-0.001%	0.064%	0.003%
90:2	10030	10459	0.959	0.142%	0.074%	0.067%	0.077%
90:3	9852	8526	1.156	-0.432%	-0.248%	-0.183%	-0.259%
90:4	10115	10889	0.929	0.208%	0.141%	0.068%	0.146%
91:1	10054	12477	0.806	0.415%	0.313%	0.102%	0.315%
91:2	10005	10244	0.977	0.046%	0.045%	0.001%	0.045%
91:3	10018	10429	0.961	0.073%	0.065%	0.008%	0.065%
91:4	10055	10497	0.958	0.205%	0.076%	0.129%	0.082%
92:1	10014	10324	0.970	0.078%	0.047%	0.031%	0.048%
92:2	10005	9723	1.029	0.013%	-0.052%	0.064%	-0.048%
92:3	10013	10392	0.964	0.051%	0.057%	-0.005%	0.057%
92:4	10015	10963	0.914	0.082%	0.146%	-0.065%	0.144%
93:1	9997	10527	0.950	-0.026%	0.082%	-0.108%	0.080%
93:2	10011	10340	0.968	0.042%	0.052%	-0.010%	0.052%
93:3	10028	10686	0.938	0.144%	0.100%	0.044%	0.101%
93:4	10013	10255	0.976	0.050%	0.033%	0.017%	0.034%
94:1	9989	9954	1.004	-0.058%	-0.010%	-0.048%	-0.011%
94:2	10009	9994	1.001	0.024%	-0.007%	0.030%	-0.005%
94:3	10019	10613	0.944	0.086%	0.089%	-0.004%	0.089%
94:4	10001	9836	1.017	0.005%	-0.031%	0.036%	-0.029%
95:1	10029	10706	0.937	0.135%	0.109%	0.026%	0.110%
95:2	10008	10873	0.920	0.055%	0.136%	-0.081%	0.134%
95:3	10010	10853	0.922	0.074%	0.132%	-0.058%	0.131%
95:4	10025	10445	0.960	0.128%	0.065%	0.063%	0.067%
96:1	10041	11027	0.911	0.252%	0.157%	0.095%	0.159%
96:2	10005	10367	0.965	0.024%	0.060%	-0.035%	0.059%
96:3	10007	10298	0.972	0.026%	0.048%	-0.023%	0.047%
96:4	10018	10817	0.926	0.118%	0.122%	-0.004%	0.122%
AVG	10017	10377	0.965	0.076%	0.054%	0.022%	0.055%

Table 3.11b
Moving Average Convergence Divergence (MAC-D) Short Return Analysis
(Average of all stocks)

Qtr	MAC-D Terminal Wealth	Buy/Hold Terminal Wealth	Relative Terminal Wealth	MAC-D Short Avg Ret	MAC-D Cash Avg Ret	MAC-D Short-Cash Avg Ret	Buy/Hold Avg Ret
85:1	10004	10142	0.986	-0.014%	0.007%	-0.021%	0.006%
85:2	9996	9700	1.031	0.020%	-0.073%	0.094%	-0.069%
85:3	10069	8889	1.133	-0.261%	-0.202%	-0.058%	-0.205%
85:4	9975	10763	0.927	0.235%	0.104%	0.131%	0.107%
86:1	9896	11428	0.866	0.300%	0.220%	0.080%	0.225%
86:2	9967	10414	0.957	0.075%	0.066%	0.009%	0.066%
86:3	10067	9175	1.097	-0.331%	-0.121%	-0.210%	-0.128%
86:4	10007	10413	0.961	-0.038%	0.073%	-0.111%	0.069%
87:1	9970	11929	0.836	0.134%	0.299%	-0.165%	0.293%
87:2	9992	10196	0.980	0.022%	0.039%	-0.017%	0.038%
87:3	9972	10408	0.958	0.116%	0.066%	0.049%	0.068%
87:4	10190	8087	1.260	-1.119%	-0.256%	-0.864%	-0.278%
88:1	9969	10989	0.907	0.134%	0.164%	-0.030%	0.163%
88:2	9948	10593	0.939	0.160%	0.096%	0.064%	0.100%
88:3	10004	10050	0.995	-0.021%	0.014%	-0.035%	0.013%
88:4	9991	10196	0.980	0.041%	0.036%	0.005%	0.037%
89:1	9972	10698	0.932	0.114%	0.112%	0.002%	0.112%
89:2	9956	10772	0.924	0.154%	0.121%	0.033%	0.122%
89:3	9942	10833	0.918	0.172%	0.129%	0.043%	0.131%
89:4	9981	9904	1.008	0.088%	-0.015%	0.103%	-0.011%
90:1	10015	9980	1.003	-0.109%	0.005%	-0.114%	0.003%
90:2	9985	10459	0.955	0.088%	0.076%	0.012%	0.077%
90:3	10070	8526	1.181	-0.358%	-0.256%	-0.102%	-0.259%
90:4	9982	10889	0.917	0.178%	0.146%	0.032%	0.146%
91:1	9941	12477	0.797	0.221%	0.319%	-0.098%	0.315%
91:2	9952	10244	0.972	0.101%	0.041%	0.060%	0.045%
91:3	9979	10429	0.957	0.094%	0.064%	0.030%	0.065%
91:4	9969	10497	0.950	0.126%	0.080%	0.046%	0.082%
92:1	10006	10324	0.969	-0.021%	0.051%	-0.072%	0.048%
92:2	10028	9723	1.031	-0.111%	-0.046%	-0.066%	-0.048%
92:3	9988	10392	0.961	0.053%	0.057%	-0.004%	0.057%
92:4	9964	10963	0.909	0.155%	0.144%	0.011%	0.144%
93:1	9967	10527	0.947	0.083%	0.079%	0.004%	0.080%
93:2	9994	10340	0.966	0.020%	0.053%	-0.033%	0.052%
93:3	9986	10686	0.934	0.063%	0.102%	-0.039%	0.101%
93:4	10017	10255	0.977	-0.069%	0.038%	-0.107%	0.034%
94:1	10004	9954	1.005	-0.014%	-0.011%	-0.003%	-0.011%
94:2	9983	9994	0.999	0.116%	-0.008%	0.124%	-0.005%
94:3	9992	10613	0.941	0.044%	0.091%	-0.047%	0.089%
94:4	10004	9836	1.017	-0.019%	-0.030%	0.011%	-0.029%
95:1	9975	10706	0.932	0.109%	0.110%	-0.001%	0.110%
95:2	9954	10873	0.915	0.144%	0.133%	0.011%	0.134%
95:3	9958	10853	0.918	0.129%	0.131%	-0.002%	0.131%
95:4	9995	10445	0.957	0.023%	0.069%	-0.046%	0.067%
96:1	9966	11027	0.904	0.126%	0.160%	-0.034%	0.159%
96:2	10000	10367	0.965	0.001%	0.061%	-0.060%	0.059%
96:3	10020	10298	0.973	-0.110%	0.052%	-0.162%	0.047%
96:4	9976	10817	0.922	0.103%	0.123%	-0.020%	0.122%
AVG	9990	10377	0.963	0.041%	0.056%	-0.015%	0.055%

only are signals generally late, they are extremely rare. Long signals occur, on average, only 3.5 percent of the time (Table 3.10a) and short signals occur 4.0 percent of the time (Table 3.10b). Optimally, these signals would occur ten times as often. With signals firing so seldom, the terminal wealth from following this strategy is less than 97 percent of the buy-and-hold terminal wealth.

However, this system has some usefulness. Whenever long signals do occur, the average return is 0.076 percent, and the average market return is 0.054 percent when cash is chosen over going long (Table 3.11a). Likewise, the market return average of only 0.041 percent when a short position is signaled is lower than the 0.056 percent return when a cash position is favored over a short position (Table 3.11b).

Like many of the other indicators, this system seems to work best during down markets. For the eleven quarters in our test in which a buy-and-hold strategy had a negative return, traders following the long-cash recommendations of the MAC-D Crossover system would outperform the market. Following the short-cash recommendations of the system would beat a buy-and-hold strategy for ten of these eleven quarters of declining stock prices.

Money Flow RSI Breakout

The Money Flow Relative Strength Index attempts to measure the flow of money into and out of an equity. It is related to the Relative Strength Index (see Chapter 4). The main difference between these two indicators is that the Relative Strength Index incorporates only price, whereas the Money Flow Relative Strength Index uses price and volume. Multiplying price by volume results in a measure of how much money is flowing into or out of the security.

This indicator looks for divergence between the indicator and the price action. If price is trending higher and the Money Flow Relative Strength Index is trending lower, volume must be trending lower. This signals an imminent price reversal. Likewise, a lower price accompanied by a higher Money Flow Relative Strength Index indicates increased volume at the falling price; the price should begin to increase.

Construction

The average of a stock's high, low, and closing prices represents the "typical price" for a trading day. This typical price for Day i is calculated as:

$$TP_i = (High_i + Low_i + Close_i)/3.$$

Multiplying the Day i's typical price by Day i's volume measures the money flow into or out of the stock for that particular day. If Day i's typical stock price (TP_i) exceeds the previous day's typical stock price (TP_{i-1}), then money is flowing into the stock and this is considered positive money flow (PMF). On the other hand, if Day i's typical stock price (TP_i) is less than the previous day's typical stock price (TP_{i-1}), then negative money flow (NMF) exists.

$$PMF_i = (TP_i \cdot Volume_i) \{if\ TP_i > Tp_{i-1}\},$$
$$NMF_i = (TP_i \cdot Volume_i) \{if\ TP_i < Tp_{i-1}\}.$$

Choose a number of periods to use for the look-back period in calculating the Money Flow Relative Strength Indicator. Then, sum all of the PMF_is and sum all of the NMF_is for this time period:

$$PSUM_t = PMF_1 + PMF_2 + \dots PMF_p,$$
$$NSUM_t = NMF_1 + NMF_2 + \dots NMF_p.$$

Finally, calculate the Money Flow Relative Strength Index for today, using the following formula:

$$MFRSI_t = 100 - [100/\{1 + (PSUM_t/NSUM_t)\}].$$

Whenever this index goes through 50 to the upside, a long signal is generated. Whenever this index falls through 50, a short signal is generated.

Results

The results shown in Table 3.12 show a hit rate of just over 60 percent for the Money Flow RSI Breakout (MFR-B) system. When choosing between long and cash positions, the system's long calls are correct 60.3 percent of the time, and the system's cash calls are correct 60.0 percent of the time (Table 3.12a). The accuracy of the system when choosing between short and cash positions is almost identical; short calls are correct 59.9 percent of the time, and cash calls are correct 60.3 percent of the time (Table 3.12b).

Table 3.13a shows that, over our twelve-year test period, the average daily market return was 0.057 percent when the system made long calls. This is higher than the average return of 0.053 percent when the system chose a cash position over a long position. By following the system, a trader is, on average, in a long position on the best days but is missing out by being out of the market on positive but relatively lower return days. An investor would ideally want to be long in the market 40.0 percent of the time. This system has the investor long in the market 56.1 percent of the time. The terminal wealth from following this strategy is lower than the terminal wealth of a buy-and-hold strategy.

Table 3.12a
Money Flow RSI Breakout (MFR-B) Long Hit Analysis
(Average of all stocks)

Qtr	Optimal Long	MFR-B Long	Long Hits	Cash Hits	Total Hits	Long Right	Long Wrong	Cash Right	Cash Wrong
85:1	32.1%	63.9%	65.8%	67.7%	66.5%	42.1%	21.9%	24.5%	11.6%
85:2	30.2%	60.1%	64.6%	69.1%	66.4%	38.8%	21.3%	27.6%	12.3%
85:3	26.3%	51.2%	60.9%	72.9%	66.8%	31.2%	20.1%	35.6%	13.2%
85:4	36.6%	67.2%	65.9%	63.7%	65.1%	44.3%	22.9%	20.9%	11.9%
86:1	44.2%	66.2%	64.2%	56.4%	61.6%	42.5%	23.7%	19.1%	14.7%
86:2	39.7%	56.2%	59.1%	59.3%	59.2%	33.2%	23.0%	26.0%	17.8%
86:3	37.0%	48.5%	56.8%	63.0%	60.0%	27.5%	21.0%	32.5%	19.1%
86:4	38.5%	57.7%	59.8%	60.9%	60.3%	34.5%	23.2%	25.8%	16.5%
87:1	44.7%	66.8%	61.6%	53.5%	58.9%	41.1%	25.6%	17.8%	15.5%
87:2	40.0%	53.5%	59.1%	58.8%	58.9%	31.6%	21.9%	27.3%	19.2%
87:3	39.5%	55.0%	59.3%	60.5%	59.8%	32.6%	22.4%	27.2%	17.8%
87:4	37.9%	42.2%	53.9%	60.9%	58.0%	22.8%	19.5%	35.2%	22.6%
88:1	41.3%	66.1%	62.5%	58.3%	61.1%	41.3%	24.8%	19.8%	14.1%
88:2	39.3%	55.8%	62.0%	60.4%	61.3%	34.6%	21.2%	26.7%	17.5%
88:3	35.9%	51.9%	61.5%	63.9%	62.6%	31.9%	20.0%	30.7%	17.4%
88:4	36.3%	54.1%	62.6%	63.6%	63.1%	33.9%	20.2%	29.2%	16.7%
89:1	39.0%	62.5%	63.1%	61.1%	62.3%	39.4%	23.1%	22.9%	14.6%
89:2	40.2%	66.4%	63.4%	60.5%	62.4%	42.0%	24.3%	20.4%	13.3%
89:3	39.9%	59.3%	62.7%	59.9%	61.6%	37.2%	22.1%	24.4%	16.3%
89:4	38.3%	48.8%	60.7%	61.7%	61.2%	29.6%	19.2%	31.6%	19.6%
90:1	36.9%	50.3%	59.3%	62.6%	61.0%	29.9%	20.5%	31.1%	18.6%
90:2	39.2%	57.0%	61.3%	60.3%	60.9%	34.9%	22.0%	26.0%	17.1%
90:3	33.5%	37.1%	55.6%	66.5%	62.4%	20.7%	16.5%	41.8%	21.1%
90:4	40.8%	55.3%	62.2%	59.7%	61.1%	34.4%	20.9%	26.7%	18.0%
91:1	44.1%	65.0%	62.2%	54.9%	59.6%	40.4%	24.6%	19.2%	15.8%
91:2	39.7%	56.7%	58.9%	59.3%	59.1%	33.4%	23.3%	25.7%	17.6%
91:3	40.4%	55.9%	59.4%	59.0%	59.3%	33.2%	22.7%	26.1%	18.1%
91:4	41.2%	51.8%	59.3%	58.7%	59.0%	30.7%	21.1%	28.3%	19.9%
92:1	40.0%	58.1%	57.1%	60.8%	58.7%	33.2%	24.9%	25.5%	16.4%
92:2	38.6%	48.6%	56.6%	60.6%	58.7%	27.5%	21.1%	31.2%	20.3%
92:3	40.3%	56.2%	60.4%	59.8%	60.1%	34.0%	22.2%	26.2%	17.6%
92:4	41.9%	59.6%	62.3%	58.2%	60.6%	37.1%	22.5%	23.5%	16.9%
93:1	42.5%	60.5%	60.4%	56.9%	59.0%	36.5%	24.0%	22.5%	17.0%
93:2	42.1%	52.0%	58.8%	57.6%	58.2%	30.6%	21.4%	27.7%	20.4%
93:3	42.5%	57.9%	60.6%	57.3%	59.2%	35.1%	22.8%	24.1%	17.9%
93:4	41.5%	51.9%	58.2%	58.2%	58.2%	30.2%	21.7%	28.0%	20.1%
94:1	40.4%	54.4%	55.9%	59.3%	57.5%	30.4%	24.0%	27.0%	18.6%
94:2	40.6%	47.0%	57.1%	58.9%	58.1%	26.9%	20.2%	31.2%	21.8%
94:3	41.8%	53.9%	60.2%	58.3%	59.3%	32.4%	21.5%	26.9%	19.2%
94:4	39.5%	45.8%	57.6%	61.0%	59.5%	26.4%	19.4%	33.1%	21.1%
95:1	43.1%	62.0%	61.0%	56.9%	59.4%	37.8%	24.2%	21.6%	16.4%
95:2	43.7%	62.0%	60.7%	56.6%	59.2%	37.7%	24.4%	21.5%	16.5%
95:3	43.9%	61.9%	60.7%	56.5%	59.1%	37.6%	24.3%	21.5%	16.6%
95:4	43.4%	54.8%	59.8%	57.5%	58.8%	32.7%	22.0%	26.0%	19.2%
96:1	45.5%	56.4%	60.7%	54.1%	57.9%	34.3%	22.2%	23.6%	20.0%
96:2	42.1%	55.4%	57.5%	57.9%	57.7%	31.8%	23.5%	25.8%	18.8%
96:3	42.6%	54.5%	59.8%	58.0%	58.9%	32.5%	21.9%	26.4%	19.2%
96:4	44.3%	59.3%	59.9%	56.1%	58.4%	35.5%	23.8%	22.8%	17.9%
AVG	40.0%	56.1%	60.3%	60.0%	60.3%	34.0%	22.2%	26.4%	17.5%

Table 3.12b
Money Flow RSI Breakout (MFR-B) Short Hit Analysis
(Average of all stocks)

Qtr	Optimal Short	MFR-B Short	Short Hits	Cash Hits	Total Hits	Short Right	Short Wrong	Cash Right	Cash Wrong
85:1	34.3%	35.2%	67.7%	65.8%	66.5%	23.8%	11.4%	42.7%	22.1%
85:2	34.6%	39.2%	69.0%	64.5%	66.3%	27.1%	12.2%	39.2%	21.6%
85:3	38.6%	48.0%	72.9%	60.9%	66.7%	35.0%	13.0%	31.7%	20.3%
85:4	33.1%	31.8%	63.6%	65.9%	65.1%	20.2%	11.6%	44.9%	23.3%
86:1	35.2%	33.2%	56.5%	64.2%	61.6%	18.8%	14.5%	42.9%	23.9%
86:2	39.8%	43.2%	59.3%	59.1%	59.2%	25.6%	17.6%	33.6%	23.2%
86:3	42.7%	50.8%	63.0%	56.8%	59.9%	32.0%	18.8%	28.0%	21.3%
86:4	38.7%	41.9%	60.9%	59.8%	60.2%	25.5%	16.4%	34.7%	23.3%
87:1	36.9%	32.7%	53.5%	61.6%	59.0%	17.5%	15.2%	41.5%	25.8%
87:2	40.0%	45.9%	58.8%	59.1%	58.9%	27.0%	18.9%	31.9%	22.1%
87:3	40.4%	44.4%	60.6%	59.3%	59.8%	26.9%	17.5%	33.0%	22.7%
87:4	45.3%	56.6%	60.9%	53.8%	57.8%	34.5%	22.1%	23.3%	20.1%
88:1	36.7%	33.4%	58.1%	62.5%	61.0%	19.4%	14.0%	41.6%	25.0%
88:2	37.4%	43.7%	60.4%	62.0%	61.3%	26.4%	17.3%	34.9%	21.4%
88:3	38.4%	47.6%	63.9%	61.5%	62.6%	30.4%	17.2%	32.2%	20.2%
88:4	37.0%	45.5%	63.5%	62.6%	63.0%	28.9%	16.6%	34.1%	20.4%
89:1	36.2%	37.3%	61.1%	63.1%	62.3%	22.8%	14.5%	39.6%	23.2%
89:2	35.9%	33.3%	60.5%	63.4%	62.4%	20.1%	13.1%	42.3%	24.4%
89:3	36.4%	40.1%	59.8%	62.7%	61.5%	24.0%	16.1%	37.5%	22.3%
89:4	39.0%	49.0%	61.8%	60.5%	61.2%	30.3%	18.7%	30.9%	20.1%
90:1	40.1%	48.9%	62.5%	59.3%	60.9%	30.6%	18.3%	30.3%	20.8%
90:2	37.8%	42.6%	60.3%	61.4%	60.9%	25.7%	16.9%	35.2%	22.2%
90:3	45.7%	62.2%	66.5%	55.6%	62.3%	41.3%	20.9%	21.0%	16.8%
90:4	37.6%	44.0%	59.7%	62.3%	61.1%	26.2%	17.7%	34.9%	21.1%
91:1	36.7%	34.4%	54.8%	62.2%	59.7%	18.9%	15.5%	40.8%	24.8%
91:2	40.4%	42.8%	59.3%	58.9%	59.1%	25.4%	17.4%	33.7%	23.5%
91:3	39.8%	43.6%	59.0%	59.4%	59.2%	25.7%	17.9%	33.5%	22.9%
91:4	40.5%	47.5%	58.7%	59.2%	59.0%	27.9%	19.6%	31.1%	21.4%
92:1	43.2%	41.6%	60.8%	57.2%	58.7%	25.3%	16.3%	33.4%	25.0%
92:2	42.9%	50.8%	60.6%	56.6%	58.6%	30.8%	20.0%	27.9%	21.4%
92:3	39.5%	43.5%	59.8%	60.4%	60.1%	26.0%	17.5%	34.1%	22.4%
92:4	37.5%	40.0%	58.2%	62.3%	60.6%	23.3%	16.7%	37.4%	22.6%
93:1	39.4%	39.1%	56.9%	60.3%	59.0%	22.3%	16.8%	36.8%	24.2%
93:2	40.9%	47.6%	57.6%	58.8%	58.2%	27.4%	20.2%	30.8%	21.6%
93:3	39.4%	41.6%	57.3%	60.5%	59.2%	23.9%	17.8%	35.3%	23.0%
93:4	41.7%	47.6%	58.2%	58.2%	58.2%	27.7%	19.9%	30.5%	21.9%
94:1	43.7%	45.3%	59.3%	55.9%	57.4%	26.8%	18.4%	30.6%	24.1%
94:2	42.7%	52.5%	58.9%	57.1%	58.0%	30.9%	21.6%	27.1%	20.4%
94:3	39.8%	45.9%	58.3%	60.1%	59.3%	26.7%	19.1%	32.5%	21.6%
94:4	42.8%	53.9%	61.1%	57.6%	59.5%	32.9%	21.0%	26.5%	19.5%
95:1	38.7%	37.7%	56.9%	60.9%	59.4%	21.5%	16.3%	37.9%	24.3%
95:2	38.9%	37.8%	56.6%	60.7%	59.2%	21.4%	16.4%	37.8%	24.5%
95:3	38.9%	37.9%	56.5%	60.8%	59.2%	21.4%	16.5%	37.8%	24.4%
95:4	40.5%	44.9%	57.6%	59.7%	58.8%	25.8%	19.0%	32.9%	22.2%
96:1	38.9%	43.2%	54.1%	60.7%	57.8%	23.4%	19.8%	34.5%	22.3%
96:2	42.4%	44.2%	57.8%	57.5%	57.6%	25.6%	18.6%	32.1%	23.7%
96:3	40.8%	45.0%	57.9%	59.7%	58.9%	26.1%	18.9%	32.8%	22.2%
96:4	39.8%	40.4%	56.0%	59.9%	58.3%	22.6%	17.7%	35.7%	23.9%
AVG	39.4%	43.3%	59.9%	60.3%	60.3%	26.0%	17.3%	34.3%	22.4%

Table 3.13a
Money Flow RSI Breakout (MFR-B) Long Return Analysis
(Average of all stocks)

Qtr	MFR-B Terminal Wealth	Buy/Hold Terminal Wealth	Relative Terminal Wealth	MFR-B Long Avg Ret	MFR-B Cash Avg Ret	MFR-B Long-Cash Avg Ret	Buy/Hold Avg Ret
85:1	10105	10142	0.996	0.016%	-0.011%	0.028%	0.006%
85:2	9696	9700	1.000	-0.093%	-0.033%	-0.060%	-0.069%
85:3	9348	8889	1.052	-0.217%	-0.192%	-0.025%	-0.205%
85:4	10401	10763	0.966	0.086%	0.148%	-0.062%	0.107%
86:1	10947	11428	0.958	0.226%	0.223%	0.003%	0.225%
86:2	10114	10414	0.971	0.032%	0.111%	-0.079%	0.066%
86:3	9541	9175	1.040	-0.150%	-0.106%	-0.044%	-0.128%
86:4	10096	10413	0.970	0.029%	0.124%	-0.094%	0.069%
87:1	11038	11929	0.925	0.243%	0.393%	-0.150%	0.293%
87:2	9990	10196	0.980	0.001%	0.080%	-0.079%	0.038%
87:3	10219	10408	0.982	0.066%	0.071%	-0.004%	0.068%
87:4	9320	8087	1.153	-0.249%	-0.299%	0.050%	-0.278%
88:1	10527	10989	0.958	0.133%	0.220%	-0.087%	0.163%
88:2	10297	10593	0.972	0.089%	0.114%	-0.025%	0.100%
88:3	10026	10050	0.998	0.012%	0.014%	-0.002%	0.013%
88:4	10088	10196	0.989	0.030%	0.044%	-0.014%	0.037%
89:1	10434	10698	0.975	0.114%	0.110%	0.004%	0.112%
89:2	10494	10772	0.974	0.118%	0.131%	-0.013%	0.122%
89:3	10442	10833	0.964	0.119%	0.149%	-0.030%	0.131%
89:4	9911	9904	1.001	-0.027%	0.004%	-0.032%	-0.011%
90:1	9943	9980	0.996	-0.015%	0.021%	-0.036%	0.003%
90:2	10248	10459	0.980	0.071%	0.084%	-0.013%	0.077%
90:3	9532	8526	1.118	-0.203%	-0.292%	0.089%	-0.259%
90:4	10502	10889	0.964	0.144%	0.150%	-0.006%	0.146%
91:1	11173	12477	0.895	0.287%	0.368%	-0.081%	0.315%
91:2	10066	10244	0.983	0.023%	0.075%	-0.053%	0.045%
91:3	10159	10429	0.974	0.042%	0.094%	-0.052%	0.065%
91:4	10171	10497	0.969	0.051%	0.115%	-0.065%	0.082%
92:1	10305	10324	0.998	0.079%	0.004%	0.075%	0.048%
92:2	9804	9723	1.008	-0.069%	-0.029%	-0.039%	-0.048%
92:3	10197	10392	0.981	0.053%	0.062%	-0.009%	0.057%
92:4	10557	10963	0.963	0.142%	0.148%	-0.006%	0.144%
93:1	10262	10527	0.975	0.066%	0.101%	-0.035%	0.080%
93:2	10163	10340	0.983	0.045%	0.059%	-0.014%	0.052%
93:3	10392	10686	0.972	0.099%	0.104%	-0.004%	0.101%
93:4	10132	10255	0.988	0.034%	0.033%	0.001%	0.034%
94:1	9928	9954	0.997	-0.023%	0.003%	-0.026%	-0.011%
94:2	9946	9994	0.995	-0.021%	0.010%	-0.031%	-0.005%
94:3	10357	10613	0.976	0.099%	0.078%	0.020%	0.089%
94:4	9961	9836	1.013	-0.014%	-0.042%	0.027%	-0.029%
95:1	10377	10706	0.969	0.096%	0.133%	-0.037%	0.110%
95:2	10532	10873	0.969	0.133%	0.135%	-0.001%	0.134%
95:3	10525	10853	0.970	0.132%	0.129%	0.003%	0.131%
95:4	10284	10445	0.985	0.079%	0.052%	0.028%	0.067%
96:1	10525	11027	0.954	0.144%	0.178%	-0.033%	0.159%
96:2	10212	10367	0.985	0.061%	0.056%	0.005%	0.059%
96:3	10217	10298	0.992	0.062%	0.030%	0.032%	0.047%
96:4	10486	10817	0.969	0.125%	0.118%	0.008%	0.122%
AVG	10208	10377	0.984	0.057%	0.053%	0.003%	0.055%

Table 3.13b
Money Flow RSI Breakout (MFR-B) Short Return Analysis
(Average of all stocks)

Qtr	MFR-B Terminal Wealth	Buy/Hold Terminal Wealth	Relative Terminal Wealth	MFR-B Short Avg Ret	MFR-B Cash Avg Ret	MFR-B Short-Cash Avg Ret	Buy/Hold Avg Ret
85:1	10046	10142	0.991	-0.012%	0.016%	-0.029%	0.006%
85:2	10127	9700	1.044	-0.033%	-0.093%	0.060%	-0.069%
85:3	10647	8889	1.198	-0.192%	-0.217%	0.025%	-0.205%
85:4	9717	10763	0.903	0.151%	0.086%	0.065%	0.107%
86:1	9556	11428	0.836	0.223%	0.226%	-0.003%	0.225%
86:2	9689	10414	0.930	0.111%	0.033%	0.078%	0.066%
86:3	10305	9175	1.123	-0.104%	-0.152%	0.049%	-0.128%
86:4	9663	10413	0.928	0.126%	0.028%	0.097%	0.069%
87:1	9248	11929	0.775	0.394%	0.244%	0.150%	0.293%
87:2	9759	10196	0.957	0.080%	0.002%	0.078%	0.038%
87:3	9798	10408	0.941	0.068%	0.068%	0.000%	0.068%
87:4	10797	8087	1.335	-0.280%	-0.276%	-0.004%	-0.278%
88:1	9538	10989	0.868	0.225%	0.132%	0.093%	0.163%
88:2	9678	10593	0.914	0.115%	0.088%	0.028%	0.100%
88:3	9941	10050	0.989	0.015%	0.011%	0.004%	0.013%
88:4	9859	10196	0.967	0.046%	0.029%	0.018%	0.037%
89:1	9749	10698	0.911	0.111%	0.113%	-0.003%	0.112%
89:2	9726	10772	0.903	0.130%	0.118%	0.011%	0.122%
89:3	9625	10833	0.888	0.151%	0.117%	0.034%	0.131%
89:4	9996	9904	1.009	-0.002%	-0.019%	0.017%	-0.011%
90:1	9912	9980	0.993	0.024%	-0.018%	0.042%	0.003%
90:2	9771	10459	0.934	0.085%	0.071%	0.014%	0.077%
90:3	11201	8526	1.314	-0.292%	-0.205%	-0.087%	-0.259%
90:4	9557	10889	0.878	0.151%	0.142%	0.009%	0.146%
91:1	9288	12477	0.744	0.366%	0.288%	0.078%	0.315%
91:2	9790	10244	0.956	0.073%	0.025%	0.048%	0.045%
91:3	9737	10429	0.934	0.096%	0.041%	0.054%	0.065%
91:4	9624	10497	0.917	0.118%	0.049%	0.070%	0.082%
92:1	9988	10324	0.967	0.004%	0.079%	-0.075%	0.048%
92:2	10086	9723	1.037	-0.027%	-0.070%	0.043%	-0.048%
92:3	9831	10392	0.946	0.062%	0.053%	0.009%	0.057%
92:4	9628	10963	0.878	0.148%	0.142%	0.007%	0.144%
93:1	9768	10527	0.928	0.100%	0.067%	0.033%	0.080%
93:2	9819	10340	0.950	0.061%	0.044%	0.017%	0.052%
93:3	9722	10686	0.910	0.106%	0.098%	0.008%	0.101%
93:4	9903	10255	0.966	0.033%	0.034%	-0.001%	0.034%
94:1	9992	9954	1.004	0.005%	-0.025%	0.030%	-0.011%
94:2	9974	9994	0.998	0.011%	-0.022%	0.033%	-0.005%
94:3	9777	10613	0.921	0.080%	0.097%	-0.018%	0.089%
94:4	10144	9836	1.031	-0.042%	-0.014%	-0.028%	-0.029%
95:1	9686	10706	0.905	0.134%	0.095%	0.039%	0.110%
95:2	9689	10873	0.891	0.135%	0.134%	0.001%	0.134%
95:3	9705	10853	0.894	0.127%	0.134%	-0.007%	0.131%
95:4	9856	10445	0.944	0.052%	0.079%	-0.027%	0.067%
96:1	9522	11027	0.863	0.181%	0.143%	0.038%	0.159%
96:2	9845	10367	0.950	0.057%	0.060%	-0.003%	0.059%
96:3	9911	10298	0.962	0.030%	0.061%	-0.031%	0.047%
96:4	9706	10817	0.897	0.119%	0.124%	-0.005%	0.122%
AVG	9852	10377	0.949	0.055%	0.056%	-0.001%	0.055%

This system does not seem to be good at distinguishing times in which the market will perform poorly. The average market return when the system gives a short signal is 0.055 percent, compared to an average market return of 0.056 percent when the system chooses cash over a short position (Table 3.13b). The 0.055 percent is smaller, but the difference between these two numbers is insignificant. Also, because 0.055 percent is a positive number, following this strategy will actually decrease terminal wealth. On average, stock prices are increasing when the investor is in a short position.

Although these results do not appear particularly useful, the Money Flow Relative Strength Index concept can be used with different trading criteria in other systems. In addition to the Money Flow RSI Breakout, we have tested the Money Flow RSI Crossover system and the Money Flow RSI Divergence system. The Divergence system is included with the other divergent indicators in Chapter 5. Next, we focus our attention on the Money Flow RSI Crossover system, to see whether it gives better trading signals.

Money Flow RSI Crossover

This system is based on the Money Flow Relative Strength Index used in the Money Flow RSI Breakout system discussed. However, this system uses overbought and oversold levels to generate trading signals. Whenever the Money Flow Relative Strength Index crosses through an overbought or oversold level on a reversal, a trading signal occurs.

Construction

The Money Flow Relative Strength Index that is used with this system is identical to the index used in the previous system, so we will not describe its calculation here. Instead, refer to page 67 for details in constructing the index.

Once the Money Flow Relative Strength Index line is drawn, we are able to draw overbought and oversold lines that will be used for signal generation. In our testing we use a lower level of 20 and an upper level of 80.

When the index moves above the overbought line and reverses, crossing back through the overbought line, a bearish short signal occurs. Bullish long signals occur whenever the index falls below the oversold line and reverses, crossing back above the oversold line.

Results

The results for this indicator are shown in Tables 3.14 and 3.15. On balance, the Money Flow RSI Crossover (MFR-C) appears to outperform the Money Flow RSI Breakout system just discussed. The MFR-C system generates, on average, long signals 35.2 percent of the time (Table 3.14a), much less often than the rate of 56.1 percent for the MFR-B system. Short signals occur 48.2 percent of the time in the MFR-C system (Table 3.14b) compared to 43.3 percent of the time in the MFR-B system. In the MFR-C system, these long calls are correct 61.6 percent of the time; the short calls are correct 60.3 percent of the time. These hit rates are slightly higher than for the MFR-B system.

When long signals are generated, the average return is 0.058 percent; this compares to an average market return of only 0.053 percent when the system chooses a cash position over a long position (Table 3.15a). Trading long with this system's recommendations results in a terminal wealth of only 97.6 percent of the terminal wealth of a buy-and-hold strategy.

The short signals for the MFR-C system are less promising. The average stock return on days when short signals are made is 0.058 percent, and the average daily return for cash signals is 0.052 percent (Table 3.15b). Thus, following the system's short calls results in investors' being short on days with above-average market appreciation—the very days when investors would want to be in a long position. In fact, the short positions recommended by this system will, on average, result in declining wealth.

Like many of the other indicators, the MFR-C system works best during declining markets. Just look at the terminal wealth from following the short strategy during the fourth quarter of 1987! The terminal wealth of $11,035 is 36.5 percent greater than the terminal wealth of $8,087 that would have resulted from a buy-and-hold strategy (see Table 3.15b).

Moving Average Crossover

Used by technicians for many years, the Moving Average Crossover (MV2-C) system is thought to generate good trades when a security begins a solid trend. With this system, two moving averages are used: a short-term moving average and a long-term moving average. The short-term moving average is the "faster" of the two averages. New price information is relatively more important with the short-term moving average because it is one piece of a relatively small set of information. The long-term moving average is the "slower" and smoother of the two averages. It incorporates new stock price information more slowly because this new information is just one piece of a larger set of information.

As a market advances, the shorter-term moving average will rise above a longer-term moving average. As this faster moving average crosses the slower moving average, a buy signal is generated. In market declines, the shorter-term moving average will cross the longer-term moving average. A sell signal is generated as the shorter-term moving average falls below the longer-term moving average.

Table 3.14a
Money Flow RSI Crossover (MFR-C) Long Hit Analysis
(Average of all stocks)

Qtr	Optimal Long	MFR-C Long	Long Hits	Cash Hits	Total Hits	Long Right	Long Wrong	Cash Right	Cash Wrong
85:1	32.1%	28.7%	68.8%	67.8%	68.1%	19.8%	9.0%	48.3%	22.9%
85:2	30.2%	34.2%	65.5%	68.9%	67.7%	22.4%	11.8%	45.3%	20.5%
85:3	26.3%	33.3%	62.3%	73.6%	69.8%	20.7%	12.5%	49.1%	17.6%
85:4	36.6%	36.4%	67.5%	62.2%	64.2%	24.6%	11.8%	39.6%	24.0%
86:1	44.2%	24.1%	66.4%	55.0%	57.8%	16.0%	8.1%	41.8%	34.1%
86:2	39.7%	27.3%	62.0%	59.9%	60.5%	16.9%	10.4%	43.6%	29.1%
86:3	37.0%	38.6%	59.1%	62.3%	61.1%	22.8%	15.8%	38.3%	23.1%
86:4	38.5%	38.7%	62.5%	61.5%	61.9%	24.2%	14.5%	37.7%	23.6%
87:1	44.7%	29.6%	65.3%	55.3%	58.3%	19.3%	10.3%	39.0%	31.5%
87:2	40.0%	35.9%	61.0%	59.3%	59.9%	21.9%	14.0%	38.0%	26.0%
87:3	39.5%	29.9%	61.4%	60.2%	60.5%	18.3%	11.6%	42.2%	27.9%
87:4	37.9%	48.8%	57.2%	62.6%	59.9%	27.9%	20.9%	32.0%	19.2%
88:1	41.3%	33.4%	65.3%	59.3%	61.3%	21.8%	11.6%	39.5%	27.1%
88:2	39.3%	36.2%	63.6%	60.8%	61.8%	23.1%	13.2%	38.8%	25.0%
88:3	35.9%	40.2%	62.4%	64.1%	63.4%	25.1%	15.1%	38.4%	21.5%
88:4	36.3%	41.3%	64.1%	63.7%	63.8%	26.5%	14.8%	37.3%	21.3%
89:1	39.0%	31.3%	64.5%	60.7%	61.9%	20.2%	11.1%	41.7%	27.0%
89:2	40.2%	27.9%	66.4%	59.4%	61.4%	18.6%	9.4%	42.8%	29.3%
89:3	39.9%	29.3%	65.4%	59.4%	61.1%	19.1%	10.1%	42.0%	28.7%
89:4	38.3%	36.8%	61.9%	60.8%	61.2%	22.8%	14.0%	38.5%	24.8%
90:1	36.9%	43.8%	60.8%	63.1%	62.1%	26.7%	17.2%	35.4%	20.7%
90:2	39.2%	36.2%	63.2%	60.5%	61.5%	22.9%	13.3%	38.6%	25.2%
90:3	33.5%	42.7%	54.4%	65.4%	60.7%	23.2%	19.5%	37.4%	19.8%
90:4	40.8%	44.7%	61.9%	58.6%	60.1%	27.6%	17.1%	32.4%	22.9%
91:1	44.1%	26.4%	65.4%	56.1%	58.5%	17.3%	9.2%	41.2%	32.3%
91:2	39.7%	28.4%	60.1%	60.0%	60.1%	17.1%	11.3%	43.0%	28.6%
91:3	40.4%	34.2%	60.5%	59.0%	59.5%	20.7%	13.5%	38.8%	27.0%
91:4	41.2%	36.8%	59.1%	58.4%	58.6%	21.7%	15.0%	36.9%	26.3%
92:1	40.0%	31.1%	57.5%	59.8%	59.1%	17.9%	13.2%	41.2%	27.7%
92:2	38.6%	41.5%	57.6%	61.6%	59.9%	23.9%	17.6%	36.0%	22.5%
92:3	40.3%	38.9%	60.4%	59.2%	59.6%	23.5%	15.4%	36.1%	24.9%
92:4	41.9%	33.7%	63.2%	58.2%	59.9%	21.3%	12.4%	38.6%	27.7%
93:1	42.5%	28.7%	60.5%	57.1%	58.1%	17.4%	11.4%	40.7%	30.6%
93:2	42.1%	36.7%	59.6%	57.6%	58.3%	21.9%	14.8%	36.5%	26.8%
93:3	42.5%	35.2%	61.0%	57.7%	58.9%	21.5%	13.7%	37.4%	27.4%
93:4	41.5%	38.2%	58.4%	58.3%	58.3%	22.3%	15.9%	36.0%	25.8%
94:1	40.4%	36.0%	56.0%	59.0%	57.9%	20.1%	15.8%	37.8%	26.3%
94:2	40.6%	42.7%	57.8%	59.0%	58.5%	24.7%	18.0%	33.8%	23.5%
94:3	41.8%	41.5%	60.4%	58.3%	59.2%	25.1%	16.4%	34.1%	24.4%
94:4	39.5%	46.5%	57.4%	60.9%	59.3%	26.7%	19.8%	32.6%	20.9%
95:1	43.1%	36.9%	61.6%	56.9%	58.6%	22.7%	14.2%	35.9%	27.2%
95:2	43.7%	30.9%	62.3%	56.1%	58.0%	19.3%	11.7%	38.7%	30.4%
95:3	43.9%	29.5%	61.8%	55.7%	57.5%	18.2%	11.2%	39.3%	31.2%
95:4	43.4%	32.4%	60.3%	56.3%	57.6%	19.6%	12.9%	38.1%	29.5%
96:1	45.5%	31.5%	61.9%	54.3%	56.7%	19.5%	12.0%	37.2%	31.3%
96:2	42.1%	31.4%	58.3%	57.8%	58.0%	18.3%	13.1%	39.7%	28.9%
96:3	42.6%	39.2%	59.9%	56.9%	58.1%	23.5%	15.7%	34.6%	26.2%
96:4	44.3%	30.9%	61.2%	55.3%	57.1%	18.9%	12.0%	38.2%	30.9%
AVG	40.0%	35.2%	61.6%	59.9%	60.3%	21.6%	13.6%	38.8%	26.1%

Table 3.14b
Money Flow RSI Crossover (MFR-C) Short Hit Analysis
(Average of all stocks)

Qtr	Optimal Short	MFR-C Short	Short Hits	Cash Hits	Total Hits	Short Right	Short Wrong	Cash Right	Cash Wrong
85:1	34.3%	54.4%	68.3%	66.6%	67.6%	37.2%	17.2%	30.4%	15.2%
85:2	34.6%	51.1%	69.6%	64.7%	67.2%	35.6%	15.6%	31.6%	17.3%
85:3	38.6%	52.2%	74.3%	61.6%	68.2%	38.8%	13.4%	29.4%	18.4%
85:4	33.1%	47.1%	62.4%	66.2%	64.4%	29.4%	17.7%	35.0%	17.9%
86:1	35.2%	51.5%	55.6%	64.0%	59.7%	28.7%	22.8%	31.0%	17.5%
86:2	39.8%	52.2%	60.3%	59.7%	60.0%	31.5%	20.7%	28.5%	19.3%
86:3	42.7%	45.2%	62.8%	58.1%	60.3%	28.4%	16.8%	31.9%	23.0%
86:4	38.7%	52.0%	61.6%	61.6%	61.6%	32.0%	20.0%	29.5%	18.4%
87:1	36.9%	51.3%	55.8%	62.9%	59.3%	28.6%	22.7%	30.6%	18.0%
87:2	40.0%	46.2%	60.1%	60.0%	60.1%	27.7%	18.4%	32.3%	21.5%
87:3	40.4%	55.9%	60.7%	59.6%	60.2%	33.9%	22.0%	26.3%	17.8%
87:4	45.3%	33.1%	63.6%	55.9%	58.4%	21.1%	12.1%	37.4%	29.5%
88:1	36.7%	57.5%	59.2%	64.2%	61.3%	34.1%	23.5%	27.3%	15.2%
88:2	37.4%	52.3%	61.1%	62.5%	61.7%	31.9%	20.3%	29.8%	17.9%
88:3	38.4%	50.6%	64.3%	61.7%	63.0%	32.5%	18.1%	30.5%	18.9%
88:4	37.0%	47.5%	64.0%	63.2%	63.6%	30.4%	17.1%	33.2%	19.3%
89:1	36.2%	55.3%	60.9%	63.3%	62.0%	33.7%	21.6%	28.3%	16.4%
89:2	35.9%	55.1%	59.7%	64.0%	61.6%	32.9%	22.2%	28.8%	16.2%
89:3	36.4%	51.3%	60.1%	63.3%	61.7%	30.8%	20.5%	30.9%	17.9%
89:4	39.0%	45.5%	61.3%	61.0%	61.1%	27.9%	17.6%	33.2%	21.3%
90:1	40.1%	41.3%	63.8%	59.8%	61.5%	26.4%	14.9%	35.1%	23.6%
90:2	37.8%	49.7%	61.4%	62.4%	61.9%	30.5%	19.2%	31.4%	18.9%
90:3	45.7%	39.3%	65.8%	54.0%	58.6%	25.9%	13.4%	32.8%	27.9%
90:4	37.6%	37.6%	58.5%	61.4%	60.4%	22.0%	15.6%	38.4%	24.1%
91:1	36.7%	54.4%	56.6%	63.7%	59.8%	30.8%	23.6%	29.0%	16.6%
91:2	40.4%	53.5%	60.6%	58.5%	59.6%	32.4%	21.1%	27.2%	19.3%
91:3	39.8%	50.5%	59.5%	59.7%	59.6%	30.0%	20.5%	29.6%	19.9%
91:4	40.5%	45.6%	59.1%	58.7%	58.9%	27.0%	18.6%	31.9%	22.5%
92:1	43.2%	48.6%	59.7%	56.3%	58.0%	29.0%	19.6%	29.0%	22.4%
92:2	42.9%	42.6%	62.1%	56.8%	59.1%	26.5%	16.2%	32.6%	24.8%
92:3	39.5%	45.7%	59.4%	60.0%	59.7%	27.1%	18.5%	32.6%	21.7%
92:4	37.5%	47.6%	58.2%	62.3%	60.4%	27.7%	19.9%	32.6%	19.7%
93:1	39.4%	51.2%	57.5%	60.0%	58.7%	29.5%	21.7%	29.3%	19.5%
93:2	40.9%	44.7%	58.0%	58.8%	58.5%	25.9%	18.8%	32.5%	22.8%
93:3	39.4%	49.1%	57.9%	60.2%	59.0%	28.4%	20.7%	30.6%	20.3%
93:4	41.7%	44.7%	58.9%	58.1%	58.5%	26.3%	18.4%	32.1%	23.2%
94:1	43.7%	46.4%	59.0%	55.4%	57.1%	27.4%	19.1%	29.7%	23.9%
94:2	42.7%	39.9%	59.4%	57.3%	58.1%	23.7%	16.2%	34.5%	25.7%
94:3	39.8%	46.8%	58.3%	60.1%	59.3%	27.3%	19.5%	32.0%	21.2%
94:4	42.8%	39.4%	61.6%	57.4%	59.0%	24.3%	15.2%	34.7%	25.8%
95:1	38.7%	48.8%	57.3%	61.2%	59.3%	28.0%	20.8%	31.3%	19.9%
95:2	38.9%	47.8%	56.3%	60.8%	58.6%	26.9%	20.9%	31.7%	20.5%
95:3	38.9%	50.3%	56.2%	60.7%	58.4%	28.3%	22.0%	30.1%	19.5%
95:4	40.5%	47.0%	56.5%	59.1%	57.9%	26.5%	20.4%	31.4%	21.7%
96:1	38.9%	47.8%	54.6%	60.5%	57.7%	26.1%	21.7%	31.6%	20.6%
96:2	42.4%	48.8%	58.1%	57.1%	57.6%	28.3%	20.4%	29.3%	22.0%
96:3	40.8%	44.8%	57.1%	59.0%	58.1%	25.6%	19.2%	32.6%	22.7%
96:4	39.8%	50.3%	55.4%	59.9%	57.7%	27.9%	22.4%	29.8%	20.0%
AVG	39.4%	48.2%	60.3%	60.5%	60.3%	29.0%	19.1%	31.3%	20.6%

Table 3.15a
Money Flow RSI Crossover (MFR-C) Long Return Analysis
(Average of all stocks)

Qtr	MFR-C Terminal Wealth	Buy/Hold Terminal Wealth	Relative Terminal Wealth	MFR-C Long Avg Ret	MFR-C Cash Avg Ret	MFR-C Long-Cash Avg Ret	Buy/Hold Avg Ret
85:1	10134	10142	0.999	0.064%	-0.017%	0.081%	0.006%
85:2	9826	9700	1.013	-0.096%	-0.055%	-0.041%	-0.069%
85:3	9640	8889	1.085	-0.185%	-0.214%	0.029%	-0.205%
85:4	10206	10763	0.948	0.079%	0.123%	-0.044%	0.107%
86:1	10339	11428	0.905	0.227%	0.224%	0.004%	0.225%
86:2	10156	10414	0.975	0.095%	0.056%	0.039%	0.066%
86:3	9760	9175	1.064	-0.090%	-0.151%	0.060%	-0.128%
86:4	10218	10413	0.981	0.090%	0.056%	0.034%	0.069%
87:1	10670	11929	0.894	0.353%	0.268%	0.086%	0.293%
87:2	10066	10196	0.987	0.034%	0.040%	-0.006%	0.038%
87:3	10175	10408	0.978	0.095%	0.057%	0.038%	0.068%
87:4	9636	8087	1.192	-0.107%	-0.441%	0.334%	-0.278%
88:1	10507	10989	0.956	0.244%	0.122%	0.121%	0.163%
88:2	10275	10593	0.970	0.127%	0.084%	0.043%	0.100%
88:3	10090	10050	1.004	0.040%	-0.006%	0.046%	0.013%
88:4	10107	10196	0.991	0.046%	0.030%	0.016%	0.037%
89:1	10201	10698	0.954	0.106%	0.115%	-0.010%	0.112%
89:2	10259	10772	0.952	0.148%	0.112%	0.035%	0.122%
89:3	10243	10833	0.946	0.134%	0.130%	0.004%	0.131%
89:4	9945	9904	1.004	-0.020%	-0.006%	-0.015%	-0.011%
90:1	10038	9980	1.006	0.018%	-0.009%	0.027%	0.003%
90:2	10233	10459	0.978	0.105%	0.061%	0.045%	0.077%
90:3	9283	8526	1.089	-0.284%	-0.240%	-0.044%	-0.259%
90:4	10361	10889	0.951	0.136%	0.154%	-0.018%	0.146%
91:1	10692	12477	0.857	0.413%	0.280%	0.133%	0.315%
91:2	10074	10244	0.983	0.044%	0.046%	-0.002%	0.045%
91:3	10113	10429	0.970	0.052%	0.072%	-0.020%	0.065%
91:4	10156	10497	0.967	0.069%	0.089%	-0.020%	0.082%
92:1	10103	10324	0.979	0.051%	0.047%	0.004%	0.048%
92:2	9938	9723	1.022	-0.023%	-0.066%	0.043%	-0.048%
92:3	10090	10392	0.971	0.032%	0.072%	-0.040%	0.057%
92:4	10369	10963	0.946	0.168%	0.133%	0.035%	0.144%
93:1	10108	10527	0.960	0.056%	0.089%	-0.033%	0.080%
93:2	10093	10340	0.976	0.040%	0.059%	-0.019%	0.052%
93:3	10270	10686	0.961	0.115%	0.093%	0.022%	0.101%
93:4	10069	10255	0.982	0.024%	0.040%	-0.017%	0.034%
94:1	9959	9954	1.001	-0.025%	-0.003%	-0.022%	-0.011%
94:2	9954	9994	0.996	-0.022%	0.008%	-0.031%	-0.005%
94:3	10262	10613	0.967	0.094%	0.086%	0.008%	0.089%
94:4	9958	9836	1.012	-0.017%	-0.040%	0.024%	-0.029%
95:1	10272	10706	0.959	0.119%	0.105%	0.015%	0.110%
95:2	10275	10873	0.945	0.139%	0.132%	0.008%	0.134%
95:3	10234	10853	0.943	0.123%	0.135%	-0.012%	0.131%
95:4	10152	10445	0.972	0.073%	0.064%	0.009%	0.067%
96:1	10380	11027	0.941	0.190%	0.145%	0.046%	0.159%
96:2	10119	10367	0.976	0.060%	0.058%	0.003%	0.059%
96:3	10105	10298	0.981	0.041%	0.051%	-0.010%	0.047%
96:4	10247	10817	0.947	0.123%	0.122%	0.002%	0.122%
AVG	10132	10377	0.976	0.058%	0.053%	0.005%	0.055%

Table 3.15b
Money Flow RSI Crossover (MFR-C) Short Return Analysis
(Average of all stocks)

Qtr	MFR-C Terminal Wealth	Buy/Hold Terminal Wealth	Relative Terminal Wealth	MFR-C Short Avg Ret	MFR-C Cash Avg Ret	MFR-C Short-Cash Avg Ret	Buy/Hold Avg Ret
85:1	10114	10142	0.997	-0.019%	0.036%	-0.055%	0.006%
85:2	10218	9700	1.053	-0.052%	-0.087%	0.034%	-0.069%
85:3	10832	8889	1.219	-0.223%	-0.185%	-0.037%	-0.205%
85:4	9622	10763	0.894	0.136%	0.081%	0.055%	0.107%
86:1	9318	11428	0.815	0.232%	0.217%	0.015%	0.225%
86:2	9801	10414	0.941	0.065%	0.068%	-0.003%	0.066%
86:3	10457	9175	1.140	-0.161%	-0.100%	-0.061%	-0.128%
86:4	9797	10413	0.941	0.058%	0.082%	-0.024%	0.069%
87:1	9161	11929	0.768	0.286%	0.301%	-0.015%	0.293%
87:2	9906	10196	0.972	0.031%	0.044%	-0.013%	0.038%
87:3	9801	10408	0.942	0.055%	0.085%	-0.030%	0.068%
87:4	11035	8087	1.365	-0.504%	-0.166%	-0.338%	-0.278%
88:1	9518	10989	0.866	0.131%	0.205%	-0.074%	0.163%
88:2	9705	10593	0.916	0.089%	0.112%	-0.024%	0.100%
88:3	9995	10050	0.994	-0.001%	0.027%	-0.028%	0.013%
88:4	9905	10196	0.971	0.029%	0.043%	-0.014%	0.037%
89:1	9578	10698	0.895	0.127%	0.094%	0.032%	0.112%
89:2	9590	10772	0.890	0.119%	0.126%	-0.006%	0.122%
89:3	9581	10833	0.884	0.135%	0.127%	0.008%	0.131%
89:4	10001	9904	1.010	-0.003%	-0.018%	0.015%	-0.011%
90:1	10017	9980	1.004	-0.008%	0.010%	-0.018%	0.003%
90:2	9829	10459	0.940	0.053%	0.100%	-0.047%	0.077%
90:3	10586	8526	1.242	-0.232%	-0.276%	0.044%	-0.259%
90:4	9594	10889	0.881	0.170%	0.132%	0.038%	0.146%
91:1	9110	12477	0.730	0.294%	0.339%	-0.045%	0.315%
91:2	9786	10244	0.955	0.058%	0.031%	0.027%	0.045%
91:3	9778	10429	0.938	0.072%	0.058%	0.014%	0.065%
91:4	9732	10497	0.927	0.088%	0.076%	0.012%	0.082%
92:1	9817	10324	0.951	0.066%	0.031%	0.036%	0.048%
92:2	10183	9723	1.047	-0.062%	-0.038%	-0.024%	-0.048%
92:3	9786	10392	0.942	0.079%	0.037%	0.042%	0.057%
92:4	9569	10963	0.873	0.149%	0.141%	0.008%	0.144%
93:1	9718	10527	0.923	0.095%	0.063%	0.032%	0.080%
93:2	9844	10340	0.952	0.059%	0.046%	0.012%	0.052%
93:3	9710	10686	0.909	0.103%	0.099%	0.003%	0.101%
93:4	9911	10255	0.967	0.036%	0.032%	0.004%	0.034%
94:1	9952	9954	1.000	0.017%	-0.036%	0.053%	-0.011%
94:2	9991	9994	1.000	0.008%	-0.013%	0.021%	-0.005%
94:3	9760	10613	0.920	0.088%	0.091%	-0.003%	0.089%
94:4	10144	9836	1.031	-0.056%	-0.012%	-0.044%	-0.029%
95:1	9707	10706	0.907	0.101%	0.119%	-0.018%	0.110%
95:2	9592	10873	0.882	0.143%	0.126%	0.016%	0.134%
95:3	9566	10853	0.881	0.144%	0.118%	0.027%	0.131%
95:4	9787	10445	0.937	0.077%	0.058%	0.018%	0.067%
96:1	9577	11027	0.868	0.149%	0.168%	-0.019%	0.159%
96:2	9797	10367	0.945	0.068%	0.049%	0.019%	0.059%
96:3	9824	10298	0.954	0.062%	0.035%	0.027%	0.047%
96:4	9585	10817	0.886	0.137%	0.107%	0.030%	0.122%
AVG	9837	10377	0.948	0.058%	0.052%	0.006%	0.055%

The MV2-C system may generate good trades when a security begins a solid trend, but, by nature, this system generates late signals. In addition, when a market consolidates sideways, this system generates "whipsaw" trades. Thus, traders express concern that using the MV2-C system will generate losses in trading range markets.

Construction

Two exponential moving averages must be constructed, using the basic technique described at the beginning of this chapter. The first moving average, EMA_1, is the shorter-period exponential moving average and, thus, the faster of the two. The second moving average, EMA_2, is the longer-period, slower one.

Long signals occur when EMA_1 crosses EMA_2 from below to the upside. Short signals occur when EMA_1 falls and crosses EMA_2.

Results

The test results for this indicator are shown in Tables 3.16 and 3.17. Across the quarters of our test period, the MV2-C system, on average, made long calls 56.2 percent of the time and short calls 43.7 percent of the time (Table 3.16). Sixty percent of both these long calls and short calls are correct.

On average, when this system makes a long call, the average daily stock return is 0.062 percent (Table 3.17a). This is indeed higher than the average daily stock return of 0.046 percent when a cash position is favored over a long position. Thus, the MV2-C system does distinguish days of above-average stock price appreciation. The main shortcoming is that when the system suggests a cash position instead of a long position, the average daily return on these days is positive. Even though an investor would be earning below-average returns on these days, the investor would earn a positive return, on average, by being in a long position. Because these positive returns are lost potential profits, trading long with this system results in a lower terminal wealth than a buy-and-hold system, which would have captured those potential profits.

Just as it distinguishes days of above-average market performance with its long calls, the MV2-C system distinguishes days of below-average market performance with its short calls. The average daily stock return is only 0.046 percent when short calls are made, compared to 0.062 percent when cash positions are favored over short positions (Table 3.17b). Unfortunately, even though the short calls are associated with below-average stock price appreciation, on average, prices are rising on these days. Therefore, following the system's short recommendations will lead to losses. In fact, for 37 of the 48 test quarters, trading short with the MV2-C system resulted in terminal wealth that was lower than the initial wealth of $10,000.

Moving Average Convergence/ Divergence Crossover

As noted earlier, the moving average convergence/divergence concept was originally developed by system writer Gerald Appel. The Moving Average Convergence/Divergence Crossover indicator (MAC-M) is based on the difference between the same two moving averages used with the MAC-D indicator discussed on page 57. However, the MAC-M indicator includes a third moving average that forms a trigger line. Whenever this trigger line is crossed, the system generates a trade signal.

Construction

The first step in constructing this system is to calculate a 12-period moving average (EMA_{12}). The second step is the calculation of a 26-period average (EMA_{26}). The MACD is then calculated as the difference in these two moving averages:

$$MACD = EMA_{12} - EMA_{26}$$

Next, a trigger line is constructed. This trigger line is the nine-period moving average of the MACD:

$$Trig = EMA_9(MACD)$$

Whenever the MACD falls below the trigger line, a short call is made. Whenever the MACD crosses above the trigger line, a long call is made.

Results

The results for the Moving Average Convergence/Divergence Crossover (MAC-M) system are shown in Tables 3.18 and 3.19. This system makes extremely frequent calls. The long call rate of 50.3 percent (Table 3.18a) and the short call rate of 49.6 percent (Table 3.18b) are among the highest calls of all the systems we have tested. The long calls have a hit rate of 60.3 percent (Table 3.18a) and the short calls have a hit rate of 59.9 percent (Table 3.18b).

The call rates are high because this system will never favor a cash position if it can choose a long or short position. Thus, when forced to choose between a long position or a cash position, the system's cash calls are identical to the system's short calls.

This system does not suffer, as do many of the systems we have seen, from making too few calls. However, the system is still not powerful enough

Table 3.16a
Moving Average Crossover (MV2-C) Long Hit Analysis
(Average of all stocks)

Qtr	Optimal Long	MV2-C Long	Long Hits	Cash Hits	Total Hits	Long Right	Long Wrong	Cash Right	Cash Wrong
85:1	32.1%	70.9%	65.6%	67.7%	66.2%	46.5%	24.4%	19.7%	9.4%
85:2	30.2%	59.8%	64.7%	70.8%	67.2%	38.7%	21.1%	28.5%	11.7%
85:3	26.3%	45.9%	60.5%	72.7%	67.1%	27.8%	18.1%	39.3%	14.8%
85:4	36.6%	69.8%	65.8%	67.1%	66.2%	45.9%	23.9%	20.3%	9.9%
86:1	44.2%	73.4%	64.1%	57.7%	62.4%	47.1%	26.3%	15.3%	11.2%
86:2	39.7%	60.0%	58.8%	59.1%	58.9%	35.3%	24.8%	23.6%	16.3%
86:3	37.0%	42.5%	55.7%	63.1%	60.0%	23.7%	18.8%	36.3%	21.2%
86:4	38.5%	54.4%	59.2%	60.8%	59.9%	32.2%	22.2%	27.7%	17.8%
87:1	44.7%	76.5%	61.5%	51.9%	59.2%	47.0%	29.5%	12.2%	11.3%
87:2	40.0%	46.1%	59.5%	59.4%	59.5%	27.4%	18.7%	32.0%	21.9%
87:3	39.5%	58.7%	58.7%	60.0%	59.2%	34.5%	24.3%	24.7%	16.5%
87:4	37.9%	23.7%	53.2%	61.5%	59.5%	12.6%	11.1%	46.9%	29.4%
88:1	41.3%	75.9%	62.5%	57.1%	61.2%	47.5%	28.5%	13.7%	10.3%
88:2	39.3%	50.4%	61.5%	60.1%	60.8%	31.0%	19.4%	29.8%	19.8%
88:3	35.9%	47.4%	60.6%	63.2%	62.0%	28.7%	18.7%	33.3%	19.4%
88:4	36.3%	49.8%	61.4%	63.2%	62.3%	30.6%	19.2%	31.8%	18.5%
89:1	39.0%	64.8%	62.8%	60.8%	62.1%	40.7%	24.1%	21.4%	13.8%
89:2	40.2%	72.1%	63.2%	60.6%	62.5%	45.5%	26.6%	16.9%	11.0%
89:3	39.9%	61.8%	62.0%	59.5%	61.0%	38.3%	23.5%	22.7%	15.5%
89:4	38.3%	43.2%	61.0%	62.4%	61.8%	26.3%	16.9%	35.5%	21.4%
90:1	36.9%	43.6%	57.8%	62.6%	60.5%	25.2%	18.4%	35.3%	21.1%
90:2	39.2%	58.5%	60.4%	60.9%	60.6%	35.3%	23.2%	25.3%	16.2%
90:3	33.5%	26.0%	54.2%	66.7%	63.5%	14.1%	11.9%	49.4%	24.7%
90:4	40.8%	54.4%	62.3%	60.7%	61.5%	33.9%	20.5%	27.7%	17.9%
91:1	44.1%	72.7%	61.8%	54.4%	59.8%	44.9%	27.8%	14.9%	12.4%
91:2	39.7%	58.6%	58.1%	58.5%	58.3%	34.1%	24.6%	24.2%	17.2%
91:3	40.4%	54.2%	59.5%	59.5%	59.5%	32.2%	21.9%	27.3%	18.6%
91:4	41.2%	50.1%	59.6%	59.3%	59.4%	29.8%	20.2%	29.6%	20.3%
92:1	40.0%	64.0%	57.4%	61.9%	59.0%	36.8%	27.3%	22.3%	13.7%
92:2	38.6%	46.9%	57.0%	61.2%	59.2%	26.7%	20.1%	32.5%	20.6%
92:3	40.3%	55.5%	60.4%	60.1%	60.3%	33.5%	22.0%	26.8%	17.7%
92:4	41.9%	63.8%	62.4%	58.7%	61.1%	39.9%	24.0%	21.2%	14.9%
93:1	42.5%	64.2%	60.5%	56.9%	59.2%	38.8%	25.4%	20.4%	15.4%
93:2	42.1%	50.5%	58.9%	58.0%	58.5%	29.7%	20.8%	28.7%	20.8%
93:3	42.5%	61.1%	60.7%	58.0%	59.7%	37.1%	24.0%	22.6%	16.4%
93:4	41.5%	50.2%	58.7%	59.0%	58.8%	29.4%	20.7%	29.4%	20.4%
94:1	40.4%	55.3%	56.5%	60.4%	58.2%	31.3%	24.0%	27.0%	17.7%
94:2	40.6%	40.8%	56.7%	59.0%	58.1%	23.1%	17.7%	35.0%	24.3%
94:3	41.8%	55.5%	59.8%	58.1%	59.1%	33.2%	22.3%	25.9%	18.7%
94:4	39.5%	39.3%	57.0%	60.3%	59.0%	22.4%	16.9%	36.6%	24.1%
95:1	43.1%	66.4%	60.9%	57.1%	59.6%	40.4%	26.0%	19.2%	14.4%
95:2	43.7%	68.7%	60.6%	56.6%	59.3%	41.6%	27.1%	17.7%	13.6%
95:3	43.9%	65.2%	60.8%	57.3%	59.6%	39.6%	25.6%	20.0%	14.9%
95:4	43.4%	55.2%	60.0%	58.2%	59.2%	33.1%	22.0%	26.1%	18.7%
96:1	45.5%	57.9%	60.7%	54.6%	58.1%	35.1%	22.7%	23.0%	19.1%
96:2	42.1%	56.6%	57.4%	58.3%	57.8%	32.5%	24.2%	25.3%	18.1%
96:3	42.6%	50.2%	60.0%	58.2%	59.1%	30.1%	20.1%	29.0%	20.8%
96:4	44.3%	63.7%	59.9%	56.6%	58.7%	38.1%	25.5%	20.5%	15.8%
AVG	40.0%	56.2%	60.0%	60.2%	60.5%	33.9%	22.2%	26.5%	17.3%

Table 3.16b
Moving Average Crossover (MV2-C) Short Hit Analysis
(Average of all stocks)

Qtr	Optimal Short	MV2-C Short	Short Hits	Cash Hits	Total Hits	Short Right	Short Wrong	Cash Right	Cash Wrong
85:1	34.3%	29.0%	67.7%	65.6%	66.2%	19.7%	9.4%	46.6%	24.4%
85:2	34.6%	40.1%	70.8%	64.7%	67.1%	28.4%	11.7%	38.8%	21.1%
85:3	38.6%	53.9%	72.7%	60.5%	67.1%	39.1%	14.7%	27.9%	18.2%
85:4	33.1%	30.1%	67.1%	65.8%	66.2%	20.2%	9.9%	46.0%	23.9%
86:1	35.2%	26.4%	57.6%	64.2%	62.4%	15.2%	11.2%	47.2%	26.4%
86:2	39.8%	39.8%	59.1%	58.8%	58.9%	23.5%	16.3%	35.4%	24.8%
86:3	42.7%	57.4%	63.1%	55.7%	60.0%	36.2%	21.2%	23.7%	18.9%
86:4	38.7%	45.5%	60.8%	59.2%	59.9%	27.7%	17.8%	32.3%	22.2%
87:1	36.9%	23.5%	51.9%	61.5%	59.2%	12.2%	11.3%	47.0%	29.5%
87:2	40.0%	53.9%	59.4%	59.5%	59.5%	32.0%	21.9%	27.5%	18.7%
87:3	40.4%	41.2%	60.0%	58.7%	59.2%	24.7%	16.5%	34.5%	24.3%
87:4	45.3%	75.7%	61.5%	53.3%	59.5%	46.5%	29.2%	13.0%	11.4%
88:1	36.7%	24.0%	57.1%	62.5%	61.2%	13.7%	10.3%	47.5%	28.5%
88:2	37.4%	49.5%	60.1%	61.5%	60.8%	29.7%	19.8%	31.0%	19.4%
88:3	38.4%	52.6%	63.2%	60.6%	62.0%	33.2%	19.3%	28.7%	18.7%
88:4	37.0%	50.2%	63.2%	61.4%	62.3%	31.8%	18.5%	30.6%	19.2%
89:1	36.2%	35.2%	60.7%	62.8%	62.1%	21.4%	13.8%	40.7%	24.1%
89:2	35.9%	27.9%	60.7%	63.2%	62.5%	16.9%	11.0%	45.5%	26.6%
89:3	36.4%	38.1%	59.5%	62.0%	61.0%	22.7%	15.5%	38.4%	23.5%
89:4	39.0%	56.1%	62.5%	60.8%	61.7%	35.0%	21.0%	26.7%	17.2%
90:1	40.1%	56.3%	62.6%	57.8%	60.5%	35.3%	21.1%	25.2%	18.4%
90:2	37.8%	41.5%	60.9%	60.3%	60.6%	25.2%	16.2%	35.3%	23.2%
90:3	45.7%	73.9%	66.7%	54.3%	63.4%	49.3%	24.6%	14.2%	11.9%
90:4	37.6%	45.5%	60.6%	62.3%	61.5%	27.6%	17.9%	34.0%	20.6%
91:1	36.7%	27.2%	54.5%	61.8%	59.8%	14.8%	12.4%	45.0%	27.8%
91:2	40.4%	41.2%	58.5%	58.1%	58.3%	24.1%	17.1%	34.1%	24.6%
91:3	39.8%	45.7%	59.5%	59.5%	59.5%	27.2%	18.5%	32.3%	22.0%
91:4	40.5%	49.8%	59.2%	59.5%	59.4%	29.5%	20.3%	29.9%	20.3%
92:1	43.2%	36.0%	61.9%	57.4%	59.0%	22.3%	13.7%	36.8%	27.3%
92:2	42.9%	52.9%	61.2%	57.0%	59.2%	32.4%	20.5%	26.8%	20.2%
92:3	39.5%	44.5%	60.2%	60.4%	60.3%	26.8%	17.7%	33.6%	22.0%
92:4	37.5%	36.1%	58.7%	62.4%	61.1%	21.2%	14.9%	39.9%	24.0%
93:1	39.4%	35.7%	56.9%	60.5%	59.2%	20.3%	15.4%	38.9%	25.4%
93:2	40.9%	49.4%	58.0%	58.9%	58.5%	28.7%	20.7%	29.8%	20.8%
93:3	39.4%	38.9%	58.0%	60.7%	59.7%	22.6%	16.3%	37.1%	24.0%
93:4	41.7%	49.8%	59.0%	58.7%	58.9%	29.4%	20.4%	29.5%	20.7%
94:1	43.7%	44.7%	60.4%	56.5%	58.2%	27.0%	17.7%	31.3%	24.1%
94:2	42.7%	59.2%	59.0%	56.7%	58.1%	34.9%	24.2%	23.1%	17.7%
94:3	39.8%	44.5%	58.1%	59.8%	59.0%	25.9%	18.6%	33.2%	22.3%
94:4	42.8%	60.7%	60.3%	57.0%	59.0%	36.6%	24.1%	22.4%	16.9%
95:1	38.7%	33.6%	57.1%	60.9%	59.6%	19.2%	14.4%	40.4%	26.0%
95:2	38.9%	31.3%	56.5%	60.6%	59.3%	17.7%	13.6%	41.7%	27.1%
95:3	38.9%	34.7%	57.3%	60.8%	59.5%	19.9%	14.8%	39.7%	25.6%
95:4	40.5%	44.8%	58.2%	60.0%	59.2%	26.1%	18.7%	33.2%	22.1%
96:1	38.9%	42.1%	54.6%	60.7%	58.1%	23.0%	19.1%	35.2%	22.8%
96:2	42.4%	43.3%	58.3%	57.4%	57.8%	25.2%	18.0%	32.5%	24.2%
96:3	40.8%	49.7%	58.2%	60.0%	59.1%	28.9%	20.8%	30.1%	20.1%
96:4	39.8%	36.3%	56.6%	59.9%	58.7%	20.5%	15.8%	38.2%	25.6%
AVG	39.4%	43.7%	60.2%	60.0%	60.5%	26.5%	17.3%	34.0%	22.3%

Table 3.17a
Moving Average Crossover (MV2-C) Long Return Analysis
(Average of all stocks)

Qtr	MV2-C Terminal Wealth	Buy/Hold Terminal Wealth	Relative Terminal Wealth	MV2-C Long Avg Ret	MV2-C Cash Avg Ret	MV2-C Long-Cash Avg Ret	Buy/Hold Avg Ret
85:1	10114	10142	0.997	0.017%	-0.019%	0.035%	0.006%
85:2	9796	9700	1.010	-0.065%	-0.076%	0.011%	-0.069%
85:3	9364	8889	1.054	-0.235%	-0.180%	-0.055%	-0.205%
85:4	10578	10763	0.983	0.124%	0.066%	0.059%	0.107%
86:1	11022	11428	0.965	0.221%	0.233%	-0.012%	0.225%
86:2	10069	10414	0.967	0.015%	0.143%	-0.128%	0.066%
86:3	9504	9175	1.036	-0.185%	-0.085%	-0.101%	-0.128%
86:4	10050	10413	0.965	0.019%	0.130%	-0.111%	0.069%
87:1	11148	11929	0.935	0.233%	0.488%	-0.255%	0.293%
87:2	10017	10196	0.982	0.009%	0.062%	-0.053%	0.038%
87:3	10143	10408	0.975	0.042%	0.106%	-0.064%	0.068%
87:4	9611	8087	1.188	-0.256%	-0.285%	0.029%	-0.278%
88:1	10537	10989	0.959	0.121%	0.296%	-0.175%	0.163%
88:2	10175	10593	0.961	0.059%	0.141%	-0.083%	0.100%
88:3	9920	10050	0.987	-0.024%	0.045%	-0.069%	0.013%
88:4	10015	10196	0.982	0.006%	0.067%	-0.061%	0.037%
89:1	10434	10698	0.975	0.109%	0.119%	-0.010%	0.112%
89:2	10509	10772	0.976	0.112%	0.149%	-0.038%	0.122%
89:3	10418	10833	0.962	0.107%	0.170%	-0.063%	0.131%
89:4	9950	9904	1.005	-0.015%	-0.008%	-0.006%	-0.011%
90:1	9869	9980	0.989	-0.045%	0.040%	-0.085%	0.003%
90:2	10204	10459	0.976	0.056%	0.106%	-0.051%	0.077%
90:3	9630	8526	1.129	-0.227%	-0.270%	0.043%	-0.259%
90:4	10544	10889	0.968	0.157%	0.133%	0.024%	0.146%
91:1	11300	12477	0.906	0.279%	0.410%	-0.130%	0.315%
91:2	9970	10244	0.973	-0.002%	0.113%	-0.116%	0.045%
91:3	10182	10429	0.976	0.048%	0.084%	-0.036%	0.065%
91:4	10211	10497	0.973	0.065%	0.098%	-0.033%	0.082%
92:1	10383	10324	1.006	0.093%	-0.032%	0.125%	0.048%
92:2	9864	9723	1.015	-0.048%	-0.049%	0.001%	-0.048%
92:3	10199	10392	0.981	0.052%	0.062%	-0.009%	0.057%
92:4	10638	10963	0.970	0.151%	0.134%	0.017%	0.144%
93:1	10280	10527	0.977	0.067%	0.103%	-0.036%	0.080%
93:2	10193	10340	0.986	0.055%	0.049%	0.006%	0.052%
93:3	10436	10686	0.977	0.106%	0.093%	0.013%	0.101%
93:4	10172	10255	0.992	0.049%	0.019%	0.030%	0.034%
94:1	10021	9954	1.007	0.005%	-0.031%	0.036%	-0.011%
94:2	9933	9994	0.994	-0.029%	0.012%	-0.040%	-0.005%
94:3	10330	10613	0.973	0.088%	0.091%	-0.003%	0.089%
94:4	9914	9836	1.008	-0.037%	-0.024%	-0.014%	-0.029%
95:1	10409	10706	0.972	0.095%	0.140%	-0.045%	0.110%
95:2	10567	10873	0.972	0.127%	0.149%	-0.022%	0.134%
95:3	10563	10853	0.973	0.134%	0.126%	0.007%	0.131%
95:4	10312	10445	0.987	0.086%	0.043%	0.043%	0.067%
96:1	10518	11027	0.954	0.139%	0.187%	-0.048%	0.159%
96:2	10232	10367	0.987	0.064%	0.052%	0.012%	0.059%
96:3	10242	10298	0.995	0.074%	0.020%	0.054%	0.047%
96:4	10548	10817	0.975	0.131%	0.108%	0.023%	0.122%
AVG	10230	10377	0.986	0.062%	0.046%	0.016%	0.055%

Table 3.17b
Moving Average Crossover (MV2-C) Short Return Analysis
(Average of all stocks)

Qtr	MV2-C Terminal Wealth	Buy/Hold Terminal Wealth	Relative Terminal Wealth	MV2-C Short Avg Ret	MV2-C Cash Avg Ret	MV2-C Short-Cash Avg Ret	Buy/Hold Avg Ret
85:1	10050	10142	0.991	-0.019%	0.016%	-0.035%	0.006%
85:2	10279	9700	1.060	-0.075%	-0.065%	-0.010%	-0.069%
85:3	10688	8889	1.202	-0.179%	-0.234%	0.055%	-0.205%
85:4	9902	10763	0.920	0.067%	0.124%	-0.056%	0.107%
86:1	9637	11428	0.843	0.233%	0.222%	0.011%	0.225%
86:2	9644	10414	0.926	0.139%	0.018%	0.120%	0.066%
86:3	10263	9175	1.119	-0.084%	-0.186%	0.101%	-0.128%
86:4	9621	10413	0.924	0.130%	0.019%	0.111%	0.069%
87:1	9324	11929	0.782	0.487%	0.233%	0.254%	0.293%
87:2	9765	10196	0.958	0.063%	0.009%	0.054%	0.038%
87:3	9719	10408	0.934	0.106%	0.042%	0.063%	0.068%
87:4	11120	8087	1.375	-0.285%	-0.258%	-0.027%	-0.278%
88:1	9558	10989	0.870	0.296%	0.121%	0.175%	0.163%
88:2	9556	10593	0.902	0.142%	0.058%	0.083%	0.100%
88:3	9838	10050	0.979	0.045%	-0.023%	0.069%	0.013%
88:4	9780	10196	0.959	0.067%	0.006%	0.061%	0.037%
89:1	9744	10698	0.911	0.119%	0.109%	0.010%	0.112%
89:2	9736	10772	0.904	0.149%	0.112%	0.037%	0.122%
89:3	9597	10833	0.886	0.171%	0.107%	0.064%	0.131%
89:4	10016	9904	1.011	-0.010%	-0.012%	0.002%	-0.011%
90:1	9834	9980	0.985	0.040%	-0.046%	0.086%	0.003%
90:2	9713	10459	0.929	0.107%	0.055%	0.052%	0.077%
90:3	11351	8526	1.331	-0.270%	-0.227%	-0.043%	-0.259%
90:4	9585	10889	0.880	0.134%	0.157%	-0.023%	0.146%
91:1	9352	12477	0.750	0.409%	0.280%	0.129%	0.315%
91:2	9699	10244	0.947	0.111%	-0.001%	0.112%	0.045%
91:3	9754	10429	0.935	0.085%	0.048%	0.038%	0.065%
91:4	9669	10497	0.921	0.100%	0.064%	0.035%	0.082%
92:1	10076	10324	0.976	-0.033%	0.093%	-0.126%	0.048%
92:2	10162	9723	1.045	-0.049%	-0.048%	0.000%	-0.048%
92:3	9834	10392	0.946	0.062%	0.052%	0.009%	0.057%
92:4	9691	10963	0.884	0.133%	0.151%	-0.017%	0.144%
93:1	9785	10527	0.929	0.104%	0.067%	0.037%	0.080%
93:2	9840	10340	0.952	0.048%	0.055%	-0.007%	0.052%
93:3	9773	10686	0.915	0.093%	0.106%	-0.013%	0.101%
93:4	9944	10255	0.970	0.018%	0.049%	-0.031%	0.034%
94:1	10094	9954	1.014	-0.031%	0.005%	-0.036%	-0.011%
94:2	9970	9994	0.998	0.012%	-0.029%	0.041%	-0.005%
94:3	9751	10613	0.919	0.091%	0.088%	0.003%	0.089%
94:4	10095	9836	1.026	-0.024%	-0.037%	0.013%	-0.029%
95:1	9711	10706	0.907	0.140%	0.095%	0.045%	0.110%
95:2	9713	10873	0.893	0.149%	0.127%	0.022%	0.134%
95:3	9726	10853	0.896	0.127%	0.133%	-0.006%	0.131%
95:4	9884	10445	0.946	0.043%	0.086%	-0.044%	0.067%
96:1	9516	11027	0.863	0.186%	0.139%	0.048%	0.159%
96:2	9863	10367	0.951	0.051%	0.064%	-0.014%	0.059%
96:3	9929	10298	0.964	0.021%	0.074%	-0.053%	0.047%
96:4	9755	10817	0.902	0.108%	0.131%	-0.023%	0.122%
AVG	9873	10377	0.951	0.046%	0.062%	-0.016%	0.055%

Table 3.18a
Moving Average Convergence Crossover (MAC-M) Long Hit Analysis
(Average of all stocks)

Qtr	Optimal Long	MAC-M Long	Long Hits	Cash Hits	Total Hits	Long Right	Long Wrong	Cash Right	Cash Wrong
85:1	32.1%	48.8%	67.0%	69.1%	68.0%	32.7%	16.1%	35.4%	15.8%
85:2	30.2%	52.9%	64.0%	69.3%	66.5%	33.8%	19.0%	32.7%	14.5%
85:3	26.3%	42.5%	61.0%	73.2%	68.0%	25.9%	16.5%	42.1%	15.4%
85:4	36.6%	63.9%	65.9%	61.6%	64.3%	42.1%	21.8%	22.2%	13.8%
86:1	44.2%	51.5%	64.0%	56.3%	60.3%	33.0%	18.6%	27.3%	21.2%
86:2	39.7%	42.3%	58.3%	59.3%	58.9%	24.7%	17.6%	34.2%	23.5%
86:3	37.0%	45.3%	57.6%	63.2%	60.6%	26.1%	19.2%	34.6%	20.1%
86:4	38.5%	55.6%	60.7%	61.1%	60.9%	33.8%	21.9%	27.1%	17.3%
87:1	44.7%	54.9%	61.6%	54.5%	58.4%	33.8%	21.1%	24.6%	20.5%
87:2	40.0%	49.6%	59.6%	59.4%	59.5%	29.6%	20.0%	29.9%	20.5%
87:3	39.5%	42.3%	59.6%	60.7%	60.2%	25.2%	17.1%	35.0%	22.7%
87:4	37.9%	62.2%	56.4%	62.1%	58.6%	35.1%	27.1%	23.4%	14.3%
88:1	41.3%	54.1%	62.8%	59.1%	61.1%	34.0%	20.1%	27.2%	18.8%
88:2	39.3%	49.0%	61.4%	60.1%	60.8%	30.1%	18.9%	30.7%	20.4%
88:3	35.9%	46.1%	61.2%	63.4%	62.4%	28.2%	17.9%	34.2%	19.7%
88:4	36.3%	49.6%	62.6%	63.5%	63.0%	31.1%	18.5%	32.0%	18.4%
89:1	39.0%	49.4%	62.4%	60.1%	61.2%	30.8%	18.6%	30.4%	20.2%
89:2	40.2%	54.8%	63.4%	59.6%	61.7%	34.7%	20.1%	26.9%	18.2%
89:3	39.9%	45.2%	61.9%	59.4%	60.5%	28.0%	17.2%	32.6%	22.2%
89:4	38.3%	50.8%	60.5%	60.6%	60.6%	30.7%	20.1%	29.9%	19.4%
90:1	36.9%	54.3%	59.9%	63.2%	61.4%	32.6%	21.8%	28.8%	16.8%
90:2	39.2%	49.5%	62.2%	61.0%	61.6%	30.8%	18.7%	30.8%	19.7%
90:3	33.5%	42.8%	53.6%	65.0%	60.1%	22.9%	19.9%	37.2%	20.0%
90:4	40.8%	64.2%	61.2%	57.1%	59.7%	39.3%	24.9%	20.4%	15.4%
91:1	44.1%	48.7%	63.2%	56.9%	60.0%	30.8%	17.9%	29.2%	22.1%
91:2	39.7%	43.6%	57.5%	59.3%	58.5%	25.0%	18.5%	33.5%	23.0%
91:3	40.4%	50.5%	59.1%	58.6%	58.9%	29.9%	20.6%	29.0%	20.5%
91:4	41.2%	50.0%	59.6%	59.5%	59.6%	29.8%	20.2%	29.8%	20.2%
92:1	40.0%	46.5%	56.4%	60.0%	58.3%	26.2%	20.3%	32.1%	21.4%
92:2	38.6%	47.1%	56.5%	60.9%	58.8%	26.6%	20.5%	32.2%	20.7%
92:3	40.3%	54.5%	59.9%	59.0%	59.5%	32.6%	21.8%	26.8%	18.7%
92:4	41.9%	54.1%	62.3%	58.3%	60.5%	33.7%	20.4%	26.8%	19.2%
93:1	42.5%	48.7%	59.9%	56.8%	58.3%	29.2%	19.5%	29.1%	22.2%
93:2	42.1%	47.5%	58.6%	57.7%	58.1%	27.8%	19.6%	30.3%	22.3%
93:3	42.5%	51.4%	60.7%	57.8%	59.3%	31.2%	20.2%	28.1%	20.5%
93:4	41.5%	49.9%	59.1%	59.1%	59.1%	29.5%	20.4%	29.6%	20.5%
94:1	40.4%	48.6%	55.8%	59.0%	57.4%	27.1%	21.5%	30.3%	21.1%
94:2	40.6%	51.5%	57.4%	58.8%	58.1%	29.6%	21.9%	28.5%	20.0%
94:3	41.8%	50.7%	60.6%	58.4%	59.5%	30.7%	20.0%	28.8%	20.5%
94:4	39.5%	48.2%	57.8%	60.9%	59.4%	27.9%	20.4%	31.5%	20.3%
95:1	43.1%	53.9%	60.3%	56.4%	58.5%	32.5%	21.4%	26.0%	20.1%
95:2	43.7%	51.2%	60.2%	55.8%	58.1%	30.8%	20.4%	27.2%	21.6%
95:3	43.9%	49.7%	60.6%	55.7%	58.1%	30.1%	19.6%	28.0%	22.3%
95:4	43.4%	49.3%	60.0%	57.3%	58.7%	29.6%	19.7%	29.0%	21.6%
96:1	45.5%	48.5%	60.9%	54.6%	57.6%	29.5%	19.0%	28.1%	23.4%
96:2	42.1%	46.6%	57.2%	57.9%	57.6%	26.7%	19.9%	30.9%	22.5%
96:3	42.6%	54.6%	60.5%	58.9%	59.8%	33.0%	21.5%	26.7%	18.7%
96:4	44.3%	49.1%	60.5%	56.1%	58.2%	29.7%	19.4%	28.6%	22.4%
AVG	40.0%	50.3%	60.3%	59.9%	60.2%	30.4%	19.9%	29.8%	19.9%

Table 3.18b
Moving Average Convergence Crossover (MAC-M) Short Hit Analysis
(Average of all stocks)

Qtr	Optimal Short	MAC-M Short	Short Hits	Cash Hits	Total Hits	Short Right	Short Wrong	Cash Right	Cash Wrong
85:1	34.3%	51.1%	69.0%	67.0%	68.0%	35.3%	15.8%	32.8%	16.1%
85:2	34.6%	47.0%	69.3%	64.0%	66.5%	32.6%	14.4%	33.9%	19.1%
85:3	38.6%	57.5%	73.2%	61.0%	68.0%	42.1%	15.4%	25.9%	16.6%
85:4	33.1%	36.0%	61.6%	65.9%	64.4%	22.2%	13.8%	42.2%	21.8%
86:1	35.2%	48.3%	56.3%	64.0%	60.3%	27.2%	21.1%	33.1%	18.6%
86:2	39.8%	57.7%	59.3%	58.4%	58.9%	34.2%	23.5%	24.7%	17.6%
86:3	42.7%	54.6%	63.2%	57.6%	60.6%	34.5%	20.1%	26.1%	19.3%
86:4	38.7%	44.3%	61.1%	60.7%	60.8%	27.1%	17.3%	33.8%	21.9%
87:1	36.9%	45.1%	54.5%	61.6%	58.4%	24.6%	20.5%	33.8%	21.1%
87:2	40.0%	50.3%	59.4%	59.6%	59.5%	29.9%	20.4%	29.6%	20.1%
87:3	40.4%	57.7%	60.7%	59.5%	60.2%	35.0%	22.7%	25.2%	17.1%
87:4	45.3%	37.5%	62.1%	56.4%	58.6%	23.3%	14.2%	35.3%	27.2%
88:1	36.7%	45.8%	59.2%	62.8%	61.1%	27.1%	18.7%	34.0%	20.1%
88:2	37.4%	50.9%	60.1%	61.4%	60.8%	30.6%	20.3%	30.2%	18.9%
88:3	38.4%	53.9%	63.4%	61.2%	62.4%	34.2%	19.7%	28.2%	17.9%
88:4	37.0%	50.4%	63.5%	62.6%	63.0%	32.0%	18.4%	31.1%	18.5%
89:1	36.2%	50.6%	60.1%	62.4%	61.2%	30.4%	20.2%	30.8%	18.6%
89:2	35.9%	45.1%	59.6%	63.4%	61.7%	26.9%	18.2%	34.8%	20.1%
89:3	36.4%	54.8%	59.4%	61.9%	60.5%	32.5%	22.2%	28.0%	17.2%
89:4	39.0%	49.1%	60.6%	60.5%	60.6%	29.8%	19.3%	30.8%	20.1%
90:1	40.1%	45.6%	63.2%	59.9%	61.4%	28.8%	16.8%	32.6%	21.8%
90:2	37.8%	50.5%	61.0%	62.2%	61.6%	30.8%	19.7%	30.8%	18.7%
90:3	45.7%	57.2%	65.0%	53.6%	60.1%	37.2%	20.0%	23.0%	19.9%
90:4	37.6%	35.5%	57.0%	61.2%	59.7%	20.3%	15.3%	39.5%	25.0%
91:1	36.7%	51.3%	56.9%	63.2%	60.0%	29.2%	22.1%	30.8%	17.9%
91:2	40.4%	56.4%	59.3%	57.5%	58.5%	33.4%	23.0%	25.1%	18.5%
91:3	39.8%	49.5%	58.6%	59.1%	58.9%	29.0%	20.5%	29.9%	20.6%
91:4	40.5%	50.0%	59.6%	59.6%	59.6%	29.8%	20.2%	29.8%	20.2%
92:1	43.2%	53.5%	60.1%	56.4%	58.3%	32.1%	21.4%	26.2%	20.3%
92:2	42.9%	52.8%	60.9%	56.5%	58.8%	32.1%	20.6%	26.7%	20.5%
92:3	39.5%	45.4%	58.9%	59.9%	59.4%	26.7%	18.7%	32.7%	21.9%
92:4	37.5%	45.9%	58.3%	62.3%	60.5%	26.7%	19.1%	33.8%	20.4%
93:1	39.4%	51.3%	56.8%	59.9%	58.3%	29.1%	22.2%	29.2%	19.5%
93:2	40.9%	52.5%	57.7%	58.6%	58.1%	30.3%	22.2%	27.8%	19.7%
93:3	39.4%	48.6%	57.8%	60.7%	59.3%	28.1%	20.5%	31.2%	20.2%
93:4	41.7%	50.1%	59.1%	59.1%	59.1%	29.6%	20.5%	29.5%	20.4%
94:1	43.7%	51.4%	59.0%	55.8%	57.4%	30.3%	21.1%	27.1%	21.5%
94:2	42.7%	48.5%	58.8%	57.4%	58.1%	28.5%	20.0%	29.6%	21.9%
94:3	39.8%	49.3%	58.4%	60.6%	59.5%	28.8%	20.5%	30.7%	20.0%
94:4	42.8%	51.8%	60.9%	57.8%	59.4%	31.5%	20.3%	27.9%	20.4%
95:1	38.7%	46.1%	56.4%	60.3%	58.5%	26.0%	20.1%	32.5%	21.4%
95:2	38.9%	48.8%	55.8%	60.2%	58.1%	27.2%	21.6%	30.8%	20.4%
95:3	38.9%	50.3%	55.7%	60.6%	58.1%	28.0%	22.3%	30.1%	19.6%
95:4	40.5%	50.7%	57.3%	60.0%	58.7%	29.0%	21.6%	29.6%	19.7%
96:1	38.9%	51.5%	54.6%	60.9%	57.6%	28.1%	23.4%	29.5%	19.0%
96:2	42.4%	53.4%	57.9%	57.2%	57.6%	30.9%	22.5%	26.7%	19.9%
96:3	40.8%	45.4%	58.9%	60.5%	59.8%	26.7%	18.7%	33.1%	21.6%
96:4	39.8%	50.9%	56.1%	60.5%	58.2%	28.6%	22.4%	29.7%	19.4%
AVG	39.4%	49.6%	59.9%	60.3%	60.2%	29.8%	19.9%	30.4%	20.0%

Table 3.19a
Moving Average Convergence Crossover (MAC-M) Long Return Analysis
(Average of all stocks)

Qtr	MAC-M Terminal Wealth	Buy/Hold Terminal Wealth	Relative Terminal Wealth	MAC-M Long Avg Ret	MAC-M Cash Avg Ret	MAC-M Long-Cash Avg Ret	Buy/Hold Avg Ret
85:1	10233	10142	1.009	0.069%	-0.053%	0.122%	0.006%
85:2	9730	9700	1.003	-0.092%	-0.044%	-0.047%	-0.069%
85:3	9467	8889	1.065	-0.215%	-0.197%	-0.018%	-0.205%
85:4	10328	10763	0.960	0.072%	0.169%	-0.098%	0.107%
86:1	10733	11428	0.939	0.231%	0.218%	0.012%	0.225%
86:2	10042	10414	0.964	0.018%	0.102%	-0.084%	0.066%
86:3	9685	9175	1.056	-0.109%	-0.143%	0.034%	-0.128%
86:4	10179	10413	0.978	0.051%	0.092%	-0.041%	0.069%
87:1	10871	11929	0.911	0.253%	0.341%	-0.088%	0.293%
87:2	10042	10196	0.985	0.017%	0.058%	-0.041%	0.038%
87:3	10242	10408	0.984	0.093%	0.050%	0.043%	0.068%
87:4	9769	8087	1.208	-0.044%	-0.664%	0.620%	-0.278%
88:1	10476	10989	0.953	0.148%	0.180%	-0.032%	0.163%
88:2	10176	10593	0.961	0.062%	0.135%	-0.073%	0.100%
88:3	9987	10050	0.994	-0.001%	0.025%	-0.026%	0.013%
88:4	10086	10196	0.989	0.030%	0.043%	-0.014%	0.037%
89:1	10304	10698	0.963	0.100%	0.125%	-0.025%	0.112%
89:2	10390	10772	0.965	0.112%	0.135%	-0.023%	0.122%
89:3	10312	10833	0.952	0.112%	0.147%	-0.035%	0.131%
89:4	9810	9904	0.990	-0.058%	0.038%	-0.096%	-0.011%
90:1	10020	9980	1.004	0.011%	-0.007%	0.018%	0.003%
90:2	10315	10459	0.986	0.103%	0.051%	0.052%	0.077%
90:3	9261	8526	1.086	-0.290%	-0.236%	-0.055%	-0.259%
90:4	10377	10889	0.953	0.099%	0.231%	-0.132%	0.146%
91:1	11329	12477	0.908	0.377%	0.256%	0.121%	0.315%
91:2	9974	10244	0.974	-0.009%	0.087%	-0.096%	0.045%
91:3	10091	10429	0.968	0.027%	0.104%	-0.077%	0.065%
91:4	10261	10497	0.977	0.084%	0.079%	0.005%	0.082%
92:1	10205	10324	0.988	0.067%	0.032%	0.035%	0.048%
92:2	9807	9723	1.009	-0.070%	-0.029%	-0.042%	-0.048%
92:3	10146	10392	0.976	0.040%	0.077%	-0.037%	0.057%
92:4	10539	10963	0.961	0.154%	0.134%	0.020%	0.144%
93:1	10193	10527	0.968	0.062%	0.096%	-0.034%	0.080%
93:2	10154	10340	0.982	0.050%	0.053%	-0.003%	0.052%
93:3	10369	10686	0.970	0.111%	0.090%	0.021%	0.101%
93:4	10215	10255	0.996	0.066%	0.002%	0.064%	0.034%
94:1	9927	9954	0.997	-0.028%	0.004%	-0.032%	-0.011%
94:2	9952	9994	0.996	-0.017%	0.008%	-0.025%	-0.005%
94:3	10358	10613	0.976	0.107%	0.071%	0.036%	0.089%
94:4	9951	9836	1.012	-0.018%	-0.040%	0.023%	-0.029%
95:1	10307	10706	0.963	0.092%	0.131%	-0.040%	0.110%
95:2	10385	10873	0.955	0.119%	0.150%	-0.032%	0.134%
95:3	10364	10853	0.955	0.115%	0.147%	-0.033%	0.131%
95:4	10288	10445	0.985	0.091%	0.043%	0.047%	0.067%
96:1	10536	11027	0.955	0.174%	0.145%	0.028%	0.159%
96:2	10188	10367	0.983	0.064%	0.054%	0.010%	0.059%
96:3	10352	10298	1.005	0.101%	-0.017%	0.118%	0.047%
96:4	10467	10817	0.968	0.149%	0.097%	0.052%	0.122%
AVG	10191	10377	0.982	0.058%	0.052%	0.006%	0.055%

Table 3.19b
Moving Average Convergence Crossover (MAC-M) Short Return Analysis
(Average of all stocks)

Qtr	MAC-M Terminal Wealth	Buy/Hold Terminal Wealth	Relative Terminal Wealth	MAC-M Short Avg Ret	MAC-M Cash Avg Ret	MAC-M Short-Cash Avg Ret	Buy/Hold Avg Ret
85:1	10200	10142	1.006	-0.053%	0.068%	-0.121%	0.006%
85:2	10186	9700	1.050	-0.044%	-0.092%	0.048%	-0.069%
85:3	10783	8889	1.213	-0.197%	-0.216%	0.019%	-0.205%
85:4	9630	10763	0.895	0.169%	0.072%	0.097%	0.107%
86:1	9382	11428	0.821	0.219%	0.230%	-0.011%	0.225%
86:2	9637	10414	0.925	0.100%	0.021%	0.079%	0.066%
86:3	10480	9175	1.142	-0.143%	-0.109%	-0.034%	-0.128%
86:4	9732	10413	0.935	0.093%	0.050%	0.043%	0.069%
87:1	9100	11929	0.763	0.341%	0.254%	0.088%	0.293%
87:2	9804	10196	0.962	0.058%	0.018%	0.040%	0.038%
87:3	9805	10408	0.942	0.050%	0.093%	-0.043%	0.068%
87:4	11456	8087	1.417	-0.669%	-0.043%	-0.626%	-0.278%
88:1	9496	10989	0.864	0.179%	0.149%	0.031%	0.163%
88:2	9576	10593	0.904	0.136%	0.063%	0.073%	0.100%
88:3	9914	10050	0.986	0.024%	-0.001%	0.026%	0.013%
88:4	9861	10196	0.967	0.043%	0.030%	0.014%	0.037%
89:1	9620	10698	0.899	0.125%	0.100%	0.025%	0.112%
89:2	9620	10772	0.893	0.134%	0.112%	0.022%	0.122%
89:3	9510	10833	0.878	0.147%	0.112%	0.035%	0.131%
89:4	9881	9904	0.998	0.037%	-0.058%	0.095%	-0.011%
90:1	10015	9980	1.004	-0.007%	0.011%	-0.018%	0.003%
90:2	9841	10459	0.941	0.051%	0.103%	-0.052%	0.077%
90:3	10859	8526	1.274	-0.235%	-0.291%	0.055%	-0.259%
90:4	9497	10889	0.872	0.232%	0.099%	0.133%	0.146%
91:1	9231	12477	0.740	0.256%	0.377%	-0.121%	0.315%
91:2	9678	10244	0.945	0.087%	-0.009%	0.096%	0.045%
91:3	9685	10429	0.929	0.104%	0.027%	0.077%	0.065%
91:4	9734	10497	0.927	0.079%	0.084%	-0.005%	0.082%
92:1	9885	10324	0.957	0.032%	0.067%	-0.035%	0.048%
92:2	10087	9723	1.037	-0.028%	-0.071%	0.042%	-0.048%
92:3	9776	10392	0.941	0.078%	0.039%	0.039%	0.057%
92:4	9618	10963	0.877	0.133%	0.154%	-0.021%	0.144%
93:1	9702	10527	0.922	0.096%	0.063%	0.033%	0.080%
93:2	9829	10340	0.951	0.053%	0.051%	0.002%	0.052%
93:3	9734	10686	0.911	0.091%	0.111%	-0.020%	0.101%
93:4	10003	10255	0.975	0.002%	0.066%	-0.064%	0.034%
94:1	9983	9954	1.003	0.004%	-0.028%	0.032%	-0.011%
94:2	9978	9994	0.998	0.008%	-0.017%	0.025%	-0.005%
94:3	9789	10613	0.922	0.071%	0.107%	-0.036%	0.089%
94:4	10133	9836	1.030	-0.040%	-0.018%	-0.023%	-0.029%
95:1	9630	10706	0.900	0.131%	0.092%	0.040%	0.110%
95:2	9555	10873	0.879	0.150%	0.119%	0.032%	0.134%
95:3	9554	10853	0.880	0.147%	0.115%	0.032%	0.131%
95:4	9872	10445	0.945	0.043%	0.091%	-0.047%	0.067%
96:1	9543	11027	0.865	0.145%	0.173%	-0.028%	0.159%
96:2	9822	10367	0.947	0.054%	0.064%	-0.010%	0.059%
96:3	10048	10298	0.976	-0.017%	0.101%	-0.119%	0.047%
96:4	9697	10817	0.896	0.097%	0.149%	-0.052%	0.122%
AVG	9843	10377	0.949	0.052%	0.058%	-0.006%	0.055%

to beat the benchmark buy-and-hold strategy. Trading long with the system results in terminal wealth that averages only 98.2 percent of the terminal wealth of a buy-and-hold strategy (Table 3.19a).

Trading short with the MAC-M system is profitable in only 11 of the 48 test quarters. On average, trading short with this system will result in losses. Traders beginning a quarter with $10,000 and following this system's short recommendations will tend to lose $157 (Table 3.19b).

Stochastic Moving Average

The stochastic systems are based on a measure of the relative position of today's closing price to the price range over a past period of trading days. Two of the systems included with the oscillator systems in Chapter 4, the Stochastic Peaks (STO-P) and the Stochastic +80/+20 Crossover (STO-C), are based on the same basic ideas as the Stochastic Moving Average (STO-M) presented here.

Construction

First, choose a time period, P, to use. Today's closing price is compared to the highest price and the lowest price that have occurred during the time period, P, using the following formula:

$$\%K = [(\text{Today's close} - \text{Low in period P})/(\text{High in period P} - \text{Low in period P})] \cdot 100.$$

Then construct an S-period moving average of %K to smooth it. This S-period moving average line is referred to as %K Slowed.

Once the %K Slowed line is calculated, apply a moving average to it. This moving average of %K Slowed is referred to as %D Trigger.

Two levels must also be chosen: an upper level that indicates overbought levels, and a lower level that indicates oversold levels.

For a long signal to occur, %K Slowed must cross up through %D Trigger while below the lower level (oversold) line. For a short signal to occur, %K Slowed must cross down through %D while above the upper level (overbought) line.

Results

As shown in Table 3.20, the Stochastic Moving Average (STO-M) system recommended a long trade 41.4 percent of the time (Table 3.20a) and a short trade 53.5 percent of the time (Table 3.20b) during our test period. The long calls are correct 61.7 percent of the time (Table 3.20a), and the short calls are correct 59.8 percent of the time (Table 3.20b).

The calls that the system is making seem to be relatively poor at distinguishing strong and weak market periods. There is no difference in the average stock return if we compare days when a long position is favored with days when a cash position is favored. Ironically, the average stock return on days when a short position is recommended exceeds the average stock return on days when cash is favored over a short position. Thus, the short calls of this system are better than the long calls at choosing days of above-average market performance.

Investors trading short, based on the Stochastic Moving Average system's recommendations, will, on average, earn negative returns (Table 3.21b). In fact, in only 10 of the 48 test quarters will trading short with the system lead to increased wealth. Trading long with the system, on average, leads to profits. However, these profits average only 97.8 percent of the profits of a simple buy-and-hold strategy (Table 3.21a).

Like most of the indicators we examine, this indicator gives profitable trading advice during declining stock markets.

Volume Accumulation Percent Breakout

The analysis of volume is a basic, yet important, element of technical analysis. Volume, the number of shares traded during a specific time frame, indicates the amount of buying and selling that is occurring for a particular security. Looking at volume provides clues as to the intensity of a given price move.

The Volume Accumulation Percent Breakout (VAP-B) system measures relative change in accumulation and distribution. By determining when traders are taking a more active role in buying and selling a stock, relative to the immediate preceding time period, users of this system detect when the market is changing its perception about the stock.

Construction

Choose a number of periods to use in constructing the Volume Accumulation Percent. Then use the following formula to calculate accumulation (ACC) for each day:

$$ACC_i = \{[(Close_i - Low_i) - (High_i - Close_i)]/(High_i - Low_i)\} \cdot Volume_i.$$

Now, sum these daily accumulations to obtain the total accumulation for the time period (TACC):

$$TACC = ACC_1 + ACC_2 + ACC_3 + \ldots + ACC_p.$$

Table 3.20a
Stochastic Moving Average (STO-M) Long Hit Analysis
(Average of all stocks)

Qtr	Optimal Long	STO-M Long	Long Hits	Cash Hits	Total Hits	Long Right	Long Wrong	Cash Right	Cash Wrong
85:1	32.1%	32.6%	68.6%	66.0%	66.9%	22.4%	10.2%	44.5%	22.9%
85:2	30.2%	44.1%	66.6%	67.8%	67.3%	29.3%	14.7%	37.9%	18.0%
85:3	26.3%	50.7%	63.0%	72.0%	67.4%	31.9%	18.8%	35.5%	13.8%
85:4	36.6%	36.8%	68.6%	60.1%	63.2%	25.2%	11.5%	38.0%	25.2%
86:1	44.2%	27.3%	66.2%	55.0%	58.1%	18.1%	9.2%	40.0%	32.7%
86:2	39.7%	36.9%	62.1%	60.2%	60.9%	22.9%	14.0%	38.0%	25.1%
86:3	37.0%	49.7%	58.7%	62.4%	60.6%	29.2%	20.5%	31.4%	18.9%
86:4	38.5%	43.7%	64.0%	61.8%	62.8%	28.0%	15.7%	34.8%	21.5%
87:1	44.7%	26.2%	67.1%	56.0%	58.9%	17.6%	8.6%	41.3%	32.5%
87:2	40.0%	48.9%	61.4%	60.3%	60.8%	30.0%	18.9%	30.9%	20.3%
87:3	39.5%	38.7%	61.3%	60.7%	61.0%	23.7%	15.0%	37.2%	24.1%
87:4	37.9%	68.0%	56.1%	64.9%	58.9%	38.2%	29.8%	20.8%	11.2%
88:1	41.3%	23.9%	66.1%	58.8%	60.6%	15.8%	8.1%	44.8%	31.3%
88:2	39.3%	49.2%	63.0%	61.1%	62.0%	31.0%	18.2%	31.0%	19.8%
88:3	35.9%	49.3%	62.3%	64.0%	63.2%	30.7%	18.6%	32.4%	18.2%
88:4	36.3%	47.2%	64.1%	63.9%	64.0%	30.3%	16.9%	33.7%	19.1%
89:1	39.0%	36.4%	64.8%	60.7%	62.2%	23.6%	12.8%	38.6%	25.0%
89:2	40.2%	32.1%	65.5%	59.2%	61.3%	21.1%	11.1%	40.2%	27.7%
89:3	39.9%	36.5%	65.1%	59.7%	61.7%	23.8%	12.7%	37.9%	25.6%
89:4	38.3%	46.0%	61.9%	60.6%	61.2%	28.5%	17.5%	32.7%	21.3%
90:1	36.9%	51.9%	61.3%	63.8%	62.5%	31.8%	20.1%	30.7%	17.4%
90:2	39.2%	40.2%	64.9%	60.8%	62.5%	26.1%	14.1%	36.4%	23.5%
90:3	33.5%	62.4%	54.9%	65.9%	59.0%	34.3%	28.2%	24.8%	12.8%
90:4	40.8%	46.8%	61.7%	57.3%	59.4%	28.9%	17.9%	30.5%	22.7%
91:1	44.1%	28.5%	67.5%	57.0%	60.0%	19.2%	9.2%	40.8%	30.8%
91:2	39.7%	39.3%	60.6%	61.2%	60.9%	23.8%	15.5%	37.2%	23.6%
91:3	40.4%	41.8%	61.0%	59.2%	59.9%	25.5%	16.3%	34.5%	23.7%
91:4	41.2%	46.8%	59.7%	58.3%	59.0%	27.9%	18.9%	31.0%	22.2%
92:1	40.0%	35.0%	55.6%	58.8%	57.7%	19.5%	15.6%	38.2%	26.8%
92:2	38.6%	48.6%	56.8%	61.4%	59.2%	27.6%	21.0%	31.6%	19.8%
92:3	40.3%	42.6%	60.2%	59.1%	59.6%	25.7%	17.0%	33.9%	23.5%
92:4	41.9%	31.6%	62.8%	58.0%	59.5%	19.9%	11.8%	39.7%	28.7%
93:1	42.5%	32.6%	60.8%	57.8%	58.8%	19.8%	12.8%	39.0%	28.5%
93:2	42.1%	43.8%	59.1%	57.8%	58.4%	25.9%	17.9%	32.5%	23.7%
93:3	42.5%	37.6%	61.0%	57.5%	58.8%	22.9%	14.6%	35.9%	26.6%
93:4	41.5%	44.7%	58.2%	58.4%	58.3%	26.0%	18.7%	32.3%	23.0%
94:1	40.4%	40.6%	56.0%	59.0%	57.8%	22.7%	17.9%	35.1%	24.3%
94:2	40.6%	52.0%	57.9%	59.8%	58.8%	30.1%	21.9%	28.7%	19.3%
94:3	41.8%	43.2%	60.7%	58.7%	59.6%	26.3%	17.0%	33.3%	23.4%
94:4	39.5%	56.8%	57.2%	60.7%	58.7%	32.5%	24.3%	26.3%	17.0%
95:1	43.1%	34.7%	62.5%	56.8%	58.8%	21.6%	13.0%	37.1%	28.2%
95:2	43.7%	31.0%	62.8%	56.2%	58.2%	19.5%	11.5%	38.7%	30.2%
95:3	43.9%	32.1%	61.4%	55.5%	57.4%	19.7%	12.4%	37.7%	30.2%
95:4	43.4%	40.8%	59.0%	55.3%	56.8%	24.1%	16.7%	32.7%	26.5%
96:1	45.5%	38.7%	61.9%	54.4%	57.3%	23.9%	14.7%	33.3%	28.0%
96:2	42.1%	38.3%	58.3%	57.7%	57.9%	22.4%	16.0%	35.6%	26.1%
96:3	42.6%	46.7%	59.1%	56.8%	57.8%	27.6%	19.1%	30.3%	23.0%
96:4	44.3%	34.3%	60.8%	55.2%	57.1%	20.9%	13.5%	36.3%	29.4%
AVG	40.0%	41.4%	61.7%	59.9%	60.3%	25.4%	16.0%	34.9%	23.7%

Table 3.20b
Stochastic Moving Average (STO-M) Short Hit Analysis
(Average of all stocks)

Qtr	Optimal Short	STO-M Short	Short Hits	Cash Hits	Total Hits	Short Right	Short Wrong	Cash Right	Cash Wrong
85:1	34.3%	61.3%	65.9%	68.0%	66.7%	40.4%	20.9%	26.3%	12.4%
85:2	34.6%	51.3%	67.3%	66.3%	66.8%	34.6%	16.8%	32.3%	16.4%
85:3	38.6%	44.7%	71.8%	62.9%	66.8%	32.1%	12.6%	34.8%	20.5%
85:4	33.1%	55.3%	59.7%	67.6%	63.3%	33.0%	22.3%	30.3%	14.5%
86:1	35.2%	64.8%	55.1%	65.2%	58.7%	35.7%	29.1%	22.9%	12.3%
86:2	39.8%	58.0%	60.3%	61.8%	60.9%	35.0%	23.0%	25.9%	16.0%
86:3	42.7%	45.4%	62.4%	58.5%	60.3%	28.4%	17.1%	31.9%	22.6%
86:4	38.7%	53.3%	61.7%	63.6%	62.6%	32.9%	20.4%	29.7%	17.0%
87:1	36.9%	66.8%	56.1%	65.4%	59.2%	37.5%	29.3%	21.7%	11.5%
87:2	40.0%	46.6%	60.3%	61.1%	60.7%	28.1%	18.5%	32.6%	20.8%
87:3	40.4%	56.6%	60.8%	60.9%	60.8%	34.4%	22.2%	26.4%	17.0%
87:4	45.3%	26.9%	65.4%	55.8%	58.4%	17.6%	9.3%	40.8%	32.3%
88:1	36.7%	72.2%	58.6%	65.1%	60.4%	42.3%	29.9%	18.1%	9.7%
88:2	37.4%	46.7%	60.9%	62.9%	62.0%	28.5%	18.2%	33.5%	19.8%
88:3	38.4%	46.9%	63.9%	62.2%	63.0%	30.0%	17.0%	33.0%	20.1%
88:4	37.0%	48.4%	63.8%	63.9%	63.8%	30.9%	17.5%	33.0%	18.6%
89:1	36.2%	57.7%	60.6%	64.2%	62.1%	35.0%	22.7%	27.1%	15.1%
89:2	35.9%	61.7%	59.1%	64.5%	61.2%	36.4%	25.2%	24.7%	13.6%
89:3	36.4%	58.0%	59.7%	64.5%	61.7%	34.6%	23.3%	27.1%	14.9%
89:4	39.0%	46.5%	60.2%	61.3%	60.8%	28.0%	18.5%	32.8%	20.7%
90:1	40.1%	44.3%	63.8%	61.2%	62.3%	28.2%	16.0%	34.1%	21.6%
90:2	37.8%	55.5%	60.6%	64.3%	62.3%	33.7%	21.8%	28.6%	15.9%
90:3	45.7%	31.2%	66.4%	54.9%	58.5%	20.7%	10.5%	37.8%	31.0%
90:4	37.6%	47.8%	56.8%	61.6%	59.3%	27.2%	20.6%	32.2%	20.0%
91:1	36.7%	64.8%	56.9%	66.0%	60.1%	36.8%	27.9%	23.2%	12.0%
91:2	40.4%	56.9%	61.1%	60.2%	60.7%	34.7%	22.1%	26.0%	17.2%
91:3	39.8%	54.4%	59.1%	60.8%	59.9%	32.2%	22.2%	27.7%	17.9%
91:4	40.5%	48.0%	58.3%	59.6%	59.0%	28.0%	20.0%	31.0%	21.0%
92:1	43.2%	60.3%	58.7%	55.7%	57.5%	35.4%	24.9%	22.1%	17.6%
92:2	42.9%	46.2%	61.6%	57.0%	59.1%	28.5%	17.8%	30.6%	23.1%
92:3	39.5%	53.0%	59.1%	60.2%	59.6%	31.3%	21.7%	28.3%	18.7%
92:4	37.5%	63.2%	57.9%	62.4%	59.5%	36.6%	26.6%	23.0%	13.8%
93:1	39.4%	61.5%	57.8%	60.4%	58.8%	35.6%	26.0%	23.2%	15.2%
93:2	40.9%	51.6%	58.1%	59.1%	58.5%	30.0%	21.6%	28.6%	19.8%
93:3	39.4%	58.0%	57.4%	60.8%	58.9%	33.3%	24.7%	25.6%	16.5%
93:4	41.7%	50.3%	58.3%	58.1%	58.2%	29.3%	21.0%	28.9%	20.8%
94:1	43.7%	54.3%	59.0%	56.0%	57.6%	32.0%	22.2%	25.6%	20.1%
94:2	42.7%	43.8%	59.7%	57.8%	58.6%	26.1%	17.7%	32.5%	23.7%
94:3	39.8%	53.0%	58.7%	60.5%	59.5%	31.1%	21.9%	28.4%	18.6%
94:4	42.8%	38.4%	61.0%	57.2%	58.7%	23.4%	15.0%	35.3%	26.3%
95:1	38.7%	61.2%	56.7%	62.1%	58.8%	34.7%	26.5%	24.1%	14.7%
95:2	38.9%	62.9%	56.2%	62.2%	58.4%	35.4%	27.5%	23.1%	14.1%
95:3	38.9%	62.3%	55.5%	61.0%	57.6%	34.6%	27.8%	23.0%	14.7%
95:4	40.5%	53.8%	55.4%	59.2%	57.1%	29.8%	24.0%	27.4%	18.8%
96:1	38.9%	56.3%	54.2%	61.2%	57.3%	30.5%	25.8%	26.7%	16.9%
96:2	42.4%	57.3%	57.8%	58.1%	57.9%	33.1%	24.2%	24.8%	17.9%
96:3	40.8%	48.6%	56.8%	59.0%	58.0%	27.6%	21.0%	30.4%	21.1%
96:4	39.8%	59.8%	55.1%	60.3%	57.2%	33.0%	26.8%	24.3%	16.0%
AVG	39.4%	53.5%	59.8%	61.3%	60.2%	31.8%	21.7%	28.4%	18.1%

Table 3.21a
Stochastic Moving Average (STO-M) Long Return Analysis
(Average of all stocks)

Qtr	STO-M Terminal Wealth	Buy/Hold Terminal Wealth	Relative Terminal Wealth	STO-M Long Avg Ret	STO-M Cash Avg Ret	STO-M Long-Cash Avg Ret	Buy/Hold Avg Ret
85:1	9985	10142	0.985	-0.026%	0.022%	-0.048%	0.006%
85:2	9809	9700	1.011	-0.090%	-0.053%	-0.037%	-0.069%
85:3	9425	8889	1.060	-0.202%	-0.208%	0.005%	-0.205%
85:4	10101	10763	0.939	0.033%	0.150%	-0.117%	0.107%
86:1	10360	11428	0.907	0.212%	0.230%	-0.018%	0.225%
86:2	10246	10414	0.984	0.104%	0.044%	0.060%	0.066%
86:3	9750	9175	1.063	-0.072%	-0.182%	0.110%	-0.128%
86:4	10327	10413	0.992	0.120%	0.030%	0.090%	0.069%
87:1	10726	11929	0.899	0.433%	0.243%	0.190%	0.293%
87:2	10219	10196	1.002	0.076%	0.002%	0.074%	0.038%
87:3	10275	10408	0.987	0.113%	0.040%	0.072%	0.068%
87:4	9468	8087	1.171	-0.103%	-0.650%	0.548%	-0.278%
88:1	10420	10989	0.948	0.285%	0.124%	0.161%	0.163%
88:2	10349	10593	0.977	0.119%	0.081%	0.038%	0.100%
88:3	10054	10050	1.000	0.023%	0.002%	0.021%	0.013%
88:4	10164	10196	0.997	0.062%	0.014%	0.049%	0.037%
89:1	10251	10698	0.958	0.113%	0.112%	0.001%	0.112%
89:2	10275	10772	0.954	0.136%	0.115%	0.021%	0.122%
89:3	10359	10833	0.956	0.157%	0.116%	0.040%	0.131%
89:4	9937	9904	1.003	-0.020%	-0.003%	-0.017%	-0.011%
90:1	10138	9980	1.016	0.048%	-0.046%	0.095%	0.003%
90:2	10291	10459	0.984	0.122%	0.047%	0.075%	0.077%
90:3	9072	8526	1.064	-0.261%	-0.256%	-0.005%	-0.259%
90:4	10246	10889	0.941	0.098%	0.188%	-0.090%	0.146%
91:1	11115	12477	0.891	0.505%	0.239%	0.265%	0.315%
91:2	10223	10244	0.998	0.094%	0.014%	0.080%	0.045%
91:3	10204	10429	0.978	0.077%	0.056%	0.020%	0.065%
91:4	10286	10497	0.980	0.102%	0.064%	0.039%	0.082%
92:1	9919	10324	0.961	-0.039%	0.095%	-0.134%	0.048%
92:2	9851	9723	1.013	-0.053%	-0.044%	-0.010%	-0.048%
92:3	10144	10392	0.976	0.051%	0.061%	-0.010%	0.057%
92:4	10312	10963	0.941	0.158%	0.138%	0.019%	0.144%
93:1	10221	10527	0.971	0.105%	0.067%	0.038%	0.080%
93:2	10142	10340	0.981	0.054%	0.050%	0.004%	0.052%
93:3	10285	10686	0.962	0.116%	0.092%	0.024%	0.101%
93:4	10101	10255	0.985	0.034%	0.034%	0.001%	0.034%
94:1	9968	9954	1.001	-0.018%	-0.007%	-0.010%	-0.011%
94:2	10025	9994	1.003	0.004%	-0.014%	0.018%	-0.005%
94:3	10280	10613	0.969	0.101%	0.081%	0.020%	0.089%
94:4	9918	9836	1.008	-0.025%	-0.035%	0.010%	-0.029%
95:1	10298	10706	0.962	0.137%	0.096%	0.041%	0.110%
95:2	10306	10873	0.948	0.156%	0.124%	0.032%	0.134%
95:3	10249	10853	0.944	0.124%	0.135%	-0.011%	0.131%
95:4	10127	10445	0.969	0.047%	0.080%	-0.033%	0.067%
96:1	10461	11027	0.949	0.190%	0.139%	0.050%	0.159%
96:2	10163	10367	0.980	0.066%	0.054%	0.012%	0.059%
96:3	10100	10298	0.981	0.035%	0.058%	-0.023%	0.047%
96:4	10247	10817	0.947	0.112%	0.127%	-0.015%	0.122%
AVG	10150	10377	0.978	0.055%	0.055%	-0.001%	0.055%

Table 3.21b
Stochastic Moving Average (STO-M) Short Return Analysis
(Average of all stocks)

Qtr	STO-M Terminal Wealth	Buy/Hold Terminal Wealth	Relative Terminal Wealth	STO-M Short Avg Ret	STO-M Cash Avg Ret	STO-M Short-Cash Avg Ret	Buy/Hold Avg Ret
85:1	9950	10142	0.981	0.022%	-0.018%	0.040%	0.006%
85:2	10163	9700	1.048	-0.042%	-0.098%	0.057%	-0.069%
85:3	10614	8889	1.194	-0.205%	-0.204%	-0.001%	-0.205%
85:4	9446	10763	0.878	0.167%	0.033%	0.134%	0.107%
86:1	9155	11428	0.801	0.228%	0.219%	0.009%	0.225%
86:2	9855	10414	0.946	0.038%	0.105%	-0.067%	0.066%
86:3	10547	9175	1.150	-0.190%	-0.076%	-0.114%	-0.128%
86:4	9886	10413	0.949	0.031%	0.113%	-0.083%	0.069%
87:1	9049	11929	0.759	0.247%	0.385%	-0.138%	0.293%
87:2	9985	10196	0.979	0.001%	0.070%	-0.069%	0.038%
87:3	9862	10408	0.948	0.036%	0.110%	-0.074%	0.068%
87:4	11119	8087	1.375	-0.637%	-0.146%	-0.491%	-0.278%
88:1	9385	10989	0.854	0.135%	0.236%	-0.101%	0.163%
88:2	9748	10593	0.920	0.084%	0.114%	-0.030%	0.100%
88:3	9978	10050	0.993	0.005%	0.019%	-0.014%	0.013%
88:4	9951	10196	0.976	0.015%	0.057%	-0.042%	0.037%
89:1	9588	10698	0.896	0.118%	0.105%	0.013%	0.112%
89:2	9524	10772	0.884	0.124%	0.120%	0.004%	0.122%
89:3	9579	10833	0.884	0.118%	0.148%	-0.030%	0.131%
89:4	9994	9904	1.009	-0.002%	-0.019%	0.017%	-0.011%
90:1	10145	9980	1.017	-0.054%	0.048%	-0.102%	0.003%
90:2	9830	10459	0.940	0.050%	0.110%	-0.059%	0.077%
90:3	10520	8526	1.234	-0.266%	-0.256%	-0.010%	-0.259%
90:4	9392	10889	0.862	0.207%	0.090%	0.117%	0.146%
91:1	9086	12477	0.728	0.248%	0.438%	-0.190%	0.315%
91:2	9928	10244	0.969	0.015%	0.085%	-0.070%	0.045%
91:3	9821	10429	0.942	0.055%	0.077%	-0.022%	0.065%
91:4	9836	10497	0.937	0.057%	0.105%	-0.048%	0.082%
92:1	9650	10324	0.935	0.096%	-0.026%	0.122%	0.048%
92:2	10175	9723	1.046	-0.055%	-0.042%	-0.013%	-0.048%
92:3	9806	10392	0.944	0.062%	0.051%	0.011%	0.057%
92:4	9464	10963	0.863	0.142%	0.149%	-0.007%	0.144%
93:1	9744	10527	0.926	0.073%	0.090%	-0.016%	0.080%
93:2	9873	10340	0.955	0.044%	0.060%	-0.016%	0.052%
93:3	9677	10686	0.906	0.095%	0.109%	-0.013%	0.101%
93:4	9909	10255	0.966	0.036%	0.032%	0.003%	0.034%
94:1	10028	9954	1.007	-0.006%	-0.017%	0.011%	-0.011%
94:2	10047	9994	1.005	-0.015%	0.004%	-0.019%	-0.005%
94:3	9740	10613	0.918	0.085%	0.095%	-0.010%	0.089%
94:4	10096	9836	1.026	-0.038%	-0.024%	-0.014%	-0.029%
95:1	9643	10706	0.901	0.098%	0.129%	-0.032%	0.110%
95:2	9541	10873	0.878	0.123%	0.152%	-0.029%	0.134%
95:3	9489	10853	0.874	0.139%	0.118%	0.021%	0.131%
95:4	9765	10445	0.935	0.075%	0.057%	0.019%	0.067%
96:1	9517	11027	0.863	0.144%	0.178%	-0.034%	0.159%
96:2	9811	10367	0.946	0.054%	0.065%	-0.011%	0.059%
96:3	9830	10298	0.955	0.057%	0.038%	0.019%	0.047%
96:4	9523	10817	0.880	0.132%	0.108%	0.024%	0.122%
AVG	9818	10377	0.946	0.058%	0.052%	0.007%	0.055%

Also, calculate the total volume for the period (TVOL) by adding together the volumes for all the days:

$$TVOL = V_1 + V_2 + V_3 + \ldots + V_p.$$

Now, calculate the Volume Accumulation Percent (VAP) using a ratio of the total accumulation and the total volume:

$$VAP = (TACC/TVOL) \cdot 100.$$

You must also choose a number of periods to look back for the trading rule; this time period is called the "peak period." In our testing, we have used a peak period of 100 days, which is considered to be the typical length. The system will trigger signals the first time the VAP goes through +50 or −50. For example, a long signal occurs the first time the VAP passes +50 during the peak period. This type of breakout shows the first time buyers have come into the market in force after a period of low activity. Conversely, a short signal occurs the first time during the peak period that the VAP falls below −50. This indicates that, after a relatively inactive period, sellers have come into the market full force.

Results

With a total hit rate of over 60 percent, the Volume Accumulation Percent Breakout system looks fairly promising, but closer examination of the results for this indicator contradicts that view. The results for this indicator appear in Tables 3.22 and 3.23. This system recommends a long position only 2.0 percent of the time, far below the 40.0 percent optimal long call rate in Table 3.22a. The call rate for the short calls—a mere 1.5 percent—is even more disappointing (Table 3.22b).

On average, the return when long signals occurred exceeded the return when cash signals occurred by 0.016 percentage point (Table 3.23a). This would seem to indicate that the system does provide some information regarding the relative strength and weakness of a market. However, this is not a very robust result. In fact, for 28 of the 48 quarters included in the test period, the average return for long calls fell below the average market return when cash calls were made.

The average market return when short signals occurred was 0.021 percentage point less than when the system recommended a cash position over a short position (Table 3.23b). This is good news in that the system is predicting relatively weaker markets by suggesting short positions. The bad news is that the market return, while relatively low, is still positive. Thus, following the system's short strategy will, on average, result in decreasing wealth.

Volume Accumulation Percent Band Crossover

This system combines the Volume Accumulation Percent concept (discussed on page 89) with the Bollinger Band Crossover (BOL-C) concept (discussed on page 39). The system makes use of the volume information that is part of the Volume Accumulation Percent model and the price volatility information that is part of the Bollinger Band Crossover model. Because two separate systems are combined, fewer signals will be generated than with either of the systems individually.

Construction

First, follow the steps on page 89 and construct the Volume Accumulation Percent. Second, construct Bollinger Bands as shown on page 39.

Long signals occur whenever the Volume Accumulation Percent goes through zero from below, coincident with a Bollinger Band Crossover signal. In essence, the low price, accompanied by increasing accumulation, indicates an oversold market. Overbought markets that will soon be reversed are indicated by high prices accompanied by declining accumulation. Therefore, short signals occur when the Volume Accumulation Percent falls through zero, coincident with a Bollinger Band crossover signal.

Results

As expected, the results for the Volume Accumulation Percent Band Crossover (VAP-C) in Table 3.24 show that combining the Volume Accumulation Percent Breakout (VAP-B) and the Bollinger Band Crossover (BOL-C) systems leads to an extremely low call rate. Long calls occur only 0.9 percent of the time (Table 3.24a), and short calls occur a mere 0.5 percent of the time (Table 3.24b). Because of these extremely low call rates, investors trading with this system will find themselves in a cash position over 99 percent of the time.

The return analysis presented in Table 3.25 shows that the average daily return of 0.066 percent for long calls (Table 3.25a) does indeed exceed the average daily return of cash calls. However, trading long with this system results in a quarterly terminal wealth of $10,004, on average. The deviation from this average for each individual quarter is extremely small. As shown in Table 3.25a the lowest terminal wealth is $9,990, which occurs in the fourth quarter of 1989; the largest terminal wealth occurs in the first quarter of 1987 and is only $10,024.

Analyzing the short return results leads to similar conclusions. The average stock return of 0.053 percent, which occurs on days when short calls are made, is slightly lower than the 0.055 percent average stock return for days when cash is favored (Table 3.25b). Because the average daily return for

Table 3.22a
Volume Accumulation Percent Breakout (VAP-B) Long Hit Analysis
(Average of all stocks)

Qtr	Optimal Long	VAP-B Long	Long Hits	Cash Hits	Total Hits	Long Right	Long Wrong	Cash Right	Cash Wrong
85:1	32.1%	2.0%	66.2%	68.1%	68.1%	1.3%	0.7%	66.8%	31.3%
85:2	30.2%	1.7%	60.8%	69.9%	69.7%	1.0%	0.7%	68.7%	29.6%
85:3	26.3%	1.6%	62.5%	73.8%	73.7%	1.0%	0.6%	72.7%	25.7%
85:4	36.6%	2.6%	63.4%	63.5%	63.5%	1.6%	0.9%	61.8%	35.6%
86:1	44.2%	2.7%	66.6%	55.8%	56.1%	1.8%	0.9%	54.3%	42.9%
86:2	39.7%	1.8%	58.1%	60.2%	60.2%	1.1%	0.8%	59.1%	39.0%
86:3	37.0%	1.6%	57.9%	63.0%	63.0%	0.9%	0.7%	62.0%	36.4%
86:4	38.5%	1.8%	59.7%	61.5%	61.4%	1.1%	0.7%	60.4%	37.8%
87:1	44.7%	2.8%	58.8%	55.1%	55.2%	1.7%	1.2%	53.6%	43.6%
87:2	40.0%	1.5%	58.8%	60.0%	60.0%	0.9%	0.6%	59.1%	39.4%
87:3	39.5%	2.2%	57.7%	60.4%	60.4%	1.3%	0.9%	59.1%	38.7%
87:4	37.9%	1.1%	50.9%	62.0%	61.9%	0.5%	0.5%	61.4%	37.6%
88:1	41.3%	2.9%	63.1%	58.6%	58.7%	1.8%	1.1%	56.9%	40.2%
88:2	39.3%	1.9%	61.0%	60.6%	60.7%	1.1%	0.7%	59.5%	38.6%
88:3	35.9%	1.4%	60.5%	64.0%	64.0%	0.9%	0.6%	63.1%	35.5%
88:4	36.3%	1.4%	63.0%	63.7%	63.7%	0.9%	0.5%	62.8%	35.8%
89:1	39.0%	2.2%	61.8%	60.9%	60.9%	1.4%	0.9%	59.5%	38.3%
89:2	40.2%	2.3%	62.1%	59.8%	59.8%	1.4%	0.9%	58.4%	39.3%
89:3	39.9%	1.8%	61.2%	60.0%	60.0%	1.1%	0.7%	58.9%	39.3%
89:4	38.3%	1.6%	58.1%	61.7%	61.6%	0.9%	0.7%	60.7%	37.7%
90:1	36.9%	1.6%	60.2%	63.1%	63.0%	1.0%	0.6%	62.1%	36.3%
90:2	39.2%	2.6%	63.1%	60.8%	60.9%	1.6%	1.0%	59.2%	38.2%
90:3	33.5%	1.1%	54.2%	66.5%	66.4%	0.6%	0.5%	65.8%	33.1%
90:4	40.8%	2.3%	66.0%	59.2%	59.3%	1.5%	0.8%	57.8%	39.9%
91:1	44.1%	2.9%	61.6%	55.9%	56.1%	1.8%	1.1%	54.3%	42.8%
91:2	39.7%	1.7%	57.2%	60.3%	60.3%	1.0%	0.7%	59.3%	39.0%
91:3	40.4%	1.9%	60.3%	59.5%	59.5%	1.1%	0.7%	58.4%	39.7%
91:4	41.2%	1.7%	56.9%	58.8%	58.7%	1.0%	0.7%	57.8%	40.5%
92:1	40.0%	2.0%	56.4%	60.1%	60.0%	1.1%	0.9%	58.9%	39.1%
92:2	38.6%	1.4%	54.3%	61.4%	61.3%	0.7%	0.6%	60.5%	38.1%
92:3	40.3%	2.3%	59.9%	59.7%	59.7%	1.4%	0.9%	58.3%	39.4%
92:4	41.9%	2.4%	61.8%	58.1%	58.2%	1.5%	0.9%	56.7%	40.8%
93:1	42.5%	2.1%	60.5%	57.5%	57.5%	1.3%	0.8%	56.3%	41.6%
93:2	42.1%	2.3%	62.1%	58.0%	58.1%	1.4%	0.9%	56.6%	41.1%
93:3	42.5%	2.9%	58.1%	57.5%	57.5%	1.7%	1.2%	55.8%	41.3%
93:4	41.5%	2.2%	60.0%	58.6%	58.6%	1.3%	0.9%	57.3%	40.5%
94:1	40.4%	1.9%	60.7%	59.6%	59.6%	1.1%	0.7%	58.5%	39.6%
94:2	40.6%	2.0%	56.3%	59.4%	59.4%	1.1%	0.9%	58.2%	39.8%
94:3	41.8%	2.6%	62.1%	58.3%	58.4%	1.6%	1.0%	56.7%	40.6%
94:4	39.5%	1.1%	58.5%	60.5%	60.5%	0.7%	0.5%	59.8%	39.0%
95:1	43.1%	2.6%	58.3%	56.8%	56.8%	1.5%	1.1%	55.3%	42.1%
95:2	43.7%	2.2%	62.0%	56.3%	56.4%	1.4%	0.8%	55.1%	42.7%
95:3	43.9%	2.5%	58.9%	56.1%	56.1%	1.5%	1.0%	54.6%	42.8%
95:4	43.4%	2.2%	59.7%	56.6%	56.7%	1.3%	0.9%	55.4%	42.4%
96:1	45.5%	2.3%	61.3%	54.5%	54.6%	1.4%	0.9%	53.2%	44.5%
96:2	42.1%	1.6%	55.3%	57.9%	57.9%	0.9%	0.7%	57.0%	41.4%
96:3	42.6%	2.0%	59.0%	57.4%	57.4%	1.2%	0.8%	56.3%	41.8%
96:4	44.3%	2.3%	60.7%	55.8%	55.9%	1.4%	0.9%	54.5%	43.2%
AVG	40.0%	2.0%	59.9%	60.1%	60.2%	1.2%	0.8%	58.9%	39.0%

Table 3.22b
Volume Accumulation Percent Breakout (VAP-B) Short Hit Analysis
(Average of all stocks)

Qtr	Optimal Short	VAP-B Short	Short Hits	Cash Hits	Total Hits	Short Right	Short Wrong	Cash Right	Cash Wrong
85:1	34.3%	1.4%	76.4%	65.7%	65.8%	1.0%	0.3%	64.8%	33.8%
85:2	34.6%	1.6%	79.7%	65.4%	65.6%	1.3%	0.3%	64.3%	34.1%
85:3	38.6%	1.9%	79.6%	61.3%	61.6%	1.5%	0.4%	60.1%	38.0%
85:4	33.1%	1.1%	65.7%	66.8%	66.8%	0.7%	0.4%	66.1%	32.8%
86:1	35.2%	0.5%	58.2%	64.8%	64.7%	0.3%	0.2%	64.4%	35.0%
86:2	39.8%	1.1%	60.6%	60.2%	60.2%	0.6%	0.4%	59.5%	39.4%
86:3	42.7%	2.1%	62.4%	57.2%	57.3%	1.3%	0.8%	56.0%	41.9%
86:4	38.7%	0.8%	63.8%	61.3%	61.3%	0.5%	0.3%	60.8%	38.4%
87:1	36.9%	0.5%	62.0%	63.1%	63.0%	0.3%	0.2%	62.7%	36.8%
87:2	40.0%	1.4%	61.5%	60.0%	60.0%	0.8%	0.5%	59.2%	39.5%
87:3	40.4%	1.3%	62.3%	59.6%	59.6%	0.8%	0.5%	58.8%	39.9%
87:4	45.3%	5.3%	60.7%	54.8%	55.1%	3.2%	2.1%	51.9%	42.8%
88:1	36.7%	2.0%	60.1%	63.3%	63.2%	1.2%	0.8%	62.0%	36.0%
88:2	37.4%	2.1%	64.1%	62.5%	62.6%	1.4%	0.8%	61.2%	36.7%
88:3	38.4%	2.5%	66.3%	61.6%	61.8%	1.7%	0.9%	60.1%	37.4%
88:4	37.0%	2.2%	62.6%	62.9%	62.9%	1.4%	0.8%	61.6%	36.3%
89:1	36.2%	1.4%	60.7%	63.8%	63.7%	0.9%	0.6%	62.9%	35.7%
89:2	35.9%	1.4%	62.5%	64.0%	64.0%	0.9%	0.5%	63.1%	35.5%
89:3	36.4%	1.4%	61.9%	63.5%	63.5%	0.9%	0.5%	62.6%	36.0%
89:4	39.0%	1.6%	63.4%	61.0%	61.0%	1.0%	0.6%	60.0%	38.4%
90:1	40.1%	1.4%	60.6%	59.8%	59.8%	0.8%	0.6%	58.9%	39.7%
90:2	37.8%	1.3%	62.8%	62.1%	62.1%	0.8%	0.5%	61.3%	37.4%
90:3	45.7%	2.6%	67.3%	54.3%	54.7%	1.8%	0.9%	52.9%	44.5%
90:4	37.6%	1.1%	60.1%	62.4%	62.4%	0.7%	0.5%	61.7%	37.2%
91:1	36.7%	0.6%	51.5%	63.3%	63.2%	0.3%	0.3%	62.9%	36.5%
91:2	40.4%	1.1%	63.4%	59.6%	59.6%	0.7%	0.4%	59.0%	40.0%
91:3	39.8%	1.8%	62.3%	60.2%	60.2%	1.1%	0.7%	59.1%	39.1%
91:4	40.5%	1.7%	60.9%	59.5%	59.5%	1.0%	0.7%	58.5%	39.8%
92:1	43.2%	1.2%	60.3%	56.7%	56.8%	0.7%	0.5%	56.0%	42.8%
92:2	42.9%	2.0%	64.1%	57.1%	57.2%	1.3%	0.7%	56.0%	42.0%
92:3	39.5%	1.5%	59.3%	60.5%	60.5%	0.9%	0.6%	59.6%	38.9%
92:4	37.5%	1.2%	61.8%	62.5%	62.5%	0.7%	0.4%	61.8%	37.0%
93:1	39.4%	0.8%	58.2%	60.6%	60.6%	0.5%	0.3%	60.1%	39.1%
93:2	40.9%	1.5%	58.8%	59.1%	59.1%	0.9%	0.6%	58.2%	40.3%
93:3	39.4%	1.4%	58.4%	60.6%	60.5%	0.8%	0.6%	59.7%	38.9%
93:4	41.7%	1.6%	60.2%	58.3%	58.4%	1.0%	0.6%	57.4%	41.0%
94:1	43.7%	1.1%	60.8%	56.3%	56.4%	0.7%	0.4%	55.7%	43.2%
94:2	42.7%	1.9%	59.2%	57.3%	57.3%	1.1%	0.8%	56.2%	41.9%
94:3	39.8%	1.7%	57.8%	60.2%	60.1%	1.0%	0.7%	59.1%	39.2%
94:4	42.8%	2.3%	62.0%	57.2%	57.3%	1.4%	0.9%	55.9%	41.9%
95:1	38.7%	0.8%	58.1%	61.3%	61.3%	0.5%	0.3%	60.8%	38.4%
95:2	38.9%	1.0%	57.0%	61.1%	61.0%	0.6%	0.4%	60.5%	38.6%
95:3	38.9%	0.8%	59.4%	61.0%	61.0%	0.5%	0.3%	60.5%	38.6%
95:4	40.5%	1.5%	60.4%	59.5%	59.5%	0.9%	0.6%	58.6%	39.9%
96:1	38.9%	0.9%	53.7%	61.1%	61.0%	0.5%	0.4%	60.6%	38.6%
96:2	42.4%	1.0%	62.1%	57.6%	57.7%	0.6%	0.4%	57.1%	42.0%
96:3	40.8%	1.5%	61.2%	59.3%	59.3%	0.9%	0.6%	58.4%	40.1%
96:4	39.8%	0.7%	55.4%	60.1%	60.1%	0.4%	0.3%	59.7%	39.6%
AVG	39.4%	1.5%	61.9%	60.7%	60.7%	0.9%	0.6%	59.8%	38.8%

Table 3.23a
Volume Accumulation Percent Breakout (VAP-B) Long Return Analysis
(Average of all stocks)

Qtr	VAP-B Terminal Wealth	Buy/Hold Terminal Wealth	Relative Terminal Wealth	VAP-B Long Avg Ret	VAP-B Cash Avg Ret	VAP-B Long-Cash Avg Ret	Buy/Hold Avg Ret
85:1	10031	10142	0.989	0.262%	0.001%	0.261%	0.006%
85:2	10004	9700	1.031	0.038%	-0.071%	0.109%	-0.069%
85:3	10003	8889	1.125	0.029%	-0.209%	0.238%	-0.205%
85:4	10023	10763	0.931	0.149%	0.106%	0.043%	0.107%
86:1	10045	11428	0.879	0.276%	0.223%	0.053%	0.225%
86:2	9991	10414	0.959	-0.072%	0.069%	-0.141%	0.066%
86:3	9993	9175	1.089	-0.070%	-0.128%	0.059%	-0.128%
86:4	10007	10413	0.961	0.071%	0.069%	0.002%	0.069%
87:1	10007	11929	0.839	0.040%	0.300%	-0.260%	0.293%
87:2	10000	10196	0.981	-0.003%	0.039%	-0.042%	0.038%
87:3	10000	10408	0.961	0.003%	0.070%	-0.066%	0.068%
87:4	9975	8087	1.233	-0.388%	-0.277%	-0.111%	-0.278%
88:1	10013	10989	0.911	0.075%	0.165%	-0.091%	0.163%
88:2	10002	10593	0.944	0.020%	0.101%	-0.081%	0.100%
88:3	9999	10050	0.995	-0.017%	0.013%	-0.030%	0.013%
88:4	10000	10196	0.981	0.005%	0.037%	-0.032%	0.037%
89:1	9994	10698	0.934	-0.039%	0.116%	-0.155%	0.112%
89:2	10013	10772	0.930	0.093%	0.123%	-0.030%	0.122%
89:3	10002	10833	0.923	0.024%	0.133%	-0.109%	0.131%
89:4	9986	9904	1.008	-0.145%	-0.009%	-0.136%	-0.011%
90:1	10004	9980	1.002	0.050%	0.002%	0.048%	0.003%
90:2	10022	10459	0.958	0.139%	0.075%	0.064%	0.077%
90:3	9984	8526	1.171	-0.228%	-0.259%	0.031%	-0.259%
90:4	10025	10889	0.921	0.172%	0.146%	0.027%	0.146%
91:1	10068	12477	0.807	0.364%	0.313%	0.051%	0.315%
91:2	10000	10244	0.976	-0.005%	0.046%	-0.051%	0.045%
91:3	9998	10429	0.959	-0.016%	0.066%	-0.083%	0.065%
91:4	9999	10497	0.953	-0.014%	0.083%	-0.098%	0.082%
92:1	10012	10324	0.970	0.106%	0.047%	0.059%	0.048%
92:2	9981	9723	1.027	-0.220%	-0.046%	-0.174%	-0.048%
92:3	10007	10392	0.963	0.042%	0.057%	-0.014%	0.057%
92:4	10022	10963	0.914	0.147%	0.144%	0.003%	0.144%
93:1	10016	10527	0.951	0.133%	0.079%	0.055%	0.080%
93:2	10021	10340	0.969	0.137%	0.050%	0.087%	0.052%
93:3	10013	10686	0.937	0.073%	0.102%	-0.028%	0.101%
93:4	10013	10255	0.976	0.094%	0.033%	0.061%	0.034%
94:1	10021	9954	1.007	0.173%	-0.015%	0.188%	-0.011%
94:2	9986	9994	0.999	-0.116%	-0.002%	-0.114%	-0.005%
94:3	10025	10613	0.945	0.146%	0.088%	0.058%	0.089%
94:4	10000	9836	1.017	0.008%	-0.030%	0.037%	-0.029%
95:1	10004	10706	0.934	0.029%	0.112%	-0.083%	0.110%
95:2	10028	10873	0.922	0.205%	0.132%	0.073%	0.134%
95:3	10021	10853	0.923	0.130%	0.131%	-0.001%	0.131%
95:4	10021	10445	0.959	0.158%	0.065%	0.093%	0.067%
96:1	10021	11027	0.909	0.143%	0.159%	-0.016%	0.159%
96:2	10005	10367	0.965	0.058%	0.059%	0.000%	0.059%
96:3	10000	10298	0.971	-0.005%	0.048%	-0.054%	0.047%
96:4	10022	10817	0.926	0.156%	0.121%	0.034%	0.122%
AVG	10009	10377	0.965	0.070%	0.055%	0.016%	0.055%

Table 3.23b
Volume Accumulation Percent Breakout (VAP-B) Short Return Analysis
(Average of all stocks)

Qtr	VAP-B Terminal Wealth	Buy/Hold Terminal Wealth	Relative Terminal Wealth	VAP-B Short Avg Ret	VAP-B Cash Avg Ret	VAP-B Short-Cash Avg Ret	Buy/Hold Avg Ret
85:1	10010	10142	0.987	-0.115%	0.008%	-0.123%	0.006%
85:2	10027	9700	1.034	-0.271%	-0.066%	-0.205%	-0.069%
85:3	10029	8889	1.128	-0.239%	-0.204%	-0.035%	-0.205%
85:4	9982	10763	0.927	0.253%	0.105%	0.148%	0.107%
86:1	9979	11428	0.873	0.685%	0.222%	0.463%	0.225%
86:2	9995	10414	0.960	0.072%	0.066%	0.006%	0.066%
86:3	9991	9175	1.089	0.069%	-0.132%	0.201%	-0.128%
86:4	9992	10413	0.960	0.201%	0.068%	0.133%	0.069%
87:1	9994	11929	0.838	0.231%	0.293%	-0.062%	0.293%
87:2	9991	10196	0.980	0.107%	0.037%	0.070%	0.038%
87:3	10000	10408	0.961	-0.001%	0.069%	-0.071%	0.068%
87:4	10014	8087	1.238	-0.092%	-0.288%	0.197%	-0.278%
38:1	9967	10989	0.907	0.269%	0.161%	0.109%	0.163%
88:2	10002	10593	0.944	-0.012%	0.102%	-0.114%	0.100%
88:3	10007	10050	0.996	-0.044%	0.014%	-0.059%	0.013%
88:4	9983	10196	0.979	0.125%	0.035%	0.091%	0.037%
89:1	9991	10698	0.934	0.103%	0.113%	-0.010%	0.112%
89:2	9992	10772	0.928	0.083%	0.123%	-0.040%	0.122%
89:3	9985	10833	0.922	0.172%	0.130%	0.041%	0.131%
89:4	9999	9904	1.010	0.005%	-0.011%	0.016%	-0.011%
90:1	9983	9980	1.000	0.198%	0.000%	0.198%	0.003%
90:2	9987	10459	0.955	0.155%	0.076%	0.079%	0.077%
90:3	10043	8526	1.178	-0.262%	-0.259%	-0.004%	-0.259%
90:4	9993	10889	0.918	0.097%	0.147%	-0.050%	0.146%
91:1	9981	12477	0.800	0.563%	0.314%	0.249%	0.315%
91:2	10003	10244	0.977	-0.047%	0.046%	-0.093%	0.045%
91:3	9993	10429	0.958	0.056%	0.065%	-0.009%	0.065%
91:4	9998	10497	0.952	0.018%	0.083%	-0.065%	0.082%
92:1	9989	10324	0.968	0.151%	0.047%	0.104%	0.048%
92:2	10009	9723	1.029	-0.077%	-0.048%	-0.030%	-0.048%
92:3	9994	10392	0.962	0.072%	0.056%	0.015%	0.057%
92:4	9989	10963	0.911	0.146%	0.144%	0.002%	0.144%
93:1	9993	10527	0.949	0.137%	0.079%	0.058%	0.080%
93:2	9990	10340	0.966	0.108%	0.051%	0.057%	0.052%
93:3	9993	10686	0.935	0.077%	0.101%	-0.024%	0.101%
93:4	10007	10255	0.976	-0.062%	0.035%	-0.097%	0.034%
94:1	10003	9954	1.005	-0.041%	-0.011%	-0.030%	-0.011%
94:2	9999	9994	1.000	0.009%	-0.005%	0.014%	-0.005%
94:3	9987	10613	0.941	0.118%	0.089%	0.030%	0.089%
94:4	10004	9836	1.017	-0.032%	-0.029%	-0.003%	-0.029%
95:1	9997	10706	0.934	0.082%	0.110%	-0.028%	0.110%
95:2	9991	10873	0.919	0.137%	0.134%	0.003%	0.134%
95:3	9996	10853	0.921	0.083%	0.131%	-0.049%	0.131%
95:4	9997	10445	0.957	0.032%	0.067%	-0.036%	0.067%
96:1	9982	11027	0.905	0.347%	0.157%	0.190%	0.159%
96:2	10007	10367	0.965	-0.113%	0.060%	-0.173%	0.059%
96:3	10005	10298	0.972	-0.060%	0.049%	-0.108%	0.047%
96:4	9992	10817	0.924	0.197%	0.122%	0.075%	0.122%
AVG	9997	10377	0.963	0.034%	0.056%	-0.021%	0.055%

Table 3.24a
Volume Accumulation Percent Crossover (VAP-C) Long Hit Analysis
(Average of all stocks)

Qtr	Optimal Long	VAP-C Long	Long Hits	Cash Hits	Total Hits	Long Right	Long Wrong	Cash Right	Cash Wrong
85:1	32.1%	0.5%	71.4%	67.9%	68.0%	0.3%	0.1%	67.6%	31.9%
85:2	30.2%	0.4%	69.7%	69.8%	69.8%	0.3%	0.1%	69.5%	30.1%
85:3	26.3%	0.3%	62.0%	73.7%	73.7%	0.2%	0.1%	73.5%	26.2%
85:4	36.6%	0.5%	69.5%	63.3%	63.4%	0.4%	0.2%	63.0%	36.5%
86:1	44.2%	0.8%	66.2%	55.8%	55.9%	0.5%	0.3%	55.4%	43.9%
86:2	39.7%	0.7%	63.0%	60.2%	60.2%	0.5%	0.3%	59.8%	39.5%
86:3	37.0%	0.8%	64.6%	63.0%	63.0%	0.5%	0.3%	62.5%	36.7%
86:4	38.5%	1.0%	64.8%	61.4%	61.5%	0.7%	0.4%	60.8%	38.2%
87:1	44.7%	1.0%	68.3%	55.3%	55.4%	0.7%	0.3%	54.8%	44.3%
87:2	40.0%	0.8%	66.2%	59.9%	60.0%	0.6%	0.3%	59.4%	39.7%
87:3	39.5%	1.2%	63.1%	60.4%	60.4%	0.7%	0.4%	59.7%	39.1%
87:4	37.9%	1.2%	55.9%	62.0%	62.0%	0.6%	0.5%	61.3%	37.5%
88:1	41.3%	0.8%	68.2%	58.6%	58.7%	0.5%	0.2%	58.2%	41.0%
88:2	39.3%	0.9%	64.2%	60.7%	60.7%	0.5%	0.3%	60.2%	39.0%
88:3	35.9%	0.9%	59.1%	64.1%	64.0%	0.5%	0.4%	63.5%	35.6%
88:4	36.3%	0.9%	63.9%	63.6%	63.6%	0.6%	0.3%	63.1%	36.0%
89:1	39.0%	0.8%	69.9%	61.0%	61.0%	0.5%	0.2%	60.5%	38.7%
89:2	40.2%	0.7%	64.6%	59.8%	59.8%	0.4%	0.2%	59.4%	39.9%
89:3	39.9%	0.9%	67.2%	60.1%	60.1%	0.6%	0.3%	59.5%	39.6%
89:4	38.3%	1.6%	57.4%	61.7%	61.6%	0.9%	0.7%	60.7%	37.7%
90:1	36.9%	1.0%	63.9%	63.1%	63.1%	0.7%	0.4%	62.5%	36.5%
90:2	39.2%	0.8%	62.5%	60.8%	60.8%	0.5%	0.3%	60.4%	38.9%
90:3	33.5%	1.1%	51.7%	66.6%	66.4%	0.6%	0.5%	65.8%	33.1%
90:4	40.8%	0.8%	62.8%	59.2%	59.2%	0.5%	0.3%	58.7%	40.4%
91:1	44.1%	0.7%	59.6%	55.9%	55.9%	0.4%	0.3%	55.5%	43.8%
91:2	39.7%	0.8%	60.7%	60.4%	60.4%	0.5%	0.3%	59.9%	39.3%
91:3	40.4%	1.2%	63.6%	59.6%	59.7%	0.7%	0.4%	58.9%	39.9%
91:4	41.2%	1.1%	58.0%	58.8%	58.8%	0.6%	0.5%	58.2%	40.8%
92:1	40.0%	0.9%	59.0%	60.0%	60.0%	0.5%	0.4%	59.5%	39.7%
92:2	38.6%	1.0%	56.2%	61.4%	61.4%	0.6%	0.5%	60.8%	38.2%
92:3	40.3%	1.0%	62.5%	59.7%	59.7%	0.6%	0.4%	59.1%	39.9%
92:4	41.9%	1.1%	59.6%	58.1%	58.1%	0.6%	0.4%	57.5%	41.4%
93:1	42.5%	0.9%	55.4%	57.4%	57.4%	0.5%	0.4%	56.9%	42.2%
93:2	42.1%	1.0%	60.0%	57.9%	57.9%	0.6%	0.4%	57.3%	41.7%
93:3	42.5%	0.9%	55.4%	57.5%	57.5%	0.5%	0.4%	57.0%	42.1%
93:4	41.5%	0.9%	57.7%	58.5%	58.5%	0.5%	0.4%	58.0%	41.1%
94:1	40.4%	1.1%	60.1%	59.6%	59.6%	0.7%	0.5%	58.9%	40.0%
94:2	40.6%	0.9%	55.6%	59.4%	59.4%	0.5%	0.4%	58.9%	40.2%
94:3	41.8%	0.8%	56.1%	58.2%	58.2%	0.5%	0.4%	57.7%	41.5%
94:4	39.5%	1.1%	59.3%	60.6%	60.5%	0.6%	0.4%	59.9%	39.0%
95:1	43.1%	0.8%	62.5%	56.9%	56.9%	0.5%	0.3%	56.4%	42.8%
95:2	43.7%	0.9%	62.7%	56.3%	56.3%	0.6%	0.3%	55.8%	43.3%
95:3	43.9%	0.9%	62.7%	56.0%	56.1%	0.6%	0.4%	55.5%	43.5%
95:4	43.4%	0.9%	60.0%	56.6%	56.6%	0.6%	0.4%	56.1%	43.0%
96:1	45.5%	0.9%	60.4%	54.5%	54.5%	0.6%	0.4%	54.0%	45.1%
96:2	42.1%	1.2%	56.8%	57.9%	57.9%	0.7%	0.5%	57.2%	41.6%
96:3	42.6%	1.1%	59.5%	57.4%	57.4%	0.6%	0.4%	56.7%	42.2%
96:4	44.3%	1.1%	63.9%	55.8%	55.9%	0.7%	0.4%	55.2%	43.7%
AVG	40.0%	0.9%	61.8%	60.1%	60.1%	0.6%	0.4%	59.6%	39.5%

Table 3.24b
Volume Accumulation Percent Crossover (VAP-C) Short Hit Analysis
(Average of all stocks)

Qtr	Optimal Short	VAP-C Short	Short Hits	Cash Hits	Total Hits	Short Right	Short Wrong	Cash Right	Cash Wrong
85:1	34.3%	0.6%	86.5%	65.6%	65.8%	0.5%	0.1%	65.3%	34.2%
85:2	34.6%	0.5%	72.7%	65.4%	65.4%	0.3%	0.1%	65.1%	34.4%
85:3	38.6%	0.3%	73.7%	61.4%	61.4%	0.3%	0.1%	61.2%	38.5%
85:4	33.1%	0.2%	65.0%	66.9%	66.9%	0.1%	0.1%	66.7%	33.0%
86:1	35.2%	0.5%	63.4%	64.8%	64.8%	0.3%	0.2%	64.4%	35.0%
86:2	39.8%	0.3%	67.9%	60.2%	60.2%	0.2%	0.1%	60.0%	39.7%
86:3	42.7%	0.3%	65.5%	57.3%	57.3%	0.2%	0.1%	57.1%	42.6%
86:4	38.7%	0.4%	71.9%	61.3%	61.3%	0.3%	0.1%	61.1%	38.6%
87:1	36.9%	0.5%	55.2%	63.1%	63.0%	0.3%	0.2%	62.8%	36.8%
87:2	40.0%	0.2%	63.2%	60.0%	60.0%	0.1%	0.1%	59.9%	39.9%
87:3	40.4%	0.3%	68.4%	59.6%	59.6%	0.2%	0.1%	59.4%	40.3%
87:4	45.3%	0.1%	75.4%	54.7%	54.8%	0.1%	0.0%	54.7%	45.2%
88:1	36.7%	0.4%	57.1%	63.3%	63.3%	0.2%	0.2%	63.0%	36.6%
88:2	37.4%	0.2%	61.8%	62.5%	62.5%	0.1%	0.1%	62.4%	37.4%
88:3	38.4%	0.5%	68.5%	61.6%	61.7%	0.3%	0.1%	61.4%	38.2%
88:4	37.0%	0.6%	61.0%	63.0%	63.0%	0.4%	0.2%	62.6%	36.8%
89:1	36.2%	0.4%	64.7%	63.8%	63.8%	0.2%	0.1%	63.6%	36.1%
89:2	35.9%	0.4%	61.5%	64.1%	64.0%	0.3%	0.2%	63.8%	35.8%
89:3	36.4%	0.4%	62.9%	63.6%	63.6%	0.3%	0.2%	63.3%	36.3%
89:4	39.0%	0.5%	68.6%	61.0%	61.1%	0.4%	0.2%	60.7%	38.8%
90:1	40.1%	0.6%	60.9%	59.8%	59.8%	0.4%	0.2%	59.5%	39.9%
90:2	37.8%	0.5%	68.5%	62.2%	62.3%	0.3%	0.2%	61.9%	37.6%
90:3	45.7%	0.2%	70.1%	54.4%	54.4%	0.2%	0.1%	54.2%	45.5%
90:4	37.6%	0.4%	64.1%	62.4%	62.4%	0.3%	0.2%	62.2%	37.4%
91:1	36.7%	0.5%	58.0%	63.3%	63.3%	0.3%	0.2%	63.0%	36.5%
91:2	40.4%	0.3%	58.0%	59.6%	59.6%	0.2%	0.1%	59.4%	40.3%
91:3	39.8%	0.8%	63.3%	60.2%	60.3%	0.5%	0.3%	59.8%	39.4%
91:4	40.5%	0.7%	52.1%	59.5%	59.4%	0.4%	0.3%	59.1%	40.2%
92:1	43.2%	0.8%	57.2%	56.8%	56.8%	0.5%	0.3%	56.3%	42.9%
92:2	42.9%	0.6%	62.0%	57.1%	57.1%	0.4%	0.2%	56.8%	42.6%
92:3	39.5%	0.7%	61.9%	60.5%	60.5%	0.4%	0.3%	60.0%	39.2%
92:4	37.5%	0.6%	61.4%	62.5%	62.5%	0.4%	0.2%	62.1%	37.2%
93:1	39.4%	0.7%	56.1%	60.6%	60.6%	0.4%	0.3%	60.2%	39.1%
93:2	40.9%	0.6%	62.7%	59.1%	59.2%	0.4%	0.2%	58.8%	40.6%
93:3	39.4%	0.6%	58.1%	60.6%	60.6%	0.4%	0.3%	60.2%	39.1%
93:4	41.7%	0.8%	57.0%	58.3%	58.3%	0.5%	0.4%	57.8%	41.3%
94:1	43.7%	0.5%	59.9%	56.3%	56.4%	0.3%	0.2%	56.0%	43.4%
94:2	42.7%	0.6%	59.5%	57.3%	57.3%	0.4%	0.2%	56.9%	42.5%
94:3	39.8%	0.6%	61.1%	60.2%	60.2%	0.4%	0.2%	59.9%	39.5%
94:4	42.8%	0.5%	61.7%	57.2%	57.2%	0.3%	0.2%	56.9%	42.6%
95:1	38.7%	0.7%	53.8%	61.3%	61.3%	0.4%	0.3%	60.9%	38.4%
95:2	38.9%	0.7%	54.5%	61.1%	61.0%	0.4%	0.3%	60.6%	38.7%
95:3	38.9%	0.8%	50.3%	61.0%	61.0%	0.4%	0.4%	60.6%	38.7%
95:4	40.5%	0.6%	60.9%	59.5%	59.5%	0.4%	0.3%	59.1%	40.3%
96:1	38.9%	0.4%	50.9%	61.1%	61.0%	0.2%	0.2%	60.8%	38.8%
96:2	42.4%	0.6%	57.0%	57.6%	57.6%	0.4%	0.3%	57.3%	42.1%
96:3	40.8%	0.5%	56.6%	59.2%	59.2%	0.3%	0.2%	58.9%	40.5%
96:4	39.8%	1.1%	57.3%	60.2%	60.2%	0.6%	0.5%	59.6%	39.4%
AVG	39.4%	0.5%	62.3%	60.7%	60.7%	0.3%	0.2%	60.4%	39.1%

Table 3.25a
Volume Accumulation Percent Crossover (VAP-C) Long Return Analysis
(Average of all stocks)

Qtr	VAP-C Terminal Wealth	Buy/Hold Terminal Wealth	Relative Terminal Wealth	VAP-C Long Avg Ret	VAP-C Cash Avg Ret	VAP-C Long-Cash Avg Ret	Buy/Hold Avg Ret
85:1	10008	10142	0.987	0.286%	0.005%	0.281%	0.006%
85:2	10000	9700	1.031	0.009%	-0.070%	0.078%	-0.069%
85:3	9999	8889	1.125	-0.025%	-0.205%	0.180%	-0.205%
85:4	10007	10763	0.930	0.224%	0.106%	0.118%	0.107%
86:1	10013	11428	0.876	0.289%	0.224%	0.065%	0.225%
86:2	10004	10414	0.961	0.101%	0.066%	0.034%	0.066%
86:3	9999	9175	1.090	-0.003%	-0.129%	0.126%	-0.128%
86:4	10006	10413	0.961	0.103%	0.069%	0.034%	0.069%
87:1	10024	11929	0.840	0.387%	0.292%	0.095%	0.293%
87:2	10001	10196	0.981	0.027%	0.038%	-0.011%	0.038%
87:3	10008	10408	0.962	0.125%	0.068%	0.057%	0.068%
87:4	9958	8087	1.231	-0.581%	-0.274%	-0.307%	-0.278%
88:1	10013	10989	0.911	0.269%	0.162%	0.107%	0.163%
88:2	10004	10593	0.944	0.074%	0.100%	-0.025%	0.100%
88:3	9996	10050	0.995	-0.075%	0.013%	-0.088%	0.013%
88:4	10000	10196	0.981	0.004%	0.037%	-0.033%	0.037%
89:1	10005	10698	0.935	0.116%	0.112%	0.003%	0.112%
89:2	10006	10772	0.929	0.139%	0.122%	0.016%	0.122%
89:3	10009	10833	0.924	0.161%	0.131%	0.030%	0.131%
89:4	9990	9904	1.009	-0.098%	-0.010%	-0.089%	-0.011%
90:1	10010	9980	1.003	0.149%	0.001%	0.148%	0.003%
90:2	10012	10459	0.957	0.243%	0.075%	0.168%	0.077%
90:3	9981	8526	1.171	-0.286%	-0.259%	-0.028%	-0.259%
90:4	10014	10889	0.920	0.246%	0.145%	0.101%	0.146%
91:1	10011	12477	0.802	0.234%	0.316%	-0.081%	0.315%
91:2	10005	10244	0.977	0.110%	0.045%	0.066%	0.045%
91:3	10016	10429	0.960	0.221%	0.063%	0.158%	0.065%
91:4	10009	10497	0.953	0.125%	0.081%	0.044%	0.082%
92:1	10008	10324	0.969	0.149%	0.047%	0.102%	0.048%
92:2	10003	9723	1.029	0.045%	-0.049%	0.094%	-0.048%
92:3	9999	10392	0.962	-0.017%	0.057%	-0.074%	0.057%
92:4	10007	10963	0.913	0.107%	0.145%	-0.038%	0.144%
93:1	9994	10527	0.949	-0.117%	0.082%	-0.198%	0.080%
93:2	10002	10340	0.967	0.044%	0.052%	-0.008%	0.052%
93:3	10001	10686	0.936	0.031%	0.102%	-0.071%	0.101%
93:4	9998	10255	0.975	-0.040%	0.035%	-0.074%	0.034%
94:1	10006	9954	1.005	0.087%	-0.012%	0.099%	-0.011%
94:2	9998	9994	1.000	-0.032%	-0.004%	-0.028%	-0.005%
94:3	10000	10613	0.942	-0.006%	0.090%	-0.096%	0.089%
94:4	10001	9836	1.017	0.016%	-0.030%	0.046%	-0.029%
95:1	10004	10706	0.934	0.083%	0.110%	-0.027%	0.110%
95:2	10016	10873	0.921	0.293%	0.133%	0.161%	0.134%
95:3	10004	10853	0.922	0.069%	0.132%	-0.063%	0.131%
95:4	10008	10445	0.958	0.146%	0.066%	0.080%	0.067%
96:1	10005	11027	0.907	0.094%	0.160%	-0.065%	0.159%
96:2	9999	10367	0.965	-0.018%	0.059%	-0.077%	0.059%
96:3	10000	10298	0.971	0.004%	0.048%	-0.044%	0.047%
96:4	10014	10817	0.926	0.202%	0.121%	0.080%	0.122%
AVG	10004	10377	0.964	0.066%	0.055%	0.011%	0.055%

Table 3.25b
Volume Accumulation Percent Crossover (VAP-C) Short Return Analysis
(Average of all stocks)

Qtr	VAP-C Terminal Wealth	Buy/Hold Terminal Wealth	Relative Terminal Wealth	VAP-C Short Avg Ret	VAP-C Cash Avg Ret	VAP-C Short-Cash Avg Ret	Buy/Hold Avg Ret
85:1	10002	10142	0.986	-0.052%	0.007%	-0.058%	0.006%
85:2	10002	9700	1.031	-0.078%	-0.069%	-0.009%	-0.069%
85:3	10010	8889	1.126	-0.411%	-0.204%	-0.207%	-0.205%
85:4	10000	10763	0.929	-0.036%	0.107%	-0.143%	0.107%
86:1	10005	11428	0.876	-0.113%	0.226%	-0.340%	0.225%
86:2	10004	10414	0.961	-0.170%	0.067%	-0.237%	0.066%
86:3	10003	9175	1.090	-0.180%	-0.127%	-0.052%	-0.128%
86:4	10006	10413	0.961	-0.243%	0.070%	-0.313%	0.069%
87:1	9993	11929	0.838	0.281%	0.293%	-0.012%	0.293%
87:2	9998	10196	0.981	0.123%	0.038%	0.086%	0.038%
87:3	10000	10408	0.961	0.012%	0.068%	-0.056%	0.068%
87:4	10001	8087	1.237	-0.162%	-0.278%	0.116%	-0.278%
88:1	9995	10989	0.910	0.184%	0.163%	0.021%	0.163%
88:2	10000	10593	0.944	-0.046%	0.100%	-0.146%	0.100%
88:3	10002	10050	0.995	-0.083%	0.013%	-0.096%	0.013%
88:4	9993	10196	0.980	0.204%	0.036%	0.168%	0.037%
89:1	9998	10698	0.935	0.090%	0.112%	-0.023%	0.112%
89:2	9997	10772	0.928	0.101%	0.122%	-0.021%	0.122%
89:3	9994	10833	0.923	0.220%	0.131%	0.090%	0.131%
89:4	10002	9904	1.010	-0.064%	-0.011%	-0.053%	-0.011%
90:1	9993	9980	1.001	0.174%	0.002%	0.172%	0.003%
90:2	10007	10459	0.957	-0.221%	0.078%	-0.299%	0.077%
90:3	10012	8526	1.174	-0.651%	-0.258%	-0.393%	-0.259%
90:4	9996	10889	0.918	0.121%	0.146%	-0.025%	0.146%
91:1	9992	12477	0.801	0.282%	0.315%	-0.033%	0.315%
91:2	9990	10244	0.975	0.541%	0.044%	0.498%	0.045%
91:3	10005	10429	0.959	-0.089%	0.066%	-0.155%	0.065%
91:4	9984	10497	0.951	0.336%	0.080%	0.256%	0.082%
92:1	9995	10324	0.968	0.142%	0.047%	0.095%	0.048%
92:2	10002	9723	1.029	-0.050%	-0.048%	-0.002%	-0.048%
92:3	10005	10392	0.963	-0.103%	0.058%	-0.161%	0.057%
92:4	10002	10963	0.912	-0.061%	0.146%	-0.207%	0.144%
93:1	9993	10527	0.949	0.158%	0.079%	0.079%	0.080%
93:2	9999	10340	0.967	0.016%	0.052%	-0.036%	0.052%
93:3	9997	10686	0.935	0.077%	0.101%	-0.024%	0.101%
93:4	9994	10255	0.975	0.122%	0.033%	0.089%	0.034%
94:1	9998	9954	1.004	0.060%	-0.012%	0.072%	-0.011%
94:2	9998	9994	1.000	0.072%	-0.005%	0.078%	-0.005%
94:3	9998	10613	0.942	0.066%	0.089%	-0.023%	0.089%
94:4	10001	9836	1.017	-0.017%	-0.029%	0.012%	-0.029%
95:1	9992	10706	0.933	0.172%	0.110%	0.062%	0.110%
95:2	9989	10873	0.919	0.251%	0.133%	0.118%	0.134%
95:3	9990	10853	0.920	0.210%	0.130%	0.080%	0.131%
95:4	10001	10445	0.957	-0.026%	0.067%	-0.094%	0.067%
96:1	9994	11027	0.906	0.239%	0.159%	0.081%	0.159%
96:2	10000	10367	0.965	-0.006%	0.059%	-0.065%	0.059%
96:3	9998	10298	0.971	0.065%	0.047%	0.018%	0.047%
96:4	9996	10817	0.924	0.063%	0.123%	-0.059%	0.122%
AVG	9998	10377	0.964	0.053%	0.055%	-0.002%	0.055%

short calls is positive, trading short with the VAP-C system leads to declining wealth. The average quarterly terminal wealth is $9,998. Again, there is very little variation in this terminal wealth from quarter to quarter. The lowest quarterly terminal wealth occurs in the fourth quarter of 1991 and is $9,984. The quarterly terminal wealth never exceeds $10,012. This small deviation from quarter to quarter is a result of the system's high cash calls. Investors following this system tend not to make much money or lose much money because they are usually in a cash position, avoiding losses but also missing out on profits.

It is obvious that combining the Bollinger Band Crossover and the Volume Accumulation Percent Breakout systems is an extremely conservative move. This combination results in very few calls.

Chapter

Oscillator Indicators

In this chapter, we focus on the group of indicators called oscillator indicators. These systems are grouped together because they are based on a common trading strategy—the idea that a stock's price oscillates between overbought and oversold levels. When the stock price reaches an overbought or oversold level, it is an indication that the price will soon change direction.

A stock is overbought when its price is too high relative to where it will be in the near future. The term *overbought* refers to a belief that many buyers have been buying the stock and the increase in demand has driven the price of the stock upward. The increased demand will not continue; thus, price will fall below its current level. This is the point at which a trader wants to enter into a short position.

A stock is *oversold* when more people have been selling the stock than will be selling it in the near future. The overselling leads to a relatively low price for the stock, and traders will want to purchase the stock at the oversold, relatively low, price. As the oversold position corrects itself, the price will rise, leading to a profitable trading strategy.

In this chapter, we analyze fifteen trading systems. You will notice that the same oscillator may be used for more than one indicator. For example, the Relative Strength Peaks (RSI-P) system and the Relative Strength Crossover (RSI-C) system are both based on the same oscillator, the Relative Strength Index. The difference between the two systems is in how each uses the oscillator to time a trade. In this case, the RSI-P system tends to call overbought and oversold levels sooner than the RSI-C version. In theory, this gives the RSI-P system a greater opportunity for profits because it makes a move faster. However, the more conservative RSI-C system waits for confirmation of a reversal before entering into a trade; an investor is therefore much less likely to enter into an incorrect trade with the RSI-C system than with the RSI-P system.

Let's turn our attention to the performance of these fifteen indicators.

Commodity Channel Index Peaks

The Commodity Channel Index (CCI), developed by Donald Lambert, measures the variation of a security's price from its statistical mean. The index is constructed so that its extreme values fall above +100 and below −100. A high value indicates that the price is unusually high compared to the average price; a low value indicates that the price is unusually low. This indicator, which was described more fully in the October 1980 issue of *Commodities* (now known as *Futures*) magazine, can be used in any market, not just the commodities market.

Construction

1. Add a trading day's high, low, and closing prices, and divide this sum by 3. This gives the typical price, TP_i, for Day i:

$$TP_i, = (H_i, + L_i, + C_i,)/3 \ \{i = 1, 2, \ldots n\},$$

where

H_i = high price for Day i,

L_i = low price for Day i,

C_i = closing price for Day i,

n = number of periods in the CCI calculation.

2. Calculate an n-period simple moving average of the typical prices computed in Step 1:

$$MV_{today} = (TP_1 + TP_2 + TP_3 + \ldots + TP_n)/n.$$

3. For each of the prior n periods, subtract today's Step 2 value (MV_{today}) from Step 1's value (TP_i):

$$R_i = TP_i - MV_{today}.$$

4. Calculate an *n*-period simple moving average of the absolute values of each of the results in Step 3. Multiply this result by 0.015:

$$MV_R = \{(R_1 + R_2 + R_3 + \ldots + R_n)/n\} \cdot 0.015.$$

5. Subtract the value in Step 2 from the value in Step 1, and divide this difference by the value in Step 4:

$$CCI_{today} = (TP_{today} - MV_{today})/MV_R.$$

A long signal is generated whenever the CCI goes below –100 and turns upward. Whenever the CCI goes above +100 and then turns downward, a bearish short signal is generated.

Results

Tables 4.1 and 4.2 present the test results for the Commodity Channel Index Peaks (CCI-P) trading system. Overall, this system seems to work as well as the typical systems in our study. The overall hit rate of this system is about 60.4 percent, and the system makes long calls 40.6 percent of the time (Table 4.1a). Short calls are made 50.2 percent of the time (Table 4.1b).

The system chooses to go long during above-average market return periods. The average daily return when the system gives a long signal is 0.057 percent (Table 4.2a), which is above the average daily market return of 0.055 percent that occurred during the twelve years of our sample.

However, the system does not choose below-average market return periods to go short. The average daily return on days when the system gives a short signal is 0.059 percent, compared to a return of 0.052 percent when the system chooses a cash position over a short position (Table 4.2b). Thus, these short calls can be viewed as perverse calls. On days when there is any stock price appreciation, investors want to be in long positions; this is especially their goal when above-average stock price appreciation occurs. Investors would have higher returns by going long when the CCI-P system recommends a short position.

In conclusion, both the long recommendations and the short recommendations of the CCI-P system result in profits lower than the profits earned from a simple buy-and-hold strategy. As with many of the other indicators, the exception to this average result occurs during quarters where there is a negative average market return.

Let's look at a sophisticated variation of the CCI-P system—the Commodity Channel Index Fibonacci Peaks (CCI-FP) system—to see whether tinkering with this system improves performance results.

Table 4.1a
Commodity Channel Index Peaks (CCI-P) Long Hit Analysis
(Average of all stocks)

Qtr	Optimal Long	CCI-P Long	Long Hits	Cash Hits	Total Hits	Long Right	Long Wrong	Cash Right	Cash Wrong
85:1	32.1%	28.0%	65.9%	68.3%	67.6%	18.5%	9.5%	49.2%	22.9%
85:2	30.2%	37.1%	66.7%	69.6%	68.5%	24.7%	12.4%	43.8%	19.1%
85:3	26.3%	48.0%	62.1%	74.7%	68.7%	29.8%	18.2%	38.9%	13.2%
85:4	36.6%	28.6%	69.1%	62.2%	64.2%	19.8%	8.8%	44.4%	27.0%
86:1	44.2%	26.0%	66.6%	55.5%	58.3%	17.3%	8.7%	41.1%	33.0%
86:2	39.7%	37.8%	62.1%	61.1%	61.4%	23.5%	14.3%	38.0%	24.2%
86:3	37.0%	49.4%	58.2%	62.6%	60.4%	28.7%	20.7%	31.7%	18.9%
86:4	38.5%	43.1%	63.3%	62.0%	62.6%	27.3%	15.8%	35.2%	21.6%
87:1	44.7%	24.2%	67.5%	56.4%	59.1%	16.3%	7.8%	42.8%	33.1%
87:2	40.0%	50.3%	60.9%	61.4%	61.1%	30.6%	19.7%	30.5%	19.2%
87:3	39.5%	38.5%	61.1%	60.9%	61.0%	23.5%	15.0%	37.5%	24.0%
87:4	37.9%	62.3%	56.2%	64.3%	59.3%	35.1%	27.3%	24.2%	13.4%
88:1	41.3%	25.1%	65.0%	59.3%	60.7%	16.3%	8.8%	44.4%	30.5%
88:2	39.3%	46.1%	63.4%	61.2%	62.3%	29.2%	16.8%	33.0%	20.9%
88:3	35.9%	47.1%	62.2%	64.3%	63.3%	29.3%	17.8%	34.1%	18.9%
88:4	36.3%	45.0%	64.0%	63.8%	63.9%	28.8%	16.2%	35.1%	19.9%
89:1	39.0%	33.9%	64.7%	60.7%	62.1%	21.9%	12.0%	40.1%	25.9%
89:2	40.2%	27.5%	65.9%	59.5%	61.3%	18.1%	9.4%	43.1%	29.4%
89:3	39.9%	36.5%	65.6%	60.3%	62.3%	23.9%	12.5%	38.3%	25.2%
89:4	38.3%	51.2%	61.2%	61.1%	61.2%	31.3%	19.9%	29.8%	19.0%
90:1	36.9%	50.2%	61.0%	63.3%	62.1%	30.6%	19.6%	31.5%	18.3%
90:2	39.2%	38.8%	64.6%	60.7%	62.2%	25.1%	13.7%	37.2%	24.0%
90:3	33.5%	62.4%	54.8%	67.2%	59.5%	34.2%	28.2%	25.3%	12.3%
90:4	40.8%	39.7%	62.8%	58.3%	60.1%	24.9%	14.8%	35.2%	25.1%
91:1	44.1%	27.3%	67.4%	56.8%	59.7%	18.4%	8.9%	41.3%	31.4%
91:2	39.7%	39.0%	61.8%	61.4%	61.6%	24.1%	14.9%	37.5%	23.5%
91:3	40.4%	43.1%	60.9%	59.9%	60.3%	26.2%	16.9%	34.1%	22.8%
91:4	41.2%	45.0%	59.4%	58.4%	58.8%	26.7%	18.3%	32.1%	22.9%
92:1	40.0%	34.3%	55.4%	58.9%	57.7%	19.0%	15.3%	38.7%	27.0%
92:2	38.6%	48.2%	57.2%	61.5%	59.4%	27.6%	20.6%	31.9%	20.0%
92:3	40.3%	41.2%	60.6%	59.6%	60.0%	24.9%	16.2%	35.1%	23.7%
92:4	41.9%	35.4%	62.9%	57.9%	59.7%	22.3%	13.1%	37.4%	27.2%
93:1	42.5%	35.0%	61.2%	58.0%	59.1%	21.4%	13.6%	37.7%	27.3%
93:2	42.1%	45.8%	59.5%	58.0%	58.6%	27.2%	18.6%	31.4%	22.8%
93:3	42.5%	36.8%	60.4%	57.5%	58.5%	22.2%	14.6%	36.3%	26.9%
93:4	41.5%	46.6%	58.2%	58.1%	58.1%	27.1%	19.5%	31.0%	22.3%
94:1	40.4%	42.0%	56.6%	59.3%	58.1%	23.8%	18.3%	34.3%	23.6%
94:2	40.6%	54.2%	57.8%	59.7%	58.6%	31.3%	22.9%	27.3%	18.5%
94:3	41.8%	41.6%	60.9%	58.6%	59.5%	25.3%	16.3%	34.2%	24.2%
94:4	39.5%	54.0%	57.3%	60.8%	58.9%	31.0%	23.1%	27.9%	18.0%
95:1	43.1%	33.6%	62.1%	56.7%	58.5%	20.9%	12.7%	37.6%	28.8%
95:2	43.7%	31.6%	61.9%	56.1%	58.0%	19.5%	12.0%	38.4%	30.0%
95:3	43.9%	33.8%	61.9%	55.6%	57.7%	20.9%	12.9%	36.8%	29.4%
95:4	43.4%	41.2%	58.9%	55.6%	57.0%	24.3%	16.9%	32.7%	26.1%
96:1	45.5%	41.0%	61.5%	54.6%	57.5%	25.2%	15.8%	32.2%	26.8%
96:2	42.1%	41.9%	57.6%	57.6%	57.6%	24.1%	17.8%	33.5%	24.6%
96:3	42.6%	44.3%	58.9%	56.9%	57.8%	26.1%	18.2%	31.7%	24.0%
96:4	44.3%	34.9%	60.6%	55.3%	57.2%	21.2%	13.8%	36.0%	29.1%
AVG	40.0%	40.6%	61.6%	60.2%	60.4%	24.8%	15.8%	35.7%	23.7%

Table 4.1b
Commodity Channel Index Peaks (CCI-P) Short Hit Analysis
(Average of all stocks)

Qtr	Optimal Short	CCI-P Short	Short Hits	Cash Hits	Total Hits	Short Right	Short Wrong	Cash Right	Cash Wrong
85:1	34.3%	56.9%	67.9%	65.3%	66.8%	38.6%	18.3%	28.1%	14.9%
85:2	34.6%	51.6%	69.1%	66.2%	67.7%	35.7%	16.0%	32.0%	16.3%
85:3	38.6%	41.9%	74.2%	61.9%	67.1%	31.1%	10.8%	36.0%	22.1%
85:4	33.1%	58.1%	62.2%	67.7%	64.5%	36.2%	22.0%	28.3%	13.5%
86:1	35.2%	60.7%	55.5%	65.3%	59.3%	33.7%	27.0%	25.6%	13.6%
86:2	39.8%	54.4%	61.3%	61.7%	61.5%	33.4%	21.1%	28.1%	17.5%
86:3	42.7%	39.1%	63.0%	58.2%	60.1%	24.6%	14.4%	35.5%	25.4%
86:4	38.7%	50.2%	61.9%	63.0%	62.5%	31.1%	19.1%	31.4%	18.4%
87:1	36.9%	63.4%	56.6%	65.7%	59.9%	35.9%	27.5%	24.0%	12.5%
87:2	40.0%	42.3%	61.4%	60.5%	60.9%	26.0%	16.3%	34.9%	22.8%
87:3	40.4%	52.7%	61.0%	60.4%	60.7%	32.2%	20.5%	28.6%	18.7%
87:4	45.3%	24.1%	65.2%	55.8%	58.1%	15.7%	8.4%	42.4%	33.5%
88:1	36.7%	66.8%	58.8%	63.3%	60.3%	39.3%	27.5%	21.0%	12.2%
88:2	37.4%	47.0%	61.1%	63.2%	62.2%	28.7%	18.2%	33.5%	19.5%
88:3	38.4%	44.9%	64.3%	61.8%	62.9%	28.8%	16.0%	34.1%	21.0%
88:4	37.0%	47.3%	64.2%	63.9%	64.0%	30.3%	16.9%	33.7%	19.0%
89:1	36.2%	57.5%	60.8%	64.1%	62.2%	35.0%	22.5%	27.3%	15.3%
89:2	35.9%	61.3%	59.4%	64.5%	61.4%	36.4%	24.9%	25.0%	13.8%
89:3	36.4%	55.3%	60.3%	64.7%	62.2%	33.3%	22.0%	28.9%	15.8%
89:4	39.0%	40.4%	61.2%	61.1%	61.1%	24.7%	15.7%	36.4%	23.2%
90:1	40.1%	41.4%	63.6%	60.8%	61.9%	26.3%	15.1%	35.6%	23.0%
90:2	37.8%	51.4%	61.1%	63.5%	62.3%	31.4%	20.0%	30.9%	17.7%
90:3	45.7%	25.5%	67.0%	54.5%	57.7%	17.1%	8.4%	40.6%	33.9%
90:4	37.6%	50.1%	58.2%	62.3%	60.2%	29.1%	20.9%	31.1%	18.8%
91:1	36.7%	58.8%	56.8%	65.2%	60.2%	33.4%	25.4%	26.8%	14.3%
91:2	40.4%	54.3%	61.5%	61.2%	61.3%	33.4%	20.9%	27.9%	17.7%
91:3	39.8%	49.8%	60.0%	60.7%	60.4%	29.9%	19.9%	30.5%	19.7%
91:4	40.5%	45.6%	58.4%	59.4%	58.9%	26.6%	18.9%	32.3%	22.1%
92:1	43.2%	55.9%	59.0%	55.8%	57.6%	33.0%	22.9%	24.6%	19.5%
92:2	42.9%	45.6%	61.7%	57.1%	59.2%	28.2%	17.5%	31.1%	23.3%
92:3	39.5%	51.3%	59.7%	60.4%	60.1%	30.7%	20.7%	29.4%	19.2%
92:4	37.5%	54.5%	57.7%	62.4%	59.9%	31.5%	23.0%	28.4%	17.1%
93:1	39.4%	56.4%	58.1%	60.9%	59.3%	32.8%	23.6%	26.5%	17.1%
93:2	40.9%	46.5%	58.0%	59.4%	58.7%	27.0%	19.5%	31.8%	21.7%
93:3	39.4%	55.0%	57.4%	60.4%	58.8%	31.6%	23.4%	27.2%	17.8%
93:4	41.7%	45.3%	58.0%	58.0%	58.0%	26.3%	19.0%	31.7%	23.0%
94:1	43.7%	50.4%	59.5%	56.5%	58.0%	30.0%	20.4%	28.0%	21.6%
94:2	42.7%	39.3%	59.9%	57.6%	58.5%	23.5%	15.8%	35.0%	25.7%
94:3	39.8%	51.2%	58.5%	60.4%	59.4%	29.9%	21.2%	29.5%	19.3%
94:4	42.8%	37.6%	61.0%	57.3%	58.7%	22.9%	14.6%	35.8%	26.7%
95:1	38.7%	59.2%	56.6%	61.6%	58.6%	33.5%	25.7%	25.1%	15.7%
95:2	38.9%	60.3%	56.3%	61.5%	58.4%	33.9%	26.4%	24.5%	15.3%
95:3	38.9%	57.0%	55.5%	61.2%	57.9%	31.6%	25.3%	26.3%	16.7%
95:4	40.5%	47.8%	55.4%	59.0%	57.2%	26.5%	21.3%	30.8%	21.4%
96:1	38.9%	51.3%	54.5%	61.1%	57.7%	27.9%	23.3%	29.8%	19.0%
96:2	42.4%	51.7%	57.7%	57.6%	57.6%	29.8%	21.9%	27.8%	20.5%
96:3	40.8%	46.2%	56.9%	58.6%	57.8%	26.3%	19.9%	31.5%	22.2%
96:4	39.8%	54.8%	55.0%	59.7%	57.2%	30.2%	24.6%	27.0%	18.2%
AVG	39.4%	50.2%	60.3%	61.1%	60.4%	30.1%	20.1%	30.3%	19.5%

Table 4.2a
Commodity Channel Index Peaks (CCI-P) Long Return Analysis
(Average of all stocks)

Qtr	CCI-P Terminal Wealth	Buy/Hold Terminal Wealth	Relative Terminal Wealth	CCI-P Long Avg Ret	CCI-P Cash Avg Ret	CCI-P Long-Cash Avg Ret	Buy/Hold Avg Ret
85:1	10016	10142	0.988	0.001%	0.008%	-0.007%	0.006%
85:2	9902	9700	1.021	-0.062%	-0.074%	0.012%	-0.069%
85:3	9500	8889	1.069	-0.179%	-0.228%	0.049%	-0.205%
85:4	10186	10763	0.946	0.094%	0.112%	-0.018%	0.107%
86:1	10405	11428	0.911	0.255%	0.214%	0.042%	0.225%
86:2	10319	10414	0.991	0.139%	0.022%	0.116%	0.066%
86:3	9677	9175	1.055	-0.098%	-0.157%	0.059%	-0.128%
86:4	10280	10413	0.987	0.104%	0.043%	0.061%	0.069%
87:1	10747	11929	0.901	0.487%	0.231%	0.255%	0.293%
87:2	10230	10196	1.003	0.079%	-0.004%	0.083%	0.038%
87:3	10275	10408	0.987	0.115%	0.039%	0.077%	0.068%
87:4	9317	8087	1.152	-0.146%	-0.496%	0.350%	-0.278%
88:1	10425	10989	0.949	0.276%	0.125%	0.151%	0.163%
88:2	10375	10593	0.979	0.135%	0.069%	0.066%	0.100%
88:3	10066	10050	1.002	0.027%	0.000%	0.028%	0.013%
88:4	10135	10196	0.994	0.052%	0.024%	0.027%	0.037%
89:1	10214	10698	0.955	0.105%	0.116%	-0.012%	0.112%
89:2	10244	10772	0.951	0.142%	0.115%	0.027%	0.122%
89:3	10364	10833	0.957	0.161%	0.114%	0.047%	0.131%
89:4	9973	9904	1.007	-0.006%	-0.017%	0.011%	-0.011%
90:1	10058	9980	1.008	0.024%	-0.019%	0.044%	0.003%
90:2	10234	10459	0.978	0.102%	0.061%	0.041%	0.077%
90:3	9091	8526	1.066	-0.251%	-0.273%	0.022%	-0.259%
90:4	10345	10889	0.950	0.147%	0.146%	0.001%	0.146%
91:1	11240	12477	0.901	0.464%	0.259%	0.205%	0.315%
91:2	10276	10244	1.003	0.114%	0.002%	0.112%	0.045%
91:3	10253	10429	0.983	0.093%	0.044%	0.049%	0.065%
91:4	10272	10497	0.979	0.100%	0.067%	0.033%	0.082%
92:1	9913	10324	0.960	-0.045%	0.096%	-0.141%	0.048%
92:2	9855	9723	1.014	-0.051%	-0.046%	-0.005%	-0.048%
92:3	10193	10392	0.981	0.067%	0.049%	0.018%	0.057%
92:4	10299	10963	0.939	0.132%	0.151%	-0.019%	0.144%
93:1	10262	10527	0.975	0.117%	0.060%	0.057%	0.080%
93:2	10175	10340	0.984	0.062%	0.043%	0.019%	0.052%
93:3	10248	10686	0.959	0.105%	0.099%	0.006%	0.101%
93:4	10076	10255	0.983	0.024%	0.042%	-0.018%	0.034%
94:1	9991	9954	1.004	-0.007%	-0.014%	0.007%	-0.011%
94:2	10024	9994	1.003	0.004%	-0.015%	0.019%	-0.005%
94:3	10266	10613	0.967	0.099%	0.083%	0.016%	0.089%
94:4	9913	9836	1.008	-0.027%	-0.032%	0.006%	-0.029%
95:1	10269	10706	0.959	0.128%	0.101%	0.027%	0.110%
95:2	10281	10873	0.946	0.142%	0.130%	0.011%	0.134%
95:3	10292	10853	0.948	0.137%	0.128%	0.009%	0.131%
95:4	10128	10445	0.970	0.048%	0.080%	-0.031%	0.067%
96:1	10470	11027	0.949	0.183%	0.142%	0.041%	0.159%
96:2	10104	10367	0.975	0.040%	0.072%	-0.032%	0.059%
96:3	10056	10298	0.977	0.021%	0.068%	-0.048%	0.047%
96:4	10243	10817	0.947	0.108%	0.130%	-0.022%	0.122%
AVG	10156	10377	0.979	0.057%	0.054%	0.004%	0.055%

Table 4.2b
Commodity Channel Index Peaks (CCI-P) Short Return Analysis
(Average of all stocks)

Qtr	CCI-P Terminal Wealth	Buy/Hold Terminal Wealth	Relative Terminal Wealth	CCI-P Short Avg Ret	CCI-P Cash Avg Ret	CCI-P Short-Cash Avg Ret	Buy/Hold Avg Ret
85:1	9975	10142	0.984	0.020%	-0.012%	0.032%	0.006%
85:2	10252	9700	1.057	-0.067%	-0.072%	0.005%	-0.069%
85:3	10629	8889	1.196	-0.221%	-0.193%	-0.029%	-0.205%
85:4	9596	10763	0.892	0.117%	0.093%	0.024%	0.107%
86:1	9237	11428	0.808	0.217%	0.236%	-0.019%	0.225%
86:2	9970	10414	0.957	0.012%	0.132%	-0.120%	0.066%
86:3	10478	9175	1.142	-0.191%	-0.087%	-0.104%	-0.128%
86:4	9868	10413	0.948	0.038%	0.101%	-0.063%	0.069%
87:1	9140	11929	0.766	0.231%	0.400%	-0.168%	0.293%
87:2	10009	10196	0.982	-0.004%	0.069%	-0.073%	0.038%
87:3	9875	10408	0.949	0.037%	0.104%	-0.067%	0.068%
87:4	10826	8087	1.339	-0.533%	-0.197%	-0.336%	-0.278%
88:1	9379	10989	0.854	0.146%	0.196%	-0.049%	0.163%
88:2	9793	10593	0.925	0.070%	0.126%	-0.055%	0.100%
88:3	9979	10050	0.993	0.005%	0.019%	-0.013%	0.013%
88:4	9954	10196	0.976	0.012%	0.058%	-0.046%	0.037%
89:1	9580	10698	0.895	0.121%	0.100%	0.021%	0.112%
89:2	9533	10772	0.885	0.122%	0.122%	0.000%	0.122%
89:3	9595	10833	0.886	0.121%	0.144%	-0.023%	0.131%
89:4	10059	9904	1.016	-0.027%	-0.001%	-0.026%	-0.011%
90:1	10074	9980	1.009	-0.030%	0.026%	-0.057%	0.003%
90:2	9814	10459	0.938	0.059%	0.096%	-0.037%	0.077%
90:3	10406	8526	1.221	-0.256%	-0.260%	0.004%	-0.259%
90:4	9486	10889	0.871	0.165%	0.128%	0.037%	0.146%
91:1	9080	12477	0.728	0.272%	0.377%	-0.105%	0.315%
91:2	9971	10244	0.973	0.005%	0.093%	-0.088%	0.045%
91:3	9890	10429	0.948	0.039%	0.091%	-0.052%	0.065%
91:4	9814	10497	0.935	0.066%	0.095%	-0.030%	0.082%
92:1	9695	10324	0.939	0.094%	-0.010%	0.104%	0.048%
92:2	10167	9723	1.046	-0.055%	-0.043%	-0.013%	-0.048%
92:3	9843	10392	0.947	0.051%	0.062%	-0.011%	0.057%
92:4	9484	10963	0.865	0.156%	0.131%	0.025%	0.144%
93:1	9808	10527	0.932	0.060%	0.106%	-0.046%	0.080%
93:2	9890	10340	0.956	0.043%	0.060%	-0.017%	0.052%
93:3	9674	10686	0.905	0.100%	0.103%	-0.003%	0.101%
93:4	9875	10255	0.963	0.049%	0.022%	0.027%	0.034%
94:1	10065	9954	1.011	-0.019%	-0.004%	-0.015%	-0.011%
94:2	10062	9994	1.007	-0.022%	0.006%	-0.028%	-0.005%
94:3	9722	10613	0.916	0.092%	0.086%	0.006%	0.089%
94:4	10090	9836	1.026	-0.036%	-0.025%	-0.011%	-0.029%
95:1	9624	10706	0.899	0.105%	0.117%	-0.012%	0.110%
95:2	9522	10873	0.876	0.133%	0.135%	-0.002%	0.134%
95:3	9548	10853	0.880	0.133%	0.129%	0.003%	0.131%
95:4	9763	10445	0.935	0.086%	0.050%	0.036%	0.067%
96:1	9539	11027	0.865	0.150%	0.168%	-0.018%	0.159%
96:2	9773	10367	0.943	0.072%	0.044%	0.028%	0.059%
96:3	9788	10298	0.950	0.075%	0.023%	0.052%	0.047%
96:4	9526	10817	0.881	0.143%	0.098%	0.045%	0.122%
AVG	9827	10377	0.947	0.059%	0.052%	0.007%	0.055%

Commodity Channel Index Fibonacci Peaks

In constructing an oscillator, the time period used for lookback values is critical. Nirvana has developed the Commodity Channel Index Fibonacci Peaks (CCI-FP) system to combine several time periods into a single oscillator, eliminating the need to optimize for the length of time allowed for lookback.

The theory behind the CCI-FP system is that by averaging an 8-period, 13-period, and 21-period CCI, signal accuracy can be increased. The values 8, 13, and 21 are taken from the Fibonacci number series.

Construction

To calculate the CCI-FP, an 8-period, a 13-period, and a 21-period CCI must first be calculated, using the calculations for the CCI-P system on page 106.

These three CCIs are added together and then divided by 3:

$$CCI\text{-}FP = (CCI_8 + CCI_{13} + CCI_{21})/3$$

A bullish long signal is triggered whenever this composite oscillator peaks above +100. A bearish short signal is triggered whenever this composite oscillator hits a trough below −100.

Results

The CCI-FP system is a more sophisticated version of the CCI-P system discussed on pages 106–107, but the added complications do not seem to be associated with better system performance. Table 4.3a shows an overall hit rate of 60.5 percent for the CCI-FP system, which is about the same as the overall hit rate for the CCI-P system presented in Table 4.1a.

The rate of calls is similar in the two systems. The CCI-P system makes long calls 41.6 percent of the time (Table 4.3a) and short calls 50.4 percent of the time (Table 4.3b). With a hit rate of 61.6 percent for long calls and 60.3 percent for short calls, the CCI-FP system is slightly more accurate at making long calls.

Table 4.4 shows that trading long or short with the more sophisticated CCI-FP system still does not beat a buy-and-hold strategy on a consistent basis. An investor trading long with the system will have an average profitability of only 97.9 percent, compared to an investor who simply buys and holds stocks. An investor who trades short with the system will fare even worse. This investor will have a terminal wealth of only 94.7 percent of the buy-and-hold profitability. Even worse, in 35 of the 48 test quarters, the CCI-FP investor will be destroying wealth since the investor will end a quarter with wealth less than the initial $10,000 invested.

Like the CCI-P system, the CCI-FP system tends to make perverse short calls. Investors should go long when either of these systems makes a short call.

Unfortunately, the sophistication the CCI-FP system adds to the trading indicator does not resolve this major shortcoming.

Chaikin Level Peaks

Developed by Marc Chaikin, the Chaikin Level Peaks (CHA-P) indicator is an oscillator based on the accumulation/distribution (AD) work pioneered by Joseph Granville and furthered by Larry Williams. The indicator rises when prices advance on higher volume and goes negative on price declines on high volume. Thus, a reversal in the indicator indicates that the current trend in accumulation or distribution could be reversing.

This indicator is based on two premises. The first premise is that accumulation occurs on days when a stock closes above its midpoint for the day. The midpoint of the day is defined as the mean average of the day's high and low. The nearer a stock's closing price is to its daily high, the more accumulation has occurred. Conversely, distribution occurs on days when a stock closes below its midpoint for the day. The nearer a stock's closing price is to its daily low, the more distribution has occurred.

The second premise is that volume is the fuel that powers rallies. Therefore, a healthy advance must be accompanied by rising volume and strong volume accumulation.

Construction

The Chaikin Oscillator is constructed by subtracting a ten-period exponential moving average of the accumulation/distribution (AD) line from the three-period exponential moving average of the same.

If

n = number of periods used in the accumulation/distribution calculation,

C_i = closing price for Day i,

L_i = low price for Day i,

H_i = high price for Day i,

V_i = volume for Day i,

then

$$ad_i = \{[(C_i - L_i) - (H_i - C_i)]/(H_i - L_i)\}/V_i,$$

$$AD = ad_1 + ad_2 + ad_3 + \ldots ad_n,$$

$$MA_1 = \text{10-period exponential moving average of AD},$$

$$MA_2 = \text{3-period exponential moving average of AD},$$

$$CHA = MA_2 - MA_1.$$

Table 4.3a
Commodity Channel Index Fibonacci Peaks (CCI-FP) Long Hit Analysis
(Average of all stocks)

Qtr	Optimal Long	CCI-FP Long	Long Hits	Cash Hits	Total Hits	Long Right	Long Wrong	Cash Right	Cash Wrong
85:1	32.1%	30.2%	65.7%	68.2%	67.5%	19.8%	10.4%	47.6%	22.2%
85:2	30.2%	38.1%	66.9%	69.7%	68.6%	25.5%	12.6%	43.1%	18.8%
85:3	26.3%	49.3%	62.2%	74.8%	68.6%	30.7%	18.7%	37.9%	12.8%
85:4	36.6%	29.3%	69.2%	62.6%	64.6%	20.3%	9.0%	44.3%	26.4%
86:1	44.2%	28.2%	66.7%	55.5%	58.7%	18.8%	9.4%	39.8%	31.9%
86:2	39.7%	40.1%	62.5%	61.5%	61.9%	25.1%	15.0%	36.8%	23.1%
86:3	37.0%	50.4%	58.1%	62.8%	60.4%	29.3%	21.1%	31.2%	18.4%
86:4	38.5%	43.0%	63.4%	62.0%	62.6%	27.2%	15.7%	35.4%	21.7%
87:1	44.7%	25.4%	67.9%	56.5%	59.4%	17.3%	8.1%	42.1%	32.5%
87:2	40.0%	49.8%	60.8%	61.3%	61.1%	30.3%	19.5%	30.7%	19.4%
87:3	39.5%	41.1%	60.6%	60.8%	60.7%	24.9%	16.2%	35.8%	23.1%
87:4	37.9%	58.1%	56.0%	63.9%	59.3%	32.5%	25.6%	26.8%	15.1%
88:1	41.3%	26.5%	64.7%	59.1%	60.6%	17.1%	9.3%	43.5%	30.1%
88:2	39.3%	45.9%	63.4%	61.1%	62.2%	29.1%	16.8%	33.1%	21.0%
88:3	35.9%	48.4%	62.2%	64.5%	63.4%	30.1%	18.3%	33.3%	18.3%
88:4	36.3%	45.5%	64.0%	63.6%	63.8%	29.1%	16.4%	34.6%	19.8%
89:1	39.0%	36.5%	64.9%	60.9%	62.4%	23.7%	12.8%	38.7%	24.8%
89:2	40.2%	28.6%	65.8%	59.6%	61.3%	18.8%	9.8%	42.6%	28.9%
89:3	39.9%	38.7%	65.6%	60.4%	62.4%	25.4%	13.3%	37.0%	24.3%
89:4	38.3%	51.7%	61.1%	61.2%	61.2%	31.6%	20.1%	29.6%	18.7%
90:1	36.9%	50.0%	60.9%	63.3%	62.1%	30.4%	19.6%	31.7%	18.3%
90:2	39.2%	40.2%	64.1%	60.6%	62.0%	25.8%	14.4%	36.2%	23.5%
90:3	33.5%	63.7%	54.8%	67.1%	59.3%	34.9%	28.8%	24.3%	11.9%
90:4	40.8%	40.1%	63.1%	58.5%	60.4%	25.3%	14.8%	35.1%	24.8%
91:1	44.1%	29.1%	66.7%	56.6%	59.5%	19.4%	9.7%	40.1%	30.8%
91:2	39.7%	40.3%	62.0%	61.6%	61.7%	25.0%	15.3%	36.7%	23.0%
91:3	40.4%	44.5%	61.1%	60.2%	60.6%	27.2%	17.3%	33.4%	22.1%
91:4	41.2%	45.4%	59.4%	58.6%	59.0%	26.9%	18.4%	32.0%	22.6%
92:1	40.0%	36.8%	55.5%	58.8%	57.6%	20.4%	16.4%	37.2%	26.0%
92:2	38.6%	49.1%	57.1%	61.4%	59.3%	28.0%	21.1%	31.2%	19.7%
92:3	40.3%	41.8%	60.7%	59.7%	60.1%	25.3%	16.4%	34.8%	23.5%
92:4	41.9%	36.2%	63.0%	57.8%	59.7%	22.8%	13.4%	36.9%	26.9%
93:1	42.5%	37.0%	61.5%	58.0%	59.3%	22.7%	14.2%	36.6%	26.4%
93:2	42.1%	47.2%	59.4%	57.9%	58.6%	28.0%	19.2%	30.6%	22.2%
93:3	42.5%	38.2%	60.6%	57.4%	58.6%	23.1%	15.1%	35.5%	26.3%
93:4	41.5%	46.8%	58.3%	58.3%	58.3%	27.3%	19.5%	31.0%	22.2%
94:1	40.4%	43.0%	56.5%	59.3%	58.1%	24.3%	18.7%	33.8%	23.2%
94:2	40.6%	54.1%	57.7%	59.8%	58.7%	31.2%	22.9%	27.4%	18.4%
94:3	41.8%	42.4%	60.8%	58.7%	59.6%	25.8%	16.6%	33.8%	23.8%
94:4	39.5%	54.4%	57.3%	60.8%	58.9%	31.2%	23.2%	27.7%	17.9%
95:1	43.1%	34.5%	62.5%	56.8%	58.8%	21.5%	12.9%	37.2%	28.3%
95:2	43.7%	32.6%	61.7%	56.1%	57.9%	20.1%	12.5%	37.8%	29.6%
95:3	43.9%	35.4%	61.5%	55.4%	57.6%	21.8%	13.6%	35.8%	28.8%
95:4	43.4%	41.9%	58.9%	55.3%	56.8%	24.7%	17.2%	32.1%	25.9%
96:1	45.5%	41.7%	61.5%	54.6%	57.5%	25.7%	16.1%	31.8%	26.5%
96:2	42.1%	43.1%	57.7%	57.6%	57.7%	24.9%	18.2%	32.8%	24.1%
96:3	42.6%	44.5%	59.0%	56.8%	57.8%	26.3%	18.3%	31.5%	23.9%
96:4	44.3%	36.7%	60.2%	55.2%	57.0%	22.1%	14.6%	34.9%	28.4%
AVG	40.0%	41.6%	61.6%	60.3%	60.5%	25.4%	16.2%	35.1%	23.3%

Table 4.3b
Commodity Channel Index Fibonacci Peaks (CCI-FP)
Short Hit Analysis (Average of all stocks)

Qtr	Optimal Short	CCI-FP Short	Short Hits	Cash Hits	Total Hits	Short Right	Short Wrong	Cash Right	Cash Wrong
85:1	34.3%	57.0%	67.7%	65.4%	66.7%	38.6%	18.4%	28.1%	14.9%
85:2	34.6%	52.8%	69.3%	66.5%	67.9%	36.6%	16.2%	31.4%	15.8%
85:3	38.6%	42.2%	74.4%	62.1%	67.3%	31.4%	10.8%	35.9%	21.9%
85:4	33.1%	59.1%	62.4%	67.9%	64.6%	36.8%	22.2%	27.8%	13.1%
86:1	35.2%	60.3%	55.6%	65.6%	59.6%	33.5%	26.8%	26.0%	13.7%
86:2	39.8%	52.6%	61.8%	62.0%	61.9%	32.5%	20.1%	29.4%	18.0%
86:3	42.7%	39.1%	63.3%	58.1%	60.2%	24.8%	14.3%	35.4%	25.5%
86:4	38.7%	50.3%	62.1%	63.0%	62.6%	31.2%	19.0%	31.4%	18.4%
87:1	36.9%	64.1%	56.6%	66.0%	60.0%	36.3%	27.8%	23.7%	12.2%
87:2	40.0%	43.1%	61.4%	60.6%	60.9%	26.5%	16.7%	34.4%	22.4%
87:3	40.4%	50.4%	60.9%	60.1%	60.5%	30.7%	19.7%	29.8%	19.7%
87:4	45.3%	26.6%	64.6%	55.5%	57.9%	17.2%	9.4%	40.8%	32.7%
88:1	36.7%	66.1%	58.7%	63.4%	60.3%	38.8%	27.3%	21.5%	12.4%
88:2	37.4%	48.1%	61.1%	63.2%	62.2%	29.4%	18.7%	32.8%	19.1%
88:3	38.4%	45.4%	64.7%	62.0%	63.2%	29.3%	16.0%	33.9%	20.8%
88:4	37.0%	47.6%	64.0%	63.9%	63.9%	30.4%	17.1%	33.5%	18.9%
89:1	36.2%	56.0%	61.0%	64.1%	62.4%	34.2%	21.8%	28.2%	15.8%
89:2	35.9%	62.5%	59.6%	64.9%	61.6%	37.3%	25.2%	24.3%	13.2%
89:3	36.4%	53.2%	60.6%	64.9%	62.6%	32.2%	21.0%	30.3%	16.4%
89:4	39.0%	40.8%	61.4%	61.0%	61.2%	25.0%	15.7%	36.1%	23.1%
90:1	40.1%	42.4%	63.7%	60.8%	62.0%	27.0%	15.4%	35.0%	22.6%
90:2	37.8%	51.3%	61.0%	63.4%	62.2%	31.3%	20.0%	30.9%	17.8%
90:3	45.7%	26.1%	67.2%	54.6%	57.9%	17.5%	8.5%	40.4%	33.6%
90:4	37.6%	51.8%	58.2%	62.6%	60.3%	30.1%	21.6%	30.2%	18.0%
91:1	36.7%	59.2%	56.7%	65.3%	60.2%	33.6%	25.7%	26.6%	14.1%
91:2	40.4%	53.7%	61.6%	61.4%	61.5%	33.1%	20.6%	28.4%	17.9%
91:3	39.8%	49.2%	60.3%	60.9%	60.6%	29.7%	19.5%	30.9%	19.9%
91:4	40.5%	46.3%	58.7%	59.5%	59.1%	27.2%	19.1%	31.9%	21.8%
92:1	43.2%	54.6%	59.1%	55.8%	57.6%	32.3%	22.4%	25.3%	20.1%
92:2	42.9%	45.1%	61.6%	57.2%	59.2%	27.8%	17.3%	31.4%	23.5%
92:3	39.5%	51.6%	59.8%	60.9%	60.3%	30.9%	20.7%	29.4%	18.9%
92:4	37.5%	55.3%	57.6%	62.5%	59.8%	31.9%	23.4%	27.9%	16.7%
93:1	39.4%	55.4%	58.1%	61.1%	59.4%	32.2%	23.2%	27.2%	17.4%
93:2	40.9%	46.2%	58.0%	59.4%	58.7%	26.8%	19.4%	31.9%	21.8%
93:3	39.4%	54.2%	57.3%	60.4%	58.7%	31.1%	23.2%	27.7%	18.1%
93:4	41.7%	47.0%	58.4%	58.1%	58.2%	27.4%	19.6%	30.8%	22.2%
94:1	43.7%	50.9%	59.4%	56.4%	58.0%	30.2%	20.6%	27.7%	21.4%
94:2	42.7%	39.9%	60.1%	57.6%	58.6%	24.0%	15.9%	34.6%	25.5%
94:3	39.8%	51.2%	58.6%	60.5%	59.5%	30.0%	21.2%	29.5%	19.3%
94:4	42.8%	39.2%	61.0%	57.3%	58.7%	23.9%	15.3%	34.8%	25.9%
95:1	38.7%	59.7%	56.6%	61.8%	58.7%	33.8%	25.9%	24.9%	15.4%
95:2	38.9%	60.2%	56.1%	61.2%	58.2%	33.8%	26.4%	24.4%	15.4%
95:3	38.9%	56.9%	55.4%	61.1%	57.8%	31.5%	25.4%	26.3%	16.8%
95:4	40.5%	48.4%	55.3%	58.8%	57.1%	26.7%	21.6%	30.4%	21.3%
96:1	38.9%	51.6%	54.4%	61.2%	57.7%	28.1%	23.5%	29.6%	18.8%
96:2	42.4%	51.5%	57.6%	57.6%	57.6%	29.6%	21.9%	28.0%	20.5%
96:3	40.8%	47.6%	56.8%	58.7%	57.8%	27.1%	20.6%	30.7%	21.6%
96:4	39.8%	54.7%	54.7%	59.6%	56.9%	29.9%	24.8%	27.0%	18.3%
AVG	39.4%	50.4%	60.3%	61.2%	60.4%	30.2%	20.2%	30.2%	19.4%

Table 4.4a
Commodity Channel Index Fibonacci Peaks (CCI-FP)
Long Return Analysis (Average of all stocks)

Qtr	CCI-FP Terminal Wealth	Buy/Hold Terminal Wealth	Relative Terminal Wealth	CCI-FP Long Avg Ret	CCI-FP Cash Avg Ret	CCI-FP Long-Cash Avg Ret	Buy/Hold Avg Ret
85:1	9999	10142	0.986	-0.009%	0.013%	-0.022%	0.006%
85:2	9909	9700	1.022	-0.057%	-0.077%	0.020%	-0.069%
85:3	9493	8889	1.068	-0.178%	-0.231%	0.053%	-0.205%
85:4	10227	10763	0.950	0.113%	0.104%	0.009%	0.107%
86:1	10453	11428	0.915	0.263%	0.210%	0.053%	0.225%
86:2	10401	10414	0.999	0.162%	0.003%	0.159%	0.066%
86:3	9676	9175	1.055	-0.095%	-0.161%	0.066%	-0.128%
86:4	10292	10413	0.988	0.107%	0.041%	0.066%	0.069%
87:1	10791	11929	0.905	0.492%	0.225%	0.267%	0.293%
87:2	10244	10196	1.005	0.083%	-0.007%	0.090%	0.038%
87:3	10256	10408	0.985	0.102%	0.045%	0.057%	0.068%
87:4	9239	8087	1.142	-0.182%	-0.411%	0.228%	-0.278%
88:1	10425	10989	0.949	0.260%	0.128%	0.133%	0.163%
88:2	10378	10593	0.980	0.136%	0.069%	0.067%	0.100%
88:3	10071	10050	1.002	0.028%	-0.001%	0.029%	0.013%
88:4	10128	10196	0.993	0.048%	0.027%	0.021%	0.037%
89:1	10249	10698	0.958	0.113%	0.112%	0.001%	0.112%
89:2	10248	10772	0.951	0.139%	0.115%	0.024%	0.122%
89:3	10383	10833	0.958	0.160%	0.113%	0.047%	0.131%
89:4	9997	9904	1.009	0.002%	-0.025%	0.027%	-0.011%
90:1	10048	9980	1.007	0.021%	-0.016%	0.037%	0.003%
90:2	10231	10459	0.978	0.097%	0.063%	0.034%	0.077%
90:3	9072	8526	1.064	-0.252%	-0.271%	0.019%	-0.259%
90:4	10411	10889	0.956	0.170%	0.130%	0.040%	0.146%
91:1	11220	12477	0.899	0.428%	0.269%	0.159%	0.315%
91:2	10274	10244	1.003	0.110%	0.001%	0.109%	0.045%
91:3	10279	10429	0.986	0.099%	0.038%	0.061%	0.065%
91:4	10283	10497	0.980	0.104%	0.063%	0.042%	0.082%
92:1	9914	10324	0.960	-0.041%	0.100%	-0.141%	0.048%
92:2	9825	9723	1.010	-0.060%	-0.037%	-0.022%	-0.048%
92:3	10203	10392	0.982	0.072%	0.045%	0.027%	0.057%
92:4	10314	10963	0.941	0.137%	0.149%	-0.012%	0.144%
93:1	10275	10527	0.976	0.117%	0.058%	0.060%	0.080%
93:2	10164	10340	0.983	0.058%	0.046%	0.012%	0.052%
93:3	10249	10686	0.959	0.101%	0.101%	0.001%	0.101%
93:4	10093	10255	0.984	0.029%	0.038%	-0.009%	0.034%
94:1	9981	9954	1.003	-0.010%	-0.012%	0.002%	-0.011%
94:2	10025	9994	1.003	0.004%	-0.015%	0.018%	-0.005%
94:3	10292	10613	0.970	0.105%	0.078%	0.027%	0.089%
94:4	9917	9836	1.008	-0.025%	-0.034%	0.010%	-0.029%
95:1	10308	10706	0.963	0.143%	0.093%	0.050%	0.110%
95:2	10275	10873	0.945	0.133%	0.134%	-0.001%	0.134%
95:3	10296	10853	0.949	0.133%	0.130%	0.003%	0.131%
95:4	10105	10445	0.967	0.039%	0.087%	-0.048%	0.067%
96:1	10483	11027	0.951	0.185%	0.140%	0.045%	0.159%
96:2	10133	10367	0.977	0.050%	0.065%	-0.015%	0.059%
96:3	10070	10298	0.978	0.026%	0.065%	-0.039%	0.047%
96:4	10247	10817	0.947	0.104%	0.133%	-0.029%	0.122%
AVG	10163	10377	0.979	0.059%	0.053%	0.006%	0.055%

Table 4.4b
Commodity Channel Index Fibonacci Peaks (CCI-FP)
Short Return Analysis (Average of all stocks)

Qtr	CCI-FP Terminal Wealth	Buy/Hold Terminal Wealth	Relative Terminal Wealth	CCI-FP Short Avg Ret	CCI-FP Cash Avg Ret	CCI-FP Short-Cash Avg Ret	Buy/Hold Avg Ret
85:1	9948	10142	0.981	0.025%	-0.018%	0.043%	0.006%
85:2	10270	9700	1.059	-0.072%	-0.067%	-0.005%	-0.069%
85:3	10647	8889	1.198	-0.227%	-0.189%	-0.039%	-0.205%
85:4	9613	10763	0.893	0.110%	0.102%	0.008%	0.107%
86:1	9240	11428	0.809	0.219%	0.234%	-0.015%	0.225%
86:2	10041	10414	0.964	-0.008%	0.149%	-0.158%	0.066%
86:3	10482	9175	1.142	-0.191%	-0.087%	-0.104%	-0.128%
86:4	9891	10413	0.950	0.031%	0.108%	-0.078%	0.069%
87:1	9144	11929	0.767	0.227%	0.410%	-0.183%	0.293%
87:2	10028	10196	0.983	-0.011%	0.075%	-0.086%	0.038%
87:3	9842	10408	0.946	0.047%	0.090%	-0.043%	0.068%
87:4	10717	8087	1.325	-0.424%	-0.225%	-0.199%	-0.278%
88:1	9387	10989	0.854	0.146%	0.196%	-0.051%	0.163%
88:2	9791	10593	0.924	0.067%	0.130%	-0.062%	0.100%
88:3	9999	10050	0.995	-0.003%	0.025%	-0.028%	0.013%
88:4	9943	10196	0.975	0.016%	0.055%	-0.039%	0.037%
89:1	9598	10698	0.897	0.119%	0.103%	0.016%	0.112%
89:2	9540	10772	0.886	0.118%	0.129%	-0.012%	0.122%
89:3	9628	10833	0.889	0.115%	0.150%	-0.035%	0.131%
89:4	10078	9904	1.018	-0.033%	0.004%	-0.038%	-0.011%
90:1	10063	9980	1.008	-0.027%	0.024%	-0.051%	0.003%
90:2	9803	10459	0.937	0.062%	0.093%	-0.031%	0.077%
90:3	10440	8526	1.224	-0.269%	-0.255%	-0.013%	-0.259%
90:4	9503	10889	0.873	0.154%	0.138%	0.015%	0.146%
91:1	9065	12477	0.727	0.274%	0.374%	-0.100%	0.315%
91:2	9971	10244	0.973	0.005%	0.093%	-0.088%	0.045%
91:3	9907	10429	0.950	0.033%	0.095%	-0.062%	0.065%
91:4	9845	10497	0.938	0.053%	0.107%	-0.054%	0.082%
92:1	9695	10324	0.939	0.094%	-0.007%	0.101%	0.048%
92:2	10146	9723	1.043	-0.048%	-0.048%	0.000%	-0.048%
92:3	9870	10392	0.950	0.042%	0.072%	-0.030%	0.057%
92:4	9476	10963	0.864	0.158%	0.127%	0.031%	0.144%
93:1	9832	10527	0.934	0.054%	0.112%	-0.058%	0.080%
93:2	9900	10340	0.957	0.040%	0.062%	-0.022%	0.052%
93:3	9669	10686	0.905	0.103%	0.098%	0.005%	0.101%
93:4	9893	10255	0.965	0.040%	0.029%	0.011%	0.034%
94:1	10048	9954	1.009	-0.013%	-0.009%	-0.004%	-0.011%
94:2	10069	9994	1.007	-0.025%	0.009%	-0.034%	-0.005%
94:3	9739	10613	0.918	0.086%	0.092%	-0.006%	0.089%
94:4	10096	9836	1.026	-0.037%	-0.024%	-0.013%	-0.029%
95:1	9640	10706	0.900	0.100%	0.124%	-0.024%	0.110%
95:2	9503	10873	0.874	0.138%	0.128%	0.010%	0.134%
95:3	9548	10853	0.880	0.132%	0.129%	0.003%	0.131%
95:4	9733	10445	0.932	0.093%	0.042%	0.051%	0.067%
96:1	9545	11027	0.866	0.147%	0.172%	-0.024%	0.159%
96:2	9794	10367	0.945	0.066%	0.051%	0.015%	0.059%
96:3	9785	10298	0.950	0.074%	0.023%	0.050%	0.047%
96:4	9513	10817	0.879	0.147%	0.093%	0.054%	0.122%
AVG	9832	10377	0.947	0.057%	0.053%	0.003%	0.055%

A level must be chosen which the oscillator must cross for a signal to be generated. The default level that we use in testing this indicator is 2000. If the Chaikin Oscillator crosses from below and forms a peak, a long signal is generated. A short signal is generated when the oscillator falls below the chosen level and forms a trough.

Results

The results for our test of the Chaikin Level Peaks (CHA-P) system are shown in Tables 4.5 and 4.6. When choosing between a long position or a cash position, the system recommends a long position 27.6 percent of the time (Table 4.5a). Long calls and short calls are correct about 60.2 percent of the time. The system makes short calls much more frequently, at a rate of 41.5 percent, and the hit rate for these short calls is 58.5 percent (Table 4.5b).

Because Table 4.5 shows an overall hit rate of about 60.2 percent for the CHA-P system, it might be tempting to conclude that, on average, trading with this system would be good. However, the return information in Table 4.6a suggests otherwise. The average stock return on days when long calls are made is only 0.046 percent. This is 0.013 percentage point below the average stock return on days when the indicator favors cash over long positions. On average, this system chooses days of above-average price appreciation to be in a cash position! These are the very days an investor does not want to be out of the market.

In Table 4.6b, look at the average stock return on days when the CHA-P system makes short calls. It is 0.067 percent, which is significantly above the average daily stock return. In all but nine of the test quarters, trading short with this system led to losses. A prudent investor would want to trade long when this system advises a short position. In fact, the system's short calls are better at predicting above-average market returns than the system's long calls are!

Commodity Channel Index +100/−100 Crossover

The Commodity Channel Index +100/−100 Crossover (CCI-C) uses the CCI index developed by Donald Lambert and used for the Commodity Channel Index Peaks (CCI-P) system. The only difference is in how a signal is generated. With the CCI-C system, trading signals are generated when the index moves through the trigger lines of +100 or −100. For example, if the index moves above +100 and then turns back down, a short signal is generated as the index crosses back down below +100. Likewise, if the index falls below −100 and then begins to rise, a long signal is generated as the index crosses back over the −100 trigger line. With the CCI-P system, trading signals occur whenever peaks are formed above the +100 trigger line or below the –100 trigger line.

Thus, using this index, the CCI-C system generates fewer and later trades than does the CCI-P system. Also, the CCI-C system has less potential for whipsaws.

Construction

Because the Commodity Channel Index used for this indicator is exactly the same as described for the Commodity Channel Index Peak system, we will not repeat the steps for its construction here. Refer to page 106 for its construction.

Results

The results for this indicator are shown in Tables 4.7 and 4.8. As expected, the CCI-C system generates fewer trades than the related CCI-P system. The CCI-C system generates long calls 22.4 percent of the time (Table 4.7a) and short calls 27.2 percent of the time (Table 4.8a). This compares to long and short calls of 40.6 percent and 50.2 percent, respectively, for the CCI-P system. Let's see whether these less frequent signals, which have less potential for whipsaws, increase trading profitability.

The hit rate for long calls is 61.3 percent (Table 4.7a), and the hit rate for short calls is 60.1 percent (Table 4.7b). Both of these numbers are slightly below the hit rates for the CCI-P system. Thus, the CCI-C system fails to outperform the CCI-P system in terms of having a higher hit rate.

However, at 0.061 percent (Table 4.8a), the average daily return for the long calls is slightly higher for the CCI-C system. This means that the CCI-C system's long calls are superior to the CCI-P system's long calls in choosing periods of high stock price appreciation. However, remember that this advantage is not without drawbacks. Investors trading long with this system earn above-average returns when they are in the market. They are in the market on the best of the best days; however, they are in the market only 22.4 percent of the time (Table 4.7a). They are often missing positive returns by being in a conservative cash position.

The short return analysis does not lead to promising conclusions. Again, as with the CCI-P system, we find a technical indicator that gives perverse short signals. The system suggests short positions on days of above-average market returns—the very days when investors want to be in a long position to capture these above-normal returns. Being in a short position, as the CCI-C system suggests, led to losses in 75 percent of our test quarters.

In conclusion, the strongest point of the CCI-C system is its ability to predict days of above-average market returns. This can be useful information

Table 4.5a
Chaikin Level Peaks (CHA-P) Long Hit Analysis
(Average of all stocks)

Qtr	Optimal Long	CHA-P Long	Long Hits	Cash Hits	Total Hits	Long Right	Long Wrong	Cash Right	Cash Wrong
85:1	32.1%	31.5%	66.3%	64.9%	65.4%	20.9%	10.6%	44.5%	24.0%
85:2	30.2%	33.1%	66.4%	66.6%	66.5%	22.0%	11.1%	44.5%	22.4%
85:3	26.3%	35.0%	61.5%	69.3%	66.6%	21.5%	13.5%	45.1%	20.0%
85:4	36.6%	32.6%	68.0%	60.2%	62.8%	22.1%	10.4%	40.6%	26.8%
86:1	44.2%	25.2%	65.1%	55.5%	57.9%	16.4%	8.8%	41.5%	33.3%
86:2	39.7%	24.5%	60.1%	60.8%	60.6%	14.7%	9.8%	45.9%	29.6%
86:3	37.0%	25.5%	56.5%	63.6%	61.8%	14.4%	11.1%	47.4%	27.1%
86:4	38.5%	23.6%	61.3%	62.2%	62.0%	14.4%	9.1%	47.6%	28.9%
87:1	44.7%	20.0%	63.4%	55.6%	57.2%	12.7%	7.3%	44.5%	35.5%
87:2	40.0%	27.7%	59.5%	61.0%	60.6%	16.5%	11.2%	44.1%	28.2%
87:3	39.5%	24.1%	58.9%	61.1%	60.5%	14.2%	9.9%	46.4%	29.6%
87:4	37.9%	34.2%	54.5%	63.3%	60.3%	18.7%	15.5%	41.6%	24.2%
88:1	41.3%	25.7%	63.4%	59.1%	60.2%	16.3%	9.4%	43.9%	30.4%
88:2	39.3%	31.7%	61.5%	61.8%	61.7%	19.5%	12.2%	42.2%	26.1%
88:3	35.9%	30.1%	60.1%	64.9%	63.5%	18.1%	12.0%	45.4%	24.5%
88:4	36.3%	27.9%	62.0%	64.4%	63.7%	17.3%	10.6%	46.4%	25.7%
89:1	39.0%	29.1%	62.3%	61.4%	61.7%	18.1%	10.9%	43.5%	27.4%
89:2	40.2%	25.5%	64.2%	60.2%	61.2%	16.4%	9.1%	44.8%	29.6%
89:3	39.9%	24.5%	64.0%	60.5%	61.4%	15.7%	8.8%	45.7%	29.8%
89:4	38.3%	25.0%	61.0%	62.2%	61.9%	15.2%	9.7%	46.7%	28.4%
90:1	36.9%	25.8%	58.8%	63.6%	62.4%	15.2%	10.6%	47.2%	27.0%
90:2	39.2%	25.2%	62.1%	61.5%	61.6%	15.6%	9.6%	46.0%	28.8%
90:3	33.5%	27.5%	53.1%	67.0%	63.2%	14.6%	12.9%	48.6%	23.9%
90:4	40.8%	23.7%	61.7%	60.0%	60.4%	14.6%	9.1%	45.8%	30.5%
91:1	44.1%	20.6%	63.2%	56.4%	57.8%	13.0%	7.6%	44.8%	34.6%
91:2	39.7%	25.0%	58.6%	61.2%	60.5%	14.7%	10.4%	45.9%	29.1%
91:3	40.4%	24.9%	59.6%	60.0%	59.9%	14.8%	10.1%	45.1%	30.1%
91:4	41.2%	25.1%	58.9%	59.2%	59.1%	14.8%	10.3%	44.3%	30.6%
92:1	40.0%	25.2%	54.9%	59.9%	58.7%	13.8%	11.3%	44.9%	30.0%
92:2	38.6%	29.0%	55.8%	62.0%	60.2%	16.2%	12.8%	44.0%	27.0%
92:3	40.3%	26.2%	58.7%	59.7%	59.5%	15.4%	10.8%	44.1%	29.7%
92:4	41.9%	21.9%	62.2%	58.3%	59.2%	13.6%	8.3%	45.6%	32.6%
93:1	42.5%	25.2%	60.0%	57.7%	58.3%	15.1%	10.1%	43.2%	31.7%
93:2	42.1%	29.0%	58.0%	58.3%	58.2%	16.8%	12.2%	41.4%	29.6%
93:3	42.5%	30.1%	60.0%	57.8%	58.5%	18.0%	12.1%	40.4%	29.5%
93:4	41.5%	31.8%	57.4%	58.7%	58.3%	18.3%	13.5%	40.0%	28.2%
94:1	40.4%	30.8%	55.9%	59.7%	58.5%	17.2%	13.6%	41.3%	27.9%
94:2	40.6%	32.4%	57.6%	59.9%	59.2%	18.7%	13.7%	40.5%	27.1%
94:3	41.8%	33.1%	59.2%	58.2%	58.6%	19.6%	13.5%	38.9%	27.9%
94:4	39.5%	37.2%	56.0%	60.9%	59.1%	20.8%	16.4%	38.2%	24.6%
95:1	43.1%	27.5%	60.9%	56.9%	58.0%	16.7%	10.8%	41.3%	31.3%
95:2	43.7%	25.8%	60.9%	56.3%	57.5%	15.7%	10.1%	41.7%	32.4%
95:3	43.9%	24.8%	61.1%	56.1%	57.3%	15.2%	9.7%	42.2%	33.0%
95:4	43.4%	26.4%	58.7%	56.6%	57.1%	15.5%	10.9%	41.6%	32.0%
96:1	45.5%	26.2%	60.0%	54.3%	55.8%	15.7%	10.5%	40.1%	33.7%
96:2	42.1%	29.1%	57.0%	57.8%	57.6%	16.6%	12.5%	41.0%	29.9%
96:3	42.6%	29.8%	58.9%	57.3%	57.8%	17.6%	12.3%	40.2%	30.0%
96:4	44.3%	31.1%	59.9%	55.6%	56.9%	18.6%	12.5%	38.3%	30.6%
AVG	40.0%	27.6%	60.2%	60.2%	60.1%	16.6%	11.0%	43.5%	28.8%

Table 4.5b
Chaikin Level Peaks (CHA-P) Short Hit Analysis
(Average of all stocks)

Qtr	Optimal Short	CHA-P Short	Short Hits	Cash Hits	Total Hits	Short Right	Short Wrong	Cash Right	Cash Wrong
85:1	34.3%	26.9%	56.8%	67.2%	64.4%	15.3%	11.6%	49.1%	24.0%
85:2	34.6%	27.8%	58.6%	66.9%	64.5%	16.3%	11.5%	48.3%	23.9%
85:3	38.6%	29.2%	62.9%	63.4%	63.3%	18.4%	10.8%	44.9%	25.9%
85:4	33.1%	30.4%	54.4%	68.2%	64.0%	16.6%	13.9%	47.4%	22.1%
86:1	35.2%	35.9%	53.0%	65.5%	61.0%	19.0%	16.9%	42.0%	22.1%
86:2	39.8%	39.6%	59.2%	61.7%	60.7%	23.4%	16.2%	37.3%	23.1%
86:3	42.7%	38.7%	62.0%	59.0%	60.2%	24.0%	14.7%	36.2%	25.1%
86:4	38.7%	46.1%	60.4%	62.8%	61.7%	27.8%	18.3%	33.8%	20.1%
87:1	36.9%	44.7%	54.1%	63.8%	59.4%	24.2%	20.5%	35.3%	20.0%
87:2	40.0%	40.6%	59.5%	61.2%	60.5%	24.1%	16.4%	36.4%	23.0%
87:3	40.4%	41.7%	59.3%	60.1%	59.8%	24.7%	17.0%	35.0%	23.2%
87:4	45.3%	33.5%	61.7%	55.5%	57.6%	20.7%	12.9%	36.9%	29.6%
88:1	36.7%	46.0%	56.6%	65.2%	61.2%	26.0%	19.9%	35.2%	18.8%
88:2	37.4%	40.7%	60.0%	63.5%	62.1%	24.4%	16.3%	37.6%	21.7%
88:3	38.4%	42.2%	63.1%	62.5%	62.8%	26.6%	15.6%	36.2%	21.7%
88:4	37.0%	44.5%	62.7%	63.9%	63.4%	27.9%	16.6%	35.5%	20.0%
89:1	36.2%	45.1%	59.7%	64.5%	62.3%	26.9%	18.2%	35.4%	19.5%
89:2	35.9%	45.3%	58.8%	65.1%	62.3%	26.7%	18.7%	35.6%	19.1%
89:3	36.4%	42.8%	59.0%	64.5%	62.1%	25.2%	17.5%	36.9%	20.3%
89:4	39.0%	42.9%	60.1%	62.4%	61.4%	25.8%	17.1%	35.6%	21.5%
90:1	40.1%	42.8%	61.4%	61.1%	61.3%	26.3%	16.5%	35.0%	22.2%
90:2	37.8%	42.8%	59.5%	63.5%	61.8%	25.4%	17.3%	36.3%	20.9%
90:3	45.7%	38.9%	65.5%	55.4%	59.3%	25.5%	13.4%	33.8%	27.3%
90:4	37.6%	41.6%	57.9%	63.5%	61.1%	24.1%	17.5%	37.1%	21.3%
91:1	36.7%	43.2%	54.5%	64.2%	60.0%	23.6%	19.7%	36.4%	20.3%
91:2	40.4%	42.7%	59.8%	60.9%	60.5%	25.5%	17.1%	34.9%	22.4%
91:3	39.8%	43.9%	58.8%	61.0%	60.1%	25.8%	18.1%	34.2%	21.9%
91:4	40.5%	43.7%	58.0%	60.0%	59.1%	25.3%	18.4%	33.8%	22.5%
92:1	43.2%	41.5%	59.2%	57.1%	58.0%	24.6%	16.9%	33.4%	25.1%
92:2	42.9%	41.8%	60.9%	57.4%	58.9%	25.4%	16.3%	33.5%	24.8%
92:3	39.5%	45.5%	58.7%	60.6%	59.8%	26.7%	18.8%	33.0%	21.5%
92:4	37.5%	48.2%	57.3%	62.9%	60.2%	27.7%	20.6%	32.5%	19.2%
93:1	39.4%	45.1%	57.4%	61.5%	59.6%	25.9%	19.2%	33.8%	21.1%
93:2	40.9%	42.5%	57.4%	59.4%	58.6%	24.4%	18.1%	34.2%	23.3%
93:3	39.4%	42.5%	57.5%	61.3%	59.7%	24.4%	18.0%	35.3%	22.3%
93:4	41.7%	41.0%	58.2%	58.5%	58.4%	23.9%	17.1%	34.5%	24.5%
94:1	43.7%	42.5%	59.8%	56.6%	58.0%	25.4%	17.1%	32.6%	24.9%
94:2	42.7%	43.2%	59.3%	57.9%	58.5%	25.6%	17.6%	32.9%	23.9%
94:3	39.8%	41.3%	57.6%	60.4%	59.2%	23.8%	17.5%	35.4%	23.3%
94:4	42.8%	36.4%	60.6%	57.4%	58.5%	22.0%	14.4%	36.5%	27.1%
95:1	38.7%	45.5%	55.7%	61.4%	58.8%	25.4%	20.2%	33.4%	21.0%
95:2	38.9%	45.3%	55.4%	61.7%	58.9%	25.1%	20.2%	33.8%	21.0%
95:3	38.9%	46.3%	55.8%	61.8%	59.0%	25.8%	20.5%	33.2%	20.5%
95:4	40.5%	43.0%	55.3%	59.5%	57.7%	23.8%	19.2%	33.9%	23.1%
96:1	38.9%	45.0%	53.2%	60.8%	57.4%	24.0%	21.1%	33.4%	21.5%
96:2	42.4%	45.7%	57.6%	58.2%	58.0%	26.3%	19.4%	31.6%	22.7%
96:3	40.8%	46.1%	56.2%	59.1%	57.8%	25.9%	20.2%	31.9%	22.0%
96:4	39.8%	41.8%	55.7%	60.8%	58.7%	23.3%	18.5%	35.4%	22.8%
AVG	39.4%	41.5%	58.5%	61.5%	60.2%	24.3%	17.3%	36.0%	22.5%

Table 4.6a
Chaikin Level Peaks (CHA-P) Long Return Analysis
(Average of all stocks)

Qtr	CHA-P Terminal Wealth	Buy/Hold Terminal Wealth	Relative Terminal Wealth	CHA-P Long Avg Ret	CHA-P Cash Avg Ret	CHA-P Long-Cash Avg Ret	Buy/Hold Avg Ret
85:1	9844	10142	0.971	-0.102%	0.056%	-0.159%	0.006%
85:2	9746	9700	1.005	-0.151%	-0.029%	-0.122%	-0.069%
85:3	9383	8889	1.056	-0.331%	-0.137%	-0.193%	-0.205%
85:4	10071	10763	0.936	0.025%	0.146%	-0.121%	0.107%
86:1	10338	11428	0.905	0.219%	0.227%	-0.008%	0.225%
86:2	10142	10414	0.974	0.090%	0.059%	0.031%	0.066%
86:3	9825	9175	1.071	-0.109%	-0.134%	0.025%	-0.128%
86:4	10185	10413	0.978	0.126%	0.052%	0.074%	0.069%
87:1	10394	11929	0.871	0.312%	0.288%	0.024%	0.293%
87:2	10110	10196	0.992	0.067%	0.027%	0.040%	0.038%
87:3	10164	10408	0.977	0.107%	0.056%	0.050%	0.068%
87:4	9625	8087	1.190	-0.159%	-0.340%	0.180%	-0.278%
88:1	10262	10989	0.934	0.168%	0.161%	0.008%	0.163%
88:2	10231	10593	0.966	0.120%	0.090%	0.030%	0.100%
88:3	10027	10050	0.998	0.016%	0.011%	0.005%	0.013%
88:4	10052	10196	0.986	0.034%	0.038%	-0.004%	0.037%
89:1	10174	10698	0.951	0.099%	0.118%	-0.019%	0.112%
89:2	10218	10772	0.949	0.135%	0.118%	0.017%	0.122%
89:3	10221	10833	0.943	0.144%	0.127%	0.017%	0.131%
89:4	10001	9904	1.010	0.003%	-0.016%	0.018%	-0.011%
90:1	10012	9980	1.003	0.012%	0.000%	0.012%	0.003%
90:2	10171	10459	0.973	0.111%	0.065%	0.046%	0.077%
90:3	9566	8526	1.122	-0.270%	-0.255%	-0.015%	-0.259%
90:4	10267	10889	0.943	0.180%	0.136%	0.044%	0.146%
91:1	10489	12477	0.841	0.374%	0.300%	0.074%	0.315%
91:2	10135	10244	0.989	0.090%	0.030%	0.060%	0.045%
91:3	10117	10429	0.970	0.073%	0.062%	0.011%	0.065%
91:4	10202	10497	0.972	0.128%	0.066%	0.062%	0.082%
92:1	10012	10324	0.970	0.005%	0.062%	-0.058%	0.048%
92:2	9939	9723	1.022	-0.033%	-0.055%	0.022%	-0.048%
92:3	10046	10392	0.967	0.029%	0.066%	-0.037%	0.057%
92:4	10200	10963	0.930	0.141%	0.146%	-0.005%	0.144%
93:1	10121	10527	0.961	0.079%	0.080%	-0.001%	0.080%
93:2	10099	10340	0.977	0.053%	0.051%	0.002%	0.052%
93:3	10218	10686	0.956	0.111%	0.097%	0.015%	0.101%
93:4	10045	10255	0.980	0.018%	0.041%	-0.023%	0.034%
94:1	9998	9954	1.004	-0.007%	-0.013%	0.006%	-0.011%
94:2	10057	9994	1.006	0.027%	-0.020%	0.047%	-0.005%
94:3	10141	10613	0.956	0.064%	0.102%	-0.038%	0.089%
94:4	9910	9836	1.008	-0.041%	-0.022%	-0.019%	-0.029%
95:1	10216	10706	0.954	0.126%	0.104%	0.022%	0.110%
95:2	10203	10873	0.938	0.124%	0.137%	-0.013%	0.134%
95:3	10203	10853	0.940	0.127%	0.132%	-0.006%	0.131%
95:4	10091	10445	0.966	0.051%	0.072%	-0.021%	0.067%
96:1	10244	11027	0.929	0.149%	0.163%	-0.014%	0.159%
96:2	10061	10367	0.971	0.032%	0.070%	-0.038%	0.059%
96:3	10104	10298	0.981	0.054%	0.045%	0.009%	0.047%
96:4	10235	10817	0.946	0.117%	0.125%	-0.008%	0.122%
AVG	10086	10377	0.972	0.046%	0.059%	-0.013%	0.055%

Table 4.6b
Chaikin Level Peaks (CHA-P) Short Return Analysis
(Average of all stocks)

Qtr	CHA-P Terminal Wealth	Buy/Hold Terminal Wealth	Relative Terminal Wealth	CHA-P Short Avg Ret	CHA-P Cash Avg Ret	CHA-P Short-Cash Avg Ret	Buy/Hold Avg Ret
85:1	9748	10142	0.961	0.157%	-0.049%	0.206%	0.006%
85:2	9874	9700	1.018	0.073%	-0.124%	0.197%	-0.069%
85:3	10167	8889	1.144	-0.091%	-0.251%	0.160%	-0.205%
85:4	9581	10763	0.890	0.226%	0.055%	0.171%	0.107%
86:1	9466	11428	0.828	0.258%	0.206%	0.052%	0.225%
86:2	9824	10414	0.943	0.069%	0.064%	0.005%	0.066%
86:3	10382	9175	1.132	-0.158%	-0.108%	-0.050%	-0.128%
86:4	9816	10413	0.943	0.061%	0.076%	-0.016%	0.069%
87:1	9175	11929	0.769	0.321%	0.270%	0.051%	0.293%
87:2	9927	10196	0.974	0.022%	0.049%	-0.027%	0.038%
87:3	9799	10408	0.941	0.073%	0.065%	0.007%	0.068%
87:4	10695	8087	1.323	-0.348%	-0.243%	-0.105%	-0.278%
88:1	9567	10989	0.871	0.148%	0.175%	-0.027%	0.163%
88:2	9787	10593	0.924	0.080%	0.113%	-0.034%	0.100%
88:3	9968	10050	0.992	0.008%	0.016%	-0.007%	0.013%
88:4	9877	10196	0.969	0.041%	0.033%	0.008%	0.037%
89:1	9673	10698	0.904	0.121%	0.105%	0.016%	0.112%
89:2	9656	10772	0.896	0.120%	0.124%	-0.004%	0.122%
89:3	9653	10833	0.891	0.133%	0.129%	0.004%	0.131%
89:4	10050	9904	1.015	-0.022%	-0.002%	-0.020%	-0.011%
90:1	9970	9980	0.999	0.006%	0.000%	0.006%	0.003%
90:2	9811	10459	0.938	0.069%	0.083%	-0.014%	0.077%
90:3	10656	8526	1.250	-0.262%	-0.257%	-0.006%	-0.259%
90:4	9610	10889	0.882	0.149%	0.144%	0.004%	0.146%
91:1	9246	12477	0.741	0.304%	0.323%	-0.019%	0.315%
91:2	9928	10244	0.969	0.021%	0.063%	-0.042%	0.045%
91:3	9876	10429	0.947	0.047%	0.079%	-0.032%	0.065%
91:4	9836	10497	0.937	0.060%	0.098%	-0.038%	0.082%
92:1	9844	10324	0.953	0.063%	0.037%	0.026%	0.048%
92:2	10148	9723	1.044	-0.053%	-0.045%	-0.007%	-0.048%
92:3	9828	10392	0.946	0.065%	0.050%	0.015%	0.057%
92:4	9585	10963	0.874	0.145%	0.144%	0.001%	0.144%
93:1	9835	10527	0.934	0.067%	0.090%	-0.024%	0.080%
93:2	9879	10340	0.955	0.048%	0.055%	-0.007%	0.052%
93:3	9789	10686	0.916	0.085%	0.113%	-0.027%	0.101%
93:4	9903	10255	0.966	0.043%	0.027%	0.016%	0.034%
94:1	10046	9954	1.009	-0.015%	-0.009%	-0.006%	-0.011%
94:2	10059	9994	1.007	-0.017%	0.004%	-0.021%	-0.005%
94:3	9752	10613	0.919	0.102%	0.081%	0.021%	0.089%
94:4	10098	9836	1.027	-0.040%	-0.023%	-0.017%	-0.029%
95:1	9669	10706	0.903	0.120%	0.101%	0.019%	0.110%
95:2	9602	10873	0.883	0.147%	0.124%	0.023%	0.134%
95:3	9641	10853	0.888	0.129%	0.133%	-0.003%	0.131%
95:4	9780	10445	0.936	0.086%	0.052%	0.034%	0.067%
96:1	9471	11027	0.859	0.197%	0.128%	0.069%	0.159%
96:2	9823	10367	0.948	0.063%	0.055%	0.009%	0.059%
96:3	9811	10298	0.953	0.066%	0.031%	0.035%	0.047%
96:4	9714	10817	0.898	0.115%	0.127%	-0.012%	0.122%
AVG	9831	10377	0.947	0.067%	0.047%	0.021%	0.055%

Table 4.7a
Commodity Channel Index Crossover (CCI-C)
Long Hit Analysis (Average of all stocks)

Qtr	Optimal Long	CCI-C Long	Long Hits	Cash Hits	Total Hits	Long Right	Long Wrong	Cash Right	Cash Wrong
85:1	32.1%	16.7%	65.4%	68.1%	67.6%	10.9%	5.8%	56.7%	26.6%
85:2	30.2%	20.3%	67.4%	69.9%	69.4%	13.7%	6.6%	55.7%	24.0%
85:3	26.3%	26.1%	61.0%	73.8%	70.5%	15.9%	10.2%	54.5%	19.3%
85:4	36.6%	15.0%	68.9%	63.1%	64.0%	10.3%	4.7%	53.7%	31.4%
86:1	44.2%	14.8%	65.4%	55.5%	56.9%	9.7%	5.1%	47.2%	37.9%
86:2	39.7%	21.0%	62.1%	60.7%	61.0%	13.1%	8.0%	47.9%	31.0%
86:3	37.0%	28.2%	58.4%	63.0%	61.7%	16.5%	11.7%	45.2%	26.6%
86:4	38.5%	19.9%	63.1%	61.6%	61.9%	12.6%	7.3%	49.3%	30.7%
87:1	44.7%	14.4%	67.3%	56.0%	57.7%	9.7%	4.7%	48.0%	37.6%
87:2	40.0%	27.6%	59.7%	60.3%	60.2%	16.5%	11.1%	43.7%	28.7%
87:3	39.5%	21.9%	59.6%	60.3%	60.2%	13.0%	8.8%	47.1%	31.0%
87:4	37.9%	30.4%	58.0%	63.9%	62.1%	17.6%	12.8%	44.5%	25.1%
88:1	41.3%	13.9%	63.0%	58.7%	59.3%	8.8%	5.1%	50.5%	35.6%
88:2	39.3%	25.3%	63.9%	61.2%	61.9%	16.2%	9.1%	45.7%	29.0%
88:3	35.9%	25.3%	61.6%	64.0%	63.4%	15.6%	9.7%	47.8%	26.9%
88:4	36.3%	24.6%	63.7%	63.6%	63.7%	15.7%	8.9%	48.0%	27.4%
89:1	39.0%	19.6%	64.4%	61.0%	61.7%	12.7%	7.0%	49.1%	31.3%
89:2	40.2%	15.6%	64.9%	59.5%	60.4%	10.1%	5.5%	50.2%	34.1%
89:3	39.9%	20.9%	65.5%	60.3%	61.4%	13.7%	7.2%	47.7%	31.5%
89:4	38.3%	26.2%	59.6%	61.1%	60.7%	15.6%	10.6%	45.0%	28.7%
90:1	36.9%	25.9%	61.2%	63.5%	62.9%	15.8%	10.0%	47.0%	27.1%
90:2	39.2%	21.5%	64.2%	60.8%	61.5%	13.8%	7.7%	47.7%	30.8%
90:3	33.5%	33.8%	54.3%	66.4%	62.3%	18.3%	15.4%	44.0%	22.2%
90:4	40.8%	22.8%	61.7%	58.5%	59.3%	14.1%	8.7%	45.2%	32.0%
91:1	44.1%	16.3%	67.7%	56.5%	58.3%	11.1%	5.3%	47.2%	36.4%
91:2	39.7%	21.6%	61.9%	60.9%	61.1%	13.3%	8.2%	47.8%	30.6%
91:3	40.4%	25.3%	61.5%	60.0%	60.4%	15.5%	9.7%	44.8%	29.9%
91:4	41.2%	24.9%	60.2%	58.9%	59.2%	15.0%	9.9%	44.2%	30.9%
92:1	40.0%	19.2%	55.8%	59.6%	58.8%	10.7%	8.5%	48.1%	32.7%
92:2	38.6%	26.7%	57.2%	61.6%	60.4%	15.3%	11.4%	45.2%	28.1%
92:3	40.3%	21.8%	60.2%	59.7%	59.8%	13.1%	8.7%	46.6%	31.5%
92:4	41.9%	20.2%	62.9%	58.2%	59.1%	12.7%	7.5%	46.4%	33.4%
93:1	42.5%	19.6%	61.9%	57.8%	58.6%	12.1%	7.5%	46.5%	33.9%
93:2	42.1%	25.4%	59.7%	58.0%	58.5%	15.1%	10.2%	43.3%	31.3%
93:3	42.5%	20.5%	60.7%	57.5%	58.2%	12.4%	8.1%	45.7%	33.8%
93:4	41.5%	24.7%	57.0%	58.3%	57.9%	14.1%	10.6%	43.8%	31.4%
94:1	40.4%	22.9%	56.3%	59.4%	58.7%	12.9%	10.0%	45.8%	31.3%
94:2	40.6%	28.2%	57.3%	59.6%	59.0%	16.2%	12.0%	42.8%	29.0%
94:3	41.8%	22.8%	60.5%	58.5%	58.9%	13.8%	9.0%	45.1%	32.1%
94:4	39.5%	30.3%	56.8%	60.3%	59.2%	17.2%	13.1%	42.0%	27.7%
95:1	43.1%	18.5%	62.7%	56.9%	57.9%	11.6%	6.9%	46.4%	35.2%
95:2	43.7%	18.3%	61.0%	56.2%	57.1%	11.1%	7.1%	45.9%	35.8%
95:3	43.9%	18.9%	62.1%	56.0%	57.1%	11.7%	7.2%	45.4%	35.7%
95:4	43.4%	23.6%	58.6%	56.2%	56.8%	13.8%	9.8%	43.0%	33.5%
96:1	45.5%	23.1%	62.2%	54.7%	56.4%	14.4%	8.7%	42.1%	34.8%
96:2	42.1%	23.3%	57.7%	57.9%	57.9%	13.5%	9.9%	44.4%	32.3%
96:3	42.6%	24.1%	57.8%	57.1%	57.3%	14.0%	10.2%	43.3%	32.6%
96:4	44.3%	21.0%	59.8%	55.5%	56.4%	12.6%	8.5%	43.8%	35.1%
AVG	40.0%	22.4%	61.3%	60.2%	60.3%	13.6%	8.7%	46.7%	31.0%

Table 4.7b
Commodity Channel Index Crossover (CCI-C)
Short Hit Analysis (Average of all stocks)

Qtr	Optimal Short	CCI-C Short	Short Hits	Cash Hits	Total Hits	Short Right	Short Wrong	Cash Right	Cash Wrong
85:1	34.3%	30.4%	68.3%	65.8%	66.5%	20.8%	9.6%	45.8%	23.8%
85:2	34.6%	28.2%	69.3%	65.8%	66.8%	19.6%	8.7%	47.3%	24.5%
85:3	38.6%	23.8%	74.0%	61.6%	64.5%	17.6%	6.2%	46.9%	29.3%
85:4	33.1%	33.9%	62.8%	67.4%	65.8%	21.3%	12.6%	44.6%	21.5%
86:1	35.2%	33.8%	55.2%	64.8%	61.6%	18.7%	15.1%	42.9%	23.3%
86:2	39.8%	27.4%	62.4%	61.3%	61.6%	17.1%	10.3%	44.5%	28.1%
86:3	42.7%	22.2%	62.6%	57.5%	58.6%	13.9%	8.3%	44.7%	33.1%
86:4	38.7%	26.3%	62.2%	62.1%	62.2%	16.3%	9.9%	45.8%	27.9%
87:1	36.9%	33.9%	56.5%	64.2%	61.6%	19.1%	14.8%	42.4%	23.7%
87:2	40.0%	23.5%	61.0%	60.2%	60.4%	14.4%	9.2%	46.0%	30.4%
87:3	40.4%	26.1%	59.5%	59.3%	59.4%	15.5%	10.6%	43.9%	30.1%
87:4	45.3%	16.4%	64.7%	55.3%	56.9%	10.6%	5.8%	46.3%	37.3%
88:1	36.7%	33.3%	57.9%	62.9%	61.2%	19.3%	14.0%	41.9%	24.8%
88:2	37.4%	25.6%	60.7%	62.6%	62.1%	15.5%	10.1%	46.6%	27.8%
88:3	38.4%	23.5%	64.1%	61.6%	62.2%	15.1%	8.4%	47.1%	29.4%
88:4	37.0%	25.6%	63.0%	63.2%	63.1%	16.1%	9.5%	47.0%	27.4%
89:1	36.2%	31.4%	61.0%	64.1%	63.1%	19.1%	12.2%	44.0%	24.6%
89:2	35.9%	32.8%	59.2%	64.2%	62.6%	19.4%	13.4%	43.1%	24.1%
89:3	36.4%	29.6%	60.2%	64.3%	63.1%	17.8%	11.8%	45.3%	25.2%
89:4	39.0%	23.3%	61.3%	61.1%	61.1%	14.3%	9.0%	46.8%	29.9%
90:1	40.1%	23.5%	63.9%	60.4%	61.2%	15.0%	8.5%	46.2%	30.3%
90:2	37.8%	26.9%	61.6%	62.9%	62.5%	16.6%	10.3%	45.9%	27.1%
90:3	45.7%	15.4%	65.4%	54.3%	56.0%	10.1%	5.3%	45.9%	38.7%
90:4	37.6%	28.2%	58.8%	62.6%	61.5%	16.6%	11.6%	44.9%	26.8%
91:1	36.7%	30.9%	56.5%	64.0%	61.7%	17.5%	13.5%	44.2%	24.9%
91:2	40.4%	28.4%	61.0%	60.1%	60.4%	17.3%	11.1%	43.0%	28.6%
91:3	39.8%	25.8%	59.8%	60.5%	60.3%	15.4%	10.4%	44.9%	29.3%
91:4	40.5%	25.6%	58.5%	59.5%	59.2%	15.0%	10.6%	44.3%	30.2%
92:1	43.2%	29.5%	57.8%	56.2%	56.7%	17.1%	12.5%	39.6%	30.9%
92:2	42.9%	24.5%	61.8%	57.2%	58.3%	15.2%	9.4%	43.2%	32.3%
92:3	39.5%	28.0%	58.9%	60.2%	59.9%	16.5%	11.5%	43.4%	28.6%
92:4	37.5%	29.1%	57.7%	62.6%	61.2%	16.8%	12.3%	44.4%	26.5%
93:1	39.4%	31.3%	58.2%	61.0%	60.1%	18.2%	13.1%	41.9%	26.8%
93:2	40.9%	25.3%	58.4%	59.4%	59.2%	14.8%	10.5%	44.4%	30.3%
93:3	39.4%	28.9%	57.1%	60.5%	59.5%	16.5%	12.4%	43.0%	28.1%
93:4	41.7%	25.0%	57.8%	58.3%	58.2%	14.5%	10.5%	43.7%	31.3%
94:1	43.7%	28.3%	59.1%	56.3%	57.1%	16.7%	11.6%	40.4%	31.3%
94:2	42.7%	21.7%	60.5%	57.5%	58.2%	13.1%	8.6%	45.1%	33.3%
94:3	39.8%	26.8%	58.3%	60.3%	59.7%	15.6%	11.2%	44.1%	29.1%
94:4	42.8%	20.9%	59.5%	56.9%	57.5%	12.5%	8.5%	45.0%	34.1%
95:1	38.7%	31.3%	56.5%	61.5%	59.9%	17.7%	13.6%	42.2%	26.5%
95:2	38.9%	32.7%	56.5%	61.3%	59.8%	18.5%	14.2%	41.3%	26.0%
95:3	38.9%	31.5%	55.5%	61.3%	59.5%	17.5%	14.0%	42.0%	26.5%
95:4	40.5%	26.1%	55.2%	59.2%	58.2%	14.4%	11.7%	43.7%	30.1%
96:1	38.9%	27.6%	54.1%	61.2%	59.3%	15.0%	12.7%	44.3%	28.0%
96:2	42.4%	27.0%	57.9%	57.8%	57.8%	15.6%	11.4%	42.2%	30.8%
96:3	40.8%	25.2%	56.8%	59.2%	58.6%	14.3%	10.9%	44.3%	30.5%
96:4	39.8%	29.5%	55.4%	60.1%	58.7%	16.3%	13.2%	42.4%	28.1%
AVG	39.4%	27.2%	60.1%	60.9%	60.5%	16.3%	10.9%	44.2%	28.6%

Table 4.8a
Commodity Channel Index Crossover (CCI-C)
Long Return Analysis (Average of all stocks)

Qtr	CCI-C Terminal Wealth	Buy/Hold Terminal Wealth	Relative Terminal Wealth	CCI-C Long Avg Ret	CCI-C Cash Avg Ret	CCI-C Long-Cash Avg Ret	Buy/Hold Avg Ret
85:1	9997	10142	0.986	-0.007%	0.009%	-0.016%	0.006%
85:2	9979	9700	1.029	-0.031%	-0.079%	0.048%	-0.069%
85:3	9678	8889	1.089	-0.205%	-0.205%	0.000%	-0.205%
85:4	10123	10763	0.941	0.127%	0.103%	0.023%	0.107%
86:1	10192	11428	0.892	0.206%	0.228%	-0.021%	0.225%
86:2	10179	10414	0.977	0.136%	0.048%	0.088%	0.066%
86:3	9866	9175	1.075	-0.069%	-0.151%	0.082%	-0.128%
86:4	10149	10413	0.975	0.122%	0.056%	0.066%	0.069%
87:1	10440	11929	0.875	0.486%	0.260%	0.225%	0.293%
87:2	10093	10196	0.990	0.058%	0.030%	0.028%	0.038%
87:3	10094	10408	0.970	0.071%	0.067%	0.004%	0.068%
87:4	10103	8087	1.249	0.062%	-0.426%	0.488%	-0.278%
88:1	10138	10989	0.923	0.164%	0.162%	0.002%	0.163%
88:2	10231	10593	0.966	0.149%	0.083%	0.067%	0.100%
88:3	10019	10050	0.997	0.017%	0.011%	0.006%	0.013%
88:4	10073	10196	0.988	0.050%	0.032%	0.018%	0.037%
89:1	10140	10698	0.948	0.119%	0.111%	0.008%	0.112%
89:2	10117	10772	0.939	0.121%	0.122%	-0.001%	0.122%
89:3	10216	10833	0.943	0.166%	0.122%	0.045%	0.131%
89:4	9920	9904	1.002	-0.047%	0.002%	-0.049%	-0.011%
90:1	10075	9980	1.009	0.049%	-0.013%	0.062%	0.003%
90:2	10100	10459	0.966	0.078%	0.077%	0.001%	0.077%
90:3	9455	8526	1.109	-0.270%	-0.253%	-0.016%	-0.259%
90:4	10091	10889	0.927	0.069%	0.169%	-0.100%	0.146%
91:1	10471	12477	0.839	0.470%	0.285%	0.186%	0.315%
91:2	10153	10244	0.991	0.114%	0.027%	0.087%	0.045%
91:3	10191	10429	0.977	0.120%	0.046%	0.073%	0.065%
91:4	10220	10497	0.974	0.153%	0.058%	0.095%	0.082%
92:1	9967	10324	0.965	-0.030%	0.066%	-0.096%	0.048%
92:2	9957	9723	1.024	-0.025%	-0.057%	0.032%	-0.048%
92:3	10075	10392	0.970	0.054%	0.057%	-0.003%	0.057%
92:4	10149	10963	0.926	0.116%	0.152%	-0.036%	0.144%
93:1	10166	10527	0.966	0.137%	0.066%	0.071%	0.080%
93:2	10105	10340	0.977	0.063%	0.048%	0.015%	0.052%
93:3	10133	10686	0.948	0.101%	0.101%	0.000%	0.101%
93:4	10004	10255	0.976	0.001%	0.045%	-0.044%	0.034%
94:1	10002	9954	1.005	-0.001%	-0.014%	0.013%	-0.011%
94:2	10011	9994	1.002	0.006%	-0.009%	0.015%	-0.005%
94:3	10146	10613	0.956	0.097%	0.087%	0.011%	0.089%
94:4	9903	9836	1.007	-0.054%	-0.019%	-0.035%	-0.029%
95:1	10170	10706	0.950	0.148%	0.101%	0.047%	0.110%
95:2	10138	10873	0.932	0.121%	0.137%	-0.016%	0.134%
95:3	10172	10853	0.937	0.146%	0.128%	0.019%	0.131%
95:4	10050	10445	0.962	0.033%	0.077%	-0.044%	0.067%
96:1	10292	11027	0.933	0.202%	0.146%	0.056%	0.159%
96:2	10066	10367	0.971	0.045%	0.063%	-0.017%	0.059%
96:3	9982	10298	0.969	-0.013%	0.066%	-0.079%	0.047%
96:4	10102	10817	0.934	0.075%	0.135%	-0.060%	0.122%
AVG	10085	10377	0.972	0.061%	0.054%	0.007%	0.055%

Table 4.8b
Commodity Channel Index Crossover (CCI-C)
Short Return Analysis (Average of all stocks)

Qtr	CCI-C Terminal Wealth	Buy/Hold Terminal Wealth	Relative Terminal Wealth	CCI-C Short Avg Ret	CCI-C Cash Avg Ret	CCI-C Short-Cash Avg Ret	Buy/Hold Avg Ret
85:1	9999	10142	0.986	0.007%	0.006%	0.001%	0.006%
85:2	10156	9700	1.047	-0.082%	-0.064%	-0.018%	-0.069%
85:3	10344	8889	1.164	-0.222%	-0.199%	-0.023%	-0.205%
85:4	9790	10763	0.910	0.100%	0.110%	-0.010%	0.107%
86:1	9556	11428	0.836	0.224%	0.225%	0.000%	0.225%
86:2	10079	10414	0.968	-0.046%	0.109%	-0.155%	0.066%
86:3	10208	9175	1.113	-0.151%	-0.121%	-0.031%	-0.128%
86:4	9951	10413	0.956	0.027%	0.084%	-0.058%	0.069%
87:1	9580	11929	0.803	0.206%	0.337%	-0.131%	0.293%
87:2	10020	10196	0.983	-0.014%	0.054%	-0.068%	0.038%
87:3	9852	10408	0.947	0.089%	0.061%	0.028%	0.068%
87:4	10468	8087	1.294	-0.440%	-0.246%	-0.194%	-0.278%
88:1	9544	10989	0.868	0.220%	0.134%	0.086%	0.163%
88:2	9861	10593	0.931	0.087%	0.104%	-0.016%	0.100%
88:3	9989	10050	0.994	0.006%	0.015%	-0.008%	0.013%
88:4	9944	10196	0.975	0.033%	0.038%	-0.004%	0.037%
89:1	9802	10698	0.916	0.103%	0.117%	-0.014%	0.112%
89:2	9749	10772	0.905	0.122%	0.122%	0.000%	0.122%
89:3	9799	10833	0.905	0.109%	0.140%	-0.031%	0.131%
89:4	10080	9904	1.018	-0.062%	0.005%	-0.067%	-0.011%
90:1	10077	9980	1.010	-0.055%	0.021%	-0.075%	0.003%
90:2	9927	10459	0.949	0.043%	0.089%	-0.046%	0.077%
90:3	10198	8526	1.196	-0.204%	-0.269%	0.065%	-0.259%
90:4	9757	10889	0.896	0.137%	0.150%	-0.013%	0.146%
91:1	9460	12477	0.758	0.297%	0.323%	-0.026%	0.315%
91:2	9963	10244	0.973	0.017%	0.057%	-0.040%	0.045%
91:3	9945	10429	0.954	0.038%	0.074%	-0.036%	0.065%
91:4	9921	10497	0.945	0.048%	0.093%	-0.045%	0.082%
92:1	9753	10324	0.945	0.139%	0.010%	0.130%	0.048%
92:2	10104	9723	1.039	-0.066%	-0.043%	-0.024%	-0.048%
92:3	9870	10392	0.950	0.075%	0.049%	0.026%	0.057%
92:4	9721	10963	0.887	0.155%	0.140%	0.015%	0.144%
93:1	9898	10527	0.940	0.056%	0.090%	-0.034%	0.080%
93:2	9962	10340	0.963	0.025%	0.061%	-0.035%	0.052%
93:3	9811	10686	0.918	0.108%	0.098%	0.009%	0.101%
93:4	9915	10255	0.967	0.057%	0.026%	0.031%	0.034%
94:1	10024	9954	1.007	-0.012%	-0.011%	0.000%	-0.011%
94:2	10065	9994	1.007	-0.047%	0.007%	-0.054%	-0.005%
94:3	9851	10613	0.928	0.091%	0.089%	0.002%	0.089%
94:4	9986	9836	1.015	0.011%	-0.040%	0.051%	-0.029%
95:1	9799	10706	0.915	0.105%	0.112%	-0.007%	0.110%
95:2	9764	10873	0.898	0.120%	0.141%	-0.021%	0.134%
95:3	9745	10853	0.898	0.133%	0.130%	0.002%	0.131%
95:4	9885	10445	0.946	0.075%	0.064%	0.011%	0.067%
96:1	9724	11027	0.882	0.163%	0.157%	0.006%	0.159%
96:2	9886	10367	0.954	0.070%	0.054%	0.015%	0.059%
96:3	9919	10298	0.963	0.052%	0.046%	0.007%	0.047%
96:4	9751	10817	0.901	0.136%	0.117%	0.019%	0.122%
AVG	9905	10377	0.955	0.058%	0.054%	0.003%	0.055%

to an investor. However, simply following the trading recommendations of this system will not beat the benchmark buy-and-hold strategy.

Momentum Peaks

Momentum measures the amount a security's price has changed during a given time span. The interpretation of the Momentum indicator is identical to that of the Rate Of Change (ROC) indicator (see page 144). Both indicators display the rate of change of a security's price; the Momentum indicator displays the rate of change as a ratio, whereas the ROC indicator displays the rate of change as a percentage.

Construction

The Momentum indicator is simply the ratio of today's close compared to the close n periods ago:

$$MOM = (Close_{today} / Close_{n\ periods\ ago}) \cdot 100.$$

Results

As shown in Table 4.9, the Momentum Peaks (MOM-P) system makes long calls 40.3 percent of the time and short calls 43.3 percent of the time. The accuracy rate for the long calls is 61.4 percent; the accuracy rate for the short calls is 60.2 percent (Table 4.9b).

The average daily return when a long signal is made is 0.067 percent, compared to an average daily return of only 0.047 percent when a cash position is favored over a long position (Table 4.10a). The 0.019 percent difference in these two average returns indicates that this system is able to distinguish between above-average market return periods and below-average market return periods when making long versus cash decisions.

Trading long with the MOM-P system is profitable in all but nine of the test quarters. However, this profitability is generally lower than the profitability of following a simple buy-and-hold strategy. On average, trading long with this system gives a terminal wealth that is only 98 percent of the buy-and-hold terminal wealth. Investors following the long calls of the system beat investors following a buy-and-hold strategy for only 25 percent of the quarters in the test sample.

The average daily return when the system gives a short signal is 0.055 percent (Table 4.10b). This positive market return indicates that prices are rising. Therefore, following the system's short recommendations will result in decreasing terminal wealth. In fact, the average quarterly terminal wealth is only $9,859, compared to a beginning investment of $10,000 and an average quarterly terminal wealth of $10,377 for a buy-and-hold strategy.

It is hard to gather much useful information from the MOM-P short calls. The average stock return on days when short calls are made is 0.055 percent, exactly the same as the average daily stock return for all days. Thus, the system does not appear to choose days that have any different return from the average return to make short calls. This is a major shortcoming for this system.

Relative Strength Index Peaks

First introduced by Welles Wilder in an article in *Commodities* (now known as *Futures*) magazine in June 1978, the Relative Strength Index (RSI) is a popular oscillator. The RSI compares "up" days with "down" days and is based on the assumption that overbought levels follow a disproportionate number of days in which the market advances, and oversold levels generally occur after the market has declined for a significant number of periods.

Construction

A number of periods *(n)* is chosen for calculation the RSI. Then:

$$\text{Ups} = (\text{Sum of gains over } n \text{ periods})/n,$$

$$\text{Downs} = (\text{Sum of losses over } n \text{ periods})/n,$$

$$\text{RS} = \text{Ups}/\text{Downs},$$

$$\text{RSI} = 100 - [100/(1 + \text{RS})].$$

The RSI can take on a value between 0 and 100. A lower level and an upper level must be chosen to indicate oversold and overbought levels for the oscillator. Typically, the upper and lower levels are recognized at 70 and 30, respectively. When the RSI moves below the lower level and reverses direction, a bullish buy signal is triggered. When the RSI moves above the upper level and peaks, a bearish sell signal occurs.

Results

The results for our tests of the Relative Strength Index Peaks (RSI-P) system are presented in Tables 4.11 and 4.12. This system produces both buy and sell signals at a relatively high rate of frequency. In fact, the long call rate of 41.0 percent and the short call rate of 49.7 percent are about one-and-a-half times the average call rate we find across all of the technical indicators in our study.

Table 4.9a
Momentum Peaks (MOM-P) Long Hit Analysis
(Average of all stocks)

Qtr	Optimal Long	MOM-P Long	Long Hits	Cash Hits	Total Hits	Long Right	Long Wrong	Cash Right	Cash Wrong
85:1	32.1%	34.3%	65.1%	68.1%	67.1%	22.3%	12.0%	44.8%	21.0%
85:2	30.2%	37.3%	66.8%	70.4%	69.1%	24.9%	12.4%	44.1%	18.5%
85:3	26.3%	44.3%	61.5%	74.5%	68.7%	27.2%	17.0%	41.5%	14.2%
85:4	36.6%	29.6%	69.1%	63.1%	64.9%	20.5%	9.2%	44.4%	26.0%
86:1	44.2%	32.2%	65.6%	55.6%	58.8%	21.1%	11.1%	37.7%	30.1%
86:2	39.7%	43.0%	61.9%	61.2%	61.5%	26.6%	16.4%	34.9%	22.1%
86:3	37.0%	42.8%	57.8%	62.8%	60.6%	24.8%	18.1%	35.9%	21.3%
86:4	38.5%	41.8%	62.7%	61.5%	62.0%	26.2%	15.6%	35.8%	22.4%
87:1	44.7%	32.2%	66.6%	56.1%	59.5%	21.4%	10.7%	38.0%	29.8%
87:2	40.0%	44.7%	61.6%	61.2%	61.4%	27.5%	17.2%	33.8%	21.5%
87:3	39.5%	44.5%	59.8%	60.5%	60.2%	26.6%	17.9%	33.6%	21.9%
87:4	37.9%	43.7%	56.4%	63.1%	60.2%	24.7%	19.1%	35.5%	20.7%
88:1	41.3%	33.3%	64.2%	58.8%	60.6%	21.4%	11.9%	39.2%	27.4%
88:2	39.3%	44.4%	62.2%	60.5%	61.2%	27.6%	16.8%	33.6%	22.0%
88:3	35.9%	46.1%	61.2%	63.9%	62.7%	28.2%	17.9%	34.4%	19.5%
88:4	36.3%	43.7%	63.5%	63.3%	63.4%	27.7%	15.9%	35.7%	20.7%
89:1	39.0%	38.6%	64.7%	61.0%	62.4%	25.0%	13.6%	37.5%	23.9%
89:2	40.2%	33.4%	65.1%	59.3%	61.2%	21.7%	11.6%	39.5%	27.1%
89:3	39.9%	40.4%	65.1%	60.2%	62.2%	26.3%	14.1%	35.9%	23.7%
89:4	38.3%	43.2%	61.7%	61.9%	61.8%	26.7%	16.6%	35.1%	21.6%
90:1	36.9%	44.4%	60.6%	63.5%	62.2%	26.9%	17.5%	35.3%	20.3%
90:2	39.2%	41.0%	63.4%	60.9%	62.0%	26.0%	15.0%	35.9%	23.0%
90:3	33.5%	45.1%	54.5%	66.5%	61.1%	24.6%	20.6%	36.5%	18.4%
90:4	40.8%	35.1%	62.6%	58.8%	60.1%	21.9%	13.1%	38.2%	26.7%
91:1	44.1%	34.8%	65.4%	56.3%	59.5%	22.8%	12.0%	36.7%	28.5%
91:2	39.7%	42.3%	60.9%	61.0%	61.0%	25.8%	16.5%	35.2%	22.5%
91:3	40.4%	43.0%	61.2%	60.2%	60.6%	26.3%	16.7%	34.3%	22.7%
91:4	41.2%	43.2%	60.3%	59.2%	59.7%	26.1%	17.1%	33.6%	23.2%
92:1	40.0%	38.7%	56.1%	59.1%	58.0%	21.7%	17.0%	36.3%	25.0%
92:2	38.6%	45.2%	57.7%	61.7%	59.9%	26.1%	19.1%	33.8%	21.0%
92:3	40.3%	39.2%	60.8%	59.8%	60.2%	23.8%	15.4%	36.3%	24.5%
92:4	41.9%	36.5%	63.5%	58.1%	60.1%	23.2%	13.3%	36.9%	26.6%
93:1	42.5%	37.4%	61.9%	58.0%	59.5%	23.1%	14.3%	36.3%	26.3%
93:2	42.1%	45.1%	59.1%	57.6%	58.3%	26.7%	18.5%	31.6%	23.3%
93:3	42.5%	38.7%	61.3%	57.7%	59.1%	23.7%	15.0%	35.4%	25.9%
93:4	41.5%	42.2%	58.3%	58.6%	58.4%	24.6%	17.6%	33.9%	24.0%
94:1	40.4%	42.5%	56.7%	59.6%	58.4%	24.1%	18.4%	34.3%	23.2%
94:2	40.6%	46.3%	58.0%	59.9%	59.0%	26.8%	19.4%	32.2%	21.5%
94:3	41.8%	42.5%	60.8%	58.5%	59.5%	25.8%	16.7%	33.7%	23.9%
94:4	39.5%	45.6%	56.7%	59.8%	58.4%	25.9%	19.7%	32.5%	21.8%
95:1	43.1%	37.1%	62.2%	56.8%	58.8%	23.1%	14.0%	35.8%	27.2%
95:2	43.7%	36.0%	61.7%	56.2%	58.2%	22.2%	13.8%	36.0%	28.0%
95:3	43.9%	37.3%	61.5%	55.7%	57.9%	23.0%	14.4%	34.9%	27.7%
95:4	43.4%	39.2%	59.2%	55.7%	57.1%	23.2%	16.0%	33.9%	26.9%
96:1	45.5%	42.5%	61.2%	54.4%	57.3%	26.0%	16.5%	31.3%	26.2%
96:2	42.1%	43.8%	58.5%	58.1%	58.3%	25.6%	18.2%	32.7%	23.5%
96:3	42.6%	39.2%	59.0%	56.7%	57.6%	23.1%	16.1%	34.5%	26.3%
96:4	44.3%	37.8%	60.4%	55.3%	57.2%	22.8%	15.0%	34.4%	27.8%
AVG	40.0%	40.3%	61.4%	60.2%	60.6%	24.7%	15.7%	35.9%	23.8%

Table 4.9b
Momentum Peaks (MOM-P) Short Hit Analysis
(Average of all stocks)

Qtr	Optimal Short	MOM-P Short	Short Hits	Cash Hits	Total Hits	Short Right	Short Wrong	Cash Right	Cash Wrong
85:1	34.3%	40.5%	65.9%	65.0%	65.4%	26.7%	13.8%	38.6%	20.8%
85:2	34.6%	43.1%	69.2%	66.1%	67.4%	29.8%	13.3%	37.6%	19.3%
85:3	38.6%	38.3%	73.3%	61.5%	66.0%	28.1%	10.2%	38.0%	23.7%
85:4	33.1%	43.2%	63.1%	66.7%	65.2%	27.2%	15.9%	37.9%	18.9%
86:1	35.2%	44.1%	55.8%	64.2%	60.5%	24.6%	19.5%	35.9%	20.0%
86:2	39.8%	42.4%	61.3%	61.0%	61.1%	25.9%	16.4%	35.1%	22.5%
86:3	42.7%	37.3%	63.4%	57.6%	59.7%	23.6%	13.7%	36.1%	26.6%
86:4	38.7%	47.7%	61.6%	62.1%	61.9%	29.4%	18.3%	32.5%	19.8%
87:1	36.9%	46.4%	56.1%	63.8%	60.2%	26.0%	20.3%	34.2%	19.4%
87:2	40.0%	42.4%	61.8%	61.3%	61.5%	26.2%	16.2%	35.3%	22.3%
87:3	40.4%	39.5%	60.6%	59.3%	59.8%	23.9%	15.5%	35.9%	24.6%
87:4	45.3%	36.1%	64.2%	55.4%	58.6%	23.2%	12.9%	35.4%	28.5%
88:1	36.7%	52.1%	58.0%	62.8%	60.3%	30.2%	21.9%	30.1%	17.8%
88:2	37.4%	43.7%	60.2%	62.1%	61.3%	26.3%	17.4%	35.0%	21.3%
88:3	38.4%	41.3%	63.6%	61.1%	62.1%	26.3%	15.0%	35.9%	22.8%
88:4	37.0%	42.5%	63.7%	63.0%	63.3%	27.1%	15.5%	36.2%	21.2%
89:1	36.2%	45.5%	61.0%	63.4%	62.3%	27.8%	17.7%	34.5%	20.0%
89:2	35.9%	46.6%	59.4%	63.8%	61.8%	27.7%	18.9%	34.1%	19.3%
89:3	36.4%	43.3%	60.0%	63.6%	62.0%	26.0%	17.3%	36.0%	20.7%
89:4	39.0%	40.4%	61.9%	61.2%	61.5%	25.0%	15.4%	36.5%	23.1%
90:1	40.1%	42.4%	63.7%	60.4%	61.8%	27.0%	15.4%	34.8%	22.8%
90:2	37.8%	42.4%	61.2%	62.3%	61.8%	25.9%	16.4%	35.9%	21.7%
90:3	45.7%	30.6%	67.7%	54.7%	58.7%	20.7%	9.9%	37.9%	31.5%
90:4	37.6%	45.4%	58.0%	62.0%	60.2%	26.4%	19.1%	33.9%	20.7%
91:1	36.7%	41.5%	55.4%	63.3%	60.0%	23.0%	18.5%	37.1%	21.5%
91:2	40.4%	45.7%	61.2%	60.4%	60.8%	28.0%	17.7%	32.8%	21.5%
91:3	39.8%	44.4%	60.5%	61.1%	60.8%	26.8%	17.5%	34.0%	21.7%
91:4	40.5%	41.7%	59.4%	60.1%	59.8%	24.8%	16.9%	35.1%	23.2%
92:1	43.2%	42.1%	59.5%	56.3%	57.7%	25.1%	17.1%	32.6%	25.3%
92:2	42.9%	42.2%	61.8%	57.6%	59.4%	26.1%	16.1%	33.3%	24.5%
92:3	39.5%	47.0%	59.9%	60.8%	60.4%	28.2%	18.8%	32.2%	20.8%
92:4	37.5%	45.4%	57.9%	62.6%	60.5%	26.3%	19.1%	34.2%	20.4%
93:1	39.4%	46.5%	58.1%	61.0%	59.7%	27.0%	19.5%	32.6%	20.9%
93:2	40.9%	42.0%	57.7%	58.9%	58.4%	24.2%	17.8%	34.1%	23.9%
93:3	39.4%	46.4%	57.6%	60.7%	59.3%	26.7%	19.7%	32.6%	21.1%
93:4	41.7%	42.8%	58.8%	58.2%	58.5%	25.2%	17.6%	33.3%	23.9%
94:1	43.7%	45.2%	59.9%	56.4%	58.0%	27.1%	18.1%	30.9%	23.9%
94:2	42.7%	41.4%	60.1%	57.6%	58.6%	24.8%	16.5%	33.8%	24.9%
94:3	39.8%	45.1%	58.6%	60.5%	59.6%	26.4%	18.7%	33.2%	21.7%
94:4	42.8%	38.7%	59.8%	56.7%	57.9%	23.1%	15.6%	34.7%	26.6%
95:1	38.7%	50.4%	56.4%	61.2%	58.8%	28.5%	22.0%	30.3%	19.2%
95:2	38.9%	49.8%	56.1%	61.0%	58.5%	27.9%	21.9%	30.6%	19.6%
95:3	38.9%	46.6%	55.9%	60.8%	58.5%	26.1%	20.5%	32.5%	20.9%
95:4	40.5%	40.7%	55.3%	59.0%	57.5%	22.5%	18.2%	35.0%	24.3%
96:1	38.9%	44.3%	54.2%	60.9%	58.0%	24.0%	20.3%	33.9%	21.7%
96:2	42.4%	45.2%	58.0%	57.9%	57.9%	26.2%	19.0%	31.7%	23.0%
96:3	40.8%	45.5%	56.6%	58.5%	57.7%	25.8%	19.7%	31.9%	22.6%
96:4	39.8%	42.4%	55.2%	59.7%	57.8%	23.4%	19.0%	34.4%	23.2%
AVG	39.4%	43.3%	60.2%	60.7%	60.4%	26.0%	17.3%	34.4%	22.3%

Table 4.10a
Momentum Peaks (MOM-P) Long Return Analysis
(Average of all stocks)

Qtr	MOM-P Terminal Wealth	Buy/Hold Terminal Wealth	Relative Terminal Wealth	MOM-P Long Avg Ret	MOM-P Cash Avg Ret	MOM-P Long-Cash Avg Ret	Buy/Hold Avg Ret
85:1	10011	10142	0.987	-0.002%	0.010%	-0.012%	0.006%
85:2	9976	9700	1.029	-0.023%	-0.097%	0.073%	-0.069%
85:3	9532	8889	1.072	-0.179%	-0.225%	0.046%	-0.205%
85:4	10244	10763	0.952	0.121%	0.101%	0.020%	0.107%
86:1	10489	11428	0.918	0.247%	0.214%	0.033%	0.225%
86:2	10382	10414	0.997	0.138%	0.012%	0.126%	0.066%
86:3	9670	9175	1.054	-0.119%	-0.134%	0.016%	-0.128%
86:4	10251	10413	0.984	0.096%	0.050%	0.046%	0.069%
87:1	10876	11929	0.912	0.427%	0.229%	0.198%	0.293%
87:2	10302	10196	1.010	0.109%	-0.020%	0.129%	0.038%
87:3	10219	10408	0.982	0.081%	0.059%	0.022%	0.068%
87:4	9510	8087	1.176	-0.161%	-0.369%	0.208%	-0.278%
88:1	10424	10989	0.949	0.207%	0.141%	0.067%	0.163%
88:2	10224	10593	0.965	0.084%	0.113%	-0.029%	0.100%
88:3	9998	10050	0.995	0.003%	0.021%	-0.018%	0.013%
88:4	10065	10196	0.987	0.028%	0.043%	-0.016%	0.037%
89:1	10264	10698	0.959	0.113%	0.112%	0.000%	0.112%
89:2	10253	10772	0.952	0.121%	0.123%	-0.002%	0.122%
89:3	10377	10833	0.958	0.149%	0.119%	0.030%	0.131%
89:4	10029	9904	1.013	0.014%	-0.030%	0.044%	-0.011%
90:1	10063	9980	1.008	0.026%	-0.016%	0.042%	0.003%
90:2	10216	10459	0.977	0.086%	0.070%	0.016%	0.077%
90:3	9249	8526	1.085	-0.281%	-0.240%	-0.041%	-0.259%
90:4	10262	10889	0.942	0.127%	0.156%	-0.029%	0.146%
91:1	10799	12477	0.866	0.367%	0.287%	0.081%	0.315%
91:2	10191	10244	0.995	0.076%	0.023%	0.053%	0.045%
91:3	10280	10429	0.986	0.100%	0.038%	0.062%	0.065%
91:4	10333	10497	0.984	0.130%	0.045%	0.085%	0.082%
92:1	9995	10324	0.968	-0.005%	0.081%	-0.086%	0.048%
92:2	9940	9723	1.022	-0.022%	-0.070%	0.049%	-0.048%
92:3	10202	10392	0.982	0.077%	0.043%	0.034%	0.057%
92:4	10380	10963	0.947	0.162%	0.134%	0.028%	0.144%
93:1	10307	10527	0.979	0.130%	0.050%	0.081%	0.080%
93:2	10136	10340	0.980	0.048%	0.054%	-0.006%	0.052%
93:3	10326	10686	0.966	0.129%	0.083%	0.046%	0.101%
93:4	10108	10255	0.986	0.038%	0.031%	0.008%	0.034%
94:1	10043	9954	1.009	0.014%	-0.030%	0.044%	-0.011%
94:2	10055	9994	1.006	0.017%	-0.024%	0.041%	-0.005%
94:3	10304	10613	0.971	0.110%	0.074%	0.036%	0.089%
94:4	9856	9836	1.002	-0.054%	-0.008%	-0.046%	-0.029%
95:1	10305	10706	0.963	0.132%	0.097%	0.036%	0.110%
95:2	10327	10873	0.950	0.146%	0.128%	0.018%	0.134%
95:3	10332	10853	0.952	0.141%	0.125%	0.016%	0.131%
95:4	10124	10445	0.969	0.048%	0.079%	-0.031%	0.067%
96:1	10451	11027	0.948	0.168%	0.152%	0.016%	0.159%
96:2	10190	10367	0.983	0.069%	0.050%	0.019%	0.059%
96:3	10064	10298	0.977	0.025%	0.062%	-0.037%	0.047%
96:4	10287	10817	0.951	0.118%	0.125%	-0.007%	0.122%
AVG	10171	10377	0.980	0.067%	0.047%	0.019%	0.055%

Table 4.10b
Momentum Peaks (MOM-P) Short Return Analysis
(Average of all stocks)

Qtr	MOM-P Terminal Wealth	Buy/Hold Terminal Wealth	Relative Terminal Wealth	MOM-P Short Avg Ret	MOM-P Cash Avg Ret	MOM-P Short-Cash Avg Ret	Buy/Hold Avg Ret
85:1	9857	10142	0.972	0.064%	-0.033%	0.098%	0.006%
85:2	10252	9700	1.057	-0.082%	-0.060%	-0.022%	-0.069%
85:3	10541	8889	1.186	-0.210%	-0.202%	-0.008%	-0.205%
85:4	9694	10763	0.901	0.117%	0.099%	0.017%	0.107%
86:1	9408	11428	0.823	0.227%	0.222%	0.005%	0.225%
86:2	9971	10414	0.957	0.015%	0.104%	-0.089%	0.066%
86:3	10397	9175	1.133	-0.166%	-0.105%	-0.061%	-0.128%
86:4	9831	10413	0.944	0.053%	0.084%	-0.031%	0.069%
87:1	9300	11929	0.780	0.254%	0.326%	-0.072%	0.293%
87:2	10107	10196	0.991	-0.040%	0.095%	-0.135%	0.038%
87:3	9817	10408	0.943	0.072%	0.066%	0.006%	0.068%
87:4	10845	8087	1.341	-0.367%	-0.228%	-0.140%	-0.278%
88:1	9405	10989	0.856	0.181%	0.143%	0.039%	0.163%
88:2	9675	10593	0.913	0.118%	0.086%	0.032%	0.100%
88:3	9917	10050	0.987	0.030%	0.001%	0.029%	0.013%
88:4	9898	10196	0.971	0.038%	0.036%	0.002%	0.037%
89:1	9626	10698	0.900	0.138%	0.091%	0.046%	0.112%
89:2	9616	10772	0.893	0.131%	0.114%	0.017%	0.122%
89:3	9637	10833	0.890	0.137%	0.127%	0.010%	0.131%
89:4	10081	9904	1.018	-0.035%	0.006%	-0.041%	-0.011%
90:1	10071	9980	1.009	-0.028%	0.026%	-0.054%	0.003%
90:2	9793	10459	0.936	0.079%	0.075%	0.004%	0.077%
90:3	10538	8526	1.236	-0.275%	-0.252%	-0.023%	-0.259%
90:4	9489	10889	0.871	0.181%	0.117%	0.064%	0.146%
91:1	9162	12477	0.734	0.355%	0.287%	0.068%	0.315%
91:2	9940	10244	0.970	0.018%	0.068%	-0.050%	0.045%
91:3	9944	10429	0.954	0.021%	0.100%	-0.078%	0.065%
91:4	9928	10497	0.946	0.032%	0.117%	-0.086%	0.082%
92:1	9809	10324	0.950	0.079%	0.025%	0.053%	0.048%
92:2	10229	9723	1.052	-0.084%	-0.023%	-0.061%	-0.048%
92:3	9893	10392	0.952	0.038%	0.073%	-0.035%	0.057%
92:4	9601	10963	0.876	0.145%	0.144%	0.001%	0.144%
93:1	9868	10527	0.937	0.052%	0.104%	-0.052%	0.080%
93:2	9860	10340	0.954	0.056%	0.049%	0.007%	0.052%
93:3	9754	10686	0.913	0.088%	0.112%	-0.024%	0.101%
93:4	9939	10255	0.969	0.028%	0.039%	-0.011%	0.034%
94:1	10099	9954	1.015	-0.033%	0.007%	-0.040%	-0.011%
94:2	10096	9994	1.010	-0.033%	0.015%	-0.048%	-0.005%
94:3	9784	10613	0.922	0.081%	0.096%	-0.015%	0.089%
94:4	10021	9836	1.019	-0.007%	-0.043%	0.036%	-0.029%
95:1	9657	10706	0.902	0.113%	0.107%	0.005%	0.110%
95:2	9596	10873	0.883	0.134%	0.134%	0.001%	0.134%
95:3	9635	10853	0.888	0.130%	0.132%	-0.002%	0.131%
95:4	9784	10445	0.937	0.089%	0.051%	0.038%	0.067%
96:1	9574	11027	0.868	0.160%	0.158%	0.002%	0.159%
96:2	9842	10367	0.949	0.058%	0.059%	0.000%	0.059%
96:3	9791	10298	0.951	0.075%	0.024%	0.050%	0.047%
96:4	9642	10817	0.891	0.137%	0.112%	0.025%	0.122%
AVG	9859	10377	0.950	0.055%	0.055%	0.000%	0.055%

Table 4.11a
Relative Strength Peaks (RSI-P) Long Hit Analysis
(Average of all stocks)

Qtr	Optimal Long	RSI-P Long	Long Hits	Cash Hits	Total Hits	Long Right	Long Wrong	Cash Right	Cash Wrong
85:1	32.1%	28.4%	67.0%	68.0%	67.7%	19.1%	9.4%	48.7%	22.9%
85:2	30.2%	39.0%	65.7%	69.4%	68.0%	25.6%	13.4%	42.4%	18.7%
85:3	26.3%	46.7%	61.7%	74.3%	68.4%	28.8%	17.9%	39.6%	13.7%
85:4	36.6%	32.2%	68.7%	61.8%	64.1%	22.1%	10.1%	41.9%	25.9%
86:1	44.2%	25.6%	67.1%	55.2%	58.3%	17.2%	8.4%	41.1%	33.3%
86:2	39.7%	38.1%	61.8%	60.9%	61.3%	23.6%	14.6%	37.7%	24.2%
86:3	37.0%	48.7%	58.5%	62.4%	60.5%	28.4%	20.2%	32.0%	19.3%
86:4	38.5%	45.4%	63.9%	62.1%	62.9%	29.0%	16.4%	33.9%	20.7%
87:1	44.7%	27.4%	67.2%	56.0%	59.1%	18.4%	9.0%	40.6%	31.9%
87:2	40.0%	49.6%	61.0%	60.7%	60.8%	30.2%	19.4%	30.6%	19.8%
87:3	39.5%	39.0%	61.3%	60.8%	61.0%	23.9%	15.1%	37.1%	23.9%
87:4	37.9%	64.6%	56.2%	64.5%	59.2%	36.3%	28.3%	22.9%	12.6%
88:1	41.3%	26.0%	66.5%	59.2%	61.1%	17.3%	8.7%	43.8%	30.2%
88:2	39.3%	46.4%	62.7%	61.1%	61.8%	29.1%	17.3%	32.7%	20.9%
88:3	35.9%	48.9%	62.0%	64.7%	63.4%	30.3%	18.6%	33.1%	18.0%
88:4	36.3%	46.7%	64.6%	64.3%	64.4%	30.1%	16.5%	34.3%	19.0%
89:1	39.0%	34.3%	65.1%	60.8%	62.2%	22.3%	12.0%	39.9%	25.8%
89:2	40.2%	31.2%	66.0%	59.4%	61.5%	20.6%	10.6%	40.9%	27.9%
89:3	39.9%	36.4%	65.4%	59.9%	61.9%	23.8%	12.6%	38.1%	25.5%
89:4	38.3%	49.5%	61.7%	61.2%	61.4%	30.5%	19.0%	30.9%	19.6%
90:1	36.9%	52.3%	61.3%	64.0%	62.5%	32.0%	20.3%	30.5%	17.2%
90:2	39.2%	38.8%	64.6%	60.8%	62.3%	25.1%	13.7%	37.2%	24.0%
90:3	33.5%	58.5%	54.6%	66.2%	59.4%	31.9%	26.5%	27.5%	14.0%
90:4	40.8%	43.4%	61.4%	58.1%	59.5%	26.7%	16.8%	32.8%	23.7%
91:1	44.1%	26.4%	67.4%	56.7%	59.5%	17.8%	8.6%	41.7%	31.9%
91:2	39.7%	38.1%	60.6%	61.0%	60.8%	23.1%	15.0%	37.7%	24.2%
91:3	40.4%	43.7%	60.8%	59.4%	60.0%	26.5%	17.1%	33.5%	22.8%
91:4	41.2%	45.8%	59.5%	58.6%	59.0%	27.3%	18.6%	31.7%	22.4%
92:1	40.0%	34.8%	55.5%	58.9%	57.7%	19.3%	15.5%	38.4%	26.8%
92:2	38.6%	49.7%	57.1%	61.5%	59.3%	28.4%	21.3%	31.0%	19.4%
92:3	40.3%	44.3%	60.6%	59.3%	59.9%	26.9%	17.4%	33.0%	22.6%
92:4	41.9%	35.9%	63.2%	57.9%	59.8%	22.7%	13.2%	37.1%	27.0%
93:1	42.5%	35.2%	60.9%	57.5%	58.7%	21.4%	13.8%	37.3%	27.6%
93:2	42.1%	45.7%	59.2%	57.5%	58.3%	27.1%	18.6%	31.2%	23.1%
93:3	42.5%	36.7%	61.0%	57.5%	58.8%	22.4%	14.3%	36.4%	26.9%
93:4	41.5%	47.2%	58.2%	58.2%	58.2%	27.5%	19.7%	30.7%	22.1%
94:1	40.4%	41.1%	56.1%	59.0%	57.8%	23.0%	18.0%	34.8%	24.1%
94:2	40.6%	54.4%	57.7%	59.6%	58.6%	31.4%	23.0%	27.2%	18.4%
94:3	41.8%	43.2%	60.9%	58.6%	59.6%	26.3%	16.9%	33.3%	23.5%
94:4	39.5%	55.6%	57.2%	60.6%	58.7%	31.8%	23.8%	26.9%	17.5%
95:1	43.1%	32.7%	62.4%	57.0%	58.8%	20.4%	12.3%	38.3%	28.9%
95:2	43.7%	30.2%	62.3%	56.1%	58.0%	18.8%	11.4%	39.2%	30.6%
95:3	43.9%	32.4%	61.4%	55.5%	57.4%	19.9%	12.5%	37.5%	30.1%
95:4	43.4%	39.7%	58.8%	55.6%	56.9%	23.3%	16.3%	33.6%	26.8%
96:1	45.5%	38.9%	62.2%	54.5%	57.5%	24.2%	14.7%	33.3%	27.8%
96:2	42.1%	39.1%	58.0%	57.8%	57.9%	22.7%	16.4%	35.2%	25.7%
96:3	42.6%	46.7%	59.4%	57.2%	58.2%	27.7%	19.0%	30.5%	22.8%
96:4	44.3%	34.9%	60.4%	55.2%	57.0%	21.1%	13.8%	35.9%	29.2%
AVG	40.0%	41.0%	61.6%	60.1%	60.4%	25.1%	16.0%	35.3%	23.6%

Relative Strength Index Peaks

Table 4.11b
Relative Strength Peaks (RSI-P) Short Hit Analysis
(Average of all stocks)

Qtr	Optimal Short	RSI-P Short	Short Hits	Cash Hits	Total Hits	Short Right	Short Wrong	Cash Right	Cash Wrong
85:1	34.3%	56.9%	67.4%	65.7%	66.6%	38.3%	18.6%	28.3%	14.8%
85:2	34.6%	51.0%	69.2%	65.5%	67.4%	35.3%	15.7%	32.1%	16.9%
85:3	38.6%	43.7%	73.8%	61.8%	67.1%	32.2%	11.5%	34.8%	21.5%
85:4	33.1%	54.1%	61.9%	67.5%	64.5%	33.5%	20.6%	31.0%	14.9%
86:1	35.2%	59.2%	55.2%	65.0%	59.2%	32.7%	26.5%	26.5%	14.3%
86:2	39.8%	52.6%	61.0%	61.3%	61.1%	32.1%	20.5%	29.0%	18.4%
86:3	42.7%	40.5%	62.7%	58.3%	60.1%	25.4%	15.1%	34.7%	24.8%
86:4	38.7%	48.6%	62.0%	63.3%	62.7%	30.1%	18.5%	32.5%	18.8%
87:1	36.9%	61.0%	56.2%	65.3%	59.7%	34.3%	26.8%	25.4%	13.5%
87:2	40.0%	43.3%	60.9%	60.6%	60.7%	26.4%	16.9%	34.4%	22.3%
87:3	40.4%	51.7%	61.1%	60.7%	60.9%	31.6%	20.1%	29.3%	19.0%
87:4	45.3%	25.8%	65.5%	55.7%	58.3%	16.9%	8.9%	41.4%	32.8%
88:1	36.7%	66.8%	58.9%	65.0%	60.9%	39.3%	27.5%	21.6%	11.6%
88:2	37.4%	45.8%	61.3%	62.6%	62.0%	28.1%	17.7%	33.9%	20.3%
88:3	38.4%	44.5%	64.9%	61.8%	63.2%	28.9%	15.6%	34.3%	21.2%
88:4	37.0%	46.5%	64.4%	64.1%	64.2%	29.9%	16.5%	34.3%	19.2%
89:1	36.2%	56.9%	60.7%	64.4%	62.3%	34.6%	22.3%	27.7%	15.4%
89:2	35.9%	58.6%	59.4%	64.4%	61.5%	34.8%	23.8%	26.7%	14.7%
89:3	36.4%	53.3%	60.2%	64.6%	62.3%	32.1%	21.2%	30.1%	16.5%
89:4	39.0%	41.3%	61.2%	61.3%	61.3%	25.3%	16.0%	36.0%	22.7%
90:1	40.1%	40.4%	64.1%	61.2%	62.4%	25.9%	14.5%	36.4%	23.1%
90:2	37.8%	52.3%	60.9%	63.9%	62.4%	31.9%	20.4%	30.5%	17.2%
90:3	45.7%	28.7%	66.7%	54.8%	58.2%	19.2%	9.6%	39.0%	32.2%
90:4	37.6%	43.8%	57.6%	61.7%	59.9%	25.2%	18.6%	34.7%	21.5%
91:1	36.7%	59.2%	56.7%	65.1%	60.1%	33.6%	25.7%	26.6%	14.2%
91:2	40.4%	54.3%	60.9%	60.5%	60.7%	33.1%	21.3%	27.6%	18.1%
91:3	39.8%	48.5%	59.3%	60.6%	60.0%	28.8%	19.8%	31.2%	20.3%
91:4	40.5%	44.5%	58.8%	59.4%	59.1%	26.1%	18.3%	33.0%	22.6%
92:1	43.2%	54.3%	59.1%	55.8%	57.6%	32.1%	22.2%	25.5%	20.2%
92:2	42.9%	43.4%	61.6%	57.2%	59.1%	26.7%	16.7%	32.4%	24.2%
92:3	39.5%	48.1%	59.2%	60.6%	59.9%	28.5%	19.6%	31.5%	20.5%
92:4	37.5%	55.0%	57.8%	62.8%	60.1%	31.8%	23.2%	28.3%	16.7%
93:1	39.4%	54.9%	57.7%	60.7%	59.1%	31.7%	23.2%	27.4%	17.7%
93:2	40.9%	46.3%	57.9%	59.1%	58.5%	26.8%	19.5%	31.7%	22.0%
93:3	39.4%	54.5%	57.6%	60.7%	59.0%	31.4%	23.1%	27.6%	17.9%
93:4	41.7%	44.9%	58.1%	58.0%	58.0%	26.1%	18.8%	32.0%	23.2%
94:1	43.7%	51.0%	59.0%	55.9%	57.5%	30.1%	20.9%	27.4%	21.6%
94:2	42.7%	38.5%	59.9%	57.6%	58.5%	23.0%	15.4%	35.4%	26.1%
94:3	39.8%	51.1%	58.5%	60.7%	59.6%	29.9%	21.2%	29.7%	19.2%
94:4	42.8%	35.4%	60.9%	57.2%	58.5%	21.5%	13.8%	37.0%	27.6%
95:1	38.7%	59.3%	57.0%	61.9%	59.0%	33.8%	25.5%	25.2%	15.5%
95:2	38.9%	60.2%	56.1%	61.5%	58.3%	33.8%	26.4%	24.5%	15.3%
95:3	38.9%	58.7%	55.6%	61.0%	57.8%	32.6%	26.0%	25.2%	16.1%
95:4	40.5%	49.6%	55.6%	58.8%	57.2%	27.6%	22.0%	29.6%	20.8%
96:1	38.9%	52.7%	54.3%	61.5%	57.7%	28.6%	24.1%	29.1%	18.2%
96:2	42.4%	54.0%	57.8%	57.9%	57.8%	31.2%	22.8%	26.6%	19.4%
96:3	40.8%	45.4%	57.1%	59.0%	58.1%	25.9%	19.5%	32.2%	22.4%
96:4	39.8%	54.1%	55.2%	59.7%	57.3%	29.9%	24.2%	27.4%	18.5%
AVG	39.4%	49.7%	60.2%	61.1%	60.4%	29.8%	19.9%	30.6%	19.7%

Table 4.12a
Relative Strength Peaks (RSI-P) Long Return Analysis
(Average of all stocks)

Qtr	RSI-P Terminal Wealth	Buy/Hold Terminal Wealth	Relative Terminal Wealth	RSI-P Long Avg Ret	RSI-P Cash Avg Ret	RSI-P Long-Cash Avg Ret	Buy/Hold Avg Ret
85:1	10052	10142	0.991	0.020%	0.001%	0.019%	0.006%
85:2	9860	9700	1.017	-0.072%	-0.068%	-0.004%	-0.069%
85:3	9511	8889	1.070	-0.184%	-0.223%	0.039%	-0.205%
85:4	10169	10763	0.945	0.073%	0.123%	-0.050%	0.107%
86:1	10384	11428	0.909	0.243%	0.218%	0.025%	0.225%
86:2	10349	10414	0.994	0.147%	0.017%	0.131%	0.066%
86:3	9711	9175	1.058	-0.090%	-0.163%	0.073%	-0.128%
86:4	10381	10413	0.997	0.132%	0.017%	0.116%	0.069%
87:1	10735	11929	0.900	0.421%	0.245%	0.176%	0.293%
87:2	10191	10196	0.999	0.066%	0.010%	0.057%	0.038%
87:3	10273	10408	0.987	0.112%	0.040%	0.072%	0.068%
87:4	9441	8087	1.167	-0.116%	-0.573%	0.457%	-0.278%
88:1	10484	10989	0.954	0.299%	0.115%	0.184%	0.163%
88:2	10320	10593	0.974	0.115%	0.087%	0.028%	0.100%
88:3	10110	10050	1.006	0.040%	-0.014%	0.054%	0.013%
88:4	10202	10196	1.001	0.074%	0.003%	0.071%	0.037%
89:1	10245	10698	0.958	0.117%	0.110%	0.007%	0.112%
89:2	10292	10772	0.955	0.150%	0.110%	0.040%	0.122%
89:3	10357	10833	0.956	0.157%	0.116%	0.042%	0.131%
89:4	9963	9904	1.006	-0.009%	-0.013%	0.004%	-0.011%
90:1	10151	9980	1.017	0.050%	-0.049%	0.098%	0.003%
90:2	10292	10459	0.984	0.124%	0.047%	0.078%	0.077%
90:3	9088	8526	1.066	-0.269%	-0.245%	-0.024%	-0.259%
90:4	10231	10889	0.939	0.098%	0.184%	-0.086%	0.146%
91:1	10756	12477	0.862	0.460%	0.263%	0.197%	0.315%
91:2	10194	10244	0.995	0.085%	0.021%	0.064%	0.045%
91:3	10200	10429	0.978	0.071%	0.060%	0.011%	0.065%
91:4	10286	10497	0.980	0.100%	0.066%	0.034%	0.082%
92:1	9932	10324	0.962	-0.036%	0.093%	-0.128%	0.048%
92:2	9854	9723	1.013	-0.051%	-0.046%	-0.006%	-0.048%
92:3	10179	10392	0.980	0.061%	0.053%	0.007%	0.057%
92:4	10356	10963	0.945	0.155%	0.138%	0.017%	0.144%
93:1	10239	10527	0.973	0.107%	0.065%	0.042%	0.080%
93:2	10168	10340	0.983	0.060%	0.045%	0.016%	0.052%
93:3	10306	10686	0.964	0.128%	0.085%	0.043%	0.101%
93:4	10073	10255	0.982	0.023%	0.043%	-0.020%	0.034%
94:1	9956	9954	1.000	-0.022%	-0.004%	-0.018%	-0.011%
94:2	10047	9994	1.005	0.009%	-0.021%	0.029%	-0.005%
94:3	10318	10613	0.972	0.112%	0.072%	0.039%	0.089%
94:4	9920	9836	1.008	-0.025%	-0.035%	0.010%	-0.029%
95:1	10288	10706	0.961	0.139%	0.096%	0.044%	0.110%
95:2	10302	10873	0.948	0.157%	0.124%	0.033%	0.134%
95:3	10257	10853	0.945	0.125%	0.134%	-0.009%	0.131%
95:4	10110	10445	0.968	0.042%	0.083%	-0.041%	0.067%
96:1	10484	11027	0.951	0.196%	0.135%	0.061%	0.159%
96:2	10168	10367	0.981	0.069%	0.052%	0.017%	0.059%
96:3	10166	10298	0.987	0.057%	0.039%	0.018%	0.047%
96:4	10241	10817	0.947	0.107%	0.130%	-0.023%	0.122%
AVG	10158	10377	0.979	0.060%	0.052%	0.009%	0.055%

Table 4.12b
Relative Strength Peaks (RSI-P) Short Return Analysis
(Average of all stocks)

Qtr	RSI-P Terminal Wealth	Buy/Hold Terminal Wealth	Relative Terminal Wealth	RSI-P Short Avg Ret	RSI-P Cash Avg Ret	RSI-P Short-Cash Avg Ret	Buy/Hold Avg Ret
85:1	9951	10142	0.981	0.024%	-0.018%	0.042%	0.006%
85:2	10239	9700	1.056	-0.062%	-0.077%	0.015%	-0.069%
85:3	10665	8889	1.200	-0.220%	-0.193%	-0.028%	-0.205%
85:4	9598	10763	0.892	0.123%	0.087%	0.036%	0.107%
86:1	9227	11428	0.807	0.227%	0.221%	0.006%	0.225%
86:2	9955	10414	0.956	0.017%	0.121%	-0.104%	0.066%
86:3	10499	9175	1.144	-0.194%	-0.082%	-0.112%	-0.128%
86:4	9938	10413	0.954	0.015%	0.121%	-0.106%	0.069%
87:1	9128	11929	0.765	0.245%	0.369%	-0.124%	0.293%
87:2	9984	10196	0.979	0.005%	0.063%	-0.058%	0.038%
87:3	9887	10408	0.950	0.032%	0.107%	-0.074%	0.068%
87:4	11001	8087	1.360	-0.598%	-0.167%	-0.432%	-0.278%
88:1	9457	10989	0.861	0.129%	0.231%	-0.103%	0.163%
88:2	9772	10593	0.923	0.078%	0.118%	-0.040%	0.100%
88:3	10041	10050	0.999	-0.017%	0.037%	-0.054%	0.013%
88:4	9997	10196	0.981	-0.001%	0.070%	-0.071%	0.037%
89:1	9602	10698	0.898	0.116%	0.108%	0.008%	0.112%
89:2	9569	10772	0.888	0.117%	0.129%	-0.012%	0.122%
89:3	9621	10833	0.888	0.117%	0.147%	-0.030%	0.131%
89:4	10041	9904	1.014	-0.018%	-0.006%	-0.012%	-0.011%
90:1	10151	9980	1.017	-0.061%	0.046%	-0.107%	0.003%
90:2	9854	10459	0.942	0.045%	0.112%	-0.067%	0.077%
90:3	10501	8526	1.232	-0.276%	-0.252%	-0.024%	-0.259%
90:4	9458	10889	0.869	0.200%	0.104%	0.096%	0.146%
91:1	9084	12477	0.728	0.277%	0.371%	-0.094%	0.315%
91:2	9923	10244	0.969	0.019%	0.077%	-0.059%	0.045%
91:3	9830	10429	0.943	0.057%	0.072%	-0.016%	0.065%
91:4	9811	10497	0.935	0.065%	0.095%	-0.031%	0.082%
92:1	9685	10324	0.938	0.099%	-0.013%	0.112%	0.048%
92:2	10164	9723	1.045	-0.058%	-0.041%	-0.018%	-0.048%
92:3	9841	10392	0.947	0.057%	0.056%	0.000%	0.057%
92:4	9524	10963	0.869	0.144%	0.145%	-0.002%	0.144%
93:1	9796	10527	0.930	0.067%	0.096%	-0.029%	0.080%
93:2	9915	10340	0.959	0.035%	0.066%	-0.031%	0.052%
93:3	9724	10686	0.910	0.086%	0.119%	-0.034%	0.101%
93:4	9868	10255	0.962	0.054%	0.018%	0.036%	0.034%
94:1	10003	9954	1.005	0.001%	-0.024%	0.025%	-0.011%
94:2	10071	9994	1.008	-0.027%	0.009%	-0.036%	-0.005%
94:3	9776	10613	0.921	0.076%	0.103%	-0.027%	0.089%
94:4	10090	9836	1.026	-0.039%	-0.024%	-0.015%	-0.029%
95:1	9663	10706	0.903	0.095%	0.132%	-0.037%	0.110%
95:2	9544	10873	0.878	0.126%	0.145%	-0.019%	0.134%
95:3	9537	10853	0.879	0.133%	0.128%	0.006%	0.131%
95:4	9754	10445	0.934	0.083%	0.051%	0.032%	0.067%
96:1	9546	11027	0.866	0.145%	0.175%	-0.030%	0.159%
96:2	9824	10367	0.948	0.053%	0.065%	-0.012%	0.059%
96:3	9856	10298	0.957	0.052%	0.043%	0.009%	0.047%
96:4	9547	10817	0.883	0.139%	0.103%	0.036%	0.122%
AVG	9844	10377	0.949	0.054%	0.056%	-0.002%	0.055%

On days when long calls are made, the return is only 0.060 percent on average (Table 4.12a). Because this return is greater than the 0.052 percent average stock return on days when a cash position is favored over a long position, the system's long calls are predicting days of above-average market return. These are days that investors definitely do want to be long. However, because there is an average return of 0.052 percent when the system recommends a cash position, following the system's cash calls means that investors lose out on positive returns. The terminal wealth figures show that this is a high price to pay. These forgone profits cause the terminal wealth of traders following the system's long and cash calls to average only 97.9 percent of the terminal wealth of investors following a buy-and-hold strategy.

The return information for the short calls also shows that the RSI-P system underperforms a simple buy-and-hold strategy. In fact, trading short with this system will lead, on average, to declining terminal wealth. This occurs because the average stock return on days when short calls are made is a positive 0.054 percent (Table 4.12b), indicating price appreciation. Even though this price appreciation is below the average price appreciation, it still indicates rising prices. Being short on these days will lead to losses.

Some useful information is found in the RSI-P system, but it is far from a perfect technical indicator. Next, let's see whether using the same RSI in a crossover system improves performance results.

Relative Strength Index Crossover

Wilder's Relative Strength Index, discussed in the previous section, can also be used in a crossover system. In the Relative Strength Index Crossover (RSI-C) system, the index must cross outside an overbought or oversold line and then return back through the same line in order for a trading signal to be generated. As with other crossover systems, this system will generate signals later than a peak system using the same index. This slower reaction to price changes can be a disadvantage, but traders may choose this system to reduce the chance of acting on false signals.

Construction

The construction of the Relative Strength Index was described in the previous section. Refer to page 129 for instructions for calculating the index.

The Relative Strength Index is defined to oscillate between 0 and 100. Typically, 70 is considered an overbought level, and 30 is considered an oversold level. With the RSI-C system, when the index crosses above 70, peaks, and then crosses through 70 again, a short signal occurs. The system generates a long signal whenever the index falls below 30, forms a valley, and rises back through 30.

Results

The results presented in Tables 4.13 and 4.14 for the Relative Strength Index Crossover (RSI-C) system are very similar to the results for the related Relative Strength Index Peaks (RSI-P) system. The RSI-C system made long calls 42.4 percent of the time and these long hits were correct 61.3 percent of the time (Table 4.13a). When this system chose a cash position over a long position, this was a correct call 60.0 percent of the time.

When a long call was made, the average daily return was 0.056 percent (Table 4.14a). This is slightly below the comparable figure for the RSI-P system but is still higher than the average daily market return when cash positions were favored. Following the long recommendations does indeed put an investor in the market during relatively strong periods. However, the main problem here is that, almost a quarter of the time, investors following this strategy are in cash when they should be in the market. The returns that the investors could be earning when they are in cash positions is the opportunity cost, or forgone profits, of following this strategy. Investors missed out on a 0.054 percent daily return on 23.2 percent of the days in our test sample (Table 4.14a). These missed profit opportunities led to an average quarterly terminal wealth of only $10,154, compared to an average quarterly terminal wealth of $10,377 for following a simple buy-and-hold strategy.

The RSI-C system made short calls 49.7 percent of the time (Table 4.13b). Of these short calls, 59.9 percent were correct. When the system chose a cash position over a short position, this call was correct 60.9 percent of the time.

The major downfall of this system is that it chooses days of above-average market returns to make short recommendations. The average daily market return when short calls occurred was 0.060 percent (Table 4.14b). On these above-average return days, investors would want to be long, not short as the RSI-C indicator recommends. Ironically, the short signals of this system are better predictors of periods of above-average market return than the long signals are!

Comparing the results from the RSI-P system with those from the RSI-C system, it is hard to conclude that there is much benefit to using the RSI-C system. The idea behind using the crossover system rather than the peaks system was to decrease false signals, even though this came at the cost of later signals. However, following the crossover system results in a lower terminal wealth than following the peaks system. A simple buy-and-hold strategy would result in greater terminal wealth than following either of the systems based on the Relative Strength Index.

Table 4.13a
Relative Strength Crossover (RSI-C) Long Hit Analysis
(Average of all stocks)

Qtr	Optimal Long	RSI-C Long	Long Hits	Cash Hits	Total Hits	Long Right	Long Wrong	Cash Right	Cash Wrong
85:1	32.1%	32.2%	67.1%	67.9%	67.6%	21.6%	10.6%	46.0%	21.8%
85:2	30.2%	42.2%	65.2%	69.0%	67.4%	27.5%	14.7%	39.9%	17.9%
85:3	26.3%	45.7%	61.5%	73.7%	68.1%	28.1%	17.6%	40.0%	14.3%
85:4	36.6%	38.1%	68.1%	61.2%	63.8%	26.0%	12.1%	37.9%	24.0%
86:1	44.2%	29.0%	66.4%	55.3%	58.5%	19.3%	9.8%	39.2%	31.7%
86:2	39.7%	38.8%	61.0%	60.5%	60.7%	23.7%	15.1%	37.0%	24.2%
86:3	37.0%	46.4%	58.1%	62.0%	60.2%	26.9%	19.5%	33.2%	20.4%
86:4	38.5%	47.3%	63.1%	61.7%	62.3%	29.8%	17.5%	32.5%	20.2%
87:1	44.7%	32.1%	65.6%	55.6%	58.8%	21.1%	11.1%	37.7%	30.1%
87:2	40.0%	51.7%	60.4%	60.4%	60.4%	31.2%	20.5%	29.2%	19.1%
87:3	39.5%	38.3%	61.3%	60.6%	60.9%	23.5%	14.8%	37.4%	24.3%
87:4	37.9%	61.9%	56.1%	62.5%	58.6%	34.8%	27.2%	23.8%	14.3%
88:1	41.3%	29.3%	65.8%	59.1%	61.1%	19.2%	10.0%	41.8%	28.9%
88:2	39.3%	48.0%	62.2%	61.0%	61.6%	29.9%	18.2%	31.7%	20.3%
88:3	35.9%	48.4%	61.9%	64.6%	63.3%	30.0%	18.4%	33.3%	18.3%
88:4	36.3%	45.8%	64.6%	64.1%	64.3%	29.6%	16.2%	34.7%	19.5%
89:1	39.0%	35.5%	64.9%	60.7%	62.2%	23.0%	12.5%	39.1%	25.4%
89:2	40.2%	34.5%	65.6%	59.5%	61.6%	22.6%	11.9%	39.0%	26.5%
89:3	39.9%	37.2%	64.8%	59.6%	61.5%	24.1%	13.1%	37.4%	25.4%
89:4	38.3%	49.8%	61.2%	60.8%	61.0%	30.5%	19.3%	30.5%	19.7%
90:1	36.9%	52.5%	61.2%	63.9%	62.5%	32.2%	20.3%	30.3%	17.1%
90:2	39.2%	41.2%	64.4%	60.7%	62.2%	26.5%	14.7%	35.7%	23.1%
90:3	33.5%	56.1%	54.8%	65.6%	59.5%	30.7%	25.4%	28.8%	15.1%
90:4	40.8%	47.9%	61.6%	57.8%	59.6%	29.5%	18.4%	30.2%	22.0%
91:1	44.1%	31.1%	66.3%	57.0%	59.9%	20.6%	10.5%	39.3%	29.7%
91:2	39.7%	38.4%	60.2%	60.7%	60.5%	23.1%	15.3%	37.4%	24.2%
91:3	40.4%	44.9%	60.4%	59.1%	59.7%	27.2%	17.8%	32.5%	22.5%
91:4	41.2%	45.9%	59.5%	58.7%	59.0%	27.3%	18.6%	31.7%	22.3%
92:1	40.0%	38.3%	55.8%	59.2%	57.9%	21.4%	16.9%	36.5%	25.1%
92:2	38.6%	48.8%	56.9%	61.2%	59.1%	27.8%	21.0%	31.4%	19.9%
92:3	40.3%	47.2%	60.3%	59.0%	59.6%	28.5%	18.7%	31.2%	21.6%
92:4	41.9%	38.4%	63.0%	58.0%	59.9%	24.2%	14.2%	35.7%	25.9%
93:1	42.5%	36.8%	60.4%	57.3%	58.4%	22.2%	14.6%	36.2%	27.0%
93:2	42.1%	45.2%	59.2%	57.7%	58.3%	26.8%	18.5%	31.6%	23.2%
93:3	42.5%	38.7%	61.1%	57.6%	58.9%	23.7%	15.1%	35.3%	26.0%
93:4	41.5%	47.8%	58.4%	58.2%	58.3%	27.9%	19.9%	30.4%	21.8%
94:1	40.4%	41.7%	56.0%	59.0%	57.8%	23.3%	18.3%	34.4%	23.9%
94:2	40.6%	53.3%	57.4%	59.0%	58.2%	30.6%	22.7%	27.5%	19.1%
94:3	41.8%	43.8%	61.1%	58.7%	59.7%	26.8%	17.1%	33.0%	23.2%
94:4	39.5%	55.7%	57.2%	60.7%	58.8%	31.9%	23.8%	26.9%	17.4%
95:1	43.1%	35.0%	61.8%	56.8%	58.6%	21.6%	13.4%	36.9%	28.1%
95:2	43.7%	32.3%	62.2%	56.2%	58.2%	20.1%	12.2%	38.1%	29.6%
95:3	43.9%	34.7%	61.3%	55.6%	57.6%	21.3%	13.4%	36.3%	29.0%
95:4	43.4%	40.7%	59.0%	55.8%	57.1%	24.0%	16.7%	33.1%	26.2%
96:1	45.5%	40.4%	62.2%	54.7%	57.7%	25.1%	15.3%	32.6%	27.0%
96:2	42.1%	39.6%	58.0%	57.8%	57.9%	23.0%	16.6%	34.9%	25.5%
96:3	42.6%	48.5%	59.6%	57.3%	58.4%	28.9%	19.6%	29.5%	22.0%
96:4	44.3%	35.9%	60.3%	55.1%	57.0%	21.6%	14.2%	35.4%	28.8%
AVG	40.0%	42.4%	61.3%	60.0%	60.3%	25.8%	16.5%	34.5%	23.2%

Table 4.13b
Relative Strength Crossover (RSI-C) Short Hit Analysis
(Average of all stocks)

Qtr	Optimal Short	RSI-C Short	Short Hits	Cash Hits	Total Hits	Short Right	Short Wrong	Cash Right	Cash Wrong
85:1	34.3%	56.7%	67.7%	66.3%	67.1%	38.4%	18.3%	28.7%	14.6%
85:2	34.6%	49.3%	68.9%	65.0%	66.9%	33.9%	15.3%	33.0%	17.8%
85:3	38.6%	46.2%	73.6%	61.7%	67.2%	34.0%	12.2%	33.2%	20.6%
85:4	33.1%	49.9%	60.9%	66.7%	63.8%	30.4%	19.5%	33.4%	16.7%
86:1	35.2%	57.1%	55.0%	64.9%	59.2%	31.4%	25.7%	27.8%	15.1%
86:2	39.8%	54.1%	60.3%	60.6%	60.4%	32.6%	21.5%	27.8%	18.1%
86:3	42.7%	44.7%	62.0%	58.0%	59.8%	27.7%	16.9%	32.1%	23.3%
86:4	38.7%	47.9%	61.3%	62.5%	61.9%	29.4%	18.5%	32.5%	19.5%
87:1	36.9%	57.6%	55.4%	63.9%	59.0%	31.9%	25.7%	27.1%	15.3%
87:2	40.0%	41.7%	60.7%	60.3%	60.4%	25.3%	16.4%	35.1%	23.2%
87:3	40.4%	54.3%	60.6%	60.4%	60.5%	32.9%	21.4%	27.6%	18.1%
87:4	45.3%	29.4%	63.6%	55.7%	58.0%	18.7%	10.7%	39.3%	31.3%
88:1	36.7%	64.8%	58.7%	64.6%	60.8%	38.0%	26.8%	22.7%	12.5%
88:2	37.4%	44.8%	61.0%	62.2%	61.7%	27.4%	17.5%	34.3%	20.9%
88:3	38.4%	46.1%	64.5%	61.6%	63.0%	29.8%	16.4%	33.2%	20.7%
88:4	37.0%	48.1%	64.1%	64.1%	64.1%	30.8%	17.3%	33.3%	18.6%
89:1	36.2%	56.8%	60.4%	64.1%	62.0%	34.3%	22.5%	27.6%	15.5%
89:2	35.9%	56.5%	59.5%	64.5%	61.7%	33.6%	22.9%	28.0%	15.4%
89:3	36.4%	54.6%	59.8%	64.1%	61.8%	32.7%	21.9%	29.1%	16.3%
89:4	39.0%	41.5%	60.7%	60.9%	60.8%	25.2%	16.3%	35.6%	22.9%
90:1	40.1%	41.6%	64.0%	61.0%	62.2%	26.6%	15.0%	35.6%	22.7%
90:2	37.8%	51.7%	60.7%	63.6%	62.1%	31.4%	20.3%	30.7%	17.6%
90:3	45.7%	32.6%	65.9%	54.7%	58.3%	21.5%	11.1%	36.9%	30.6%
90:4	37.6%	42.2%	57.4%	61.5%	59.8%	24.2%	18.0%	35.6%	22.2%
91:1	36.7%	58.5%	56.9%	65.0%	60.3%	33.3%	25.2%	27.0%	14.5%
91:2	40.4%	55.1%	60.5%	59.6%	60.1%	33.3%	21.7%	26.8%	18.2%
91:3	39.8%	49.1%	59.0%	60.3%	59.7%	28.9%	20.1%	30.7%	20.2%
91:4	40.5%	45.5%	58.7%	59.2%	59.0%	26.7%	18.8%	32.3%	22.2%
92:1	43.2%	54.1%	59.2%	55.8%	57.7%	32.0%	22.1%	25.6%	20.3%
92:2	42.9%	44.9%	61.3%	56.9%	58.9%	27.5%	17.4%	31.4%	23.7%
92:3	39.5%	47.0%	58.9%	60.4%	59.7%	27.7%	19.3%	32.0%	21.0%
92:4	37.5%	53.1%	57.7%	62.4%	59.9%	30.7%	22.5%	29.3%	17.6%
93:1	39.4%	54.7%	57.3%	60.1%	58.6%	31.4%	23.4%	27.2%	18.1%
93:2	40.9%	47.6%	57.9%	59.1%	58.5%	27.6%	20.0%	31.0%	21.4%
93:3	39.4%	53.9%	57.7%	60.8%	59.1%	31.1%	22.8%	28.0%	18.1%
93:4	41.7%	44.8%	58.2%	58.2%	58.2%	26.1%	18.7%	32.1%	23.1%
94:1	43.7%	50.8%	58.9%	55.8%	57.4%	29.9%	20.9%	27.5%	21.7%
94:2	42.7%	39.2%	59.3%	57.5%	58.2%	23.2%	15.9%	35.0%	25.9%
94:3	39.8%	50.6%	58.5%	60.7%	59.6%	29.6%	21.0%	30.0%	19.4%
94:4	42.8%	37.0%	60.9%	57.2%	58.6%	22.5%	14.4%	36.1%	27.0%
95:1	38.7%	58.3%	56.7%	61.2%	58.6%	33.1%	25.2%	25.5%	16.1%
95:2	38.9%	59.0%	56.0%	61.1%	58.1%	33.1%	25.9%	25.1%	15.9%
95:3	38.9%	56.8%	55.7%	60.8%	57.9%	31.6%	25.2%	26.3%	16.9%
95:4	40.5%	50.5%	55.9%	59.1%	57.5%	28.2%	22.2%	29.3%	20.3%
96:1	38.9%	52.5%	54.6%	61.7%	58.0%	28.7%	23.8%	29.3%	18.2%
96:2	42.4%	54.6%	57.6%	57.6%	57.6%	31.4%	23.2%	26.2%	19.3%
96:3	40.8%	44.6%	57.2%	59.1%	58.3%	25.5%	19.1%	32.8%	22.7%
96:4	39.8%	54.5%	55.2%	59.8%	57.3%	30.1%	24.4%	27.2%	18.3%
AVG	39.4%	49.7%	59.9%	60.9%	60.2%	29.7%	20.0%	30.5%	19.8%

Table 4.14a
Relative Strength Crossover (RSI-C) Long Return Analysis
(Average of all stocks)

Qtr	RSI-C Terminal Wealth	Buy/Hold Terminal Wealth	Relative Terminal Wealth	RSI-C Long Avg Ret	RSI-C Cash Avg Ret	RSI-C Long-Cash Avg Ret	Buy/Hold Avg Ret
85:1	10074	10142	0.993	0.022%	-0.001%	0.024%	0.006%
85:2	9807	9700	1.011	-0.086%	-0.057%	-0.029%	-0.069%
85:3	9494	8889	1.068	-0.195%	-0.213%	0.018%	-0.205%
85:4	10180	10763	0.946	0.064%	0.133%	-0.069%	0.107%
86:1	10412	11428	0.911	0.229%	0.223%	0.006%	0.225%
86:2	10256	10414	0.985	0.107%	0.041%	0.067%	0.066%
86:3	9689	9175	1.056	-0.103%	-0.149%	0.047%	-0.128%
86:4	10313	10413	0.990	0.106%	0.036%	0.069%	0.069%
87:1	10744	11929	0.901	0.366%	0.258%	0.107%	0.293%
87:2	10138	10196	0.994	0.049%	0.026%	0.022%	0.038%
87:3	10270	10408	0.987	0.112%	0.041%	0.071%	0.068%
87:4	9446	8087	1.168	-0.130%	-0.519%	0.389%	-0.278%
88:1	10496	10989	0.955	0.274%	0.117%	0.157%	0.163%
88:2	10296	10593	0.972	0.104%	0.096%	0.008%	0.100%
88:3	10099	10050	1.005	0.037%	-0.010%	0.047%	0.013%
88:4	10191	10196	1.000	0.072%	0.007%	0.065%	0.037%
89:1	10258	10698	0.959	0.118%	0.109%	0.008%	0.112%
89:2	10319	10772	0.958	0.147%	0.109%	0.038%	0.122%
89:3	10342	10833	0.955	0.148%	0.121%	0.027%	0.131%
89:4	9891	9904	0.999	-0.031%	0.009%	-0.040%	-0.011%
90:1	10121	9980	1.014	0.041%	-0.040%	0.081%	0.003%
90:2	10315	10459	0.986	0.125%	0.043%	0.083%	0.077%
90:3	9120	8526	1.070	-0.269%	-0.246%	-0.024%	-0.259%
90:4	10250	10889	0.941	0.095%	0.193%	-0.098%	0.146%
91:1	10852	12477	0.870	0.438%	0.259%	0.179%	0.315%
91:2	10153	10244	0.991	0.068%	0.031%	0.037%	0.045%
91:3	10157	10429	0.974	0.055%	0.073%	-0.019%	0.065%
91:4	10290	10497	0.980	0.101%	0.066%	0.035%	0.082%
92:1	9992	10324	0.968	-0.009%	0.083%	-0.092%	0.048%
92:2	9814	9723	1.009	-0.067%	-0.030%	-0.037%	-0.048%
92:3	10156	10392	0.977	0.048%	0.064%	-0.017%	0.057%
92:4	10387	10963	0.948	0.156%	0.137%	0.019%	0.144%
93:1	10190	10527	0.968	0.081%	0.079%	0.002%	0.080%
93:2	10158	10340	0.982	0.055%	0.049%	0.007%	0.052%
93:3	10319	10686	0.966	0.127%	0.085%	0.042%	0.101%
93:4	10093	10255	0.984	0.028%	0.039%	-0.010%	0.034%
94:1	9955	9954	1.000	-0.023%	-0.003%	-0.020%	-0.011%
94:2	9979	9994	0.999	-0.011%	0.003%	-0.014%	-0.005%
94:3	10341	10613	0.974	0.117%	0.068%	0.049%	0.089%
94:4	9907	9836	1.007	-0.028%	-0.030%	0.002%	-0.029%
95:1	10274	10706	0.960	0.125%	0.102%	0.023%	0.110%
95:2	10318	10873	0.949	0.154%	0.124%	0.030%	0.134%
95:3	10295	10853	0.949	0.133%	0.130%	0.003%	0.131%
95:4	10137	10445	0.970	0.053%	0.077%	-0.024%	0.067%
96:1	10506	11027	0.953	0.196%	0.134%	0.063%	0.159%
96:2	10181	10367	0.982	0.073%	0.049%	0.025%	0.059%
96:3	10160	10298	0.987	0.053%	0.042%	0.011%	0.047%
96:4	10257	10817	0.948	0.111%	0.129%	-0.018%	0.122%
AVG	10154	10377	0.979	0.056%	0.054%	0.002%	0.055%

Table 4.14b
Relative Strength Crossover (RSI-C) Short Return Analysis
(Average of all stocks)

Qtr	RSI-C Terminal Wealth	Buy/Hold Terminal Wealth	Relative Terminal Wealth	RSI-C Short Avg Ret	RSI-C Cash Avg Ret	RSI-C Short-Cash Avg Ret	Buy/Hold Avg Ret
85:1	10033	10142	0.989	0.001%	0.013%	-0.012%	0.006%
85:2	10187	9700	1.050	-0.048%	-0.090%	0.043%	-0.069%
85:3	10668	8889	1.200	-0.210%	-0.200%	-0.011%	-0.205%
85:4	9551	10763	0.887	0.150%	0.064%	0.086%	0.107%
86:1	9226	11428	0.807	0.236%	0.209%	0.027%	0.225%
86:2	9831	10414	0.944	0.050%	0.085%	-0.035%	0.066%
86:3	10475	9175	1.142	-0.170%	-0.093%	-0.077%	-0.128%
86:4	9852	10413	0.946	0.044%	0.092%	-0.048%	0.069%
87:1	9071	11929	0.760	0.279%	0.312%	-0.034%	0.293%
87:2	9949	10196	0.976	0.017%	0.053%	-0.037%	0.038%
87:3	9845	10408	0.946	0.044%	0.097%	-0.053%	0.068%
87:4	10955	8087	1.355	-0.531%	-0.172%	-0.358%	-0.278%
88:1	9452	10989	0.860	0.135%	0.213%	-0.078%	0.163%
88:2	9739	10593	0.919	0.092%	0.106%	-0.015%	0.100%
88:3	10010	10050	0.996	-0.006%	0.029%	-0.035%	0.013%
88:4	9977	10196	0.978	0.005%	0.066%	-0.061%	0.037%
89:1	9587	10698	0.896	0.121%	0.101%	0.019%	0.112%
89:2	9589	10772	0.890	0.116%	0.130%	-0.014%	0.122%
89:3	9592	10833	0.885	0.123%	0.141%	-0.018%	0.131%
89:4	9964	9904	1.006	0.012%	-0.027%	0.039%	-0.011%
90:1	10112	9980	1.013	-0.045%	0.037%	-0.082%	0.003%
90:2	9850	10459	0.942	0.047%	0.108%	-0.061%	0.077%
90:3	10525	8526	1.234	-0.253%	-0.262%	0.008%	-0.259%
90:4	9445	10889	0.867	0.215%	0.096%	0.119%	0.146%
91:1	9127	12477	0.731	0.267%	0.382%	-0.115%	0.315%
91:2	9856	10244	0.962	0.037%	0.055%	-0.018%	0.045%
91:3	9790	10429	0.939	0.070%	0.060%	0.010%	0.065%
91:4	9800	10497	0.934	0.067%	0.094%	-0.026%	0.082%
92:1	9721	10324	0.942	0.086%	0.003%	0.083%	0.048%
92:2	10115	9723	1.040	-0.039%	-0.056%	0.017%	-0.048%
92:3	9811	10392	0.944	0.066%	0.048%	0.019%	0.057%
92:4	9516	10963	0.868	0.152%	0.137%	0.015%	0.144%
93:1	9741	10527	0.925	0.083%	0.076%	0.007%	0.080%
93:2	9887	10340	0.956	0.042%	0.060%	-0.018%	0.052%
93:3	9740	10686	0.911	0.083%	0.122%	-0.039%	0.101%
93:4	9896	10255	0.965	0.044%	0.026%	0.018%	0.034%
94:1	9997	9954	1.004	0.003%	-0.026%	0.028%	-0.011%
94:2	10020	9994	1.003	-0.006%	-0.004%	-0.002%	-0.005%
94:3	9772	10613	0.921	0.078%	0.101%	-0.023%	0.089%
94:4	10086	9836	1.025	-0.036%	-0.025%	-0.011%	-0.029%
95:1	9613	10706	0.898	0.111%	0.109%	0.002%	0.110%
95:2	9512	10873	0.875	0.138%	0.128%	0.010%	0.134%
95:3	9542	10853	0.879	0.137%	0.124%	0.013%	0.131%
95:4	9785	10445	0.937	0.073%	0.061%	0.012%	0.067%
96:1	9562	11027	0.867	0.139%	0.181%	-0.041%	0.159%
96:2	9814	10367	0.947	0.056%	0.061%	-0.005%	0.059%
96:3	9855	10298	0.957	0.054%	0.042%	0.011%	0.047%
96:4	9559	10817	0.884	0.135%	0.107%	0.029%	0.122%
AVG	9825	10377	0.947	0.060%	0.050%	0.010%	0.055%

Rate of Change Crossover

The Rate of Change Crossover (ROC-C) system measures the amount a stock's price has changed over a given number of past periods. This indicator measures essentially the same phenomenon as the Momentum Peaks (MOM-P) system (see page 128). The difference in the two indicators is that the change in price is expressed as a *percentage* of the price for the ROC-C system and as a *proportion* for the MOM-P system. Most short-term rallies will move about 6 percent, which is the level typically used to generate signals for this trading rule. Many short-term trading signals are generated by this rule.

Construction

In determining the rate of change, a past time period must be chosen. The rate of change is calculated by first subtracting the close for the chosen past period from the close today, which results in a value for the price change in absolute terms. This value is then divided by the close from the earlier period, and the answer is multiplied by 100. Thus:

$$\text{ROC} = [(\text{Close}_{\text{today}} - \text{Close}_{\text{P periods ago}})/\text{Close}_{\text{P periods ago}}] \cdot 100.$$

Trading signals are triggered whenever this ROC-C oscillator forms a peak above a given level or a trough below a given level. When a 6 percent level is used, a long signal is generated whenever the ROC falls below –6 percent and then reverses direction. If the ROC goes above 6 percent and then reverses direction, a short signal occurs.

Results

As might be expected, the results for this indicator, shown in Tables 4.15 and 4.16, are very similar to the results presented for the Momentum Peaks (MOM-P) indicator (see Tables 4.9 and 4.10). The ROC-C system makes long calls 37.5 percent of the time (Table 4.15a), slightly less often than the MOM-P system. However, the converse is true for the short calls. The ROC-C system makes short calls 52.4 percent of the time (Table 4.15b), which is more often than the MOM-P system.

When choosing between long and cash positions, this system's long calls are correct 61.5 percent of the time, and its cash calls are correct 60.2 percent of the time (Table 4.15a). When choosing between short and cash positions, this system's short calls are correct 60.2 percent of the time, and its cash calls are correct 61.0 percent of the time (Table 4.15b).

At 0.060 percent, the average daily return when a long call is made is greater than the average daily market return of 0.052 percent when cash is chosen over a long position (Table 4.16a). The 0.055 percent average daily market return when short calls are made is slightly below the average daily market return of 0.056 percent when cash is chosen over a short position (Table 4.16b). Therefore, this system is able, to some degree, to distinguish market periods of above-average performance and below-average performance.

The system is able to predict market periods of above- and below-average performance, but this information alone is not usually enough to generate trading profits greater than the profits of a buy-and-hold strategy. Trading long with the system results in profits that are only 97.8 percent of the buy-and-hold profits (Table 4.16a). For trading short with this indicator, the profitability drops to only 94.8 percent the buy-and-hold strategy's return.

The next indicator we will examine, the Rate of Change +6/−6 Crossover (ROC-X), is a variation of this system. Let's see whether this variation proves to be any more profitable.

Rate of Change +6/−6 Crossover

The previous system, the Rate of Change Crossover (ROC-C), traded on reversals. This system trades on crossovers through levels. Both of these systems use the same calculation to measure the rate at which price is changing per period.

For example, if the price increases begin to accelerate and then surpass 6 percent, the Rate of Change (ROC) oscillator will break through a 6 percent ROC line. This price acceleration may peak at 7 percent and then decelerate to a rate of below 6 percent. When the rate of the price increase falls below 6 percent, the oscillator will again pass through the 6 percent ROC line. At this point, a long trading signal will be generated. (Note that the previous system, the Rate of Change Crossover (ROC-C), would have traded earlier when price acceleration peaked at 7 percent.)

This same type of acceleration/deceleration of price can also occur. An accelerating price fall is represented by a negative ROC calculation that is growing in absolute value. For example, if the price of a stock is falling at a rate of 5 percent but begins to fall faster, the ROC calculation will fall from −5 percent to perhaps −7 percent. As this occurs, a −6 percent ROC line will be crossed. As soon as the price decrease slows to a rate of less than −6 percent, a trade will be triggered. As the −6 percent ROC line is crossed to the upside, a bullish, long signal occurs.

Construction

The details for constructing the oscillator for this system are exactly the same as for the construction of the ROC-C system just described. Refer to page 144 for detailed instructions.

Table 4.15a
Rate of Change Crossover (ROC-C) Long Hit Analysis
(Average of all stocks)

Qtr	Optimal Long	ROC-C Long	Long Hits	Cash Hits	Total Hits	Long Right	Long Wrong	Cash Right	Cash Wrong
85:1	32.1%	23.1%	66.0%	67.8%	67.4%	15.3%	7.9%	52.1%	24.8%
85:2	30.2%	34.2%	66.3%	69.1%	68.1%	22.7%	11.5%	45.4%	20.3%
85:3	26.3%	45.3%	61.6%	74.1%	68.4%	27.9%	17.4%	40.5%	14.2%
85:4	36.6%	30.9%	69.0%	62.2%	64.3%	21.3%	9.6%	43.0%	26.1%
86:1	44.2%	23.4%	66.6%	55.2%	57.8%	15.6%	7.8%	42.3%	34.4%
86:2	39.7%	35.8%	61.8%	60.7%	61.1%	22.1%	13.7%	38.9%	25.3%
86:3	37.0%	47.9%	58.5%	62.8%	60.8%	28.0%	19.9%	32.7%	19.4%
86:4	38.5%	41.8%	64.0%	62.3%	63.0%	26.8%	15.0%	36.3%	21.9%
87:1	44.7%	23.9%	67.5%	56.0%	58.7%	16.1%	7.8%	42.6%	33.5%
87:2	40.0%	49.1%	61.1%	61.3%	61.2%	30.0%	19.1%	31.2%	19.7%
87:3	39.5%	36.3%	60.8%	60.6%	60.7%	22.1%	14.2%	38.6%	25.1%
87:4	37.9%	54.8%	56.2%	64.4%	59.9%	30.8%	24.0%	29.1%	16.1%
88:1	41.3%	26.8%	65.5%	59.3%	61.0%	17.6%	9.2%	43.4%	29.8%
88:2	39.3%	43.9%	62.7%	61.0%	61.8%	27.6%	16.4%	34.2%	21.8%
88:3	35.9%	43.9%	62.1%	64.5%	63.4%	27.2%	16.6%	36.2%	19.9%
88:4	36.3%	43.7%	64.4%	64.5%	64.4%	28.1%	15.6%	36.3%	20.0%
89:1	39.0%	29.2%	64.6%	60.8%	61.9%	18.9%	10.3%	43.1%	27.7%
89:2	40.2%	27.3%	65.5%	59.6%	61.2%	17.9%	9.4%	43.3%	29.4%
89:3	39.9%	28.6%	65.0%	60.0%	61.5%	18.6%	10.0%	42.9%	28.5%
89:4	38.3%	47.9%	61.0%	61.1%	61.1%	29.2%	18.7%	31.8%	20.3%
90:1	36.9%	51.3%	61.4%	64.1%	62.7%	31.5%	19.8%	31.2%	17.5%
90:2	39.2%	36.6%	64.5%	60.4%	61.9%	23.6%	13.0%	38.3%	25.1%
90:3	33.5%	53.8%	54.4%	66.3%	59.9%	29.2%	24.5%	30.6%	15.6%
90:4	40.8%	37.8%	61.7%	58.1%	59.5%	23.3%	14.5%	36.1%	26.0%
91:1	44.1%	25.3%	67.2%	56.6%	59.3%	17.0%	8.3%	42.2%	32.5%
91:2	39.7%	34.8%	60.6%	60.9%	60.8%	21.1%	13.7%	39.7%	25.5%
91:3	40.4%	39.4%	60.7%	59.5%	60.0%	23.9%	15.5%	36.1%	24.5%
91:4	41.2%	42.9%	59.6%	58.6%	59.0%	25.6%	17.3%	33.5%	23.6%
92:1	40.0%	32.7%	55.3%	59.2%	57.9%	18.1%	14.6%	39.8%	27.5%
92:2	38.6%	46.3%	57.2%	61.4%	59.5%	26.5%	19.8%	33.0%	20.7%
92:3	40.3%	38.9%	61.0%	59.9%	60.3%	23.7%	15.2%	36.6%	24.5%
92:4	41.9%	31.7%	63.2%	58.2%	59.8%	20.0%	11.7%	39.8%	28.5%
93:1	42.5%	31.2%	60.9%	57.5%	58.6%	19.0%	12.2%	39.6%	29.2%
93:2	42.1%	40.8%	59.3%	57.7%	58.4%	24.2%	16.6%	34.2%	25.0%
93:3	42.5%	33.3%	60.7%	57.4%	58.5%	20.2%	13.1%	38.3%	28.4%
93:4	41.5%	42.0%	58.7%	58.6%	58.6%	24.7%	17.4%	34.0%	24.0%
94:1	40.4%	38.7%	56.0%	58.9%	57.8%	21.7%	17.0%	36.1%	25.2%
94:2	40.6%	51.3%	57.8%	59.7%	58.7%	29.7%	21.6%	29.1%	19.7%
94:3	41.8%	40.0%	61.2%	58.5%	59.6%	24.5%	15.5%	35.1%	24.9%
94:4	39.5%	53.3%	57.6%	60.8%	59.1%	30.7%	22.6%	28.4%	18.3%
95:1	43.1%	30.2%	61.9%	56.8%	58.4%	18.7%	11.5%	39.7%	30.1%
95:2	43.7%	26.2%	61.9%	56.0%	57.5%	16.2%	10.0%	41.3%	32.5%
95:3	43.9%	26.0%	61.3%	55.7%	57.2%	15.9%	10.1%	41.2%	32.8%
95:4	43.4%	36.5%	58.7%	55.7%	56.8%	21.5%	15.1%	35.4%	28.1%
96:1	45.5%	34.0%	61.6%	54.5%	56.9%	21.0%	13.1%	36.0%	30.0%
96:2	42.1%	36.3%	57.7%	57.7%	57.7%	20.9%	15.3%	36.8%	27.0%
96:3	42.6%	41.7%	59.3%	57.3%	58.1%	24.7%	17.0%	33.4%	24.9%
96:4	44.3%	31.3%	60.6%	55.3%	56.9%	19.0%	12.3%	38.0%	30.7%
AVG	40.0%	37.5%	61.5%	60.2%	60.4%	22.9%	14.6%	37.4%	25.0%

Table 4.15b
Rate of Change Crossover (ROC-C) Short Hit Analysis
(Average of all stocks)

Qtr	Optimal Short	ROC-C Short	Short Hits	Cash Hits	Total Hits	Short Right	Short Wrong	Cash Right	Cash Wrong
85:1	34.3%	60.4%	67.2%	65.2%	66.4%	40.6%	19.8%	25.8%	13.8%
85:2	34.6%	55.2%	68.6%	66.1%	67.5%	37.9%	17.3%	29.6%	15.2%
85:3	38.6%	46.1%	73.8%	61.7%	67.3%	34.0%	12.1%	33.2%	20.6%
85:4	33.1%	57.1%	62.3%	67.5%	64.6%	35.6%	21.5%	29.0%	13.9%
86:1	35.2%	62.9%	55.4%	64.9%	58.9%	34.8%	28.1%	24.1%	13.0%
86:2	39.8%	55.5%	60.7%	61.2%	61.0%	33.7%	21.8%	27.3%	17.2%
86:3	42.7%	43.1%	63.1%	58.3%	60.4%	27.2%	15.9%	33.2%	23.7%
86:4	38.7%	53.0%	62.4%	63.5%	62.9%	33.1%	19.9%	29.8%	17.2%
87:1	36.9%	63.9%	56.1%	64.9%	59.3%	35.8%	28.1%	23.5%	12.7%
87:2	40.0%	44.6%	61.4%	60.8%	61.1%	27.4%	17.2%	33.7%	21.7%
87:3	40.4%	54.5%	60.9%	60.0%	60.5%	33.2%	21.3%	27.3%	18.2%
87:4	45.3%	35.9%	65.1%	55.8%	59.1%	23.4%	12.5%	35.8%	28.3%
88:1	36.7%	64.9%	58.9%	63.9%	60.7%	38.3%	26.7%	22.4%	12.7%
88:2	37.4%	49.2%	61.1%	62.5%	61.8%	30.0%	19.1%	31.8%	19.1%
88:3	38.4%	48.4%	64.4%	61.8%	63.1%	31.2%	17.2%	31.9%	19.7%
88:4	37.0%	48.5%	64.5%	63.9%	64.2%	31.2%	17.2%	32.9%	18.6%
89:1	36.2%	61.2%	60.9%	64.2%	62.1%	37.2%	23.9%	24.9%	13.9%
89:2	35.9%	60.0%	59.7%	64.3%	61.6%	35.8%	24.2%	25.7%	14.3%
89:3	36.4%	58.0%	60.3%	64.0%	61.8%	34.9%	23.0%	26.9%	15.1%
89:4	39.0%	42.4%	61.5%	61.2%	61.3%	26.1%	16.3%	35.2%	22.4%
90:1	40.1%	41.6%	64.2%	60.9%	62.3%	26.7%	14.9%	35.6%	22.8%
90:2	37.8%	53.8%	60.6%	63.7%	62.0%	32.6%	21.2%	29.4%	16.8%
90:3	45.7%	33.0%	66.9%	54.7%	58.7%	22.1%	10.9%	36.6%	30.4%
90:4	37.6%	50.0%	57.7%	61.5%	59.6%	28.9%	21.2%	30.7%	19.2%
91:1	36.7%	56.5%	56.3%	64.3%	59.8%	31.8%	24.7%	28.0%	15.5%
91:2	40.4%	56.7%	60.9%	60.4%	60.6%	34.5%	22.2%	26.1%	17.1%
91:3	39.8%	52.9%	59.7%	61.0%	60.3%	31.5%	21.3%	28.7%	18.4%
91:4	40.5%	47.0%	58.9%	59.8%	59.4%	27.7%	19.3%	31.7%	21.3%
92:1	43.2%	55.1%	58.9%	55.3%	57.3%	32.4%	22.6%	24.8%	20.1%
92:2	42.9%	47.0%	61.6%	57.2%	59.3%	29.0%	18.1%	30.3%	22.7%
92:3	39.5%	52.4%	59.8%	60.7%	60.3%	31.4%	21.1%	28.9%	18.7%
92:4	37.5%	56.3%	58.0%	62.7%	60.1%	32.7%	23.7%	27.4%	16.3%
93:1	39.4%	56.6%	57.9%	61.3%	59.4%	32.7%	23.8%	26.6%	16.8%
93:2	40.9%	49.2%	58.0%	59.4%	58.7%	28.5%	20.7%	30.2%	20.6%
93:3	39.4%	56.1%	57.7%	61.2%	59.2%	32.3%	23.7%	26.9%	17.1%
93:4	41.7%	48.4%	58.6%	58.2%	58.4%	28.3%	20.1%	30.0%	21.6%
94:1	43.7%	52.5%	59.2%	56.2%	57.8%	31.1%	21.4%	26.7%	20.8%
94:2	42.7%	41.2%	59.7%	57.5%	58.4%	24.6%	16.6%	33.8%	25.0%
94:3	39.8%	53.1%	58.6%	60.7%	59.6%	31.1%	22.0%	28.5%	18.4%
94:4	42.8%	38.7%	61.1%	57.5%	58.9%	23.7%	15.1%	35.2%	26.1%
95:1	38.7%	61.5%	57.0%	61.8%	58.8%	35.0%	26.4%	23.8%	14.7%
95:2	38.9%	61.5%	55.9%	61.0%	57.9%	34.4%	27.1%	23.5%	15.0%
95:3	38.9%	62.2%	56.0%	60.8%	57.8%	34.8%	27.4%	23.0%	14.8%
95:4	40.5%	51.6%	55.7%	58.9%	57.3%	28.8%	22.8%	28.5%	19.9%
96:1	38.9%	55.2%	54.4%	61.1%	57.4%	30.0%	25.2%	27.4%	17.4%
96:2	42.4%	55.3%	57.5%	57.6%	57.6%	31.8%	23.5%	25.7%	19.0%
96:3	40.8%	49.8%	57.0%	58.7%	57.9%	28.4%	21.4%	29.5%	20.7%
96:4	39.8%	57.3%	55.5%	60.0%	57.4%	31.8%	25.5%	25.6%	17.1%
AVG	39.4%	52.4%	60.2%	61.0%	60.4%	31.5%	21.0%	28.9%	18.7%

Table 4.16a
Rate of Change Crossover (ROC-C) Long Return Analysis
(Average of all stocks)

Qtr	ROC-C Terminal Wealth	Buy/Hold Terminal Wealth	Relative Terminal Wealth	ROC-C Long Avg Ret	ROC-C Cash Avg Ret	ROC-C Long-Cash Avg Ret	Buy/Hold Avg Ret
85:1	10001	10142	0.986	-0.011%	0.012%	-0.023%	0.006%
85:2	9864	9700	1.017	-0.081%	-0.063%	-0.018%	-0.069%
85:3	9507	8889	1.070	-0.190%	-0.217%	0.028%	-0.205%
85:4	10183	10763	0.946	0.083%	0.117%	-0.034%	0.107%
86:1	10328	11428	0.904	0.226%	0.224%	0.002%	0.225%
86:2	10314	10414	0.990	0.142%	0.024%	0.117%	0.066%
86:3	9736	9175	1.061	-0.081%	-0.170%	0.089%	-0.128%
86:4	10346	10413	0.994	0.130%	0.025%	0.105%	0.069%
87:1	10706	11929	0.897	0.465%	0.239%	0.226%	0.293%
87:2	10282	10196	1.008	0.095%	-0.017%	0.112%	0.038%
87:3	10235	10408	0.983	0.105%	0.047%	0.058%	0.068%
87:4	9441	8087	1.167	-0.142%	-0.443%	0.301%	-0.278%
88:1	10466	10989	0.952	0.283%	0.119%	0.164%	0.163%
88:2	10313	10593	0.974	0.119%	0.085%	0.034%	0.100%
88:3	10097	10050	1.005	0.040%	-0.009%	0.049%	0.013%
88:4	10173	10196	0.998	0.068%	0.012%	0.057%	0.037%
89:1	10196	10698	0.953	0.112%	0.112%	0.000%	0.112%
89:2	10224	10772	0.949	0.132%	0.118%	0.014%	0.122%
89:3	10304	10833	0.951	0.170%	0.115%	0.054%	0.131%
89:4	9957	9904	1.005	-0.013%	-0.009%	-0.004%	-0.011%
90:1	10151	9980	1.017	0.052%	-0.049%	0.101%	0.003%
90:2	10234	10459	0.979	0.107%	0.059%	0.048%	0.077%
90:3	9137	8526	1.072	-0.278%	-0.237%	-0.040%	-0.259%
90:4	10210	10889	0.938	0.102%	0.174%	-0.072%	0.146%
91:1	10737	12477	0.861	0.468%	0.263%	0.205%	0.315%
91:2	10169	10244	0.993	0.083%	0.025%	0.057%	0.045%
91:3	10207	10429	0.979	0.082%	0.054%	0.029%	0.065%
91:4	10296	10497	0.981	0.120%	0.053%	0.067%	0.082%
92:1	9956	10324	0.964	-0.026%	0.084%	-0.109%	0.048%
92:2	9856	9723	1.014	-0.051%	-0.046%	-0.005%	-0.048%
92:3	10230	10392	0.984	0.090%	0.035%	0.055%	0.057%
92:4	10328	10963	0.942	0.163%	0.136%	0.027%	0.144%
93:1	10240	10527	0.973	0.120%	0.061%	0.059%	0.080%
93:2	10155	10340	0.982	0.063%	0.044%	0.019%	0.052%
93:3	10246	10686	0.959	0.114%	0.095%	0.020%	0.101%
93:4	10111	10255	0.986	0.041%	0.029%	0.012%	0.034%
94:1	9950	9954	1.000	-0.024%	-0.003%	-0.021%	-0.011%
94:2	10025	9994	1.003	0.004%	-0.014%	0.019%	-0.005%
94:3	10291	10613	0.970	0.111%	0.075%	0.036%	0.089%
94:4	9957	9836	1.012	-0.015%	-0.045%	0.030%	-0.029%
95:1	10264	10706	0.959	0.139%	0.097%	0.042%	0.110%
95:2	10244	10873	0.942	0.147%	0.130%	0.017%	0.134%
95:3	10206	10853	0.940	0.125%	0.133%	-0.008%	0.131%
95:4	10132	10445	0.970	0.057%	0.072%	-0.015%	0.067%
96:1	10416	11027	0.945	0.193%	0.141%	0.051%	0.159%
96:2	10114	10367	0.976	0.050%	0.064%	-0.014%	0.059%
96:3	10118	10298	0.983	0.046%	0.048%	-0.003%	0.047%
96:4	10233	10817	0.946	0.116%	0.125%	-0.009%	0.122%
AVG	10143	10377	0.978	0.060%	0.052%	0.008%	0.055%

Table 4.16b
Rate of Change Crossover (ROC-C) Short Return Analysis
(Average of all stocks)

Qtr	ROC-C Terminal Wealth	Buy/Hold Terminal Wealth	Relative Terminal Wealth	ROC-C Short Avg Ret	ROC-C Cash Avg Ret	ROC-C Short-Cash Avg Ret	Buy/Hold Avg Ret
85:1	9899	10142	0.976	0.036%	-0.039%	0.074%	0.006%
85:2	10233	9700	1.055	-0.055%	-0.087%	0.032%	-0.069%
85:3	10671	8889	1.200	-0.214%	-0.197%	-0.017%	-0.205%
85:4	9585	10763	0.891	0.121%	0.088%	0.034%	0.107%
86:1	9177	11428	0.803	0.226%	0.221%	0.005%	0.225%
86:2	9919	10414	0.952	0.028%	0.115%	-0.087%	0.066%
86:3	10529	9175	1.148	-0.191%	-0.079%	-0.112%	-0.128%
86:4	9913	10413	0.952	0.022%	0.122%	-0.100%	0.069%
87:1	9094	11929	0.762	0.243%	0.382%	-0.139%	0.293%
87:2	10054	10196	0.986	-0.021%	0.085%	-0.106%	0.038%
87:3	9832	10408	0.945	0.047%	0.094%	-0.047%	0.068%
87:4	11026	8087	1.363	-0.446%	-0.184%	-0.263%	-0.278%
88:1	9421	10989	0.857	0.141%	0.203%	-0.063%	0.163%
88:2	9731	10593	0.919	0.086%	0.113%	-0.026%	0.100%
88:3	10013	10050	0.996	-0.007%	0.031%	-0.038%	0.013%
88:4	9975	10196	0.978	0.006%	0.065%	-0.059%	0.037%
89:1	9551	10698	0.893	0.122%	0.097%	0.025%	0.112%
89:2	9545	10772	0.886	0.122%	0.122%	0.000%	0.122%
89:3	9573	10833	0.884	0.122%	0.144%	-0.022%	0.131%
89:4	10060	9904	1.016	-0.026%	0.000%	-0.026%	-0.011%
90:1	10132	9980	1.015	-0.053%	0.043%	-0.096%	0.003%
90:2	9809	10459	0.938	0.057%	0.099%	-0.042%	0.077%
90:3	10569	8526	1.240	-0.272%	-0.252%	-0.020%	-0.259%
90:4	9385	10889	0.862	0.200%	0.092%	0.109%	0.146%
91:1	9060	12477	0.726	0.295%	0.340%	-0.045%	0.315%
91:2	9896	10244	0.966	0.025%	0.072%	-0.047%	0.045%
91:3	9849	10429	0.944	0.047%	0.085%	-0.038%	0.065%
91:4	9868	10497	0.940	0.048%	0.112%	-0.064%	0.082%
92:1	9696	10324	0.939	0.094%	-0.008%	0.102%	0.048%
92:2	10156	9723	1.045	-0.051%	-0.046%	-0.004%	-0.048%
92:3	9887	10392	0.951	0.038%	0.077%	-0.039%	0.057%
92:4	9506	10963	0.867	0.146%	0.142%	0.005%	0.144%
93:1	9840	10527	0.935	0.051%	0.117%	-0.066%	0.080%
93:2	9907	10340	0.958	0.034%	0.069%	-0.036%	0.052%
93:3	9690	10686	0.907	0.094%	0.110%	-0.016%	0.101%
93:4	9904	10255	0.966	0.038%	0.030%	0.009%	0.034%
94:1	10033	9954	1.008	-0.008%	-0.015%	0.007%	-0.011%
94:2	10050	9994	1.006	-0.015%	0.002%	-0.017%	-0.005%
94:3	9755	10613	0.919	0.079%	0.100%	-0.021%	0.089%
94:4	10128	9836	1.030	-0.051%	-0.016%	-0.035%	-0.029%
95:1	9649	10706	0.901	0.095%	0.133%	-0.038%	0.110%
95:2	9496	10873	0.873	0.136%	0.131%	0.005%	0.134%
95:3	9523	10853	0.877	0.129%	0.134%	-0.005%	0.131%
95:4	9771	10445	0.935	0.076%	0.057%	0.020%	0.067%
96:1	9508	11027	0.862	0.151%	0.169%	-0.018%	0.159%
96:2	9780	10367	0.943	0.065%	0.051%	0.013%	0.059%
96:3	9806	10298	0.952	0.064%	0.031%	0.033%	0.047%
96:4	9558	10817	0.884	0.127%	0.115%	0.012%	0.122%
AVG	9834	10377	0.948	0.055%	0.056%	-0.001%	0.055%

Results

Overall, judging from the results presented in Tables 4.17 and 4.18, the Rate of Change +6/−6 Crossover (ROC-X) system does not appear to perform as well as the ROC-C system discussed in the previous section. The ROC-X system makes long calls 38.4 percent of the time (Table 4.17a), or slightly more than the 37.5 percent long call rate for the ROC-C system. These calls are correct 61.1 percent of the time, which is slightly less than the hit rate of 61.5 percent for long calls in the ROC-C system. Using the ROC-X system to choose long or cash positions during our test period resulted in an average quarterly terminal wealth of $10,137 (Table 4.18a). This is slightly less than the average quarterly terminal wealth of $10,143 achieved with the ROC-C system.

When the decision is between a short position or a cash position, the ROC-X system chooses a short position 51.6 percent of the time (Table 4.17b). This is slightly less than the 52.4 percent short call rate for the ROC-C system. These short calls are correct 59.9 percent of the time, which is just under the 60.1 percent hit rate for short calls in the ROC-C system. Using the ROC-X system to choose between short and cash positions results in an average quarterly terminal wealth of only $9,814 (Table 4.18b), which is $20 below the average quarterly terminal wealth of the ROC-C system. The quarterly terminal wealth with either of these systems is, on average, below the quarterly terminal wealth of a simple buy-and-hold strategy.

Our test results did not provide much evidence to support trading based solely on the ROC-X system.

Stochastic Peaks

George C. Lane, the developer of this system, based his work on the theory that prices tend to close near the end of a trading range before reversing. In other words, a stock's price will tend to close near the upper end of a trading range during an uptrend. As the trend matures, closes tend to occur farther away from the upper end of the trading range. The reverse movement often occurs in downtrending markets. Therefore, the movement of the closing price within the trading range gives clues as to future market movements and price reversals.

Construction

First, choose a time period, P. Today's closing price will be compared to the highest price and the lowest price that have occurred during the time period, P, using the following formula:

$$\%K = [(\text{Today's close} - \text{Low in period P})/(\text{High in period P} - \text{Low in period P})] \cdot 100.$$

Next, construct an S-period moving average of %K to smooth it. This S-period moving average line is referred to as %K Slowed.

After the %K Slowed line is calculated, apply a moving average to it. This moving average of %K Slowed is referred to as %D Trigger.

Choose a lower level to indicate an "oversold" market level. Whenever %D Trigger crosses under this lower level and turns back, forming a trough, a long signal is generated.

Finally, choose an upper level to indicate an "overbought" market condition. Whenever %D Trigger crosses above this upper level and turns down, forming a peak, a short signal is generated.

Results

The test results for the Stochastic Peaks (STO-P) system are shown in Tables 4.19 and 4.20. When choosing between long and cash positions, the indicator chooses a cash position 59.0 percent of the time. The hit rate for these cash calls is 60.0 percent (Table 4.19a), so, the majority of the time, these cash calls are correct. The system chooses a long position only 41.0 percent of the time. The hit rate for these long calls averages 61.6 percent.

The average daily return for long calls is 0.060 percent (Table 4.20a), which is indeed higher than the average daily return of 0.055 percent for our test period. The higher average daily return for long calls shows that this system is making long calls during periods of strong market returns. However, the average daily return when a cash position is taken is 0.052 percent. Therefore, investors following this strategy find themselves missing out on an average 0.052 percent return the majority of the time. Following the system's recommendations yields lower terminal wealth, on average, than investors would have had if they had followed a simple buy-and-hold strategy.

When choosing between short and cash positions, the indicator is about as likely to choose a short position as a cash position. The STO-P indicator chooses a short position 49.9 percent of the time, and the hit rate for these short calls is 60.1 percent (Table 4.19b). When a cash position is favored over a short position, this cash position is a correct call 61.1 percent of the time.

A close look at the results in Table 4.20 indicates a real problem with using this system's short calls as a trading strategy. On average, the market return on days when short calls are made is a positive 0.055 percent (Table 4.20b). Stock prices are rising when short calls are made. Thus, traders who have entered into short positions when this system has made short calls will find that their wealth is declining. Table 4.20b shows an average quarterly terminal wealth of only $9,838 for the short-versus-cash trading strategy. In addition, this average daily return on short call days is exactly the same as for cash call days. Therefore, the short calls of this system appear to be random. On any particular day, there is a 50 percent chance of getting a short call. If a

Table 4.17a
Rate of Change +6/−6 Crossover (ROC-X) Long Hit Analysis
(Average of all stocks)

Qtr	Optimal Long	ROC-X Long	Long Hits	Cash Hits	Total Hits	Long Right	Long Wrong	Cash Right	Cash Wrong
85:1	32.1%	25.9%	66.3%	67.7%	67.4%	17.1%	8.7%	50.2%	23.9%
85:2	30.2%	35.6%	65.3%	68.8%	67.5%	23.2%	12.3%	44.3%	20.1%
85:3	26.3%	43.7%	61.2%	73.5%	68.1%	26.8%	17.0%	41.4%	14.9%
85:4	36.6%	35.5%	67.6%	61.5%	63.6%	24.0%	11.5%	39.6%	24.8%
86:1	44.2%	26.6%	65.6%	55.3%	58.0%	17.5%	9.2%	40.6%	32.8%
86:2	39.7%	36.4%	60.8%	60.2%	60.4%	22.1%	14.3%	38.3%	25.3%
86:3	37.0%	42.1%	57.6%	61.9%	60.1%	24.2%	17.9%	35.8%	22.0%
86:4	38.5%	44.8%	63.1%	61.9%	62.4%	28.3%	16.6%	34.1%	21.0%
87:1	44.7%	30.7%	65.3%	55.6%	58.5%	20.0%	10.6%	38.5%	30.8%
87:2	40.0%	50.5%	60.3%	60.3%	60.3%	30.5%	20.1%	29.9%	19.6%
87:3	39.5%	36.7%	60.7%	60.6%	60.6%	22.2%	14.4%	38.4%	25.0%
87:4	37.9%	45.0%	55.4%	61.7%	58.8%	24.9%	20.1%	33.9%	21.1%
88:1	41.3%	33.5%	64.7%	59.3%	61.1%	21.7%	11.8%	39.4%	27.1%
88:2	39.3%	46.6%	62.0%	60.8%	61.4%	28.9%	17.7%	32.4%	20.9%
88:3	35.9%	43.3%	61.6%	64.3%	63.2%	26.7%	16.6%	36.5%	20.2%
88:4	36.3%	42.9%	64.3%	64.2%	64.3%	27.6%	15.3%	36.7%	20.4%
89:1	39.0%	30.7%	64.2%	60.7%	61.8%	19.7%	11.0%	42.1%	27.2%
89:2	40.2%	29.0%	65.2%	59.6%	61.2%	18.9%	10.1%	42.3%	28.7%
89:3	39.9%	29.8%	64.3%	59.8%	61.2%	19.2%	10.6%	42.0%	28.2%
89:4	38.3%	46.5%	60.5%	60.5%	60.5%	28.2%	18.4%	32.4%	21.1%
90:1	36.9%	51.2%	61.3%	63.8%	62.5%	31.4%	19.8%	31.1%	17.7%
90:2	39.2%	38.3%	63.9%	60.3%	61.7%	24.5%	13.8%	37.2%	24.5%
90:3	33.5%	47.5%	54.6%	65.9%	60.5%	25.9%	21.5%	34.6%	17.9%
90:4	40.8%	40.2%	61.5%	58.0%	59.4%	24.7%	15.5%	34.7%	25.1%
91:1	44.1%	33.2%	65.6%	56.9%	59.8%	21.8%	11.4%	38.0%	28.8%
91:2	39.7%	35.7%	59.5%	60.5%	60.1%	21.2%	14.4%	38.9%	25.4%
91:3	40.4%	39.5%	60.1%	59.1%	59.5%	23.7%	15.8%	35.7%	24.8%
91:4	41.2%	41.9%	59.6%	58.8%	59.1%	25.0%	16.9%	34.2%	23.9%
92:1	40.0%	38.2%	56.0%	59.6%	58.3%	21.4%	16.8%	36.8%	24.9%
92:2	38.6%	44.3%	56.9%	61.2%	59.3%	25.2%	19.1%	34.1%	21.6%
92:3	40.3%	40.9%	60.6%	59.7%	60.0%	24.8%	16.1%	35.3%	23.8%
92:4	41.9%	33.7%	63.0%	58.3%	59.9%	21.2%	12.5%	38.7%	27.6%
93:1	42.5%	32.2%	60.6%	57.3%	58.4%	19.5%	12.7%	38.8%	28.9%
93:2	42.1%	39.9%	59.4%	57.7%	58.4%	23.7%	16.2%	34.7%	25.4%
93:3	42.5%	35.0%	60.6%	57.5%	58.6%	21.2%	13.8%	37.4%	27.7%
93:4	41.5%	41.5%	58.7%	58.5%	58.6%	24.4%	17.2%	34.2%	24.2%
94:1	40.4%	39.9%	56.0%	58.9%	57.7%	22.3%	17.5%	35.4%	24.7%
94:2	40.6%	48.8%	57.5%	59.1%	58.4%	28.1%	20.7%	30.3%	20.9%
94:3	41.8%	41.5%	61.2%	58.6%	59.7%	25.4%	16.1%	34.3%	24.2%
94:4	39.5%	52.0%	57.6%	60.6%	59.1%	30.0%	22.0%	29.1%	18.9%
95:1	43.1%	32.3%	61.5%	56.7%	58.3%	19.9%	12.4%	38.4%	29.3%
95:2	43.7%	27.5%	61.4%	55.9%	57.5%	16.9%	10.6%	40.6%	32.0%
95:3	43.9%	27.4%	60.7%	55.6%	57.0%	16.6%	10.8%	40.4%	32.2%
95:4	43.4%	36.1%	58.9%	55.9%	57.0%	21.3%	14.8%	35.7%	28.2%
96:1	45.5%	36.1%	61.5%	54.6%	57.1%	22.2%	13.9%	34.9%	29.1%
96:2	42.1%	37.6%	57.9%	57.8%	57.9%	21.8%	15.8%	36.1%	26.3%
96:3	42.6%	42.2%	59.7%	57.5%	58.4%	25.2%	17.0%	33.3%	24.5%
96:4	44.3%	32.0%	60.7%	55.2%	57.0%	19.4%	12.6%	37.6%	30.5%
AVG	40.0%	38.4%	61.1%	60.0%	60.2%	23.3%	15.0%	36.9%	24.8%

Table 4.17b
Rate of Change +6/−6 Crossover (ROC-X) Short Hit Analysis
(Average of all stocks)

Qtr	Optimal Short	ROC-X Short	Short Hits	Cash Hits	Total Hits	Short Right	Short Wrong	Cash Right	Cash Wrong
85:1	34.3%	58.1%	66.9%	65.9%	66.5%	38.9%	19.2%	27.6%	14.3%
85:2	34.6%	52.8%	68.3%	65.2%	66.8%	36.0%	16.8%	30.8%	16.4%
85:3	38.6%	47.0%	73.1%	61.6%	67.0%	34.4%	12.6%	32.6%	20.4%
85:4	33.1%	50.9%	60.8%	66.1%	63.4%	30.9%	20.0%	32.4%	16.7%
86:1	35.2%	57.4%	55.3%	64.0%	59.0%	31.8%	25.7%	27.3%	15.3%
86:2	39.8%	54.9%	60.1%	59.9%	60.0%	33.0%	21.9%	27.0%	18.1%
86:3	42.7%	48.3%	62.1%	57.5%	59.7%	30.0%	18.3%	29.7%	22.0%
86:4	38.7%	50.5%	61.6%	62.4%	62.0%	31.1%	19.4%	30.9%	18.6%
87:1	36.9%	56.5%	55.5%	63.2%	58.9%	31.4%	25.1%	27.5%	16.0%
87:2	40.0%	43.0%	60.6%	60.2%	60.4%	26.1%	16.9%	34.3%	22.7%
87:3	40.4%	54.7%	60.6%	59.7%	60.2%	33.1%	21.6%	27.0%	18.3%
87:4	45.3%	42.1%	62.6%	55.0%	58.2%	26.3%	15.8%	31.9%	26.0%
88:1	36.7%	59.7%	58.7%	63.6%	60.7%	35.1%	24.7%	25.6%	14.7%
88:2	37.4%	46.5%	60.7%	61.9%	61.3%	28.2%	18.3%	33.2%	20.4%
88:3	38.4%	49.9%	64.2%	61.7%	63.0%	32.1%	17.9%	30.9%	19.2%
88:4	37.0%	49.2%	64.1%	63.8%	64.0%	31.5%	17.6%	32.4%	18.4%
89:1	36.2%	58.3%	60.3%	63.2%	61.6%	35.2%	23.1%	26.4%	15.3%
89:2	35.9%	57.6%	59.6%	64.0%	61.5%	34.4%	23.3%	27.1%	15.3%
89:3	36.4%	57.6%	59.8%	63.3%	61.3%	34.5%	23.2%	26.8%	15.5%
89:4	39.0%	42.0%	60.7%	60.6%	60.7%	25.5%	16.5%	35.2%	22.8%
90:1	40.1%	41.8%	63.7%	60.7%	62.0%	26.7%	15.2%	35.3%	22.8%
90:2	37.8%	52.5%	60.3%	63.2%	61.7%	31.7%	20.8%	30.0%	17.5%
90:3	45.7%	40.0%	66.2%	54.5%	59.2%	26.5%	13.5%	32.7%	27.3%
90:4	37.6%	48.4%	57.4%	61.2%	59.4%	27.8%	20.6%	31.6%	20.0%
91:1	36.7%	53.8%	56.6%	64.3%	60.1%	30.5%	23.4%	29.7%	16.5%
91:2	40.4%	55.5%	60.4%	59.1%	59.8%	33.6%	22.0%	26.3%	18.2%
91:3	39.8%	52.1%	59.3%	60.4%	59.8%	30.9%	21.2%	28.9%	19.0%
91:4	40.5%	48.1%	59.3%	59.7%	59.5%	28.5%	19.6%	31.0%	20.9%
92:1	43.2%	51.9%	59.5%	55.8%	57.7%	30.9%	21.0%	26.8%	21.3%
92:2	42.9%	48.0%	61.3%	56.9%	59.0%	29.4%	18.6%	29.6%	22.4%
92:3	39.5%	51.1%	59.7%	60.7%	60.2%	30.5%	20.6%	29.7%	19.2%
92:4	37.5%	54.2%	58.0%	62.4%	60.0%	31.4%	22.7%	28.6%	17.2%
93:1	39.4%	55.2%	57.6%	60.8%	59.0%	31.8%	23.4%	27.2%	17.5%
93:2	40.9%	50.4%	57.9%	59.5%	58.7%	29.2%	21.2%	29.5%	20.1%
93:3	39.4%	54.0%	57.7%	61.2%	59.3%	31.1%	22.9%	28.1%	17.9%
93:4	41.7%	48.4%	58.5%	58.3%	58.4%	28.3%	20.1%	30.1%	21.5%
94:1	43.7%	51.2%	58.9%	55.8%	57.4%	30.2%	21.1%	27.2%	21.5%
94:2	42.7%	43.1%	59.4%	57.5%	58.3%	25.6%	17.5%	32.7%	24.2%
94:3	39.8%	52.1%	58.7%	60.9%	59.8%	30.6%	21.5%	29.1%	18.7%
94:4	42.8%	39.9%	61.0%	57.5%	58.9%	24.4%	15.6%	34.6%	25.5%
95:1	38.7%	59.1%	56.6%	61.0%	58.4%	33.5%	25.7%	24.9%	16.0%
95:2	38.9%	59.7%	55.8%	60.5%	57.7%	33.3%	26.4%	24.4%	15.9%
95:3	38.9%	59.8%	56.0%	60.6%	57.8%	33.5%	26.3%	24.4%	15.9%
95:4	40.5%	52.1%	56.0%	59.2%	57.5%	29.1%	22.9%	28.4%	19.6%
96:1	38.9%	53.5%	54.5%	61.0%	57.5%	29.2%	24.4%	28.4%	18.1%
96:2	42.4%	54.5%	57.6%	57.5%	57.6%	31.4%	23.1%	26.2%	19.3%
96:3	40.8%	49.6%	57.4%	59.1%	58.2%	28.5%	21.1%	29.8%	20.6%
96:4	39.8%	57.0%	55.2%	60.0%	57.2%	31.5%	25.6%	25.8%	17.2%
AVG	39.4%	51.6%	59.9%	60.7%	60.1%	30.8%	20.7%	29.3%	19.1%

Table 4.18a
Rate of Change +6/−6 Crossover (ROC-X) Long Return Analysis
(Average of all stocks)

Qtr	ROC-X Terminal Wealth	Buy/Hold Terminal Wealth	Relative Terminal Wealth	ROC-X Long Avg Ret	ROC-X Cash Avg Ret	ROC-X Long-Cash Avg Ret	Buy/Hold Avg Ret
85:1	10031	10142	0.989	0.001%	0.008%	-0.007%	0.006%
85:2	9795	9700	1.010	-0.106%	-0.049%	-0.057%	-0.069%
85:3	9491	8889	1.068	-0.203%	-0.206%	0.003%	-0.205%
85:4	10130	10763	0.941	0.045%	0.141%	-0.095%	0.107%
86:1	10379	11428	0.908	0.226%	0.224%	0.001%	0.225%
86:2	10183	10414	0.978	0.081%	0.058%	0.022%	0.066%
86:3	9647	9175	1.052	-0.129%	-0.126%	-0.003%	-0.128%
86:4	10278	10413	0.987	0.097%	0.046%	0.051%	0.069%
87:1	10758	11929	0.902	0.387%	0.251%	0.136%	0.293%
87:2	10141	10196	0.995	0.050%	0.025%	0.025%	0.038%
87:3	10237	10408	0.984	0.104%	0.048%	0.056%	0.068%
87:4	9417	8087	1.165	-0.204%	-0.338%	0.134%	-0.278%
88:1	10517	10989	0.957	0.252%	0.118%	0.135%	0.163%
88:2	10262	10593	0.969	0.096%	0.103%	-0.008%	0.100%
88:3	10074	10050	1.002	0.033%	-0.003%	0.036%	0.013%
88:4	10158	10196	0.996	0.064%	0.016%	0.047%	0.037%
89:1	10207	10698	0.954	0.110%	0.114%	-0.004%	0.112%
89:2	10241	10772	0.951	0.133%	0.118%	0.015%	0.122%
89:3	10295	10833	0.950	0.157%	0.120%	0.037%	0.131%
89:4	9884	9904	0.998	-0.038%	0.012%	-0.050%	-0.011%
90:1	10112	9980	1.013	0.040%	-0.037%	0.077%	0.003%
90:2	10218	10459	0.977	0.095%	0.065%	0.030%	0.077%
90:3	9274	8526	1.088	-0.258%	-0.259%	0.001%	-0.259%
90:4	10196	10889	0.936	0.089%	0.185%	-0.096%	0.146%
91:1	10965	12477	0.879	0.459%	0.243%	0.216%	0.315%
91:2	10114	10244	0.987	0.058%	0.039%	0.019%	0.045%
91:3	10109	10429	0.969	0.044%	0.079%	-0.035%	0.065%
91:4	10275	10497	0.979	0.104%	0.066%	0.038%	0.082%
92:1	10041	10324	0.973	0.011%	0.070%	-0.059%	0.048%
92:2	9829	9723	1.011	-0.065%	-0.035%	-0.030%	-0.048%
92:3	10206	10392	0.982	0.073%	0.045%	0.028%	0.057%
92:4	10395	10963	0.948	0.178%	0.127%	0.050%	0.144%
93:1	10218	10527	0.971	0.103%	0.068%	0.035%	0.080%
93:2	10175	10340	0.984	0.071%	0.039%	0.032%	0.052%
93:3	10243	10686	0.959	0.108%	0.097%	0.010%	0.101%
93:4	10113	10255	0.986	0.041%	0.029%	0.012%	0.034%
94:1	9948	9954	0.999	-0.024%	-0.003%	-0.021%	-0.011%
94:2	9965	9994	0.997	-0.015%	0.005%	-0.020%	-0.005%
94:3	10309	10613	0.971	0.113%	0.073%	0.040%	0.089%
94:4	9949	9836	1.011	-0.019%	-0.040%	0.021%	-0.029%
95:1	10246	10706	0.957	0.123%	0.104%	0.019%	0.110%
95:2	10247	10873	0.942	0.140%	0.132%	0.009%	0.134%
95:3	10210	10853	0.941	0.121%	0.135%	-0.014%	0.131%
95:4	10136	10445	0.970	0.059%	0.071%	-0.012%	0.067%
96:1	10448	11027	0.948	0.195%	0.139%	0.056%	0.159%
96:2	10148	10367	0.979	0.063%	0.056%	0.006%	0.059%
96:3	10137	10298	0.984	0.051%	0.044%	0.007%	0.047%
96:4	10245	10817	0.947	0.120%	0.123%	-0.003%	0.122%
AVG	10137	10377	0.977	0.055%	0.055%	0.000%	0.055%

Table 4.18b
Rate of Change +6/−6 Crossover (ROC-X) Short Return Analysis
(Average of all stocks)

Qtr	ROC-X Terminal Wealth	Buy/Hold Terminal Wealth	Relative Terminal Wealth	ROC-X Short Avg Ret	ROC-X Cash Avg Ret	ROC-X Short-Cash Avg Ret	Buy/Hold Avg Ret
85:1	9934	10142	0.979	0.028%	-0.024%	0.052%	0.006%
85:2	10184	9700	1.050	-0.039%	-0.103%	0.065%	-0.069%
85:3	10641	8889	1.197	-0.200%	-0.209%	0.008%	-0.205%
85:4	9477	10763	0.881	0.172%	0.039%	0.132%	0.107%
86:1	9213	11428	0.806	0.238%	0.207%	0.031%	0.225%
86:2	9781	10414	0.939	0.067%	0.066%	0.001%	0.066%
86:3	10441	9175	1.138	-0.145%	-0.112%	-0.033%	-0.128%
86:4	9822	10413	0.943	0.052%	0.087%	-0.035%	0.069%
87:1	9120	11929	0.764	0.268%	0.325%	-0.057%	0.293%
87:2	9954	10196	0.976	0.014%	0.056%	-0.042%	0.038%
87:3	9809	10408	0.942	0.054%	0.086%	-0.031%	0.068%
87:4	10818	8087	1.338	-0.342%	-0.231%	-0.111%	-0.278%
88:1	9468	10989	0.862	0.143%	0.193%	-0.050%	0.163%
88:2	9676	10593	0.913	0.112%	0.089%	0.023%	0.100%
88:3	10002	10050	0.995	-0.003%	0.028%	-0.031%	0.013%
88:4	9952	10196	0.976	0.014%	0.059%	-0.045%	0.037%
89:1	9544	10698	0.892	0.131%	0.087%	0.044%	0.112%
89:2	9557	10772	0.887	0.124%	0.120%	0.003%	0.122%
89:3	9547	10833	0.881	0.130%	0.133%	-0.003%	0.131%
89:4	9946	9904	1.004	0.016%	-0.031%	0.047%	-0.011%
90:1	10091	9980	1.011	-0.037%	0.031%	-0.068%	0.003%
90:2	9805	10459	0.937	0.061%	0.095%	-0.034%	0.077%
90:3	10689	8526	1.254	-0.266%	-0.254%	-0.012%	-0.259%
90:4	9346	10889	0.858	0.219%	0.078%	0.142%	0.146%
91:1	9219	12477	0.739	0.261%	0.378%	-0.118%	0.315%
91:2	9826	10244	0.959	0.046%	0.045%	0.002%	0.045%
91:3	9773	10429	0.937	0.072%	0.057%	0.014%	0.065%
91:4	9793	10497	0.933	0.066%	0.096%	-0.030%	0.082%
92:1	9767	10324	0.946	0.074%	0.019%	0.055%	0.048%
92:2	10123	9723	1.041	-0.039%	-0.057%	0.018%	-0.048%
92:3	9873	10392	0.950	0.042%	0.071%	-0.029%	0.057%
92:4	9528	10963	0.869	0.143%	0.146%	-0.003%	0.144%
93:1	9805	10527	0.931	0.060%	0.104%	-0.043%	0.080%
93:2	9892	10340	0.957	0.037%	0.067%	-0.030%	0.052%
93:3	9708	10686	0.908	0.091%	0.113%	-0.022%	0.101%
93:4	9913	10255	0.967	0.035%	0.033%	0.002%	0.034%
94:1	9997	9954	1.004	0.004%	-0.027%	0.031%	-0.011%
94:2	10019	9994	1.002	-0.002%	-0.007%	0.005%	-0.005%
94:3	9771	10613	0.921	0.076%	0.104%	-0.029%	0.089%
94:4	10127	9836	1.030	-0.049%	-0.016%	-0.032%	-0.029%
95:1	9599	10706	0.897	0.113%	0.106%	0.008%	0.110%
95:2	9489	10873	0.873	0.142%	0.122%	0.021%	0.134%
95:3	9515	10853	0.877	0.136%	0.123%	0.013%	0.131%
95:4	9794	10445	0.938	0.068%	0.065%	0.004%	0.067%
96:1	9528	11027	0.864	0.148%	0.171%	-0.023%	0.159%
96:2	9787	10367	0.944	0.065%	0.051%	0.013%	0.059%
96:3	9833	10298	0.955	0.055%	0.040%	0.015%	0.047%
96:4	9567	10817	0.884	0.127%	0.116%	0.011%	0.122%
AVG	9814	10377	0.946	0.061%	0.049%	0.012%	0.055%

Table 4.19a
Stochastic Peaks (STO-P) Long Hit Analysis
(Average of all stocks)

Qtr	Optimal Long	STO-P Long	Long Hits	Cash Hits	Total Hits	Long Right	Long Wrong	Cash Right	Cash Wrong
85:1	32.1%	33.3%	67.3%	66.6%	66.8%	22.4%	10.9%	44.4%	22.3%
85:2	30.2%	41.2%	66.9%	68.8%	68.0%	27.5%	13.6%	40.4%	18.4%
85:3	26.3%	49.4%	62.3%	73.4%	67.9%	30.7%	18.6%	37.2%	13.5%
85:4	36.6%	31.8%	69.2%	61.5%	63.9%	22.0%	9.8%	41.9%	26.3%
86:1	44.2%	29.8%	66.2%	55.1%	58.5%	19.8%	10.1%	38.7%	31.5%
86:2	39.7%	40.4%	62.6%	61.0%	61.7%	25.3%	15.1%	36.4%	23.2%
86:3	37.0%	47.7%	58.3%	62.6%	60.5%	27.8%	19.9%	32.7%	19.6%
86:4	38.5%	43.3%	63.6%	61.9%	62.7%	27.6%	15.8%	35.1%	21.6%
87:1	44.7%	27.7%	67.8%	56.3%	59.5%	18.8%	8.9%	40.7%	31.6%
87:2	40.0%	48.5%	61.3%	60.8%	61.0%	29.7%	18.8%	31.3%	20.2%
87:3	39.5%	42.2%	60.5%	60.4%	60.4%	25.5%	16.7%	34.9%	22.9%
87:4	37.9%	56.5%	55.7%	63.4%	59.0%	31.5%	25.1%	27.6%	15.9%
88:1	41.3%	27.8%	64.8%	58.6%	60.4%	18.0%	9.8%	42.4%	29.9%
88:2	39.3%	47.3%	63.0%	61.0%	61.9%	29.8%	17.5%	32.1%	20.5%
88:3	35.9%	48.3%	61.8%	64.0%	62.9%	29.8%	18.5%	33.1%	18.6%
88:4	36.3%	45.1%	64.1%	63.2%	63.6%	28.9%	16.2%	34.7%	20.2%
89:1	39.0%	37.9%	64.4%	60.9%	62.2%	24.4%	13.5%	37.8%	24.3%
89:2	40.2%	32.4%	65.2%	59.4%	61.3%	21.1%	11.3%	40.2%	27.4%
89:3	39.9%	39.1%	65.5%	60.1%	62.2%	25.6%	13.5%	36.6%	24.3%
89:4	38.3%	45.1%	61.9%	60.9%	61.3%	27.9%	17.2%	33.4%	21.5%
90:1	36.9%	47.7%	61.1%	63.6%	62.4%	29.2%	18.6%	33.3%	19.0%
90:2	39.2%	40.2%	64.0%	60.9%	62.2%	25.7%	14.5%	36.5%	23.4%
90:3	33.5%	56.2%	54.8%	66.9%	60.1%	30.8%	25.4%	29.3%	14.5%
90:4	40.8%	39.4%	62.5%	58.3%	59.9%	24.6%	14.8%	35.3%	25.3%
91:1	44.1%	31.0%	66.6%	56.6%	59.7%	20.7%	10.3%	39.0%	29.9%
91:2	39.7%	41.1%	61.2%	61.3%	61.3%	25.1%	15.9%	36.1%	22.8%
91:3	40.4%	41.7%	61.5%	59.8%	60.5%	25.6%	16.0%	34.9%	23.5%
91:4	41.2%	45.0%	59.9%	58.8%	59.3%	26.9%	18.0%	32.3%	22.7%
92:1	40.0%	37.1%	55.7%	59.0%	57.8%	20.7%	16.5%	37.1%	25.8%
92:2	38.6%	46.5%	57.5%	61.8%	59.8%	26.7%	19.8%	33.0%	20.4%
92:3	40.3%	40.6%	60.5%	59.3%	59.7%	24.5%	16.1%	35.2%	24.2%
92:4	41.9%	33.0%	63.0%	57.8%	59.6%	20.8%	12.2%	38.7%	28.2%
93:1	42.5%	35.0%	61.5%	58.0%	59.2%	21.5%	13.5%	37.7%	27.3%
93:2	42.1%	45.4%	59.5%	57.9%	58.6%	27.0%	18.4%	31.6%	23.0%
93:3	42.5%	37.1%	60.8%	57.5%	58.7%	22.5%	14.5%	36.2%	26.8%
93:4	41.5%	44.3%	58.2%	58.1%	58.2%	25.8%	18.5%	32.4%	23.3%
94:1	40.4%	40.6%	56.2%	59.3%	58.1%	22.8%	17.8%	35.2%	24.2%
94:2	40.6%	49.8%	58.1%	60.0%	59.1%	28.9%	20.9%	30.1%	20.1%
94:3	41.8%	42.8%	60.5%	58.5%	59.4%	25.9%	16.9%	33.5%	23.7%
94:4	39.5%	52.9%	57.0%	60.5%	58.7%	30.2%	22.7%	28.5%	18.6%
95:1	43.1%	34.7%	62.5%	57.0%	58.9%	21.7%	13.0%	37.2%	28.1%
95:2	43.7%	32.7%	62.3%	56.1%	58.2%	20.4%	12.3%	37.8%	29.5%
95:3	43.9%	34.7%	61.6%	55.6%	57.7%	21.4%	13.3%	36.3%	29.0%
95:4	43.4%	40.5%	59.0%	55.5%	56.9%	23.9%	16.6%	33.0%	26.5%
96:1	45.5%	41.0%	61.7%	54.6%	57.5%	25.3%	15.7%	32.2%	26.8%
96:2	42.1%	41.3%	58.1%	57.7%	57.8%	24.0%	17.3%	33.8%	24.8%
96:3	42.6%	42.5%	58.7%	56.5%	57.4%	25.0%	17.6%	32.5%	25.0%
96:4	44.3%	37.4%	60.3%	55.3%	57.2%	22.5%	14.8%	34.6%	28.0%
AVG	40.0%	41.0%	61.6%	60.0%	60.4%	25.1%	15.9%	35.3%	23.7%

Table 4.19b
Stochastic Peaks (STO-P) Short Hit Analysis
(Average of all stocks)

Qtr	Optimal Short	STO-P Short	Short Hits	Cash Hits	Total Hits	Short Right	Short Wrong	Cash Right	Cash Wrong
85:1	34.3%	52.4%	65.8%	66.2%	66.0%	34.5%	17.9%	31.5%	16.1%
85:2	34.6%	48.1%	68.2%	66.3%	67.2%	32.8%	15.3%	34.4%	17.5%
85:3	38.6%	40.8%	72.5%	62.3%	66.5%	29.6%	11.2%	36.9%	22.3%
85:4	33.1%	53.6%	61.3%	68.0%	64.4%	32.8%	20.7%	31.6%	14.8%
86:1	35.2%	56.8%	55.1%	64.8%	59.3%	31.3%	25.5%	28.0%	15.2%
86:2	39.8%	51.4%	61.1%	61.7%	61.4%	31.4%	20.0%	30.0%	18.6%
86:3	42.7%	40.9%	63.1%	58.1%	60.2%	25.8%	15.1%	34.4%	24.8%
86:4	38.7%	50.6%	62.0%	63.2%	62.6%	31.3%	19.2%	31.2%	18.2%
87:1	36.9%	60.5%	56.5%	65.4%	60.0%	34.2%	26.3%	25.9%	13.7%
87:2	40.0%	44.8%	60.9%	60.8%	60.9%	27.3%	17.5%	33.6%	21.6%
87:3	40.4%	48.5%	60.5%	60.0%	60.3%	29.3%	19.1%	30.9%	20.6%
87:4	45.3%	30.9%	64.3%	55.4%	58.1%	19.9%	11.0%	38.2%	30.8%
88:1	36.7%	64.1%	58.1%	63.4%	60.0%	37.3%	26.8%	22.8%	13.2%
88:2	37.4%	46.2%	61.1%	62.9%	62.1%	28.2%	18.0%	33.8%	19.9%
88:3	38.4%	44.3%	63.8%	61.7%	62.6%	28.2%	16.0%	34.4%	21.4%
88:4	37.0%	46.8%	63.5%	63.8%	63.7%	29.7%	17.1%	34.0%	19.3%
89:1	36.2%	54.3%	60.9%	63.8%	62.2%	33.1%	21.2%	29.2%	16.5%
89:2	35.9%	57.5%	59.4%	64.3%	61.5%	34.2%	23.4%	27.3%	15.2%
89:3	36.4%	51.3%	60.3%	64.6%	62.4%	30.9%	20.4%	31.4%	17.3%
89:4	39.0%	45.3%	60.8%	61.5%	61.2%	27.5%	17.8%	33.7%	21.1%
90:1	40.1%	44.5%	63.9%	61.1%	62.3%	28.4%	16.0%	33.9%	21.6%
90:2	37.8%	50.8%	61.2%	63.2%	62.2%	31.1%	19.7%	31.1%	18.1%
90:3	45.7%	30.9%	67.3%	54.8%	58.7%	20.8%	10.1%	37.9%	31.2%
90:4	37.6%	49.8%	57.5%	62.1%	59.8%	28.6%	21.2%	31.2%	19.0%
91:1	36.7%	55.3%	56.6%	64.7%	60.2%	31.3%	24.0%	28.9%	15.8%
91:2	40.4%	52.5%	61.3%	60.9%	61.1%	32.2%	20.3%	29.0%	18.6%
91:3	39.8%	51.2%	60.0%	61.5%	60.7%	30.7%	20.5%	30.0%	18.8%
91:4	40.5%	46.0%	59.1%	59.7%	59.4%	27.2%	18.8%	32.3%	21.8%
92:1	43.2%	52.7%	59.3%	56.1%	57.8%	31.3%	21.5%	26.5%	20.8%
92:2	42.9%	46.9%	62.0%	57.4%	59.5%	29.1%	17.8%	30.5%	22.6%
92:3	39.5%	51.9%	59.3%	60.4%	59.8%	30.8%	21.1%	29.0%	19.0%
92:4	37.5%	57.5%	57.8%	62.5%	59.8%	33.2%	24.3%	26.6%	15.9%
93:1	39.4%	55.7%	58.2%	61.2%	59.5%	32.4%	23.3%	27.1%	17.2%
93:2	40.9%	47.6%	58.3%	59.3%	58.8%	27.7%	19.8%	31.1%	21.3%
93:3	39.4%	54.7%	57.4%	60.6%	58.9%	31.4%	23.3%	27.5%	17.9%
93:4	41.7%	48.3%	57.9%	57.9%	57.9%	28.0%	20.3%	30.0%	21.7%
94:1	43.7%	52.3%	59.5%	56.3%	58.0%	31.1%	21.1%	26.9%	20.9%
94:2	42.7%	43.5%	60.2%	57.9%	58.9%	26.2%	17.3%	32.7%	23.8%
94:3	39.8%	50.0%	58.6%	60.3%	59.4%	29.3%	20.7%	30.1%	19.8%
94:4	42.8%	38.9%	60.5%	57.0%	58.4%	23.6%	15.4%	34.8%	26.3%
95:1	38.7%	58.5%	56.9%	61.9%	59.0%	33.3%	25.2%	25.7%	15.8%
95:2	38.9%	58.6%	56.2%	61.8%	58.6%	33.0%	25.7%	25.6%	15.8%
95:3	38.9%	56.8%	55.7%	61.2%	58.1%	31.6%	25.2%	26.5%	16.7%
95:4	40.5%	48.1%	55.2%	58.8%	57.1%	26.6%	21.6%	30.5%	21.4%
96:1	38.9%	51.4%	54.5%	61.3%	57.8%	28.0%	23.4%	29.8%	18.8%
96:2	42.4%	52.2%	58.0%	58.1%	58.0%	30.3%	22.0%	27.8%	20.0%
96:3	40.8%	48.0%	56.1%	58.4%	57.3%	27.0%	21.1%	30.3%	21.6%
96:4	39.8%	51.9%	55.0%	59.6%	57.2%	28.6%	23.3%	28.7%	19.4%
AVG	39.4%	49.9%	60.1%	61.1%	60.3%	29.8%	20.1%	30.5%	19.6%

Table 4.20a
Stochastic Peaks (STO-P) Long Return Analysis
(Average of all stocks)

Qtr	STO-P Terminal Wealth	Buy/Hold Terminal Wealth	Relative Terminal Wealth	STO-P Long Avg Ret	STO-P Cash Avg Ret	STO-P Long-Cash Avg Ret	Buy/Hold Avg Ret
85:1	9955	10142	0.982	-0.034%	0.027%	-0.061%	0.006%
85:2	9859	9700	1.016	-0.076%	-0.065%	-0.011%	-0.069%
85:3	9449	8889	1.063	-0.195%	-0.214%	0.019%	-0.205%
85:4	10173	10763	0.945	0.074%	0.122%	-0.048%	0.107%
86:1	10440	11428	0.914	0.236%	0.220%	0.016%	0.225%
86:2	10357	10414	0.995	0.137%	0.018%	0.119%	0.066%
86:3	9705	9175	1.058	-0.091%	-0.161%	0.070%	-0.128%
86:4	10331	10413	0.992	0.122%	0.029%	0.093%	0.069%
87:1	10827	11929	0.908	0.466%	0.227%	0.240%	0.293%
87:2	10257	10196	1.006	0.087%	-0.008%	0.095%	0.038%
87:3	10254	10408	0.985	0.097%	0.047%	0.050%	0.068%
87:4	9360	8087	1.157	-0.159%	-0.433%	0.275%	-0.278%
88:1	10393	10989	0.946	0.233%	0.136%	0.097%	0.163%
88:2	10341	10593	0.976	0.120%	0.081%	0.039%	0.100%
88:3	10048	10050	1.000	0.020%	0.006%	0.014%	0.013%
88:4	10108	10196	0.991	0.044%	0.030%	0.014%	0.037%
89:1	10272	10698	0.960	0.118%	0.109%	0.009%	0.112%
89:2	10280	10772	0.954	0.138%	0.115%	0.024%	0.122%
89:3	10383	10833	0.958	0.156%	0.115%	0.042%	0.131%
89:4	9981	9904	1.008	-0.004%	-0.016%	0.012%	-0.011%
90:1	10093	9980	1.011	0.036%	-0.028%	0.064%	0.003%
90:2	10230	10459	0.978	0.096%	0.064%	0.032%	0.077%
90:3	9152	8526	1.073	-0.261%	-0.256%	-0.005%	-0.259%
90:4	10279	10889	0.944	0.121%	0.163%	-0.041%	0.146%
91:1	11306	12477	0.906	0.446%	0.256%	0.189%	0.315%
91:2	10244	10244	1.000	0.098%	0.009%	0.089%	0.045%
91:3	10273	10429	0.985	0.103%	0.037%	0.066%	0.065%
91:4	10306	10497	0.982	0.114%	0.055%	0.059%	0.082%
92:1	9948	10324	0.964	-0.025%	0.091%	-0.116%	0.048%
92:2	9912	9723	1.019	-0.032%	-0.063%	0.031%	-0.048%
92:3	10153	10392	0.977	0.057%	0.056%	0.002%	0.057%
92:4	10286	10963	0.938	0.139%	0.147%	-0.008%	0.144%
93:1	10277	10527	0.976	0.125%	0.055%	0.070%	0.080%
93:2	10155	10340	0.982	0.057%	0.047%	0.010%	0.052%
93:3	10288	10686	0.963	0.120%	0.090%	0.030%	0.101%
93:4	10086	10255	0.984	0.028%	0.038%	-0.010%	0.034%
94:1	9996	9954	1.004	-0.004%	-0.016%	0.012%	-0.011%
94:2	10086	9994	1.009	0.024%	-0.033%	0.057%	-0.005%
94:3	10260	10613	0.967	0.094%	0.086%	0.008%	0.089%
94:4	9909	9836	1.007	-0.028%	-0.030%	0.002%	-0.029%
95:1	10307	10706	0.963	0.142%	0.093%	0.048%	0.110%
95:2	10316	10873	0.949	0.153%	0.125%	0.029%	0.134%
95:3	10306	10853	0.950	0.141%	0.126%	0.015%	0.131%
95:4	10107	10445	0.968	0.042%	0.084%	-0.042%	0.067%
96:1	10487	11027	0.951	0.189%	0.138%	0.051%	0.159%
96:2	10159	10367	0.980	0.061%	0.057%	0.004%	0.059%
96:3	10044	10298	0.975	0.017%	0.070%	-0.053%	0.047%
96:4	10263	10817	0.949	0.109%	0.130%	-0.021%	0.122%
AVG	10167	10377	0.980	0.060%	0.052%	0.009%	0.055%

Table 4.20b
Stochastic Peaks (STO-P) Short Return Analysis
(Average of all stocks)

Qtr	STO-P Terminal Wealth	Buy/Hold Terminal Wealth	Relative Terminal Wealth	STO-P Short Avg Ret	STO-P Cash Avg Ret	STO-P Short-Cash Avg Ret	Buy/Hold Avg Ret
85:1	9888	10142	0.975	0.044%	-0.035%	0.079%	0.006%
85:2	10191	9700	1.051	-0.055%	-0.083%	0.028%	-0.069%
85:3	10567	8889	1.189	-0.206%	-0.204%	-0.002%	-0.205%
85:4	9587	10763	0.891	0.127%	0.083%	0.044%	0.107%
86:1	9245	11428	0.809	0.229%	0.219%	0.009%	0.225%
86:2	9945	10414	0.955	0.018%	0.117%	-0.099%	0.066%
86:3	10485	9175	1.143	-0.186%	-0.087%	-0.099%	-0.128%
86:4	9908	10413	0.951	0.025%	0.114%	-0.089%	0.069%
87:1	9163	11929	0.768	0.236%	0.380%	-0.144%	0.293%
87:2	10015	10196	0.982	-0.010%	0.076%	-0.086%	0.038%
87:3	9845	10408	0.946	0.049%	0.087%	-0.038%	0.068%
87:4	10893	8087	1.347	-0.445%	-0.203%	-0.241%	-0.278%
88:1	9355	10989	0.851	0.159%	0.170%	-0.011%	0.163%
88:2	9774	10593	0.923	0.077%	0.119%	-0.042%	0.100%
88:3	9969	10050	0.992	0.009%	0.016%	-0.007%	0.013%
88:4	9922	10196	0.973	0.025%	0.046%	-0.021%	0.037%
89:1	9614	10698	0.899	0.117%	0.107%	0.010%	0.112%
89:2	9570	10772	0.888	0.119%	0.126%	-0.007%	0.122%
89:3	9623	10833	0.888	0.119%	0.144%	-0.025%	0.131%
89:4	10060	9904	1.016	-0.024%	0.000%	-0.024%	-0.011%
90:1	10130	9980	1.015	-0.048%	0.044%	-0.092%	0.003%
90:2	9804	10459	0.937	0.062%	0.092%	-0.031%	0.077%
90:3	10538	8526	1.236	-0.278%	-0.251%	-0.027%	-0.259%
90:4	9426	10889	0.866	0.187%	0.106%	0.081%	0.146%
91:1	9132	12477	0.732	0.273%	0.367%	-0.095%	0.315%
91:2	9973	10244	0.974	0.004%	0.091%	-0.087%	0.045%
91:3	9919	10429	0.951	0.029%	0.103%	-0.074%	0.065%
91:4	9880	10497	0.941	0.042%	0.116%	-0.074%	0.082%
92:1	9715	10324	0.941	0.093%	-0.003%	0.096%	0.048%
92:2	10201	9723	1.049	-0.065%	-0.034%	-0.031%	-0.048%
92:3	9820	10392	0.945	0.060%	0.053%	0.007%	0.057%
92:4	9478	10963	0.865	0.151%	0.136%	0.015%	0.144%
93:1	9846	10527	0.935	0.053%	0.113%	-0.060%	0.080%
93:2	9902	10340	0.958	0.037%	0.065%	-0.028%	0.052%
93:3	9701	10686	0.908	0.093%	0.111%	-0.019%	0.101%
93:4	9890	10255	0.964	0.042%	0.026%	0.016%	0.034%
94:1	10062	9954	1.011	-0.018%	-0.004%	-0.014%	-0.011%
94:2	10114	9994	1.012	-0.038%	0.021%	-0.059%	-0.005%
94:3	9739	10613	0.918	0.088%	0.090%	-0.002%	0.089%
94:4	10069	9836	1.024	-0.027%	-0.031%	0.003%	-0.029%
95:1	9661	10706	0.902	0.097%	0.128%	-0.031%	0.110%
95:2	9567	10873	0.880	0.123%	0.150%	-0.027%	0.134%
95:3	9577	10853	0.882	0.125%	0.139%	-0.014%	0.131%
95:4	9742	10445	0.933	0.092%	0.043%	0.049%	0.067%
96:1	9562	11027	0.867	0.143%	0.176%	-0.033%	0.159%
96:2	9843	10367	0.949	0.049%	0.069%	-0.021%	0.059%
96:3	9751	10298	0.947	0.085%	0.012%	0.072%	0.047%
96:4	9559	10817	0.884	0.140%	0.103%	0.037%	0.122%
AVG	9838	10377	0.948	0.055%	0.055%	0.000%	0.055%

short call does occur, investors cannot expect the return on that day to be distinguishable from an average day.

Overall, using the STO-P system alone to make trading decisions will not lead to above-average profits. Let's now look at the Stochastic +80/+20 Crossover, another system based on the same stochastic oscillator, to see how trading might be improved.

Stochastic +80/+20 Crossover

This system is based on the same stochastic oscillator as the Stochastic Peaks (STO-P) system just discussed. The only differences between these two systems are the criteria for and the timing of signal generation. For the Stochastic +80/+20 Crossover (STO-C) system, the oscillator must move beyond a level, form a peak or valley, turn back, and cross through the same level before a trade is signaled. (Remember that trades were generated as peaks or valleys were formed in the STO-P system.)

Long signals occur when the stochastic oscillator moves below a lower level of +20 and then moves back up through the same level. Short signals occur as the stochastic oscillator moves above an upper level of +80 and then falls back through this same level.

Construction

Because the stochastic oscillator used with this system is the same oscillator that is used with the STO-P system described earlier, we will not repeat the details here. Refer to page 150 to review its construction.

Results

The results for this indicator are shown in Tables 4.21 and 4.22. The Stochastic +80/+20 Crossover (STO-C) system generates long and short calls much less frequently than the STO-P system. As shown in Table 4.21a, when choosing to go long or be in cash, the system chooses long positions 24.7 percent of the time. This rate is far below the optimal long rate of 40.0 percent, but it is about the average long call rate of the sixty technical indicators included in this book. The long calls for the STO-C system are correct 61.1 percent of the time. (Recall that the long hit rate for the STO-P system was very similar: 61.6 percent.) The cash decisions the STO-C system makes are correct 60.1 percent of the time. This means that investors who follow this system are in a correct long or cash position 60.2 percent of the time.

Unfortunately, when long calls are made by the system, the average daily return is less than when the system favors a cash position. The average daily return for long calls is only 0.051 percent (Table 4.22a). When investors following this system are in a cash position, the average daily return is 0.056 percent; so these investors are missing some of the most important days to be in the market. As a consequence, the terminal wealth of the STO-C system tends to be lower than the terminal wealth of the STO-P system. The average quarterly terminal wealth of $10,080 (Table 4.22a) is only 97.1 percent of the average terminal wealth of a buy-and-hold strategy.

When choosing to go short or be in cash, the STO-C system chooses short positions 29.3 percent of the time (Table 4.21b). This number is much lower than the 49.9 percent short call rate of the STO-P system. Despite the difference in frequency of short calls between the two systems, the accuracy of the systems' calls is very similar. The hit rate for short calls is 59.8 percent for the STO-C system, compared to the short call hit rate of 60.1 percent for the STO-P model.

The STO-C system appears to have an advantage over the STO-P system when we compare the average quarterly terminal wealth realized. On average, trading short with the STO-C system will result in terminal wealth of $9,900 (Table 4.22b); trading short with the STO-P system will result in terminal wealth of only $9,838. However, it is hard to see this as a great advantage. Both systems have average quarterly terminal wealth amounts that fall below the initial investment of $10,000. Wise investors should not depend solely on either of these systems to make short-position decisions.

TRIX Momentum Peaks

Traders use moving averages to smooth daily data; this smoothing helps them to see real underlying trends and not be distracted by insignificant daily price movements. By taking moving averages of moving averages, data are smoothed even more. One popular system that makes use of this technique is the Triple Exponential Moving Average (TRIX) system, in which an exponential moving average of an exponential moving average of an exponential moving average is calculated to smooth data.

Nirvana has taken the TRIX system one step farther by calculating the momentum of the TRIX oscillator and measuring the rate at which the TRIX is gaining or losing strength. Therefore, it gives early warning signals—turning down before the TRIX itself turns down, and turning up before the TRIX itself turns up. In our study, we tested Nirvana's advanced version of the TRIX Momentum Peaks (TXM-P) indicator.

Construction

TRIX is constructed by calculating three moving averages. The first (EMA_1) is a P-period exponential moving average of the closing price. The

Table 4.21a
Stochastic Crossover (STO-C) Long Hit Analysis
(Average of all stocks)

Qtr	Optimal Long	STO-C Long	Long Hits	Cash Hits	Total Hits	Long Right	Long Wrong	Cash Right	Cash Wrong
85:1	32.1%	20.0%	66.1%	67.7%	67.4%	13.2%	6.8%	54.2%	25.8%
85:2	30.2%	25.4%	66.3%	69.6%	68.8%	16.8%	8.5%	51.9%	22.7%
85:3	26.3%	29.2%	61.0%	73.2%	69.7%	17.8%	11.4%	51.9%	19.0%
85:4	36.6%	20.1%	68.7%	62.5%	63.8%	13.8%	6.3%	49.9%	29.9%
86:1	44.2%	18.7%	64.6%	55.5%	57.2%	12.1%	6.6%	45.1%	36.2%
86:2	39.7%	24.8%	61.6%	60.7%	60.9%	15.3%	9.5%	45.6%	29.5%
86:3	37.0%	28.7%	57.2%	62.8%	61.2%	16.4%	12.3%	44.8%	26.5%
86:4	38.5%	24.4%	63.5%	61.9%	62.3%	15.5%	8.9%	46.8%	28.8%
87:1	44.7%	18.9%	67.6%	56.0%	58.2%	12.8%	6.1%	45.4%	35.6%
87:2	40.0%	28.7%	59.4%	59.9%	59.8%	17.1%	11.7%	42.7%	28.6%
87:3	39.5%	25.0%	59.6%	60.2%	60.0%	14.9%	10.1%	45.1%	29.9%
87:4	37.9%	33.2%	56.9%	63.4%	61.2%	18.9%	14.3%	42.4%	24.5%
88:1	41.3%	16.3%	63.2%	58.4%	59.2%	10.3%	6.0%	48.9%	34.8%
88:2	39.3%	28.8%	62.4%	60.7%	61.2%	17.9%	10.8%	43.2%	28.0%
88:3	35.9%	28.1%	61.1%	63.7%	63.0%	17.1%	10.9%	45.8%	26.1%
88:4	36.3%	26.2%	64.5%	63.7%	63.9%	16.9%	9.3%	47.0%	26.8%
89:1	39.0%	22.0%	63.7%	60.8%	61.4%	14.0%	8.0%	47.4%	30.6%
89:2	40.2%	19.4%	64.3%	59.6%	60.5%	12.5%	6.9%	48.1%	32.5%
89:3	39.9%	23.4%	65.2%	60.1%	61.3%	15.2%	8.1%	46.1%	30.6%
89:4	38.3%	26.9%	60.7%	61.1%	61.0%	16.4%	10.6%	44.6%	28.4%
90:1	36.9%	27.9%	61.7%	63.8%	63.2%	17.2%	10.7%	46.0%	26.1%
90:2	39.2%	23.8%	64.3%	61.1%	61.8%	15.3%	8.5%	46.5%	29.7%
90:3	33.5%	34.2%	55.0%	66.6%	62.7%	18.8%	15.4%	43.9%	21.9%
90:4	40.8%	25.2%	60.0%	58.0%	58.5%	15.1%	10.1%	43.4%	31.4%
91:1	44.1%	19.4%	66.2%	56.2%	58.2%	12.8%	6.5%	45.3%	35.3%
91:2	39.7%	24.8%	60.6%	60.7%	60.7%	15.0%	9.8%	45.6%	29.5%
91:3	40.4%	26.4%	61.2%	59.6%	60.0%	16.1%	10.2%	43.9%	29.7%
91:4	41.2%	27.5%	59.7%	58.9%	59.1%	16.4%	11.1%	42.7%	29.8%
92:1	40.0%	22.2%	55.1%	59.4%	58.4%	12.2%	10.0%	46.2%	31.6%
92:2	38.6%	27.1%	57.1%	61.5%	60.3%	15.5%	11.6%	44.9%	28.1%
92:3	40.3%	24.9%	59.5%	59.3%	59.4%	14.8%	10.1%	44.6%	30.6%
92:4	41.9%	20.5%	62.8%	58.2%	59.1%	12.8%	7.6%	46.3%	33.3%
93:1	42.5%	21.0%	61.9%	57.9%	58.7%	13.0%	8.0%	45.7%	33.3%
93:2	42.1%	27.2%	58.9%	58.1%	58.3%	16.0%	11.2%	42.3%	30.5%
93:3	42.5%	22.8%	60.8%	57.6%	58.4%	13.8%	8.9%	44.5%	32.7%
93:4	41.5%	26.6%	57.5%	58.3%	58.1%	15.3%	11.3%	42.8%	30.7%
94:1	40.4%	23.9%	56.5%	59.5%	58.8%	13.5%	10.4%	45.3%	30.8%
94:2	40.6%	29.2%	57.1%	59.5%	58.8%	16.7%	12.5%	42.1%	28.7%
94:3	41.8%	25.4%	60.4%	58.4%	58.9%	15.3%	10.0%	43.5%	31.1%
94:4	39.5%	32.6%	56.0%	60.3%	58.9%	18.3%	14.4%	40.6%	26.8%
95:1	43.1%	20.8%	62.2%	56.9%	58.0%	13.0%	7.9%	45.1%	34.1%
95:2	43.7%	19.4%	61.5%	56.2%	57.2%	11.9%	7.5%	45.3%	35.3%
95:3	43.9%	20.1%	61.8%	55.8%	57.0%	12.4%	7.7%	44.6%	35.3%
95:4	43.4%	25.1%	59.1%	56.2%	56.9%	14.8%	10.3%	42.1%	32.8%
96:1	45.5%	25.3%	61.8%	54.7%	56.5%	15.6%	9.7%	40.9%	33.9%
96:2	42.1%	24.2%	57.6%	57.8%	57.7%	14.0%	10.3%	43.8%	32.0%
96:3	42.6%	26.2%	57.7%	56.8%	57.0%	15.1%	11.1%	41.9%	31.9%
96:4	44.3%	22.8%	59.9%	55.5%	56.5%	13.6%	9.1%	42.8%	34.4%
AVG	40.0%	24.7%	61.1%	60.1%	60.2%	15.0%	9.7%	45.2%	30.1%

Table 4.21b
Stochastic Crossover (STO-C) Short Hit Analysis
(Average of all stocks)

Qtr	Optimal Short	STO-C Short	Short Hits	Cash Hits	Total Hits	Short Right	Short Wrong	Cash Right	Cash Wrong
85:1	34.3%	31.8%	66.1%	66.1%	66.1%	21.0%	10.8%	45.0%	23.1%
85:2	34.6%	29.5%	68.0%	65.7%	66.4%	20.1%	9.4%	46.3%	24.2%
85:3	38.6%	25.9%	72.6%	62.0%	64.7%	18.8%	7.1%	46.0%	28.2%
85:4	33.1%	33.5%	60.5%	67.2%	64.9%	20.3%	13.3%	44.6%	21.8%
86:1	35.2%	33.4%	54.9%	64.8%	61.5%	18.3%	15.0%	43.2%	23.5%
86:2	39.8%	30.4%	61.0%	60.9%	60.9%	18.5%	11.9%	42.4%	27.2%
86:3	42.7%	25.9%	63.3%	58.0%	59.3%	16.4%	9.5%	42.9%	31.1%
86:4	38.7%	29.3%	60.7%	61.8%	61.5%	17.8%	11.5%	43.7%	27.0%
87:1	36.9%	34.1%	56.3%	63.9%	61.3%	19.2%	14.9%	42.1%	23.8%
87:2	40.0%	25.8%	60.8%	60.3%	60.4%	15.7%	10.1%	44.7%	29.4%
87:3	40.4%	28.8%	59.9%	59.5%	59.6%	17.3%	11.6%	42.3%	28.8%
87:4	45.3%	18.2%	65.8%	55.4%	57.3%	12.0%	6.2%	45.3%	36.4%
88:1	36.7%	37.6%	57.6%	62.9%	60.9%	21.6%	15.9%	39.3%	23.1%
88:2	37.4%	26.4%	60.0%	62.5%	61.8%	15.8%	10.6%	46.0%	27.6%
88:3	38.4%	26.0%	63.5%	61.4%	62.0%	16.5%	9.5%	45.5%	28.6%
88:4	37.0%	27.5%	62.6%	63.1%	63.0%	17.2%	10.3%	45.8%	26.8%
89:1	36.2%	32.2%	60.0%	63.6%	62.4%	19.3%	12.9%	43.1%	24.7%
89:2	35.9%	33.3%	58.9%	64.0%	62.3%	19.6%	13.7%	42.6%	24.0%
89:3	36.4%	30.4%	60.1%	64.1%	62.9%	18.3%	12.1%	44.6%	25.0%
89:4	39.0%	26.2%	60.3%	61.0%	60.8%	15.8%	10.4%	45.1%	28.8%
90:1	40.1%	27.0%	64.7%	60.7%	61.7%	17.5%	9.5%	44.3%	28.7%
90:2	37.8%	29.6%	60.9%	62.8%	62.2%	18.0%	11.6%	44.2%	26.2%
90:3	45.7%	19.4%	67.2%	54.6%	57.0%	13.0%	6.4%	44.0%	36.6%
90:4	37.6%	29.4%	56.6%	62.0%	60.4%	16.7%	12.8%	43.7%	26.8%
91:1	36.7%	33.5%	57.1%	64.1%	61.8%	19.1%	14.4%	42.6%	23.8%
91:2	40.4%	31.0%	60.7%	60.0%	60.2%	18.8%	12.2%	41.4%	27.6%
91:3	39.8%	29.3%	58.9%	60.4%	60.0%	17.3%	12.0%	42.7%	28.0%
91:4	40.5%	27.7%	58.6%	59.5%	59.3%	16.2%	11.5%	43.0%	29.3%
92:1	43.2%	31.7%	58.4%	56.3%	56.9%	18.5%	13.2%	38.4%	29.9%
92:2	42.9%	27.4%	61.7%	57.3%	58.5%	16.9%	10.5%	41.6%	31.0%
92:3	39.5%	30.6%	58.4%	60.0%	59.5%	17.9%	12.7%	41.7%	27.8%
92:4	37.5%	32.8%	57.3%	62.5%	60.8%	18.8%	14.0%	42.0%	25.2%
93:1	39.4%	33.1%	58.1%	61.2%	60.2%	19.3%	13.9%	40.9%	25.9%
93:2	40.9%	27.8%	57.4%	59.1%	58.6%	16.0%	11.8%	42.6%	29.5%
93:3	39.4%	31.2%	57.7%	60.8%	59.8%	18.0%	13.2%	41.8%	27.0%
93:4	41.7%	28.1%	57.9%	58.1%	58.0%	16.2%	11.8%	41.8%	30.1%
94:1	43.7%	30.7%	59.0%	56.2%	57.0%	18.1%	12.6%	38.9%	30.4%
94:2	42.7%	25.7%	60.4%	57.7%	58.4%	15.6%	10.2%	42.8%	31.4%
94:3	39.8%	29.1%	58.5%	60.2%	59.7%	17.0%	12.1%	42.7%	28.2%
94:4	42.8%	22.2%	59.6%	56.9%	57.5%	13.2%	9.0%	44.3%	33.5%
95:1	38.7%	32.9%	56.5%	61.4%	59.8%	18.6%	14.3%	41.2%	25.9%
95:2	38.9%	33.3%	55.6%	61.1%	59.3%	18.5%	14.8%	40.8%	25.9%
95:3	38.9%	32.2%	55.5%	61.2%	59.3%	17.9%	14.3%	41.5%	26.3%
95:4	40.5%	28.3%	55.3%	59.3%	58.2%	15.6%	12.6%	42.5%	29.2%
96:1	38.9%	29.5%	54.5%	61.3%	59.3%	16.1%	13.4%	43.3%	27.3%
96:2	42.4%	30.1%	57.2%	57.6%	57.5%	17.2%	12.9%	40.3%	29.6%
96:3	40.8%	26.3%	56.9%	59.2%	58.6%	15.0%	11.3%	43.7%	30.0%
96:4	39.8%	30.4%	55.8%	60.3%	58.9%	17.0%	13.4%	42.0%	27.6%
AVG	39.4%	29.3%	59.8%	60.8%	60.4%	17.4%	11.9%	42.9%	27.8%

Table 4.22a
Stochastic Crossover (STO-C) Long Return Analysis
(Average of all stocks)

Qtr	STO-C Terminal Wealth	Buy/Hold Terminal Wealth	Relative Terminal Wealth	STO-C Long Avg Ret	STO-C Cash Avg Ret	STO-C Long-Cash Avg Ret	Buy/Hold Avg Ret
85:1	10003	10142	0.986	-0.004%	0.009%	-0.013%	0.006%
85:2	9909	9700	1.022	-0.073%	-0.068%	-0.005%	-0.069%
85:3	9621	8889	1.082	-0.219%	-0.199%	-0.021%	-0.205%
85:4	10106	10763	0.939	0.077%	0.114%	-0.037%	0.107%
86:1	10201	11428	0.893	0.174%	0.236%	-0.063%	0.225%
86:2	10217	10414	0.981	0.137%	0.043%	0.094%	0.066%
86:3	9808	9175	1.069	-0.100%	-0.139%	0.039%	-0.128%
86:4	10216	10413	0.981	0.143%	0.045%	0.097%	0.069%
87:1	10536	11929	0.883	0.447%	0.257%	0.190%	0.293%
87:2	10075	10196	0.988	0.046%	0.035%	0.011%	0.038%
87:3	10100	10408	0.970	0.067%	0.069%	-0.001%	0.068%
87:4	9780	8087	1.209	-0.082%	-0.375%	0.293%	-0.278%
88:1	10165	10989	0.925	0.169%	0.162%	0.007%	0.163%
88:2	10169	10593	0.960	0.098%	0.100%	-0.002%	0.100%
88:3	9995	10050	0.994	0.001%	0.017%	-0.016%	0.013%
88:4	10093	10196	0.990	0.061%	0.028%	0.033%	0.037%
89:1	10138	10698	0.948	0.104%	0.115%	-0.011%	0.112%
89:2	10143	10772	0.942	0.118%	0.123%	-0.005%	0.122%
89:3	10222	10833	0.944	0.155%	0.124%	0.032%	0.131%
89:4	9963	9904	1.006	-0.018%	-0.008%	-0.010%	-0.011%
90:1	10111	9980	1.013	0.068%	-0.022%	0.090%	0.003%
90:2	10153	10459	0.971	0.106%	0.068%	0.039%	0.077%
90:3	9510	8526	1.115	-0.244%	-0.266%	0.022%	-0.259%
90:4	9994	10889	0.918	-0.002%	0.196%	-0.198%	0.146%
91:1	10500	12477	0.842	0.418%	0.290%	0.128%	0.315%
91:2	10126	10244	0.989	0.083%	0.033%	0.051%	0.045%
91:3	10145	10429	0.973	0.089%	0.056%	0.033%	0.065%
91:4	10151	10497	0.967	0.086%	0.080%	0.005%	0.082%
92:1	9957	10324	0.964	-0.035%	0.071%	-0.106%	0.048%
92:2	9926	9723	1.021	-0.048%	-0.048%	0.000%	-0.048%
92:3	10036	10392	0.966	0.023%	0.068%	-0.045%	0.057%
92:4	10182	10963	0.929	0.139%	0.146%	-0.007%	0.144%
93:1	10177	10527	0.967	0.134%	0.065%	0.068%	0.080%
93:2	10053	10340	0.972	0.032%	0.059%	-0.027%	0.052%
93:3	10174	10686	0.952	0.119%	0.096%	0.024%	0.101%
93:4	10021	10255	0.977	0.011%	0.042%	-0.031%	0.034%
94:1	9992	9954	1.004	-0.006%	-0.013%	0.006%	-0.011%
94:2	10005	9994	1.001	0.001%	-0.007%	0.008%	-0.005%
94:3	10149	10613	0.956	0.091%	0.089%	0.002%	0.089%
94:4	9888	9836	1.005	-0.058%	-0.016%	-0.042%	-0.029%
95:1	10194	10706	0.952	0.149%	0.100%	0.050%	0.110%
95:2	10157	10873	0.934	0.129%	0.135%	-0.006%	0.134%
95:3	10174	10853	0.938	0.138%	0.129%	0.009%	0.131%
95:4	10093	10445	0.966	0.057%	0.070%	-0.013%	0.067%
96:1	10305	11027	0.935	0.193%	0.147%	0.045%	0.159%
96:2	10093	10367	0.974	0.061%	0.058%	0.003%	0.059%
96:3	9963	10298	0.968	-0.022%	0.072%	-0.093%	0.047%
96:4	10155	10817	0.939	0.107%	0.127%	-0.020%	0.122%
AVG	10080	10377	0.971	0.051%	0.056%	-0.005%	0.055%

Table 4.22b
Stochastic Crossover (STO-C) Short Return Analysis
(Average of all stocks)

Qtr	STO-C Terminal Wealth	Buy/Hold Terminal Wealth	Relative Terminal Wealth	STO-C Short Avg Ret	STO-C Cash Avg Ret	STO-C Short-Cash Avg Ret	Buy/Hold Avg Ret
85:1	9949	10142	0.981	0.032%	-0.006%	0.037%	0.006%
85:2	10107	9700	1.042	-0.053%	-0.076%	0.023%	-0.069%
85:3	10379	8889	1.168	-0.222%	-0.199%	-0.023%	-0.205%
85:4	9714	10763	0.903	0.140%	0.090%	0.051%	0.107%
86:1	9538	11428	0.835	0.235%	0.219%	0.016%	0.225%
86:2	9999	10414	0.960	0.001%	0.095%	-0.094%	0.066%
86:3	10346	9175	1.128	-0.213%	-0.097%	-0.116%	-0.128%
86:4	9905	10413	0.951	0.048%	0.078%	-0.030%	0.069%
87:1	9557	11929	0.801	0.219%	0.331%	-0.112%	0.293%
87:2	9985	10196	0.979	0.007%	0.049%	-0.042%	0.038%
87:3	9888	10408	0.950	0.060%	0.072%	-0.012%	0.068%
87:4	10707	8087	1.324	-0.597%	-0.207%	-0.390%	-0.278%
88:1	9559	10989	0.870	0.187%	0.148%	0.038%	0.163%
88:2	9847	10593	0.930	0.093%	0.102%	-0.010%	0.100%
88:3	9962	10050	0.991	0.022%	0.009%	0.012%	0.013%
88:4	9932	10196	0.974	0.038%	0.036%	0.002%	0.037%
89:1	9734	10698	0.910	0.136%	0.101%	0.035%	0.112%
89:2	9728	10772	0.903	0.130%	0.118%	0.012%	0.122%
89:3	9797	10833	0.904	0.108%	0.141%	-0.033%	0.131%
89:4	10007	9904	1.010	-0.007%	-0.013%	0.006%	-0.011%
90:1	10114	9980	1.013	-0.069%	0.029%	-0.098%	0.003%
90:2	9905	10459	0.947	0.051%	0.088%	-0.037%	0.077%
90:3	10322	8526	1.211	-0.266%	-0.257%	-0.008%	-0.259%
90:4	9590	10889	0.881	0.225%	0.114%	0.111%	0.146%
91:1	9517	12477	0.763	0.247%	0.349%	-0.103%	0.315%
91:2	9980	10244	0.974	0.005%	0.063%	-0.058%	0.045%
91:3	9893	10429	0.949	0.059%	0.067%	-0.008%	0.065%
91:4	9913	10497	0.944	0.050%	0.094%	-0.044%	0.082%
92:1	9786	10324	0.948	0.111%	0.018%	0.093%	0.048%
92:2	10119	9723	1.041	-0.068%	-0.041%	-0.027%	-0.048%
92:3	9870	10392	0.950	0.070%	0.051%	0.019%	0.057%
92:4	9693	10963	0.884	0.156%	0.139%	0.018%	0.144%
93:1	9938	10527	0.944	0.034%	0.102%	-0.068%	0.080%
93:2	9909	10340	0.958	0.055%	0.050%	0.005%	0.052%
93:3	9819	10686	0.919	0.095%	0.104%	-0.008%	0.101%
93:4	9905	10255	0.966	0.057%	0.025%	0.032%	0.034%
94:1	10003	9954	1.005	-0.001%	-0.016%	0.014%	-0.011%
94:2	10062	9994	1.007	-0.037%	0.006%	-0.043%	-0.005%
94:3	9836	10613	0.927	0.094%	0.087%	0.006%	0.089%
94:4	9982	9836	1.015	0.015%	-0.042%	0.056%	-0.029%
95:1	9791	10706	0.915	0.107%	0.112%	-0.005%	0.110%
95:2	9731	10873	0.895	0.133%	0.135%	-0.002%	0.134%
95:3	9729	10853	0.896	0.140%	0.127%	0.013%	0.131%
95:4	9861	10445	0.944	0.084%	0.060%	0.025%	0.067%
96:1	9750	11027	0.884	0.141%	0.166%	-0.025%	0.159%
96:2	9869	10367	0.952	0.069%	0.054%	0.015%	0.059%
96:3	9916	10298	0.963	0.052%	0.046%	0.006%	0.047%
96:4	9782	10817	0.904	0.116%	0.125%	-0.009%	0.122%
AVG	9900	10377	0.954	0.057%	0.055%	0.002%	0.055%

second (EMA$_2$) is the P-period exponential moving average of EMA$_1$. The third (TRIX) is the P-period exponential moving average of EMA$_2$.

The momentum of TRIX (TXM) is calculated as follows:

$$TXM = \text{Today's TRIX} - \text{Yesterday's TRIX}.$$

Whenever the TRIX Momentum forms a valley below zero, trade long. Trade short whenever the TRIX Momentum forms a peak above zero.

Results

The test results of the TRIX Momentum Peaks (TXM-P) system shown in Tables 4.23 and 4.24 indicate that, compared to the average call rates for the indicators in our study, this system makes a relatively large number of long and short calls. When choosing between a long position or a cash position, the system favors a long position 45.8 percent of the time (Table 4.23a). On average, the hit rate for these long calls is 60.8 percent. The cash recommendations for this system have a hit rate of 60.2 percent.

The results for the system's recommendations between short and cash positions are very similar to those for its long-versus-cash recommendations. Short calls are made 42.6 percent of the time, and the hit rate for these short calls is 60.2 percent (Table 4.23b). When the system chooses a cash position over a short position, the call is correct 60.6 percent of the time.

These results show a total hit rate of approximately 60.4 percent for the TXM-P system. Thus, an investor following this system would be making the correct decision over half of the time. But, the returns that can be expected from following this trading system are lower than the returns of a simple buy-and-hold strategy. Thus, being in the correct market position for the majority of the time is not enough to make a trading system profitable.

From the data in Table 4.24, we see that the average stock return is 0.045 percent on days when the system favors a cash position over a long position. This return is the opportunity cost, or missed potential return, of following the system's cash recommendations rather than entering into long positions. Even though the cash positions are, on average, correct calls, the missed returns are so high on the incorrect call days that an investor's total average return would be higher just staying in the market.

The story for the short-versus-long calls is even worse. Not only is the terminal wealth less, on average, than the terminal wealth of a buy-and-hold strategy, it is less than the beginning wealth. This occurs because of the positive average return that occurs when short positions are taken. Entering into short positions when stock prices are rising will lead to losses.

Like most of the systems in this study, the TXM-P system outperforms a buy-and-hold strategy during periods of negative market returns. Since there does, however, seem to be some value to this indicator, let's look at a system that builds on the TXM-P system: the TRIX Momentum Fibonacci Peaks system.

TRIX Momentum Fibonacci Peaks

This system builds on the TRIX Momentum Peaks (TXM-P) system just discussed. The TRIX is based on a triple exponential moving average. The TRIX Momentum Fibonacci Peaks (TXM-FP) system takes the triple concept one step farther by calculating the average of three TRIXs. In this system, an 8-period, a 13-period, and a 21-period TRIX Momentum oscillator are averaged together to form one indicator.

Construction

Calculate three separate TRIX Momentums—an 8-period (TXM_8), a 13-period (TXM_{13}), and a 21-period (TXM_{21})—following the steps outlined under the TXM-P system on page 161. A composite oscillator is created by averaging these three:

$$TXM\text{-}FP = (TXM_8 + TXM_{13} + TXM_{21})/3.$$

Long signals occur when the TXM-FP forms a valley. Short signals occur when the TXM-FP forms a peak.

Results

The results in Tables 4.25 and 4.26 show that the TRIX Momentum Fibonacci Peaks (TXM-FP) system makes slightly more calls than the simpler TRIX Momentum Peaks (TXM-P) system we discussed in the previous section. The TXM-FP system has a long call rate of 46.9 percent (Table 4.25a) and a short call rate of 44.1 percent (Table 4.25b).

The hit rate for the long calls in the TXM-FP system is 61.0 percent. When the system chooses a cash position over a long position, there is a slightly lower hit rate of 60.3 percent. Six times out of ten, this system will make a correct call between long or cash positions. The long return analysis suggests that these are fairly good calls. Trading long with this system leads to an average quarterly terminal wealth of $10,217 (Table 4.26a). This average terminal wealth figure is relatively high for the sixty technical indicators included in this book, but it still falls short of the $10,377 average quarterly terminal wealth of the buy-and-hold strategy.

We see a similar pattern when using the TXM-FP system to choose between short and cash positions (Table 4.25b). With hit rates of 60.4 percent for

Table 4.23a
TRIX Peaks (TXM-P) Long Hit Analysis
(Average of all stocks)

Qtr	Optimal Long	TXM-P Long	Long Hits	Cash Hits	Total Hits	Long Right	Long Wrong	Cash Right	Cash Wrong
85:1	32.1%	48.0%	64.2%	67.3%	65.8%	30.8%	17.2%	35.0%	17.0%
85:2	30.2%	43.3%	66.4%	70.5%	68.7%	28.7%	14.5%	40.0%	16.8%
85:3	26.3%	47.9%	61.7%	74.2%	68.2%	29.6%	18.4%	38.7%	13.4%
85:4	36.6%	38.1%	67.3%	63.9%	65.2%	25.6%	12.5%	39.6%	22.3%
86:1	44.2%	47.9%	64.8%	55.7%	60.0%	31.0%	16.9%	29.0%	23.1%
86:2	39.7%	52.9%	61.4%	62.0%	61.7%	32.5%	20.4%	29.2%	17.9%
86:3	37.0%	42.4%	58.1%	63.3%	61.1%	24.6%	17.8%	36.4%	21.1%
86:4	38.5%	42.2%	61.2%	61.1%	61.1%	25.8%	16.4%	35.3%	22.5%
87:1	44.7%	48.8%	64.6%	56.5%	60.4%	31.5%	17.3%	28.9%	22.3%
87:2	40.0%	45.1%	60.0%	59.9%	59.9%	27.0%	18.0%	32.9%	22.0%
87:3	39.5%	51.9%	59.4%	60.2%	59.8%	30.8%	21.1%	29.0%	19.1%
87:4	37.9%	30.9%	55.9%	62.6%	60.5%	17.3%	13.6%	43.3%	25.8%
88:1	41.3%	45.0%	62.1%	57.5%	59.5%	28.0%	17.1%	31.6%	23.4%
88:2	39.3%	49.4%	62.2%	60.4%	61.3%	30.7%	18.7%	30.6%	20.0%
88:3	35.9%	48.8%	60.4%	63.6%	62.0%	29.5%	19.3%	32.5%	18.6%
88:4	36.3%	45.7%	62.2%	62.6%	62.4%	28.5%	17.3%	34.0%	20.3%
89:1	39.0%	47.7%	63.2%	60.7%	61.8%	30.1%	17.6%	31.7%	20.6%
89:2	40.2%	45.1%	63.6%	59.7%	61.5%	28.7%	16.4%	32.8%	22.1%
89:3	39.9%	49.7%	64.1%	60.1%	62.1%	31.9%	17.8%	30.2%	20.1%
89:4	38.3%	44.2%	60.7%	61.7%	61.3%	26.8%	17.4%	34.4%	21.4%
90:1	36.9%	41.3%	59.7%	63.1%	61.7%	24.6%	16.6%	37.1%	21.7%
90:2	39.2%	46.2%	62.2%	60.6%	61.3%	28.7%	17.5%	32.6%	21.2%
90:3	33.5%	41.7%	55.2%	66.9%	62.0%	23.0%	18.7%	39.0%	19.3%
90:4	40.8%	38.6%	62.2%	59.4%	60.5%	24.0%	14.6%	36.5%	24.9%
91:1	44.1%	49.4%	63.5%	55.6%	59.5%	31.4%	18.0%	28.1%	22.5%
91:2	39.7%	50.9%	60.3%	60.9%	60.6%	30.7%	20.2%	29.9%	19.2%
91:3	40.4%	47.8%	60.7%	60.1%	60.4%	29.0%	18.8%	31.4%	20.8%
91:4	41.2%	46.6%	60.5%	59.2%	59.8%	28.2%	18.4%	31.6%	21.8%
92:1	40.0%	48.8%	56.8%	59.4%	58.1%	27.7%	21.1%	30.5%	20.8%
92:2	38.6%	46.0%	57.2%	61.5%	59.5%	26.3%	19.7%	33.2%	20.8%
92:3	40.3%	43.0%	60.4%	59.6%	59.9%	26.0%	17.0%	33.9%	23.0%
92:4	41.9%	44.8%	63.1%	58.0%	60.3%	28.3%	16.6%	32.0%	23.2%
93:1	42.5%	46.9%	61.8%	58.1%	59.8%	29.0%	17.9%	30.9%	22.3%
93:2	42.1%	47.5%	59.4%	58.2%	58.7%	28.2%	19.3%	30.5%	21.9%
93:3	42.5%	45.0%	60.5%	57.2%	58.7%	27.2%	17.8%	31.5%	23.5%
93:4	41.5%	45.1%	58.3%	58.6%	58.5%	26.3%	18.8%	32.1%	22.7%
94:1	40.4%	46.9%	56.8%	59.9%	58.4%	26.6%	20.3%	31.8%	21.3%
94:2	40.6%	43.6%	58.1%	60.1%	59.2%	25.3%	18.2%	33.9%	22.5%
94:3	41.8%	46.8%	60.2%	58.3%	59.2%	28.1%	18.6%	31.1%	22.2%
94:4	39.5%	44.8%	56.3%	59.9%	58.3%	25.2%	19.6%	33.1%	22.2%
95:1	43.1%	44.9%	62.0%	57.1%	59.3%	27.8%	17.0%	31.5%	23.6%
95:2	43.7%	46.5%	61.2%	56.2%	58.5%	28.5%	18.1%	30.1%	23.4%
95:3	43.9%	47.9%	61.5%	56.2%	58.7%	29.5%	18.4%	29.3%	22.8%
95:4	43.4%	44.8%	59.2%	56.0%	57.5%	26.5%	18.3%	31.0%	24.3%
96:1	45.5%	49.4%	60.9%	54.3%	57.6%	30.1%	19.3%	27.5%	23.1%
96:2	42.1%	49.5%	58.3%	58.3%	58.3%	28.9%	20.6%	29.4%	21.1%
96:3	42.6%	40.2%	59.1%	57.1%	57.9%	23.7%	16.4%	34.2%	25.7%
96:4	44.3%	48.0%	60.3%	56.0%	58.0%	28.9%	19.1%	29.1%	22.9%
AVG	40.0%	45.8%	60.8%	60.2%	60.5%	27.9%	17.9%	32.7%	21.6%

Table 4.23b
TRIX Peaks (TXM-P) Short Hit Analysis
(Average of all stocks)

Qtr	Optimal Short	TXM-P Short	Short Hits	Cash Hits	Total Hits	Short Right	Short Wrong	Cash Right	Cash Wrong
85:1	34.3%	35.6%	66.0%	64.5%	65.1%	23.5%	12.1%	41.6%	22.8%
85:2	34.6%	43.1%	69.6%	65.9%	67.5%	30.0%	13.1%	37.5%	19.4%
85:3	38.6%	39.3%	73.5%	61.8%	66.4%	28.9%	10.4%	37.5%	23.2%
85:4	33.1%	44.2%	63.4%	66.8%	65.3%	28.0%	16.1%	37.3%	18.6%
86:1	35.2%	39.0%	55.9%	64.5%	61.1%	21.8%	17.2%	39.4%	21.7%
86:2	39.8%	38.8%	62.2%	61.3%	61.7%	24.1%	14.7%	37.5%	23.7%
86:3	42.7%	41.3%	64.0%	57.9%	60.4%	26.4%	14.9%	34.0%	24.7%
86:4	38.7%	48.2%	61.0%	60.9%	60.9%	29.4%	18.8%	31.6%	20.3%
87:1	36.9%	40.3%	56.7%	64.0%	61.0%	22.9%	17.5%	38.2%	21.5%
87:2	40.0%	43.6%	60.3%	59.9%	60.1%	26.3%	17.3%	33.8%	22.6%
87:3	40.4%	36.1%	60.1%	59.0%	59.4%	21.7%	14.4%	37.7%	26.2%
87:4	45.3%	54.0%	62.9%	54.8%	59.2%	33.9%	20.0%	25.3%	20.8%
88:1	36.7%	44.5%	56.4%	61.9%	59.5%	25.1%	19.4%	34.3%	21.2%
88:2	37.4%	41.6%	60.6%	62.4%	61.7%	25.2%	16.4%	36.4%	22.0%
88:3	38.4%	41.2%	63.3%	60.5%	61.7%	26.1%	15.1%	35.6%	23.2%
88:4	37.0%	43.3%	62.9%	62.3%	62.6%	27.2%	16.0%	35.3%	21.4%
89:1	36.2%	40.8%	60.3%	63.1%	62.0%	24.6%	16.2%	37.3%	21.8%
89:2	35.9%	43.7%	59.5%	63.2%	61.6%	26.0%	17.7%	35.6%	20.7%
89:3	36.4%	38.9%	60.1%	63.5%	62.2%	23.4%	15.5%	38.8%	22.3%
89:4	39.0%	43.8%	61.7%	60.4%	61.0%	27.0%	16.8%	34.0%	22.2%
90:1	40.1%	47.7%	63.3%	59.7%	61.4%	30.2%	17.5%	31.2%	21.1%
90:2	37.8%	40.6%	60.9%	61.8%	61.4%	24.7%	15.9%	36.7%	22.7%
90:3	45.7%	40.4%	68.5%	55.5%	60.8%	27.7%	12.7%	33.1%	26.5%
90:4	37.6%	49.2%	59.1%	62.2%	60.7%	29.0%	20.1%	31.6%	19.2%
91:1	36.7%	35.1%	55.3%	63.2%	60.4%	19.4%	15.7%	41.0%	23.9%
91:2	40.4%	42.0%	61.0%	60.2%	60.5%	25.6%	16.4%	34.9%	23.1%
91:3	39.8%	42.2%	60.7%	60.8%	60.7%	25.6%	16.6%	35.1%	22.7%
91:4	40.5%	42.4%	59.6%	60.1%	59.9%	25.2%	17.1%	34.7%	23.0%
92:1	43.2%	36.9%	60.2%	56.9%	58.1%	22.2%	14.7%	35.9%	27.2%
92:2	42.9%	43.6%	61.9%	57.3%	59.3%	27.0%	16.6%	32.3%	24.1%
92:3	39.5%	47.1%	59.5%	60.4%	60.0%	28.0%	19.0%	32.0%	21.0%
92:4	37.5%	43.4%	57.9%	62.7%	60.6%	25.2%	18.3%	35.5%	21.1%
93:1	39.4%	42.8%	58.2%	61.3%	60.0%	24.9%	17.9%	35.0%	22.1%
93:2	40.9%	42.5%	58.4%	59.3%	58.9%	24.8%	17.7%	34.1%	23.4%
93:3	39.4%	43.6%	57.1%	60.2%	58.8%	24.9%	18.7%	33.9%	22.5%
93:4	41.7%	43.1%	58.4%	58.0%	58.2%	25.2%	17.9%	33.0%	23.9%
94:1	43.7%	44.3%	60.1%	56.5%	58.1%	26.6%	17.7%	31.5%	24.2%
94:2	42.7%	47.4%	60.4%	57.6%	58.9%	28.6%	18.8%	30.3%	22.3%
94:3	39.8%	43.4%	58.4%	59.9%	59.3%	25.3%	18.1%	33.9%	22.7%
94:4	42.8%	42.3%	59.9%	56.5%	57.9%	25.3%	17.0%	32.6%	25.1%
95:1	38.7%	45.6%	56.8%	61.4%	59.3%	25.9%	19.7%	33.4%	21.0%
95:2	38.9%	44.4%	56.1%	60.8%	58.7%	24.9%	19.5%	33.8%	21.8%
95:3	38.9%	42.5%	56.4%	61.2%	59.2%	24.0%	18.5%	35.2%	22.3%
95:4	40.5%	40.5%	55.9%	59.0%	57.8%	22.7%	17.9%	35.1%	24.4%
96:1	38.9%	40.9%	54.4%	60.9%	58.2%	22.3%	18.6%	36.0%	23.1%
96:2	42.4%	42.7%	58.2%	58.1%	58.1%	24.8%	17.8%	33.3%	24.0%
96:3	40.8%	46.7%	56.9%	58.5%	57.8%	26.6%	20.1%	31.2%	22.1%
96:4	39.8%	39.8%	55.6%	59.6%	58.0%	22.1%	17.7%	35.9%	24.3%
AVG	39.4%	42.6%	60.2%	60.6%	60.4%	25.6%	17.0%	34.8%	22.6%

Table 4.24a
TRIX Peaks (TXM-P) Long Return Analysis
(Average of all stocks)

Qtr	TXM-P Terminal Wealth	Buy/Hold Terminal Wealth	Relative Terminal Wealth	TXM-P Long Avg Ret	TXM-P Cash Avg Ret	TXM-P Long-Cash Avg Ret	Buy/Hold Avg Ret
85:1	9923	10142	0.978	-0.034%	0.043%	-0.077%	0.006%
85:2	9967	9700	1.028	-0.026%	-0.103%	0.077%	-0.069%
85:3	9475	8889	1.066	-0.187%	-0.221%	0.034%	-0.205%
85:4	10380	10763	0.964	0.151%	0.079%	0.072%	0.107%
86:1	10672	11428	0.934	0.229%	0.221%	0.008%	0.225%
86:2	10455	10414	1.004	0.133%	-0.009%	0.142%	0.066%
86:3	9736	9175	1.061	-0.098%	-0.149%	0.051%	-0.128%
86:4	10161	10413	0.976	0.063%	0.074%	-0.011%	0.069%
87:1	11159	11929	0.935	0.368%	0.222%	0.146%	0.293%
87:2	10151	10196	0.996	0.056%	0.023%	0.034%	0.038%
87:3	10232	10408	0.983	0.073%	0.064%	0.009%	0.068%
87:4	9655	8087	1.194	-0.169%	-0.327%	0.158%	-0.278%
88:1	10324	10989	0.940	0.121%	0.197%	-0.076%	0.163%
88:2	10292	10593	0.972	0.096%	0.103%	-0.007%	0.100%
88:3	9961	10050	0.991	-0.010%	0.035%	-0.045%	0.013%
88:4	10013	10196	0.982	0.006%	0.063%	-0.057%	0.037%
89:1	10292	10698	0.962	0.100%	0.124%	-0.024%	0.112%
89:2	10349	10772	0.961	0.124%	0.121%	0.003%	0.122%
89:3	10430	10833	0.963	0.137%	0.126%	0.011%	0.131%
89:4	9990	9904	1.009	-0.002%	-0.018%	0.017%	-0.011%
90:1	10001	9980	1.002	0.002%	0.004%	-0.002%	0.003%
90:2	10185	10459	0.974	0.064%	0.087%	-0.023%	0.077%
90:3	9382	8526	1.100	-0.248%	-0.266%	0.018%	-0.259%
90:4	10323	10889	0.948	0.133%	0.155%	-0.022%	0.146%
91:1	10952	12477	0.878	0.304%	0.326%	-0.022%	0.315%
91:2	10225	10244	0.998	0.073%	0.017%	0.056%	0.045%
91:3	10263	10429	0.984	0.085%	0.046%	0.039%	0.065%
91:4	10353	10497	0.986	0.122%	0.046%	0.076%	0.082%
92:1	10077	10324	0.976	0.024%	0.071%	-0.047%	0.048%
92:2	9886	9723	1.017	-0.041%	-0.055%	0.014%	-0.048%
92:3	10175	10392	0.979	0.061%	0.053%	0.007%	0.057%
92:4	10422	10963	0.951	0.147%	0.143%	0.004%	0.144%
93:1	10353	10527	0.983	0.117%	0.047%	0.070%	0.080%
93:2	10170	10340	0.984	0.055%	0.048%	0.007%	0.052%
93:3	10309	10686	0.965	0.105%	0.098%	0.007%	0.101%
93:4	10107	10255	0.986	0.035%	0.033%	0.002%	0.034%
94:1	10069	9954	1.012	0.022%	-0.040%	0.062%	-0.011%
94:2	10099	9994	1.010	0.035%	-0.035%	0.071%	-0.005%
94:3	10270	10613	0.968	0.088%	0.091%	-0.003%	0.089%
94:4	9852	9836	1.002	-0.056%	-0.008%	-0.049%	-0.029%
95:1	10365	10706	0.968	0.130%	0.093%	0.037%	0.110%
95:2	10396	10873	0.956	0.135%	0.133%	0.002%	0.134%
95:3	10456	10853	0.963	0.149%	0.115%	0.034%	0.131%
95:4	10164	10445	0.973	0.056%	0.076%	-0.020%	0.067%
96:1	10440	11027	0.947	0.139%	0.178%	-0.039%	0.159%
96:2	10222	10367	0.986	0.071%	0.046%	0.025%	0.059%
96:3	10129	10298	0.984	0.049%	0.046%	0.002%	0.047%
96:4	10388	10817	0.960	0.122%	0.123%	-0.001%	0.122%
AVG	10201	10377	0.983	0.068%	0.045%	0.023%	0.055%

Table 4.24b
TRIX Peaks (TXM-P) Short Return Analysis
Average of all stocks)

Qtr	TXM-P Terminal Wealth	Buy/Hold Terminal Wealth	Relative Terminal Wealth	TXM-P Short Avg Ret	TXM-P Cash Avg Ret	TXM-P Short-Cash Avg Ret	Buy/Hold Avg Ret
85:1	9822	10142	0.968	0.088%	-0.039%	0.128%	0.006%
85:2	10287	9700	1.061	-0.093%	-0.051%	-0.042%	-0.069%
85:3	10580	8889	1.190	-0.219%	-0.196%	-0.023%	-0.205%
85:4	9749	10763	0.906	0.094%	0.117%	-0.022%	0.107%
86:1	9475	11428	0.829	0.229%	0.222%	0.007%	0.225%
86:2	10059	10414	0.966	-0.020%	0.121%	-0.141%	0.066%
86:3	10462	9175	1.140	-0.173%	-0.096%	-0.077%	-0.128%
86:4	9757	10413	0.937	0.079%	0.060%	0.019%	0.069%
87:1	9463	11929	0.793	0.220%	0.342%	-0.122%	0.293%
87:2	9963	10196	0.977	0.010%	0.059%	-0.049%	0.038%
87:3	9815	10408	0.943	0.080%	0.062%	0.019%	0.068%
87:4	11057	8087	1.367	-0.311%	-0.239%	-0.072%	-0.278%
88:1	9331	10989	0.849	0.242%	0.100%	0.142%	0.163%
88:2	9752	10593	0.921	0.095%	0.103%	-0.008%	0.100%
88:3	9874	10050	0.982	0.047%	-0.012%	0.059%	0.013%
88:4	9844	10196	0.965	0.057%	0.021%	0.036%	0.037%
89:1	9642	10698	0.901	0.145%	0.090%	0.055%	0.112%
89:2	9634	10772	0.894	0.134%	0.113%	0.020%	0.122%
89:3	9672	10833	0.893	0.137%	0.127%	0.009%	0.131%
89:4	10052	9904	1.015	-0.022%	-0.002%	-0.020%	-0.011%
90:1	10015	9980	1.003	-0.007%	0.012%	-0.019%	0.003%
90:2	9777	10459	0.935	0.090%	0.068%	0.022%	0.077%
90:3	10883	8526	1.276	-0.338%	-0.206%	-0.132%	-0.259%
90:4	9459	10889	0.869	0.174%	0.120%	0.054%	0.146%
91:1	9283	12477	0.744	0.357%	0.292%	0.065%	0.315%
91:2	9960	10244	0.972	0.013%	0.069%	-0.056%	0.045%
91:3	9933	10429	0.952	0.025%	0.094%	-0.069%	0.065%
91:4	9894	10497	0.943	0.039%	0.113%	-0.074%	0.082%
92:1	9910	10324	0.960	0.042%	0.051%	-0.009%	0.048%
92:2	10201	9723	1.049	-0.071%	-0.031%	-0.040%	-0.048%
92:3	9836	10392	0.947	0.056%	0.057%	-0.001%	0.057%
92:4	9610	10963	0.877	0.147%	0.142%	0.005%	0.144%
93:1	9893	10527	0.940	0.045%	0.105%	-0.060%	0.080%
93:2	9895	10340	0.957	0.042%	0.059%	-0.017%	0.052%
93:3	9717	10686	0.909	0.107%	0.096%	0.011%	0.101%
93:4	9905	10255	0.966	0.038%	0.031%	0.007%	0.034%
94:1	10120	9954	1.017	-0.042%	0.013%	-0.055%	-0.011%
94:2	10135	9994	1.014	-0.043%	0.029%	-0.072%	-0.005%
94:3	9751	10613	0.919	0.096%	0.084%	0.012%	0.089%
94:4	10018	9836	1.018	-0.007%	-0.046%	0.039%	-0.029%
95:1	9701	10706	0.906	0.109%	0.111%	-0.002%	0.110%
95:2	9614	10873	0.884	0.143%	0.127%	0.017%	0.134%
95:3	9712	10853	0.895	0.111%	0.146%	-0.035%	0.131%
95:4	9791	10445	0.937	0.083%	0.055%	0.028%	0.067%
96:1	9561	11027	0.867	0.176%	0.147%	0.029%	0.159%
96:2	9863	10367	0.951	0.051%	0.064%	-0.013%	0.059%
96:3	9824	10298	0.954	0.062%	0.034%	0.028%	0.047%
96:4	9623	10817	0.890	0.153%	0.102%	0.052%	0.122%
AVG	9879	10377	0.952	0.048%	0.060%	-0.012%	0.055%

Table 4.25a
TRIX Fibonacci Peaks (TXM-FP) Long Hit Analysis
(Average of all stocks)

Qtr	Optimal Long	TXM-FP Long	Long Hits	Cash Hits	Total Hits	Long Right	Long Wrong	Cash Right	Cash Wrong
85:1	32.1%	49.0%	64.7%	67.4%	66.1%	31.7%	17.3%	34.4%	16.6%
85:2	30.2%	45.7%	66.7%	70.8%	68.9%	30.5%	15.2%	38.4%	15.8%
85:3	26.3%	48.1%	61.4%	73.8%	67.8%	29.5%	18.6%	38.4%	13.6%
85:4	36.6%	39.8%	67.4%	64.2%	65.5%	26.9%	13.0%	38.6%	21.5%
86:1	44.2%	48.2%	64.9%	55.7%	60.1%	31.3%	16.9%	28.9%	23.0%
86:2	39.7%	53.1%	61.9%	61.8%	61.9%	32.9%	20.2%	29.0%	17.9%
86:3	37.0%	44.2%	58.3%	63.5%	61.2%	25.7%	18.4%	35.4%	20.4%
86:4	38.5%	43.1%	61.0%	61.0%	61.0%	26.3%	16.8%	34.7%	22.2%
87:1	44.7%	48.2%	64.7%	56.6%	60.5%	31.2%	17.0%	29.3%	22.4%
87:2	40.0%	45.4%	60.8%	60.2%	60.5%	27.6%	17.8%	32.9%	21.7%
87:3	39.5%	52.0%	59.0%	60.2%	59.6%	30.7%	21.3%	28.9%	19.1%
87:4	37.9%	29.5%	53.4%	61.8%	59.3%	15.8%	13.7%	43.6%	26.9%
88:1	41.3%	47.7%	62.7%	57.8%	60.2%	29.9%	17.8%	30.3%	22.1%
88:2	39.3%	48.8%	62.5%	60.7%	61.6%	30.5%	18.3%	31.1%	20.1%
88:3	35.9%	49.5%	60.9%	63.7%	62.3%	30.2%	19.4%	32.2%	18.3%
88:4	36.3%	47.0%	61.7%	62.3%	62.0%	29.0%	18.0%	33.0%	20.0%
89:1	39.0%	49.1%	63.5%	60.8%	62.1%	31.1%	17.9%	31.0%	20.0%
89:2	40.2%	46.7%	64.2%	59.6%	61.8%	30.0%	16.7%	31.8%	21.5%
89:3	39.9%	50.8%	64.1%	60.2%	62.1%	32.5%	18.2%	29.6%	19.6%
89:4	38.3%	45.4%	60.9%	61.8%	61.4%	27.7%	17.7%	33.7%	20.9%
90:1	36.9%	42.9%	59.6%	63.1%	61.6%	25.6%	17.3%	36.0%	21.1%
90:2	39.2%	47.7%	62.1%	60.6%	61.3%	29.7%	18.1%	31.7%	20.6%
90:3	33.5%	43.1%	55.1%	67.0%	61.9%	23.8%	19.4%	38.1%	18.8%
90:4	40.8%	41.1%	63.5%	60.3%	61.6%	26.1%	15.0%	35.5%	23.4%
91:1	44.1%	49.8%	63.4%	55.3%	59.4%	31.6%	18.2%	27.8%	22.4%
91:2	39.7%	51.8%	60.5%	61.2%	60.8%	31.4%	20.5%	29.5%	18.7%
91:3	40.4%	48.2%	61.0%	60.1%	60.6%	29.4%	18.8%	31.1%	20.6%
91:4	41.2%	47.4%	60.9%	59.8%	60.3%	28.9%	18.5%	31.5%	21.1%
92:1	40.0%	49.3%	57.2%	59.8%	58.6%	28.2%	21.1%	30.3%	20.4%
92:2	38.6%	49.6%	57.2%	61.6%	59.4%	28.4%	21.2%	31.0%	19.4%
92:3	40.3%	44.1%	60.8%	59.8%	60.2%	26.8%	17.3%	33.4%	22.5%
92:4	41.9%	46.5%	63.3%	58.1%	60.5%	29.5%	17.0%	31.1%	22.4%
93:1	42.5%	47.8%	61.3%	58.0%	59.6%	29.3%	18.5%	30.3%	21.9%
93:2	42.1%	48.3%	60.0%	58.6%	59.2%	29.0%	19.3%	30.3%	21.4%
93:3	42.5%	46.5%	60.6%	57.4%	58.9%	28.2%	18.3%	30.7%	22.8%
93:4	41.5%	46.3%	58.4%	58.5%	58.5%	27.1%	19.2%	31.4%	22.3%
94:1	40.4%	47.8%	57.0%	60.0%	58.6%	27.3%	20.5%	31.3%	20.9%
94:2	40.6%	45.1%	58.2%	60.6%	59.5%	26.3%	18.9%	33.2%	21.6%
94:3	41.8%	47.4%	60.6%	58.8%	59.7%	28.7%	18.7%	30.9%	21.6%
94:4	39.5%	46.0%	57.2%	60.5%	59.0%	26.3%	19.7%	32.7%	21.3%
95:1	43.1%	46.8%	62.4%	57.6%	59.8%	29.2%	17.6%	30.6%	22.6%
95:2	43.7%	47.2%	61.2%	56.3%	58.6%	28.9%	18.3%	29.7%	23.1%
95:3	43.9%	49.2%	61.4%	56.0%	58.7%	30.2%	19.0%	28.4%	22.4%
95:4	43.4%	46.6%	59.2%	56.5%	57.8%	27.6%	19.0%	30.1%	23.2%
96:1	45.5%	48.4%	61.3%	54.4%	57.7%	29.7%	18.7%	28.0%	23.6%
96:2	42.1%	50.8%	58.7%	58.6%	58.7%	29.8%	21.0%	28.9%	20.3%
96:3	42.6%	42.0%	59.1%	57.0%	57.9%	24.8%	17.2%	33.1%	24.9%
96:4	44.3%	49.7%	59.9%	55.7%	57.8%	29.8%	19.9%	28.0%	22.3%
AVG	40.0%	46.9%	61.0%	60.3%	60.7%	28.6%	18.3%	32.1%	21.1%

Table 4.25b
TRIX Fibonacci Peaks (TXM-FP) Short Hit Analysis
(Average of all stocks)

Qtr	Optimal Short	TXM-FP Short	Short Hits	Cash Hits	Total Hits	Short Right	Short Wrong	Cash Right	Cash Wrong
85:1	34.3%	37.6%	66.8%	65.0%	65.6%	25.1%	12.5%	40.5%	21.9%
85:2	34.6%	43.4%	70.1%	66.4%	68.0%	30.5%	13.0%	37.6%	19.0%
85:3	38.6%	41.3%	73.3%	61.4%	66.3%	30.2%	11.0%	36.1%	22.6%
85:4	33.1%	46.7%	63.4%	66.7%	65.2%	29.6%	17.1%	35.6%	17.8%
86:1	35.2%	41.3%	55.7%	64.5%	60.9%	23.0%	18.3%	37.8%	20.8%
86:2	39.8%	39.9%	62.3%	61.8%	62.0%	24.8%	15.0%	37.1%	23.0%
86:3	42.7%	41.6%	64.0%	57.9%	60.5%	26.6%	15.0%	33.8%	24.6%
86:4	38.7%	50.0%	60.8%	60.8%	60.8%	30.4%	19.6%	30.4%	19.6%
87:1	36.9%	42.7%	56.7%	64.1%	60.9%	24.2%	18.5%	36.7%	20.6%
87:2	40.0%	45.6%	60.6%	60.5%	60.6%	27.6%	18.0%	32.9%	21.5%
87:3	40.4%	38.2%	60.1%	58.8%	59.3%	23.0%	15.2%	36.3%	25.4%
87:4	45.3%	53.9%	62.4%	53.2%	58.2%	33.7%	20.3%	24.5%	21.6%
88:1	36.7%	44.9%	57.1%	62.4%	60.0%	25.6%	19.3%	34.4%	20.7%
88:2	37.4%	42.9%	61.0%	62.4%	61.8%	26.2%	16.8%	35.6%	21.4%
88:3	38.4%	43.3%	63.6%	60.9%	62.1%	27.5%	15.8%	34.6%	22.2%
88:4	37.0%	44.9%	62.6%	61.8%	62.2%	28.1%	16.8%	34.0%	21.0%
89:1	36.2%	43.0%	60.8%	63.3%	62.2%	26.2%	16.9%	36.1%	20.9%
89:2	35.9%	44.9%	59.5%	63.7%	61.8%	26.7%	18.2%	35.1%	20.0%
89:3	36.4%	41.1%	60.4%	63.6%	62.3%	24.8%	16.3%	37.5%	21.5%
89:4	39.0%	45.1%	61.8%	60.7%	61.2%	27.8%	17.2%	33.3%	21.6%
90:1	40.1%	48.3%	63.3%	59.6%	61.4%	30.5%	17.7%	30.9%	20.9%
90:2	37.8%	41.8%	60.7%	61.9%	61.4%	25.4%	16.4%	36.0%	22.2%
90:3	45.7%	44.2%	68.0%	55.4%	61.0%	30.1%	14.1%	30.9%	24.9%
90:4	37.6%	50.0%	60.3%	63.5%	61.9%	30.2%	19.9%	31.7%	18.2%
91:1	36.7%	37.8%	55.5%	63.2%	60.3%	20.9%	16.8%	39.3%	22.9%
91:2	40.4%	42.1%	61.2%	60.4%	60.7%	25.7%	16.3%	35.0%	22.9%
91:3	39.8%	44.5%	60.7%	61.1%	60.9%	27.0%	17.5%	33.9%	21.6%
91:4	40.5%	43.9%	60.3%	60.7%	60.5%	26.5%	17.4%	34.1%	22.0%
92:1	43.2%	40.0%	60.9%	57.4%	58.8%	24.4%	15.6%	34.4%	25.6%
92:2	42.9%	42.9%	61.8%	57.3%	59.2%	26.5%	16.4%	32.7%	24.4%
92:3	39.5%	48.4%	60.1%	60.8%	60.5%	29.1%	19.3%	31.4%	20.2%
92:4	37.5%	44.5%	58.1%	62.8%	60.7%	25.9%	18.6%	34.8%	20.6%
93:1	39.4%	44.4%	57.9%	60.9%	59.6%	25.7%	18.7%	33.9%	21.8%
93:2	40.9%	44.8%	58.5%	59.6%	59.1%	26.2%	18.6%	32.9%	22.3%
93:3	39.4%	44.9%	57.3%	60.4%	59.0%	25.7%	19.1%	33.3%	21.8%
93:4	41.7%	44.9%	58.7%	58.3%	58.5%	26.3%	18.5%	32.1%	23.0%
94:1	43.7%	45.7%	60.2%	56.9%	58.4%	27.5%	18.2%	30.9%	23.4%
94:2	42.7%	48.0%	60.9%	57.8%	59.3%	29.2%	18.8%	30.1%	22.0%
94:3	39.8%	45.4%	58.9%	60.3%	59.7%	26.7%	18.7%	33.0%	21.7%
94:4	42.8%	45.1%	60.4%	57.0%	58.5%	27.3%	17.9%	31.3%	23.6%
95:1	38.7%	46.6%	57.4%	61.9%	59.8%	26.8%	19.9%	33.0%	20.3%
95:2	38.9%	46.0%	56.1%	60.8%	58.7%	25.8%	20.2%	32.9%	21.1%
95:3	38.9%	43.3%	56.1%	61.3%	59.1%	24.3%	19.0%	34.8%	21.9%
95:4	40.5%	42.5%	56.4%	59.1%	57.9%	24.0%	18.5%	34.0%	23.5%
96:1	38.9%	43.9%	54.4%	61.2%	58.2%	23.9%	20.0%	34.3%	21.8%
96:2	42.4%	43.4%	58.5%	58.4%	58.4%	25.4%	18.0%	33.0%	23.6%
96:3	40.8%	48.3%	56.8%	58.7%	57.8%	27.4%	20.9%	30.4%	21.4%
96:4	39.8%	40.8%	55.6%	59.5%	57.9%	22.7%	18.1%	35.2%	24.0%
AVG	39.4%	44.1%	60.4%	60.7%	60.6%	26.6%	17.5%	34.0%	21.9%

Table 4.26a
TRIX Fibonacci Peaks (TXM-FP) Long Return Analysis
(Average of all stocks)

Qtr	TXM-FP Terminal Wealth	Buy/Hold Terminal Wealth	Relative Terminal Wealth	TXM-FP Long Avg Ret	TXM-FP Cash Avg Ret	TXM-FP Long-Cash Avg Ret	Buy/Hold Avg Ret
85:1	9954	10142	0.981	-0.023%	0.034%	-0.057%	0.006%
85:2	9960	9700	1.027	-0.027%	-0.105%	0.079%	-0.069%
85:3	9436	8889	1.062	-0.200%	-0.209%	0.009%	-0.205%
85:4	10424	10763	0.969	0.162%	0.070%	0.092%	0.107%
86:1	10708	11428	0.937	0.238%	0.212%	0.025%	0.225%
86:2	10461	10414	1.005	0.134%	-0.010%	0.144%	0.066%
86:3	9696	9175	1.057	-0.106%	-0.145%	0.039%	-0.128%
86:4	10141	10413	0.974	0.054%	0.081%	-0.028%	0.069%
87:1	11157	11929	0.935	0.371%	0.220%	0.151%	0.293%
87:2	10226	10196	1.003	0.081%	0.002%	0.078%	0.038%
87:3	10203	10408	0.980	0.063%	0.074%	-0.012%	0.068%
87:4	9196	8087	1.137	-0.424%	-0.217%	-0.207%	-0.278%
88:1	10396	10989	0.946	0.137%	0.186%	-0.049%	0.163%
88:2	10311	10593	0.973	0.104%	0.096%	0.008%	0.100%
88:3	9982	10050	0.993	-0.003%	0.028%	-0.031%	0.013%
88:4	9989	10196	0.980	-0.002%	0.071%	-0.072%	0.037%
89:1	10326	10698	0.965	0.108%	0.117%	-0.009%	0.112%
89:2	10390	10772	0.965	0.132%	0.114%	0.018%	0.122%
89:3	10431	10833	0.963	0.135%	0.127%	0.008%	0.131%
89:4	10025	9904	1.012	0.010%	-0.028%	0.038%	-0.011%
90:1	9978	9980	1.000	-0.007%	0.010%	-0.016%	0.003%
90:2	10181	10459	0.973	0.062%	0.090%	-0.029%	0.077%
90:3	9358	8526	1.098	-0.250%	-0.266%	0.015%	-0.259%
90:4	10599	10889	0.973	0.226%	0.090%	0.136%	0.146%
91:1	10903	12477	0.874	0.290%	0.340%	-0.049%	0.315%
91:2	10238	10244	0.999	0.074%	0.015%	0.059%	0.045%
91:3	10316	10429	0.989	0.101%	0.031%	0.070%	0.065%
91:4	10458	10497	0.996	0.155%	0.016%	0.139%	0.082%
92:1	10128	10324	0.981	0.039%	0.057%	-0.018%	0.048%
92:2	9885	9723	1.017	-0.038%	-0.059%	0.021%	-0.048%
92:3	10200	10392	0.982	0.070%	0.046%	0.023%	0.057%
92:4	10443	10963	0.953	0.149%	0.141%	0.008%	0.144%
93:1	10309	10527	0.979	0.101%	0.061%	0.040%	0.080%
93:2	10247	10340	0.991	0.080%	0.025%	0.054%	0.052%
93:3	10354	10686	0.969	0.116%	0.088%	0.028%	0.101%
93:4	10121	10255	0.987	0.038%	0.031%	0.007%	0.034%
94:1	10071	9954	1.012	0.022%	-0.042%	0.064%	-0.011%
94:2	10145	9994	1.015	0.051%	-0.050%	0.101%	-0.005%
94:3	10327	10613	0.973	0.105%	0.075%	0.031%	0.089%
94:4	9953	9836	1.012	-0.019%	-0.038%	0.020%	-0.029%
95:1	10428	10706	0.974	0.145%	0.079%	0.066%	0.110%
95:2	10419	10873	0.958	0.140%	0.129%	0.011%	0.134%
95:3	10474	10853	0.965	0.150%	0.113%	0.037%	0.131%
95:4	10223	10445	0.979	0.073%	0.061%	0.012%	0.067%
96:1	10466	11027	0.949	0.150%	0.167%	-0.017%	0.159%
96:2	10266	10367	0.990	0.083%	0.033%	0.050%	0.059%
96:3	10131	10298	0.984	0.049%	0.046%	0.002%	0.047%
96:4	10376	10817	0.959	0.115%	0.129%	-0.013%	0.122%
AVG	10217	10377	0.985	0.071%	0.041%	0.030%	0.055%

Table 4.26b
TRIX Fibonacci Peaks (TXM-FP) Short Return Analysis
(Average of all stocks)

Qtr	TXM-FP Terminal Wealth	Buy/Hold Terminal Wealth	Relative Terminal Wealth	TXM-FP Short Avg Ret	TXM-FP Cash Avg Ret	TXM-FP Short-Cash Avg Ret	Buy/Hold Avg Ret
85:1	9883	10142	0.974	0.059%	-0.025%	0.084%	0.006%
85:2	10305	9700	1.062	-0.100%	-0.046%	-0.055%	-0.069%
85:3	10567	8889	1.189	-0.204%	-0.205%	0.001%	-0.205%
85:4	9744	10763	0.905	0.092%	0.120%	-0.029%	0.107%
86:1	9469	11428	0.829	0.220%	0.228%	-0.008%	0.225%
86:2	10069	10414	0.967	-0.023%	0.126%	-0.149%	0.066%
86:3	10444	9175	1.138	-0.166%	-0.100%	-0.065%	-0.128%
86:4	9715	10413	0.933	0.091%	0.048%	0.043%	0.069%
87:1	9431	11929	0.791	0.224%	0.345%	-0.121%	0.293%
87:2	10028	10196	0.983	-0.014%	0.081%	-0.095%	0.038%
87:3	9793	10408	0.941	0.085%	0.058%	0.027%	0.068%
87:4	10590	8087	1.310	-0.183%	-0.390%	0.207%	-0.278%
88:1	9386	10989	0.854	0.220%	0.116%	0.104%	0.163%
88:2	9747	10593	0.920	0.094%	0.104%	-0.011%	0.100%
88:3	9894	10050	0.984	0.038%	-0.007%	0.045%	0.013%
88:4	9813	10196	0.962	0.066%	0.012%	0.054%	0.037%
89:1	9671	10698	0.904	0.127%	0.101%	0.027%	0.112%
89:2	9645	10772	0.895	0.126%	0.119%	0.006%	0.122%
89:3	9674	10833	0.893	0.129%	0.132%	-0.003%	0.131%
89:4	10078	9904	1.018	-0.030%	0.005%	-0.035%	-0.011%
90:1	9988	9980	1.001	0.003%	0.003%	0.000%	0.003%
90:2	9756	10459	0.933	0.094%	0.064%	0.030%	0.077%
90:3	10892	8526	1.278	-0.309%	-0.219%	-0.090%	-0.259%
90:4	9698	10889	0.891	0.092%	0.200%	-0.108%	0.146%
91:1	9238	12477	0.740	0.357%	0.289%	0.068%	0.315%
91:2	9973	10244	0.974	0.010%	0.071%	-0.061%	0.045%
91:3	9968	10429	0.956	0.012%	0.107%	-0.095%	0.065%
91:4	9999	10497	0.953	0.000%	0.146%	-0.146%	0.082%
92:1	9962	10324	0.965	0.018%	0.068%	-0.049%	0.048%
92:2	10201	9723	1.049	-0.071%	-0.031%	-0.040%	-0.048%
92:3	9880	10392	0.951	0.042%	0.071%	-0.029%	0.057%
92:4	9602	10963	0.876	0.146%	0.143%	0.003%	0.144%
93:1	9849	10527	0.936	0.062%	0.094%	-0.033%	0.080%
93:2	9932	10340	0.961	0.027%	0.072%	-0.046%	0.052%
93:3	9751	10686	0.912	0.093%	0.108%	-0.015%	0.101%
93:4	9923	10255	0.968	0.029%	0.038%	-0.009%	0.034%
94:1	10138	9954	1.019	-0.047%	0.018%	-0.065%	-0.011%
94:2	10193	9994	1.020	-0.061%	0.047%	-0.108%	-0.005%
94:3	9787	10613	0.922	0.078%	0.099%	-0.021%	0.089%
94:4	10097	9836	1.026	-0.033%	-0.026%	-0.007%	-0.029%
95:1	9743	10706	0.910	0.091%	0.126%	-0.035%	0.110%
95:2	9623	10873	0.885	0.134%	0.134%	0.000%	0.134%
95:3	9713	10853	0.895	0.109%	0.148%	-0.039%	0.131%
95:4	9821	10445	0.940	0.070%	0.064%	0.006%	0.067%
96:1	9559	11027	0.867	0.162%	0.156%	0.006%	0.159%
96:2	9901	10367	0.955	0.037%	0.075%	-0.039%	0.059%
96:3	9810	10298	0.953	0.062%	0.033%	0.029%	0.047%
96:4	9646	10817	0.892	0.141%	0.109%	0.032%	0.122%
AVG	9887	10377	0.953	0.043%	0.064%	-0.021%	0.055%

short calls and 60.7 percent for cash calls, these calls are also correct the majority of the time. The average quarterly terminal wealth of investors trading short with this system is $9,887 (Table 4.26b), the average for all of the technical indicators in this book. However, as with almost all of our indicators, trading short with the TXM-FP system results in declining terminal wealth. Therefore, investors would not want to rely solely on this indicator when they make short-position decisions.

In summary, the TXM-FP system makes calls more often than the average system and has above-average returns for all of the systems. It does indeed provide slightly better results than the related, simpler TRIX Peaks systems. However, especially when it comes to making short calls, investors desire a better performing system.

Williams %R Peaks

The Williams %R Peaks (WLR-P) system is almost identical to the Stochastic Peaks (STO-P) system discussed earlier in this chapter. In fact, the WLR-P system is basically an "inverted, nonsmoothed" stochastic oscillator.

The system is "inverted" in that the difference between the high of a trading range and a daily close is calculated. In the STO-P system, the difference between the low of a trading range and a daily close is calculated. Thus, one model tells whether a stock is at a relatively high point in its trading range, and the other tells whether a stock is at a relatively low point in its trading range.

The WLR-P is "nonsmoothed": no moving average is calculated.

Construction

First, choose a period, P, to use for the lookback period. Then calculate the WLR using the formula:

WLR = (High in period P – Today's close)/(High in period P – Low in period P).

Choose a level for an upper signal line and a level for a lower signal line. Whenever the WLR-P oscillator moves below the lower signal line and forms a valley, a bullish, long signal occurs. Whenever the WLR-P oscillator moves above the upper signal line and forms a peak, a bearish, short signal occurs.

Results

The test results for the WLR-P system are shown in Tables 4.27 and 4.28. Comparing these results with the results of the STO-P system discussed earlier, we see that this system makes both long and short calls slightly more frequently than the STO-P system did.

The WLR-P system makes long calls 44.2 percent of the time (Table 4.27a), and short calls 54.2 percent of the time (Table 4.27b). The hit rates for these calls are marginally better than the hit rates for the STO-P indicator. When choosing between long and cash positions, the WLR-P system has a 61.5 percent hit rate for long calls (Table 4.27a) and a 60.2 percent hit rate for short calls (Table 4.27b). When choosing between short and cash positions, the system has a 60.2 percent hit rate for short calls and a 61.4 percent hit rate for cash calls.

Using the WLR-P system for long-versus-cash decisions results in about the same terminal wealth as with the STO-P system. Trading long with the WLR-P system leads to an average quarterly terminal wealth of $10,168 (Table 4.28a), one dollar more than the $10,167 figure for the STO-P system.

However, traders using the WLR-P system for short-versus-cash decisions fare slightly worse than traders who use the STO-P system. The average quarterly terminal wealth for the WLR-P system is only $9,825 (Table 4.28b), compared to the average quarterly terminal wealth of $9,838 for the STO-P system.

It is hard to see how the short calls of the WLR-P system are of much use to traders. The average daily return for the short call days is exactly the same as it is for cash call days (Table 4.28b). The short calls do not appear to distinguish between periods of market strength or weakness, nor do they contain much useful information for an investor.

On balance, the WLR-P system outperforms its nonsmoothed, inverse counterpart, the STO-P system, for long calls, but underperforms it for short calls.

Williams %R Crossover

The Williams %R Crossover (WLR-C) system is based on the same oscillator as the WLR-P system we have just analyzed. Therefore, this indicator can be thought of as an inverted, nonsmoothed version of the Stochastic Crossover (STO-C) system discussed earlier in this chapter (see page 160). The WLR-C is a version of the STO-C indicator, but it tends to be less time-intensive to calculate.

Construction

The Williams %R Crossover (WLR-C) is based on the Williams %R oscillator. To calculate this oscillator, first choose a lookback period, P. Then calculate the oscillator, using this formula:

WLR-C = (High in period P – Today's close)/(High in period P – Low in period P).

Table 4.27a
Williams %R Peaks (WLR-P) Long Hit Analysis
(Average of all stocks)

Qtr	Optimal Long	WLR-P Long	Long Hits	Cash Hits	Total Hits	Long Right	Long Wrong	Cash Right	Cash Wrong
85:1	32.1%	37.3%	66.8%	67.0%	66.9%	24.9%	12.4%	42.0%	20.7%
85:2	30.2%	42.5%	67.3%	69.4%	68.5%	28.6%	13.9%	40.0%	17.6%
85:3	26.3%	53.1%	61.9%	73.7%	67.4%	32.9%	20.2%	34.5%	12.3%
85:4	36.6%	32.5%	69.2%	62.1%	64.4%	22.5%	10.0%	42.0%	25.6%
86:1	44.2%	32.6%	66.3%	55.3%	58.8%	21.6%	11.0%	37.3%	30.2%
86:2	39.7%	44.1%	62.8%	61.4%	62.0%	27.7%	16.4%	34.3%	21.6%
86:3	37.0%	54.6%	58.4%	63.3%	60.6%	31.9%	22.7%	28.8%	16.7%
86:4	38.5%	44.3%	63.3%	61.9%	62.5%	28.1%	16.3%	34.5%	21.2%
87:1	44.7%	29.2%	67.4%	56.1%	59.4%	19.7%	9.5%	39.7%	31.1%
87:2	40.0%	50.0%	61.2%	61.0%	61.1%	30.6%	19.4%	30.5%	19.5%
87:3	39.5%	46.0%	60.0%	60.3%	60.2%	27.6%	18.4%	32.6%	21.4%
87:4	37.9%	61.8%	55.4%	63.8%	58.6%	34.2%	27.6%	24.4%	13.8%
88:1	41.3%	32.8%	64.2%	58.7%	60.5%	21.0%	11.8%	39.4%	27.8%
88:2	39.3%	48.6%	63.2%	61.2%	62.2%	30.7%	17.9%	31.4%	20.0%
88:3	35.9%	51.2%	61.8%	64.0%	62.9%	31.7%	19.6%	31.2%	17.5%
88:4	36.3%	48.2%	63.4%	63.2%	63.3%	30.6%	17.6%	32.7%	19.1%
89:1	39.0%	39.7%	64.6%	60.9%	62.4%	25.7%	14.1%	36.7%	23.6%
89:2	40.2%	33.2%	65.1%	59.4%	61.3%	21.6%	11.6%	39.7%	27.1%
89:3	39.9%	42.2%	65.4%	60.2%	62.4%	27.6%	14.6%	34.8%	23.0%
89:4	38.3%	50.9%	61.6%	61.5%	61.5%	31.4%	19.5%	30.2%	18.9%
90:1	36.9%	51.0%	61.1%	63.8%	62.4%	31.1%	19.8%	31.3%	17.8%
90:2	39.2%	44.4%	63.6%	60.6%	61.9%	28.2%	16.2%	33.7%	21.9%
90:3	33.5%	63.7%	54.5%	67.1%	59.1%	34.7%	29.0%	24.3%	12.0%
90:4	40.8%	42.5%	63.4%	58.9%	60.8%	26.9%	15.6%	33.8%	23.7%
91:1	44.1%	34.2%	66.1%	56.5%	59.7%	22.6%	11.6%	37.1%	28.6%
91:2	39.7%	43.6%	61.1%	61.3%	61.2%	26.6%	17.0%	34.6%	21.8%
91:3	40.4%	44.8%	61.7%	60.3%	60.9%	27.7%	17.1%	33.3%	21.9%
91:4	41.2%	48.8%	60.0%	58.9%	59.5%	29.3%	19.5%	30.2%	21.0%
92:1	40.0%	39.9%	56.0%	59.1%	57.9%	22.3%	17.5%	35.6%	24.6%
92:2	38.6%	50.8%	57.5%	62.0%	59.8%	29.2%	21.6%	30.5%	18.7%
92:3	40.3%	42.4%	60.7%	59.8%	60.2%	25.8%	16.7%	34.4%	23.2%
92:4	41.9%	37.0%	63.2%	57.8%	59.8%	23.4%	13.6%	36.4%	26.6%
93:1	42.5%	38.2%	61.3%	57.9%	59.2%	23.4%	14.8%	35.8%	26.0%
93:2	42.1%	48.3%	59.9%	58.4%	59.1%	29.0%	19.4%	30.2%	21.5%
93:3	42.5%	40.8%	60.8%	57.4%	58.8%	24.8%	16.0%	34.0%	25.2%
93:4	41.5%	47.7%	58.1%	58.2%	58.1%	27.7%	20.0%	30.5%	21.9%
94:1	40.4%	44.6%	56.3%	59.3%	58.0%	25.1%	19.5%	32.8%	22.6%
94:2	40.6%	53.9%	57.9%	60.5%	59.1%	31.2%	22.7%	27.9%	18.2%
94:3	41.8%	45.0%	60.6%	58.6%	59.5%	27.2%	17.7%	32.2%	22.8%
94:4	39.5%	56.3%	57.2%	60.5%	58.6%	32.2%	24.1%	26.5%	17.3%
95:1	43.1%	37.6%	62.6%	57.1%	59.1%	23.5%	14.1%	35.6%	26.8%
95:2	43.7%	35.8%	61.7%	56.2%	58.1%	22.1%	13.7%	36.1%	28.1%
95:3	43.9%	36.9%	62.2%	55.8%	58.2%	22.9%	14.0%	35.2%	27.9%
95:4	43.4%	45.0%	58.5%	55.2%	56.7%	26.3%	18.7%	30.3%	24.6%
96:1	45.5%	43.7%	61.9%	54.6%	57.8%	27.0%	16.6%	30.7%	25.6%
96:2	42.1%	45.3%	58.1%	57.9%	58.0%	26.3%	19.0%	31.7%	23.0%
96:3	42.6%	46.6%	58.4%	56.6%	57.4%	27.2%	19.4%	30.2%	23.2%
96:4	44.3%	40.5%	60.3%	55.1%	57.2%	24.4%	16.1%	32.8%	26.7%
AVG	40.0%	44.2%	61.5%	60.2%	60.5%	27.1%	17.2%	33.4%	22.3%

Table 4.27b
Williams %R Peaks (WLR-P) Short Hit Analysis
(Average of all stocks)

Qtr	Optimal Short	WLR-P Short	Short Hits	Cash Hits	Total Hits	Short Right	Short Wrong	Cash Right	Cash Wrong
85:1	34.3%	60.6%	66.8%	66.6%	66.8%	40.5%	20.1%	26.2%	13.1%
85:2	34.6%	55.8%	69.3%	67.2%	68.4%	38.7%	17.1%	29.7%	14.5%
85:3	38.6%	44.9%	73.5%	62.0%	67.2%	33.0%	11.9%	34.2%	20.9%
85:4	33.1%	65.0%	62.0%	68.8%	64.4%	40.3%	24.7%	24.1%	10.9%
86:1	35.2%	65.2%	55.3%	66.0%	59.0%	36.0%	29.2%	22.9%	11.8%
86:2	39.8%	54.5%	61.5%	62.7%	62.1%	33.5%	21.0%	28.5%	17.0%
86:3	42.7%	43.7%	63.4%	58.2%	60.5%	27.7%	16.0%	32.8%	23.5%
86:4	38.7%	54.8%	62.0%	63.2%	62.5%	34.0%	20.8%	28.6%	16.6%
87:1	36.9%	69.0%	56.1%	67.1%	59.5%	38.7%	30.3%	20.8%	10.2%
87:2	40.0%	48.7%	61.0%	61.1%	61.1%	29.7%	19.0%	31.4%	19.9%
87:3	40.4%	52.4%	60.3%	60.0%	60.2%	31.6%	20.8%	28.6%	19.1%
87:4	45.3%	35.9%	63.8%	55.1%	58.2%	22.9%	13.0%	35.3%	28.8%
88:1	36.7%	65.7%	58.6%	63.9%	60.4%	38.5%	27.2%	21.9%	12.4%
88:2	37.4%	50.2%	61.2%	63.1%	62.1%	30.7%	19.5%	31.4%	18.3%
88:3	38.4%	47.7%	64.0%	61.8%	62.9%	30.6%	17.2%	32.3%	20.0%
88:4	37.0%	50.4%	63.1%	63.4%	63.2%	31.8%	18.6%	31.5%	18.2%
89:1	36.2%	58.8%	60.9%	64.4%	62.4%	35.8%	23.0%	26.5%	14.6%
89:2	35.9%	65.1%	59.4%	64.9%	61.3%	38.7%	26.4%	22.6%	12.3%
89:3	36.4%	56.3%	60.2%	65.1%	62.4%	33.9%	22.4%	28.5%	15.2%
89:4	39.0%	47.4%	61.5%	61.6%	61.6%	29.1%	18.2%	32.4%	20.2%
90:1	40.1%	47.7%	63.9%	61.1%	62.4%	30.5%	17.2%	31.9%	20.4%
90:2	37.8%	54.2%	60.6%	63.5%	61.9%	32.8%	21.4%	29.1%	16.7%
90:3	45.7%	33.6%	67.4%	54.5%	58.8%	22.7%	11.0%	36.2%	30.2%
90:4	37.6%	55.7%	58.8%	63.2%	60.7%	32.8%	22.9%	28.0%	16.3%
91:1	36.7%	63.7%	56.5%	65.9%	59.9%	36.0%	27.7%	23.9%	12.4%
91:2	40.4%	55.1%	61.4%	61.0%	61.2%	33.8%	21.3%	27.4%	17.5%
91:3	39.8%	53.8%	60.3%	61.7%	61.0%	32.5%	21.3%	28.5%	17.7%
91:4	40.5%	49.6%	59.1%	60.0%	59.6%	29.3%	20.3%	30.3%	20.2%
92:1	43.2%	58.6%	59.2%	56.0%	57.9%	34.7%	23.9%	23.2%	18.2%
92:2	42.9%	47.9%	62.0%	57.4%	59.6%	29.7%	18.2%	29.9%	22.2%
92:3	39.5%	56.5%	59.8%	60.7%	60.2%	33.8%	22.7%	26.4%	17.1%
92:4	37.5%	61.2%	57.8%	63.1%	59.8%	35.4%	25.9%	24.5%	14.3%
93:1	39.4%	60.3%	58.0%	61.4%	59.3%	35.0%	25.3%	24.3%	15.3%
93:2	40.9%	50.2%	58.5%	59.8%	59.2%	29.4%	20.9%	29.8%	20.0%
93:3	39.4%	57.7%	57.4%	60.7%	58.8%	33.2%	24.6%	25.7%	16.6%
93:4	41.7%	51.0%	58.3%	58.0%	58.1%	29.7%	21.3%	28.4%	20.6%
94:1	43.7%	54.1%	59.4%	56.4%	58.0%	32.2%	22.0%	25.9%	20.0%
94:2	42.7%	45.0%	60.6%	57.9%	59.1%	27.3%	17.7%	31.8%	23.2%
94:3	39.8%	53.7%	58.6%	60.5%	59.5%	31.5%	22.2%	28.0%	18.3%
94:4	42.8%	42.3%	60.4%	57.1%	58.5%	25.6%	16.7%	32.9%	24.8%
95:1	38.7%	61.2%	57.0%	62.3%	59.1%	34.9%	26.3%	24.2%	14.6%
95:2	38.9%	62.5%	56.2%	61.6%	58.2%	35.2%	27.4%	23.1%	14.4%
95:3	38.9%	61.6%	55.8%	62.0%	58.2%	34.3%	27.2%	23.8%	14.6%
95:4	40.5%	53.4%	55.2%	58.6%	56.8%	29.5%	23.9%	27.3%	19.3%
96:1	38.9%	54.8%	54.6%	61.8%	57.8%	29.9%	24.9%	27.9%	17.3%
96:2	42.4%	53.6%	57.8%	58.0%	57.9%	31.0%	22.6%	26.9%	19.5%
96:3	40.8%	52.0%	56.5%	58.3%	57.4%	29.4%	22.6%	28.0%	20.0%
96:4	39.8%	57.7%	55.1%	60.1%	57.2%	31.8%	25.9%	25.4%	16.9%
AVG	39.4%	54.2%	60.2%	61.4%	60.5%	32.5%	21.7%	28.0%	17.8%

Table 4.28a
Williams %R Peaks (WLR-P) Long Return Analysis
(Average of all stocks)

Qtr	WLR-P Terminal Wealth	Buy/Hold Terminal Wealth	Relative Terminal Wealth	WLR-P Long Avg Ret	WLR-P Cash Avg Ret	WLR-P Long-Cash Avg Ret	Buy/Hold Avg Ret
85:1	9964	10142	0.982	-0.027%	0.026%	-0.054%	0.006%
85:2	9904	9700	1.021	-0.056%	-0.079%	0.023%	-0.069%
85:3	9411	8889	1.059	-0.194%	-0.217%	0.023%	-0.205%
85:4	10217	10763	0.949	0.095%	0.112%	-0.017%	0.107%
86:1	10459	11428	0.915	0.231%	0.222%	0.010%	0.225%
86:2	10427	10414	1.001	0.151%	-0.001%	0.152%	0.066%
86:3	9685	9175	1.056	-0.084%	-0.180%	0.096%	-0.128%
86:4	10297	10413	0.989	0.106%	0.040%	0.067%	0.069%
87:1	10807	11929	0.906	0.437%	0.234%	0.203%	0.293%
87:2	10251	10196	1.005	0.082%	-0.007%	0.089%	0.038%
87:3	10218	10408	0.982	0.078%	0.060%	0.018%	0.068%
87:4	8947	8087	1.106	-0.238%	-0.342%	0.104%	-0.278%
88:1	10395	10989	0.946	0.198%	0.146%	0.052%	0.163%
88:2	10389	10593	0.981	0.131%	0.070%	0.060%	0.100%
88:3	10029	10050	0.998	0.012%	0.014%	-0.002%	0.013%
88:4	10075	10196	0.988	0.028%	0.045%	-0.017%	0.037%
89:1	10240	10698	0.957	0.100%	0.121%	-0.021%	0.112%
89:2	10270	10772	0.953	0.130%	0.118%	0.012%	0.122%
89:3	10398	10833	0.960	0.152%	0.116%	0.036%	0.131%
89:4	10010	9904	1.011	0.007%	-0.030%	0.037%	-0.011%
90:1	10084	9980	1.010	0.033%	-0.028%	0.061%	0.003%
90:2	10188	10459	0.974	0.072%	0.080%	-0.008%	0.077%
90:3	9034	8526	1.060	-0.265%	-0.248%	-0.016%	-0.259%
90:4	10452	10889	0.960	0.173%	0.126%	0.047%	0.146%
91:1	11276	12477	0.904	0.393%	0.274%	0.118%	0.315%
91:2	10224	10244	0.998	0.084%	0.015%	0.069%	0.045%
91:3	10335	10429	0.991	0.117%	0.023%	0.094%	0.065%
91:4	10363	10497	0.987	0.125%	0.040%	0.085%	0.082%
92:1	9983	10324	0.967	-0.009%	0.085%	-0.094%	0.048%
92:2	9925	9723	1.021	-0.025%	-0.072%	0.047%	-0.048%
92:3	10225	10392	0.984	0.084%	0.036%	0.047%	0.057%
92:4	10346	10963	0.944	0.150%	0.141%	0.008%	0.144%
93:1	10266	10527	0.975	0.113%	0.059%	0.053%	0.080%
93:2	10221	10340	0.988	0.075%	0.030%	0.044%	0.052%
93:3	10286	10686	0.962	0.109%	0.095%	0.014%	0.101%
93:4	10068	10255	0.982	0.021%	0.046%	-0.025%	0.034%
94:1	9984	9954	1.003	-0.009%	-0.013%	0.004%	-0.011%
94:2	10107	9994	1.011	0.030%	-0.045%	0.076%	-0.005%
94:3	10270	10613	0.968	0.092%	0.087%	0.005%	0.089%
94:4	9911	9836	1.008	-0.028%	-0.032%	0.004%	-0.029%
95:1	10350	10706	0.967	0.150%	0.086%	0.064%	0.110%
95:2	10310	10873	0.948	0.138%	0.132%	0.007%	0.134%
95:3	10372	10853	0.956	0.160%	0.114%	0.045%	0.131%
95:4	10105	10445	0.967	0.037%	0.091%	-0.054%	0.067%
96:1	10507	11027	0.953	0.186%	0.138%	0.048%	0.159%
96:2	10194	10367	0.983	0.068%	0.051%	0.017%	0.059%
96:3	10038	10298	0.975	0.014%	0.077%	-0.063%	0.047%
96:4	10268	10817	0.949	0.105%	0.134%	-0.030%	0.122%
AVG	10168	10377	0.980	0.057%	0.054%	0.003%	0.055%

Table 4.28b
Williams %R Peaks (WLR-P) Short Return Analysis
(Average of all stocks)

Qtr	WLR-P Terminal Wealth	Buy/Hold Terminal Wealth	Relative Terminal Wealth	WLR-P Short Avg Ret	WLR-P Cash Avg Ret	WLR-P Short-Cash Avg Ret	Buy/Hold Avg Ret
85:1	9915	10142	0.978	0.031%	-0.032%	0.063%	0.006%
85:2	10299	9700	1.062	-0.076%	-0.061%	-0.015%	-0.069%
85:3	10655	8889	1.199	-0.215%	-0.196%	-0.019%	-0.205%
85:4	9555	10763	0.888	0.116%	0.090%	0.025%	0.107%
86:1	9170	11428	0.802	0.220%	0.233%	-0.012%	0.225%
86:2	10014	10414	0.962	-0.003%	0.150%	-0.153%	0.066%
86:3	10496	9175	1.144	-0.180%	-0.087%	-0.092%	-0.128%
86:4	9863	10413	0.947	0.037%	0.108%	-0.071%	0.069%
87:1	9064	11929	0.760	0.234%	0.424%	-0.190%	0.293%
87:2	10019	10196	0.983	-0.009%	0.082%	-0.091%	0.038%
87:3	9793	10408	0.941	0.060%	0.078%	-0.018%	0.068%
87:4	10630	8087	1.314	-0.278%	-0.278%	0.001%	-0.278%
88:1	9374	10989	0.853	0.151%	0.186%	-0.035%	0.163%
88:2	9770	10593	0.922	0.072%	0.127%	-0.055%	0.100%
88:3	9953	10050	0.990	0.015%	0.011%	0.004%	0.013%
88:4	9856	10196	0.967	0.046%	0.027%	0.019%	0.037%
89:1	9568	10698	0.894	0.123%	0.097%	0.027%	0.112%
89:2	9525	10772	0.884	0.118%	0.130%	-0.012%	0.122%
89:3	9600	10833	0.886	0.117%	0.149%	-0.032%	0.131%
89:4	10096	9904	1.019	-0.035%	0.011%	-0.046%	-0.011%
90:1	10088	9980	1.011	-0.032%	0.034%	-0.066%	0.003%
90:2	9730	10459	0.930	0.081%	0.071%	0.010%	0.077%
90:3	10523	8526	1.234	-0.250%	-0.263%	0.014%	-0.259%
90:4	9554	10889	0.877	0.129%	0.168%	-0.038%	0.146%
91:1	9017	12477	0.723	0.270%	0.394%	-0.125%	0.315%
91:2	9942	10244	0.971	0.012%	0.086%	-0.074%	0.045%
91:3	9942	10429	0.953	0.020%	0.117%	-0.096%	0.065%
91:4	9885	10497	0.942	0.038%	0.125%	-0.087%	0.082%
92:1	9718	10324	0.941	0.083%	-0.002%	0.085%	0.048%
92:2	10208	9723	1.050	-0.069%	-0.030%	-0.039%	-0.048%
92:3	9885	10392	0.951	0.036%	0.083%	-0.047%	0.057%
92:4	9471	10963	0.864	0.144%	0.145%	-0.001%	0.144%
93:1	9816	10527	0.932	0.055%	0.117%	-0.062%	0.080%
93:2	9926	10340	0.960	0.028%	0.076%	-0.048%	0.052%
93:3	9653	10686	0.903	0.100%	0.102%	-0.002%	0.101%
93:4	9870	10255	0.963	0.046%	0.021%	0.024%	0.034%
94:1	10064	9954	1.011	-0.017%	-0.004%	-0.013%	-0.011%
94:2	10141	9994	1.015	-0.047%	0.030%	-0.077%	-0.005%
94:3	9722	10613	0.916	0.087%	0.092%	-0.005%	0.089%
94:4	10079	9836	1.025	-0.028%	-0.030%	0.001%	-0.029%
95:1	9676	10706	0.904	0.088%	0.144%	-0.056%	0.110%
95:2	9511	10873	0.875	0.131%	0.139%	-0.008%	0.134%
95:3	9576	10853	0.882	0.116%	0.155%	-0.039%	0.131%
95:4	9724	10445	0.931	0.089%	0.041%	0.049%	0.067%
96:1	9547	11027	0.866	0.138%	0.185%	-0.047%	0.159%
96:2	9831	10367	0.948	0.053%	0.065%	-0.013%	0.059%
96:3	9746	10298	0.946	0.080%	0.012%	0.068%	0.047%
96:4	9525	10817	0.881	0.136%	0.104%	0.032%	0.122%
AVG	9825	10377	0.947	0.055%	0.055%	0.000%	0.055%

Table 4.29a
Williams %R Crossover (WLR-C) Long Hit Analysis
(Average of all stocks)

Qtr	Optimal Long	WLR-C Long	Long Hits	Cash Hits	Total Hits	Long Right	Long Wrong	Cash Right	Cash Wrong
85:1	32.1%	38.0%	66.5%	67.2%	66.9%	25.2%	12.7%	41.7%	20.4%
85:2	30.2%	43.3%	66.5%	69.5%	68.2%	28.8%	14.5%	39.4%	17.3%
85:3	26.3%	50.7%	61.8%	73.5%	67.6%	31.3%	19.3%	36.3%	13.0%
85:4	36.6%	35.8%	68.4%	62.0%	64.3%	24.5%	11.3%	39.8%	24.4%
86:1	44.2%	35.4%	66.2%	55.4%	59.2%	23.4%	12.0%	35.8%	28.8%
86:2	39.7%	44.9%	61.6%	61.2%	61.4%	27.7%	17.2%	33.7%	21.4%
86:3	37.0%	50.2%	58.2%	62.9%	60.6%	29.2%	21.0%	31.3%	18.5%
86:4	38.5%	45.8%	62.5%	61.6%	62.0%	28.6%	17.2%	33.4%	20.8%
87:1	44.7%	35.2%	66.1%	56.2%	59.7%	23.3%	11.9%	36.4%	28.3%
87:2	40.0%	50.9%	60.7%	60.6%	60.7%	30.9%	20.0%	29.7%	19.3%
87:3	39.5%	45.3%	60.0%	60.4%	60.2%	27.2%	18.1%	33.0%	21.7%
87:4	37.9%	60.4%	55.7%	63.4%	58.8%	33.6%	26.7%	25.1%	14.5%
88:1	41.3%	33.8%	63.6%	58.5%	60.2%	21.5%	12.3%	38.7%	27.5%
88:2	39.3%	50.3%	62.5%	60.9%	61.7%	31.4%	18.9%	30.3%	19.5%
88:3	35.9%	49.9%	61.5%	63.8%	62.7%	30.7%	19.2%	32.0%	18.1%
88:4	36.3%	46.5%	63.2%	62.9%	63.1%	29.4%	17.1%	33.7%	19.8%
89:1	39.0%	40.1%	64.0%	60.7%	62.0%	25.6%	14.4%	36.4%	23.6%
89:2	40.2%	35.4%	64.3%	59.3%	61.1%	22.8%	12.6%	38.3%	26.3%
89:3	39.9%	43.2%	64.7%	60.1%	62.1%	28.0%	15.3%	34.1%	22.6%
89:4	38.3%	51.2%	61.2%	61.2%	61.2%	31.3%	19.9%	29.9%	19.0%
90:1	36.9%	50.4%	60.8%	63.8%	62.3%	30.7%	19.8%	31.6%	17.9%
90:2	39.2%	44.3%	63.8%	61.0%	62.2%	28.2%	16.0%	34.0%	21.7%
90:3	33.5%	58.3%	54.8%	67.1%	59.9%	32.0%	26.4%	28.0%	13.7%
90:4	40.8%	42.7%	62.6%	58.4%	60.2%	26.7%	15.9%	33.5%	23.9%
91:1	44.1%	37.2%	65.9%	56.9%	60.2%	24.5%	12.7%	35.7%	27.1%
91:2	39.7%	44.5%	60.7%	61.1%	60.9%	27.0%	17.5%	33.9%	21.6%
91:3	40.4%	45.7%	61.3%	60.1%	60.6%	28.0%	17.7%	32.6%	21.7%
91:4	41.2%	49.0%	60.0%	59.0%	59.5%	29.4%	19.6%	30.1%	20.9%
92:1	40.0%	40.9%	55.9%	59.2%	57.9%	22.9%	18.0%	35.0%	24.1%
92:2	38.6%	49.0%	57.1%	61.5%	59.3%	27.9%	21.0%	31.4%	19.7%
92:3	40.3%	43.8%	60.3%	59.5%	59.8%	26.4%	17.3%	33.4%	22.8%
92:4	41.9%	39.1%	62.9%	57.8%	59.8%	24.6%	14.5%	35.2%	25.7%
93:1	42.5%	39.7%	61.4%	58.1%	59.4%	24.4%	15.3%	35.0%	25.3%
93:2	42.1%	47.8%	59.7%	58.3%	59.0%	28.5%	19.2%	30.4%	21.8%
93:3	42.5%	41.4%	60.9%	57.6%	58.9%	25.2%	16.2%	33.7%	24.9%
93:4	41.5%	47.4%	57.9%	58.2%	58.1%	27.5%	19.9%	30.6%	22.0%
94:1	40.4%	44.5%	56.4%	59.4%	58.1%	25.1%	19.4%	33.0%	22.5%
94:2	40.6%	52.9%	57.7%	60.0%	58.8%	30.5%	22.4%	28.2%	18.9%
94:3	41.8%	44.7%	60.7%	58.7%	59.6%	27.1%	17.6%	32.5%	22.8%
94:4	39.5%	54.5%	57.0%	60.5%	58.6%	31.1%	23.4%	27.5%	18.0%
95:1	43.1%	38.7%	62.0%	56.9%	58.9%	24.0%	14.7%	34.8%	26.4%
95:2	43.7%	37.6%	61.3%	56.2%	58.1%	23.1%	14.6%	35.0%	27.3%
95:3	43.9%	38.5%	61.8%	55.7%	58.0%	23.8%	14.7%	34.3%	27.3%
95:4	43.4%	44.5%	58.5%	55.2%	56.7%	26.0%	18.5%	30.6%	24.8%
96:1	45.5%	45.6%	61.7%	54.8%	57.9%	28.2%	17.5%	29.8%	24.6%
96:2	42.1%	45.6%	58.1%	57.9%	58.0%	26.5%	19.1%	31.5%	22.9%
96:3	42.6%	48.4%	59.0%	57.2%	58.1%	28.5%	19.9%	29.5%	22.1%
96:4	44.3%	41.1%	60.3%	55.2%	57.3%	24.8%	16.3%	32.5%	26.4%
AVG	40.0%	44.7%	61.2%	60.1%	60.4%	27.2%	17.4%	33.2%	22.2%

Table 4.29b
Williams %R Crossover (WLR-C) Short Hit Analysis
(Average of all stocks)

Qtr	Optimal Short	WLR-C Short	Short Hits	Cash Hits	Total Hits	Short Right	Short Wrong	Cash Right	Cash Wrong
85:1	34.3%	55.7%	66.9%	66.0%	66.5%	37.2%	18.5%	29.2%	15.1%
85:2	34.6%	52.0%	69.2%	66.1%	67.7%	36.0%	16.0%	31.7%	16.3%
85:3	38.6%	44.7%	73.2%	62.0%	67.0%	32.8%	12.0%	34.2%	21.0%
85:4	33.1%	57.2%	61.6%	67.3%	64.0%	35.2%	22.0%	28.8%	14.0%
86:1	35.2%	58.2%	55.4%	65.2%	59.5%	32.3%	26.0%	27.2%	14.5%
86:2	39.8%	51.8%	61.4%	61.4%	61.4%	31.8%	20.0%	29.6%	18.6%
86:3	42.7%	44.6%	63.1%	58.0%	60.3%	28.1%	16.5%	32.1%	23.2%
86:4	38.7%	51.8%	61.6%	62.2%	61.9%	31.9%	19.9%	30.0%	18.2%
87:1	36.9%	60.1%	56.2%	65.2%	59.8%	33.8%	26.3%	26.0%	13.9%
87:2	40.0%	46.1%	60.7%	60.6%	60.7%	28.0%	18.1%	32.7%	21.3%
87:3	40.4%	50.7%	60.3%	59.6%	60.0%	30.6%	20.1%	29.4%	19.9%
87:4	45.3%	35.5%	63.9%	55.6%	58.5%	22.6%	12.8%	35.9%	28.7%
88:1	36.7%	62.5%	58.2%	63.1%	60.1%	36.4%	26.1%	23.6%	13.8%
88:2	37.4%	46.8%	60.9%	62.4%	61.7%	28.5%	18.3%	33.2%	20.0%
88:3	38.4%	47.6%	63.8%	61.4%	62.6%	30.4%	17.2%	32.2%	20.2%
88:4	37.0%	50.2%	62.9%	62.9%	62.9%	31.6%	18.6%	31.4%	18.5%
89:1	36.2%	56.1%	60.7%	63.7%	62.0%	34.1%	22.1%	27.9%	15.9%
89:2	35.9%	59.8%	59.3%	63.7%	61.1%	35.4%	24.3%	25.6%	14.6%
89:3	36.4%	53.4%	60.1%	64.2%	62.0%	32.1%	21.3%	29.9%	16.7%
89:4	39.0%	45.0%	61.3%	61.1%	61.2%	27.6%	17.4%	33.6%	21.4%
90:1	40.1%	46.6%	63.8%	60.7%	62.2%	29.7%	16.8%	32.5%	21.0%
90:2	37.8%	52.0%	61.0%	63.3%	62.1%	31.7%	20.3%	30.4%	17.6%
90:3	45.7%	35.9%	67.7%	54.7%	59.4%	24.3%	11.6%	35.0%	29.0%
90:4	37.6%	52.7%	58.2%	62.4%	60.2%	30.7%	22.0%	29.5%	17.8%
91:1	36.7%	57.7%	56.9%	65.1%	60.4%	32.8%	24.9%	27.5%	14.7%
91:2	40.4%	52.8%	61.0%	60.4%	60.7%	32.2%	20.6%	28.5%	18.7%
91:3	39.8%	51.1%	60.1%	61.1%	60.5%	30.7%	20.4%	29.9%	19.0%
91:4	40.5%	47.4%	59.4%	60.0%	59.7%	28.1%	19.3%	31.6%	21.0%
92:1	43.2%	55.0%	59.3%	55.9%	57.7%	32.6%	22.4%	25.2%	19.9%
92:2	42.9%	47.7%	61.5%	57.0%	59.2%	29.3%	18.3%	29.8%	22.5%
92:3	39.5%	53.2%	59.5%	60.3%	59.9%	31.6%	21.5%	28.3%	18.6%
92:4	37.5%	56.6%	57.6%	62.3%	59.7%	32.6%	24.0%	27.1%	16.4%
93:1	39.4%	56.5%	58.1%	61.1%	59.4%	32.8%	23.7%	26.6%	16.9%
93:2	40.9%	49.3%	58.3%	59.5%	58.9%	28.7%	20.5%	30.2%	20.5%
93:3	39.4%	54.9%	57.5%	60.7%	59.0%	31.6%	23.3%	27.4%	17.7%
93:4	41.7%	49.2%	58.3%	57.9%	58.1%	28.7%	20.5%	29.4%	21.4%
94:1	43.7%	52.5%	59.4%	56.3%	57.9%	31.2%	21.3%	26.7%	20.7%
94:2	42.7%	44.7%	60.2%	57.7%	58.8%	26.9%	17.8%	31.9%	23.4%
94:3	39.8%	52.2%	58.7%	60.5%	59.6%	30.6%	21.6%	28.9%	18.9%
94:4	42.8%	42.4%	60.6%	56.9%	58.5%	25.7%	16.7%	32.8%	24.8%
95:1	38.7%	58.2%	56.7%	61.6%	58.8%	33.0%	25.2%	25.8%	16.1%
95:2	38.9%	58.8%	56.2%	61.0%	58.2%	33.0%	25.8%	25.1%	16.0%
95:3	38.9%	57.4%	55.7%	61.4%	58.1%	32.0%	25.4%	26.1%	16.5%
95:4	40.5%	50.9%	55.2%	58.6%	56.8%	28.1%	22.8%	28.8%	20.4%
96:1	38.9%	51.5%	54.6%	61.3%	57.9%	28.1%	23.4%	29.7%	18.7%
96:2	42.4%	51.6%	57.9%	57.8%	57.8%	29.9%	21.7%	28.0%	20.4%
96:3	40.8%	48.3%	57.2%	58.8%	58.0%	27.6%	20.7%	30.4%	21.3%
96:4	39.8%	54.4%	55.1%	59.9%	57.3%	30.0%	24.4%	27.3%	18.3%
AVG	39.4%	51.5%	60.1%	61.0%	60.3%	30.8%	20.6%	29.5%	19.0%

Table 4.30a
Williams %R Crossover (WLR-C) Long Return Analysis
(Average of all stocks)

Qtr	WLR-C Terminal Wealth	Buy/Hold Terminal Wealth	Relative Terminal Wealth	WLR-C Long Avg Ret	WLR-C Cash Avg Ret	WLR-C Long-Cash Avg Ret	Buy/Hold Avg Ret
85:1	9987	10142	0.985	-0.018%	0.021%	-0.039%	0.006%
85:2	9867	9700	1.017	-0.067%	-0.071%	0.004%	-0.069%
85:3	9437	8889	1.062	-0.193%	-0.217%	0.023%	-0.205%
85:4	10217	10763	0.949	0.087%	0.118%	-0.030%	0.107%
86:1	10521	11428	0.921	0.236%	0.218%	0.017%	0.225%
86:2	10340	10414	0.993	0.118%	0.025%	0.093%	0.066%
86:3	9670	9175	1.054	-0.099%	-0.157%	0.058%	-0.128%
86:4	10251	10413	0.984	0.088%	0.054%	0.034%	0.069%
87:1	10908	11929	0.914	0.406%	0.232%	0.174%	0.293%
87:2	10189	10196	0.999	0.062%	0.013%	0.050%	0.038%
87:3	10250	10408	0.985	0.089%	0.051%	0.039%	0.068%
87:4	9277	8087	1.147	-0.172%	-0.440%	0.268%	-0.278%
88:1	10348	10989	0.942	0.172%	0.158%	0.014%	0.163%
88:2	10318	10593	0.974	0.105%	0.094%	0.011%	0.100%
88:3	10019	10050	0.997	0.009%	0.016%	-0.007%	0.013%
88:4	10053	10196	0.986	0.021%	0.050%	-0.029%	0.037%
89:1	10224	10698	0.956	0.092%	0.126%	-0.034%	0.112%
89:2	10266	10772	0.953	0.120%	0.123%	-0.003%	0.122%
89:3	10385	10833	0.959	0.143%	0.122%	0.021%	0.131%
89:4	9974	9904	1.007	-0.004%	-0.018%	0.013%	-0.011%
90:1	10081	9980	1.010	0.032%	-0.027%	0.059%	0.003%
90:2	10257	10459	0.981	0.096%	0.061%	0.035%	0.077%
90:3	9145	8526	1.073	-0.254%	-0.266%	0.012%	-0.259%
90:4	10354	10889	0.951	0.141%	0.150%	-0.009%	0.146%
91:1	11333	12477	0.908	0.413%	0.257%	0.156%	0.315%
91:2	10204	10244	0.996	0.075%	0.022%	0.053%	0.045%
91:3	10289	10429	0.987	0.099%	0.036%	0.063%	0.065%
91:4	10348	10497	0.986	0.113%	0.052%	0.061%	0.082%
92:1	9997	10324	0.968	-0.004%	0.084%	-0.089%	0.048%
92:2	9875	9723	1.016	-0.043%	-0.053%	0.010%	-0.048%
92:3	10201	10392	0.982	0.070%	0.046%	0.023%	0.057%
92:4	10353	10963	0.944	0.143%	0.145%	-0.002%	0.144%
93:1	10302	10527	0.979	0.121%	0.053%	0.068%	0.080%
93:2	10194	10340	0.986	0.065%	0.039%	0.026%	0.052%
93:3	10289	10686	0.963	0.107%	0.097%	0.011%	0.101%
93:4	10069	10255	0.982	0.021%	0.046%	-0.025%	0.034%
94:1	9998	9954	1.004	-0.005%	-0.017%	0.012%	-0.011%
94:2	10062	9994	1.007	0.018%	-0.030%	0.048%	-0.005%
94:3	10289	10613	0.969	0.099%	0.082%	0.017%	0.089%
94:4	9890	9836	1.005	-0.035%	-0.022%	-0.012%	-0.029%
95:1	10329	10706	0.965	0.136%	0.093%	0.043%	0.110%
95:2	10307	10873	0.948	0.130%	0.137%	-0.007%	0.134%
95:3	10364	10853	0.955	0.150%	0.120%	0.030%	0.131%
95:4	10111	10445	0.968	0.039%	0.089%	-0.050%	0.067%
96:1	10506	11027	0.953	0.177%	0.144%	0.033%	0.159%
96:2	10181	10367	0.982	0.063%	0.055%	0.009%	0.059%
96:3	10096	10298	0.980	0.033%	0.061%	-0.028%	0.047%
96:4	10272	10817	0.950	0.104%	0.135%	-0.031%	0.122%
AVG	10171	10377	0.980	0.057%	0.054%	0.003%	0.055%

Table 4.30b
Williams %R Crossover (WLR-C) Short Return Analysis
(Average of all stocks)

Qtr	WLR-C Terminal Wealth	Buy/Hold Terminal Wealth	Relative Terminal Wealth	WLR-C Short Avg Ret	WLR-C Cash Avg Ret	WLR-C Short-Cash Avg Ret	Buy/Hold Avg Ret
85:1	9919	10142	0.978	0.033%	-0.027%	0.059%	0.006%
85:2	10243	9700	1.056	-0.063%	-0.076%	0.012%	-0.069%
85:3	10645	8889	1.198	-0.212%	-0.199%	-0.013%	-0.205%
85:4	9551	10763	0.887	0.132%	0.073%	0.059%	0.107%
86:1	9247	11428	0.809	0.225%	0.225%	0.000%	0.225%
86:2	9945	10414	0.955	0.016%	0.120%	-0.104%	0.066%
86:3	10469	9175	1.141	-0.168%	-0.095%	-0.073%	-0.128%
86:4	9817	10413	0.943	0.053%	0.086%	-0.033%	0.069%
87:1	9165	11929	0.768	0.239%	0.374%	-0.135%	0.293%
87:2	9966	10196	0.977	0.008%	0.063%	-0.055%	0.038%
87:3	9820	10408	0.944	0.055%	0.082%	-0.027%	0.068%
87:4	10912	8087	1.349	-0.410%	-0.205%	-0.205%	-0.278%
88:1	9324	10989	0.848	0.173%	0.146%	0.027%	0.163%
88:2	9715	10593	0.917	0.098%	0.102%	-0.004%	0.100%
88:3	9943	10050	0.989	0.018%	0.008%	0.011%	0.013%
88:4	9830	10196	0.964	0.054%	0.019%	0.035%	0.037%
89:1	9560	10698	0.894	0.132%	0.088%	0.044%	0.112%
89:2	9531	10772	0.885	0.127%	0.115%	0.012%	0.122%
89:3	9592	10833	0.885	0.126%	0.137%	-0.011%	0.131%
89:4	10061	9904	1.016	-0.025%	0.000%	-0.025%	-0.011%
90:1	10085	9980	1.011	-0.030%	0.031%	-0.062%	0.003%
90:2	9794	10459	0.936	0.066%	0.089%	-0.023%	0.077%
90:3	10645	8526	1.249	-0.280%	-0.247%	-0.032%	-0.259%
90:4	9473	10889	0.870	0.163%	0.128%	0.034%	0.146%
91:1	9125	12477	0.731	0.265%	0.383%	-0.118%	0.315%
91:2	9920	10244	0.968	0.021%	0.073%	-0.053%	0.045%
91:3	9889	10429	0.948	0.037%	0.094%	-0.057%	0.065%
91:4	9854	10497	0.939	0.041%	0.118%	-0.077%	0.082%
92:1	9730	10324	0.942	0.085%	0.002%	0.083%	0.048%
92:2	10161	9723	1.045	-0.054%	-0.043%	-0.011%	-0.048%
92:3	9857	10392	0.949	0.045%	0.069%	-0.024%	0.057%
92:4	9467	10963	0.864	0.157%	0.128%	0.029%	0.144%
93:1	9831	10527	0.934	0.055%	0.112%	-0.057%	0.080%
93:2	9900	10340	0.957	0.036%	0.067%	-0.031%	0.052%
93:3	9656	10686	0.904	0.105%	0.096%	0.010%	0.101%
93:4	9877	10255	0.963	0.045%	0.023%	0.022%	0.034%
94:1	10049	9954	1.010	-0.014%	-0.008%	-0.006%	-0.011%
94:2	10104	9994	1.011	-0.033%	0.018%	-0.051%	-0.005%
94:3	9731	10613	0.917	0.087%	0.092%	-0.005%	0.089%
94:4	10061	9836	1.023	-0.021%	-0.036%	0.015%	-0.029%
95:1	9653	10706	0.902	0.100%	0.124%	-0.024%	0.110%
95:2	9511	10873	0.875	0.139%	0.127%	0.011%	0.134%
95:3	9579	10853	0.883	0.123%	0.143%	-0.020%	0.131%
95:4	9736	10445	0.932	0.089%	0.043%	0.046%	0.067%
96:1	9545	11027	0.866	0.147%	0.171%	-0.024%	0.159%
96:2	9826	10367	0.948	0.056%	0.061%	-0.005%	0.059%
96:3	9797	10298	0.951	0.068%	0.028%	0.040%	0.047%
96:4	9551	10817	0.883	0.138%	0.103%	0.035%	0.122%
AVG	9826	10377	0.947	0.058%	0.053%	0.005%	0.055%

Next, upper and lower threshold levels must be chosen. Typically, the upper-level threshold is set at 20 and the lower-level threshold is set at 80.

Whenever the WLR falls below the lower-level threshold, turns up, and then crosses through the lower-level threshold for a second time, a long, bullish signal is generated. Likewise, for a short signal to occur, the WLR-C must cross above the upper-level threshold, turn down, and then cross the threshold to the downside.

Results

The hit results in Table 4.29 show that the WLR-C makes calls at a rate similar to the related Williams %R Peaks (WLR-P) system. This indicator has a long call rate of 44.7 percent and a short call rate of 51.5 percent. Thus, this system makes both long and short calls more frequently than the optimal call rates. The long calls for the WLR-C system have a hit rate of 61.2 percent (Table 4.29a), and the short calls have a hit rate of 60.1 percent (Table 4.29b).

The return results presented in Table 4.30 are somewhat mixed. First, looking at the long call return analysis, we see that the long calls tend to be associated with above-average returns. The average return for long call days is 0.057 percent, or 0.003 percent higher than the return on days when the system favors a cash position over a long position (Table 4.30a). Thus, when trading long with this system, investors end up earning above-average returns on the days when they are in the market. Trading long with this system is profitable. An investor who begins a quarter with $10,000 and trades long following the WLR-C recommendations will, on average, end the quarter with a wealth of $10,171. The downside, however, is that even though this system's long strategy is profitable, it is not as profitable as a simple buy-and-hold strategy. In fact, the results show that this system tends to have returns that are only 98 percent of the returns of a buy-and-hold investment strategy.

The short return analysis is even more disappointing. First, the average daily return on long call days exceeds the average daily return when cash recommendations are made. Unfortunately, this system tends to make short calls on days of above-average stock price appreciation—the exact days when investors would want to be in a long position. Second, because the average daily return on long call days is positive, trading short with this system tends to be unprofitable. In fact, in 37 of the 48 test quarters, investors trading short with this system had losses. On average, an investor beginning with $10,000 to invest had only $9,826 after trading short with this system.

In conclusion, the results for the WLR-C system are similar to the WLR-P system discussed earlier. Neither system appears to provide traders with an advantage over the benchmark buy-and-hold strategy. In fact, trading short with either of these systems tends to be unprofitable and leads to losses.

Chapter

5

Divergence Indicators

Divergence

Divergence occurs when the trend of a stock's price and the trend of an indicator do not agree. For example, divergence occurs when a stock's price is reaching new highs but an indicator is not reaching new highs. When this occurs, price will usually reverse direction and confirm the direction of the indicator. Thus, divergence indicators are said to be better predictors of price trends than the prices themselves.

We include nine divergence indicators in this chapter. You will notice that some of these divergent indicators, such as the Commodity Channel Index Divergence system, look at the same oscillators that we considered in Chapter 4. We will see how these divergent indicators perform relative to the oscillator indicators.

Commodity Channel Index Divergence

Despite its name, the Commodity Channel Index Divergence (CCI-D) system can be used effectively in any type of security market, not just commodities. This system is based on measuring a security's price from its statistical mean. This indicator and the Commodity Channel Index Peaks (CCI-P) indicator, which is discussed on page 106, use the Commodity Channel Index developed by Donald Lambert. Lambert provided a complete description and interpretation of the Commodity Channel Index in the October 1980 issue of *Commodities* (now *Futures*) magazine.

Analysts who use this indicator assume that when a stock's prices are reaching new highs while the Commodity Channel Index is falling, a correction in the security's price will occur.

Construction

After determining a lookback period, P, calculate the typical price (TP) for each of the days in the lookback period, as follows:

$$TP_i = (H_i + L_i + C_i)/3 \ \{i = 1, 2, \ldots, P\}.$$

Then, calculate an average of the typical prices in the lookback period:

$$MV_{today} = (TP_1 + TP_2 + TP_3 + \ldots + TP_P)/P.$$

Next, calculate the absolute value of the daily deviation from this average:

$$R_i = |\ TP_i - MV_{today}\ | \ \{i = 1, 2, \ldots, P\}.$$

Calculate a simple moving average of these deviations and multiply this moving average by 0.015:

$$MV_R = [(R_1 + R_2 + R_3 + \ldots + R_P)/P] \cdot 0.015.$$

Finally, construct the CCI by dividing the difference between today's typical price and the moving average of the price by MV_R:

$$CCI_{today} = (TP_{today} - MV_{today})/MV_R.$$

Results

The Commodity Channel Index Divergence (CCI-D) system makes both long and short calls much less frequently than the related Commodity Channel Index Peaks (CCI-P) system. As seen in Table 5.1, the CCI-D system makes long calls only 4.8 percent of the time and short calls only 10.3 percent of the time, as opposed to the 40.6 percent long-call rate and the 50.2 percent short-call rate of the CCI-P system. The CCI-D system has a long hit rate of 61.5 percent (Table 5.1a). The system's short hit rate is slightly lower: 59.7 percent (Table 5.1b).

Table 5.2 gives the long and short return analysis for the CCI-D indicator. These results show that, when judged by the average daily return, the system makes excellent long calls. The average return of 0.077 percent on days when long calls are made is almost 25 percent higher than the average stock return of 0.054 percent when a cash position is favored over a long position. This shows that the long calls of the system are good at predicting periods of above-average market return.

Trading long with the system's recommendations was profitable in all but eight of the test quarters. On average, the quarterly terminal wealth of trading long with this indicator was $10,023 (Table 5.2a). Unfortunately, this terminal wealth was only 96.6 percent of the buy-and-hold terminal wealth. The disadvantage of using this system to determine long positions is that, on average, investors will have a lower terminal wealth than if they bought and held stocks. Investors trading with this system underperformed traders following a buy-and-hold strategy in all but eleven quarters.

Trading short with the CCI-D system also results in terminal wealth lower than the buy-and-hold terminal wealth. More than 75 percent of the time, trading short with this system will lead to losses. This occurs because, on average, the CCI-D system makes short calls on days when stock prices are appreciating by 0.038 percent. These are indeed days of below-average market performance, but they are days of positive stock price movement. Therefore, being in a short position means losses for investors.

On balance, we conclude that the CCI-D system makes some good calls that contain some information for investors, but these calls alone are not good enough to beat a simple buy-and-hold strategy.

Chaikin Level Divergence

Technical analysts have always mentioned volume as an important consideration, but little consequential volume work was done until the 1960s, when Joseph Granville and Larry Williams began to use volume information in new ways. In developing the Chaikin Oscillator, Mark Chaikin has extended the work of Granville and Williams. The Chaikin Oscillator is used in the Chaikin Level Divergence (CHA-D) trading system as well as the Chaikin Level Peaks (CHA-P) trading system described in Chapter 4.

The basis for this oscillator is threefold:

1. Accumulation is said to occur when a stock closes above its midpoint for the day [calculated as (high + low)/2]. The closer the closing price is to the day's high, the more accumulation has occurred. On the other hand, distribution occurs whenever the stock closes below its midpoint for the day. This distribution is greater as the stock closes closer to its low.

2. Volume is viewed as the fuel that powers rallies. Therefore, a healthy advance is powered by rising volume and a strong volume accumulation. If low volume accompanies rising stock prices, not much fuel exists to push

Table 5.1a
Commodity Channel Index Divergence (CCI-D)
Long Hit Analysis (Average of all stocks)

Qtr	Optimal Long	CCI-D Long	Long Hits	Cash Hits	Total Hits	Long Right	Long Wrong	Cash Right	Cash Wrong
85:1	32.1%	2.4%	66.2%	67.9%	67.8%	1.6%	0.8%	66.3%	31.4%
85:2	30.2%	3.9%	64.6%	69.9%	69.7%	2.5%	1.4%	67.1%	29.0%
85:3	26.3%	5.1%	62.2%	73.9%	73.3%	3.2%	1.9%	70.1%	24.8%
85:4	36.6%	3.8%	66.2%	63.3%	63.4%	2.5%	1.3%	60.9%	35.3%
86:1	44.2%	2.5%	67.1%	55.9%	56.2%	1.7%	0.8%	54.5%	43.0%
86:2	39.7%	3.6%	64.2%	60.4%	60.6%	2.3%	1.3%	58.3%	38.1%
86:3	37.0%	6.2%	60.7%	63.0%	62.9%	3.7%	2.4%	59.2%	34.7%
86:4	38.5%	5.5%	65.4%	61.8%	62.0%	3.6%	1.9%	58.4%	36.1%
87:1	44.7%	3.0%	70.7%	55.6%	56.0%	2.1%	0.9%	53.9%	43.1%
87:2	40.0%	5.9%	60.4%	60.0%	60.1%	3.5%	2.3%	56.5%	37.6%
87:3	39.5%	4.8%	60.8%	60.7%	60.7%	2.9%	1.9%	57.8%	37.4%
87:4	37.9%	7.7%	57.6%	62.2%	61.8%	4.4%	3.2%	57.4%	34.9%
88:1	41.3%	2.1%	65.3%	58.8%	58.9%	1.4%	0.7%	57.5%	40.3%
88:2	39.3%	5.1%	63.6%	60.9%	61.0%	3.3%	1.9%	57.8%	37.1%
88:3	35.9%	5.5%	62.2%	64.2%	64.1%	3.4%	2.1%	60.6%	33.8%
88:4	36.3%	5.1%	64.3%	63.7%	63.7%	3.3%	1.8%	60.4%	34.5%
89:1	39.0%	3.6%	64.0%	61.0%	61.1%	2.3%	1.3%	58.8%	37.6%
89:2	40.2%	2.6%	66.5%	59.9%	60.1%	1.7%	0.9%	58.3%	39.1%
89:3	39.9%	4.0%	66.0%	60.1%	60.4%	2.6%	1.4%	57.7%	38.3%
89:4	38.3%	8.4%	59.1%	61.6%	61.4%	5.0%	3.4%	56.4%	35.2%
90:1	36.9%	7.0%	62.9%	63.3%	63.2%	4.4%	2.6%	58.8%	34.2%
90:2	39.2%	4.3%	65.8%	60.8%	61.1%	2.9%	1.5%	58.2%	37.5%
90:3	33.5%	9.4%	55.7%	66.7%	65.7%	5.2%	4.1%	60.5%	30.2%
90:4	40.8%	6.0%	59.7%	59.1%	59.2%	3.6%	2.4%	55.6%	38.4%
91:1	44.1%	2.6%	66.9%	56.0%	56.3%	1.8%	0.9%	54.5%	42.9%
91:2	39.7%	3.8%	60.0%	60.5%	60.5%	2.3%	1.5%	58.2%	38.0%
91:3	40.4%	4.8%	61.1%	59.6%	59.6%	2.9%	1.9%	56.7%	38.5%
91:4	41.2%	6.5%	57.3%	58.7%	58.6%	3.7%	2.8%	54.9%	38.6%
92:1	40.0%	3.3%	54.0%	59.9%	59.7%	1.8%	1.5%	57.9%	38.8%
92:2	38.6%	6.0%	58.9%	61.5%	61.4%	3.5%	2.5%	57.8%	36.2%
92:3	40.3%	5.0%	60.5%	59.7%	59.8%	3.0%	2.0%	56.7%	38.3%
92:4	41.9%	3.4%	64.4%	58.2%	58.4%	2.2%	1.2%	56.2%	40.4%
93:1	42.5%	3.3%	59.6%	57.5%	57.6%	2.0%	1.3%	55.6%	41.1%
93:2	42.1%	5.5%	59.2%	57.9%	58.0%	3.2%	2.2%	54.8%	39.8%
93:3	42.5%	4.3%	60.9%	57.6%	57.7%	2.6%	1.7%	55.1%	40.6%
93:4	41.5%	6.2%	57.3%	58.5%	58.4%	3.6%	2.7%	54.9%	38.9%
94:1	40.4%	5.1%	56.3%	59.5%	59.4%	2.9%	2.2%	56.5%	38.4%
94:2	40.6%	7.4%	56.9%	59.4%	59.2%	4.2%	3.2%	55.0%	37.6%
94:3	41.8%	4.8%	61.9%	58.3%	58.5%	3.0%	1.8%	55.5%	39.6%
94:4	39.5%	8.4%	58.3%	60.7%	60.5%	4.9%	3.5%	55.6%	36.0%
95:1	43.1%	3.0%	60.5%	56.9%	57.0%	1.8%	1.2%	55.2%	41.9%
95:2	43.7%	2.7%	60.9%	56.2%	56.4%	1.6%	1.1%	54.7%	42.6%
95:3	43.9%	3.2%	61.7%	56.0%	56.2%	1.9%	1.2%	54.3%	42.6%
95:4	43.4%	4.8%	58.9%	56.5%	56.7%	2.8%	2.0%	53.9%	41.4%
96:1	45.5%	4.4%	61.1%	54.5%	54.8%	2.7%	1.7%	52.1%	43.5%
96:2	42.1%	3.8%	57.5%	57.9%	57.9%	2.2%	1.6%	55.7%	40.5%
96:3	42.6%	6.1%	57.6%	57.3%	57.3%	3.5%	2.6%	53.9%	40.1%
96:4	44.3%	2.8%	59.3%	55.7%	55.8%	1.7%	1.1%	54.1%	43.1%
AVG	40.0%	4.8%	61.5%	60.2%	60.2%	2.9%	1.9%	57.3%	37.9%

Table 5.1b
Commodity Channel Index Divergence (CCI-D)
Short Hit Analysis (Average of all stocks)

Qtr	Optimal Short	CCI-D Short	Short Hits	Cash Hits	Total Hits	Short Right	Short Wrong	Cash Right	Cash Wrong
85:1	34.3%	15.2%	68.5%	66.0%	66.4%	10.4%	4.8%	56.0%	28.8%
85:2	34.6%	11.2%	68.4%	65.7%	66.0%	7.7%	3.6%	58.3%	30.4%
85:3	38.6%	8.5%	74.2%	61.7%	62.7%	6.3%	2.2%	56.4%	35.1%
85:4	33.1%	12.6%	58.2%	67.0%	65.9%	7.3%	5.3%	58.6%	28.8%
86:1	35.2%	15.7%	55.1%	65.2%	63.6%	8.7%	7.1%	55.0%	29.3%
86:2	39.8%	10.1%	60.9%	60.5%	60.5%	6.2%	4.0%	54.4%	35.5%
86:3	42.7%	8.2%	63.4%	57.7%	58.1%	5.2%	3.0%	53.0%	38.9%
86:4	38.7%	8.1%	60.8%	61.5%	61.4%	4.9%	3.2%	56.5%	35.4%
87:1	36.9%	15.3%	55.7%	63.4%	62.3%	8.5%	6.8%	53.8%	31.0%
87:2	40.0%	7.0%	58.7%	60.1%	60.0%	4.1%	2.9%	55.9%	37.0%
87:3	40.4%	12.7%	62.6%	60.2%	60.5%	7.9%	4.7%	52.5%	34.8%
87:4	45.3%	4.5%	62.3%	54.9%	55.2%	2.8%	1.7%	52.4%	43.1%
88:1	36.7%	17.8%	59.7%	64.0%	63.2%	10.6%	7.2%	52.6%	29.6%
88:2	37.4%	8.2%	60.4%	62.8%	62.6%	5.0%	3.2%	57.7%	34.2%
88:3	38.4%	8.3%	65.2%	61.8%	62.1%	5.4%	2.9%	56.7%	35.0%
88:4	37.0%	8.1%	62.7%	63.2%	63.1%	5.1%	3.0%	58.0%	33.8%
89:1	36.2%	12.2%	60.1%	64.0%	63.6%	7.3%	4.9%	56.2%	31.6%
89:2	35.9%	13.0%	58.8%	64.3%	63.6%	7.6%	5.3%	56.0%	31.0%
89:3	36.4%	10.3%	59.2%	64.0%	63.5%	6.1%	4.2%	57.4%	32.3%
89:4	39.0%	6.7%	59.5%	61.1%	61.0%	4.0%	2.7%	57.0%	36.3%
90:1	40.1%	6.5%	64.1%	60.1%	60.4%	4.2%	2.3%	56.2%	37.3%
90:2	37.8%	11.1%	59.2%	62.6%	62.2%	6.6%	4.5%	55.6%	33.3%
90:3	45.7%	4.0%	63.5%	54.4%	54.7%	2.6%	1.5%	52.2%	43.8%
90:4	37.6%	8.6%	56.5%	62.4%	61.9%	4.9%	3.7%	57.0%	34.4%
91:1	36.7%	14.5%	57.8%	63.9%	63.0%	8.4%	6.1%	54.6%	30.9%
91:2	40.4%	10.0%	61.7%	59.9%	60.1%	6.2%	3.8%	53.9%	36.1%
91:3	39.8%	8.9%	58.1%	60.2%	60.0%	5.2%	3.7%	54.8%	36.2%
91:4	40.5%	8.0%	58.0%	59.6%	59.5%	4.6%	3.4%	54.8%	37.2%
92:1	43.2%	14.2%	58.7%	56.7%	57.0%	8.3%	5.9%	48.7%	37.1%
92:2	42.9%	7.3%	60.6%	57.1%	57.4%	4.4%	2.9%	52.9%	39.8%
92:3	39.5%	9.7%	59.6%	60.5%	60.4%	5.8%	3.9%	54.6%	35.7%
92:4	37.5%	12.3%	57.9%	62.6%	62.0%	7.1%	5.2%	54.9%	32.8%
93:1	39.4%	12.5%	57.2%	60.7%	60.3%	7.2%	5.4%	53.1%	34.4%
93:2	40.9%	9.1%	57.0%	59.2%	59.0%	5.2%	3.9%	53.8%	37.1%
93:3	39.4%	11.8%	57.6%	60.7%	60.3%	6.8%	5.0%	53.5%	34.7%
93:4	41.7%	8.9%	58.4%	58.4%	58.4%	5.2%	3.7%	53.2%	37.9%
94:1	43.7%	10.3%	57.5%	56.3%	56.5%	5.9%	4.4%	50.5%	39.2%
94:2	42.7%	6.5%	59.5%	57.4%	57.6%	3.9%	2.6%	53.7%	39.8%
94:3	39.8%	9.8%	59.5%	60.5%	60.4%	5.8%	4.0%	54.6%	35.7%
94:4	42.8%	5.9%	61.1%	57.3%	57.5%	3.6%	2.3%	53.9%	40.2%
95:1	38.7%	11.8%	56.6%	61.6%	61.0%	6.7%	5.1%	54.4%	33.9%
95:2	38.9%	12.1%	56.1%	61.2%	60.6%	6.8%	5.3%	53.8%	34.1%
95:3	38.9%	12.3%	55.6%	61.2%	60.5%	6.9%	5.5%	53.7%	34.0%
95:4	40.5%	11.6%	55.0%	59.4%	58.9%	6.4%	5.2%	52.5%	35.9%
96:1	38.9%	10.9%	54.5%	61.2%	60.5%	6.0%	5.0%	54.5%	34.5%
96:2	42.4%	10.3%	58.4%	57.7%	57.8%	6.0%	4.3%	51.8%	37.9%
96:3	40.8%	8.1%	57.6%	59.3%	59.2%	4.7%	3.4%	54.5%	37.4%
96:4	39.8%	13.7%	55.6%	60.4%	59.8%	7.6%	6.1%	52.2%	34.2%
AVG	39.4%	10.3%	59.7%	60.9%	60.7%	6.1%	4.2%	54.5%	35.1%

Table 5.2a
Commodity Channel Index Divergence (CCI-D)
Long Return Analysis (Average of all stocks)

Qtr	CCI-D Terminal Wealth	Buy/Hold Terminal Wealth	Relative Terminal Wealth	CCI-D Long Avg Ret	CCI-D Cash Avg Ret	CCI-D Long-Cash Avg Ret	Buy/Hold Avg Ret
85:1	9992	10142	0.985	-0.057%	0.008%	-0.065%	0.006%
85:2	9997	9700	1.031	-0.016%	-0.071%	0.056%	-0.069%
85:3	9965	8889	1.121	-0.112%	-0.210%	0.098%	-0.205%
85:4	10024	10763	0.931	0.100%	0.107%	-0.007%	0.107%
86:1	10059	11428	0.880	0.388%	0.220%	0.168%	0.225%
86:2	10055	10414	0.966	0.242%	0.060%	0.182%	0.066%
86:3	10003	9175	1.090	0.011%	-0.137%	0.147%	-0.128%
86:4	10074	10413	0.967	0.217%	0.061%	0.156%	0.069%
87:1	10119	11929	0.848	0.633%	0.282%	0.351%	0.293%
87:2	10018	10196	0.983	0.051%	0.037%	0.014%	0.038%
87:3	10052	10408	0.966	0.173%	0.063%	0.110%	0.068%
87:4	9957	8087	1.231	-0.085%	-0.294%	0.209%	-0.278%
88:1	10044	10989	0.914	0.329%	0.159%	0.170%	0.163%
88:2	10057	10593	0.949	0.181%	0.095%	0.086%	0.100%
88:3	10013	10050	0.996	0.040%	0.011%	0.029%	0.013%
88:4	10029	10196	0.984	0.093%	0.034%	0.059%	0.037%
89:1	10019	10698	0.937	0.089%	0.113%	-0.025%	0.112%
89:2	10034	10772	0.931	0.206%	0.120%	0.087%	0.122%
89:3	10056	10833	0.928	0.231%	0.127%	0.104%	0.131%
89:4	9973	9904	1.007	-0.050%	-0.007%	-0.042%	-0.011%
90:1	10031	9980	1.005	0.073%	-0.003%	0.075%	0.003%
90:2	10034	10459	0.959	0.126%	0.075%	0.052%	0.077%
90:3	9888	8526	1.160	-0.192%	-0.266%	0.074%	-0.259%
90:4	10059	10889	0.924	0.131%	0.147%	-0.017%	0.146%
91:1	10073	12477	0.807	0.448%	0.311%	0.137%	0.315%
91:2	10029	10244	0.979	0.123%	0.042%	0.081%	0.045%
91:3	10023	10429	0.961	0.079%	0.064%	0.015%	0.065%
91:4	10018	10497	0.954	0.044%	0.084%	-0.040%	0.082%
92:1	9988	10324	0.967	-0.054%	0.051%	-0.105%	0.048%
92:2	10005	9723	1.029	0.010%	-0.052%	0.062%	-0.048%
92:3	10035	10392	0.966	0.107%	0.054%	0.053%	0.057%
92:4	10046	10963	0.916	0.217%	0.142%	0.075%	0.144%
93:1	10034	10527	0.953	0.169%	0.077%	0.093%	0.080%
93:2	10043	10340	0.971	0.129%	0.047%	0.082%	0.052%
93:3	10040	10686	0.940	0.145%	0.099%	0.046%	0.101%
93:4	10004	10255	0.976	0.009%	0.036%	-0.027%	0.034%
94:1	10009	9954	1.006	0.031%	-0.014%	0.045%	-0.011%
94:2	10001	9994	1.001	0.003%	-0.005%	0.009%	-0.005%
94:3	10035	10613	0.946	0.112%	0.088%	0.024%	0.089%
94:4	10007	9836	1.017	0.015%	-0.033%	0.048%	-0.029%
95:1	10027	10706	0.937	0.145%	0.109%	0.036%	0.110%
95:2	10018	10873	0.921	0.105%	0.135%	-0.030%	0.134%
95:3	10029	10853	0.924	0.148%	0.131%	0.018%	0.131%
95:4	10018	10445	0.959	0.059%	0.067%	-0.008%	0.067%
96:1	10055	11027	0.912	0.203%	0.157%	0.046%	0.159%
96:2	10004	10367	0.965	0.012%	0.060%	-0.048%	0.059%
96:3	9998	10298	0.971	-0.005%	0.051%	-0.056%	0.047%
96:4	10016	10817	0.926	0.091%	0.123%	-0.032%	0.122%
AVG	10023	10377	0.966	0.077%	0.054%	0.023%	0.055%

Table 5.2b
Commodity Channel Index Divergence (CCI-D)
Short Return Analysis (Average of all stocks)

Qtr	CCI-D Terminal Wealth	Buy/Hold Terminal Wealth	Relative Terminal Wealth	CCI-D Short Avg Ret	CCI-D Cash Avg Ret	CCI-D Short-Cash Avg Ret	Buy/Hold Avg Ret
85:1	10030	10142	0.989	-0.031%	0.013%	-0.043%	0.006%
85:2	10071	9700	1.038	-0.094%	-0.066%	-0.027%	-0.069%
85:3	10164	8889	1.143	-0.288%	-0.197%	-0.091%	-0.205%
85:4	9860	10763	0.916	0.179%	0.096%	0.082%	0.107%
86:1	9827	11428	0.860	0.187%	0.232%	-0.044%	0.225%
86:2	9991	10414	0.959	0.015%	0.072%	-0.057%	0.066%
86:3	10167	9175	1.108	-0.320%	-0.110%	-0.210%	-0.128%
86:4	9977	10413	0.958	0.042%	0.072%	-0.030%	0.069%
87:1	9791	11929	0.821	0.225%	0.305%	-0.080%	0.293%
87:2	9999	10196	0.981	-0.003%	0.041%	-0.044%	0.038%
87:3	10041	10408	0.965	-0.051%	0.086%	-0.136%	0.068%
87:4	10133	8087	1.253	-0.474%	-0.269%	-0.206%	-0.278%
88:1	10001	10989	0.910	-0.009%	0.200%	-0.209%	0.163%
88:2	9978	10593	0.942	0.041%	0.105%	-0.064%	0.100%
88:3	10020	10050	0.997	-0.040%	0.017%	-0.057%	0.013%
88:4	9980	10196	0.979	0.039%	0.036%	0.003%	0.037%
89:1	9925	10698	0.928	0.099%	0.114%	-0.015%	0.112%
89:2	9921	10772	0.921	0.096%	0.126%	-0.030%	0.122%
89:3	9947	10833	0.918	0.083%	0.137%	-0.054%	0.131%
89:4	9996	9904	1.009	0.006%	-0.012%	0.019%	-0.011%
90:1	10041	9980	1.006	-0.100%	0.010%	-0.110%	0.003%
90:2	9983	10459	0.955	0.023%	0.083%	-0.060%	0.077%
90:3	10057	8526	1.180	-0.223%	-0.260%	0.038%	-0.259%
90:4	9887	10889	0.908	0.209%	0.140%	0.069%	0.146%
91:1	9853	12477	0.790	0.168%	0.340%	-0.172%	0.315%
91:2	10042	10244	0.980	-0.069%	0.058%	-0.127%	0.045%
91:3	9952	10429	0.954	0.086%	0.063%	0.024%	0.065%
91:4	9982	10497	0.951	0.035%	0.086%	-0.050%	0.082%
92:1	9930	10324	0.962	0.076%	0.043%	0.033%	0.048%
92:2	10006	9723	1.029	-0.014%	-0.051%	0.037%	-0.048%
92:3	9989	10392	0.961	0.017%	0.061%	-0.044%	0.057%
92:4	9897	10963	0.903	0.134%	0.146%	-0.012%	0.144%
93:1	9971	10527	0.947	0.042%	0.085%	-0.044%	0.080%
93:2	9979	10340	0.965	0.034%	0.054%	-0.020%	0.052%
93:3	9938	10686	0.930	0.086%	0.103%	-0.017%	0.101%
93:4	9997	10255	0.975	0.004%	0.037%	-0.033%	0.034%
94:1	9988	9954	1.003	0.023%	-0.015%	0.038%	-0.011%
94:2	10026	9994	1.003	-0.065%	-0.001%	-0.064%	-0.005%
94:3	9971	10613	0.940	0.047%	0.094%	-0.047%	0.089%
94:4	10017	9836	1.018	-0.049%	-0.028%	-0.021%	-0.029%
95:1	9952	10706	0.930	0.067%	0.116%	-0.049%	0.110%
95:2	9915	10873	0.912	0.114%	0.137%	-0.023%	0.134%
95:3	9927	10853	0.915	0.099%	0.136%	-0.036%	0.131%
95:4	9939	10445	0.952	0.087%	0.064%	0.023%	0.067%
96:1	9910	11027	0.899	0.135%	0.162%	-0.027%	0.159%
96:2	9976	10367	0.962	0.038%	0.061%	-0.023%	0.059%
96:3	9975	10298	0.969	0.049%	0.047%	0.002%	0.047%
96:4	9926	10817	0.918	0.087%	0.128%	-0.041%	0.122%
AVG	9976	10377	0.961	0.038%	0.057%	-0.019%	0.055%

stock prices higher. In addition, low volume will usually accompany stock price declines. Toward the end of the decline, volume may rise as worried institutional investors liquidate.

3. Analysts can monitor the flow of volume into and out of the market using the Chaikin Oscillator. Chaikin claims that comparing this flow to price movements can help identify both short-term and intermediate-term tops and bottoms.

Construction

Accumulation/distribution (ad) is calculated as follows:

$$ad_i = \{[(Close_i - Low_i) - (High_i - Close_i)] / (High_i - Low_i)\} / V_i.$$

Next, an accumulation/distribution line (AD) for time period, P, is formed:

$$AD = ad_1 + ad_2 + \ldots + ad_P.$$

Then, a ten-period exponential moving average and a three-period exponential moving average of the accumulation/distribution lines are calculated. The Chaikin Oscillator is the difference of these two exponential moving averages:

$$CHA = 3\text{-period moving average} - 10\text{-period moving average.}$$

When price movement and the Chaikin Oscillator movement diverge, a trading signal is generated. When price is reaching higher highs but the Chaikin Oscillator is falling, a short signal is generated. When lower or flat prices are accompanied by a rising Chaikin Oscillator, a long signal is generated.

Results

The hit results for the Chaikin Level Divergence (CHA-D) system in Table 5.3 show that this system makes long and short calls at less than one-third the rate achieved by the related Chaikin Level Peaks (CHA-P) system. The CHA-D system makes long and short calls at rates of 8.8 percent and 11.5 percent, respectively. The long and short call rates for the CHA-P system were 27.6 percent and 41.9 percent, respectively. Table 5.3 also indicates that the CHA-D indicator's hit rates (61.7 percent for long calls and 60.1 percent for short calls) are slightly higher than the hit rates of the CHA-P system.

The analysis in Table 5.4 creates a toss-up as to whether the CHA-D system is better or worse than the CHA-P system. From the average quarterly terminal wealth for long signals, it appears that the CHA-P system performs better. Looking at the average quarterly terminal wealth for short signals, the Chaikin Level Divergence system seems to perform better. However, both systems' short calls are unprofitable, and the long-call terminal wealth for both systems falls short of the buy-and-hold terminal wealth.

Because the CHA-D indicator does not outperform a buy-and-hold strategy for terminal wealth, its main benefit to investors would be an ability to signal periods of above- and below-average market performance. With a daily average stock return of 0.058 percent (Table 5.4a), the system's long calls do predict periods of slightly above-average price appreciation. The average stock return on days when short calls are made is 0.047 percent (Table 5.4b). This return is below the average daily stock return of 0.055 percent, so the short calls do provide a prediction of below-average market return days.

Rate of Change Divergence

The Rate of Change Divergence (ROC-D) system is based on the same concept as the Rate of Change Crossover (ROC-C) indicator, one of the oscillator indicators in Chapter 4. This system considers the relative price movement (expressed as a percentage) of a stock's price. The divergence system then looks for the direction of the stock price movement to diverge from its relative price movement. This divergence will signal market trades.

Construction

The ROC-D indicator expresses the change in stock price over a period of time as a percentage of the stock price at the beginning of the time period. This is calculated as follows:

$$ROC = [(Close_{today} - Close_{p\ periods\ ago})/Close_{p\ periods\ ago}] \cdot 100.$$

If the ROC rises while the stock price is falling, a long signal is triggered. The system makes short calls when a fall in the ROC is accompanied by a rise in the stock's price.

Results

The hit analysis results in Table 5.5 show that the Rate of Change Divergence (ROC-D) system rarely makes calls. Long calls occur only 3.4 percent of the time; short recommendations, with a call rate of 7.6 percent, occur more than twice as often. The hit rates for the long and short calls are 60.2 percent and 59.7 percent, respectively.

Table 5.3a
Chaikin Level Divergence (CHA-D) Long Hit Analysis
(Average of all stocks)

Qtr	Optimal Long	CHA-D Long	Long Hits	Cash Hits	Total Hits	Long Right	Long Wrong	Cash Right	Cash Wrong
85:1	32.1%	8.8%	67.6%	67.6%	67.6%	5.9%	2.9%	61.6%	29.6%
85:2	30.2%	10.1%	66.5%	69.2%	69.0%	6.7%	3.4%	62.2%	27.7%
85:3	26.3%	11.7%	63.4%	73.1%	72.0%	7.4%	4.3%	64.6%	23.7%
85:4	36.6%	8.8%	68.7%	62.9%	63.4%	6.0%	2.8%	57.4%	33.8%
86:1	44.2%	6.2%	66.0%	55.8%	56.5%	4.1%	2.1%	52.4%	41.4%
86:2	39.7%	8.3%	63.3%	60.4%	60.6%	5.3%	3.1%	55.4%	36.3%
86:3	37.0%	10.4%	59.9%	62.9%	62.6%	6.2%	4.2%	56.4%	33.3%
86:4	38.5%	9.5%	64.4%	61.6%	61.8%	6.1%	3.4%	55.7%	34.8%
87:1	44.7%	6.3%	67.2%	55.5%	56.2%	4.2%	2.1%	52.0%	41.7%
87:2	40.0%	10.3%	61.4%	60.0%	60.1%	6.3%	4.0%	53.8%	35.9%
87:3	39.5%	7.7%	61.7%	60.5%	60.6%	4.7%	2.9%	55.9%	36.4%
87:4	37.9%	12.4%	56.8%	62.3%	61.6%	7.0%	5.3%	54.6%	33.0%
88:1	41.3%	6.2%	64.5%	58.8%	59.1%	4.0%	2.2%	55.1%	38.7%
88:2	39.3%	10.8%	63.0%	60.8%	61.0%	6.8%	4.0%	54.2%	35.0%
88:3	35.9%	11.3%	62.5%	64.1%	63.9%	7.1%	4.2%	56.8%	31.9%
88:4	36.3%	9.5%	62.4%	63.4%	63.3%	5.9%	3.6%	57.4%	33.1%
89:1	39.0%	7.7%	63.5%	60.9%	61.1%	4.9%	2.8%	56.2%	36.1%
89:2	40.2%	6.1%	64.1%	59.7%	60.0%	3.9%	2.2%	56.1%	37.8%
89:3	39.9%	7.9%	66.6%	60.0%	60.6%	5.3%	2.6%	55.3%	36.8%
89:4	38.3%	11.3%	60.1%	61.5%	61.4%	6.8%	4.5%	54.6%	34.1%
90:1	36.9%	10.6%	61.9%	63.2%	63.1%	6.6%	4.0%	56.5%	32.9%
90:2	39.2%	7.9%	63.8%	60.5%	60.8%	5.0%	2.9%	55.7%	36.3%
90:3	33.5%	14.4%	54.4%	66.5%	64.8%	7.8%	6.6%	57.0%	28.7%
90:4	40.8%	8.6%	63.5%	59.2%	59.5%	5.5%	3.2%	54.0%	37.3%
91:1	44.1%	5.2%	65.7%	55.8%	56.3%	3.4%	1.8%	52.9%	41.9%
91:2	39.7%	8.6%	61.4%	60.4%	60.5%	5.3%	3.3%	55.2%	36.2%
91:3	40.4%	8.8%	61.8%	59.5%	59.7%	5.4%	3.4%	54.2%	37.0%
91:4	41.2%	9.4%	59.7%	58.8%	58.9%	5.6%	3.8%	53.3%	37.3%
92:1	40.0%	7.3%	55.1%	59.7%	59.4%	4.0%	3.3%	55.4%	37.3%
92:2	38.6%	10.3%	57.5%	61.5%	61.1%	5.9%	4.4%	55.1%	34.6%
92:3	40.3%	8.2%	61.7%	59.8%	60.0%	5.1%	3.1%	54.9%	36.9%
92:4	41.9%	7.0%	62.3%	58.1%	58.4%	4.3%	2.6%	54.1%	39.0%
93:1	42.5%	6.8%	61.7%	57.5%	57.7%	4.2%	2.6%	53.6%	39.7%
93:2	42.1%	8.5%	60.8%	57.9%	58.2%	5.2%	3.3%	53.0%	38.5%
93:3	42.5%	7.2%	60.5%	57.5%	57.7%	4.4%	2.9%	53.4%	39.4%
93:4	41.5%	9.4%	58.8%	58.5%	58.6%	5.5%	3.9%	53.0%	37.6%
94:1	40.4%	8.4%	56.6%	59.6%	59.3%	4.7%	3.6%	54.6%	37.1%
94:2	40.6%	10.7%	57.9%	59.5%	59.3%	6.2%	4.5%	53.1%	36.1%
94:3	41.8%	8.3%	59.2%	58.1%	58.2%	4.9%	3.4%	53.3%	38.4%
94:4	39.5%	12.0%	58.7%	60.8%	60.6%	7.0%	4.9%	53.5%	34.5%
95:1	43.1%	7.5%	63.4%	56.9%	57.4%	4.8%	2.8%	52.6%	39.9%
95:2	43.7%	6.9%	59.9%	56.2%	56.4%	4.1%	2.8%	52.3%	40.8%
95:3	43.9%	7.4%	63.5%	56.1%	56.7%	4.7%	2.7%	52.0%	40.6%
95:4	43.4%	8.1%	60.4%	56.6%	56.9%	4.9%	3.2%	52.1%	39.9%
96:1	45.5%	7.9%	61.9%	54.4%	55.0%	4.9%	3.0%	50.1%	42.0%
96:2	42.1%	8.7%	58.7%	57.9%	57.9%	5.1%	3.6%	52.8%	38.5%
96:3	42.6%	10.0%	58.0%	57.3%	57.3%	5.8%	4.2%	51.5%	38.5%
96:4	44.3%	7.3%	60.9%	55.7%	56.0%	4.5%	2.9%	51.6%	41.1%
AVG	40.0%	8.8%	61.7%	60.1%	60.2%	5.4%	3.4%	54.8%	36.4%

Table 5.3b
Chaikin Level Divergence (CHA-D) Short Hit Analysis
(Average of all stocks)

Qtr	Optimal Short	CHA-D Short	Short Hits	Cash Hits	Total Hits	Short Right	Short Wrong	Cash Right	Cash Wrong
85:1	34.3%	14.7%	67.4%	65.7%	65.9%	9.9%	4.8%	56.0%	29.3%
85:2	34.6%	11.8%	69.0%	65.4%	65.8%	8.1%	3.6%	57.7%	30.5%
85:3	38.6%	10.0%	74.3%	61.4%	62.7%	7.4%	2.6%	55.3%	34.7%
85:4	33.1%	12.8%	61.5%	67.0%	66.3%	7.9%	4.9%	58.4%	28.8%
86:1	35.2%	14.9%	54.2%	64.8%	63.2%	8.0%	6.8%	55.2%	30.0%
86:2	39.8%	12.3%	60.7%	60.5%	60.5%	7.5%	4.8%	53.0%	34.7%
86:3	42.7%	9.7%	63.4%	57.6%	58.2%	6.1%	3.5%	52.1%	38.3%
86:4	38.7%	10.0%	60.6%	61.3%	61.3%	6.1%	3.9%	55.2%	34.8%
87:1	36.9%	15.5%	54.4%	63.1%	61.7%	8.4%	7.1%	53.3%	31.2%
87:2	40.0%	9.5%	60.8%	60.1%	60.1%	5.7%	3.7%	54.4%	36.2%
87:3	40.4%	11.2%	61.1%	59.7%	59.8%	6.9%	4.4%	53.0%	35.8%
87:4	45.3%	6.1%	63.1%	54.8%	55.3%	3.9%	2.3%	51.4%	42.4%
88:1	36.7%	16.4%	59.6%	63.5%	62.9%	9.8%	6.6%	53.1%	30.5%
88:2	37.4%	9.1%	61.3%	62.6%	62.5%	5.6%	3.5%	56.9%	33.9%
88:3	38.4%	9.8%	65.2%	61.8%	62.1%	6.4%	3.4%	55.7%	34.5%
88:4	37.0%	10.8%	62.5%	63.0%	63.0%	6.7%	4.0%	56.3%	33.0%
89:1	36.2%	12.7%	59.6%	63.8%	63.3%	7.6%	5.1%	55.7%	31.5%
89:2	35.9%	14.7%	58.7%	64.1%	63.3%	8.6%	6.1%	54.7%	30.6%
89:3	36.4%	11.9%	60.0%	63.6%	63.2%	7.1%	4.8%	56.0%	32.1%
89:4	39.0%	9.6%	60.0%	61.0%	60.9%	5.8%	3.8%	55.2%	35.2%
90:1	40.1%	8.9%	64.4%	59.9%	60.3%	5.7%	3.2%	54.5%	36.6%
90:2	37.8%	11.9%	61.4%	62.4%	62.3%	7.3%	4.6%	55.0%	33.1%
90:3	45.7%	7.2%	63.5%	54.2%	54.9%	4.6%	2.6%	50.3%	42.5%
90:4	37.6%	10.2%	58.3%	62.4%	62.0%	6.0%	4.3%	56.0%	33.7%
91:1	36.7%	14.6%	58.2%	63.7%	62.9%	8.5%	6.1%	54.4%	31.0%
91:2	40.4%	11.2%	61.1%	59.6%	59.8%	6.9%	4.4%	52.9%	35.9%
91:3	39.8%	10.5%	59.4%	60.2%	60.1%	6.3%	4.3%	53.8%	35.6%
91:4	40.5%	10.2%	57.9%	59.5%	59.3%	5.9%	4.3%	53.4%	36.4%
92:1	43.2%	13.1%	60.4%	56.8%	57.3%	7.9%	5.2%	49.4%	37.5%
92:2	42.9%	9.6%	62.6%	57.1%	57.6%	6.0%	3.6%	51.6%	38.8%
92:3	39.5%	11.4%	60.1%	60.5%	60.5%	6.9%	4.6%	53.6%	35.0%
92:4	37.5%	13.5%	57.8%	62.5%	61.9%	7.8%	5.7%	54.1%	32.4%
93:1	39.4%	13.5%	57.1%	60.8%	60.3%	7.7%	5.8%	52.6%	33.9%
93:2	40.9%	10.2%	58.2%	59.2%	59.1%	5.9%	4.3%	53.2%	36.6%
93:3	39.4%	12.7%	57.2%	60.7%	60.3%	7.3%	5.4%	53.0%	34.3%
93:4	41.7%	10.9%	59.4%	58.5%	58.5%	6.5%	4.4%	52.1%	37.0%
94:1	43.7%	11.6%	59.0%	56.3%	56.6%	6.8%	4.7%	49.8%	38.7%
94:2	42.7%	9.0%	61.1%	57.4%	57.8%	5.5%	3.5%	52.2%	38.7%
94:3	39.8%	10.6%	58.7%	60.3%	60.1%	6.2%	4.4%	53.9%	35.5%
94:4	42.8%	8.2%	61.5%	57.2%	57.6%	5.0%	3.2%	52.6%	39.3%
95:1	38.7%	13.2%	57.2%	61.5%	60.9%	7.6%	5.7%	53.4%	33.4%
95:2	38.9%	13.7%	55.2%	61.1%	60.3%	7.5%	6.1%	52.7%	33.6%
95:3	38.9%	13.4%	56.0%	61.1%	60.4%	7.5%	5.9%	52.9%	33.7%
95:4	40.5%	11.9%	55.0%	59.3%	58.8%	6.5%	5.3%	52.3%	35.8%
96:1	38.9%	12.2%	54.9%	61.3%	60.6%	6.7%	5.5%	53.8%	33.9%
96:2	42.4%	12.4%	58.4%	57.8%	57.9%	7.2%	5.2%	50.6%	37.0%
96:3	40.8%	10.3%	56.4%	59.2%	58.9%	5.8%	4.5%	53.1%	36.6%
96:4	39.8%	13.3%	55.6%	60.3%	59.7%	7.4%	5.9%	52.3%	34.4%
AVG	39.4%	11.5%	60.1%	60.7%	60.6%	6.9%	4.6%	53.7%	34.8%

Table 5.4a
Chaikin Level Divergence (CHA-D) Long Return Analysis
(Average of all stocks)

Qtr	CHA-D Terminal Wealth	Buy/Hold Terminal Wealth	Relative Terminal Wealth	CHA-D Long Avg Ret	CHA-D Cash Avg Ret	CHA-D Long-Cash Avg Ret	Buy/Hold Avg Ret
85:1	9977	10142	0.984	-0.047%	0.011%	-0.058%	0.006%
85:2	9913	9700	1.022	-0.148%	-0.060%	-0.088%	-0.069%
85:3	9835	8889	1.106	-0.234%	-0.201%	-0.033%	-0.205%
85:4	10029	10763	0.932	0.047%	0.113%	-0.066%	0.107%
86:1	10094	11428	0.883	0.248%	0.223%	0.025%	0.225%
86:2	10084	10414	0.968	0.161%	0.058%	0.103%	0.066%
86:3	9940	9175	1.083	-0.090%	-0.132%	0.042%	-0.128%
86:4	10084	10413	0.968	0.141%	0.062%	0.079%	0.069%
87:1	10177	11929	0.853	0.448%	0.283%	0.166%	0.293%
87:2	10048	10196	0.986	0.078%	0.033%	0.045%	0.038%
87:3	10054	10408	0.966	0.113%	0.065%	0.048%	0.068%
87:4	9948	8087	1.230	-0.071%	-0.307%	0.237%	-0.278%
88:1	10078	10989	0.917	0.207%	0.160%	0.047%	0.163%
88:2	10103	10593	0.954	0.159%	0.093%	0.066%	0.100%
88:3	10025	10050	0.997	0.036%	0.010%	0.027%	0.013%
88:4	9993	10196	0.980	-0.008%	0.041%	-0.049%	0.037%
89:1	10043	10698	0.939	0.094%	0.114%	-0.020%	0.112%
89:2	10048	10772	0.933	0.128%	0.122%	0.006%	0.122%
89:3	10088	10833	0.931	0.181%	0.127%	0.055%	0.131%
89:4	9977	9904	1.007	-0.029%	-0.009%	-0.020%	-0.011%
90:1	10029	9980	1.005	0.047%	-0.003%	0.050%	0.003%
90:2	10023	10459	0.958	0.049%	0.079%	-0.030%	0.077%
90:3	9764	8526	1.145	-0.274%	-0.256%	-0.018%	-0.259%
90:4	10097	10889	0.927	0.164%	0.145%	0.020%	0.146%
91:1	10104	12477	0.810	0.327%	0.314%	0.012%	0.315%
91:2	10029	10244	0.979	0.056%	0.044%	0.011%	0.045%
91:3	10047	10429	0.963	0.084%	0.063%	0.021%	0.065%
91:4	10070	10497	0.959	0.118%	0.078%	0.040%	0.082%
92:1	10000	10324	0.969	0.000%	0.052%	-0.051%	0.048%
92:2	9990	9723	1.027	-0.013%	-0.052%	0.039%	-0.048%
92:3	10064	10392	0.968	0.119%	0.051%	0.068%	0.057%
92:4	10063	10963	0.918	0.146%	0.144%	0.002%	0.144%
93:1	10053	10527	0.955	0.126%	0.076%	0.050%	0.080%
93:2	10050	10340	0.972	0.097%	0.047%	0.050%	0.052%
93:3	10055	10686	0.941	0.119%	0.100%	0.020%	0.101%
93:4	10028	10255	0.978	0.044%	0.033%	0.011%	0.034%
94:1	10000	9954	1.005	0.001%	-0.012%	0.013%	-0.011%
94:2	10040	9994	1.005	0.060%	-0.012%	0.073%	-0.005%
94:3	10034	10613	0.945	0.063%	0.092%	-0.029%	0.089%
94:4	10019	9836	1.019	0.026%	-0.037%	0.063%	-0.029%
95:1	10076	10706	0.941	0.165%	0.106%	0.059%	0.110%
95:2	10058	10873	0.925	0.136%	0.134%	0.002%	0.134%
95:3	10090	10853	0.930	0.194%	0.126%	0.068%	0.131%
95:4	10070	10445	0.964	0.136%	0.061%	0.075%	0.067%
96:1	10064	11027	0.913	0.131%	0.161%	-0.030%	0.159%
96:2	10029	10367	0.967	0.053%	0.059%	-0.006%	0.059%
96:3	10000	10298	0.971	-0.003%	0.053%	-0.056%	0.047%
96:4	10064	10817	0.930	0.136%	0.121%	0.015%	0.122%
AVG	10032	10377	0.967	0.058%	0.055%	0.003%	0.055%

Table 5.4b
Chaikin Level Divergence (CHA-D) Short Return Analysis
(Average of all stocks)

Qtr	CHA-D Terminal Wealth	Buy/Hold Terminal Wealth	Relative Terminal Wealth	CHA-D Short Avg Ret	CHA-D Cash Avg Ret	CHA-D Short-Cash Avg Ret	Buy/Hold Avg Ret
85:1	9991	10142	0.985	0.016%	0.005%	0.012%	0.006%
85:2	10035	9700	1.035	-0.045%	-0.073%	0.028%	-0.069%
85:3	10158	8889	1.143	-0.244%	-0.200%	-0.043%	-0.205%
85:4	9903	10763	0.920	0.121%	0.105%	0.016%	0.107%
86:1	9802	11428	0.858	0.225%	0.225%	0.000%	0.225%
86:2	9977	10414	0.958	0.027%	0.072%	-0.045%	0.066%
86:3	10139	9175	1.105	-0.230%	-0.117%	-0.114%	-0.128%
86:4	9964	10413	0.957	0.054%	0.071%	-0.018%	0.069%
87:1	9749	11929	0.817	0.270%	0.297%	-0.027%	0.293%
87:2	10008	10196	0.982	-0.016%	0.043%	-0.059%	0.038%
87:3	9976	10408	0.958	0.035%	0.073%	-0.038%	0.068%
87:4	10131	8087	1.253	-0.332%	-0.274%	-0.057%	-0.278%
88:1	9903	10989	0.901	0.093%	0.176%	-0.083%	0.163%
88:2	9955	10593	0.940	0.078%	0.102%	-0.023%	0.100%
88:3	10024	10050	0.997	-0.038%	0.018%	-0.056%	0.013%
88:4	9986	10196	0.979	0.022%	0.038%	-0.016%	0.037%
89:1	9900	10698	0.925	0.130%	0.110%	0.020%	0.112%
89:2	9899	10772	0.919	0.109%	0.125%	-0.016%	0.122%
89:3	9914	10833	0.915	0.118%	0.133%	-0.015%	0.131%
89:4	9982	9904	1.008	0.029%	-0.015%	0.044%	-0.011%
90:1	10011	9980	1.003	-0.016%	0.005%	-0.021%	0.003%
90:2	9997	10459	0.956	0.003%	0.087%	-0.084%	0.077%
90:3	10076	8526	1.182	-0.171%	-0.266%	0.094%	-0.259%
90:4	9903	10889	0.909	0.151%	0.146%	0.006%	0.146%
91:1	9829	12477	0.788	0.198%	0.335%	-0.137%	0.315%
91:2	9989	10244	0.975	0.011%	0.050%	-0.039%	0.045%
91:3	9976	10429	0.957	0.037%	0.068%	-0.031%	0.065%
91:4	9964	10497	0.949	0.060%	0.084%	-0.024%	0.082%
92:1	9964	10324	0.965	0.048%	0.048%	0.000%	0.048%
92:2	10047	9723	1.033	-0.080%	-0.045%	-0.035%	-0.048%
92:3	9978	10392	0.960	0.030%	0.060%	-0.030%	0.057%
92:4	9888	10963	0.902	0.133%	0.146%	-0.014%	0.144%
93:1	9973	10527	0.947	0.034%	0.087%	-0.053%	0.080%
93:2	9993	10340	0.966	0.012%	0.056%	-0.044%	0.052%
93:3	9956	10686	0.932	0.060%	0.107%	-0.047%	0.101%
93:4	10006	10255	0.976	-0.008%	0.039%	-0.047%	0.034%
94:1	10014	9954	1.006	-0.020%	-0.010%	-0.009%	-0.011%
94:2	10047	9994	1.005	-0.084%	0.003%	-0.087%	-0.005%
94:3	9951	10613	0.938	0.074%	0.091%	-0.017%	0.089%
94:4	10042	9836	1.021	-0.080%	-0.025%	-0.055%	-0.029%
95:1	9944	10706	0.929	0.069%	0.116%	-0.047%	0.110%
95:2	9877	10873	0.908	0.147%	0.132%	0.015%	0.134%
95:3	9912	10853	0.913	0.110%	0.134%	-0.024%	0.131%
95:4	9932	10445	0.951	0.094%	0.063%	0.031%	0.067%
96:1	9927	11027	0.900	0.097%	0.167%	-0.070%	0.159%
96:2	9963	10367	0.961	0.049%	0.060%	-0.011%	0.059%
96:3	9959	10298	0.967	0.064%	0.045%	0.018%	0.047%
96:4	9908	10817	0.916	0.113%	0.124%	-0.011%	0.122%
AVG	9967	10377	0.961	0.047%	0.056%	-0.009%	0.055%

Table 5.5a
Rate of Change Divergence (ROC-D) Long Hit Analysis
(Average of all stocks)

Qtr	Optimal Long	ROC-D Long	Long Hits	Cash Hits	Total Hits	Long Right	Long Wrong	Cash Right	Cash Wrong
85:1	32.1%	2.3%	64.4%	68.0%	67.9%	1.5%	0.8%	66.4%	31.3%
85:2	30.2%	3.5%	65.5%	69.9%	69.8%	2.3%	1.2%	67.5%	29.0%
85:3	26.3%	4.0%	59.5%	73.8%	73.3%	2.4%	1.6%	70.9%	25.1%
85:4	36.6%	2.9%	67.9%	63.5%	63.6%	2.0%	0.9%	61.7%	35.4%
86:1	44.2%	2.2%	62.6%	55.8%	56.0%	1.4%	0.8%	54.6%	43.2%
86:2	39.7%	3.5%	59.0%	60.3%	60.2%	2.1%	1.4%	58.2%	38.3%
86:3	37.0%	3.7%	57.1%	63.0%	62.8%	2.1%	1.6%	60.6%	35.7%
86:4	38.5%	4.3%	62.5%	61.7%	61.7%	2.7%	1.6%	59.0%	36.7%
87:1	44.7%	2.3%	66.2%	55.5%	55.7%	1.5%	0.8%	54.2%	43.5%
87:2	40.0%	4.2%	59.0%	60.0%	59.9%	2.5%	1.7%	57.5%	38.4%
87:3	39.5%	2.6%	60.9%	60.5%	60.5%	1.6%	1.0%	58.9%	38.5%
87:4	37.9%	5.1%	53.7%	62.0%	61.6%	2.7%	2.3%	58.9%	36.0%
88:1	41.3%	2.7%	66.9%	58.8%	59.1%	1.8%	0.9%	57.3%	40.1%
88:2	39.3%	4.5%	60.5%	60.8%	60.8%	2.7%	1.8%	58.0%	37.5%
88:3	35.9%	3.7%	61.4%	64.2%	64.1%	2.3%	1.4%	61.8%	34.5%
88:4	36.3%	2.4%	58.3%	63.6%	63.5%	1.4%	1.0%	62.1%	35.5%
89:1	39.0%	2.6%	63.6%	61.1%	61.1%	1.7%	0.9%	59.5%	37.9%
89:2	40.2%	2.0%	65.6%	59.9%	60.0%	1.3%	0.7%	58.7%	39.3%
89:3	39.9%	3.7%	63.9%	60.0%	60.2%	2.4%	1.3%	57.8%	38.5%
89:4	38.3%	4.2%	58.6%	61.7%	61.5%	2.5%	1.8%	59.1%	36.7%
90:1	36.9%	3.7%	57.7%	63.1%	62.9%	2.1%	1.6%	60.8%	35.5%
90:2	39.2%	2.3%	60.5%	60.8%	60.8%	1.4%	0.9%	59.4%	38.3%
90:3	33.5%	5.4%	52.0%	66.4%	65.6%	2.8%	2.6%	62.8%	31.8%
90:4	40.8%	4.0%	65.4%	59.4%	59.6%	2.6%	1.4%	57.0%	39.0%
91:1	44.1%	2.2%	62.9%	55.9%	56.0%	1.4%	0.8%	54.6%	43.2%
91:2	39.7%	3.7%	60.4%	60.4%	60.4%	2.2%	1.5%	58.2%	38.1%
91:3	40.4%	3.4%	58.8%	59.6%	59.5%	2.0%	1.4%	57.5%	39.1%
91:4	41.2%	4.0%	58.1%	58.8%	58.8%	2.3%	1.7%	56.5%	39.5%
92:1	40.0%	3.0%	53.1%	59.9%	59.7%	1.6%	1.4%	58.1%	38.9%
92:2	38.6%	4.7%	58.3%	61.5%	61.3%	2.7%	2.0%	58.6%	36.7%
92:3	40.3%	3.4%	59.2%	59.7%	59.7%	2.0%	1.4%	57.6%	38.9%
92:4	41.9%	2.5%	61.6%	58.1%	58.2%	1.6%	1.0%	56.6%	40.8%
93:1	42.5%	3.1%	59.6%	57.5%	57.5%	1.8%	1.3%	55.7%	41.2%
93:2	42.1%	3.7%	61.8%	58.1%	58.2%	2.3%	1.4%	55.9%	40.4%
93:3	42.5%	2.7%	60.6%	57.6%	57.6%	1.6%	1.0%	56.0%	41.3%
93:4	41.5%	4.1%	56.9%	58.5%	58.4%	2.4%	1.8%	56.1%	39.8%
94:1	40.4%	3.7%	56.1%	59.6%	59.5%	2.1%	1.6%	57.4%	38.9%
94:2	40.6%	4.5%	55.4%	59.4%	59.2%	2.5%	2.0%	56.7%	38.8%
94:3	41.8%	3.2%	61.8%	58.3%	58.4%	2.0%	1.2%	56.5%	40.4%
94:4	39.5%	3.9%	56.6%	60.5%	60.4%	2.2%	1.7%	58.2%	37.9%
95:1	43.1%	3.0%	60.6%	56.9%	57.0%	1.8%	1.2%	55.1%	41.8%
95:2	43.7%	2.8%	62.2%	56.3%	56.5%	1.7%	1.1%	54.7%	42.5%
95:3	43.9%	3.2%	60.5%	56.0%	56.2%	1.9%	1.2%	54.3%	42.6%
95:4	43.4%	2.9%	59.4%	56.6%	56.7%	1.7%	1.2%	55.0%	42.2%
96:1	45.5%	3.6%	59.4%	54.5%	54.6%	2.1%	1.4%	52.5%	43.9%
96:2	42.1%	3.9%	58.7%	58.0%	58.1%	2.3%	1.6%	55.8%	40.3%
96:3	42.6%	3.8%	56.2%	57.3%	57.2%	2.1%	1.7%	55.1%	41.1%
96:4	44.3%	2.1%	58.0%	55.7%	55.7%	1.2%	0.9%	54.5%	43.4%
AVG	40.0%	3.4%	60.2%	60.2%	60.2%	2.0%	1.4%	58.1%	38.5%

Table 5.5b
Rate of Change Divergence (ROC-D) Short Hit Analysis
(Average of all stocks)

Qtr	Optimal Short	ROC-D Short	Short Hits	Cash Hits	Total Hits	Short Right	Short Wrong	Cash Right	Cash Wrong
85:1	34.3%	11.0%	69.0%	66.1%	66.4%	7.6%	3.4%	58.8%	30.2%
85:2	34.6%	8.3%	69.2%	65.7%	66.0%	5.8%	2.6%	60.2%	31.5%
85:3	38.6%	5.9%	71.0%	61.5%	62.0%	4.2%	1.7%	57.8%	36.2%
85:4	33.1%	9.5%	56.8%	66.9%	65.9%	5.4%	4.1%	60.5%	30.0%
86:1	35.2%	11.1%	54.6%	65.2%	64.0%	6.0%	5.0%	58.0%	31.0%
86:2	39.8%	7.9%	60.0%	60.3%	60.3%	4.7%	3.2%	55.6%	36.5%
86:3	42.7%	6.1%	63.3%	57.7%	58.0%	3.8%	2.2%	54.2%	39.8%
86:4	38.7%	7.1%	61.1%	61.5%	61.5%	4.3%	2.8%	57.1%	35.7%
87:1	36.9%	10.1%	55.8%	63.4%	62.7%	5.6%	4.5%	57.0%	32.9%
87:2	40.0%	5.7%	59.9%	60.1%	60.1%	3.4%	2.3%	56.7%	37.6%
87:3	40.4%	8.0%	61.2%	59.9%	60.0%	4.9%	3.1%	55.1%	36.9%
87:4	45.3%	5.2%	62.9%	54.9%	55.3%	3.3%	1.9%	52.1%	42.8%
88:1	36.7%	13.0%	59.2%	63.8%	63.2%	7.7%	5.3%	55.5%	31.5%
88:2	37.4%	6.5%	62.4%	62.8%	62.8%	4.0%	2.4%	58.8%	34.8%
88:3	38.4%	7.1%	64.4%	61.7%	61.9%	4.6%	2.5%	57.4%	35.6%
88:4	37.0%	6.4%	62.0%	63.1%	63.1%	3.9%	2.4%	59.1%	34.5%
89:1	36.2%	8.8%	58.6%	63.8%	63.4%	5.1%	3.6%	58.2%	33.0%
89:2	35.9%	9.5%	59.2%	64.3%	63.8%	5.6%	3.9%	58.2%	32.3%
89:3	36.4%	7.6%	59.3%	63.6%	63.3%	4.5%	3.1%	58.8%	33.6%
89:4	39.0%	5.1%	59.8%	61.0%	60.9%	3.1%	2.1%	57.8%	37.0%
90:1	40.1%	4.9%	62.4%	59.9%	60.0%	3.0%	1.8%	57.0%	38.1%
90:2	37.8%	8.3%	59.2%	62.4%	62.1%	4.9%	3.4%	57.2%	34.5%
90:3	45.7%	3.5%	64.1%	54.4%	54.7%	2.2%	1.2%	52.5%	44.1%
90:4	37.6%	7.1%	57.1%	62.4%	62.0%	4.1%	3.0%	57.9%	35.0%
91:1	36.7%	10.9%	60.2%	64.0%	63.6%	6.6%	4.3%	57.0%	32.1%
91:2	40.4%	7.1%	62.9%	59.8%	60.1%	4.5%	2.7%	55.6%	37.3%
91:3	39.8%	6.9%	58.1%	60.2%	60.1%	4.0%	2.9%	56.0%	37.0%
91:4	40.5%	6.0%	61.0%	59.7%	59.8%	3.7%	2.3%	56.1%	37.9%
92:1	43.2%	9.2%	58.3%	56.7%	56.8%	5.4%	3.9%	51.4%	39.3%
92:2	42.9%	6.1%	61.3%	57.1%	57.4%	3.7%	2.4%	53.7%	40.3%
92:3	39.5%	6.5%	57.7%	60.4%	60.3%	3.7%	2.7%	56.5%	37.0%
92:4	37.5%	8.7%	56.8%	62.6%	62.1%	4.9%	3.7%	57.2%	34.2%
93:1	39.4%	9.0%	57.1%	60.6%	60.3%	5.2%	3.9%	55.2%	35.8%
93:2	40.9%	7.8%	58.1%	59.3%	59.2%	4.5%	3.3%	54.7%	37.5%
93:3	39.4%	8.6%	57.5%	60.6%	60.3%	4.9%	3.7%	55.4%	36.0%
93:4	41.7%	6.7%	58.3%	58.3%	58.3%	3.9%	2.8%	54.4%	38.9%
94:1	43.7%	7.9%	56.8%	56.3%	56.3%	4.5%	3.4%	51.9%	40.3%
94:2	42.7%	6.1%	62.2%	57.6%	57.9%	3.8%	2.3%	54.1%	39.8%
94:3	39.8%	6.9%	59.8%	60.3%	60.3%	4.2%	2.8%	56.1%	36.9%
94:4	42.8%	4.5%	62.0%	57.2%	57.5%	2.8%	1.7%	54.7%	40.8%
95:1	38.7%	8.9%	57.1%	61.4%	61.0%	5.1%	3.8%	56.0%	35.2%
95:2	38.9%	8.7%	54.7%	61.1%	60.5%	4.7%	3.9%	55.8%	35.5%
95:3	38.9%	8.2%	53.5%	61.0%	60.4%	4.4%	3.8%	56.0%	35.8%
95:4	40.5%	7.8%	55.0%	59.5%	59.2%	4.3%	3.5%	54.9%	37.4%
96:1	38.9%	8.0%	54.6%	61.3%	60.8%	4.4%	3.7%	56.4%	35.6%
96:2	42.4%	7.1%	59.0%	57.7%	57.8%	4.2%	2.9%	53.6%	39.3%
96:3	40.8%	6.0%	57.7%	59.3%	59.2%	3.4%	2.5%	55.8%	38.3%
96:4	39.8%	8.4%	54.3%	60.3%	59.8%	4.5%	3.8%	55.2%	36.4%
AVG	39.4%	7.6%	59.7%	60.8%	60.7%	4.5%	3.1%	56.1%	36.2%

The return results in Table 5.6 are not very promising. The ROC-D system does not make good long calls: the average return for long calls is exactly equal to the average market return. The system seems to be randomly choosing average days to make its long calls. Because of the infrequency of these calls, profitability of trading with this system is extremely low. Investors beginning a quarter with $10,000 and trading long with this system will make an average of only $12 for the quarter because they are so seldom in the market.

On balance, the short return results are no better. The short calls do seem to distinguish between below-average and above-average market periods. The average stock return is only 0.040 percent (Table 5.6b) on days when this system makes short calls. Unfortunately, these days of below-average stock market performance are still characterized by stock price appreciation. Therefore, trading short with this system is, on average, unprofitable. In fact, investors trading short with this system during our test quarters had losses in all but 16 quarters.

Thus, the ROC-D system does not appear to be extremely useful for trading decisions. The infrequency of call rates, coupled with the relatively low information content of the calls, results in marginal, if any, profits.

Relative Strength Index Divergence

Welles Wilder introduced his Relative Strength Index in June 1978, in an article in *Commodities* (now known as *Futures*) magazine. The Relative Strength Index Divergence (RSI-D) indicator described here, along with the Relative Strength Index Peaks indicator (page 129) and the Relative Strength Index Crossover indicator (page 138) described in Chapter 4, use this index. As with other trading systems described in this chapter, trades are triggered whenever price movement and the movement in the value of an indicator diverge. For example, whenever stock price is rising to new highs but the Relative Strength Index is falling, analysts using this system expect that price will correct and move in the direction of the Relative Strength Index.

Construction

A number of periods *(n)* is chosen for which to calculate the RSI. Then:

$$\text{Ups} = (\text{Sum of gains over } n \text{ periods})/n,$$

$$\text{Downs} = (\text{Sum of losses over } n \text{ periods})/n,$$

$$\text{RS} = \text{Ups}/\text{Downs},$$

$$\text{RSI} = 100 - [100/(1 + \text{RS})].$$

The RSI can take on a value between 0 and 100.

Results

In Table 5.7, the long hit analysis and the short hit analysis for the Relative Strength Index Divergence (RSI-D) system show that this system makes calls much less frequently than the Relative Strength Index Peaks and Relative Strength Index Crossover systems do. This indicator has a long call rate of only 6.5 percent and a short call rate of only 7.3 percent.

When choosing between long and cash positions, the RSI-D system makes correct long calls 61.5 percent of the time and correct cash calls 60.2 percent of the time (Table 5.7a). When the choice is between a short position or a cash position, the system has a 59.2 percent hit rate for short calls and a 60.7 percent hit rate for cash calls (Table 5.7b).

The return results presented in Table 5.8 show that this system does a good job of distinguishing days in which the market is particularly strong with its long calls. The daily stock return for long calls averages 0.063 percent (Table 5.8a). Because this is above the average daily stock return of 0.055 percent for the entire test period, the RSI-D system does suggest a long position on days of above-average returns. However, an investor does not want to be in the market only on above-average return days; for maximum profits, the investor wants to be in the market on *all* positive return days. Taking a long position when the RSI-D system recommends is not profitable enough to beat a buy-and-hold strategy. In fact, an investor following this strategy would end up with an average wealth that is only 96.6 percent of the wealth a buy-and-hold investor would have.

Unfortunately, the short calls for this system also predict days of above-average stock market performance. A desirable short call indicator signals days of below-average, negative returns. This indicator advises short positions on the very days investors would want to be in a long position. By not taking a long position, investors are missing out on potential profits; by taking a short position, they are setting themselves up for losses.

Trading short with this system is profitable only 25 percent of the time. Even during the thirteen profitable quarters, however, the system's results are not strong. Table 5.8b shows that the highest quarterly terminal wealth an investor trading short with this system would have is $10,155, occurring during the fourth-quarter market crash period of 1987. This $155 profit on a $10,000 initial investment is only about half of the $377 expected quarterly profit of buying and holding securities.

Given the infrequency of its trading calls and the unprofitability of its short calls, the main benefit of the RSI-D system is the informational content of its calls; whether long or short, they tend to predict periods of above-average stock appreciation. We now turn our attention to the Money Flow Relative Strength Index Divergence system, which is similar to this indicator but also considers volume in making its calls.

Table 5.6a
Rate of Change Divergence (ROC-D) Long Return Analysis
(Average of all stocks)

Qtr	ROC-D Terminal Wealth	Buy/Hold Terminal Wealth	Relative Terminal Wealth	ROC-D Long Avg Ret	ROC-D Cash Avg Ret	ROC-D Long-Cash Avg Ret	Buy/Hold Avg Ret
85:1	10017	10142	0.988	0.119%	0.004%	0.115%	0.006%
85:2	10002	9700	1.031	0.008%	-0.072%	0.080%	-0.069%
85:3	9960	8889	1.121	-0.162%	-0.207%	0.045%	-0.205%
85:4	10045	10763	0.933	0.239%	0.103%	0.136%	0.107%
86:1	10033	11428	0.878	0.247%	0.224%	0.023%	0.225%
86:2	10024	10414	0.963	0.107%	0.065%	0.042%	0.066%
86:3	9983	9175	1.088	-0.072%	-0.130%	0.058%	-0.128%
86:4	10041	10413	0.964	0.153%	0.066%	0.087%	0.069%
87:1	10070	11929	0.844	0.477%	0.289%	0.189%	0.293%
87:2	10005	10196	0.981	0.018%	0.039%	-0.021%	0.038%
87:3	10028	10408	0.963	0.169%	0.066%	0.103%	0.068%
87:4	9937	8087	1.229	-0.212%	-0.282%	0.070%	-0.278%
88:1	10071	10989	0.916	0.424%	0.156%	0.269%	0.163%
88:2	10025	10593	0.946	0.090%	0.100%	-0.010%	0.100%
88:3	10016	10050	0.997	0.072%	0.010%	0.062%	0.013%
88:4	9989	10196	0.980	-0.072%	0.039%	-0.112%	0.037%
89:1	10020	10698	0.937	0.125%	0.112%	0.013%	0.112%
89:2	10020	10772	0.930	0.162%	0.121%	0.041%	0.122%
89:3	10023	10833	0.925	0.102%	0.132%	-0.030%	0.131%
89:4	9981	9904	1.008	-0.069%	-0.008%	-0.061%	-0.011%
90:1	9993	9980	1.001	-0.032%	0.004%	-0.036%	0.003%
90:2	10011	10459	0.957	0.076%	0.077%	0.000%	0.077%
90:3	9877	8526	1.158	-0.375%	-0.252%	-0.122%	-0.259%
90:4	10077	10889	0.925	0.301%	0.140%	0.161%	0.146%
91:1	10043	12477	0.805	0.313%	0.315%	-0.002%	0.315%
91:2	10013	10244	0.978	0.055%	0.045%	0.010%	0.045%
91:3	10017	10429	0.961	0.084%	0.064%	0.020%	0.065%
91:4	10032	10497	0.956	0.125%	0.080%	0.045%	0.082%
92:1	9989	10324	0.967	-0.047%	0.051%	-0.098%	0.048%
92:2	10003	9723	1.029	0.009%	-0.051%	0.061%	-0.048%
92:3	10012	10392	0.963	0.055%	0.057%	-0.002%	0.057%
92:4	10015	10963	0.914	0.089%	0.146%	-0.057%	0.144%
93:1	10015	10527	0.951	0.078%	0.080%	-0.002%	0.080%
93:2	10035	10340	0.970	0.151%	0.048%	0.103%	0.052%
93:3	10023	10686	0.938	0.136%	0.100%	0.036%	0.101%
93:4	10005	10255	0.976	0.018%	0.035%	-0.016%	0.034%
94:1	9994	9954	1.004	-0.025%	-0.011%	-0.015%	-0.011%
94:2	9980	9994	0.999	-0.075%	-0.001%	-0.073%	-0.005%
94:3	10032	10613	0.945	0.159%	0.087%	0.073%	0.089%
94:4	9985	9836	1.015	-0.061%	-0.028%	-0.032%	-0.029%
95:1	10016	10706	0.936	0.082%	0.111%	-0.029%	0.110%
95:2	10025	10873	0.922	0.143%	0.134%	0.009%	0.134%
95:3	10026	10853	0.924	0.134%	0.131%	0.003%	0.131%
95:4	10020	10445	0.959	0.112%	0.065%	0.046%	0.067%
96:1	10028	11027	0.909	0.124%	0.160%	-0.036%	0.159%
96:2	10033	10367	0.968	0.133%	0.056%	0.078%	0.059%
96:3	9981	10298	0.969	-0.083%	0.052%	-0.135%	0.047%
96:4	10001	10817	0.925	0.011%	0.125%	-0.114%	0.122%
AVG	10012	10377	0.965	0.055%	0.055%	-0.001%	0.055%

Table 5.6b
Rate of Change Divergence (ROC-D) Short Return Analysis
(Average of all stocks)

Qtr	ROC-D Terminal Wealth	Buy/Hold Terminal Wealth	Relative Terminal Wealth	ROC-D Short Avg Ret	ROC-D Cash Avg Ret	ROC-D Short-Cash Avg Ret	Buy/Hold Avg Ret
85:1	10038	10142	0.990	-0.050%	0.013%	-0.063%	0.006%
85:2	10049	9700	1.036	-0.085%	-0.068%	-0.017%	-0.069%
85:3	10074	8889	1.133	-0.191%	-0.206%	0.015%	-0.205%
85:4	9871	10763	0.917	0.219%	0.095%	0.125%	0.107%
86:1	9879	11428	0.864	0.185%	0.230%	-0.045%	0.225%
86:2	9997	10414	0.960	0.009%	0.071%	-0.062%	0.066%
86:3	10120	9175	1.103	-0.311%	-0.116%	-0.195%	-0.128%
86:4	9990	10413	0.959	0.020%	0.073%	-0.053%	0.069%
87:1	9862	11929	0.827	0.226%	0.300%	-0.074%	0.293%
87:2	9997	10196	0.980	0.010%	0.040%	-0.030%	0.038%
87:3	10022	10408	0.963	-0.041%	0.078%	-0.119%	0.068%
87:4	10127	8087	1.252	-0.392%	-0.272%	-0.121%	-0.278%
88:1	9983	10989	0.908	0.017%	0.185%	-0.168%	0.163%
88:2	10001	10593	0.944	-0.007%	0.107%	-0.114%	0.100%
88:3	10008	10050	0.996	-0.020%	0.015%	-0.035%	0.013%
88:4	9996	10196	0.980	0.009%	0.038%	-0.030%	0.037%
89:1	9928	10698	0.928	0.135%	0.110%	0.025%	0.112%
89:2	9941	10772	0.923	0.098%	0.125%	-0.027%	0.122%
89:3	9931	10833	0.917	0.150%	0.129%	0.021%	0.131%
89:4	9980	9904	1.008	0.063%	-0.015%	0.078%	-0.011%
90:1	10010	9980	1.003	-0.032%	0.005%	-0.036%	0.003%
90:2	9965	10459	0.953	0.067%	0.078%	-0.011%	0.077%
90:3	10050	8526	1.179	-0.222%	-0.260%	0.038%	-0.259%
90:4	9905	10889	0.910	0.209%	0.141%	0.068%	0.146%
91:1	9962	12477	0.798	0.063%	0.346%	-0.283%	0.315%
91:2	10014	10244	0.978	-0.035%	0.052%	-0.087%	0.045%
91:3	9934	10429	0.953	0.154%	0.058%	0.096%	0.065%
91:4	10037	10497	0.956	-0.102%	0.093%	-0.195%	0.082%
92:1	9957	10324	0.964	0.076%	0.045%	0.031%	0.048%
92:2	10030	9723	1.032	-0.078%	-0.046%	-0.032%	-0.048%
92:3	9967	10392	0.959	0.081%	0.055%	0.026%	0.057%
92:4	9919	10963	0.905	0.152%	0.144%	0.008%	0.144%
93:1	9964	10527	0.947	0.064%	0.081%	-0.018%	0.080%
93:2	9999	10340	0.967	0.002%	0.056%	-0.054%	0.052%
93:3	9959	10686	0.932	0.078%	0.103%	-0.025%	0.101%
93:4	10010	10255	0.976	-0.020%	0.038%	-0.058%	0.034%
94:1	9981	9954	1.003	0.040%	-0.016%	0.055%	-0.011%
94:2	10054	9994	1.006	-0.141%	0.004%	-0.145%	-0.005%
94:3	9983	10613	0.941	0.040%	0.093%	-0.053%	0.089%
94:4	10022	9836	1.019	-0.081%	-0.027%	-0.054%	-0.029%
95:1	9951	10706	0.930	0.090%	0.112%	-0.022%	0.110%
95:2	9912	10873	0.912	0.165%	0.131%	0.034%	0.134%
95:3	9918	10853	0.914	0.164%	0.128%	0.036%	0.131%
95:4	9948	10445	0.952	0.109%	0.063%	0.046%	0.067%
96:1	9955	11027	0.903	0.090%	0.165%	-0.075%	0.159%
96:2	9982	10367	0.963	0.043%	0.060%	-0.017%	0.059%
96:3	9990	10298	0.970	0.027%	0.049%	-0.021%	0.047%
96:4	9939	10817	0.919	0.117%	0.123%	-0.005%	0.122%
AVG	9981	10377	0.962	0.040%	0.056%	-0.016%	0.055%

Table 5.7a
Relative Strength Divergence (RSI-D) Long Hit Analysis
(Average of all stocks)

Qtr	Optimal Long	RSI-D Long	Long Hits	Cash Hits	Total Hits	Long Right	Long Wrong	Cash Right	Cash Wrong
85:1	32.1%	4.2%	66.5%	67.9%	67.9%	2.8%	1.4%	65.1%	30.7%
85:2	30.2%	6.7%	64.5%	69.8%	69.5%	4.3%	2.4%	65.1%	28.1%
85:3	26.3%	7.0%	61.4%	73.7%	72.8%	4.3%	2.7%	68.5%	24.5%
85:4	36.6%	6.3%	67.8%	63.5%	63.7%	4.3%	2.0%	59.4%	34.2%
86:1	44.2%	4.0%	66.2%	55.8%	56.2%	2.7%	1.4%	53.6%	42.4%
86:2	39.7%	5.4%	60.8%	60.3%	60.3%	3.3%	2.1%	57.0%	37.6%
86:3	37.0%	7.7%	59.8%	62.9%	62.7%	4.6%	3.1%	58.1%	34.2%
86:4	38.5%	6.3%	65.0%	61.6%	61.8%	4.1%	2.2%	57.7%	36.0%
87:1	44.7%	3.6%	67.0%	55.4%	55.8%	2.4%	1.2%	53.4%	43.0%
87:2	40.0%	8.1%	60.1%	60.0%	60.0%	4.9%	3.2%	55.1%	36.7%
87:3	39.5%	5.0%	60.7%	60.5%	60.5%	3.1%	2.0%	57.5%	37.5%
87:4	37.9%	10.0%	56.7%	62.1%	61.6%	5.7%	4.3%	55.9%	34.1%
88:1	41.3%	3.0%	65.2%	58.7%	58.9%	1.9%	1.0%	57.0%	40.0%
88:2	39.3%	7.8%	61.9%	60.7%	60.8%	4.8%	3.0%	56.0%	36.2%
88:3	35.9%	7.4%	62.4%	64.2%	64.0%	4.6%	2.8%	59.4%	33.2%
88:4	36.3%	6.4%	64.0%	63.7%	63.7%	4.1%	2.3%	59.6%	34.0%
89:1	39.0%	4.3%	64.7%	60.9%	61.1%	2.8%	1.5%	58.3%	37.4%
89:2	40.2%	4.7%	64.8%	59.8%	60.0%	3.1%	1.7%	57.0%	38.3%
89:3	39.9%	5.1%	65.1%	60.0%	60.3%	3.3%	1.8%	57.0%	37.9%
89:4	38.3%	9.9%	58.3%	61.5%	61.2%	5.8%	4.1%	55.4%	34.6%
90:1	36.9%	7.9%	62.2%	63.3%	63.3%	4.9%	3.0%	58.3%	33.8%
90:2	39.2%	5.1%	66.0%	60.7%	61.0%	3.4%	1.7%	57.6%	37.3%
90:3	33.5%	10.9%	54.4%	66.4%	65.1%	5.9%	5.0%	59.2%	29.9%
90:4	40.8%	9.7%	61.6%	59.1%	59.3%	5.9%	3.7%	53.4%	37.0%
91:1	44.1%	3.1%	64.2%	55.8%	56.1%	2.0%	1.1%	54.0%	42.8%
91:2	39.7%	5.5%	60.3%	60.5%	60.5%	3.3%	2.2%	57.2%	37.3%
91:3	40.4%	7.1%	59.5%	59.5%	59.5%	4.2%	2.9%	55.3%	37.6%
91:4	41.2%	8.5%	60.0%	58.9%	59.0%	5.1%	3.4%	53.9%	37.6%
92:1	40.0%	5.5%	57.1%	59.9%	59.8%	3.1%	2.3%	56.7%	37.9%
92:2	38.6%	8.7%	57.5%	61.5%	61.2%	5.0%	3.7%	56.1%	35.1%
92:3	40.3%	6.4%	60.5%	59.7%	59.7%	3.9%	2.5%	55.8%	37.7%
92:4	41.9%	5.3%	62.7%	58.1%	58.3%	3.3%	2.0%	55.0%	39.7%
93:1	42.5%	4.8%	61.8%	57.5%	57.7%	3.0%	1.8%	54.7%	40.5%
93:2	42.1%	7.4%	58.0%	57.8%	57.9%	4.3%	3.1%	53.6%	39.0%
93:3	42.5%	5.8%	62.1%	57.6%	57.9%	3.6%	2.2%	54.3%	39.9%
93:4	41.5%	7.8%	57.3%	58.5%	58.4%	4.5%	3.3%	53.9%	38.3%
94:1	40.4%	6.7%	57.3%	59.6%	59.4%	3.8%	2.9%	55.6%	37.7%
94:2	40.6%	9.7%	58.8%	59.5%	59.4%	5.7%	4.0%	53.7%	36.6%
94:3	41.8%	6.3%	60.3%	58.3%	58.4%	3.8%	2.5%	54.6%	39.1%
94:4	39.5%	9.2%	58.8%	60.8%	60.6%	5.4%	3.8%	55.2%	35.6%
95:1	43.1%	5.0%	62.0%	56.8%	57.1%	3.1%	1.9%	54.0%	41.0%
95:2	43.7%	4.4%	61.7%	56.2%	56.5%	2.7%	1.7%	53.7%	41.8%
95:3	43.9%	4.9%	61.3%	56.1%	56.3%	3.0%	1.9%	53.3%	41.8%
95:4	43.4%	6.6%	60.1%	56.5%	56.7%	4.0%	2.6%	52.8%	40.6%
96:1	45.5%	5.9%	62.4%	54.6%	55.0%	3.7%	2.2%	51.4%	42.7%
96:2	42.1%	6.7%	60.0%	58.1%	58.2%	4.0%	2.7%	54.2%	39.1%
96:3	42.6%	8.8%	58.4%	57.3%	57.4%	5.2%	3.7%	52.2%	39.0%
96:4	44.3%	5.0%	61.6%	55.7%	56.0%	3.1%	1.9%	52.9%	42.0%
AVG	40.0%	6.5%	61.5%	60.2%	60.2%	4.0%	2.5%	56.2%	37.3%

Table 5.7b
Relative Strength Divergence (RSI-D) Short Hit Analysis
(Average of all stocks)

Qtr	Optimal Short	RSI-D Short	Short Hits	Cash Hits	Total Hits	Short Right	Short Wrong	Cash Right	Cash Wrong
85:1	34.3%	9.7%	68.5%	66.1%	66.3%	6.6%	3.1%	59.7%	30.6%
85:2	34.6%	6.8%	67.8%	65.2%	65.4%	4.6%	2.2%	60.8%	32.4%
85:3	38.6%	6.9%	72.2%	61.5%	62.2%	4.9%	1.9%	57.3%	35.9%
85:4	33.1%	6.1%	56.9%	66.8%	66.2%	3.5%	2.6%	62.7%	31.1%
86:1	35.2%	9.8%	54.2%	64.8%	63.8%	5.3%	4.5%	58.4%	31.7%
86:2	39.8%	9.9%	59.2%	60.3%	60.1%	5.8%	4.0%	54.3%	35.8%
86:3	42.7%	6.2%	63.2%	57.5%	57.9%	3.9%	2.3%	54.0%	39.8%
86:4	38.7%	6.5%	60.2%	61.3%	61.3%	3.9%	2.6%	57.3%	36.2%
87:1	36.9%	9.1%	56.0%	63.3%	62.6%	5.1%	4.0%	57.6%	33.4%
87:2	40.0%	5.8%	60.3%	60.1%	60.1%	3.5%	2.3%	56.6%	37.6%
87:3	40.4%	8.1%	59.1%	59.5%	59.5%	4.8%	3.3%	54.7%	37.2%
87:4	45.3%	5.0%	61.4%	54.8%	55.1%	3.1%	1.9%	52.1%	42.9%
88:1	36.7%	9.1%	57.8%	63.4%	62.9%	5.3%	3.8%	57.6%	33.3%
88:2	37.4%	6.6%	60.7%	62.5%	62.4%	4.0%	2.6%	58.4%	35.0%
88:3	38.4%	6.3%	65.5%	61.8%	62.1%	4.1%	2.2%	58.0%	35.8%
88:4	37.0%	6.1%	63.9%	63.2%	63.2%	3.9%	2.2%	59.3%	34.6%
89:1	36.2%	8.1%	58.5%	63.8%	63.3%	4.7%	3.4%	58.6%	33.3%
89:2	35.9%	7.6%	58.3%	64.2%	63.7%	4.4%	3.2%	59.3%	33.1%
89:3	36.4%	8.7%	58.7%	63.6%	63.2%	5.1%	3.6%	58.0%	33.2%
89:4	39.0%	5.1%	58.4%	60.9%	60.8%	3.0%	2.1%	57.8%	37.0%
90:1	40.1%	5.2%	64.3%	60.1%	60.3%	3.4%	1.9%	57.0%	37.8%
90:2	37.8%	7.2%	59.8%	62.3%	62.1%	4.3%	2.9%	57.8%	35.0%
90:3	45.7%	4.4%	63.3%	54.3%	54.7%	2.8%	1.6%	51.9%	43.7%
90:4	37.6%	5.1%	55.1%	62.3%	61.9%	2.8%	2.3%	59.1%	35.8%
91:1	36.7%	10.3%	56.9%	63.5%	62.9%	5.8%	4.4%	57.0%	32.7%
91:2	40.4%	8.3%	58.3%	59.4%	59.3%	4.9%	3.5%	54.4%	37.2%
91:3	39.8%	6.9%	56.4%	60.1%	59.9%	3.9%	3.0%	55.9%	37.1%
91:4	40.5%	6.5%	58.3%	59.5%	59.4%	3.8%	2.7%	55.6%	37.9%
92:1	43.2%	8.8%	61.0%	56.8%	57.2%	5.4%	3.4%	51.8%	39.4%
92:2	42.9%	6.6%	61.3%	57.2%	57.5%	4.0%	2.5%	53.5%	40.0%
92:3	39.5%	6.8%	59.1%	60.5%	60.4%	4.0%	2.8%	56.4%	36.8%
92:4	37.5%	8.1%	57.4%	62.5%	62.1%	4.6%	3.4%	57.4%	34.5%
93:1	39.4%	9.0%	57.5%	60.7%	60.4%	5.2%	3.8%	55.3%	35.8%
93:2	40.9%	7.5%	56.9%	59.1%	58.9%	4.2%	3.2%	54.7%	37.9%
93:3	39.4%	7.4%	54.9%	60.5%	60.1%	4.1%	3.4%	56.0%	36.5%
93:4	41.7%	6.9%	59.6%	58.4%	58.5%	4.1%	2.8%	54.4%	38.7%
94:1	43.7%	7.8%	58.1%	56.3%	56.4%	4.5%	3.2%	51.9%	40.3%
94:2	42.7%	4.6%	58.7%	57.3%	57.4%	2.7%	1.9%	54.7%	40.7%
94:3	39.8%	6.7%	58.5%	60.2%	60.1%	3.9%	2.8%	56.2%	37.1%
94:4	42.8%	5.4%	58.6%	57.1%	57.2%	3.2%	2.2%	54.0%	40.6%
95:1	38.7%	7.7%	54.7%	61.3%	60.8%	4.2%	3.5%	56.6%	35.8%
95:2	38.9%	9.0%	54.8%	61.1%	60.6%	4.9%	4.1%	55.7%	35.4%
95:3	38.9%	8.2%	54.4%	61.1%	60.5%	4.5%	3.7%	56.0%	35.7%
95:4	40.5%	6.9%	57.8%	59.7%	59.5%	4.0%	2.9%	55.5%	37.6%
96:1	38.9%	8.4%	54.0%	61.2%	60.6%	4.5%	3.9%	56.0%	35.6%
96:2	42.4%	7.6%	58.7%	57.7%	57.8%	4.5%	3.2%	53.3%	39.1%
96:3	40.8%	5.0%	56.1%	59.3%	59.2%	2.8%	2.2%	56.4%	38.6%
96:4	39.8%	8.4%	55.5%	60.3%	59.9%	4.7%	3.7%	55.2%	36.4%
AVG	39.4%	7.3%	59.2%	60.7%	60.6%	4.3%	3.0%	56.3%	36.5%

Table 5.8a
Relative Strength Divergence (RSI-D) Long Return Analysis
(Average of all stocks)

Qtr	RSI-D Terminal Wealth	Buy/Hold Terminal Wealth	Relative Terminal Wealth	RSI-D Long Avg Ret	RSI-D Cash Avg Ret	RSI-D Long-Cash Avg Ret	Buy/Hold Avg Ret
85:1	10015	10142	0.987	0.051%	0.004%	0.047%	0.006%
85:2	9964	9700	1.027	-0.092%	-0.068%	-0.025%	-0.069%
85:3	9925	8889	1.117	-0.174%	-0.207%	0.034%	-0.205%
85:4	10056	10763	0.934	0.138%	0.105%	0.034%	0.107%
86:1	10079	11428	0.882	0.314%	0.221%	0.094%	0.225%
86:2	10050	10414	0.965	0.144%	0.062%	0.082%	0.066%
86:3	9991	9175	1.089	-0.012%	-0.137%	0.125%	-0.128%
86:4	10048	10413	0.965	0.120%	0.066%	0.054%	0.069%
87:1	10099	11929	0.847	0.441%	0.288%	0.153%	0.293%
87:2	10013	10196	0.982	0.029%	0.039%	-0.009%	0.038%
87:3	10041	10408	0.965	0.128%	0.065%	0.063%	0.068%
87:4	9928	8087	1.228	-0.113%	-0.296%	0.183%	-0.278%
88:1	10063	10989	0.916	0.342%	0.157%	0.185%	0.163%
88:2	10054	10593	0.949	0.115%	0.098%	0.017%	0.100%
88:3	10039	10050	0.999	0.088%	0.007%	0.082%	0.013%
88:4	10031	10196	0.984	0.079%	0.034%	0.045%	0.037%
89:1	10044	10698	0.939	0.166%	0.110%	0.056%	0.112%
89:2	10039	10772	0.932	0.132%	0.122%	0.010%	0.122%
89:3	10048	10833	0.927	0.151%	0.130%	0.021%	0.131%
89:4	9948	9904	1.005	-0.085%	-0.003%	-0.082%	-0.011%
90:1	10051	9980	1.007	0.105%	-0.006%	0.111%	0.003%
90:2	10041	10459	0.960	0.129%	0.074%	0.055%	0.077%
90:3	9817	8526	1.151	-0.276%	-0.257%	-0.019%	-0.259%
90:4	10069	10889	0.925	0.116%	0.149%	-0.033%	0.146%
91:1	10070	12477	0.807	0.368%	0.313%	0.055%	0.315%
91:2	10046	10244	0.981	0.132%	0.040%	0.092%	0.045%
91:3	10034	10429	0.962	0.071%	0.064%	0.006%	0.065%
91:4	10083	10497	0.961	0.153%	0.075%	0.077%	0.082%
92:1	9999	10324	0.968	0.000%	0.051%	-0.051%	0.048%
92:2	9989	9723	1.027	-0.022%	-0.051%	0.028%	-0.048%
92:3	10035	10392	0.966	0.085%	0.055%	0.030%	0.057%
92:4	10030	10963	0.915	0.092%	0.147%	-0.056%	0.144%
93:1	10022	10527	0.952	0.072%	0.080%	-0.008%	0.080%
93:2	10010	10340	0.968	0.023%	0.054%	-0.031%	0.052%
93:3	10058	10686	0.941	0.151%	0.098%	0.053%	0.101%
93:4	10011	10255	0.976	0.019%	0.035%	-0.016%	0.034%
94:1	10014	9954	1.006	0.031%	-0.014%	0.045%	-0.011%
94:2	10025	9994	1.003	0.042%	-0.010%	0.052%	-0.005%
94:3	10016	10613	0.944	0.036%	0.093%	-0.056%	0.089%
94:4	10012	9836	1.018	0.022%	-0.034%	0.056%	-0.029%
95:1	10045	10706	0.938	0.145%	0.108%	0.037%	0.110%
95:2	10029	10873	0.922	0.104%	0.135%	-0.031%	0.134%
95:3	10038	10853	0.925	0.124%	0.131%	-0.007%	0.131%
95:4	10033	10445	0.961	0.083%	0.066%	0.017%	0.067%
96:1	10087	11027	0.915	0.235%	0.154%	0.081%	0.159%
96:2	10046	10367	0.969	0.114%	0.055%	0.059%	0.059%
96:3	10006	10298	0.972	0.012%	0.051%	-0.038%	0.047%
96:4	10043	10817	0.928	0.133%	0.122%	0.011%	0.122%
AVG	10026	10377	0.966	0.063%	0.055%	0.008%	0.055%

Table 5.8b
Relative Strength Divergence (RSI-D) Short Return Analysis
(Average of all stocks)

Qtr	RSI-D Terminal Wealth	Buy/Hold Terminal Wealth	Relative Terminal Wealth	RSI-D Short Avg Ret	RSI-D Cash Avg Ret	RSI-D Short-Cash Avg Ret	Buy/Hold Avg Ret
85:1	10038	10142	0.990	-0.060%	0.013%	-0.073%	0.006%
85:2	10005	9700	1.032	-0.009%	-0.074%	0.065%	-0.069%
85:3	10095	8889	1.136	-0.209%	-0.205%	-0.004%	-0.205%
85:4	9920	10763	0.922	0.210%	0.100%	0.110%	0.107%
86:1	9848	11428	0.862	0.260%	0.221%	0.040%	0.225%
86:2	9949	10414	0.955	0.081%	0.065%	0.016%	0.066%
86:3	10106	9175	1.101	-0.270%	-0.118%	-0.152%	-0.128%
86:4	9955	10413	0.956	0.106%	0.067%	0.039%	0.069%
87:1	9886	11929	0.829	0.211%	0.301%	-0.090%	0.293%
87:2	9994	10196	0.980	0.011%	0.040%	-0.028%	0.038%
87:3	9954	10408	0.956	0.091%	0.066%	0.024%	0.068%
87:4	10155	8087	1.256	-0.492%	-0.267%	-0.225%	-0.278%
88:1	9915	10989	0.902	0.147%	0.164%	-0.018%	0.163%
88:2	9949	10593	0.939	0.121%	0.098%	0.023%	0.100%
88:3	10024	10050	0.997	-0.061%	0.018%	-0.079%	0.013%
88:4	10002	10196	0.981	-0.005%	0.039%	-0.044%	0.037%
89:1	9928	10698	0.928	0.145%	0.109%	0.036%	0.112%
89:2	9951	10772	0.924	0.102%	0.124%	-0.022%	0.122%
89:3	9923	10833	0.916	0.141%	0.130%	0.011%	0.131%
89:4	9972	9904	1.007	0.088%	-0.016%	0.105%	-0.011%
90:1	10033	9980	1.005	-0.103%	0.009%	-0.111%	0.003%
90:2	9985	10459	0.955	0.032%	0.080%	-0.048%	0.077%
90:3	10041	8526	1.178	-0.149%	-0.264%	0.115%	-0.259%
90:4	9921	10889	0.911	0.253%	0.141%	0.112%	0.146%
91:1	9874	12477	0.791	0.207%	0.327%	-0.120%	0.315%
91:2	9932	10244	0.970	0.128%	0.038%	0.091%	0.045%
91:3	9951	10429	0.954	0.116%	0.061%	0.055%	0.065%
91:4	9964	10497	0.949	0.090%	0.081%	0.009%	0.082%
92:1	9995	10324	0.968	0.008%	0.052%	-0.044%	0.048%
92:2	10035	9723	1.032	-0.085%	-0.046%	-0.040%	-0.048%
92:3	9974	10392	0.960	0.061%	0.056%	0.004%	0.057%
92:4	9933	10963	0.906	0.136%	0.145%	-0.009%	0.144%
93:1	9964	10527	0.946	0.065%	0.081%	-0.016%	0.080%
93:2	9979	10340	0.965	0.044%	0.052%	-0.009%	0.052%
93:3	9930	10686	0.929	0.153%	0.097%	0.056%	0.101%
93:4	10002	10255	0.975	-0.006%	0.037%	-0.043%	0.034%
94:1	9980	9954	1.003	0.041%	-0.016%	0.057%	-0.011%
94:2	9986	9994	0.999	0.049%	-0.007%	0.056%	-0.005%
94:3	9978	10613	0.940	0.052%	0.092%	-0.040%	0.089%
94:4	10009	9836	1.018	-0.027%	-0.029%	0.002%	-0.029%
95:1	9938	10706	0.928	0.131%	0.108%	0.022%	0.110%
95:2	9920	10873	0.912	0.145%	0.133%	0.012%	0.134%
95:3	9909	10853	0.913	0.178%	0.127%	0.051%	0.131%
95:4	10007	10445	0.958	-0.017%	0.073%	-0.090%	0.067%
96:1	9926	11027	0.900	0.143%	0.160%	-0.018%	0.159%
96:2	9997	10367	0.964	0.007%	0.063%	-0.056%	0.059%
96:3	9994	10298	0.970	0.018%	0.049%	-0.031%	0.047%
96:4	9960	10817	0.921	0.078%	0.126%	-0.049%	0.122%
AVG	9973	10377	0.961	0.061%	0.055%	0.007%	0.055%

Money Flow Relative Strength Index Divergence

The Money Flow Relative Strength Index is similar to Wilder's Relative Strength Index measure. Both indexes consider "up" days and "down" days in their calculations to determine the flow of money into and out of an equity. The difference is that the Money Flow Relative Strength Index incorporates volume, and Wilder's index considers only price.

In the Money Flow Relative Strength Index Divergence (MFR-D) model, the index is used to indicate price reversals. Whenever the direction of the index and the direction of stock price movement diverge, a signal is triggered.

Construction

Calculate the money flow (MF) by finding the typical, or average, stock price for the day (AVG) and multiplying this value by the day's volume (V):

$$AVG = (H_i + L_i + C_i)/3,$$

$$MF_i = AVG \cdot V_i.$$

If today's average price is higher than yesterday's average price, there is positive money flow (PMF). Negative money flow (NMF) occurs when today's average price is lower than yesterday's average price.

The positive money flow for a specified time period, P, is the sum of the daily positive money flows occurring during that time period. Likewise, negative money flow for the time period is the sum of the daily negative money flows:

$$PMFSUM = PMF_1 + PMF_2 + \ldots + PMF_P,$$

$$NMFSUM = NMF_1 + NMF_2 + \ldots + NMF_P.$$

To calculate the money flow ratio (MFR), divide the positive money flow by the negative money flow:

$$MFR = PMFSUM/NMFSUM$$

Finally, calculate the Money Flow Relative Strength Index using the following formula:

$$Money\ Flow\ RSI = 100 - [100/(1 + MFR)].$$

Long signals occur whenever the Money Flow RSI is rising and price is falling. Short signals occur when a fall in the Money Flow RSI is accompanied by rising price.

Results

Table 5.9 shows that the Money Flow Relative Strength Index Divergence (MFR-D) system, which incorporates both price and volume, makes many more long and short calls than the Relative Strength Index Divergence (RSI-D) system, which only looks at price. The long call rate for the MFR-D system is 39.5 percent, and these long calls are correct 61.1 percent of the time (Table 5.9a). The system makes short calls 33.4 percent of the time and these calls also have a hit rate of 59.7 percent (Table 5.9b).

From the long return analysis in Table 5.10, we see that this increased frequency of calls is not without cost. The MFR-D system is still choosing relatively high return days for a long position, but the average strength of these days has declined. The average return on days when long calls are made is 0.060 percent for this system, compared to 0.063 percent for the previous system (Table 5.8a). The RSI-D system chooses a few "great" days; the MFR-D system chooses many "good" days. The average daily return for long days is lower with the MFR-D system, but the average quarterly terminal wealth is higher because of increased market participation. In fact, the MFR-D system's average quarterly terminal wealth of $10,168 (Table 5.10a), which is 98.0 percent of the buy-and-hold average quarterly terminal wealth, is one of the highest terminal wealth figures for any of the indicators we tested.

Unfortunately, we cannot say the same about the short return analysis. Because the average stock return on days when short calls are made is a positive 0.061 percent (Table 5.10b), trading short with this system leads to losses and declining wealth. Coincidentally, this average return for short call days is exactly the same as with the RSI-D system.

Stochastic Divergence

This trading system uses the same Stochastic Oscillator employed in the Stochastic Peaks system (page 150) and the Stochastic +80/+20 Crossover system (page 160). However, instead of looking for a particular level of the Stochastic Oscillator, this model looks for divergences in the direction of the Stochastic Oscillator and the direction of stock price movement.

The Stochastic Oscillator compares a stock's closing price to the range of prices over a given lookback period. A basic premise is that the stock price will typically extend to the end of a price range before reversing direction.

Table 5.9a
Money Flow RSI Divergence (MFR-D) Long Hit Analysis
(Average of all stocks)

Qtr	Optimal Long	MFR-D Long	Long Hits	Cash Hits	Total Hits	Long Right	Long Wrong	Cash Right	Cash Wrong
85:1	32.1%	35.9%	66.8%	68.0%	67.6%	24.0%	11.9%	43.5%	20.5%
85:2	30.2%	36.5%	65.0%	68.9%	67.5%	23.7%	12.8%	43.8%	19.7%
85:3	26.3%	34.0%	62.1%	73.0%	69.3%	21.1%	12.9%	48.2%	17.8%
85:4	36.6%	44.2%	67.3%	63.2%	65.0%	29.8%	14.4%	35.3%	20.5%
86:1	44.2%	27.3%	64.3%	55.0%	57.6%	17.5%	9.8%	40.0%	32.7%
86:2	39.7%	27.8%	61.6%	59.8%	60.3%	17.1%	10.7%	43.2%	29.0%
86:3	37.0%	38.3%	58.0%	62.4%	60.7%	22.2%	16.1%	38.5%	23.2%
86:4	38.5%	42.9%	62.0%	60.9%	61.4%	26.6%	16.3%	34.8%	22.4%
87:1	44.7%	34.3%	63.7%	54.8%	57.8%	21.9%	12.4%	36.0%	29.7%
87:2	40.0%	37.8%	61.5%	59.8%	60.4%	23.3%	14.6%	37.2%	25.0%
87:3	39.5%	40.3%	60.2%	60.2%	60.2%	24.3%	16.1%	35.9%	23.8%
87:4	37.9%	40.3%	56.0%	61.9%	59.5%	22.6%	17.8%	36.9%	22.7%
88:1	41.3%	49.8%	63.3%	58.9%	61.1%	31.5%	18.3%	29.6%	20.6%
88:2	39.3%	40.4%	62.7%	61.0%	61.7%	25.3%	15.1%	36.4%	23.2%
88:3	35.9%	45.6%	61.7%	64.5%	63.2%	28.2%	17.5%	35.1%	19.3%
88:4	36.3%	46.0%	63.4%	63.5%	63.5%	29.2%	16.8%	34.3%	19.7%
89:1	39.0%	41.5%	64.1%	60.8%	62.2%	26.6%	14.9%	35.6%	22.9%
89:2	40.2%	36.7%	64.7%	59.6%	61.5%	23.7%	12.9%	37.7%	25.6%
89:3	39.9%	32.1%	63.6%	59.2%	60.6%	20.4%	11.7%	40.2%	27.7%
89:4	38.3%	39.1%	61.7%	61.2%	61.4%	24.1%	14.9%	37.3%	23.7%
90:1	36.9%	44.7%	60.7%	63.2%	62.1%	27.1%	17.6%	34.9%	20.3%
90:2	39.2%	44.3%	62.0%	60.2%	61.0%	27.5%	16.9%	33.5%	22.2%
90:3	33.5%	38.5%	55.1%	65.8%	61.7%	21.2%	17.3%	40.4%	21.1%
90:4	40.8%	51.3%	62.9%	58.9%	60.9%	32.2%	19.0%	28.7%	20.0%
91:1	44.1%	38.8%	64.4%	55.3%	58.8%	25.0%	13.8%	33.8%	27.3%
91:2	39.7%	27.8%	60.8%	59.8%	60.1%	16.9%	10.9%	43.2%	29.0%
91:3	40.4%	40.4%	60.0%	58.8%	59.3%	24.2%	16.2%	35.1%	24.5%
91:4	41.2%	39.4%	59.5%	58.0%	58.6%	23.5%	16.0%	35.1%	25.4%
92:1	40.0%	37.3%	57.4%	59.6%	58.8%	21.4%	15.9%	37.4%	25.4%
92:2	38.6%	42.0%	57.5%	60.5%	59.3%	24.2%	17.9%	35.1%	22.9%
92:3	40.3%	42.5%	60.6%	59.5%	60.0%	25.8%	16.7%	34.2%	23.3%
92:4	41.9%	39.6%	63.2%	57.9%	60.0%	25.0%	14.6%	35.0%	25.4%
93:1	42.5%	34.6%	61.3%	57.1%	58.6%	21.2%	13.4%	37.4%	28.1%
93:2	42.1%	36.4%	59.2%	57.8%	58.3%	21.6%	14.9%	36.7%	26.8%
93:3	42.5%	40.1%	60.6%	57.3%	58.6%	24.3%	15.8%	34.3%	25.6%
93:4	41.5%	39.6%	58.9%	58.6%	58.7%	23.3%	16.3%	35.4%	25.0%
94:1	40.4%	40.8%	56.5%	59.0%	58.0%	23.1%	17.7%	34.9%	24.3%
94:2	40.6%	46.5%	57.3%	58.8%	58.1%	26.6%	19.9%	31.5%	22.0%
94:3	41.8%	44.6%	60.1%	57.8%	58.8%	26.8%	17.8%	32.0%	23.4%
94:4	39.5%	44.1%	57.2%	59.9%	58.7%	25.2%	18.9%	33.5%	22.4%
95:1	43.1%	44.0%	61.7%	56.4%	58.7%	27.2%	16.9%	31.6%	24.4%
95:2	43.7%	36.9%	61.2%	55.5%	57.6%	22.6%	14.3%	35.0%	28.1%
95:3	43.9%	32.1%	61.8%	55.6%	57.6%	19.9%	12.3%	37.7%	30.1%
95:4	43.4%	34.8%	60.4%	56.2%	57.7%	21.0%	13.8%	36.6%	28.6%
96:1	45.5%	38.4%	61.7%	53.9%	56.9%	23.7%	14.7%	33.2%	28.4%
96:2	42.1%	41.9%	58.2%	57.6%	57.9%	24.4%	17.5%	33.4%	24.6%
96:3	42.6%	43.9%	60.4%	57.3%	58.6%	26.5%	17.4%	32.1%	24.0%
96:4	44.3%	39.0%	60.8%	55.0%	57.3%	23.7%	15.3%	33.6%	27.5%
AVG	40.0%	39.5%	61.1%	59.8%	60.3%	24.1%	15.4%	36.1%	24.4%

Table 5.9b
Money Flow RSI Divergence (MFR-D) Short Hit Analysis
(Average of all stocks)

Qtr	Optimal Short	MFR-D Short	Short Hits	Cash Hits	Total Hits	Short Right	Short Wrong	Cash Right	Cash Wrong
85:1	34.3%	30.3%	67.8%	65.5%	66.2%	20.6%	9.8%	45.6%	24.1%
85:2	34.6%	33.6%	69.3%	64.7%	66.2%	23.3%	10.3%	42.9%	23.5%
85:3	38.6%	36.6%	72.4%	61.1%	65.3%	26.5%	10.1%	38.8%	24.6%
85:4	33.1%	26.4%	63.6%	66.6%	65.8%	16.8%	9.6%	49.0%	24.6%
86:1	35.2%	35.0%	55.1%	64.0%	60.9%	19.3%	15.7%	41.6%	23.4%
86:2	39.8%	38.6%	60.0%	59.8%	59.9%	23.2%	15.4%	36.7%	24.7%
86:3	42.7%	31.4%	63.8%	57.2%	59.2%	20.1%	11.4%	39.2%	29.4%
86:4	38.7%	32.6%	61.8%	61.3%	61.5%	20.2%	12.4%	41.3%	26.1%
87:1	36.9%	33.1%	54.5%	62.6%	59.9%	18.0%	15.0%	41.9%	25.0%
87:2	40.0%	36.1%	59.7%	60.5%	60.2%	21.6%	14.5%	38.6%	25.3%
87:3	40.4%	33.5%	60.1%	59.4%	59.7%	20.1%	13.4%	39.5%	27.0%
87:4	45.3%	27.7%	62.2%	55.4%	57.3%	17.2%	10.5%	40.1%	32.2%
88:1	36.7%	30.7%	58.4%	63.1%	61.6%	17.9%	12.8%	43.7%	25.6%
88:2	37.4%	40.5%	60.8%	62.7%	61.9%	24.6%	15.9%	37.3%	22.2%
88:3	38.4%	37.7%	64.4%	61.5%	62.6%	24.3%	13.4%	38.3%	24.0%
88:4	37.0%	37.4%	63.4%	62.8%	63.0%	23.7%	13.7%	39.3%	23.3%
89:1	36.2%	35.9%	60.5%	63.3%	62.3%	21.7%	14.2%	40.6%	23.5%
89:2	35.9%	33.9%	59.8%	63.7%	62.3%	20.2%	13.6%	42.1%	24.0%
89:3	36.4%	36.4%	59.4%	62.9%	61.6%	21.6%	14.8%	40.0%	23.6%
89:4	39.0%	31.2%	61.1%	60.8%	60.9%	19.0%	12.1%	41.9%	27.0%
90:1	40.1%	29.2%	62.9%	59.7%	60.6%	18.4%	10.8%	42.3%	28.5%
90:2	37.8%	28.8%	59.8%	61.7%	61.2%	17.2%	11.6%	43.9%	27.3%
90:3	45.7%	30.9%	65.6%	54.5%	57.9%	20.3%	10.6%	37.7%	31.4%
90:4	37.6%	19.8%	58.5%	62.4%	61.6%	11.6%	8.2%	50.0%	30.2%
91:1	36.7%	28.7%	55.0%	63.2%	60.8%	15.8%	12.9%	45.0%	26.2%
91:2	40.4%	43.4%	59.6%	59.7%	59.7%	25.9%	17.5%	33.8%	22.8%
91:3	39.8%	33.8%	59.0%	60.0%	59.7%	19.9%	13.8%	39.7%	26.5%
91:4	40.5%	31.4%	57.7%	59.1%	58.7%	18.1%	13.3%	40.6%	28.0%
92:1	43.2%	30.0%	60.8%	56.9%	58.0%	18.2%	11.8%	39.8%	30.2%
92:2	42.9%	35.1%	60.4%	57.0%	58.2%	21.2%	13.9%	37.0%	27.9%
92:3	39.5%	32.1%	59.5%	60.3%	60.1%	19.1%	13.0%	40.9%	26.9%
92:4	37.5%	33.1%	58.2%	62.3%	60.9%	19.2%	13.8%	41.7%	25.2%
93:1	39.4%	34.9%	56.8%	60.2%	59.0%	19.8%	15.1%	39.2%	25.9%
93:2	40.9%	36.9%	58.2%	58.7%	58.5%	21.5%	15.4%	37.0%	26.1%
93:3	39.4%	34.9%	57.3%	60.3%	59.2%	20.0%	14.9%	39.2%	25.9%
93:4	41.7%	35.7%	58.2%	58.2%	58.2%	20.7%	14.9%	37.4%	26.9%
94:1	43.7%	35.2%	58.8%	56.0%	57.0%	20.7%	14.5%	36.3%	28.5%
94:2	42.7%	27.6%	58.2%	57.1%	57.4%	16.0%	11.5%	41.4%	31.0%
94:3	39.8%	32.0%	57.9%	59.9%	59.3%	18.6%	13.5%	40.7%	27.3%
94:4	42.8%	33.1%	59.8%	57.1%	58.0%	19.8%	13.3%	38.2%	28.7%
95:1	38.7%	31.4%	56.3%	61.1%	59.6%	17.7%	13.7%	41.9%	26.7%
95:2	38.9%	35.3%	55.8%	60.8%	59.0%	19.7%	15.6%	39.3%	25.4%
95:3	38.9%	37.4%	56.2%	61.0%	59.2%	21.0%	16.4%	38.1%	24.4%
95:4	40.5%	35.4%	56.2%	59.5%	58.3%	19.9%	15.5%	38.5%	26.2%
96:1	38.9%	34.3%	53.4%	60.7%	58.2%	18.3%	16.0%	39.9%	25.8%
96:2	42.4%	36.6%	57.5%	57.7%	57.7%	21.0%	15.5%	36.6%	26.8%
96:3	40.8%	33.6%	57.0%	59.7%	58.8%	19.2%	14.4%	39.6%	26.8%
96:4	39.8%	33.3%	54.9%	59.9%	58.3%	18.3%	15.0%	40.0%	26.7%
AVG	39.4%	33.4%	59.7%	60.5%	60.2%	19.9%	13.4%	40.3%	26.3%

Table 5.10a
Money Flow RSI Divergence (MFR-D) Long Return Analysis
(Average of all stocks)

Qtr	MFR-D Terminal Wealth	Buy/Hold Terminal Wealth	Relative Terminal Wealth	MFR-D Long Avg Ret	MFR-D Cash Avg Ret	MFR-D Long-Cash Avg Ret	Buy/Hold Avg Ret
85:1	10087	10142	00001	0.019%	-0.001%	0.020%	0.006%
85:2	9792	9700	00001	-0.115%	-0.043%	-0.072%	-0.069%
85:3	9586	8889	00001	-0.219%	-0.197%	-0.022%	-0.205%
85:4	10326	10763	00001	0.103%	0.110%	-0.006%	0.107%
86:1	10331	11428	00001	0.194%	0.236%	-0.043%	0.225%
86:2	10102	10414	00001	0.060%	0.069%	-0.008%	0.066%
86:3	9680	9175	00001	-0.131%	-0.125%	-0.006%	-0.128%
86:4	10172	10413	00001	0.067%	0.071%	-0.004%	0.069%
87:1	10650	11929	00001	0.291%	0.294%	-0.003%	0.293%
87:2	10106	10196	00001	0.050%	0.030%	0.020%	0.038%
87:3	10164	10408	00001	0.067%	0.069%	-0.002%	0.068%
87:4	9540	8087	00001	-0.176%	-0.347%	0.171%	-0.278%
88:1	10548	10989	00001	0.181%	0.145%	0.036%	0.163%
88:2	10268	10593	00001	0.112%	0.091%	0.021%	0.100%
88:3	10072	10050	00001	0.030%	-0.001%	0.031%	0.013%
88:4	10100	10196	00001	0.041%	0.033%	0.008%	0.037%
89:1	10325	10698	00001	0.126%	0.103%	0.023%	0.112%
89:2	10328	10772	00001	0.140%	0.112%	0.029%	0.122%
89:3	10250	10833	00001	0.122%	0.135%	-0.013%	0.131%
89:4	9984	9904	00001	-0.004%	-0.016%	0.012%	-0.011%
90:1	10045	9980	00001	0.018%	-0.010%	0.028%	0.003%
90:2	10180	10459	00001	0.068%	0.084%	-0.016%	0.077%
90:3	9379	8526	00001	-0.272%	-0.251%	-0.021%	-0.259%
90:4	10553	10889	00001	0.173%	0.118%	0.055%	0.146%
91:1	11329	12477	00001	0.349%	0.294%	0.055%	0.315%
91:2	10092	10244	00001	0.060%	0.040%	0.020%	0.045%
91:3	10169	10429	00001	0.062%	0.067%	-0.005%	0.065%
91:4	10142	10497	00001	0.057%	0.098%	-0.040%	0.082%
92:1	10159	10324	00001	0.066%	0.037%	0.029%	0.048%
92:2	9831	9723	00001	-0.070%	-0.033%	-0.038%	-0.048%
92:3	10182	10392	00001	0.061%	0.053%	0.008%	0.057%
92:4	10445	10963	00001	0.164%	0.132%	0.032%	0.144%
93:1	10231	10527	00001	0.100%	0.069%	0.030%	0.080%
93:2	10172	10340	00001	0.071%	0.041%	0.031%	0.052%
93:3	10303	10686	00001	0.113%	0.093%	0.021%	0.101%
93:4	10117	10255	00001	0.042%	0.029%	0.013%	0.034%
94:1	9987	9954	00001	-0.010%	-0.012%	0.003%	-0.011%
94:2	9953	9994	00001	-0.020%	0.008%	-0.028%	-0.005%
94:3	10251	10613	00001	0.085%	0.093%	-0.009%	0.089%
94:4	9875	9836	00001	-0.047%	-0.015%	-0.032%	-0.029%
95:1	10304	10706	00001	0.109%	0.111%	-0.002%	0.110%
95:2	10323	10873	00001	0.135%	0.133%	0.002%	0.134%
95:3	10262	10853	00001	0.125%	0.134%	-0.009%	0.131%
95:4	10199	10445	00001	0.087%	0.056%	0.032%	0.067%
96:1	10436	11027	00001	0.175%	0.149%	0.026%	0.159%
96:2	10193	10367	00001	0.072%	0.049%	0.024%	0.059%
96:3	10208	10298	00001	0.070%	0.030%	0.040%	0.047%
96:4	10331	10817	00001	0.129%	0.118%	0.011%	0.122%
AVG	10168	10377	00001	0.060%	0.052%	0.008%	0.055%

Table 5.10b
Money Flow RSI Divergence (MFR-D) Short Return Analysis
(Average of all stocks)

Qtr	MFR-D Terminal Wealth	Buy/Hold Terminal Wealth	Relative Terminal Wealth	MFR-D Short Avg Ret	MFR-D Cash Avg Ret	MFR-D Short-Cash Avg Ret	Buy/Hold Avg Ret
85:1	10008	10142	0.987	0.007%	0.006%	0.001%	0.006%
85:2	10116	9700	1.043	-0.037%	-0.086%	0.049%	-0.069%
85:3	10466	8889	1.177	-0.181%	-0.219%	0.038%	-0.205%
85:4	9822	10763	0.913	0.115%	0.104%	0.012%	0.107%
86:1	9480	11428	0.830	0.255%	0.208%	0.047%	0.225%
86:2	9790	10414	0.940	0.091%	0.051%	0.040%	0.066%
86:3	10269	9175	1.119	-0.139%	-0.122%	-0.017%	-0.128%
86:4	9887	10413	0.949	0.054%	0.076%	-0.022%	0.069%
87:1	9358	11929	0.784	0.332%	0.274%	0.058%	0.293%
87:2	9925	10196	0.973	0.034%	0.040%	-0.006%	0.038%
87:3	9844	10408	0.946	0.075%	0.065%	0.009%	0.068%
87:4	10662	8087	1.318	-0.406%	-0.229%	-0.177%	-0.278%
88:1	9684	10989	0.881	0.165%	0.162%	0.003%	0.163%
88:2	9758	10593	0.921	0.095%	0.103%	-0.008%	0.100%
88:3	9972	10050	0.992	0.010%	0.014%	-0.004%	0.013%
88:4	9919	10196	0.973	0.033%	0.039%	-0.006%	0.037%
89:1	9746	10698	0.911	0.117%	0.110%	0.007%	0.112%
89:2	9726	10772	0.903	0.129%	0.119%	0.010%	0.122%
89:3	9675	10833	0.893	0.146%	0.122%	0.023%	0.131%
89:4	10019	9904	1.012	-0.012%	-0.011%	-0.001%	-0.011%
90:1	9999	9980	1.002	-0.002%	0.005%	-0.007%	0.003%
90:2	9797	10459	0.937	0.114%	0.062%	0.052%	0.077%
90:3	10480	8526	1.229	-0.240%	-0.267%	0.027%	-0.259%
90:4	9837	10889	0.903	0.133%	0.150%	-0.017%	0.146%
91:1	9459	12477	0.758	0.325%	0.311%	0.015%	0.315%
91:2	9852	10244	0.962	0.049%	0.042%	0.007%	0.045%
91:3	9867	10429	0.946	0.066%	0.064%	0.002%	0.065%
91:4	9752	10497	0.929	0.123%	0.063%	0.060%	0.082%
92:1	9992	10324	0.968	0.009%	0.064%	-0.055%	0.048%
92:2	10044	9723	1.033	-0.020%	-0.064%	0.044%	-0.048%
92:3	9882	10392	0.951	0.059%	0.055%	0.003%	0.057%
92:4	9724	10963	0.887	0.135%	0.149%	-0.014%	0.144%
93:1	9800	10527	0.931	0.099%	0.069%	0.030%	0.080%
93:2	9901	10340	0.958	0.045%	0.056%	-0.011%	0.052%
93:3	9809	10686	0.918	0.093%	0.105%	-0.012%	0.101%
93:4	9910	10255	0.966	0.046%	0.027%	0.019%	0.034%
94:1	9991	9954	1.004	0.007%	-0.021%	0.029%	-0.011%
94:2	9953	9994	0.996	0.030%	-0.018%	0.047%	-0.005%
94:3	9820	10613	0.925	0.096%	0.086%	0.010%	0.089%
94:4	10008	9836	1.017	-0.001%	-0.043%	0.042%	-0.029%
95:1	9758	10706	0.911	0.127%	0.102%	0.025%	0.110%
95:2	9687	10873	0.891	0.144%	0.128%	0.016%	0.134%
95:3	9697	10853	0.894	0.134%	0.129%	0.004%	0.131%
95:4	9902	10445	0.948	0.048%	0.077%	-0.029%	0.067%
96:1	9640	11027	0.874	0.175%	0.150%	0.025%	0.159%
96:2	9880	10367	0.953	0.055%	0.061%	-0.005%	0.059%
96:3	9939	10298	0.965	0.029%	0.056%	-0.027%	0.047%
96:4	9733	10817	0.900	0.131%	0.118%	0.013%	0.122%
AVG	9880	10377	0.952	0.061%	0.053%	0.008%	0.055%

Construction

First, choose a time period, P, to use. Today's closing price will be compared to the highest price and the lowest price that have occurred during the time period, P, using the following formula:

%K = [(Today's close – Low in period P)/(High in period P – Low in period P)] · 100.

Construct an S-period moving average of %K to smooth it. This S-period moving average line is referred to as %K Slowed.

After the %K Slowed line is calculated, apply a moving average to it. This moving average of %K Slowed is referred to as %D Trigger and serves as the trigger line for this system.

Results

The test results for the Stochastic Divergence (STO-D) indicator are shown in Tables 5.11 and 5.12. This indicator makes long calls 7.7 percent of the time with an accuracy rate of 61.2 percent (Table 5.11a). When the system favors a cash position over a long position, this call is correct 60.2 percent of the time.

These calls seem to be fairly good calls in that they are choosing days with above-average market returns. The average stock return on days when long calls are made is 0.071 percent (Table 5.12a). This return is significantly greater than the 0.054 percent average daily stock return for cash positions. However, this higher return is not enough to compensate for the infrequency of long calls, which causes investors to miss out on the potential profits of many positive return days.

The STO-D system makes short calls 8.4 percent of the time, with an average accuracy rate of 59.2 percent (Table 5.11b). When this system favors a cash position over a short position, this call is correct 60.7 percent of the time. Unfortunately, these short calls are not very good calls. The average daily stock return on the days they occur is higher than the average daily stock return on days when cash positions are favored. Following this indicator's advice and taking a short position will lead to losses. On average, an investor starting a quarter with $10,000 and investing with this indicator's short calls will lose $35 during that quarter.

The main problem with the STO-D system is the infrequency of calls. Because calls are so rare with this system, investors find themselves in a wrong cash position more frequently than once every three days. In these cash positions, they are earning no returns and are forgoing potential returns. Therefore, trading with this system leads to a lower terminal wealth, on average, than the terminal wealth of a buy-and-hold strategy.

TRIX Divergence

TRIX stands for Triple Exponential Moving Average. This system uses TRIX as a divergent indicator; the TRIX Momentum Peaks indicator presented on page 161 also uses TRIX, but as an oscillator.

TRIX is based on taking a moving average of a moving average of a moving average. Using a triple exponentially smoothed moving average of a stock's price eliminates whipsaws and filters.

When price direction diverges from the direction of this smoothed trend, trading signals occur.

Construction

TRIX is constructed by calculating three moving averages. The first (EMA_1) is a P-period exponential moving average of the closing price. The second (EMA_2) is the P-period exponential moving average of EMA_1. The third (TRIX) is the P-period exponential moving average of EMA_2. This third moving average gives the TRIX oscillator.

If TRIX is rising while price is falling, a price reversal is assumed to be imminent and a long signal is triggered. If TRIX falls while price rises, a short signal is triggered.

Results

Table 5.13 contains the long and short hit analysis and Table 5.14 contains the long and short return analysis for the TRIX Divergence (TRX-D) system. Comparing the hit results for this system to the hit results in Table 4.23 for the related TRIX Momentum Peaks (TXM-P) system, we see that the TRX-D system makes calls less frequently. In fact, with a long call rate of 3.7 percent and a short call rate of 4.3 percent, the call rate for the TRX-D system is only about 13 percent of the call rate of the TXM-P system.

The TRX-D system makes fewer long and short calls, but the system tends to make superior calls. The long hit rate is 61.8 percent and the short hit rate is 59.8 percent. The hit rates for long and short calls for the TXM-P system are 60.8 percent and 60.2 percent, respectively.

This system is especially good at predicting periods when stock returns are greatly above average and far below average. Thus, the system is good at picking the best and strongest times to be long, and the weakest times of the market. On days when the indicator makes long calls, the average stock return is 0.095 percent (Table 5.14a). This is significantly above the average daily stock return of 0.054 percent when the system favors a cash position over a long position. Only a couple of the technical indicators we tested have long average returns that exceed this system's returns. Despite the high long average

Table 5.11a
Stochastic Divergence (STO-D) Long Hit Analysis
(Average of all stocks)

Qtr	Optimal Long	STO-D Long	Long Hits	Cash Hits	Total Hits	Long Right	Long Wrong	Cash Right	Cash Wrong
85:1	32.1%	4.1%	67.7%	68.1%	68.1%	2.8%	1.3%	65.3%	30.6%
85:2	30.2%	6.6%	63.2%	69.7%	69.3%	4.2%	2.4%	65.1%	28.3%
85:3	26.3%	7.8%	60.2%	73.8%	72.7%	4.7%	3.1%	68.0%	24.2%
85:4	36.6%	7.2%	65.8%	63.3%	63.5%	4.7%	2.5%	58.8%	34.0%
86:1	44.2%	5.0%	66.0%	55.9%	56.4%	3.3%	1.7%	53.1%	41.9%
86:2	39.7%	6.3%	62.3%	60.4%	60.5%	3.9%	2.4%	56.5%	37.1%
86:3	37.0%	9.3%	58.6%	63.1%	62.7%	5.5%	3.9%	57.2%	33.5%
86:4	38.5%	8.3%	63.0%	61.5%	61.7%	5.2%	3.1%	56.4%	35.3%
87:1	44.7%	4.9%	66.1%	55.5%	56.0%	3.2%	1.7%	52.7%	42.4%
87:2	40.0%	9.2%	60.1%	60.0%	60.0%	5.5%	3.7%	54.5%	36.3%
87:3	39.5%	6.9%	61.4%	60.6%	60.7%	4.2%	2.7%	56.5%	36.6%
87:4	37.9%	14.1%	55.2%	62.4%	61.4%	7.8%	6.3%	53.6%	32.3%
88:1	41.3%	4.1%	63.5%	58.8%	58.9%	2.6%	1.5%	56.3%	39.6%
88:2	39.3%	9.2%	62.5%	60.8%	60.9%	5.7%	3.4%	55.2%	35.6%
88:3	35.9%	9.1%	61.7%	64.2%	63.9%	5.6%	3.5%	58.3%	32.6%
88:4	36.3%	8.1%	64.4%	63.7%	63.8%	5.2%	2.9%	58.6%	33.3%
89:1	39.0%	5.2%	64.6%	61.0%	61.2%	3.3%	1.8%	57.8%	37.0%
89:2	40.2%	5.0%	64.3%	59.8%	60.0%	3.2%	1.8%	56.8%	38.2%
89:3	39.9%	6.2%	64.2%	60.1%	60.4%	4.0%	2.2%	56.4%	37.4%
89:4	38.3%	11.2%	58.5%	61.5%	61.1%	6.6%	4.7%	54.6%	34.2%
90:1	36.9%	9.3%	62.6%	63.4%	63.3%	5.8%	3.5%	57.5%	33.2%
90:2	39.2%	6.4%	64.2%	60.7%	60.9%	4.1%	2.3%	56.8%	36.8%
90:3	33.5%	13.5%	53.9%	66.5%	64.8%	7.3%	6.2%	57.5%	29.0%
90:4	40.8%	8.8%	62.0%	59.2%	59.5%	5.5%	3.4%	54.0%	37.2%
91:1	44.1%	3.4%	67.5%	55.9%	56.3%	2.3%	1.1%	54.0%	42.6%
91:2	39.7%	5.9%	61.8%	60.6%	60.6%	3.6%	2.3%	57.0%	37.1%
91:3	40.4%	8.0%	60.2%	59.6%	59.6%	4.8%	3.2%	54.8%	37.2%
91:4	41.2%	9.6%	59.7%	58.8%	58.9%	5.7%	3.9%	53.2%	37.2%
92:1	40.0%	6.1%	55.4%	59.9%	59.6%	3.4%	2.7%	56.2%	37.7%
92:2	38.6%	10.2%	58.1%	61.5%	61.2%	5.9%	4.3%	55.3%	34.5%
92:3	40.3%	7.6%	60.4%	59.7%	59.8%	4.6%	3.0%	55.2%	37.2%
92:4	41.9%	6.2%	62.8%	58.1%	58.4%	3.9%	2.3%	54.5%	39.3%
93:1	42.5%	5.3%	60.7%	57.4%	57.6%	3.2%	2.1%	54.4%	40.3%
93:2	42.1%	8.6%	59.8%	57.9%	58.1%	5.1%	3.4%	52.9%	38.5%
93:3	42.5%	7.1%	60.0%	57.5%	57.7%	4.3%	2.8%	53.4%	39.5%
93:4	41.5%	9.5%	57.7%	58.5%	58.4%	5.5%	4.0%	52.9%	37.5%
94:1	40.4%	7.4%	56.6%	59.5%	59.3%	4.2%	3.2%	55.1%	37.5%
94:2	40.6%	11.4%	59.3%	59.6%	59.6%	6.8%	4.6%	52.8%	35.8%
94:3	41.8%	7.8%	61.7%	58.3%	58.6%	4.8%	3.0%	53.8%	38.4%
94:4	39.5%	12.2%	58.1%	60.8%	60.4%	7.1%	5.1%	53.3%	34.4%
95:1	43.1%	6.0%	61.1%	56.8%	57.1%	3.7%	2.3%	53.4%	40.6%
95:2	43.7%	5.5%	61.0%	56.2%	56.5%	3.4%	2.2%	53.1%	41.3%
95:3	43.9%	6.1%	62.4%	56.1%	56.4%	3.8%	2.3%	52.7%	41.3%
95:4	43.4%	8.3%	59.6%	56.5%	56.8%	5.0%	3.4%	51.8%	39.8%
96:1	45.5%	7.2%	61.6%	54.5%	55.0%	4.4%	2.8%	50.6%	42.2%
96:2	42.1%	7.1%	58.8%	58.0%	58.1%	4.2%	2.9%	53.9%	39.0%
96:3	42.6%	9.6%	58.1%	57.4%	57.4%	5.6%	4.0%	51.9%	38.5%
96:4	44.3%	5.3%	61.1%	55.8%	56.0%	3.3%	2.1%	52.8%	41.9%
AVG	40.0%	7.7%	61.2%	60.2%	60.2%	4.6%	3.0%	55.6%	36.8%

Table 5.11b
Stochastic Divergence (STO-D) Short Hit Analysis
(Average of all stocks)

Qtr	Optimal Short	STO-D Short	Short Hits	Cash Hits	Total Hits	Short Right	Short Wrong	Cash Right	Cash Wrong
85:1	34.3%	10.1%	67.8%	65.9%	66.1%	6.8%	3.2%	59.3%	30.7%
85:2	34.6%	7.5%	67.2%	65.3%	65.4%	5.0%	2.5%	60.4%	32.1%
85:3	38.6%	8.4%	73.8%	61.6%	62.6%	6.2%	2.2%	56.4%	35.2%
85:4	33.1%	8.0%	57.4%	66.9%	66.2%	4.6%	3.4%	61.6%	30.4%
86:1	35.2%	11.2%	54.1%	64.8%	63.6%	6.0%	5.1%	57.6%	31.3%
86:2	39.8%	10.9%	59.0%	60.2%	60.1%	6.4%	4.5%	53.7%	35.5%
86:3	42.7%	6.8%	63.9%	57.6%	58.0%	4.3%	2.5%	53.7%	39.5%
86:4	38.7%	7.1%	59.6%	61.4%	61.2%	4.2%	2.9%	57.0%	35.9%
87:1	36.9%	11.0%	55.1%	63.2%	62.3%	6.1%	4.9%	56.2%	32.8%
87:2	40.0%	7.1%	59.2%	60.1%	60.1%	4.2%	2.9%	55.9%	37.1%
87:3	40.4%	9.6%	60.0%	59.7%	59.7%	5.8%	3.9%	53.9%	36.4%
87:4	45.3%	2.8%	65.6%	54.9%	55.2%	1.8%	1.0%	53.4%	43.9%
88:1	36.7%	11.7%	59.8%	63.4%	63.0%	7.0%	4.7%	56.0%	32.3%
88:2	37.4%	6.9%	60.7%	62.4%	62.3%	4.2%	2.7%	58.2%	35.0%
88:3	38.4%	8.1%	66.0%	61.9%	62.2%	5.3%	2.8%	56.9%	35.0%
88:4	37.0%	7.5%	63.2%	63.2%	63.2%	4.7%	2.8%	58.5%	34.0%
89:1	36.2%	11.0%	57.2%	63.8%	63.0%	6.3%	4.7%	56.7%	32.2%
89:2	35.9%	9.8%	58.5%	64.1%	63.6%	5.7%	4.1%	57.9%	32.4%
89:3	36.4%	10.4%	59.4%	63.5%	63.1%	6.2%	4.2%	56.9%	32.7%
89:4	39.0%	6.0%	59.2%	61.0%	60.9%	3.6%	2.5%	57.3%	36.6%
90:1	40.1%	6.1%	64.4%	60.1%	60.4%	3.9%	2.2%	56.4%	37.4%
90:2	37.8%	9.6%	60.1%	62.5%	62.3%	5.7%	3.8%	56.5%	33.9%
90:3	45.7%	4.3%	62.8%	54.2%	54.6%	2.7%	1.6%	51.8%	43.8%
90:4	37.6%	5.7%	55.6%	62.3%	61.9%	3.2%	2.5%	58.7%	35.6%
91:1	36.7%	12.6%	57.8%	63.7%	63.0%	7.3%	5.3%	55.7%	31.7%
91:2	40.4%	9.2%	59.8%	59.4%	59.5%	5.5%	3.7%	54.0%	36.9%
91:3	39.8%	7.7%	59.1%	60.2%	60.1%	4.5%	3.1%	55.6%	36.8%
91:4	40.5%	8.0%	58.1%	59.5%	59.4%	4.7%	3.4%	54.7%	37.3%
92:1	43.2%	9.9%	59.6%	56.7%	57.0%	5.9%	4.0%	51.1%	39.0%
92:2	42.9%	7.1%	60.8%	57.1%	57.4%	4.3%	2.8%	53.0%	39.8%
92:3	39.5%	7.5%	57.8%	60.4%	60.2%	4.4%	3.2%	55.8%	36.6%
92:4	37.5%	8.5%	57.3%	62.5%	62.1%	4.8%	3.6%	57.2%	34.3%
93:1	39.4%	10.1%	58.0%	60.7%	60.4%	5.9%	4.2%	54.6%	35.4%
93:2	40.9%	9.1%	56.7%	59.1%	58.9%	5.2%	3.9%	53.7%	37.2%
93:3	39.4%	9.7%	56.8%	60.5%	60.1%	5.5%	4.2%	54.6%	35.7%
93:4	41.7%	7.7%	57.1%	58.2%	58.1%	4.4%	3.3%	53.7%	38.6%
94:1	43.7%	8.9%	56.9%	56.1%	56.2%	5.1%	3.8%	51.1%	39.9%
94:2	42.7%	5.3%	57.6%	57.3%	57.3%	3.0%	2.2%	54.2%	40.5%
94:3	39.8%	7.5%	58.3%	60.2%	60.0%	4.4%	3.1%	55.6%	36.8%
94:4	42.8%	6.0%	58.2%	57.2%	57.2%	3.5%	2.5%	53.7%	40.3%
95:1	38.7%	9.0%	56.0%	61.3%	60.8%	5.0%	4.0%	55.8%	35.2%
95:2	38.9%	9.9%	55.0%	61.1%	60.5%	5.4%	4.5%	55.1%	35.0%
95:3	38.9%	9.7%	54.7%	61.1%	60.5%	5.3%	4.4%	55.2%	35.2%
95:4	40.5%	8.5%	55.3%	59.5%	59.2%	4.7%	3.8%	54.5%	37.0%
96:1	38.9%	9.5%	53.4%	61.1%	60.4%	5.1%	4.4%	55.3%	35.2%
96:2	42.4%	8.4%	57.7%	57.7%	57.7%	4.9%	3.6%	52.8%	38.8%
96:3	40.8%	5.7%	56.9%	59.3%	59.2%	3.2%	2.4%	56.0%	38.4%
96:4	39.8%	10.4%	55.6%	60.3%	59.8%	5.8%	4.6%	54.0%	35.6%
AVG	39.4%	8.4%	59.2%	60.7%	60.5%	5.0%	3.4%	55.6%	36.0%

Table 5.12a
Stochastic Divergence (STO-D) Long Return Analysis
(Average of all stocks)

Qtr	STO-D Terminal Wealth	Buy/Hold Terminal Wealth	Relative Terminal Wealth	STO-D Long Avg Ret	STO-D Cash Avg Ret	STO-D Long-Cash Avg Ret	Buy/Hold Avg Ret
85:1	10030	10142	0.989	0.117%	0.002%	0.115%	0.006%
85:2	9966	9700	1.027	-0.088%	-0.068%	-0.020%	-0.069%
85:3	9905	8889	1.114	-0.200%	-0.205%	0.005%	-0.205%
85:4	10034	10763	0.932	0.074%	0.109%	-0.035%	0.107%
86:1	10076	11428	0.882	0.257%	0.223%	0.034%	0.225%
86:2	10072	10414	0.967	0.184%	0.058%	0.125%	0.066%
86:3	9988	9175	1.089	-0.020%	-0.139%	0.119%	-0.128%
86:4	10059	10413	0.966	0.114%	0.065%	0.049%	0.069%
87:1	10144	11929	0.850	0.464%	0.284%	0.180%	0.293%
87:2	10021	10196	0.983	0.041%	0.038%	0.003%	0.038%
87:3	10078	10408	0.968	0.180%	0.060%	0.120%	0.068%
87:4	9918	8087	1.226	-0.084%	-0.310%	0.226%	-0.278%
88:1	10064	10989	0.916	0.258%	0.159%	0.099%	0.163%
88:2	10068	10593	0.950	0.121%	0.098%	0.023%	0.100%
88:3	10021	10050	0.997	0.041%	0.010%	0.031%	0.013%
88:4	10034	10196	0.984	0.070%	0.034%	0.037%	0.037%
89:1	10045	10698	0.939	0.145%	0.111%	0.035%	0.112%
89:2	10048	10772	0.933	0.155%	0.120%	0.035%	0.122%
89:3	10062	10833	0.929	0.161%	0.129%	0.032%	0.131%
89:4	9948	9904	1.004	-0.071%	-0.003%	-0.067%	-0.011%
90:1	10068	9980	1.009	0.119%	-0.009%	0.128%	0.003%
90:2	10029	10459	0.959	0.073%	0.077%	-0.004%	0.077%
90:3	9781	8526	1.147	-0.268%	-0.258%	-0.010%	-0.259%
90:4	10107	10889	0.928	0.185%	0.143%	0.043%	0.146%
91:1	10105	12477	0.810	0.508%	0.308%	0.200%	0.315%
91:2	10060	10244	0.982	0.163%	0.038%	0.126%	0.045%
91:3	10038	10429	0.963	0.077%	0.064%	0.013%	0.065%
91:4	10083	10497	0.961	0.144%	0.075%	0.069%	0.082%
92:1	9992	10324	0.968	-0.018%	0.052%	-0.070%	0.048%
92:2	10004	9723	1.029	0.009%	-0.055%	0.064%	-0.048%
92:3	10029	10392	0.965	0.059%	0.056%	. 0.002%	0.057%
92:4	10058	10963	0.917	0.148%	0.144%	0.004%	0.144%
93:1	10022	10527	0.952	0.069%	0.080%	-0.011%	0.080%
93:2	10032	10340	0.970	0.062%	0.051%	0.011%	0.052%
93:3	10048	10686	0.940	0.106%	0.101%	0.005%	0.101%
93:4	10017	10255	0.977	0.026%	0.035%	-0.009%	0.034%
94:1	10006	9954	1.005	0.013%	-0.013%	0.026%	-0.011%
94:2	10048	9994	1.005	0.066%	-0.014%	0.080%	-0.005%
94:3	10074	10613	0.949	0.152%	0.084%	0.068%	0.089%
94:4	10022	9836	1.019	0.028%	-0.037%	0.066%	-0.029%
95:1	10041	10706	0.938	0.113%	0.110%	0.003%	0.110%
95:2	10049	10873	0.924	0.145%	0.133%	0.011%	0.134%
95:3	10057	10853	0.927	0.150%	0.130%	0.020%	0.131%
95:4	10059	10445	0.963	0.114%	0.062%	0.051%	0.067%
96:1	10097	11027	0.916	0.215%	0.155%	0.061%	0.159%
96:2	10037	10367	0.968	0.085%	0.057%	0.028%	0.059%
96:3	10033	10298	0.974	0.052%	0.047%	0.005%	0.047%
96:4	10042	10817	0.928	0.125%	0.122%	0.002%	0.122%
AVG	10034	10377	0.967	0.071%	0.054%	0.017%	0.055%

Table 5.12b
Stochastic Divergence (STO-D) Short Return Analysis
(Average of all stocks)

Qtr	STO-D Terminal Wealth	Buy/Hold Terminal Wealth	Relative Terminal Wealth	STO-D Short Avg Ret	STO-D Cash Avg Ret	STO-D Short-Cash Avg Ret	Buy/Hold Avg Ret
85:1	10029	10142	0.989	-0.042%	0.012%	-0.054%	0.006%
85:2	10003	9700	1.031	-0.005%	-0.075%	0.070%	-0.069%
85:3	10125	8889	1.139	-0.228%	-0.203%	-0.026%	-0.205%
85:4	9883	10763	0.918	0.234%	0.096%	0.138%	0.107%
86:1	9842	11428	0.861	0.240%	0.223%	0.017%	0.225%
86:2	9957	10414	0.956	0.062%	0.067%	-0.004%	0.066%
86:3	10132	9175	1.104	-0.306%	-0.115%	-0.191%	-0.128%
86:4	9968	10413	0.957	0.070%	0.069%	0.001%	0.069%
87:1	9829	11929	0.824	0.257%	0.297%	-0.040%	0.293%
87:2	9983	10196	0.979	0.035%	0.038%	-0.003%	0.038%
87:3	9987	10408	0.960	0.022%	0.073%	-0.052%	0.068%
87:4	10167	8087	1.257	-0.931%	-0.259%	-0.671%	-0.278%
88:1	9914	10989	0.902	0.117%	0.169%	-0.051%	0.163%
88:2	9932	10593	0.938	0.157%	0.096%	0.062%	0.100%
88:3	10043	10050	0.999	-0.086%	0.021%	-0.108%	0.013%
88:4	9994	10196	0.980	0.010%	0.039%	-0.029%	0.037%
89:1	9894	10698	0.925	0.159%	0.107%	0.052%	0.112%
89:2	9911	10772	0.920	0.144%	0.120%	0.024%	0.122%
89:3	9918	10833	0.915	0.129%	0.131%	-0.002%	0.131%
89:4	9987	9904	1.008	0.031%	-0.014%	0.044%	-0.011%
90:1	10030	9980	1.005	-0.079%	0.008%	-0.087%	0.003%
90:2	9987	10459	0.955	0.021%	0.083%	-0.061%	0.077%
90:3	10031	8526	1.177	-0.116%	-0.265%	0.150%	-0.259%
90:4	9910	10889	0.910	0.251%	0.140%	0.111%	0.146%
91:1	9863	12477	0.790	0.182%	0.334%	-0.152%	0.315%
91:2	9939	10244	0.970	0.101%	0.040%	0.061%	0.045%
91:3	9953	10429	0.954	0.102%	0.062%	0.040%	0.065%
91:4	9974	10497	0.950	0.051%	0.084%	-0.033%	0.082%
92:1	9971	10324	0.966	0.047%	0.048%	-0.001%	0.048%
92:2	10028	9723	1.031	-0.061%	-0.047%	-0.013%	-0.048%
92:3	9958	10392	0.958	0.091%	0.054%	0.037%	0.057%
92:4	9927	10963	0.906	0.139%	0.145%	-0.006%	0.144%
93:1	9971	10527	0.947	0.047%	0.083%	-0.036%	0.080%
93:2	9970	10340	0.964	0.056%	0.051%	0.004%	0.052%
93:3	9926	10686	0.929	0.126%	0.098%	0.028%	0.101%
93:4	9974	10255	0.973	0.053%	0.032%	0.021%	0.034%
94:1	9983	9954	1.003	0.030%	-0.015%	0.046%	-0.011%
94:2	9986	9994	0.999	0.045%	-0.007%	0.052%	-0.005%
94:3	9950	10613	0.938	0.109%	0.088%	0.021%	0.089%
94:4	9991	9836	1.016	0.022%	-0.033%	0.055%	-0.029%
95:1	9928	10706	0.927	0.130%	0.108%	0.022%	0.110%
95:2	9903	10873	0.911	0.159%	0.131%	0.027%	0.134%
95:3	9897	10853	0.912	0.174%	0.126%	0.048%	0.131%
95:4	9961	10445	0.954	0.074%	0.066%	0.008%	0.067%
96:1	9906	11027	0.898	0.162%	0.159%	0.004%	0.159%
96:2	9970	10367	0.962	0.060%	0.058%	0.002%	0.059%
96:3	9990	10298	0.970	0.027%	0.048%	-0.021%	0.047%
96:4	9948	10817	0.920	0.082%	0.127%	-0.045%	0.122%
AVG	9965	10377	0.960	0.068%	0.054%	0.014%	0.055%

Table 5.13a
TRIX Divergence (TRX-D) Long Hit Analysis
(Average of all stocks)

Qtr	Optimal Long	TRX-D Long	Long Hits	Cash Hits	Total Hits	Long Right	Long Wrong	Cash Right	Cash Wrong
85:1	32.1%	1.8%	71.3%	68.0%	68.1%	1.3%	0.5%	66.8%	31.4%
85:2	30.2%	3.2%	65.4%	69.8%	69.7%	2.1%	1.1%	67.6%	29.2%
85:3	26.3%	3.3%	63.3%	73.6%	73.3%	2.1%	1.2%	71.2%	25.5%
85:4	36.6%	5.0%	67.8%	63.3%	63.6%	3.4%	1.6%	60.2%	34.8%
86:1	44.2%	2.2%	64.3%	55.8%	56.0%	1.4%	0.8%	54.6%	43.2%
86:2	39.7%	2.6%	60.6%	60.2%	60.2%	1.6%	1.0%	58.6%	38.8%
86:3	37.0%	3.7%	57.9%	62.9%	62.8%	2.1%	1.5%	60.6%	35.7%
86:4	38.5%	4.7%	61.3%	61.5%	61.5%	2.9%	1.8%	58.6%	36.7%
87:1	44.7%	2.1%	64.6%	55.4%	55.6%	1.4%	0.7%	54.2%	43.7%
87:2	40.0%	4.8%	63.3%	60.2%	60.4%	3.0%	1.8%	57.3%	37.9%
87:3	39.5%	2.8%	63.0%	60.5%	60.5%	1.8%	1.0%	58.8%	38.4%
87:4	37.9%	8.2%	63.3%	62.9%	62.9%	5.2%	3.0%	57.8%	34.0%
88:1	41.3%	2.7%	67.9%	58.7%	59.0%	1.8%	0.9%	57.2%	40.1%
88:2	39.3%	4.2%	63.3%	60.7%	60.8%	2.7%	1.5%	58.2%	37.7%
88:3	35.9%	3.7%	62.9%	64.0%	64.0%	2.3%	1.4%	61.7%	34.6%
88:4	36.3%	4.2%	65.6%	63.6%	63.7%	2.7%	1.4%	61.0%	34.8%
89:1	39.0%	3.2%	67.3%	60.9%	61.1%	2.1%	1.0%	59.0%	37.8%
89:2	40.2%	2.7%	66.2%	59.8%	59.9%	1.8%	0.9%	58.1%	39.1%
89:3	39.9%	2.5%	64.2%	60.0%	60.1%	1.6%	0.9%	58.5%	39.0%
89:4	38.3%	3.6%	62.7%	61.6%	61.7%	2.2%	1.3%	59.4%	37.0%
90:1	36.9%	5.7%	62.3%	63.2%	63.2%	3.5%	2.1%	59.6%	34.7%
90:2	39.2%	3.6%	63.6%	60.7%	60.8%	2.3%	1.3%	58.6%	37.9%
90:3	33.5%	3.6%	52.1%	66.4%	65.9%	1.9%	1.7%	64.0%	32.4%
90:4	40.8%	8.8%	57.7%	58.8%	58.7%	5.1%	3.7%	53.6%	37.6%
91:1	44.1%	2.5%	68.4%	55.9%	56.2%	1.7%	0.8%	54.5%	43.0%
91:2	39.7%	2.6%	59.1%	60.3%	60.3%	1.5%	1.1%	58.7%	38.7%
91:3	40.4%	4.1%	61.0%	59.5%	59.5%	2.5%	1.6%	57.0%	38.9%
91:4	41.2%	4.1%	60.6%	58.8%	58.9%	2.5%	1.6%	56.4%	39.5%
92:1	40.0%	2.4%	54.9%	59.9%	59.8%	1.3%	1.1%	58.5%	39.1%
92:2	38.6%	4.9%	56.8%	61.4%	61.2%	2.8%	2.1%	58.4%	36.7%
92:3	40.3%	4.5%	60.0%	59.7%	59.7%	2.7%	1.8%	57.0%	38.5%
92:4	41.9%	3.4%	62.8%	58.0%	58.2%	2.1%	1.3%	56.1%	40.5%
93:1	42.5%	2.2%	58.7%	57.5%	57.5%	1.3%	0.9%	56.2%	41.6%
93:2	42.1%	4.3%	58.9%	57.9%	57.9%	2.6%	1.8%	55.4%	40.3%
93:3	42.5%	3.5%	60.5%	57.5%	57.6%	2.1%	1.4%	55.5%	41.0%
93:4	41.5%	3.5%	60.0%	58.6%	58.6%	2.1%	1.4%	56.5%	39.9%
94:1	40.4%	4.0%	55.8%	59.5%	59.3%	2.3%	1.8%	57.1%	38.9%
94:2	40.6%	6.2%	58.2%	59.5%	59.4%	3.6%	2.6%	55.8%	38.0%
94:3	41.8%	4.3%	62.6%	58.3%	58.5%	2.7%	1.6%	55.8%	39.9%
94:4	39.5%	4.8%	58.1%	60.7%	60.5%	2.8%	2.0%	57.7%	37.4%
95:1	43.1%	3.4%	61.7%	56.9%	57.0%	2.1%	1.3%	54.9%	41.6%
95:2	43.7%	2.3%	61.6%	56.2%	56.3%	1.4%	0.9%	54.9%	42.8%
95:3	43.9%	2.1%	63.0%	56.0%	56.2%	1.4%	0.8%	54.8%	43.0%
95:4	43.4%	3.0%	59.7%	56.6%	56.7%	1.8%	1.2%	54.9%	42.1%
96:1	45.5%	3.0%	60.7%	54.5%	54.7%	1.8%	1.2%	52.8%	44.2%
96:2	42.1%	3.7%	60.2%	58.0%	58.0%	2.2%	1.5%	55.8%	40.5%
96:3	42.6%	3.7%	59.2%	57.3%	57.4%	2.2%	1.5%	55.2%	41.1%
96:4	44.3%	2.7%	62.8%	55.7%	55.9%	1.7%	1.0%	54.2%	43.1%
AVG	40.0%	3.7%	61.8%	60.1%	60.2%	2.3%	1.4%	57.9%	38.4%

Table 5.13b
TRIX Divergence (TRX-D) Short Hit Analysis
(Average of all stocks)

Qtr	Optimal Short	TRX-D Short	Short Hits	Cash Hits	Total Hits	Short Right	Short Wrong	Cash Right	Cash Wrong
85:1	34.3%	3.1%	65.1%	65.6%	65.6%	2.0%	1.1%	63.5%	33.3%
85:2	34.6%	4.8%	66.6%	65.3%	65.3%	3.2%	1.6%	62.1%	33.1%
85:3	38.6%	4.7%	73.8%	61.5%	62.1%	3.4%	1.2%	58.6%	36.7%
85:4	33.1%	1.9%	64.7%	66.9%	66.8%	1.2%	0.7%	65.6%	32.5%
86:1	35.2%	5.4%	52.3%	64.7%	64.0%	2.8%	2.6%	61.2%	33.4%
86:2	39.8%	6.7%	57.9%	60.1%	60.0%	3.9%	2.8%	56.1%	37.2%
86:3	42.7%	3.9%	63.1%	57.4%	57.6%	2.5%	1.4%	55.2%	40.9%
86:4	38.7%	2.9%	61.5%	61.3%	61.3%	1.8%	1.1%	59.6%	37.6%
87:1	36.9%	2.8%	56.6%	63.0%	62.9%	1.6%	1.2%	61.3%	35.9%
87:2	40.0%	5.7%	59.7%	60.1%	60.1%	3.4%	2.3%	56.7%	37.6%
87:3	40.4%	3.9%	60.7%	59.6%	59.6%	2.3%	1.5%	57.3%	38.9%
87:4	45.3%	5.6%	61.1%	54.9%	55.2%	3.4%	2.2%	51.8%	42.6%
88:1	36.7%	5.9%	59.2%	63.4%	63.2%	3.5%	2.4%	59.7%	34.4%
88:2	37.4%	7.3%	60.5%	62.6%	62.4%	4.4%	2.9%	58.0%	34.7%
88:3	38.4%	4.9%	64.2%	61.8%	61.9%	3.1%	1.7%	58.8%	36.3%
88:4	37.0%	3.8%	63.4%	63.1%	63.1%	2.4%	1.4%	60.7%	35.5%
89:1	36.2%	3.9%	60.0%	63.8%	63.7%	2.3%	1.5%	61.4%	34.8%
89:2	35.9%	4.9%	59.4%	64.0%	63.8%	2.9%	2.0%	60.9%	34.2%
89:3	36.4%	6.3%	58.8%	63.6%	63.3%	3.7%	2.6%	59.6%	34.1%
89:4	39.0%	4.4%	60.9%	61.2%	61.2%	2.7%	1.7%	58.5%	37.1%
90:1	40.1%	2.6%	64.1%	59.9%	60.0%	1.7%	0.9%	58.4%	39.0%
90:2	37.8%	3.2%	60.5%	62.2%	62.1%	2.0%	1.3%	60.2%	36.6%
90:3	45.7%	3.5%	66.0%	54.5%	54.9%	2.3%	1.2%	52.6%	44.0%
90:4	37.6%	1.6%	63.1%	62.5%	62.5%	1.0%	0.6%	61.5%	36.9%
91:1	36.7%	3.6%	54.3%	63.3%	63.0%	1.9%	1.6%	61.0%	35.4%
91:2	40.4%	8.3%	60.2%	59.6%	59.6%	5.0%	3.3%	54.6%	37.0%
91:3	39.8%	4.0%	57.2%	60.2%	60.1%	2.3%	1.7%	57.8%	38.2%
91:4	40.5%	4.1%	58.2%	59.4%	59.4%	2.4%	1.7%	57.0%	38.9%
92:1	43.2%	3.9%	60.5%	56.7%	56.9%	2.3%	1.5%	54.6%	41.6%
92:2	42.9%	4.3%	58.9%	57.1%	57.2%	2.5%	1.7%	54.7%	41.1%
92:3	39.5%	3.2%	59.7%	60.5%	60.5%	1.9%	1.3%	58.5%	38.2%
92:4	37.5%	3.7%	58.5%	62.5%	62.4%	2.2%	1.5%	60.2%	36.1%
93:1	39.4%	5.5%	56.8%	60.7%	60.4%	3.1%	2.4%	57.3%	37.2%
93:2	40.9%	5.4%	57.6%	59.1%	59.0%	3.1%	2.3%	55.9%	38.7%
93:3	39.4%	3.7%	57.5%	60.6%	60.5%	2.1%	1.6%	58.4%	37.9%
93:4	41.7%	3.7%	59.8%	58.4%	58.5%	2.2%	1.5%	56.2%	40.0%
94:1	43.7%	3.9%	57.3%	56.2%	56.3%	2.3%	1.7%	54.0%	42.0%
94:2	42.7%	2.8%	57.5%	57.3%	57.3%	1.6%	1.2%	55.7%	41.5%
94:3	39.8%	3.0%	59.9%	60.3%	60.3%	1.8%	1.2%	58.5%	38.5%
94:4	42.8%	3.4%	61.0%	57.2%	57.3%	2.0%	1.3%	55.2%	41.4%
95:1	38.7%	3.1%	57.7%	61.4%	61.3%	1.8%	1.3%	59.5%	37.4%
95:2	38.9%	5.2%	57.1%	61.2%	61.0%	3.0%	2.2%	58.0%	36.8%
95:3	38.9%	5.0%	55.2%	61.0%	60.7%	2.8%	2.2%	57.9%	37.0%
95:4	40.5%	4.4%	56.4%	59.5%	59.4%	2.5%	1.9%	56.9%	38.7%
96:1	38.9%	5.0%	52.9%	61.1%	60.7%	2.7%	2.4%	58.0%	37.0%
96:2	42.4%	5.5%	57.3%	57.6%	57.6%	3.2%	2.4%	54.5%	40.0%
96:3	40.8%	3.1%	60.0%	59.3%	59.4%	1.9%	1.3%	57.5%	39.4%
96:4	39.8%	4.3%	56.7%	60.3%	60.1%	2.4%	1.9%	57.7%	38.0%
AVG	39.4%	4.3%	59.8%	60.7%	60.7%	2.6%	1.7%	58.1%	37.6%

Table 5.14a
TRIX Divergence (TRX-D) Long Return Analysis
(Average of all stocks)

Qtr	TRX-D Terminal Wealth	Buy/Hold Terminal Wealth	Relative Terminal Wealth	TRX-D Long Avg Ret	TRX-D Cash Avg Ret	TRX-D Long-Cash Avg Ret	Buy/Hold Avg Ret
85:1	10034	10142	0.989	0.318%	0.001%	0.317%	0.006%
85:2	9988	9700	1.030	-0.062%	-0.070%	0.007%	-0.069%
85:3	9963	8889	1.121	-0.194%	-0.205%	0.011%	-0.205%
85:4	10038	10763	0.933	0.119%	0.106%	0.013%	0.107%
86:1	10026	11428	0.877	0.205%	0.225%	-0.020%	0.225%
86:2	10000	10414	0.960	-0.001%	0.068%	-0.069%	0.066%
86:3	9981	9175	1.088	-0.094%	-0.129%	0.035%	-0.128%
86:4	10025	10413	0.963	0.091%	0.068%	0.023%	0.069%
87:1	10055	11929	0.843	0.416%	0.290%	0.126%	0.293%
87:2	10057	10196	0.986	0.196%	0.030%	0.166%	0.038%
87:3	10025	10408	0.963	0.150%	0.066%	0.084%	0.068%
87:4	10230	8087	1.265	0.437%	-0.342%	0.779%	-0.278%
88:1	10061	10989	0.916	0.363%	0.157%	0.206%	0.163%
88:2	10031	10593	0.947	0.119%	0.099%	0.020%	0.100%
88:3	10010	10050	0.996	0.044%	0.011%	0.033%	0.013%
88:4	10016	10196	0.982	0.069%	0.035%	0.034%	0.037%
89:1	10027	10698	0.937	0.144%	0.111%	0.033%	0.112%
89:2	10032	10772	0.931	0.187%	0.120%	0.066%	0.122%
89:3	10020	10833	0.925	0.132%	0.131%	0.001%	0.131%
89:4	9982	9904	1.008	-0.076%	-0.009%	-0.067%	-0.011%
90:1	10030	9980	1.005	0.084%	-0.002%	0.086%	0.003%
90:2	10026	10459	0.959	0.119%	0.075%	0.043%	0.077%
90:3	9934	8526	1.165	-0.309%	-0.257%	-0.052%	-0.259%
90:4	9947	10889	0.913	-0.096%	0.170%	-0.266%	0.146%
91:1	10070	12477	0.807	0.437%	0.312%	0.125%	0.315%
91:2	10009	10244	0.977	0.059%	0.045%	0.014%	0.045%
91:3	10022	10429	0.961	0.083%	0.064%	0.019%	0.065%
91:4	10030	10497	0.956	0.119%	0.080%	0.039%	0.082%
92:1	9996	10324	0.968	-0.032%	0.050%	-0.082%	0.048%
92:2	9990	9723	1.027	-0.032%	-0.049%	0.017%	-0.048%
92:3	10023	10392	0.965	0.086%	0.055%	0.030%	0.057%
92:4	10031	10963	0.915	0.142%	0.145%	-0.003%	0.144%
93:1	10001	10527	0.950	0.005%	0.081%	-0.077%	0.080%
93:2	9996	10340	0.967	-0.020%	0.055%	-0.075%	0.052%
93:3	10041	10686	0.940	0.185%	0.098%	0.087%	0.101%
93:4	10034	10255	0.978	0.148%	0.030%	0.118%	0.034%
94:1	9990	9954	1.004	-0.046%	-0.010%	-0.036%	-0.011%
94:2	10021	9994	1.003	0.056%	-0.009%	0.065%	-0.005%
94:3	10041	10613	0.946	0.151%	0.086%	0.065%	0.089%
94:4	10007	9836	1.017	0.023%	-0.032%	0.055%	-0.029%
95:1	10039	10706	0.938	0.179%	0.107%	0.072%	0.110%
95:2	10025	10873	0.922	0.173%	0.133%	0.039%	0.134%
95:3	10027	10853	0.924	0.198%	0.130%	0.069%	0.131%
95:4	10018	10445	0.959	0.097%	0.066%	0.031%	0.067%
96:1	10051	11027	0.911	0.274%	0.155%	0.119%	0.159%
96:2	10029	10367	0.967	0.131%	0.056%	0.075%	0.059%
96:3	10015	10298	0.973	0.065%	0.047%	0.018%	0.047%
96:4	10027	10817	0.927	0.154%	0.121%	0.032%	0.122%
AVG	10022	10377	0.966	0.095%	0.054%	0.041%	0.055%

Table 5.14b
TRIX Divergence (TRX-D) Short Return Analysis
(Average of all stocks)

Qtr	TRX-D Terminal Wealth	Buy/Hold Terminal Wealth	Relative Terminal Wealth	TRX-D Short Avg Ret	TRX-D Cash Avg Ret	TRX-D Short-Cash Avg Ret	Buy/Hold Avg Ret
85:1	9980	10142	0.984	0.109%	0.003%	0.106%	0.006%
85:2	9988	9700	1.030	0.044%	-0.075%	0.119%	-0.069%
85:3	10068	8889	1.133	-0.230%	-0.204%	-0.026%	-0.205%
85:4	9990	10763	0.928	0.083%	0.107%	-0.025%	0.107%
86:1	9892	11428	0.866	0.336%	0.218%	0.118%	0.225%
86:2	9949	10414	0.955	0.124%	0.062%	0.061%	0.066%
86:3	10055	9175	1.096	-0.219%	-0.124%	-0.095%	-0.128%
86:4	9988	10413	0.959	0.066%	0.069%	-0.003%	0.069%
87:1	9947	11929	0.834	0.306%	0.293%	0.014%	0.293%
87:2	9996	10196	0.980	0.010%	0.040%	-0.030%	0.038%
87:3	9992	10408	0.960	0.032%	0.070%	-0.037%	0.068%
87:4	10186	8087	1.260	-0.564%	-0.261%	-0.303%	-0.278%
88:1	9986	10989	0.909	0.036%	0.171%	-0.134%	0.163%
88:2	9954	10593	0.940	0.098%	0.100%	-0.002%	0.100%
88:3	10006	10050	0.996	-0.020%	0.014%	-0.034%	0.013%
88:4	10000	10196	0.981	0.001%	0.038%	-0.037%	0.037%
89:1	9970	10698	0.932	0.128%	0.112%	0.017%	0.112%
89:2	9958	10772	0.924	0.131%	0.122%	0.009%	0.122%
89:3	9949	10833	0.918	0.134%	0.131%	0.003%	0.131%
89:4	10003	9904	1.010	-0.013%	-0.011%	-0.002%	-0.011%
90:1	10020	9980	1.004	-0.118%	0.006%	-0.124%	0.003%
90:2	9992	10459	0.955	0.043%	0.078%	-0.035%	0.077%
90:3	10077	8526	1.182	-0.353%	-0.256%	-0.098%	-0.259%
90:4	10006	10889	0.919	-0.062%	0.150%	-0.211%	0.146%
91:1	9943	12477	0.797	0.266%	0.317%	-0.051%	0.315%
91:2	9974	10244	0.974	0.049%	0.045%	0.004%	0.045%
91:3	9970	10429	0.956	0.124%	0.062%	0.062%	0.065%
91:4	9968	10497	0.950	0.123%	0.080%	0.043%	0.082%
92:1	10001	10324	0.969	-0.001%	0.050%	-0.051%	0.048%
92:2	10000	9723	1.028	0.005%	-0.051%	0.055%	-0.048%
92:3	9999	10392	0.962	0.006%	0.058%	-0.052%	0.057%
92:4	9978	10963	0.910	0.093%	0.146%	-0.053%	0.144%
93:1	9981	10527	0.948	0.056%	0.081%	-0.025%	0.080%
93:2	9987	10340	0.966	0.038%	0.053%	-0.015%	0.052%
93:3	9977	10686	0.934	0.107%	0.101%	0.006%	0.101%
93:4	10019	10255	0.977	-0.077%	0.038%	-0.115%	0.034%
94:1	9992	9954	1.004	0.032%	-0.013%	0.045%	-0.011%
94:2	9990	9994	1.000	0.055%	-0.006%	0.061%	-0.005%
94:3	9992	10613	0.941	0.047%	0.091%	-0.044%	0.089%
94:4	10004	9836	1.017	-0.012%	-0.030%	0.018%	-0.029%
95:1	9985	10706	0.933	0.081%	0.111%	-0.030%	0.110%
95:2	9980	10873	0.918	0.064%	0.138%	-0.074%	0.134%
95:3	9961	10853	0.918	0.125%	0.131%	-0.007%	0.131%
95:4	9991	10445	0.957	0.033%	0.068%	-0.036%	0.067%
96:1	9959	11027	0.903	0.133%	0.160%	-0.027%	0.159%
96:2	9979	10367	0.963	0.060%	0.058%	0.002%	0.059%
96:3	10004	10298	0.971	-0.018%	0.049%	-0.067%	0.047%
96:4	9973	10817	0.922	0.100%	0.123%	-0.023%	0.122%
AVG	9991	10377	0.963	0.034%	0.056%	-0.022%	0.055%

return, trading long with this system does not result in profitability greater than that of the buy-and-hold strategy. Because of the infrequency of long calls—and, thus, the infrequent opportunities to earn returns—the terminal wealth of the TRX-D system's strategy is only 96.6 percent of the wealth of a buy-and-hold strategy.

The results for the short calls are not quite as significant as for the long calls, but we see some similar return results. The short calls provide some information to investors in that they predict days of below-average stock returns. In fact, the average stock return on days when short calls are made is only 0.034 percent (Table 5.14b). This information alone, however, is not enough to lead to profitable results from a short trading strategy. In all but 14 of the 48 test quarters, trading short with the TRX-D system led to losses. Like many of the other technical indicators, this indicator's best performance occurs during market downturns. The largest profit for this system occurred during the fourth quarter of 1987, a period of record dropping stock prices.

Volume Accumulation Percent Divergence

Like the Chaikin Level Divergence system discussed earlier in this chapter, this system is based on the volume work pioneered by Joseph Granville and Larry Williams. This system looks at changes in volume as clues to traders' perceptions about a stock. More active buying or selling of a stock, relative to the immediately preceding time period, indicates changed perceptions.

Construction

Choose a number of periods to use in constructing the Volume Accumulation Percent (VAP). Then use the following formula to calculate accumulation (ACC) for each day:

$$ACC_i = \{[(Close_i - Low_i) - (High_i - Close_i)]/(High_i - Low_i)\} \cdot Volume_i.$$

Sum these daily accumulations to obtain the total accumulation for the time period (TACC):

$$TACC = ACC_1 + ACC_2 + ACC_3 + \ldots + ACC_p.$$

Calculate the total volume for the period (TVOL) by adding together the volume for each day:

$$TVOL = V_1 + V_2 + V_3 + \ldots + V_p.$$

Now, calculate the Volume Accumulation Percent (VAP) using a ratio of the total accumulation and the total volume:

$$VAP = (TACC/TVOL) \cdot 100.$$

If price falls while the VAP is rising, a long signal is generated to benefit from the expected price reversal. Conversely, if price rises, accompanied by a fall in the VAP, a short signal is generated.

Results

The theory behind the Volume Accumulation Percent Divergence (VAP-D) indicator is similar to the theory behind the Chaikin Level Divergence (CHA-D) indicator; so are the results for the two systems. Table 5.15 contains the long and short hit analysis for the VAP-D system. The system makes long calls 5.7 percent of the time and has an accuracy rate of 61.5 percent. Short calls are made 9.0 percent of the time and have an accuracy rate of 60.0 percent. Overall, this system makes calls a little less frequently and with about the same accuracy as the CHA-D system.

Table 5.16 contains the long and short return analysis for the VAP-D system. Overall, the system tends to choose good days to be in a long position; the average stock return on these long call days is 0.064 percent. This is above the average daily stock return of 0.055 percent for the entire test period, so this technical indicator is choosing days of above-average stock price appreciation to be in long positions. Investors definitely want to follow this indicator's advice and be long on these days. The indicator's downfall, however, is that it fails to make long calls on many days on which a long position would lead to positive returns. The above-average returns of the long call days do not compensate investors for all of the opportunities for profits that they miss by remaining in cash as often as the system recommends. Because of this infrequency of long positions, the quarterly terminal wealth of trading long with this system averages only 96.6 percent of the quarterly terminal wealth of a buy-and-hold strategy.

From the short return analysis, we see that this system's short recommendations were profitable in only 13 test quarters. For the remaining 35 test quarters, trading short with this system actually led to losses and decreasing wealth. On average, an investor who begins a quarter with a $10,000 initial investment and trades short with this system will end the quarter with only $9,972 (Table 5.16b). This investor loses $28 by following the VAP-D system's short strategy.

This technical indicator may provide investors with some useful information, but, alone, it is not powerful enough to beat a buy-and-hold strategy.

Table 5.15a
Volume Accumulation Percent Divergence (VAP-D)
Long Hit Analysis (Average of all stocks)

Qtr	Optimal Long	VAP-D Long	Long Hits	Cash Hits	Total Hits	Long Right	Long Wrong	Cash Right	Cash Wrong
85:1	32.1%	3.9%	65.4%	68.1%	68.0%	2.6%	1.4%	65.4%	30.7%
85:2	30.2%	5.2%	66.5%	69.9%	69.7%	3.4%	1.7%	66.3%	28.5%
85:3	26.3%	5.9%	61.6%	73.8%	73.0%	3.6%	2.3%	69.4%	24.7%
85:4	36.6%	4.8%	67.4%	63.4%	63.6%	3.2%	1.6%	60.4%	34.8%
86:1	44.2%	3.6%	65.1%	55.8%	56.1%	2.3%	1.3%	53.8%	42.6%
86:2	39.7%	5.0%	62.7%	60.3%	60.5%	3.1%	1.9%	57.3%	37.7%
86:3	37.0%	6.5%	59.9%	63.0%	62.8%	3.9%	2.6%	59.0%	34.6%
86:4	38.5%	6.1%	62.4%	61.6%	61.6%	3.8%	2.3%	57.8%	36.1%
87:1	44.7%	4.2%	65.8%	55.5%	56.0%	2.8%	1.4%	53.2%	42.6%
87:2	40.0%	6.2%	60.2%	60.1%	60.1%	3.7%	2.5%	56.4%	37.5%
87:3	39.5%	4.5%	61.3%	60.5%	60.5%	2.8%	1.7%	57.8%	37.7%
87:4	37.9%	7.4%	55.6%	62.2%	61.7%	4.1%	3.3%	57.6%	35.0%
88:1	41.3%	3.7%	64.4%	58.8%	59.0%	2.4%	1.3%	56.6%	39.7%
88:2	39.3%	6.5%	62.8%	60.8%	61.0%	4.1%	2.4%	56.9%	36.6%
88:3	35.9%	5.4%	64.4%	64.2%	64.2%	3.5%	1.9%	60.7%	33.9%
88:4	36.3%	5.7%	63.8%	63.6%	63.6%	3.6%	2.1%	60.0%	34.3%
89:1	39.0%	4.3%	65.7%	61.1%	61.3%	2.8%	1.5%	58.4%	37.2%
89:2	40.2%	4.0%	63.9%	59.8%	60.0%	2.6%	1.4%	57.4%	38.6%
89:3	39.9%	5.5%	65.8%	60.1%	60.4%	3.6%	1.9%	56.8%	37.7%
89:4	38.3%	6.8%	59.6%	61.7%	61.5%	4.0%	2.7%	57.5%	35.7%
90:1	36.9%	6.0%	60.9%	63.1%	63.0%	3.7%	2.3%	59.3%	34.7%
90:2	39.2%	4.2%	63.4%	60.7%	60.8%	2.7%	1.5%	58.1%	37.7%
90:3	33.5%	8.4%	52.1%	66.3%	65.1%	4.4%	4.0%	60.8%	30.8%
90:4	40.8%	6.1%	65.6%	59.4%	59.8%	4.0%	2.1%	55.8%	38.1%
91:1	44.1%	3.6%	63.7%	55.8%	56.1%	2.3%	1.3%	53.7%	42.6%
91:2	39.7%	6.0%	62.0%	60.5%	60.6%	3.7%	2.3%	56.9%	37.1%
91:3	40.4%	5.7%	61.3%	59.6%	59.7%	3.5%	2.2%	56.2%	38.1%
91:4	41.2%	7.2%	58.3%	58.7%	58.7%	4.2%	3.0%	54.5%	38.3%
92:1	40.0%	4.3%	55.1%	59.9%	59.7%	2.4%	1.9%	57.3%	38.4%
92:2	38.6%	7.1%	58.0%	61.5%	61.2%	4.1%	3.0%	57.1%	35.8%
92:3	40.3%	5.6%	61.9%	59.7%	59.8%	3.4%	2.1%	56.4%	38.1%
92:4	41.9%	4.8%	63.3%	58.1%	58.3%	3.1%	1.8%	55.2%	39.9%
93:1	42.5%	5.3%	60.9%	57.5%	57.7%	3.2%	2.1%	54.4%	40.2%
93:2	42.1%	7.1%	60.1%	58.0%	58.1%	4.2%	2.8%	53.9%	39.1%
93:3	42.5%	5.8%	61.8%	57.6%	57.8%	3.6%	2.2%	54.3%	40.0%
93:4	41.5%	6.5%	59.4%	58.6%	58.6%	3.8%	2.6%	54.8%	38.7%
94:1	40.4%	6.2%	56.6%	59.5%	59.3%	3.5%	2.7%	55.8%	38.0%
94:2	40.6%	8.0%	57.4%	59.4%	59.2%	4.6%	3.4%	54.6%	37.4%
94:3	41.8%	5.9%	59.8%	58.2%	58.3%	3.6%	2.4%	54.8%	39.3%
94:4	39.5%	7.8%	58.3%	60.6%	60.4%	4.5%	3.2%	55.9%	36.3%
95:1	43.1%	5.1%	63.2%	56.8%	57.2%	3.2%	1.9%	53.9%	41.0%
95:2	43.7%	4.9%	62.0%	56.3%	56.6%	3.0%	1.9%	53.5%	41.6%
95:3	43.9%	5.1%	61.6%	56.0%	56.3%	3.1%	1.9%	53.2%	41.8%
95:4	43.4%	6.0%	60.1%	56.5%	56.7%	3.6%	2.4%	53.1%	40.9%
96:1	45.5%	6.6%	60.7%	54.4%	54.8%	4.0%	2.6%	50.8%	42.6%
96:2	42.1%	6.7%	59.0%	58.0%	58.1%	4.0%	2.8%	54.1%	39.2%
96:3	42.6%	7.0%	57.8%	57.3%	57.3%	4.0%	3.0%	53.2%	39.7%
96:4	44.3%	4.7%	61.9%	55.8%	56.1%	2.9%	1.8%	53.1%	42.1%
AVG	40.0%	5.7%	61.5%	60.2%	60.2%	3.5%	2.2%	56.7%	37.6%

Table 5.15b
Volume Accumulation Percent Divergence (VAP-D)
Short Hit Analysis (Average of all stocks)

Qtr	Optimal Short	VAP-D Short	Short Hits	Cash Hits	Total Hits	Short Right	Short Wrong	Cash Right	Cash Wrong
85:1	34.3%	11.3%	68.9%	65.9%	66.2%	7.8%	3.5%	58.4%	30.3%
85:2	34.6%	9.3%	69.5%	65.5%	65.9%	6.5%	2.8%	59.4%	31.3%
85:3	38.6%	6.6%	72.0%	61.4%	62.1%	4.8%	1.9%	57.3%	36.1%
85:4	33.1%	9.2%	58.2%	67.0%	66.1%	5.4%	3.8%	60.8%	30.0%
86:1	35.2%	12.9%	55.4%	65.1%	63.8%	7.1%	5.7%	56.7%	30.4%
86:2	39.8%	10.2%	59.4%	60.2%	60.1%	6.0%	4.1%	54.1%	35.8%
86:3	42.7%	7.1%	64.8%	57.7%	58.2%	4.6%	2.5%	53.6%	39.4%
86:4	38.7%	7.8%	61.5%	61.4%	61.4%	4.8%	3.0%	56.6%	35.6%
87:1	36.9%	11.1%	55.6%	63.3%	62.5%	6.2%	4.9%	56.3%	32.6%
87:2	40.0%	7.1%	61.0%	60.1%	60.1%	4.3%	2.8%	55.8%	37.1%
87:3	40.4%	10.2%	62.4%	59.9%	60.1%	6.4%	3.8%	53.8%	36.0%
87:4	45.3%	4.3%	61.8%	54.8%	55.1%	2.7%	1.6%	52.4%	43.3%
88:1	36.7%	13.4%	59.9%	63.5%	63.0%	8.0%	5.4%	55.0%	31.7%
88:2	37.4%	7.6%	61.3%	62.8%	62.7%	4.7%	2.9%	58.0%	34.4%
88:3	38.4%	8.2%	64.5%	61.8%	62.0%	5.3%	2.9%	56.7%	35.1%
88:4	37.0%	7.8%	63.0%	63.0%	63.0%	4.9%	2.9%	58.1%	34.1%
89:1	36.2%	10.7%	60.0%	63.8%	63.4%	6.4%	4.3%	57.0%	32.3%
89:2	35.9%	11.0%	60.3%	64.3%	63.9%	6.7%	4.4%	57.2%	31.7%
89:3	36.4%	9.2%	59.8%	63.8%	63.4%	5.5%	3.7%	57.9%	32.9%
89:4	39.0%	5.8%	60.3%	61.0%	61.0%	3.5%	2.3%	57.5%	36.7%
90:1	40.1%	5.4%	63.2%	60.0%	60.2%	3.4%	2.0%	56.7%	37.9%
90:2	37.8%	9.4%	60.2%	62.4%	62.2%	5.7%	3.8%	56.6%	34.0%
90:3	45.7%	4.5%	65.2%	54.3%	54.7%	2.9%	1.6%	51.8%	43.7%
90:4	37.6%	8.6%	58.0%	62.4%	62.0%	5.0%	3.6%	57.0%	34.4%
91:1	36.7%	12.3%	58.2%	63.7%	63.1%	7.2%	5.1%	55.9%	31.8%
91:2	40.4%	9.2%	61.3%	59.7%	59.9%	5.6%	3.6%	54.2%	36.6%
91:3	39.8%	8.6%	59.2%	60.3%	60.2%	5.1%	3.5%	55.1%	36.3%
91:4	40.5%	7.4%	58.0%	59.4%	59.3%	4.3%	3.1%	55.0%	37.6%
92:1	43.2%	10.7%	59.5%	56.7%	57.0%	6.4%	4.3%	50.6%	38.7%
92:2	42.9%	7.0%	61.8%	57.1%	57.4%	4.3%	2.7%	53.1%	39.9%
92:3	39.5%	8.3%	59.3%	60.5%	60.4%	4.9%	3.4%	55.4%	36.2%
92:4	37.5%	9.7%	57.9%	62.5%	62.1%	5.6%	4.1%	56.5%	33.8%
93:1	39.4%	11.3%	58.2%	60.7%	60.4%	6.6%	4.7%	53.8%	34.9%
93:2	40.9%	9.3%	59.5%	59.3%	59.3%	5.5%	3.8%	53.8%	36.9%
93:3	39.4%	9.8%	57.5%	60.6%	60.3%	5.6%	4.2%	54.7%	35.6%
93:4	41.7%	8.7%	58.4%	58.3%	58.3%	5.1%	3.6%	53.2%	38.1%
94:1	43.7%	9.7%	58.3%	56.3%	56.5%	5.7%	4.1%	50.8%	39.5%
94:2	42.7%	7.1%	60.0%	57.4%	57.6%	4.3%	2.8%	53.3%	39.6%
94:3	39.8%	8.4%	58.4%	60.2%	60.1%	4.9%	3.5%	55.2%	36.4%
94:4	42.8%	5.8%	60.9%	57.2%	57.4%	3.5%	2.3%	53.9%	40.4%
95:1	38.7%	10.4%	57.5%	61.4%	61.0%	6.0%	4.4%	55.0%	34.6%
95:2	38.9%	11.3%	56.2%	61.0%	60.5%	6.4%	5.0%	54.1%	34.5%
95:3	38.9%	11.1%	55.2%	61.2%	60.5%	6.1%	5.0%	54.4%	34.5%
95:4	40.5%	9.7%	55.9%	59.5%	59.2%	5.4%	4.3%	53.8%	36.5%
96:1	38.9%	10.6%	54.6%	61.3%	60.6%	5.8%	4.8%	54.8%	34.6%
96:2	42.4%	9.6%	59.6%	57.7%	57.9%	5.7%	3.9%	52.2%	38.2%
96:3	40.8%	7.6%	56.3%	59.2%	58.9%	4.3%	3.3%	54.6%	37.7%
96:4	39.8%	10.7%	54.5%	60.2%	59.6%	5.8%	4.9%	53.7%	35.6%
AVG	39.4%	9.0%	60.0%	60.8%	60.6%	5.4%	3.6%	55.3%	35.7%

Table 5.16a
Volume Accumulation Percent Divergence (VAP-D)
Long Return Analysis (Average of all stocks)

Qtr	VAP-D Terminal Wealth	Buy/Hold Terminal Wealth	Relative Terminal Wealth	VAP-D Long Avg Ret	VAP-D Cash Avg Ret	VAP-D Long-Cash Avg Ret	Buy/Hold Avg Ret
85:1	10023	10142	0.988	0.093%	0.003%	0.090%	0.006%
85:2	9984	9700	1.029	-0.053%	-0.070%	0.017%	-0.069%
85:3	9942	8889	1.118	-0.160%	-0.208%	0.048%	-0.205%
85:4	10052	10763	0.934	0.166%	0.104%	0.063%	0.107%
86:1	10058	11428	0.880	0.264%	0.223%	0.040%	0.225%
86:2	10052	10414	0.965	0.165%	0.061%	0.104%	0.066%
86:3	10000	9175	1.090	-0.004%	-0.136%	0.132%	-0.128%
86:4	10028	10413	0.963	0.075%	0.069%	0.006%	0.069%
87:1	10113	11929	0.848	0.431%	0.287%	0.144%	0.293%
87:2	10023	10196	0.983	0.058%	0.037%	0.021%	0.038%
87:3	10020	10408	0.963	0.071%	0.068%	0.003%	0.068%
87:4	9905	8087	1.225	-0.217%	-0.283%	0.065%	-0.278%
88:1	10073	10989	0.917	0.323%	0.157%	0.167%	0.163%
88:2	10053	10593	0.949	0.135%	0.097%	0.037%	0.100%
88:3	10030	10050	0.998	0.089%	0.008%	0.081%	0.013%
88:4	10008	10196	0.982	0.022%	0.037%	-0.016%	0.037%
89:1	10042	10698	0.939	0.155%	0.110%	0.045%	0.112%
89:2	10031	10772	0.931	0.124%	0.122%	0.002%	0.122%
89:3	10060	10833	0.929	0.178%	0.128%	0.050%	0.131%
89:4	9984	9904	1.008	-0.038%	-0.009%	-0.029%	-0.011%
90:1	9997	9980	1.002	-0.008%	0.003%	-0.011%	0.003%
90:2	10009	10459	0.957	0.036%	0.079%	-0.043%	0.077%
90:3	9811	8526	1.151	-0.372%	-0.249%	-0.124%	-0.259%
90:4	10103	10889	0.928	0.272%	0.138%	0.134%	0.146%
91:1	10051	12477	0.806	0.229%	0.318%	-0.089%	0.315%
91:2	10053	10244	0.981	0.143%	0.039%	0.103%	0.045%
91:3	10061	10429	0.965	0.163%	0.059%	0.104%	0.065%
91:4	10052	10497	0.958	0.148%	0.077%	0.072%	0.082%
92:1	9989	10324	0.968	-0.032%	0.051%	-0.083%	0.048%
92:2	9974	9723	1.026	-0.059%	-0.048%	-0.012%	-0.048%
92:3	10032	10392	0.965	0.087%	0.055%	0.033%	0.057%
92:4	10035	10963	0.915	0.114%	0.146%	-0.032%	0.144%
93:1	10033	10527	0.953	0.099%	0.079%	0.020%	0.080%
93:2	10029	10340	0.970	0.065%	0.051%	0.014%	0.052%
93:3	10055	10686	0.941	0.147%	0.098%	0.049%	0.101%
93:4	10030	10255	0.978	0.072%	0.031%	0.041%	0.034%
94:1	9995	9954	1.004	-0.014%	-0.011%	-0.002%	-0.011%
94:2	9999	9994	1.000	-0.004%	-0.005%	0.001%	-0.005%
94:3	10035	10613	0.946	0.090%	0.089%	0.001%	0.089%
94:4	10011	9836	1.018	0.021%	-0.034%	0.054%	-0.029%
95:1	10033	10706	0.937	0.106%	0.110%	-0.004%	0.110%
95:2	10049	10873	0.924	0.161%	0.133%	0.028%	0.134%
95:3	10032	10853	0.924	0.101%	0.133%	-0.032%	0.131%
95:4	10028	10445	0.960	0.075%	0.066%	0.009%	0.067%
96:1	10048	11027	0.911	0.116%	0.162%	-0.046%	0.159%
96:2	10044	10367	0.969	0.103%	0.055%	0.047%	0.059%
96:3	9999	10298	0.971	-0.001%	0.051%	-0.052%	0.047%
96:4	10035	10817	0.928	0.118%	0.122%	-0.005%	0.122%
AVG	10023	10377	0.966	0.064%	0.055%	0.010%	0.055%

Table 5.16b
Volume Accumulation Percent Divergence (VAP-D)
Short Return Analysis (Average of all stocks)

Qtr	VAP-D Terminal Wealth	Buy/Hold Terminal Wealth	Relative Terminal Wealth	VAP-D Short Avg Ret	VAP-D Cash Avg Ret	VAP-D Short-Cash Avg Ret	Buy/Hold Avg Ret
85:1	10009	10142	0.987	-0.009%	0.008%	-0.018%	0.006%
85:2	10035	9700	1.035	-0.058%	-0.070%	0.013%	-0.069%
85:3	10077	8889	1.134	-0.181%	-0.207%	0.026%	-0.205%
85:4	9893	10763	0.919	0.186%	0.099%	0.087%	0.107%
86:1	9846	11428	0.862	0.200%	0.228%	-0.028%	0.225%
86:2	9943	10414	0.955	0.094%	0.063%	0.031%	0.066%
86:3	10141	9175	1.105	-0.316%	-0.113%	-0.202%	-0.128%
86:4	9979	10413	0.958	0.038%	0.072%	-0.034%	0.069%
87:1	9834	11929	0.824	0.248%	0.299%	-0.051%	0.293%
87:2	9993	10196	0.980	0.018%	0.039%	-0.022%	0.038%
87:3	10009	10408	0.962	-0.014%	0.078%	-0.092%	0.068%
87:4	10093	8087	1.248	-0.342%	-0.275%	-0.067%	-0.278%
88:1	9936	10989	0.904	0.073%	0.177%	-0.103%	0.163%
88:2	9972	10593	0.941	0.058%	0.103%	-0.045%	0.100%
88:3	10010	10050	0.996	-0.020%	0.016%	-0.036%	0.013%
88:4	9978	10196	0.979	0.045%	0.036%	0.009%	0.037%
89:1	9923	10698	0.928	0.119%	0.112%	0.007%	0.112%
89:2	9950	10772	0.924	0.070%	0.129%	-0.058%	0.122%
89:3	9929	10833	0.917	0.124%	0.132%	-0.007%	0.131%
89:4	9980	9904	1.008	0.056%	-0.015%	0.071%	-0.011%
90:1	10025	9980	1.005	-0.075%	0.007%	-0.083%	0.003%
90:2	9979	10459	0.954	0.036%	0.081%	-0.045%	0.077%
90:3	10055	8526	1.179	-0.194%	-0.262%	0.068%	-0.259%
90:4	9900	10889	0.909	0.184%	0.143%	0.042%	0.146%
91:1	9886	12477	0.792	0.159%	0.337%	-0.178%	0.315%
91:2	9989	10244	0.975	0.016%	0.048%	-0.032%	0.045%
91:3	9963	10429	0.955	0.070%	0.064%	0.006%	0.065%
91:4	9971	10497	0.950	0.061%	0.083%	-0.022%	0.082%
92:1	9958	10324	0.965	0.063%	0.046%	0.017%	0.048%
92:2	10036	9723	1.032	-0.070%	-0.047%	-0.023%	-0.048%
92:3	9987	10392	0.961	0.024%	0.059%	-0.035%	0.057%
92:4	9904	10963	0.903	0.150%	0.144%	0.006%	0.144%
93:1	9991	10527	0.949	0.017%	0.088%	-0.071%	0.080%
93:2	10013	10340	0.968	-0.018%	0.059%	-0.077%	0.052%
93:3	9935	10686	0.930	0.108%	0.100%	0.008%	0.101%
93:4	9981	10255	0.973	0.036%	0.034%	0.002%	0.034%
94:1	9997	9954	1.004	0.004%	-0.013%	0.017%	-0.011%
94:2	10024	9994	1.003	-0.056%	-0.001%	-0.055%	-0.005%
94:3	9962	10613	0.939	0.072%	0.091%	-0.019%	0.089%
94:4	10020	9836	1.019	-0.059%	-0.027%	-0.032%	-0.029%
95:1	9944	10706	0.929	0.087%	0.113%	-0.026%	0.110%
95:2	9896	10873	0.910	0.149%	0.132%	0.017%	0.134%
95:3	9916	10853	0.914	0.125%	0.132%	-0.006%	0.131%
95:4	9972	10445	0.955	0.048%	0.069%	-0.020%	0.067%
96:1	9939	11027	0.901	0.094%	0.167%	-0.072%	0.159%
96:2	9979	10367	0.963	0.034%	0.061%	-0.027%	0.059%
96:3	9970	10298	0.968	0.065%	0.046%	0.019%	0.047%
96:4	9919	10817	0.917	0.122%	0.122%	0.000%	0.122%
AVG	9972	10377	0.961	0.051%	0.056%	-0.004%	0.055%

Let's now turn our attention to the final divergence technical indicator, the Williams %R Divergence system.

Williams %R Divergence

This system uses the Williams %R Oscillator developed by Larry Williams. This oscillator is very similar to the Stochastic Oscillator described earlier in this chapter. There are two main differences in the construction of these two indicators: (1) the Stochastic Oscillator has internal smoothing, and the Williams %R Oscillator is nonsmoothed; and (2) the Williams %R Oscillator is the inverse of the Stochastic Oscillator. Both of these oscillators compare today's closing price to the prices that have occurred over a given period. The Williams %R considers the difference between today's close and the highest high of the period, and compares it to the trading range of the period. The Stochastic Oscillator considers the difference between today's close and the lowest low of the period, and compares it to the trading range of the period.

Construction

Choose a period, P, to use for the lookback period. Then calculate the Williams %R, using this formula:

WLR = (High in period P − Today's close)/(High in period P − Low in period P).

If the price falls while the Williams %R is rising, trade long. Trade short whenever a price increase is accompanied by a decrease in the Williams %R.

Results

Table 5.17 contains the hit analysis and Table 5.18 contains the return analysis for the Williams %R Divergence (WLR-D) indicator. This indicator produces fewer calls than the similar, nonsmoothed Stochastic Divergence (STO-D) system discussed earlier in this chapter. Overall, the accuracy of the two systems is quite similar.

The WLR-D system makes long calls only 1.6 percent of the time (Table 5.17a). The accuracy rate of these long calls is 59.4 percent. When the indicator favors a cash position over a long position, this call is correct 60.2 percent of the time.

With a short call rate of 3.0 percent, the indicator makes short calls more often than long calls. The hit rate for these short calls is 59.4 percent.

The system has an accuracy rate of 60.7 percent when it chooses a cash position over a short position (Table 5.17b).

The return analysis for this indicator shows that the system makes "good" long calls: it chooses periods of very high daily returns to go long. The average daily stock return for long calls is 0.097 percent (Table 5.18a). This is almost twice as high as the average daily stock return of 0.055 percent, which occurs on days when a cash position is favored over a long position.

Trading long with this system is profitable, but not as profitable as following a simple buy-and-hold strategy. The WLR-D system beat a buy-and-hold strategy in only ten quarters of our test sample. Each of these quarters was characterized by negative average stock returns. In fact, this system performed its best relative to a buy-and-hold strategy during the market crash period of 1987; during the fourth quarter of that year, the long strategy of the WLR-D had a terminal wealth that was more than 25 percent greater than the terminal wealth of the buy-and-hold strategy.

The short return analysis also shows this system falling short of a buy-and-hold strategy. On average, trading short with this system leads to a wealth level that is only 96.8 percent of a buy-and-hold strategy's terminal wealth. In fact, for all but seventeen of the test quarters, the short strategy of the WLR-D system led to losses. On average, an investor beginning a quarter with a $10,000 investment will lose $7 of this capital by the end of the quarter.

On a more positive note, the WLR-D system does seem to be able to distinguish between periods of above- and below-average market performance with its short calls. The average stock return on days when short calls are made is only 0.039 percent (Table 5.18b). The daily stock return over the test period averages 0.055 percent, so this system is predicting days of below-average market performance with its short calls. The problem is that even though these days are characterized by below-average market performance, they are still characterized by positive stock price returns. Thus, being short on these days leads to losses.

Trading long with the WLR-D system is profitable, but it is less profitable than a simple buy-and-hold strategy. Again, we have found a system that makes reasonably good calls but makes calls so infrequently that trading with the system has an extremely high cost of missed profit opportunities.

Table 5.17a
Williams %R Divergence (WLR-D) Long Hit Analysis
(Average of all stocks)

Qtr	Optimal Long	WLR-D Long	Long Hits	Cash Hits	Total Hits	Long Right	Long Wrong	Cash Right	Cash Wrong
85:1	32.1%	0.6%	60.1%	67.9%	67.9%	0.4%	0.3%	67.5%	31.9%
85:2	30.2%	1.1%	59.2%	69.8%	69.7%	0.7%	0.5%	69.0%	29.8%
85:3	26.3%	1.6%	58.2%	73.9%	73.6%	0.9%	0.7%	72.7%	25.7%
85:4	36.6%	0.9%	62.6%	63.4%	63.4%	0.6%	0.3%	62.9%	36.2%
86:1	44.2%	0.9%	63.3%	55.8%	55.9%	0.6%	0.3%	55.3%	43.7%
86:2	39.7%	1.4%	59.4%	60.3%	60.3%	0.8%	0.6%	59.5%	39.1%
86:3	37.0%	2.3%	56.2%	63.1%	62.9%	1.3%	1.0%	61.6%	36.1%
86:4	38.5%	1.2%	61.6%	61.6%	61.6%	0.7%	0.5%	60.8%	38.0%
87:1	44.7%	0.8%	69.3%	55.4%	55.5%	0.5%	0.2%	55.0%	44.3%
87:2	40.0%	2.3%	60.3%	60.1%	60.1%	1.4%	0.9%	58.7%	38.9%
87:3	39.5%	2.0%	59.6%	60.5%	60.5%	1.2%	0.8%	59.3%	38.7%
87:4	37.9%	4.6%	59.4%	62.5%	62.3%	2.7%	1.9%	59.6%	35.8%
88:1	41.3%	0.8%	62.6%	58.7%	58.7%	0.5%	0.3%	58.2%	41.0%
88:2	39.3%	1.6%	59.3%	60.7%	60.7%	1.0%	0.7%	59.8%	38.6%
88:3	35.9%	1.5%	60.2%	64.1%	64.1%	0.9%	0.6%	63.2%	35.3%
88:4	36.3%	1.3%	63.3%	63.7%	63.7%	0.9%	0.5%	62.9%	35.8%
89:1	39.0%	1.1%	63.9%	61.0%	61.0%	0.7%	0.4%	60.3%	38.6%
89:2	40.2%	0.8%	65.6%	59.9%	59.9%	0.5%	0.3%	59.4%	39.8%
89:3	39.9%	1.1%	66.6%	60.1%	60.2%	0.7%	0.4%	59.5%	39.4%
89:4	38.3%	1.9%	63.9%	61.8%	61.8%	1.2%	0.7%	60.6%	37.5%
90:1	36.9%	2.1%	61.7%	63.3%	63.2%	1.3%	0.8%	61.9%	36.0%
90:2	39.2%	1.5%	61.2%	60.9%	60.9%	0.9%	0.6%	60.0%	38.6%
90:3	33.5%	3.1%	52.3%	66.6%	66.1%	1.6%	1.5%	64.5%	32.4%
90:4	40.8%	1.8%	59.3%	59.3%	59.3%	1.0%	0.7%	58.2%	40.0%
91:1	44.1%	0.8%	63.5%	55.9%	56.0%	0.5%	0.3%	55.4%	43.7%
91:2	39.7%	1.4%	57.3%	60.4%	60.4%	0.8%	0.6%	59.6%	39.0%
91:3	40.4%	1.5%	56.0%	59.6%	59.5%	0.8%	0.6%	58.7%	39.8%
91:4	41.2%	2.0%	60.0%	58.9%	58.9%	1.2%	0.8%	57.7%	40.3%
92:1	40.0%	1.3%	51.0%	60.0%	59.8%	0.7%	0.7%	59.1%	39.5%
92:2	38.6%	1.8%	56.0%	61.4%	61.4%	1.0%	0.8%	60.3%	37.8%
92:3	40.3%	1.5%	59.2%	59.8%	59.8%	0.9%	0.6%	58.9%	39.6%
92:4	41.9%	1.2%	61.7%	58.1%	58.2%	0.7%	0.4%	57.4%	41.4%
93:1	42.5%	1.5%	58.1%	57.5%	57.5%	0.9%	0.6%	56.6%	41.8%
93:2	42.1%	1.9%	53.9%	57.9%	57.8%	1.0%	0.9%	56.8%	41.3%
93:3	42.5%	1.4%	59.2%	57.5%	57.6%	0.8%	0.6%	56.8%	41.9%
93:4	41.5%	2.0%	59.1%	58.6%	58.6%	1.2%	0.8%	57.4%	40.6%
94:1	40.4%	1.8%	55.4%	59.6%	59.5%	1.0%	0.8%	58.5%	39.7%
94:2	40.6%	2.5%	56.1%	59.4%	59.3%	1.4%	1.1%	57.9%	39.6%
94:3	41.8%	1.4%	56.1%	58.2%	58.2%	0.8%	0.6%	57.4%	41.2%
94:4	39.5%	3.0%	57.0%	60.6%	60.5%	1.7%	1.3%	58.8%	38.2%
95:1	43.1%	1.4%	60.2%	56.9%	56.9%	0.8%	0.5%	56.1%	42.5%
95:2	43.7%	1.1%	59.2%	56.3%	56.3%	0.7%	0.5%	55.7%	43.2%
95:3	43.9%	1.2%	55.7%	56.0%	56.0%	0.7%	0.5%	55.4%	43.4%
95:4	43.4%	1.5%	57.0%	56.6%	56.6%	0.8%	0.6%	55.7%	42.8%
96:1	45.5%	1.7%	60.5%	54.5%	54.6%	1.1%	0.7%	53.6%	44.7%
96:2	42.1%	1.5%	54.7%	57.9%	57.9%	0.8%	0.7%	57.1%	41.5%
96:3	42.6%	3.0%	58.1%	57.5%	57.5%	1.8%	1.3%	55.7%	41.2%
96:4	44.3%	1.0%	57.6%	55.7%	55.8%	0.6%	0.4%	55.2%	43.8%
AVG	40.0%	1.6%	59.4%	60.2%	60.2%	1.0%	0.7%	59.2%	39.2%

Table 5.17b
Williams %R Divergence (WLR-D) Short Hit Analysis
(Average of all stocks)

Qtr	Optimal Short	WLR-D Short	Short Hits	Cash Hits	Total Hits	Short Right	Short Wrong	Cash Right	Cash Wrong
85:1	34.3%	3.8%	67.5%	65.8%	65.9%	2.6%	1.2%	63.3%	32.9%
85:2	34.6%	3.0%	66.3%	65.4%	65.5%	2.0%	1.0%	63.5%	33.5%
85:3	38.6%	2.2%	74.1%	61.5%	61.8%	1.7%	0.6%	60.1%	37.6%
85:4	33.1%	3.5%	56.5%	67.0%	66.6%	2.0%	1.5%	64.7%	31.9%
86:1	35.2%	4.4%	55.0%	65.0%	64.6%	2.4%	2.0%	62.1%	33.4%
86:2	39.8%	3.4%	60.9%	60.3%	60.3%	2.1%	1.3%	58.3%	38.3%
86:3	42.7%	2.7%	61.9%	57.4%	57.5%	1.7%	1.0%	55.9%	41.4%
86:4	38.7%	2.5%	59.7%	61.4%	61.3%	1.5%	1.0%	59.8%	37.6%
87:1	36.9%	3.5%	56.9%	63.1%	62.9%	2.0%	1.5%	61.0%	35.6%
87:2	40.0%	2.1%	62.7%	60.1%	60.2%	1.3%	0.8%	58.9%	39.1%
87:3	40.4%	2.9%	62.8%	59.7%	59.8%	1.8%	1.1%	58.0%	39.2%
87:4	45.3%	1.7%	61.7%	54.8%	54.9%	1.1%	0.7%	53.8%	44.5%
88:1	36.7%	5.7%	60.1%	63.5%	63.3%	3.4%	2.3%	59.9%	34.4%
88:2	37.4%	2.6%	59.8%	62.6%	62.5%	1.6%	1.0%	60.9%	36.5%
88:3	38.4%	2.3%	66.5%	61.7%	61.8%	1.5%	0.8%	60.3%	37.4%
88:4	37.0%	2.5%	63.4%	63.1%	63.1%	1.6%	0.9%	61.5%	36.0%
89:1	36.2%	3.1%	58.4%	63.8%	63.7%	1.8%	1.3%	61.8%	35.0%
89:2	35.9%	3.1%	58.5%	64.1%	63.9%	1.8%	1.3%	62.1%	34.8%
89:3	36.4%	2.6%	59.6%	63.7%	63.5%	1.6%	1.1%	62.0%	35.4%
89:4	39.0%	2.5%	57.9%	61.1%	61.0%	1.5%	1.1%	59.5%	38.0%
90:1	40.1%	2.4%	63.3%	60.0%	60.1%	1.5%	0.9%	58.5%	39.1%
90:2	37.8%	3.0%	59.4%	62.3%	62.2%	1.8%	1.2%	60.4%	36.5%
90:3	45.7%	1.2%	62.8%	54.4%	54.5%	0.7%	0.4%	53.7%	45.1%
90:4	37.6%	2.8%	57.5%	62.4%	62.3%	1.6%	1.2%	60.7%	36.5%
91:1	36.7%	3.8%	57.4%	63.4%	63.2%	2.2%	1.6%	61.0%	35.2%
91:2	40.4%	2.8%	60.6%	59.7%	59.7%	1.7%	1.1%	58.0%	39.2%
91:3	39.8%	2.7%	58.7%	60.3%	60.2%	1.6%	1.1%	58.6%	38.6%
91:4	40.5%	2.1%	56.7%	59.5%	59.4%	1.2%	0.9%	58.3%	39.6%
92:1	43.2%	4.6%	55.1%	56.7%	56.7%	2.5%	2.1%	54.1%	41.3%
92:2	42.9%	2.7%	60.4%	57.1%	57.2%	1.6%	1.1%	55.6%	41.7%
92:3	39.5%	2.8%	58.8%	60.5%	60.4%	1.6%	1.1%	58.8%	38.4%
92:4	37.5%	3.1%	57.8%	62.6%	62.4%	1.8%	1.3%	60.6%	36.3%
93:1	39.4%	3.6%	59.9%	60.7%	60.7%	2.1%	1.4%	58.5%	37.9%
93:2	40.9%	2.5%	56.6%	59.2%	59.1%	1.4%	1.1%	57.6%	39.8%
93:3	39.4%	3.3%	58.8%	60.7%	60.6%	2.0%	1.4%	58.7%	38.0%
93:4	41.7%	2.7%	55.8%	58.3%	58.2%	1.5%	1.2%	56.8%	40.6%
94:1	43.7%	2.8%	58.1%	56.4%	56.4%	1.6%	1.2%	54.8%	42.4%
94:2	42.7%	2.2%	59.2%	57.3%	57.4%	1.3%	0.9%	56.1%	41.7%
94:3	39.8%	2.9%	57.4%	60.3%	60.2%	1.7%	1.3%	58.5%	38.6%
94:4	42.8%	1.8%	62.2%	57.3%	57.4%	1.1%	0.7%	56.2%	42.0%
95:1	38.7%	3.6%	55.6%	61.4%	61.2%	2.0%	1.6%	59.2%	37.2%
95:2	38.9%	3.7%	55.7%	61.2%	61.0%	2.0%	1.6%	58.9%	37.4%
95:3	38.9%	3.5%	55.9%	61.2%	61.0%	2.0%	1.6%	59.0%	37.5%
95:4	40.5%	3.4%	54.6%	59.5%	59.3%	1.9%	1.5%	57.5%	39.1%
96:1	38.9%	3.1%	54.0%	61.2%	60.9%	1.7%	1.4%	59.3%	37.6%
96:2	42.4%	2.6%	56.5%	57.6%	57.6%	1.5%	1.1%	56.1%	41.3%
96:3	40.8%	2.1%	58.9%	59.2%	59.2%	1.2%	0.9%	58.0%	39.9%
96:4	39.8%	3.7%	55.6%	60.3%	60.1%	2.1%	1.6%	58.0%	38.3%
AVG	39.4%	3.0%	59.4%	60.7%	60.7%	1.7%	1.2%	58.9%	38.1%

Table 5.18a
Williams %R Divergence (WLR-D) Long Return Analysis
(Average of all stocks)

Qtr	WLR-D Terminal Wealth	Buy/Hold Terminal Wealth	Relative Terminal Wealth	WLR-D Long Avg Ret	WLR-D Cash Avg Ret	WLR-D Long-Cash Avg Ret	Buy/Hold Avg Ret
85:1	10001	10142	0.986	0.039%	0.006%	0.033%	0.006%
85:2	9997	9700	1.031	-0.044%	-0.070%	0.026%	-0.069%
85:3	9997	8889	1.125	-0.024%	-0.208%	0.184%	-0.205%
85:4	10020	10763	0.931	0.327%	0.105%	0.222%	0.107%
86:1	10006	11428	0.876	0.098%	0.226%	-0.128%	0.225%
86:2	10015	10414	0.962	0.162%	0.065%	0.097%	0.066%
86:3	10000	9175	1.090	0.006%	-0.131%	0.137%	-0.128%
86:4	10015	10413	0.962	0.190%	0.068%	0.122%	0.069%
87:1	10031	11929	0.841	0.631%	0.290%	0.340%	0.293%
87:2	10014	10196	0.982	0.101%	0.036%	0.064%	0.038%
87:3	10019	10408	0.963	0.145%	0.067%	0.078%	0.068%
87:4	10123	8087	1.252	0.439%	-0.313%	0.751%	-0.278%
88:1	10010	10989	0.911	0.189%	0.163%	0.026%	0.163%
88:2	10011	10593	0.945	0.110%	0.100%	0.010%	0.100%
88:3	10007	10050	0.996	0.070%	0.012%	0.058%	0.013%
88:4	10014	10196	0.982	0.166%	0.035%	0.131%	0.037%
89:1	10005	10698	0.935	0.078%	0.113%	-0.035%	0.112%
89:2	10007	10772	0.929	0.136%	0.122%	0.014%	0.122%
89:3	10020	10833	0.925	0.294%	0.129%	0.164%	0.131%
89:4	10017	9904	1.011	0.141%	-0.014%	0.155%	-0.011%
90:1	10022	9980	1.004	0.173%	-0.001%	0.174%	0.003%
90:2	10006	10459	0.957	0.064%	0.077%	-0.013%	0.077%
90:3	9947	8526	1.167	-0.284%	-0.258%	-0.026%	-0.259%
90:4	10010	10889	0.919	0.090%	0.147%	-0.058%	0.146%
91:1	10018	12477	0.803	0.361%	0.315%	0.047%	0.315%
91:2	10009	10244	0.977	0.106%	0.045%	0.062%	0.045%
91:3	10008	10429	0.960	0.088%	0.065%	0.023%	0.065%
91:4	10025	10497	0.955	0.198%	0.079%	0.119%	0.082%
92:1	9990	10324	0.968	-0.118%	0.050%	-0.168%	0.048%
92:2	9996	9723	1.028	-0.036%	-0.049%	0.012%	-0.048%
92:3	10010	10392	0.963	0.105%	0.056%	0.049%	0.057%
92:4	10009	10963	0.913	0.131%	0.145%	-0.014%	0.144%
93:1	10008	10527	0.951	0.092%	0.080%	0.012%	0.080%
93:2	9992	10340	0.966	-0.066%	0.054%	-0.120%	0.052%
93:3	10005	10686	0.936	0.063%	0.102%	-0.039%	0.101%
93:4	10018	10255	0.977	0.149%	0.032%	0.117%	0.034%
94:1	9996	9954	1.004	-0.046%	-0.011%	-0.036%	-0.011%
94:2	9991	9994	1.000	-0.057%	-0.003%	-0.054%	-0.005%
94:3	10006	10613	0.943	0.064%	0.090%	-0.026%	0.089%
94:4	9997	9836	1.016	-0.016%	-0.030%	0.014%	-0.029%
95:1	10010	10706	0.935	0.120%	0.110%	0.010%	0.110%
95:2	10009	10873	0.921	0.134%	0.134%	0.000%	0.134%
95:3	9999	10853	0.921	-0.010%	0.133%	-0.143%	0.131%
95:4	10007	10445	0.958	0.079%	0.067%	0.012%	0.067%
96:1	10024	11027	0.909	0.217%	0.158%	0.059%	0.159%
96:2	9995	10367	0.964	-0.054%	0.060%	-0.115%	0.059%
96:3	10036	10298	0.975	0.179%	0.043%	0.136%	0.047%
96:4	9999	10817	0.924	-0.010%	0.124%	-0.133%	0.122%
AVG	10010	10377	0.965	0.097%	0.055%	0.043%	0.055%

Table 5.18b
Williams %R Divergence (WLR-D) Short Return Analysis
(Average of all stocks)

Qtr	WLR-D Terminal Wealth	Buy/Hold Terminal Wealth	Relative Terminal Wealth	WLR-D Short Avg Ret	WLR-D Cash Avg Ret	WLR-D Short-Cash Avg Ret	Buy/Hold Avg Ret
85:1	10002	10142	0.986	-0.006%	0.007%	-0.013%	0.006%
85:2	10005	9700	1.032	-0.027%	-0.071%	0.044%	-0.069%
85:3	10038	8889	1.129	-0.263%	-0.203%	-0.059%	-0.205%
85:4	9952	10763	0.925	0.221%	0.103%	0.118%	0.107%
86:1	9947	11428	0.870	0.202%	0.226%	-0.024%	0.225%
86:2	9994	10414	0.960	0.026%	0.068%	-0.041%	0.066%
86:3	10047	9175	1.095	-0.271%	-0.124%	-0.147%	-0.128%
86:4	9998	10413	0.960	0.011%	0.071%	-0.059%	0.069%
87:1	9961	11929	0.835	0.187%	0.297%	-0.110%	0.293%
87:2	10026	10196	0.983	-0.197%	0.043%	-0.240%	0.038%
87:3	10001	10408	0.961	-0.002%	0.070%	-0.072%	0.068%
87:4	10042	8087	1.242	-0.391%	-0.276%	-0.115%	-0.278%
88:1	9990	10989	0.909	0.021%	0.171%	-0.150%	0.163%
88:2	9984	10593	0.943	0.095%	0.100%	-0.005%	0.100%
88:3	10006	10050	0.996	-0.044%	0.014%	-0.058%	0.013%
88:4	9999	10196	0.981	0.006%	0.037%	-0.032%	0.037%
89:1	9978	10698	0.933	0.112%	0.112%	0.000%	0.112%
89:2	9973	10772	0.926	0.142%	0.122%	0.020%	0.122%
89:3	9987	10833	0.922	0.080%	0.132%	-0.053%	0.131%
89:4	10004	9904	1.010	-0.032%	-0.010%	-0.022%	-0.011%
90:1	10013	9980	1.003	-0.088%	0.005%	-0.093%	0.003%
90:2	9995	10459	0.956	0.026%	0.078%	-0.052%	0.077%
90:3	10021	8526	1.175	-0.277%	-0.259%	-0.018%	-0.259%
90:4	9964	10889	0.915	0.203%	0.145%	0.059%	0.146%
91:1	9954	12477	0.798	0.201%	0.319%	-0.118%	0.315%
91:2	10002	10244	0.976	-0.020%	0.047%	-0.067%	0.045%
91:3	9994	10429	0.958	0.032%	0.066%	-0.034%	0.065%
91:4	9981	10497	0.951	0.147%	0.080%	0.067%	0.082%
92:1	9961	10324	0.965	0.144%	0.043%	0.100%	0.048%
92:2	10004	9723	1.029	-0.028%	-0.049%	0.021%	-0.048%
92:3	9993	10392	0.962	0.039%	0.057%	-0.018%	0.057%
92:4	9973	10963	0.910	0.140%	0.145%	-0.005%	0.144%
93:1	10012	10527	0.951	-0.045%	0.084%	-0.130%	0.080%
93:2	9988	10340	0.966	0.073%	0.051%	0.022%	0.052%
93:3	9996	10686	0.935	0.021%	0.104%	-0.082%	0.101%
93:4	9989	10255	0.974	0.067%	0.033%	0.034%	0.034%
94:1	10000	9954	1.005	-0.004%	-0.012%	0.007%	-0.011%
94:2	10007	9994	1.001	-0.050%	-0.004%	-0.046%	-0.005%
94:3	9995	10613	0.942	0.033%	0.091%	-0.058%	0.089%
94:4	10016	9836	1.018	-0.138%	-0.027%	-0.111%	-0.029%
95:1	9983	10706	0.933	0.074%	0.111%	-0.037%	0.110%
95:2	9973	10873	0.917	0.121%	0.134%	-0.013%	0.134%
95:3	9976	10853	0.919	0.109%	0.132%	-0.023%	0.131%
95:4	9981	10445	0.955	0.092%	0.066%	0.027%	0.067%
96:1	9987	11027	0.906	0.068%	0.162%	-0.093%	0.159%
96:2	9983	10367	0.963	0.106%	0.057%	0.048%	0.059%
96:3	9996	10298	0.971	0.024%	0.048%	-0.023%	0.047%
96:4	9988	10817	0.923	0.051%	0.125%	-0.074%	0.122%
AVG	9993	10377	0.963	0.039%	0.056%	-0.017%	0.055%

Chapter

6

Trend Indicators

Trends

One of the basic tenets of the Dow Theory is that security prices do trend. The indicators presented in this chapter are based on this belief. The price of a stock fluctuates on a daily basis, but there also tends to be an upward or downward trend to the stock price. Technical analysts believe that once a trend is formed it will remain intact until broken. Investors can invest with the current trend until it is broken, or they can wait for the trend to be broken and then invest in the direction of the new trend.

Trends are often measured and identified by "trendlines"—lines drawn on charts by connecting two or more prominent points. These prominent points are either troughs or peaks. Low daily prices during an upward trend are troughs. High daily prices during downward trends are peaks. When two or more trough points are connected in an upward trending market, the rising trendline identifies price support. Note that this rising trendline is drawn below the stock prices. When two or more peak points are connected in a downward trending market, the falling trendline identifies price resistance. This falling trendline is drawn above the stock prices.

In this chapter, we explore these trend indicators and test how well they performed over our twelve-year test period. In all, twelve technical indicators are described in this chapter. They range from the extremely conservative Bollinger Bands with ADX (Average Directional Index) system, which makes extremely infrequent calls, to the Stop and Reverse system that is always in the market.

Average Directional Index Breakout

In his book, *New Concepts in Technical Trading Systems*, Welles Wilder describes the concept of directional movement. This system attempts to define an "average" direction for the market and helps to determine whether a stock is trending.

Like the Directional Movement Crossover, discussed in Chapter 3, the Average Directional Index Breakout (ADX-B) is based on two oscillators: +DI, based on an accumulation of higher highs and showing positive directional movement, and –DI, based on lower lows and showing negative directional movement.

Construction

First calculate +DI and –DI, using the technique described under the Directional Movement Crossover indicator in Chapter 3 (page 51). Recall that +DI is the Positive Directional Index and –DI is the Negative Directional Index. Next, form a ratio using the following steps:

$$DIF_i = (+DI_i) - (-DI_i),$$

$$SUM_i = (+DI_i) + (-DI_i),$$

$$AVG_i = (DIF_i/SUM_i) \cdot 100.$$

Calculate the Average Directional Movement Index line:

$$ADX = (AVG_1 + AVG_2 + AVG_3 + \ldots + AVG_P)/P$$

where P is the number of periods.

Choose a level of ADX to use as a trigger line. Typically, an ADX value of 30 is used.

A +DI and –DI crossover is a necessary precondition for trading with the ADX-B system. A long call occurs when +DI crosses above –DI and is followed by the ADX line going above the chosen ADX trigger level. Short calls occur when –DI crosses over +DI and is followed by the ADX line going above the chosen ADX trigger level.

Results

Table 6.1 shows much different results for the Average Directional Index Breakout (ADX-B) system than for the typical system in our sample. The

Table 6.1a
Average Directional Index Breakout (ADX-B)
Long Hit Analysis (Average of all stocks)

Qtr	Optimal Long	ADX-B Long	Long Hits	Cash Hits	Total Hits	Long Right	Long Wrong	Cash Right	Cash Wrong
85:1	32.1%	71.4%	64.3%	71.3%	66.3%	45.9%	25.5%	20.4%	8.2%
85:2	30.2%	62.3%	64.9%	74.8%	68.7%	40.4%	21.8%	28.2%	9.5%
85:3	26.3%	57.0%	60.0%	76.8%	67.2%	34.2%	22.8%	33.1%	10.0%
85:4	36.6%	54.2%	65.6%	66.9%	66.2%	35.6%	18.6%	30.6%	15.2%
86:1	44.2%	77.8%	64.5%	59.0%	63.3%	50.2%	27.7%	13.1%	9.1%
86:2	39.7%	75.6%	59.8%	61.2%	60.2%	45.2%	30.4%	14.9%	9.5%
86:3	37.0%	51.5%	56.4%	62.9%	59.5%	29.1%	22.5%	30.5%	18.0%
86:4	38.5%	48.2%	60.0%	61.0%	60.5%	28.9%	19.3%	31.6%	20.2%
87:1	44.7%	71.8%	61.9%	54.8%	59.9%	44.4%	27.4%	15.4%	12.7%
87:2	40.0%	58.8%	59.2%	58.6%	58.9%	34.8%	24.0%	24.1%	17.1%
87:3	39.5%	68.1%	58.9%	61.1%	59.6%	40.1%	27.9%	19.5%	12.4%
87:4	37.9%	26.1%	50.1%	60.1%	57.5%	13.1%	13.0%	44.4%	29.4%
88:1	41.3%	51.7%	62.8%	56.3%	59.7%	32.5%	19.3%	27.2%	21.1%
88:2	39.3%	63.9%	62.5%	59.0%	61.2%	39.9%	24.0%	21.3%	14.8%
88:3	35.9%	58.4%	61.3%	62.9%	62.0%	35.8%	22.6%	26.2%	15.4%
88:4	36.3%	55.0%	62.7%	62.4%	62.6%	34.5%	20.5%	28.1%	16.9%
89:1	39.0%	68.0%	63.1%	61.0%	62.4%	42.9%	25.1%	19.5%	12.5%
89:2	40.2%	75.2%	63.4%	60.8%	62.8%	47.7%	27.5%	15.1%	9.7%
89:3	39.9%	78.0%	63.0%	61.6%	62.7%	49.1%	28.9%	13.6%	8.5%
89:4	38.3%	53.0%	61.2%	62.3%	61.7%	32.4%	20.6%	29.3%	17.7%
90:1	36.9%	43.0%	59.5%	62.1%	61.0%	25.6%	17.4%	35.4%	21.6%
90:2	39.2%	56.8%	61.6%	60.9%	61.3%	35.0%	21.9%	26.3%	16.9%
90:3	33.5%	43.5%	55.2%	67.7%	62.2%	24.0%	19.5%	38.2%	18.2%
90:4	40.8%	35.4%	62.9%	59.0%	60.4%	22.3%	13.1%	38.1%	26.5%
91:1	44.1%	74.2%	62.6%	55.7%	60.8%	46.4%	27.8%	14.4%	11.5%
91:2	39.7%	79.5%	59.3%	61.2%	59.7%	47.2%	32.3%	12.5%	8.0%
91:3	40.4%	61.3%	60.3%	60.6%	60.4%	37.0%	24.4%	23.4%	15.2%
91:4	41.2%	53.8%	60.0%	59.5%	59.8%	32.3%	21.6%	27.5%	18.7%
92:1	40.0%	66.3%	56.4%	60.5%	57.8%	37.4%	28.9%	20.4%	13.3%
92:2	38.6%	54.2%	57.0%	61.1%	58.9%	30.9%	23.3%	28.0%	17.8%
92:3	40.3%	53.1%	60.4%	60.5%	60.4%	32.1%	21.0%	28.3%	18.5%
92:4	41.9%	57.3%	62.3%	57.5%	60.3%	35.7%	21.6%	24.5%	18.1%
93:1	42.5%	70.9%	60.8%	58.6%	60.1%	43.1%	27.8%	17.0%	12.0%
93:2	42.1%	56.8%	59.0%	58.1%	58.6%	33.5%	23.3%	25.1%	18.1%
93:3	42.5%	58.7%	60.8%	57.9%	59.6%	35.7%	23.0%	23.9%	17.4%
93:4	41.5%	55.2%	57.9%	58.5%	58.2%	32.0%	23.2%	26.2%	18.6%
94:1	40.4%	54.0%	56.7%	61.0%	58.7%	30.6%	23.4%	28.1%	17.9%
94:2	40.6%	33.9%	57.0%	59.4%	58.6%	19.3%	14.6%	39.2%	26.9%
94:3	41.8%	49.2%	59.7%	58.1%	58.9%	29.4%	19.9%	29.5%	21.3%
94:4	39.5%	46.1%	56.6%	60.2%	58.6%	26.1%	20.0%	32.4%	21.4%
95:1	43.1%	57.4%	61.0%	56.9%	59.3%	35.0%	22.4%	24.3%	18.4%
95:2	43.7%	73.8%	60.7%	57.1%	59.7%	44.8%	29.0%	15.0%	11.3%
95:3	43.9%	75.4%	60.6%	57.2%	59.8%	45.7%	29.7%	14.1%	10.5%
95:4	43.4%	63.0%	59.7%	57.9%	59.0%	37.6%	25.4%	21.4%	15.6%
96:1	45.5%	65.1%	60.9%	54.9%	58.8%	39.6%	25.5%	19.2%	15.7%
96:2	42.1%	64.0%	57.2%	58.3%	57.6%	36.6%	27.4%	21.0%	15.0%
96:3	42.6%	41.9%	58.3%	56.8%	57.4%	24.4%	17.5%	33.0%	25.1%
96:4	44.3%	63.9%	59.6%	56.9%	58.6%	38.0%	25.8%	20.6%	15.6%
AVG	40.0%	59.0%	60.2%	60.6%	60.6%	35.7%	23.3%	24.9%	16.1%

Table 6.1b
Average Directional Index Breakout (ADX-B)
Short Hit Analysis (Average of all stocks)

Qtr	Optimal Short	ADX-B Short	Short Hits	Cash Hits	Total Hits	Short Right	Short Wrong	Cash Right	Cash Wrong
85:1	34.3%	28.6%	71.3%	64.3%	66.3%	20.4%	8.2%	45.9%	25.5%
85:2	34.6%	37.7%	74.8%	64.9%	68.7%	28.2%	9.5%	40.4%	21.8%
85:3	38.6%	43.0%	76.8%	60.0%	67.2%	33.1%	10.0%	34.2%	22.8%
85:4	33.1%	45.8%	66.9%	65.6%	66.2%	30.6%	15.2%	35.6%	18.6%
86:1	35.2%	22.2%	59.0%	64.5%	63.3%	13.1%	9.1%	50.2%	27.7%
86:2	39.8%	24.4%	61.2%	59.8%	60.2%	14.9%	9.5%	45.2%	30.4%
86:3	42.7%	48.5%	62.9%	56.4%	59.5%	30.5%	18.0%	29.1%	22.5%
86:4	38.7%	51.8%	61.0%	60.0%	60.5%	31.6%	20.2%	28.9%	19.3%
87:1	36.9%	28.2%	54.8%	61.9%	59.9%	15.4%	12.7%	44.4%	27.4%
87:2	40.0%	41.2%	58.6%	59.2%	58.9%	24.1%	17.1%	34.8%	24.0%
87:3	40.4%	31.9%	61.1%	58.9%	59.6%	19.5%	12.4%	40.1%	27.9%
87:4	45.3%	73.9%	60.1%	50.1%	57.5%	44.4%	29.4%	13.1%	13.0%
88:1	36.7%	48.3%	56.3%	62.8%	59.7%	27.2%	21.1%	32.5%	19.3%
88:2	37.4%	36.1%	59.0%	62.5%	61.2%	21.3%	14.8%	39.9%	24.0%
88:3	38.4%	41.6%	62.9%	61.3%	62.0%	26.2%	15.4%	35.8%	22.6%
88:4	37.0%	45.0%	62.4%	62.7%	62.6%	28.1%	16.9%	34.5%	20.5%
89:1	36.2%	32.0%	61.0%	63.1%	62.4%	19.5%	12.5%	42.9%	25.1%
89:2	35.9%	24.8%	60.8%	63.4%	62.8%	15.1%	9.7%	47.7%	27.5%
89:3	36.4%	22.0%	61.6%	63.0%	62.7%	13.6%	8.5%	49.1%	28.9%
89:4	39.0%	47.0%	62.3%	61.2%	61.7%	29.3%	17.7%	32.4%	20.6%
90:1	40.1%	57.0%	62.1%	59.5%	61.0%	35.4%	21.6%	25.6%	17.4%
90:2	37.8%	43.2%	60.9%	61.6%	61.3%	26.3%	16.9%	35.0%	21.9%
90:3	45.7%	56.5%	67.7%	55.2%	62.2%	38.2%	18.2%	24.0%	19.5%
90:4	37.6%	64.6%	59.0%	62.9%	60.4%	38.1%	26.5%	22.3%	13.1%
91:1	36.7%	25.8%	55.7%	62.6%	60.8%	14.4%	11.5%	46.4%	27.8%
91:2	40.4%	20.5%	61.2%	59.3%	59.7%	12.5%	8.0%	47.2%	32.3%
91:3	39.8%	38.7%	60.6%	60.3%	60.4%	23.4%	15.2%	37.0%	24.4%
91:4	40.5%	46.2%	59.5%	60.0%	59.8%	27.5%	18.7%	32.3%	21.6%
92:1	43.2%	33.7%	60.5%	56.4%	57.8%	20.4%	13.3%	37.4%	28.9%
92:2	42.9%	45.8%	61.1%	57.0%	58.9%	28.0%	17.8%	30.9%	23.3%
92:3	39.5%	46.9%	60.5%	60.4%	60.4%	28.3%	18.5%	32.1%	21.0%
92:4	37.5%	42.7%	57.5%	62.3%	60.3%	24.5%	18.1%	35.7%	21.6%
93:1	39.4%	29.1%	58.6%	60.8%	60.1%	17.0%	12.0%	43.1%	27.8%
93:2	40.9%	43.2%	58.1%	59.0%	58.6%	25.1%	18.1%	33.5%	23.3%
93:3	39.4%	41.3%	57.9%	60.8%	59.6%	23.9%	17.4%	35.7%	23.0%
93:4	41.7%	44.8%	58.5%	57.9%	58.2%	26.2%	18.6%	32.0%	23.2%
94:1	43.7%	46.0%	61.0%	56.7%	58.7%	28.1%	17.9%	30.6%	23.4%
94:2	42.7%	66.1%	59.4%	57.0%	58.6%	39.2%	26.9%	19.3%	14.6%
94:3	39.8%	50.8%	58.1%	59.7%	58.9%	29.5%	21.3%	29.4%	19.9%
94:4	42.8%	53.9%	60.2%	56.6%	58.6%	32.4%	21.4%	26.1%	20.0%
95:1	38.7%	42.6%	56.9%	61.0%	59.3%	24.3%	18.4%	35.0%	22.4%
95:2	38.9%	26.2%	57.1%	60.7%	59.7%	15.0%	11.3%	44.8%	29.0%
95:3	38.9%	24.6%	57.2%	60.6%	59.8%	14.1%	10.5%	45.7%	29.7%
95:4	40.5%	37.0%	57.9%	59.7%	59.0%	21.4%	15.6%	37.6%	25.4%
96:1	38.9%	34.9%	54.9%	60.9%	58.8%	19.2%	15.7%	39.6%	25.5%
96:2	42.4%	36.0%	58.3%	57.2%	57.6%	21.0%	15.0%	36.6%	27.4%
96:3	40.8%	58.1%	56.8%	58.3%	57.4%	33.0%	25.1%	24.4%	17.5%
96:4	39.8%	36.1%	56.9%	59.6%	58.6%	20.6%	15.6%	38.0%	25.8%
AVG	39.4%	41.0%	60.6%	60.2%	60.6%	24.9%	16.1%	35.7%	23.3%

Table 6.2a
Average Directional Index Breakout (ADX-B)
Long Return Analysis (Average of all stocks)

Qtr	ADX-B Terminal Wealth	Buy/Hold Terminal Wealth	Relative Terminal Wealth	ADX-B Long Avg Ret	ADX-B Cash Avg Ret	ADX-B Long-Cash Avg Ret	Buy/Hold Avg Ret
85:1	10100	10142	0.996	0.012%	-0.008%	0.020%	0.006%
85:2	9991	9700	1.030	-0.011%	-0.166%	0.155%	-0.069%
85:3	9437	8889	1.062	-0.170%	-0.251%	0.081%	-0.205%
85:4	10540	10763	0.979	0.151%	0.054%	0.098%	0.107%
86:1	11159	11428	0.976	0.235%	0.189%	0.045%	0.225%
86:2	10303	10414	0.989	0.066%	0.069%	-0.003%	0.066%
86:3	9421	9175	1.027	-0.176%	-0.076%	-0.100%	-0.128%
86:4	10092	10413	0.969	0.035%	0.102%	-0.067%	0.069%
87:1	11192	11929	0.938	0.256%	0.386%	-0.130%	0.293%
87:2	10056	10196	0.986	0.019%	0.065%	-0.047%	0.038%
87:3	10248	10408	0.985	0.060%	0.085%	-0.025%	0.068%
87:4	8803	8087	1.089	-0.748%	-0.112%	-0.636%	-0.278%
88:1	10344	10989	0.941	0.109%	0.220%	-0.111%	0.163%
88:2	10304	10593	0.973	0.078%	0.138%	-0.060%	0.100%
88:3	9933	10050	0.988	-0.017%	0.054%	-0.070%	0.013%
88:4	10042	10196	0.985	0.014%	0.064%	-0.051%	0.037%
89:1	10430	10698	0.975	0.102%	0.134%	-0.031%	0.112%
89:2	10542	10772	0.979	0.114%	0.147%	-0.033%	0.122%
89:3	10612	10833	0.980	0.124%	0.154%	-0.029%	0.131%
89:4	9947	9904	1.004	-0.012%	-0.010%	-0.003%	-0.011%
90:1	9894	9980	0.991	-0.036%	0.032%	-0.068%	0.003%
90:2	10225	10459	0.978	0.064%	0.094%	-0.030%	0.077%
90:3	9431	8526	1.106	-0.216%	-0.292%	0.076%	-0.259%
90:4	10284	10889	0.944	0.126%	0.157%	-0.031%	0.146%
91:1	11341	12477	0.909	0.282%	0.409%	-0.126%	0.315%
91:2	10190	10244	0.995	0.044%	0.051%	-0.007%	0.045%
91:3	10313	10429	0.989	0.076%	0.047%	0.029%	0.065%
91:4	10284	10497	0.980	0.087%	0.076%	0.011%	0.082%
92:1	10189	10324	0.987	0.044%	0.056%	-0.013%	0.048%
92:2	9834	9723	1.011	-0.052%	-0.044%	-0.008%	-0.048%
92:3	10223	10392	0.984	0.063%	0.049%	0.014%	0.057%
92:4	10501	10963	0.958	0.131%	0.162%	-0.031%	0.144%
93:1	10375	10527	0.986	0.081%	0.077%	0.003%	0.080%
93:2	10151	10340	0.982	0.038%	0.070%	-0.032%	0.052%
93:3	10448	10686	0.978	0.111%	0.087%	0.024%	0.101%
93:4	10083	10255	0.983	0.017%	0.055%	-0.038%	0.034%
94:1	10029	9954	1.008	0.007%	-0.033%	0.040%	-0.011%
94:2	9978	9994	0.998	-0.012%	-0.001%	-0.011%	-0.005%
94:3	10273	10613	0.968	0.081%	0.097%	-0.016%	0.089%
94:4	9869	9836	1.003	-0.050%	-0.012%	-0.038%	-0.029%
95:1	10364	10706	0.968	0.099%	0.125%	-0.027%	0.110%
95:2	10615	10873	0.976	0.128%	0.152%	-0.024%	0.134%
95:3	10644	10853	0.981	0.132%	0.128%	0.003%	0.131%
95:4	10288	10445	0.985	0.070%	0.061%	0.009%	0.067%
96:1	10596	11027	0.961	0.141%	0.192%	-0.050%	0.159%
96:2	10195	10367	0.983	0.049%	0.076%	-0.028%	0.059%
96:3	9986	10298	0.970	-0.008%	0.087%	-0.095%	0.047%
96:4	10512	10817	0.972	0.121%	0.124%	-0.003%	0.122%
AVG	10221	10377	0.985	0.056%	0.053%	0.003%	0.055%

Table 6.2b
Average Directional Index Breakout (ADX-B)
Short Return Analysis (Average of all stocks)

Qtr	ADX-B Terminal Wealth	Buy/Hold Terminal Wealth	Relative Terminal Wealth	ADX-B Short Avg Ret	ADX-B Cash Avg Ret	ADX-B Short-Cash Avg Ret	Buy/Hold Avg Ret
85:1	10071	10142	0.993	-0.008%	0.012%	-0.020%	0.006%
85:2	10529	9700	1.085	-0.166%	-0.011%	-0.155%	-0.069%
85:3	10836	8889	1.219	-0.251%	-0.170%	-0.081%	-0.205%
85:4	9901	10763	0.920	0.054%	0.151%	-0.098%	0.107%
86:1	9769	11428	0.855	0.189%	0.235%	-0.045%	0.225%
86:2	9916	10414	0.952	0.069%	0.066%	0.003%	0.066%
86:3	10211	9175	1.113	-0.076%	-0.176%	0.100%	-0.128%
86:4	9672	10413	0.929	0.102%	0.035%	0.067%	0.069%
87:1	9379	11929	0.786	0.386%	0.256%	0.130%	0.293%
87:2	9824	10196	0.964	0.065%	0.019%	0.047%	0.038%
87:3	9826	10408	0.944	0.085%	0.060%	0.025%	0.068%
87:4	10330	8087	1.277	-0.112%	-0.748%	0.636%	-0.278%
88:1	9327	10989	0.849	0.220%	0.109%	0.111%	0.163%
88:2	9680	10593	0.914	0.138%	0.078%	0.060%	0.100%
88:3	9846	10050	0.980	0.054%	-0.017%	0.070%	0.013%
88:4	9803	10196	0.961	0.064%	0.014%	0.051%	0.037%
89:1	9744	10698	0.911	0.134%	0.102%	0.031%	0.112%
89:2	9771	10772	0.907	0.147%	0.114%	0.033%	0.122%
89:3	9795	10833	0.904	0.154%	0.124%	0.029%	0.131%
89:4	10014	9904	1.011	-0.010%	-0.012%	0.003%	-0.011%
90:1	9867	9980	0.989	0.032%	-0.036%	0.068%	0.003%
90:2	9739	10459	0.931	0.094%	0.064%	0.030%	0.077%
90:3	11111	8526	1.303	-0.292%	-0.216%	-0.076%	-0.259%
90:4	9326	10889	0.856	0.157%	0.126%	0.031%	0.146%
91:1	9419	12477	0.755	0.409%	0.282%	0.126%	0.315%
91:2	9927	10244	0.969	0.051%	0.044%	0.007%	0.045%
91:3	9887	10429	0.948	0.047%	0.076%	-0.029%	0.065%
91:4	9765	10497	0.930	0.076%	0.087%	-0.011%	0.082%
92:1	9894	10324	0.958	0.056%	0.044%	0.013%	0.048%
92:2	10133	9723	1.042	-0.044%	-0.052%	0.008%	-0.048%
92:3	9866	10392	0.949	0.049%	0.063%	-0.014%	0.057%
92:4	9568	10963	0.873	0.162%	0.131%	0.031%	0.144%
93:1	9871	10527	0.938	0.077%	0.081%	-0.003%	0.080%
93:2	9815	10340	0.949	0.070%	0.038%	0.032%	0.052%
93:3	9777	10686	0.915	0.087%	0.111%	-0.024%	0.101%
93:4	9854	10255	0.961	0.055%	0.017%	0.038%	0.034%
94:1	10107	9954	1.015	-0.033%	0.007%	-0.040%	-0.011%
94:2	10018	9994	1.002	-0.001%	-0.012%	0.011%	-0.005%
94:3	9711	10613	0.915	0.097%	0.081%	0.016%	0.089%
94:4	10041	9836	1.021	-0.012%	-0.050%	0.038%	-0.029%
95:1	9672	10706	0.903	0.125%	0.099%	0.027%	0.110%
95:2	9760	10873	0.898	0.152%	0.128%	0.024%	0.134%
95:3	9811	10853	0.904	0.128%	0.132%	-0.003%	0.131%
95:4	9867	10445	0.945	0.061%	0.070%	-0.009%	0.067%
96:1	9592	11027	0.870	0.192%	0.141%	0.050%	0.159%
96:2	9833	10367	0.948	0.076%	0.049%	0.028%	0.059%
96:3	9686	10298	0.941	0.087%	-0.008%	0.095%	0.047%
96:4	9727	10817	0.899	0.124%	0.121%	0.003%	0.122%
AVG	9873	10377	0.951	0.053%	0.056%	-0.003%	0.055%

ADX-B system makes many long and short calls. With a long call rate of 59.0 percent (Table 6.1a), this indicator makes long calls more than twice as often as our other indicators. (The average call rate is 27.9 percent.) The hit rate for these long calls is 60.2 percent.

The main shortfall of most of the systems we tested was that they make calls too infrequently. This system definitely does not follow that pattern; it makes more than the optimal number of long calls. In Table 6.2a, we see that the average daily return for long calls is 0.056 percent, which is only slightly above the average return of 0.053 percent for days when cash calls are made. The system is choosing, on average, slightly above-average performance days to go long.

The average quarterly terminal wealth for trading long with this system is $10,221. The long strategy of the ADX-B system was profitable for 75 percent of the test quarters, but it tends not to be as profitable as a buy-and-hold strategy. The terminal wealth of the indicator's strategy averages only 98.5 percent of the terminal wealth of a buy-and-hold strategy.

The ADX-B system's performance for short calls follows the same general pattern (Table 6.1b). Making short calls 41.0 percent of the time, this system exceeds the average system in our test sample. These short calls have a hit rate of 60.6 percent.

These short calls are, on average, correct calls, but trading with them is unprofitable. Table 6.2b shows that the average stock return on the days when these short calls are made is a positive 0.053 percent. The average short call is correct six out of ten times, since the stock's price is depreciating. However, the four times it is not depreciating are characterized by greater positive price movement than the negative price movement that characterizes the other six days.

An investor beginning a quarter with $10,000 and trading short with the ADX-B system will tend to end the quarter with only $9,873. This system's short strategy was unprofitable in all but eleven of the test quarters.

The ADX-B system makes many long and short calls. The system's main problem is its inability, in its calls, to distinguish between above-average and below-average performing periods.

Gap Breakout

Gaps occur when there is a "hole" in price action. For example, if today's low is $30 per share and yesterday's high was $28 per share, prices between $28 and $30 were skipped. When today's low is higher than yesterday's high, forming a hole, a "gap-up" occurs. The size of this gap-up is measured by subtracting yesterday's high from today's low. (In the example above, the gap-up would be $30 – $28 or $2.) This gap, or hole, appears as an empty vertical space between today's prices and yesterday's prices on a bar chart. Gap-downs occur when today's high is below yesterday's low.

The Gap Breakout (GAP-B) system uses gaps to indicate market strength in the direction of the gap. A gap-up suggests that upward price movement will continue; a gap-down suggests that downward price movement will continue.

Construction

Choose an absolute percentage of current price to use as a benchmark. For example, if you choose 5 percent, then today's low must be 5 percent above yesterday's high in order for a signal to be generated by the gap-up. Using an absolute percentage causes the dollar amount of the gap to be larger for a signal to be generated whenever the price is higher.

A long signal is generated whenever today's low exceeds yesterday's high by the chosen percentage amount. A short signal occurs whenever yesterday's low exceeds today's high by the chosen percentage.

Results

Table 6.3 shows that the Gap Breakout (GAP-B) system makes a relatively high number of long and short calls, but at a rate still below the optimal rate. The system makes long calls 37.8 percent of the time and has an accuracy rate of 59.8 percent. Short calls are made 31.5 percent of the time, with a hit rate of 60.6 percent.

Table 6.4 considers the returns an investor trading with this system would reap. The results are disappointing. The system seems to make neither good long nor good short calls. For example, the average daily stock return for long calls is 0.044 percent (Table 6.4a). The average return on days when the system favors a cash position over a long position is 0.062 percent. Thus, the GAP-B system chooses to be in a cash position when there is the greatest amount of stock price appreciation. Traders would do better with actions that directly oppose this system's suggestions—for example, going long when the system suggests cash. Investors would be in the market more often and at a higher daily average return than if they follow the system's suggestions.

We see the same type of perverse calls when we look at the short return analysis (Table 6.4b). The average return of 0.057 percent for short call days exceeds the average daily return of 0.054 percent on days when a cash position is favored over a short position. Thus, this system chooses days of above-average stock price appreciation to go short. Investors do not want to be short on days of positive stock price appreciation; they certainly do not want to follow a rule that puts them in short positions on days of above-average positive stock price appreciation. Because of the tendency of this indicator to make short calls on days with positive returns, trading with this system led to losses in all but ten of the test quarters.

Table 6.3a
Gap Breakout (GAP-B) Long Hit Analysis
(Average of all stocks)

Qtr	Optimal Long	GAP-B Long	Long Hits	Cash Hits	Total Hits	Long Right	Long Wrong	Cash Right	Cash Wrong
85:1	32.1%	54.2%	65.6%	64.4%	65.0%	35.5%	18.6%	29.5%	16.3%
85:2	30.2%	52.1%	65.1%	65.6%	65.4%	33.9%	18.2%	31.4%	16.5%
85:3	26.3%	45.1%	61.6%	69.6%	66.0%	27.8%	17.3%	38.2%	16.7%
85:4	36.6%	52.4%	66.3%	59.2%	62.9%	34.7%	17.7%	28.1%	19.4%
86:1	44.2%	49.5%	64.2%	55.4%	59.8%	31.8%	17.8%	28.0%	22.5%
86:2	39.7%	47.0%	59.1%	60.4%	59.8%	27.8%	19.2%	32.0%	21.0%
86:3	37.0%	29.5%	56.8%	62.8%	61.0%	16.8%	12.7%	44.2%	26.2%
86:4	38.5%	35.0%	60.4%	60.9%	60.7%	21.1%	13.9%	39.6%	25.4%
87:1	44.7%	47.3%	61.9%	55.5%	58.5%	29.3%	18.0%	29.3%	23.5%
87:2	40.0%	32.5%	59.3%	59.7%	59.6%	19.3%	13.3%	40.3%	27.2%
87:3	39.5%	43.5%	57.9%	60.8%	59.5%	25.2%	18.3%	34.3%	22.2%
87:4	37.9%	28.9%	53.5%	61.4%	59.1%	15.5%	13.4%	43.6%	27.5%
88:1	41.3%	52.0%	61.9%	58.4%	60.2%	32.2%	19.8%	28.1%	20.0%
88:2	39.3%	37.4%	62.0%	59.9%	60.7%	23.2%	14.2%	37.5%	25.1%
88:3	35.9%	33.8%	60.1%	63.7%	62.5%	20.3%	13.5%	42.2%	24.0%
88:4	36.3%	29.2%	62.3%	63.3%	63.0%	18.2%	11.0%	44.8%	26.0%
89:1	39.0%	33.2%	63.0%	60.8%	61.6%	20.9%	12.3%	40.6%	26.1%
89:2	40.2%	40.9%	62.8%	59.8%	61.0%	25.7%	15.2%	35.3%	23.8%
89:3	39.9%	41.4%	62.5%	60.5%	61.4%	25.9%	15.5%	35.5%	23.1%
89:4	38.3%	27.9%	60.4%	61.7%	61.3%	16.9%	11.0%	44.5%	27.6%
90:1	36.9%	24.0%	59.5%	62.9%	62.1%	14.3%	9.7%	47.8%	28.2%
90:2	39.2%	32.3%	61.4%	60.6%	60.8%	19.8%	12.5%	41.0%	26.7%
90:3	33.5%	30.1%	54.0%	66.9%	63.0%	16.2%	13.9%	46.7%	23.2%
90:4	40.8%	40.1%	61.2%	59.3%	60.1%	24.5%	15.5%	35.6%	24.4%
91:1	44.1%	57.5%	62.9%	57.5%	60.6%	36.2%	21.4%	24.4%	18.0%
91:2	39.7%	46.9%	58.8%	60.8%	59.9%	27.6%	19.3%	32.3%	20.8%
91:3	40.4%	37.2%	58.4%	59.2%	58.9%	21.7%	15.5%	37.2%	25.6%
91:4	41.2%	33.5%	59.2%	59.2%	59.2%	19.8%	13.6%	39.4%	27.2%
92:1	40.0%	45.5%	56.0%	60.1%	58.2%	25.4%	20.0%	32.8%	21.8%
92:2	38.6%	36.3%	55.4%	61.0%	59.0%	20.1%	16.2%	38.9%	24.8%
92:3	40.3%	35.2%	59.3%	59.4%	59.3%	20.8%	14.3%	38.5%	26.3%
92:4	41.9%	38.4%	62.4%	58.5%	60.0%	23.9%	14.4%	36.0%	25.6%
93:1	42.5%	39.8%	59.7%	57.3%	58.3%	23.8%	16.0%	34.5%	25.7%
93:2	42.1%	33.3%	58.0%	57.8%	57.9%	19.3%	14.0%	38.6%	28.1%
93:3	42.5%	35.2%	59.5%	57.5%	58.3%	21.0%	14.3%	37.3%	27.5%
93:4	41.5%	34.3%	57.6%	58.7%	58.3%	19.7%	14.5%	38.6%	27.1%
94:1	40.4%	34.7%	55.9%	60.0%	58.6%	19.4%	15.3%	39.2%	26.1%
94:2	40.6%	29.8%	56.3%	59.3%	58.4%	16.8%	13.0%	41.6%	28.6%
94:3	41.8%	33.1%	59.1%	58.1%	58.4%	19.6%	13.6%	38.9%	28.0%
94:4	39.5%	26.3%	56.2%	60.5%	59.4%	14.8%	11.5%	44.6%	29.1%
95:1	43.1%	34.0%	60.5%	56.7%	58.0%	20.5%	13.4%	37.4%	28.6%
95:2	43.7%	35.9%	60.1%	56.4%	57.7%	21.6%	14.3%	36.2%	27.9%
95:3	43.9%	37.9%	59.8%	56.5%	57.8%	22.7%	15.2%	35.1%	27.0%
95:4	43.4%	34.4%	59.1%	56.8%	57.6%	20.3%	14.1%	37.3%	28.4%
96:1	45.5%	32.5%	59.4%	54.0%	55.8%	19.3%	13.2%	36.5%	31.0%
96:2	42.1%	34.0%	57.2%	58.1%	57.8%	19.4%	14.5%	38.4%	27.7%
96:3	42.6%	29.2%	59.5%	57.5%	58.1%	17.4%	11.8%	40.7%	30.1%
96:4	44.3%	38.4%	59.5%	56.0%	57.3%	22.9%	15.6%	34.5%	27.1%
AVG	40.0%	37.8%	59.8%	59.8%	59.9%	22.7%	15.0%	37.2%	25.0%

Table 6.3b
Gap Breakout (GAP-B) Short Hit Analysis
(Average of all stocks)

Qtr	Optimal Short	GAP-B Short	Short Hits	Cash Hits	Total Hits	Short Right	Short Wrong	Cash Right	Cash Wrong
85:1	34.3%	29.0%	66.4%	65.5%	65.8%	19.3%	9.7%	46.5%	24.5%
85:2	34.6%	31.3%	68.9%	64.7%	66.0%	21.5%	9.7%	44.5%	24.3%
85:3	38.6%	34.9%	72.6%	60.5%	64.8%	25.4%	9.6%	39.4%	25.7%
85:4	33.1%	25.0%	63.2%	65.7%	65.1%	15.8%	9.2%	49.3%	25.7%
86:1	35.2%	23.2%	57.5%	64.2%	62.7%	13.3%	9.8%	49.4%	27.5%
86:2	39.8%	24.3%	62.6%	59.7%	60.4%	15.2%	9.1%	45.2%	30.5%
86:3	42.7%	36.4%	63.7%	56.3%	59.0%	23.2%	13.2%	35.8%	27.8%
86:4	38.7%	31.2%	61.5%	60.3%	60.6%	19.2%	12.0%	41.5%	27.3%
87:1	36.9%	18.3%	57.2%	62.4%	61.5%	10.5%	7.9%	51.0%	30.7%
87:2	40.0%	42.5%	59.3%	59.8%	59.6%	25.2%	17.3%	34.4%	23.1%
87:3	40.4%	23.6%	60.6%	58.6%	59.1%	14.3%	9.3%	44.7%	31.6%
87:4	45.3%	54.2%	59.7%	52.2%	56.2%	32.3%	21.8%	23.9%	21.9%
88:1	36.7%	29.3%	57.7%	62.2%	60.9%	16.9%	12.4%	44.0%	26.7%
88:2	37.4%	37.0%	59.7%	62.0%	61.2%	22.1%	14.9%	39.1%	23.9%
88:3	38.4%	31.7%	64.7%	60.7%	62.0%	20.5%	11.2%	41.5%	26.8%
88:4	37.0%	35.4%	64.1%	62.1%	62.8%	22.7%	12.7%	40.1%	24.5%
89:1	36.2%	28.4%	61.9%	62.7%	62.4%	17.6%	10.8%	44.8%	26.7%
89:2	35.9%	23.4%	60.6%	63.0%	62.4%	14.2%	9.2%	48.2%	28.4%
89:3	36.4%	22.6%	62.6%	62.7%	62.7%	14.2%	8.5%	48.5%	28.8%
89:4	39.0%	38.6%	63.5%	60.2%	61.5%	24.5%	14.1%	37.0%	24.4%
90:1	40.1%	45.7%	63.2%	58.4%	60.6%	28.9%	16.8%	31.7%	22.6%
90:2	37.8%	34.6%	62.2%	61.2%	61.5%	21.5%	13.1%	40.0%	25.4%
90:3	45.7%	47.6%	67.7%	54.1%	60.6%	32.2%	15.4%	28.3%	24.1%
90:4	37.6%	40.3%	59.7%	61.7%	60.9%	24.0%	16.2%	36.8%	22.9%
91:1	36.7%	24.2%	58.3%	62.8%	61.7%	14.1%	10.1%	47.6%	28.2%
91:2	40.4%	29.8%	61.6%	59.0%	59.8%	18.4%	11.5%	41.4%	28.8%
91:3	39.8%	38.7%	59.6%	59.3%	59.4%	23.0%	15.6%	36.4%	25.0%
91:4	40.5%	35.8%	60.3%	59.7%	59.9%	21.6%	14.2%	38.3%	25.9%
92:1	43.2%	24.2%	61.0%	56.6%	57.7%	14.7%	9.4%	42.9%	32.9%
92:2	42.9%	33.1%	61.2%	56.2%	57.9%	20.3%	12.8%	37.6%	29.3%
92:3	39.5%	32.8%	60.1%	59.7%	59.8%	19.7%	13.1%	40.1%	27.1%
92:4	37.5%	29.2%	59.3%	62.3%	61.5%	17.3%	11.9%	44.1%	26.6%
93:1	39.4%	26.5%	57.5%	60.5%	59.7%	15.2%	11.2%	44.5%	29.0%
93:2	40.9%	34.6%	57.7%	58.9%	58.5%	20.0%	14.6%	38.5%	26.9%
93:3	39.4%	27.0%	57.9%	60.2%	59.6%	15.6%	11.4%	43.9%	29.1%
93:4	41.7%	26.7%	58.9%	58.1%	58.3%	15.7%	11.0%	42.6%	30.7%
94:1	43.7%	28.2%	59.6%	56.1%	57.1%	16.8%	11.4%	40.3%	31.5%
94:2	42.7%	38.7%	60.0%	57.1%	58.2%	23.2%	15.5%	35.0%	26.3%
94:3	39.8%	33.1%	57.8%	59.5%	58.9%	19.2%	14.0%	39.8%	27.1%
94:4	42.8%	35.7%	60.5%	56.6%	58.0%	21.6%	14.1%	36.4%	27.9%
95:1	38.7%	27.1%	57.8%	61.1%	60.2%	15.7%	11.5%	44.5%	28.3%
95:2	38.9%	24.5%	57.0%	60.7%	59.8%	14.0%	10.5%	45.8%	29.7%
95:3	38.9%	23.0%	57.1%	60.7%	59.9%	13.2%	9.9%	46.7%	30.2%
95:4	40.5%	29.2%	58.8%	59.7%	59.4%	17.2%	12.0%	42.2%	28.5%
96:1	38.9%	29.7%	54.7%	60.7%	58.9%	16.2%	13.5%	42.7%	27.6%
96:2	42.4%	33.3%	57.9%	57.6%	57.7%	19.3%	14.0%	38.4%	28.3%
96:3	40.8%	35.2%	57.5%	59.1%	58.5%	20.2%	14.9%	38.3%	26.5%
96:4	39.8%	24.9%	56.9%	60.0%	59.2%	14.2%	10.7%	45.0%	30.0%
AVG	39.4%	31.5%	60.6%	60.1%	60.4%	19.2%	12.3%	41.2%	27.2%

Table 6.4a
Gap Breakout (GAP-B) Long Return Analysis
(Average of all stocks)

Qtr	GAP-B Terminal Wealth	Buy/Hold Terminal Wealth	Relative Terminal Wealth	GAP-B Long Avg Ret	GAP-B Cash Avg Ret	GAP-B Long-Cash Avg Ret	Buy/Hold Avg Ret
85:1	9895	10142	0.976	-0.048%	0.071%	-0.119%	0.006%
85:2	9618	9700	0.992	-0.142%	0.010%	-0.152%	-0.069%
85:3	9282	8889	1.044	-0.287%	-0.137%	-0.150%	-0.205%
85:4	10155	10763	0.944	0.036%	0.185%	-0.149%	0.107%
86:1	10664	11428	0.933	0.213%	0.236%	-0.022%	0.225%
86:2	10134	10414	0.973	0.045%	0.086%	-0.041%	0.066%
86:3	9664	9175	1.053	-0.181%	-0.105%	-0.076%	-0.128%
86:4	10077	10413	0.968	0.039%	0.086%	-0.047%	0.069%
87:1	10851	11929	0.910	0.275%	0.309%	-0.034%	0.293%
87:2	10027	10196	0.983	0.017%	0.048%	-0.031%	0.038%
87:3	10128	10408	0.973	0.051%	0.082%	-0.031%	0.068%
87:4	9538	8087	1.179	-0.257%	-0.286%	0.029%	-0.278%
88:1	10387	10989	0.945	0.124%	0.204%	-0.080%	0.163%
88:2	10140	10593	0.957	0.063%	0.121%	-0.058%	0.100%
88:3	9953	10050	0.990	-0.021%	0.030%	-0.050%	0.013%
88:4	10026	10196	0.983	0.015%	0.046%	-0.031%	0.037%
89:1	10187	10698	0.952	0.091%	0.123%	-0.032%	0.112%
89:2	10269	10772	0.953	0.105%	0.134%	-0.030%	0.122%
89:3	10333	10833	0.954	0.128%	0.133%	-0.006%	0.131%
89:4	9924	9904	1.002	-0.041%	0.001%	-0.042%	-0.011%
90:1	9995	9980	1.001	-0.001%	0.004%	-0.004%	0.003%
90:2	10161	10459	0.972	0.078%	0.076%	0.002%	0.077%
90:3	9554	8526	1.121	-0.244%	-0.265%	0.021%	-0.259%
90:4	10302	10889	0.946	0.120%	0.164%	-0.045%	0.146%
91:1	11643	12477	0.933	0.324%	0.303%	0.020%	0.315%
91:2	10123	10244	0.988	0.048%	0.043%	0.005%	0.045%
91:3	10119	10429	0.970	0.049%	0.074%	-0.025%	0.065%
91:4	10180	10497	0.970	0.078%	0.084%	-0.006%	0.082%
92:1	10089	10324	0.977	0.025%	0.067%	-0.041%	0.048%
92:2	9824	9723	1.010	-0.084%	-0.028%	-0.056%	-0.048%
92:3	10046	10392	0.967	0.019%	0.077%	-0.059%	0.057%
92:4	10418	10963	0.950	0.165%	0.132%	0.033%	0.144%
93:1	10156	10527	0.965	0.059%	0.094%	-0.035%	0.080%
93:2	10085	10340	0.975	0.034%	0.061%	-0.027%	0.052%
93:3	10249	10686	0.959	0.105%	0.099%	0.006%	0.101%
93:4	10052	10255	0.980	0.020%	0.041%	-0.020%	0.034%
94:1	9976	9954	1.002	-0.013%	-0.010%	-0.003%	-0.011%
94:2	9933	9994	0.994	-0.040%	0.010%	-0.050%	-0.005%
94:3	10186	10613	0.960	0.082%	0.093%	-0.010%	0.089%
94:4	9902	9836	1.007	-0.061%	-0.018%	-0.043%	-0.029%
95:1	10210	10706	0.954	0.097%	0.117%	-0.020%	0.110%
95:2	10286	10873	0.946	0.124%	0.140%	-0.016%	0.134%
95:3	10301	10853	0.949	0.125%	0.135%	-0.009%	0.131%
95:4	10127	10445	0.969	0.055%	0.073%	-0.018%	0.067%
96:1	10220	11027	0.927	0.103%	0.186%	-0.084%	0.159%
96:2	10136	10367	0.978	0.064%	0.056%	0.009%	0.059%
96:3	10145	10298	0.985	0.076%	0.036%	0.040%	0.047%
96:4	10299	10817	0.952	0.118%	0.125%	-0.007%	0.122%
AVG	10124	10377	0.976	0.044%	0.062%	-0.019%	0.055%

Table 6.4b
Gap Breakout (GAP-B) Short Return Analysis
(Average of all stocks)

Qtr	GAP-B Terminal Wealth	Buy/Hold Terminal Wealth	Relative Terminal Wealth	GAP-B Short Avg Ret	GAP-B Cash Avg Ret	GAP-B Short-Cash Avg Ret	Buy/Hold Avg Ret
85:1	9952	10142	0.981	0.033%	-0.005%	0.038%	0.006%
85:2	10080	9700	1.039	-0.033%	-0.086%	0.053%	-0.069%
85:3	10367	8889	1.166	-0.157%	-0.230%	0.073%	-0.205%
85:4	9776	10763	0.908	0.148%	0.093%	0.055%	0.107%
86:1	9712	11428	0.850	0.220%	0.226%	-0.006%	0.225%
86:2	9914	10414	0.952	0.061%	0.068%	-0.008%	0.066%
86:3	10162	9175	1.108	-0.073%	-0.159%	0.085%	-0.128%
86:4	9772	10413	0.938	0.116%	0.048%	0.068%	0.069%
87:1	9670	11929	0.811	0.309%	0.289%	0.019%	0.293%
87:2	9854	10196	0.966	0.051%	0.028%	0.022%	0.038%
87:3	9813	10408	0.943	0.125%	0.051%	0.074%	0.068%
87:4	10230	8087	1.265	-0.103%	-0.485%	0.383%	-0.278%
88:1	9538	10989	0.868	0.255%	0.124%	0.131%	0.163%
88:2	9696	10593	0.915	0.130%	0.082%	0.048%	0.100%
88:3	9925	10050	0.987	0.035%	0.002%	0.033%	0.013%
88:4	9864	10196	0.967	0.059%	0.025%	0.034%	0.037%
89:1	9790	10698	0.915	0.121%	0.109%	0.012%	0.112%
89:2	9765	10772	0.907	0.160%	0.111%	0.050%	0.122%
89:3	9813	10833	0.906	0.133%	0.130%	0.002%	0.131%
89:4	10017	9904	1.011	-0.011%	-0.011%	0.000%	-0.011%
90:1	9925	9980	0.994	0.023%	-0.014%	0.037%	0.003%
90:2	9835	10459	0.940	0.074%	0.078%	-0.004%	0.077%
90:3	10882	8526	1.276	-0.278%	-0.241%	-0.037%	-0.259%
90:4	9523	10889	0.875	0.182%	0.122%	0.060%	0.146%
91:1	9575	12477	0.767	0.298%	0.320%	-0.022%	0.315%
91:2	9917	10244	0.968	0.039%	0.048%	-0.009%	0.045%
91:3	9812	10429	0.941	0.077%	0.057%	0.020%	0.065%
91:4	9807	10497	0.934	0.076%	0.085%	-0.009%	0.082%
92:1	9941	10324	0.963	0.042%	0.050%	-0.008%	0.048%
92:2	10049	9723	1.033	-0.021%	-0.062%	0.041%	-0.048%
92:3	9829	10392	0.946	0.084%	0.043%	0.041%	0.057%
92:4	9795	10963	0.894	0.110%	0.159%	-0.049%	0.144%
93:1	9836	10527	0.934	0.101%	0.072%	0.029%	0.080%
93:2	9876	10340	0.955	0.056%	0.049%	0.007%	0.052%
93:3	9831	10686	0.920	0.103%	0.100%	0.003%	0.101%
93:4	9918	10255	0.967	0.051%	0.028%	0.023%	0.034%
94:1	10039	9954	1.009	-0.018%	-0.009%	-0.009%	-0.011%
94:2	10041	9994	1.005	-0.014%	0.001%	-0.014%	-0.005%
94:3	9799	10613	0.923	0.101%	0.083%	0.018%	0.089%
94:4	10025	9836	1.019	-0.011%	-0.040%	0.029%	-0.029%
95:1	9819	10706	0.917	0.109%	0.110%	-0.001%	0.110%
95:2	9800	10873	0.901	0.135%	0.134%	0.001%	0.134%
95:3	9797	10853	0.903	0.144%	0.127%	0.017%	0.131%
95:4	9927	10445	0.950	0.039%	0.078%	-0.040%	0.067%
96:1	9657	11027	0.876	0.189%	0.146%	0.042%	0.159%
96:2	9900	10367	0.955	0.050%	0.063%	-0.013%	0.059%
96:3	9907	10298	0.962	0.042%	0.050%	-0.009%	0.047%
96:4	9831	10817	0.909	0.109%	0.127%	-0.017%	0.122%
AVG	9888	10377	0.953	0.057%	0.054%	0.003%	0.055%

Because of the perverse nature of the GAP-B system's long and short calls, it is difficult to see how investors can consistently profit from using this indicator.

Random Walk Breakout

Michael Poulos defines the "Random Walk Breakout System" in the January 1992 and September 1992 issues of *Technical Analysis of Stocks and Commodities*. Based on the idea that a certain amount of price volatility may occur randomly, this system attempts to measure how much price activity can be attributed to purely random movements. If the stock price moves out of this random walk range, then price is assumed to be trending.

Construction

The Random Walk Breakout System is based on two different plots, the Random Walk of the Highs (RWH) and the Random Walk of the Lows (RWL). To calculate these two plots, first pick a time period, P, to use for lookback.

Let TR_i represent Day i's true range. This true range is calculated as $High_i - Low_i$.

To construct the Random Walk of the Highs (RWH):

$$RWH_i = (H_{i-P+1} - L_i)/(((TR_{i-1} + TR_{i-2} + \ldots + TR_{i-p})/P) \cdot SQRT(P)).$$

To construct the Random Walk of the Lows (RWL):

$$RWL_i = (H_i - L_{i-P+1})/(((TR_{i-1} + TR_{i-2} + \ldots + TR_{i-p})/P) \cdot SQRT(P)).$$

If RWH is less than 1.0 and RWL is greater than −1.0, price movements are considered to be random movements or changes. The Random Walk indicator must move past 1.0 or −1.0 in order to signal that a trend is occurring. The Random Walk Breakout (RWI-B) system makes long calls whenever the RWH goes above 1.0 as long as the RWL is not below −1.0. It trades short when the RWL falls below −1.0 as long as RWH is not above 1.0.

Results

Because the Random Walk Breakout (RWI-B) system will always choose a long or a short position over a neutral cash position, this indicator has a high call rate. Table 6.5 shows that long calls occur 56.2 percent of the time and have a hit rate of 60.1 percent. Short calls occur 43.8 percent of the time and have a hit rate of 60.3 percent.

Table 6.6 shows the return analysis for the RWI-B system. From the results for the long calls, we see that this indicator is good at predicting days when above-average stock price appreciation occurs. The average daily return for long calls is 0.064 percent, almost 50 percent higher than the average return of 0.044 percent when a cash position is favored over a long position.

Even though investors trading long with this indicator have an above-average return on the days when they are in the market, this strategy does not beat a buy-and-hold investment strategy. Trading long with this system results in a quarterly terminal wealth that averages only 98.6 percent of the buy-and-hold terminal wealth. The RWI-B system beats the buy-and-hold strategy in only ten of the test quarters.

In the short return analysis, we see results that parallel the long return analysis. The days when this system favored a short position are the same days when the system did not make long calls. Thus, the short average return of 0.044 percent (Table 6.6b) is identical to the cash average return when the system chose only between long and cash positions. Likewise, the average daily cash return of 0.064 percent when the system chose only between short and cash positions is identical to the average daily return for long positions.

Unfortunately, trading short with this system will be unprofitable. Because the average daily return for short call days is a positive number, shorting securities on these days will lead to losses. An investor trading short with this system over the 48-quarter test period would have lost money in 38 of the quarters. On average, an investor beginning a quarter with $10,000 and trading wholly with the RWI-B system would lose $120.

We now turn our attention to another trend indicator, the Stop and Reverse Crossover system.

Stop and Reverse Crossover

The Stop and Reverse Crossover (SAR-C) technique is another technique developed by Welles Wilder. It is described in his book *New Concepts in Technical Trading Systems* under the title "Parabolic Time/Price System." With this system, a trader is always in a long or short position. Suppose, for example, that you enter into a long position. You remain in that position until a stop and reverse (SAR) signal is generated, at which time you reverse from a long position to a short position. The level of the SAR changes daily and is a function of both price and time. The general idea behind this system is that, for the first few days after a trade is entered into, more room is allowed for market movement. For this time period, a relatively low SAR is used, which tends to keep the trader in the long position. However, as the time horizon expands, the SAR, or the price level at which a reversal will be triggered, increases. This

Table 6.5a
Random Walk Breakout System (RWI-B) Long Hit Analysis
(Average of all stocks)

Qtr	Optimal Long	RWI-B Long	Long Hits	Cash Hits	Total Hits	Long Right	Long Wrong	Cash Right	Cash Wrong
85:1	32.1%	71.8%	65.0%	67.0%	65.6%	46.7%	25.1%	18.9%	9.3%
85:2	30.2%	59.6%	65.0%	70.3%	67.1%	38.7%	20.9%	28.4%	12.0%
85:3	26.3%	46.8%	60.9%	73.0%	67.4%	28.5%	18.3%	38.9%	14.4%
85:4	36.6%	69.4%	65.8%	67.4%	66.3%	45.6%	23.7%	20.6%	10.0%
86:1	44.2%	73.3%	64.2%	58.2%	62.6%	47.1%	26.2%	15.5%	11.2%
86:2	39.7%	60.6%	58.7%	59.7%	59.1%	35.6%	25.0%	23.5%	15.9%
86:3	37.0%	41.6%	55.8%	63.5%	60.3%	23.2%	18.4%	37.1%	21.3%
86:4	38.5%	53.3%	58.9%	60.4%	59.6%	31.4%	21.9%	28.2%	18.5%
87:1	44.7%	77.2%	61.7%	53.5%	59.8%	47.6%	29.6%	12.2%	10.6%
87:2	40.0%	47.0%	59.4%	59.4%	59.4%	27.9%	19.1%	31.5%	21.5%
87:3	39.5%	60.1%	58.9%	60.5%	59.5%	35.4%	24.7%	24.2%	15.8%
87:4	37.9%	23.4%	52.7%	61.4%	59.4%	12.3%	11.1%	47.1%	29.6%
88:1	41.3%	75.6%	62.6%	56.9%	61.2%	47.3%	28.3%	13.9%	10.5%
88:2	39.3%	52.4%	61.7%	60.0%	60.9%	32.3%	20.1%	28.6%	19.0%
88:3	35.9%	48.0%	60.5%	63.3%	62.0%	29.0%	19.0%	32.9%	19.1%
88:4	36.3%	48.8%	61.8%	63.4%	62.6%	30.1%	18.7%	32.4%	18.8%
89:1	39.0%	64.4%	63.0%	61.0%	62.3%	40.5%	23.8%	21.8%	13.9%
89:2	40.2%	70.7%	63.1%	61.0%	62.5%	44.7%	26.1%	17.9%	11.4%
89:3	39.9%	63.1%	62.2%	59.7%	61.2%	39.2%	23.9%	22.0%	14.9%
89:4	38.3%	42.6%	61.2%	62.5%	61.9%	26.1%	16.6%	35.9%	21.5%
90:1	36.9%	43.0%	58.1%	62.5%	60.6%	25.0%	18.0%	35.6%	21.4%
90:2	39.2%	58.0%	60.7%	61.6%	61.1%	35.2%	22.8%	25.9%	16.1%
90:3	33.5%	27.8%	55.5%	67.1%	63.8%	15.4%	12.4%	48.4%	23.8%
90:4	40.8%	52.1%	62.0%	60.5%	61.3%	32.3%	19.8%	29.0%	18.9%
91:1	44.1%	74.8%	62.3%	54.8%	60.4%	46.6%	28.2%	13.8%	11.4%
91:2	39.7%	59.4%	58.7%	58.9%	58.8%	34.8%	24.5%	23.9%	16.7%
91:3	40.4%	53.2%	59.5%	59.4%	59.5%	31.7%	21.5%	27.8%	19.0%
91:4	41.2%	50.6%	59.7%	59.4%	59.6%	30.2%	20.4%	29.4%	20.1%
92:1	40.0%	64.7%	57.5%	61.8%	59.0%	37.2%	27.5%	21.8%	13.5%
92:2	38.6%	46.6%	56.6%	60.8%	58.8%	26.3%	20.2%	32.5%	20.9%
92:3	40.3%	55.5%	60.5%	60.3%	60.4%	33.6%	21.9%	26.8%	17.7%
92:4	41.9%	63.3%	62.4%	58.9%	61.1%	39.5%	23.8%	21.6%	15.1%
93:1	42.5%	64.2%	60.5%	57.2%	59.3%	38.8%	25.4%	20.5%	15.3%
93:2	42.1%	50.9%	58.6%	57.7%	58.1%	29.8%	21.1%	28.3%	20.8%
93:3	42.5%	60.5%	60.7%	57.8%	59.6%	36.7%	23.7%	22.9%	16.7%
93:4	41.5%	50.8%	58.8%	59.1%	58.9%	29.8%	20.9%	29.1%	20.2%
94:1	40.4%	55.1%	56.7%	60.6%	58.4%	31.2%	23.9%	27.2%	17.7%
94:2	40.6%	40.1%	56.5%	59.0%	58.0%	22.7%	17.4%	35.4%	24.5%
94:3	41.8%	54.7%	60.0%	58.1%	59.1%	32.8%	21.9%	26.3%	19.0%
94:4	39.5%	39.6%	56.8%	60.5%	59.0%	22.5%	17.1%	36.5%	23.9%
95:1	43.1%	64.9%	60.7%	57.0%	59.4%	39.4%	25.5%	20.0%	15.1%
95:2	43.7%	67.8%	60.4%	56.7%	59.2%	40.9%	26.9%	18.2%	13.9%
95:3	43.9%	64.9%	60.7%	57.1%	59.5%	39.4%	25.5%	20.0%	15.1%
95:4	43.4%	55.4%	59.8%	58.0%	59.0%	33.2%	22.3%	25.8%	18.7%
96:1	45.5%	59.3%	60.5%	54.6%	58.1%	35.9%	23.4%	22.2%	18.5%
96:2	42.1%	57.0%	57.5%	58.6%	58.0%	32.8%	24.3%	25.2%	17.8%
96:3	42.6%	49.7%	59.9%	58.4%	59.1%	29.8%	20.0%	29.4%	20.9%
96:4	44.3%	63.5%	59.9%	56.7%	58.7%	38.1%	25.5%	20.7%	15.8%
AVG	40.0%	56.2%	60.1%	60.3%	60.6%	34.0%	22.2%	26.6%	17.2%

Table 6.5b
Random Walk Breakout System (RWI-B) Short Hit Analysis
(Average of all stocks)

Qtr	Optimal Short	RWI-B Short	Short Hits	Cash Hits	Total Hits	Short Right	Short Wrong	Cash Right	Cash Wrong
85:1	34.3%	27.6%	66.3%	65.2%	65.5%	18.3%	9.3%	47.2%	25.2%
85:2	34.6%	40.4%	70.3%	65.0%	67.1%	28.4%	12.0%	38.8%	20.9%
85:3	38.6%	53.1%	73.0%	61.0%	67.3%	38.7%	14.3%	28.6%	18.3%
85:4	33.1%	30.6%	67.4%	65.8%	66.3%	20.6%	10.0%	45.7%	23.7%
86:1	35.2%	26.7%	58.2%	64.2%	62.6%	15.5%	11.1%	47.1%	26.3%
86:2	39.8%	39.3%	59.5%	58.8%	59.1%	23.4%	15.9%	35.7%	25.0%
86:3	42.7%	58.3%	63.5%	55.8%	60.3%	37.0%	21.3%	23.2%	18.4%
86:4	38.7%	46.7%	60.4%	58.9%	59.6%	28.2%	18.5%	31.4%	21.9%
87:1	36.9%	22.8%	53.5%	61.7%	59.8%	12.2%	10.6%	47.7%	29.6%
87:2	40.0%	53.0%	59.4%	59.4%	59.4%	31.5%	21.5%	27.9%	19.1%
87:3	40.4%	39.9%	60.5%	58.9%	59.6%	24.2%	15.8%	35.4%	24.7%
87:4	45.3%	76.5%	61.4%	52.7%	59.4%	47.0%	29.5%	12.4%	11.1%
88:1	36.7%	24.4%	56.9%	62.6%	61.2%	13.9%	10.5%	47.3%	28.3%
88:2	37.4%	47.5%	60.1%	61.7%	60.9%	28.6%	19.0%	32.4%	20.1%
88:3	38.4%	52.0%	63.3%	60.5%	62.0%	32.9%	19.1%	29.1%	19.0%
88:4	37.0%	51.1%	63.3%	61.8%	62.6%	32.4%	18.7%	30.2%	18.7%
89:1	36.2%	35.6%	61.0%	63.0%	62.3%	21.7%	13.9%	40.5%	23.8%
89:2	35.9%	29.2%	61.0%	63.1%	62.5%	17.8%	11.4%	44.7%	26.1%
89:3	36.4%	36.9%	59.7%	62.2%	61.2%	22.0%	14.9%	39.2%	23.9%
89:4	39.0%	57.2%	62.5%	61.1%	61.9%	35.7%	21.4%	26.2%	16.6%
90:1	40.1%	56.9%	62.5%	58.1%	60.6%	35.6%	21.3%	25.0%	18.0%
90:2	37.8%	41.9%	61.6%	60.7%	61.1%	25.8%	16.1%	35.3%	22.8%
90:3	45.7%	72.1%	67.1%	55.5%	63.8%	48.4%	23.8%	15.5%	12.4%
90:4	37.6%	47.8%	60.5%	62.0%	61.3%	28.9%	18.9%	32.3%	19.8%
91:1	36.7%	25.2%	54.8%	62.3%	60.4%	13.8%	11.4%	46.6%	28.2%
91:2	40.4%	40.6%	58.8%	58.7%	58.8%	23.9%	16.7%	34.8%	24.5%
91:3	39.8%	46.8%	59.4%	59.5%	59.5%	27.8%	19.0%	31.7%	21.5%
91:4	40.5%	49.4%	59.4%	59.7%	59.6%	29.4%	20.0%	30.2%	20.4%
92:1	43.2%	35.2%	61.8%	57.5%	59.0%	21.8%	13.4%	37.2%	27.6%
92:2	42.9%	53.4%	60.8%	56.5%	58.8%	32.5%	20.9%	26.4%	20.3%
92:3	39.5%	44.5%	60.3%	60.5%	60.4%	26.8%	17.6%	33.6%	21.9%
92:4	37.5%	36.7%	58.9%	62.4%	61.1%	21.6%	15.1%	39.5%	23.8%
93:1	39.4%	35.8%	57.2%	60.5%	59.3%	20.5%	15.3%	38.8%	25.4%
93:2	40.9%	49.0%	57.7%	58.6%	58.1%	28.3%	20.7%	29.9%	21.1%
93:3	39.4%	39.5%	57.8%	60.7%	59.6%	22.8%	16.6%	36.8%	23.8%
93:4	41.7%	49.2%	59.1%	58.8%	58.9%	29.1%	20.1%	29.9%	20.9%
94:1	43.7%	44.9%	60.6%	56.7%	58.4%	27.2%	17.7%	31.2%	23.9%
94:2	42.7%	59.9%	59.0%	56.5%	58.0%	35.4%	24.5%	22.7%	17.4%
94:3	39.8%	45.3%	58.1%	60.0%	59.1%	26.3%	19.0%	32.8%	21.9%
94:4	42.8%	60.4%	60.5%	56.8%	59.0%	36.5%	23.9%	22.5%	17.1%
95:1	38.7%	35.0%	57.0%	60.7%	59.4%	20.0%	15.1%	39.5%	25.5%
95:2	38.9%	32.2%	56.7%	60.4%	59.2%	18.2%	13.9%	41.0%	26.9%
95:3	38.9%	35.1%	57.1%	60.7%	59.5%	20.0%	15.0%	39.4%	25.5%
95:4	40.5%	44.5%	58.0%	59.8%	59.0%	25.8%	18.7%	33.2%	22.3%
96:1	38.9%	40.6%	54.6%	60.5%	58.1%	22.2%	18.4%	35.9%	23.4%
96:2	42.4%	42.9%	58.7%	57.5%	58.0%	25.2%	17.8%	32.8%	24.3%
96:3	40.8%	50.3%	58.4%	59.8%	59.1%	29.4%	20.9%	29.8%	20.0%
96:4	39.8%	36.4%	56.7%	59.9%	58.7%	20.7%	15.8%	38.1%	25.5%
AVG	39.4%	43.8%	60.3%	60.1%	60.6%	26.5%	17.2%	34.0%	22.2%

Table 6.6a
Random Walk Breakout System (RWI-B) Long Return Analysis
(Average of all stocks)

Qtr	RWI-B Terminal Wealth	Buy/Hold Terminal Wealth	Relative Terminal Wealth	RWI-B Long Avg Ret	RWI-B Cash Avg Ret	RWI-B Long-Cash Avg Ret	Buy/Hold Avg Ret
85:1	10027	10142	0.989	-0.004%	0.032%	-0.036%	0.006%
85:2	9790	9700	1.009	-0.067%	-0.072%	0.005%	-0.069%
85:3	9407	8889	1.058	-0.216%	-0.195%	-0.022%	-0.205%
85:4	10587	10763	0.984	0.127%	0.061%	0.066%	0.107%
86:1	11036	11428	0.966	0.224%	0.225%	-0.001%	0.225%
86:2	10119	10414	0.972	0.031%	0.121%	-0.091%	0.066%
86:3	9558	9175	1.042	-0.168%	-0.099%	-0.069%	-0.128%
86:4	9991	10413	0.959	0.002%	0.146%	-0.144%	0.069%
87:1	11235	11929	0.942	0.248%	0.445%	-0.198%	0.293%
87:2	10025	10196	0.983	0.012%	0.061%	-0.049%	0.038%
87:3	10188	10408	0.979	0.054%	0.090%	-0.037%	0.068%
87:4	9614	8087	1.189	-0.257%	-0.284%	0.027%	-0.278%
88:1	10516	10989	0.957	0.116%	0.308%	-0.192%	0.163%
88:2	10212	10593	0.964	0.068%	0.135%	-0.067%	0.100%
88:3	9929	10050	0.988	-0.020%	0.043%	-0.063%	0.013%
88:4	10043	10196	0.985	0.016%	0.056%	-0.040%	0.037%
89:1	10432	10698	0.975	0.109%	0.118%	-0.009%	0.112%
89:2	10503	10772	0.975	0.112%	0.146%	-0.033%	0.122%
89:3	10426	10833	0.962	0.107%	0.172%	-0.065%	0.131%
89:4	9963	9904	1.006	-0.010%	-0.012%	0.002%	-0.011%
90:1	9887	9980	0.991	-0.039%	0.035%	-0.074%	0.003%
90:2	10246	10459	0.980	0.069%	0.087%	-0.018%	0.077%
90:3	9688	8526	1.136	-0.177%	-0.291%	0.114%	-0.259%
90:4	10509	10889	0.965	0.155%	0.137%	0.017%	0.146%
91:1	11339	12477	0.909	0.281%	0.415%	-0.134%	0.315%
91:2	10042	10244	0.980	0.017%	0.087%	-0.070%	0.045%
91:3	10156	10429	0.974	0.043%	0.090%	-0.048%	0.065%
91:4	10221	10497	0.974	0.066%	0.098%	-0.031%	0.082%
92:1	10346	10324	1.002	0.084%	-0.018%	0.102%	0.048%
92:2	9825	9723	1.010	-0.063%	-0.036%	-0.027%	-0.048%
92:3	10213	10392	0.983	0.056%	0.057%	-0.001%	0.057%
92:4	10639	10963	0.970	0.152%	0.131%	0.022%	0.144%
93:1	10313	10527	0.980	0.074%	0.090%	-0.016%	0.080%
93:2	10164	10340	0.983	0.043%	0.061%	-0.018%	0.052%
93:3	10414	10686	0.974	0.102%	0.100%	0.001%	0.101%
93:4	10190	10255	0.994	0.053%	0.014%	0.039%	0.034%
94:1	10042	9954	1.009	0.009%	-0.037%	0.046%	-0.011%
94:2	9933	9994	0.994	-0.030%	0.012%	-0.042%	-0.005%
94:3	10339	10613	0.974	0.092%	0.086%	0.006%	0.089%
94:4	9909	9836	1.007	-0.040%	-0.022%	-0.018%	-0.029%
95:1	10393	10706	0.971	0.093%	0.141%	-0.048%	0.110%
95:2	10534	10873	0.969	0.122%	0.160%	-0.038%	0.134%
95:3	10566	10853	0.974	0.134%	0.125%	0.009%	0.131%
95:4	10290	10445	0.985	0.079%	0.052%	0.027%	0.067%
96:1	10505	11027	0.953	0.132%	0.199%	-0.067%	0.159%
96:2	10247	10367	0.988	0.068%	0.046%	0.022%	0.059%
96:3	10249	10298	0.995	0.077%	0.018%	0.059%	0.047%
96:4	10543	10817	0.975	0.130%	0.109%	0.020%	0.122%
AVG	10236	10377	0.986	0.064%	0.044%	0.020%	0.055%

Table 6.6b
Random Walk Breakout System (RWI-B) Short Return Analysis
(Average of all stocks)

Qtr	RWI-B Terminal Wealth	Buy/Hold Terminal Wealth	Relative Terminal Wealth	RWI-B Short Avg Ret	RWI-B Cash Avg Ret	RWI-B Short-Cash Avg Ret	Buy/Hold Avg Ret
85:1	9960	10142	0.982	0.037%	-0.005%	0.042%	0.006%
85:2	10272	9700	1.059	-0.072%	-0.067%	-0.005%	-0.069%
85:3	10739	8889	1.208	-0.196%	-0.215%	0.019%	-0.205%
85:4	9911	10763	0.921	0.061%	0.127%	-0.066%	0.107%
86:1	9659	11428	0.845	0.225%	0.224%	0.001%	0.225%
86:2	9683	10414	0.930	0.128%	0.027%	0.101%	0.066%
86:3	10328	9175	1.126	-0.097%	-0.170%	0.072%	-0.128%
86:4	9575	10413	0.920	0.147%	0.002%	0.145%	0.069%
87:1	9405	11929	0.788	0.444%	0.249%	0.195%	0.293%
87:2	9786	10196	0.960	0.061%	0.012%	0.049%	0.038%
87:3	9766	10408	0.938	0.090%	0.054%	0.037%	0.068%
87:4	11112	8087	1.374	-0.284%	-0.258%	-0.026%	-0.278%
88:1	9534	10989	0.868	0.308%	0.116%	0.192%	0.163%
88:2	9588	10593	0.905	0.135%	0.068%	0.067%	0.100%
88:3	9842	10050	0.979	0.043%	-0.020%	0.063%	0.013%
88:4	9804	10196	0.962	0.056%	0.016%	0.039%	0.037%
89:1	9741	10698	0.911	0.119%	0.109%	0.010%	0.112%
89:2	9728	10772	0.903	0.146%	0.112%	0.034%	0.122%
89:3	9605	10833	0.887	0.173%	0.107%	0.066%	0.131%
89:4	10027	9904	1.012	-0.012%	-0.009%	-0.003%	-0.011%
90:1	9853	9980	0.987	0.034%	-0.039%	0.073%	0.003%
90:2	9758	10459	0.933	0.088%	0.069%	0.019%	0.077%
90:3	11424	8526	1.340	-0.291%	-0.176%	-0.115%	-0.259%
90:4	9543	10889	0.876	0.138%	0.154%	-0.016%	0.146%
91:1	9411	12477	0.754	0.416%	0.281%	0.135%	0.315%
91:2	9761	10244	0.953	0.087%	0.017%	0.070%	0.045%
91:3	9733	10429	0.933	0.090%	0.043%	0.047%	0.065%
91:4	9663	10497	0.921	0.099%	0.065%	0.034%	0.082%
92:1	10042	10324	0.973	-0.019%	0.084%	-0.103%	0.048%
92:2	10127	9723	1.042	-0.035%	-0.063%	0.028%	-0.048%
92:3	9844	10392	0.947	0.057%	0.056%	0.001%	0.057%
92:4	9696	10963	0.884	0.131%	0.152%	-0.021%	0.144%
93:1	9805	10527	0.931	0.090%	0.074%	0.016%	0.080%
93:2	9803	10340	0.948	0.061%	0.043%	0.018%	0.052%
93:3	9755	10686	0.913	0.101%	0.101%	0.000%	0.101%
93:4	9959	10255	0.971	0.014%	0.053%	-0.039%	0.034%
94:1	10113	9954	1.016	-0.037%	0.009%	-0.046%	-0.011%
94:2	9970	9994	0.998	0.012%	-0.029%	0.041%	-0.005%
94:3	9765	10613	0.920	0.086%	0.092%	-0.006%	0.089%
94:4	10087	9836	1.025	-0.022%	-0.040%	0.019%	-0.029%
95:1	9694	10706	0.905	0.141%	0.093%	0.048%	0.110%
95:2	9686	10873	0.891	0.160%	0.122%	0.039%	0.134%
95:3	9728	10853	0.896	0.125%	0.134%	-0.009%	0.131%
95:4	9860	10445	0.944	0.052%	0.079%	-0.027%	0.067%
96:1	9504	11027	0.862	0.199%	0.132%	0.067%	0.159%
96:2	9879	10367	0.953	0.045%	0.068%	-0.023%	0.059%
96:3	9934	10298	0.965	0.018%	0.077%	-0.059%	0.047%
96:4	9756	10817	0.902	0.109%	0.130%	-0.020%	0.122%
AVG	9880	10377	0.952	0.044%	0.064%	-0.020%	0.055%

causes a narrowing of the range in which the stock price can fluctuate before a reversal is signaled.

Construction

First, an initial SAR (SAR_1) is set to be equal to the highest high (if long) or lowest low (if short) price of the previous trade. This highest high or lowest low is referred to as the extreme price (EP).

$$SAR_1 = EP \text{ for the previous trade.}$$

Second, an initial acceleration factor (AF_1) must be chosen. This acceleration factor is what makes the SAR tighten as time progresses. Typically, AF_1 is set equal to .02. A second SAR is created using the following formula:

$$SAR_2 = SAR_1 + AF_1 \cdot (EP_1 - SAR_1).$$

SAR_2 will exceed SAR_1 because of the time factor considered in the acceleration function. This upward movement on the stop and reverse calculation occurs independently of what is happening to price. SAR_2 may also move because the price has reached a new high (if in a long position).

Each day, the acceleration factor increases, until it reaches some maximum level. Typically, the AF increases by .02 each day. The amount by which the acceleration factor increases each day is referred to as the "Step." Once a maximum level of AF is reached (typically 2), the AF remains at that level until a reversal is signaled. This gives the following formula to calculate the AF each day:

If AF < the maximum level, then $AF_i = AF_{i-1} + Step$; otherwise, $AF_i = AF_{i-1}$.

Each day, a new SAR is calculated using the general formula:

$$SAR_i = SAR_{i-1} + AF_{i-1} \cdot (EP_{i-1} - SAR_{i-1}).$$

This process of calculating a new SAR each day continues until the price penetrates the SAR. At that point, a reversal signal is generated, AF and SAR are reset to initial levels, and the process starts over.

Results

Like the Random Walk Breakout system, the Stop and Reverse Crossover (SAR-C) system always favors a long or a short position over a neutral cash position. This leads to extremely high call rates, as seen in Table 6.7. The system favors long calls more often than short calls. The long call rate is 53.1

percent, and the short call rate is almost 47.0 percent. In addition, the long calls, with a hit rate of 60.4 percent, have a slightly higher accuracy rate than the short calls do.

From the results in Table 6.8, we again see a similarity to the Random Walk Breakout system. The calls of the SAR-C system contain helpful information in that they predict periods of above-average and below-average stock price appreciation. The average daily return for long calls is 0.068 percent; on days when short calls are made, stock prices appreciate by only 0.041 percent.

Unfortunately, this information by itself is not helpful enough for an investor to earn above-average profits. In fact, trading long with this system leads to a terminal wealth that is only 98.6 percent of the terminal wealth of the buy-and-hold investment strategy. Even worse, trading short with the SAR-C system leads to losses.

We have uncovered another technical indicator that is able to give us information by predicting periods of market strength, but is not as strong as we would desire when we look at the returns it brings.

Trendline Break—Long Term

The Trendline Break system creates a trading band around a trendline. The closing stock price must move outside of this band to signal a trend reversal. For example, during an upward trending market, the close must penetrate the lower band to indicate a price reversal and signal a short trade. The wider the band, the lower the price must fall before this reversal is signaled.

In the Trendline Break trading system, trend lines for different lengths of time can be used. For the long-term trendline we are considering here, the trendline is drawn connecting prominent (peak or trough) points spanning one to three months.

Construction

The Trendline Break—Long Term (TLN-BL) trading system is constructed using trendlines that are derived from an advanced Pivot Point algorithm. The Pivot Point algorithm finds consecutive higher lows during the past one to three months and connects them to create upward-sloping lines. Consecutive lower highs are connected to create downward sloping lines.

Bands are drawn around the trendlines to represent the amounts by which prices must pass the trendline before a signal is generated. The system generates long trades when a stock's closing price passes through the upward band of a downward sloping trendline. Short signals occur when a stock's closing price falls through the lower band of an upward sloping trendline.

Table 6.7a
Stop and Reverse Crossover (SAR-C) Long Hit Analysis
(Average of all stocks)

Qtr	Optimal Long	SAR-C Long	Long Hits	Cash Hits	Total Hits	Long Right	Long Wrong	Cash Right	Cash Wrong
85:1	32.1%	57.8%	66.1%	68.2%	67.0%	38.2%	19.6%	28.8%	13.4%
85:2	30.2%	55.5%	64.6%	69.5%	66.8%	35.8%	19.6%	31.0%	13.6%
85:3	26.3%	45.7%	61.5%	73.7%	68.1%	28.1%	17.6%	40.0%	14.3%
85:4	36.6%	64.4%	65.8%	63.4%	64.9%	42.4%	22.0%	22.5%	13.0%
86:1	44.2%	61.1%	64.4%	56.8%	61.5%	39.4%	21.8%	22.1%	16.8%
86:2	39.7%	51.3%	59.0%	59.6%	59.3%	30.3%	21.0%	29.0%	19.7%
86:3	37.0%	44.1%	57.4%	63.3%	60.7%	25.3%	18.8%	35.4%	20.5%
86:4	38.5%	55.1%	60.2%	61.5%	60.8%	33.2%	21.9%	27.6%	17.3%
87:1	44.7%	64.7%	62.1%	54.4%	59.4%	40.2%	24.6%	19.2%	16.1%
87:2	40.0%	49.6%	59.1%	59.1%	59.1%	29.3%	20.3%	29.8%	20.6%
87:3	39.5%	50.2%	59.8%	61.3%	60.5%	30.0%	20.2%	30.5%	19.3%
87:4	37.9%	49.0%	55.5%	61.5%	58.6%	27.2%	21.8%	31.4%	19.6%
88:1	41.3%	59.1%	63.1%	58.6%	61.3%	37.3%	21.8%	24.0%	17.0%
88:2	39.3%	51.4%	61.8%	60.3%	61.1%	31.8%	19.6%	29.3%	19.3%
88:3	35.9%	47.0%	61.3%	63.5%	62.5%	28.8%	18.2%	33.6%	19.3%
88:4	36.3%	49.5%	62.7%	64.1%	63.4%	31.1%	18.5%	32.4%	18.1%
89:1	39.0%	54.9%	63.0%	60.9%	62.1%	34.6%	20.3%	27.5%	17.7%
89:2	40.2%	61.3%	63.7%	60.6%	62.5%	39.0%	22.3%	23.5%	15.3%
89:3	39.9%	53.4%	62.5%	59.6%	61.2%	33.4%	20.0%	27.8%	18.8%
89:4	38.3%	45.9%	60.8%	61.5%	61.2%	27.9%	18.0%	33.2%	20.8%
90:1	36.9%	49.7%	59.3%	63.3%	61.3%	29.5%	20.2%	31.8%	18.5%
90:2	39.2%	51.3%	62.4%	61.8%	62.1%	32.0%	19.3%	30.1%	18.6%
90:3	33.5%	38.9%	54.7%	66.5%	61.9%	21.3%	17.6%	40.7%	20.5%
90:4	40.8%	57.1%	61.3%	58.6%	60.2%	35.0%	22.1%	25.2%	17.7%
91:1	44.1%	59.5%	63.2%	56.7%	60.6%	37.6%	21.9%	23.0%	17.5%
91:2	39.7%	52.5%	58.7%	59.6%	59.1%	30.8%	21.7%	28.3%	19.2%
91:3	40.4%	53.2%	58.7%	58.2%	58.5%	31.2%	21.9%	27.2%	19.6%
91:4	41.2%	50.8%	59.8%	59.9%	59.9%	30.4%	20.4%	29.5%	19.7%
92:1	40.0%	53.9%	56.5%	60.0%	58.1%	30.5%	23.5%	27.6%	18.4%
92:2	38.6%	47.7%	56.4%	60.9%	58.7%	26.9%	20.8%	31.8%	20.5%
92:3	40.3%	55.3%	60.0%	59.3%	59.7%	33.2%	22.1%	26.5%	18.2%
92:4	41.9%	57.5%	62.5%	58.6%	60.9%	36.0%	21.5%	24.9%	17.6%
93:1	42.5%	57.2%	60.5%	57.0%	59.0%	34.6%	22.6%	24.4%	18.4%
93:2	42.1%	49.0%	58.7%	57.6%	58.1%	28.7%	20.2%	29.4%	21.6%
93:3	42.5%	54.9%	60.8%	58.1%	59.6%	33.4%	21.5%	26.2%	18.9%
93:4	41.5%	51.7%	58.7%	58.6%	58.6%	30.3%	21.4%	28.3%	20.0%
94:1	40.4%	51.5%	56.1%	59.7%	57.8%	28.9%	22.6%	28.9%	19.6%
94:2	40.6%	46.8%	56.4%	58.5%	57.5%	26.4%	20.4%	31.1%	22.0%
94:3	41.8%	52.3%	60.4%	58.6%	59.5%	31.6%	20.7%	27.9%	19.7%
94:4	39.5%	47.6%	57.6%	61.1%	59.4%	27.4%	20.2%	32.0%	20.4%
95:1	43.1%	57.4%	61.0%	57.1%	59.3%	.35.0%	22.4%	24.3%	18.3%
95:2	43.7%	58.6%	60.5%	56.1%	58.7%	35.5%	23.1%	23.2%	18.2%
95:3	43.9%	57.0%	60.8%	56.3%	58.9%	34.7%	22.3%	24.2%	18.8%
95:4	43.4%	52.0%	59.9%	57.5%	58.7%	31.1%	20.9%	27.6%	20.4%
96:1	45.5%	53.6%	60.6%	54.3%	57.7%	32.5%	21.1%	25.2%	21.2%
96:2	42.1%	50.5%	57.6%	58.6%	58.1%	29.1%	21.4%	29.0%	20.5%
96:3	42.6%	53.3%	60.2%	58.7%	59.5%	32.1%	21.2%	27.4%	19.2%
96:4	44.3%	55.4%	60.5%	56.7%	58.8%	33.5%	21.9%	25.3%	19.3%
AVG	40.0%	53.1%	60.4%	60.2%	60.5%	32.1%	20.9%	28.3%	18.6%

Table 6.7b
Stop and Reverse Crossover (SAR-C) Short Hit Analysis
(Average of all stocks)

Qtr	Optimal Short	SAR-C Short	Short Hits	Cash Hits	Total Hits	Short Right	Short Wrong	Cash Right	Cash Wrong
85:1	34.3%	42.2%	68.2%	66.1%	67.0%	28.8%	13.4%	38.2%	19.6%
85:2	34.6%	44.5%	69.5%	64.6%	66.8%	31.0%	13.6%	35.8%	19.6%
85:3	38.6%	54.2%	73.6%	61.5%	68.1%	39.9%	14.3%	28.2%	17.6%
85:4	33.1%	35.5%	63.4%	65.8%	64.9%	22.5%	13.0%	42.4%	22.1%
86:1	35.2%	38.8%	56.8%	64.4%	61.5%	22.0%	16.8%	39.4%	21.8%
86:2	39.8%	48.6%	59.5%	59.1%	59.3%	28.9%	19.7%	30.3%	21.0%
86:3	42.7%	55.9%	63.3%	57.4%	60.7%	35.4%	20.5%	25.3%	18.8%
86:4	38.7%	44.9%	61.5%	60.2%	60.8%	27.6%	17.3%	33.2%	21.9%
87:1	36.9%	35.3%	54.4%	62.1%	59.4%	19.2%	16.1%	40.2%	24.6%
87:2	40.0%	50.4%	59.1%	59.1%	59.1%	29.8%	20.6%	29.3%	20.3%
87:3	40.4%	49.8%	61.3%	59.8%	60.5%	30.5%	19.3%	30.0%	20.2%
87:4	45.3%	50.9%	61.6%	55.5%	58.6%	31.3%	19.6%	27.2%	21.9%
88:1	36.7%	40.9%	58.6%	63.2%	61.3%	24.0%	16.9%	37.3%	21.8%
88:2	37.4%	48.6%	60.3%	61.8%	61.1%	29.3%	19.3%	31.8%	19.6%
88:3	38.4%	53.0%	63.5%	61.3%	62.5%	33.6%	19.3%	28.8%	18.2%
88:4	37.0%	50.5%	64.1%	62.7%	63.4%	32.4%	18.1%	31.1%	18.5%
89:1	36.2%	45.1%	60.9%	63.0%	62.1%	27.5%	17.7%	34.6%	20.3%
89:2	35.9%	38.7%	60.6%	63.7%	62.5%	23.5%	15.3%	39.0%	22.3%
89:3	36.4%	46.6%	59.6%	62.5%	61.2%	27.8%	18.8%	33.4%	20.0%
89:4	39.0%	54.1%	61.5%	60.8%	61.2%	33.2%	20.8%	27.9%	18.0%
90:1	40.1%	50.3%	63.3%	59.3%	61.3%	31.8%	18.5%	29.5%	20.2%
90:2	37.8%	48.7%	61.8%	62.4%	62.1%	30.1%	18.6%	32.0%	19.3%
90:3	45.7%	61.0%	66.5%	54.8%	61.9%	40.6%	20.4%	21.4%	17.6%
90:4	37.6%	42.8%	58.5%	61.4%	60.2%	25.0%	17.7%	35.1%	22.1%
91:1	36.7%	40.5%	56.7%	63.2%	60.6%	23.0%	17.5%	37.6%	21.9%
91:2	40.4%	47.5%	59.6%	58.7%	59.1%	28.3%	19.2%	30.8%	21.7%
91:3	39.8%	46.8%	58.2%	58.7%	58.5%	27.2%	19.6%	31.2%	21.9%
91:4	40.5%	49.2%	59.9%	59.8%	59.9%	29.5%	19.7%	30.4%	20.4%
92:1	43.2%	46.0%	60.0%	56.5%	58.1%	27.6%	18.4%	30.5%	23.5%
92:2	42.9%	52.2%	60.9%	56.4%	58.7%	31.8%	20.5%	26.9%	20.8%
92:3	39.5%	44.7%	59.3%	60.0%	59.7%	26.5%	18.2%	33.2%	22.1%
92:4	37.5%	42.5%	58.6%	62.5%	60.9%	24.9%	17.6%	36.0%	21.5%
93:1	39.4%	42.8%	57.0%	60.5%	59.0%	24.4%	18.4%	34.6%	22.6%
93:2	40.9%	51.0%	57.6%	58.7%	58.1%	29.4%	21.6%	28.7%	20.2%
93:3	39.4%	45.1%	58.1%	60.8%	59.6%	26.2%	18.9%	33.4%	21.5%
93:4	41.7%	48.3%	58.6%	58.7%	58.6%	28.3%	20.0%	30.3%	21.4%
94:1	43.7%	48.5%	59.7%	56.1%	57.8%	28.9%	19.6%	28.9%	22.6%
94:2	42.7%	53.2%	58.5%	56.4%	57.5%	31.1%	22.0%	26.4%	20.4%
94:3	39.8%	47.7%	58.6%	60.4%	59.5%	27.9%	19.7%	31.6%	20.7%
94:4	42.8%	52.4%	61.1%	57.6%	59.4%	32.0%	20.4%	27.4%	20.2%
95:1	38.7%	42.6%	57.1%	61.0%	59.3%	24.3%	18.3%	35.0%	22.4%
95:2	38.9%	41.4%	56.1%	60.5%	58.7%	23.2%	18.2%	35.5%	23.1%
95:3	38.9%	43.0%	56.3%	60.8%	58.9%	24.2%	18.8%	34.7%	22.3%
95:4	40.5%	48.0%	57.5%	59.9%	58.7%	27.6%	20.4%	31.1%	20.9%
96:1	38.9%	46.4%	54.3%	60.6%	57.7%	25.2%	21.2%	32.5%	21.1%
96:2	42.4%	49.5%	58.6%	57.6%	58.1%	29.0%	20.5%	29.1%	21.4%
96:3	40.8%	46.7%	58.7%	60.2%	59.5%	27.4%	19.2%	32.1%	21.2%
96:4	39.8%	44.6%	56.7%	60.5%	58.8%	25.3%	19.3%	33.5%	21.9%
AVG	39.4%	46.9%	60.2%	60.4%	60.5%	28.3%	18.6%	32.1%	20.9%

Table 6.8a
Stop and Reverse Crossover (SAR-C) Long Return Analysis
(Average of all stocks)

Qtr	SAR-C Terminal Wealth	Buy/Hold Terminal Wealth	Relative Terminal Wealth	SAR-C Long Avg Ret	SAR-C Cash Avg Ret	SAR-C Long-Cash Avg Ret	Buy/Hold Avg Ret
85:1	10135	10142	0.999	0.029%	-0.025%	0.054%	0.006%
85:2	9773	9700	1.008	-0.075%	-0.062%	-0.013%	-0.069%
85:3	9489	8889	1.068	-0.190%	-0.217%	0.027%	-0.205%
85:4	10415	10763	0.968	0.096%	0.126%	-0.030%	0.107%
86:1	10885	11428	0.952	0.232%	0.213%	0.019%	0.225%
86:2	10128	10414	0.973	0.039%	0.095%	-0.056%	0.066%
86:3	9703	9175	1.058	-0.106%	-0.145%	0.039%	-0.128%
86:4	10173	10413	0.977	0.053%	0.089%	-0.037%	0.069%
87:1	11091	11929	0.930	0.266%	0.343%	-0.077%	0.293%
87:2	10024	10196	0.983	0.011%	0.064%	-0.053%	0.038%
87:3	10339	10408	0.993	0.110%	0.026%	0.083%	0.068%
87:4	9667	8087	1.195	-0.094%	-0.455%	0.361%	-0.278%
88:1	10542	10989	0.959	0.154%	0.176%	-0.022%	0.163%
88:2	10256	10593	0.968	0.085%	0.115%	-0.030%	0.100%
88:3	10010	10050	0.996	0.006%	0.019%	-0.013%	0.013%
88:4	10153	10196	0.996	0.052%	0.022%	0.030%	0.037%
89:1	10417	10698	0.974	0.123%	0.099%	0.024%	0.112%
89:2	10500	10772	0.975	0.129%	0.112%	0.017%	0.122%
89:3	10418	10833	0.962	0.123%	0.140%	-0.017%	0.131%
89:4	9844	9904	0.994	-0.053%	0.025%	-0.078%	-0.011%
90:1	10007	9980	1.003	0.006%	0.000%	0.007%	0.003%
90:2	10367	10459	0.991	0.116%	0.035%	0.081%	0.077%
90:3	9481	8526	1.112	-0.216%	-0.286%	0.070%	-0.259%
90:4	10390	10889	0.954	0.110%	0.195%	-0.085%	0.146%
91:1	11292	12477	0.905	0.347%	0.268%	0.078%	0.315%
91:2	10107	10244	0.987	0.036%	0.056%	-0.021%	0.045%
91:3	10059	10429	0.965	0.016%	0.120%	-0.104%	0.065%
91:4	10307	10497	0.982	0.093%	0.070%	0.023%	0.082%
92:1	10187	10324	0.987	0.053%	0.042%	0.011%	0.048%
92:2	9784	9723	1.006	-0.074%	-0.025%	-0.049%	-0.048%
92:3	10145	10392	0.976	0.037%	0.080%	-0.043%	0.057%
92:4	10604	10963	0.967	0.161%	0.123%	0.038%	0.144%
93:1	10300	10527	0.978	0.082%	0.077%	0.005%	0.080%
93:2	10149	10340	0.982	0.045%	0.058%	-0.013%	0.052%
93:3	10408	10686	0.974	0.113%	0.087%	0.026%	0.101%
93:4	10184	10255	0.993	0.052%	0.014%	0.039%	0.034%
94:1	9969	9954	1.002	-0.012%	-0.010%	-0.002%	-0.011%
94:2	9876	9994	0.988	-0.046%	0.032%	-0.078%	-0.005%
94:3	10361	10613	0.976	0.105%	0.072%	0.033%	0.089%
94:4	9946	9836	1.011	-0.019%	-0.039%	0.020%	-0.029%
95:1	10384	10706	0.970	0.106%	0.116%	-0.010%	0.110%
95:2	10456	10873	0.962	0.123%	0.150%	-0.028%	0.134%
95:3	10464	10853	0.964	0.127%	0.137%	-0.010%	0.131%
95:4	10300	10445	0.986	0.089%	0.043%	0.046%	0.067%
96:1	10505	11027	0.953	0.149%	0.170%	-0.021%	0.159%
96:2	10227	10367	0.987	0.070%	0.047%	0.023%	0.059%
96:3	10333	10298	1.003	0.097%	-0.009%	0.106%	0.047%
96:4	10550	10817	0.975	0.152%	0.085%	0.067%	0.122%
AVG	10231	10377	0.986	0.068%	0.041%	0.027%	0.055%

Table 6.8b
Stop and Reverse Crossover (SAR-C) Short Return Analysis
(Average of all stocks)

Qtr	SAR-C Terminal Wealth	Buy/Hold Terminal Wealth	Relative Terminal Wealth	SAR-C Short Avg Ret	SAR-C Cash Avg Ret	SAR-C Short-Cash Avg Ret	Buy/Hold Avg Ret
85:1	10092	10142	0.995	-0.025%	0.029%	-0.054%	0.006%
85:2	10246	9700	1.056	-0.062%	-0.075%	0.013%	-0.069%
85:3	10815	8889	1.217	-0.216%	-0.191%	-0.025%	-0.205%
85:4	9735	10763	0.905	0.126%	0.096%	0.030%	0.107%
86:1	9507	11428	0.832	0.213%	0.232%	-0.018%	0.225%
86:2	9708	10414	0.932	0.095%	0.039%	0.056%	0.066%
86:3	10492	9175	1.144	-0.145%	-0.106%	-0.039%	-0.128%
86:4	9737	10413	0.935	0.089%	0.053%	0.037%	0.069%
87:1	9282	11929	0.778	0.343%	0.266%	0.077%	0.293%
87:2	9784	10196	0.960	0.064%	0.011%	0.053%	0.038%
87:3	9906	10408	0.952	0.026%	0.110%	-0.083%	0.068%
87:4	11277	8087	1.394	-0.456%	-0.093%	-0.363%	-0.278%
88:1	9553	10989	0.869	0.176%	0.154%	0.022%	0.163%
88:2	9650	10593	0.911	0.115%	0.085%	0.030%	0.100%
88:3	9926	10050	0.988	0.019%	0.006%	0.013%	0.013%
88:4	9918	10196	0.973	0.022%	0.052%	-0.030%	0.037%
89:1	9722	10698	0.909	0.099%	0.123%	-0.024%	0.112%
89:2	9722	10772	0.902	0.112%	0.129%	-0.017%	0.122%
89:3	9594	10833	0.886	0.140%	0.123%	0.017%	0.131%
89:4	9907	9904	1.000	0.025%	-0.053%	0.077%	-0.011%
90:1	9983	9980	1.000	-0.001%	0.006%	-0.007%	0.003%
90:2	9882	10459	0.945	0.035%	0.116%	-0.081%	0.077%
90:3	11164	8526	1.309	-0.287%	-0.215%	-0.071%	-0.259%
90:4	9467	10889	0.869	0.195%	0.110%	0.086%	0.146%
91:1	9385	12477	0.752	0.269%	0.346%	-0.078%	0.315%
91:2	9813	10244	0.958	0.056%	0.036%	0.020%	0.045%
91:3	9651	10429	0.925	0.120%	0.016%	0.104%	0.065%
91:4	9764	10497	0.930	0.070%	0.093%	-0.024%	0.082%
92:1	9875	10324	0.956	0.042%	0.053%	-0.011%	0.048%
92:2	10079	9723	1.037	-0.025%	-0.074%	0.049%	-0.048%
92:3	9782	10392	0.941	0.080%	0.037%	0.043%	0.057%
92:4	9669	10963	0.882	0.123%	0.161%	-0.038%	0.144%
93:1	9798	10527	0.931	0.077%	0.082%	-0.005%	0.080%
93:2	9814	10340	0.949	0.058%	0.045%	0.013%	0.052%
93:3	9763	10686	0.914	0.087%	0.113%	-0.026%	0.101%
93:4	9964	10255	0.972	0.014%	0.052%	-0.039%	0.034%
94:1	10032	9954	1.008	-0.010%	-0.012%	0.002%	-0.011%
94:2	9907	9994	0.991	0.032%	-0.046%	0.078%	-0.005%
94:3	9794	10613	0.923	0.072%	0.105%	-0.033%	0.089%
94:4	10132	9836	1.030	-0.039%	-0.019%	-0.020%	-0.029%
95:1	9694	10706	0.906	0.116%	0.106%	0.010%	0.110%
95:2	9619	10873	0.885	0.150%	0.123%	0.028%	0.134%
95:3	9643	10853	0.889	0.137%	0.127%	0.010%	0.131%
95:4	9874	10445	0.945	0.043%	0.089%	-0.046%	0.067%
96:1	9519	11027	0.863	0.170%	0.149%	0.021%	0.159%
96:2	9856	10367	0.951	0.047%	0.070%	-0.023%	0.059%
96:3	10023	10298	0.973	-0.009%	0.097%	-0.106%	0.047%
96:4	9768	10817	0.903	0.085%	0.152%	-0.067%	0.122%
AVG	9881	10377	0.952	0.041%	0.068%	-0.027%	0.055%

Table 6.9a
Trendline Break—Long Term (TLN-BL) Long Hit Analysis
(Average of all stocks)

Qtr	Optimal Long	TLN-BL Long	Long Hits	Cash Hits	Total Hits	Long Right	Long Wrong	Cash Right	Cash Wrong
85:1	32.1%	45.9%	64.6%	66.4%	65.6%	29.6%	16.2%	36.0%	18.2%
85:2	30.2%	41.0%	65.2%	68.9%	67.4%	26.7%	14.3%	40.6%	18.4%
85:3	26.3%	38.5%	61.3%	73.5%	68.8%	23.6%	14.9%	45.2%	16.3%
85:4	36.6%	39.9%	66.1%	63.4%	64.4%	26.4%	13.6%	38.1%	22.0%
86:1	44.2%	50.0%	64.6%	55.8%	60.2%	32.3%	17.7%	27.9%	22.1%
86:2	39.7%	44.0%	60.2%	59.5%	59.8%	26.5%	17.5%	33.3%	22.7%
86:3	37.0%	28.7%	58.6%	62.8%	61.6%	16.8%	11.9%	44.8%	26.6%
86:4	38.5%	35.8%	60.4%	60.6%	60.5%	21.6%	14.2%	38.9%	25.3%
87:1	44.7%	63.1%	62.0%	54.0%	59.0%	39.1%	24.0%	19.9%	17.0%
87:2	40.0%	48.7%	59.4%	59.2%	59.3%	28.9%	19.8%	30.4%	21.0%
87:3	39.5%	47.5%	59.0%	60.0%	59.5%	28.1%	19.5%	31.5%	21.0%
87:4	37.9%	18.2%	52.6%	61.2%	59.6%	9.6%	8.6%	50.0%	31.7%
88:1	41.3%	32.1%	63.1%	57.7%	59.5%	20.3%	11.9%	39.2%	28.7%
88:2	39.3%	39.3%	62.9%	59.6%	60.9%	24.7%	14.6%	36.2%	24.6%
88:3	35.9%	36.9%	62.0%	63.7%	63.0%	22.9%	14.0%	40.1%	22.9%
88:4	36.3%	39.2%	62.4%	63.3%	62.9%	24.4%	14.7%	38.5%	22.3%
89:1	39.0%	51.1%	63.2%	60.6%	62.0%	32.3%	18.8%	29.7%	19.3%
89:2	40.2%	58.5%	63.2%	59.9%	61.9%	37.0%	21.5%	24.9%	16.6%
89:3	39.9%	58.5%	62.9%	60.0%	61.7%	36.8%	21.7%	24.9%	16.6%
89:4	38.3%	37.4%	61.1%	61.6%	61.4%	22.8%	14.5%	38.6%	24.0%
90:1	36.9%	32.6%	59.6%	62.6%	61.6%	19.4%	13.2%	42.2%	25.2%
90:2	39.2%	45.2%	61.2%	60.4%	60.8%	27.7%	17.5%	33.1%	21.7%
90:3	33.5%	33.2%	53.7%	66.8%	62.4%	17.8%	15.4%	44.6%	22.2%
90:4	40.8%	32.9%	63.0%	59.8%	60.8%	20.7%	12.2%	40.1%	27.0%
91:1	44.1%	57.7%	63.1%	55.6%	59.9%	36.4%	21.3%	23.5%	18.8%
91:2	39.7%	56.6%	59.9%	60.0%	59.9%	33.9%	22.7%	26.0%	17.4%
91:3	40.4%	39.2%	60.5%	59.6%	60.0%	23.7%	15.5%	36.3%	24.5%
91:4	41.2%	35.1%	60.2%	59.1%	59.4%	21.1%	14.0%	38.3%	26.6%
92:1	40.0%	50.5%	56.4%	60.0%	58.2%	28.5%	22.0%	29.7%	19.8%
92:2	38.6%	40.0%	56.9%	61.2%	59.5%	22.8%	17.2%	36.7%	23.3%
92:3	40.3%	41.4%	61.3%	60.0%	60.5%	25.3%	16.0%	35.2%	23.5%
92:4	41.9%	50.2%	62.6%	57.6%	60.1%	31.4%	18.8%	28.7%	21.1%
93:1	42.5%	55.3%	61.0%	57.5%	59.4%	33.8%	21.6%	25.7%	19.0%
93:2	42.1%	43.3%	59.9%	57.7%	58.6%	25.9%	17.4%	32.8%	24.0%
93:3	42.5%	41.4%	61.1%	57.5%	59.0%	25.3%	16.1%	33.7%	24.9%
93:4	41.5%	41.8%	58.5%	58.4%	58.4%	24.4%	17.3%	34.0%	24.2%
94:1	40.4%	39.9%	57.3%	60.2%	59.0%	22.9%	17.0%	36.2%	23.9%
94:2	40.6%	30.2%	57.5%	59.6%	59.0%	17.4%	12.8%	41.6%	28.2%
94:3	41.8%	44.5%	59.5%	57.9%	58.6%	26.5%	18.0%	32.1%	23.4%
94:4	39.5%	40.1%	57.1%	60.4%	59.1%	22.9%	17.2%	36.2%	23.7%
95:1	43.1%	46.6%	61.3%	57.0%	59.0%	28.6%	18.0%	30.4%	23.0%
95:2	43.7%	55.7%	60.6%	55.9%	58.5%	33.8%	21.9%	24.8%	19.5%
95:3	43.9%	52.6%	61.4%	56.4%	59.0%	32.3%	20.3%	26.8%	20.6%
95:4	43.4%	42.0%	60.0%	57.3%	58.5%	25.2%	16.8%	33.3%	24.8%
96:1	45.5%	44.6%	61.4%	54.6%	57.6%	27.4%	17.2%	30.3%	25.2%
96:2	42.1%	45.1%	57.5%	57.8%	57.6%	25.9%	19.2%	31.7%	23.2%
96:3	42.6%	33.5%	59.5%	57.4%	58.1%	19.9%	13.5%	38.2%	28.3%
96:4	44.3%	48.6%	60.3%	56.2%	58.2%	29.3%	19.3%	28.9%	22.5%
AVG	40.0%	43.2%	60.6%	59.9%	60.4%	26.3%	16.9%	34.2%	22.6%

Table 6.9b
Trendline Break—Long Term (TLN-BL) Short Hit Analysis
(Average of all stocks)

Qtr	Optimal Short	TLN-BL Short	Short Hits	Cash Hits	Total Hits	Short Right	Short Wrong	Cash Right	Cash Wrong
85:1	34.3%	17.8%	63.3%	65.3%	64.9%	11.2%	6.5%	53.7%	28.6%
85:2	34.6%	26.3%	68.2%	65.5%	66.2%	17.9%	8.4%	48.2%	25.4%
85:3	38.6%	36.2%	72.2%	61.2%	65.2%	26.2%	10.1%	39.0%	24.8%
85:4	33.1%	36.9%	62.4%	66.0%	64.7%	23.0%	13.9%	41.6%	21.5%
86:1	35.2%	17.9%	57.5%	64.7%	63.4%	10.3%	7.6%	53.1%	29.0%
86:2	39.8%	22.5%	60.2%	60.0%	60.0%	13.6%	9.0%	46.5%	31.0%
86:3	42.7%	47.5%	62.8%	56.9%	59.7%	29.8%	17.7%	29.9%	22.7%
86:4	38.7%	49.2%	60.5%	60.6%	60.6%	29.7%	19.4%	30.8%	20.0%
87:1	36.9%	20.4%	52.6%	61.9%	60.0%	10.7%	9.7%	49.3%	30.3%
87:2	40.0%	35.8%	59.0%	59.1%	59.1%	21.1%	14.7%	38.0%	26.2%
87:3	40.4%	32.8%	60.1%	58.7%	59.2%	19.7%	13.1%	39.5%	27.8%
87:4	45.3%	68.1%	60.6%	53.0%	58.1%	41.2%	26.8%	16.9%	15.0%
88:1	36.7%	58.2%	57.4%	63.1%	59.8%	33.4%	24.8%	26.4%	15.4%
88:2	37.4%	51.1%	59.4%	62.6%	61.0%	30.4%	20.7%	30.6%	18.3%
88:3	38.4%	50.7%	63.4%	61.7%	62.6%	32.2%	18.5%	30.4%	18.9%
88:4	37.0%	48.5%	63.4%	62.4%	62.9%	30.8%	17.8%	32.1%	19.3%
89:1	36.2%	34.2%	60.9%	63.0%	62.3%	20.8%	13.3%	41.5%	24.3%
89:2	35.9%	23.0%	60.5%	63.0%	62.5%	13.9%	9.1%	48.6%	28.5%
89:3	36.4%	20.1%	60.9%	62.9%	62.5%	12.2%	7.9%	50.2%	29.7%
89:4	39.0%	45.1%	61.8%	60.9%	61.3%	27.9%	17.2%	33.4%	21.5%
90:1	40.1%	51.3%	62.3%	59.4%	60.9%	32.0%	19.3%	28.9%	19.8%
90:2	37.8%	38.0%	60.9%	61.7%	61.4%	23.1%	14.9%	38.3%	23.8%
90:3	45.7%	47.6%	67.0%	54.2%	60.3%	31.9%	15.7%	28.4%	24.0%
90:4	37.6%	48.5%	59.7%	62.7%	61.2%	28.9%	19.5%	32.3%	19.2%
91:1	36.7%	25.7%	56.1%	63.1%	61.3%	14.4%	11.3%	46.9%	27.4%
91:2	40.4%	24.1%	59.7%	59.1%	59.3%	14.4%	9.7%	44.9%	31.0%
91:3	39.8%	42.9%	60.2%	60.2%	60.2%	25.8%	17.1%	34.4%	22.8%
91:4	40.5%	45.8%	59.5%	59.7%	59.6%	27.3%	18.5%	32.3%	21.8%
92:1	43.2%	27.1%	60.4%	56.6%	57.6%	16.4%	10.7%	41.2%	31.6%
92:2	42.9%	42.6%	61.0%	56.9%	58.6%	26.0%	16.6%	32.7%	24.8%
92:3	39.5%	42.9%	59.8%	61.0%	60.5%	25.7%	17.2%	34.8%	22.3%
92:4	37.5%	33.7%	57.6%	62.4%	60.8%	19.4%	14.3%	41.4%	24.9%
93:1	39.4%	26.8%	58.0%	61.0%	60.2%	15.5%	11.2%	44.7%	28.6%
93:2	40.9%	39.2%	58.2%	59.4%	58.9%	22.8%	16.4%	36.1%	24.7%
93:3	39.4%	39.7%	57.9%	60.5%	59.5%	23.0%	16.7%	36.5%	23.8%
93:4	41.7%	42.4%	58.1%	58.1%	58.1%	24.6%	17.8%	33.5%	24.1%
94:1	43.7%	44.2%	60.6%	56.9%	58.5%	26.8%	17.4%	31.7%	24.1%
94:2	42.7%	56.5%	59.8%	57.5%	58.8%	33.8%	22.7%	25.0%	18.5%
94:3	39.8%	42.6%	57.9%	59.6%	58.9%	24.6%	17.9%	34.2%	23.2%
94:4	42.8%	44.9%	60.4%	57.2%	58.6%	27.1%	17.8%	31.5%	23.6%
95:1	38.7%	38.6%	57.1%	61.2%	59.6%	22.0%	16.6%	37.6%	23.8%
95:2	38.9%	27.3%	56.4%	60.6%	59.5%	15.4%	11.9%	44.1%	28.6%
95:3	38.9%	27.1%	57.1%	60.7%	59.7%	15.5%	11.6%	44.2%	28.7%
95:4	40.5%	36.8%	58.3%	59.6%	59.1%	21.5%	15.3%	37.7%	25.5%
96:1	38.9%	34.9%	54.7%	60.6%	58.5%	19.1%	15.8%	39.5%	25.6%
96:2	42.4%	37.2%	58.0%	57.1%	57.4%	21.5%	15.6%	35.9%	27.0%
96:3	40.8%	50.1%	57.2%	59.2%	58.2%	28.6%	21.4%	29.6%	20.4%
96:4	39.8%	31.9%	56.5%	59.9%	58.8%	18.0%	13.9%	40.8%	27.3%
AVG	39.4%	38.2%	59.9%	60.4%	60.4%	22.9%	15.2%	37.5%	24.4%

Table 6.10a
Trendline Break—Long Term (TLN-BL) Long Return Analysis
(Average of all stocks)

Qtr	TLN-BL Terminal Wealth	Buy/Hold Terminal Wealth	Relative Terminal Wealth	TLN-BL Long Avg Ret	TLN-BL Cash Avg Ret	TLN-BL Long-Cash Avg Ret	Buy/Hold Avg Ret
85:1	9895	10142	0.976	-0.054%	0.058%	-0.112%	0.006%
85:2	9799	9700	1.010	-0.097%	-0.050%	-0.048%	-0.069%
85:3	9530	8889	1.072	-0.218%	-0.196%	-0.022%	-0.205%
85:4	10238	10763	0.951	0.085%	0.121%	-0.037%	0.107%
86:1	10687	11428	0.935	0.217%	0.232%	-0.015%	0.225%
86:2	10109	10414	0.971	0.034%	0.092%	-0.057%	0.066%
86:3	9745	9175	1.062	-0.144%	-0.121%	-0.023%	-0.128%
86:4	10063	10413	0.966	0.031%	0.091%	-0.060%	0.069%
87:1	11057	11929	0.927	0.256%	0.357%	-0.101%	0.293%
87:2	10029	10196	0.984	0.011%	0.063%	-0.052%	0.038%
87:3	10165	10408	0.977	0.057%	0.078%	-0.021%	0.068%
87:4	9401	8087	1.162	-0.539%	-0.220%	-0.319%	-0.278%
88:1	10256	10989	0.933	0.131%	0.178%	-0.046%	0.163%
88:2	10191	10593	0.962	0.083%	0.110%	-0.027%	0.100%
88:3	9989	10050	0.994	0.000%	0.020%	-0.019%	0.013%
88:4	10032	10196	0.984	0.017%	0.049%	-0.032%	0.037%
89:1	10294	10698	0.962	0.096%	0.130%	-0.034%	0.112%
89:2	10403	10772	0.966	0.110%	0.140%	-0.030%	0.122%
89:3	10426	10833	0.962	0.113%	0.156%	-0.043%	0.131%
89:4	9952	9904	1.005	-0.018%	-0.007%	-0.011%	-0.011%
90:1	9980	9980	1.000	-0.007%	0.008%	-0.015%	0.003%
90:2	10194	10459	0.975	0.070%	0.082%	-0.013%	0.077%
90:3	9487	8526	1.113	-0.256%	-0.260%	0.004%	-0.259%
90:4	10343	10889	0.950	0.167%	0.136%	0.032%	0.146%
91:1	11565	12477	0.927	0.299%	0.337%	-0.037%	0.315%
91:2	10135	10244	0.989	0.044%	0.047%	-0.003%	0.045%
91:3	10155	10429	0.974	0.059%	0.069%	-0.010%	0.065%
91:4	10206	10497	0.972	0.103%	0.070%	0.033%	0.082%
92:1	10109	10324	0.979	0.036%	0.061%	-0.025%	0.048%
92:2	9880	9723	1.016	-0.049%	-0.048%	-0.001%	-0.048%
92:3	10206	10392	0.982	0.071%	0.046%	0.025%	0.057%
92:4	10514	10963	0.959	0.150%	0.139%	0.011%	0.144%
93:1	10362	10527	0.984	0.101%	0.054%	0.047%	0.080%
93:2	10207	10340	0.987	0.070%	0.038%	0.033%	0.052%
93:3	10274	10686	0.961	0.098%	0.103%	-0.006%	0.101%
93:4	10128	10255	0.988	0.044%	0.027%	0.017%	0.034%
94:1	10043	9954	1.009	0.015%	-0.029%	0.043%	-0.011%
94:2	9999	9994	1.001	-0.001%	-0.006%	0.005%	-0.005%
94:3	10227	10613	0.964	0.075%	0.101%	-0.025%	0.089%
94:4	9923	9836	1.009	-0.035%	-0.026%	-0.009%	-0.029%
95:1	10321	10706	0.964	0.107%	0.113%	-0.006%	0.110%
95:2	10406	10873	0.957	0.111%	0.162%	-0.051%	0.134%
95:3	10472	10853	0.965	0.138%	0.124%	0.014%	0.131%
95:4	10248	10445	0.981	0.088%	0.051%	0.037%	0.067%
96:1	10441	11027	0.947	0.153%	0.163%	-0.010%	0.159%
96:2	10174	10367	0.981	0.061%	0.057%	0.004%	0.059%
96:3	10093	10298	0.980	0.042%	0.050%	-0.008%	0.047%
96:4	10423	10817	0.964	0.131%	0.114%	0.018%	0.122%
AVG	10183	10377	0.981	0.060%	0.052%	0.008%	0.055%

Table 6.10b
Trendline Break—Long Term (TLN-BL) Short Return Analysis
(Average of all stocks)

Qtr	TLN-BL Terminal Wealth	Buy/Hold Terminal Wealth	Relative Terminal Wealth	TLN-BL Short Avg Ret	TLN-BL Cash Avg Ret	TLN-BL Short-Cash Avg Ret	Buy/Hold Avg Ret
85:1	9903	10142	0.976	0.103%	-0.015%	0.118%	0.006%
85:2	10138	9700	1.045	-0.054%	-0.075%	0.021%	-0.069%
85:3	10462	8889	1.177	-0.175%	-0.222%	0.047%	-0.205%
85:4	9682	10763	0.900	0.147%	0.083%	0.064%	0.107%
86:1	9760	11428	0.854	0.221%	0.225%	-0.005%	0.225%
86:2	9840	10414	0.945	0.107%	0.055%	0.052%	0.066%
86:3	10219	9175	1.114	-0.083%	-0.168%	0.085%	-0.128%
86:4	9683	10413	0.930	0.101%	0.039%	0.062%	0.069%
87:1	9478	11929	0.795	0.439%	0.255%	0.184%	0.293%
87:2	9806	10196	0.962	0.081%	0.014%	0.066%	0.038%
87:3	9789	10408	0.940	0.101%	0.052%	0.049%	0.068%
87:4	10622	8087	1.313	-0.190%	-0.466%	0.277%	-0.278%
88:1	9349	10989	0.851	0.180%	0.139%	0.042%	0.163%
88:2	9632	10593	0.909	0.113%	0.086%	0.027%	0.100%
88:3	9895	10050	0.985	0.028%	-0.003%	0.031%	0.013%
88:4	9827	10196	0.964	0.052%	0.022%	0.031%	0.037%
89:1	9720	10698	0.909	0.137%	0.099%	0.038%	0.112%
89:2	9768	10772	0.907	0.161%	0.111%	0.050%	0.122%
89:3	9789	10833	0.904	0.171%	0.121%	0.050%	0.131%
89:4	9987	9904	1.008	0.002%	-0.021%	0.023%	-0.011%
90:1	9925	9980	0.994	0.017%	-0.012%	0.029%	0.003%
90:2	9815	10459	0.938	0.075%	0.078%	-0.003%	0.077%
90:3	10826	8526	1.270	-0.261%	-0.257%	-0.004%	-0.259%
90:4	9578	10889	0.880	0.134%	0.158%	-0.024%	0.146%
91:1	9501	12477	0.762	0.336%	0.308%	0.028%	0.315%
91:2	9883	10244	0.965	0.073%	0.037%	0.036%	0.045%
91:3	9837	10429	0.943	0.061%	0.068%	-0.007%	0.065%
91:4	9798	10497	0.933	0.070%	0.092%	-0.022%	0.082%
92:1	9885	10324	0.957	0.076%	0.037%	0.039%	0.048%
92:2	10112	9723	1.040	-0.043%	-0.053%	0.010%	-0.048%
92:3	9858	10392	0.949	0.053%	0.059%	-0.007%	0.057%
92:4	9689	10963	0.884	0.146%	0.144%	0.003%	0.144%
93:1	9936	10527	0.944	0.044%	0.093%	-0.049%	0.080%
93:2	9894	10340	0.957	0.041%	0.058%	-0.017%	0.052%
93:3	9751	10686	0.912	0.105%	0.098%	0.006%	0.101%
93:4	9905	10255	0.966	0.039%	0.030%	0.008%	0.034%
94:1	10099	9954	1.015	-0.031%	0.004%	-0.035%	-0.011%
94:2	10037	9994	1.004	-0.006%	-0.003%	-0.003%	-0.005%
94:3	9730	10613	0.917	0.107%	0.076%	0.031%	0.089%
94:4	10094	9836	1.026	-0.033%	-0.026%	-0.006%	-0.029%
95:1	9738	10706	0.910	0.111%	0.109%	0.002%	0.110%
95:2	9722	10873	0.894	0.169%	0.121%	0.048%	0.134%
95:3	9791	10853	0.902	0.127%	0.133%	-0.006%	0.131%
95:4	9919	10445	0.950	0.038%	0.084%	-0.046%	0.067%
96:1	9605	11027	0.871	0.187%	0.144%	0.043%	0.159%
96:2	9845	10367	0.950	0.068%	0.053%	0.015%	0.059%
96:3	9828	10298	0.954	0.055%	0.040%	0.015%	0.047%
96:4	9776	10817	0.904	0.117%	0.125%	-0.008%	0.122%
AVG	9869	10377	0.951	0.055%	0.055%	0.000%	0.055%

Results

Tables 6.9 and 6.10 provide the results for the Trendline Break—Long Term (TLN-BL) system. This system makes a relatively high number of long and short calls. In fact, the long call rate of 43.2 percent for this system exceeds the optimal long call rate of 40.0 percent.

The hit rate for this system's long calls is 60.6 percent. When the system favors a cash position over a long position, this call is correct 59.9 percent of the time. The system predicts days of above-average strength to go long; the average return for long calls exceeds the overall average return. Trading long with this system was profitable in all but twelve of the test quarters. However, trading with this system is less profitable than simply buying and holding stocks. On average, an investor trading long with this system will have profits of only 98.1 percent of the profits of an investor who follows a buy-and-hold strategy.

The Trendline Break—Long Term system makes short calls 38.2 percent of the time and has a hit rate of 59.9 percent. These short calls appear to be of minimal use. The average stock return of 0.055 percent for short calls is identical to the overall average return. Thus, there does not appear to be any distinction being made by this system's short calls.

Because the average stock is appreciating in price when short calls are made, following this system will usually result in losses. In fact, in all but nine of the test quarters, terminal wealth fell short of the beginning wealth of $10,000.

Let's investigate whether a medium-term or short-term Trendline Break system generates more promising results.

Trendline Break—Medium Term

This is a shorter-term version of the Trendline Break system we just discussed. With this system, a trading band is created around a trendline. The closing stock price must move outside of this band to signal a trend reversal. For example, during a upward trending market the close must penetrate the lower band to indicate a price reversal and signal a short trade. The wider the band, the lower the price must fall before this reversal is signaled.

With a medium-term system, a two-week to one-month time horizon is considered when constructing the trendline. Therefore, the upward sloping trendlines connect the extreme low prices that have occurred for a stock over the past two weeks to one month. Likewise, the downward sloping trendlines connect the extreme high prices that have occurred over this time period.

Construction

The Trendline Break—Medium Term (TLN-BM) trading system is constructed using trendlines that are derived from an advanced Pivot Point algorithm. This Pivot Point algorithm finds consecutive higher lows during the past two-week to one-month time horizon, and connects them to create upward-sloping lines. Consecutive lower highs are connected to create downward sloping lines.

Bands are drawn around the trendline to represent the amount by which prices must pass the trendline before a signal is generated. The system generates long trades when a stock's closing price passes through the upward band of a downward sloping trend line. Short signals occur when a stock's closing price falls through the lower band of an upward sloping trendline.

Results

Table 6.11 indicates that the Trendline Break—Medium Term (TLN-BM) system makes more long and more short calls than the Trendline Break—Long Term system discussed in the previous section. With a long call rate of 47.7 percent and a short call rate of 40.8 percent, this system has one of the highest call rates of any of the systems described in this book. The hit rate for the long calls is 60.5 percent. The short calls have a slightly lower hit rate of 60.0 percent.

The return analysis in Table 6.12 shows that the TLN-BM system predicts above- and below-average market periods through its long and short calls. The average daily return for long calls is 0.064 percent, which is significantly higher than the average daily return of 0.055 percent for all days in our twelve-year study. Likewise, the average stock return of 0.046 percent for short call days falls below this overall average.

The information provided by this indicator's long and short calls can help investors predict days of above-average stock price appreciation and days of below-average stock price appreciation. However, looking more closely at Table 6.12, we see that this information alone cannot be exploited to earn above-average stock returns.

Investors who begin each quarter with $10,000 and trade long with this system will end the quarter, on average, with $10,205. Thus, the long strategy of the TLN-BM system is profitable, but not as profitable as the buy-and-hold strategy, which gives an average terminal wealth of $10,377. The TLN-BM system's long strategy outperformed the buy-and-hold strategy in only nine of the test quarters.

Let's see whether a shorter-term system based on this same idea produces any better results.

Table 6.11a
Trendline Break—Medium Term (TLN-BM) Long Hit Analysis
(Average of all stocks)

Qtr	Optimal Long	TLN-BM Long	Long Hits	Cash Hits	Total Hits	Long Right	Long Wrong	Cash Right	Cash Wrong
85:1	32.1%	58.5%	65.1%	67.6%	66.1%	38.1%	20.5%	28.0%	13.4%
85:2	30.2%	50.1%	65.0%	70.8%	67.9%	32.6%	17.5%	35.3%	14.6%
85:3	26.3%	43.1%	61.6%	73.5%	68.3%	26.6%	16.6%	41.8%	15.1%
85:4	36.6%	55.4%	65.5%	65.5%	65.5%	36.3%	19.1%	29.2%	15.4%
86:1	44.2%	56.1%	64.0%	55.7%	60.4%	35.9%	20.2%	24.5%	19.4%
86:2	39.7%	43.5%	59.8%	59.9%	59.9%	26.0%	17.5%	33.8%	22.6%
86:3	37.0%	35.3%	56.7%	63.1%	60.8%	20.0%	15.3%	40.8%	23.9%
86:4	38.5%	49.2%	60.4%	60.9%	60.6%	29.7%	19.5%	30.9%	19.8%
87:1	44.7%	63.5%	62.7%	54.7%	59.8%	39.8%	23.7%	20.0%	16.5%
87:2	40.0%	36.9%	59.9%	59.1%	59.4%	22.1%	14.8%	37.3%	25.8%
87:3	39.5%	56.2%	59.2%	60.1%	59.6%	33.2%	22.9%	26.3%	17.5%
87:4	37.9%	21.6%	54.9%	61.8%	60.3%	11.8%	9.7%	48.4%	30.0%
88:1	41.3%	49.7%	63.0%	57.5%	60.3%	31.3%	18.4%	29.0%	21.4%
88:2	39.3%	39.0%	62.6%	60.2%	61.1%	24.4%	14.6%	36.7%	24.3%
88:3	35.9%	47.1%	60.7%	63.5%	62.2%	28.6%	18.5%	33.6%	19.3%
88:4	36.3%	49.5%	61.5%	62.9%	62.2%	30.4%	19.1%	31.8%	18.7%
89:1	39.0%	57.1%	63.3%	60.9%	62.3%	36.1%	20.9%	26.1%	16.8%
89:2	40.2%	59.5%	63.4%	60.4%	62.2%	37.8%	21.8%	24.4%	16.0%
89:3	39.9%	53.5%	62.8%	59.6%	61.3%	33.6%	19.9%	27.7%	18.8%
89:4	38.3%	34.8%	61.5%	61.8%	61.7%	21.4%	13.4%	40.3%	24.9%
90:1	36.9%	43.2%	58.6%	62.7%	60.9%	25.3%	17.9%	35.6%	21.2%
90:2	39.2%	54.2%	61.2%	61.2%	61.2%	33.2%	21.0%	28.0%	17.8%
90:3	33.5%	29.6%	54.6%	66.7%	63.1%	16.2%	13.4%	47.0%	23.5%
90:4	40.8%	53.2%	62.5%	60.5%	61.6%	33.2%	19.9%	28.3%	18.5%
91:1	44.1%	56.2%	62.8%	55.0%	59.4%	35.3%	20.9%	24.1%	19.7%
91:2	39.7%	40.2%	59.3%	59.7%	59.5%	23.8%	16.4%	35.7%	24.1%
91:3	40.4%	44.5%	59.8%	59.5%	59.6%	26.6%	17.9%	33.0%	22.4%
91:4	41.2%	45.5%	60.3%	59.2%	59.7%	27.4%	18.1%	32.3%	22.3%
92:1	40.0%	53.1%	57.0%	60.5%	58.6%	30.3%	22.8%	28.4%	18.6%
92:2	38.6%	42.4%	57.3%	61.1%	59.5%	24.3%	18.1%	35.2%	22.4%
92:3	40.3%	50.1%	60.6%	59.7%	60.1%	30.4%	19.8%	29.8%	20.1%
92:4	41.9%	52.5%	62.6%	58.1%	60.5%	32.8%	19.6%	27.6%	19.9%
93:1	42.5%	52.5%	61.5%	57.9%	59.8%	32.3%	20.2%	27.5%	20.0%
93:2	42.1%	43.4%	59.5%	57.8%	58.5%	25.8%	17.6%	32.7%	23.9%
93:3	42.5%	50.9%	60.9%	57.5%	59.2%	31.0%	19.9%	28.2%	20.9%
93:4	41.5%	42.6%	58.1%	58.6%	58.4%	24.7%	17.9%	33.6%	23.8%
94:1	40.4%	46.0%	56.4%	59.6%	58.2%	26.0%	20.1%	32.2%	21.8%
94:2	40.6%	38.2%	57.0%	59.1%	58.3%	21.8%	16.4%	36.5%	25.3%
94:3	41.8%	51.9%	59.9%	57.8%	58.9%	31.1%	20.8%	27.8%	20.3%
94:4	39.5%	37.8%	57.2%	60.1%	59.0%	21.7%	16.2%	37.3%	24.8%
95:1	43.1%	56.2%	61.2%	56.8%	59.2%	34.4%	21.8%	24.9%	18.9%
95:2	43.7%	55.1%	61.0%	56.5%	59.0%	33.6%	21.5%	25.4%	19.5%
95:3	43.9%	52.6%	61.3%	56.6%	59.1%	32.2%	20.3%	26.8%	20.6%
95:4	43.4%	46.3%	59.9%	57.4%	58.5%	27.7%	18.6%	30.8%	22.9%
96:1	45.5%	50.9%	60.9%	54.4%	57.7%	31.0%	19.9%	26.7%	22.4%
96:2	42.1%	49.4%	57.5%	57.6%	57.5%	28.4%	21.0%	29.1%	21.5%
96:3	42.6%	38.1%	59.3%	57.3%	58.0%	22.6%	15.5%	35.4%	26.4%
96:4	44.3%	54.2%	60.3%	56.5%	58.6%	32.7%	21.5%	25.9%	19.9%
AVG	40.0%	47.7%	60.5%	60.1%	60.5%	29.0%	18.7%	31.5%	20.8%

Table 6.11b
Trendline Break—Medium Term (TLN-BM) Short Hit Analysis
(Average of all stocks)

Qtr	Optimal Short	TLN-BM Short	Short Hits	Cash Hits	Total Hits	Short Right	Short Wrong	Cash Right	Cash Wrong
85:1	34.3%	26.6%	66.4%	65.2%	65.5%	17.6%	8.9%	47.9%	25.5%
85:2	34.6%	35.8%	70.7%	65.1%	67.1%	25.3%	10.5%	41.8%	22.4%
85:3	38.6%	43.9%	72.2%	61.7%	66.3%	31.7%	12.2%	34.6%	21.5%
85:4	33.1%	32.7%	65.0%	65.8%	65.6%	21.2%	11.4%	44.3%	23.0%
86:1	35.2%	25.1%	56.1%	64.1%	62.1%	14.1%	11.0%	48.0%	26.9%
86:2	39.8%	38.0%	60.0%	59.7%	59.8%	22.8%	15.2%	37.0%	25.0%
86:3	42.7%	52.2%	63.2%	56.7%	60.1%	33.0%	19.2%	27.1%	20.7%
86:4	38.7%	42.7%	60.8%	60.5%	60.6%	26.0%	16.8%	34.7%	22.6%
87:1	36.9%	23.1%	53.2%	62.2%	60.1%	12.3%	10.8%	47.8%	29.1%
87:2	40.0%	53.4%	58.8%	59.5%	59.1%	31.4%	22.0%	27.7%	18.9%
87:3	40.4%	33.2%	60.2%	58.9%	59.3%	20.0%	13.2%	39.3%	27.4%
87:4	45.3%	67.7%	61.5%	54.8%	59.3%	41.6%	26.0%	17.7%	14.6%
88:1	36.7%	42.6%	57.2%	63.0%	60.5%	24.4%	18.2%	36.2%	21.2%
88:2	37.4%	52.2%	59.9%	62.6%	61.2%	31.3%	20.9%	29.9%	17.9%
88:3	38.4%	45.1%	63.3%	60.7%	61.9%	28.5%	16.5%	33.3%	21.6%
88:4	37.0%	42.0%	62.5%	61.5%	62.0%	26.3%	15.8%	35.7%	22.3%
89:1	36.2%	33.3%	61.2%	63.1%	62.5%	20.4%	12.9%	42.1%	24.6%
89:2	35.9%	27.9%	60.3%	63.4%	62.6%	16.8%	11.1%	45.7%	26.4%
89:3	36.4%	32.1%	59.5%	62.7%	61.7%	19.1%	13.0%	42.6%	25.3%
89:4	39.0%	53.3%	61.7%	61.0%	61.4%	32.9%	20.4%	28.5%	18.2%
90:1	40.1%	45.6%	62.5%	59.1%	60.7%	28.5%	17.1%	32.1%	22.2%
90:2	37.8%	34.2%	61.3%	61.5%	61.4%	21.0%	13.3%	40.4%	25.3%
90:3	45.7%	60.4%	66.6%	54.6%	61.8%	40.2%	20.1%	21.6%	18.0%
90:4	37.6%	37.1%	60.1%	62.3%	61.5%	22.3%	14.8%	39.2%	23.7%
91:1	36.7%	27.2%	54.2%	62.6%	60.4%	14.7%	12.4%	45.6%	27.2%
91:2	40.4%	42.4%	59.3%	59.3%	59.3%	25.1%	17.2%	34.1%	23.5%
91:3	39.8%	43.7%	59.7%	60.0%	59.8%	26.0%	17.6%	33.8%	22.6%
91:4	40.5%	43.1%	59.4%	59.9%	59.7%	25.6%	17.5%	34.1%	22.8%
92:1	43.2%	34.0%	60.8%	56.9%	58.3%	20.7%	13.3%	37.6%	28.4%
92:2	42.9%	48.5%	61.3%	57.1%	59.1%	29.7%	18.7%	29.4%	22.1%
92:3	39.5%	40.6%	59.6%	60.4%	60.1%	24.2%	16.4%	35.9%	23.5%
92:4	37.5%	36.3%	58.3%	62.4%	60.9%	21.2%	15.1%	39.8%	24.0%
93:1	39.4%	35.4%	58.0%	61.2%	60.1%	20.5%	14.8%	39.5%	25.1%
93:2	40.9%	46.3%	57.7%	59.0%	58.4%	26.8%	19.6%	31.6%	22.0%
93:3	39.4%	37.2%	57.5%	60.7%	59.5%	21.4%	15.8%	38.1%	24.7%
93:4	41.7%	46.1%	58.5%	58.1%	58.3%	27.0%	19.2%	31.3%	22.6%
94:1	43.7%	43.1%	59.9%	56.3%	57.9%	25.8%	17.3%	32.1%	24.9%
94:2	42.7%	51.7%	59.0%	57.0%	58.0%	30.5%	21.2%	27.6%	20.8%
94:3	39.8%	39.4%	58.2%	60.1%	59.3%	22.9%	16.5%	36.4%	24.2%
94:4	42.8%	53.6%	60.2%	57.3%	58.8%	32.3%	21.4%	26.5%	19.8%
95:1	38.7%	34.9%	57.0%	61.0%	59.6%	19.9%	15.0%	39.7%	25.4%
95:2	38.9%	33.1%	56.8%	60.6%	59.4%	18.8%	14.3%	40.5%	26.3%
95:3	38.9%	34.3%	56.7%	60.7%	59.3%	19.4%	14.8%	39.9%	25.8%
95:4	40.5%	41.3%	57.8%	59.7%	58.9%	23.9%	17.4%	35.1%	23.6%
96:1	38.9%	37.4%	54.5%	60.8%	58.4%	20.4%	17.0%	38.1%	24.6%
96:2	42.4%	40.5%	57.7%	57.7%	57.7%	23.4%	17.1%	34.3%	25.2%
96:3	40.8%	52.2%	56.9%	59.0%	57.9%	29.7%	22.5%	28.2%	19.6%
96:4	39.8%	33.5%	56.7%	60.1%	59.0%	19.0%	14.5%	40.0%	26.5%
AVG	39.4%	40.8%	60.0%	60.4%	60.5%	24.5%	16.2%	35.9%	23.3%

Table 6.12a
Trendline Break—Medium Term (TLN-BM) Long Return Analysis
(Average of all stocks)

Qtr	TLN-BM Terminal Wealth	Buy/Hold Terminal Wealth	Relative Terminal Wealth	TLN-BM Long Avg Ret	TLN-BM Cash Avg Ret	TLN-BM Long-Cash Avg Ret	Buy/Hold Avg Ret
85:1	10048	10142	0.991	0.001%	0.014%	-0.013%	0.006%
85:2	9866	9700	1.017	-0.057%	-0.081%	0.024%	-0.069%
85:3	9498	8889	1.069	-0.202%	-0.207%	0.006%	-0.205%
85:4	10458	10763	0.972	0.124%	0.086%	0.038%	0.107%
86:1	10734	11428	0.939	0.204%	0.251%	-0.048%	0.225%
86:2	10121	10414	0.972	0.038%	0.088%	-0.050%	0.066%
86:3	9632	9175	1.050	-0.165%	-0.107%	-0.057%	-0.128%
86:4	10099	10413	0.970	0.036%	0.101%	-0.065%	0.069%
87:1	11114	11929	0.932	0.267%	0.339%	-0.072%	0.293%
87:2	10035	10196	0.984	0.016%	0.051%	-0.035%	0.038%
87:3	10210	10408	0.981	0.061%	0.077%	-0.016%	0.068%
87:4	9645	8087	1.193	-0.255%	-0.284%	0.029%	-0.278%
88:1	10423	10989	0.949	0.143%	0.182%	-0.038%	0.163%
88:2	10206	10593	0.964	0.089%	0.106%	-0.017%	0.100%
88:3	9968	10050	0.992	-0.007%	0.030%	-0.036%	0.013%
88:4	9981	10196	0.979	-0.001%	0.074%	-0.075%	0.037%
89:1	10379	10698	0.970	0.109%	0.117%	-0.009%	0.112%
89:2	10418	10772	0.967	0.111%	0.139%	-0.027%	0.122%
89:3	10398	10833	0.960	0.114%	0.150%	-0.036%	0.131%
89:4	9958	9904	1.005	-0.017%	-0.008%	-0.009%	-0.011%
90:1	9932	9980	0.995	-0.024%	0.023%	-0.048%	0.003%
90:2	10217	10459	0.977	0.065%	0.091%	-0.026%	0.077%
90:3	9583	8526	1.124	-0.230%	-0.271%	0.041%	-0.259%
90:4	10573	10889	0.971	0.170%	0.120%	0.050%	0.146%
91:1	11105	12477	0.890	0.284%	0.355%	-0.071%	0.315%
91:2	10023	10244	0.978	0.016%	0.065%	-0.049%	0.045%
91:3	10165	10429	0.975	0.056%	0.072%	-0.016%	0.065%
91:4	10248	10497	0.976	0.083%	0.080%	0.003%	0.082%
92:1	10207	10324	0.989	0.059%	0.035%	0.024%	0.048%
92:2	9864	9723	1.014	-0.055%	-0.043%	-0.012%	-0.048%
92:3	10171	10392	0.979	0.049%	0.065%	-0.016%	0.057%
92:4	10530	10963	0.960	0.151%	0.137%	0.014%	0.144%
93:1	10307	10527	0.979	0.091%	0.067%	0.024%	0.080%
93:2	10158	10340	0.982	0.054%	0.050%	0.004%	0.052%
93:3	10382	10686	0.972	0.108%	0.093%	0.015%	0.101%
93:4	10111	10255	0.986	0.034%	0.033%	0.001%	0.034%
94:1	10000	9954	1.005	-0.004%	-0.017%	0.013%	-0.011%
94:2	9938	9994	0.994	-0.028%	0.009%	-0.037%	-0.005%
94:3	10313	10613	0.972	0.089%	0.089%	0.000%	0.089%
94:4	9903	9836	1.007	-0.046%	-0.019%	-0.026%	-0.029%
95:1	10389	10706	0.970	0.108%	0.113%	-0.005%	0.110%
95:2	10500	10873	0.966	0.138%	0.129%	0.009%	0.134%
95:3	10487	10853	0.966	0.141%	0.120%	0.021%	0.131%
95:4	10269	10445	0.983	0.089%	0.047%	0.042%	0.067%
96:1	10494	11027	0.952	0.151%	0.167%	-0.015%	0.159%
96:2	10190	10367	0.983	0.060%	0.057%	0.003%	0.059%
96:3	10098	10298	0.981	0.038%	0.053%	-0.015%	0.047%
96:4	10471	10817	0.968	0.131%	0.112%	0.020%	0.122%
AVG	10205	10377	0.983	0.064%	0.047%	0.017%	0.055%

Table 6.12b
Trendline Break—Medium Term (TLN-BM) Short Return Analysis
(Average of all stocks)

Qtr	TLN-BM Terminal Wealth	Buy/Hold Terminal Wealth	Relative Terminal Wealth	TLN-BM Short Avg Ret	TLN-BM Cash Avg Ret	TLN-BM Short-Cash Avg Ret	Buy/Hold Avg Ret
85:1	9986	10142	0.985	0.023%	0.000%	0.023%	0.006%
85:2	10268	9700	1.059	-0.094%	-0.056%	-0.038%	-0.069%
85:3	10605	8889	1.193	-0.189%	-0.217%	0.029%	-0.205%
85:4	9828	10763	0.913	0.095%	0.112%	-0.017%	0.107%
86:1	9582	11428	0.838	0.282%	0.205%	0.076%	0.225%
86:2	9741	10414	0.935	0.104%	0.043%	0.060%	0.066%
86:3	10313	9175	1.124	-0.102%	-0.155%	0.053%	-0.128%
86:4	9716	10413	0.933	0.104%	0.043%	0.061%	0.069%
87:1	9437	11929	0.791	0.421%	0.255%	0.166%	0.293%
87:2	9783	10196	0.959	0.059%	0.013%	0.046%	0.038%
87:3	9810	10408	0.943	0.088%	0.058%	0.030%	0.068%
87:4	11077	8087	1.370	-0.290%	-0.253%	-0.037%	-0.278%
88:1	9504	10989	0.865	0.188%	0.144%	0.044%	0.163%
88:2	9632	10593	0.909	0.110%	0.089%	0.021%	0.100%
88:3	9890	10050	0.984	0.036%	-0.006%	0.042%	0.013%
88:4	9782	10196	0.959	0.079%	0.005%	0.074%	0.037%
89:1	9773	10698	0.914	0.113%	0.112%	0.000%	0.112%
89:2	9733	10772	0.904	0.151%	0.111%	0.041%	0.122%
89:3	9664	10833	0.892	0.170%	0.113%	0.057%	0.131%
89:4	9991	9904	1.009	-0.001%	-0.022%	0.021%	-0.011%
90:1	9918	9980	0.994	0.025%	-0.016%	0.040%	0.003%
90:2	9805	10459	0.937	0.088%	0.071%	0.017%	0.077%
90:3	11110	8526	1.303	-0.272%	-0.239%	-0.032%	-0.259%
90:4	9693	10889	0.890	0.122%	0.160%	-0.038%	0.146%
91:1	9392	12477	0.753	0.393%	0.286%	0.107%	0.315%
91:2	9782	10244	0.955	0.077%	0.022%	0.054%	0.045%
91:3	9810	10429	0.941	0.068%	0.062%	0.006%	0.065%
91:4	9784	10497	0.932	0.077%	0.086%	-0.009%	0.082%
92:1	9960	10324	0.965	0.022%	0.061%	-0.039%	0.048%
92:2	10153	9723	1.044	-0.048%	-0.049%	0.001%	-0.048%
92:3	9833	10392	0.946	0.069%	0.048%	0.021%	0.057%
92:4	9693	10963	0.884	0.137%	0.149%	-0.012%	0.144%
93:1	9868	10527	0.937	0.067%	0.087%	-0.020%	0.080%
93:2	9832	10340	0.951	0.059%	0.045%	0.014%	0.052%
93:3	9792	10686	0.916	0.090%	0.108%	-0.018%	0.101%
93:4	9924	10255	0.968	0.030%	0.038%	-0.008%	0.034%
94:1	10054	9954	1.010	-0.018%	-0.006%	-0.012%	-0.011%
94:2	9968	9994	0.997	0.013%	-0.024%	0.037%	-0.005%
94:3	9806	10613	0.924	0.082%	0.094%	-0.011%	0.089%
94:4	10097	9836	1.026	-0.028%	-0.031%	0.003%	-0.029%
95:1	9752	10706	0.911	0.116%	0.107%	0.009%	0.110%
95:2	9716	10873	0.894	0.138%	0.132%	0.006%	0.134%
95:3	9724	10853	0.896	0.131%	0.131%	-0.001%	0.131%
95:4	9918	10445	0.950	0.036%	0.089%	-0.053%	0.067%
96:1	9600	11027	0.871	0.176%	0.149%	0.027%	0.159%
96:2	9866	10367	0.952	0.054%	0.061%	-0.007%	0.059%
96:3	9791	10298	0.951	0.063%	0.030%	0.033%	0.047%
96:4	9779	10817	0.904	0.108%	0.129%	-0.021%	0.122%
AVG	9886	10377	0.953	0.046%	0.062%	-0.016%	0.055%

Trendline Break—Short Term

This is the shortest version of the three Trendline Break systems. Here, a trading band is created around a trendline considering an eight- to sixteen-day time horizon. The closing stock price must move outside of this band to signal a trend reversal. For example, during a upward trending market, the close must penetrate the lower band to indicate a price reversal and signal a short trade. The wider the band, the lower the price must fall before this reversal is signaled.

The upward sloping trendlines in this system connect the extreme low prices that have occurred for a stock over the past eight to sixteen days. The downward sloping trendlines connect the extreme high prices that have occurred over this time period.

Construction

The Trendline Break Short Term (TLN-BS) trading system is constructed using trendlines that are derived using an advanced Pivot Point algorithm. This Pivot Point algorithm finds consecutive higher lows during the last eight-to sixteen-day time horizon and connects them to create upward sloping lines. Consecutive lower highs are connected to create downward sloping lines.

Bands are drawn around the trendline to represent the amount by which prices must pass the trendline before a signal is generated. The system generates long trades when a stock's closing price passes through the upward band of a downward sloping trend line. Short signals occur when a stock's closing price falls through the lower band of an upward sloping trendline.

Results

Table 6.13 shows that the TLN-BS system makes calls more frequently than its longer-term counterparts. The system chooses a long position 53.1 percent of the time and a short position 46.0 percent of the time. The long and short hit rates for the TLN-BS system are 60.3 percent and 59.9 percent, respectively.

The return results for the TLN-BS system are shown in Table 6.14. Like its longer-term counterparts, this system underperforms relative to a buy-and-hold strategy. The long strategy of the TLN-BS system averages only 98.4 percent of the buy-and-hold strategy's terminal wealth. The short strategy performs even worse: terminal wealth averages only 95.0 percent of the buy-and-hold terminal wealth.

Although it does not appear that this system can be used alone to capture above-normal profits, let's look at the results a little more closely to discern whether any useful information is being provided by its calls. The system does appear to be making a good number of long calls on days of above-average stock price appreciation. The average return on these days is 0.060 percent. Thus, traders following this system earn above-average returns when they are in the market. The shortcoming of this system is that it misses some days of positive stock price appreciation by choosing a cash position over a long position. Although this happens less than twice in every ten days, the forgone profits are large enough to make trading with this system less profitable than the buy-and-hold strategy.

At 0.051 percent, the average stock return on days when short calls are made is below the average daily stock return for the test period. Therefore, we can conclude that the TLN-BS system does predict periods of below-average stock price appreciation. The main shortcoming here is that even though the stock price appreciation is below average, it is still positive. Being in a short position when stock prices are rising leads to losses.

Like its two longer-term counterparts, the TLN-BS system can provide some useful information in terms of predicting above- and below-average market periods. But this information, by itself, is not powerful enough to match or beat the benchmark buy-and-hold strategy.

Trend Rule Trading

The Trend Rule Trading (TRU) system, developed by Nirvana, attempts to recognize trend changes. The system is based on a medium-term lookback period; that is, the system looks at the last two weeks to one month to discern trends. The system is similar to the Trendline Reversal systems discussed later in this chapter.

Construction

The Trend Rule Trading (TRU) system is constructed using trendlines derived from an advanced Pivot Point algorithm. This Pivot Point algorithm finds consecutive higher lows during the last two weeks to one month and connects them to create upward-sloping lines. Consecutive lower highs are connected to create downward sloping lines.

Whenever price falls through one of the upward-sloping medium-term trend lines, a reversal in trend is signaled. Because the price is falling through a positively sloped trend, this signals a falling trend in the stock's price. Therefore, a short signal will be generated.

Whenever price crosses through one of the downward-sloping medium-term trendlines to the upside, a reversal in trend is also signaled. In this case, a reversal from a declining stock price to an appreciating stock price is predicted. Therefore, a long signal occurs.

Table 6.13a
Trendline Break—Short Term (TLN-BS) Long Hit Analysis
(Average of all stocks)

Qtr	Optimal Long	TLN-BS Long	Long Hits	Cash Hits	Total Hits	Long Right	Long Wrong	Cash Right	Cash Wrong
85:1	32.1%	52.4%	66.2%	69.5%	67.8%	34.7%	17.7%	33.1%	14.5%
85:2	30.2%	51.9%	64.3%	71.1%	67.6%	33.4%	18.5%	34.2%	13.9%
85:3	26.3%	47.8%	60.8%	74.0%	67.7%	29.1%	18.7%	38.6%	13.6%
85:4	36.6%	60.7%	66.1%	63.7%	65.1%	40.1%	20.6%	25.0%	14.3%
86:1	44.2%	57.6%	64.2%	56.5%	60.9%	37.0%	20.6%	23.9%	18.4%
86:2	39.7%	51.7%	59.2%	59.7%	59.4%	30.6%	21.1%	28.8%	19.5%
86:3	37.0%	49.5%	57.0%	62.8%	60.0%	28.2%	21.2%	31.8%	18.8%
86:4	38.5%	53.9%	60.8%	61.2%	61.0%	32.8%	21.1%	28.2%	17.9%
87:1	44.7%	59.7%	62.1%	54.8%	59.1%	37.1%	22.7%	22.1%	18.2%
87:2	40.0%	50.9%	59.6%	59.3%	59.5%	30.4%	20.6%	29.1%	20.0%
87:3	39.5%	50.1%	58.6%	60.4%	59.5%	29.3%	20.7%	30.2%	19.7%
87:4	37.9%	43.0%	55.8%	61.8%	59.2%	24.0%	19.0%	35.2%	21.8%
88:1	41.3%	53.9%	63.1%	58.8%	61.1%	34.0%	19.9%	27.1%	19.0%
88:2	39.3%	55.9%	61.5%	60.5%	61.0%	34.4%	21.6%	26.7%	17.4%
88:3	35.9%	50.0%	61.6%	63.2%	62.4%	30.8%	19.2%	31.6%	18.4%
88:4	36.3%	54.0%	62.5%	63.6%	63.0%	33.8%	20.3%	29.2%	16.7%
89:1	39.0%	56.2%	62.7%	60.2%	61.6%	35.3%	20.9%	26.3%	17.4%
89:2	40.2%	61.2%	63.5%	60.3%	62.2%	38.8%	22.3%	23.4%	15.4%
89:3	39.9%	55.0%	62.7%	59.9%	61.4%	34.5%	20.5%	27.0%	18.1%
89:4	38.3%	51.9%	60.8%	61.4%	61.1%	31.6%	20.3%	29.5%	18.6%
90:1	36.9%	51.5%	59.4%	62.9%	61.1%	30.6%	20.9%	30.5%	18.0%
90:2	39.2%	52.9%	61.8%	60.9%	61.4%	32.7%	20.2%	28.7%	18.4%
90:3	33.5%	43.8%	54.0%	65.7%	60.6%	23.7%	20.2%	36.9%	19.3%
90:4	40.8%	57.5%	61.9%	57.8%	60.2%	35.6%	21.9%	24.6%	17.9%
91:1	44.1%	52.6%	62.9%	55.7%	59.5%	33.1%	19.5%	26.4%	21.0%
91:2	39.7%	51.2%	58.6%	59.8%	59.2%	30.0%	21.2%	29.2%	19.6%
91:3	40.4%	53.2%	59.1%	59.1%	59.1%	31.5%	21.7%	27.7%	19.1%
91:4	41.2%	52.0%	60.1%	59.7%	59.9%	31.2%	20.8%	28.6%	19.3%
92:1	40.0%	52.6%	56.4%	60.1%	58.2%	29.7%	22.9%	28.5%	18.9%
92:2	38.6%	50.8%	56.9%	60.8%	58.8%	28.9%	21.9%	29.9%	19.3%
92:3	40.3%	55.3%	60.4%	59.3%	59.9%	33.4%	21.9%	26.5%	18.2%
92:4	41.9%	57.3%	62.5%	58.3%	60.7%	35.8%	21.5%	24.9%	17.8%
93:1	42.5%	53.9%	60.4%	57.1%	58.9%	32.5%	21.4%	26.3%	19.8%
93:2	42.1%	48.8%	59.4%	58.0%	58.7%	29.0%	19.8%	29.7%	21.5%
93:3	42.5%	55.8%	60.8%	57.5%	59.3%	33.9%	21.9%	25.4%	18.8%
93:4	41.5%	50.4%	58.6%	58.5%	58.6%	29.5%	20.9%	29.0%	20.5%
94:1	40.4%	54.3%	55.8%	59.1%	57.3%	30.3%	24.0%	27.0%	18.7%
94:2	40.6%	48.9%	57.1%	58.7%	57.9%	27.9%	21.0%	30.0%	21.1%
94:3	41.8%	54.2%	60.1%	57.9%	59.1%	32.6%	21.6%	26.5%	19.3%
94:4	39.5%	48.0%	57.3%	60.3%	58.9%	27.5%	20.5%	31.4%	20.7%
95:1	43.1%	57.0%	60.8%	56.5%	58.9%	34.6%	22.4%	24.3%	18.7%
95:2	43.7%	57.0%	60.4%	55.9%	58.4%	34.4%	22.6%	24.0%	19.0%
95:3	43.9%	56.3%	60.8%	56.3%	58.9%	34.2%	22.0%	24.6%	19.1%
95:4	43.4%	53.9%	59.8%	57.5%	58.7%	32.2%	21.7%	26.5%	19.6%
96:1	45.5%	53.8%	60.8%	54.3%	57.8%	32.7%	21.1%	25.1%	21.1%
96:2	42.1%	50.8%	57.6%	57.8%	57.7%	29.3%	21.5%	28.5%	20.8%
96:3	42.6%	52.9%	59.6%	57.6%	58.6%	31.5%	21.4%	27.1%	20.0%
96:4	44.3%	53.6%	60.0%	55.8%	58.1%	32.2%	21.4%	25.9%	20.5%
AVG	40.0%	53.1%	60.3%	60.0%	60.3%	32.1%	21.0%	28.2%	18.7%

Table 6.13b
Trendline Break—Short Term (TLN-BS) Short Hit Analysis
(Average of all stocks)

Qtr	Optimal Short	TLN-BS Short	Short Hits	Cash Hits	Total Hits	Short Right	Short Wrong	Cash Right	Cash Wrong
85:1	34.3%	45.5%	69.0%	66.3%	67.5%	31.4%	14.1%	36.1%	18.4%
85:2	34.6%	46.6%	70.6%	64.5%	67.4%	32.9%	13.7%	34.4%	18.9%
85:3	38.6%	50.8%	73.7%	60.9%	67.4%	37.4%	13.4%	30.0%	19.2%
85:4	33.1%	37.4%	63.2%	66.0%	64.9%	23.6%	13.8%	41.3%	21.3%
86:1	35.2%	40.0%	56.2%	64.2%	61.0%	22.5%	17.5%	38.5%	21.5%
86:2	39.8%	46.9%	59.5%	59.3%	59.4%	27.9%	19.0%	31.5%	21.6%
86:3	42.7%	49.5%	62.8%	57.2%	59.9%	31.1%	18.4%	28.8%	21.6%
86:4	38.7%	45.7%	61.2%	60.8%	61.0%	28.0%	17.8%	33.0%	21.3%
87:1	36.9%	38.7%	54.6%	62.0%	59.1%	21.1%	17.6%	38.0%	23.3%
87:2	40.0%	48.1%	59.3%	59.7%	59.5%	28.5%	19.6%	31.0%	20.9%
87:3	40.4%	48.9%	60.4%	58.6%	59.5%	29.5%	19.3%	30.0%	21.2%
87:4	45.3%	54.4%	61.8%	55.7%	59.0%	33.6%	20.8%	25.4%	20.2%
88:1	36.7%	45.3%	58.7%	63.1%	61.1%	26.6%	18.7%	34.5%	20.2%
88:2	37.4%	43.5%	60.4%	61.4%	61.0%	26.3%	17.2%	34.7%	21.8%
88:3	38.4%	49.5%	63.2%	61.6%	62.4%	31.3%	18.2%	31.1%	19.4%
88:4	37.0%	45.2%	63.4%	62.5%	62.9%	28.6%	16.5%	34.3%	20.6%
89:1	36.2%	43.2%	60.2%	62.7%	61.6%	26.0%	17.2%	35.6%	21.2%
89:2	35.9%	37.6%	60.1%	63.5%	62.3%	22.6%	15.0%	39.6%	22.7%
89:3	36.4%	43.8%	59.8%	62.8%	61.5%	26.2%	17.6%	35.3%	20.9%
89:4	39.0%	47.1%	61.2%	60.9%	61.0%	28.9%	18.3%	32.2%	20.7%
90:1	40.1%	47.7%	62.7%	59.5%	61.0%	29.9%	17.8%	31.1%	21.2%
90:2	37.8%	46.1%	60.8%	61.9%	61.4%	28.1%	18.1%	33.3%	20.5%
90:3	45.7%	54.7%	65.6%	54.0%	60.4%	35.9%	18.8%	24.5%	20.8%
90:4	37.6%	41.4%	57.7%	62.0%	60.2%	23.9%	17.5%	36.3%	22.3%
91:1	36.7%	46.1%	55.6%	62.9%	59.5%	25.7%	20.5%	33.9%	20.0%
91:2	40.4%	48.0%	59.8%	58.6%	59.2%	28.7%	19.3%	30.4%	21.5%
91:3	39.8%	46.4%	59.1%	59.2%	59.2%	27.4%	19.0%	31.7%	21.9%
91:4	40.5%	47.4%	59.7%	60.1%	59.9%	28.3%	19.1%	31.6%	21.0%
92:1	43.2%	46.5%	60.0%	56.4%	58.1%	27.9%	18.6%	30.2%	23.3%
92:2	42.9%	48.9%	60.8%	56.9%	58.8%	29.7%	19.2%	29.1%	22.0%
92:3	39.5%	44.3%	59.3%	60.4%	59.9%	26.3%	18.1%	33.6%	22.1%
92:4	37.5%	41.9%	58.3%	62.5%	60.7%	24.4%	17.5%	36.3%	21.8%
93:1	39.4%	45.1%	57.0%	60.4%	58.9%	25.7%	19.4%	33.1%	21.7%
93:2	40.9%	50.7%	58.0%	59.4%	58.7%	29.4%	21.3%	29.3%	20.0%
93:3	39.4%	43.5%	57.5%	60.8%	59.4%	25.1%	18.5%	34.3%	22.1%
93:4	41.7%	49.1%	58.6%	58.6%	58.6%	28.7%	20.3%	29.8%	21.1%
94:1	43.7%	45.3%	59.1%	55.9%	57.3%	26.8%	18.5%	30.6%	24.1%
94:2	42.7%	50.7%	58.7%	57.1%	57.9%	29.7%	20.9%	28.1%	21.2%
94:3	39.8%	45.4%	57.9%	60.1%	59.1%	26.3%	19.1%	32.8%	21.8%
94:4	42.8%	51.6%	60.3%	57.4%	58.9%	31.1%	20.5%	27.8%	20.6%
95:1	38.7%	42.5%	56.5%	60.8%	58.9%	24.0%	18.5%	34.9%	22.6%
95:2	38.9%	42.4%	55.8%	60.4%	58.5%	23.7%	18.7%	34.8%	22.8%
95:3	38.9%	42.5%	56.3%	60.9%	58.9%	23.9%	18.6%	35.0%	22.5%
95:4	40.5%	45.5%	57.5%	59.8%	58.8%	26.2%	19.3%	32.6%	21.9%
96:1	38.9%	45.6%	54.3%	60.8%	57.8%	24.7%	20.8%	33.1%	21.3%
96:2	42.4%	48.8%	57.8%	57.6%	57.7%	28.2%	20.6%	29.5%	21.7%
96:3	40.8%	46.9%	57.6%	59.6%	58.7%	27.0%	19.9%	31.7%	21.5%
96:4	39.8%	45.4%	55.9%	60.0%	58.1%	25.4%	20.0%	32.7%	21.9%
AVG	39.4%	46.0%	59.9%	60.4%	60.3%	27.6%	18.4%	32.7%	21.3%

Table 6.14a
Trendline Break—Short Term (TLN-BS) Long Return Analysis
(Average of all stocks)

Qtr	TLN-BS Terminal Wealth	Buy/Hold Terminal Wealth	Relative Terminal Wealth	TLN-BS Long Avg Ret	TLN-BS Cash Avg Ret	TLN-BS Long-Cash Avg Ret	Buy/Hold Avg Ret
85:1	10200	10142	1.006	0.053%	-0.045%	0.097%	0.006%
85:2	09834	09700	1.014	-0.063%	-0.076%	0.014%	-0.069%
85:3	09439	08889	1.062	-0.201%	-0.208%	0.008%	-0.205%
85:4	10415	10763	0.968	0.102%	0.114%	-0.013%	0.107%
86:1	10837	11428	0.948	0.233%	0.213%	0.020%	0.225%
86:2	10109	10414	0.971	0.034%	0.101%	-0.068%	0.066%
86:3	09601	09175	1.046	-0.125%	-0.130%	0.005%	-0.128%
86:4	10196	10413	0.979	0.063%	0.077%	-0.014%	0.069%
87:1	10996	11929	0.922	0.263%	0.338%	-0.075%	0.293%
87:2	10050	10196	0.986	0.018%	0.058%	-0.040%	0.038%
87:3	10195	10408	0.979	0.063%	0.073%	-0.010%	0.068%
87:4	09670	08087	1.196	-0.111%	-0.404%	0.293%	-0.278%
88:1	10517	10989	0.957	0.158%	0.168%	-0.009%	0.163%
88:2	10254	10593	0.968	0.076%	0.129%	-0.053%	0.100%
88:3	10001	10050	0.995	0.004%	0.021%	-0.017%	0.013%
88:4	10100	10196	0.991	0.035%	0.038%	-0.003%	0.037%
89:1	10329	10698	0.966	0.095%	0.134%	-0.039%	0.112%
89:2	10440	10772	0.969	0.114%	0.135%	-0.021%	0.122%
89:3	10421	10833	0.962	0.121%	0.143%	-0.022%	0.131%
89:4	09886	09904	0.998	-0.032%	0.012%	-0.044%	-0.011%
90:1	09988	09980	1.001	0.000%	0.006%	-0.005%	0.003%
90:2	10298	10459	0.985	0.093%	0.059%	0.034%	0.077%
90:3	09301	08526	1.091	-0.269%	-0.251%	-0.019%	-0.259%
90:4	10416	10889	0.957	0.122%	0.180%	-0.058%	0.146%
91:1	11111	12477	0.891	0.335%	0.293%	0.042%	0.315%
91:2	10055	10244	0.982	0.022%	0.070%	-0.049%	0.045%
91:3	10140	10429	0.972	0.042%	0.091%	-0.049%	0.065%
91:4	10358	10497	0.987	0.109%	0.052%	0.057%	0.082%
92:1	10208	10324	0.989	0.062%	0.033%	0.029%	0.048%
92:2	09806	09723	1.008	-0.066%	-0.030%	-0.035%	-0.048%
92:3	10140	10392	0.976	0.039%	0.079%	-0.040%	0.057%
92:4	10566	10963	0.964	0.148%	0.139%	0.009%	0.144%
93:1	10259	10527	0.974	0.074%	0.086%	-0.011%	0.080%
93:2	10207	10340	0.987	0.065%	0.039%	0.027%	0.052%
93:3	10386	10686	0.972	0.104%	0.097%	0.007%	0.101%
93:4	10167	10255	0.991	0.047%	0.020%	0.027%	0.034%
94:1	09931	09954	0.998	-0.024%	0.003%	-0.027%	-0.011%
94:2	09945	09994	0.995	-0.021%	0.011%	-0.032%	-0.005%
94:3	10326	10613	0.973	0.088%	0.091%	-0.002%	0.089%
94:4	09890	09836	1.005	-0.037%	-0.022%	-0.016%	-0.029%
95:1	10329	10706	0.965	0.093%	0.133%	-0.040%	0.110%
95:2	10445	10873	0.961	0.122%	0.150%	-0.027%	0.134%
95:3	10467	10853	0.964	0.129%	0.134%	-0.005%	0.131%
95:4	10294	10445	0.985	0.084%	0.046%	0.038%	0.067%
96:1	10500	11027	0.952	0.147%	0.173%	-0.026%	0.159%
96:2	10211	10367	0.985	0.064%	0.053%	0.011%	0.059%
96:3	10222	10298	0.993	0.065%	0.028%	0.037%	0.047%
96:4	10465	10817	0.967	0.134%	0.109%	0.025%	0.122%
AVG	10207	10377	0.984	0.060%	0.049%	0.011%	0.055%

Table 6.14b
Trendline Break—Short Term (TLN-BS) Short Return Analysis
(Average of all stocks)

Qtr	TLN-BS Terminal Wealth	Buy/Hold Terminal Wealth	Relative Terminal Wealth	TLN-BS Short Avg Ret	TLN-BS Cash Avg Ret	TLN-BS Short-Cash Avg Ret	Buy/Hold Avg Ret
85:1	10154	10142	1.001	-0.039%	0.044%	-0.083%	0.006%
85:2	10251	9700	1.057	-0.069%	-0.070%	0.001%	-0.069%
85:3	10730	8889	1.207	-0.204%	-0.206%	0.002%	-0.205%
85:4	9728	10763	0.904	0.131%	0.092%	0.038%	0.107%
86:1	9469	11428	0.829	0.224%	0.225%	0.000%	0.225%
86:2	9678	10414	0.929	0.107%	0.031%	0.076%	0.066%
86:3	10401	9175	1.134	-0.131%	-0.124%	-0.007%	-0.128%
86:4	9779	10413	0.939	0.076%	0.064%	0.013%	0.069%
87:1	9231	11929	0.774	0.345%	0.260%	0.086%	0.293%
87:2	9820	10196	0.963	0.056%	0.021%	0.036%	0.038%
87:3	9764	10408	0.938	0.074%	0.063%	0.011%	0.068%
87:4	11325	8087	1.400	-0.415%	-0.115%	-0.300%	-0.278%
88:1	9519	10989	0.866	0.170%	0.157%	0.014%	0.163%
88:2	9641	10593	0.910	0.131%	0.075%	0.056%	0.100%
88:3	9924	10050	0.987	0.020%	0.005%	0.015%	0.013%
88:4	9884	10196	0.969	0.039%	0.035%	0.004%	0.037%
89:1	9647	10698	0.902	0.135%	0.095%	0.039%	0.112%
89:2	9679	10772	0.899	0.137%	0.114%	0.023%	0.122%
89:3	9615	10833	0.887	0.143%	0.122%	0.021%	0.131%
89:4	9952	9904	1.005	0.012%	-0.032%	0.044%	-0.011%
90:1	9966	9980	0.999	0.006%	-0.001%	0.007%	0.003%
90:2	9826	10459	0.939	0.060%	0.091%	-0.032%	0.077%
90:3	10888	8526	1.277	-0.250%	-0.270%	0.020%	-0.259%
90:4	9528	10889	0.875	0.183%	0.120%	0.063%	0.146%
91:1	9234	12477	0.740	0.297%	0.330%	-0.034%	0.315%
91:2	9771	10244	0.954	0.070%	0.022%	0.048%	0.045%
91:3	9748	10429	0.935	0.088%	0.045%	0.044%	0.065%
91:4	9812	10497	0.935	0.054%	0.106%	-0.052%	0.082%
92:1	9899	10324	0.959	0.037%	0.058%	-0.021%	0.048%
92:2	10091	9723	1.038	-0.029%	-0.066%	0.037%	-0.048%
92:3	9795	10392	0.943	0.077%	0.040%	0.037%	0.057%
92:4	9644	10963	0.880	0.137%	0.150%	-0.013%	0.144%
93:1	9770	10527	0.928	0.085%	0.075%	0.010%	0.080%
93:2	9886	10340	0.956	0.037%	0.067%	-0.030%	0.052%
93:3	9749	10686	0.912	0.095%	0.106%	-0.011%	0.101%
93:4	9951	10255	0.970	0.019%	0.049%	-0.030%	0.034%
94:1	9996	9954	1.004	0.003%	-0.023%	0.027%	-0.011%
94:2	9970	9994	0.998	0.012%	-0.021%	0.033%	-0.005%
94:3	9752	10613	0.919	0.090%	0.088%	0.002%	0.089%
94:4	10080	9836	1.025	-0.023%	-0.036%	0.012%	-0.029%
95:1	9659	10706	0.902	0.132%	0.094%	0.038%	0.110%
95:2	9612	10873	0.884	0.151%	0.122%	0.029%	0.134%
95:3	9663	10853	0.890	0.132%	0.130%	0.001%	0.131%
95:4	9881	10445	0.946	0.044%	0.085%	-0.041%	0.067%
96:1	9520	11027	0.863	0.174%	0.147%	0.027%	0.159%
96:2	9830	10367	0.948	0.055%	0.062%	-0.007%	0.059%
96:3	9916	10298	0.963	0.028%	0.064%	-0.036%	0.047%
96:4	9700	10817	0.897	0.109%	0.133%	-0.024%	0.122%
AVG	9861	10377	0.950	0.051%	0.059%	-0.009%	0.055%

Results

The results for the TRU indicator are presented in Tables 6.15 and 6.16. This system makes a relatively large number of long and short calls. Long calls occur 49.7 percent of the time, and they are correct 60.3 percent of the time.

The average daily return when long calls are made is 0.063 percent. This exceeds the average daily return for cash calls by 0.016 percent point. Thus, the TRU system is signaling days that, on average, have above-average market performance. However, these calls are still not good enough to lead to terminal wealth that exceeds buy-and-hold terminal wealth.

The system's short call rate of 40.0 percent (Table 6.15b) is slightly above the optimal short call rate. The hit rate for these short calls is 60.1 percent. This indicator is choosing to make short calls on days that have slightly below-average returns. Note the short average return of 0.046 percent falls 0.015 percentage point below the cash average return. The main problem with this system's short calls is that even though short-call days are days of below-average stock price appreciation, there is still stock price appreciation. On average, stock prices are increasing when short calls are made, so trading short with the system leads to losses. Trading short with the TRU system leads to an average quarterly wealth of $9,886, which is less than the beginning wealth of $10,000 and is only 95.3 percent of the average terminal wealth of a simple buy-and-hold strategy.

Bollinger Bands with ADX

Developed by Linda Bradford Raschke, the Bollinger Bands with ADX indicator is based on two other systems: the Average Directional Index (ADX) and the Bollinger Bands. The ADX is used to detect a retracement from the trend. The Bollinger Bands concept is used to establish entry and exit points.

Because it combines two other indicators, this is a conservative system. Traders must wait for confirmation by both of these systems before making a trade. Calls are infrequent, but traders using this type of system count on the correctness of the calls to make money.

Construction

The first step for constructing this system is to create 20-period Bollinger Bands. (The method for drawing Bollinger Bands is thoroughly described in Chapter 3.)

The second step is to construct a 30-period ADX line. Construction of the ADX line has been described earlier in this chapter.

The system waits for the ADX to rise above 30 before making a trade. After the ADX passes that level, the system waits for the ADX line to drop slightly, indicating a momentary change in trend. After this occurs, the system takes a position when the price line moves back to the exponential moving average that forms the center of the Bollinger Band.

Results

As expected, the results in Table 6.17 show that this system makes infrequent calls. The long call rate for this system is only 13.4 percent. The short call rate is even lower: 9.7 percent. These long and short calls have hit rates of 61.0 percent and 61.3 percent, respectively.

In Table 6.18, the return results for the Bollinger Band with ADX (BOL-T) system show that not only are this system's long and short calls usually correct, but they are also good at distinguishing between above- and below-average market periods. For example, at 0.078 percent, the average return for long calls is 0.026 percentage point greater than the average return for cash calls. Likewise, the average stock return on the days when the system makes short calls is only 0.039 percent. Thus, the system tends to predict days of above-average stock price appreciation with its long calls, and days of below-average stock price appreciation with its short calls.

Unfortunately, these strengths of the BOL-T system are not enough to bring returns that exceed the benchmark buy-and-hold strategy. The terminal wealth from following the system's long calls averages only 97 percent of the terminal wealth of a buy-and-hold strategy. Investors following this system's long calls make above-average returns on the days when they are in the market; however, they are out of the market so often, missing positive return days, that their overall profit level suffers.

The short return analysis gives an even bleaker picture. Investors following the short strategy of this system average only 96.2 percent of the profitability of buy-and-hold investors. Worse yet, those trading short with the BOL-T system lost money in all but 15 of the test quarters. On average, investors beginning a quarter with $10,000 and trading short with the system ended the quarter with only $9,977.

This system was designed to be a conservative system; the confirmation of two indicators is needed to make a trade. The long and short calls are correct more often than they are wrong, but trading with this system does not beat a buy-and-hold strategy.

Trendline Reversal—Long Term

The Trendline Reversal—Long Term (TLN-RL) system is based on a stock's price relative to the stock's long-term trend. In this case, "long term" is defined as a one-month to three-month time span. The system is used to detect reversals in trend.

Table 6.15a
Trend Rule Trading (TRU) Long Hit Analysis
(Average of all stocks)

Qtr	Optimal Long	TRU Long	Long Hits	Cash Hits	Total Hits	Long Right	Long Wrong	Cash Right	Cash Wrong
85:1	32.1%	63.2%	64.7%	66.8%	65.5%	40.9%	22.3%	24.6%	12.2%
85:2	30.2%	52.0%	65.0%	70.5%	67.7%	33.8%	18.2%	33.9%	14.1%
85:3	26.3%	46.0%	61.5%	73.4%	67.9%	28.3%	17.7%	39.6%	14.4%
85:4	36.6%	58.6%	65.5%	66.4%	65.8%	38.4%	20.2%	27.5%	13.9%
86:1	44.2%	63.1%	64.2%	55.5%	61.0%	40.5%	22.6%	20.5%	16.4%
86:2	39.7%	52.4%	59.9%	59.6%	59.8%	31.4%	21.0%	28.4%	19.2%
86:3	37.0%	39.1%	56.6%	63.0%	60.5%	22.1%	17.0%	38.4%	22.5%
86:4	38.5%	48.9%	60.4%	60.8%	60.6%	29.6%	19.3%	31.1%	20.0%
87:1	44.7%	68.0%	62.1%	54.0%	59.5%	42.2%	25.7%	17.3%	14.7%
87:2	40.0%	38.6%	59.8%	59.4%	59.5%	23.1%	15.5%	36.5%	25.0%
87:3	39.5%	58.3%	59.0%	60.4%	59.6%	34.4%	23.9%	25.2%	16.5%
87:4	37.9%	22.7%	55.6%	62.3%	60.8%	12.6%	10.1%	48.2%	29.1%
88:1	41.3%	66.5%	62.4%	57.7%	60.8%	41.5%	25.0%	19.3%	14.2%
88:2	39.3%	41.8%	62.1%	60.5%	61.2%	25.9%	15.9%	35.2%	23.0%
88:3	35.9%	47.9%	60.6%	63.6%	62.2%	29.0%	18.9%	33.1%	19.0%
88:4	36.3%	48.9%	61.4%	63.1%	62.2%	30.0%	18.9%	32.2%	18.9%
89:1	39.0%	60.5%	63.2%	60.8%	62.3%	38.2%	22.2%	24.0%	15.5%
89:2	40.2%	61.2%	63.0%	60.2%	61.9%	38.6%	22.6%	23.3%	15.4%
89:3	39.9%	59.6%	62.8%	59.7%	61.5%	37.4%	22.2%	24.1%	16.3%
89:4	38.3%	33.6%	61.4%	61.6%	61.5%	20.6%	13.0%	40.9%	25.5%
90:1	36.9%	40.1%	58.9%	62.7%	61.2%	23.7%	16.5%	37.5%	22.3%
90:2	39.2%	52.8%	60.7%	60.4%	60.6%	32.0%	20.7%	28.5%	18.7%
90:3	33.5%	28.9%	55.2%	66.8%	63.5%	15.9%	12.9%	47.5%	23.6%
90:4	40.8%	52.3%	62.2%	60.2%	61.3%	32.6%	19.8%	28.7%	19.0%
91:1	44.1%	63.7%	62.1%	54.1%	59.2%	39.6%	24.1%	19.6%	16.7%
91:2	39.7%	46.5%	58.8%	59.8%	59.3%	27.4%	19.2%	32.0%	21.5%
91:3	40.4%	44.9%	59.6%	59.6%	59.6%	26.8%	18.2%	32.8%	22.3%
91:4	41.2%	44.4%	59.8%	58.9%	59.3%	26.5%	17.9%	32.7%	22.9%
92:1	40.0%	59.5%	57.0%	60.2%	58.3%	33.9%	25.6%	24.4%	16.1%
92:2	38.6%	44.1%	57.0%	61.0%	59.2%	25.2%	19.0%	34.1%	21.8%
92:3	40.3%	47.4%	60.3%	59.6%	59.9%	28.5%	18.8%	31.4%	21.2%
92:4	41.9%	51.9%	62.4%	58.0%	60.3%	32.4%	19.5%	27.9%	20.2%
93:1	42.5%	52.6%	61.1%	57.2%	59.2%	32.1%	20.5%	27.1%	20.3%
93:2	42.1%	45.5%	59.1%	58.0%	58.5%	26.9%	18.6%	31.6%	22.8%
93:3	42.5%	53.3%	60.6%	57.2%	59.0%	32.3%	21.0%	26.7%	20.0%
93:4	41.5%	45.2%	58.1%	58.5%	58.3%	26.3%	18.9%	32.0%	22.8%
94:1	40.4%	48.1%	56.8%	60.0%	58.5%	27.4%	20.8%	31.1%	20.7%
94:2	40.6%	36.3%	56.9%	59.2%	58.4%	20.7%	15.6%	37.7%	26.0%
94:3	41.8%	51.0%	59.8%	57.6%	58.7%	30.5%	20.5%	28.2%	20.8%
94:4	39.5%	35.8%	57.2%	60.1%	59.1%	20.4%	15.3%	38.6%	25.6%
95:1	43.1%	57.1%	61.1%	56.8%	59.3%	34.9%	22.2%	24.3%	18.5%
95:2	43.7%	59.4%	60.8%	56.6%	59.1%	36.1%	23.2%	23.0%	17.6%
95:3	43.9%	55.0%	60.7%	56.4%	58.8%	33.4%	21.6%	25.4%	19.6%
95:4	43.4%	46.6%	59.7%	57.2%	58.4%	27.8%	18.8%	30.5%	22.8%
96:1	45.5%	54.1%	60.6%	54.2%	57.7%	32.8%	21.3%	24.9%	21.0%
96:2	42.1%	49.7%	57.8%	58.0%	57.9%	28.7%	20.9%	29.2%	21.1%
96:3	42.6%	34.4%	58.9%	56.8%	57.5%	20.3%	14.1%	37.2%	28.3%
96:4	44.3%	56.2%	60.2%	56.3%	58.5%	33.8%	22.4%	24.7%	19.1%
AVG	40.0%	49.7%	60.3%	60.0%	60.4%	30.2%	19.6%	30.3%	20.0%

Table 6.15b
Trend Rule Trading (TRU) Short Hit Analysis
(Average of all stocks)

Qtr	Optimal Short	TRU Short	Short Hits	Cash Hits	Total Hits	Short Right	Short Wrong	Cash Right	Cash Wrong
85:1	34.3%	23.9%	67.0%	65.1%	65.6%	16.0%	7.9%	49.6%	26.5%
85:2	34.6%	34.8%	71.1%	65.0%	67.1%	24.8%	10.1%	42.3%	22.8%
85:3	38.6%	41.2%	72.3%	61.7%	66.1%	29.8%	11.4%	36.3%	22.5%
85:4	33.1%	30.7%	66.0%	65.8%	65.9%	20.3%	10.4%	45.6%	23.7%
86:1	35.2%	25.1%	56.1%	64.5%	62.4%	14.1%	11.0%	48.3%	26.6%
86:2	39.8%	37.2%	59.9%	59.8%	59.8%	22.3%	14.9%	37.6%	25.3%
86:3	42.7%	51.5%	63.0%	56.5%	59.8%	32.4%	19.1%	27.4%	21.1%
86:4	38.7%	42.2%	61.0%	60.4%	60.6%	25.7%	16.5%	34.9%	22.9%
87:1	36.9%	22.5%	53.3%	62.2%	60.2%	12.0%	10.5%	48.2%	29.3%
87:2	40.0%	52.7%	59.0%	59.8%	59.4%	31.1%	21.6%	28.3%	19.0%
87:3	40.4%	31.8%	60.3%	58.9%	59.3%	19.2%	12.6%	40.1%	28.0%
87:4	45.3%	72.9%	61.9%	54.6%	59.9%	45.1%	27.8%	14.8%	12.3%
88:1	36.7%	28.9%	57.4%	62.5%	61.0%	16.6%	12.3%	44.5%	26.7%
88:2	37.4%	50.6%	60.2%	62.1%	61.2%	30.5%	20.1%	30.7%	18.7%
88:3	38.4%	42.9%	63.4%	60.8%	61.9%	27.2%	15.7%	34.7%	22.4%
88:4	37.0%	40.3%	62.8%	61.7%	62.1%	25.3%	15.0%	36.8%	22.9%
89:1	36.2%	29.2%	61.1%	63.2%	62.6%	17.8%	11.3%	44.7%	26.1%
89:2	35.9%	27.7%	60.7%	63.2%	62.6%	16.8%	10.9%	45.8%	26.6%
89:3	36.4%	29.0%	59.8%	62.8%	61.9%	17.3%	11.7%	44.6%	26.4%
89:4	39.0%	54.4%	61.8%	61.4%	61.6%	33.6%	20.8%	28.0%	17.6%
90:1	40.1%	47.1%	62.2%	59.0%	60.5%	29.3%	17.8%	31.2%	21.7%
90:2	37.8%	34.8%	60.7%	61.1%	61.0%	21.1%	13.7%	39.9%	25.4%
90:3	45.7%	61.5%	66.8%	55.0%	62.3%	41.1%	20.4%	21.2%	17.3%
90:4	37.6%	38.3%	60.3%	62.5%	61.6%	23.1%	15.2%	38.5%	23.2%
91:1	36.7%	24.6%	53.3%	62.3%	60.1%	13.1%	11.5%	47.0%	28.4%
91:2	40.4%	42.6%	59.5%	59.1%	59.3%	25.3%	17.2%	33.9%	23.5%
91:3	39.8%	44.0%	60.0%	59.9%	59.9%	26.4%	17.6%	33.5%	22.5%
91:4	40.5%	44.2%	59.0%	59.8%	59.5%	26.1%	18.1%	33.4%	22.4%
92:1	43.2%	28.9%	61.4%	57.1%	58.3%	17.7%	11.1%	40.6%	30.5%
92:2	42.9%	46.7%	61.2%	57.1%	59.0%	28.6%	18.1%	30.4%	22.9%
92:3	39.5%	40.7%	59.7%	60.4%	60.1%	24.3%	16.4%	35.8%	23.5%
92:4	37.5%	36.6%	58.4%	62.3%	60.9%	21.4%	15.3%	39.5%	23.9%
93:1	39.4%	35.1%	57.6%	61.0%	59.8%	20.2%	14.9%	39.6%	25.3%
93:2	40.9%	45.5%	57.8%	58.8%	58.4%	26.3%	19.2%	32.1%	22.5%
93:3	39.4%	36.8%	57.2%	60.4%	59.2%	21.1%	15.8%	38.2%	25.0%
93:4	41.7%	45.1%	58.4%	57.9%	58.1%	26.3%	18.8%	31.8%	23.1%
94:1	43.7%	42.6%	60.1%	56.4%	58.0%	25.6%	17.0%	32.4%	25.0%
94:2	42.7%	55.0%	59.5%	57.1%	58.4%	32.7%	22.3%	25.7%	19.3%
94:3	39.8%	38.6%	57.7%	59.8%	59.0%	22.3%	16.3%	36.7%	24.7%
94:4	42.8%	54.8%	60.0%	57.0%	58.7%	32.9%	21.9%	25.7%	19.4%
95:1	38.7%	32.9%	57.0%	61.0%	59.7%	18.7%	14.1%	41.0%	26.2%
95:2	38.9%	32.4%	56.7%	60.7%	59.4%	18.4%	14.0%	41.0%	26.6%
95:3	38.9%	35.4%	56.7%	60.8%	59.3%	20.0%	15.3%	39.3%	25.3%
95:4	40.5%	42.2%	57.4%	59.7%	58.8%	24.2%	17.9%	34.5%	23.3%
96:1	38.9%	35.3%	54.7%	60.8%	58.6%	19.3%	16.0%	39.3%	25.4%
96:2	42.4%	41.1%	58.4%	57.9%	58.1%	24.0%	17.1%	34.1%	24.8%
96:3	40.8%	55.2%	56.8%	59.3%	57.9%	31.3%	23.9%	26.6%	18.2%
96:4	39.8%	32.9%	56.6%	60.1%	58.9%	18.6%	14.3%	40.3%	26.8%
AVG	39.4%	40.0%	60.1%	60.3%	60.5%	24.1%	15.9%	36.4%	23.6%

Table 6.16a
Trend Rule Trading (TRU) Long Return Analysis
(Average of all stocks)

Qtr	TRU Terminal Wealth	Buy/Hold Terminal Wealth	Relative Terminal Wealth	TRU Long Avg Ret	TRU Cash Avg Ret	TRU Long-Cash Avg Ret	Buy/Hold Avg Ret
85:1	9991	10142	0.985	-0.015%	0.042%	-0.057%	0.006%
85:2	9818	9700	1.012	-0.072%	-0.066%	-0.005%	-0.069%
85:3	9450	8889	1.063	-0.207%	-0.203%	-0.004%	-0.205%
85:4	10499	10763	0.976	0.127%	0.078%	0.049%	0.107%
86:1	10814	11428	0.946	0.203%	0.261%	-0.058%	0.225%
86:2	10149	10414	0.975	0.044%	0.091%	-0.047%	0.066%
86:3	9547	9175	1.041	-0.184%	-0.091%	-0.092%	-0.128%
86:4	10108	10413	0.971	0.038%	0.099%	-0.062%	0.069%
87:1	11125	11929	0.933	0.255%	0.372%	-0.117%	0.293%
87:2	10038	10196	0.985	0.019%	0.050%	-0.031%	0.038%
87:3	10184	10408	0.978	0.053%	0.090%	-0.036%	0.068%
87:4	9744	8087	1.205	-0.183%	-0.306%	0.122%	-0.278%
88:1	10553	10989	0.960	0.138%	0.212%	-0.074%	0.163%
88:2	10225	10593	0.965	0.090%	0.107%	-0.016%	0.100%
88:3	9965	10050	0.992	-0.007%	0.031%	-0.038%	0.013%
88:4	10005	10196	0.981	0.005%	0.067%	-0.063%	0.037%
89:1	10393	10698	0.971	0.106%	0.122%	-0.016%	0.112%
89:2	10426	10772	0.968	0.109%	0.142%	-0.033%	0.122%
89:3	10430	10833	0.963	0.114%	0.156%	-0.042%	0.131%
89:4	9925	9904	1.002	-0.033%	0.000%	-0.033%	-0.011%
90:1	9921	9980	0.994	-0.031%	0.025%	-0.056%	0.003%
90:2	10165	10459	0.972	0.051%	0.106%	-0.055%	0.077%
90:3	9596	8526	1.125	-0.228%	-0.272%	0.044%	-0.259%
90:4	10555	10889	0.969	0.167%	0.123%	0.044%	0.146%
91:1	11231	12477	0.900	0.278%	0.380%	-0.103%	0.315%
91:2	10029	10244	0.979	0.016%	0.071%	-0.054%	0.045%
91:3	10167	10429	0.975	0.055%	0.073%	-0.019%	0.065%
91:4	10195	10497	0.971	0.077%	0.086%	-0.009%	0.082%
92:1	10230	10324	0.991	0.062%	0.027%	0.034%	0.048%
92:2	9856	9723	1.014	-0.059%	-0.040%	-0.019%	-0.048%
92:3	10151	10392	0.977	0.046%	0.066%	-0.019%	0.057%
92:4	10534	10963	0.961	0.153%	0.135%	0.018%	0.144%
93:1	10289	10527	0.977	0.085%	0.074%	0.010%	0.080%
93:2	10159	10340	0.982	0.049%	0.054%	-0.005%	0.052%
93:3	10383	10686	0.972	0.105%	0.097%	0.008%	0.101%
93:4	10120	10255	0.987	0.036%	0.032%	0.004%	0.034%
94:1	10030	9954	1.008	0.006%	-0.028%	0.034%	-0.011%
94:2	9955	9994	0.996	-0.022%	0.005%	-0.027%	-0.005%
94:3	10294	10613	0.970	0.085%	0.093%	-0.008%	0.089%
94:4	9913	9836	1.008	-0.043%	-0.022%	-0.021%	-0.029%
95:1	10392	10706	0.971	0.107%	0.114%	-0.008%	0.110%
95:2	10548	10873	0.970	0.141%	0.124%	0.017%	0.134%
95:3	10474	10853	0.965	0.132%	0.129%	0.003%	0.131%
95:4	10230	10445	0.979	0.072%	0.062%	0.011%	0.067%
96:1	10513	11027	0.953	0.145%	0.175%	-0.030%	0.159%
96:2	10241	10367	0.988	0.076%	0.042%	0.034%	0.059%
96:3	10033	10298	0.974	0.013%	0.065%	-0.052%	0.047%
96:4	10497	10817	0.970	0.133%	0.108%	0.025%	0.122%
AVG	10210	10377	0.984	0.063%	0.047%	0.016%	0.055%

Table 6.16b
Trend Rule Trading (TRU) Short Return Analysis
(Average of all stocks)

Qtr	TRU Terminal Wealth	Buy/Hold Terminal Wealth	Relative Terminal Wealth	TRU Short Avg Ret	TRU Cash Avg Ret	TRU Short-Cash Avg Ret	Buy/Hold Avg Ret
85:1	9982	10142	0.984	0.022%	0.001%	0.021%	0.006%
85:2	10227	9700	1.054	-0.083%	-0.062%	-0.021%	-0.069%
85:3	10585	8889	1.191	-0.201%	-0.208%	0.007%	-0.205%
85:4	9872	10763	0.917	0.079%	0.119%	-0.040%	0.107%
86:1	9624	11428	0.842	0.251%	0.216%	0.036%	0.225%
86:2	9777	10414	0.939	0.097%	0.048%	0.049%	0.066%
86:3	10252	9175	1.117	-0.086%	-0.172%	0.086%	-0.128%
86:4	9724	10413	0.934	0.103%	0.045%	0.059%	0.069%
87:1	9443	11929	0.792	0.422%	0.256%	0.166%	0.293%
87:2	9803	10196	0.961	0.053%	0.022%	0.031%	0.038%
87:3	9778	10408	0.939	0.109%	0.049%	0.059%	0.068%
87:4	11067	8087	1.368	-0.266%	-0.310%	0.043%	-0.278%
88:1	9591	10989	0.873	0.229%	0.136%	0.093%	0.163%
88:2	9631	10593	0.909	0.113%	0.086%	0.027%	0.100%
88:3	9889	10050	0.984	0.038%	-0.007%	0.045%	0.013%
88:4	9802	10196	0.961	0.075%	0.011%	0.064%	0.037%
89:1	9778	10698	0.914	0.126%	0.107%	0.019%	0.112%
89:2	9739	10772	0.904	0.148%	0.112%	0.036%	0.122%
89:3	9700	10833	0.895	0.170%	0.115%	0.054%	0.131%
89:4	10004	9904	1.010	-0.006%	-0.017%	0.011%	-0.011%
90:1	9869	9980	0.989	0.040%	-0.030%	0.070%	0.003%
90:2	9758	10459	0.933	0.110%	0.059%	0.050%	0.077%
90:3	11146	8526	1.307	-0.279%	-0.227%	-0.051%	-0.259%
90:4	9695	10889	0.890	0.120%	0.162%	-0.042%	0.146%
91:1	9406	12477	0.754	0.418%	0.281%	0.137%	0.315%
91:2	9780	10244	0.955	0.074%	0.024%	0.050%	0.045%
91:3	9805	10429	0.940	0.068%	0.062%	0.006%	0.065%
91:4	9753	10497	0.929	0.085%	0.079%	0.007%	0.082%
92:1	9996	10324	0.968	0.007%	0.065%	-0.058%	0.048%
92:2	10131	9723	1.042	-0.044%	-0.052%	0.008%	-0.048%
92:3	9853	10392	0.948	0.064%	0.052%	0.012%	0.057%
92:4	9677	10963	0.883	0.141%	0.147%	-0.006%	0.144%
93:1	9853	10527	0.936	0.073%	0.083%	-0.011%	0.080%
93:2	9812	10340	0.949	0.066%	0.040%	0.026%	0.052%
93:3	9776	10686	0.915	0.098%	0.103%	-0.006%	0.101%
93:4	9895	10255	0.965	0.039%	0.029%	0.010%	0.034%
94:1	10052	9954	1.010	-0.017%	-0.007%	-0.011%	-0.011%
94:2	9995	9994	1.000	0.005%	-0.016%	0.021%	-0.005%
94:3	9788	10613	0.922	0.092%	0.088%	0.004%	0.089%
94:4	10072	9836	1.024	-0.020%	-0.041%	0.020%	-0.029%
95:1	9761	10706	0.912	0.120%	0.105%	0.014%	0.110%
95:2	9739	10873	0.896	0.132%	0.135%	-0.002%	0.134%
95:3	9721	10853	0.896	0.129%	0.132%	-0.003%	0.131%
95:4	9852	10445	0.943	0.059%	0.072%	-0.013%	0.067%
96:1	9604	11027	0.871	0.183%	0.146%	0.037%	0.159%
96:2	9917	10367	0.957	0.034%	0.076%	-0.042%	0.059%
96:3	9781	10298	0.950	0.062%	0.029%	0.034%	0.047%
96:4	9761	10817	0.902	0.117%	0.125%	-0.008%	0.122%
AVG	9886	10377	0.953	0.046%	0.061%	-0.015%	0.055%

Table 6.17a
Bollinger Band with ADX (BOL-T) Long Hit Analysis
(Average of all stocks)

Qtr	Optimal Long	BOL-T Long	Long Hits	Cash Hits	Total Hits	Long Right	Long Wrong	Cash Right	Cash Wrong
85:1	32.1%	17.2%	61.7%	67.9%	66.9%	10.6%	6.6%	56.2%	26.5%
85:2	30.2%	14.0%	65.8%	70.2%	69.6%	9.2%	4.8%	60.4%	25.6%
85:3	26.3%	14.8%	60.6%	73.9%	71.9%	8.9%	5.8%	63.0%	22.2%
85:4	36.6%	9.6%	66.8%	63.8%	64.1%	6.4%	3.2%	57.7%	32.7%
86:1	44.2%	20.6%	66.3%	56.2%	58.2%	13.6%	6.9%	44.6%	34.8%
86:2	39.7%	20.3%	61.3%	60.6%	60.7%	12.5%	7.9%	48.3%	31.4%
86:3	37.0%	11.9%	57.1%	62.9%	62.2%	6.8%	5.1%	55.4%	32.7%
86:4	38.5%	11.5%	62.6%	61.4%	61.5%	7.2%	4.3%	54.3%	34.2%
87:1	44.7%	18.0%	64.2%	55.4%	57.0%	11.6%	6.4%	45.4%	36.6%
87:2	40.0%	12.1%	60.4%	59.6%	59.7%	7.3%	4.8%	52.4%	35.5%
87:3	39.5%	18.1%	59.0%	60.5%	60.2%	10.7%	7.4%	49.5%	32.4%
87:4	37.9%	3.2%	46.2%	61.8%	61.3%	1.5%	1.7%	59.8%	37.0%
88:1	41.3%	10.9%	63.0%	58.1%	58.7%	6.9%	4.0%	51.8%	37.3%
88:2	39.3%	15.3%	64.2%	60.5%	61.1%	9.8%	5.5%	51.3%	33.4%
88:3	35.9%	15.3%	61.0%	63.7%	63.3%	9.3%	6.0%	53.9%	30.8%
88:4	36.3%	13.7%	62.0%	63.7%	63.5%	8.5%	5.2%	55.0%	31.3%
89:1	39.0%	17.1%	63.7%	61.0%	61.5%	10.9%	6.2%	50.6%	32.3%
89:2	40.2%	16.2%	63.4%	59.9%	60.4%	10.3%	5.9%	50.1%	33.6%
89:3	39.9%	20.2%	64.4%	60.3%	61.1%	13.0%	7.2%	48.1%	31.7%
89:4	38.3%	10.7%	62.1%	61.9%	61.9%	6.6%	4.1%	55.2%	34.1%
90:1	36.9%	11.3%	58.8%	63.0%	62.5%	6.6%	4.7%	55.9%	32.8%
90:2	39.2%	13.4%	62.1%	61.0%	61.1%	8.3%	5.1%	52.8%	33.8%
90:3	33.5%	11.3%	54.8%	66.8%	65.5%	6.2%	5.1%	59.3%	29.4%
90:4	40.8%	4.9%	66.2%	59.2%	59.5%	3.3%	1.7%	56.3%	38.8%
91:1	44.1%	19.2%	65.2%	56.4%	58.0%	12.5%	6.7%	45.5%	35.3%
91:2	39.7%	18.0%	60.6%	60.5%	60.6%	10.9%	7.1%	49.7%	32.4%
91:3	40.4%	12.1%	61.8%	59.7%	59.9%	7.5%	4.6%	52.5%	35.4%
91:4	41.2%	13.2%	61.6%	58.8%	59.1%	8.1%	5.1%	51.0%	35.8%
92:1	40.0%	18.5%	56.2%	60.0%	59.3%	10.4%	8.1%	48.9%	32.6%
92:2	38.6%	9.3%	58.3%	61.5%	61.2%	5.4%	3.9%	55.8%	34.9%
92:3	40.3%	10.7%	61.5%	59.8%	60.0%	6.6%	4.1%	53.4%	35.9%
92:4	41.9%	10.6%	63.7%	57.9%	58.5%	6.7%	3.9%	51.7%	37.7%
93:1	42.5%	17.5%	62.8%	57.8%	58.7%	11.0%	6.5%	47.7%	34.8%
93:2	42.1%	10.9%	60.9%	58.0%	58.3%	6.7%	4.3%	51.7%	37.4%
93:3	42.5%	12.9%	61.8%	57.5%	58.0%	8.0%	4.9%	50.0%	37.0%
93:4	41.5%	12.1%	59.4%	58.6%	58.7%	7.2%	4.9%	51.5%	36.4%
94:1	40.4%	11.8%	59.1%	59.8%	59.8%	7.0%	4.8%	52.8%	35.4%
94:2	40.6%	6.4%	56.4%	59.3%	59.1%	3.6%	2.8%	55.5%	38.1%
94:3	41.8%	11.4%	60.6%	58.3%	58.6%	6.9%	4.5%	51.6%	36.9%
94:4	39.5%	10.0%	57.2%	60.5%	60.1%	5.7%	4.3%	54.4%	35.6%
95:1	43.1%	12.8%	61.8%	56.8%	57.5%	7.9%	4.9%	49.6%	37.7%
95:2	43.7%	14.6%	61.3%	56.4%	57.1%	9.0%	5.7%	48.2%	37.2%
95:3	43.9%	14.5%	60.9%	55.9%	56.6%	8.8%	5.7%	47.8%	37.7%
95:4	43.4%	15.0%	60.1%	56.6%	57.1%	9.0%	6.0%	48.1%	36.9%
96:1	45.5%	14.9%	62.5%	54.6%	55.7%	9.3%	5.6%	46.4%	38.7%
96:2	42.1%	11.4%	58.2%	57.9%	58.0%	6.6%	4.8%	51.3%	37.3%
96:3	42.6%	7.4%	59.3%	57.3%	57.4%	4.4%	3.0%	53.0%	39.6%
96:4	44.3%	15.8%	59.8%	55.9%	56.5%	9.5%	6.4%	47.0%	37.1%
AVG	40.0%	13.4%	61.0%	60.2%	60.4%	8.2%	5.2%	52.1%	34.5%

Table 6.17b
Bollinger Band with ADX (BOL-T) Short Hit Analysis
(Average of all stocks)

Qtr	Optimal Short	BOL-T Short	Short Hits	Cash Hits	Total Hits	Short Right	Short Wrong	Cash Right	Cash Wrong
85:1	34.3%	5.1%	66.8%	65.5%	65.6%	3.4%	1.7%	62.2%	32.7%
85:2	34.6%	9.3%	74.7%	65.4%	66.3%	6.9%	2.3%	59.4%	31.4%
85:3	38.6%	9.9%	78.4%	61.3%	63.0%	7.7%	2.1%	55.3%	34.9%
85:4	33.1%	12.3%	66.5%	66.7%	66.7%	8.2%	4.1%	58.5%	29.2%
86:1	35.2%	4.0%	58.6%	64.8%	64.6%	2.4%	1.7%	62.2%	33.8%
86:2	39.8%	5.3%	62.7%	60.1%	60.2%	3.3%	2.0%	56.9%	37.8%
86:3	42.7%	13.3%	64.2%	57.2%	58.2%	8.5%	4.8%	49.6%	37.1%
86:4	38.7%	13.6%	59.6%	61.1%	60.9%	8.1%	5.5%	52.8%	33.6%
87:1	36.9%	4.9%	56.5%	63.0%	62.7%	2.8%	2.1%	59.9%	35.2%
87:2	40.0%	12.0%	61.1%	59.9%	60.0%	7.3%	4.7%	52.7%	35.3%
87:3	40.4%	7.4%	62.6%	59.5%	59.7%	4.7%	2.8%	55.0%	37.5%
87:4	45.3%	21.1%	62.0%	54.3%	55.9%	13.1%	8.0%	42.9%	36.1%
88:1	36.7%	10.9%	55.6%	63.0%	62.2%	6.1%	4.8%	56.1%	33.0%
88:2	37.4%	6.8%	60.1%	62.5%	62.3%	4.1%	2.7%	58.2%	35.0%
88:3	38.4%	9.5%	63.2%	61.4%	61.5%	6.0%	3.5%	55.6%	35.0%
88:4	37.0%	10.4%	63.7%	62.9%	62.9%	6.7%	3.8%	56.3%	33.3%
89:1	36.2%	6.9%	60.4%	63.6%	63.4%	4.2%	2.7%	59.2%	33.9%
89:2	35.9%	5.8%	60.2%	63.8%	63.6%	3.5%	2.3%	60.1%	34.1%
89:3	36.4%	5.3%	62.2%	63.4%	63.3%	3.3%	2.0%	60.1%	34.7%
89:4	39.0%	13.1%	62.4%	61.0%	61.2%	8.1%	4.9%	53.1%	33.9%
90:1	40.1%	17.4%	63.6%	59.8%	60.5%	11.1%	6.3%	49.4%	33.2%
90:2	37.8%	11.5%	62.0%	62.0%	62.0%	7.1%	4.4%	54.8%	33.6%
90:3	45.7%	11.9%	70.2%	54.6%	56.4%	8.3%	3.6%	48.1%	40.0%
90:4	37.6%	18.1%	59.8%	62.5%	62.0%	10.8%	7.3%	51.2%	30.7%
91:1	36.7%	4.1%	57.3%	63.2%	62.9%	2.4%	1.8%	60.6%	35.3%
91:2	40.4%	4.3%	64.3%	59.6%	59.8%	2.8%	1.5%	57.1%	38.6%
91:3	39.8%	8.1%	62.8%	60.2%	60.4%	5.1%	3.0%	55.4%	36.6%
91:4	40.5%	10.1%	60.3%	59.5%	59.5%	6.1%	4.0%	53.5%	36.5%
92:1	43.2%	7.8%	58.5%	56.6%	56.7%	4.6%	3.2%	52.2%	40.0%
92:2	42.9%	9.1%	63.1%	57.1%	57.7%	5.8%	3.4%	51.9%	39.0%
92:3	39.5%	10.9%	62.3%	60.5%	60.7%	6.8%	4.1%	53.9%	35.2%
92:4	37.5%	10.2%	58.9%	62.6%	62.2%	6.0%	4.2%	56.2%	33.6%
93:1	39.4%	6.3%	61.1%	60.8%	60.8%	3.8%	2.4%	57.0%	36.8%
93:2	40.9%	9.7%	58.5%	59.1%	59.0%	5.7%	4.0%	53.3%	36.9%
93:3	39.4%	10.4%	58.7%	60.6%	60.4%	6.1%	4.3%	54.3%	35.3%
93:4	41.7%	11.0%	58.6%	58.0%	58.1%	6.5%	4.6%	51.6%	37.4%
94:1	43.7%	10.1%	62.1%	56.4%	57.0%	6.3%	3.8%	50.7%	39.2%
94:2	42.7%	16.2%	60.3%	57.4%	57.8%	9.8%	6.4%	48.1%	35.7%
94:3	39.8%	10.7%	58.7%	60.0%	59.8%	6.3%	4.4%	53.6%	35.7%
94:4	42.8%	12.8%	60.9%	57.2%	57.7%	7.8%	5.0%	49.9%	37.3%
95:1	38.7%	9.3%	57.5%	61.3%	61.0%	5.3%	3.9%	55.6%	35.1%
95:2	38.9%	5.8%	56.5%	61.0%	60.7%	3.3%	2.5%	57.5%	36.8%
95:3	38.9%	5.0%	57.8%	61.0%	60.8%	2.9%	2.1%	58.0%	37.1%
95:4	40.5%	9.7%	57.3%	59.4%	59.2%	5.6%	4.1%	53.6%	36.7%
96:1	38.9%	8.4%	56.9%	61.2%	60.9%	4.8%	3.6%	56.1%	35.5%
96:2	42.4%	6.5%	58.9%	57.6%	57.7%	3.8%	2.7%	53.9%	39.6%
96:3	40.8%	16.6%	55.5%	58.8%	58.3%	9.2%	7.4%	49.1%	34.3%
96:4	39.8%	6.6%	56.7%	60.1%	59.8%	3.7%	2.9%	56.1%	37.3%
AVG	39.4%	9.7%	61.3%	60.6%	60.7%	6.0%	3.7%	54.8%	35.5%

Table 6.18a
Bollinger Band with ADX (BOL-T) Long Return Analysis
(Average of all stocks)

Qtr	BOL-T Terminal Wealth	Buy/Hold Terminal Wealth	Relative Terminal Wealth	BOL-T Long Avg Ret	BOL-T Cash Avg Ret	BOL-T Long-Cash Avg Ret	Buy/Hold Avg Ret
85:1	9942	10142	0.980	-0.060%	0.020%	-0.080%	0.006%
85:2	9992	9700	1.030	-0.011%	-0.079%	0.068%	-0.069%
85:3	9855	8889	1.109	-0.161%	-0.212%	0.052%	-0.205%
85:4	10121	10763	0.940	0.198%	0.097%	0.101%	0.107%
86:1	10334	11428	0.904	0.263%	0.215%	0.049%	0.225%
86:2	10148	10414	0.975	0.113%	0.054%	0.059%	0.066%
86:3	9854	9175	1.074	-0.194%	-0.119%	-0.075%	-0.128%
86:4	10051	10413	0.965	0.074%	0.069%	0.006%	0.069%
87:1	10331	11929	0.866	0.298%	0.292%	0.006%	0.293%
87:2	10003	10196	0.981	0.004%	0.042%	-0.038%	0.038%
87:3	10043	10408	0.965	0.041%	0.074%	-0.033%	0.068%
87:4	9797	8087	1.212	-1.039%	-0.252%	-0.787%	-0.278%
88:1	10066	10989	0.916	0.102%	0.170%	-0.068%	0.163%
88:2	10125	10593	0.956	0.133%	0.094%	0.039%	0.100%
88:3	9958	10050	0.991	-0.043%	0.023%	-0.065%	0.013%
88:4	10005	10196	0.981	0.008%	0.041%	-0.033%	0.037%
89:1	10115	10698	0.945	0.111%	0.113%	-0.002%	0.112%
89:2	10114	10772	0.939	0.111%	0.124%	-0.013%	0.122%
89:3	10199	10833	0.941	0.156%	0.125%	0.032%	0.131%
89:4	10032	9904	1.013	0.047%	-0.018%	0.065%	-0.011%
90:1	9958	9980	0.998	-0.055%	0.010%	-0.065%	0.003%
90:2	10061	10459	0.962	0.075%	0.077%	-0.003%	0.077%
90:3	9887	8526	1.160	-0.165%	-0.271%	0.106%	-0.259%
90:4	10066	10889	0.924	0.212%	0.143%	0.069%	0.146%
91:1	10433	12477	0.836	0.363%	0.304%	0.060%	0.315%
91:2	10066	10244	0.983	0.061%	0.042%	0.019%	0.045%
91:3	10078	10429	0.966	0.102%	0.060%	0.042%	0.065%
91:4	10149	10497	0.967	0.194%	0.065%	0.130%	0.082%
92:1	10027	10324	0.971	0.021%	0.054%	-0.033%	0.048%
92:2	9984	9723	1.027	-0.031%	-0.050%	0.019%	-0.048%
92:3	10060	10392	0.968	0.087%	0.053%	0.034%	0.057%
92:4	10110	10963	0.922	0.159%	0.143%	0.016%	0.144%
93:1	10126	10527	0.962	0.115%	0.072%	0.043%	0.080%
93:2	10063	10340	0.973	0.089%	0.047%	0.042%	0.052%
93:3	10107	10686	0.946	0.127%	0.097%	0.030%	0.101%
93:4	10035	10255	0.979	0.043%	0.033%	0.011%	0.034%
94:1	10060	9954	1.011	0.079%	-0.023%	0.103%	-0.011%
94:2	9995	9994	1.000	-0.017%	-0.004%	-0.013%	-0.005%
94:3	10070	10613	0.949	0.094%	0.089%	0.006%	0.089%
94:4	9979	9836	1.015	-0.036%	-0.029%	-0.007%	-0.029%
95:1	10104	10706	0.944	0.132%	0.107%	0.025%	0.110%
95:2	10144	10873	0.933	0.156%	0.130%	0.026%	0.134%
95:3	10113	10853	0.932	0.122%	0.133%	-0.011%	0.131%
95:4	10071	10445	0.964	0.074%	0.065%	0.008%	0.067%
96:1	10155	11027	0.921	0.163%	0.158%	0.005%	0.159%
96:2	10050	10367	0.969	0.069%	0.057%	0.011%	0.059%
96:3	10003	10298	0.971	0.006%	0.051%	-0.045%	0.047%
96:4	10136	10817	0.937	0.132%	0.120%	0.012%	0.122%
AVG	10066	10377	0.970	0.078%	0.052%	0.026%	0.055%

Table 6.18b
Bollinger Band with ADX (BOL-T) Short Return Analysis
(Average of all stocks)

Qtr	BOL-T Terminal Wealth	Buy/Hold Terminal Wealth	Relative Terminal Wealth	BOL-T Short Avg Ret	BOL-T Cash Avg Ret	BOL-T Short-Cash Avg Ret	Buy/Hold Avg Ret
85:1	9953	10142	0.981	0.161%	-0.002%	0.163%	0.006%
85:2	10113	9700	1.043	-0.182%	-0.058%	-0.124%	-0.069%
85:3	10212	8889	1.149	-0.306%	-0.194%	-0.113%	-0.205%
85:4	9956	10763	0.925	0.062%	0.113%	-0.051%	0.107%
86:1	9951	11428	0.871	0.191%	0.226%	-0.035%	0.225%
86:2	9989	10414	0.959	0.026%	0.069%	-0.043%	0.066%
86:3	10109	9175	1.102	-0.131%	-0.127%	-0.004%	-0.128%
86:4	9882	10413	0.949	0.138%	0.058%	0.080%	0.069%
87:1	9892	11929	0.829	0.372%	0.289%	0.083%	0.293%
87:2	9972	10196	0.978	0.034%	0.038%	-0.004%	0.038%
87:3	9984	10408	0.959	0.029%	0.071%	-0.042%	0.068%
87:4	10057	8087	1.244	-0.047%	-0.340%	0.293%	-0.278%
88:1	9835	10989	0.895	0.234%	0.154%	0.080%	0.163%
88:2	9942	10593	0.939	0.134%	0.097%	0.037%	0.100%
88:3	9968	10050	0.992	0.051%	0.009%	0.043%	0.013%
88:4	9971	10196	0.978	0.040%	0.036%	0.004%	0.037%
89:1	9939	10698	0.929	0.146%	0.110%	0.036%	0.112%
89:2	9951	10772	0.924	0.134%	0.121%	0.013%	0.122%
89:3	9955	10833	0.919	0.137%	0.131%	0.007%	0.131%
89:4	10002	9904	1.010	-0.003%	-0.012%	0.009%	-0.011%
90:1	10000	9980	1.002	-0.001%	0.004%	-0.005%	0.003%
90:2	9930	10459	0.949	0.095%	0.074%	0.020%	0.077%
90:3	10271	8526	1.205	-0.361%	-0.245%	-0.116%	-0.259%
90:4	9820	10889	0.902	0.159%	0.143%	0.016%	0.146%
91:1	9916	12477	0.795	0.354%	0.313%	0.041%	0.315%
91:2	10011	10244	0.977	-0.039%	0.049%	-0.089%	0.045%
91:3	10002	10429	0.959	-0.010%	0.071%	-0.082%	0.065%
91:4	9961	10497	0.949	0.066%	0.084%	-0.017%	0.082%
92:1	9934	10324	0.962	0.142%	0.040%	0.102%	0.048%
92:2	10076	9723	1.036	-0.124%	-0.041%	-0.083%	-0.048%
92:3	10018	10392	0.964	-0.027%	0.067%	-0.094%	0.057%
92:4	9903	10963	0.903	0.156%	0.143%	0.013%	0.144%
93:1	10018	10527	0.952	-0.041%	0.088%	-0.129%	0.080%
93:2	9992	10340	0.966	0.014%	0.056%	-0.041%	0.052%
93:3	9958	10686	0.932	0.064%	0.105%	-0.041%	0.101%
93:4	9955	10255	0.971	0.068%	0.030%	0.038%	0.034%
94:1	10031	9954	1.008	-0.047%	-0.007%	-0.040%	-0.011%
94:2	10049	9994	1.005	-0.049%	0.004%	-0.052%	-0.005%
94:3	9931	10613	0.936	0.109%	0.087%	0.022%	0.089%
94:4	10016	9836	1.018	-0.022%	-0.030%	0.008%	-0.029%
95:1	9934	10706	0.928	0.113%	0.110%	0.004%	0.110%
95:2	9936	10873	0.914	0.179%	0.131%	0.048%	0.134%
95:3	9963	10853	0.918	0.125%	0.131%	-0.007%	0.131%
95:4	9942	10445	0.952	0.101%	0.063%	0.037%	0.067%
96:1	9924	11027	0.900	0.149%	0.160%	-0.011%	0.159%
96:2	9971	10367	0.962	0.075%	0.057%	0.017%	0.059%
96:3	9872	10298	0.959	0.124%	0.032%	0.092%	0.047%
96:4	9945	10817	0.919	0.141%	0.121%	0.020%	0.122%
AVG	9977	10377	0.962	0.039%	0.057%	-0.018%	0.055%

Table 6.19a
Trendline Reversal—Long Term (TLN-RL) Long Hit Analysis
(Average of all stocks)

Qtr	Optimal Long	TLN-RL Long	Long Hits	Cash Hits	Total Hits	Long Right	Long Wrong	Cash Right	Cash Wrong
85:1	32.1%	5.2%	66.5%	68.2%	68.1%	3.5%	1.7%	64.6%	30.2%
85:2	30.2%	6.2%	63.8%	69.9%	69.5%	4.0%	2.3%	65.5%	28.2%
85:3	26.3%	6.3%	59.7%	73.7%	72.9%	3.8%	2.5%	69.1%	24.6%
85:4	36.6%	5.3%	65.8%	63.3%	63.5%	3.5%	1.8%	60.0%	34.7%
86:1	44.2%	6.5%	64.2%	56.0%	56.5%	4.2%	2.3%	52.3%	41.2%
86:2	39.7%	7.7%	60.8%	60.3%	60.3%	4.7%	3.0%	55.6%	36.7%
86:3	37.0%	7.3%	57.0%	63.1%	62.6%	4.2%	3.1%	58.5%	34.2%
86:4	38.5%	5.8%	60.7%	61.6%	61.6%	3.5%	2.3%	58.0%	36.2%
87:1	44.7%	5.8%	62.7%	55.3%	55.8%	3.6%	2.2%	52.1%	42.1%
87:2	40.0%	6.4%	61.2%	60.1%	60.1%	3.9%	2.5%	56.2%	37.4%
87:3	39.5%	6.7%	60.6%	60.4%	60.4%	4.1%	2.7%	56.4%	36.9%
87:4	37.9%	4.1%	52.9%	62.0%	61.6%	2.2%	1.9%	59.5%	36.4%
88:1	41.3%	3.9%	61.6%	58.5%	58.7%	2.4%	1.5%	56.2%	39.8%
88:2	39.3%	6.5%	61.1%	60.7%	60.7%	4.0%	2.5%	56.8%	36.8%
88:3	35.9%	6.9%	61.9%	64.1%	64.0%	4.3%	2.6%	59.7%	33.4%
88:4	36.3%	6.1%	62.5%	63.7%	63.6%	3.8%	2.3%	59.8%	34.1%
89:1	39.0%	6.9%	62.9%	61.0%	61.2%	4.4%	2.6%	56.8%	36.3%
89:2	40.2%	7.0%	62.8%	60.0%	60.2%	4.4%	2.6%	55.8%	37.3%
89:3	39.9%	7.8%	63.5%	60.2%	60.5%	4.9%	2.8%	55.5%	36.7%
89:4	38.3%	8.2%	59.9%	61.8%	61.6%	4.9%	3.3%	56.7%	35.1%
90:1	36.9%	6.3%	58.3%	63.1%	62.8%	3.7%	2.6%	59.1%	34.6%
90:2	39.2%	5.7%	62.1%	60.8%	60.9%	3.5%	2.1%	57.4%	37.0%
90:3	33.5%	4.7%	55.6%	66.6%	66.1%	2.6%	2.1%	63.5%	31.8%
90:4	40.8%	2.7%	62.1%	59.3%	59.4%	1.7%	1.0%	57.7%	39.6%
91:1	44.1%	3.2%	64.7%	55.9%	56.2%	2.1%	1.1%	54.2%	42.7%
91:2	39.7%	5.0%	56.2%	60.3%	60.1%	2.8%	2.2%	57.3%	37.7%
91:3	40.4%	6.6%	59.6%	59.7%	59.7%	4.0%	2.7%	55.7%	37.7%
91:4	41.2%	5.6%	59.7%	58.9%	59.0%	3.4%	2.3%	55.6%	38.8%
92:1	40.0%	5.5%	57.8%	60.1%	59.9%	3.2%	2.3%	56.7%	37.7%
92:2	38.6%	5.3%	55.5%	61.4%	61.1%	2.9%	2.3%	58.2%	36.6%
92:3	40.3%	4.9%	59.7%	59.8%	59.8%	2.9%	2.0%	56.9%	38.2%
92:4	41.9%	5.3%	61.7%	58.2%	58.4%	3.3%	2.0%	55.1%	39.6%
93:1	42.5%	5.3%	60.5%	57.6%	57.7%	3.2%	2.1%	54.5%	40.2%
93:2	42.1%	5.7%	59.2%	57.9%	57.9%	3.4%	2.3%	54.5%	39.7%
93:3	42.5%	5.5%	60.1%	57.5%	57.6%	3.3%	2.2%	54.3%	40.2%
93:4	41.5%	5.4%	55.8%	58.5%	58.4%	3.0%	2.4%	55.4%	39.2%
94:1	40.4%	5.6%	56.2%	59.6%	59.4%	3.1%	2.4%	56.2%	38.2%
94:2	40.6%	4.7%	56.9%	59.4%	59.3%	2.7%	2.0%	56.7%	38.7%
94:3	41.8%	4.8%	58.3%	58.2%	58.2%	2.8%	2.0%	55.4%	39.8%
94:4	39.5%	5.0%	57.8%	60.6%	60.4%	2.9%	2.1%	57.5%	37.5%
95:1	43.1%	5.4%	61.4%	56.8%	57.1%	3.3%	2.1%	53.8%	40.8%
95:2	43.7%	7.4%	60.7%	56.3%	56.6%	4.5%	2.9%	52.1%	40.4%
95:3	43.9%	7.3%	62.1%	56.0%	56.5%	4.5%	2.7%	52.0%	40.8%
95:4	43.4%	6.7%	58.5%	56.6%	56.7%	3.9%	2.8%	52.8%	40.5%
96:1	45.5%	7.7%	61.1%	54.5%	55.0%	4.7%	3.0%	50.3%	41.9%
96:2	42.1%	7.4%	57.9%	57.9%	57.9%	4.3%	3.1%	53.6%	39.0%
96:3	42.6%	6.7%	60.3%	57.5%	57.6%	4.0%	2.6%	53.6%	39.7%
96:4	44.3%	6.3%	59.8%	55.7%	56.0%	3.7%	2.5%	52.2%	41.5%
AVG	40.0%	5.9%	60.3%	60.2%	60.2%	3.6%	2.3%	56.6%	37.5%

Table 6.19b
Trendline Reversal—Long Term (TLN-RL) Short Hit Analysis
(Average of all stocks)

Qtr	Optimal Short	TLN-RL Short	Short Hits	Cash Hits	Total Hits	Short Right	Short Wrong	Cash Right	Cash Wrong
85:1	34.3%	1.9%	62.7%	65.7%	65.7%	1.2%	0.7%	64.5%	33.6%
85:2	34.6%	1.8%	67.0%	65.5%	65.5%	1.2%	0.6%	64.3%	33.9%
85:3	38.6%	2.4%	70.4%	61.4%	61.6%	1.7%	0.7%	59.9%	37.7%
85:4	33.1%	3.2%	59.9%	66.8%	66.6%	1.9%	1.3%	64.7%	32.1%
86:1	35.2%	1.9%	56.1%	64.8%	64.7%	1.1%	0.8%	63.6%	34.5%
86:2	39.8%	1.6%	61.9%	60.2%	60.3%	1.0%	0.6%	59.3%	39.1%
86:3	42.7%	2.5%	65.8%	57.3%	57.5%	1.7%	0.9%	55.9%	41.6%
86:4	38.7%	5.0%	61.1%	61.4%	61.4%	3.0%	1.9%	58.4%	36.7%
87:1	36.9%	3.0%	51.7%	62.9%	62.6%	1.5%	1.4%	61.1%	36.0%
87:2	40.0%	2.8%	61.3%	60.0%	60.0%	1.7%	1.1%	58.3%	38.9%
87:3	40.4%	3.4%	61.7%	59.6%	59.6%	2.1%	1.3%	57.5%	39.1%
87:4	45.3%	5.5%	61.9%	54.7%	55.1%	3.4%	2.1%	51.7%	42.8%
88:1	36.7%	5.9%	59.0%	63.2%	63.0%	3.5%	2.4%	59.5%	34.6%
88:2	37.4%	6.0%	59.7%	62.4%	62.3%	3.6%	2.4%	58.7%	35.3%
88:3	38.4%	5.8%	63.2%	61.5%	61.6%	3.7%	2.2%	57.9%	36.2%
88:4	37.0%	5.6%	62.8%	63.0%	63.0%	3.5%	2.1%	59.5%	35.0%
89:1	36.2%	4.5%	60.4%	63.7%	63.5%	2.7%	1.8%	60.8%	34.7%
89:2	35.9%	3.1%	58.2%	63.9%	63.8%	1.8%	1.3%	62.0%	35.0%
89:3	36.4%	2.4%	60.5%	63.6%	63.5%	1.5%	1.0%	62.0%	35.5%
89:4	39.0%	2.5%	61.5%	61.0%	61.0%	1.5%	1.0%	59.5%	38.0%
90:1	40.1%	3.7%	63.4%	59.9%	60.0%	2.4%	1.4%	57.7%	38.6%
90:2	37.8%	4.6%	63.3%	62.2%	62.2%	2.9%	1.7%	59.3%	36.1%
90:3	45.7%	5.1%	67.1%	54.3%	54.9%	3.4%	1.7%	51.5%	43.4%
90:4	37.6%	4.9%	58.5%	62.4%	62.2%	2.8%	2.0%	59.4%	35.8%
91:1	36.7%	3.3%	57.3%	63.3%	63.1%	1.9%	1.4%	61.2%	35.5%
91:2	40.4%	2.6%	58.8%	59.5%	59.5%	1.5%	1.1%	58.0%	39.4%
91:3	39.8%	3.7%	61.3%	60.3%	60.3%	2.2%	1.4%	58.1%	38.3%
91:4	40.5%	3.4%	59.4%	59.6%	59.5%	2.0%	1.4%	57.5%	39.1%
92:1	43.2%	2.8%	58.6%	56.7%	56.8%	1.6%	1.2%	55.1%	42.1%
92:2	42.9%	3.1%	61.2%	57.1%	57.2%	1.9%	1.2%	55.3%	41.6%
92:3	39.5%	3.9%	59.7%	60.4%	60.4%	2.4%	1.6%	58.1%	38.0%
92:4	37.5%	3.8%	57.0%	62.6%	62.3%	2.2%	1.6%	60.2%	36.0%
93:1	39.4%	2.4%	58.7%	60.6%	60.6%	1.4%	1.0%	59.1%	38.4%
93:2	40.9%	3.1%	59.3%	59.1%	59.1%	1.8%	1.2%	57.3%	39.6%
93:3	39.4%	3.8%	57.8%	60.5%	60.4%	2.2%	1.6%	58.2%	38.0%
93:4	41.7%	3.5%	58.2%	58.3%	58.3%	2.1%	1.5%	56.2%	40.2%
94:1	43.7%	4.4%	59.6%	56.3%	56.4%	2.6%	1.8%	53.8%	41.8%
94:2	42.7%	5.4%	59.6%	57.3%	57.4%	3.2%	2.2%	54.2%	40.4%
94:3	39.8%	5.7%	59.0%	60.2%	60.1%	3.4%	2.4%	56.7%	37.5%
94:4	42.8%	5.0%	61.6%	57.3%	57.5%	3.1%	1.9%	54.4%	40.6%
95:1	38.7%	4.7%	56.4%	61.3%	61.0%	2.7%	2.1%	58.4%	36.9%
95:2	38.9%	3.4%	56.9%	61.0%	60.9%	1.9%	1.5%	59.0%	37.7%
95:3	38.9%	2.1%	55.2%	61.0%	60.9%	1.2%	1.0%	59.7%	38.1%
95:4	40.5%	3.0%	57.5%	59.5%	59.4%	1.7%	1.3%	57.7%	39.3%
96:1	38.9%	3.1%	54.9%	61.1%	60.9%	1.7%	1.4%	59.1%	37.7%
96:2	42.4%	2.9%	56.9%	57.6%	57.5%	1.6%	1.2%	55.9%	41.2%
96:3	40.8%	4.5%	57.6%	59.2%	59.1%	2.6%	1.9%	56.5%	39.0%
96:4	39.8%	3.5%	55.0%	60.0%	59.8%	1.9%	1.6%	57.9%	38.6%
AVG	39.4%	3.7%	59.9%	60.6%	60.6%	2.2%	1.5%	58.4%	37.9%

Table 6.20a
Trendline Reversal—Long Term (TLN-RL) Long Return Analysis
(Average of all stocks)

Qtr	TLN-RL Terminal Wealth	Buy/Hold Terminal Wealth	Relative Terminal Wealth	TLN-RL Long Avg Ret	TLN-RL Cash Avg Ret	TLN-RL Long-Cash Avg Ret	Buy/Hold Avg Ret
85:1	10050	10142	0.991	0.155%	-0.002%	0.157%	0.006%
85:2	9995	9700	1.030	-0.020%	-0.073%	0.053%	-0.069%
85:3	9937	8889	1.118	-0.163%	-0.208%	0.045%	-0.205%
85:4	10027	10763	0.932	0.078%	0.108%	-0.030%	0.107%
86:1	10096	11428	0.883	0.242%	0.223%	0.019%	0.225%
86:2	10045	10414	0.965	0.092%	0.064%	0.028%	0.066%
86:3	9952	9175	1.085	-0.103%	-0.129%	0.026%	-0.128%
86:4	10023	10413	0.963	0.065%	0.070%	-0.004%	0.069%
87:1	10103	11929	0.847	0.284%	0.293%	-0.009%	0.293%
87:2	10037	10196	0.984	0.097%	0.034%	0.063%	0.038%
87:3	10036	10408	0.964	0.090%	0.067%	0.023%	0.068%
87:4	9880	8087	1.222	-0.462%	-0.270%	-0.192%	-0.278%
88:1	10021	10989	0.912	0.081%	0.166%	-0.086%	0.163%
88:2	10033	10593	0.947	0.086%	0.101%	-0.015%	0.100%
88:3	9997	10050	0.995	-0.005%	0.014%	-0.019%	0.013%
88:4	10002	10196	0.981	0.007%	0.038%	-0.031%	0.037%
89:1	10052	10698	0.940	0.125%	0.111%	0.014%	0.112%
89:2	10057	10772	0.934	0.131%	0.122%	0.009%	0.122%
89:3	10086	10833	0.931	0.174%	0.127%	0.047%	0.131%
89:4	9985	9904	1.008	-0.028%	-0.010%	-0.018%	-0.011%
90:1	9977	9980	1.000	-0.056%	0.007%	-0.062%	0.003%
90:2	10033	10459	0.959	0.095%	0.076%	0.019%	0.077%
90:3	9945	8526	1.166	-0.192%	-0.262%	0.071%	-0.259%
90:4	10020	10889	0.920	0.116%	0.147%	-0.031%	0.146%
91:1	10062	12477	0.806	0.320%	0.315%	0.005%	0.315%
91:2	9992	10244	0.975	-0.024%	0.049%	-0.073%	0.045%
91:3	10042	10429	0.963	0.101%	0.062%	0.039%	0.065%
91:4	10029	10497	0.955	0.081%	0.082%	-0.001%	0.082%
92:1	10020	10324	0.971	0.053%	0.048%	0.006%	0.048%
92:2	9976	9723	1.026	-0.074%	-0.047%	-0.027%	-0.048%
92:3	10022	10392	0.964	0.074%	0.056%	0.018%	0.057%
92:4	10040	10963	0.916	0.117%	0.146%	-0.029%	0.144%
93:1	10017	10527	0.952	0.052%	0.081%	-0.029%	0.080%
93:2	10014	10340	0.968	0.037%	0.053%	-0.016%	0.052%
93:3	10032	10686	0.939	0.091%	0.102%	-0.011%	0.101%
93:4	10007	10255	0.976	0.017%	0.035%	-0.018%	0.034%
94:1	10003	9954	1.005	0.010%	-0.013%	0.022%	-0.011%
94:2	9992	9994	1.000	-0.028%	-0.004%	-0.025%	-0.005%
94:3	10013	10613	0.943	0.042%	0.092%	-0.049%	0.089%
94:4	9996	9836	1.016	-0.012%	-0.030%	0.018%	-0.029%
95:1	10031	10706	0.937	0.094%	0.111%	-0.017%	0.110%
95:2	10064	10873	0.926	0.137%	0.134%	0.003%	0.134%
95:3	10056	10853	0.927	0.125%	0.132%	-0.006%	0.131%
95:4	10016	10445	0.959	0.038%	0.069%	-0.031%	0.067%
96:1	10063	11027	0.913	0.129%	0.161%	-0.032%	0.159%
96:2	10022	10367	0.967	0.049%	0.059%	-0.010%	0.059%
96:3	10030	10298	0.974	0.069%	0.046%	0.023%	0.047%
96:4	10041	10817	0.928	0.102%	0.124%	-0.021%	0.122%
AVG	10020	10377	0.966	0.054%	0.055%	-0.001%	0.055%

Table 6.20b
Trendline Reversal—Long Term (TLN-RL)
Short Return Analysis (Average of all stocks)

Qtr	TLN-RL Terminal Wealth	Buy/Hold Terminal Wealth	Relative Terminal Wealth	TLN-RL Short Avg Ret	TLN-RL Cash Avg Ret	TLN-RL Short-Cash Avg Ret	Buy/Hold Avg Ret
85:1	9983	10142	0.984	0.150%	0.004%	0.146%	0.006%
85:2	10015	9700	1.033	-0.131%	-0.068%	-0.063%	-0.069%
85:3	10025	8889	1.128	-0.160%	-0.206%	0.046%	-0.205%
85:4	9963	10763	0.926	0.188%	0.104%	0.084%	0.107%
86:1	9978	11428	0.873	0.216%	0.225%	-0.009%	0.225%
86:2	10004	10414	0.961	-0.044%	0.068%	-0.112%	0.066%
86:3	10026	9175	1.093	-0.170%	-0.126%	-0.043%	-0.128%
86:4	9986	10413	0.959	0.041%	0.071%	-0.030%	0.069%
87:1	9923	11929	0.832	0.436%	0.289%	0.147%	0.293%
87:2	9992	10196	0.980	0.038%	0.038%	0.000%	0.038%
87:3	9990	10408	0.960	0.043%	0.069%	-0.027%	0.068%
87:4	10111	8087	1.250	-0.344%	-0.274%	-0.069%	-0.278%
88:1	9940	10989	0.905	0.168%	0.162%	0.005%	0.163%
88:2	9952	10593	0.940	0.131%	0.098%	0.033%	0.100%
88:3	9968	10050	0.992	0.085%	0.008%	0.077%	0.013%
88:4	9972	10196	0.978	0.082%	0.034%	0.048%	0.037%
89:1	9961	10698	0.931	0.139%	0.111%	0.028%	0.112%
89:2	9959	10772	0.925	0.215%	0.119%	0.096%	0.122%
89:3	9975	10833	0.921	0.158%	0.130%	0.028%	0.131%
89:4	9995	9904	1.009	0.035%	-0.012%	0.047%	-0.011%
90:1	10006	9980	1.003	-0.022%	0.004%	-0.026%	0.003%
90:2	9996	10459	0.956	0.013%	0.080%	-0.067%	0.077%
90:3	10064	8526	1.180	-0.203%	-0.262%	0.059%	-0.259%
90:4	9947	10889	0.913	0.168%	0.145%	0.023%	0.146%
91:1	9942	12477	0.797	0.295%	0.316%	-0.020%	0.315%
91:2	9977	10244	0.974	0.138%	0.043%	0.095%	0.045%
91:3	9994	10429	0.958	0.029%	0.066%	-0.037%	0.065%
91:4	9990	10497	0.952	0.047%	0.083%	-0.036%	0.082%
92:1	9987	10324	0.967	0.075%	0.047%	0.028%	0.048%
92:2	10004	9723	1.029	-0.013%	-0.050%	0.037%	-0.048%
92:3	9981	10392	0.960	0.080%	0.056%	0.025%	0.057%
92:4	9961	10963	0.909	0.162%	0.144%	0.018%	0.144%
93:1	9981	10527	0.948	0.152%	0.078%	0.074%	0.080%
93:2	9988	10340	0.966	0.084%	0.051%	0.033%	0.052%
93:3	9962	10686	0.932	0.159%	0.099%	0.060%	0.101%
93:4	9983	10255	0.973	0.077%	0.032%	0.045%	0.034%
94:1	10003	9954	1.005	-0.009%	-0.011%	0.002%	-0.011%
94:2	9991	9994	1.000	0.025%	-0.006%	0.032%	-0.005%
94:3	9980	10613	0.940	0.056%	0.091%	-0.035%	0.089%
94:4	10025	9836	1.019	-0.083%	-0.027%	-0.056%	-0.029%
95:1	9965	10706	0.931	0.119%	0.110%	0.010%	0.110%
95:2	9973	10873	0.917	0.132%	0.134%	-0.002%	0.134%
95:3	9982	10853	0.920	0.137%	0.131%	0.006%	0.131%
95:4	9999	10445	0.957	0.000%	0.069%	-0.069%	0.067%
96:1	9962	11027	0.903	0.198%	0.158%	0.040%	0.159%
96:2	9982	10367	0.963	0.100%	0.057%	0.043%	0.059%
96:3	9987	10298	0.970	0.054%	0.047%	0.007%	0.047%
96:4	9958	10817	0.921	0.200%	0.119%	0.081%	0.122%
AVG	9985	10377	0.962	0.066%	0.055%	0.011%	0.055%

Construction

Omni-Trader generates an automatic trendline using an advanced Pivot Point algorithm. This algorithm determines the relatively high points and the relatively low points for the stock price in the past one-month to three-month time span. The relatively high points are connected to form a trendline, and the relatively low points are connected to form a trendline.

Bands are constructed around these high trendlines and low trendlines. A bandwidth of 2 percent indicates that the stock's price must move within 2 percent of the trendline before a signal will be generated.

Results

The results in Table 6.19 for the Trendline Reversal—Long Term (TLN-RL) indicator show that this system makes relatively few calls. The long call rate for the system is only 5.9 percent. The short call rate is even lower, 3.7 percent. The long calls have an accuracy rate of 60.3 percent, and the short calls have an accuracy rate of 59.9 percent.

The return results in Table 6.20 are disappointing. The system is not good at predicting days of above-average and below-average stock price appreciation. The average return for long calls is only 0.054 percent, which is slightly less than the average overall stock return for the sample period. Traders using this system are seldom in the market; when they are in the market, they receive below-average returns. Thus, trading long with this system leads to a profit of only 96.6 percent of the profit of a buy-and-hold investment strategy.

The return results for the long calls were not promising, but the return results for the short calls appear to be even worse. The average stock appreciates in price by 0.066 percent on the days when the TLN-RL system recommends a short position. This means the system is recommending a short position on some of the market's strongest days—the very days when investors would want to be long and definitely would not want to be short. Going short on these days leads to losses. In fact, investors who followed this system's short recommendations for the test quarters had losses in all but ten of the quarters. On average, by following this system's short strategy, these investors lost $15 for each $10,000 invested.

These results leave much to be desired. Let's turn to a shorter-term version of this system to see whether performance results improve.

Trendline Reversal—Medium Term

The Trendline Reversal—Medium Term (TLN-RM) system is based on the same strategy as the Trendline Reversal—Long Term system we just investigated. The only difference in the two systems is the lookback period on which the trend is calculated. This medium-term system uses two weeks to one month as the lookback period, compared to the one-month to three-month lookback period of its longer-term counterpart.

Construction

The construction for the TLN-RM system is identical to the construction of the Trendline Reversal—Long Term system, except for one factor. For the medium-term system, high points and low points are chosen over a time frame of two weeks to one month, as opposed to the one-month to three-months time frame of the longer-term strategy.

After Omni-Trader generates a trendline based on this one-week to one-month time period, a band is drawn 2 percent away from this trend. This system will generate trading signals whenever the price moves outside this band.

Results

Tables 6.21 and 6.22 show that the performance of the TLN-RM system is fairly similar to that of its longer-term counterpart. The TLN-RM system does make calls slightly more frequently than the long-term system. The long call rate for this system is 7.1 percent, compared to 5.9 percent for the long-term system. The short call rate of 5.2 percent for the TLN-RM system is also slightly higher than the short call rate of 3.7 percent for the long-term system. The hit rates of 60.1 percent for the long calls and 59.8 percent for the short calls of the TLN-RM system fall just short of the hit rates for the long-term system.

The TLN-RM indicator does choose days of slightly above-average stock price appreciation to make its long calls. The average return on these days is 0.058 percent. However, profits from trading long with this system still fall short of the profits of a buy-and-hold investment strategy. Traders following this system's long calls average only 96.6 percent of the profits of investors who buy and hold securities.

Trendline Reversal—Short Term

This indicator, the Trendline Reversal—Short Term (TLN-RS) system, is a shorter-term version of the two systems that we have just analyzed. This system looks at a period spanning only eight to sixteen days. The idea behind this indicator is that whenever the price of a stock begins to trade outside a band around its trend, a reversal is signaled.

Table 6.21a
Trendline Reversal—Medium Term (TLN-RM)
Long Hit Analysis (Average of all stocks)

Qtr	Optimal Long	TLN-RM Long	Long Hits	Cash Hits	Total Hits	Long Right	Long Wrong	Cash Right	Cash Wrong
85:1	32.1%	7.3%	65.1%	68.0%	67.8%	4.7%	2.5%	63.1%	29.7%
85:2	30.2%	6.8%	64.0%	70.1%	69.7%	4.3%	2.4%	65.3%	27.9%
85:3	26.3%	7.0%	60.3%	73.6%	72.7%	4.2%	2.8%	68.5%	24.6%
85:4	36.6%	6.6%	66.7%	63.3%	63.5%	4.4%	2.2%	59.1%	34.3%
86:1	44.2%	9.9%	64.6%	56.1%	56.9%	6.4%	3.5%	50.5%	39.6%
86:2	39.7%	9.2%	59.4%	60.2%	60.2%	5.5%	3.7%	54.7%	36.1%
86:3	37.0%	6.6%	57.3%	63.0%	62.6%	3.8%	2.8%	58.8%	34.5%
86:4	38.5%	6.7%	59.0%	61.4%	61.2%	3.9%	2.7%	57.3%	36.0%
87:1	44.7%	7.7%	63.0%	55.4%	56.0%	4.9%	2.9%	51.2%	41.1%
87:2	40.0%	5.9%	58.7%	59.9%	59.8%	3.4%	2.4%	56.4%	37.7%
87:3	39.5%	7.5%	59.5%	60.4%	60.4%	4.4%	3.0%	55.9%	36.6%
87:4	37.9%	2.9%	53.5%	62.0%	61.8%	1.6%	1.4%	60.2%	36.9%
88:1	41.3%	5.9%	62.0%	58.6%	58.8%	3.7%	2.2%	55.1%	39.0%
88:2	39.3%	6.3%	62.1%	60.6%	60.7%	3.9%	2.4%	56.8%	36.9%
88:3	35.9%	7.5%	60.6%	64.1%	63.8%	4.6%	3.0%	59.2%	33.2%
88:4	36.3%	7.0%	62.1%	63.6%	63.5%	4.3%	2.6%	59.2%	33.8%
89:1	39.0%	8.7%	64.8%	61.0%	61.3%	5.7%	3.1%	55.7%	35.6%
89:2	40.2%	9.0%	64.1%	59.9%	60.3%	5.8%	3.2%	54.5%	36.4%
89:3	39.9%	9.2%	63.9%	60.3%	60.6%	5.9%	3.3%	54.8%	36.1%
89:4	38.3%	6.6%	59.6%	61.7%	61.5%	3.9%	2.7%	57.6%	35.8%
90:1	36.9%	5.5%	57.9%	63.1%	62.8%	3.2%	2.3%	59.6%	34.9%
90:2	39.2%	7.7%	61.3%	60.8%	60.8%	4.7%	3.0%	56.1%	36.2%
90:3	33.5%	5.3%	52.6%	66.5%	65.8%	2.8%	2.5%	62.9%	31.7%
90:4	40.8%	4.7%	61.9%	59.3%	59.4%	2.9%	1.8%	56.5%	38.8%
91:1	44.1%	6.7%	63.0%	55.9%	56.4%	4.2%	2.5%	52.1%	41.1%
91:2	39.7%	7.7%	58.7%	60.3%	60.2%	4.6%	3.2%	55.7%	36.6%
91:3	40.4%	6.9%	60.9%	59.6%	59.7%	4.2%	2.7%	55.5%	37.6%
91:4	41.2%	7.4%	60.8%	59.0%	59.1%	4.5%	2.9%	54.6%	38.0%
92:1	40.0%	7.0%	56.8%	60.0%	59.8%	4.0%	3.0%	55.8%	37.2%
92:2	38.6%	5.9%	56.4%	61.5%	61.2%	3.3%	2.6%	57.9%	36.2%
92:3	40.3%	7.0%	61.0%	59.9%	59.9%	4.3%	2.7%	55.7%	37.3%
92:4	41.9%	6.7%	62.2%	58.2%	58.4%	4.1%	2.5%	54.3%	39.0%
93:1	42.5%	7.5%	60.5%	57.6%	57.9%	4.6%	3.0%	53.3%	39.2%
93:2	42.1%	6.9%	57.8%	57.9%	57.9%	4.0%	2.9%	53.9%	39.2%
93:3	42.5%	6.9%	60.2%	57.5%	57.7%	4.2%	2.7%	53.5%	39.6%
93:4	41.5%	5.7%	56.8%	58.5%	58.4%	3.3%	2.5%	55.2%	39.1%
94:1	40.4%	7.1%	55.6%	59.6%	59.3%	4.0%	3.2%	55.3%	37.5%
94:2	40.6%	5.2%	59.3%	59.5%	59.5%	3.1%	2.1%	56.4%	38.4%
94:3	41.8%	6.9%	59.2%	58.2%	58.3%	4.1%	2.8%	54.2%	38.9%
94:4	39.5%	5.9%	56.4%	60.5%	60.2%	3.3%	2.6%	56.9%	37.2%
95:1	43.1%	7.5%	62.4%	57.0%	57.4%	4.7%	2.8%	52.7%	39.8%
95:2	43.7%	9.6%	60.8%	56.3%	56.7%	5.8%	3.7%	50.9%	39.5%
95:3	43.9%	10.0%	60.8%	56.1%	56.5%	6.1%	3.9%	50.5%	39.6%
95:4	43.4%	8.4%	58.2%	56.6%	56.8%	4.9%	3.5%	51.9%	39.7%
96:1	45.5%	8.3%	61.0%	54.6%	55.1%	5.1%	3.2%	50.0%	41.7%
96:2	42.1%	8.3%	57.4%	58.0%	57.9%	4.8%	3.5%	53.1%	38.5%
96:3	42.6%	6.1%	57.1%	57.3%	57.3%	3.5%	2.6%	53.8%	40.1%
96:4	44.3%	8.7%	59.6%	55.7%	56.0%	5.2%	3.5%	50.8%	40.5%
AVG	40.0%	7.1%	60.1%	60.2%	60.2%	4.3%	2.8%	55.9%	37.0%

Table 6.21b
Trendline Reversal—Medium Term (TLN-RM)
Short Hit Analysis (Average of all stocks)

Qtr	Optimal Short	TLN-RM Short	Short Hits	Cash Hits	Total Hits	Short Right	Short Wrong	Cash Right	Cash Wrong
85:1	34.3%	3.2%	60.0%	65.6%	65.4%	1.9%	1.3%	63.5%	33.3%
85:2	34.6%	4.3%	66.9%	65.4%	65.5%	2.9%	1.4%	62.6%	33.1%
85:3	38.6%	4.4%	72.2%	61.4%	61.9%	3.2%	1.2%	58.8%	36.9%
85:4	33.1%	4.6%	61.7%	66.8%	66.6%	2.8%	1.8%	63.8%	31.6%
86:1	35.2%	2.3%	55.0%	64.8%	64.5%	1.3%	1.0%	63.3%	34.4%
86:2	39.8%	3.2%	60.7%	60.2%	60.2%	2.0%	1.3%	58.2%	38.6%
86:3	42.7%	5.2%	63.0%	57.2%	57.5%	3.3%	1.9%	54.3%	40.6%
86:4	38.7%	5.0%	60.5%	61.3%	61.2%	3.0%	2.0%	58.2%	36.8%
87:1	36.9%	2.8%	54.7%	63.0%	62.8%	1.5%	1.3%	61.2%	36.0%
87:2	40.0%	4.9%	59.9%	60.0%	60.0%	2.9%	2.0%	57.0%	38.1%
87:3	40.4%	3.8%	61.2%	59.5%	59.5%	2.3%	1.5%	57.2%	39.0%
87:4	45.3%	6.0%	61.9%	54.8%	55.2%	3.7%	2.3%	51.5%	42.5%
88:1	36.7%	5.8%	58.5%	63.4%	63.1%	3.4%	2.4%	59.7%	34.4%
88:2	37.4%	7.0%	57.9%	62.5%	62.2%	4.1%	3.0%	58.1%	34.9%
88:3	38.4%	6.6%	61.3%	61.5%	61.5%	4.1%	2.6%	57.4%	36.0%
88:4	37.0%	6.5%	62.9%	63.0%	63.0%	4.1%	2.4%	58.9%	34.6%
89:1	36.2%	5.5%	59.5%	63.8%	63.5%	3.3%	2.2%	60.3%	34.2%
89:2	35.9%	4.1%	60.7%	64.0%	63.8%	2.5%	1.6%	61.3%	34.5%
89:3	36.4%	4.0%	59.7%	63.4%	63.3%	2.4%	1.6%	60.9%	35.1%
89:4	39.0%	5.6%	61.9%	61.1%	61.1%	3.5%	2.1%	57.6%	36.7%
90:1	40.1%	6.3%	63.7%	59.8%	60.0%	4.0%	2.3%	56.0%	37.7%
90:2	37.8%	5.6%	62.0%	62.2%	62.1%	3.5%	2.1%	58.6%	35.7%
90:3	45.7%	6.5%	67.6%	54.3%	55.2%	4.4%	2.1%	50.8%	42.7%
90:4	37.6%	5.3%	59.0%	62.4%	62.2%	3.1%	2.2%	59.1%	35.6%
91:1	36.7%	3.0%	57.9%	63.3%	63.1%	1.7%	1.2%	61.4%	35.7%
91:2	40.4%	4.4%	60.3%	59.6%	59.7%	2.7%	1.8%	57.0%	38.6%
91:3	39.8%	6.4%	59.9%	60.4%	60.4%	3.8%	2.6%	56.6%	37.1%
91:4	40.5%	6.0%	58.4%	59.6%	59.5%	3.5%	2.5%	56.0%	38.0%
92:1	43.2%	4.6%	59.2%	56.7%	56.9%	2.7%	1.9%	54.1%	41.3%
92:2	42.9%	5.7%	60.7%	57.1%	57.3%	3.5%	2.2%	53.8%	40.5%
92:3	39.5%	5.9%	60.0%	60.5%	60.5%	3.5%	2.3%	57.0%	37.1%
92:4	37.5%	5.5%	57.3%	62.5%	62.2%	3.2%	2.4%	59.0%	35.4%
93:1	39.4%	4.5%	58.0%	60.7%	60.6%	2.6%	1.9%	58.0%	37.5%
93:2	40.9%	5.8%	58.8%	59.2%	59.2%	3.4%	2.4%	55.7%	38.5%
93:3	39.4%	5.1%	57.3%	60.5%	60.4%	2.9%	2.2%	57.4%	37.4%
93:4	41.7%	5.3%	57.9%	58.3%	58.3%	3.1%	2.2%	55.2%	39.5%
94:1	43.7%	5.6%	60.6%	56.3%	56.6%	3.4%	2.2%	53.2%	41.2%
94:2	42.7%	6.6%	58.1%	57.2%	57.3%	3.8%	2.7%	53.5%	39.9%
94:3	39.8%	5.4%	58.3%	60.2%	60.1%	3.2%	2.3%	56.9%	37.6%
94:4	42.8%	7.1%	60.4%	57.2%	57.4%	4.3%	2.8%	53.1%	39.7%
95:1	38.7%	5.5%	57.1%	61.4%	61.1%	3.1%	2.4%	58.0%	36.5%
95:2	38.9%	4.6%	56.5%	61.0%	60.8%	2.6%	2.0%	58.2%	37.2%
95:3	38.9%	4.5%	57.8%	61.1%	60.9%	2.6%	1.9%	58.3%	37.2%
95:4	40.5%	5.1%	58.3%	59.5%	59.4%	3.0%	2.1%	56.4%	38.5%
96:1	38.9%	5.0%	55.1%	61.0%	60.7%	2.7%	2.2%	58.0%	37.0%
96:2	42.4%	6.4%	57.6%	57.6%	57.6%	3.7%	2.7%	53.9%	39.7%
96:3	40.8%	6.8%	58.2%	59.3%	59.3%	4.0%	2.9%	55.3%	37.9%
96:4	39.8%	4.9%	56.2%	60.0%	59.9%	2.7%	2.1%	57.1%	38.0%
AVG	39.4%	5.2%	59.8%	60.7%	60.6%	3.1%	2.1%	57.5%	37.3%

Table 6.22a
Trendline Reversal—Medium Term (TLN-RM)
Long Return Analysis (Average of all stocks)

Qtr	TLN-RM Terminal Wealth	Buy/Hold Terminal Wealth	Relative Terminal Wealth	TLN-RM Long Avg Ret	TLN-RM Cash Avg Ret	TLN-RM Long-Cash Avg Ret	Buy/Hold Avg Ret
85:1	10023	10142	0.988	0.049%	0.003%	0.046%	0.006%
85:2	10004	9700	1.031	0.004%	-0.075%	0.079%	-0.069%
85:3	9911	8889	1.115	-0.212%	-0.204%	-0.007%	-0.205%
85:4	10031	10763	0.932	0.072%	0.109%	-0.037%	0.107%
86:1	10133	11428	0.887	0.218%	0.225%	-0.007%	0.225%
86:2	10038	10414	0.964	0.063%	0.067%	-0.004%	0.066%
86:3	9953	9175	1.085	-0.110%	-0.129%	0.018%	-0.128%
86:4	10000	10413	0.960	0.000%	0.074%	-0.074%	0.069%
87:1	10142	11929	0.850	0.294%	0.293%	0.001%	0.293%
87:2	9996	10196	0.980	-0.010%	0.041%	-0.050%	0.038%
87:3	10027	10408	0.963	0.060%	0.069%	-0.009%	0.068%
87:4	9917	8087	1.226	-0.455%	-0.273%	-0.183%	-0.278%
88:1	10059	10989	0.915	0.158%	0.163%	-0.005%	0.163%
88:2	10028	10593	0.947	0.075%	0.101%	-0.026%	0.100%
88:3	9999	10050	0.995	-0.002%	0.014%	-0.016%	0.013%
88:4	10010	10196	0.982	0.022%	0.038%	-0.016%	0.037%
89:1	10073	10698	0.942	0.138%	0.110%	0.028%	0.112%
89:2	10063	10772	0.934	0.111%	0.123%	-0.012%	0.122%
89:3	10104	10833	0.933	0.181%	0.126%	0.055%	0.131%
89:4	9976	9904	1.007	-0.061%	-0.008%	-0.053%	-0.011%
90:1	9970	9980	0.999	-0.089%	0.008%	-0.097%	0.003%
90:2	10033	10459	0.959	0.068%	0.077%	-0.010%	0.077%
90:3	9917	8526	1.163	-0.256%	-0.259%	0.004%	-0.259%
90:4	10050	10889	0.923	0.170%	0.145%	0.025%	0.146%
91:1	10121	12477	0.811	0.298%	0.316%	-0.018%	0.315%
91:2	10014	10244	0.978	0.030%	0.047%	-0.017%	0.045%
91:3	10026	10429	0.961	0.061%	0.065%	-0.004%	0.065%
91:4	10046	10497	0.957	0.097%	0.081%	0.016%	0.082%
92:1	10002	10324	0.969	0.005%	0.051%	-0.046%	0.048%
92:2	9994	9723	1.028	-0.016%	-0.050%	0.034%	-0.048%
92:3	10025	10392	0.965	0.056%	0.057%	-0.001%	0.057%
92:4	10046	10963	0.916	0.106%	0.147%	-0.042%	0.144%
93:1	10042	10527	0.954	0.089%	0.079%	0.010%	0.080%
93:2	9996	10340	0.967	-0.011%	0.056%	-0.068%	0.052%
93:3	10040	10686	0.940	0.091%	0.102%	-0.011%	0.101%
93:4	10010	10255	0.976	0.026%	0.034%	-0.008%	0.034%
94:1	9985	9954	1.003	-0.037%	-0.009%	-0.027%	-0.011%
94:2	10020	9994	1.003	0.063%	-0.008%	0.071%	-0.005%
94:3	10035	10613	0.946	0.076%	0.090%	-0.015%	0.089%
94:4	9975	9836	1.014	-0.070%	-0.027%	-0.043%	-0.029%
95:1	10072	10706	0.941	0.149%	0.107%	0.043%	0.110%
95:2	10083	10873	0.927	0.140%	0.133%	0.007%	0.134%
95:3	10086	10853	0.929	0.138%	0.130%	0.007%	0.131%
95:4	10028	10445	0.960	0.053%	0.068%	-0.015%	0.067%
96:1	10070	11027	0.913	0.138%	0.161%	-0.023%	0.159%
96:2	10032	10367	0.968	0.063%	0.058%	0.005%	0.059%
96:3	9994	10298	0.971	-0.013%	0.051%	-0.064%	0.047%
96:4	10060	10817	0.930	0.107%	0.124%	-0.017%	0.122%
AVG	10026	10377	0.966	0.058%	0.055%	0.003%	0.055%

Table 6.22b
Trendline Reversal—Medium Term (TLN-RM)
Short Return Analysis (Average of all stocks)

Qtr	TLN-RM Terminal Wealth	Buy/Hold Terminal Wealth	Relative Terminal Wealth	TLN-RM Short Avg Ret	TLN-RM Cash Avg Ret	TLN-RM Short-Cash Avg Ret	Buy/Hold Avg Ret
85:1	9971	10142	0.983	0.156%	0.001%	0.154%	0.006%
85:2	10019	9700	1.033	-0.058%	-0.070%	0.012%	-0.069%
85:3	10047	8889	1.130	-0.162%	-0.207%	0.045%	-0.205%
85:4	9952	10763	0.925	0.172%	0.104%	0.069%	0.107%
86:1	9960	11428	0.872	0.293%	0.223%	0.070%	0.225%
86:2	9983	10414	0.959	0.085%	0.066%	0.019%	0.066%
86:3	10046	9175	1.095	-0.141%	-0.127%	-0.014%	-0.128%
86:4	9964	10413	0.957	0.114%	0.067%	0.047%	0.069%
87:1	9943	11929	0.833	0.343%	0.292%	0.052%	0.293%
87:2	9991	10196	0.980	0.030%	0.038%	-0.008%	0.038%
87:3	9986	10408	0.959	0.058%	0.069%	-0.011%	0.068%
87:4	10135	8087	1.253	-0.375%	-0.272%	-0.104%	-0.278%
88:1	9968	10989	0.907	0.081%	0.168%	-0.086%	0.163%
88:2	9940	10593	0.938	0.136%	0.097%	0.039%	0.100%
88:3	9976	10050	0.993	0.056%	0.010%	0.046%	0.013%
88:4	9983	10196	0.979	0.042%	0.036%	0.006%	0.037%
89:1	9959	10698	0.931	0.123%	0.112%	0.011%	0.112%
89:2	9971	10772	0.926	0.110%	0.123%	-0.012%	0.122%
89:3	9952	10833	0.919	0.195%	0.128%	0.066%	0.131%
89:4	9992	9904	1.009	0.021%	-0.013%	0.033%	-0.011%
90:1	9996	9980	1.002	0.010%	0.002%	0.007%	0.003%
90:2	9984	10459	0.955	0.047%	0.079%	-0.032%	0.077%
90:3	10113	8526	1.186	-0.276%	-0.258%	-0.018%	-0.259%
90:4	9940	10889	0.913	0.175%	0.145%	0.031%	0.146%
91:1	9959	12477	0.798	0.237%	0.317%	-0.080%	0.315%
91:2	9982	10244	0.974	0.064%	0.045%	0.019%	0.045%
91:3	9988	10429	0.958	0.031%	0.067%	-0.036%	0.065%
91:4	9983	10497	0.951	0.052%	0.084%	-0.032%	0.082%
92:1	9986	10324	0.967	0.054%	0.048%	0.006%	0.048%
92:2	10012	9723	1.030	-0.031%	-0.049%	0.019%	-0.048%
92:3	9998	10392	0.962	0.014%	0.059%	-0.045%	0.057%
92:4	9941	10963	0.907	0.172%	0.143%	0.029%	0.144%
93:1	9989	10527	0.949	0.044%	0.081%	-0.037%	0.080%
93:2	9993	10340	0.966	0.022%	0.054%	-0.032%	0.052%
93:3	9950	10686	0.931	0.156%	0.098%	0.057%	0.101%
93:4	9972	10255	0.972	0.084%	0.031%	0.053%	0.034%
94:1	10004	9954	1.005	-0.010%	-0.011%	0.001%	-0.011%
94:2	9984	9994	0.999	0.043%	-0.008%	0.051%	-0.005%
94:3	9976	10613	0.940	0.069%	0.090%	-0.021%	0.089%
94:4	10002	9836	1.017	-0.003%	-0.031%	0.029%	-0.029%
95:1	9970	10706	0.931	0.087%	0.111%	-0.024%	0.110%
95:2	9947	10873	0.915	0.184%	0.132%	0.052%	0.134%
95:3	9975	10853	0.919	0.089%	0.133%	-0.044%	0.131%
95:4	9992	10445	0.957	0.026%	0.069%	-0.043%	0.067%
96:1	9944	11027	0.902	0.189%	0.157%	0.031%	0.159%
96:2	9972	10367	0.962	0.073%	0.058%	0.016%	0.059%
96:3	9990	10298	0.970	0.024%	0.049%	-0.025%	0.047%
96:4	9954	10817	0.920	0.148%	0.121%	0.027%	0.122%
AVG	9984	10377	0.962	0.051%	0.055%	-0.005%	0.055%

Table 6.23a
Trendline Reversal—Short Term (TLN-RS)
Long Hit Analysis (Average of all stocks)

Qtr	Optimal Long	TLN-RS Long	Long Hits	Cash Hits	Total Hits	Long Right	Long Wrong	Cash Right	Cash Wrong
85:1	32.1%	14.3%	66.9%	67.3%	67.2%	9.6%	4.7%	57.7%	28.0%
85:2	30.2%	13.5%	65.8%	69.5%	69.0%	8.9%	4.6%	60.2%	26.4%
85:3	26.3%	12.2%	62.5%	73.1%	71.8%	7.6%	4.6%	64.2%	23.7%
85:4	36.6%	16.4%	67.5%	62.6%	63.4%	11.1%	5.3%	52.3%	31.2%
86:1	44.2%	14.6%	64.4%	56.0%	57.2%	9.4%	5.2%	47.9%	37.6%
86:2	39.7%	11.8%	60.9%	60.3%	60.4%	7.2%	4.6%	53.2%	35.1%
86:3	37.0%	8.8%	56.6%	63.1%	62.5%	5.0%	3.8%	57.5%	33.6%
86:4	38.5%	10.2%	60.9%	61.6%	61.5%	6.2%	4.0%	55.3%	34.5%
87:1	44.7%	10.6%	61.2%	55.3%	55.9%	6.5%	4.1%	49.5%	39.9%
87:2	40.0%	9.2%	59.4%	59.8%	59.8%	5.5%	3.7%	54.3%	36.5%
87:3	39.5%	9.9%	59.8%	60.6%	60.5%	5.9%	4.0%	54.6%	35.5%
87:4	37.9%	5.3%	54.3%	62.0%	61.6%	2.9%	2.4%	58.7%	36.0%
88:1	41.3%	10.3%	62.8%	58.6%	59.1%	6.5%	3.8%	52.6%	37.1%
88:2	39.3%	10.2%	62.0%	60.8%	60.9%	6.4%	3.9%	54.5%	35.2%
88:3	35.9%	10.7%	60.2%	64.0%	63.6%	6.4%	4.3%	57.2%	32.1%
88:4	36.3%	11.0%	62.0%	63.6%	63.4%	6.8%	4.2%	56.6%	32.4%
89:1	39.0%	13.0%	63.0%	61.0%	61.3%	8.2%	4.8%	53.1%	33.9%
89:2	40.2%	14.7%	63.6%	60.1%	60.6%	9.4%	5.4%	51.3%	34.0%
89:3	39.9%	11.7%	63.2%	60.0%	60.4%	7.4%	4.3%	53.0%	35.3%
89:4	38.3%	10.0%	61.6%	61.9%	61.9%	6.2%	3.9%	55.7%	34.3%
90:1	36.9%	9.3%	59.5%	63.2%	62.9%	5.5%	3.8%	57.3%	33.4%
90:2	39.2%	10.7%	61.7%	60.8%	60.9%	6.6%	4.1%	54.3%	35.0%
90:3	33.5%	6.7%	53.2%	66.4%	65.5%	3.6%	3.2%	61.9%	31.4%
90:4	40.8%	8.9%	64.5%	59.4%	59.8%	5.7%	3.1%	54.1%	37.0%
91:1	44.1%	10.6%	63.3%	55.9%	56.7%	6.7%	3.9%	50.0%	39.4%
91:2	39.7%	10.7%	58.8%	60.3%	60.2%	6.3%	4.4%	53.9%	35.4%
91:3	40.4%	11.1%	59.7%	59.6%	59.6%	6.6%	4.5%	53.0%	35.9%
91:4	41.2%	10.1%	60.9%	59.0%	59.2%	6.2%	4.0%	53.0%	36.9%
92:1	40.0%	10.5%	55.6%	59.9%	59.4%	5.8%	4.6%	53.6%	35.9%
92:2	38.6%	10.1%	57.9%	61.5%	61.1%	5.8%	4.2%	55.3%	34.7%
92:3	40.3%	10.9%	60.7%	59.8%	59.9%	6.6%	4.3%	53.3%	35.9%
92:4	41.9%	11.7%	62.9%	58.3%	58.8%	7.3%	4.3%	51.5%	36.9%
93:1	42.5%	11.4%	61.3%	57.6%	58.0%	7.0%	4.4%	51.0%	37.5%
93:2	42.1%	10.5%	59.6%	58.0%	58.2%	6.3%	4.3%	51.9%	37.5%
93:3	42.5%	11.6%	60.8%	57.7%	58.0%	7.1%	4.6%	51.0%	37.4%
93:4	41.5%	10.3%	58.3%	58.6%	58.6%	6.0%	4.3%	52.6%	37.1%
94:1	40.4%	12.2%	55.4%	59.6%	59.1%	6.7%	5.4%	52.4%	35.5%
94:2	40.6%	8.8%	56.9%	59.4%	59.2%	5.0%	3.8%	54.2%	37.0%
94:3	41.8%	11.4%	60.4%	58.4%	58.6%	6.9%	4.5%	51.7%	36.9%
94:4	39.5%	9.7%	58.4%	60.8%	60.6%	5.6%	4.0%	55.0%	35.4%
95:1	43.1%	12.9%	61.6%	57.1%	57.6%	7.9%	4.9%	49.7%	37.4%
95:2	43.7%	14.0%	60.4%	56.2%	56.8%	8.5%	5.5%	48.3%	37.7%
95:3	43.9%	12.7%	62.5%	56.4%	57.2%	8.0%	4.8%	49.2%	38.1%
95:4	43.4%	11.8%	60.7%	56.8%	57.3%	7.2%	4.6%	50.1%	38.1%
96:1	45.5%	11.2%	61.0%	54.5%	55.2%	6.8%	4.4%	48.4%	40.4%
96:2	42.1%	10.8%	58.4%	57.9%	58.0%	6.3%	4.5%	51.7%	37.5%
96:3	42.6%	10.3%	59.3%	57.4%	57.6%	6.1%	4.2%	51.5%	38.2%
96:4	44.3%	11.3%	59.3%	55.8%	56.2%	6.7%	4.6%	49.5%	39.2%
AVG	40.0%	11.0%	60.7%	60.2%	60.3%	6.7%	4.3%	53.5%	35.4%

Table 6.23b
Trendline Reversal—Short Term (TLN-RS)
Short Hit Analysis (Average of all stocks)

Qtr	Optimal Short	TLN-RS Short	Short Hits	Cash Hits	Total Hits	Short Right	Short Wrong	Cash Right	Cash Wrong
85:1	34.3%	8.1%	65.5%	66.0%	66.0%	5.3%	2.8%	60.7%	31.2%
85:2	34.6%	9.7%	67.9%	65.4%	65.6%	6.6%	3.1%	59.0%	31.3%
85:3	38.6%	10.4%	71.3%	61.4%	62.4%	7.4%	3.0%	55.0%	34.6%
85:4	33.1%	7.5%	62.8%	66.7%	66.4%	4.7%	2.8%	61.7%	30.8%
86:1	35.2%	7.0%	54.0%	64.7%	63.9%	3.8%	3.2%	60.1%	32.8%
86:2	39.8%	8.4%	58.4%	60.2%	60.1%	4.9%	3.5%	55.1%	36.4%
86:3	42.7%	9.1%	64.0%	57.4%	58.0%	5.8%	3.3%	52.2%	38.7%
86:4	38.7%	9.7%	61.7%	61.3%	61.3%	6.0%	3.7%	55.3%	35.0%
87:1	36.9%	7.2%	52.6%	63.0%	62.2%	3.8%	3.4%	58.4%	34.4%
87:2	40.0%	9.8%	59.0%	60.0%	59.9%	5.8%	4.0%	54.2%	36.1%
87:3	40.4%	9.3%	60.6%	59.6%	59.7%	5.7%	3.7%	54.1%	36.6%
87:4	45.3%	13.1%	62.2%	54.8%	55.8%	8.2%	4.9%	47.6%	39.3%
88:1	36.7%	10.5%	58.5%	63.2%	62.7%	6.2%	4.4%	56.6%	32.9%
88:2	37.4%	10.9%	59.7%	62.4%	62.1%	6.5%	4.4%	55.6%	33.5%
88:3	38.4%	12.2%	62.6%	61.5%	61.6%	7.6%	4.6%	54.0%	33.8%
88:4	37.0%	11.4%	62.7%	62.9%	62.9%	7.1%	4.2%	55.7%	32.9%
89:1	36.2%	10.4%	59.5%	63.6%	63.2%	6.2%	4.2%	57.0%	32.6%
89:2	35.9%	7.5%	60.1%	64.0%	63.7%	4.5%	3.0%	59.2%	33.3%
89:3	36.4%	9.0%	58.5%	63.3%	62.9%	5.2%	3.7%	57.6%	33.4%
89:4	39.0%	10.5%	61.8%	60.9%	61.0%	6.5%	4.0%	54.5%	35.0%
90:1	40.1%	11.1%	64.1%	59.8%	60.3%	7.1%	4.0%	53.2%	35.7%
90:2	37.8%	9.6%	62.0%	62.1%	62.1%	5.9%	3.6%	56.2%	34.3%
90:3	45.7%	12.8%	65.4%	54.2%	55.6%	8.4%	4.4%	47.3%	39.9%
90:4	37.6%	8.4%	60.9%	62.2%	62.1%	5.1%	3.3%	57.0%	34.6%
91:1	36.7%	8.3%	56.4%	63.2%	62.7%	4.7%	3.6%	58.0%	33.7%
91:2	40.4%	10.1%	59.6%	59.5%	59.6%	6.0%	4.1%	53.5%	36.4%
91:3	39.8%	11.3%	57.3%	60.0%	59.7%	6.5%	4.8%	53.2%	35.5%
91:4	40.5%	8.9%	61.3%	59.8%	59.9%	5.4%	3.4%	54.5%	36.7%
92:1	43.2%	8.7%	61.0%	56.8%	57.1%	5.3%	3.4%	51.8%	39.5%
92:2	42.9%	11.7%	61.1%	57.0%	57.5%	7.1%	4.5%	50.3%	38.0%
92:3	39.5%	10.4%	59.5%	60.5%	60.4%	6.2%	4.2%	54.2%	35.4%
92:4	37.5%	9.8%	58.2%	62.5%	62.1%	5.7%	4.1%	56.4%	33.8%
93:1	39.4%	9.4%	57.8%	60.7%	60.4%	5.5%	4.0%	54.9%	35.6%
93:2	40.9%	11.3%	58.1%	59.1%	59.0%	6.6%	4.7%	52.4%	36.3%
93:3	39.4%	10.4%	57.7%	60.7%	60.3%	6.0%	4.4%	54.4%	35.3%
93:4	41.7%	11.4%	58.1%	58.3%	58.3%	6.6%	4.8%	51.6%	37.0%
94:1	43.7%	10.6%	59.6%	56.4%	56.7%	6.3%	4.3%	50.4%	39.0%
94:2	42.7%	10.9%	59.1%	57.2%	57.4%	6.5%	4.5%	51.0%	38.1%
94:3	39.8%	11.6%	57.8%	60.3%	60.0%	6.7%	4.9%	53.3%	35.1%
94:4	42.8%	11.4%	61.5%	57.3%	57.8%	7.0%	4.4%	50.8%	37.8%
95:1	38.7%	8.9%	55.9%	61.3%	60.8%	5.0%	3.9%	55.8%	35.3%
95:2	38.9%	8.8%	56.5%	61.1%	60.7%	5.0%	3.9%	55.7%	35.4%
95:3	38.9%	9.1%	55.8%	61.0%	60.5%	5.1%	4.0%	55.4%	35.5%
95:4	40.5%	10.5%	57.1%	59.5%	59.2%	6.0%	4.5%	53.2%	36.3%
96:1	38.9%	10.6%	54.0%	61.0%	60.3%	5.7%	4.9%	54.6%	34.9%
96:2	42.4%	11.0%	58.5%	57.6%	57.7%	6.5%	4.6%	51.3%	37.7%
96:3	40.8%	11.1%	58.3%	59.4%	59.3%	6.5%	4.6%	52.8%	36.1%
96:4	39.8%	10.0%	56.3%	60.1%	59.7%	5.6%	4.4%	54.1%	35.9%
AVG	39.4%	10.0%	59.8%	60.6%	60.6%	6.0%	4.0%	54.6%	35.4%

Table 6.24a
Trendline Reversal—Short Term (TLN-RS)
Long Return Analysis (Average of all stocks)

Qtr	TLN-RS Terminal Wealth	Buy/Hold Terminal Wealth	Relative Terminal Wealth	TLN-RS Long Avg Ret	TLN-RS Cash Avg Ret	TLN-RS Long-Cash Avg Ret	Buy/Hold Avg Ret
85:1	9998	10142	0.986	-0.008%	0.009%	-0.017%	0.006%
85:2	9938	9700	1.025	-0.078%	-0.068%	-0.010%	-0.069%
85:3	9822	8889	1.105	-0.252%	-0.198%	-0.054%	-0.205%
85:4	10051	10763	0.934	0.045%	0.119%	-0.074%	0.107%
86:1	10203	11428	0.893	0.231%	0.224%	0.007%	0.225%
86:2	10064	10414	0.966	0.085%	0.064%	0.021%	0.066%
86:3	9933	9175	1.083	-0.122%	-0.128%	0.006%	-0.128%
86:4	10041	10413	0.964	0.062%	0.070%	-0.009%	0.069%
87:1	10164	11929	0.852	0.250%	0.298%	-0.048%	0.293%
87:2	9987	10196	0.980	-0.024%	0.044%	-0.068%	0.038%
87:3	10050	10408	0.966	0.082%	0.067%	0.015%	0.068%
87:4	9919	8087	1.227	-0.249%	-0.280%	0.030%	-0.278%
88:1	10091	10989	0.918	0.143%	0.165%	-0.022%	0.163%
88:2	10065	10593	0.950	0.103%	0.099%	0.003%	0.100%
88:3	9976	10050	0.993	-0.034%	0.018%	-0.052%	0.013%
88:4	10004	10196	0.981	0.006%	0.040%	-0.035%	0.037%
89:1	10087	10698	0.943	0.110%	0.113%	-0.002%	0.112%
89:2	10124	10772	0.940	0.133%	0.120%	0.012%	0.122%
89:3	10093	10833	0.932	0.130%	0.131%	-0.001%	0.131%
89:4	10006	9904	1.010	0.012%	-0.014%	0.025%	-0.011%
90:1	10004	9980	1.002	0.006%	0.002%	0.004%	0.003%
90:2	10065	10459	0.962	0.098%	0.074%	0.024%	0.077%
90:3	9882	8526	1.159	-0.287%	-0.257%	-0.030%	-0.259%
90:4	10096	10889	0.927	0.174%	0.144%	0.031%	0.146%
91:1	10213	12477	0.819	0.329%	0.313%	0.016%	0.315%
91:2	10026	10244	0.979	0.039%	0.046%	-0.008%	0.045%
91:3	10031	10429	0.962	0.044%	0.067%	-0.023%	0.065%
91:4	10070	10497	0.959	0.110%	0.079%	0.032%	0.082%
92:1	9987	10324	0.967	-0.023%	0.056%	-0.079%	0.048%
92:2	9993	9723	1.028	-0.011%	-0.053%	0.041%	-0.048%
92:3	10050	10392	0.967	0.074%	0.054%	0.020%	0.057%
92:4	10122	10963	0.923	0.163%	0.142%	0.021%	0.144%
93:1	10068	10527	0.956	0.093%	0.078%	0.015%	0.080%
93:2	10040	10340	0.971	0.061%	0.051%	0.010%	0.052%
93:3	10097	10686	0.945	0.130%	0.097%	0.033%	0.101%
93:4	10033	10255	0.978	0.047%	0.032%	0.015%	0.034%
94:1	9982	9954	1.003	-0.023%	-0.010%	-0.014%	-0.011%
94:2	10005	9994	1.001	0.009%	-0.006%	0.015%	-0.005%
94:3	10097	10613	0.951	0.130%	0.084%	0.046%	0.089%
94:4	10009	9836	1.018	0.014%	-0.034%	0.048%	-0.029%
95:1	10105	10706	0.944	0.129%	0.107%	0.022%	0.110%
95:2	10083	10873	0.927	0.095%	0.140%	-0.045%	0.134%
95:3	10129	10853	0.933	0.161%	0.127%	0.034%	0.131%
95:4	10071	10445	0.964	0.097%	0.063%	0.034%	0.067%
96:1	10104	11027	0.916	0.148%	0.160%	-0.012%	0.159%
96:2	10051	10367	0.970	0.075%	0.057%	0.018%	0.059%
96:3	10033	10298	0.974	0.051%	0.047%	0.005%	0.047%
96:4	10109	10817	0.934	0.152%	0.118%	0.033%	0.122%
AVG	10045	10377	0.968	0.064%	0.054%	0.010%	0.055%

Table 6.24b
Trendline Reversal—Short Term (TLN-RS)
Short Return Analysis (Average of all stocks)

Qtr	TLN-RS Terminal Wealth	Buy/Hold Terminal Wealth	Relative Terminal Wealth	TLN-RS Short Avg Ret	TLN-RS Cash Avg Ret	TLN-RS Short-Cash Avg Ret	Buy/Hold Avg Ret
85:1	10009	10142	0.987	-0.014%	0.008%	-0.022%	0.006%
85:2	10018	9700	1.033	-0.025%	-0.074%	0.049%	-0.069%
85:3	10120	8889	1.139	-0.177%	-0.208%	0.032%	-0.205%
85:4	9938	10763	0.923	0.135%	0.105%	0.030%	0.107%
86:1	9884	11428	0.865	0.276%	0.221%	0.055%	0.225%
86:2	9950	10414	0.955	0.091%	0.064%	0.027%	0.066%
86:3	10107	9175	1.102	-0.188%	-0.121%	-0.067%	-0.128%
86:4	9974	10413	0.958	0.043%	0.072%	-0.029%	0.069%
87:1	9837	11929	0.825	0.379%	0.286%	0.093%	0.293%
87:2	9968	10196	0.978	0.052%	0.036%	0.015%	0.038%
87:3	9976	10408	0.959	0.037%	0.072%	-0.035%	0.068%
87:4	10272	8087	1.270	-0.341%	-0.268%	-0.073%	-0.278%
88:1	9912	10989	0.902	0.133%	0.166%	-0.034%	0.163%
88:2	9912	10593	0.936	0.129%	0.096%	0.032%	0.100%
88:3	9960	10050	0.991	0.051%	0.007%	0.044%	0.013%
88:4	9963	10196	0.977	0.052%	0.035%	0.018%	0.037%
89:1	9912	10698	0.927	0.139%	0.109%	0.030%	0.112%
89:2	9937	10772	0.922	0.135%	0.121%	0.014%	0.122%
89:3	9914	10833	0.915	0.155%	0.129%	0.026%	0.131%
89:4	9991	9904	1.009	0.012%	-0.014%	0.026%	-0.011%
90:1	10024	9980	1.004	-0.037%	0.008%	-0.045%	0.003%
90:2	9972	10459	0.953	0.047%	0.080%	-0.033%	0.077%
90:3	10186	8526	1.195	-0.226%	-0.264%	0.037%	-0.259%
90:4	9919	10889	0.911	0.153%	0.146%	0.007%	0.146%
91:1	9865	12477	0.791	0.284%	0.318%	-0.034%	0.315%
91:2	9962	10244	0.972	0.057%	0.044%	0.013%	0.045%
91:3	9911	10429	0.950	0.127%	0.057%	0.070%	0.065%
91:4	10005	10497	0.953	-0.009%	0.091%	-0.100%	0.082%
92:1	10016	10324	0.970	-0.029%	0.055%	-0.084%	0.048%
92:2	10004	9723	1.029	-0.008%	-0.054%	0.045%	-0.048%
92:3	9965	10392	0.959	0.051%	0.057%	-0.007%	0.057%
92:4	9938	10963	0.907	0.100%	0.149%	-0.049%	0.144%
93:1	9976	10527	0.948	0.043%	0.084%	-0.040%	0.080%
93:2	9972	10340	0.964	0.043%	0.053%	-0.010%	0.052%
93:3	9938	10686	0.930	0.097%	0.102%	-0.005%	0.101%
93:4	9980	10255	0.973	0.029%	0.035%	-0.006%	0.034%
94:1	10014	9954	1.006	-0.018%	-0.010%	-0.008%	-0.011%
94:2	9997	9994	1.000	0.008%	-0.006%	0.014%	-0.005%
94:3	9965	10613	0.939	0.050%	0.094%	-0.045%	0.089%
94:4	10042	9836	1.021	-0.060%	-0.025%	-0.035%	-0.029%
95:1	9919	10706	0.927	0.147%	0.106%	0.041%	0.110%
95:2	9929	10873	0.913	0.132%	0.134%	-0.003%	0.134%
95:3	9921	10853	0.914	0.141%	0.130%	0.011%	0.131%
95:4	9970	10445	0.954	0.049%	0.069%	-0.019%	0.067%
96:1	9896	11027	0.897	0.161%	0.159%	0.003%	0.159%
96:2	9971	10367	0.962	0.042%	0.061%	-0.019%	0.059%
96:3	9992	10298	0.970	0.013%	0.052%	-0.039%	0.047%
96:4	9939	10817	0.919	0.097%	0.125%	-0.028%	0.122%
AVG	9974	10377	0.961	0.043%	0.057%	-0.014%	0.055%

Construction

The construction for the TLN-RS system is identical to that for the previous two systems except for the lookback period used for constructing the trendlines. For this short-term system, a period of only eight to sixteen days is used to calculate high points and low points. Trends are based on these high points and low points.

Results

Table 6.23 shows that the TLN-RS system makes both long and short calls more often than its longer-term counterparts. Still, the long call rate of 11 percent and the short call rate of 10 percent fall far below the optimal call rates. The system's long calls, with a hit rate of 60.7 percent, are slightly more accurate than its short calls, which have a hit rate of 59.8 percent.

The TLN-RS system appears to be slightly better than the longer-term versions at distinguishing between periods of above-average market returns and below-average market returns. The average return for long call days is 0.064 percent, as shown in Table 6.24a. This represents a return higher than the average return of 0.055 percent for all days included in our test sample.

The average stock return on days when short calls are made is only 0.043 percent. This is below the average daily stock return for the test period, so the system's short calls do predict days of below-average market strength.

However, from the terminal wealth results, we see that this system's ability to predict periods of above-average and below-average market performance is not enough, by itself, to earn above-average returns. Trading long with the system results in terminal wealth averaging only 96.8 percent of the terminal wealth of a buy-and-hold investment strategy. Worse yet, trading short with the system led to losses in 75 percent of the test quarters. On average, an investor who begins a quarter with $10,000 and trades short based on the TLN-RS system's recommendations will have only $9,974 by the end of the quarter.

Thus, even though this shorter-term version of the Trendline Reversal concept may outperform the longer-term versions, investors would not want to rely on this system alone to determine long and short positions.

Chapter

7

Patterns

Candlestick Patterns

Most of the patterns in this chapter are candlestick patterns. Before discussing the individual results for the nine candlestick indicators that we examined, we will briefly explain candlesticks in general. Figure 7.1 illustrates some examples of candlesticks.

Let's start by explaining how candlesticks are formed. Four numbers are used in forming candlesticks: the open, high, low, and closing prices for the time period, which in this case is one day. Consider candle number 1 in Figure 7.1. The opening price is 11, the high is 18, the low is 10, and the closing price is 17. The body of the candle is formed from the opening and closing prices; this is the white candle body between 11 and 17. The body is white because the stock closed higher than the opening price. In candle number 2, the reverse is true; it closed lower than the opening price so the body is black. White bodies signal price rises, and black bodies signal price declines. The small lines that extend above and below the body represent the high and low prices. The thin line extending from 17 to 18 for candle number 1 shows that the high was above the close. The thin line extending down from 11 to 10 shows that the low was below the opening price.

Certain price relationships result in some odd candle patterns. Candle number 3 has no body because the open was equal to the close. Candle number 4 has no lower "wick" because the low was equal to the open. Similarly, a

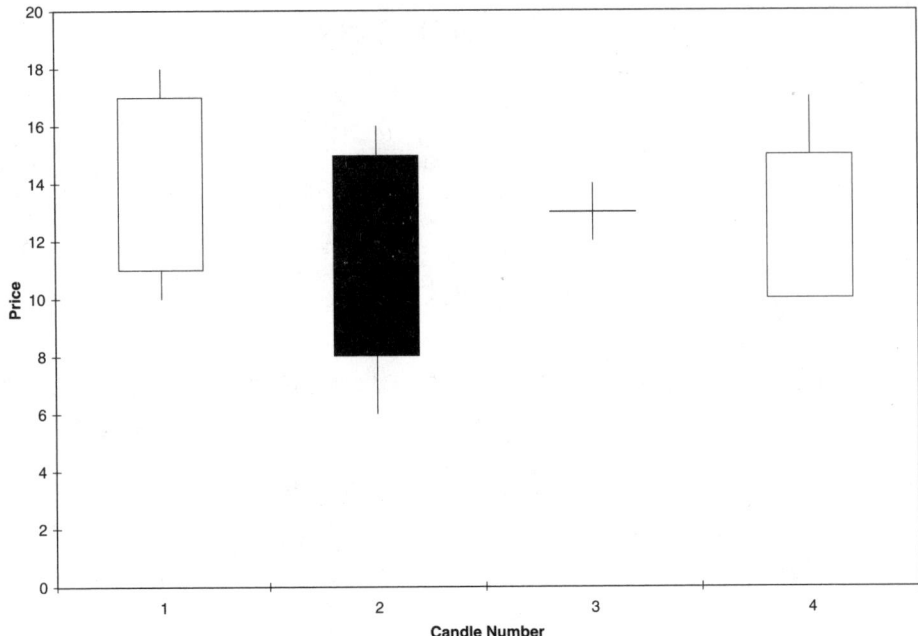

Figure 7.1 Candlestick examples.

candle might not have an upper wick if price relationships occurred on the high side.

Some of the candlestick indicator patterns are determined from just one candle. Other indicators require two or three candles to form the particular pattern. Of the nine candle indicators we examined, four are based on the prices for only one day, four are based on two-day price relationships, and one is based on three-day price relationships. Candlesticks are focused only on the very short run. Price history more than three days in the past is irrelevant when using daily candlesticks.

Candle Belt Hold

A Belt Hold indicates that a strong move in a given direction has occurred during a particular day, with slight hesitation at the end of the day. Belt Holds occur frequently. Usually, price moves in the direction of the close following a Belt Hold. Belt Holds indicate a continuation of the current trend and are not generally used for forecasting reversals.

Construction

A bearish Belt Hold occurs when a stock opens at its high, then the stock price falls during the day but reverses before the end of the trading day. This results in a low that is below the close.

A bullish Belt Hold occurs when the low equals the open, but the stock trades higher during the day. However, the stock cannot maintain its high and reverses by day's end, so that the close is below the high. See Figure 7.2 for an example of this pattern.

Results

Trading long with the Candle Belt Hold (CN-BH) system results in a higher terminal wealth than trading with any of the other technical indicators included in this book. Let's examine the data in Tables 7.1 and 7.2 to uncover the underlying reasons for this system's superior performance.

When choosing between long positions and cash positions, the Candle Belt Hold chooses long positions 36.4 percent of the time (Table 7.1a). This falls just short of the optimal 40.0 percent long call rate. These long recommendations are correct 60.7 percent of the time, and the cash recommendations are correct 61.3 percent of the time.

The average stock return that occurs on days when long calls are made is the underlying strength of this system. As shown in Table 7.2a, this return is 0.110 percent, twice the average daily stock return of 0.055 percent for all days in our test period. Thus, the Candle Belt Hold system chooses days of extremely high market returns to make its long calls. With this system, investors are long on the "best of the best" trading days.

Unfortunately, however, even though trading with this indicator leads to a higher average terminal wealth than any other indicator in this book, the system is not powerful enough to outperform a simple buy-and-hold strategy. The Candle Belt Hold's average quarterly terminal wealth of $10,255 falls $122 short of the buy-and-hold terminal wealth of $10,377. The buy-and-hold

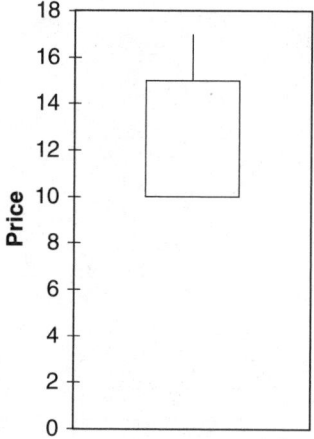

Figure 7.2 Candle belt hold.

Table 7.1a
Candle Belt Hold (CN-BH) Long Hit Analysis
(Average of all stocks)

Qtr	Optimal Long	CN-BH Long	Long Hits	Cash Hits	Total Hits	Long Right	Long Wrong	Cash Right	Cash Wrong
85:1	32.1%	32.8%	64.3%	71.9%	69.4%	21.1%	11.7%	48.3%	18.9%
85:2	30.2%	31.3%	63.8%	74.1%	70.9%	20.0%	11.3%	50.9%	17.8%
85:3	26.3%	25.7%	59.1%	77.6%	72.8%	15.2%	10.5%	57.7%	16.7%
85:4	36.6%	34.2%	65.5%	68.2%	67.2%	22.4%	11.8%	44.9%	21.0%
86:1	44.2%	40.9%	64.3%	57.3%	60.2%	26.3%	14.6%	33.9%	25.2%
86:2	39.7%	37.2%	60.9%	61.9%	61.5%	22.6%	14.5%	38.9%	24.0%
86:3	37.0%	34.0%	57.8%	64.6%	62.3%	19.6%	14.3%	42.6%	23.4%
86:4	38.5%	33.9%	61.4%	62.7%	62.2%	20.8%	13.1%	41.5%	24.7%
87:1	44.7%	41.4%	63.1%	57.0%	59.5%	26.1%	15.3%	33.4%	25.2%
87:2	40.0%	38.9%	59.6%	61.4%	60.7%	23.2%	15.7%	37.5%	23.6%
87:3	39.5%	37.4%	59.1%	61.5%	60.6%	22.1%	15.3%	38.5%	24.1%
87:4	37.9%	33.8%	54.7%	62.7%	60.0%	18.5%	15.3%	41.5%	24.7%
88:1	41.3%	40.3%	62.2%	59.4%	60.5%	25.1%	15.2%	35.5%	24.2%
88:2	39.3%	38.8%	61.3%	61.7%	61.6%	23.8%	15.0%	37.7%	23.4%
88:3	35.9%	33.5%	60.9%	65.0%	63.7%	20.4%	13.1%	43.2%	23.2%
88:4	36.3%	33.8%	62.4%	64.7%	63.9%	21.1%	12.7%	42.8%	23.4%
89:1	39.0%	39.2%	63.7%	62.5%	63.0%	25.0%	14.3%	38.0%	22.8%
89:2	40.2%	40.9%	63.7%	61.5%	62.4%	26.1%	14.8%	36.3%	22.8%
89:3	39.9%	37.0%	63.3%	61.1%	61.9%	23.4%	13.6%	38.5%	24.5%
89:4	38.3%	35.9%	60.8%	62.9%	62.2%	21.8%	14.1%	40.3%	23.8%
90:1	36.9%	33.7%	59.8%	64.2%	62.7%	20.2%	13.6%	42.6%	23.7%
90:2	39.2%	37.6%	62.9%	62.6%	62.7%	23.6%	14.0%	39.0%	23.3%
90:3	33.5%	30.4%	56.2%	67.8%	64.3%	17.1%	13.3%	47.2%	22.4%
90:4	40.8%	37.7%	61.9%	60.1%	60.8%	23.4%	14.4%	37.4%	24.9%
91:1	44.1%	41.3%	63.5%	57.1%	59.7%	26.2%	15.1%	33.5%	25.2%
91:2	39.7%	37.2%	59.6%	61.5%	60.8%	22.2%	15.0%	38.6%	24.2%
91:3	40.4%	33.3%	60.3%	60.1%	60.2%	20.1%	13.2%	40.1%	26.6%
91:4	41.2%	30.7%	60.8%	59.7%	60.0%	18.7%	12.0%	41.4%	27.9%
92:1	40.0%	33.5%	56.8%	60.3%	59.1%	19.0%	14.5%	40.1%	26.4%
92:2	38.6%	30.1%	57.6%	61.9%	60.6%	17.3%	12.8%	43.2%	26.7%
92:3	40.3%	32.7%	60.1%	60.1%	60.1%	19.6%	13.0%	40.5%	26.9%
92:4	41.9%	33.0%	63.1%	58.8%	60.2%	20.8%	12.2%	39.4%	27.6%
93:1	42.5%	36.1%	60.7%	58.1%	59.0%	21.9%	14.2%	37.1%	26.8%
93:2	42.1%	37.0%	59.3%	58.2%	58.6%	22.0%	15.1%	36.6%	26.3%
93:3	42.5%	40.0%	61.0%	57.9%	59.2%	24.4%	15.6%	34.8%	25.3%
93:4	41.5%	37.1%	59.6%	59.5%	59.5%	22.1%	15.0%	37.4%	25.5%
94:1	40.4%	36.4%	56.9%	59.9%	58.8%	20.7%	15.7%	38.1%	25.5%
94:2	40.6%	35.0%	58.1%	59.8%	59.2%	20.4%	14.7%	38.8%	26.1%
94:3	41.8%	38.7%	60.8%	59.1%	59.7%	23.6%	15.2%	36.2%	25.1%
94:4	39.5%	38.2%	57.7%	61.1%	59.8%	22.1%	16.2%	37.8%	24.0%
95:1	43.1%	40.1%	61.9%	57.5%	59.3%	24.8%	15.3%	34.4%	25.4%
95:2	43.7%	39.0%	61.3%	56.5%	58.4%	23.9%	15.1%	34.4%	26.5%
95:3	43.9%	38.8%	61.8%	56.6%	58.6%	24.0%	14.8%	34.6%	26.6%
95:4	43.4%	38.9%	60.2%	57.2%	58.4%	23.4%	15.5%	34.9%	26.2%
96:1	45.5%	41.8%	61.4%	54.8%	57.5%	25.7%	16.1%	31.9%	26.3%
96:2	42.1%	38.1%	58.4%	58.5%	58.5%	22.3%	15.8%	36.2%	25.7%
96:3	42.6%	38.8%	61.0%	58.5%	59.5%	23.7%	15.1%	35.8%	25.4%
96:4	44.3%	41.2%	61.1%	56.7%	58.5%	25.2%	16.0%	33.3%	25.4%
AVG	40.0%	36.4%	60.7%	61.3%	61.3%	22.1%	14.3%	39.1%	24.5%

Table 7.1b
Candle Belt Hold (CN-BH) Short Hit Analysis
(Average of all stocks)

Qtr	Optimal Short	CN-BH Short	Short Hits	Cash Hits	Total Hits	Short Right	Short Wrong	Cash Right	Cash Wrong
85:1	34.3%	30.9%	62.7%	67.6%	66.1%	19.3%	11.5%	46.8%	22.4%
85:2	34.6%	29.9%	63.4%	66.9%	65.8%	19.0%	11.0%	46.9%	23.2%
85:3	38.6%	32.1%	65.4%	63.5%	64.1%	21.0%	11.1%	43.1%	24.8%
85:4	33.1%	30.1%	57.2%	68.0%	64.7%	17.2%	12.9%	47.5%	22.4%
86:1	35.2%	36.6%	55.4%	65.7%	61.9%	20.3%	16.3%	41.7%	21.8%
86:2	39.8%	39.2%	60.7%	62.1%	61.5%	23.8%	15.4%	37.7%	23.1%
86:3	42.7%	42.2%	63.0%	59.5%	61.0%	26.6%	15.6%	34.4%	23.4%
86:4	38.7%	41.4%	61.0%	62.7%	62.0%	25.2%	16.1%	36.7%	21.9%
87:1	36.9%	36.3%	55.6%	64.1%	61.0%	20.2%	16.1%	40.8%	22.9%
87:2	40.0%	39.0%	59.7%	61.1%	60.6%	23.3%	15.7%	37.2%	23.7%
87:3	40.4%	40.1%	60.5%	60.9%	60.8%	24.3%	15.8%	36.5%	23.4%
87:4	45.3%	47.5%	62.0%	56.0%	58.9%	29.4%	18.1%	29.4%	23.1%
88:1	36.7%	37.3%	57.8%	64.1%	61.8%	21.6%	15.7%	40.2%	22.5%
88:2	37.4%	38.0%	59.7%	63.7%	62.2%	22.7%	15.3%	39.4%	22.5%
88:3	38.4%	40.1%	62.7%	63.2%	63.0%	25.2%	14.9%	37.9%	22.0%
88:4	37.0%	40.9%	62.7%	64.6%	63.8%	25.7%	15.3%	38.1%	20.9%
89:1	36.2%	37.5%	61.3%	65.3%	63.8%	23.0%	14.5%	40.8%	21.7%
89:2	35.9%	35.6%	59.7%	65.2%	63.2%	21.3%	14.3%	42.0%	22.4%
89:3	36.4%	38.7%	59.0%	64.4%	62.3%	22.8%	15.9%	39.5%	21.9%
89:4	39.0%	40.7%	61.3%	62.4%	61.9%	24.9%	15.8%	37.0%	22.3%
90:1	40.1%	42.5%	62.9%	61.8%	62.3%	26.7%	15.8%	35.5%	22.0%
90:2	37.8%	39.3%	61.3%	64.0%	62.9%	24.1%	15.2%	38.8%	21.9%
90:3	45.7%	49.1%	66.2%	56.9%	61.5%	32.5%	16.6%	29.0%	21.9%
90:4	37.6%	38.7%	58.1%	63.3%	61.3%	22.5%	16.2%	38.8%	22.5%
91:1	36.7%	37.9%	56.4%	64.3%	61.3%	21.4%	16.5%	39.9%	22.1%
91:2	40.4%	41.4%	61.0%	61.2%	61.1%	25.3%	16.2%	35.8%	22.7%
91:3	39.8%	41.4%	59.4%	61.0%	60.3%	24.5%	16.8%	35.8%	22.9%
91:4	40.5%	43.6%	59.4%	60.8%	60.2%	25.9%	17.7%	34.3%	22.1%
92:1	43.2%	41.0%	60.4%	57.0%	58.4%	24.7%	16.2%	33.6%	25.4%
92:2	42.9%	45.5%	61.5%	57.8%	59.5%	28.0%	17.5%	31.5%	23.0%
92:3	39.5%	43.1%	59.3%	60.9%	60.2%	25.6%	17.5%	34.6%	22.2%
92:4	37.5%	43.9%	58.4%	63.3%	61.2%	25.7%	18.3%	35.5%	20.6%
93:1	39.4%	43.5%	57.9%	61.2%	59.8%	25.2%	18.3%	34.6%	22.0%
93:2	40.9%	43.0%	58.3%	59.7%	59.1%	25.1%	17.9%	34.0%	22.9%
93:3	39.4%	40.4%	57.8%	61.1%	59.8%	23.4%	17.0%	36.4%	23.1%
93:4	41.7%	43.7%	59.7%	59.4%	59.5%	26.1%	17.6%	33.4%	22.9%
94:1	43.7%	44.1%	60.1%	56.7%	58.2%	26.5%	17.6%	31.7%	24.2%
94:2	42.7%	44.1%	60.0%	58.0%	58.9%	26.5%	17.7%	32.4%	23.5%
94:3	39.8%	41.9%	59.0%	61.0%	60.2%	24.8%	17.2%	35.4%	22.6%
94:4	42.8%	41.6%	61.2%	57.9%	59.3%	25.5%	16.1%	33.8%	24.6%
95:1	38.7%	39.6%	57.4%	61.8%	60.0%	22.7%	16.9%	37.3%	23.1%
95:2	38.9%	40.6%	56.4%	61.5%	59.5%	22.9%	17.7%	36.6%	22.9%
95:3	38.9%	41.4%	56.8%	61.9%	59.8%	23.5%	17.9%	36.3%	22.3%
95:4	40.5%	40.9%	57.1%	60.1%	58.9%	23.4%	17.6%	35.5%	23.5%
96:1	38.9%	38.3%	55.1%	61.6%	59.1%	21.1%	17.2%	38.0%	23.7%
96:2	42.4%	41.6%	58.2%	58.1%	58.2%	24.2%	17.4%	34.0%	24.5%
96:3	40.8%	41.7%	58.7%	60.6%	59.8%	24.5%	17.2%	35.3%	23.0%
96:4	39.8%	38.0%	57.0%	60.9%	59.4%	21.7%	16.4%	37.7%	24.2%
AVG	39.4%	40.1%	59.7%	61.8%	61.0%	24.0%	16.2%	37.1%	22.8%

Table 7.2a
Candle Belt Hold (CN-BH) Long Return Analysis
(Average of all stocks)

Qtr	CN-BH Terminal Wealth	Buy/Hold Terminal Wealth	Relative Terminal Wealth	CN-BH Long Avg Ret	CN-BH Cash Avg Ret	CN-BH Long-Cash Avg Ret	Buy/Hold Avg Ret
85:1	10300	10142	1.016	0.146%	-0.062%	0.207%	0.006%
85:2	10170	9700	1.049	0.086%	-0.140%	0.226%	-0.069%
85:3	9955	8889	1.120	-0.027%	-0.266%	0.239%	-0.205%
85:4	10578	10763	0.983	0.264%	0.025%	0.239%	0.107%
86:1	10663	11428	0.933	0.262%	0.199%	0.063%	0.225%
86:2	10326	10414	0.992	0.137%	0.024%	0.113%	0.066%
86:3	9893	9175	1.078	-0.047%	-0.169%	0.122%	-0.128%
86:4	10269	10413	0.986	0.128%	0.039%	0.089%	0.069%
87:1	10908	11929	0.914	0.343%	0.257%	0.086%	0.293%
87:2	10195	10196	1.000	0.082%	0.010%	0.072%	0.038%
87:3	10252	10408	0.985	0.107%	0.045%	0.062%	0.068%
87:4	9785	8087	1.210	-0.087%	-0.375%	0.288%	-0.278%
88:1	10327	10989	0.940	0.135%	0.181%	-0.046%	0.163%
88:2	10257	10593	0.968	0.111%	0.092%	0.019%	0.100%
88:3	10072	10050	1.002	0.036%	0.001%	0.034%	0.013%
88:4	10143	10196	0.995	0.070%	0.019%	0.051%	0.037%
89:1	10360	10698	0.968	0.149%	0.088%	0.061%	0.112%
89:2	10382	10772	0.964	0.147%	0.105%	0.042%	0.122%
89:3	10365	10833	0.957	0.157%	0.115%	0.042%	0.131%
89:4	10086	9904	1.018	0.041%	-0.040%	0.081%	-0.011%
90:1	10114	9980	1.013	0.056%	-0.024%	0.081%	0.003%
90:2	10350	10459	0.990	0.148%	0.034%	0.115%	0.077%
90:3	9736	8526	1.142	-0.140%	-0.311%	0.171%	-0.259%
90:4	10487	10889	0.963	0.202%	0.112%	0.090%	0.146%
91:1	10913	12477	0.875	0.357%	0.285%	0.071%	0.315%
91:2	10242	10244	1.000	0.107%	0.009%	0.098%	0.045%
91:3	10191	10429	0.977	0.087%	0.054%	0.033%	0.065%
91:4	10267	10497	0.978	0.135%	0.058%	0.076%	0.082%
92:1	10147	10324	0.983	0.068%	0.038%	0.031%	0.048%
92:2	9981	9723	1.027	-0.009%	-0.066%	0.057%	-0.048%
92:3	10145	10392	0.976	0.064%	0.053%	0.011%	0.057%
92:4	10404	10963	0.949	0.188%	0.123%	0.065%	0.144%
93:1	10218	10527	0.971	0.095%	0.071%	0.023%	0.080%
93:2	10147	10340	0.981	0.063%	0.045%	0.018%	0.052%
93:3	10295	10686	0.963	0.114%	0.093%	0.021%	0.101%
93:4	10240	10255	0.999	0.097%	-0.004%	0.101%	0.034%
94:1	10061	9954	1.011	0.021%	-0.030%	0.051%	-0.011%
94:2	10060	9994	1.007	0.027%	-0.022%	0.049%	-0.005%
94:3	10318	10613	0.972	0.126%	0.066%	0.060%	0.089%
94:4	9993	9836	1.016	-0.004%	-0.045%	0.041%	-0.029%
95:1	10340	10706	0.966	0.135%	0.093%	0.042%	0.110%
95:2	10362	10873	0.953	0.145%	0.127%	0.019%	0.134%
95:3	10375	10853	0.956	0.152%	0.118%	0.034%	0.131%
95:4	10228	10445	0.979	0.092%	0.051%	0.041%	0.067%
96:1	10439	11027	0.947	0.164%	0.156%	0.008%	0.159%
96:2	10179	10367	0.982	0.074%	0.049%	0.024%	0.059%
96:3	10259	10298	0.996	0.102%	0.012%	0.090%	0.047%
96:4	10448	10817	0.966	0.167%	0.091%	0.076%	0.122%
AVG	10255	10377	0.988	0.110%	0.024%	0.087%	0.055%

Table 7.2b
Candle Belt Hold (CN-BH) Short Return Analysis
(Average of all stocks)

Qtr	CN-BH Terminal Wealth	Buy/Hold Terminal Wealth	Relative Terminal Wealth	CN-BH Short Avg Ret	CN-BH Cash Avg Ret	CN-BH Short-Cash Avg Ret	Buy/Hold Avg Ret
85:1	9949	10142	0.981	0.028%	-0.004%	0.032%	0.006%
85:2	10008	9700	1.032	-0.004%	-0.097%	0.093%	-0.069%
85:3	10239	8889	1.152	-0.119%	-0.246%	0.127%	-0.205%
85:4	9677	10763	0.899	0.172%	0.078%	0.094%	0.107%
86:1	9565	11428	0.837	0.199%	0.239%	-0.041%	0.225%
86:2	9965	10414	0.957	0.012%	0.102%	-0.090%	0.066%
86:3	10536	9175	1.148	-0.203%	-0.072%	-0.131%	-0.128%
86:4	9891	10413	0.950	0.038%	0.091%	-0.053%	0.069%
87:1	9438	11929	0.791	0.260%	0.312%	-0.051%	0.293%
87:2	10001	10196	0.981	-0.006%	0.066%	-0.073%	0.038%
87:3	9924	10408	0.953	0.028%	0.095%	-0.067%	0.068%
87:4	11213	8087	1.387	-0.434%	-0.137%	-0.296%	-0.278%
88:1	9625	10989	0.876	0.159%	0.165%	-0.007%	0.163%
88:2	9821	10593	0.927	0.074%	0.115%	-0.041%	0.100%
88:3	10021	10050	0.997	-0.012%	0.029%	-0.042%	0.013%
88:4	9977	10196	0.979	0.005%	0.058%	-0.053%	0.037%
89:1	9858	10698	0.921	0.061%	0.143%	-0.083%	0.112%
89:2	9788	10772	0.909	0.093%	0.139%	-0.046%	0.122%
89:3	9709	10833	0.896	0.121%	0.137%	-0.016%	0.131%
89:4	10126	9904	1.022	-0.056%	0.019%	-0.075%	-0.011%
90:1	10123	9980	1.014	-0.051%	0.043%	-0.094%	0.003%
90:2	9952	10459	0.952	0.017%	0.115%	-0.098%	0.077%
90:3	11052	8526	1.296	-0.327%	-0.193%	-0.134%	-0.259%
90:4	9707	10889	0.891	0.122%	0.161%	-0.039%	0.146%
91:1	9427	12477	0.756	0.259%	0.349%	-0.090%	0.315%
91:2	10072	10244	0.983	-0.032%	0.100%	-0.133%	0.045%
91:3	9890	10429	0.948	0.043%	0.081%	-0.038%	0.065%
91:4	9885	10497	0.942	0.041%	0.113%	-0.073%	0.082%
92:1	9918	10324	0.961	0.033%	0.058%	-0.025%	0.048%
92:2	10197	9723	1.049	-0.070%	-0.030%	-0.040%	-0.048%
92:3	9821	10392	0.945	0.065%	0.050%	0.014%	0.057%
92:4	9706	10963	0.885	0.110%	0.172%	-0.062%	0.144%
93:1	9849	10527	0.936	0.058%	0.096%	-0.038%	0.080%
93:2	9926	10340	0.960	0.029%	0.069%	-0.040%	0.052%
93:3	9777	10686	0.915	0.089%	0.109%	-0.020%	0.101%
93:4	10066	10255	0.982	-0.022%	0.077%	-0.099%	0.034%
94:1	10117	9954	1.016	-0.042%	0.013%	-0.054%	-0.011%
94:2	10111	9994	1.012	-0.038%	0.021%	-0.059%	-0.005%
94:3	9872	10613	0.930	0.051%	0.117%	-0.066%	0.089%
94:4	10133	9836	1.030	-0.050%	-0.014%	-0.036%	-0.029%
95:1	9784	10706	0.914	0.089%	0.123%	-0.034%	0.110%
95:2	9692	10873	0.891	0.124%	0.141%	-0.016%	0.134%
95:3	9751	10853	0.898	0.098%	0.154%	-0.056%	0.131%
95:4	9904	10445	0.948	0.039%	0.086%	-0.047%	0.067%
96:1	9658	11027	0.876	0.147%	0.167%	-0.020%	0.159%
96:2	9856	10367	0.951	0.056%	0.060%	-0.005%	0.059%
96:3	10018	10298	0.973	-0.007%	0.086%	-0.093%	0.047%
96:4	9809	10817	0.907	0.081%	0.147%	-0.066%	0.122%
AVG	9946	10377	0.959	0.021%	0.078%	-0.057%	0.055%

strategy consistently outperforms the Candle Belt Hold, earning a higher return in just over two-thirds of the test quarters.

Also, the performance of the short calls of this system falls short of the performance of the long calls. The indicator favors a short position over a cash position 40.1 percent of the time (Table 7.1b). The hit rate for the short calls is 59.7 percent, and the hit rate for the cash calls is 61.8 percent.

These short calls are good at predicting periods of below-average stock returns. On days when short calls are made, the average stock return (Table 7.2b) is only 0.021 percent, far below the 0.078 percent return on days when cash positions are favored over short positions. However, because there are positive returns, on average, on the days when the indicator recommends a short position, trading short with the system will result in losses. In fact, trading short with this system resulted in a quarterly terminal wealth less than the beginning wealth of $10,000 for all but sixteen of the test quarters.

This system is the strongest tested system in making long calls. The system's real strength is its ability to predict periods of above-average and below-average stock returns.

Candle Counterattack

The Candle Counterattack Line is a two-day pattern. This pattern occurs when the close on two consecutive trading days is approximately the same, but the direction for the second day is the opposite of the direction for the first day. On one day the stock price is rising and on the other day the stock price is falling, but the resulting close is roughly the same. Thus, a Counterattack is seen when the market reverses direction violently from the previous day and arrives at the same valuation as the day before. Counterattack Lines are reversal patterns and are considered to be of moderate significance at the end of intermediate trends.

Construction

A bearish Counterattack Line occurs when a stock opens at a price higher than the prior day's close, but moves down during the day to close at the closing price of the prior day. Figure 7.3 shows an example of this pattern.

When the market opens lower than the previous day but strengthens during the day to close at the previous day's close, a bullish Counterattack Line is formed.

Results

The results for the Candle Counterattack (CN-CA) trading system in Tables 7.3 and 7.4 show that signals from this system are rare. Long signals and short

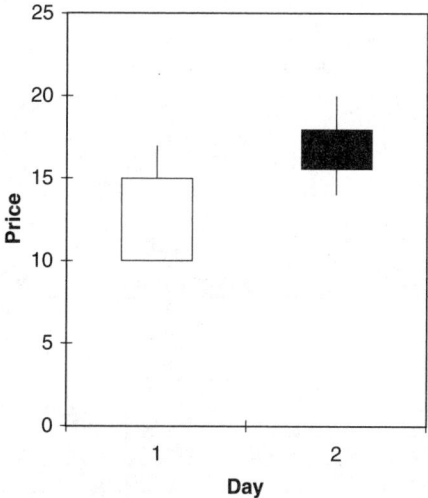

Figure 7.3 Candle counterattack line.

signals each occur only 0.6 percent of the time. Interestingly, no long or short signals occurred during the entire first half of the test period. They first appeared in the third quarter of 1991, and, thereafter, short and long calls occurred in every subsequent quarter. During this later time period, call rates averaged close to 1.5 percent.

The hit rates for the system's long and short calls are 28.9 percent and 27.9 percent, respectively. However, these hit rates are somewhat misleading. For over half of the test period, the system made no long or short calls. Therefore, the hit rate for long and short calls until the third quarter of 1991 was 0 percent. For the time period in which this system was making calls, the hit rate greatly exceeded 60 percent. In fact, the lowest hit rate for long calls during this time period was the 57.7 percent hit rate that occurred in the second quarter of 1996. The lowest hit rate for short calls, 57.0 percent, occurred in the first quarter of 1995.

The long return analysis (Table 7.4a) does not offer much support for using the Candle Counterattack system. The average quarterly terminal wealth from following this system's long recommendations is significantly lower than the terminal wealth of a buy-and-hold strategy. Because investors trading with this system are almost always in a zero-return cash position, they have few opportunities for gains. During our twelve-year test period, the largest possible quarterly profit for an investor trading long with this system would have been $20 on a $10,000 initial investment.

The short return analysis for the Candle Counterattack system (Table 7.4b) indicates that trading short when the system made short calls, on average, led to decreasing wealth. For all but six of the quarters in which short calls were made, trading with the system led to a quarterly terminal wealth below the initial wealth of $10,000.

Table 7.3a
Candle Counter Attack (CN-CA) Long Hit Analysis
(Average of all stocks)

Qtr	Optimal Long	CN-CA Long	Long Hits	Cash Hits	Total Hits	Long Right	Long Wrong	Cash Right	Cash Wrong
85:1	32.1%	0.0%	0.0%	67.9%	67.9%	0.0%	0.0%	67.9%	32.1%
85:2	30.2%	0.0%	0.0%	69.8%	69.8%	0.0%	0.0%	69.8%	30.2%
85:3	26.3%	0.0%	0.0%	73.7%	73.7%	0.0%	0.0%	73.7%	26.3%
85:4	36.6%	0.0%	0.0%	63.4%	63.4%	0.0%	0.0%	63.4%	36.6%
86:1	44.2%	0.0%	0.0%	55.8%	55.8%	0.0%	0.0%	55.8%	44.2%
86:2	39.7%	0.0%	0.0%	60.3%	60.3%	0.0%	0.0%	60.3%	39.7%
86:3	37.0%	0.0%	0.0%	63.0%	63.0%	0.0%	0.0%	63.0%	37.0%
86:4	38.5%	0.0%	0.0%	61.5%	61.5%	0.0%	0.0%	61.5%	38.5%
87:1	44.7%	0.0%	0.0%	55.3%	55.3%	0.0%	0.0%	55.3%	44.7%
87:2	40.0%	0.0%	0.0%	60.0%	60.0%	0.0%	0.0%	60.0%	40.0%
87:3	39.5%	0.0%	0.0%	60.5%	60.5%	0.0%	0.0%	60.5%	39.5%
87:4	37.9%	0.0%	0.0%	62.1%	62.1%	0.0%	0.0%	62.1%	37.9%
88:1	41.3%	0.0%	0.0%	58.7%	58.7%	0.0%	0.0%	58.7%	41.3%
88:2	39.3%	0.0%	0.0%	60.7%	60.7%	0.0%	0.0%	60.7%	39.3%
88:3	35.9%	0.0%	0.0%	64.1%	64.1%	0.0%	0.0%	64.1%	35.9%
88:4	36.3%	0.0%	0.0%	63.7%	63.7%	0.0%	0.0%	63.7%	36.3%
89:1	39.0%	0.0%	0.0%	61.0%	61.0%	0.0%	0.0%	61.0%	39.0%
89:2	40.2%	0.0%	0.0%	59.8%	59.8%	0.0%	0.0%	59.8%	40.2%
89:3	39.9%	0.0%	0.0%	60.1%	60.1%	0.0%	0.0%	60.1%	39.9%
89:4	38.3%	0.0%	0.0%	61.7%	61.7%	0.0%	0.0%	61.7%	38.3%
90:1	36.9%	0.0%	0.0%	63.1%	63.1%	0.0%	0.0%	63.1%	36.9%
90:2	39.2%	0.0%	0.0%	60.8%	60.8%	0.0%	0.0%	60.8%	39.2%
90:3	33.5%	0.0%	0.0%	66.5%	66.5%	0.0%	0.0%	66.5%	33.5%
90:4	40.8%	0.0%	0.0%	59.2%	59.2%	0.0%	0.0%	59.2%	40.8%
91:1	44.1%	0.0%	0.0%	55.9%	55.9%	0.0%	0.0%	55.9%	44.1%
91:2	39.7%	0.0%	0.0%	60.3%	60.3%	0.0%	0.0%	60.3%	39.7%
91:3	40.4%	1.0%	62.5%	59.5%	59.6%	0.6%	0.4%	58.9%	40.1%
91:4	41.2%	1.2%	65.5%	58.8%	58.9%	0.8%	0.4%	58.1%	40.7%
92:1	40.0%	0.9%	64.6%	60.0%	60.0%	0.6%	0.3%	59.4%	39.6%
92:2	38.6%	1.3%	59.8%	61.4%	61.3%	0.8%	0.5%	60.5%	38.1%
92:3	40.3%	1.5%	64.9%	59.7%	59.8%	1.0%	0.5%	58.8%	39.7%
92:4	41.9%	1.1%	68.7%	58.1%	58.2%	0.8%	0.3%	57.5%	41.4%
93:1	42.5%	1.2%	64.0%	57.4%	57.5%	0.8%	0.4%	56.7%	42.0%
93:2	42.1%	1.6%	63.7%	57.9%	58.0%	1.0%	0.6%	57.0%	41.5%
93:3	42.5%	1.3%	65.7%	57.5%	57.6%	0.8%	0.4%	56.8%	42.0%
93:4	41.5%	1.2%	60.1%	58.5%	58.5%	0.7%	0.5%	57.8%	41.0%
94:1	40.4%	1.5%	61.8%	59.6%	59.6%	0.9%	0.6%	58.7%	39.8%
94:2	40.6%	1.6%	59.2%	59.3%	59.3%	0.9%	0.6%	58.4%	40.0%
94:3	41.8%	1.8%	63.5%	58.2%	58.3%	1.1%	0.6%	57.2%	41.1%
94:4	39.5%	1.4%	61.7%	60.5%	60.5%	0.9%	0.5%	59.7%	38.9%
95:1	43.1%	1.4%	66.8%	56.9%	57.0%	0.9%	0.5%	56.1%	42.5%
95:2	43.7%	1.5%	65.4%	56.3%	56.4%	1.0%	0.5%	55.4%	43.1%
95:3	43.9%	1.6%	64.0%	56.0%	56.1%	1.0%	0.6%	55.1%	43.3%
95:4	43.4%	1.7%	61.0%	56.6%	56.6%	1.0%	0.6%	55.6%	42.7%
96:1	45.5%	1.5%	63.0%	54.5%	54.6%	0.9%	0.5%	53.7%	44.9%
96:2	42.1%	1.5%	57.7%	57.9%	57.9%	0.9%	0.6%	57.0%	41.5%
96:3	42.6%	1.7%	61.1%	57.4%	57.4%	1.0%	0.6%	56.4%	41.9%
96:4	44.3%	1.4%	64.1%	55.7%	55.8%	0.9%	0.5%	54.9%	43.7%
AVG	40.0%	0.6%	28.9%	60.1%	60.2%	0.4%	0.2%	59.8%	39.6%

Table 7.3b
Candle Counter Attack (CN-CA) Short Hit Analysis
(Average of all stocks)

Qtr	Optimal Short	CN-CA Short	Short Hits	Cash Hits	Total Hits	Short Right	Short Wrong	Cash Right	Cash Wrong
85:1	34.3%	0.0%	0.0%	65.7%	65.7%	0.0%	0.0%	65.7%	34.3%
85:2	34.6%	0.0%	0.0%	65.4%	65.4%	0.0%	0.0%	65.4%	34.6%
85:3	38.6%	0.0%	0.0%	61.4%	61.4%	0.0%	0.0%	61.4%	38.6%
85:4	33.1%	0.0%	0.0%	66.9%	66.9%	0.0%	0.0%	66.9%	33.1%
86:1	35.2%	0.0%	0.0%	64.8%	64.8%	0.0%	0.0%	64.8%	35.2%
86:2	39.8%	0.0%	0.0%	60.2%	60.2%	0.0%	0.0%	60.2%	39.8%
86:3	42.7%	0.0%	0.0%	57.3%	57.3%	0.0%	0.0%	57.3%	42.7%
86:4	38.7%	0.0%	0.0%	61.3%	61.3%	0.0%	0.0%	61.3%	38.7%
87:1	36.9%	0.0%	0.0%	63.1%	63.1%	0.0%	0.0%	63.1%	36.9%
87:2	40.0%	0.0%	0.0%	60.0%	60.0%	0.0%	0.0%	60.0%	40.0%
87:3	40.4%	0.0%	0.0%	59.6%	59.6%	0.0%	0.0%	59.6%	40.4%
87:4	45.3%	0.0%	0.0%	54.7%	54.7%	0.0%	0.0%	54.7%	45.3%
88:1	36.7%	0.0%	0.0%	63.3%	63.3%	0.0%	0.0%	63.3%	36.7%
88:2	37.4%	0.0%	0.0%	62.6%	62.6%	0.0%	0.0%	62.6%	37.4%
88:3	38.4%	0.0%	0.0%	61.6%	61.6%	0.0%	0.0%	61.6%	38.4%
88:4	37.0%	0.0%	0.0%	63.0%	63.0%	0.0%	0.0%	63.0%	37.0%
89:1	36.2%	0.0%	0.0%	63.8%	63.8%	0.0%	0.0%	63.8%	36.2%
89:2	35.9%	0.0%	0.0%	64.1%	64.1%	0.0%	0.0%	64.1%	35.9%
89:3	36.4%	0.0%	0.0%	63.6%	63.6%	0.0%	0.0%	63.6%	36.4%
89:4	39.0%	0.0%	0.0%	61.0%	61.0%	0.0%	0.0%	61.0%	39.0%
90:1	40.1%	0.0%	0.0%	59.9%	59.9%	0.0%	0.0%	59.9%	40.1%
90:2	37.8%	0.0%	0.0%	62.2%	62.2%	0.0%	0.0%	62.2%	37.8%
90:3	45.7%	0.0%	0.0%	54.3%	54.3%	0.0%	0.0%	54.3%	45.7%
90:4	37.6%	0.0%	0.0%	62.4%	62.4%	0.0%	0.0%	62.4%	37.6%
91:1	36.7%	0.0%	0.0%	63.3%	63.3%	0.0%	0.0%	63.3%	36.7%
91:2	40.4%	0.0%	0.0%	59.6%	59.6%	0.0%	0.0%	59.6%	40.4%
91:3	39.8%	1.2%	62.1%	60.2%	60.2%	0.8%	0.5%	59.5%	39.3%
91:4	40.5%	1.3%	63.3%	59.5%	59.5%	0.8%	0.5%	58.7%	40.0%
92:1	43.2%	1.2%	67.6%	56.7%	56.9%	0.8%	0.4%	56.1%	42.7%
92:2	42.9%	1.2%	65.1%	57.1%	57.2%	0.8%	0.4%	56.4%	42.4%
92:3	39.5%	1.9%	60.8%	60.5%	60.5%	1.1%	0.7%	59.3%	38.8%
92:4	37.5%	1.4%	62.5%	62.5%	62.5%	0.9%	0.5%	61.6%	37.0%
93:1	39.4%	1.4%	59.6%	60.6%	60.6%	0.9%	0.6%	59.7%	38.9%
93:2	40.9%	1.3%	57.5%	59.1%	59.1%	0.8%	0.6%	58.3%	40.3%
93:3	39.4%	1.6%	59.7%	60.6%	60.5%	0.9%	0.6%	59.6%	38.8%
93:4	41.7%	1.4%	60.4%	58.3%	58.3%	0.8%	0.5%	57.5%	41.2%
94:1	43.7%	1.4%	63.2%	56.4%	56.5%	0.9%	0.5%	55.6%	43.0%
94:2	42.7%	1.3%	62.4%	57.3%	57.4%	0.8%	0.5%	56.6%	42.2%
94:3	39.8%	1.6%	60.8%	60.2%	60.2%	1.0%	0.6%	59.2%	39.2%
94:4	42.8%	1.7%	64.1%	57.2%	57.3%	1.1%	0.6%	56.2%	42.1%
95:1	38.7%	1.6%	57.0%	61.3%	61.2%	0.9%	0.7%	60.3%	38.1%
95:2	38.9%	1.5%	55.4%	61.0%	60.9%	0.9%	0.7%	60.0%	38.4%
95:3	38.9%	1.3%	54.5%	61.0%	60.9%	0.7%	0.6%	60.2%	38.5%
95:4	40.5%	0.9%	61.6%	59.4%	59.5%	0.6%	0.4%	58.9%	40.2%
96:1	38.9%	1.2%	58.8%	61.1%	61.1%	0.7%	0.5%	60.4%	38.4%
96:2	42.4%	1.3%	61.9%	57.6%	57.6%	0.8%	0.5%	56.9%	41.9%
96:3	40.8%	1.2%	61.4%	59.3%	59.3%	0.7%	0.5%	58.5%	40.3%
96:4	39.8%	1.5%	57.1%	60.1%	60.1%	0.9%	0.7%	59.2%	39.3%
AVG	39.4%	0.6%	27.9%	60.7%	60.7%	0.4%	0.2%	60.3%	39.1%

Table 7.4a
Candle Counter Attack (CN-CA) Long Return Analysis
(Average of all stocks)

Qtr	CN-CA Terminal Wealth	Buy/Hold Terminal Wealth	Relative Terminal Wealth	CN-CA Long Avg Ret	CN-CA Cash Avg Ret	CN-CA Long-Cash Avg Ret	Buy/Hold Avg Ret
85:1	10000	10142	0.986	0.000%	0.006%	-0.006%	0.006%
85:2	10000	9700	1.031	0.000%	-0.069%	0.069%	-0.069%
85:3	10000	8889	1.125	0.000%	-0.205%	0.205%	-0.205%
85:4	10000	10763	0.929	0.000%	0.107%	-0.107%	0.107%
86:1	10000	11428	0.875	0.000%	0.225%	-0.225%	0.225%
86:2	10000	10414	0.960	0.000%	0.066%	-0.066%	0.066%
86:3	10000	9175	1.090	0.000%	-0.128%	0.128%	-0.128%
86:4	10000	10413	0.960	0.000%	0.069%	-0.069%	0.069%
87:1	10000	11929	0.838	0.000%	0.293%	-0.293%	0.293%
87:2	10000	10196	0.981	0.000%	0.038%	-0.038%	0.038%
87:3	10000	10408	0.961	0.000%	0.068%	-0.068%	0.068%
87:4	10000	8087	1.237	0.000%	-0.278%	0.278%	-0.278%
88:1	10000	10989	0.910	0.000%	0.163%	-0.163%	0.163%
88:2	10000	10593	0.944	0.000%	0.100%	-0.100%	0.100%
88:3	10000	10050	0.995	0.000%	0.013%	-0.013%	0.013%
88:4	10000	10196	0.981	0.000%	0.037%	-0.037%	0.037%
89:1	10000	10698	0.935	0.000%	0.112%	-0.112%	0.112%
89:2	10000	10772	0.928	0.000%	0.122%	-0.122%	0.122%
89:3	10000	10833	0.923	0.000%	0.131%	-0.131%	0.131%
89:4	10000	9904	1.010	0.000%	-0.011%	0.011%	-0.011%
90:1	10000	9980	1.002	0.000%	0.003%	-0.003%	0.003%
90:2	10000	10459	0.956	0.000%	0.077%	-0.077%	0.077%
90:3	10000	8526	1.173	0.000%	-0.259%	0.259%	-0.259%
90:4	10000	10889	0.918	0.000%	0.146%	-0.146%	0.146%
91:1	10000	12477	0.801	0.000%	0.315%	-0.315%	0.315%
91:2	10000	10244	0.976	0.000%	0.045%	-0.045%	0.045%
91:3	10000	10429	0.959	-0.001%	0.066%	-0.067%	0.065%
91:4	10014	10497	0.954	0.178%	0.081%	0.097%	0.082%
92:1	10012	10324	0.970	0.200%	0.046%	0.154%	0.048%
92:2	10001	9723	1.029	0.005%	-0.049%	0.054%	-0.048%
92:3	10010	10392	0.963	0.110%	0.056%	0.054%	0.057%
92:4	10016	10963	0.914	0.218%	0.144%	0.074%	0.144%
93:1	10000	10527	0.950	0.020%	0.080%	-0.060%	0.080%
93:2	10010	10340	0.968	0.098%	0.051%	0.048%	0.052%
93:3	10013	10686	0.937	0.157%	0.100%	0.057%	0.101%
93:4	10005	10255	0.976	0.054%	0.034%	0.021%	0.034%
94:1	10010	9954	1.006	0.106%	-0.013%	0.119%	-0.011%
94:2	9992	9994	1.000	-0.081%	-0.003%	-0.078%	-0.005%
94:3	10014	10613	0.944	0.119%	0.089%	0.030%	0.089%
94:4	9999	9836	1.017	-0.007%	-0.030%	0.023%	-0.029%
95:1	10020	10706	0.936	0.235%	0.108%	0.127%	0.110%
95:2	10018	10873	0.921	0.190%	0.133%	0.056%	0.134%
95:3	10016	10853	0.923	0.160%	0.131%	0.030%	0.131%
95:4	10006	10445	0.958	0.054%	0.067%	-0.013%	0.067%
96:1	10012	11027	0.908	0.136%	0.159%	-0.023%	0.159%
96:2	10000	10367	0.965	-0.009%	0.060%	-0.068%	0.059%
96:3	9996	10298	0.971	-0.039%	0.049%	-0.088%	0.047%
96:4	10015	10817	0.926	0.170%	0.122%	0.049%	0.122%
AVG	10004	10377	0.964	0.091%	0.055%	0.036%	0.055%

Table 7.4b
Candle Counter Attack (CN-CA) Short Return Analysis
(Average of all stocks)

Qtr	CN-CA Terminal Wealth	Buy/Hold Terminal Wealth	Relative Terminal Wealth	CN-CA Short Avg Ret	CN-CA Cash Avg Ret	CN-CA Short-Cash Avg Ret	Buy/Hold Avg Ret
85:1	10000	10142	0.986	0.000%	0.006%	-0.006%	0.006%
85:2	10000	9700	1.031	0.000%	-0.069%	0.069%	-0.069%
85:3	10000	8889	1.125	0.000%	-0.205%	0.205%	-0.205%
85:4	10000	10763	0.929	0.000%	0.107%	-0.107%	0.107%
86:1	10000	11428	0.875	0.000%	0.225%	-0.225%	0.225%
86:2	10000	10414	0.960	0.000%	0.066%	-0.066%	0.066%
86:3	10000	9175	1.090	0.000%	-0.128%	0.128%	-0.128%
86:4	10000	10413	0.960	0.000%	0.069%	-0.069%	0.069%
87:1	10000	11929	0.838	0.000%	0.293%	-0.293%	0.293%
87:2	10000	10196	0.981	0.000%	0.038%	-0.038%	0.038%
87:3	10000	10408	0.961	0.000%	0.068%	-0.068%	0.068%
87:4	10000	8087	1.237	0.000%	-0.278%	0.278%	-0.278%
88:1	10000	10989	0.910	0.000%	0.163%	-0.163%	0.163%
88:2	10000	10593	0.944	0.000%	0.100%	-0.100%	0.100%
88:3	10000	10050	0.995	0.000%	0.013%	-0.013%	0.013%
88:4	10000	10196	0.981	0.000%	0.037%	-0.037%	0.037%
89:1	10000	10698	0.935	0.000%	0.112%	-0.112%	0.112%
89:2	10000	10772	0.928	0.000%	0.122%	-0.122%	0.122%
89:3	10000	10833	0.923	0.000%	0.131%	-0.131%	0.131%
89:4	10000	9904	1.010	0.000%	-0.011%	0.011%	-0.011%
90:1	10000	9980	1.002	0.000%	0.003%	-0.003%	0.003%
90:2	10000	10459	0.956	0.000%	0.077%	-0.077%	0.077%
90:3	10000	8526	1.173	0.000%	-0.259%	0.259%	-0.259%
90:4	10000	10889	0.918	0.000%	0.146%	-0.146%	0.146%
91:1	10000	12477	0.801	0.000%	0.315%	-0.315%	0.315%
91:2	10000	10244	0.976	0.000%	0.045%	-0.045%	0.045%
91:3	9992	10429	0.958	0.098%	0.064%	0.034%	0.065%
91:4	9999	10497	0.953	0.011%	0.083%	-0.072%	0.082%
92:1	10004	10324	0.969	-0.054%	0.049%	-0.103%	0.048%
92:2	10007	9723	1.029	-0.094%	-0.048%	-0.046%	-0.048%
92:3	9989	10392	0.961	0.090%	0.056%	0.034%	0.057%
92:4	9993	10963	0.912	0.086%	0.145%	-0.060%	0.144%
93:1	9989	10527	0.949	0.128%	0.079%	0.049%	0.080%
93:2	9992	10340	0.966	0.112%	0.051%	0.061%	0.052%
93:3	9992	10686	0.935	0.089%	0.101%	-0.012%	0.101%
93:4	9989	10255	0.974	0.125%	0.033%	0.092%	0.034%
94:1	10019	9954	1.007	-0.214%	-0.008%	-0.206%	-0.011%
94:2	9998	9994	1.000	0.019%	-0.005%	0.024%	-0.005%
94:3	9992	10613	0.942	0.078%	0.089%	-0.011%	0.089%
94:4	10008	9836	1.017	-0.075%	-0.029%	-0.047%	-0.029%
95:1	9982	10706	0.932	0.183%	0.109%	0.075%	0.110%
95:2	9974	10873	0.917	0.283%	0.132%	0.151%	0.134%
95:3	9986	10853	0.920	0.181%	0.130%	0.051%	0.131%
95:4	10003	10445	0.958	-0.038%	0.068%	-0.105%	0.067%
96:1	9997	11027	0.907	0.036%	0.160%	-0.125%	0.159%
96:2	9994	10367	0.964	0.074%	0.058%	0.015%	0.059%
96:3	10006	10298	0.972	-0.071%	0.049%	-0.119%	0.047%
96:4	9985	10817	0.923	0.170%	0.122%	0.049%	0.122%
AVG	9998	10377	0.963	0.061%	0.055%	0.006%	0.055%

The Candle Counterattack system is not a system that should be followed for profitable trading. In fact, it is difficult to see how a trader could make much use of the information provided by the system. Call rates for the system are extremely low and often lead to unprofitable trades.

Candle Doji Star

A doji star occurs when a security opens and closes at the same price—an indication of indecision in the market. Price fluctuates during the day, but at the end of the day the valuation is the same as at the beginning of the day.

Stars indicate reversals. The open-to-close range on one day is relatively large compared to the open-to-close range on the following day, and the open-to-close ranges of the two days do not overlap.

When the second day of the star pattern is a doji (see below), a doji star is formed. The doji star can be a precursor to a reversal at the end of an intermediate uptrend or downtrend. However, markets typically trading in a narrow range generate many doji stars, lessening their significance.

Construction

Dojis are candles with no bodies (see Figure 7.4). The open and close are the same value, resulting in a horizontal line that intersects a vertical line representing the day's trading range. A doji star occurs when this horizontal line lies outside the range of the previous day's open-to-close range. A bearish doji star occurs when a open-bodied candle is followed by a doji that opens and closes above the first day's open-to-close range. A bullish doji star is formed when a black candle is followed by a doji that has a horizontal line below the black candle's body.

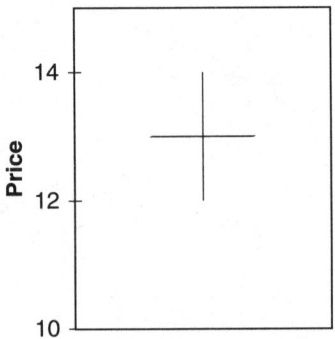

Figure 7.4 Candle doji.

Results

Table 7.5 shows that the Candle Doji Star (CN-DS) system makes fewer long and short calls than the Candle Counterattack pattern discussed earlier. With both long and short call rates of 0.5 percent, the CN-DS system makes fewer long calls than any of the tested indicators. Only the Candle Inverted Hammer system, discussed later in the chapter, makes fewer short calls than the CN-DS system.

When the system is used to decide between long and cash positions, the system's hit rate for long calls is 61.2 percent and its hit rate for cash calls is 60.1 percent (Table 7.5a). When choosing between short and cash positions, the system's hit rate for short calls is 60.1 percent and its hit rate for cash calls is 60.7 percent (Table 7.5b).

Table 7.6 shows that the return results for the CN-DS system were worse than for the Candle Counterattack, previously discussed. Trading long with the CN-DS system led to an average quarterly terminal wealth of $10,002, only $2 higher than an initial investment of $10,000. The highest quarterly terminal wealth an investor trading with this system could attain was only $10,017 (for a $10,000 investment), and trading long with this system would have led to losses in 14 of the test quarters.

The results from the short return analysis are even worse. For 28 of the 48 quarters tested, following the system's short calls yielded ending wealth that was less than the beginning wealth. The average ending quarterly wealth was only $9,999. On average, trading short with this system will decrease wealth.

The results for the Candle Doji Star leave much to be desired.

Candle Engulfing Lines

This two-day trading pattern is one of the most important and powerful candle patterns. A Candle Engulfing Line (CN-EL) occurs when one day's range encloses or "engulfs" the prior day's range. An engulfing line indicates that the market opened in the same direction as the prior day's market move, but reversed direction during the day to close strongly in the opposite direction. Thus, the market moved in opposite directions during the two trading days. A CN-EL indicates great market strength in the direction of today's close. It often forecasts major moves when it occurs opposite the current intermediate-term or long-term trend.

Construction

Because the market moves in opposite directions on two consecutive days, a candle engulfing pattern results in two bodies of opposite colors. The

Table 7.5a
Candle Doji Star (CN-DS) Long Hit Analysis
(Average of all stocks)

Qtr	Optimal Long	CN-DS Long	Long Hits	Cash Hits	Total Hits	Long Right	Long Wrong	Cash Right	Cash Wrong
85:1	32.1%	0.2%	57.3%	67.9%	67.9%	0.1%	0.1%	67.8%	32.0%
85:2	30.2%	0.2%	67.0%	69.8%	69.8%	0.1%	0.1%	69.6%	30.2%
85:3	26.3%	0.2%	55.8%	73.7%	73.6%	0.1%	0.1%	73.5%	26.3%
85:4	36.6%	0.1%	71.6%	63.4%	63.4%	0.1%	0.0%	63.3%	36.6%
86:1	44.2%	0.2%	67.1%	55.8%	55.9%	0.1%	0.1%	55.7%	44.1%
86:2	39.7%	0.1%	54.1%	60.3%	60.3%	0.1%	0.1%	60.2%	39.7%
86:3	37.0%	0.2%	56.7%	63.0%	63.0%	0.1%	0.1%	62.9%	36.9%
86:4	38.5%	0.2%	58.6%	61.5%	61.5%	0.1%	0.1%	61.4%	38.4%
87:1	44.7%	0.1%	64.6%	55.3%	55.3%	0.1%	0.0%	55.3%	44.6%
87:2	40.0%	0.2%	59.1%	60.0%	60.0%	0.1%	0.1%	59.9%	39.9%
87:3	39.5%	0.2%	64.8%	60.5%	60.5%	0.1%	0.1%	60.4%	39.5%
87:4	37.9%	0.2%	53.7%	62.1%	62.1%	0.1%	0.1%	62.0%	37.8%
88:1	41.3%	0.1%	71.0%	58.7%	58.7%	0.1%	0.0%	58.6%	41.3%
88:2	39.3%	0.3%	62.8%	60.7%	60.7%	0.2%	0.1%	60.5%	39.2%
88:3	35.9%	0.2%	72.4%	64.1%	64.1%	0.2%	0.1%	63.9%	35.9%
88:4	36.3%	0.2%	78.4%	63.7%	63.7%	0.1%	0.0%	63.5%	36.3%
89:1	39.0%	0.3%	61.9%	61.0%	61.0%	0.2%	0.1%	60.8%	38.9%
89:2	40.2%	0.2%	62.7%	59.9%	59.9%	0.1%	0.1%	59.7%	40.1%
89:3	39.9%	0.2%	71.2%	60.1%	60.1%	0.2%	0.1%	59.9%	39.8%
89:4	38.3%	0.3%	62.4%	61.7%	61.7%	0.2%	0.1%	61.5%	38.2%
90:1	36.9%	0.2%	61.9%	63.1%	63.1%	0.2%	0.1%	63.0%	36.8%
90:2	39.2%	0.2%	66.9%	60.8%	60.8%	0.2%	0.1%	60.6%	39.1%
90:3	33.5%	0.3%	60.0%	66.5%	66.5%	0.2%	0.1%	66.4%	33.4%
90:4	40.8%	0.3%	62.1%	59.2%	59.2%	0.2%	0.1%	59.0%	40.7%
91:1	44.1%	0.2%	65.6%	55.9%	55.9%	0.1%	0.1%	55.8%	44.0%
91:2	39.7%	0.2%	56.5%	60.3%	60.3%	0.1%	0.1%	60.2%	39.6%
91:3	40.4%	0.8%	62.0%	59.6%	59.6%	0.5%	0.3%	59.1%	40.1%
91:4	41.2%	0.6%	53.4%	58.7%	58.7%	0.3%	0.3%	58.4%	41.0%
92:1	40.0%	0.6%	61.7%	60.0%	60.0%	0.3%	0.2%	59.6%	39.8%
92:2	38.6%	0.9%	57.2%	61.4%	61.4%	0.5%	0.4%	60.8%	38.2%
92:3	40.3%	1.0%	61.2%	59.8%	59.8%	0.6%	0.4%	59.2%	39.9%
92:4	41.9%	0.7%	60.3%	58.1%	58.1%	0.4%	0.3%	57.7%	41.6%
93:1	42.5%	0.8%	58.8%	57.5%	57.5%	0.4%	0.3%	57.1%	42.2%
93:2	42.1%	0.8%	59.2%	57.9%	57.9%	0.4%	0.3%	57.4%	41.8%
93:3	42.5%	0.6%	58.8%	57.5%	57.5%	0.3%	0.2%	57.2%	42.2%
93:4	41.5%	0.9%	60.7%	58.5%	58.6%	0.5%	0.3%	58.0%	41.1%
94:1	40.4%	0.9%	53.8%	59.5%	59.5%	0.5%	0.4%	59.0%	40.1%
94:2	40.6%	0.8%	62.4%	59.4%	59.4%	0.5%	0.3%	58.9%	40.2%
94:3	41.8%	0.8%	59.9%	58.2%	58.2%	0.5%	0.3%	57.8%	41.5%
94:4	39.5%	0.8%	53.3%	60.5%	60.5%	0.4%	0.4%	60.0%	39.2%
95:1	43.1%	0.7%	56.1%	56.9%	56.9%	0.4%	0.3%	56.5%	42.8%
95:2	43.7%	0.8%	56.2%	56.2%	56.2%	0.5%	0.4%	55.8%	43.4%
95:3	43.9%	0.9%	59.4%	56.1%	56.1%	0.5%	0.3%	55.6%	43.5%
95:4	43.4%	0.9%	60.0%	56.6%	56.6%	0.5%	0.3%	56.1%	43.0%
96:1	45.5%	1.0%	63.4%	54.5%	54.6%	0.6%	0.4%	54.0%	45.0%
96:2	42.1%	1.1%	58.6%	57.9%	57.9%	0.6%	0.5%	57.3%	41.6%
96:3	42.6%	0.8%	60.4%	57.4%	57.4%	0.5%	0.3%	56.9%	42.3%
96:4	44.3%	1.0%	56.1%	55.7%	55.7%	0.6%	0.4%	55.2%	43.8%
AVG	40.0%	0.5%	61.2%	60.1%	60.1%	0.3%	0.2%	59.9%	39.7%

Table 7.5b
Candle Doji Star (CN-DS) Short Hit Analysis
(Average of all stocks)

Qtr	Optimal Short	CN-DS Short	Short Hits	Cash Hits	Total Hits	Short Right	Short Wrong	Cash Right	Cash Wrong
85:1	34.3%	0.2%	70.5%	65.7%	65.7%	0.2%	0.1%	65.5%	34.2%
85:2	34.6%	0.2%	76.6%	65.4%	65.4%	0.2%	0.1%	65.2%	34.5%
85:3	38.6%	0.1%	75.0%	61.4%	61.4%	0.1%	0.0%	61.3%	38.6%
85:4	33.1%	0.1%	53.6%	66.9%	66.9%	0.1%	0.0%	66.8%	33.1%
86:1	35.2%	0.1%	56.7%	64.8%	64.8%	0.1%	0.1%	64.7%	35.1%
86:2	39.8%	0.1%	68.0%	60.2%	60.2%	0.1%	0.0%	60.2%	39.7%
86:3	42.7%	0.1%	53.2%	57.3%	57.3%	0.1%	0.1%	57.2%	42.7%
86:4	38.7%	0.1%	58.3%	61.3%	61.3%	0.1%	0.1%	61.2%	38.6%
87:1	36.9%	0.2%	45.7%	63.1%	63.0%	0.1%	0.1%	63.0%	36.9%
87:2	40.0%	0.2%	67.6%	60.0%	60.0%	0.1%	0.1%	59.9%	39.9%
87:3	40.4%	0.1%	49.0%	59.6%	59.5%	0.0%	0.0%	59.5%	40.4%
87:4	45.3%	0.2%	68.5%	54.7%	54.8%	0.1%	0.1%	54.6%	45.2%
88:1	36.7%	0.1%	62.1%	63.3%	63.3%	0.1%	0.0%	63.2%	36.7%
88:2	37.4%	0.2%	65.2%	62.5%	62.6%	0.1%	0.1%	62.4%	37.4%
88:3	38.4%	0.1%	45.3%	61.6%	61.6%	0.0%	0.1%	61.6%	38.3%
88:4	37.0%	0.1%	65.0%	63.0%	63.0%	0.0%	0.0%	63.0%	37.0%
89:1	36.2%	0.1%	58.1%	63.8%	63.8%	0.1%	0.0%	63.7%	36.2%
89:2	35.9%	0.1%	55.0%	64.1%	64.0%	0.0%	0.0%	64.0%	35.9%
89:3	36.4%	0.1%	62.9%	63.6%	63.6%	0.1%	0.0%	63.5%	36.4%
89:4	39.0%	0.1%	54.0%	61.0%	61.0%	0.0%	0.0%	61.0%	39.0%
90:1	40.1%	0.1%	77.4%	59.9%	59.9%	0.1%	0.0%	59.8%	40.1%
90:2	37.8%	0.1%	70.3%	62.2%	62.2%	0.1%	0.0%	62.1%	37.8%
90:3	45.7%	0.1%	71.6%	54.3%	54.4%	0.1%	0.0%	54.3%	45.6%
90:4	37.6%	0.2%	67.5%	62.4%	62.4%	0.2%	0.1%	62.3%	37.5%
91:1	36.7%	0.1%	62.7%	63.3%	63.3%	0.1%	0.1%	63.2%	36.6%
91:2	40.4%	0.2%	57.1%	59.6%	59.6%	0.1%	0.1%	59.5%	40.3%
91:3	39.8%	0.7%	58.3%	60.2%	60.2%	0.4%	0.3%	59.8%	39.5%
91:4	40.5%	0.6%	55.0%	59.5%	59.5%	0.3%	0.3%	59.1%	40.3%
92:1	43.2%	0.7%	58.1%	56.8%	56.8%	0.4%	0.3%	56.4%	43.0%
92:2	42.9%	0.8%	61.5%	57.1%	57.2%	0.5%	0.3%	56.6%	42.5%
92:3	39.5%	1.1%	58.3%	60.5%	60.5%	0.6%	0.5%	59.9%	39.1%
92:4	37.5%	1.1%	59.0%	62.6%	62.5%	0.7%	0.5%	61.8%	37.0%
93:1	39.4%	1.2%	56.4%	60.6%	60.6%	0.7%	0.5%	59.9%	38.9%
93:2	40.9%	1.0%	60.0%	59.1%	59.2%	0.6%	0.4%	58.6%	40.4%
93:3	39.4%	0.9%	54.1%	60.6%	60.5%	0.5%	0.4%	60.1%	39.1%
93:4	41.7%	0.9%	54.3%	58.3%	58.3%	0.5%	0.4%	57.8%	41.3%
94:1	43.7%	1.0%	59.4%	56.3%	56.4%	0.6%	0.4%	55.7%	43.2%
94:2	42.7%	0.9%	60.6%	57.3%	57.4%	0.6%	0.4%	56.8%	42.3%
94:3	39.8%	0.8%	60.9%	60.2%	60.3%	0.5%	0.3%	59.8%	39.4%
94:4	42.8%	1.0%	56.6%	57.2%	57.2%	0.6%	0.4%	56.6%	42.4%
95:1	38.7%	0.8%	55.3%	61.3%	61.3%	0.4%	0.3%	60.9%	38.4%
95:2	38.9%	1.0%	54.9%	61.1%	61.0%	0.5%	0.4%	60.5%	38.5%
95:3	38.9%	1.0%	57.9%	61.1%	61.0%	0.6%	0.4%	60.5%	38.5%
95:4	40.5%	0.9%	59.7%	59.5%	59.5%	0.6%	0.4%	58.9%	40.1%
96:1	38.9%	0.9%	57.8%	61.1%	61.1%	0.5%	0.4%	60.6%	38.5%
96:2	42.4%	0.7%	58.3%	57.6%	57.6%	0.4%	0.3%	57.2%	42.1%
96:3	40.8%	0.8%	53.9%	59.2%	59.2%	0.4%	0.4%	58.8%	40.5%
96:4	39.8%	0.9%	59.2%	60.2%	60.2%	0.5%	0.4%	59.7%	39.4%
AVG	39.4%	0.5%	60.1%	60.7%	60.7%	0.3%	0.2%	60.4%	39.1%

Table 7.6a
Candle Doji Star (CN-DS) Long Return Analysis
(Average of all stocks)

Qtr	CN-DS Terminal Wealth	Buy/Hold Terminal Wealth	Relative Terminal Wealth	CN-DS Long Avg Ret	CN-DS Cash Avg Ret	CN-DS Long-Cash Avg Ret	Buy/Hold Avg Ret
85:1	10002	10142	0.986	0.226%	0.006%	0.220%	0.006%
85:2	10000	9700	1.031	-0.019%	-0.069%	0.050%	-0.069%
85:3	9998	8889	1.125	-0.130%	-0.205%	0.075%	-0.205%
85:4	10002	10763	0.929	0.303%	0.107%	0.197%	0.107%
86:1	10001	11428	0.875	0.143%	0.225%	-0.082%	0.225%
86:2	10002	10414	0.960	0.271%	0.066%	0.205%	0.066%
86:3	9998	9175	1.090	-0.195%	-0.127%	-0.068%	-0.128%
86:4	10000	10413	0.960	-0.008%	0.069%	-0.077%	0.069%
87:1	10000	11929	0.838	0.070%	0.293%	-0.223%	0.293%
87:2	10000	10196	0.981	-0.033%	0.038%	-0.071%	0.038%
87:3	10004	10408	0.961	0.412%	0.068%	0.344%	0.068%
87:4	9998	8087	1.236	-0.150%	-0.278%	0.128%	-0.278%
88:1	10001	10989	0.910	0.067%	0.163%	-0.096%	0.163%
88:2	10002	10593	0.944	0.137%	0.100%	0.038%	0.100%
88:3	10001	10050	0.995	0.050%	0.013%	0.038%	0.013%
88:4	10003	10196	0.981	0.275%	0.036%	0.239%	0.037%
89:1	10000	10698	0.935	0.027%	0.113%	-0.086%	0.112%
89:2	10001	10772	0.928	0.084%	0.122%	-0.038%	0.122%
89:3	10001	10833	0.923	0.093%	0.131%	-0.038%	0.131%
89:4	9999	9904	1.010	-0.042%	-0.011%	-0.031%	-0.011%
90:1	9999	9980	1.002	-0.034%	0.003%	-0.037%	0.003%
90:2	10000	10459	0.956	0.020%	0.077%	-0.057%	0.077%
90:3	9997	8526	1.173	-0.161%	-0.259%	0.099%	-0.259%
90:4	9999	10889	0.918	-0.079%	0.147%	-0.226%	0.146%
91:1	10008	12477	0.802	0.651%	0.314%	0.336%	0.315%
91:2	9999	10244	0.976	-0.054%	0.046%	-0.100%	0.045%
91:3	10007	10429	0.960	0.132%	0.064%	0.067%	0.065%
91:4	9999	10497	0.953	-0.019%	0.082%	-0.102%	0.082%
92:1	10004	10324	0.969	0.105%	0.048%	0.058%	0.048%
92:2	9993	9723	1.028	-0.126%	-0.048%	-0.078%	-0.048%
92:3	10011	10392	0.963	0.188%	0.055%	0.133%	0.057%
92:4	10002	10963	0.912	0.062%	0.145%	-0.083%	0.144%
93:1	10001	10527	0.950	0.021%	0.080%	-0.060%	0.080%
93:2	10001	10340	0.967	0.020%	0.052%	-0.032%	0.052%
93:3	10005	10686	0.936	0.133%	0.101%	0.032%	0.101%
93:4	10010	10255	0.976	0.180%	0.033%	0.148%	0.034%
94:1	9995	9954	1.004	-0.080%	-0.011%	-0.069%	-0.011%
94:2	10004	9994	1.001	0.082%	-0.005%	0.087%	-0.005%
94:3	10003	10613	0.943	0.057%	0.090%	-0.032%	0.089%
94:4	9994	9836	1.016	-0.129%	-0.028%	-0.100%	-0.029%
95:1	9999	10706	0.934	-0.012%	0.111%	-0.122%	0.110%
95:2	10008	10873	0.920	0.153%	0.134%	0.019%	0.134%
95:3	10011	10853	0.922	0.204%	0.130%	0.073%	0.131%
95:4	10005	10445	0.958	0.108%	0.066%	0.041%	0.067%
96:1	10017	11027	0.908	0.277%	0.158%	0.119%	0.159%
96:2	10000	10367	0.965	0.003%	0.059%	-0.056%	0.059%
96:3	10005	10298	0.972	0.109%	0.047%	0.062%	0.047%
96:4	9998	10817	0.924	-0.024%	0.124%	-0.148%	0.122%
AVG	10002	10377	0.964	0.063%	0.055%	0.008%	0.055%

Table 7.6b
Candle Doji Star (CN-DS) Short Return Analysis
(Average of all stocks)

Qtr	CN-DS Terminal Wealth	Buy/Hold Terminal Wealth	Relative Terminal Wealth	CN-DS Short Avg Ret	CN-DS Cash Avg Ret	CN-DS Short-Cash Avg Ret	Buy/Hold Avg Ret
85:1	9999	10142	0.986	0.063%	0.006%	0.056%	0.006%
85:2	10003	9700	1.031	-0.194%	-0.069%	-0.125%	-0.069%
85:3	10000	8889	1.125	0.007%	-0.205%	0.211%	-0.205%
85:4	9997	10763	0.929	0.535%	0.106%	0.428%	0.107%
86:1	9999	11428	0.875	0.122%	0.225%	-0.103%	0.225%
86:2	10001	10414	0.960	-0.119%	0.067%	-0.186%	0.066%
86:3	9998	9175	1.090	0.247%	-0.128%	0.375%	-0.128%
86:4	9999	10413	0.960	0.073%	0.069%	0.004%	0.069%
87:1	9993	11929	0.838	0.797%	0.292%	0.505%	0.293%
87:2	10001	10196	0.981	-0.103%	0.038%	-0.141%	0.038%
87:3	9998	10408	0.961	0.285%	0.068%	0.217%	0.068%
87:4	10001	8087	1.237	-0.134%	-0.278%	0.145%	-0.278%
88:1	10000	10989	0.910	0.002%	0.163%	-0.161%	0.163%
88:2	10000	10593	0.944	-0.037%	0.100%	-0.137%	0.100%
88:3	9998	10050	0.995	0.344%	0.012%	0.332%	0.013%
88:4	9998	10196	0.981	0.468%	0.036%	0.432%	0.037%
89:1	9999	10698	0.935	0.194%	0.112%	0.082%	0.112%
89:2	9999	10772	0.928	0.144%	0.122%	0.021%	0.122%
89:3	9999	10833	0.923	0.091%	0.131%	-0.040%	0.131%
89:4	9999	9904	1.010	0.207%	-0.011%	0.218%	-0.011%
90:1	10001	9980	1.002	-0.147%	0.003%	-0.150%	0.003%
90:2	10001	10459	0.956	-0.126%	0.077%	-0.203%	0.077%
90:3	10001	8526	1.173	-0.146%	-0.259%	0.113%	-0.259%
90:4	10001	10889	0.918	-0.066%	0.147%	-0.213%	0.146%
91:1	9994	12477	0.801	0.649%	0.314%	0.334%	0.315%
91:2	9998	10244	0.976	0.191%	0.045%	0.146%	0.045%
91:3	9996	10429	0.959	0.079%	0.065%	0.014%	0.065%
91:4	9995	10497	0.952	0.135%	0.081%	0.053%	0.082%
92:1	10000	10324	0.969	-0.001%	0.048%	-0.049%	0.048%
92:2	9996	9723	1.028	0.066%	-0.049%	0.115%	-0.048%
92:3	9998	10392	0.962	0.040%	0.057%	-0.016%	0.057%
92:4	10000	10963	0.912	-0.005%	0.146%	-0.151%	0.144%
93:1	9999	10527	0.950	0.011%	0.081%	-0.069%	0.080%
93:2	10002	10340	0.967	-0.036%	0.053%	-0.089%	0.052%
93:3	9990	10686	0.935	0.183%	0.100%	0.083%	0.101%
93:4	9994	10255	0.975	0.102%	0.033%	0.069%	0.034%
94:1	10000	9954	1.005	0.004%	-0.011%	0.015%	-0.011%
94:2	10003	9994	1.001	-0.044%	-0.004%	-0.039%	-0.005%
94:3	10001	10613	0.942	-0.014%	0.090%	-0.104%	0.089%
94:4	9997	9836	1.016	0.048%	-0.030%	0.078%	-0.029%
95:1	9995	10706	0.934	0.102%	0.110%	-0.008%	0.110%
95:2	9995	10873	0.919	0.079%	0.135%	-0.056%	0.134%
95:3	10006	10853	0.922	-0.067%	0.133%	-0.200%	0.131%
95:4	10002	10445	0.958	-0.032%	0.068%	-0.100%	0.067%
96:1	9995	11027	0.906	0.088%	0.160%	-0.071%	0.159%
96:2	10001	10367	0.965	-0.036%	0.059%	-0.095%	0.059%
96:3	9988	10298	0.970	0.251%	0.046%	0.206%	0.047%
96:4	9997	10817	0.924	0.051%	0.123%	-0.072%	0.122%
AVG	9999	10377	0.964	0.050%	0.055%	-0.005%	0.055%

difference between the open and close on the first day is smaller than the difference between the open and close on the second day. Thus, the first body is shorter than the second body.

A bullish CN-EL line, as shown in Figure 7.5, is formed when yesterday's market closed lower, today's open is below yesterday's close, and today's close is above yesterday's open. With the bullish indicator, the white body of today "engulfs" the black body of yesterday. A bearish CN-EL is formed when the price of a stock closed higher yesterday, today's open is higher than yesterday's close, and today's close is lower than yesterday's close. In this case, today's black body would engulf yesterday's white body.

Results

The test results for the Candle Engulfing Lines are shown in Tables 7.7 and 7.8.

This system chooses a long position over a cash position only 25.7 percent of the time (Table 7.7a). The hit rate for long calls is 60.0 percent. When the indicator chooses a cash position over a long position, it is correct 60.4 percent of the time.

How useful these long calls are is questionable. The system's ending wealth averages only 97.5 percent of the buy-and-hold terminal wealth and exceeds a buy-and-hold strategy's ending wealth in only ten test quarters.

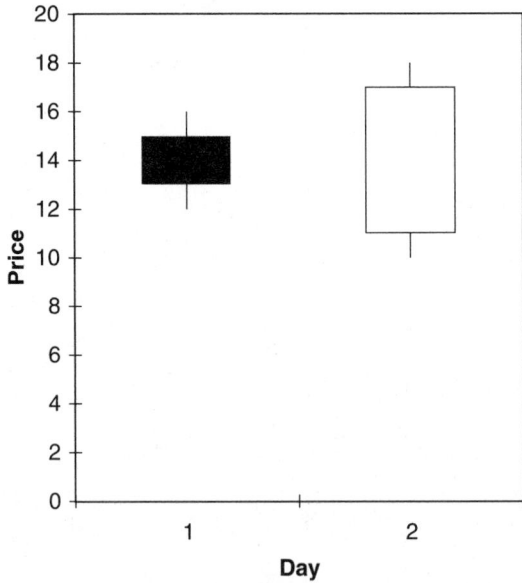

Figure 7.5 Bullish candle engulfing line.

The system makes short calls slightly less often than it makes long calls. The system favors a short position 22.8 percent of the time. The hit rate for these short calls is 59.0 percent, and the hit rate for cash calls is 60.7 percent.

Using this system's short calls to make trading decisions is more unprofitable than using the system's long calls. In all but nine of the test quarters, the terminal wealth from trading short is less than the beginning wealth of $10,000. In an average quarter, an investor with a $10,000 investment would lose $90 trading short with this system.

Table 7.8b reveals that the average daily stock return when the system recommends a short position is 0.064 percent. This is significantly larger than the average daily stock return of 0.052 percent when the system favors a cash position. This system is poor at making short calls. It advises a short position during some of the strongest market periods—the days when investors definitely want to be in long positions.

Let's turn our attention to another two-day candle pattern, the Candle Harami Pattern, to see whether trading results are improved.

Candle Harami Pattern

Another two-day pattern, the Candle Harami Pattern (CN-HAM), is just the opposite of the Candle Engulfing Line (CN-EL). The CN-HAM takes its name from the Japanese word for "pregnant." With the CN-HAM, today's body is engulfed by yesterday's body and is of opposite color. Its opposite, the CN-EL, represents market strength in the direction of the second day's direction. The CN-HAM represents market indecision. Although typically not as powerful a reversal predictor as the CN-EL, the CN-HAM can be a good forecaster of reversals at the end of intermediate-term and long-term trends.

Construction

A CN-HAM is formed when today's open and close are entirely within the prior day's open and close range, but the market moved in the opposite direction. A bearish CN-HAM, shown in Figure 7.6, is formed when the market moves up one day, opens the following day at a price below the previous day's close, and then moves down during the day but closes above the previous day's opening. The first day's open-to-close range is larger than the second day's open-to-close range, resulting in a relatively large open body followed by a relatively small black body. A bullish CN-HAM is characterized by a large black body on Day 1, followed by a small open body on Day 2. With the bullish indicator, the second day's opening is above the first day's close, and the second day's close is higher than the second day's opening but below the previous day's opening.

Table 7.7a
Candle Engulfing Lines (CN-EL) Long Hit Analysis
(Average of all stocks)

Qtr	Optimal Long	CN-EL Long	Long Hits	Cash Hits	Total Hits	Long Right	Long Wrong	Cash Right	Cash Wrong
85:1	32.1%	23.1%	62.3%	69.8%	68.0%	14.4%	8.7%	53.6%	23.3%
85:2	30.2%	20.4%	63.1%	71.8%	70.0%	12.9%	7.5%	57.1%	22.4%
85:3	26.3%	19.6%	58.1%	76.2%	72.6%	11.4%	8.2%	61.2%	19.2%
85:4	36.6%	25.3%	64.7%	65.9%	65.6%	16.4%	8.9%	49.2%	25.5%
86:1	44.2%	28.7%	63.8%	56.4%	58.5%	18.3%	10.4%	40.2%	31.1%
86:2	39.7%	27.0%	59.6%	60.4%	60.2%	16.1%	10.9%	44.1%	28.9%
86:3	37.0%	25.1%	56.5%	63.3%	61.6%	14.2%	10.9%	47.4%	27.5%
86:4	38.5%	28.9%	59.3%	61.4%	60.8%	17.1%	11.8%	43.7%	27.4%
87:1	44.7%	31.0%	61.6%	55.1%	57.1%	19.1%	11.9%	38.0%	31.0%
87:2	40.0%	26.4%	58.2%	59.5%	59.2%	15.4%	11.1%	43.8%	29.8%
87:3	39.5%	26.6%	59.0%	60.6%	60.1%	15.7%	10.9%	44.4%	28.9%
87:4	37.9%	23.1%	55.5%	62.3%	60.7%	12.8%	10.3%	47.9%	29.0%
88:1	41.3%	25.6%	62.1%	58.5%	59.5%	15.9%	9.7%	43.5%	30.8%
88:2	39.3%	28.9%	61.5%	60.5%	60.8%	17.8%	11.1%	43.1%	28.1%
88:3	35.9%	29.1%	59.6%	63.8%	62.6%	17.3%	11.7%	45.2%	25.7%
88:4	36.3%	29.6%	61.5%	63.4%	62.9%	18.2%	11.4%	44.6%	25.7%
89:1	39.0%	31.5%	61.5%	60.7%	61.0%	19.4%	12.2%	41.6%	26.9%
89:2	40.2%	29.8%	62.4%	59.5%	60.3%	18.6%	11.2%	41.7%	28.4%
89:3	39.9%	29.7%	61.7%	59.7%	60.3%	18.3%	11.4%	42.0%	28.3%
89:4	38.3%	25.9%	60.4%	61.5%	61.2%	15.7%	10.3%	45.6%	28.5%
90:1	36.9%	29.0%	58.6%	63.3%	61.9%	17.0%	12.0%	44.9%	26.1%
90:2	39.2%	28.0%	61.0%	60.9%	60.9%	17.1%	10.9%	43.9%	28.2%
90:3	33.5%	25.0%	52.9%	66.3%	63.0%	13.3%	11.8%	49.7%	25.2%
90:4	40.8%	29.0%	61.8%	59.8%	60.4%	18.0%	11.1%	42.4%	28.5%
91:1	44.1%	29.9%	62.6%	56.2%	58.1%	18.7%	11.2%	39.4%	30.7%
91:2	39.7%	26.7%	58.2%	60.2%	59.6%	15.6%	11.2%	44.1%	29.2%
91:3	40.4%	23.8%	59.5%	59.5%	59.5%	14.1%	9.6%	45.3%	30.9%
91:4	41.2%	23.4%	59.2%	59.1%	59.1%	13.8%	9.5%	45.3%	31.4%
92:1	40.0%	24.6%	57.0%	60.3%	59.5%	14.0%	10.6%	45.5%	30.0%
92:2	38.6%	22.7%	57.0%	61.4%	60.4%	12.9%	9.7%	47.5%	29.8%
92:3	40.3%	23.9%	61.0%	60.1%	60.3%	14.6%	9.3%	45.7%	30.3%
92:4	41.9%	25.1%	62.3%	58.3%	59.3%	15.6%	9.5%	43.6%	31.3%
93:1	42.5%	24.2%	60.6%	57.6%	58.3%	14.7%	9.5%	43.6%	32.2%
93:2	42.1%	23.2%	60.1%	58.2%	58.6%	13.9%	9.3%	44.7%	32.1%
93:3	42.5%	24.6%	60.5%	57.5%	58.3%	14.9%	9.7%	43.4%	32.0%
93:4	41.5%	23.4%	59.0%	58.7%	58.7%	13.8%	9.6%	44.9%	31.7%
94:1	40.4%	22.9%	56.7%	59.8%	59.1%	13.0%	9.9%	46.1%	31.0%
94:2	40.6%	22.1%	57.0%	59.3%	58.8%	12.6%	9.5%	46.2%	31.7%
94:3	41.8%	24.4%	61.0%	58.5%	59.1%	14.9%	9.5%	44.2%	31.3%
94:4	39.5%	22.9%	57.7%	60.6%	59.9%	13.2%	9.7%	46.7%	30.4%
95:1	43.1%	24.8%	62.0%	57.1%	58.3%	15.4%	9.4%	42.9%	32.3%
95:2	43.7%	25.4%	61.3%	56.4%	57.6%	15.6%	9.8%	42.1%	32.6%
95:3	43.9%	24.6%	60.9%	56.1%	57.3%	15.0%	9.6%	42.3%	33.1%
95:4	43.4%	25.2%	59.6%	56.8%	57.5%	15.0%	10.2%	42.5%	32.3%
96:1	45.5%	25.3%	61.7%	54.8%	56.5%	15.6%	9.7%	40.9%	33.8%
96:2	42.1%	25.3%	58.2%	58.1%	58.1%	14.7%	10.6%	43.4%	31.3%
96:3	42.6%	22.5%	60.0%	57.6%	58.1%	13.5%	9.0%	44.6%	32.9%
96:4	44.3%	25.1%	60.2%	55.8%	56.9%	15.1%	10.0%	41.8%	33.1%
AVG	40.0%	25.7%	60.0%	60.4%	60.3%	15.4%	10.2%	44.9%	29.4%

Table 7.7b
Candle Engulfing Lines (CN-EL) Short Hit Analysis
(Average of all stocks)

Qtr	Optimal Short	CN-EL Short	Short Hits	Cash Hits	Total Hits	Short Right	Short Wrong	Cash Right	Cash Wrong
85:1	34.3%	19.5%	62.0%	66.2%	65.4%	12.1%	7.4%	53.3%	27.2%
85:2	34.6%	18.4%	63.4%	65.8%	65.3%	11.7%	6.7%	53.7%	27.9%
85:3	38.6%	17.9%	63.4%	61.8%	62.1%	11.3%	6.5%	50.8%	31.3%
85:4	33.1%	18.5%	54.3%	66.9%	64.6%	10.0%	8.4%	54.6%	27.0%
86:1	35.2%	23.6%	54.9%	64.8%	62.5%	12.9%	10.6%	49.5%	26.9%
86:2	39.8%	25.2%	59.5%	60.2%	60.1%	15.0%	10.2%	45.1%	29.8%
86:3	42.7%	24.1%	63.3%	57.6%	59.0%	15.2%	8.8%	43.7%	32.2%
86:4	38.7%	25.0%	60.2%	61.1%	60.9%	15.1%	9.9%	45.8%	29.1%
87:1	36.9%	23.3%	53.1%	62.6%	60.4%	12.4%	10.9%	48.0%	28.7%
87:2	40.0%	24.5%	58.4%	60.0%	59.6%	14.3%	10.2%	45.3%	30.2%
87:3	40.4%	25.8%	60.1%	59.5%	59.6%	15.5%	10.3%	44.1%	30.1%
87:4	45.3%	25.8%	60.9%	54.6%	56.2%	15.7%	10.1%	40.5%	33.7%
88:1	36.7%	24.7%	57.6%	63.2%	61.8%	14.2%	10.5%	47.6%	27.7%
88:2	37.4%	23.6%	59.5%	62.4%	61.7%	14.1%	9.6%	47.6%	28.7%
88:3	38.4%	27.1%	62.4%	61.1%	61.4%	16.9%	10.2%	44.5%	28.4%
88:4	37.0%	25.2%	62.2%	62.7%	62.6%	15.7%	9.5%	46.9%	27.9%
89:1	36.2%	24.5%	58.4%	63.0%	61.9%	14.3%	10.2%	47.6%	27.9%
89:2	35.9%	25.5%	58.3%	63.5%	62.2%	14.9%	10.6%	47.3%	27.2%
89:3	36.4%	25.4%	58.7%	63.0%	61.9%	14.9%	10.5%	47.0%	27.6%
89:4	39.0%	24.6%	60.6%	60.6%	60.6%	14.9%	9.7%	45.7%	29.7%
90:1	40.1%	25.1%	62.0%	60.0%	60.5%	15.5%	9.5%	44.9%	30.0%
90:2	37.8%	24.5%	60.3%	62.1%	61.7%	14.8%	9.7%	46.9%	28.6%
90:3	45.7%	24.2%	65.9%	54.4%	57.2%	15.9%	8.3%	41.2%	34.5%
90:4	37.6%	21.1%	57.6%	61.9%	61.0%	12.2%	9.0%	48.8%	30.0%
91:1	36.7%	23.0%	55.8%	63.5%	61.7%	12.8%	10.2%	48.9%	28.1%
91:2	40.4%	26.4%	58.9%	59.2%	59.1%	15.6%	10.9%	43.6%	30.0%
91:3	39.8%	22.6%	58.6%	60.2%	59.9%	13.3%	9.3%	46.6%	30.8%
91:4	40.5%	21.8%	58.7%	59.6%	59.4%	12.8%	9.0%	46.6%	31.6%
92:1	43.2%	21.1%	60.7%	57.0%	57.8%	12.8%	8.3%	45.0%	33.9%
92:2	42.9%	22.6%	60.7%	57.0%	57.9%	13.7%	8.9%	44.2%	33.2%
92:3	39.5%	21.2%	59.1%	60.6%	60.3%	12.5%	8.7%	47.8%	31.1%
92:4	37.5%	20.0%	57.7%	62.5%	61.6%	11.6%	8.5%	50.0%	30.0%
93:1	39.4%	22.5%	57.5%	60.8%	60.1%	13.0%	9.6%	47.1%	30.4%
93:2	40.9%	21.6%	58.2%	59.3%	59.1%	12.6%	9.0%	46.5%	31.9%
93:3	39.4%	21.4%	57.3%	60.7%	60.0%	12.2%	9.1%	47.7%	30.9%
93:4	41.7%	22.4%	59.1%	58.7%	58.8%	13.3%	9.2%	45.6%	32.0%
94:1	43.7%	22.7%	59.5%	56.4%	57.1%	13.5%	9.2%	43.6%	33.7%
94:2	42.7%	21.6%	59.7%	57.4%	57.9%	12.9%	8.7%	44.9%	33.4%
94:3	39.8%	21.9%	58.4%	60.3%	59.9%	12.8%	9.1%	47.1%	31.0%
94:4	42.8%	22.7%	60.3%	57.4%	58.1%	13.7%	9.0%	44.4%	32.9%
95:1	38.7%	21.8%	57.1%	61.5%	60.5%	12.4%	9.4%	48.1%	30.1%
95:2	38.9%	21.0%	56.9%	61.3%	60.3%	12.0%	9.1%	48.4%	30.6%
95:3	38.9%	22.0%	55.7%	60.9%	59.8%	12.3%	9.7%	47.5%	30.5%
95:4	40.5%	21.8%	57.8%	59.7%	59.3%	12.6%	9.2%	46.7%	31.5%
96:1	38.9%	20.5%	55.7%	61.4%	60.2%	11.4%	9.1%	48.8%	30.7%
96:2	42.4%	21.6%	57.9%	57.7%	57.7%	12.5%	9.1%	45.2%	33.2%
96:3	40.8%	21.5%	58.5%	59.4%	59.2%	12.6%	8.9%	46.7%	31.9%
96:4	39.8%	21.3%	55.6%	60.3%	59.3%	11.9%	9.4%	47.4%	31.3%
AVG	39.4%	22.8%	59.0%	60.7%	60.3%	13.5%	9.3%	46.8%	30.4%

Table 7.8a
Candle Engulfing Lines (CN-EL) Long Return Analysis
(Average of all stocks)

Qtr	CN-EL Terminal Wealth	Buy/Hold Terminal Wealth	Relative Terminal Wealth	CN-EL Long Avg Ret	CN-EL Cash Avg Ret	CN-EL Long-Cash Avg Ret	Buy/Hold Avg Ret
85:1	10117	10142	0.997	0.082%	-0.016%	0.098%	0.006%
85:2	10059	9700	1.037	0.044%	-0.098%	0.142%	-0.069%
85:3	9949	8889	1.119	-0.039%	-0.245%	0.206%	-0.205%
85:4	10361	10763	0.963	0.222%	0.068%	0.155%	0.107%
86:1	10461	11428	0.915	0.259%	0.211%	0.049%	0.225%
86:2	10120	10414	0.972	0.074%	0.063%	0.011%	0.066%
86:3	9804	9175	1.069	-0.124%	-0.129%	0.005%	-0.128%
86:4	10026	10413	0.963	0.016%	0.091%	-0.075%	0.069%
87:1	10525	11929	0.882	0.270%	0.303%	-0.034%	0.293%
87:2	10012	10196	0.982	0.009%	0.048%	-0.040%	0.038%
87:3	10128	10408	0.973	0.077%	0.065%	0.012%	0.068%
87:4	9811	8087	1.213	-0.128%	-0.323%	0.195%	-0.278%
88:1	10193	10989	0.928	0.127%	0.175%	-0.048%	0.163%
88:2	10164	10593	0.960	0.091%	0.103%	-0.012%	0.100%
88:3	9961	10050	0.991	-0.019%	0.026%	-0.044%	0.013%
88:4	10028	10196	0.984	0.017%	0.045%	-0.028%	0.037%
89:1	10133	10698	0.947	0.070%	0.132%	-0.062%	0.112%
89:2	10185	10772	0.946	0.099%	0.132%	-0.033%	0.122%
89:3	10192	10833	0.941	0.103%	0.143%	-0.040%	0.131%
89:4	9947	9904	1.004	-0.031%	-0.004%	-0.027%	-0.011%
90:1	9973	9980	0.999	-0.013%	0.009%	-0.023%	0.003%
90:2	10102	10459	0.966	0.060%	0.083%	-0.023%	0.077%
90:3	9563	8526	1.122	-0.289%	-0.249%	-0.041%	-0.259%
90:4	10316	10889	0.947	0.170%	0.136%	0.034%	0.146%
91:1	10667	12477	0.855	0.357%	0.297%	0.060%	0.315%
91:2	10027	10244	0.979	0.018%	0.056%	-0.038%	0.045%
91:3	10071	10429	0.966	0.047%	0.071%	-0.024%	0.065%
91:4	10162	10497	0.968	0.105%	0.075%	0.031%	0.082%
92:1	10133	10324	0.981	0.084%	0.036%	0.047%	0.048%
92:2	9967	9723	1.025	-0.028%	-0.054%	0.026%	-0.048%
92:3	10134	10392	0.975	0.086%	0.047%	0.039%	0.057%
92:4	10250	10963	0.935	0.156%	0.141%	0.015%	0.144%
93:1	10142	10527	0.963	0.093%	0.075%	0.018%	0.080%
93:2	10131	10340	0.980	0.090%	0.040%	0.049%	0.052%
93:3	10178	10686	0.952	0.110%	0.098%	0.013%	0.101%
93:4	10093	10255	0.984	0.061%	0.026%	0.035%	0.034%
94:1	10054	9954	1.010	0.036%	-0.025%	0.062%	-0.011%
94:2	10001	9994	1.001	0.001%	-0.006%	0.007%	-0.005%
94:3	10161	10613	0.957	0.102%	0.085%	0.017%	0.089%
94:4	9958	9836	1.012	-0.032%	-0.029%	-0.003%	-0.029%
95:1	10207	10706	0.953	0.133%	0.102%	0.031%	0.110%
95:2	10231	10873	0.941	0.144%	0.131%	0.013%	0.134%
95:3	10242	10853	0.944	0.154%	0.124%	0.031%	0.131%
95:4	10135	10445	0.970	0.084%	0.061%	0.023%	0.067%
96:1	10305	11027	0.935	0.190%	0.149%	0.041%	0.159%
96:2	10113	10367	0.976	0.070%	0.055%	0.015%	0.059%
96:3	10108	10298	0.982	0.075%	0.039%	0.036%	0.047%
96:4	10220	10817	0.945	0.137%	0.117%	0.020%	0.122%
AVG	10121	10377	0.975	0.074%	0.049%	0.026%	0.055%

Table 7.8b
Candle Engulfing Lines (CN-EL) Short Return Analysis
(Average of all stocks)

Qtr	CN-EL Terminal Wealth	Buy/Hold Terminal Wealth	Relative Terminal Wealth	CN-EL Short Avg Ret	CN-EL Cash Avg Ret	CN-EL Short-Cash Avg Ret	Buy/Hold Avg Ret
85:1	9918	10142	0.978	0.075%	-0.011%	0.086%	0.006%
85:2	9971	9700	1.028	0.028%	-0.091%	0.119%	-0.069%
85:3	10065	8889	1.132	-0.056%	-0.237%	0.181%	-0.205%
85:4	9697	10763	0.901	0.263%	0.071%	0.191%	0.107%
86:1	9674	11428	0.847	0.235%	0.221%	0.013%	0.225%
86:2	9885	10414	0.949	0.070%	0.065%	0.005%	0.066%
86:3	10293	9175	1.122	-0.189%	-0.108%	-0.081%	-0.128%
86:4	9811	10413	0.942	0.118%	0.053%	0.065%	0.069%
87:1	9520	11929	0.798	0.347%	0.277%	0.070%	0.293%
87:2	9951	10196	0.976	0.031%	0.040%	-0.009%	0.038%
87:3	9896	10408	0.951	0.061%	0.071%	-0.010%	0.068%
87:4	10434	8087	1.290	-0.280%	-0.277%	-0.002%	-0.278%
88:1	9679	10989	0.881	0.207%	0.148%	0.059%	0.163%
88:2	9830	10593	0.928	0.116%	0.095%	0.021%	0.100%
88:3	9916	10050	0.987	0.048%	-0.001%	0.049%	0.013%
88:4	9894	10196	0.970	0.066%	0.027%	0.039%	0.037%
89:1	9732	10698	0.910	0.185%	0.089%	0.097%	0.112%
89:2	9757	10772	0.906	0.153%	0.112%	0.041%	0.122%
89:3	9756	10833	0.901	0.156%	0.122%	0.034%	0.131%
89:4	9946	9904	1.004	0.034%	-0.026%	0.060%	-0.011%
90:1	9998	9980	1.002	0.001%	0.003%	-0.002%	0.003%
90:2	9871	10459	0.944	0.085%	0.074%	0.011%	0.077%
90:3	10433	8526	1.224	-0.278%	-0.253%	-0.025%	-0.259%
90:4	9666	10889	0.888	0.256%	0.117%	0.139%	0.146%
91:1	9611	12477	0.770	0.291%	0.322%	-0.031%	0.315%
91:2	9869	10244	0.963	0.077%	0.034%	0.043%	0.045%
91:3	9910	10429	0.950	0.062%	0.066%	-0.004%	0.065%
91:4	9899	10497	0.943	0.072%	0.084%	-0.012%	0.082%
92:1	9980	10324	0.967	0.013%	0.057%	-0.044%	0.048%
92:2	10113	9723	1.040	-0.078%	-0.040%	-0.038%	-0.048%
92:3	9928	10392	0.955	0.054%	0.057%	-0.003%	0.057%
92:4	9830	10963	0.897	0.136%	0.147%	-0.010%	0.144%
93:1	9922	10527	0.942	0.058%	0.086%	-0.028%	0.080%
93:2	9956	10340	0.963	0.036%	0.056%	-0.020%	0.052%
93:3	9862	10686	0.923	0.104%	0.100%	0.004%	0.101%
93:4	10021	10255	0.977	-0.012%	0.047%	-0.059%	0.034%
94:1	10020	9954	1.007	-0.013%	-0.011%	-0.002%	-0.011%
94:2	10048	9994	1.005	-0.030%	0.002%	-0.033%	-0.005%
94:3	9913	10613	0.934	0.067%	0.095%	-0.028%	0.089%
94:4	10051	9836	1.022	-0.035%	-0.027%	-0.008%	-0.029%
95:1	9875	10706	0.922	0.093%	0.115%	-0.022%	0.110%
95:2	9868	10873	0.908	0.101%	0.143%	-0.042%	0.134%
95:3	9836	10853	0.906	0.121%	0.134%	-0.013%	0.131%
95:4	9961	10445	0.954	0.030%	0.077%	-0.047%	0.067%
96:1	9852	11027	0.893	0.118%	0.170%	-0.052%	0.159%
96:2	9932	10367	0.958	0.051%	0.061%	-0.010%	0.059%
96:3	9981	10298	0.969	0.014%	0.056%	-0.043%	0.047%
96:4	9860	10817	0.911	0.106%	0.127%	-0.020%	0.122%
AVG	9910	10377	0.955	0.064%	0.052%	0.012%	0.055%

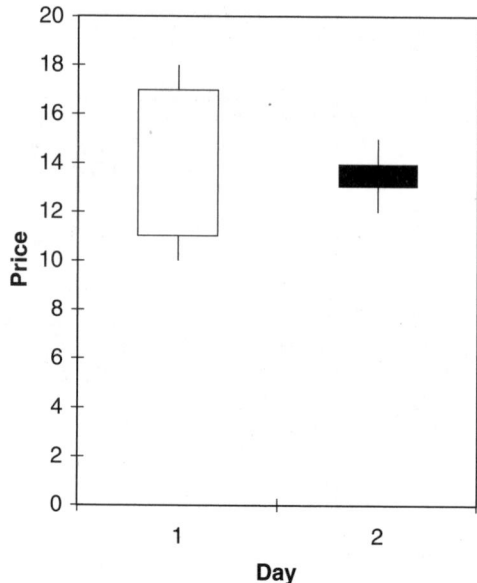

Figure 7.6   Candle Harami pattern.

Results

The call rates for the CN-HAM indicator are far below the optimal call rates. In Table 7.9, the long call rate for the system is 17.8 percent, compared to an optimal long call rate of 40.0 percent. The system's short call rate is 20.6 percent, far below the optimal 39.4 percent call rate.

Overall, the hit rate for this system is just about 60.5 percent. The hit rate for long calls is 59.5 percent, while the hit rate for short calls is 58.8 percent.

The return analysis for long and short calls of the CN-HAM is shown in Table 7.10. The average daily stock return of 0.069 percent for long calls shows that the indicator is able to predict days when above-average stock returns will occur with long calls. This can be useful information for an investor. However, this information alone is not enough for an investor to beat a buy-and-hold strategy. In fact, because of the infrequency of long calls, the return to an investor using this strategy would average only 97.1 percent of the returns with a buy-and-hold strategy. Trading long with the CN-HAM, an investor will be in the market during some of the most important time periods; however, the system makes many cash calls on positive return days. An investor who trades with this system forgoes these profits.

The short return analysis projects an even bleaker picture. Trading short with this system leads to losses in all but eleven of the test quarters. The average quarterly terminal wealth when trading short with this system is $9,940, which is $60 below the initial wealth level and 95.8 percent of the buy-and-hold terminal wealth.

The Candle Harami Pattern system has failed to provide a candle pattern that can be consistently used for profitable trading.

Candle Hammer

A hammer pattern is formed when a short body is at the top of a long tail. The body can be either open or black. Figure 7.7 is an example of this pattern. A hammer indicates that the daily trading range for a stock was much greater than the open-to-close range. To have meaning, a hammer must occur at the end of a significant trend. Hammers indicate indecision in the direction of the trend. Therefore, traders should wait for the next session to confirm a bullish or bearish hammer.

Construction

A hammer occurs when the high, open, and close prices are roughly the same, but the low of the day is far below the other prices. A "hanging man" occurs when a black-bodied hammer shows up at the end of an uptrend. The hanging man hammer indicates the market's propensity to sell off sharply if the next session confirms the bearish mood by opening below the close of the hammer.

A bullish hammer is an open-bodied hammer that occurs at the end of a downtrend. This hammer indicates strength for a reversal to the upside.

Results

Table 7.11 shows that the Candle Hammer (CN-HMR) indicator makes many more long calls than short calls, but, overall, the system makes far too few long and short calls. The long call rate for this system is 5.9 percent, and the

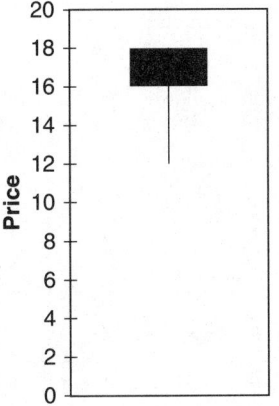

Figure 7.7   Candle hammer.

Table 7.9a
Candle Harami Pattern (CN-HAM) Long Hit Analysis
(Average of all stocks)

Qtr	Optimal Long	CN-HAM Long	Long Hits	Cash Hits	Total Hits	Long Right	Long Wrong	Cash Right	Cash Wrong
85:1	32.1%	14.7%	62.0%	69.7%	68.6%	9.1%	5.6%	59.5%	25.9%
85:2	30.2%	14.6%	63.7%	71.9%	70.8%	9.3%	5.3%	61.5%	24.0%
85:3	26.3%	15.3%	57.5%	75.7%	73.0%	8.8%	6.5%	64.2%	20.5%
85:4	36.6%	15.1%	65.4%	65.2%	65.2%	9.9%	5.2%	55.3%	29.5%
86:1	44.2%	19.1%	63.7%	56.5%	57.9%	12.2%	6.9%	45.7%	35.2%
86:2	39.7%	20.1%	59.6%	60.8%	60.5%	12.0%	8.1%	48.6%	31.3%
86:3	37.0%	20.7%	54.7%	63.3%	61.5%	11.3%	9.4%	50.2%	29.1%
86:4	38.5%	19.9%	60.7%	62.3%	62.0%	12.1%	7.8%	49.9%	30.2%
87:1	44.7%	18.6%	62.6%	55.7%	57.0%	11.7%	7.0%	45.3%	36.1%
87:2	40.0%	21.3%	58.7%	60.5%	60.1%	12.5%	8.8%	47.6%	31.1%
87:3	39.5%	22.1%	58.9%	61.0%	60.5%	13.0%	9.1%	47.5%	30.4%
87:4	37.9%	21.5%	54.5%	62.8%	61.0%	11.7%	9.8%	49.3%	29.2%
88:1	41.3%	20.0%	61.3%	59.3%	59.7%	12.3%	7.7%	47.4%	32.6%
88:2	39.3%	20.3%	60.6%	61.4%	61.2%	12.3%	8.0%	48.9%	30.8%
88:3	35.9%	20.3%	58.9%	64.7%	63.5%	12.0%	8.3%	51.5%	28.2%
88:4	36.3%	19.0%	60.0%	64.1%	63.3%	11.4%	7.6%	52.0%	29.1%
89:1	39.0%	18.1%	61.7%	61.6%	61.6%	11.2%	6.9%	50.4%	31.5%
89:2	40.2%	18.6%	62.4%	60.5%	60.9%	11.6%	7.0%	49.2%	32.1%
89:3	39.9%	19.7%	62.1%	60.5%	60.9%	12.2%	7.5%	48.6%	31.7%
89:4	38.3%	19.4%	60.0%	62.2%	61.8%	11.6%	7.7%	50.2%	30.4%
90:1	36.9%	20.8%	57.5%	63.6%	62.3%	11.9%	8.8%	50.4%	28.8%
90:2	39.2%	19.5%	60.3%	61.2%	61.0%	11.8%	7.7%	49.2%	31.3%
90:3	33.5%	21.9%	53.5%	67.1%	64.1%	11.7%	10.2%	52.4%	25.7%
90:4	40.8%	18.6%	62.3%	60.0%	60.4%	11.6%	7.0%	48.8%	32.6%
91:1	44.1%	19.4%	62.4%	56.2%	57.4%	12.1%	7.3%	45.3%	35.3%
91:2	39.7%	22.2%	59.1%	61.0%	60.6%	13.1%	9.1%	47.4%	30.4%
91:3	40.4%	16.5%	59.5%	59.8%	59.7%	9.8%	6.7%	49.9%	33.6%
91:4	41.2%	17.1%	58.4%	59.0%	58.9%	10.0%	7.1%	48.9%	34.0%
92:1	40.0%	15.9%	55.9%	60.1%	59.4%	8.9%	7.0%	50.5%	33.6%
92:2	38.6%	17.2%	56.6%	61.7%	60.8%	9.8%	7.5%	51.1%	31.7%
92:3	40.3%	15.1%	60.0%	59.9%	59.9%	9.1%	6.0%	50.9%	34.1%
92:4	41.9%	15.8%	61.9%	58.3%	58.9%	9.8%	6.0%	49.1%	35.1%
93:1	42.5%	16.1%	59.9%	57.6%	58.0%	9.6%	6.4%	48.4%	35.6%
93:2	42.1%	15.8%	58.7%	58.1%	58.2%	9.3%	6.5%	48.9%	35.3%
93:3	42.5%	16.0%	59.8%	57.7%	58.0%	9.6%	6.4%	48.4%	35.5%
93:4	41.5%	16.7%	58.1%	58.7%	58.6%	9.7%	7.0%	48.9%	34.4%
94:1	40.4%	16.5%	55.6%	59.6%	58.9%	9.2%	7.3%	49.8%	33.7%
94:2	40.6%	16.5%	56.9%	59.6%	59.2%	9.4%	7.1%	49.8%	33.7%
94:3	41.8%	16.4%	59.3%	58.3%	58.5%	9.7%	6.7%	48.8%	34.9%
94:4	39.5%	17.0%	56.4%	60.7%	59.9%	9.6%	7.4%	50.3%	32.6%
95:1	43.1%	16.1%	61.5%	57.0%	57.8%	9.9%	6.2%	47.9%	36.1%
95:2	43.7%	14.7%	60.4%	56.4%	57.0%	8.9%	5.8%	48.2%	37.2%
95:3	43.9%	15.8%	60.5%	56.1%	56.8%	9.6%	6.3%	47.2%	37.0%
95:4	43.4%	15.5%	58.5%	56.7%	57.0%	9.1%	6.4%	47.9%	36.6%
96:1	45.5%	14.6%	60.5%	54.5%	55.4%	8.8%	5.7%	46.6%	38.9%
96:2	42.1%	15.8%	56.0%	58.0%	57.7%	8.8%	6.9%	48.9%	35.4%
96:3	42.6%	15.3%	58.3%	57.3%	57.4%	8.9%	6.4%	48.5%	36.2%
96:4	44.3%	15.4%	58.8%	55.7%	56.2%	9.0%	6.3%	47.2%	37.5%
AVG	40.0%	17.8%	59.5%	60.6%	60.4%	10.6%	7.2%	49.8%	32.4%

Table 7.9b
Candle Harami Pattern (CN-HAM) Short Hit Analysis
(Average of all stocks)

Qtr	Optimal Short	CN-HAM Short	Short Hits	Cash Hits	Total Hits	Short Right	Short Wrong	Cash Right	Cash Wrong
85:1	34.3%	18.4%	58.2%	66.7%	65.2%	10.7%	7.7%	54.4%	27.1%
85:2	34.6%	16.0%	60.3%	66.4%	65.4%	9.6%	6.4%	55.7%	28.3%
85:3	38.6%	16.1%	63.1%	62.3%	62.4%	10.2%	6.0%	52.3%	31.6%
85:4	33.1%	20.6%	55.6%	67.9%	65.4%	11.4%	9.1%	54.0%	25.5%
86:1	35.2%	24.6%	54.3%	65.4%	62.7%	13.4%	11.3%	49.3%	26.0%
86:2	39.8%	23.4%	60.0%	60.9%	60.7%	14.1%	9.4%	46.7%	29.9%
86:3	42.7%	20.8%	62.5%	58.0%	58.9%	13.0%	7.8%	45.9%	33.3%
86:4	38.7%	23.0%	61.4%	62.4%	62.2%	14.1%	8.9%	48.1%	29.0%
87:1	36.9%	26.5%	55.3%	64.2%	61.8%	14.7%	11.8%	47.2%	26.3%
87:2	40.0%	23.2%	58.9%	60.7%	60.3%	13.7%	9.5%	46.6%	30.2%
87:3	40.4%	22.7%	59.9%	60.2%	60.2%	13.6%	9.1%	46.6%	30.7%
87:4	45.3%	24.9%	61.4%	55.0%	56.6%	15.3%	9.6%	41.3%	33.7%
88:1	36.7%	23.9%	58.0%	64.1%	62.7%	13.9%	10.0%	48.8%	27.3%
88:2	37.4%	22.7%	59.2%	63.1%	62.3%	13.4%	9.3%	48.8%	28.5%
88:3	38.4%	21.8%	62.5%	62.6%	62.6%	13.6%	8.2%	49.0%	29.2%
88:4	37.0%	20.5%	61.8%	63.8%	63.3%	12.7%	7.8%	50.7%	28.8%
89:1	36.2%	23.8%	60.2%	64.6%	63.5%	14.3%	9.5%	49.2%	27.0%
89:2	35.9%	23.7%	58.2%	64.7%	63.2%	13.8%	9.9%	49.4%	26.9%
89:3	36.4%	22.5%	58.8%	64.2%	63.0%	13.3%	9.3%	49.8%	27.7%
89:4	39.0%	23.1%	61.6%	61.9%	61.8%	14.2%	8.9%	47.6%	29.3%
90:1	40.1%	21.7%	61.1%	60.4%	60.5%	13.2%	8.4%	47.3%	31.0%
90:2	37.8%	22.5%	59.6%	62.9%	62.2%	13.4%	9.1%	48.8%	28.7%
90:3	45.7%	19.9%	65.6%	55.0%	57.1%	13.0%	6.8%	44.1%	36.1%
90:4	37.6%	23.8%	58.8%	63.4%	62.3%	14.0%	9.8%	48.3%	27.9%
91:1	36.7%	25.3%	54.5%	63.7%	61.4%	13.8%	11.5%	47.6%	27.1%
91:2	40.4%	23.2%	60.7%	60.6%	60.6%	14.1%	9.1%	46.5%	30.3%
91:3	39.8%	18.7%	59.0%	60.4%	60.2%	11.0%	7.7%	49.2%	32.2%
91:4	40.5%	18.4%	58.0%	59.7%	59.4%	10.7%	7.7%	48.7%	32.9%
92:1	43.2%	19.6%	59.7%	56.9%	57.5%	11.7%	7.9%	45.7%	34.6%
92:2	42.9%	17.0%	61.2%	57.4%	58.1%	10.4%	6.6%	47.7%	35.3%
92:3	39.5%	18.6%	59.6%	60.9%	60.7%	11.1%	7.5%	49.6%	31.8%
92:4	37.5%	18.2%	57.0%	62.8%	61.7%	10.4%	7.8%	51.3%	30.4%
93:1	39.4%	19.4%	57.8%	60.7%	60.1%	11.2%	8.2%	48.9%	31.7%
93:2	40.9%	17.8%	57.0%	59.3%	58.9%	10.2%	7.7%	48.7%	33.5%
93:3	39.4%	18.1%	57.0%	60.8%	60.1%	10.3%	7.8%	49.8%	32.1%
93:4	41.7%	17.5%	58.5%	58.5%	58.5%	10.2%	7.2%	48.3%	34.2%
94:1	43.7%	18.7%	59.6%	56.6%	57.2%	11.2%	7.6%	46.0%	35.3%
94:2	42.7%	18.6%	59.2%	57.3%	57.6%	11.0%	7.6%	46.6%	34.8%
94:3	39.8%	18.3%	58.6%	60.6%	60.2%	10.7%	7.6%	49.5%	32.2%
94:4	42.8%	16.7%	60.1%	57.4%	57.8%	10.0%	6.7%	47.8%	35.5%
95:1	38.7%	18.9%	56.4%	61.5%	60.6%	10.6%	8.2%	49.9%	31.2%
95:2	38.9%	20.2%	56.4%	61.4%	60.4%	11.4%	8.8%	49.0%	30.8%
95:3	38.9%	18.9%	56.5%	61.3%	60.4%	10.7%	8.2%	49.7%	31.4%
95:4	40.5%	19.1%	56.0%	59.5%	58.8%	10.7%	8.4%	48.1%	32.8%
96:1	38.9%	19.5%	54.2%	61.2%	59.8%	10.6%	9.0%	49.3%	31.2%
96:2	42.4%	18.6%	58.3%	57.9%	57.9%	10.9%	7.8%	47.1%	34.3%
96:3	40.8%	18.5%	56.8%	59.3%	58.8%	10.5%	8.0%	48.3%	33.2%
96:4	39.8%	18.6%	55.1%	60.2%	59.3%	10.2%	8.3%	49.0%	32.4%
AVG	39.4%	20.6%	58.8%	61.2%	60.7%	12.1%	8.5%	48.6%	30.9%

Table 7.10a
Candle Harami Pattern (CN-HAM) Long Return Analysis
(Average of all stocks)

Qtr	CN-HAM Terminal Wealth	Buy/Hold Terminal Wealth	Relative Terminal Wealth	CN-HAM Long Avg Ret	CN-HAM Cash Avg Ret	CN-HAM Long-Cash Avg Ret	Buy/Hold Avg Ret
85:1	10120	10142	0.998	0.132%	-0.015%	0.147%	0.006%
85:2	10115	9700	1.043	0.125%	-0.102%	0.228%	-0.069%
85:3	9947	8889	1.119	-0.055%	-0.232%	0.177%	-0.205%
85:4	10260	10763	0.953	0.268%	0.078%	0.191%	0.107%
86:1	10290	11428	0.900	0.250%	0.219%	0.031%	0.225%
86:2	10129	10414	0.973	0.103%	0.057%	0.045%	0.066%
86:3	9787	9175	1.067	-0.166%	-0.118%	-0.048%	-0.128%
86:4	10132	10413	0.973	0.108%	0.060%	0.048%	0.069%
87:1	10377	11929	0.870	0.325%	0.286%	0.039%	0.293%
87:2	10056	10196	0.986	0.044%	0.036%	0.008%	0.038%
87:3	10116	10408	0.972	0.083%	0.064%	0.019%	0.068%
87:4	9705	8087	1.200	-0.212%	-0.296%	0.084%	-0.278%
88:1	10215	10989	0.930	0.176%	0.159%	0.017%	0.163%
88:2	10154	10593	0.959	0.124%	0.094%	0.031%	0.100%
88:3	10021	10050	0.997	0.019%	0.011%	0.007%	0.013%
88:4	10009	10196	0.982	0.010%	0.043%	-0.033%	0.037%
89:1	10104	10698	0.944	0.094%	0.116%	-0.022%	0.112%
89:2	10172	10772	0.944	0.146%	0.117%	0.029%	0.122%
89:3	10151	10833	0.937	0.124%	0.133%	-0.009%	0.131%
89:4	9990	9904	1.009	-0.006%	-0.012%	0.006%	-0.011%
90:1	9958	9980	0.998	-0.030%	0.011%	-0.042%	0.003%
90:2	10072	10459	0.963	0.061%	0.081%	-0.020%	0.077%
90:3	9682	8526	1.136	-0.239%	-0.265%	0.026%	-0.259%
90:4	10296	10889	0.945	0.243%	0.124%	0.119%	0.146%
91:1	10357	12477	0.830	0.298%	0.319%	-0.021%	0.315%
91:2	10095	10244	0.985	0.070%	0.038%	0.032%	0.045%
91:3	10073	10429	0.966	0.071%	0.064%	0.007%	0.065%
91:4	10069	10497	0.959	0.062%	0.086%	-0.024%	0.082%
92:1	10033	10324	0.972	0.031%	0.051%	-0.020%	0.048%
92:2	9970	9723	1.025	-0.030%	-0.052%	0.022%	-0.048%
92:3	10064	10392	0.968	0.067%	0.055%	0.012%	0.057%
92:4	10144	10963	0.925	0.144%	0.145%	-0.001%	0.144%
93:1	10081	10527	0.958	0.082%	0.079%	0.003%	0.080%
93:2	10064	10340	0.973	0.066%	0.049%	0.017%	0.052%
93:3	10081	10686	0.943	0.077%	0.106%	-0.028%	0.101%
93:4	10055	10255	0.981	0.050%	0.031%	0.020%	0.034%
94:1	9994	9954	1.004	-0.007%	-0.012%	0.006%	-0.011%
94:2	9996	9994	1.000	-0.005%	-0.005%	-0.001%	-0.005%
94:3	10091	10613	0.951	0.087%	0.090%	-0.003%	0.089%
94:4	9959	9836	1.012	-0.041%	-0.027%	-0.014%	-0.029%
95:1	10109	10706	0.944	0.108%	0.110%	-0.002%	0.110%
95:2	10131	10873	0.932	0.144%	0.132%	0.012%	0.134%
95:3	10111	10853	0.932	0.113%	0.135%	-0.022%	0.131%
95:4	10092	10445	0.966	0.096%	0.061%	0.035%	0.067%
96:1	10124	11027	0.918	0.137%	0.163%	-0.026%	0.159%
96:2	10038	10367	0.968	0.038%	0.063%	-0.025%	0.059%
96:3	10012	10298	0.972	0.013%	0.054%	-0.041%	0.047%
96:4	10095	10817	0.933	0.097%	0.127%	-0.030%	0.122%
AVG	10077	10377	0.971	0.069%	0.052%	0.017%	0.055%

Table 7.10b
Candle Harami Pattern (CN-HAM) Short Return Analysis
(Average of all stocks)

Qtr	CN-HAM Terminal Wealth	Buy/Hold Terminal Wealth	Relative Terminal Wealth	CN-HAM Short Avg Ret	CN-HAM Cash Avg Ret	CN-HAM Short-Cash Avg Ret	Buy/Hold Avg Ret
85:1	9862	10142	0.972	0.123%	-0.020%	0.143%	0.006%
85:2	9977	9700	1.029	0.023%	-0.087%	0.110%	-0.069%
85:3	10081	8889	1.134	-0.081%	-0.229%	0.148%	-0.205%
85:4	9764	10763	0.907	0.182%	0.087%	0.095%	0.107%
86:1	9685	11428	0.847	0.219%	0.227%	-0.008%	0.225%
86:2	9982	10414	0.959	0.011%	0.083%	-0.072%	0.066%
86:3	10211	9175	1.113	-0.161%	-0.119%	-0.043%	-0.128%
86:4	9986	10413	0.959	0.006%	0.088%	-0.082%	0.069%
87:1	9657	11929	0.809	0.217%	0.320%	-0.103%	0.293%
87:2	9983	10196	0.979	0.007%	0.047%	-0.040%	0.038%
87:3	9951	10408	0.956	0.033%	0.079%	-0.046%	0.068%
87:4	10352	8087	1.280	-0.239%	-0.291%	0.052%	-0.278%
88:1	9825	10989	0.894	0.113%	0.178%	-0.066%	0.163%
88:2	9892	10593	0.934	0.076%	0.107%	-0.031%	0.100%
88:3	10012	10050	0.996	-0.010%	0.019%	-0.029%	0.013%
88:4	9963	10196	0.977	0.028%	0.039%	-0.011%	0.037%
89:1	9869	10698	0.923	0.090%	0.119%	-0.030%	0.112%
89:2	9830	10772	0.913	0.114%	0.125%	-0.010%	0.122%
89:3	9842	10833	0.908	0.114%	0.136%	-0.022%	0.131%
89:4	10098	9904	1.020	-0.071%	0.007%	-0.078%	-0.011%
90:1	9997	9980	1.002	0.000%	0.003%	-0.003%	0.003%
90:2	9913	10459	0.948	0.064%	0.080%	-0.016%	0.077%
90:3	10363	8526	1.215	-0.286%	-0.252%	-0.034%	-0.259%
90:4	9858	10889	0.905	0.095%	0.162%	-0.068%	0.146%
91:1	9537	12477	0.764	0.314%	0.315%	-0.002%	0.315%
91:2	10034	10244	0.980	-0.026%	0.067%	-0.093%	0.045%
91:3	9942	10429	0.953	0.049%	0.068%	-0.019%	0.065%
91:4	9917	10497	0.945	0.072%	0.084%	-0.013%	0.082%
92:1	9959	10324	0.965	0.031%	0.052%	-0.021%	0.048%
92:2	10062	9723	1.035	-0.058%	-0.046%	-0.012%	-0.048%
92:3	9985	10392	0.961	0.014%	0.066%	-0.053%	0.057%
92:4	9845	10963	0.898	0.137%	0.146%	-0.009%	0.144%
93:1	9907	10527	0.941	0.082%	0.079%	0.003%	0.080%
93:2	9953	10340	0.963	0.044%	0.053%	-0.010%	0.052%
93:3	9897	10686	0.926	0.093%	0.103%	-0.010%	0.101%
93:4	9990	10255	0.974	0.009%	0.039%	-0.030%	0.034%
94:1	10027	9954	1.007	-0.022%	-0.009%	-0.013%	-0.011%
94:2	10028	9994	1.003	-0.022%	-0.001%	-0.021%	-0.005%
94:3	9937	10613	0.936	0.055%	0.097%	-0.042%	0.089%
94:4	10038	9836	1.021	-0.036%	-0.028%	-0.008%	-0.029%
95:1	9896	10706	0.924	0.091%	0.114%	-0.023%	0.110%
95:2	9871	10873	0.908	0.106%	0.141%	-0.036%	0.134%
95:3	9873	10853	0.910	0.109%	0.136%	-0.027%	0.131%
95:4	9912	10445	0.949	0.078%	0.064%	0.014%	0.067%
96:1	9817	11027	0.890	0.155%	0.160%	-0.005%	0.159%
96:2	9971	10367	0.962	0.027%	0.066%	-0.038%	0.059%
96:3	9948	10298	0.966	0.045%	0.048%	-0.003%	0.047%
96:4	9831	10817	0.909	0.145%	0.117%	0.028%	0.122%
AVG	9940	10377	0.958	0.047%	0.057%	-0.010%	0.055%

Table 7.11a
Candle Hammer (CN-HMR) Long Hit Analysis
(Average of all stocks)

Qtr	Optimal Long	CN-HMR Long	Long Hits	Cash Hits	Total Hits	Long Right	Long Wrong	Cash Right	Cash Wrong
85:1	32.1%	4.5%	59.1%	68.4%	67.9%	2.7%	1.8%	65.3%	30.2%
85:2	30.2%	5.0%	60.9%	70.5%	70.0%	3.1%	2.0%	67.0%	28.0%
85:3	26.3%	5.2%	56.9%	74.3%	73.4%	2.9%	2.2%	70.5%	24.3%
85:4	36.6%	4.2%	62.5%	63.8%	63.7%	2.6%	1.6%	61.1%	34.7%
86:1	44.2%	4.8%	62.5%	56.1%	56.4%	3.0%	1.8%	53.4%	41.8%
86:2	39.7%	6.9%	58.5%	60.6%	60.5%	4.1%	2.9%	56.4%	36.7%
86:3	37.0%	7.9%	56.0%	63.4%	62.8%	4.4%	3.5%	58.4%	33.7%
86:4	38.5%	7.0%	57.6%	61.8%	61.5%	4.0%	3.0%	57.5%	35.6%
87:1	44.7%	6.5%	62.4%	55.6%	56.1%	4.0%	2.4%	52.0%	41.5%
87:2	40.0%	8.2%	57.2%	60.4%	60.1%	4.7%	3.5%	55.4%	36.4%
87:3	39.5%	6.2%	55.5%	60.7%	60.3%	3.5%	2.8%	56.9%	36.9%
87:4	37.9%	8.4%	52.8%	62.4%	61.6%	4.4%	4.0%	57.2%	34.4%
88:1	41.3%	6.6%	59.8%	58.9%	58.9%	3.9%	2.6%	55.0%	38.4%
88:2	39.3%	7.0%	59.2%	61.0%	60.9%	4.2%	2.9%	56.7%	36.3%
88:3	35.9%	5.2%	57.1%	64.3%	63.9%	3.0%	2.2%	61.0%	33.8%
88:4	36.3%	5.3%	57.9%	63.8%	63.5%	3.1%	2.2%	60.5%	34.2%
89:1	39.0%	5.3%	60.9%	61.2%	61.2%	3.3%	2.1%	57.9%	36.7%
89:2	40.2%	4.6%	59.6%	60.0%	60.0%	2.7%	1.9%	57.3%	38.1%
89:3	39.9%	5.9%	61.4%	60.3%	60.3%	3.6%	2.3%	56.7%	37.4%
89:4	38.3%	7.2%	56.7%	62.0%	61.6%	4.1%	3.1%	57.6%	35.3%
90:1	36.9%	8.0%	55.4%	63.4%	62.8%	4.4%	3.6%	58.4%	33.6%
90:2	39.2%	5.9%	59.4%	61.1%	61.0%	3.5%	2.4%	57.5%	36.6%
90:3	33.5%	10.7%	50.6%	67.0%	65.2%	5.4%	5.3%	59.8%	29.5%
90:4	40.8%	6.6%	61.2%	59.5%	59.6%	4.0%	2.6%	55.6%	37.8%
91:1	44.1%	5.9%	59.5%	56.0%	56.2%	3.5%	2.4%	52.7%	41.5%
91:2	39.7%	5.7%	57.0%	60.5%	60.3%	3.3%	2.5%	57.0%	37.3%
91:3	40.4%	4.8%	59.0%	59.7%	59.7%	2.8%	2.0%	56.9%	38.3%
91:4	41.2%	6.1%	56.9%	58.9%	58.8%	3.4%	2.6%	55.3%	38.6%
92:1	40.0%	5.5%	54.2%	60.0%	59.7%	3.0%	2.5%	56.7%	37.8%
92:2	38.6%	5.6%	56.3%	61.6%	61.3%	3.1%	2.4%	58.2%	36.3%
92:3	40.3%	5.2%	59.4%	59.9%	59.9%	3.1%	2.1%	56.8%	38.0%
92:4	41.9%	5.9%	59.9%	58.2%	58.3%	3.5%	2.4%	54.8%	39.3%
93:1	42.5%	5.5%	58.9%	57.5%	57.6%	3.2%	2.2%	54.4%	40.1%
93:2	42.1%	5.7%	58.4%	58.0%	58.0%	3.3%	2.4%	54.7%	39.6%
93:3	42.5%	4.4%	57.7%	57.6%	57.6%	2.5%	1.8%	55.1%	40.5%
93:4	41.5%	6.1%	55.3%	58.5%	58.4%	3.4%	2.7%	55.0%	38.9%
94:1	40.4%	6.4%	54.7%	59.7%	59.4%	3.5%	2.9%	55.9%	37.8%
94:2	40.6%	7.1%	56.9%	59.7%	59.5%	4.0%	3.1%	55.4%	37.5%
94:3	41.8%	5.0%	56.2%	58.2%	58.1%	2.8%	2.2%	55.3%	39.7%
94:4	39.5%	6.1%	56.5%	60.7%	60.5%	3.4%	2.6%	57.0%	36.9%
95:1	43.1%	4.3%	60.2%	56.9%	57.1%	2.6%	1.7%	54.5%	41.2%
95:2	43.7%	4.2%	56.9%	56.2%	56.3%	2.4%	1.8%	53.9%	41.9%
95:3	43.9%	5.1%	59.5%	56.2%	56.3%	3.0%	2.0%	53.3%	41.6%
95:4	43.4%	6.3%	55.7%	56.7%	56.6%	3.5%	2.8%	53.1%	40.6%
96:1	45.5%	5.3%	59.0%	54.5%	54.8%	3.1%	2.2%	51.6%	43.0%
96:2	42.1%	5.6%	56.4%	58.0%	58.0%	3.2%	2.5%	54.8%	39.6%
96:3	42.6%	6.2%	56.9%	57.5%	57.4%	3.5%	2.7%	53.9%	39.9%
96:4	44.3%	4.6%	57.9%	55.8%	55.9%	2.7%	1.9%	53.2%	42.2%
AVG	40.0%	5.9%	57.9%	60.4%	60.2%	3.4%	2.5%	56.8%	37.3%

Table 7.11b
Candle Hammer (CN-HMR) Short Hit Analysis
(Average of all stocks)

Qtr	Optimal Short	CN-HMR Short	Short Hits	Cash Hits	Total Hits	Short Right	Short Wrong	Cash Right	Cash Wrong
85:1	34.3%	0.5%	56.7%	65.7%	65.7%	0.3%	0.2%	65.4%	34.1%
85:2	34.6%	0.5%	59.2%	65.4%	65.4%	0.3%	0.2%	65.1%	34.4%
85:3	38.6%	0.4%	58.6%	61.4%	61.4%	0.3%	0.2%	61.1%	38.4%
85:4	33.1%	0.7%	51.7%	66.9%	66.8%	0.4%	0.4%	66.4%	32.9%
86:1	35.2%	0.9%	56.1%	64.8%	64.7%	0.5%	0.4%	64.2%	34.9%
86:2	39.8%	0.8%	62.4%	60.2%	60.2%	0.5%	0.3%	59.8%	39.5%
86:3	42.7%	0.8%	63.5%	57.3%	57.4%	0.5%	0.3%	56.8%	42.3%
86:4	38.7%	0.9%	61.1%	61.3%	61.3%	0.5%	0.3%	60.8%	38.3%
87:1	36.9%	0.6%	53.8%	63.1%	63.0%	0.3%	0.3%	62.7%	36.7%
87:2	40.0%	0.5%	53.6%	60.0%	59.9%	0.3%	0.2%	59.6%	39.8%
87:3	40.4%	0.6%	60.6%	59.6%	59.6%	0.4%	0.2%	59.2%	40.2%
87:4	45.3%	0.8%	62.5%	54.7%	54.8%	0.5%	0.3%	54.3%	44.9%
88:1	36.7%	0.9%	57.7%	63.3%	63.3%	0.5%	0.4%	62.8%	36.4%
88:2	37.4%	0.7%	57.3%	62.6%	62.5%	0.4%	0.3%	62.1%	37.2%
88:3	38.4%	0.5%	60.7%	61.7%	61.7%	0.3%	0.2%	61.4%	38.2%
88:4	37.0%	0.6%	56.2%	63.0%	63.0%	0.3%	0.3%	62.6%	36.7%
89:1	36.2%	0.5%	55.6%	63.8%	63.7%	0.3%	0.2%	63.5%	36.0%
89:2	35.9%	0.6%	58.5%	64.1%	64.0%	0.3%	0.2%	63.7%	35.7%
89:3	36.4%	0.5%	54.5%	63.6%	63.6%	0.3%	0.2%	63.3%	36.2%
89:4	39.0%	0.5%	54.8%	61.0%	61.0%	0.3%	0.2%	60.7%	38.8%
90:1	40.1%	0.7%	60.8%	59.9%	59.9%	0.4%	0.3%	59.5%	39.8%
90:2	37.8%	0.5%	56.8%	62.2%	62.2%	0.3%	0.2%	61.9%	37.6%
90:3	45.7%	0.5%	66.3%	54.4%	54.4%	0.3%	0.2%	54.1%	45.4%
90:4	37.6%	0.6%	58.4%	62.4%	62.4%	0.4%	0.3%	62.0%	37.3%
91:1	36.7%	0.9%	51.0%	63.3%	63.2%	0.5%	0.4%	62.8%	36.4%
91:2	40.4%	0.8%	61.2%	59.7%	59.7%	0.5%	0.3%	59.2%	40.0%
91:3	39.8%	1.2%	59.9%	60.3%	60.3%	0.7%	0.5%	59.5%	39.2%
91:4	40.5%	1.4%	55.6%	59.5%	59.4%	0.8%	0.6%	58.6%	39.9%
92:1	43.2%	1.2%	56.4%	56.8%	56.8%	0.7%	0.5%	56.1%	42.7%
92:2	42.9%	1.0%	66.4%	57.2%	57.2%	0.7%	0.3%	56.6%	42.4%
92:3	39.5%	1.3%	56.1%	60.5%	60.4%	0.7%	0.6%	59.7%	39.0%
92:4	37.5%	1.1%	58.7%	62.6%	62.5%	0.7%	0.5%	61.9%	37.0%
93:1	39.4%	1.4%	56.4%	60.7%	60.6%	0.8%	0.6%	59.8%	38.8%
93:2	40.9%	1.2%	57.8%	59.1%	59.1%	0.7%	0.5%	58.4%	40.3%
93:3	39.4%	1.0%	57.3%	60.6%	60.6%	0.6%	0.4%	60.0%	39.0%
93:4	41.7%	1.2%	58.6%	58.4%	58.4%	0.7%	0.5%	57.7%	41.2%
94:1	43.7%	1.2%	57.4%	56.3%	56.3%	0.7%	0.5%	55.6%	43.2%
94:2	42.7%	0.9%	59.2%	57.3%	57.3%	0.6%	0.4%	56.8%	42.3%
94:3	39.8%	0.9%	57.9%	60.2%	60.2%	0.5%	0.4%	59.7%	39.5%
94:4	42.8%	0.9%	59.5%	57.2%	57.2%	0.5%	0.4%	56.7%	42.4%
95:1	38.7%	0.9%	59.1%	61.4%	61.3%	0.5%	0.4%	60.8%	38.3%
95:2	38.9%	1.3%	59.0%	61.1%	61.1%	0.7%	0.5%	60.4%	38.4%
95:3	38.9%	1.4%	52.6%	61.1%	60.9%	0.7%	0.7%	60.2%	38.4%
95:4	40.5%	0.8%	58.3%	59.5%	59.5%	0.5%	0.3%	59.0%	40.2%
96:1	38.9%	1.1%	54.5%	61.1%	61.1%	0.6%	0.5%	60.5%	38.5%
96:2	42.4%	1.1%	58.8%	57.7%	57.7%	0.6%	0.5%	57.0%	41.9%
96:3	40.8%	1.2%	57.5%	59.3%	59.2%	0.7%	0.5%	58.6%	40.3%
96:4	39.8%	1.1%	53.0%	60.2%	60.1%	0.6%	0.5%	59.5%	39.4%
AVG	39.4%	0.9%	57.9%	60.7%	60.7%	0.5%	0.4%	60.2%	39.0%

short call rate is only 0.9 percent. The long calls and the short calls are equally accurate; the hit rate for both signals is 57.9 percent.

The return summary statistics for the CN-HMR indicator, presented in Table 7.12, do not look very promising. With a technical indicator that makes such infrequent calls, we might expect a system that makes very good calls when calls are made. This expectation is not fulfilled.

There is no difference in the average daily stock return, whether cash is preferred over a long position or a long position is recommended. No useful information is apparent in the system's calls. The average returns for long call days, coupled with the infrequency of long calls, led to an average quarterly wealth for the CN-HMR system that is only 96.6 percent of the buy-and-hold terminal wealth.

For the short calls, we do see a difference in average daily stock returns for long recommendations and cash recommendations. However, the direction of this difference is opposite to what we hope for when looking at short calls. The short call average daily return of 0.064 percent indicates that the CN-HMR indicator is choosing above-average return days to recommend a short position. On these days, an investor would want to be in a long position; they are the worst possible, most unprofitable days to be in a short position.

These results could be considered perverse. The short calls of the system are better at predicting strong days to be long in the market than the long calls themselves are. Investors should be extremely cautious about using this system for trading advice.

Next, let's see whether the opposite of the Candle Hammer system, the Candle Inverted Hammer, is a stronger trading system.

Candle Inverted Hammer

Candle Inverted Hammers occur when a small body appears at the bottom of a long tail. Thus, the inverted hammer is the opposite of the hammer. The longer the tail, the more significant the inverted hammer is in terms of forecasting a reversal.

Construction

When the open, close, and low prices are approximately the same and the high price is significantly above, an inverted hammer is formed, as shown in Figure 7.8. When a black-bodied inverted hammer occurs at the end of an uptrend, it is clearly a bearish signal; the market has failed in its attempt to rally higher and is closing near the open. However, when on open-bodied hammer occurs at the end of a downtrend, a bullish day following the hammer is needed to confirm the reversal.

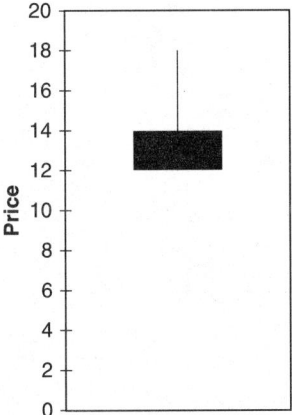

Figure 7.8   Candle inverted hammer.

Results

Table 7.13 shows that the Candle Inverted Hammer (CN-IHM) makes long calls almost four times as often as the opposite Candle Hammer system we just discussed. When choosing between a long or a cash position, the system chooses a long position 22.8 percent of the time. In addition, the accuracy of these long calls is slightly higher than the accuracy for the Candle Hammer system. With the CN-IHM system, the hit rate for long calls is 60.0 percent. When a cash position is favored over a long position, the hit rate is 60.5 percent. This gives an overall accuracy rate of 60.4 percent for this system, when choosing between long and cash positions.

The return analysis in Table 7.14 indicates that trading with this system can be more profitable than trading with the Candle Hammer system. The average quarterly terminal wealth with the CN-IHM system is $10,090. (It was only $10,021 with the Candle Hammer system.)

During the entire test period, the CN-IHM indicator never made a short call for any stock. Investors following this system would have found themselves always in a cash position. The cash position was the correct position almost 60 percent of the time, but these investors' terminal wealth of $10,000 would then have been exactly equal to their initial investment. This may sound ironic at first: the investors following this system were correct to take short positions the majority of the time, but they made no returns. For anyone who remains in a conservative cash position for the entire investment period, this is exactly what will occur.

The Candle Inverted Hammer is of no use in helping an investor decide when to take short positions. The long calls of this system may contain some useful information, but, because of its conservative design, investors will not

Table 7.12a
Candle Hammer (CN-HMR) Long Return Analysis
(Average of all stocks)

Qtr	CN-HMR Terminal Wealth	Buy/Hold Terminal Wealth	Relative Terminal Wealth	CN-HMR Long Avg Ret	CN-HMR Cash Avg Ret	CN-HMR Long-Cash Avg Ret	Buy/Hold Avg Ret
85:1	10032	10142	0.989	0.116%	0.001%	0.115%	0.006%
85:2	10026	9700	1.034	0.084%	-0.077%	0.162%	-0.069%
85:3	9982	8889	1.123	-0.054%	-0.213%	0.159%	-0.205%
85:4	10068	10763	0.935	0.253%	0.100%	0.153%	0.107%
86:1	10085	11428	0.882	0.284%	0.222%	0.063%	0.225%
86:2	10069	10414	0.967	0.156%	0.060%	0.096%	0.066%
86:3	9987	9175	1.089	-0.027%	-0.136%	0.109%	-0.128%
86:4	10052	10413	0.965	0.119%	0.066%	0.054%	0.069%
87:1	10135	11929	0.850	0.333%	0.290%	0.042%	0.293%
87:2	10032	10196	0.984	0.067%	0.035%	0.032%	0.038%
87:3	10017	10408	0.962	0.044%	0.070%	-0.026%	0.068%
87:4	9836	8087	1.216	-0.315%	-0.275%	-0.040%	-0.278%
88:1	10026	10989	0.912	0.065%	0.170%	-0.105%	0.163%
88:2	10042	10593	0.948	0.099%	0.100%	-0.001%	0.100%
88:3	10007	10050	0.996	0.022%	0.012%	0.009%	0.013%
88:4	10005	10196	0.981	0.016%	0.038%	-0.022%	0.037%
89:1	10029	10698	0.937	0.092%	0.114%	-0.022%	0.112%
89:2	10027	10772	0.931	0.094%	0.124%	-0.030%	0.122%
89:3	10058	10833	0.928	0.156%	0.129%	0.026%	0.131%
89:4	9988	9904	1.008	-0.026%	-0.010%	-0.016%	-0.011%
90:1	9986	9980	1.001	-0.025%	0.005%	-0.030%	0.003%
90:2	10026	10459	0.959	0.073%	0.077%	-0.004%	0.077%
90:3	9825	8526	1.152	-0.268%	-0.258%	-0.010%	-0.259%
90:4	10089	10889	0.927	0.219%	0.141%	0.078%	0.146%
91:1	10079	12477	0.808	0.223%	0.321%	-0.098%	0.315%
91:2	10008	10244	0.977	0.021%	0.047%	-0.025%	0.045%
91:3	10039	10429	0.963	0.132%	0.062%	0.070%	0.065%
91:4	10028	10497	0.955	0.073%	0.082%	-0.010%	0.082%
92:1	10007	10324	0.969	0.019%	0.050%	-0.031%	0.048%
92:2	10001	9723	1.029	0.004%	-0.051%	0.056%	-0.048%
92:3	10034	10392	0.966	0.100%	0.054%	0.046%	0.057%
92:4	10040	10963	0.916	0.105%	0.147%	-0.042%	0.144%
93:1	10030	10527	0.953	0.089%	0.079%	0.010%	0.080%
93:2	10026	10340	0.970	0.075%	0.050%	0.024%	0.052%
93:3	10023	10686	0.938	0.085%	0.102%	-0.017%	0.101%
93:4	9990	10255	0.974	-0.029%	0.038%	-0.067%	0.034%
94:1	10016	9954	1.006	0.039%	-0.015%	0.054%	-0.011%
94:2	10014	9994	1.002	0.027%	-0.007%	0.034%	-0.005%
94:3	10008	10613	0.943	0.021%	0.093%	-0.072%	0.089%
94:4	10008	9836	1.018	0.021%	-0.033%	0.054%	-0.029%
95:1	10021	10706	0.936	0.079%	0.111%	-0.032%	0.110%
95:2	10018	10873	0.921	0.070%	0.137%	-0.067%	0.134%
95:3	10051	10853	0.926	0.162%	0.129%	0.032%	0.131%
95:4	10001	10445	0.957	0.002%	0.071%	-0.069%	0.067%
96:1	10069	11027	0.913	0.206%	0.156%	0.050%	0.159%
96:2	10025	10367	0.967	0.071%	0.058%	0.014%	0.059%
96:3	10007	10298	0.972	0.017%	0.049%	-0.033%	0.047%
96:4	10021	10817	0.926	0.071%	0.125%	-0.053%	0.122%
AVG	10021	10377	0.966	0.055%	0.055%	0.000%	0.055%

Table 7.12b
Candle Hammer (CN-HMR) Short Return Analysis
(Average of all stocks)

Qtr	CN-HMR Terminal Wealth	Buy/Hold Terminal Wealth	Relative Terminal Wealth	CN-HMR Short Avg Ret	CN-HMR Cash Avg Ret	CN-HMR Short-Cash Avg Ret	Buy/Hold Avg Ret
85:1	9996	10142	0.986	0.147%	0.006%	0.141%	0.006%
85:2	9997	9700	1.031	0.092%	-0.070%	0.162%	-0.069%
85:3	10000	8889	1.125	-0.003%	-0.206%	0.203%	-0.205%
85:4	9988	10763	0.928	0.266%	0.106%	0.160%	0.107%
86:1	9989	11428	0.874	0.203%	0.225%	-0.022%	0.225%
86:2	10000	10414	0.960	0.001%	0.067%	-0.066%	0.066%
86:3	10003	9175	1.090	-0.061%	-0.128%	0.067%	-0.128%
86:4	9997	10413	0.960	0.051%	0.069%	-0.019%	0.069%
87:1	9989	11929	0.837	0.285%	0.293%	-0.008%	0.293%
87:2	9993	10196	0.980	0.212%	0.037%	0.175%	0.038%
87:3	9998	10408	0.961	0.047%	0.068%	-0.022%	0.068%
87:4	10000	8087	1.237	-0.014%	-0.280%	0.266%	-0.278%
88:1	9996	10989	0.910	0.069%	0.164%	-0.094%	0.163%
88:2	10001	10593	0.944	-0.019%	0.101%	-0.120%	0.100%
88:3	10001	10050	0.995	-0.021%	0.013%	-0.033%	0.013%
88:4	9996	10196	0.980	0.113%	0.036%	0.077%	0.037%
89:1	9995	10698	0.934	0.179%	0.112%	0.067%	0.112%
89:2	9998	10772	0.928	0.058%	0.123%	-0.065%	0.122%
89:3	9994	10833	0.923	0.179%	0.131%	0.048%	0.131%
89:4	9995	9904	1.009	0.147%	-0.012%	0.159%	-0.011%
90:1	10005	9980	1.002	-0.102%	0.004%	-0.106%	0.003%
90:2	9995	10459	0.956	0.147%	0.076%	0.070%	0.077%
90:3	10010	8526	1.174	-0.313%	-0.259%	-0.054%	-0.259%
90:4	9995	10889	0.918	0.126%	0.146%	-0.020%	0.146%
91:1	9982	12477	0.800	0.352%	0.315%	0.038%	0.315%
91:2	10008	10244	0.977	-0.164%	0.047%	-0.211%	0.045%
91:3	9993	10429	0.958	0.093%	0.065%	0.029%	0.065%
91:4	9986	10497	0.951	0.154%	0.081%	0.073%	0.082%
92:1	9992	10324	0.968	0.110%	0.047%	0.063%	0.048%
92:2	10013	9723	1.030	-0.217%	-0.047%	-0.170%	-0.048%
92:3	9999	10392	0.962	0.009%	0.057%	-0.048%	0.057%
92:4	9986	10963	0.911	0.199%	0.144%	0.055%	0.144%
93:1	9999	10527	0.950	0.009%	0.081%	-0.072%	0.080%
93:2	10005	10340	0.968	-0.063%	0.053%	-0.117%	0.052%
93:3	9996	10686	0.935	0.061%	0.101%	-0.040%	0.101%
93:4	10000	10255	0.975	0.011%	0.034%	-0.023%	0.034%
94:1	10002	9954	1.005	-0.024%	-0.011%	-0.013%	-0.011%
94:2	9999	9994	1.000	0.015%	-0.005%	0.019%	-0.005%
94:3	9990	10613	0.941	0.189%	0.088%	0.101%	0.089%
94:4	9998	9836	1.016	0.043%	-0.030%	0.073%	-0.029%
95:1	9998	10706	0.934	0.045%	0.111%	-0.066%	0.110%
95:2	9994	10873	0.919	0.078%	0.135%	-0.057%	0.134%
95:3	9989	10853	0.920	0.132%	0.131%	0.001%	0.131%
95:4	9997	10445	0.957	0.058%	0.067%	-0.009%	0.067%
96:1	9986	11027	0.906	0.202%	0.158%	0.044%	0.159%
96:2	10000	10367	0.965	0.003%	0.059%	-0.056%	0.059%
96:3	10005	10298	0.972	-0.074%	0.049%	-0.122%	0.047%
96:4	9987	10817	0.923	0.185%	0.122%	0.063%	0.122%
AVG	9997	10377	0.963	0.064%	0.055%	0.009%	0.055%

Table 7.13a
Candle Inverted Hammer (CN-IHM) Long Hit Analysis
(Average of all stocks)

Qtr	Optimal Long	CN-IHM Long	Long Hits	Cash Hits	Total Hits	Long Right	Long Wrong	Cash Right	Cash Wrong
85:1	32.1%	22.0%	67.2%	68.2%	68.0%	14.8%	7.2%	53.2%	24.8%
85:2	30.2%	21.7%	65.2%	70.3%	69.2%	14.1%	7.6%	55.0%	23.3%
85:3	26.3%	19.8%	60.7%	73.8%	71.2%	12.0%	7.8%	59.2%	21.0%
85:4	36.6%	21.3%	66.0%	63.8%	64.2%	14.1%	7.3%	50.2%	28.5%
86:1	44.2%	23.6%	64.7%	56.3%	58.2%	15.3%	8.4%	43.0%	33.4%
86:2	39.7%	22.8%	59.6%	60.4%	60.2%	13.6%	9.2%	46.7%	30.6%
86:3	37.0%	20.9%	56.9%	63.1%	61.8%	11.9%	9.0%	49.9%	29.2%
86:4	38.5%	22.2%	60.8%	61.9%	61.6%	13.5%	8.7%	48.1%	29.7%
87:1	44.7%	23.7%	62.7%	55.8%	57.5%	14.9%	8.8%	42.6%	33.7%
87:2	40.0%	25.4%	58.5%	60.5%	60.0%	14.9%	10.5%	45.1%	29.5%
87:3	39.5%	24.7%	58.8%	60.9%	60.4%	14.5%	10.2%	45.9%	29.4%
87:4	37.9%	23.7%	54.2%	62.4%	60.4%	12.9%	10.9%	47.6%	28.7%
88:1	41.3%	25.8%	61.6%	59.3%	59.9%	15.9%	9.9%	44.0%	30.2%
88:2	39.3%	24.6%	60.8%	61.3%	61.2%	15.0%	9.7%	46.2%	29.1%
88:3	35.9%	21.0%	60.0%	64.5%	63.6%	12.6%	8.4%	51.0%	28.0%
88:4	36.3%	20.4%	61.7%	64.2%	63.7%	12.6%	7.8%	51.1%	28.5%
89:1	39.0%	22.3%	62.7%	61.8%	62.0%	14.0%	8.3%	48.0%	29.7%
89:2	40.2%	23.6%	63.3%	60.6%	61.2%	15.0%	8.7%	46.3%	30.1%
89:3	39.9%	22.8%	62.3%	60.3%	60.8%	14.2%	8.6%	46.6%	30.6%
89:4	38.3%	21.6%	60.8%	62.2%	61.9%	13.2%	8.5%	48.8%	29.6%
90:1	36.9%	22.2%	59.4%	63.8%	62.9%	13.2%	9.0%	49.7%	28.2%
90:2	39.2%	23.4%	62.1%	61.6%	61.7%	14.5%	8.9%	47.2%	29.4%
90:3	33.5%	22.1%	54.3%	66.9%	64.1%	12.0%	10.1%	52.1%	25.8%
90:4	40.8%	23.0%	61.4%	59.5%	60.0%	14.1%	8.9%	45.8%	31.2%
91:1	44.1%	26.0%	62.8%	56.4%	58.0%	16.3%	9.7%	41.7%	32.3%
91:2	39.7%	24.1%	58.4%	60.9%	60.3%	14.1%	10.0%	46.2%	29.7%
91:3	40.4%	20.5%	59.0%	59.9%	59.7%	12.1%	8.4%	47.6%	31.9%
91:4	41.2%	19.9%	58.6%	59.1%	59.0%	11.6%	8.2%	47.4%	32.8%
92:1	40.0%	21.6%	56.0%	60.1%	59.2%	12.1%	9.5%	47.2%	31.3%
92:2	38.6%	19.4%	55.4%	61.6%	60.4%	10.7%	8.6%	49.7%	31.0%
92:3	40.3%	19.2%	58.7%	59.9%	59.7%	11.3%	7.9%	48.4%	32.4%
92:4	41.9%	19.8%	62.3%	58.7%	59.4%	12.3%	7.5%	47.1%	33.1%
93:1	42.5%	22.0%	59.0%	57.5%	57.8%	13.0%	9.0%	44.9%	33.2%
93:2	42.1%	21.7%	58.4%	58.3%	58.3%	12.7%	9.0%	45.7%	32.6%
93:3	42.5%	23.2%	59.5%	57.6%	58.0%	13.8%	9.4%	44.2%	32.6%
93:4	41.5%	24.7%	57.6%	58.6%	58.3%	14.2%	10.5%	44.1%	31.2%
94:1	40.4%	24.1%	56.2%	59.7%	58.9%	13.6%	10.6%	45.3%	30.6%
94:2	40.6%	23.5%	56.8%	59.5%	58.9%	13.4%	10.1%	45.5%	31.0%
94:3	41.8%	24.4%	59.3%	58.5%	58.7%	14.5%	9.9%	44.2%	31.4%
94:4	39.5%	24.4%	57.0%	60.9%	59.9%	13.9%	10.5%	46.0%	29.6%
95:1	43.1%	23.6%	61.8%	57.3%	58.4%	14.6%	9.0%	43.8%	32.6%
95:2	43.7%	22.4%	61.0%	56.5%	57.5%	13.6%	8.7%	43.9%	33.7%
95:3	43.9%	22.3%	60.9%	56.4%	57.4%	13.5%	8.7%	43.8%	33.9%
95:4	43.4%	23.5%	58.9%	56.8%	57.3%	13.8%	9.7%	43.5%	33.1%
96:1	45.5%	25.5%	60.5%	54.4%	56.0%	15.4%	10.1%	40.5%	33.9%
96:2	42.1%	25.0%	57.4%	58.2%	58.0%	14.4%	10.7%	43.6%	31.3%
96:3	42.6%	25.0%	59.7%	57.8%	58.3%	15.0%	10.1%	43.4%	31.6%
96:4	44.3%	24.8%	59.2%	56.1%	56.8%	14.7%	10.1%	42.1%	33.0%
AVG	40.0%	22.8%	60.0%	60.5%	60.4%	13.7%	9.1%	46.7%	30.5%

Table 7.13b
Candle Inverted Hammer (CN-IHM) Short Hit Analysis
(Average of all stocks)

Qtr	Optimal Short	CN-IHM Short	Short Hits	Cash Hits	Total Hits	Short Right	Short Wrong	Cash Right	Cash Wrong
85:1	34.3%	0.0%	0.0%	65.7%	65.7%	0.0%	0.0%	65.7%	34.3%
85:2	34.6%	0.0%	0.0%	65.4%	65.4%	0.0%	0.0%	65.4%	34.6%
85:3	38.6%	0.0%	0.0%	61.4%	61.4%	0.0%	0.0%	61.4%	38.6%
85:4	33.1%	0.0%	0.0%	66.9%	66.9%	0.0%	0.0%	66.9%	33.1%
86:1	35.2%	0.0%	0.0%	64.8%	64.8%	0.0%	0.0%	64.8%	35.2%
86:2	39.8%	0.0%	0.0%	60.2%	60.2%	0.0%	0.0%	60.2%	39.8%
86:3	42.7%	0.0%	0.0%	57.3%	57.3%	0.0%	0.0%	57.3%	42.7%
86:4	38.7%	0.0%	0.0%	61.3%	61.3%	0.0%	0.0%	61.3%	38.7%
87:1	36.9%	0.0%	0.0%	63.1%	63.1%	0.0%	0.0%	63.1%	36.9%
87:2	40.0%	0.0%	0.0%	60.0%	60.0%	0.0%	0.0%	60.0%	40.0%
87:3	40.4%	0.0%	0.0%	59.6%	59.6%	0.0%	0.0%	59.6%	40.4%
87:4	45.3%	0.0%	0.0%	54.7%	54.7%	0.0%	0.0%	54.7%	45.3%
88:1	36.7%	0.0%	0.0%	63.3%	63.3%	0.0%	0.0%	63.3%	36.7%
88:2	37.4%	0.0%	0.0%	62.6%	62.6%	0.0%	0.0%	62.6%	37.4%
88:3	38.4%	0.0%	0.0%	61.6%	61.6%	0.0%	0.0%	61.6%	38.4%
88:4	37.0%	0.0%	0.0%	63.0%	63.0%	0.0%	0.0%	63.0%	37.0%
89:1	36.2%	0.0%	0.0%	63.8%	63.8%	0.0%	0.0%	63.8%	36.2%
89:2	35.9%	0.0%	0.0%	64.1%	64.1%	0.0%	0.0%	64.1%	35.9%
89:3	36.4%	0.0%	0.0%	63.6%	63.6%	0.0%	0.0%	63.6%	36.4%
89:4	39.0%	0.0%	0.0%	61.0%	61.0%	0.0%	0.0%	61.0%	39.0%
90:1	40.1%	0.0%	0.0%	59.9%	59.9%	0.0%	0.0%	59.9%	40.1%
90:2	37.8%	0.0%	0.0%	62.2%	62.2%	0.0%	0.0%	62.2%	37.8%
90:3	45.7%	0.0%	0.0%	54.3%	54.3%	0.0%	0.0%	54.3%	45.7%
90:4	37.6%	0.0%	0.0%	62.4%	62.4%	0.0%	0.0%	62.4%	37.6%
91:1	36.7%	0.0%	0.0%	63.3%	63.3%	0.0%	0.0%	63.3%	36.7%
91:2	40.4%	0.0%	0.0%	59.6%	59.6%	0.0%	0.0%	59.6%	40.4%
91:3	39.8%	0.0%	0.0%	60.2%	60.2%	0.0%	0.0%	60.2%	39.8%
91:4	40.5%	0.0%	0.0%	59.5%	59.5%	0.0%	0.0%	59.5%	40.5%
92:1	43.2%	0.0%	0.0%	56.8%	56.8%	0.0%	0.0%	56.8%	43.2%
92:2	42.9%	0.0%	0.0%	57.1%	57.1%	0.0%	0.0%	57.1%	42.9%
92:3	39.5%	0.0%	0.0%	60.5%	60.5%	0.0%	0.0%	60.5%	39.5%
92:4	37.5%	0.0%	0.0%	62.5%	62.5%	0.0%	0.0%	62.5%	37.5%
93:1	39.4%	0.0%	0.0%	60.6%	60.6%	0.0%	0.0%	60.6%	39.4%
93:2	40.9%	0.0%	0.0%	59.1%	59.1%	0.0%	0.0%	59.1%	40.9%
93:3	39.4%	0.0%	0.0%	60.6%	60.6%	0.0%	0.0%	60.6%	39.4%
93:4	41.7%	0.0%	0.0%	58.3%	58.3%	0.0%	0.0%	58.3%	41.7%
94:1	43.7%	0.0%	0.0%	56.3%	56.3%	0.0%	0.0%	56.3%	43.7%
94:2	42.7%	0.0%	0.0%	57.3%	57.3%	0.0%	0.0%	57.3%	42.7%
94:3	39.8%	0.0%	0.0%	60.2%	60.2%	0.0%	0.0%	60.2%	39.8%
94:4	42.8%	0.0%	0.0%	57.2%	57.2%	0.0%	0.0%	57.2%	42.8%
95:1	38.7%	0.0%	0.0%	61.3%	61.3%	0.0%	0.0%	61.3%	38.7%
95:2	38.9%	0.0%	0.0%	61.1%	61.1%	0.0%	0.0%	61.1%	38.9%
95:3	38.9%	0.0%	0.0%	61.1%	61.1%	0.0%	0.0%	61.1%	38.9%
95:4	40.5%	0.0%	0.0%	59.5%	59.5%	0.0%	0.0%	59.5%	40.5%
96:1	38.9%	0.0%	0.0%	61.1%	61.1%	0.0%	0.0%	61.1%	38.9%
96:2	42.4%	0.0%	0.0%	57.6%	57.6%	0.0%	0.0%	57.6%	42.4%
96:3	40.8%	0.0%	0.0%	59.2%	59.2%	0.0%	0.0%	59.2%	40.8%
96:4	39.8%	0.0%	0.0%	60.2%	60.2%	0.0%	0.0%	60.2%	39.8%
AVG	39.4%	0.0%	0.0%	60.7%	60.7%	0.0%	0.0%	60.7%	39.3%

Table 7.14a
Candle Inverted Hammer (CN-IHM) Long Return Analysis
(Average of all stocks)

Qtr	CN-IHM Terminal Wealth	Buy/Hold Terminal Wealth	Relative Terminal Wealth	CN-IHM Long Avg Ret	CN-IHM Cash Avg Ret	CN-IHM Long-Cash Avg Ret	Buy/Hold Avg Ret
85:1	10078	10142	0.994	0.050%	-0.006%	0.057%	0.006%
85:2	9934	9700	1.024	-0.056%	-0.073%	0.018%	-0.069%
85:3	9747	8889	1.097	-0.220%	-0.201%	-0.019%	-0.205%
85:4	10155	10763	0.944	0.111%	0.106%	0.005%	0.107%
86:1	10353	11428	0.906	0.241%	0.219%	0.022%	0.225%
86:2	10042	10414	0.964	0.025%	0.078%	-0.053%	0.066%
86:3	9817	9175	1.070	-0.138%	-0.125%	-0.013%	-0.128%
86:4	10108	10413	0.971	0.079%	0.066%	0.013%	0.069%
87:1	10457	11929	0.877	0.304%	0.289%	0.015%	0.293%
87:2	10030	10196	0.984	0.021%	0.044%	-0.022%	0.038%
87:3	10105	10408	0.971	0.069%	0.068%	0.001%	0.068%
87:4	9699	8087	1.199	-0.197%	-0.303%	0.106%	-0.278%
88:1	10205	10989	0.929	0.134%	0.173%	-0.039%	0.163%
88:2	10119	10593	0.955	0.081%	0.106%	-0.025%	0.100%
88:3	10008	10050	0.996	0.008%	0.014%	-0.006%	0.013%
88:4	10045	10196	0.985	0.038%	0.036%	0.002%	0.037%
89:1	10177	10698	0.951	0.130%	0.107%	0.023%	0.112%
89:2	10184	10772	0.945	0.124%	0.122%	0.002%	0.122%
89:3	10169	10833	0.939	0.117%	0.135%	-0.018%	0.131%
89:4	9999	9904	1.010	0.002%	-0.015%	0.016%	-0.011%
90:1	10047	9980	1.007	0.037%	-0.007%	0.044%	0.003%
90:2	10156	10459	0.971	0.108%	0.067%	0.040%	0.077%
90:3	9687	8526	1.136	-0.236%	-0.266%	0.030%	-0.259%
90:4	10214	10889	0.938	0.147%	0.146%	0.001%	0.146%
91:1	10514	12477	0.843	0.316%	0.315%	0.001%	0.315%
91:2	10063	10244	0.982	0.045%	0.045%	0.000%	0.045%
91:3	10096	10429	0.968	0.072%	0.063%	0.009%	0.065%
91:4	10078	10497	0.960	0.060%	0.087%	-0.027%	0.082%
92:1	10045	10324	0.973	0.031%	0.052%	-0.021%	0.048%
92:2	9938	9723	1.022	-0.054%	-0.047%	-0.007%	-0.048%
92:3	10022	10392	0.964	0.018%	0.066%	-0.048%	0.057%
92:4	10229	10963	0.933	0.180%	0.136%	0.044%	0.144%
93:1	10069	10527	0.957	0.046%	0.089%	-0.043%	0.080%
93:2	10046	10340	0.972	0.034%	0.057%	-0.023%	0.052%
93:3	10124	10686	0.947	0.081%	0.107%	-0.026%	0.101%
93:4	10043	10255	0.979	0.026%	0.036%	-0.010%	0.034%
94:1	10014	9954	1.006	0.008%	-0.018%	0.026%	-0.011%
94:2	9974	9994	0.998	-0.020%	0.000%	-0.021%	-0.005%
94:3	10160	10613	0.957	0.100%	0.086%	0.014%	0.089%
94:4	9962	9836	1.013	-0.028%	-0.030%	0.002%	-0.029%
95:1	10187	10706	0.952	0.124%	0.106%	0.019%	0.110%
95:2	10210	10873	0.939	0.148%	0.130%	0.018%	0.134%
95:3	10205	10853	0.940	0.146%	0.127%	0.019%	0.131%
95:4	10105	10445	0.967	0.070%	0.066%	0.005%	0.067%
96:1	10228	11027	0.928	0.139%	0.166%	-0.027%	0.159%
96:2	10124	10367	0.977	0.081%	0.051%	0.030%	0.059%
96:3	10135	10298	0.984	0.082%	0.036%	0.046%	0.047%
96:4	10196	10817	0.943	0.123%	0.122%	0.001%	0.122%
AVG	10090	10377	0.972	0.061%	0.053%	0.007%	0.055%

Table 7.14b
Candle Inverted Hammer (CN-IHM) Short Return Analysis
(Average of all stocks)

Qtr	CN-IHM Terminal Wealth	Buy/Hold Terminal Wealth	Relative Terminal Wealth	CN-IHM Short Avg Ret	CN-IHM Cash Avg Ret	CN-IHM Short-Cash Avg Ret	Buy/Hold Avg Ret
85:1	10000	10142	0.986	0.000%	0.006%	-0.006%	0.006%
85:2	10000	9700	1.031	0.000%	-0.069%	0.069%	-0.069%
85:3	10000	8889	1.125	0.000%	-0.205%	0.205%	-0.205%
85:4	10000	10763	0.929	0.000%	0.107%	-0.107%	0.107%
86:1	10000	11428	0.875	0.000%	0.225%	-0.225%	0.225%
86:2	10000	10414	0.960	0.000%	0.066%	-0.066%	0.066%
86:3	10000	9175	1.090	0.000%	-0.128%	0.128%	-0.128%
86:4	10000	10413	0.960	0.000%	0.069%	-0.069%	0.069%
87:1	10000	11929	0.838	0.000%	0.293%	-0.293%	0.293%
87:2	10000	10196	0.981	0.000%	0.038%	-0.038%	0.038%
87:3	10000	10408	0.961	0.000%	0.068%	-0.068%	0.068%
87:4	10000	8087	1.237	0.000%	-0.278%	0.278%	-0.278%
88:1	10000	10989	0.910	0.000%	0.163%	-0.163%	0.163%
88:2	10000	10593	0.944	0.000%	0.100%	-0.100%	0.100%
88:3	10000	10050	0.995	0.000%	0.013%	-0.013%	0.013%
88:4	10000	10196	0.981	0.000%	0.037%	-0.037%	0.037%
89:1	10000	10698	0.935	0.000%	0.112%	-0.112%	0.112%
89:2	10000	10772	0.928	0.000%	0.122%	-0.122%	0.122%
89:3	10000	10833	0.923	0.000%	0.131%	-0.131%	0.131%
89:4	10000	9904	1.010	0.000%	-0.011%	0.011%	-0.011%
90:1	10000	9980	1.002	0.000%	0.003%	-0.003%	0.003%
90:2	10000	10459	0.956	0.000%	0.077%	-0.077%	0.077%
90:3	10000	8526	1.173	0.000%	-0.259%	0.259%	-0.259%
90:4	10000	10889	0.918	0.000%	0.146%	-0.146%	0.146%
91:1	10000	12477	0.801	0.000%	0.315%	-0.315%	0.315%
91:2	10000	10244	0.976	0.000%	0.045%	-0.045%	0.045%
91:3	10000	10429	0.959	0.000%	0.065%	-0.065%	0.065%
91:4	10000	10497	0.953	0.000%	0.082%	-0.082%	0.082%
92:1	10000	10324	0.969	0.000%	0.048%	-0.048%	0.048%
92:2	10000	9723	1.028	0.000%	-0.048%	0.048%	-0.048%
92:3	10000	10392	0.962	0.000%	0.057%	-0.057%	0.057%
92:4	10000	10963	0.912	0.000%	0.144%	-0.144%	0.144%
93:1	10000	10527	0.950	0.000%	0.080%	-0.080%	0.080%
93:2	10000	10340	0.967	0.000%	0.052%	-0.052%	0.052%
93:3	10000	10686	0.936	0.000%	0.101%	-0.101%	0.101%
93:4	10000	10255	0.975	0.000%	0.034%	-0.034%	0.034%
94:1	10000	9954	1.005	0.000%	-0.011%	0.011%	-0.011%
94:2	10000	9994	1.001	0.000%	-0.005%	0.005%	-0.005%
94:3	10000	10613	0.942	0.000%	0.089%	-0.089%	0.089%
94:4	10000	9836	1.017	0.000%	-0.029%	0.029%	-0.029%
95:1	10000	10706	0.934	0.000%	0.110%	-0.110%	0.110%
95:2	10000	10873	0.920	0.000%	0.134%	-0.134%	0.134%
95:3	10000	10853	0.921	0.000%	0.131%	-0.131%	0.131%
95:4	10000	10445	0.957	0.000%	0.067%	-0.067%	0.067%
96:1	10000	11027	0.907	0.000%	0.159%	-0.159%	0.159%
96:2	10000	10367	0.965	0.000%	0.059%	-0.059%	0.059%
96:3	10000	10298	0.971	0.000%	0.047%	-0.047%	0.047%
96:4	10000	10817	0.924	0.000%	0.122%	-0.122%	0.122%
AVG	10000	10377	0.964	0.000%	0.055%	-0.055%	0.055%

be able to reap large returns by relying solely on the advice of this technical indicator.

Candle Morning-Evening Star

A Morning Star is a three-day pattern formed when a star (a small-bodied candle) is located between two other bodies so that it appears above or below the other two. The body of the star can be open or black. Rarely seen, Morning and Evening Stars are of moderate significance but can signify key reversals in markets.

Construction

The Morning Star pattern, a bullish indicator, can be seen in Figure 7.9. The price activity on one day forms an "island" below the price activity of the two surrounding days. This occurs when a down day is followed by a star below the range of the first day's black candle, and then the third day opens above the range of the star and continues up, forming an open candle.

An Evening Star, a bearish indicator, occurs when three trading days occur in a particular fashion. The first day is an up day, characterized by an open-bodied candle. The second day has a small open-to-close range,

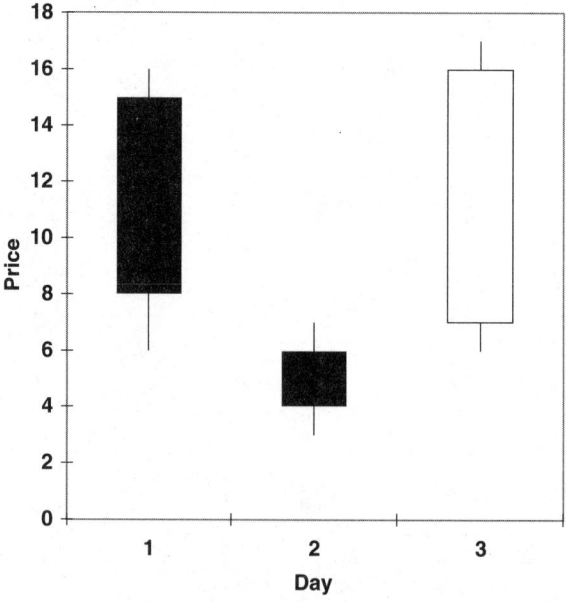

Figure 7.9 Candle morning star.

characterized by a small-bodied candle or a star; the range of the star's body lies above the open-to-close range of the first day. The third day opens below the body of the star and continues down to form a black candle. The middle day forms an "island" of price activity above the two surrounding days.

Results

As our description of the Candle Morning-Evening Star (CN-MES) indicator predicted, this pattern is seldom seen in the market. The bullish Morning Star occurred 1.1 percent of the time during our test period, as can be seen in Table 7.15a. The bearish Evening Star occurred only 0.8 percent of the time (Table 7.15b).

When the Morning Star occurred and signaled a long position, the signal was correct 61.1 percent of the time. When the Evening Star occurred and signaled a short position, the signal was correct 58.5 percent of the time.

The return analysis in Table 7.16 indicates some real problems with the CN-MES indicator. First, let's look at the long return analysis. The average daily return when a long signal occurs is 0.057 percent, only slightly higher than the overall average daily stock return of 0.055 percent. Long calls do occur on days when investors want to be in the market, but the system misses many additional days when investors would want to be in the market. In fact, investors following the recommendations of this system find themselves in a zero-return cash position on days when investing in the market would have been profitable 39.4 percent of the time. The infrequency of long positions led to an average quarterly terminal wealth of $10,004, only slightly above the initial wealth level of $10,000.

Looking at the short return analysis, we see similar, or even worse, results. The average daily stock return when this indicator recommends a short position is 0.041 percent. This is indeed below the average daily stock return, but stock prices are still, on average, appreciating on days when the short calls are made. Losses result when trading short with the system; however, because the system makes short calls so seldom, the losses are contained. On average, an investor who begins a quarter with a $10,000 investment and trades short with the CN-MES system will lose $2.

Candle Piercing Line

The Candle Piercing Line is a two-day pattern that occurs when today's candle "pierces" the range of the prior day and is opposite in direction. Piercing lines occur when the market opens in the same direction as the previous day, then reverses direction to close within the range of the previous day. Often signaling that a powerful reversal is about to take place, the Candle Piercing Line pattern is of major significance.

Table 7.15a
Candle Morning-Evening Star (CN-MES) Long Hit Analysis
(Average of all stocks)

Qtr	Optimal Long	CN-MES Long	Long Hits	Cash Hits	Total Hits	Long Right	Long Wrong	Cash Right	Cash Wrong
85:1	32.1%	0.5%	62.2%	67.9%	67.9%	0.3%	0.2%	67.6%	31.9%
85:2	30.2%	0.4%	64.6%	69.8%	69.8%	0.3%	0.2%	69.5%	30.1%
85:3	26.3%	0.4%	62.6%	73.7%	73.7%	0.2%	0.1%	73.5%	26.2%
85:4	36.6%	0.4%	71.4%	63.4%	63.4%	0.3%	0.1%	63.2%	36.5%
86:1	44.2%	0.4%	65.2%	55.9%	55.9%	0.3%	0.1%	55.6%	44.0%
86:2	39.7%	0.7%	60.9%	60.3%	60.3%	0.4%	0.3%	59.9%	39.4%
86:3	37.0%	0.6%	58.2%	63.0%	63.0%	0.4%	0.3%	62.6%	36.8%
86:4	38.5%	0.7%	60.4%	61.5%	61.5%	0.4%	0.3%	61.1%	38.2%
87:1	44.7%	0.5%	59.8%	55.3%	55.3%	0.3%	0.2%	55.1%	44.5%
87:2	40.0%	0.5%	57.3%	60.0%	60.0%	0.3%	0.2%	59.7%	39.8%
87:3	39.5%	0.6%	55.2%	60.5%	60.4%	0.3%	0.2%	60.1%	39.3%
87:4	37.9%	0.7%	50.4%	62.1%	62.0%	0.4%	0.3%	61.6%	37.7%
88:1	41.3%	0.6%	70.9%	58.7%	58.7%	0.4%	0.2%	58.3%	41.1%
88:2	39.3%	0.9%	61.4%	60.7%	60.7%	0.5%	0.3%	60.2%	39.0%
88:3	35.9%	0.7%	64.6%	64.0%	64.0%	0.4%	0.2%	63.6%	35.7%
88:4	36.3%	0.6%	67.8%	63.6%	63.6%	0.4%	0.2%	63.2%	36.2%
89:1	39.0%	0.7%	66.3%	61.0%	61.0%	0.5%	0.2%	60.5%	38.8%
89:2	40.2%	0.7%	66.4%	59.8%	59.9%	0.4%	0.2%	59.5%	39.9%
89:3	39.9%	0.7%	68.1%	60.0%	60.1%	0.5%	0.2%	59.6%	39.7%
89:4	38.3%	0.7%	67.6%	61.7%	61.7%	0.5%	0.2%	61.2%	38.0%
90:1	36.9%	0.8%	68.6%	63.1%	63.2%	0.6%	0.3%	62.6%	36.6%
90:2	39.2%	0.8%	61.9%	60.7%	60.7%	0.5%	0.3%	60.2%	38.9%
90:3	33.5%	0.9%	54.9%	66.5%	66.4%	0.5%	0.4%	65.9%	33.2%
90:4	40.8%	0.8%	61.3%	59.2%	59.2%	0.5%	0.3%	58.7%	40.5%
91:1	44.1%	0.7%	65.6%	55.8%	55.9%	0.4%	0.2%	55.5%	43.9%
91:2	39.7%	0.7%	63.4%	60.3%	60.3%	0.4%	0.2%	59.9%	39.4%
91:3	40.4%	1.4%	62.4%	59.6%	59.6%	0.9%	0.5%	58.7%	39.9%
91:4	41.2%	1.5%	55.9%	58.7%	58.7%	0.8%	0.7%	57.9%	40.7%
92:1	40.0%	1.7%	55.3%	60.0%	59.9%	0.9%	0.8%	58.9%	39.3%
92:2	38.6%	2.1%	56.0%	61.5%	61.4%	1.2%	0.9%	60.2%	37.7%
92:3	40.3%	1.8%	61.1%	59.8%	59.8%	1.1%	0.7%	58.7%	39.5%
92:4	41.9%	1.7%	61.6%	58.1%	58.2%	1.0%	0.6%	57.1%	41.2%
93:1	42.5%	1.5%	58.0%	57.5%	57.5%	0.9%	0.6%	56.6%	41.9%
93:2	42.1%	1.7%	59.9%	57.9%	57.9%	1.0%	0.7%	56.9%	41.4%
93:3	42.5%	1.6%	60.6%	57.5%	57.6%	0.9%	0.6%	56.6%	41.8%
93:4	41.5%	1.8%	56.7%	58.5%	58.5%	1.0%	0.8%	57.5%	40.7%
94:1	40.4%	1.9%	57.9%	59.6%	59.5%	1.1%	0.8%	58.4%	39.7%
94:2	40.6%	2.0%	59.2%	59.4%	59.4%	1.2%	0.8%	58.3%	39.8%
94:3	41.8%	1.7%	61.9%	58.2%	58.3%	1.0%	0.6%	57.3%	41.1%
94:4	39.5%	1.6%	55.2%	60.5%	60.4%	0.9%	0.7%	59.5%	38.9%
95:1	43.1%	1.2%	59.2%	56.9%	56.9%	0.7%	0.5%	56.2%	42.6%
95:2	43.7%	1.6%	59.6%	56.3%	56.3%	1.0%	0.7%	55.4%	43.0%
95:3	43.9%	1.8%	59.8%	56.1%	56.1%	1.1%	0.7%	55.1%	43.1%
95:4	43.4%	1.8%	58.6%	56.6%	56.6%	1.1%	0.7%	55.6%	42.6%
96:1	45.5%	1.7%	62.0%	54.5%	54.7%	1.1%	0.7%	53.6%	44.7%
96:2	42.1%	1.6%	56.7%	57.9%	57.9%	0.9%	0.7%	57.0%	41.4%
96:3	42.6%	1.6%	58.2%	57.4%	57.4%	0.9%	0.7%	56.5%	41.9%
96:4	44.3%	2.0%	58.6%	55.7%	55.8%	1.2%	0.8%	54.6%	43.4%
AVG	40.0%	1.1%	61.1%	60.1%	60.1%	0.7%	0.4%	59.5%	39.4%

Table 7.15b
Candle Morning-Evening Star (CN-MES) Short Hit Analysis
(Average of all stocks)

Qtr	Optimal Short	CN-MES Short	Short Hits	Cash Hits	Total Hits	Short Right	Short Wrong	Cash Right	Cash Wrong
85:1	34.3%	0.7%	69.4%	65.7%	65.8%	0.5%	0.2%	65.3%	34.0%
85:2	34.6%	0.7%	69.1%	65.4%	65.5%	0.5%	0.2%	64.9%	34.3%
85:3	38.6%	0.3%	63.9%	61.4%	61.4%	0.2%	0.1%	61.2%	38.5%
85:4	33.1%	0.4%	48.6%	66.9%	66.8%	0.2%	0.2%	66.6%	33.0%
86:1	35.2%	0.3%	60.2%	64.8%	64.8%	0.2%	0.1%	64.6%	35.1%
86:2	39.8%	0.3%	58.5%	60.2%	60.2%	0.2%	0.1%	60.1%	39.7%
86:3	42.7%	0.4%	59.4%	57.3%	57.3%	0.3%	0.2%	57.1%	42.5%
86:4	38.7%	0.2%	67.6%	61.3%	61.3%	0.1%	0.1%	61.2%	38.6%
87:1	36.9%	0.4%	46.0%	63.1%	63.0%	0.2%	0.2%	62.9%	36.8%
87:2	40.0%	0.4%	57.5%	60.0%	60.0%	0.2%	0.2%	59.8%	39.8%
87:3	40.4%	0.3%	54.1%	59.5%	59.5%	0.2%	0.1%	59.4%	40.3%
87:4	45.3%	0.3%	63.0%	54.7%	54.8%	0.2%	0.1%	54.6%	45.1%
88:1	36.7%	0.4%	51.4%	63.3%	63.3%	0.2%	0.2%	63.1%	36.6%
88:2	37.4%	0.4%	55.8%	62.5%	62.5%	0.2%	0.2%	62.3%	37.3%
88:3	38.4%	0.2%	61.3%	61.6%	61.6%	0.1%	0.1%	61.5%	38.3%
88:4	37.0%	0.2%	63.4%	63.0%	63.0%	0.2%	0.1%	62.8%	36.9%
89:1	36.2%	0.4%	56.7%	63.8%	63.7%	0.2%	0.2%	63.5%	36.1%
89:2	35.9%	0.3%	52.9%	64.0%	64.0%	0.2%	0.2%	63.8%	35.8%
89:3	36.4%	0.3%	56.9%	63.6%	63.6%	0.2%	0.1%	63.4%	36.3%
89:4	39.0%	0.2%	64.4%	61.0%	61.0%	0.2%	0.1%	60.9%	38.9%
90:1	40.1%	0.3%	66.2%	59.9%	59.9%	0.2%	0.1%	59.7%	40.0%
90:2	37.8%	0.3%	63.4%	62.2%	62.2%	0.2%	0.1%	62.0%	37.7%
90:3	45.7%	0.5%	64.2%	54.4%	54.4%	0.3%	0.2%	54.1%	45.4%
90:4	37.6%	0.6%	61.2%	62.5%	62.5%	0.4%	0.2%	62.1%	37.3%
91:1	36.7%	0.4%	59.1%	63.3%	63.3%	0.2%	0.1%	63.1%	36.5%
91:2	40.4%	0.4%	59.8%	59.6%	59.6%	0.2%	0.1%	59.4%	40.2%
91:3	39.8%	1.1%	59.3%	60.3%	60.3%	0.7%	0.5%	59.6%	39.3%
91:4	40.5%	1.2%	59.3%	59.6%	59.5%	0.7%	0.5%	58.8%	40.0%
92:1	43.2%	1.2%	56.4%	56.8%	56.7%	0.7%	0.5%	56.1%	42.7%
92:2	42.9%	1.2%	58.5%	57.1%	57.1%	0.7%	0.5%	56.4%	42.4%
92:3	39.5%	1.3%	57.8%	60.5%	60.5%	0.8%	0.6%	59.7%	39.0%
92:4	37.5%	1.3%	57.0%	62.6%	62.5%	0.7%	0.5%	61.8%	37.0%
93:1	39.4%	1.3%	58.2%	60.7%	60.6%	0.7%	0.5%	59.9%	38.8%
93:2	40.9%	1.3%	59.4%	59.2%	59.2%	0.8%	0.5%	58.4%	40.3%
93:3	39.4%	1.2%	55.9%	60.6%	60.6%	0.7%	0.5%	59.9%	38.9%
93:4	41.7%	1.2%	56.0%	58.3%	58.3%	0.6%	0.5%	57.6%	41.2%
94:1	43.7%	1.5%	59.8%	56.3%	56.4%	0.9%	0.6%	55.5%	43.0%
94:2	42.7%	1.1%	58.4%	57.3%	57.3%	0.6%	0.4%	56.7%	42.2%
94:3	39.8%	1.2%	58.8%	60.2%	60.2%	0.7%	0.5%	59.5%	39.3%
94:4	42.8%	1.4%	60.3%	57.2%	57.3%	0.9%	0.6%	56.4%	42.2%
95:1	38.7%	1.0%	55.0%	61.3%	61.3%	0.5%	0.4%	60.8%	38.3%
95:2	38.9%	1.4%	55.5%	61.1%	61.0%	0.8%	0.6%	60.3%	38.4%
95:3	38.9%	1.4%	56.3%	61.1%	61.0%	0.8%	0.6%	60.2%	38.3%
95:4	40.5%	1.2%	56.9%	59.5%	59.5%	0.7%	0.5%	58.8%	40.0%
96:1	38.9%	1.5%	53.4%	61.1%	61.0%	0.8%	0.7%	60.2%	38.3%
96:2	42.4%	1.4%	54.8%	57.6%	57.6%	0.8%	0.6%	56.8%	41.8%
96:3	40.8%	1.2%	55.3%	59.3%	59.2%	0.7%	0.6%	58.6%	40.2%
96:4	39.8%	1.7%	52.6%	60.2%	60.1%	0.9%	0.8%	59.2%	39.2%
AVG	39.4%	0.8%	58.5%	60.7%	60.7%	0.5%	0.3%	60.2%	39.0%

Table 7.16a
Candle Morning-Evening Star (CN-MES) Long Return Analysis
(Average of all stocks)

Qtr	CN-MES Terminal Wealth	Buy/Hold Terminal Wealth	Relative Terminal Wealth	CN-MES Long Avg Ret	CN-MES Cash Avg Ret	CN-MES Long-Cash Avg Ret	Buy/Hold Avg Ret
85:1	10004	10142	0.986	0.121%	0.006%	0.116%	0.006%
85:2	10001	9700	1.031	0.048%	-0.070%	0.118%	-0.069%
85:3	10001	8889	1.125	0.059%	-0.206%	0.264%	-0.205%
85:4	10007	10763	0.930	0.314%	0.106%	0.208%	0.107%
86:1	10007	11428	0.876	0.261%	0.224%	0.037%	0.225%
86:2	10011	10414	0.961	0.254%	0.065%	0.189%	0.066%
86:3	9994	9175	1.089	-0.152%	-0.127%	-0.025%	-0.128%
86:4	10006	10413	0.961	0.146%	0.069%	0.077%	0.069%
87:1	10007	11929	0.839	0.239%	0.293%	-0.054%	0.293%
87:2	9999	10196	0.981	-0.028%	0.038%	-0.066%	0.038%
87:3	10001	10408	0.961	0.023%	0.069%	-0.045%	0.068%
87:4	9989	8087	1.235	-0.269%	-0.278%	0.009%	-0.278%
88:1	10007	10989	0.911	0.199%	0.163%	0.036%	0.163%
88:2	10005	10593	0.945	0.086%	0.100%	-0.014%	0.100%
88:3	9998	10050	0.995	-0.042%	0.013%	-0.055%	0.013%
88:4	10001	10196	0.981	0.034%	0.037%	-0.002%	0.037%
89:1	10003	10698	0.935	0.068%	0.113%	-0.045%	0.112%
89:2	10005	10772	0.929	0.113%	0.122%	-0.009%	0.122%
89:3	10005	10833	0.923	0.101%	0.131%	-0.030%	0.131%
89:4	10000	9904	1.010	0.001%	-0.011%	0.012%	-0.011%
90:1	10005	9980	1.003	0.101%	0.002%	0.099%	0.003%
90:2	9995	10459	0.956	-0.096%	0.078%	-0.174%	0.077%
90:3	9984	8526	1.171	-0.287%	-0.259%	-0.028%	-0.259%
90:4	9996	10889	0.918	-0.101%	0.148%	-0.249%	0.146%
91:1	10008	12477	0.802	0.209%	0.316%	-0.107%	0.315%
91:2	10006	10244	0.977	0.127%	0.045%	0.082%	0.045%
91:3	10016	10429	0.960	0.156%	0.064%	0.092%	0.065%
91:4	9996	10497	0.952	-0.046%	0.084%	-0.130%	0.082%
92:1	10000	10324	0.969	-0.004%	0.049%	-0.053%	0.048%
92:2	10001	9723	1.029	0.011%	-0.050%	0.061%	-0.048%
92:3	10006	10392	0.963	0.054%	0.057%	-0.003%	0.057%
92:4	10016	10963	0.914	0.153%	0.144%	0.009%	0.144%
93:1	9997	10527	0.950	-0.041%	0.082%	-0.122%	0.080%
93:2	10000	10340	0.967	-0.002%	0.053%	-0.054%	0.052%
93:3	10007	10686	0.936	0.073%	0.101%	-0.029%	0.101%
93:4	10003	10255	0.975	0.030%	0.034%	-0.004%	0.034%
94:1	10004	9954	1.005	0.024%	-0.012%	0.036%	-0.011%
94:2	10012	9994	1.002	0.097%	-0.007%	0.104%	-0.005%
94:3	10016	10613	0.944	0.148%	0.088%	0.059%	0.089%
94:4	9994	9836	1.016	-0.057%	-0.029%	-0.028%	-0.029%
95:1	10000	10706	0.934	-0.006%	0.111%	-0.117%	0.110%
95:2	10017	10873	0.921	0.172%	0.133%	0.038%	0.134%
95:3	10024	10853	0.924	0.222%	0.129%	0.093%	0.131%
95:4	10000	10445	0.957	0.009%	0.068%	-0.058%	0.067%
96:1	10027	11027	0.909	0.256%	0.157%	0.099%	0.159%
96:2	9999	10367	0.964	-0.013%	0.060%	-0.073%	0.059%
96:3	10006	10298	0.972	0.065%	0.047%	0.018%	0.047%
96:4	10012	10817	0.926	0.096%	0.123%	-0.026%	0.122%
AVG	10004	10377	0.964	0.057%	0.055%	0.002%	0.055%

Table 7.16b
Candle Morning-Evening Star (CN-MES) Short Return Analysis
(Average of all stocks)

Qtr	CN-MES Terminal Wealth	Buy/Hold Terminal Wealth	Relative Terminal Wealth	CN-MES Short Avg Ret	CN-MES Cash Avg Ret	CN-MES Short-Cash Avg Ret	Buy/Hold Avg Ret
85:1	10001	10142	0.986	-0.029%	0.007%	-0.036%	0.006%
85:2	10004	9700	1.031	-0.076%	-0.069%	-0.007%	-0.069%
85:3	10004	8889	1.125	-0.194%	-0.205%	0.011%	-0.205%
85:4	9991	10763	0.928	0.367%	0.106%	0.262%	0.107%
86:1	9997	11428	0.875	0.163%	0.225%	-0.062%	0.225%
86:2	9999	10414	0.960	0.071%	0.066%	0.005%	0.066%
86:3	10004	9175	1.090	-0.154%	-0.127%	-0.026%	-0.128%
86:4	10001	10413	0.960	-0.077%	0.070%	-0.146%	0.069%
87:1	9992	11929	0.838	0.371%	0.293%	0.078%	0.293%
87:2	9999	10196	0.981	0.057%	0.038%	0.019%	0.038%
87:3	9995	10408	0.960	0.287%	0.068%	0.219%	0.068%
87:4	10006	8087	1.237	-0.270%	-0.278%	0.008%	-0.278%
88:1	9996	10989	0.910	0.176%	0.163%	0.013%	0.163%
88:2	9992	10593	0.943	0.336%	0.099%	0.237%	0.100%
88:3	10000	10050	0.995	-0.014%	0.013%	-0.027%	0.013%
88:4	9996	10196	0.980	0.248%	0.036%	0.212%	0.037%
89:1	9996	10698	0.934	0.165%	0.112%	0.053%	0.112%
89:2	9998	10772	0.928	0.096%	0.122%	-0.026%	0.122%
89:3	9998	10833	0.923	0.130%	0.131%	-0.001%	0.131%
89:4	9998	9904	1.010	0.103%	-0.011%	0.114%	-0.011%
90:1	10000	9980	1.002	-0.021%	0.003%	-0.023%	0.003%
90:2	10004	10459	0.957	-0.252%	0.078%	-0.329%	0.077%
90:3	10010	8526	1.174	-0.349%	-0.259%	-0.091%	-0.259%
90:4	10003	10889	0.919	-0.082%	0.148%	-0.229%	0.146%
91:1	9993	12477	0.801	0.323%	0.315%	0.009%	0.315%
91:2	10001	10244	0.976	-0.070%	0.046%	-0.116%	0.045%
91:3	9995	10429	0.958	0.081%	0.065%	0.016%	0.065%
91:4	9992	10497	0.952	0.100%	0.082%	0.018%	0.082%
92:1	9996	10324	0.968	0.055%	0.048%	0.007%	0.048%
92:2	9994	9723	1.028	0.073%	-0.050%	0.123%	-0.048%
92:3	9994	10392	0.962	0.070%	0.056%	0.014%	0.057%
92:4	10001	10963	0.912	-0.011%	0.146%	-0.157%	0.144%
93:1	9998	10527	0.950	0.019%	0.081%	-0.061%	0.080%
93:2	10008	10340	0.968	-0.096%	0.054%	-0.150%	0.052%
93:3	9987	10686	0.935	0.169%	0.100%	0.069%	0.101%
93:4	9997	10255	0.975	0.042%	0.034%	0.008%	0.034%
94:1	10002	9954	1.005	-0.022%	-0.011%	-0.011%	-0.011%
94:2	10002	9994	1.001	-0.040%	-0.004%	-0.035%	-0.005%
94:3	9997	10613	0.942	0.040%	0.090%	-0.050%	0.089%
94:4	10008	9836	1.018	-0.096%	-0.028%	-0.067%	-0.029%
95:1	9989	10706	0.933	0.188%	0.109%	0.079%	0.110%
95:2	9988	10873	0.919	0.138%	0.134%	0.004%	0.134%
95:3	10007	10853	0.922	-0.056%	0.134%	-0.190%	0.131%
95:4	10000	10445	0.957	-0.001%	0.068%	-0.068%	0.067%
96:1	9992	11027	0.906	0.083%	0.160%	-0.077%	0.159%
96:2	9996	10367	0.964	0.045%	0.059%	-0.014%	0.059%
96:3	10001	10298	0.971	-0.002%	0.048%	-0.050%	0.047%
96:4	9983	10817	0.923	0.163%	0.122%	0.041%	0.122%
AVG	9998	10377	0.964	0.041%	0.055%	-0.014%	0.055%

Construction

The bearish Candle Piercing Line is also called the Dark Cloud Cover. It occurs when the market opens above the previous day's closing, confirming the previous day's positive movement, but then reverses direction to close within the previous day's open-to-close range. This movement is characterized by an open candle followed by a black candle of which the body top and bottom are each higher than the open candle's top and bottom. Figure 7.10 gives an example of this pattern.

The bullish Candle Piercing Line appears when yesterday's market was down (characterized by a black-bodied candle) and today's market is up (characterized by an open-bodied candle), with today's open below yesterday's close and today's close below yesterday's open-to-close. The market opened down in the direction of yesterday's close, but the daily movement was positive. While the rally was not large enough to reach the price of the previous day's open, the price has been pushed back up into the previous day's territory, indicating strength in today's positive direction.

Results

The test results for the Candle Piercing Line (CN-PL) system are shown in Tables 7.17 and 7.18. Like many of the other candle indicators, the CN-PL system makes very few long and short calls. The indicator chooses a long position only 2.3 percent of the time and a short position only 2.7 percent of the

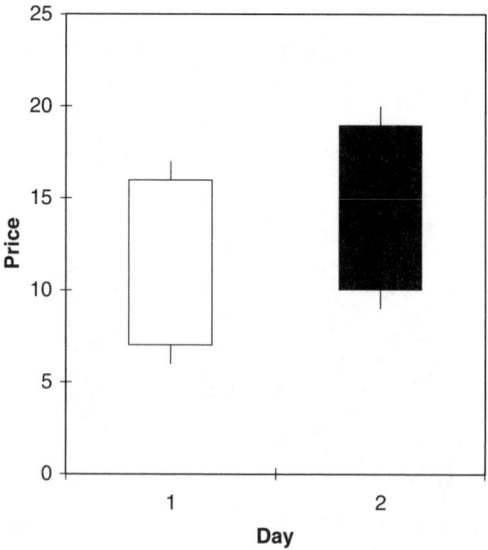

Figure 7.10 Candle piercing line.

time. Surprisingly, the call pattern is the same as for the Candle Counterattack system: no long or short calls were made by the system until the third quarter of 1991. After that time, the system made long calls at least 2.5 percent of the time and short calls at least 4.5 percent of the time.

Because of the absence of any long or short calls during the first half of the test period, the 26.9 percent long call hit rate and the 26.5 percent short call hit rate are misleading. During the time period when long calls are occurring, the quarterly long hit rates range from a low of 55.1 percent to a high of 61.5 percent. The quarterly short hit rates range from a low of 55.0 percent to a high of 61.5 percent.

The problems with the CN-PL system go beyond the infrequent call rates. Look closely at the long return analysis in Table 7.18a. The largest profit an investor trading long with this system would have made occurs in the first quarter of 1996. The $10,061 this investor would have is only 91.2 percent of the terminal wealth an investor using a buy-and-hold strategy would have realized during the same quarter.

Similar problems are evident with the short calls. In only six of the test quarters does the terminal wealth of trading short with the system exceed the initial investment. For fifteen of the test quarters, there are losses from trading short with the indicator. During the remaining quarters, there are no losses or profits because there are no short positions taken. Recall that, until the third quarter of 1991, investors using the CN-PL system remained in a zero-return cash position.

In short, our analysis indicates that not only does the Candle Piercing Line significantly underperform a buy-and-hold strategy, but following the system can lead to losses.

Volatility Breakout System

The Volatility Breakout (VTY-B) system makes use of current volatility and range movements to signal new highs and new lows. This system is based on the premise that when new highs or new lows occur in a market, the market is usually characterized by increased volatility and range.

Construction

The construction of a Volatility Breakout system involves the construction of volatility bands. To construct volatility bands, two parameters must be chosen: periods and range. The number of periods (P) determines the number of days back information will be gathered to calculate price volatility. The range determines how much volatility is needed, on a specific day, for a trading signal to be generated; that is, if the range value is 150, today's close must rise 150 percent or fall 150 percent.

Table 7.17a
Candle Piercing Line (CN-PL) Long Hit Analysis
(Average of all stocks)

Qtr	Optimal Long	CN-PL Long	Long Hits	Cash Hits	Total Hits	Long Right	Long Wrong	Cash Right	Cash Wrong
85:1	32.1%	0.0%	0.0%	67.9%	67.9%	0.0%	0.0%	67.9%	32.1%
85:2	30.2%	0.0%	0.0%	69.8%	69.8%	0.0%	0.0%	69.8%	30.2%
85:3	26.3%	0.0%	0.0%	73.7%	73.7%	0.0%	0.0%	73.7%	26.3%
85:4	36.6%	0.0%	0.0%	63.4%	63.4%	0.0%	0.0%	63.4%	36.6%
86:1	44.2%	0.0%	0.0%	55.8%	55.8%	0.0%	0.0%	55.8%	44.2%
86:2	39.7%	0.0%	0.0%	60.3%	60.3%	0.0%	0.0%	60.3%	39.7%
86:3	37.0%	0.0%	0.0%	63.0%	63.0%	0.0%	0.0%	63.0%	37.0%
86:4	38.5%	0.0%	0.0%	61.5%	61.5%	0.0%	0.0%	61.5%	38.5%
87:1	44.7%	0.0%	0.0%	55.3%	55.3%	0.0%	0.0%	55.3%	44.7%
87:2	40.0%	0.0%	0.0%	60.0%	60.0%	0.0%	0.0%	60.0%	40.0%
87:3	39.5%	0.0%	0.0%	60.5%	60.5%	0.0%	0.0%	60.5%	39.5%
87:4	37.9%	0.0%	0.0%	62.1%	62.1%	0.0%	0.0%	62.1%	37.9%
88:1	41.3%	0.0%	0.0%	58.7%	58.7%	0.0%	0.0%	58.7%	41.3%
88:2	39.3%	0.0%	0.0%	60.7%	60.7%	0.0%	0.0%	60.7%	39.3%
88:3	35.9%	0.0%	0.0%	64.1%	64.1%	0.0%	0.0%	64.1%	35.9%
88:4	36.3%	0.0%	0.0%	63.7%	63.7%	0.0%	0.0%	63.7%	36.3%
89:1	39.0%	0.0%	0.0%	61.0%	61.0%	0.0%	0.0%	61.0%	39.0%
89:2	40.2%	0.0%	0.0%	59.8%	59.8%	0.0%	0.0%	59.8%	40.2%
89:3	39.9%	0.0%	0.0%	60.1%	60.1%	0.0%	0.0%	60.1%	39.9%
89:4	38.3%	0.0%	0.0%	61.7%	61.7%	0.0%	0.0%	61.7%	38.3%
90:1	36.9%	0.0%	0.0%	63.1%	63.1%	0.0%	0.0%	63.1%	36.9%
90:2	39.2%	0.0%	0.0%	60.8%	60.8%	0.0%	0.0%	60.8%	39.2%
90:3	33.5%	0.0%	0.0%	66.5%	66.5%	0.0%	0.0%	66.5%	33.5%
90:4	40.8%	0.0%	0.0%	59.2%	59.2%	0.0%	0.0%	59.2%	40.8%
91:1	44.1%	0.0%	0.0%	55.9%	55.9%	0.0%	0.0%	55.9%	44.1%
91:2	39.7%	0.0%	0.0%	60.3%	60.3%	0.0%	0.0%	60.3%	39.7%
91:3	40.4%	2.5%	57.8%	59.6%	59.5%	1.5%	1.1%	58.0%	39.4%
91:4	41.2%	3.7%	58.8%	58.8%	58.8%	2.2%	1.5%	56.7%	39.6%
92:1	40.0%	4.1%	56.2%	60.1%	59.9%	2.3%	1.8%	57.7%	38.3%
92:2	38.6%	4.1%	56.5%	61.5%	61.3%	2.3%	1.8%	59.0%	36.9%
92:3	40.3%	4.2%	60.3%	59.8%	59.8%	2.5%	1.7%	57.3%	38.5%
92:4	41.9%	3.7%	61.5%	58.2%	58.3%	2.3%	1.4%	56.0%	40.3%
93:1	42.5%	4.4%	59.0%	57.5%	57.5%	2.6%	1.8%	54.9%	40.7%
93:2	42.1%	5.2%	59.2%	57.9%	58.0%	3.1%	2.1%	55.0%	39.9%
93:3	42.5%	4.3%	59.7%	57.5%	57.6%	2.6%	1.7%	55.0%	40.7%
93:4	41.5%	5.2%	58.5%	58.5%	58.5%	3.0%	2.1%	55.5%	39.3%
94:1	40.4%	6.7%	55.1%	59.6%	59.3%	3.7%	3.0%	55.6%	37.7%
94:2	40.6%	5.5%	55.3%	59.4%	59.1%	3.0%	2.4%	56.1%	38.4%
94:3	41.8%	4.9%	61.0%	58.4%	58.5%	3.0%	1.9%	55.5%	39.6%
94:4	39.5%	5.6%	58.3%	60.8%	60.6%	3.2%	2.3%	57.4%	37.1%
95:1	43.1%	4.4%	61.2%	56.9%	57.1%	2.7%	1.7%	54.4%	41.1%
95:2	43.7%	5.0%	61.2%	56.4%	56.6%	3.0%	1.9%	53.6%	41.5%
95:3	43.9%	4.9%	58.4%	56.1%	56.2%	2.8%	2.0%	53.4%	41.8%
95:4	43.4%	5.9%	58.8%	56.6%	56.8%	3.5%	2.4%	53.3%	40.8%
96:1	45.5%	7.0%	60.7%	54.5%	55.0%	4.2%	2.7%	50.7%	42.3%
96:2	42.1%	5.7%	55.3%	57.9%	57.7%	3.1%	2.5%	54.6%	39.8%
96:3	42.6%	5.7%	60.5%	57.6%	57.7%	3.5%	2.3%	54.3%	40.0%
96:4	44.3%	6.3%	59.0%	55.9%	56.1%	3.7%	2.6%	52.3%	41.4%
AVG	40.0%	2.3%	26.9%	60.2%	60.2%	1.3%	0.9%	58.9%	38.9%

Table 7.17b
Candle Piercing Line (CN-PL) Short Hit Analysis
(Average of all stocks)

Qtr	Optimal Short	CN-PL Short	Short Hits	Cash Hits	Total Hits	Short Right	Short Wrong	Cash Right	Cash Wrong
85:1	34.3%	0.0%	0.0%	65.7%	65.7%	0.0%	0.0%	65.7%	34.3%
85:2	34.6%	0.0%	0.0%	65.4%	65.4%	0.0%	0.0%	65.4%	34.6%
85:3	38.6%	0.0%	0.0%	61.4%	61.4%	0.0%	0.0%	61.4%	38.6%
85:4	33.1%	0.0%	0.0%	66.9%	66.9%	0.0%	0.0%	66.9%	33.1%
86:1	35.2%	0.0%	0.0%	64.8%	64.8%	0.0%	0.0%	64.8%	35.2%
86:2	39.8%	0.0%	0.0%	60.2%	60.2%	0.0%	0.0%	60.2%	39.8%
86:3	42.7%	0.0%	0.0%	57.3%	57.3%	0.0%	0.0%	57.3%	42.7%
86:4	38.7%	0.0%	0.0%	61.3%	61.3%	0.0%	0.0%	61.3%	38.7%
87:1	36.9%	0.0%	0.0%	63.1%	63.1%	0.0%	0.0%	63.1%	36.9%
87:2	40.0%	0.0%	0.0%	60.0%	60.0%	0.0%	0.0%	60.0%	40.0%
87:3	40.4%	0.0%	0.0%	59.6%	59.6%	0.0%	0.0%	59.6%	40.4%
87:4	45.3%	0.0%	0.0%	54.7%	54.7%	0.0%	0.0%	54.7%	45.3%
88:1	36.7%	0.0%	0.0%	63.3%	63.3%	0.0%	0.0%	63.3%	36.7%
88:2	37.4%	0.0%	0.0%	62.6%	62.6%	0.0%	0.0%	62.6%	37.4%
88:3	38.4%	0.0%	0.0%	61.6%	61.6%	0.0%	0.0%	61.6%	38.4%
88:4	37.0%	0.0%	0.0%	63.0%	63.0%	0.0%	0.0%	63.0%	37.0%
89:1	36.2%	0.0%	0.0%	63.8%	63.8%	0.0%	0.0%	63.8%	36.2%
89:2	35.9%	0.0%	0.0%	64.1%	64.1%	0.0%	0.0%	64.1%	35.9%
89:3	36.4%	0.0%	0.0%	63.6%	63.6%	0.0%	0.0%	63.6%	36.4%
89:4	39.0%	0.0%	0.0%	61.0%	61.0%	0.0%	0.0%	61.0%	39.0%
90:1	40.1%	0.0%	0.0%	59.9%	59.9%	0.0%	0.0%	59.9%	40.1%
90:2	37.8%	0.0%	0.0%	62.2%	62.2%	0.0%	0.0%	62.2%	37.8%
90:3	45.7%	0.0%	0.0%	54.3%	54.3%	0.0%	0.0%	54.3%	45.7%
90:4	37.6%	0.0%	0.0%	62.4%	62.4%	0.0%	0.0%	62.4%	37.6%
91:1	36.7%	0.0%	0.0%	63.3%	63.3%	0.0%	0.0%	63.3%	36.7%
91:2	40.4%	0.0%	0.0%	59.6%	59.6%	0.0%	0.0%	59.6%	40.4%
91:3	39.8%	4.5%	58.6%	60.4%	60.3%	2.7%	1.9%	57.6%	37.8%
91:4	40.5%	4.6%	59.0%	59.6%	59.6%	2.7%	1.9%	56.8%	38.5%
92:1	43.2%	5.2%	59.0%	56.9%	57.0%	3.1%	2.1%	53.9%	40.9%
92:2	42.9%	5.1%	59.8%	57.2%	57.4%	3.1%	2.1%	54.3%	40.6%
92:3	39.5%	5.5%	59.3%	60.6%	60.5%	3.3%	2.3%	57.2%	37.2%
92:4	37.5%	5.7%	57.3%	62.6%	62.3%	3.2%	2.4%	59.0%	35.3%
93:1	39.4%	4.8%	55.9%	60.7%	60.5%	2.7%	2.1%	57.8%	37.4%
93:2	40.9%	5.7%	57.3%	59.2%	59.1%	3.3%	2.4%	55.8%	38.5%
93:3	39.4%	5.4%	56.5%	60.6%	60.3%	3.0%	2.3%	57.3%	37.3%
93:4	41.7%	6.3%	57.7%	58.4%	58.4%	3.6%	2.6%	54.8%	39.0%
94:1	43.7%	6.5%	59.0%	56.4%	56.6%	3.8%	2.7%	52.8%	40.7%
94:2	42.7%	5.9%	59.7%	57.5%	57.6%	3.5%	2.4%	54.1%	40.0%
94:3	39.8%	5.5%	58.2%	60.3%	60.2%	3.2%	2.3%	57.0%	37.5%
94:4	42.8%	6.1%	61.5%	57.3%	57.6%	3.8%	2.4%	53.8%	40.0%
95:1	38.7%	6.0%	57.7%	61.4%	61.2%	3.5%	2.5%	57.8%	36.2%
95:2	38.9%	6.4%	55.0%	61.2%	60.8%	3.5%	2.9%	57.3%	36.4%
95:3	38.9%	6.9%	56.0%	61.2%	60.8%	3.9%	3.0%	57.0%	36.2%
95:4	40.5%	6.4%	57.8%	59.7%	59.6%	3.7%	2.7%	55.9%	37.8%
96:1	38.9%	5.6%	55.1%	61.2%	60.9%	3.1%	2.5%	57.8%	36.6%
96:2	42.4%	7.4%	58.1%	57.7%	57.7%	4.3%	3.1%	53.5%	39.2%
96:3	40.8%	5.6%	56.0%	59.2%	59.1%	3.2%	2.5%	55.9%	38.5%
96:4	39.8%	7.7%	55.9%	60.3%	60.0%	4.3%	3.4%	55.7%	36.6%
AVG	39.4%	2.7%	26.5%	60.7%	60.7%	1.5%	1.1%	59.1%	38.2%

Table 7.18a
Candle Piercing Line (CN-PL) Long Return Analysis
(Average of all stocks)

Qtr	CN-PL Terminal Wealth	Buy/Hold Terminal Wealth	Relative Terminal Wealth	CN-PL Long Avg Ret	CN-PL Cash Avg Ret	CN-PL Long-Cash Avg Ret	Buy/Hold Avg Ret
85:1	10000	10142	0.986	0.000%	0.006%	-0.006%	0.006%
85:2	10000	9700	1.031	0.000%	-0.069%	0.069%	-0.069%
85:3	10000	8889	1.125	0.000%	-0.205%	0.205%	-0.205%
85:4	10000	10763	0.929	0.000%	0.107%	-0.107%	0.107%
86:1	10000	11428	0.875	0.000%	0.225%	-0.225%	0.225%
86:2	10000	10414	0.960	0.000%	0.066%	-0.066%	0.066%
86:3	10000	9175	1.090	0.000%	-0.128%	0.128%	-0.128%
86:4	10000	10413	0.960	0.000%	0.069%	-0.069%	0.069%
87:1	10000	11929	0.838	0.000%	0.293%	-0.293%	0.293%
87:2	10000	10196	0.981	0.000%	0.038%	-0.038%	0.038%
87:3	10000	10408	0.961	0.000%	0.068%	-0.068%	0.068%
87:4	10000	8087	1.237	0.000%	-0.278%	0.278%	-0.278%
88:1	10000	10989	0.910	0.000%	0.163%	-0.163%	0.163%
88:2	10000	10593	0.944	0.000%	0.100%	-0.100%	0.100%
88:3	10000	10050	0.995	0.000%	0.013%	-0.013%	0.013%
88:4	10000	10196	0.981	0.000%	0.037%	-0.037%	0.037%
89:1	10000	10698	0.935	0.000%	0.112%	-0.112%	0.112%
89:2	10000	10772	0.928	0.000%	0.122%	-0.122%	0.122%
89:3	10000	10833	0.923	0.000%	0.131%	-0.131%	0.131%
89:4	10000	9904	1.010	0.000%	-0.011%	0.011%	-0.011%
90:1	10000	9980	1.002	0.000%	0.003%	-0.003%	0.003%
90:2	10000	10459	0.956	0.000%	0.077%	-0.077%	0.077%
90:3	10000	8526	1.173	0.000%	-0.259%	0.259%	-0.259%
90:4	10000	10889	0.918	0.000%	0.146%	-0.146%	0.146%
91:1	10000	12477	0.801	0.000%	0.315%	-0.315%	0.315%
91:2	10000	10244	0.976	0.000%	0.045%	-0.045%	0.045%
91:3	9996	10429	0.959	-0.022%	0.067%	-0.089%	0.065%
91:4	10019	10497	0.954	0.081%	0.082%	0.000%	0.082%
92:1	10021	10324	0.971	0.086%	0.046%	0.040%	0.048%
92:2	9991	9723	1.028	-0.034%	-0.049%	0.015%	-0.048%
92:3	10027	10392	0.965	0.104%	0.054%	0.050%	0.057%
92:4	10035	10963	0.915	0.149%	0.144%	0.005%	0.144%
93:1	10005	10527	0.950	0.014%	0.083%	-0.069%	0.080%
93:2	10034	10340	0.970	0.105%	0.049%	0.057%	0.052%
93:3	10023	10686	0.938	0.084%	0.102%	-0.017%	0.101%
93:4	10011	10255	0.976	0.031%	0.034%	-0.003%	0.034%
94:1	10001	9954	1.005	0.002%	-0.012%	0.014%	-0.011%
94:2	9988	9994	0.999	-0.036%	-0.003%	-0.034%	-0.005%
94:3	10052	10613	0.947	0.163%	0.085%	0.077%	0.089%
94:4	10017	9836	1.018	0.049%	-0.034%	0.083%	-0.029%
95:1	10030	10706	0.937	0.107%	0.110%	-0.003%	0.110%
95:2	10041	10873	0.923	0.133%	0.134%	-0.001%	0.134%
95:3	10038	10853	0.925	0.123%	0.131%	-0.008%	0.131%
95:4	10036	10445	0.961	0.100%	0.065%	0.036%	0.067%
96:1	10061	11027	0.912	0.138%	0.160%	-0.022%	0.159%
96:2	9988	10367	0.963	-0.033%	0.064%	-0.097%	0.059%
96:3	10044	10298	0.975	0.120%	0.043%	0.077%	0.047%
96:4	10046	10817	0.929	0.115%	0.123%	-0.008%	0.122%
AVG	10011	10377	0.965	0.073%	0.055%	0.019%	0.055%

Table 7.18b
Candle Piercing Line (CN-PL) Short Return Analysis
(Average of all stocks)

Qtr	CN-PL Terminal Wealth	Buy/Hold Terminal Wealth	Relative Terminal Wealth	CN-PL Short Avg Ret	CN-PL Cash Avg Ret	CN-PL Short-Cash Avg Ret	Buy/Hold Avg Ret
85:1	10000	10142	0.986	0.000%	0.006%	-0.006%	0.006%
85:2	10000	9700	1.031	0.000%	-0.069%	0.069%	-0.069%
85:3	10000	8889	1.125	0.000%	-0.205%	0.205%	-0.205%
85:4	10000	10763	0.929	0.000%	0.107%	-0.107%	0.107%
86:1	10000	11428	0.875	0.000%	0.225%	-0.225%	0.225%
86:2	10000	10414	0.960	0.000%	0.066%	-0.066%	0.066%
86:3	10000	9175	1.090	0.000%	-0.128%	0.128%	-0.128%
86:4	10000	10413	0.960	0.000%	0.069%	-0.069%	0.069%
87:1	10000	11929	0.838	0.000%	0.293%	-0.293%	0.293%
87:2	10000	10196	0.981	0.000%	0.038%	-0.038%	0.038%
87:3	10000	10408	0.961	0.000%	0.068%	-0.068%	0.068%
87:4	10000	8087	1.237	0.000%	-0.278%	0.278%	-0.278%
88:1	10000	10989	0.910	0.000%	0.163%	-0.163%	0.163%
88:2	10000	10593	0.944	0.000%	0.100%	-0.100%	0.100%
88:3	10000	10050	0.995	0.000%	0.013%	-0.013%	0.013%
88:4	10000	10196	0.981	0.000%	0.037%	-0.037%	0.037%
89:1	10000	10698	0.935	0.000%	0.112%	-0.112%	0.112%
89:2	10000	10772	0.928	0.000%	0.122%	-0.122%	0.122%
89:3	10000	10833	0.923	0.000%	0.131%	-0.131%	0.131%
89:4	10000	9904	1.010	0.000%	-0.011%	0.011%	-0.011%
90:1	10000	9980	1.002	0.000%	0.003%	-0.003%	0.003%
90:2	10000	10459	0.956	0.000%	0.077%	-0.077%	0.077%
90:3	10000	8526	1.173	0.000%	-0.259%	0.259%	-0.259%
90:4	10000	10889	0.918	0.000%	0.146%	-0.146%	0.146%
91:1	10000	12477	0.801	0.000%	0.315%	-0.315%	0.315%
91:2	10000	10244	0.976	0.000%	0.045%	-0.045%	0.045%
91:3	9991	10429	0.958	0.029%	0.067%	-0.038%	0.065%
91:4	10006	10497	0.953	-0.023%	0.087%	-0.110%	0.082%
92:1	10000	10324	0.969	0.001%	0.050%	-0.050%	0.048%
92:2	10025	9723	1.031	-0.074%	-0.047%	-0.027%	-0.048%
92:3	9992	10392	0.961	0.020%	0.059%	-0.038%	0.057%
92:4	9959	10963	0.908	0.114%	0.146%	-0.033%	0.144%
93:1	9985	10527	0.948	0.053%	0.081%	-0.028%	0.080%
93:2	9986	10340	0.966	0.041%	0.052%	-0.011%	0.052%
93:3	9952	10686	0.931	0.141%	0.099%	0.042%	0.101%
93:4	9996	10255	0.975	0.014%	0.035%	-0.021%	0.034%
94:1	10008	9954	1.005	-0.019%	-0.011%	-0.008%	-0.011%
94:2	10020	9994	1.003	-0.055%	-0.002%	-0.053%	-0.005%
94:3	9972	10613	0.940	0.081%	0.090%	-0.008%	0.089%
94:4	10034	9836	1.020	-0.090%	-0.025%	-0.065%	-0.029%
95:1	9979	10706	0.932	0.060%	0.113%	-0.053%	0.110%
95:2	9951	10873	0.915	0.123%	0.135%	-0.011%	0.134%
95:3	9957	10853	0.917	0.104%	0.133%	-0.030%	0.131%
95:4	10021	10445	0.959	-0.048%	0.075%	-0.122%	0.067%
96:1	9967	11027	0.904	0.099%	0.163%	-0.064%	0.159%
96:2	9975	10367	0.962	0.056%	0.059%	-0.003%	0.059%
96:3	9976	10298	0.969	0.068%	0.046%	0.022%	0.047%
96:4	9963	10817	0.921	0.075%	0.126%	-0.051%	0.122%
AVG	9994	10377	0.963	0.036%	0.056%	-0.019%	0.055%

Table 7.19a
Volatility Breakout System (VTY-B) Long Hit Analysis
(Average of all stocks)

Qtr	Optimal Long	VTY-B Long	Long Hits	Cash Hits	Total Hits	Long Right	Long Wrong	Cash Right	Cash Wrong
85:1	32.1%	56.9%	65.2%	68.2%	66.5%	37.1%	19.8%	29.4%	13.7%
85:2	30.2%	55.5%	64.7%	70.9%	67.5%	35.9%	19.6%	31.5%	13.0%
85:3	26.3%	47.7%	60.8%	73.5%	67.4%	29.0%	18.7%	38.4%	13.8%
85:4	36.6%	61.2%	65.3%	63.1%	64.5%	40.0%	21.2%	24.4%	14.3%
86:1	44.2%	60.3%	64.1%	56.5%	61.0%	38.7%	21.7%	22.4%	17.3%
86:2	39.7%	53.0%	59.5%	60.5%	59.9%	31.5%	21.5%	28.4%	18.6%
86:3	37.0%	46.2%	57.6%	63.7%	60.9%	26.6%	19.6%	34.2%	19.5%
86:4	38.5%	54.1%	59.7%	60.8%	60.2%	32.3%	21.8%	27.9%	18.0%
87:1	44.7%	63.9%	62.4%	55.2%	59.8%	39.9%	24.0%	19.9%	16.2%
87:2	40.0%	51.5%	59.4%	59.5%	59.4%	30.6%	20.9%	28.9%	19.6%
87:3	39.5%	53.1%	59.0%	60.2%	59.6%	31.3%	21.8%	28.2%	18.6%
87:4	37.9%	46.9%	55.1%	62.1%	58.8%	25.8%	21.1%	33.0%	20.1%
88:1	41.3%	57.6%	61.9%	57.1%	59.9%	35.6%	21.9%	24.2%	18.2%
88:2	39.3%	52.5%	61.1%	60.1%	60.6%	32.1%	20.4%	28.5%	18.9%
88:3	35.9%	50.9%	59.6%	62.8%	61.2%	30.3%	20.6%	30.8%	18.3%
88:4	36.3%	50.1%	61.2%	62.2%	61.7%	30.7%	19.4%	31.0%	18.9%
89:1	39.0%	54.4%	61.7%	59.4%	60.7%	33.6%	20.8%	27.1%	18.5%
89:2	40.2%	60.8%	62.6%	59.1%	61.2%	38.0%	22.8%	23.2%	16.1%
89:3	39.9%	54.3%	62.0%	59.0%	60.6%	33.7%	20.6%	26.9%	18.7%
89:4	38.3%	50.6%	60.6%	61.6%	61.1%	30.6%	19.9%	30.4%	19.0%
90:1	36.9%	48.8%	59.5%	63.3%	61.5%	29.0%	19.8%	32.4%	18.8%
90:2	39.2%	52.9%	61.5%	61.1%	61.3%	32.5%	20.3%	28.8%	18.3%
90:3	33.5%	40.4%	55.3%	66.8%	62.2%	22.4%	18.1%	39.8%	19.7%
90:4	40.8%	56.7%	61.6%	59.3%	60.6%	34.9%	21.8%	25.7%	17.6%
91:1	44.1%	59.7%	63.4%	56.9%	60.8%	37.9%	21.9%	22.9%	17.4%
91:2	39.7%	51.6%	58.4%	59.7%	59.0%	30.1%	21.5%	28.9%	19.5%
91:3	40.4%	54.1%	59.6%	59.3%	59.4%	32.2%	21.9%	27.2%	18.7%
91:4	41.2%	52.6%	60.7%	61.0%	60.9%	32.0%	20.7%	28.9%	18.5%
92:1	40.0%	55.4%	56.4%	60.0%	58.0%	31.3%	24.2%	26.7%	17.8%
92:2	38.6%	48.6%	56.7%	61.3%	59.0%	27.5%	21.1%	31.5%	19.9%
92:3	40.3%	54.6%	60.2%	59.6%	59.9%	32.9%	21.7%	27.0%	18.4%
92:4	41.9%	57.8%	62.6%	58.4%	60.9%	36.2%	21.6%	24.7%	17.6%
93:1	42.5%	55.3%	61.0%	57.9%	59.6%	33.7%	21.5%	25.9%	18.8%
93:2	42.1%	51.3%	59.4%	58.6%	59.0%	30.5%	20.8%	28.5%	20.1%
93:3	42.5%	55.3%	61.0%	58.4%	59.8%	33.7%	21.6%	26.1%	18.6%
93:4	41.5%	51.6%	58.9%	59.3%	59.1%	30.4%	21.2%	28.7%	19.7%
94:1	40.4%	51.0%	56.6%	60.1%	58.3%	28.9%	22.1%	29.4%	19.6%
94:2	40.6%	49.5%	58.0%	60.1%	59.0%	28.7%	20.8%	30.3%	20.1%
94:3	41.8%	53.6%	60.5%	59.0%	59.8%	32.4%	21.2%	27.3%	19.0%
94:4	39.5%	48.1%	57.1%	60.6%	58.9%	27.4%	20.6%	31.5%	20.5%
95:1	43.1%	55.9%	61.3%	57.5%	59.6%	34.3%	21.6%	25.3%	18.7%
95:2	43.7%	58.4%	60.4%	56.0%	58.6%	35.3%	23.1%	23.3%	18.3%
95:3	43.9%	56.8%	60.8%	56.1%	58.8%	34.5%	22.2%	24.2%	19.0%
95:4	43.4%	53.8%	59.6%	57.1%	58.5%	32.1%	21.7%	26.4%	19.8%
96:1	45.5%	55.1%	60.5%	54.6%	57.8%	33.3%	21.7%	24.5%	20.4%
96:2	42.1%	52.5%	57.8%	58.3%	58.1%	30.4%	22.1%	27.7%	19.8%
96:3	42.6%	52.5%	59.8%	58.2%	59.0%	31.4%	21.1%	27.7%	19.9%
96:4	44.3%	57.2%	60.4%	56.7%	58.8%	34.5%	22.7%	24.3%	18.5%
AVG	40.0%	53.6%	60.3%	60.2%	60.4%	32.4%	21.2%	28.0%	18.4%

Table 7.19b
Volatility Breakout System (VTY-B) Short Hit Analysis
(Average of all stocks)

Qtr	Optimal Short	VTY-B Short	Short Hits	Cash Hits	Total Hits	Short Right	Short Wrong	Cash Right	Cash Wrong
85:1	34.3%	43.1%	68.2%	65.2%	66.5%	29.4%	13.7%	37.1%	19.8%
85:2	34.6%	44.5%	70.9%	64.7%	67.4%	31.5%	13.0%	35.9%	19.6%
85:3	38.6%	52.3%	73.5%	60.8%	67.4%	38.4%	13.8%	29.0%	18.7%
85:4	33.1%	38.7%	63.1%	65.3%	64.4%	24.4%	14.3%	40.0%	21.2%
86:1	35.2%	39.6%	56.4%	64.1%	61.0%	22.4%	17.3%	38.7%	21.7%
86:2	39.8%	46.9%	60.5%	59.5%	60.0%	28.4%	18.5%	31.6%	21.5%
86:3	42.7%	53.7%	63.7%	57.6%	60.9%	34.2%	19.5%	26.7%	19.6%
86:4	38.7%	45.9%	60.8%	59.7%	60.2%	27.9%	18.0%	32.3%	21.8%
87:1	36.9%	36.1%	55.2%	62.4%	59.8%	19.9%	16.2%	39.9%	24.0%
87:2	40.0%	48.5%	59.5%	59.4%	59.4%	28.8%	19.6%	30.6%	20.9%
87:3	40.4%	46.9%	60.2%	59.0%	59.6%	28.2%	18.6%	31.3%	21.8%
87:4	45.3%	53.1%	62.1%	55.1%	58.8%	32.9%	20.1%	25.8%	21.1%
88:1	36.7%	42.4%	57.1%	61.9%	59.9%	24.2%	18.2%	35.6%	21.9%
88:2	37.4%	47.4%	60.1%	61.1%	60.6%	28.5%	18.9%	32.1%	20.4%
88:3	38.4%	49.1%	62.8%	59.6%	61.2%	30.8%	18.3%	30.4%	20.6%
88:4	37.0%	49.9%	62.2%	61.2%	61.7%	31.0%	18.9%	30.7%	19.4%
89:1	36.2%	45.6%	59.4%	61.8%	60.7%	27.1%	18.5%	33.6%	20.8%
89:2	35.9%	39.2%	59.1%	62.6%	61.2%	23.2%	16.1%	38.0%	22.8%
89:3	36.4%	45.6%	59.0%	62.0%	60.6%	26.9%	18.7%	33.7%	20.6%
89:4	39.0%	49.4%	61.6%	60.6%	61.1%	30.4%	19.0%	30.7%	19.9%
90:1	40.1%	51.2%	63.3%	59.5%	61.5%	32.4%	18.8%	29.0%	19.8%
90:2	37.8%	47.1%	61.1%	61.5%	61.3%	28.8%	18.3%	32.6%	20.3%
90:3	45.7%	59.6%	66.8%	55.3%	62.2%	39.8%	19.7%	22.4%	18.1%
90:4	37.6%	43.3%	59.3%	61.6%	60.6%	25.7%	17.6%	34.9%	21.8%
91:1	36.7%	40.3%	56.9%	63.4%	60.8%	22.9%	17.4%	37.9%	21.9%
91:2	40.4%	48.4%	59.7%	58.4%	59.0%	28.9%	19.5%	30.1%	21.5%
91:3	39.8%	45.9%	59.3%	59.6%	59.4%	27.2%	18.7%	32.2%	21.9%
91:4	40.5%	47.4%	61.0%	60.7%	60.9%	28.9%	18.4%	32.0%	20.7%
92:1	43.2%	44.6%	60.0%	56.4%	58.0%	26.7%	17.8%	31.3%	24.2%
92:2	42.9%	51.4%	61.3%	56.7%	59.0%	31.5%	19.9%	27.6%	21.1%
92:3	39.5%	45.4%	59.5%	60.2%	59.9%	27.0%	18.4%	32.9%	21.7%
92:4	37.5%	42.2%	58.4%	62.6%	60.9%	24.7%	17.5%	36.2%	21.6%
93:1	39.4%	44.7%	58.0%	61.0%	59.7%	25.9%	18.8%	33.7%	21.5%
93:2	40.9%	48.7%	58.6%	59.4%	59.0%	28.5%	20.1%	30.5%	20.8%
93:3	39.4%	44.7%	58.4%	61.0%	59.8%	26.1%	18.6%	33.7%	21.6%
93:4	41.7%	48.4%	59.3%	58.9%	59.1%	28.7%	19.7%	30.4%	21.2%
94:1	43.7%	49.0%	60.1%	56.6%	58.3%	29.4%	19.6%	28.9%	22.2%
94:2	42.7%	50.4%	60.1%	58.0%	59.0%	30.3%	20.1%	28.7%	20.8%
94:3	39.8%	46.4%	59.0%	60.5%	59.8%	27.3%	19.0%	32.4%	21.2%
94:4	42.8%	51.9%	60.6%	57.1%	58.9%	31.5%	20.5%	27.4%	20.6%
95:1	38.7%	44.1%	57.5%	61.3%	59.6%	25.3%	18.7%	34.3%	21.6%
95:2	38.9%	41.6%	56.0%	60.4%	58.6%	23.3%	18.3%	35.3%	23.1%
95:3	38.9%	43.2%	56.1%	60.8%	58.8%	24.2%	19.0%	34.5%	22.2%
95:4	40.5%	46.2%	57.1%	59.6%	58.4%	26.4%	19.8%	32.1%	21.7%
96:1	38.9%	44.9%	54.6%	60.5%	57.9%	24.5%	20.4%	33.3%	21.7%
96:2	42.4%	47.5%	58.3%	57.8%	58.1%	27.7%	19.8%	30.4%	22.1%
96:3	40.8%	47.5%	58.2%	59.8%	59.0%	27.6%	19.9%	31.4%	21.1%
96:4	39.8%	42.8%	56.7%	60.4%	58.8%	24.3%	18.5%	34.5%	22.7%
AVG	39.4%	46.4%	60.2%	60.3%	60.4%	28.0%	18.4%	32.4%	21.2%

Table 7.20a
Volatility Breakout System (VTY-B) Long Return Analysis
(Average of all stocks)

Qtr	VTY-B Terminal Wealth	Buy/Hold Terminal Wealth	Relative Terminal Wealth	VTY-B Long Avg Ret	VTY-B Cash Avg Ret	VTY-B Long-Cash Avg Ret	Buy/Hold Avg Ret
85:1	10093	10142	0.995	0.016%	-0.007%	0.024%	0.006%
85:2	9863	9700	1.017	-0.051%	-0.093%	0.042%	-0.069%
85:3	9442	8889	1.062	-0.203%	-0.206%	0.003%	-0.205%
85:4	10380	10763	0.964	0.089%	0.136%	-0.047%	0.107%
86:1	10882	11428	0.952	0.231%	0.215%	0.017%	0.225%
86:2	10269	10414	0.986	0.077%	0.055%	0.022%	0.066%
86:3	9723	9175	1.060	-0.095%	-0.155%	0.060%	-0.128%
86:4	10103	10413	0.970	0.029%	0.117%	-0.088%	0.069%
87:1	11175	11929	0.937	0.287%	0.304%	-0.018%	0.293%
87:2	10109	10196	0.991	0.035%	0.040%	-0.005%	0.038%
87:3	10251	10408	0.985	0.076%	0.060%	0.016%	0.068%
87:4	9734	8087	1.204	-0.080%	-0.453%	0.373%	-0.278%
88:1	10287	10989	0.936	0.086%	0.267%	-0.181%	0.163%
88:2	10204	10593	0.963	0.062%	0.141%	-0.079%	0.100%
88:3	9889	10050	0.984	-0.037%	0.064%	-0.101%	0.013%
88:4	9984	10196	0.979	-0.008%	0.081%	-0.089%	0.037%
89:1	10274	10698	0.960	0.081%	0.150%	-0.070%	0.112%
89:2	10393	10772	0.965	0.100%	0.156%	-0.056%	0.122%
89:3	10375	10833	0.958	0.109%	0.157%	-0.049%	0.131%
89:4	9933	9904	1.003	-0.020%	-0.002%	-0.018%	-0.011%
90:1	10011	9980	1.003	0.006%	0.000%	0.007%	0.003%
90:2	10280	10459	0.983	0.084%	0.069%	0.015%	0.077%
90:3	9506	8526	1.115	-0.204%	-0.296%	0.092%	-0.259%
90:4	10429	10889	0.958	0.120%	0.180%	-0.060%	0.146%
91:1	11702	12477	0.938	0.354%	0.257%	0.098%	0.315%
91:2	10090	10244	0.985	0.026%	0.066%	-0.040%	0.045%
91:3	10187	10429	0.977	0.053%	0.079%	-0.027%	0.065%
91:4	10482	10497	0.999	0.140%	0.017%	0.124%	0.082%
92:1	10203	10324	0.988	0.055%	0.039%	0.016%	0.048%
92:2	9852	9723	1.013	-0.052%	-0.045%	-0.007%	-0.048%
92:3	10208	10392	0.982	0.056%	0.057%	-0.001%	0.057%
92:4	10594	10963	0.966	0.157%	0.127%	0.030%	0.144%
93:1	10360	10527	0.984	0.102%	0.052%	0.050%	0.080%
93:2	10286	10340	0.995	0.087%	0.015%	0.072%	0.052%
93:3	10461	10686	0.979	0.128%	0.068%	0.059%	0.101%
93:4	10219	10255	0.996	0.063%	0.002%	0.061%	0.034%
94:1	10068	9954	1.011	0.018%	-0.041%	0.059%	-0.011%
94:2	10082	9994	1.009	0.028%	-0.037%	0.066%	-0.005%
94:3	10402	10613	0.980	0.113%	0.062%	0.051%	0.089%
94:4	9922	9836	1.009	-0.029%	-0.030%	0.002%	-0.029%
95:1	10434	10706	0.975	0.123%	0.094%	0.029%	0.110%
95:2	10480	10873	0.964	0.128%	0.142%	-0.014%	0.134%
95:3	10502	10853	0.968	0.138%	0.122%	0.016%	0.131%
95:4	10294	10445	0.986	0.082%	0.049%	0.033%	0.067%
96:1	10546	11027	0.956	0.154%	0.164%	-0.010%	0.159%
96:2	10272	10367	0.991	0.082%	0.033%	0.048%	0.059%
96:3	10285	10298	0.999	0.085%	0.006%	0.079%	0.047%
96:4	10551	10817	0.975	0.147%	0.090%	0.057%	0.122%
AVG	10252	10377	0.988	0.069%	0.039%	0.030%	0.055%

Table 7.20b
Volatility Breakout System (VTY-B) Short Return Analysis
(Average of all stocks)

Qtr	VTY-B Terminal Wealth	Buy/Hold Terminal Wealth	Relative Terminal Wealth	VTY-B Short Avg Ret	VTY-B Cash Avg Ret	VTY-B Short-Cash Avg Ret	Buy/Hold Avg Ret
85:1	10051	10142	0.991	-0.007%	0.016%	-0.024%	0.006%
85:2	10314	9700	1.063	-0.093%	-0.051%	-0.042%	-0.069%
85:3	10755	8889	1.210	-0.206%	-0.203%	-0.003%	-0.205%
85:4	9694	10763	0.901	0.136%	0.088%	0.047%	0.107%
86:1	9519	11428	0.833	0.215%	0.231%	-0.016%	0.225%
86:2	9874	10414	0.948	0.054%	0.077%	-0.022%	0.066%
86:3	10531	9175	1.148	-0.155%	-0.095%	-0.060%	-0.128%
86:4	9689	10413	0.930	0.117%	0.029%	0.088%	0.069%
87:1	9354	11929	0.784	0.304%	0.287%	0.017%	0.293%
87:2	9871	10196	0.968	0.041%	0.035%	0.005%	0.038%
87:3	9824	10408	0.944	0.060%	0.076%	-0.016%	0.068%
87:4	11391	8087	1.409	-0.454%	-0.079%	-0.374%	-0.278%
88:1	9329	10989	0.849	0.266%	0.087%	0.179%	0.163%
88:2	9599	10593	0.906	0.141%	0.063%	0.078%	0.100%
88:3	9814	10050	0.976	0.064%	-0.037%	0.101%	0.013%
88:4	9760	10196	0.957	0.081%	-0.008%	0.089%	0.037%
89:1	9600	10698	0.897	0.150%	0.081%	0.070%	0.112%
89:2	9628	10772	0.894	0.156%	0.100%	0.056%	0.122%
89:3	9564	10833	0.883	0.158%	0.109%	0.049%	0.131%
89:4	10006	9904	1.010	-0.002%	-0.020%	0.017%	-0.011%
90:1	9997	9980	1.002	-0.001%	0.006%	-0.007%	0.003%
90:2	9805	10459	0.937	0.069%	0.084%	-0.015%	0.077%
90:3	11185	8526	1.312	-0.296%	-0.204%	-0.092%	-0.259%
90:4	9505	10889	0.873	0.181%	0.120%	0.061%	0.146%
91:1	9396	12477	0.753	0.257%	0.354%	-0.098%	0.315%
91:2	9803	10244	0.957	0.066%	0.026%	0.040%	0.045%
91:3	9770	10429	0.937	0.079%	0.053%	0.026%	0.065%
91:4	9926	10497	0.946	0.016%	0.140%	-0.124%	0.082%
92:1	9895	10324	0.958	0.039%	0.055%	-0.016%	0.048%
92:2	10145	9723	1.043	-0.045%	-0.052%	0.006%	-0.048%
92:3	9837	10392	0.947	0.057%	0.056%	0.001%	0.057%
92:4	9661	10963	0.881	0.127%	0.157%	-0.030%	0.144%
93:1	9863	10527	0.937	0.050%	0.103%	-0.053%	0.080%
93:2	9950	10340	0.962	0.015%	0.087%	-0.072%	0.052%
93:3	9816	10686	0.919	0.068%	0.128%	-0.060%	0.101%
93:4	10001	10255	0.975	0.002%	0.063%	-0.061%	0.034%
94:1	10129	9954	1.018	-0.041%	0.018%	-0.059%	-0.011%
94:2	10133	9994	1.014	-0.037%	0.028%	-0.065%	-0.005%
94:3	9825	10613	0.926	0.062%	0.113%	-0.051%	0.089%
94:4	10100	9836	1.027	-0.030%	-0.028%	-0.002%	-0.029%
95:1	9744	10706	0.910	0.094%	0.123%	-0.029%	0.110%
95:2	9639	10873	0.886	0.142%	0.128%	0.014%	0.134%
95:3	9679	10853	0.892	0.122%	0.138%	-0.016%	0.131%
95:4	9864	10445	0.944	0.049%	0.082%	-0.033%	0.067%
96:1	9554	11027	0.866	0.164%	0.155%	0.010%	0.159%
96:2	9903	10367	0.955	0.033%	0.082%	-0.048%	0.059%
96:3	9978	10298	0.969	0.006%	0.084%	-0.078%	0.047%
96:4	9762	10817	0.902	0.090%	0.147%	-0.057%	0.122%
AVG	9897	10377	0.954	0.039%	0.069%	-0.030%	0.055%

Results

The results presented in Tables 7.19 and 7.20 show that the Volatility Break-out (VTY-B) system performs slightly better than the average system in our indicator sample.

With a long call rate of 53.6 percent, this system chooses to be in the market the majority of the time. These long calls have a hit rate of 60.3 percent. This indicator also frequently chooses a short position; the short call rate is 46.4 percent, and these short calls have a hit rate of 60.2 percent.

Relative to the other technical indicators we tested, the VTY-B system has strong long return results. The system tends to choose periods of above-average stock price appreciation to recommend long positions. The average daily stock return for long positions is 0.069 percent, compared to an average stock return of 0.039 percent for cash call days. With an initial investment of $10,000, trading long with this system results in an average quarterly terminal wealth of $10,252. This number falls short of the $10,377 terminal wealth that would be expected from a buy-and-hold-strategy, but, of the sixty technical indicators we tested, it yields the second highest terminal wealth from following a long strategy. Only the Candle Belt Hold, with an average quarterly terminal wealth of $10,252, has a higher return.

The short return results for this system are not as strong as the long re-turn results, but they are slightly stronger than for the average technical indicator. The average stock return on days when short calls are made is 0.039 percent. This is below the average stock return of 0.069 percent when long calls are made, so the system does choose days of below-average market performance to be in a short position. Unfortunately, even though these days are characterized by below-average market performance, they are still, on aver-age, characterized by stock price appreciation. Therefore, being in a short position on these days will lead to losses and declining terminal wealth. Be-ginning each quarter with an initial investment of $10,000 and trading short with this system results in terminal wealth of only $9,897.

Trading short with this system led to a loss in 75 percent of the test quarters. This strategy beat a buy-and-hold strategy in only eleven of the test quarters.

For the most part, trading short with the VTY-B system is unprof-itable. Trading long with this system is more profitable than any other system except the Candle Belt Hold system, but it is not as profitable, on average, as following a buy-and-hold strategy.

Volume Climax

The Volume Climax is based on the premise that as markets reach peaks or valleys in price there is often a panic "sell-off" or "short-covering" move. For example, at market lows, holders of a security fear lower lows; thus, they quickly sell off their holdings. As these holdings are dumped into the market, prices are driven lower and volume is heavy. Likewise, at market highs, short traders fear higher highs and begin to cover their positions. The increased demand for a security drives its price up higher and increases volume. After the fearful traders have made their moves, volume declines and the price reverses.

Construction

Using the Volume Climax (VOL-C) system depends on identifying periods in which volume increased as price increased or decreased. This movement is followed by volume and price reversals that occur at the same time. Constructing a VOL-C system involves using an exponential moving average of volume. Volume spikes that occur a certain percentage above this moving average are volume peaks. Coincident price motion is examined to validate peaks that occur at the same time as price.

Results

The results for the VOL-C indicator in Tables 7.21 and 7.22 point to a major problem with this system—the infrequency of long and short calls. This system makes long calls only 3.7 percent of the time, far below the 40.0 percent optimal long call rate. Short calls occur slightly more often, but the 5.5 percent short call rate is also far below the optimal 39.4 percent short call rate. The hit rate of 59.1 percent for long calls is slightly higher than the 58.7 percent hit rate for short calls. When the hit rate for cash calls is considered, the VOL-C system's recommendations are correct just over three out of five times.

Looking more closely at the test results, we find another shortcoming in this technical indicator's performance. This system fails to predict strong market periods with its long calls, and weak market conditions with its short calls. In fact, the daily return when the indicator makes a long call—0.050 percent—falls short of the 0.055 percent return when the system recommends a cash position over a long position. On average, the system's longs are correct, but the system misses too many times when investors would reap positive returns from being in the market. On average, investors trading long with this system are missing out on a positive 0.055 percent return when they are in cash positions instead of in the market. This is a high price to pay for following the system.

Turning to the short return analysis (Table 7.22b), we see an even bleaker picture. Not only are there missed profitable opportunities, there are actually losses from trading with the system. On average, an investor who begins with $10,000 and trades short with the system for a quarter will lose $19. In only eleven test quarters would this short trading strategy result in

Table 7.21a
Volatility Climax (VOL-C) Long Hit Analysis
(Average of all stocks)

Qtr	Optimal Long	VOL-C Long	Long Hits	Cash Hits	Total Hits	Long Right	Long Wrong	Cash Right	Cash Wrong
85:1	32.1%	2.8%	63.7%	68.1%	67.9%	1.8%	1.0%	66.1%	31.0%
85:2	30.2%	2.8%	62.2%	69.9%	69.7%	1.8%	1.1%	67.9%	29.3%
85:3	26.3%	3.5%	59.1%	73.8%	73.3%	2.1%	1.4%	71.2%	25.3%
85:4	36.6%	2.9%	66.5%	63.4%	63.5%	2.0%	1.0%	61.6%	35.5%
86:1	44.2%	3.5%	62.5%	55.9%	56.2%	2.2%	1.3%	54.0%	42.5%
86:2	39.7%	3.6%	56.1%	60.2%	60.0%	2.0%	1.6%	58.0%	38.4%
86:3	37.0%	4.3%	55.8%	63.1%	62.8%	2.4%	1.9%	60.4%	35.3%
86:4	38.5%	3.0%	59.1%	61.6%	61.5%	1.8%	1.2%	59.7%	37.3%
87:1	44.7%	3.8%	63.6%	55.4%	55.7%	2.4%	1.4%	53.3%	42.9%
87:2	40.0%	4.5%	58.1%	60.1%	60.0%	2.6%	1.9%	57.4%	38.1%
87:3	39.5%	3.3%	57.4%	60.5%	60.4%	1.9%	1.4%	58.5%	38.2%
87:4	37.9%	4.8%	56.4%	62.3%	62.0%	2.7%	2.1%	59.3%	35.9%
88:1	41.3%	3.5%	62.4%	58.8%	58.9%	2.2%	1.3%	56.7%	39.8%
88:2	39.3%	3.2%	60.0%	60.8%	60.8%	1.9%	1.3%	58.8%	37.9%
88:3	35.9%	3.2%	58.8%	64.1%	64.0%	1.9%	1.3%	62.1%	34.7%
88:4	36.3%	3.2%	59.9%	63.7%	63.6%	1.9%	1.3%	61.7%	35.1%
89:1	39.0%	2.7%	61.0%	61.0%	61.0%	1.7%	1.1%	59.3%	37.9%
89:2	40.2%	2.8%	60.9%	59.9%	59.9%	1.7%	1.1%	58.2%	39.0%
89:3	39.9%	2.8%	60.7%	60.1%	60.1%	1.7%	1.1%	58.4%	38.8%
89:4	38.3%	3.2%	59.9%	61.8%	61.7%	1.9%	1.3%	59.8%	37.0%
90:1	36.9%	3.8%	58.6%	63.2%	63.1%	2.3%	1.6%	60.8%	35.4%
90:2	39.2%	2.8%	61.0%	60.9%	60.9%	1.7%	1.1%	59.2%	38.0%
90:3	33.5%	4.7%	51.3%	66.6%	65.9%	2.4%	2.3%	63.5%	31.8%
90:4	40.8%	4.1%	60.6%	59.2%	59.3%	2.5%	1.6%	56.8%	39.1%
91:1	44.1%	3.4%	63.5%	56.0%	56.2%	2.2%	1.2%	54.1%	42.5%
91:2	39.7%	3.5%	59.0%	60.4%	60.4%	2.1%	1.4%	58.3%	38.2%
91:3	40.4%	4.3%	59.0%	59.6%	59.6%	2.6%	1.8%	57.0%	38.6%
91:4	41.2%	3.9%	58.2%	58.9%	58.9%	2.3%	1.6%	56.6%	39.5%
92:1	40.0%	3.7%	56.3%	60.0%	59.8%	2.1%	1.6%	57.8%	38.6%
92:2	38.6%	4.7%	55.2%	61.5%	61.2%	2.6%	2.1%	58.6%	36.7%
92:3	40.3%	4.1%	57.0%	59.7%	59.6%	2.3%	1.8%	57.2%	38.7%
92:4	41.9%	3.8%	60.2%	58.1%	58.2%	2.3%	1.5%	55.9%	40.3%
93:1	42.5%	4.2%	60.0%	57.5%	57.6%	2.5%	1.7%	55.1%	40.8%
93:2	42.1%	4.0%	58.3%	58.0%	58.0%	2.3%	1.7%	55.7%	40.3%
93:3	42.5%	4.0%	59.2%	57.5%	57.6%	2.4%	1.6%	55.2%	40.8%
93:4	41.5%	4.4%	58.5%	58.5%	58.5%	2.6%	1.8%	55.9%	39.6%
94:1	40.4%	3.7%	56.1%	59.6%	59.4%	2.1%	1.6%	57.4%	38.9%
94:2	40.6%	3.4%	55.2%	59.4%	59.2%	1.9%	1.5%	57.4%	39.2%
94:3	41.8%	3.6%	59.8%	58.3%	58.3%	2.1%	1.4%	56.2%	40.2%
94:4	39.5%	4.1%	56.3%	60.5%	60.4%	2.3%	1.8%	58.0%	37.8%
95:1	43.1%	3.3%	59.8%	56.9%	57.0%	2.0%	1.3%	55.0%	41.7%
95:2	43.7%	3.7%	59.0%	56.2%	56.4%	2.2%	1.5%	54.2%	42.1%
95:3	43.9%	3.9%	61.3%	56.2%	56.3%	2.4%	1.5%	54.0%	42.2%
95:4	43.4%	3.9%	57.2%	56.5%	56.6%	2.3%	1.7%	54.3%	41.7%
96:1	45.5%	4.4%	59.1%	54.5%	54.7%	2.6%	1.8%	52.1%	43.5%
96:2	42.1%	4.0%	56.3%	57.9%	57.9%	2.2%	1.7%	55.7%	40.4%
96:3	42.6%	4.4%	57.6%	57.4%	57.4%	2.6%	1.9%	54.8%	40.7%
96:4	44.3%	3.8%	59.6%	55.8%	55.9%	2.3%	1.5%	53.6%	42.6%
AVG	40.0%	3.7%	59.1%	60.2%	60.2%	2.2%	1.5%	58.0%	38.3%

Table 7.21b
Volatility Climax (VOL-C) Short Hit Analysis
(Average of all stocks)

Qtr	Optimal Short	VOL-C Short	Short Hits	Cash Hits	Total Hits	Short Right	Short Wrong	Cash Right	Cash Wrong
85:1	34.3%	4.2%	65.3%	66.0%	65.9%	2.7%	1.5%	63.2%	32.6%
85:2	34.6%	4.5%	64.0%	65.6%	65.5%	2.9%	1.6%	62.6%	32.9%
85:3	38.6%	4.7%	70.6%	61.6%	62.0%	3.3%	1.4%	58.7%	36.6%
85:4	33.1%	5.9%	58.6%	67.0%	66.5%	3.5%	2.4%	63.1%	31.0%
86:1	35.2%	6.0%	54.1%	64.8%	64.2%	3.3%	2.8%	60.9%	33.0%
86:2	39.8%	4.7%	59.5%	60.4%	60.3%	2.8%	1.9%	57.6%	37.8%
86:3	42.7%	5.0%	61.3%	57.5%	57.6%	3.1%	1.9%	54.6%	40.4%
86:4	38.7%	5.7%	59.2%	61.5%	61.4%	3.4%	2.3%	58.0%	36.3%
87:1	36.9%	5.5%	55.1%	63.3%	62.8%	3.0%	2.5%	59.8%	34.7%
87:2	40.0%	5.1%	59.1%	60.1%	60.1%	3.0%	2.1%	57.1%	37.8%
87:3	40.4%	5.9%	59.6%	59.7%	59.7%	3.5%	2.4%	56.2%	37.9%
87:4	45.3%	7.1%	60.3%	54.9%	55.3%	4.3%	2.8%	51.0%	41.9%
88:1	36.7%	6.1%	55.6%	63.4%	62.9%	3.4%	2.7%	59.5%	34.4%
88:2	37.4%	6.4%	58.2%	62.7%	62.4%	3.7%	2.7%	58.7%	34.9%
88:3	38.4%	5.5%	61.2%	61.8%	61.7%	3.3%	2.1%	58.4%	36.2%
88:4	37.0%	5.1%	61.0%	63.1%	63.0%	3.1%	2.0%	59.9%	35.0%
89:1	36.2%	5.3%	57.6%	63.9%	63.5%	3.0%	2.2%	60.5%	34.2%
89:2	35.9%	5.4%	56.9%	64.2%	63.8%	3.1%	2.3%	60.7%	33.9%
89:3	36.4%	5.4%	57.8%	63.7%	63.4%	3.1%	2.3%	60.3%	34.3%
89:4	39.0%	5.4%	60.8%	61.2%	61.1%	3.3%	2.1%	57.9%	36.8%
90:1	40.1%	5.3%	60.9%	60.0%	60.0%	3.2%	2.1%	56.8%	37.9%
90:2	37.8%	5.4%	59.9%	62.3%	62.2%	3.2%	2.2%	58.9%	35.7%
90:3	45.7%	4.8%	64.6%	54.4%	54.9%	3.1%	1.7%	51.8%	43.4%
90:4	37.6%	5.0%	58.0%	62.6%	62.3%	2.9%	2.1%	59.4%	35.6%
91:1	36.7%	4.9%	55.4%	63.3%	62.9%	2.7%	2.2%	60.2%	34.9%
91:2	40.4%	5.9%	61.4%	59.8%	59.9%	3.6%	2.3%	56.3%	37.8%
91:3	39.8%	5.5%	60.1%	60.4%	60.4%	3.3%	2.2%	57.1%	37.4%
91:4	40.5%	5.6%	58.6%	59.6%	59.5%	3.3%	2.3%	56.3%	38.1%
92:1	43.2%	5.9%	59.1%	56.8%	56.9%	3.5%	2.4%	53.5%	40.7%
92:2	42.9%	6.0%	60.1%	57.2%	57.3%	3.6%	2.4%	53.7%	40.2%
92:3	39.5%	5.3%	57.9%	60.5%	60.4%	3.1%	2.2%	57.3%	37.3%
92:4	37.5%	5.1%	57.4%	62.6%	62.3%	2.9%	2.2%	59.4%	35.5%
93:1	39.4%	5.2%	53.7%	60.5%	60.2%	2.8%	2.4%	57.4%	37.4%
93:2	40.9%	6.1%	55.3%	59.1%	58.9%	3.4%	2.7%	55.5%	38.4%
93:3	39.4%	5.9%	57.8%	60.8%	60.6%	3.4%	2.5%	57.2%	36.9%
93:4	41.7%	5.4%	59.7%	58.4%	58.5%	3.2%	2.2%	55.3%	39.3%
94:1	43.7%	5.9%	59.4%	56.4%	56.5%	3.5%	2.4%	53.1%	41.1%
94:2	42.7%	5.4%	58.9%	57.4%	57.4%	3.2%	2.2%	54.3%	40.3%
94:3	39.8%	4.9%	57.4%	60.2%	60.1%	2.8%	2.1%	57.3%	37.8%
94:4	42.8%	5.2%	59.7%	57.3%	57.4%	3.1%	2.1%	54.3%	40.5%
95:1	38.7%	5.4%	56.1%	61.4%	61.1%	3.0%	2.4%	58.1%	36.5%
95:2	38.9%	5.8%	55.2%	61.1%	60.7%	3.2%	2.6%	57.5%	36.7%
95:3	38.9%	5.3%	55.3%	61.1%	60.8%	2.9%	2.4%	57.9%	36.8%
95:4	40.5%	5.4%	55.9%	59.5%	59.3%	3.0%	2.4%	56.3%	38.3%
96:1	38.9%	5.3%	53.5%	61.1%	60.7%	2.8%	2.4%	57.9%	36.8%
96:2	42.4%	6.0%	58.5%	57.8%	57.8%	3.5%	2.5%	54.3%	39.7%
96:3	40.8%	5.6%	58.2%	59.3%	59.3%	3.3%	2.4%	56.0%	38.4%
96:4	39.8%	5.6%	56.0%	60.2%	60.0%	3.2%	2.5%	56.8%	37.5%
AVG	39.4%	5.5%	58.7%	60.8%	60.7%	3.2%	2.3%	57.5%	37.1%

Table 7.22a
Volatility Climax (VOL-C) Long Return Analysis
(Average of all stocks)

Qtr	VOL-C Terminal Wealth	Buy/Hold Terminal Wealth	Relative Terminal Wealth	VOL-C Long Avg Ret	VOL-C Cash Avg Ret	VOL-C Long-Cash Avg Ret	Buy/Hold Avg Ret
85:1	10011	10142	0.987	0.063%	0.005%	0.059%	0.006%
85:2	9994	9700	1.030	-0.038%	-0.070%	0.032%	-0.069%
85:3	9965	8889	1.121	-0.166%	-0.206%	0.041%	-0.205%
85:4	10029	10763	0.932	0.157%	0.105%	0.052%	0.107%
86:1	10044	11428	0.879	0.206%	0.225%	-0.019%	0.225%
86:2	10000	10414	0.960	0.000%	0.069%	-0.069%	0.066%
86:3	9976	9175	1.087	-0.088%	-0.129%	0.041%	-0.128%
86:4	10015	10413	0.962	0.081%	0.069%	0.012%	0.069%
87:1	10081	11929	0.845	0.346%	0.291%	0.055%	0.293%
87:2	10023	10196	0.983	0.084%	0.036%	0.048%	0.038%
87:3	10016	10408	0.962	0.075%	0.068%	0.007%	0.068%
87:4	10014	8087	1.238	0.053%	-0.295%	0.347%	-0.278%
88:1	10034	10989	0.913	0.162%	0.163%	-0.001%	0.163%
88:2	10015	10593	0.945	0.071%	0.101%	-0.030%	0.100%
88:3	10000	10050	0.995	0.001%	0.013%	-0.012%	0.013%
88:4	9992	10196	0.980	-0.040%	0.039%	-0.079%	0.037%
89:1	10010	10698	0.936	0.062%	0.114%	-0.051%	0.112%
89:2	10009	10772	0.929	0.057%	0.124%	-0.067%	0.122%
89:3	10022	10833	0.925	0.128%	0.131%	-0.003%	0.131%
89:4	9996	9904	1.009	-0.019%	-0.011%	-0.008%	-0.011%
90:1	10014	9980	1.003	0.061%	0.000%	0.060%	0.003%
90:2	10015	10459	0.958	0.088%	0.076%	0.012%	0.077%
90:3	9925	8526	1.164	-0.267%	-0.259%	-0.009%	-0.259%
90:4	10024	10889	0.921	0.087%	0.149%	-0.062%	0.146%
91:1	10072	12477	0.807	0.356%	0.314%	0.042%	0.315%
91:2	10008	10244	0.977	0.037%	0.046%	-0.009%	0.045%
91:3	10015	10429	0.960	0.058%	0.065%	-0.007%	0.065%
91:4	10041	10497	0.957	0.168%	0.078%	0.090%	0.082%
92:1	10004	10324	0.969	0.013%	0.049%	-0.036%	0.048%
92:2	9984	9723	1.027	-0.055%	-0.048%	-0.007%	-0.048%
92:3	9995	10392	0.962	-0.020%	0.060%	-0.080%	0.057%
92:4	10028	10963	0.915	0.112%	0.146%	-0.034%	0.144%
93:1	10013	10527	0.951	0.052%	0.081%	-0.029%	0.080%
93:2	10016	10340	0.969	0.064%	0.051%	0.013%	0.052%
93:3	10015	10686	0.937	0.058%	0.103%	-0.045%	0.101%
93:4	9996	10255	0.975	-0.012%	0.036%	-0.048%	0.034%
94:1	10004	9954	1.005	0.013%	-0.012%	0.025%	-0.011%
94:2	9983	9994	0.999	-0.085%	-0.002%	-0.083%	-0.005%
94:3	10028	10613	0.945	0.123%	0.088%	0.034%	0.089%
94:4	9991	9836	1.016	-0.038%	-0.029%	-0.009%	-0.029%
95:1	10017	10706	0.936	0.081%	0.111%	-0.030%	0.110%
95:2	10025	10873	0.922	0.109%	0.135%	-0.026%	0.134%
95:3	10040	10853	0.925	0.165%	0.130%	0.035%	0.131%
95:4	10002	10445	0.958	0.008%	0.069%	-0.061%	0.067%
96:1	10036	11027	0.910	0.129%	0.160%	-0.031%	0.159%
96:2	10001	10367	0.965	0.007%	0.061%	-0.054%	0.059%
96:3	10001	10298	0.971	0.004%	0.049%	-0.045%	0.047%
96:4	10016	10817	0.926	0.066%	0.124%	-0.058%	0.122%
AVG	10012	10377	0.965	0.050%	0.055%	-0.005%	0.055%

Table 7.22b
Volume Climax (VOL-C) Short Return Analysis
(Average of all stocks)

Qtr	VOL-C Terminal Wealth	Buy/Hold Terminal Wealth	Relative Terminal Wealth	VOL-C Short Avg Ret	VOL-C Cash Avg Ret	VOL-C Short-Cash Avg Ret	Buy/Hold Avg Ret
85:1	9998	10142	0.986	0.009%	0.006%	0.003%	0.006%
85:2	10003	9700	1.031	-0.010%	-0.072%	0.063%	-0.069%
85:3	10061	8889	1.132	-0.201%	-0.205%	0.004%	-0.205%
85:4	9936	10763	0.923	0.175%	0.102%	0.073%	0.107%
86:1	9908	11428	0.867	0.258%	0.222%	0.036%	0.225%
86:2	9999	10414	0.960	0.000%	0.070%	-0.070%	0.066%
86:3	10055	9175	1.096	-0.173%	-0.125%	-0.048%	-0.128%
86:4	9973	10413	0.958	0.071%	0.069%	0.002%	0.069%
87:1	9920	11929	0.832	0.243%	0.296%	-0.053%	0.293%
87:2	10004	10196	0.981	-0.018%	0.041%	-0.059%	0.038%
87:3	9977	10408	0.959	0.062%	0.069%	-0.006%	0.068%
87:4	10115	8087	1.251	-0.286%	-0.277%	-0.009%	-0.278%
88:1	9933	10989	0.904	0.177%	0.162%	0.015%	0.163%
88:2	9959	10593	0.940	0.102%	0.100%	0.002%	0.100%
88:3	9984	10050	0.993	0.047%	0.011%	0.036%	0.013%
88:4	9986	10196	0.979	0.042%	0.036%	0.005%	0.037%
89:1	9959	10698	0.931	0.123%	0.112%	0.011%	0.112%
89:2	9948	10772	0.924	0.154%	0.120%	0.034%	0.122%
89:3	9960	10833	0.919	0.119%	0.132%	-0.013%	0.131%
89:4	10027	9904	1.012	-0.081%	-0.007%	-0.074%	-0.011%
90:1	9995	9980	1.002	0.013%	0.002%	0.011%	0.003%
90:2	9976	10459	0.954	0.074%	0.077%	-0.003%	0.077%
90:3	10092	8526	1.184	-0.291%	-0.257%	-0.034%	-0.259%
90:4	9964	10889	0.915	0.104%	0.149%	-0.045%	0.146%
91:1	9896	12477	0.793	0.368%	0.312%	0.055%	0.315%
91:2	10002	10244	0.976	-0.013%	0.049%	-0.062%	0.045%
91:3	9991	10429	0.958	0.024%	0.067%	-0.044%	0.065%
91:4	9979	10497	0.951	0.061%	0.083%	-0.022%	0.082%
92:1	9966	10324	0.965	0.102%	0.045%	0.057%	0.048%
92:2	10024	9723	1.031	-0.064%	-0.047%	-0.017%	-0.048%
92:3	9971	10392	0.959	0.088%	0.055%	0.034%	0.057%
92:4	9957	10963	0.908	0.133%	0.145%	-0.013%	0.144%
93:1	9941	10527	0.944	0.193%	0.074%	0.120%	0.080%
93:2	9966	10340	0.964	0.098%	0.049%	0.049%	0.052%
93:3	9964	10686	0.932	0.099%	0.101%	-0.002%	0.101%
93:4	9998	10255	0.975	0.000%	0.036%	-0.036%	0.034%
94:1	10002	9954	1.005	-0.003%	-0.012%	0.009%	-0.011%
94:2	10004	9994	1.001	-0.012%	-0.004%	-0.008%	-0.005%
94:3	9977	10613	0.940	0.075%	0.090%	-0.015%	0.089%
94:4	10011	9836	1.018	-0.032%	-0.029%	-0.003%	-0.029%
95:1	9982	10706	0.932	0.057%	0.113%	-0.056%	0.110%
95:2	9944	10873	0.915	0.157%	0.133%	0.025%	0.134%
95:3	9937	10853	0.916	0.193%	0.128%	0.065%	0.131%
95:4	9963	10445	0.954	0.109%	0.064%	0.045%	0.067%
96:1	9947	11027	0.902	0.167%	0.158%	0.009%	0.159%
96:2	10000	10367	0.965	-0.001%	0.062%	-0.063%	0.059%
96:3	9981	10298	0.969	0.052%	0.047%	0.005%	0.047%
96:4	9957	10817	0.920	0.125%	0.122%	0.003%	0.122%
AVG	9981	10377	0.962	0.056%	0.055%	0.001%	0.055%

positive profits. (The largest profit, $115, would have occurred in the fourth quarter of 1987.)

The VOL-C system appears to provide little helpful information for investors. First, it makes calls infrequently. Second, the quality of the calls is mediocre to poor.

Volume Trend

The Volume Trend (VOL-T) system is based on the idea that price moves and volume are interrelated. This system assumes that increases in volume indicate support for the market. Therefore, an increase in price accompanied by an increase in volume shows that traders are supporting the market price through increased trading. Likewise, a decrease in price accompanied by an increase in volume indicates market support for the decline.

Construction

The VOL-T system is constructed by defining the average volume move over a period of time. To do this, a lookback time period is chosen, and the moving average of volume over that time period is calculated. Next, the percentage of change in volume that is necessary for detection of a volume trend must be chosen. Finally, a delay period is chosen. This delay period determines how many days the trend must continue before a signal is generated.

As an example, let's say a five-day delay period is chosen. If volume rises for five days in a row and is accompanied by price rising, then an upward trend is detected. The system will generate a long call. If volume rises for five days in a row and is accompanied by price falling, a downward trend is detected and the system generates a bearish, short call.

Results

The results in Tables 7.23 and 7.24 indicate that the VOL-T system underperforms most of the systems in our sample. Surprisingly, the system makes short calls much more frequently—about five times as often—than long calls. The long call rate for this indicator is only 6.1 percent; the short call rate is 31.6 percent.

The results also show that the VOL-T system is slightly more accurate at making short calls than it is at making long calls. The short calls are correct 58.2 percent of the time, and the long calls are correct only 56.8 percent of the time.

Turning to the return analysis for this technical indicator, let's see whether trading with this system can be considered profitable. Trading long with the system is profitable in only 27 of the test quarters. On average, a $10,000 initial investment will yield only a $10 profit per quarter. A major weakness of the VOL-T system is that it chooses a cash position over a long position on days of above-average market performance. These are the days when an investor would definitely want to be in the market. In fact, an investor would have a higher return by trading long when this system suggested a cash position, and remaining in cash when the system suggested a long position!

The short return analysis (Table 7.24b) reveals even worse performance. The average daily stock return when short calls are made is 0.057 percent, which is higher than the average daily stock return of 0.055 percent. The VOL-T system makes short calls during periods of above-average market strength; during these times, investors would want to be in a long position, not a short position. In addition, because the average stock return for short call days is positive, trading short with the system will lead to declining wealth. In fact, for all but nine of the test quarters, the terminal wealth was less than the beginning wealth of $10,000. On average, the quarterly ending wealth is only $9,889, less than the beginning wealth and only 95.3 percent of buy-and-hold terminal wealth.

Using the Volume Trend system alone for trading decisions will not prove to be profitable.

Table 7.23a
Volume Trend (VOL-T) Long Hit Analysis
(Average of all stocks)

Qtr	Optimal Long	VOL-T Long	Long Hits	Cash Hits	Total Hits	Long Right	Long Wrong	Cash Right	Cash Wrong
85:1	32.1%	6.9%	60.9%	68.4%	67.9%	4.2%	2.7%	63.7%	29.4%
85:2	30.2%	5.9%	60.5%	70.1%	69.5%	3.6%	2.3%	65.9%	28.2%
85:3	26.3%	4.8%	56.2%	73.9%	73.0%	2.7%	2.1%	70.4%	24.9%
85:4	36.6%	7.1%	61.7%	63.7%	63.6%	4.4%	2.7%	59.2%	33.7%
86:1	44.2%	8.4%	60.2%	56.0%	56.3%	5.0%	3.3%	51.3%	40.4%
86:2	39.7%	6.5%	56.4%	60.4%	60.1%	3.7%	2.9%	56.4%	37.0%
86:3	37.0%	5.2%	52.2%	63.1%	62.5%	2.7%	2.5%	59.8%	35.0%
86:4	38.5%	6.0%	55.3%	61.6%	61.2%	3.3%	2.7%	57.9%	36.1%
87:1	44.7%	9.1%	58.2%	55.5%	55.7%	5.3%	3.8%	50.5%	40.5%
87:2	40.0%	5.7%	56.8%	60.2%	60.0%	3.2%	2.4%	56.8%	37.6%
87:3	39.5%	6.4%	56.1%	60.6%	60.4%	3.6%	2.8%	56.7%	36.8%
87:4	37.9%	5.1%	56.1%	62.4%	62.1%	2.8%	2.2%	59.2%	35.7%
88:1	41.3%	7.5%	57.1%	58.5%	58.4%	4.3%	3.2%	54.2%	38.4%
88:2	39.3%	5.5%	57.9%	60.7%	60.6%	3.2%	2.3%	57.4%	37.1%
88:3	35.9%	4.1%	55.3%	64.1%	63.7%	2.3%	1.8%	61.4%	34.5%
88:4	36.3%	4.0%	56.0%	63.7%	63.4%	2.2%	1.7%	61.2%	34.9%
89:1	39.0%	5.3%	59.0%	61.2%	61.1%	3.1%	2.2%	57.9%	36.7%
89:2	40.2%	6.3%	58.0%	59.8%	59.7%	3.6%	2.6%	56.1%	37.6%
89:3	39.9%	5.8%	57.8%	60.2%	60.1%	3.4%	2.5%	56.7%	37.5%
89:4	38.3%	4.6%	57.4%	61.9%	61.7%	2.7%	2.0%	59.1%	36.3%
90:1	36.9%	5.2%	53.6%	63.2%	62.7%	2.8%	2.4%	59.9%	34.9%
90:2	39.2%	6.3%	59.0%	61.0%	60.9%	3.7%	2.6%	57.2%	36.6%
90:3	33.5%	4.3%	51.4%	66.7%	66.0%	2.2%	2.1%	63.8%	31.9%
90:4	40.8%	6.4%	56.0%	59.1%	58.9%	3.6%	2.8%	55.4%	38.2%
91:1	44.1%	8.1%	60.6%	56.1%	56.5%	4.9%	3.2%	51.6%	40.3%
91:2	39.7%	6.6%	54.5%	60.4%	60.0%	3.6%	3.0%	56.4%	37.0%
91:3	40.4%	5.6%	55.1%	59.5%	59.3%	3.1%	2.5%	56.2%	38.2%
91:4	41.2%	6.1%	56.2%	58.8%	58.7%	3.4%	2.7%	55.2%	38.6%
92:1	40.0%	7.5%	54.0%	60.1%	59.6%	4.1%	3.5%	55.5%	36.9%
92:2	38.6%	5.0%	53.4%	61.4%	61.0%	2.7%	2.3%	58.3%	36.7%
92:3	40.3%	6.0%	58.3%	59.8%	59.7%	3.5%	2.5%	56.2%	37.8%
92:4	41.9%	6.9%	59.3%	58.2%	58.2%	4.1%	2.8%	54.1%	38.9%
93:1	42.5%	7.0%	57.4%	57.6%	57.5%	4.0%	3.0%	53.5%	39.5%
93:2	42.1%	5.8%	54.3%	57.9%	57.7%	3.1%	2.6%	54.6%	39.7%
93:3	42.5%	5.8%	59.0%	57.6%	57.7%	3.4%	2.4%	54.2%	39.9%
93:4	41.5%	5.8%	55.4%	58.5%	58.3%	3.2%	2.6%	55.1%	39.1%
94:1	40.4%	6.1%	53.0%	59.6%	59.2%	3.3%	2.9%	55.9%	38.0%
94:2	40.6%	5.0%	54.7%	59.4%	59.2%	2.7%	2.2%	56.5%	38.5%
94:3	41.8%	6.0%	55.5%	58.2%	58.0%	3.3%	2.7%	54.7%	39.3%
94:4	39.5%	5.3%	54.0%	60.6%	60.2%	2.9%	2.4%	57.4%	37.3%
95:1	43.1%	6.3%	58.5%	56.9%	57.0%	3.7%	2.6%	53.3%	40.4%
95:2	43.7%	6.5%	58.7%	56.4%	56.5%	3.8%	2.7%	52.7%	40.8%
95:3	43.9%	6.6%	58.4%	56.1%	56.3%	3.9%	2.7%	52.4%	41.0%
95:4	43.4%	5.7%	56.6%	56.6%	56.6%	3.2%	2.5%	53.4%	40.9%
96:1	45.5%	6.9%	58.6%	54.6%	54.9%	4.0%	2.9%	50.8%	42.3%
96:2	42.1%	5.9%	56.3%	58.0%	57.9%	3.3%	2.6%	54.6%	39.6%
96:3	42.6%	6.0%	57.8%	57.4%	57.4%	3.5%	2.6%	54.0%	40.0%
96:4	44.3%	6.9%	58.4%	55.8%	56.0%	4.0%	2.9%	52.0%	41.2%
AVG	40.0%	6.1%	56.8%	60.2%	60.1%	3.5%	2.6%	56.6%	37.3%

Table 7.23b
Volume Trend (VOL-T) Short Hit Analysis
(Average of all stocks)

Qtr	Optimal Short	VOL-T Short	Short Hits	Cash Hits	Total Hits	Short Right	Short Wrong	Cash Right	Cash Wrong
85:1	34.3%	25.2%	63.3%	66.9%	66.0%	15.9%	9.2%	50.1%	24.7%
85:2	34.6%	26.3%	64.9%	66.1%	65.8%	17.1%	9.2%	48.7%	25.0%
85:3	38.6%	29.1%	69.2%	62.3%	64.3%	20.1%	9.0%	44.1%	26.7%
85:4	33.1%	23.7%	59.1%	67.3%	65.3%	14.0%	9.7%	51.3%	25.0%
86:1	35.2%	27.7%	52.8%	64.8%	61.5%	14.7%	13.1%	46.8%	25.4%
86:2	39.8%	31.8%	58.2%	61.1%	60.1%	18.5%	13.3%	41.6%	26.6%
86:3	42.7%	33.9%	60.7%	58.0%	58.9%	20.5%	13.3%	38.3%	27.8%
86:4	38.7%	30.1%	58.3%	61.6%	60.6%	17.5%	12.5%	43.1%	26.9%
87:1	36.9%	27.3%	52.6%	63.2%	60.3%	14.3%	13.0%	46.0%	26.8%
87:2	40.0%	34.1%	57.4%	60.9%	59.7%	19.6%	14.5%	40.2%	25.8%
87:3	40.4%	33.6%	57.9%	60.1%	59.4%	19.5%	14.2%	39.9%	26.5%
87:4	45.3%	47.5%	60.4%	56.0%	58.1%	28.7%	18.8%	29.4%	23.1%
88:1	36.7%	34.6%	55.8%	63.7%	61.0%	19.3%	15.3%	41.7%	23.7%
88:2	37.4%	31.5%	57.7%	63.0%	61.3%	18.1%	13.3%	43.2%	25.4%
88:3	38.4%	30.1%	61.1%	62.6%	62.1%	18.4%	11.7%	43.7%	26.2%
88:4	37.0%	28.5%	60.9%	63.6%	62.9%	17.4%	11.1%	45.5%	26.0%
89:1	36.2%	26.5%	58.1%	64.1%	62.5%	15.4%	11.1%	47.2%	26.4%
89:2	35.9%	24.5%	57.1%	64.5%	62.7%	14.0%	10.5%	48.6%	26.8%
89:3	36.4%	28.1%	57.2%	63.7%	61.9%	16.1%	12.0%	45.8%	26.1%
89:4	39.0%	32.1%	60.2%	61.8%	61.3%	19.3%	12.8%	42.0%	25.9%
90:1	40.1%	31.8%	61.6%	60.7%	61.0%	19.6%	12.2%	41.4%	26.8%
90:2	37.8%	28.9%	59.8%	63.0%	62.0%	17.3%	11.6%	44.8%	26.3%
90:3	45.7%	37.4%	64.2%	55.1%	58.5%	24.0%	13.4%	34.5%	28.1%
90:4	37.6%	32.2%	56.5%	62.8%	60.8%	18.2%	14.0%	42.6%	25.2%
91:1	36.7%	29.3%	55.0%	63.8%	61.2%	16.1%	13.2%	45.1%	25.6%
91:2	40.4%	31.6%	58.1%	60.2%	59.5%	18.4%	13.2%	41.1%	27.2%
91:3	39.8%	30.9%	57.2%	60.5%	59.5%	17.7%	13.2%	41.8%	27.3%
91:4	40.5%	32.4%	57.9%	60.3%	59.5%	18.7%	13.6%	40.8%	26.8%
92:1	43.2%	33.3%	58.4%	57.0%	57.5%	19.5%	13.9%	38.0%	28.7%
92:2	42.9%	35.5%	59.8%	57.5%	58.3%	21.2%	14.3%	37.1%	27.4%
92:3	39.5%	30.3%	58.1%	60.6%	59.9%	17.6%	12.7%	42.2%	27.4%
92:4	37.5%	30.3%	57.2%	63.1%	61.3%	17.4%	13.0%	44.0%	25.7%
93:1	39.4%	32.1%	56.9%	61.2%	59.9%	18.3%	13.8%	41.6%	26.3%
93:2	40.9%	34.5%	56.8%	59.6%	58.6%	19.6%	14.9%	39.0%	26.5%
93:3	39.4%	31.9%	57.3%	61.4%	60.1%	18.3%	13.6%	41.8%	26.3%
93:4	41.7%	33.3%	57.9%	58.8%	58.5%	19.3%	14.0%	39.2%	27.5%
94:1	43.7%	34.0%	58.4%	56.4%	57.1%	19.8%	14.1%	37.2%	28.8%
94:2	42.7%	35.9%	58.2%	57.6%	57.8%	20.9%	15.0%	36.9%	27.2%
94:3	39.8%	29.7%	57.8%	60.6%	59.8%	17.2%	12.5%	42.6%	27.7%
94:4	42.8%	34.6%	59.7%	57.6%	58.3%	20.6%	13.9%	37.7%	27.8%
95:1	38.7%	30.5%	55.0%	61.1%	59.3%	16.8%	13.7%	42.5%	27.0%
95:2	38.9%	30.1%	54.3%	61.0%	59.0%	16.3%	13.8%	42.7%	27.2%
95:3	38.9%	30.5%	55.7%	61.7%	59.9%	17.0%	13.5%	42.9%	26.6%
95:4	40.5%	33.6%	56.0%	60.1%	58.7%	18.8%	14.8%	39.9%	26.5%
96:1	38.9%	32.9%	53.7%	61.4%	58.9%	17.7%	15.3%	41.2%	25.9%
96:2	42.4%	34.8%	57.3%	58.0%	57.7%	19.9%	14.9%	37.8%	27.4%
96:3	40.8%	34.7%	56.7%	59.8%	58.7%	19.7%	15.0%	39.0%	26.3%
96:4	39.8%	32.0%	55.0%	60.5%	58.8%	17.6%	14.4%	41.2%	26.8%
AVG	39.4%	31.6%	58.2%	61.2%	60.3%	18.4%	13.2%	42.0%	26.5%

Table 7.24a
Volume Trend (VOL-T) Long Return Analysis
(Average of all stocks)

Qtr	VOL-T Terminal Wealth	Buy/Hold Terminal Wealth	Relative Terminal Wealth	VOL-T Long Avg Ret	VOL-T Cash Avg Ret	VOL-T Long-Cash Avg Ret	Buy/Hold Avg Ret
85:1	10036	10142	0.990	0.082%	0.001%	0.081%	0.006%
85:2	9966	9700	1.028	-0.093%	-0.068%	-0.025%	-0.069%
85:3	9938	8889	1.118	-0.209%	-0.205%	-0.004%	-0.205%
85:4	10048	10763	0.934	0.107%	0.107%	0.000%	0.107%
86:1	10082	11428	0.882	0.162%	0.230%	-0.069%	0.225%
86:2	10016	10414	0.962	0.041%	0.068%	-0.027%	0.066%
86:3	9939	9175	1.083	-0.185%	-0.124%	-0.061%	-0.128%
86:4	10013	10413	0.962	0.033%	0.072%	-0.039%	0.069%
87:1	10147	11929	0.851	0.261%	0.296%	-0.035%	0.293%
87:2	10003	10196	0.981	0.013%	0.039%	-0.027%	0.038%
87:3	10031	10408	0.964	0.078%	0.068%	0.010%	0.068%
87:4	10024	8087	1.240	0.079%	-0.297%	0.376%	-0.278%
88:1	9962	10989	0.907	-0.076%	0.182%	-0.258%	0.163%
88:2	10000	10593	0.944	0.000%	0.106%	-0.105%	0.100%
88:3	9986	10050	0.994	-0.053%	0.015%	-0.069%	0.013%
88:4	9995	10196	0.980	-0.019%	0.039%	-0.058%	0.037%
89:1	10034	10698	0.938	0.105%	0.113%	-0.008%	0.112%
89:2	10022	10772	0.930	0.056%	0.127%	-0.070%	0.122%
89:3	10032	10833	0.926	0.090%	0.134%	-0.044%	0.131%
89:4	9996	9904	1.009	-0.010%	-0.011%	0.001%	-0.011%
90:1	9975	9980	0.999	-0.076%	0.007%	-0.083%	0.003%
90:2	10028	10459	0.959	0.072%	0.077%	-0.005%	0.077%
90:3	9941	8526	1.166	-0.226%	-0.260%	0.034%	-0.259%
90:4	9986	10889	0.917	-0.031%	0.158%	-0.189%	0.146%
91:1	10171	12477	0.815	0.347%	0.312%	0.035%	0.315%
91:2	9993	10244	0.976	-0.015%	0.050%	-0.065%	0.045%
91:3	9996	10429	0.959	-0.012%	0.069%	-0.081%	0.065%
91:4	9980	10497	0.951	-0.048%	0.090%	-0.138%	0.082%
92:1	10009	10324	0.969	0.021%	0.050%	-0.029%	0.048%
92:2	9952	9723	1.024	-0.156%	-0.043%	-0.114%	-0.048%
92:3	9994	10392	0.962	-0.015%	0.061%	-0.076%	0.057%
92:4	10031	10963	0.915	0.072%	0.150%	-0.078%	0.144%
93:1	10028	10527	0.953	0.064%	0.081%	-0.017%	0.080%
93:2	9977	10340	0.965	-0.066%	0.059%	-0.125%	0.052%
93:3	10026	10686	0.938	0.069%	0.103%	-0.034%	0.101%
93:4	9992	10255	0.974	-0.022%	0.037%	-0.059%	0.034%
94:1	9968	9954	1.001	-0.085%	-0.006%	-0.079%	-0.011%
94:2	9988	9994	0.999	-0.044%	-0.003%	-0.041%	-0.005%
94:3	9993	10613	0.942	-0.022%	0.096%	-0.118%	0.089%
94:4	9972	9836	1.014	-0.087%	-0.026%	-0.061%	-0.029%
95:1	10027	10706	0.937	0.072%	0.112%	-0.040%	0.110%
95:2	10037	10873	0.923	0.091%	0.137%	-0.046%	0.134%
95:3	10022	10853	0.923	0.053%	0.137%	-0.083%	0.131%
95:4	10016	10445	0.959	0.044%	0.068%	-0.024%	0.067%
96:1	10040	11027	0.910	0.092%	0.164%	-0.072%	0.159%
96:2	10020	10367	0.967	0.055%	0.059%	-0.004%	0.059%
96:3	10012	10298	0.972	0.030%	0.048%	-0.019%	0.047%
96:4	10042	10817	0.928	0.098%	0.124%	-0.026%	0.122%
AVG	10010	10377	0.965	0.027%	0.057%	-0.030%	0.055%

Table 7.24b
Volume Trend (VOL-T) Short Return Analysis
(Average of all stocks)

Qtr	VOL-T Terminal Wealth	Buy/Hold Terminal Wealth	Relative Terminal Wealth	VOL-T Short Avg Ret	VOL-T Cash Avg Ret	VOL-T Short-Cash Avg Ret	Buy/Hold Avg Ret
85:1	9964	10142	0.982	0.031%	-0.002%	0.033%	0.006%
85:2	10047	9700	1.036	-0.019%	-0.087%	0.068%	-0.069%
85:3	10317	8889	1.161	-0.161%	-0.223%	0.061%	-0.205%
85:4	9738	10763	0.905	0.181%	0.084%	0.098%	0.107%
86:1	9545	11428	0.835	0.282%	0.203%	0.079%	0.225%
86:2	9884	10414	0.949	0.057%	0.071%	-0.013%	0.066%
86:3	10262	9175	1.119	-0.123%	-0.130%	0.006%	-0.128%
86:4	9783	10413	0.939	0.113%	0.050%	0.063%	0.069%
87:1	9493	11929	0.796	0.313%	0.286%	0.027%	0.293%
87:2	9908	10196	0.972	0.038%	0.038%	0.000%	0.038%
87:3	9832	10408	0.945	0.078%	0.063%	0.015%	0.068%
87:4	10918	8087	1.350	-0.336%	-0.225%	-0.111%	-0.278%
88:1	9584	10989	0.872	0.193%	0.147%	0.046%	0.163%
88:2	9747	10593	0.920	0.128%	0.087%	0.042%	0.100%
88:3	9958	10050	0.991	0.020%	0.009%	0.011%	0.013%
88:4	9922	10196	0.973	0.042%	0.034%	0.007%	0.037%
89:1	9785	10698	0.915	0.134%	0.104%	0.030%	0.112%
89:2	9790	10772	0.909	0.136%	0.118%	0.019%	0.122%
89:3	9730	10833	0.898	0.158%	0.120%	0.038%	0.131%
89:4	10028	9904	1.013	-0.016%	-0.009%	-0.007%	-0.011%
90:1	10023	9980	1.004	-0.014%	0.011%	-0.025%	0.003%
90:2	9910	10459	0.948	0.050%	0.088%	-0.037%	0.077%
90:3	10572	8526	1.240	-0.240%	-0.271%	0.031%	-0.259%
90:4	9618	10889	0.883	0.187%	0.127%	0.060%	0.146%
91:1	9496	12477	0.761	0.296%	0.323%	-0.026%	0.315%
91:2	9872	10244	0.964	0.061%	0.038%	0.023%	0.045%
91:3	9787	10429	0.938	0.111%	0.044%	0.067%	0.065%
91:4	9866	10497	0.940	0.067%	0.089%	-0.023%	0.082%
92:1	9887	10324	0.958	0.055%	0.044%	0.011%	0.048%
92:2	10079	9723	1.037	-0.036%	-0.055%	0.019%	-0.048%
92:3	9854	10392	0.948	0.080%	0.046%	0.034%	0.057%
92:4	9763	10963	0.891	0.124%	0.153%	-0.030%	0.144%
93:1	9895	10527	0.940	0.054%	0.092%	-0.038%	0.080%
93:2	9906	10340	0.958	0.044%	0.056%	-0.012%	0.052%
93:3	9833	10686	0.920	0.085%	0.109%	-0.024%	0.101%
93:4	9973	10255	0.972	0.014%	0.044%	-0.030%	0.034%
94:1	9980	9954	1.003	0.009%	-0.022%	0.031%	-0.011%
94:2	9983	9994	0.999	0.008%	-0.012%	0.020%	-0.005%
94:3	9858	10613	0.929	0.080%	0.093%	-0.013%	0.089%
94:4	10017	9836	1.018	-0.007%	-0.041%	0.034%	-0.029%
95:1	9760	10706	0.912	0.129%	0.102%	0.027%	0.110%
95:2	9686	10873	0.891	0.171%	0.118%	0.054%	0.134%
95:3	9737	10853	0.897	0.143%	0.126%	0.017%	0.131%
95:4	9874	10445	0.945	0.063%	0.069%	-0.006%	0.067%
96:1	9667	11027	0.877	0.165%	0.156%	0.009%	0.159%
96:2	9865	10367	0.952	0.063%	0.056%	0.008%	0.059%
96:3	9897	10298	0.961	0.047%	0.048%	-0.001%	0.047%
96:4	9801	10817	0.906	0.101%	0.132%	-0.031%	0.122%
AVG	9889	10377	0.953	0.057%	0.054%	0.002%	0.055%

Chapter

8

Individual Stock Results

Averaging always masks variation. In the earlier chapters, we have presented results for various indicators averaged across 878 stocks. For the indicators that generally worked well, there were many stocks for which they did not work well. On the other hand, for some stocks, the indicators worked extremely well. In this chapter, we examine some of the details concerning individual stocks. In particular, we focus on stocks for which one or more of the technical indicators provided extremely good trading signals.

Earlier, we encountered certain difficulties in trying to decide whether a particular indicator was performing well. When we examine individual stocks, we also encounter difficulties. We had to ask: Are we most interested in the stocks that had the highest returns for all sixty technical indicators or the stocks that had the highest returns using just one indicator? We have chosen to focus on the latter question because averaging across all sixty indicators would be making use of some indicators that we already know are not very useful.

We also had to decide what return figure to use. Should we focus on the stocks with the highest average returns per long signal or the stocks with the highest average daily return over and above that of a buy-and-hold strategy? Here too, we have chosen the latter path. We focus on the stock/indicator combinations that outperformed the buy-and-hold strategy by the widest margin over the entire testing period. This overlooks some stock/indicator combinations that did even better over a single quarter, or some other shorter time period.

Long-Signal Results

Table 8.1 shows the sorted results for the top 40 stock/indicator combinations for the long signals. First, let's make sure we understand the numbers in the table. Table 8.1 considers only long versus cash allocations. If the indicator says to go long, then we buy the stock and hold it as long as we are getting a long indication. When we do not have a long indication, then we hold cash, earning no interest. The best overall combination was for Enzo Biochem stock (ticker symbol ENZ) using the Bollinger Band with ADX (BOL-T) indicator.

The column labeled *%Long* shows that an investor following the BOL-T signals over the entire 1985–1996 time period for ENZ stock would have averaged being long only 8.9 percent of the time. During the other 91.1 percent of the time, the investor would have been invested in cash. The column labeled *Long Signals Average Return* shows the average daily return for the days when BOL-T signaled to go long. This figure, 1.246 percent, is extremely high as a daily return. For comparison purposes, keep in mind that the average daily return for all 878 stocks over the entire time period was 0.055 percent. The next column, labeled *Overall Average Return*, shows the average daily return for the entire time period. Because the investor would have been in cash 91.1 percent of the time, earning no return, the overall average is roughly one-tenth that of the average return for the long signal days. The final column is labeled *Excess Average Return*. Entries here represent the amount that the overall average return exceeded the average daily return for a buy-and-hold strategy. As can be seen, the excess return for ENZ using BOL-T was 0.106 percent. Beating the buy-and-hold return by roughly one-tenth of a percent per day is a substantial performance. Given the low percentage of long signals, the risk is also lower, if risk is defined as the time the investor's capital is exposed to market forces.

A scanning of the *Technical Indicator* column reveals that four indicators appear in about half the list. They are: (1) Volatility Breakout (VTY-B), which appears eight times; (2) Candle Belt Hold (CN-BH), which appears six times; (3) Average Directional Index Breakout (ADX-B), which appears four times, and (4) Stop and Reverse Crossover (SAR-C), which also appears four times. Three of these four indicators appeared in the upper quartile of overall indicator performance that we discussed in Chapter 2. However, ADX-B was not, in general, a very good indicator for the stocks as a whole. The rest of the indicators that appear in the list occur only once or twice. The tickers for GPS (Gap Inc.) and NATR (Nature's Sunshine) appear four times in Table 8.1. KWD (Kellwood Company) appears three times in the list. The remaining stocks

Table 8.1
Top 40 Long Stock/Indicator Combinations
(Average Daily Returns 1985–1996)

Stock Ticker	Technical Indicator	% Long	Long Signals Average Return	Overall Average Return	Excess Average Return
ENZ	BOL-T	8.905%	1.246%	0.111%	0.106%
MDC	CHA-P	44.359%	0.363%	0.161%	0.084%
SCOR	BND-C	42.718%	0.282%	0.120%	0.082%
LBNA	ADX-B	61.466%	0.204%	0.125%	0.078%
LBNA	MFR-B	54.369%	0.220%	0.120%	0.072%
CNTO	CN-BH	40.007%	0.326%	0.131%	0.072%
INSUA	CN-BH	34.617%	0.340%	0.118%	0.068%
CKR	MV2-C	52.829%	0.193%	0.102%	0.067%
MXM	VTY-B	51.858%	0.243%	0.126%	0.064%
AOS	VTY-B	52.025%	0.222%	0.115%	0.064%
GNT	TXM-FP	45.832%	0.289%	0.133%	0.061%
NATR	CCI-FP	40.978%	0.329%	0.135%	0.061%
ASAI	TRU	49.314%	0.234%	0.115%	0.060%
BMET	ADX-B	61.265%	0.202%	0.123%	0.059%
NATR	CN-BH	30.465%	0.435%	0.133%	0.058%
KWD	VTY-B	52.293%	0.215%	0.112%	0.054%
BQR	CN-BH	41.078%	0.244%	0.100%	0.049%
MIR	CN-BH	38.935%	0.311%	0.121%	0.046%
KWD	MAC-M	51.925%	0.199%	0.103%	0.045%
REY	VTY-B	56.177%	0.194%	0.109%	0.044%
KWD	CN-BH	38.400%	0.266%	0.102%	0.044%
BBN	SAR-C	46.502%	0.220%	0.102%	0.043%
FLK	VTY-B	55.038%	0.227%	0.125%	0.041%
NATR	ROC-C	41.078%	0.278%	0.114%	0.040%
RJF	VTY-B	54.302%	0.200%	0.108%	0.040%
WHX	BOL-C	53.699%	0.484%	0.260%	0.040%
GPS	MFR-B	56.210%	0.243%	0.137%	0.038%
IGT	VAP-B	43.522%	0.243%	0.106%	0.037%
CAS	VTY-B	51.590%	0.200%	0.103%	0.036%
NATR	MOM-P	39.270%	0.274%	0.108%	0.034%
PIOS	SAR-C	54.938%	0.184%	0.101%	0.033%
GPS	RWI-B	60.663%	0.216%	0.131%	0.033%
APOG	SAR-C	55.373%	0.205%	0.114%	0.029%
GNT	TXM-P	47.305%	0.211%	0.100%	0.029%
GPS	MV2-C	60.462%	0.209%	0.127%	0.028%
PD	VTY-B	55.574%	0.193%	0.107%	0.027%
FJC	TRU	51.289%	0.264%	0.135%	0.027%
GPS	SAR-C	55.172%	0.223%	0.123%	0.024%
MDC	ADX-B	55.909%	0.179%	0.100%	0.024%
SYMM	ADX-B	62.136%	0.242%	0.150%	0.023%

appear only once or twice. Almost all of the other stocks appear only once. All in all, the table contains a fairly well mixed group of indicators and stocks.

All of the top 40 stock/indicator combinations in Table 8.1 are quite attractive. All 40 have an average excess return of 0.023 percent or greater. Long signals are occurring roughly half of the time for these combinations.

The summary figures are intriguing, but they raise some questions. The overall result for the entire time period is quite good, but how much consistency existed from one quarter to the next? Is it likely that an investor could have spotted the great performance of these combinations and then jumped on the train early enough to do well? To address this issue, we look at three of the best combinations in more detail.

Table 8.2 shows detailed results for the ENZ/BOL-T combination. The results are presented by quarter and show the same figures as were presented in Table 8.1, with the addition of *Buy-Hold Terminal Wealth* and *Relative Terminal Wealth*. The *Buy-Hold Terminal Wealth* figures provide a quarterly account of how ENZ stock was performing. The stock's price volatility was high. Terminal wealth ranged from a low of $4,014 to a high of $20,028. The many zeros in the *%Long* column provide a warning that something is very unusual. The most unusual entry occurs in the fourth quarter of 1991: the long signals' average return is an astronomical 21.172 percent. This extremely high figure indicates that the price of this stock shot up from a $1–$2 per-share range to a $5–$8 per-share range during that particular quarter. The indicator signaled to go long on some of these extreme days, so the average return was huge.

The unusual result for the ENZ/BOL-T combination is normal in a certain sense. If we examine a large group of stocks over a long time period, there are bound to be some stocks that exhibit some very unusual behavior. Using statistical jargon, these might be considered *outliers*—outcomes that do not seem to match the general behavior of what is being studied. They are not just rare outcomes, but outcomes that are being driven by some circumstance that is not considered typical. We could examine some other statistical properties of the entire results in an effort to determine whether the result for ENZ/BOL-T is an outlier. However, we are trying to follow a more commonsense approach with this book. This result looks unusual. This combination seems to be at the top of the list due to some atypical circumstances and the results are probably not what we could normally expect. Looking back at the results before the end of 1991, we can see that any investor who had been using BOL-T to trade this stock in prior years probably would have decided that it wasn't useful and would have given up.

Some of the other combinations among the top 40 also have patterns that seem to be unusual in one way or another. Again, this is probably to be expected because we are sorting all the results based on one simple criterion: highest excess returns. For stocks that are always falling in price, the best "long" strategy is not to go long. If the price is falling, then the average

Table 8.2
Best Stock Results—Summary Results for
ENZ/BOL-T Combination

Qtr	Buy-Hold Terminal Wealth	Relative Terminal Wealth	% Long	Long Signals Avg Ret	Overall Avg Ret	Excess Avg Ret
85:1	6318	1.583	0.0%	0.000%	0.000%	0.720%
85:2	4924	2.333	0.0%	0.000%	0.000%	1.121%
85:3	4898	2.210	3.2%	-3.007%	-0.095%	1.018%
85:4	7397	1.352	0.0%	0.000%	0.000%	0.427%
86:1	12282	0.814	0.0%	0.000%	0.000%	-0.392%
86:2	9197	1.087	50.8%	-0.335%	-0.170%	-0.077%
86:3	8555	1.249	0.0%	0.000%	0.000%	0.179%
86:4	7684	1.301	0.0%	0.000%	0.000%	0.389%
87:1	12120	0.757	26.2%	0.177%	0.047%	-0.336%
87:2	8947	1.118	0.0%	0.000%	0.000%	0.149%
87:3	6889	1.452	0.0%	0.000%	0.000%	0.567%
87:4	6443	1.700	0.0%	0.000%	0.000%	0.495%
88:1	9443	1.004	0.0%	0.000%	0.000%	0.035%
88:2	13025	0.745	54.8%	0.266%	0.146%	-0.333%
88:3	10561	0.947	74.6%	-0.100%	-0.075%	-0.185%
88:4	6905	1.448	0.0%	0.000%	0.000%	0.517%
89:1	8140	1.229	0.0%	0.000%	0.000%	0.262%
89:2	13272	0.753	0.0%	0.000%	0.000%	-0.502%
89:3	12108	0.826	25.8%	-0.306%	-0.079%	-0.469%
89:4	9018	1.109	0.0%	0.000%	0.000%	0.120%
90:1	10268	0.974	0.0%	0.000%	0.000%	-0.102%
90:2	9657	1.036	0.0%	0.000%	0.000%	0.026%
90:3	8489	1.105	0.0%	0.000%	0.000%	0.137%
90:4	10207	0.945	0.0%	0.000%	0.000%	-0.178%
91:1	8149	1.227	0.0%	0.000%	0.000%	0.114%
91:2	4014	2.491	0.0%	0.000%	0.000%	1.165%
91:3	20028	0.326	0.0%	0.000%	0.000%	-1.535%
91:4	9292	1.076	23.8%	21.172%	5.041%	1.455%
92:1	4402	2.272	0.0%	0.000%	0.000%	0.869%
92:2	6268	1.595	0.0%	0.000%	0.000%	0.649%
92:3	10718	0.862	22.2%	1.156%	0.257%	0.076%
92:4	19694	0.379	6.3%	0.051%	0.003%	-1.160%
93:1	8669	1.154	0.0%	0.000%	0.000%	0.144%
93:2	11473	0.872	22.6%	0.238%	0.054%	-0.210%
93:3	13461	0.743	15.9%	0.683%	0.108%	-0.442%
93:4	9111	1.098	12.7%	-0.208%	-0.026%	0.057%
94:1	7528	1.441	0.0%	0.000%	0.000%	0.390%
94:2	6481	1.457	0.0%	0.000%	0.000%	0.639%
94:3	14442	0.692	14.3%	0.151%	0.022%	-0.618%
94:4	7617	1.387	12.9%	0.805%	0.104%	0.499%
95:1	8381	1.129	0.0%	0.000%	0.000%	0.263%
95:2	10775	0.928	3.2%	0.564%	0.018%	-0.125%
95:3	15179	0.659	6.5%	3.546%	0.229%	-0.495%
95:4	7752	1.290	50.0%	-0.632%	-0.316%	-0.009%
96:1	9858	1.014	0.0%	0.000%	0.000%	-0.032%
96:2	8616	1.161	0.0%	0.000%	0.000%	0.219%
96:3	11281	0.886	0.0%	0.000%	0.000%	-0.262%
96:4	10555	0.947	0.0%	0.000%	0.000%	-0.110%

Table 8.3
Best Stock Results—Summary Results for
CNTO/CN-BH Combination

Qtr	Buy-Hold Terminal Wealth	Relative Terminal Wealth	% Long	Long Signals Avg Ret	Overall Avg Ret	Excess Avg Ret
85:1	6824	1.654	13.1%	-0.319%	-0.042%	0.562%
85:2	6360	1.746	8.1%	-0.576%	-0.046%	0.665%
85:3	5618	1.924	0.0%	0.000%	0.000%	0.903%
85:4	8563	1.083	19.0%	-0.132%	-0.025%	0.198%
86:1	15996	0.458	31.7%	0.941%	0.298%	-0.530%
86:2	12846	0.753	42.9%	0.710%	0.304%	-0.163%
86:3	6224	2.116	14.3%	0.918%	0.131%	0.798%
86:4	9730	1.057	34.9%	-0.359%	-0.125%	-0.123%
87:1	14702	0.537	42.6%	0.510%	0.217%	-0.454%
87:2	9750	1.068	54.8%	0.109%	0.060%	0.079%
87:3	9552	1.200	44.4%	0.305%	0.135%	0.177%
87:4	6245	2.412	65.1%	-0.084%	-0.054%	0.568%
88:1	11467	0.714	30.6%	0.033%	0.010%	-0.243%
88:2	9310	1.122	38.7%	-0.189%	-0.073%	0.027%
88:3	8385	1.297	33.3%	-0.303%	-0.101%	0.169%
88:4	8341	1.276	12.9%	-1.155%	-0.149%	0.113%
89:1	13000	0.750	55.7%	0.629%	0.351%	-0.101%
89:2	8832	1.192	55.6%	-0.060%	-0.033%	0.152%
89:3	12814	0.589	50.0%	0.109%	0.055%	-0.381%
89:4	10302	1.053	50.0%	0.478%	0.239%	0.155%
90:1	12137	0.682	43.5%	-0.154%	-0.067%	-0.428%
90:2	12476	0.700	40.3%	0.532%	0.214%	-0.183%
90:3	8021	1.344	29.0%	-0.089%	-0.026%	0.279%
90:4	12099	0.773	50.8%	0.460%	0.233%	-0.115%
91:1	15775	0.498	41.7%	1.216%	0.507%	-0.293%
91:2	9154	0.958	49.2%	-0.494%	-0.243%	-0.152%
91:3	9093	1.028	14.3%	-0.473%	-0.068%	0.019%
91:4	8645	1.110	25.4%	-0.328%	-0.083%	0.113%
92:1	5037	2.933	24.2%	-0.026%	-0.006%	1.023%
92:2	8376	1.160	51.6%	-0.148%	-0.076%	0.030%
92:3	6817	1.983	36.5%	-0.028%	-0.010%	0.565%
92:4	16583	0.557	57.1%	1.245%	0.711%	-0.179%
93:1	16622	0.536	60.7%	1.430%	0.868%	-0.088%
93:2	15735	0.718	56.5%	1.247%	0.704%	-0.108%
93:3	15504	0.578	50.8%	0.848%	0.431%	-0.340%
93:4	10205	1.221	54.0%	0.549%	0.296%	0.170%
94:1	9397	1.108	53.2%	0.262%	0.139%	0.195%
94:2	9264	1.474	47.5%	1.179%	0.561%	0.565%
94:3	18335	0.424	33.3%	2.181%	0.727%	-0.291%
94:4	6592	1.700	33.9%	-0.855%	-0.290%	0.340%
95:1	10192	1.040	56.5%	0.130%	0.073%	-0.009%
95:2	8605	1.126	33.9%	-0.399%	-0.135%	0.058%
95:3	8292	1.483	40.3%	0.145%	0.058%	0.332%
95:4	19097	0.394	62.9%	1.033%	0.650%	-0.491%
96:1	13087	0.777	75.8%	0.418%	0.317%	-0.172%
96:2	7665	1.341	53.2%	-0.457%	-0.243%	0.143%
96:3	10818	0.767	20.6%	-0.372%	-0.077%	-0.291%
96:4	8591	1.323	27.0%	-0.008%	-0.002%	0.167%

buy-and-hold return will be negative. If the return from "long" signals is zero, then the excess return is positive. If the stock is falling severely in price and the indicator signals to stay in cash, then the excess return will be strongly positive. Some of these outcomes occurred with the ENZ/BOL-T combination.

Let's examine the Centocor Inc./Candle Belt Hold (CNTO/CN-BH) combination, which is sixth among the top 40. The results for this combination are shown in Table 8.3. This stock has some pretty large swings in price, as revealed in the *Buy-Hold Terminal Wealth* column. Large movements also create investment opportunities. For the four quarters of 1985, the stock fell in price and the CN-BH indicator primarily signaled to be in cash, as evidenced by the low *%Long* figures. As we discussed in the previous paragraph, this leads to a good excess figure. In the first two quarters of 1986, the stock moved up in price. The *Long Signals Average Return* was high for these quarters, but because the average buy-and-hold return was also quite high, the excess return was negative. Notice how low the *Relative Terminal Wealth* was for these two quarters.

Rather than continue this research quarter by quarter, we can look at Figure 8.1 to see that the pattern of excess return is highly volatile. Cover up the right side of the graph from 1991 on. Now, imagine that you are an investor at the beginning of 1991, and you are looking at the left side of the graph. Would you be saying: "This looks like a great indicator to use for this

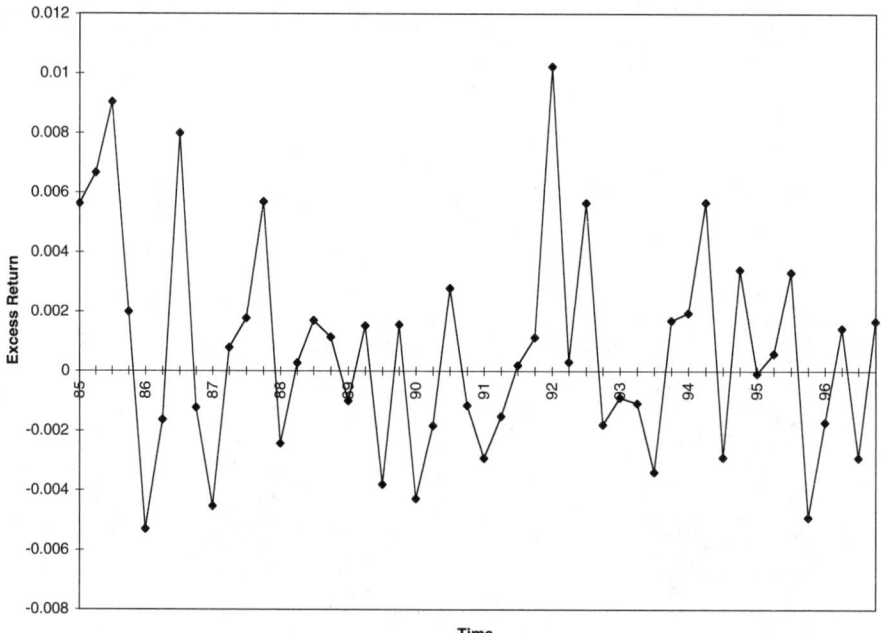

Figure 8.1 CNTO/CN-BH long combination.

Table 8.4
Best Stock Results—Summary Results for
MXM/VTY-B Combination

Qtr	Buy-Hold Terminal Wealth	Relative Terminal Wealth	% Long	Long Signals Avg Ret	Overall Avg Ret	Excess Avg Ret
85:1	9435	1.081	62.3%	-0.096%	-0.060%	0.033%
85:2	9548	1.015	37.1%	-0.320%	-0.119%	-0.048%
85:3	11437	0.784	57.1%	0.078%	0.044%	-0.172%
85:4	10569	0.886	33.3%	-0.035%	-0.012%	-0.104%
86:1	11239	0.910	56.7%	0.428%	0.243%	0.040%
86:2	9104	1.212	33.3%	0.042%	0.014%	0.159%
86:3	9799	1.037	42.9%	-0.001%	-0.001%	0.028%
86:4	7206	1.917	30.2%	0.143%	0.043%	0.536%
87:1	13082	0.749	75.4%	0.563%	0.425%	-0.033%
87:2	11368	0.853	64.5%	0.265%	0.171%	-0.046%
87:3	10713	0.875	69.8%	0.023%	0.016%	-0.099%
87:4	6549	2.079	31.7%	-0.391%	-0.124%	0.516%
88:1	11487	0.876	46.8%	0.536%	0.251%	0.014%
88:2	11545	1.064	50.0%	1.252%	0.626%	0.341%
88:3	12693	0.801	84.1%	0.505%	0.425%	0.028%
88:4	15317	0.531	85.5%	0.488%	0.417%	-0.318%
89:1	12273	0.853	42.6%	1.139%	0.485%	0.094%
89:2	11755	0.804	36.5%	0.516%	0.188%	-0.086%
89:3	11566	0.865	46.8%	0.558%	0.261%	0.009%
89:4	10093	1.052	71.0%	0.278%	0.197%	0.123%
90:1	8843	1.252	30.6%	0.064%	0.020%	0.186%
90:2	9863	1.051	71.0%	0.090%	0.064%	0.066%
90:3	15127	0.679	72.6%	1.076%	0.781%	0.063%
90:4	6388	1.919	25.4%	-0.978%	-0.248%	0.371%
91:1	13528	0.735	61.7%	0.936%	0.577%	0.000%
91:2	9530	1.040	54.0%	-0.115%	-0.062%	-0.006%
91:3	7562	1.547	30.2%	-0.592%	-0.179%	0.256%
91:4	8435	1.438	39.7%	0.183%	0.072%	0.319%
92:1	11285	0.790	64.5%	0.071%	0.046%	-0.179%
92:2	7898	1.456	22.6%	-0.537%	-0.121%	0.241%
92:3	8208	1.527	30.2%	0.255%	0.077%	0.370%
92:4	10723	0.816	57.1%	-0.124%	-0.071%	-0.201%
93:1	10630	0.863	52.5%	0.005%	0.003%	-0.131%
93:2	8926	1.208	35.5%	-0.066%	-0.023%	0.136%
93:3	10893	0.764	61.9%	-0.192%	-0.119%	-0.283%
93:4	12143	0.770	79.4%	0.287%	0.228%	-0.099%
94:1	9574	1.114	48.4%	0.099%	0.048%	0.107%
94:2	9895	1.022	44.3%	0.039%	0.017%	0.025%
94:3	10576	0.940	47.6%	0.231%	0.110%	0.003%
94:4	9184	1.180	43.5%	0.018%	0.008%	0.134%
95:1	9283	1.056	32.3%	-0.431%	-0.139%	-0.027%
95:2	11711	0.812	74.2%	0.243%	0.180%	-0.080%
95:3	16238	0.532	67.7%	0.915%	0.620%	-0.217%
95:4	5775	2.792	46.8%	-0.070%	-0.033%	0.806%
96:1	13256	0.707	71.0%	0.523%	0.371%	-0.100%
96:2	8709	1.319	43.5%	0.032%	0.014%	0.229%
96:3	10577	0.943	50.8%	0.214%	0.109%	0.005%
96:4	11196	0.920	74.6%	0.335%	0.250%	0.056%

stock"? Probably not. The ideal situation from an investments perspective is to have a consistent pattern. We would like to be finding situations where an indicator has consistently good performance.

Another long combination, MAXXAM INC./Volatility Breakout (MXM/VTY-B), is shown in Table 8.4 and Figure 8.2. Here again, the performance is fairly erratic, as can be seen in Figure 8.2. However, positive excess returns are more frequent than negative excess returns and also seem to be larger in absolute value. In other words, when the news is good, it is generally more good than the bad news is bad. The worst excess return is –0.318 percent, but the best excess return is 0.806 percent. The results for this stock and this indicator may not be telling you to rush out and start using technical indicators for trading. However, we have to keep in mind that any advantage we are going to gain is probably going to be narrow. Apparently, we will need to be content with results that are just slightly better than average and are not always consistent.

Short-Signal Results

Summary results for the best short combinations can be seen in Table 8.5. The columns and their interpretation are the same as for Table 8.1, with one

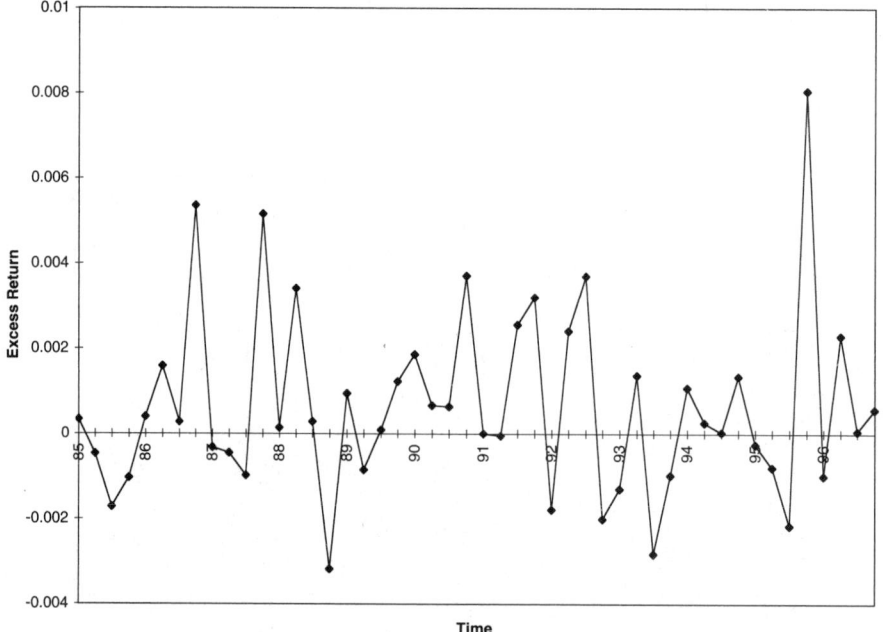

Figure 8.2 MXM/VTY-B long combination.

Table 8.5
Top 40 Short Stock/Indicator Combinations
(Average Daily Returns 1985–1996)

Stock Ticker	Technical Indicator	% Short	Short Signals Average Return	Overall Average Return	Excess Average Return
BRR	RWI-B	52.461%	-0.475%	0.249%	0.494%
BRR	ADX-B	43.689%	-0.563%	0.246%	0.491%
BRR	KBA-C	45.497%	-0.485%	0.221%	0.466%
BRR	GAP-B	41.078%	-0.501%	0.206%	0.451%
BRR	VTY-B	54.972%	-0.337%	0.185%	0.431%
BRR	CCI-P	51.992%	-0.314%	0.163%	0.408%
BRR	MFR-C	52.159%	-0.304%	0.159%	0.404%
BRR	SAR-C	49.381%	-0.318%	0.157%	0.402%
BRR	TXM-FP	44.426%	-0.334%	0.148%	0.394%
BRR	CCI-FP	48.945%	-0.295%	0.144%	0.390%
BRR	BOL-C	50.017%	-0.274%	0.137%	0.383%
BRR	MFR-B	43.488%	-0.305%	0.133%	0.378%
BRR	TXM-P	47.372%	-0.277%	0.131%	0.376%
BRR	TLN-BS	43.689%	-0.269%	0.117%	0.363%
BRR	RSI-P	49.280%	-0.232%	0.115%	0.360%
BRR	MV2-C	46.535%	-0.242%	0.113%	0.358%
BRR	MAC-M	49.012%	-0.217%	0.106%	0.352%
BRR	MOM-P	44.258%	-0.235%	0.104%	0.350%
BRR	RSI-C	49.883%	-0.199%	0.099%	0.345%
BRR	ROC-C	48.845%	-0.193%	0.094%	0.340%
PLX	RWI-B	55.005%	-0.271%	0.149%	0.242%
PLX	ADX-B	48.477%	-0.290%	0.141%	0.234%
NAV	CHA-P	56.512%	-0.212%	0.120%	0.217%
PLX	MFR-B	45.765%	-0.242%	0.111%	0.204%
OHM	MFR-C	41.748%	-0.250%	0.104%	0.199%
AAPL	MV2-C	47.941%	-0.253%	0.121%	0.194%
PLX	TLN-BS	50.418%	-0.192%	0.097%	0.190%
VLSI	ADX-B	44.861%	-0.243%	0.109%	0.190%
NAV	CN-BH	39.973%	-0.230%	0.092%	0.189%
AAPL	RWI-B	46.870%	-0.247%	0.116%	0.188%
PLX	TLN-BM	37.864%	-0.249%	0.094%	0.188%
NAV	MFR-B	49.782%	-0.181%	0.090%	0.187%
VLSI	MFR-B	41.915%	-0.248%	0.104%	0.185%
NAV	RWI-B	57.549%	-0.152%	0.088%	0.185%
MB	WLR-P	49.012%	-0.209%	0.103%	0.181%
NAV	MV2-C	58.185%	-0.143%	0.083%	0.180%
NAV	TRU	48.611%	-0.171%	0.083%	0.180%
NAV	SAR-C	54.603%	-0.147%	0.080%	0.177%
VLSI	MV2-C	46.669%	-0.201%	0.094%	0.175%
DIGI	RWI-B	47.874%	-0.230%	0.110%	0.174%

minor qualification. The column labeled *Short Signals Average Return* contains negative values because these are the corresponding returns, or price changes. If, however, we had sold the stock short, then these negative signs would have been reversed and delivered good news instead of bad news. The overall average return takes this into account; effectively, it flips the negative returns on short signal days to positive values and considers all other days to have a zero return owing to a cash position. The *Excess Average Return* column is the difference between the overall average return from the shorting strategy and the return from a buy-and-hold (long) strategy. Therefore, the excess return figures are all positive. The fact that all of the *Short Signals Average Return* figures are negative is encouraging; this is what we want. Remember that we did not see this when we looked at the overall indicator summary results in Table 2.2.

A review of Table 8.5 reveals that four indicators appear three times or more. The Random Walk Breakout (RWI-B) shows up five times and is followed by four appearances of the Moving Average Crossover (MV2-C). Average Directional Index Breakout (ADX-B) and Money Flow RSI Breakout (MFR-B) show up three times in the list. The remaining indicators all appear either once or twice. Therefore, the clumping of indicators in this list is similar to what we saw for the long signals in Table 8.1, although the specific indicators are different. The ticker list, however, is completely dominated by BRR (Barrett Resources), which shows up in the first 20 entries (half of this top 40 list). There are only eight different companies in the entire list. One immediately suspects that some or all of these eight stocks experienced especially sharp downturns that created large potential gains for shorting strategies. Further investigation shows that this was indeed the case.

Table 8.6 shows the quarterly results for the Barrett Resources/Random Walk Breakout (BRR/RWI-B) short combination. Because BRR appeared in half of the top 40 list, the first thing to examine is the underlying performance of this stock. Indeed, we see that this stock was experiencing great trouble over the first eleven quarters of the time period. A $10,000 initial long investment at the start of each of these quarters was being cut in half or reduced more on a quarterly basis. That situation gets old very fast. However, for investors on the short side, this is a golden opportunity. The severe drops in these first eleven quarters (and a few later bad quarters) provided an opportunity for almost any substantial shorting of the stock in those periods to be quite lucrative. That is why so many combinations that include this stock show up in Table 8.5.

However, the Random Walk Breakout (RWI-B) indicator did not just blindly signal to always go short for this stock. In quarters three through eleven, it did signal 100 percent to be short, leading to high returns. But, in later periods, the *%Short* is at low levels—sometimes when the stock was rising

Table 8.6
Best Stock Results—Summary Results for
BRR/RWI-B Combination

Qtr	Buy-Hold Terminal Wealth	Relative Terminal Wealth	% Short	Short Signals Avg Ret	Overall Avg Ret	Excess Avg Ret
85:1	3657	2.735	0.0%	0.000%	0.000%	1.538%
85:2	4572	2.342	33.9%	-0.337%	0.114%	1.325%
85:3	5279	3.400	100.0%	-0.969%	0.969%	1.937%
85:4	3570	6.710	100.0%	-1.497%	1.497%	2.993%
86:1	2367	13.925	100.0%	-2.169%	2.169%	4.337%
86:2	2167	16.159	100.0%	-2.179%	2.179%	4.359%
86:3	2822	9.031	100.0%	-1.733%	1.733%	3.466%
86:4	2265	15.001	100.0%	-2.122%	2.122%	4.245%
87:1	3251	7.696	100.0%	-1.650%	1.650%	3.300%
87:2	2865	10.261	100.0%	-1.864%	1.864%	3.728%
87:3	4035	4.016	82.5%	-0.989%	0.816%	2.164%
87:4	10119	0.853	81.0%	0.166%	-0.134%	-0.250%
88:1	17408	0.478	17.7%	1.579%	-0.280%	-1.207%
88:2	13258	0.659	66.1%	0.304%	-0.201%	-0.682%
88:3	8567	1.319	55.6%	-0.422%	0.234%	0.416%
88:4	12186	0.771	62.9%	0.131%	-0.082%	-0.429%
89:1	10244	0.966	24.6%	-0.009%	0.002%	-0.073%
89:2	11864	0.782	3.2%	3.619%	-0.115%	-0.459%
89:3	10765	0.828	79.0%	0.209%	-0.165%	-0.317%
89:4	13757	0.667	17.7%	0.659%	-0.117%	-0.717%
90:1	11509	0.753	16.1%	1.266%	-0.204%	-0.484%
90:2	10156	0.985	0.0%	0.000%	0.000%	-0.044%
90:3	11919	0.824	8.1%	0.325%	-0.026%	-0.331%
90:4	9269	1.086	69.8%	-0.037%	0.026%	0.125%
91:1	9976	0.959	81.7%	0.047%	-0.038%	-0.070%
91:2	9346	0.877	79.4%	0.345%	-0.274%	-0.226%
91:3	13042	0.551	88.9%	0.547%	-0.486%	-0.946%
91:4	6429	1.954	49.2%	-0.793%	0.390%	1.046%
92:1	7549	1.778	85.5%	-0.588%	0.503%	0.922%
92:2	8568	0.973	58.1%	0.455%	-0.264%	-0.062%
92:3	13460	0.743	0.0%	0.000%	0.000%	-0.527%
92:4	10149	0.840	28.6%	0.749%	-0.214%	-0.311%
93:1	13301	0.583	59.0%	0.630%	-0.372%	-0.902%
93:2	9250	1.157	16.1%	-0.730%	0.118%	0.210%
93:3	11794	0.687	69.8%	0.425%	-0.297%	-0.600%
93:4	8848	1.135	81.0%	-0.035%	0.029%	0.197%
94:1	15531	0.571	8.1%	2.362%	-0.190%	-0.928%
94:2	10992	0.953	37.7%	-0.221%	0.083%	-0.100%
94:3	14009	0.634	6.3%	2.878%	-0.183%	-0.747%
94:4	10869	0.813	32.3%	0.602%	-0.194%	-0.357%
95:1	9391	1.013	62.9%	0.108%	-0.068%	0.012%
95:2	10628	0.820	41.9%	0.512%	-0.215%	-0.335%
95:3	10387	0.922	54.8%	0.105%	-0.058%	-0.136%
95:4	12635	0.747	22.6%	0.407%	-0.092%	-0.486%
96:1	9184	1.033	82.3%	0.085%	-0.070%	0.048%
96:2	10205	0.996	24.2%	-0.121%	0.029%	-0.023%
96:3	11711	0.782	17.5%	0.772%	-0.135%	-0.408%
96:4	12404	0.758	11.1%	0.881%	-0.098%	-0.458%

Table 8.7
Best Stock Results—Summary Results for
PLX/RWI-B Combination

Qtr	Buy-Hold Terminal Wealth	Relative Terminal Wealth	% Short	Short Signals Avg Ret	Overall Avg Ret	Excess Avg Ret
85:1	4727	3.376	83.6%	-0.958%	0.801%	1.978%
85:2	5990	2.701	100.0%	-0.800%	0.800%	1.600%
85:3	3961	5.847	100.0%	-1.396%	1.396%	2.793%
85:4	4105	5.577	100.0%	-1.361%	1.361%	2.723%
86:1	5003	3.728	100.0%	-1.092%	1.092%	2.184%
86:2	6313	1.584	44.4%	0.000%	0.000%	0.695%
86:3	5589	1.920	20.6%	-0.562%	0.116%	1.010%
86:4	5649	1.770	9.5%	0.000%	0.000%	0.864%
87:1	4649	2.916	54.1%	-0.973%	0.526%	1.728%
87:2	5246	3.487	100.0%	-1.006%	1.006%	2.011%
87:3	13001	0.522	17.5%	3.267%	-0.570%	-1.132%
87:4	3796	3.755	100.0%	-1.043%	1.043%	2.087%
88:1	19578	0.411	12.9%	2.321%	-0.299%	-1.602%
88:2	20676	0.421	14.5%	1.335%	-0.194%	-1.479%
88:3	7922	1.263	69.8%	-0.248%	0.173%	0.330%
88:4	11236	0.625	79.0%	0.431%	-0.341%	-0.796%
89:1	12253	0.771	68.9%	0.078%	-0.054%	-0.516%
89:2	13112	0.736	4.8%	1.177%	-0.056%	-0.535%
89:3	10652	0.909	35.5%	0.087%	-0.031%	-0.178%
89:4	11923	0.623	85.5%	0.497%	-0.425%	-0.775%
90:1	12906	0.674	32.3%	0.667%	-0.215%	-0.717%
90:2	9400	1.115	100.0%	-0.088%	0.088%	0.175%
90:3	10542	0.883	6.5%	1.755%	-0.113%	-0.214%
90:4	8503	1.290	84.1%	-0.207%	0.174%	0.404%
91:1	10951	0.875	25.0%	0.281%	-0.070%	-0.233%
91:2	8580	1.338	100.0%	-0.231%	0.231%	0.463%
91:3	29251	0.316	12.7%	0.943%	-0.120%	-1.965%
91:4	6413	2.113	44.4%	-1.179%	0.524%	1.133%
92:1	9038	0.826	69.4%	0.608%	-0.422%	-0.330%
92:2	10493	1.045	38.7%	-0.464%	0.180%	0.011%
92:3	7016	1.695	76.2%	-0.429%	0.327%	0.810%
92:4	8050	1.503	71.4%	-0.512%	0.365%	0.633%
93:1	9335	1.263	50.8%	-0.564%	0.286%	0.351%
93:2	10994	0.865	14.5%	0.540%	-0.078%	-0.265%
93:3	9377	1.105	98.4%	-0.081%	0.080%	0.159%
93:4	8143	1.276	65.1%	-0.134%	0.087%	0.382%
94:1	7415	1.645	82.3%	-0.414%	0.340%	0.800%
94:2	9832	0.975	41.0%	0.129%	-0.053%	-0.067%
94:3	10368	1.039	39.7%	-0.317%	0.126%	0.039%
94:4	10226	0.935	100.0%	0.054%	-0.054%	-0.108%
95:1	11799	0.833	43.5%	0.037%	-0.016%	-0.311%
95:2	11028	0.776	25.8%	0.850%	-0.219%	-0.422%
95:3	10455	0.900	40.3%	0.220%	-0.089%	-0.233%
95:4	10078	1.001	64.5%	-0.046%	0.030%	-0.024%
96:1	11152	0.874	40.3%	0.077%	-0.031%	-0.229%
96:2	15653	0.538	24.2%	1.112%	-0.269%	-1.023%
96:3	10181	0.901	11.1%	1.208%	-0.134%	-0.192%
96:4	11523	0.792	38.1%	0.365%	-0.139%	-0.385%

in value, which would be desirable. Nevertheless, the early quarters tell most of the story for this stock, with this indicator and other indicators.

In Table 8.7 and Figure 8.3, we look at the Plains Resources/Random Walk Breakout (PLX/RWI-B) short combination. This stock has a price pattern similar to that of BRR; the first ten quarters are all periods of declining price. However, something interesting occurs during the second and third quarters of 1987. The recommendation switches from 100.0 percent short to only 17.5 percent short while the *Buy-Hold Terminal Wealth* is changing from $5,246 to $13,001. In general terms, this change is what we would like to see. Unfortunately, even though there were a few short signals in the third quarter of 1987, they were generally very bad calls, as can be seen by the high level of the short signal average return, 2.321 percent. The pre- and post-1988 performance of this combination is quite different, as can be seen in Figure 8.3. Some things appear to be happening correctly with this indicator for this stock, but an overall inconsistency is troubling.

The OHM Corp./Money Flow RSI Crossover (OHM/MFR-C) short combination is shown in Table 8.8 and Figure 8.4. Once again the performance is fairly erratic; however, there are some periods of amazing performance. In the third quarter of 1985, the *Excess Average Return* is over 2 percent. Looking at just the left side of Figure 8.4 doesn't inspire confidence in the consistency of this indicator, although most of the negative excess returns are followed by enough positive outcomes to offset the negative

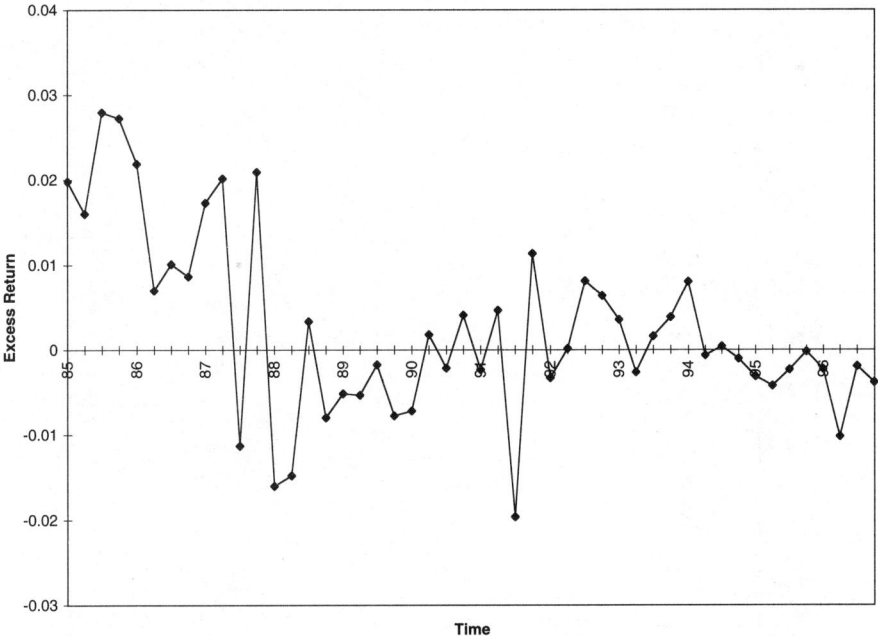

Figure 8.3   PLX/RWI-B short combination.

Table 8.8
Best Stock Results—Summary Results for
OHM/MFR-C Combination

Qtr	Buy-Hold Terminal Wealth	Relative Terminal Wealth	% Short	Short Signals Avg Ret	Overall Avg Ret	Excess Avg Ret
85:1	4945	3.245	78.7%	-1.008%	0.793%	1.921%
85:2	7355	1.662	61.3%	-0.535%	0.328%	0.817%
85:3	4815	3.903	92.1%	-1.109%	1.021%	2.157%
85:4	8759	1.235	93.7%	-0.148%	0.139%	0.335%
86:1	10263	0.993	50.0%	-0.095%	0.048%	-0.037%
86:2	8878	1.314	66.7%	-0.384%	0.256%	0.426%
86:3	7420	1.629	71.4%	-0.459%	0.328%	0.769%
86:4	13531	0.727	69.8%	0.002%	-0.002%	-0.525%
87:1	10629	0.946	41.0%	-0.064%	0.026%	-0.108%
87:2	9291	1.005	3.2%	3.376%	-0.109%	-0.021%
87:3	12152	0.749	28.6%	0.501%	-0.143%	-0.476%
87:4	4740	4.280	63.5%	-1.879%	1.193%	2.263%
88:1	12518	0.746	27.4%	0.378%	-0.104%	-0.499%
88:2	7961	1.350	62.9%	-0.207%	0.130%	0.469%
88:3	11914	0.722	36.5%	0.636%	-0.232%	-0.533%
88:4	9076	1.142	8.1%	-0.746%	0.060%	0.201%
89:1	8922	1.208	95.1%	-0.155%	0.148%	0.310%
89:2	10269	1.050	34.9%	-0.361%	0.126%	0.066%
89:3	11454	0.805	29.0%	0.426%	-0.124%	-0.367%
89:4	7583	1.319	0.0%	0.000%	0.000%	0.414%
90:1	9405	1.063	0.0%	0.000%	0.000%	0.087%
90:2	14384	0.547	35.5%	1.048%	-0.372%	-0.989%
90:3	6948	1.994	100.0%	-0.556%	0.556%	1.112%
90:4	11245	0.853	44.4%	0.115%	-0.051%	-0.261%
91:1	11556	0.937	48.3%	-0.290%	0.140%	-0.126%
91:2	8161	1.225	0.0%	0.000%	0.000%	0.299%
91:3	8465	1.241	11.1%	-0.709%	0.079%	0.320%
91:4	10542	0.879	41.3%	0.228%	-0.094%	-0.226%
92:1	11300	0.804	80.6%	0.169%	-0.136%	-0.361%
92:2	10039	0.887	35.5%	0.494%	-0.175%	-0.206%
92:3	8912	1.122	0.0%	0.000%	0.000%	0.150%
92:4	8848	1.153	19.0%	-0.215%	0.041%	0.203%
93:1	12784	0.772	26.2%	0.049%	-0.013%	-0.447%
93:2	12472	0.739	8.1%	1.540%	-0.124%	-0.513%
93:3	10902	0.831	58.7%	0.227%	-0.133%	-0.301%
93:4	9363	1.166	90.5%	-0.164%	0.148%	0.243%
94:1	14006	0.653	14.5%	0.952%	-0.138%	-0.723%
94:2	5547	2.046	45.9%	-0.491%	0.226%	1.150%
94:3	9673	1.085	71.4%	-0.135%	0.096%	0.120%
94:4	6559	1.703	46.8%	-0.411%	0.192%	0.824%
95:1	7984	1.451	41.9%	-0.659%	0.276%	0.577%
95:2	11862	0.834	12.9%	0.087%	-0.011%	-0.321%
95:3	7317	1.626	58.1%	-0.511%	0.297%	0.752%
95:4	7971	1.255	0.0%	0.000%	0.000%	0.334%
96:1	11519	0.868	0.0%	0.000%	0.000%	-0.258%
96:2	8111	1.501	71.0%	-0.509%	0.361%	0.649%
96:3	10872	0.905	1.6%	1.626%	-0.026%	-0.185%
96:4	9192	1.066	27.0%	0.062%	-0.017%	0.074%

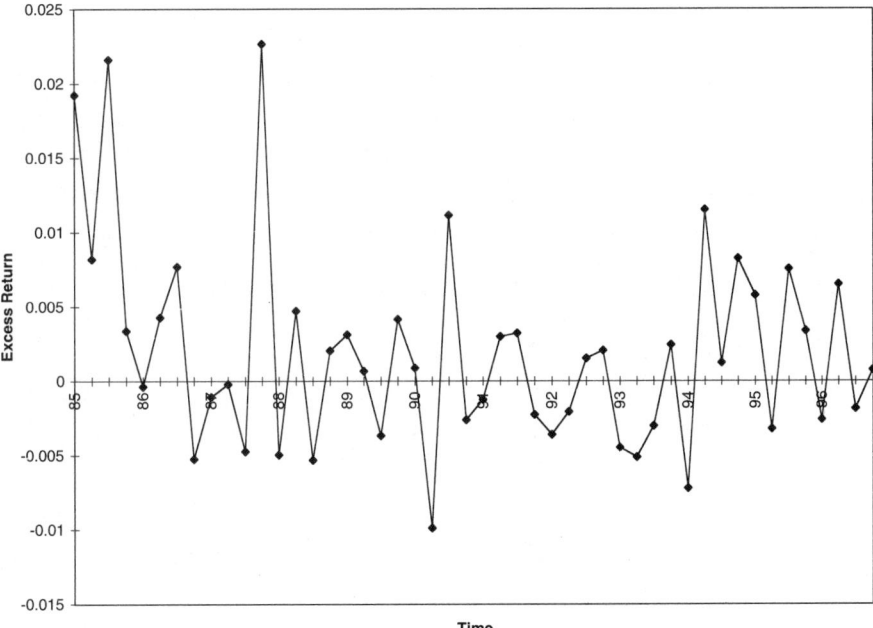

Figure 8.4   OHM/MFR-C short combination.

outcomes. After 1991, the performance does not gyrate as wildly, but the 1991–1994 results are poor. From 1994 on, the performance is better.

Conclusions

Some important lessons can be learned from the individual stock results. The potential gains shown in the top 40 tables are intriguing. However, closer examination reveals that extraordinarily high returns are usually linked to some extreme circumstance that would probably be difficult to foresee; it is always easy to spot great opportunities with hindsight.

The question is: Would an investor have been able to spot these opportunities at the time they occurred? The tables and graphs for the stocks that we examined in detail all look substantially different. There are no easy or obvious patterns that would have pointed to big profits. However, we probably need to look for opportunities that are somewhat subtle. All we can realistically hope for is to gain just a slight edge. For this reason, we may need to look closely at some patterns that look somewhat erratic but have a tendency to produce a slight edge.

In the aggregate results, the indicators did not work well on the short side. But, there are definitely some situations that present very lucrative opportunities, as we saw in this chapter. Some stocks do experience severe problems, with precipitous falls. It takes much work to create a beautiful lawn or garden, but just a little neglect can cause it to look horrible. In a similar vein, it takes much work to build a successful business, but businesses can fall apart quickly. Stocks can reflect these quick downfalls, presenting incredible opportunities for shorting.

We will examine all these issues, and more, in greater detail in Chapter 10, where we list and describe all the major conclusions from our research.

Chapter

9

Combination Results

Two heads are better than one, right? Two indicators are better than one, right? Maybe. The idea of combining indicators has intuitive appeal. It would seem that looking at two good indicators in some type of combination might produce a highly reliable signal. However, combinations are not so simple. There is no free lunch; the full cost of combining indicators may not be readily apparent. In this chapter, we examine the best two-way combinations of the sixty indicators we have already analyzed.

For each of the sixty indicators, there are three possible signals each day: (1) long, (2) cash, or (3) short. In the earlier chapters, we treated the short signals as cash signals when we were examining long/cash positions, and we treated the long signals as cash signals when we were examining short/cash positions. If each of two indicators has three possible signals, then there are nine possible combinations. When considering whether to go long when we are getting input from two signals, we can take various approaches. The simplest approach is to only go long when both of the indicators have a long signal. This is equivalent to a logical AND operation. Both conditions must be true. Another approach would be to go long when either of the two indicators signaled to go long. This would be equivalent to a logical OR operation. Similar considerations would apply to the short signals. In our analysis, we found that only the AND type combination was particularly worthwhile, so that is what we will discuss.

Summary Results: Long Combinations

With sixty indicators taken two at a time in combination, there are 1,770 possible combinations. We analyzed all 1,770, but will report only the best performing combinations. Table 9.1 shows some "top 40" results similar to those we reported in Chapter 8. The Volume Accumulation Percent Crossover/Williams %R Divergence (VAP-C/WLR-D) combination has the highest average return for its long signals. Again, as per the previous discussion, we are focusing only where both indicators must agree with a long signal. The other eight possible outcomes are assumed to be a cash position. A major complication is readily apparent in the *%Long* column. Requiring agreement between both indicators results in few long positions. So, even though the average return for the VAP-C/WLR-D combination is highly attractive at 0.312 percent, this only occurs 0.017 percent of the time. To put that percentage of long calls in perspective, that represents 447 occurrences for the entire group of 878 stocks over the twelve-year period. On average, that is about ten signals per quarter. The last column shows the *Overall Average Return*, which is the product of the average long return and the *%Long* figure. The overall return reflects the fact that this strategy would result in a cash position earning no return about 99.8 percent of the time. In the aggregate, this extremely cautious strategy is missing many days of positive returns. The average daily overall return is 0.00005 percent, which is minuscule. (We report the overall return to five decimal places in all the tables of this chapter in order to make comparisons, even though it looks somewhat ridiculous to be measuring percentages to five decimal places.)

In any ranking of average long return, you get outcomes with high returns at the top of the list, but generally very low levels of long positions. Table 9.2 reports a different "top 40"; the ranking is based on overall average return, so we see combinations with much higher frequency of long calls, but more modest average long return values. The Moving Average Crossover/Random Walk Breakout (MV2-C/RWI-B) combination at the top of the list signals long trades about 50 percent of the time, but has a modest 0.062 percent average long return. Recall that the overall average buy-and-hold return for our sample was 0.055 percent, so this combination is providing long signals that have only a very narrow advantage over the average buy-and-hold return. Even though the frequency is high at about 50 percent, that still knocks the overall return down to 0.03137 percent, as seen in the last column. Again, we should compare this 0.032 percent (rounding to three decimals) to the 0.055 percent buy-and-hold return. Since this is the best combination of the entire 40, we see that there are no combination strategies that outperform the buy-and-hold strategy on the basis of overall return. This is, as they say, the rub.

Table 9.2 clearly shows the major problem with combining indicators. Yes, two indicators are better than one—if we're only considering the basic

Table 9.1
Top 40 Long Indicator Combinations Ranked by Long
Signal Average Return (Average Daily Returns 1985–1996)

Rank	Technical Indicator 1	Technical Indicator 2	% Long	Long Signals Average Return	Overall Average Return
1	VAP-C	WLR-D	0.017%	0.312%	0.00005%
2	CN-CA	CN-MES	0.006%	0.240%	0.00002%
3	VAP-B	VAP-C	0.024%	0.229%	0.00006%
4	CN-CA	TLN-RS	0.050%	0.226%	0.00011%
5	CN-CA	WLR-D	0.010%	0.226%	0.00002%
6	CN-MES	VAP-B	0.023%	0.221%	0.00005%
7	CN-CA	TLN-RL	0.027%	0.220%	0.00006%
8	CN-CA	CN-HMR	0.027%	0.217%	0.00006%
9	CN-PL	WLR-D	0.051%	0.183%	0.00009%
10	CN-MES	TRX-D	0.051%	0.179%	0.00009%
11	CN-MES	VAP-C	0.009%	0.170%	0.00002%
12	CCI-D	CN-CA	0.034%	0.170%	0.00006%
13	MAC-D	VAP-B	0.040%	0.169%	0.00007%
14	CN-CA	ROC-D	0.032%	0.167%	0.00005%
15	CN-CA	CN-PL	0.017%	0.165%	0.00003%
16	MAC-D	WLR-D	0.161%	0.162%	0.00026%
17	CN-DS	CN-PL	0.009%	0.159%	0.00001%
18	CN-CA	DMI-C	0.121%	0.157%	0.00019%
19	CCI-D	TLN-RM	0.189%	0.155%	0.00029%
20	CN-CA	RSI-D	0.047%	0.152%	0.00007%
21	STO-P	VAP-B	0.262%	0.151%	0.00039%
22	CN-DS	CN-HAM	0.055%	0.150%	0.00008%
23	CN-BH	TRX-D	1.508%	0.148%	0.00224%
24	TRX-D	WLR-D	0.093%	0.148%	0.00014%
25	CN-BH	MAC-D	1.332%	0.148%	0.00197%
26	CN-CA	STO-C	0.176%	0.144%	0.00025%
27	STO-D	WLR-D	0.433%	0.143%	0.00062%
28	CN-BH	VAP-C	0.286%	0.143%	0.00041%
29	CN-CA	VTY-B	0.282%	0.143%	0.00040%
30	CN-HMR	WLR-D	0.153%	0.142%	0.00022%
31	ROC-D	VAP-B	0.033%	0.140%	0.00005%
32	CN-BH	VAP-D	2.065%	0.139%	0.00287%
33	STO-C	WLR-D	0.737%	0.137%	0.00101%
34	CN-DS	ROC-D	0.022%	0.137%	0.00003%
35	DMI-C	TRX-D	1.376%	0.137%	0.00188%
36	CN-HAM	CN-MES	0.121%	0.137%	0.00016%
37	CN-BH	DMI-C	10.856%	0.137%	0.01485%
38	CCI-FP	DMI-C	8.322%	0.136%	0.01132%
39	CCI-P	VAP-B	0.274%	0.136%	0.00037%
40	CN-CA	MAC-M	0.242%	0.136%	0.00033%

Table 9.2
Top 40 Long Indicator Combinations Ranked by Long
Overall Average Return (Average Daily Returns 1985–1996)

Rank	Technical Indicator 1	Technical Indicator 2	% Long	Long Signals Average Return	Overall Average Return
1	MV2-C	RWI-B	50.323%	0.062%	0.03137%
2	CN-BH	VTY-B	23.451%	0.122%	0.02853%
3	SAR-C	VTY-B	37.546%	0.075%	0.02810%
4	RWI-B	SAR-C	40.772%	0.069%	0.02799%
5	MV2-C	SAR-C	40.795%	0.067%	0.02736%
6	TXM-FP	TXM-P	36.429%	0.074%	0.02682%
7	MAC-M	SAR-C	41.606%	0.063%	0.02636%
8	MFR-B	MV2-C	43.359%	0.060%	0.02593%
9	MFR-B	RWI-B	42.648%	0.060%	0.02578%
10	CN-BH	SAR-C	23.095%	0.111%	0.02566%
11	RWI-B	VTY-B	35.816%	0.071%	0.02555%
12	ADX-B	RWI-B	39.741%	0.064%	0.02531%
13	MFR-B	SAR-C	39.448%	0.064%	0.02510%
14	MV2-C	VTY-B	35.538%	0.069%	0.02469%
15	SAR-C	TLN-BS	35.822%	0.069%	0.02462%
16	ADX-B	MV2-C	39.699%	0.062%	0.02458%
17	CN-BH	RWI-B	22.709%	0.107%	0.02437%
18	CN-BH	TXM-FP	18.037%	0.133%	0.02407%
19	MAC-M	VTY-B	36.273%	0.066%	0.02406%
20	CN-BH	MV2-C	22.194%	0.108%	0.02400%
21	TLN-BS	VTY-B	33.493%	0.071%	0.02381%
22	ADX-B	CN-BH	22.122%	0.107%	0.02374%
23	RWI-B	TLN-BS	36.230%	0.064%	0.02325%
24	CN-BH	TLN-BS	21.293%	0.109%	0.02316%
25	CN-BH	MFR-B	22.569%	0.102%	0.02309%
26	MV2-C	TLN-BS	36.917%	0.062%	0.02300%
27	MV2-C	TLN-BM	34.894%	0.066%	0.02299%
28	RWI-B	TRU	36.876%	0.062%	0.02294%
29	TLN-BM	TRU	36.564%	0.063%	0.02292%
30	RWI-B	TLN-BM	34.386%	0.067%	0.02291%
31	MV2-C	TRU	37.511%	0.061%	0.02290%
32	CN-BH	TXM-P	18.266%	0.125%	0.02288%
33	CN-BH	MAC-M	21.721%	0.105%	0.02286%
34	ADX-B	VTY-B	32.663%	0.070%	0.02274%
35	WLR-C	WLR-P	39.567%	0.057%	0.02252%
36	MFR-B	VTY-B	34.306%	0.065%	0.02222%
37	MAC-M	MV2-C	36.082%	0.061%	0.02208%
38	RSI-C	RSI-P	36.889%	0.060%	0.02206%
39	TXM-FP	VTY-B	24.696%	0.089%	0.02203%
40	MAC-M	RWI-B	35.404%	0.062%	0.02199%

quality of the signals they generate. The quality may be high; when both agree that it's a good time to go long, it probably is. But the problem is not with quality, it's with quantity. If you rarely take a long position, it is hard to make up for all the highly conservative cash positions. Cash has an opportunity cost. The basic question here is: How do we exploit these attractive but infrequent opportunities? We will discuss this in the next chapter, as part of our concluding comments.

Summary Results: Short Combinations

Table 9.3 is the short-signal equivalent of Table 9.1; combinations are ranked based on short signals' average return. In earlier chapters, we identified a major problem with the short signals from all sixty of the indicators: The average return was positive. Here, we see that all combinations in the top 40 list do have negative values, which is what we would like to see. As in Table 9.1, the frequency of calls is extremely low. The best performing combination, Candle Counterattack/Candle Morning-Evening Star (CN-CA/CN/MES), occurs only 0.004 percent of the time. Using these signals to take short positions flips the actual return from negative values to positive values, but the low frequency of calls leads to extremely low overall rates of return, as seen in the last column. The best performing combination has an overall average return of one one-hundred-thousandth (1/100,000) percent!

Even the best performing combinations based on overall average return have exceptionally low overall returns. This can be seen in Table 9.4. Notice that there is quite a bit of overlap in the combinations that appear in Tables 9.3 and 9.4. This is because only a limited number of the short combinations result in negative values for the average return from short signals. We did not see this much overlap in Tables 9.1 and 9.2, the corresponding tables for the long signals. Looking down the *%Short* column, you can see that the *%Short* figures are primarily responsible for the overall return ranking.

The overall return for the best long combination was 0.03137 percent, which was disappointing. For the best short signal combination, the overall return was a paltry 0.00075 percent. The figure for the long signals is about forty times larger, and yet we were calling that disappointing. The short signals are clearly problematic. We will address this issue in the next chapter.

A More Detailed Picture

In the preceding tables, we looked at aggregate results over the entire time period. Now we will examine two of the combinations on a quarterly basis. The goal here is consistency. Is there a reliable pattern of good performance?

Table 9.3
**Top 40 Short Indicator Combinations Ranked by Short
Signal Average Return (Average Daily Returns 1985–1996)**

Rank	Technical Indicator 1	Technical Indicator 2	% Short	Short Signals Average Return	Overall Average Return
1	CN-CA	CN-MES	0.004%	-0.128%	0.00001%
2	CN-CA	WLR-D	0.015%	-0.124%	0.00002%
3	CHA-D	VAP-B	0.082%	-0.089%	0.00007%
4	CN-HMR	WLR-D	0.030%	-0.088%	0.00003%
5	CN-DS	TLN-RL	0.014%	-0.073%	0.00001%
6	MAC-D	VAP-B	0.052%	-0.071%	0.00004%
7	VAP-B	WLR-D	0.013%	-0.065%	0.00001%
8	VAP-B	VAP-D	0.074%	-0.056%	0.00004%
9	CN-CA	CN-PL	0.020%	-0.050%	0.00001%
10	DMI-C	VAP-C	0.075%	-0.049%	0.00004%
11	SAR-C	VAP-C	0.144%	-0.048%	0.00007%
12	CN-DS	CN-HMR	0.003%	-0.045%	0.00000%
13	CN-HMR	MAC-D	0.025%	-0.034%	0.00001%
14	CN-MES	ROC-D	0.080%	-0.033%	0.00003%
15	ROC-D	VAP-C	0.067%	-0.032%	0.00002%
16	CN-CA	CN-DS	0.004%	-0.027%	0.00000%
17	VAP-B	VOL-C	0.041%	-0.024%	0.00001%
18	DMI-C	VAP-B	0.387%	-0.021%	0.00008%
19	BOL-T	CN-DS	0.051%	-0.018%	0.00001%
20	CN-MES	VAP-D	0.095%	-0.015%	0.00001%
21	CN-HMR	ROC-D	0.074%	-0.013%	0.00001%
22	CN-MES	TLN-RL	0.027%	-0.013%	0.00000%
23	CN-HMR	DMI-C	0.106%	-0.011%	0.00001%
24	CCI-D	CN-DS	0.060%	-0.011%	0.00001%
25	TLN-RS	VAP-B	0.204%	-0.011%	0.00002%
26	CN-CA	VAP-D	0.068%	-0.010%	0.00001%
27	CN-BH	TRX-D	1.885%	-0.010%	0.00018%
28	DMI-C	MAC-D	1.744%	-0.009%	0.00016%
29	DMI-C	MOM-P	8.446%	-0.009%	0.00075%
30	CN-DS	VAP-D	0.057%	-0.007%	0.00000%
31	CN-HAM	CN-MES	0.102%	-0.007%	0.00001%
32	STO-C	VAP-B	0.159%	-0.006%	0.00001%
33	DMI-C	TXM-FP	8.270%	-0.005%	0.00043%
34	CCI-D	CN-CA	0.052%	-0.005%	0.00000%
35	DMI-C	TRX-D	1.944%	-0.005%	0.00009%
36	TLN-RM	TRX-D	0.227%	-0.003%	0.00001%
37	BOL-T	ROC-D	0.595%	-0.003%	0.00002%
38	CCI-D	CN-MES	0.108%	-0.003%	0.00000%
39	CN-HAM	DMI-C	3.435%	-0.003%	0.00010%
40	RSI-D	VAP-B	0.077%	-0.002%	0.00000%

Table 9.4
Top 40 Short Indicator Combinations Ranked by Short
Overall Average Return (Average Daily Returns 1985–1996)

Rank	Technical Indicator 1	Technical Indicator 2	% Short	Short Signals Average Return	Overall Average Return
1	DMI-C	MOM-P	8.446%	-0.009%	0.00075%
2	DMI-C	TXM-FP	8.270%	-0.005%	0.00043%
3	CN-BH	DMI-C	11.365%	-0.002%	0.00021%
4	CN-BH	TRX-D	1.885%	-0.010%	0.00018%
5	DMI-C	MAC-D	1.744%	-0.009%	0.00016%
6	DMI-C	WLR-P	8.110%	-0.002%	0.00014%
7	CN-HAM	DMI-C	3.435%	-0.003%	0.00010%
8	DMI-C	TRX-D	1.944%	-0.005%	0.00009%
9	DMI-C	VAP-B	0.387%	-0.021%	0.00008%
10	DMI-C	TXM-P	9.804%	-0.001%	0.00008%
11	CHA-D	VAP-B	0.082%	-0.089%	0.00007%
12	SAR-C	VAP-C	0.144%	-0.048%	0.00007%
13	VAP-B	VAP-D	0.074%	-0.056%	0.00004%
14	MAC-D	VAP-B	0.052%	-0.071%	0.00004%
15	DMI-C	VAP-C	0.075%	-0.049%	0.00004%
16	BND-C	DMI-C	8.147%	0.000%	0.00003%
17	CN-HMR	WLR-D	0.030%	-0.088%	0.00003%
18	CN-MES	ROC-D	0.080%	-0.033%	0.00003%
19	TLN-RS	VAP-B	0.204%	-0.011%	0.00002%
20	DMI-C	TRU	9.897%	0.000%	0.00002%
21	ROC-D	VAP-C	0.067%	-0.032%	0.00002%
22	BOL-T	ROC-D	0.595%	-0.003%	0.00002%
23	CN-CA	WLR-D	0.015%	-0.124%	0.00002%
24	CN-MES	VAP-D	0.095%	-0.015%	0.00001%
25	CN-HMR	DMI-C	0.106%	-0.011%	0.00001%
26	VAP-B	VOL-C	0.041%	-0.024%	0.00001%
27	CN-CA	CN-PL	0.020%	-0.050%	0.00001%
28	CN-DS	TLN-RL	0.014%	-0.073%	0.00001%
29	CN-HMR	ROC-D	0.074%	-0.013%	0.00001%
30	BOL-T	CN-DS	0.051%	-0.018%	0.00001%
31	STO-C	VAP-B	0.159%	-0.006%	0.00001%
32	CN-HMR	MAC-D	0.025%	-0.034%	0.00001%
33	VAP-B	WLR-D	0.013%	-0.065%	0.00001%
34	BOL-T	VOL-C	0.461%	-0.002%	0.00001%
35	CN-HAM	CN-MES	0.102%	-0.007%	0.00001%
36	TLN-RM	TRX-D	0.227%	-0.003%	0.00001%
37	CN-CA	VAP-D	0.068%	-0.010%	0.00001%
38	CCI-D	CN-DS	0.060%	-0.011%	0.00001%
39	CN-CA	CN-MES	0.004%	-0.128%	0.00001%
40	CN-DS	VAP-D	0.057%	-0.007%	0.00000%

Table 9.5
Best Combination Results—Summary Results for
CN-BH/VTY-B Combination

Qtr	Buy/Hold Return	% Long	Long Signals Avg Ret	Overall Avg Ret	Excess Avg Ret
85:1	0.006%	22.65%	0.164%	0.037%	0.031%
85:2	-0.070%	21.37%	0.092%	0.020%	0.089%
85:3	-0.205%	15.40%	-0.015%	-0.002%	0.203%
85:4	0.107%	24.47%	0.253%	0.062%	-0.045%
86:1	0.225%	28.70%	0.276%	0.079%	-0.145%
86:2	0.067%	23.95%	0.168%	0.040%	-0.026%
86:3	-0.128%	20.48%	-0.029%	-0.006%	0.122%
86:4	0.069%	22.33%	0.122%	0.027%	-0.042%
87:1	0.293%	30.82%	0.351%	0.108%	-0.184%
87:2	0.038%	24.45%	0.073%	0.018%	-0.020%
87:3	0.068%	24.05%	0.119%	0.029%	-0.040%
87:4	-0.278%	20.25%	-0.020%	-0.004%	0.274%
88:1	0.163%	27.19%	0.097%	0.026%	-0.137%
88:2	0.100%	24.26%	0.089%	0.022%	-0.078%
88:3	0.013%	20.61%	0.014%	0.003%	-0.010%
88:4	0.037%	20.59%	0.058%	0.012%	-0.025%
89:1	0.112%	25.15%	0.124%	0.031%	-0.081%
89:2	0.122%	28.98%	0.132%	0.038%	-0.084%
89:3	0.131%	24.07%	0.152%	0.037%	-0.094%
89:4	-0.011%	22.55%	0.047%	0.011%	0.022%
90:1	0.003%	20.45%	0.063%	0.013%	0.010%
90:2	0.077%	24.27%	0.157%	0.038%	-0.038%
90:3	-0.259%	17.09%	-0.120%	-0.020%	0.238%
90:4	0.146%	25.58%	0.175%	0.045%	-0.102%
91:1	0.315%	29.60%	0.381%	0.113%	-0.203%
91:2	0.046%	23.54%	0.105%	0.025%	-0.021%
91:3	0.065%	20.87%	0.080%	0.017%	-0.048%
91:4	0.081%	20.12%	0.187%	0.038%	-0.044%
92:1	0.048%	21.82%	0.084%	0.018%	-0.030%
92:2	-0.048%	18.28%	-0.012%	-0.002%	0.046%
92:3	0.056%	20.91%	0.055%	0.012%	-0.045%
92:4	0.145%	22.59%	0.209%	0.047%	-0.097%
93:1	0.080%	23.39%	0.107%	0.025%	-0.055%
93:2	0.051%	22.61%	0.088%	0.020%	-0.032%
93:3	0.101%	25.67%	0.127%	0.033%	-0.069%
93:4	0.034%	23.41%	0.119%	0.028%	-0.006%
94:1	-0.011%	22.17%	0.044%	0.010%	0.021%
94:2	-0.005%	21.03%	0.053%	0.011%	0.016%
94:3	0.089%	24.64%	0.142%	0.035%	-0.054%
94:4	-0.030%	22.22%	-0.006%	-0.001%	0.028%
95:1	0.110%	26.12%	0.149%	0.039%	-0.071%
95:2	0.134%	26.04%	0.126%	0.033%	-0.101%
95:3	0.131%	25.35%	0.164%	0.042%	-0.089%
95:4	0.067%	24.94%	0.107%	0.027%	-0.040%
96:1	0.159%	26.48%	0.157%	0.042%	-0.117%
96:2	0.058%	23.48%	0.094%	0.022%	-0.036%
96:3	0.047%	24.21%	0.125%	0.030%	-0.017%
96:4	0.122%	27.06%	0.192%	0.052%	-0.070%

For the long combinations, we chose to examine the Candle Belt Hold/Volatility Breakout (CN-BH/VTY-B) combination in more detail. This combination ranked second in overall return. A logical question is: Why not look at number one instead of number two? The reason is that the average return for the best combination—MV2-C/RWI-B, discussed earlier—was only slightly better than the average buy-and-hold return. That combination just doesn't seem to be clearly identifying strong return situations. The CN-BH/VTY-B combination, in contrast, has a healthy 0.122 percent average return for long signals; furthermore, this combination occurs 23.451 percent of the time, so a respectable number of long signals are being generated.

Table 9.5 shows the quarterly performance of this combination. The *Buy/Hold Return* and *Excess Average Return* are also reported, unlike Tables 9.1 through 9.4. For those earlier tables, the buy/hold return was identical for all entries because we were aggregating all 878 stocks for the entire twelve-year period. If Tables 9.2 and 9.4 had been based on a ranking of excess return, the ranking would have been the same as the one shown, because we would have been subtracting the same constant buy/hold return from each entry. But, on a quarterly basis, the buy/hold return will vary. Therefore, we report it, and the excess return figures, in Table 9.5.

Let's look back at Table 9.2 for a minute. The overall return, based on the entire time period, was 0.029 percent (rounded) for the CN-BH/VTY-B combination. Comparing this to the 0.055 percent buy-and-hold return for all stocks over the twelve-year period, we can see that this combination, on average, has a negative excess return. Looking at the last column in Table 9.5, we can see that most of the excess returns are indeed negative. This is not good news.

Let's go back to the issue of the quality of the basic signals. Something we might want to look at is the relationship between the long signal average return and the buy/hold return. The question here would be: Are the returns on the days for long signals generally higher than just the average day, as represented by the buy/hold return? The answer here is: Yes, and it is a fairly consistent pattern.

To see this pattern, turn to Figure 9.1, which shows the two return figures over time. The pattern is intriguing. The average long signal return exceeds the buy/hold return in all but five of the sixty quarters. The only periods of negative returns for the long signals occur in market downturns when the buy/hold return is even more strongly negative. This combination appears to offer long signals, which are pretty consistent good advice.

Similar detail is shown for the Directional Movement Crossover/Momentum Peaks (DMI-C/MOM-P) short combination in Table 9.6 and Figure 9.2. This combination, which was at the top of the Table 9.4 list, was chosen because it had negative short returns and one of the higher call rates, leading to the best overall return for the short combinations. The detailed

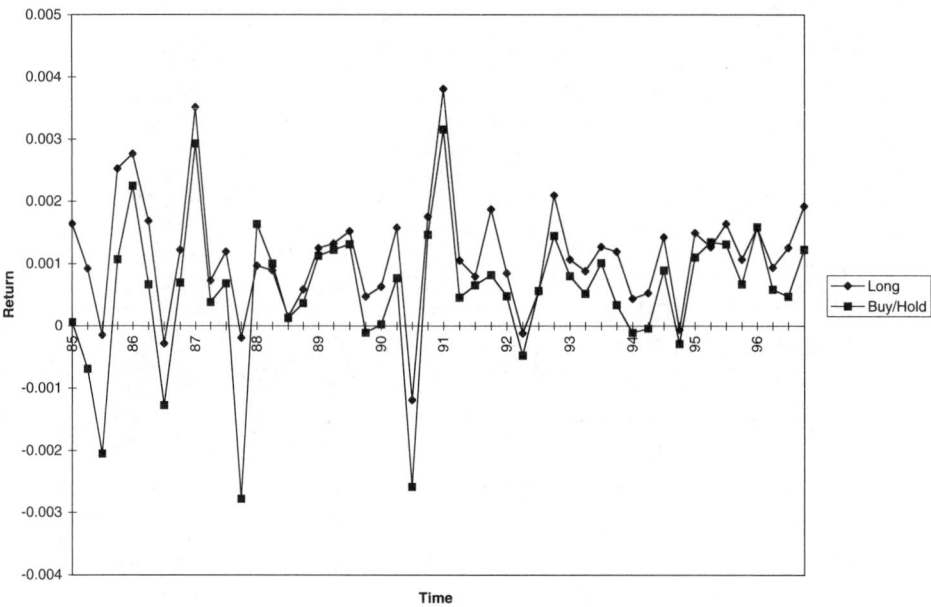

Figure 9.1   Average returns: CN-BH/VTY-B combination.

results require some explanation because they are somewhat confusing. Figure 9.2 is a graph of the negative of the short signals average return, along with the buy/hold return. Because these are signals for possible short positions, the negatives become positives from a short perspective.

What would we like to see? If the average buy/hold return is 0.055 percent, then we would like to have a short combination that generates short signals on days that have an average return of, say, −0.075 percent. If this were true, then we could go short on those days and average a +0.075 percent return, beating the average buy/hold return by +0.020 percent. What would Figure 9.2 look like if this were true? We are plotting the negative of the short signal returns, so we would see the short signal points plotting above the buy/hold return points by an average of +0.020 percent (+0.075 percent minus +0.055 percent). This difference would fluctuate from quarter to quarter, but, on average, the short signals would plot above the buy/hold signals.

What do we actually see in Figure 9.2? Not anything close to what we just described as our ideal. At first glance, the two series seem to plot as mirror images about the horizontal axis, but they are not exactly mirrored. Let's consider the two most extreme quarters in the entire time period. In the third quarter of 1987, the quarter of the famous October 1987 crash, the average return for the short signals was −0.801 percent, so a short position would have resulted in a +0.801 percent return. The buy/hold return was −0.278 percent, so the DMI-C/MOM-P short combination performed outstandingly well.

Table 9.6
Best Combination Results—Summary Results for
DMI-C/MOM-P Combination

Qtr	Buy/Hold Return	% Short	Short Signals Avg Ret	Overall Avg Ret	Excess Avg Ret
85:1	0.006%	7.01%	-0.016%	0.001%	-0.005%
85:2	-0.070%	8.77%	-0.129%	0.011%	0.081%
85:3	-0.205%	9.76%	-0.299%	0.029%	0.234%
85:4	0.107%	6.42%	0.053%	-0.003%	-0.110%
86:1	0.225%	5.48%	0.213%	-0.012%	-0.236%
86:2	0.067%	8.74%	-0.026%	0.002%	-0.064%
86:3	-0.128%	10.15%	-0.283%	0.029%	0.156%
86:4	0.069%	9.74%	0.126%	-0.012%	-0.082%
87:1	0.293%	5.51%	0.180%	-0.010%	-0.303%
87:2	0.038%	9.39%	-0.108%	0.010%	-0.028%
87:3	0.068%	7.47%	0.014%	-0.001%	-0.069%
87:4	-0.278%	10.76%	-0.801%	0.086%	0.364%
88:1	0.163%	7.75%	0.394%	-0.031%	-0.194%
88:2	0.100%	8.46%	0.144%	-0.012%	-0.112%
88:3	0.013%	8.61%	0.022%	-0.002%	-0.015%
88:4	0.037%	8.22%	0.020%	-0.002%	-0.038%
89:1	0.112%	7.51%	0.098%	-0.007%	-0.120%
89:2	0.122%	5.74%	0.095%	-0.005%	-0.127%
89:3	0.131%	7.32%	0.135%	-0.010%	-0.141%
89:4	-0.011%	9.25%	0.040%	-0.004%	0.008%
90:1	0.003%	10.50%	-0.114%	0.012%	0.009%
90:2	0.077%	7.95%	-0.013%	0.001%	-0.075%
90:3	-0.259%	8.44%	-0.397%	0.033%	0.292%
90:4	0.146%	8.51%	0.222%	-0.019%	-0.165%
91:1	0.315%	5.50%	0.205%	-0.011%	-0.327%
91:2	0.046%	9.22%	0.007%	-0.001%	-0.046%
91:3	0.065%	9.67%	0.041%	-0.004%	-0.069%
91:4	0.081%	9.15%	-0.075%	0.007%	-0.075%
92:1	0.048%	7.15%	0.043%	-0.003%	-0.051%
92:2	-0.048%	9.91%	-0.082%	0.008%	0.056%
92:3	0.056%	8.99%	0.054%	-0.005%	-0.061%
92:4	0.145%	8.16%	0.103%	-0.008%	-0.153%
93:1	0.080%	8.86%	-0.011%	0.001%	-0.079%
93:2	0.051%	9.54%	0.000%	0.000%	-0.051%
93:3	0.101%	8.12%	0.031%	-0.003%	-0.104%
93:4	0.034%	8.69%	-0.036%	0.003%	-0.030%
94:1	-0.011%	10.19%	-0.094%	0.010%	0.021%
94:2	-0.005%	10.32%	-0.098%	0.010%	0.015%
94:3	0.089%	8.79%	0.023%	-0.002%	-0.091%
94:4	-0.030%	8.55%	-0.011%	0.001%	0.031%
95:1	0.110%	8.23%	0.073%	-0.006%	-0.116%
95:2	0.134%	7.98%	0.187%	-0.015%	-0.149%
95:3	0.131%	8.29%	0.134%	-0.011%	-0.142%
95:4	0.067%	7.30%	0.015%	-0.001%	-0.068%
96:1	0.159%	8.50%	0.138%	-0.012%	-0.170%
96:2	0.058%	9.74%	0.033%	-0.003%	-0.062%
96:3	0.047%	9.56%	0.017%	-0.002%	-0.049%
96:4	0.122%	7.27%	0.067%	-0.005%	-0.127%

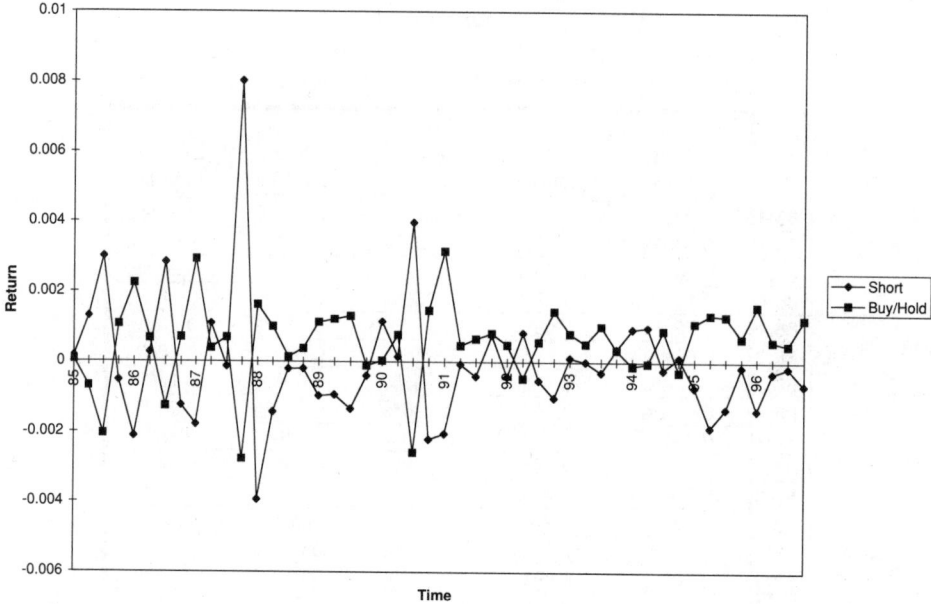

Figure 9.2   Average returns: DMI-C/MOM-P combination.

However, in the very next quarter, the market rebounded with a +0.163 percent buy/hold return. The return for the days when both indicators signaled to go short was +0.394 percent. The return from the short position in that quarter was –0.394 percent. The only apparent consistency is that there is a strong negative correlation between the two series; the correlation coefficient is –0.88. In the vast majority of the cases, the buy/hold return plots above the return from the short position. This is bad news.

However, there is still some good news here. Look at Table 9.6. If you compare the *Buy/Hold Return* to the *Short Signals Average Return*, you will see that the latter is less than the buy/hold return in all but eight quarters. This combination is indeed fairly consistently alerting us to days when return performance will be lower than the average day. This combination is, in fact, holding up a fairly good yellow caution flag.

Conclusions

A red/yellow/green analogy characterizes the combination results fairly well. We would like to see the long combinations giving us good reliable green flags for days that will have positive returns. For the better combinations, we are pretty safe in proceeding when we get a green flag, in the form of a long signal. We will probably be pleased with the results from proceeding. The problem is that we see few flags. Most of the time there is no flag at all and we are driving blindly. For the short combinations, we would like to have good reliable red flags when it looks like negative returns are just around the corner. What we are actually getting is more like a yellow flag. The return may not be negative, it may just be lower than normal.

The biggest point to take away from this chapter is that there is a price to pay when you use indicators in combination. Two indicators may be better than one, but they will agree infrequently. If you watch two indicators for long signals and only go long when both give you a long signal, you may be pleased when you go long, but you won't go long very often. The situation is similar for short signals. If you keep waiting for agreement, you will mostly be waiting. If you are neither long or short, then you are in cash and earning nothing. The opportunity cost of cash is high. There *is* a price to pay.

The news concerning the combination signals was, however, not all bad. The two combinations that we examined in detail did have a quite consistent ability to provide valuable information. When the long combination says to go long, that advice is probably worth heeding. When the short combination says to go short, that warning is probably at least valuable. In the next chapter, we will have more comments about how all this information might be exploited.

Chapter

10

Conclusions

We have made many general summarizing comments at various points in the book. In this chapter, we bring them all together. What follows is a list of twelve major conclusions from our tests. Before you launch into technically based trading, we think that each point needs to be fully understood. Technical analysis can quickly become a sinkhole of time and money. We hope these points will save you many hours and many dollars. Each point will be briefly explained. For a complete understanding of each point, refer back to the relevant section of the book.

Major Conclusions

1. **If you trade strictly following the signals from technical indicators, you will, on average, do worse than a buy-and-hold strategy.**

This is a sweeping conclusion, based on average results. What we are saying here is that if you were to just randomly pick one of the sixty indicators, randomly pick a stock, and begin trading, then you will probably not fare as well as you would have with a buy-and-hold strategy. You might get lucky and beat a buy-and-hold strategy. You might even have a string of successful results, just as a few people do from Las Vegas slot machines. But, on average, you are likely to be disappointed. If you keep playing a random picking game long enough, you will probably lose. The odds for the technical analysis slot machine are against you. Conclusion 2, below, partially explains what is causing the underperformance, relative to a buy-and-hold strategy. Before you write off technical analysis as a complete waste of time, however, see Conclusion 4.

2. Technical indicators are, on average, conservative; they signal a high proportion of cash positions.

This is, perhaps, a surprising conclusion. Many people view technical analysis as fairly risky. However, most indicators seem to provide definite buy or sell signals only when reasonably restrictive criteria are met. They are not just saying buy or sell in a willy-nilly manner. Therefore, they are actually somewhat cautious. Imagine that Joe is a technical analyst who strictly follows the Bollinger Band Crossover indicator in making his buy and sell recommendations. When Joe says buy or sell, he is probably worth listening to. However, much of the time, he throws up his hands and says, "I don't know what to do here; maybe you should just park your money in cash until the situation gets a little clearer." Joe's behavior is basically what is going on with most of the technical indicators. There are many "I don't know" messages.

You might ask: "What's the harm?" The problem is that, on average, stock prices rise. The long-run historical performance of stocks is quite good. There is an opportunity cost to sitting on the sidelines, staying in cash. The opportunity cost is the forgone return. Because the forgone return is generally positive, holding cash too frequently hurts overall performance. The balance between positive and negative returns is somewhat delicate. For the stocks we examined and the time period we examined, the optimal percentage of long positions was 45.6 percent. This, coupled with the fact that the magnitude of positive returns is greater than the magnitude of negative returns, means that it is beneficial, on average, to be long. The opportunity cost of a cash position is significant.

3. Technical indicators generally outperform a buy-and-hold strategy for stocks that are declining in price, and they underperform stocks that are rising in price.

Part of the explanation here goes back to Conclusion 2. If the strategy you are using tends to leave you invested in cash much of the time, then you will miss many good days in rising markets and avoid many bad days in falling markets. Thus, you will underperform a buy-and-hold strategy in rising markets and outperform it during falling markets. This is, in fact, what we observed. It could also be true that technical indicators inherently have this tendency, even above and beyond what happens from the tendency toward cash positions. Our results point in this direction, but we need to do more analysis before we could feel comfortable making a definite assertion in this regard. Our advice here is mainly to be somewhat cautious about good results you might be getting in falling markets.

4. The trading signals from technical indicators do, on average, contain information that may be of value in trading.

The easiest way to understand this conclusion is to go back to the buy-and-hold strategy and its underlying philosophy. Buy-and-hold is a simple no-brainer approach; you just buy the stock and continue holding the stock throughout your investment horizon. This approach will give you a certain average daily return, which for our sample of stocks and time period was 0.055 percent per day. The buy-and-hold strategy treats all days as equal, essentially settling for the average return over time. There will be some good days and some bad days, but they will all average out to a decent return; that's the philosophy.

If you use technical indicators, then you are assuming that you can differentiate between good and bad days. If the indicator says to go long, then you expect to receive an above-average return for that day; you expect something better than the average daily return you would get from the buy-and-hold return. At least, that's what you expect on average. You know that some days might have a return lower than 0.055 percent and some days will have a return higher than 0.055 percent, but you expect the overall average return on days that are marked with long signals to be higher than 0.055 percent. Our results show that this appears to be a reasonable expectation, at least using certain indicators.

Many of the technical indicators do seem to be providing useful information concerning days to go long. The best overall summary of this is Table 2.2, which shows the average return for long signal days for all sixty of the indicators we tested. Fifty of the sixty indicators had an average daily long return above the 0.055 percent buy-and-hold average return. Twelve had averages above 0.070 percent, which is more than one-fourth, or 25 percent, greater than the buy-and-hold average.

The results concerning short signals were not as strong, but the short signals still contain value. Ideally, if a technical indicator signals to go short, you would want the stock price to be going down, resulting in a negative return. If you have shorted the stock, then this negative change in price leads to positive returns on your short position. Unfortunately, the average daily return on days of short signals was positive, not negative, as can be seen in Table 2.3. However, the average short signal return is lower than the average buy-and-hold return for more than half of the sixty indicators. Therefore, the short signals do contain information. Essentially, they are saying: "It looks like a worse-than-average day ahead." They seem to be pointing toward days when the average return is likely to be below the buy-and-hold return; you will likely earn less than 0.055 percent on days when a short signal has occurred.

We have qualified our remarks above with phrases like "seem to be." The reason is that we tested a certain sample of stocks over a certain time period. Results for other stocks might point to a different conclusion. Results in other time periods might point toward other conclusions. Future results for our sample of stocks may be different. There is always some uncertainty with these types of investigations. However, our sample was quite broad and did cover a reasonably extensive period of time. The signals from the technical indicators do, in general, seem to contain valuable information.

5. Trading only long positions or only short positions with technical indicators generally will not beat a buy-and-hold strategy; you must be willing to utilize both long and short signals.

As discussed above, following only the long signals or only the short signals leaves you doing nothing a high proportion of the time. The returns on days when long signals have occurred are generally above average. The problem is that those signals don't occur frequently enough. If you are not long and not short, then you must be in a cash position. The opportunity cost of cash, the forgone return, is high when the return for an average day is 0.055 percent.

Therefore, something more is required, other than just acting on either the long signals or the short signals. The problem is: What is the *something more?* As we have explained above, the short signals do contain information, but the information is not as good as one would like. Because the average return on days when short signals occur is positive, the issue is not simply a matter of going short on those days and long on the days when long signals occur.

To beat a buy-and-hold strategy, you will have to somehow use the information from the short signals. This is not easy to do without creating other problems. Conclusions 6 and 12 have more thoughts along these lines.

6. Portfolio management is an important issue in technically based trading systems.

Portfolio management has many different aspects. There are many different things to consider in the construction and implementation of a trading system. However, we will focus on one specific portfolio management issue.

Earlier, we talked about how the low frequency of long and short signals creates problems. To see the problems, let's look first at a situation that would be easy to manage. Assume that you only want to trade long signals with one indicator, you are going to trade just five different stocks, and you are starting with $10,000. For Monday, your indicator signals a long position only for stock A. You invest all your money in stock A. For Tuesday, you receive a long signal only for stock B, so you close out your position in A and move your money into stock B. For Wednesday, you receive a long signal only for stock C. You repeat the earlier actions, moving your money out of B into C. For Thursday you receive a long signal only for stock D, and you follow the actions along the same lines as before. For Friday, the same thing occurs with stock E. If this pattern occurred repeatedly, week after week, and you were getting good average returns from your long positions, then life would be relatively simple. The problem that we have discussed concerning the low frequency of long signals would be solved, owing to the distribution of the signals. You would be getting one signal per day, so you could have a long position 100 percent of the days. But you would be invested in different stocks on different days.

The situation we just described is quite unrealistic. There are numerous possible complications. For example, what if, on Tuesday, you had received long signals for stocks A and B? Would you sell some of stock A and split your money between A and B, or just ignore the signal about B and continue with all of your money in A? Or, what if long signals always occurred on Monday for all five stocks and there were no long signals during the rest of the week? You would still have the problem that on 80 percent of the days you would be uninvested, holding your money in cash. These examples show that the distribution of the long signals, day by day, for the stocks that you are considering will be quite important.

Deciding how you will manage a portfolio of stocks when faced with a variety of long and/or short signal patterns is what we are referring to here as a portfolio management issue. There are many different ways you could decide to approach this issue, and your approach will have a major bearing on your overall results. We have not tested various methods of handling this problem. Our purpose here is just to alert you to an important issue that should be considered.

7. Results vary widely from stock to stock.

The performance of different indicators varies considerably from stock to stock. Just because an indicator has good average results over the entire sample does not mean that it will have that same performance for each stock. One indicator may work extremely well for one stock and somewhat poorly for another stock. Averaging across the two stocks, we might say the performance is moderately good.

It would be nice to be able to predict the performance of a particular indicator for a particular stock. We have no guidance to offer about that. Our primary results deal with *average* performance. In Chapter 8, we examined some results for particular stocks and saw that certain indicators work extremely well for certain stocks. If we had looked at the other end of the spectrum, we could have described results that were miserable for certain stocks. Results vary considerably from stock to stock.

8. For a single stock, results can vary significantly from one time period to the next.

As we saw in the Chapter 8 results, the performance of a particular indicator for a particular stock can vary widely from one time period to the next. It would be nice to find a stock/indicator combination that performs well consistently. We examined the individual stock/indicator combinations that performed best on an overall basis. These combinations had only limited consistency of attractive returns. It is possible that some combinations have overall results that are not as good as the ones we focused on, but show more consistency in their patterns. Consistency is certainly an important issue to consider.

9. Transactions costs, slippage, and interest need to be considered.

Our results represent somewhat of a best-case scenario because we have totally ignored transactions costs. Our results do not give technical indicators a rave review, but rather a more modest positive review, and this is disturbing for those wanting to implement technically based trading systems. We are looking at daily long/short signals, so it might seem that transactions costs would be extremely high as a result of a lot of switching in and out of positions. However, the technical indicators generally give signals in streaks. For example, consider a twenty-day trading period. If an indicator gives ten long signals over this period, it is more likely to come in the form of seven days long, ten days in cash, followed by three days long, and not long/cash/long/cash/long/cash, and so on. The signals tend to come in runs or streaks, so the transactions costs issue is not the major concern that it potentially could be.

Slippage refers to the ability to transact at the prices we were using. This too is a definite problem. If, on average, you were only able to buy at higher prices than we used and sell at lower prices, the results would be much worse. Omni-Trader and some other technical analysis software packages allow the user to explicitly factor in a user-defined level of slippage when performing historical backtesting.

We have ignored the possibility of earning interest in the cash positions. This extra return would improve the performance of all of the indicators we tested. However, even in quarters with money market rates of 12 percent annually, this would only raise the overall return by about 1½ percent (assuming 3 percent quarterly and a 50 percent cash position). This is still not enough extra return to outperform a buy-and-hold strategy in most cases.

The bottom line here is that transactions costs and slippage will probably dampen our results. This is clearly worrisome to those wanting to implement technically based systems.

10. Combining indicators may result in better signals, but they will be less frequent.

You may have heard the free lunch theorem: There is no free lunch. As we saw in Chapter 9, two indicators may be better than one, but the extra reliability comes with a price: frequency. As you try to combine indicators in an effort to get a more reliable signal, you will sacrifice frequency. The combined signal may be great when it comes, but what do you do while you wait for it to arrive? If you are parked in a cash position while you wait, you are forgoing opportunities. Because the average daily return for stocks is a decent positive return, cash positions carry an opportunity cost. The high frequency of cash positions when using indicator combinations creates a major drag on overall return.

11. Changing the interpretation of signals may be useful in some cases.

Assume that Joe gives you investment advice on a regular basis. You notice that nine times out of ten he is dead wrong. When he says to buy, it would have been better to sell, and vice versa. Is Joe's investment advice valuable? Yes. Just do the opposite of what Joe says to do. As long as Joe gives consistently bad advice, then you should pay attention to his recommendations. We can carry this same idea over to our interpretation of signals from indicators.

Some of the indicators actually had returns, on days of short signals, that were higher than the average buy-and-hold return. One way to use these signals would be to consider the short signals to actually be long signals.

Based on our results, the short signals generally should be viewed more as a yellow caution flag than a red flag saying "Stop." If you are going to go short, then you want the price change in the stock to be negative, not positive. Our results showed that the price changes, or returns, on days when short signals occurred, were generally positive. However, the returns were lower than average on those days. Thus, the short signals may need to be interpreted as days of gentle warning.

The indicators give one of three signals: long, cash, or short. When you combine two indicators, there are nine possible outcomes: short/short, short/cash, short/long, cash/short, cash/cash, cash/long, long/short, long/cash, and long/long. If, in studying the returns for each of these nine possibilities, you saw that only the cash/cash combination had returns that were, on average, negative, then you might want to use a cash/cash combination signal to mean "Go short" and interpret the other eight combinations as "Go long."

12. Leveraged positions may be necessary to exploit certain opportunities.

What do we mean by a leveraged position? We mean a position that involves using borrowed funds, such as buying stocks on margin. Let's assume that you have $10,000 to invest. Let's also assume that you have found an indicator that gives good long signals. The returns on days of long signals from this indicator average 0.130 percent, which is more than twice that of the average buy-and-hold return of 0.055 percent. The problem is that these signals occur only 50 percent of the time. To keep things simple, assume that you can borrow at no cost. So, every time you go long, you invest your $10,000 and another $10,000 that you have borrowed. Because you are doubling the amount invested, this will compensate for the fact that these signals occur only 50 percent of the time. You would be using leverage to capitalize on the long signals from your indicator.

One way to leverage an investment is through buying on margin. Another possibility is using options. Options contracts have inherent leverage. So, if the stock you are following has options traded on it, you might be able to implement an options-based strategy that would allow you to capitalize on indicators that give good, but infrequent, signals.

The basic idea here definitely has merit, but we want to issue several caveats.

1. Make sure that you thoroughly understand any leveraged strategy that you try to employ. Many people lose money in options because they simply do not understand the characteristics of what they have bought.

2. Based on our results, fairly high levels of leverage might be necessary. For example, the Directional Movement Crossover (DMI-C) indicator had an average long signal return of 0.100 percent, which is not quite twice that of the buy-and-hold average return of 0.055 percent. But, this signal only occurs 22.3 percent of the time. Therefore, you would need to employ significant leverage, more than just doubling up your capital, to compensate for the low frequency of signals. The higher the leverage, the higher the risk.

3. As a former colleague once said, repeated games of Russian roulette have a certain, not an uncertain, outcome. Leverage magnifies outcomes. If you are highly leveraged during a severe market downturn such as the crash of October 1987, then you may lose all of your capital. Borrower, beware!

Final Thoughts

The main purpose of this book has been to inform you about the likely performance of certain technical indicators based on our tests, which were conducted using a broad sample of stocks across a fairly long (twelve-year) period that encompassed varying market conditions. The reporting of these results took up most of the text and tables. However, there was another purpose: to alert you to the many different issues that must be addressed if you decide to use technical indicators for trading decisions. We have discussed issues such as performance measurement criteria, consistency of results, combining indicators, portfolio considerations, and leveraging. We have purposely omitted some things that seemed beyond the scope of the book. Unintentionally, or through our own ignorance, we have, no doubt, omitted other issues. There is much to consider. The best single piece of advice we can offer is: Keep learning and keep thinking!

Bibliography

Achelis, Steven B., *Technical Analysis From A to Z*, Irwin, 1995.

In this book, Achelis describes over 100 technical indicators. Both classic indicators and newer, more complex indicators are included in this reference tool.

Block, Stanley B., and Geoffrey A. Hirt, *Investment Management*, Fifth Edition, Irwin, 1996.

Block and Hirt present the basic assumptions and methods of technical analysis. Also, a thorough discussion of the efficient market hypothesis challenges the use of technical analysis.

Bodie, Zvi, Alex Kane, and Alan J. Marcus, *Investments*, Third Edition, Irwin, 1996.

While the focus of this book is extremely broad, these authors include a brief discussion of technical analysis. The focus is on how the support of technical analysis is diametrically opposed to the notion of an efficient market.

Chande, Tushar S., and Stanley Kroll, *The New Technical Trader*, John Wiley & Sons, Inc., 1994.

These authors present, in a step-by-step tutorial style, an array of new technical indicators that can be used in a variety of markets.

Cherian, Samuel, and I. Malakkal, "Leading-Edge Investors Downplay Debate on Fundamental vs. Technical Analysis," *Wall Street Computer Review*, November 1989.

This article discusses the emerging trend of viewing fundamental and technical analysis as complementary tools rather than opposing philosophies.

Colby, Robert W., and Thomas A. Meyers, *The Encyclopedia of Technical Market Indicators*, Irwin, 1988.

This reference book contains a comprehensive description of technical stock market indicators.

Cootner, Paul H. (ed.), *The Random Character of Stock Market Prices*, MIT Press, 1964.

This book popularized the random walk theory that claims stock price movement is random and unpredictable.

DeMark, Thomas R., *The New Science of Technical Analysis*, John Wiley & Sons, Inc., 1994.

DeMark describes some of the sophisticated market timing techniques that he has developed. They include some novel concepts that are unconventional and unorthodox.

Edwards, Robert D., and John Magee, Jr., *Technical Analysis of Stock Trends*, Fifth Edition, Springfield, MA: John Magee, 1966.

This book has been widely used by technical analysts. It is a good basic reference even though it is more than 30 years old.

Eng, William F., *The Technical Analysis of Stocks, Options & Futures*, Irwin, 1988.

Eng examines fifteen trading systems and reports on their effectiveness in various types of market environments.

Fama, Eugene, "The Behavior of Stock Market Prices," *Journal of Business*, January 1965, pp. 34–105.

Galant, Debbie, "Fast Cars and Loose Exchange Rates," *Institutional Investor*, May 1992, pp. 103–104.

This article tells how David Morrison, chief international economist at Goldman Sachs International in London, placed first in currency forecasting on 1992's All-Europe Research Team. His success was based, in part, on his use of technical analysis.

Helzner, Jerry, "Confessions of a Trader: In the Long Run, He'll Buy the Short Term," *Barron's*, October 27, 1986, pp. 30–32.

Helzner describes society's bias against technical analysis and short-term trading. He also provides helpful tips for those who want to break through this negative stereotype and try their hand at trading.

Jagadeesh, Narasimhan, "Evidence of Predictable Behavior of Security Returns," *Journal of Finance*, July 1990, pp. 881–898.

Jagadeesh finds predictable stock price patterns when looking at monthly returns during the 1934–1987 time period. This article presents evidence that stocks that experience large increases or decreases in price during one month are likely to reverse significantly during the following month. This type of pattern suggests that investors can profit from technical trading strategies.

Joy, O. Maurice, "Hunting the Stock Market Snark," *Sloan Management Review*, Spring 1987, pp. 17–24.

In this delightful article, Joy compares the search for stock market inefficiencies to hunting the snark, a mysterious, rarely seen beast from a Lewis Carroll poem.

Joy, O. Maurice, "Should We Believe the Tests of the Market Efficiency?" *Journal of Portfolio Management*, Summer 1986, pp. 49–54.

Maurice claims that, contrary to popular belief, technical analysis has not been adequately tested. He suggests that until there is incontrovertible knowledge of the true state of market efficiency, traders are justified in their consideration of technical analysis.

Kamara, Avraham, "Issues in Futures Markets: A Survey," *Journal of Futures Markets*, Fall 1982, pp. 275–278.

In this survey article, Kamara cites research that both rejects the random walk hypothesis and supports the hypothesis.

Laderman, Jeffrey M., "Watching the Bull Through a Technician's Eyes," *Business Week*, September 28, 1987.

Laderman points to increased interest in technical analysis and indicates that this interest is based on the fact that the technicians correctly predicted a continued bull market, despite corrections. The increased interest is also attributed to the growing relationship between the stock market and the options and futures markets.

Lehmann, Bruce N., "Fads, Martingales, and Market Efficiency," *The Quarterly Journal of Economics*, February 1990, pp. 1–28.

In this article, Lehmann detects patterns in stock price movements. He observes that stocks that experience a significant price rise or fall in one week often have a significant reversal the following week. This empirical evidence supports the idea that stock price trends occur frequently enough to create profit opportunities for technical traders.

Levy, Haim, *Introduction to Investments*, South-Western College Publishing, 1996.

With an entire chapter of this book devoted to technical analysis, it provides much broader coverage of the subject than the typical introductory investments book. Haim provides arguments in support of and against the use of technical analysis, and introduces some of the empirical literature in the area.

Malkiel, Burton G., *A Random Walk Down Wall Street*, Norton, 1990.

In this popular book, Malkiel explains some basic investment theories to individual investors. While the book contains descriptions of both technical and fundamental analysis, technical analysis is portrayed in a negative light. Throughout the book, Malkiel provides both intuitive, theoretical arguments against the use of technical analysis, and examples from his experience of technical analysts' failing to do what they claimed to do.

"Mountain View's Dinesh Desai Enjoys Mountaintop Experiences," *Futures: The Magazine of Commodities & Options*, March 1988, pp. 53, 57.

This article points to Desai's use of technical analysis to trade futures. Using technical analysis for 85 percent of his trades, Desai managed seven of the top eight performing public futures funds in 1987.

Murphy, J. Austin, "Futures Fund Performance: A Test of the Effectiveness of Technical Analysis," *Journal of Futures Markets*, Summer 1986, pp. 175–185.

The performance of sixteen purely technical futures funds during the period from May 1980 to April 1985 is analyzed. No statistically significant evidence is found to support the idea that technical funds can outperform a benchmark buy-and-hold strategy.

Murphy, John J., "Intermarket Analysis," *InterMarket*, May 1988, pp. 20–21.

Murphy discusses the role that technical analysis has played in the linkage among markets. He claims that technical analysis is the preferred method for intermarket analysis because it does not require vast amounts of knowledge about economic fundamentals.

Murphy, John J., *Intermarket Technical Analysis*, John Wiley & Sons, Inc., 1991.

This book focuses on the interdependency of the stock, bond, commodities, and currencies markets. Emphasis is placed on how these intermarket relationships impact technical trading.

Murphy, John J., *Technical Analysis of the Futures Markets: A Comprehensive Guide to Trading Methods and Applications*, New York Institute of Finance, 1986.

In this thorough reference book, Murphy describes the concepts of technical analysis and their application to the futures markets.

Murphy, John J., *The Visual Investor: How to Spot Market Trends*, John Wiley & Sons, Inc., 1996.

In this book, Murphy helps readers develop an ability to visually analyze trading charts. Using this visual analysis, traders can quickly and simply determine price trends without complicated mathematical formulas.

Neftci, Salih N., "Naive Trading Rules in Financial Markets and Wiener–Kolmogorov Prediction Theory: A Study of 'Technical Analysis'," *Journal of Business*, October 1991, pp. 549–571.

Based on a study using the Dow Jones Industrials from 1911 to 1976, Neftci concludes that using a moving average technical indicator may provide some information.

"On The Fundamentals of Technical Analysis: Andrew Lo," *Stocks & Commodities*, December 1997, p. 50.

In this interview, Andrew Lo discusses the value of technical analysis and stresses the need to be open-minded and creative when it comes to investing. However, he also warns of misapplied statistics and the limits of forecasting models that are based on physical laws.

Pardo, Robert, *Design, Testing, and Optimization of Trading Systems*, John Wiley & Sons, Inc., 1992.

For those who are interested in designing their own technical trading systems, Pardo provides a step-by-step guide. He offers practical guidance for setting up, testing, and implementing mechanical trading systems.

Pring, Martin J., *Technical Analysis Explained: The Successful Investor's Guide to Spotting Investment Trends and Turning Points*, Third Edition, McGraw-Hill, 1991.

In this book, Pring provides an in-depth description of the basic types of technical indicators.

Pruitt, Stephen W., and Richard E. White, "The CRISMA Trading System: Who Says Technical Analysis Can't Beat the Market?" *Journal of Portfolio Management*, Spring 1998, pp. 55–58.

This test of the CRISMA trading system suggests that trading with the system results in profits greater than would be attributed to chance. These results argue against market efficiency.

Schwager, Jack D., *Schwager on Futures: Technical Analysis*, John Wiley & Sons, Inc., 1996.

Written from a trader's perspective, this book provides a comprehensive guide for using technical analysis for futures trading.

Stein, Jon, and Ginger Szala, "Hot, New Traders," *Futures: The Magazine of Commodities & Options*, October 1993, pp. 28–31.

Two of the traders selected for *Futures'* emerging commodity trading advisor designation report using technical analysis.

Strong, Robert A., "A Behavioral Investigation of Three Paradigms in Finance," *Northeast Journal of Business & Economics*, Spring/Summer 1988, pp. 1–28.

Strong presents the results of a survey of the attitudes of investment professionals and academics toward the use of technical analysis. The study finds that although the majority of professionals support the use of technical analysis, the majority of academics do not view technical analysis as a useful investment tool.

Szala, Ginger, "Shahrokh Nikkah: Scalping for Singles in Home-Run Market," *Futures: The Magazine of Commodities & Options*, February 1998, p. 106.

Nikkah, vice-president of futures at Shearson Lehman Brothers Inc. in New York, is reported to earn impressive returns for his clients in the energy markets. He claims that his trades are based 95 percent on technical analysis.

Taylor, Mark P., and Helen Allen, "The Use of Technical Analysis in the Foreign Exchange Market," *Journal of International Money & Finance*, June 1992, pp. 304–314.

The results of a survey of foreign exchange dealers conducted by the Bank of England are discussed. The vast majority of the respondents report placing some weight on technical analysis.

Warnecke, Steven J., "Hear This, Bob Prechter! A Critic Attacks the Elliot Wave Theory," *Barron's*, January 26, 1987, p. 13.

Warnecke criticizes the Elliot Wave Theory, claiming that there is no rational proof for it.

Wilder, J. Welles, *New Concepts in Technical Trading Systems*, Greensboro, NC: Trend Research, 1978.

In this classic book, Wilder develops eight technical trading systems. Many of the technical indicators used today are based on Wilder's work. Written before the widespread use of computers, this book provides simple, easy-to-follow explanations for developing technical trading systems.

Index